Picture yourself getting more value.

Your Days Inn® CAA/AAA Member discount gives you a nice, warm feeling.
So does our free Daybreak® Café breakfast*with Kellogg's® cereals and
Minute Maid® juices.** And you'll earn more rewards to brighten
your day with TripRewards.®† CAA/AAA Members
always get more on the Sunny Side.

Show Your Card & Save

**CAA/AAA Members: Save up to 10%††
at more than 10 CAA
approved Days Inn® hotels
in Atlantic Canada & Quebec.**

For specific locations and reservations, call
**1-800-432-9755 or
daysinn.ca**

*Daybreak Café not available at all hotels. **Minute Maid is a registered trademark of The Coca-Cola Company. †Days Inn is a participating hotel chain in the TripRewards program, the largest hotel rewards program based on total number of participating hotels. ††Discount is off standard room rates and may not be combined with any other discounts or special offers. Discounts and amenities vary by property. Some restrictions may apply. All Days Inn hotels are independently owned and operated. ©2006 Days Inns Worldwide, Inc.

Atlantic Provinces & Québec

Are we meeting your travel needs?
Send written comments to:

AAA Member Comments
1000 AAA Drive, Box 61
Heathrow, FL 32746-5063

Published by AAA Publishing
1000 AAA Drive
Heathrow, FL 32746-5063
Copyright AAA 2007

**Advertising Rate and Circulation
Information: (407) 444-8280**

**Printed in the USA by
Quebecor World, Buffalo, NY**

Photo Credit: (Cover & Title Page)
*Newfoundland, north of
Gros Morne National Park*
© *Eero Sorila*

 Printed on recyclable paper.
Please recycle whenever possible.

 Mixed Sources
Product group from well-managed
forests and other controlled sources
www.fsc.org Cert no. SW-COC-1610
© 1996 Forest Stewardship Council

Stock #4604

Atlantic Provinces & Québec

Prince Edward Island

Featured Information

Québec

Photos courtesy of Nova Scotia Tourism and Culture.

Getting away just got better.

Sheraton

FOUR ✕ POINTS
BY SHERATON

WESTIN

W
HOTELS

Le **MERIDIEN**

Le Centre Sheraton Montréal Hotel, Québec

Sheraton Laval Hotel, Québec

Four Points by Sheraton Halifax, Nova Scotia

Four Points by Sheraton Conference Centre, Gatineau-Ottawa

Four Points by Sheraton Québec

Four Points by Sheraton Montréal Airport, Québec

Four Points by Sheraton Montréal Centre-Ville, Québec

Le Westin Resort & Spa, Tremblant, Québec

The Westin Nova Scotian, Halifax, Nova Scotia

W Montréal, Québec

Le Méridien Versailles, Montréal, Québec

Whether you travel by plane, train, or automobile, simply show your
AAA card and receive exclusive savings at Starwood Hotels & Resorts worldwide.

For hotel reservations and vacation planning, get right to the point on *aaa*•*com*. Reserve AAA approved and Diamond rated hotels at the lowest online prices. Plus, enjoy these additional tools and benefits:

AAA.com TourBook® – Find thousands of AAA Approved and Diamond rated hotels and restaurants, plus destinations, attractions, & events.

AAA.com TripTik® – Get complete trip routings with hotel reservations, sightseeing stops, member discount locations, and more.

AAA Drive Trips – Enjoy nearly 100 flexible, preplanned driving itineraries for popular destinations.

Vacation Getaways – Get exclusive benefits on flights, tours, cruises, and Disney vacation packages from AAA's Preferred Travel Partners.

Hertz – Save up to 20% on car rental.

Show Your Card & Save® – Search for exclusive member savings at 150,000 locations worldwide at AAA.com/save.

AAA Travel Money – Get no-fee travelers cheques, foreign currency, and prepaid cards.

Books – Save 5% on AAA travel publications at aaa.com/barnesandnoble.

AAA Credit Card – Get up to 5% gas rebate.

AAA Approved Auto Repair – Find reliable service facilities at home and away.

Plan your next trip on *aaa*•*com* — the only
travel Web site backed by thousands of highly trained
travel professionals at more than 1,000 AAA/CAA offices!

aaa•*com*
Plan to go.

Attractions, lodgings and restaurants are listed on the basis of merit alone after careful evaluation and approval by one of AAA/CAA's full-time, professionally trained Tourism Editors. Evaluations are unannounced to ensure that we see an establishment just as you would see it.

An establishment's decision to advertise in the TourBook guide has no bearing on its evaluation or rating. Advertising for services or products does not imply AAA endorsement.

All information in this guide was reviewed for accuracy before publication. However, since changes inevitably occur between annual editions, we suggest you work with your AAA travel professional or check on AAA.com to confirm prices and schedules.

How the TourBook Guide is Organized

The TourBook guide is organized into three distinct sections.

The **Points of Interest** section helps you plan daily activities and sightseeing excursions and provides details about the city or attraction you are visiting.

The **Lodgings and Restaurants** section helps you select AAA Approved accommodations and dining facilities meeting your specific needs and expectations.

The **Reference** section provides indexes for locating information within this guide and items to aid the trip planning process.

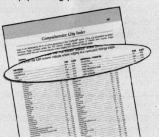

Locating the Attractions, Lodgings and Restaurants

Attractions, lodgings and restaurants are listed under the city in which they physically are located - or in some cases under the nearest recognized city. Most listings are alphabetically organized by state, province, region or island, then by city and establishment name.

A color is assigned to each state or province so that you can match the color bars at the top of the page to switch from the **Points of Interest** section to the **Lodgings and Restaurants** section.

Spotting maps help you physically locate points of interest, lodgings and restaurants in the major destinations.

The Comprehensive City Index located in the **Reference** section contains an A-to-Z list of cities.

Destination Cities and Destination Areas

Destination cities, established based on government models and local expertise, include metropolitan areas plus nearby vicinity cities. **Destination areas** are regions with broad tourist appeal; several cities will comprise the area.

If a city falls within a destination's vicinity, the city name will appear at its alphabetical location in the book, and a cross reference will give you the exact page on which listings for that city begin.

An orientation map appears at the beginning of each destination section to orient you to that destination.

Understanding the Points of Interest Listing

GEM Designation

A 🔻GEM indicates the attraction has been rated a AAA GEM, a "must see" point of interest that offers a *Great Experience for Members®*. These attractions have been judged to be of exceptional interest and quality by AAA Tourism Editors.

A GEM listing page with a brief description of individual GEM attractions follows the Orientation map near the beginning of each state or province Points of Interest section. Cross-references guide the reader to the attraction's listing page.

Discount Savings

The 🅢🅐🅥🅔 icon denotes those attractions offering AAA/CAA, AAA MasterCard, AAA VISA or international Show Your Card & Save discount cardholders a discount off the attraction's standard admission. Present your card at the attraction's admission desk.

A list of participating points of interest appears in the Reference section of this guide.

Shopping establishments preceded by a 🅢🅐🅥🅔 icon also provide to AAA/CAA members a discount and/or gift with purchase; present your card at the mall's customer service center to receive your benefit.

Exceptions

- Members should inquire in advance concerning the validity of the discount for special rates.
- The 🅢🅐🅥🅔 discount may not be used in conjunction with other discounts.
- Attractions that already provide a reduced senior or child rate may not honor the 🅢🅐🅥🅔 discount for those age groups.
- All offers are subject to change and may not apply during special events, particular days or seasons or for the entire validity period of the TourBook guide.

Shopping areas: Mast General Store, 630 W. King St., operates out of a 1913 building, stocked with a variety of goods, incl. Swair Box

🔻GEM 🅢🅐🅥🅔 **RED OAK,** is off I-95 exit 4A, just n. to Dogwoo restored 1812 house has eight 60-foot columns and Allow 1 hour minimum. Daily 9-5, Apr. 1-Labor D Labor Day-Nov. 30; by appointment rest of year. C 6-12, $5; ages 2-5, $4; family rate (two adults and two chil 5555 or (800) 555-5555.

🔻GEM 🅢🅐🅥🅔 **RED OAK,** is off I-95 exit 4A, just n. to Dogwood Dr., then 2 mi. e. to 610 Magno- lia St. The restored 1812 house has eight 60-foot columns and is furnished in period. Costumed guides demonstrate the 1812 lifestyle. Allow 1 hour minimum. Daily 9-5, Apr. 1-Labor Day; Thurs.-Sun. 9-5, Feb.-Mar. 31 and day after Labor Day-Nov. 30; by appointment rest of year. Closed holidays. Admission $8; over 65 and ages 6-12, $5; ages 2-5, $4; family rate (two adults and two children) $12. DS, MC, VI. ($10). Phone (828) 555-5555 or (800) 555-5555.

RECREATIONAL ACTIVITIES

White-water Rafting

- **River Adventures,** 1 mi. s. on SR 50. Write P.O. Box 1012, Gale, NC 35244. Trips daily May-Oct. Phone (828) 555-5555.

BREVARD (F-3) pop. 6,789, elev. 2,229′

The town is a popular summer resort at the en- trance to Pisgah National Forest *(see place listing p. 165).* Brevard is in an area known as the "Land of Waterfalls," sporting more than 250 named wa- terfalls such as Laughing Falls and Courthouse Falls. Brevard Music Center offers concerts nightly last weekend in June to mid-August.

Brevard is ... portio...

RECREATIONAL ACTIVIT

White-water Rafting

- **River Adventures,** 1 mi. s. Box 1012, Gale, NC 35244. Phone (828) 555-5555.

Directions

Unless otherwise specified, directions are given from the center of town, using the following highway designations:

I=interstate highway	**US**=federal highway
SR=state route	**CR**=county road
FM=farm to market	**FR**=forest road
Mex.=Mexican highway	**Hwy.**=Canadian or Caribbean highway

Prices and Dates of Operations

Admission prices are quoted without sales tax. Children under the lowest age specified are admitted free when accompanied by an adult. Days, months and age groups written with a hyphen are inclusive.

Prices pertaining to points of interest in the United States are quoted in U.S. dollars; points of interest in Canada are quoted in Canadian dollars; prices for points of interest in Mexico and the Caribbean are quoted as an approximate U.S. dollar equivalent.

Credit Cards Accepted

AX=American Express	**JC**=Japan Credit Bureau
CB=Carte Blanche	**MC**=MasterCard
DC=Diners Club	**VI**=VISA
DS=Discover	

Bulleted Listings

Casino gambling establishments are visited by AAA personnel to ensure safety; casinos within hotels are presented for member information regardless of whether the lodging is AAA Approved.

Recreational activities of a participatory nature (requiring physical exertion or special skills) are not inspected.

Wineries are inspected by AAA Tourism Editors to ensure they meet listing requirements and offer tours.

All are presented in an abbreviated bulleted format for informational purposes.

Sample listing (partial, illustrative):

NE — BURLINGTON, NC   125

Chamber of Commerce: P.O.
on City, NC 28713; phone (828)
-057-0246.

hen 2 mi. e. to 610 Magnolia St. The
shed in period. Costumed guided tours.
s.-Sun. 9-5, Feb.-Mar. 31 and day after
lidays. Admission $8; over 65 and ages
2. DS, MC, VI. ($10). Phone (828) 555-

wy. 19W. Write
wy. 19W, Bryson City, NC 28713. Trips
y-Sept. Phone (828) 488-9366 or (800)

aft, 12 mi. s. on US 19W. Write 11044
W, Bryson City, NC 28713. Trips daily
pt. Phone (828) 488-3316 or (800)
8.

ater Ltd., 12 mi. s.w. on US 19/74W.
P.O. Box 309, Long Creek, SC 29658.
daily Apr.-Oct. Phone (828) 488-2384 or
451-9972. See color ads starting on p. 146.

INGTON (B-5) pop. 44,917, elev. 656'
ngton is a textile industry center with nu-
factory outlet shops that attract bargain
from nearby states. Clothing, leather goods,
blankets, sheets, carpets and furniture are
· products.

centerpiece of 76-acre City Park, at South
n Street and Overbrook Road, is a 1910 Dent-
enagerie Carousel. Known for their detail and
ate carvings, only 14 such carousels still exist
wide. In addition to 26 horses, the hand-
d animals include a lion, tiger, giraffe and re-
r, four pigs, rabbits, ostriches and cats. The
usel operates seasonally and hours vary; phone
) 222-5030.

ington/Alamance County Convention and
eau: 610 S. Lexington Ave., P.O.
ington, NC 27216-0519; phone
-637-3804.

ington Manufacturer's
145, houses more

TATE HISTORIC
mi. s.w. on SR
between Royal-
tia and an inexpe-
mers known as the
axes, corrupt officials
ohn Allen house, a log

50. Write P.O.
daily May-Oct.

Understanding the Lodging Listing

Official Appointment

AAA or CAA indicates our Official Appointment (OA) lodgings. These properties guarantee members the lowest public rate available at the time of booking for the dates of stay or a minimum 10% discount off the standard room rates published in TourBook guides. We highlight these properties with red and a SAVE icon to help you quickly identify them.

Diamond Rating

The number of diamonds informs you of the overall complexity of a lodging's amenities and service. Red indicates an Official Appointment lodging. An fyi in place of diamonds indicates the property has not been rated but is included as an "information only" service. A detailed description of each rating level appears on page 20.

Classification

All diamond rated lodgings are classified using three key elements: style of operation, overall concept and service level. See pages 22-23 for details on our classifications.

Online Reservations

This notation indicates AAA/CAA members can conveniently check room availability, validate room rates and make reservations for this property in a secure online environment at AAA.com.

Rates

Shown from left to right: dates the rates are effective; any meal plan included in the rates (see below); standard room rates for 1 person (1P) or 2 persons (2P); extra person charge (XP); and any applicable family plan indicator (see below).

Rates are provided to AAA by each lodging and represent the regular (rack) rate ranges for a standard room. Rates are rounded to the nearest dollar and do not include taxes. U.S., Mexican and Caribbean rates are in U.S. dollars; rates for Canadian lodgings are in Canadian dollars.

Meal Plan Indicators

AP = American Plan of three meals daily
BP = Breakfast Plan of full hot breakfast
CP = Continental Plan of pastry, juice and another beverage
ECP = Expanded Continental Plan, which offers a wider variety of breakfast items
MAP = Modified American Plan of two meals daily

See individual listing "Terms" for additional meal plans not included in the room rate.

Family Plan Indicators

F = Children stay free
D = Discounts for children
F17 = Children 17 and under stay free
D17 = Discount for children 17 or under

The number displayed will reflect the property's age policy.

Credit Cards Accepted

AX=American Express
CB=Carte Blanche
DC=Diners Club
DS=Discover

JC=Japan Credit Bureau
MC=MasterCard
VI=VISA

Spotting Symbol

Black ovals with white numbers are used to locate, or "spot," lodgings on maps we provide for larger cities.

Service Availability

Unit types, amenities and room features preceded by the word "Some" indicate the item is available on a limited basis, potentially within only one unit.

Free Special Amenities

Some OA properties offer special amenities such as Continental breakfast; expanded Continental breakfast or full breakfast; early check-in and late check-out; room upgrade or preferred room; local phone calls; or daily newspaper. This does not imply that only these properties offer these amenities.

Icons

Lodging icons represent some of the member values, services and facilities offered.

Discounts

(ASK) May offer discount

(S/D) Offers minimum 10% senior discount to members over 59

Member Services

Airport transportation

Pets allowed

Restaurant on premises

Restaurant off premises (walking distance)

(24) 24-hour room service

Cocktail lounge

Child care

Accessibility Features

(&M) Accessible features

Hearing-impaired equipment available

Roll-in showers

In-Room Amenities

Designated non-smoking rooms

(VCR) VCR

Movies

Refrigerator

Microwave

Coffee maker

No air conditioning

No TV

No cable TV

No telephones

Leisure Activities

Full-service casino

Pool

Health club on premises

Health club off premises

Recreational activities

Safety Features (see page 24)

(Mexico and Caribbean only)

(S) Sprinklers

(D) Smoke detectors

SOME UNITS printed above the icons indicates the amenity is available on a limited basis, potentially in only one unit. **FEE** appearing below an icon indicates that an extra charge applies.

Official Appointment

or indicates our Official Appointment (OA) restaurants. The OA program permits properties to display and advertise the AAA or CAA emblem. We highlight these properties in red to help you quickly identify them. The AAA or CAA Approved sign helps traveling members find restaurants that want member business.

Diamond Rating

The number of diamonds informs you of the overall complexity of food, presentation, service and ambience. Red indicates an Official Appointment restaurant. A detailed description of each diamond level appears on page 21.

Cuisine Type

The cuisine type helps you select a dining facility that caters to your individual taste. AAA currently recognizes more than 90 different cuisine types.

Menus

This notation indicates AAA/CAA members can conveniently view the restaurant's menu in a secure online environment at AAA.com.

Credit Cards Accepted

AX=American Express
CB=Carte Blanche
DC=Diners Club
DS=Discover
JC=Japan Credit Bureau
MC=MasterCard
VI=VISA

GREENSBORO, NC 62:

9-$99
9-$79
Rd), just n; exit 210 eastbound, just e on Albert Pick Rd, then just n on
s: 336/931-1496. **Facility:** 116 one-bedroom standard units. 7 sto-
on-site. **Terms:** cancellation fee imposed. **Amenities:** dual phone
Guest Services: valet and coin laundry. **Business Services:** fax

2P: $64-$104
2P: $54-$84

Phone: (236)961-1272
XP: $5   F18
XP: $5   F18

SOME UNITS

Dinner: $16-$36   **Phone:** 336/555-5555   (5)
802. 1000 Ocean Blvd 35244. **Hours:** 6 pm-10 pm. Closed:
sted. **Features:** Guests are in for a treat at this top-notch
able experience—from the wait staff's casually elegant
g to the striking grounds views from the cozy dining area.
s seasonally and regionally available, into mouthwatering
n mark on the meal. Dressy casual attire; cocktails;
, DS, MC, VI. **Classic**

DINE

Dinner: $8-$19   **Phone:** 336/273-1386
Wendover Ave. 1628 Battleground Ave 27408. **Hours:** 11 am-10
d major holidays; also 12/24 & Sun. **Features:** This eatery
rustic Italian theme with black and white table cloths and
ar dining area. Famous for its lasagna, it also features a
Cards: AX, MC, VI.

: $18-$30   **Phone:** 336/299-1003
and Patterson St. 1200 S Holden Rd 27407. **Hours:** 5 pm-10
. Closed: 11/25, 12/24, 12/25. **Reservations:** suggested;
teak, chicken, shrimp and sauteed vegetables prepared
ing cooked right at your table and enjoy huge portions
ling: on-site. **Cards:** AX, MC, VI.

$19-$30   **Phone:** 336/333-9833
Ave; in Irving Park Plaza. 1720 Battleground Ave 27408.
major holidays; also Sun. **Reservations:** suggested.
rom the wood-burning oven and reach diners as they
dipped in olive oil is one small example of the delicious
asual dress; cocktails; entertainment. **Parking:** on-site.

n just s. 616 Dolley Madison Rd 27410. **Hours:** 5 pm-10   **Phone:** 336/855-1313
: suggested. **Features:** Elegant but not stuffy, this is
te French cuisine served by extremely helpful and
res. The Bistro was a house that has been converted
Cards: AX, DC, MC, VI.

nner: $19-$30   **Phone:** 336/294-1800
on Grandover Pkwy; in Grandover Resort & Conference
10:30 pm, Sun 6-11 am, 11:30-2:30 & 6-10 pm.
ting, which reflects the ambience of a European
ed the 18th hole of the east course. Casual dress;
, DS, MC, VI.

Dinner: $19-$30   **Phone:** 336/294-9977
n. 106 S Holden Rd 27407. **Hours:** 11:30 am-10 pm,
, 12/25; also Sun. **Reservations:** suggested.
is upscale bistro, which features a private dining
o and end your meal with the creamy, mile-high
AX, DC, DS, MC, VI.

Dinner: $4-$10   **Phone:** 336/856-0070
ut. 435B Dolly Madison Rd 27410. **Hours:** 11 am-8
arian entrees, fresh fruits and vegetable juices;
n dishes. Casual dress; beer only. **Parking:**

Prices

Rates shown represent the minimum and maximum entree cost per person. Exceptions may include one-of-a-kind or special market priced items. Rates are rounded to the nearest dollar and do not include taxes. U.S., Mexican and Caribbean rates are in U.S. dollars; rates for Canadian restaurants are in Canadian dollars.

Spotting Symbol

White ovals with black numbers serve as restaurant locators and are used to locate, or "spot," restaurants on maps we provide for larger cities.

Icons

Icons provide additional information about services and facilities.

   No air-conditioning

   Accessible features

   Cocktail lounge

   Designated smoking section available

Classifications

If applicable, a restaurant may be defined as:

Classic - renowned and/or landmark restaurant in business longer than 25 years, known for unique style and ambience.

Historic - properties must meet one of the following criteria:

- Listed on the U.S. National Register of Historic Places
- Designated a U.S. National Historic Landmark
- Located in a U.S. National Register Historic District

Separate criteria designate historic properties in Canada, Mexico and the Caribbean.

Lodging Rates Guaranteed

AAA/CAA members are guaranteed they will not be charged more than the maximum regular rate printed in the TourBook guide in each rate range for a standard room. Rates may vary within the range, depending on season and room type. Listed rates are based on last standard room availability. Obtain current AAA/CAA member rates and make reservations at AAA.com.

Discounts

Member discounts will apply to rates quoted within the rate range and are applicable at the time of booking. Special rates used in advertising, as well as special short-term promotional rates lower than the lowest listed rate in the range, are not subject to additional member discounts.

Exceptions

Rates for properties operating as concessionaires for the U.S. National Park Service are not guaranteed due to governing regulations. Rates in the Mexico TourBook are not guaranteed and may fluctuate based on the exchange rate of the peso.

Lodgings may temporarily increase room rates, not recognize discounts or modify pricing policies during special events. Examples of special events range from Mardi Gras and the Kentucky Derby (including pre-Derby events) to college football games, holidays, holiday periods and state fairs. Although some special events are listed in AAA/CAA TourBook guides and on AAA.com, it is always wise to check in advance with AAA travel professionals for specific dates.

Get the Room You Reserved

When making your reservation, identify yourself as a AAA or CAA member and request written confirmation to guarantee: type of room, rate, dates of stay, and cancellation and refund policies. At registration, show your membership card.

When you find your room is not as specified, and you have written confirmation of reservations for a certain type of accommodation, you should be given the option of choosing a different room or finding one elsewhere. Should you choose to go elsewhere and a refund is refused or resisted, submit the matter to AAA/CAA within 30 days, along with complete documentation, including your reasons for refusing the room and copies of your written confirmation and any receipts or canceled checks associated with this problem.

If you are charged more than the maximum rate listed in the TourBook guide for a standard

room, question the additional charge. If management refuses to adhere to the published rate, pay for the room and submit your receipt and membership number to AAA/CAA within 30 days. Include all pertinent information: dates of stay, rate paid, itemized paid receipts, number of persons in your party and the room number you occupied, and list any extra room equipment used. A refund of the amount paid in excess of the stated maximum will be made if our investigation indicates that unjustified charging occurred.

Deposit, Refund and Cancellation Policies

Most establishments give full deposit refunds if they have been notified at least 48 hours before the normal check-in time. Listing prose will note if more than 48 hours' notice is required for cancellation. Some properties may charge a cancellation or handling fee. When this applies, "cancellation fee imposed" will appear in the listing. If you cancel too late, you have little recourse if a refund is denied.

When an establishment requires full or partial payment in advance and your trip is cut short, a refund may not be given.

When canceling a reservation, phone the lodging immediately. Make a note of the date and time you called, the cancellation number if there is one, and the name of the person who handled the cancellation. If your AAA/CAA club made your reservation, allow them to make the cancellation for you as well, so you will have proof of cancellation.

Check-in and Check-out Times

Check-in and check-out times are shown in the lodging listings, under Terms, only if they are before 10 a.m. or after 3 p.m. respectively.

Members Save With Our Partners

These National Show Your Card & Save® partners provide the listed member benefits. Admission tickets that offer greater discounts may be available for purchase at the local AAA/CAA club. A maximum of six tickets is available at the discount price at the gate. Visit AAA.com to discover all the great Show Your Card & Save® discounts in your area.

SeaWorld/Busch Gardens AAA.com/SeaWorld

- Save $5 on 1-day gate admission at SeaWorld, Busch Gardens, and Sesame Place
- Save $3 on 1-day admission at Water Country USA and Adventure Island

- Save 10% on select up-close dining. Reservations are required; visit Guest Relations for details   AAA.com/BuschGardens

Six Flags Theme Parks

- 10% OFF Brunch with Bugs
- 10% OFF merchandise purchases of $15 or more at all Six Flags operated locations.

Universal Orlando AAA.com/Universal

- Save $4 on a 2-day/2-park pass at Universal Orlando's theme parks (savings apply to tickets purchased at the gate)
- Save 10% on select dining and souvenirs at both Universal Orlando theme parks and at select Universal CityWalk Orlando restaurants (excludes Emeril's)

Universal Studios Hollywood

- Save $3 on a 1-day Universal Studios Hollywood pass (savings applies to tickets purchased at the gate)   AAA.com/Universal
- Save 10% on select dining and souvenirs at Universal Studios Hollywood and Universal CityWalk

Gray Line
AAA.com/GrayLine

- Save 10% on sightseeing tours of 1 day or less

Landry's Seafood House, The Crab House, Chart House, Muer Seafood Restaurants, Joe's Crab Shack and Aquarium and Downtown Aquarium Restaurants

- 10% discount on food and non-alcoholic beverages at all of the above restaurants.
- 10% discount on novelty merchandise at Joe's Crab Shacks and Aquarium and Downtown Aquarium Restaurants.

Hard Rock Cafe

- Save 10% on food, beverage and merchandise at all U.S. and select Canadian and international locations

Restaurant Partner Savings applies to AAA/CAA members and up to five guests.

Tanger Outlet Centers www.tangeroutlet.com

- Save up to 20% on total purchase at select merchants with AAA/CAA coupon booklet
- Member BONUS: FREE $5 gift card for each additional Tanger Outlet Center visited after first within same calendar year
- Show membership card and register at the AAA customer service desk when you visit

Lodging Partners

SAVINGS. SELECTION. SATISFACTION.—When contacting one of these lodging partners, you will be given AAA/CAA's best rates for your dates of stay. Your valid membership card must be presented at check-in. Select the chain you want and have your membership card available when making a reservation and checking in. Let the property know if you are dissatisfied with any part of your stay. If the matter cannot be resolved, you are entitled to recompense (see page 17).

Offer good at time of publication; chains and offers may change without notice. Lodging partners offering discounts to AAA/CAA members may vary in Mexico and the Caribbean.

Visit	Over 1,000 AAA/CAA Offices	Click	AAA.com	Call	866-AAA-SAVE

CHOICE HOTELS INTERNATIONAL ™

Understanding the Diamond Ratings

AAA/CAA Tourism Editors have evaluated and rated each of the 60,000 lodging and restaurant establishments in the TourBook series to ensure quality travel information for our members. All properties must meet AAA's 27 minimum requirements (for lodgings) concerning cleanliness, comfort and security - or - AAA's 12 minimum requirements (for restaurants) pertaining to cleanliness, food preparation and service.

Eligible applicants receive an unannounced evaluation by a AAA/CAA Tourism Editor that includes two distinct components:

- AAA Approval: The Tourism Editor first must determine whether the property meets the criteria required to be AAA Approved. Every establishment that meets these strict guidelines offers AAA members the assurance that, regardless of the diamond rating, it provides acceptable quality, cleanliness, service and value.
- AAA Diamond Rating: Once an establishment becomes AAA Approved, it is then assigned a rating of one to five diamonds, indicating the extensiveness of its facilities, amenities and services, from basic to moderate to luxury. These diamond ratings guide members in selecting establishments appropriately matched to their needs and expectations.

LODGINGS

1 Diamond

One diamond lodgings typically appeal to the budget-minded traveler. They provide essential, no-frills accommodations and basic comfort and hospitality.

2 Diamond

Two diamond lodgings appeal to family travelers seeking affordable yet more than the basic accommodations. Facilities, decor and amenities are modestly enhanced.

3 Diamond

Three diamond lodgings offer a distinguished style. Properties are

multi-faceted, with marked upgrades in physical attributes, amenities and guest comforts.

4 Diamond

Four diamond lodgings are refined and stylish. Physical attributes are upscale. The fundamental hallmarks at this level include an extensive array of amenities combined with a high degree of hospitality, service and attention to detail.

5 Diamond

Five diamond lodgings provide the ultimate in luxury and sophistication. Physical attributes are extraordinary in every manner. Service is meticulous, exceeding guest expectations and maintaining impeccable standards of excellence. Extensive personalized services and amenities provide first-class comfort.

fyi The lodging listings with **fyi** in place of diamonds are included as an *information only* service for members. The icon indicates that a property has not been rated for one or more of the following reasons: too new to rate, under construction, under major renovation, not evaluated, may not meet all AAA requirements.

A property not meeting all AAA requirements is included for either its member value or because it may be the only accommodation available in the area. Listing prose will give insight as to why the **fyi** designation was assigned.

4 Diamond

Four diamond restaurants provide a distinctive fine-dining experience that is typically expensive. Surroundings are highly refined with upscale enhancements throughout. Highly creative chefs use imaginative presentations to augment fresh, top-quality ingredients. A proficient service staff meets or exceeds guest expectations. A wine steward may offer menu-specific knowledge to guide selection.

5 Diamond

Five diamond restaurants are luxurious and renowned for consistently providing a world-class experience. Highly acclaimed chefs offer artistic menu selections that are imaginative and unique, using only the finest ingredients available. A maitre d' leads an expert service staff in exceeding guest expectations, attending to every detail in an effortless and unobtrusive manner.

RESTAURANTS

1 Diamond

One diamond restaurants provide simple, familiar specialty food (such as burgers, chicken, pizza or tacos) at an economical price. Often self-service, basic surroundings complement a no-nonsense approach.

2 Diamond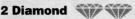

Two diamond restaurants offer a familiar, family-oriented experience. Menu selection includes home-style foods and family favorites, often cooked to order, modestly enhanced and reasonably priced. Service is accommodating yet relaxed, a perfect complement to casual surroundings.

fyi The restaurants with **fyi** in place of diamonds are included as an *information only* service for members. These listings provide additional dining choices but have not yet been evaluated.

3 Diamond

Three diamond restaurants convey an entry into fine dining and are often positioned as adult-oriented experiences. The atypical menu may feature the latest cooking trends and/or traditional cuisine. Expanded beverage offerings complement the menu. The ambience is well coordinated, comfortable and enhanced by a professional service staff.

Understanding the Lodging Classifications

To ensure that your lodging needs and preferences are met, we recommend that you consider an establishment's classification when making your travel choices. While the quality and comfort at properties with the same diamond rating should be consistent (regardless of the classification), there are differences in typical decor/theme elements, range of facilities and service levels.

Large-scale Hotel

A multistory establishment with interior room entrances. A variety of guest unit styles is offered. Public areas are spacious and include a variety of facilities such as a restaurant, fitness center, spa, business center, shops or meeting rooms.

Hotel Royal Plaza, Lake Buena Vista, FL

Small-scale Hotel

A multistory establishment typically with interior room entrances. A variety of guest unit styles is offered. Public areas are limited in size and/or the variety of facilities available.

Baymont Inn, Dallas Ft. Worth-Airport N, TX

Motel

A 1- to 3-story establishment typically with exterior room entrances facilitating convenient access to parking. The standard guest units have one bedroom with a bathroom and are typically similar in decor and design throughout. Public areas are limited in size and/or the variety of facilities available.

Best Western Deltona Inn, Deltona, FL

Country Inn

Similar in definition to a bed and breakfast but usually larger in scale, with spacious public areas offering a dining facility that serves at least breakfast and dinner.

Greenville Inn, Greenville, ME

Bed & Breakfast

Small-scale properties emphasizing a high degree of personal touches that provide guests an "at home" feeling. Guest units tend to be individually decorated. Rooms may not include some modern amenities such as televisions and telephones, and may have a shared bathroom. Usually owner-operated with a common room or parlor separate from the innkeeper's living quarters, where guests and operators can interact during evening and breakfast hours. Evening office closures are normal. A Continental or full, hot breakfast is served and is included in the room rate.

1884 Paxton House Inn, Thomasville, GA

Condominium

Vacation-oriented or extended-stay, apartment-style accommodations that are routinely available for rent through a management company. Units vary in design and decor and often contain one or more bedrooms, a living room, full kitchen and an eating area. Studio-type models combine the sleeping and living areas into one room. Typically, basic cleaning supplies, kitchen utensils and complete bed and bath linens are supplied. The guest registration area may be located off-site.

Sands of Kahana, Kahana, Maui, HI

Cabin/Cottage

Vacation-oriented, small-scale, freestanding houses or cabins. Units vary in design and decor and often contain one or more bedrooms, a living room, kitchen, dining area and bathroom. Studio-type models combine the sleeping and living areas into one room. Typically, basic cleaning supplies, kitchen utensils, and complete bed and bath linens are supplied. The guest registration area may be located off-site.

Desert Rose Inn, Bluff, UT

Ranch

Typically a working ranch with an obvious rustic, Western theme. In general, equestrian-related activities are featured, but

Lost Valley Ranch, Deckers, CO

ranches may include other animals and activities as well. A variety of guest unit styles is offered in a family-oriented atmosphere.

Vacation Home

Vacation-oriented or extended-stay, large-scale, freestanding houses that are routinely available for rent through a

ResortQuest, Hilton Head Island, SC

management company. Houses vary in design and decor and often contain two or more bedrooms, a living room, full kitchen, dining room and multiple bathrooms. Typically, basic cleaning supplies, kitchen utensils, and complete bed and bath linens are supplied. The guest registration area may be located off-site.

Lodging Subclassifications

The following are subclassifications that may appear along with the classifications listed previously to provide a more specific description of the lodging.

Casino

Extensive gaming facilities are available such as blackjack, craps, keno and slot machines. Note: This subclassification will not appear beneath its diamond rating in the listing. It will be indicated by a 🎲 icon and will be included in the row of icons immediately below the lodging listing.

Classic

Renowned and landmark properties, older than 50 years, well-known for their unique style and ambience.

Historic

These properties are typically over 75 years of age and exhibit many features of a historic nature with respect to architecture, design, furnishings, public record or acclaim. Properties must meet one of the following criteria:

- Maintained the integrity of the historical aspect
- Listed on the U.S. National Register of Historic Places
- Designated a U.S. National Historic Landmark
- Located in a U.S. National Register Historic District

Separate criteria designate historic properties in Canada, Mexico and the Caribbean.

Vacation Rental

Typically houses, condos, cottages or cabins; these properties are a "home away from home" offering more room and greater value for the money and generally provide the conveniences of home, such as full kitchens and washers/dryers. They are located in resort or popular destination areas within close proximity to major points of interest, attractions, or recreation areas. These properties may require a pre-arranged reservation and check-in at an off-site location. Housekeeping services may be limited or not included.

Resort

Recreation-oriented, geared to vacation travelers seeking a specific destination experience. Travel packages, meal plans, themed entertainment, and social and recreational programs are typically available. Recreational facilities are extensive and may include spa treatments, golf, tennis, skiing, fishing, water sports, etc. Larger resorts may offer a variety of guest accommodations.

Guest Safety

Room Security

In order to be approved for listing in AAA/CAA TourBook guides for the United States and Canada, accommodations must have dead-bolt locks on all guest room entry doors and connecting room doors.

If the area outside the guest room door is not visible from inside the room through a window or door panel, viewports must be installed on all guest room entry doors. Bed and breakfast properties and country inns are not required to have viewports. Ground floor and easily accessible sliding doors must be equipped with some type of secondary security locks.

Even with those approval requirements, AAA cannot guarantee guest safety. Tourism Editors view a percentage of rooms at each property since it is not feasible to evaluate every room in every lodging establishment. Therefore, AAA cannot guarantee that there are working locks on all doors and windows in all guest rooms.

Fire Safety

Because of the highly specialized skills needed to conduct professional fire safety inspections, AAA/CAA Tourism Editors cannot assess fire safety.

Properties must meet all federal, state and local fire codes. Each guest unit in all U.S. and Canadian lodging properties must be equipped with an operational, single-station smoke detector. A AAA/CAA Tourism Editor has evaluated a sampling of the rooms to verify this equipment is in place.

Mexico and the Caribbean

Requirements for some features, such as door locks and smoke detectors/sprinkler systems, differ in Mexico and the Caribbean. If a property met AAA's security requirements at the time of the evaluation, the phrase "Meets AAA guest room security requirements" appears in the listing.

Service Animals

The Americans with Disabilities Act (ADA) prohibits U.S. businesses that serve the public from discriminating against persons with disabilities. Some businesses have mistakenly denied access to persons who use service animals. Businesses must permit entry to guests and their service animals, as well as allow service animals to accompany guests to all public areas of a property.

A property is permitted to ask whether the animal is a service animal or a pet, and whether the guest has a disability. The property may not, however, ask questions about the nature of the disability, the service provided by the animal or require proof of a disability or certification that the animal is a service animal. These regulations may not apply in Canada, Mexico or the Caribbean.

No fees or deposits, even those normally charged for pets, may be charged for service animals. Service animals fulfill a critical need for their owners—they are not pets.

Frank Frand with his seeing eye dog, Cardinal.
Todd Masinter © 2006

Savings for all Seasons

Hertz rents Fords and other fine cars. ® REG. U.S. PAT. OFF © HERTZ SYSTEM INC., 1999/2006-99.

No matter the season, Hertz offers CAA members exclusive discounts and benefits.

Operating in 150 countries at over 8,100 locations, Hertz makes traveling more convenient and efficient wherever and whenever you go. Hertz offers CAA members discounts up to 20% on car rentals worldwide.

To receive your exclusive CAA member discounts and benefits, mention your CAA membership card at time of reservation and present it at time of rental. **In addition**, to receive a free one car class upgrade on daily, weekly or weekend rental in the United States and Canada, mention PC# 969194 and in Puerto Rico mention PC# 969183 at the time of reservation. Offer available through 12/15/07.

For reservations and program details, call your CAA Travel centre or the Hertz/CAA Desk at **1-800-263-0600**; **Toronto (416) 620-9620.**

A reflection of how you travel today.

How you take a vacation hasn't changed—your travel money choices have.

Today there are many ways to take your vacation money with you, and the prepaid CAA Visa TravelMoney® card is the most secure, convenient way to carry your funds. Simply preload your card with your travel funds before you leave, and you are ready to use your card for payment at any Visa® debit merchant or withdraw local currency at any Visa® Interlink/PLUS ATM around the world. Vacation with the Visa TravelMoney card—it is safer than cash.

The CAA Visa TravelMoney Card:

- Accepted at millions of Visa® debit merchants and hundreds of thousands of Visa® Interlink/PLUS ATMs worldwide
- More secure because it is not linked to your other cards or accounts
- Reloadable to help you track spending
- Refund/Replacement service if card is lost or stolen.

CAA Visa TravelMoney card...safer than cash.

*Terms and conditions apply, see detailed terms and conditions provided with your card fulfillment kit. Information correct at time of printing, subject to change.

 Visit Participating CAA offices
Call 866-339-3378

Other Travel Money products include:

Foreign Currency

Travelers Cheques

New Brunswick

Kouchibouguac National Park
Warm sand beaches, dunes, salt marshes, meadows and forests

A Whale of a Time
More types of whales breed and feed here than anywhere else

Joie de Vivre
Acadian Historical Village recalls French heritage and tenacity

Fundy National Park
Rugged shoreline, steep cliffs and rocky coves surround the Bay of Fundy

Mount Carleton
The last tier of the Appalachian Mountain Range

Riverside-Albert
© Walter Bibikow
Danita Delimont Agency

a timeless land

Hopewell Rocks Ocean Tidal Exploration Site, Hopewell Cape / Canadian Tourism Commission

Fed up with the appointments, schedules, deadlines and frenetic pace of modern life? Then head for New Brunswick, where you can forget your wristwatch and measure time in a more natural, leisurely fashion.

Spawned by lunar gravity and synchronized to the moon's orbit of Earth, massive tides ebb and flow like clockwork in the Bay of Fundy,

sculpting islands into streamlined works of art. At low tide, visit Fundy National Park to explore tidal pools along the bay's silty bottom, then retreat to higher ground to observe the sea slowly pour back in.

Calendars are equally superfluous in this land of dramatic seasonal change. You'll know spring has sprung when delicious fiddleheads thrust their

succulent tendrils from moist riverbank soil. In late summer, look for rare right whales courting offshore.

Autumn's arrival is heralded by a crazy quilt of color in coastal peat bogs, where green is juxtaposed against patches of crimson, orange and gold. The top of Miscou Island's historic lighthouse offers a particularly good view of this spectacle. Winter snowfalls cloak the province's hilly northern quarter in white, much to the delight of skiers.

The only time you may need to keep here is while tapping your toes to Acadian folk music. So leave your day planner at home, and let New Brunswick's natural rhythms count the hours for you.

With the Gulf of St. Lawrence and Fundy and Chaleur bays lapping its shores on three sides, New Brunswick has literally been shaped by the sea. That rich heritage is still evident today: Lighthouses send protective beams from harborside hilltops; 19th-century clapboard houses with widow's walks stand as sentinels from a bygone era; sandy beaches invite leisurely strolls along the surf; and the interior of Saint John's historic farmers market resembles an inverted ship's hull.

The Phenomenal Fundy

The Bay of Fundy tides, said to be the world's highest, have been known to reach 14 metres (48 ft.), the height of a four-story building. An interesting tale explains this anomaly. According to a Mi'kmaq legend, a giant whale, angered by the god Glooscap, slammed its powerful tail into the water, causing the tremendous ebb and flow. Although the bay's tidal fluctuations are attributable to science rather than lore, they do create some pretty amazing phenomena.

Take the Hopewell Rocks, near the mouth of the Petitcodiac River at Hopewell Cape. These whimsical sandstone sculptures, carved over centuries by the force of the tides, are topped by fir and spruce outcroppings. At low tide the columns resemble flowerpots and can be explored by merely walking along the beach. At high tide, however, when only the upper portions are visible, they appear to be tree-topped islands and can be viewed from lookout points along nature trails or, for the more adventurous, by kayak.

The old Loyalist seaport of Saint John is the site of another astounding event, the Reversing Falls. At the narrow, rocky gorge where the Saint John River's rapids meet the Bay of Fundy, the bay's immense tides actually overpower the river twice each day, causing the rapids to flow backward.

And caves—created by the enormous pressure of the Fundy tides—can be reached from crescent-shaped beaches near St. Martins. Once a bustling 1800s shipbuilding center, this seaside fishing village is now an access point for the Fundy Trail, which includes a low-speed roadway as well as walking and bicycling trails.

A Whale of a Place

Whales absolutely love this place—about 15 species flock to the waters near Grand Manan and Deer islands and just off the coast of St. Andrews to feed on the watery buffet

Jacques Cartier explores the coast of New Brunswick.
1534

Acadians who choose neutrality are deported; many find refuge in the interior of New Brunswick.
1755

The first French settlement in North America is founded on St. Croix Island.
1604

© Bettmann/Corbis

1713
France cedes Acadia to Great Britain in the Treaty of Utrecht.

1783
Populated by loyalists fleeing the American Revolution, St. John becomes the first incorporated city in Canada.

New Brunswick Historical Timeline

churned up by the bay's tidal currents. If you can arrange your visit between July and September, by all means schedule a whale-watching excursion for an up-close glimpse of these magnificent mammals breaching and frolicking. Remember to bring a jacket—sea breezes can be quite chilly.

Travel up the coast to Shediac, not for whales, but for lobsters: The town calls itself the lobster capital of the world. Join in the celebration during early July at the Lobster Festival and help devour the tons of succulent crustaceans served up to festival attendees.

Living by the Sea

You can get a true feel for the Acadian way of life near the coastal town of Caraquet, the 18th-century Capital de l'Acadie, where the annual Blessing of the Fleet is a treasured link to the past. Caught in a power struggle between France and Great Britain, French-speaking Acadians unwilling to swear allegiance to the British crown were deported in 1755; the event was immortalized by Henry Wadsworth Longfellow's narrative poem "Evangeline." Many of the exiles returned, however, reestablishing their culture and *joie de vivre*.

Caraquet's Acadian Historical Village preserves the traditions and the humble everyday existence of those people. Restored buildings—including a general store, print shop, gristmill, tavern and chapel—relocated from throughout the province comprise the settlement, where transportation is by ox-drawn cart, and homespun interpreters are busily engaged in daily chores.

For generations Acadians have relied on the Gulf of St. Lawrence's waters for their livelihood. That bond is illustrated at the New Brunswick Aquarium and Marine Centre, overlooking the Baie des Chaleurs in Shippagan, where the region's nautical ties can be examined through exhibits about ships and fishermen, and aquariums teeming with marine life.

Like a breath of fresh sea air, this largest of the Maritime Provinces invigorates you. For a true taste of New Brunswick visit the Saint John City Market. There you'll find just-caught salmon, lobster and scallops; fresh produce and baked goods; and the local delicacy known as dulse, sun-dried seaweed gathered from rocks along the Bay of Fundy. You'll have a whale of a good time.

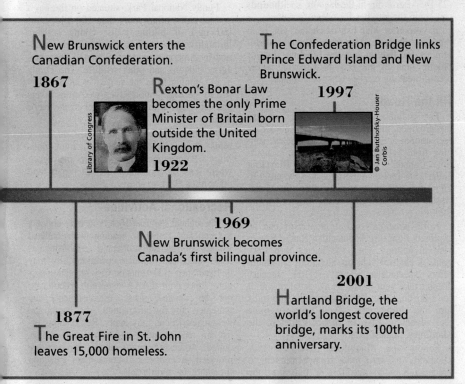

New Brunswick enters the Canadian Confederation.

1867

Rexton's Bonar Law becomes the only Prime Minister of Britain born outside the United Kingdom.

1922

Library of Congress

The Confederation Bridge links Prince Edward Island and New Brunswick.

1997

© Jan Butchofsky-Houser Corbis

1969

New Brunswick becomes Canada's first bilingual province.

2001

Hartland Bridge, the world's longest covered bridge, marks its 100th anniversary.

1877

The Great Fire in St. John leaves 15,000 homeless.

Recreation

Water, water, everywhere—Canada's largest Maritime Province has 2,400 kilometres (1,500 mi.) of coastline, making aquatic adventure a prime diversion. Surrounded on three sides by water, New Brunswick's shores are lapped by the Bay of Fundy on the south, the Gulf of St. Lawrence on the northeast and the Bay of Chaleur on the north.

Sea kayaking past the Flower Pot Rocks near the Petitcodiac River's mouth is thrilling, and so is a ride on the world's highest tides in the Bay of Fundy. Paddle past grey seals in Kouchibouguac Bay, or don your flippers and **scuba dive** the waters off Deer Island.

One of the best ways to experience the Reversing Falls at Saint John is to hop aboard a jet boat; various outfitters provide tours. Here, the Bay of Fundy's forceful tides push against the Saint John River's current, causing the river to run backwards and resulting in a wild ride.

Sail away on scenic Passamaquoddy Bay, or head inland and cruise the waters of Mactaquac Lake and the Saint John River. Make a splash at the lagoon in Kouchibouguac National Park, where the **swimming** is refreshing in summer waters that are 24 degrees Celsius (75 F). After a dip in the lagoon, **rockhounds** can comb the beaches for ocean treasures.

If salmon is your fish of choice, you're in the right place; the Miramichi River is world-famous for **fishing** out the big one. Jig for bluefin tuna in the Bay of Chaleur, where record-breaking catches have been made.

Hit the Road

For landlubbers, five scenic drives traverse the province, all offering access to numerous recreational activities. The River Valley, running from St-Jacques to Saint John, is maritime Canada's most picturesque. **Bicycling** enthusiasts cruise in Edmundston, where 130 kilometres (81 mi.) of trails line the Madawaska River in Petit Témis Interprovincial Park.

North America's oldest mountains can be explored along the Appalachian Range Route; visit in autumn when the leaves turn fiery gold. A chairlift ride up Sugarloaf Mountain offers spectacular views; if the scenery doesn't take your breath away, pedal downhill for a thrilling ride. When snow falls, the trails turn into **skiing** runs. If you're up for some real adventure, hike to Mount Carleton, the Maritimes' highest peak.

Follow the Miramichi River, a 182-kilometre (113-mi.) route from Miramichi to Fredericton. Stop and toss a line into the salmon-filled waters, stroll past waterfalls and over a suspension footbridge, or while away the hours **canoeing** down a stretch of this pristine waterway.

For a coastal adventure tour the Fundy Coastal Drive from St. Stephen to Aulac, where recreational opportunities prevail along the rugged coastline. **Spelunkers** can get lost in the sandstone caves of St. Martins, while **rock climbers** can rappel cliffs overlooking the bay.

If you'd like to explore more of New Brunswick's coast, travel the Acadian Coastal Drive from Aulac to Campbellton. **Camping** next to the ocean in Murray Corner is fun, or you can explore the dunes along boardwalks in Kouchibouguac National Park.

Bountiful Bay

The Bay of Fundy is a **wildlife viewing** paradise. One of the marine wonders of the world, the bay's powerful tides churn up nutrient-rich waters, attracting varied sea life. Late August to early September is the best time to view the endangered right whale breaching in the tidal waters. Up to 15 other species abound here too.

Fundy National Park, situated on the bay's coastal cliffs, offers more than 100 kilometres (60 mi.) of **hiking** trails, taking walkers through wooded valleys and highlands inhabited by American martens, whitetail deer, peregrine falcons and other wildlife. The Fundy Trail, running from the sea caves of St. Martins to the Big Salmon River, welcomes hikers and bicyclists who want to revel in the bay's beauty.

Autumn is the best time to see migrating birds dining in the bay's rich mud flats. Mary's Point attracts bird watchers in August, when tens of thousands of sandpipers and other birds flock to shore.

Recreational Activities

Throughout the TourBook, you may notice a Recreational Activities heading with bulleted listings of recreation-oriented establishments listed underneath. Similar operations also may be mentioned in Destination City recreation sections. Since normal AAA inspection criteria cannot be applied, these establishments are presented only for information. Age, height and weight restrictions may apply. Reservations often are recommended and sometimes are required. Addresses and/or phone numbers are provided so visitors can contact the attraction for additional information.

Fast Facts

POPULATION: 729,498.

AREA: 72,908 sq km (28,150 sq mi); ranks 11th.

CAPITAL: Fredericton.

HIGHEST POINT: 820 m/2,690 ft., Mount Carleton.

LOWEST POINT: Sea level, Atlantic Ocean.

TIME ZONE(S): Atlantic. DST.

MINIMUM AGE FOR UNRESTRICTED DRIVER'S LICENSE: 16 years and 4 months.

SEAT BELT/CHILD RESTRAINT LAWS: Seat belts required for driver and all passengers 16 and older. Children ages 5-15 and over 18 kg (40 lbs.) are required to be in a seat belt. Child restraints required for children under age 5 and under 18 kg.

HELMETS FOR MOTORCYCLISTS: Required for all riders.

RADAR DETECTORS: Not permitted.

FIREARMS LAWS: By federal law, all nonresidents entering Canada with a firearm must declare their weapon in writing and pay a fee of $25 (Canadian). Contact the Canadian Firearms Centre at (800) 731-4000 to receive a declaration form or for additional information.

HOLIDAYS: Jan. 1; Good Friday; Easter; Easter Monday; Victoria Day, May 24 or closest prior Mon.; Canada Day, July 1; New Brunswick Day, Aug. (1st Mon.); Labour Day, Sept. (1st Mon.); Thanksgiving, Oct. (2nd Mon.); Remembrance Day, Nov. 11; Christmas, Dec. 25; Boxing Day, Dec. 26.

TAXES: New Brunswick's harmonized sales tax is 14 percent—8 percent provincial tax and 6 percent federal goods and services tax; it is applied to most goods and services.

INFORMATION CENTERS: Provincial welcome centers that provide details about attractions, accommodations, historic sites, parks, Outdoor Network Properties (formerly known as provincial parks), Day Adventure Centres and events are at Aulac, Campbellton, Cape Jourimain in Bayfield, Prince William, St-Jacques, St. Stephen and Woodstock. All centers are open daily May 15 through the second Monday in October. For further information phone (800) 561-0123.

FURTHER INFORMATION FOR VISITORS:

Department of Tourism and Parks
P.O. Box 6000
Fredericton, NB, Canada E3B 5H1
(800) 561-0123

FISHING AND HUNTING REGULATIONS:

Department of Natural Resources
Fish and Wildlife Branch
P.O. Box 6000
Fredericton, NB, Canada E3B 5H1
(506) 453-2440

INTERPROVINCE FERRY INFORMATION:

Bay Ferries Terminals
600 Lancaster St.
Saint John, NB, Canada E2M 7Y6
(506) 649-7777
(888) 249-7245

ALCOHOL CONSUMPTION: Legal age 19.

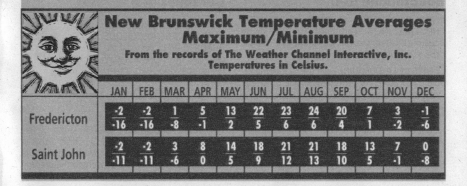

New Brunswick Temperature Averages Maximum/Minimum

From the records of The Weather Channel Interactive, Inc.
Temperatures in Celsius.

	JAN	FEB	MAR	APR	MAY	JUN	JUL	AUG	SEP	OCT	NOV	DEC
Fredericton	-2	-2	1	5	13	22	23	24	20	7	3	-1
	-16	-16	-8	-1	2	5	6	6	4	1	-2	-6
Saint John	-2	-2	3	8	14	18	21	21	18	13	7	0
	-11	-11	-6	0	5	9	12	13	10	5	-1	-8

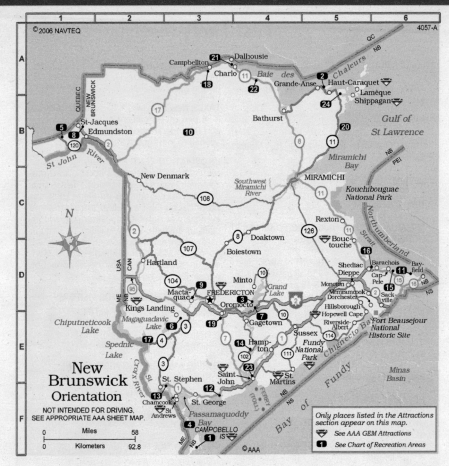

© 2006 NAVTEQ

4057-A

New Brunswick Orientation

NOT INTENDED FOR DRIVING.
SEE APPROPRIATE AAA SHEET MAP.

| Miles | 58 |
| Kilometers | 92.8 |

Only places listed in the Attractions section appear on this map.

See AAA GEM Attractions

See Chart of Recreation Areas

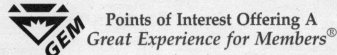

Points of Interest Offering A
Great Experience for Members®

Bouctouche (D-5)

IRVING ECO-CENTRE, "LA DUNE DE BOUCTOU-CHE"—This white sand dune stretches across Bouctouche Bay, sheltering aquatic and marine flora and fauna. See p. 37.

LE PAYS DE LA SAGOUINE—On this island, the Acadian characters of Antonine Maillet's famous story come to life. See p. 38.

Campobello Island (F-3)

ROOSEVELT CAMPOBELLO INTERNATIONAL PARK—Visit the 34-room summer home of Franklin D. Roosevelt and see the coves, cliffs and beaches where he and his family once roamed. See p. 38.

Caraquet (A-5)

ACADIAN HISTORICAL VILLAGE (VILLAGE HISTORIQUE ACADIEN)—Discover what life was like in an 18th-century French-speaking settlement. See p. 39.

Fredericton (D-3)

THE BEAVERBROOK ART GALLERY—The gallery features works by British and Canadian artists as well as furniture, paintings, porcelain and sculpture dating from the 14th century to the present. See p. 42.

Fundy National Park of Canada (E-5)

FUNDY NATIONAL PARK OF CANADA—Several ecosystems coexist in this park marked by beaches, seaside cliffs, lakes, waterfalls and wildflower meadows; hiking, cross-country skiing and snowshoeing are popular diversions. See p. 43.

Hopewell Cape (E-5)

HOPEWELL ROCKS OCEAN TIDAL EXPLORATION SITE—Formed by ocean tides, the Flower Pot Rocks are featured; visitors may walk on the ocean's floor at low tide. See p. 46.

Kings Landing (E-3)

KINGS LANDING HISTORICAL SETTLEMENT—This detailed re-creation of a 19th-century Loyalist village even includes oxen pulling hay rigs. See p. 46.

St. Andrews (F-3)

KINGSBRAE GARDEN—This 11-hectare (27-acre) horticultural garden features more than 50,000 flowers, shrubs and trees as well as a labyrinth and woodland trail. See p. 52.

Saint John (E-4)

NEW BRUNSWICK MUSEUM—Explore the entire province without ever leaving town in one of the oldest museums in Canada. See p. 55.

St. Martins (E-4)

FUNDY TRAIL—Drive, pedal or hike along the Bay of Fundy, where the views are spectacular. See p. 56.

Shippagan (A-5)

NEW BRUNSWICK AQUARIUM AND MARINE CENTRE—Learn how the sea has affected the inhabitants of New Brunswick since the 16th century. See p. 57.

RECREATION AREAS	MAP LOCATION	CAMPING	PICNICKING	HIKING TRAILS	BOATING	BOAT RAMP	BOAT RENTAL	FISHING	SWIMMING	PETS ON LEASH	BICYCLE TRAILS	WINTER SPORTS	VISITOR CENTER	LODGE/CABINS	FOOD SERVICE
NATIONAL PARKS *(See place listings)*															
Fundy (E-5) 206 square kilometres on Hwy. 114, 130 km s.w. of Moncton. Nonmotorized boats only.		•	•	•	•		•	•	•	•	•	•	•	•	•
Kouchibouguac (C-5) 238 square kilometres on Rte. 134, n. of Moncton.		•	•	•	•		•	•	•	•	•		•		•
PROVINCIAL															
Anchorage (F-3) 181 hectares on Grand Manan Island, off Hwy. 776 s.w. of Grand Harbour.	❶	•	•	•	•			•	•	•			•		
Caraquet (A-5) 3 hectares 10 km w. of Caraquet on Hwy. 11.	❷	•	•					•	•						
Grand Lake (D-4) 54 hectares 31 km e. of Fredericton on Hwy. 2 and 23 km n. on Hwy. 690, on n. shore of Grand Lake.	❸	•	•		•	•		•	•	•					•
Herring Cove (F-3) 423 hectares on Campobello Island. Golf (nine holes), sea kayaking, whale watching; interpretive programs, playground.	❹	•	•	•	•			•	•				•		•
Lac Baker (B-1) 5 hectares 3.25 km n.w. of Lac Baker on Hwy. 120. Tennis.	❺	•		•				•	•						
Lake George (E-3) 10 hectares 9.75 km n.w. of Harvey Station via hwys. 3 and 636.	❻		•						•						
Lakeside (E-4) 50 hectares 17.75 km e. of Jemseq.	❼	•	•		•	•		•	•						
Les Jardins de la République (B-1) 44 hectares 8 km n. of Edmundston on Rt. 2. Tennis; museum.	❽	•	•	•	•			•	•	•					•
Mactaquac (D-3) 550 hectares 24.5 km w. of Fredericton on Hwy. 105. Cross-country skiing, golf, snowmobiling.	❾	•	•	•	•	•		•	•			•	•		
Mount Carleton (B-3) 17,000 hectares 85 km n.w. of Plaster Rock on Hwy. 385, then on gravel road. Wilderness.	❿	•	•	•	•			•	•	•		•			

RECREATION AREAS

RECREATION AREAS	MAP LOCATION	CAMPING	PICNICKING	HIKING TRAILS	BOATING	BOAT RAMP	BOAT RENTAL	FISHING	SWIMMING	PETS ON LEASH	BICYCLE TRAILS	WINTER SPORTS	VISITOR CENTER	LODGE/CABINS	FOOD SERVICE
Murray Beach (D-6) 26 hectares 16 km n.w. of Cape Tormentine on Hwy. 955.	11	•	•	•	•	•			•	•					
New River Beach (F-3) 8 hectares e. of Pennfield off Hwy. 1. Interpretive programs.	12	•	•	•	•	•		•	•	•			•		•
Oak Bay (F-2) 11 hectares 8 km n.e. of St. Stephen on Hwy. 1.	13	•	•	•				•	•	•			•		
Oak Point (E-4) 10 hectares 8 km w. of Evandale off Hwy. 102.	14	•	•					•	•	•			•		
Parc de L'Aboiteau (D-6) 18 hectares w. of Cap-Pelé on Rte. 15.	15								•	•	•		•		•
Parlee Beach (D-5) 30 hectares 1.5 km e. of Shediac off Hwy. 15.	16	•	•		•				•	•			•		•
Spednic Lake (E-2) 347 hectares 20 km w. of McAdam off Hwy. 650. Canoeing.	17	•	•	•	•	•		•	•	•					
Sugarloaf (A-3) 1,142 hectares s.w. of Campbellton on Hwy. 11. Alpine slide, cross-country and downhill skiing, ice skating, snowmobiling, tennis.	18	•	•	•			•		•	•	•	•	•	•	•
Sunbury-Oromocto (E-3) 7 hectares 30 km s.e. of Fredericton off Hwy. 2.	19	•	•	•	•	•		•	•	•	•				
Val Comeau (B-5) 24 hectares 9.75 km s. of Tracadie-Sheila off Hwy. 11.	20	•	•						•	•					
OTHER															
Chaleur (A-3) 135 hectares 5 km e. of Dalhousie on Hwy. 11. Windsurfing.	21	•	•						•	•					
Jacquet River (A-4) 2 hectares 51.5 km n. of Bathurst on Hwy. 11.	22	•	•		•				•	•					
Rockwood Park (E-4) 870 hectares 2 km n. of Saint John. Golf. *(See Saint John p. 56)*	23	•	•					•	•	•	•	•	•		
Shippagan (B-5) 20 hectares 3.25 km w. of Shippagan off Hwy. 113.	24	•	•					•	•	•					

Points of Interest

BARACHOIS (D-6) pop. 700

Barachois comes from an old French word for "sandbar," appearing dozens of times in Canadian place names. In the Atlantic Provinces, the word has come to mean a salt pond cut off from a larger body of water.

HISTORIC CHURCH OF ST. HENRI-DE-BARACHOIS is at 1350 Rte. 133. Built in 1824, the structure is believed to be the oldest surviving Acadian wooden church in North America. Restored and converted into a museum and cultural center, it houses displays depicting the region's Acadian background. Various cultural activities are presented. Guided 15-minute tours are given upon request Mon.-Fri. 10-6, late June-Aug. 31. Donations. Phone (506) 532-2976 to verify schedule.

BATHURST (B-4) pop. 12,924

Explorer Jacques Cartier reached the Bathurst area and established trade with the local Mi'kmaq Indians in 1534. Nicholas Denys, governor of the Acadian coast and author of one of the first local histories, lived in Bathurst a century later; his memorial is downtown. The city, established in 1826, was named for the then colonial secretary of Great Britain, the Earl of Bathurst.

Now a tourist center on Bathurst Harbour at the mouth of Nepisiguit River, Bathurst also is a city of heavy industries, especially mining and papermaking.

Nearby Youghall Beach Park offers warm-water swimming in the Chaleur and Nepisiguit bays. Boating and fishing are popular pastimes.

Bathurst Parks, Recreation and Tourism Department: 850 St. Anne St., Bathurst, NB, Canada E2A 6X2; phone (506) 548-0410.

ROYAL CANADIAN LEGION WAR MUSEUM is at 575 St. Peter Ave. This museum of the Royal Canadian Legion Branch 18 displays artifacts of the North Shore Regiment and weapons and uniforms from the World Wars. Other exhibits depict the Boer, Korean and Persian Gulf wars. A replica of the Victoria Cross Medal stands in the museum. Daily 10-5, July-Aug.; by appointment rest of year. Donations. Phone (506) 546-3135.

BAYFIELD (D-6) pop. 56

On the eastern tip of the province, Bayfield was the staging area for construction of the Confederation Bridge, built in 1997 to link Borden-Carleton, Prince Edward Island, with Cape Jourimain, New Brunswick, and the mainland. Construction cost $1 billion. The 12.9-kilometre (8-mi.) span is the world's longest over ice-covered waters. A $39.50 toll is charged per private vehicle.

It is believed that centuries before the bridge was built, Mi'kmaq Indians launched their canoes from Cape Jourimain to cross the Northumberland Strait. In the 19th century, winter crossings were made with iceboats equipped with runners; passengers had to get out and push the boats over frozen stretches.

Cape Jourimain Provincial Visitor Information Centre: 5039 Hwy. 16, P.O. Box 1006, Bayfield, NB, Canada E4M 3Z2; phone (506) 538-2133.

CAPE JOURIMAIN NATURE CENTRE is off Hwy. 16 exit 51. This 675-hectare (1,668-acre) wildlife area is a major stop-over for migratory birds along the Atlantic flyway. More than 200 species visit or live in the area. The center at the mainland end of the Confederation Bridge includes an exhibit hall, a four-story observation tower, a lighthouse and 13 kilometres (8 mi.) of nature trails.

Food is available. Allow 1 hour minimum. Daily 9-5, mid-May to mid-Oct. (with extended hours in summer). Admission $6; over 60, $5; students with ID $4; under 5 free; family rate $12.50. Phone (506) 538-2220 or (866) 538-2220.

BOIESTOWN (D-3) pop. 300

Founded at the junction of the Miramichi and Taxis rivers, Boiestown was named for an American settler from New Hampshire. Thomas Boies ran a lumber mill, one of a half dozen that opened here to take advantage of abundant trees and water power. Boiestown is considered the geographical center of the province.

SAVE **CENTRAL NEW BRUNSWICK WOODMEN'S MUSEUM** is 1.6 km (1 mi.) e. on Hwy. 8. Frontier life in early New Brunswick is depicted at this 6-hectare (15-acre) exhibition area, which chronicles the woods industry and local history with tools, documents, photographs, a restored trapper's cabin and a man-made lake. Self-guiding trails also are available. Allow 1 hour minimum. Daily 9:30-5, mid-May to mid-Oct. Admission $5; over 55, $4; ages 6-16, $2.50; family rate $12. VI. Phone (506) 369-7214.

BOUCTOUCHE (D-5) pop. 2,426

François and Charlitte LeBlanc arrived in Bouctouche in 1785, soon followed by other deported Acadian settlers. The area was called "Chebooktoosk," or "big little harbor" by the Mi'kmaq Indians. Bouctouche was the birthplace of industrialist K.C. Irving, the founding father of one of Canada's biggest conglomerates.

GEM **IRVING ECO-CENTRE, "LA DUNE DE BOUCTOUCHE"** is 10 km (6 mi.) n. on Hwy. 475. One of the few remaining sand dunes on the northeast coast of North America is preserved here. The dune extends 12 kilometres (7.5

mi.) across Bouctouche Bay, providing a vital marine habitat. A 2-kilometre (1.2 mi.) boardwalk enables visitors to observe the dune's flora and fauna; they may also hike a forested nature trail from the dune to the town of Bouctouche. An interpretive center contains interactive displays for all ages.

Ongoing scientific studies are conducted at the site and bilingual interpreters are available. Picnicking is permitted. Dogs are not allowed on the grounds; kennel services are available. Allow 2 hours minimum. Daily 10-8, late June-early Sept.; Mon.-Thurs. noon-5, Fri. noon-6, Sat.-Sun. 10-6, mid-May to late June and early Sept.-late Oct. Free. Phone (506) 743-2600.

KENT MUSEUM is 2.5 km (1.5 mi.) n.e. of Hwy. 11 on Hwy. 475 at 150 du Couvent Rd. This museum occupies a restored three-story Victorian building that served as a convent and educational center 1880-1969. The Gothic Revival chapel and a quilt exhibition are of interest. Exhibits depict Kent's Acadian culture and display the works of local artists. Guided tours Mon.-Sat. 9-5:30, Sun. noon-6, late June-Labour Day; by appointment rest of year. Admission $3; over 64, $2; students with ID $1; under 6 free. Phone (506) 743-5005.

LE PAYS DE LA SAGOUINE is off Hwy. 11 exit 32A to 57 Acadie St. This island recreates the Acadian setting and French-speaking characters of Antonine Maillet's story, "Le Pays de la Sagouine." Live performances, children's activities and Acadian food and music are offered throughout the day. Actress Viola Léger has played the part of la Sagouine, the storytelling scrubwoman, for more than 30 years.

All plays and performances on the island are in French; guided tours in English are available. Allow 2 hours minimum. Daily 9:30-5:30, mid-June to mid-Sept. Admission $15; over 65, $14; students with ID $10; ages 5-16, $9. Evening show $35; under 12, $17. MC, VI. Phone (506) 743-1400 or (800) 561-9188.

CAMPBELLTON (A-3) pop. 7,798

Campbellton began as a British land grant along the Restigouche River; the first settlers were Scottish. Its early economy focused on a lucrative salmon industry, followed by farming and lumbering eras. In the early 1900s Campbellton became an important railroad center.

Restigouche Theatre, one of New Brunswick's finest, is used for many of Campbellton's cultural activities. Residents and visitors enjoy the ski trails and other recreational facilities of nearby Sugarloaf Provincial Park (see Recreation Chart and the AAA/CAA Eastern Canada CampBook), which features 304-metre (997-ft.) Sugarloaf Mountain. Many hunters and anglers pursuing the riches of the Restigouche and Upsalquitch rivers are outfitted in Campbellton.

Campbellton Provincial Visitor Information Centre: 56 Salmon Blvd., Campbellton, NB, Canada E3N 3H4; phone (506) 789-2376.

GALERIE RESTIGOUCHE is at 39 Andrew St. This national exhibition center features local, regional, national and international exhibits dealing with art, history, science and nature. A permanent display chronicles the Mi'kmaq, French, Acadian and Scottish heritage of the Restigouche region. Mon.-Sat. 9-5, mid-June to early Sept. Guided tour $3. Gallery admission $2. Phone (506) 753-5750.

CAMPOBELLO ISLAND (F-3) pop. 1,300

For more than a century, 1767-1881, Campobello Island belonged to the Owen family. The 1835 home of Adm. William F. Owen, who so loved the sea that he reputedly built a quarterdeck on which to pace, is preserved at Deer Point. A picturesque lighthouse stands at East Quoddy Head; whales and porpoises can be seen swimming nearby.

James Roosevelt went to Campobello in 1883 when his son Franklin was 1 year old. From then until 1921, Franklin D. Roosevelt spent most of his summers on the island. A small collection of items relating to the Roosevelt family is among the displays at Campobello Public Library and Museum, in the village of Welshpool; phone (506) 752-7082.

Campobello Chamber of Commerce: 916 Hwy. 774, Welshpool, Campobello Island, NB, Canada E5E 1B1; phone (506) 752-2233.

ROOSEVELT CAMPOBELLO INTERNATIONAL PARK is linked to the mainland by the Franklin D. Roosevelt Memorial Bridge at Lubec, Maine, and also can be reached by ferry from Deer Island in July and August. The centerpiece of the 1,134-hectare (2,741-acre) memorial is a 34-room "cottage" occupied 1905-21 by the soon-to-be president. The house contains furniture, photographs, toys and other items belonging to the Roosevelt family.

A 15-minute videotape is presented at the visitor center. The surrounding area features scenic drives and walking trails along coves, bogs, beaches and cliffs. Picnicking is permitted. Self-guiding tours of the cottage are available daily 10-6, Sat. after Victoria Day-second Mon. in Oct. Last admission is 15 minutes before closing. Visitor center daily 10-6, Sat. after Victoria Day-Oct. 31. Nature areas and trails open year-round. Donations. Phone (506) 752-2922.

CAP-PELÉ (D-6) pop. 2,200

Fishing is the main industry in Cap-Pelé, where more than 95 percent of the world's smoked herring is said to be produced. West of town on Rte. 15 is Parc de L'Aboiteau, a scenic beach with boardwalks, cottages, volleyball courts and evening concerts during the summer; phone (506) 577-2005.

CARAQUET (A-5) pop. 4,442

Established in 1758 as Capital de l'Acadie, Caraquet is the oldest French settlement in northern New Brunswick. A monument just west of town honors the area's first Acadian settlers, originally expelled by the British in 1755. The Shrine of Sainte Anne du Bocage overlooks the burial ground of many of these early settlers.

This picturesque and culturally vibrant community is headquarters for a huge fishing fleet. A popular event, the Blessing of the Fleet takes place during the Acadian Festival in early August.

La Chambre de Commerce de Grand Caraquet: 25-48 Boulevard St. Pierre W., Caraquet, NB, Canada E1W 1B8; phone (506) 727-2931.

ACADIAN HISTORICAL VILLAGE (VILLAGE HISTORIQUE ACADIEN) is 10 km (6 mi.) w. on Hwy. 11. This historic site interprets the lives of the Acadians, New Brunswick's "marsh settlers," from 1770 through the industrial development and modernization of Acadia in 1939. More than 40 authentic Acadian structures, transported to the site and restored, include houses, a chapel, a school, a general store, a printing house, a cobbler's shop, a tinsmith shop, a smithy, a gristmill, a tavern and the 1910 Château-Albert Hotel. Interpreters in period costumes bring ancestral customs and traditional trades to life.

A visitor center offers an 18-minute slide presentation about Acadian history. Allow 2 hours minimum. Daily 10-6, early June-early Sept.; 10-5, early Sept.-early Oct. Admission $15; over 64, $13; students over 16 with ID $11; ages 6-16, $10; family rate $34. MC, VI. Phone (506) 726-2600 to confirm fall schedule, or (877) 721-2200.

ACADIAN WAX MUSEUM is at 14311 Hwy. 11 at entrance to Acadian Historical Village. Some 90 wax figures in 23 scenes represent Acadian history from the arrival of the continent's first Acadian settlers in 1604 to the return of Acadians reported in 1755. A self-guiding audiotape tour is offered. Allow 30 minutes minimum. Daily 9-7, July-Aug.; 9-6 in June and Sept. 1-25. Admission $9; over 65, $7; ages 6-18, $5; family rate $20. MC, VI. Phone (506) 727-6424.

MUSÉE ACADIEN is off Hwy. 11 at 15 St. Pierre Blvd. E. Historical artifacts depict the general history of the Acadian peninsula. Mon.-Sat. 10-8, Sun. 1-6, June 15-Sept. 15. Admission $3; over 59, $2; students with ID $1; under 12 free. Phone (506) 727-2812, (506) 726-2682, or (506) 726-2727 in the off-season.

CHAMCOOK (F-3) pop. 547

Dangerous shoals, scattered islands and record-breaking tides make the Bay of Fundy a difficult passage to navigate. The highest concentration of lighthouses once ringed Passamaquoddy Bay; more than 16 beacons guided mariners from both the American and Canadian shores. The wooden Chamcook lighthouse was destroyed by lightning in 1945.

CHARLO (A-3) pop. 1,449

Though this small town on the Bay of Chaleur wasn't incorporated until 1966, Charlo is one of the

AAA and Motorsports

AAA, a pioneer in the development and growth of auto racing during the first half of the 20th century, has returned to the racetrack. Today the association is the "Official Auto Club" and "Official Roadside Assistance Provider" of 11 tracks owned and operated by the International Speedway Corporation (ISC), which hosts the NASCAR NEXTEL Cup Series and Indy Racing League (IRL) events.

As part of an agreement with ISC, AAA's widely recognized logo appears on track safety and recovery vehicles as well as on track signs, in racing programs and at other promotional venues. ISC, a leading promoter of motorsports activities in the United States, conducts more than 100 events annually. ISC/AAA facilities include California Speedway in Fontana, Calif.; Darlington Raceway in Darlington, S.C.; Daytona International Speedway in Daytona Beach, Fla.; Homestead-Miami Speedway in Homestead, Fla.; Kansas Speedway in Kansas City, Kan.; Martinsville Speedway in Martinsville, Va.; Michigan International Speedway in Cambridge Junction, Mich.; Phoenix International Raceway in Phoenix, Ariz.; Richmond International Raceway in Richmond, Va.; Talladega Superspeedway in Talladega, Ala.; and Watkins Glen International in Watkins Glen, N.Y.

© International Speedway Corporation

older settlements in Restigouche County. The first last grant was issued here in 1799; a Catholic parish had been established by 1853.

CHARLO SALMONID ENHANCEMENT CENTRE AND FISH HATCHERY is off Hwy. 11 exit 375, on McPherson St. Speckled trout and Atlantic salmon are bred and raised for release into their natural habitat. Daily 9-4. Free. Phone (506) 684-3050.

DALHOUSIE (A-4) pop. 3,975

A year-round port at the mouth of the Restigouche River, Dalhousie offers deep-sea fishing and swimming in the sheltered Bay of Chaleur. The town is the home of the Bowater Paper Co., one of the province's largest industries. The Bon Ami Festival is a 10-day event held in late July and features a parade, fireworks, sporting events and local arts and crafts exhibits.

RESTIGOUCHE REGIONAL MUSEUM is just off Hwy. 11 at 115 George St. at Adelaide St. The facility contains an art gallery and a museum with displays about pioneers, farming, commercial fishing and the Canada Winter Games. Mon.-Fri. 9-5, Sat. 9-1, Sun. 1-5. Donations. Phone (506) 684-7490.

DEER ISLAND (F-3)

Deer Island is at the entrance to Passamaquoddy Bay, 10 kilometres (6 mi.) by water from St. Andrews *(see place listing p. 51).* It can be reached by free automobile ferry from the mainland south of St. George at Letete and, during the summer, from Eastport, Maine; the ferry also runs to Campobello Island July through August.

Deer Island Point has a 16-hectare (40-acre) park and beaches. An enormous whirlpool, "Old Sow," can be seen offshore 3 hours before high tide. Currents rushing through the Western Passage between Deer Island Point and Dog Island create this whirling vortex, one of the world's largest. The name comes from the smaller "piglet" whirlpools that spin away from their mother. Access to the best lookout is through a private campground; check with the office before entering.

DIEPPE (D-5) pop. 14,951, elev. 16 m/52′

This suburb of Moncton on the Petitcodiac River was named in honor of Canadian soldiers killed in the 1942 raid on Dieppe, France, during World War II. Marketing itself as an industrial hub, Dieppe is now one of the fastest-growing cities in New Brunswick.

Shopping areas: Champlain Place at 477 Paul St. has more than 150 shops, including Sears.

CRYSTAL PALACE AMUSEMENT PARK is w. on Hwy. 15 to exit 10 (Paul St.). This 1.1-hectare (2.8-acre) entertainment complex includes an indoor amusement park, an eight-cinema theater and a hotel. Indoor rides include a roller coaster, a wave swinger, an antique carousel and a miniature golf course. An outdoor park is open in summer.

Food is available. Amusement park open daily 10-10, late June-Labour Day; Mon.-Thurs. noon-8, Fri. noon-9, Sat. 10-9, Sun. 10-8, rest of year. Closed Dec. 25. Admission free; fees are charged per ride. Summer all-day pass $19.95, under 48 inches tall $16.95, family pass (four people) $62 ($15.50 each additional person). Rest of year all-day pass $15.50, under 48 inches tall $13.50, family pass (four people) $49.95 ($12.50 each additional person). Rates may vary; phone ahead. MC, VI. Phone (506) 859-4386, or (877) 856-4386 in Canada.

DOAKTOWN (C-4) pop. 955

Doaktown was named after Squire Robert Doak, who brought his family from Scotland to New Brunswick in 1815. After settling on a farm in the Miramichi region, he built a carding mill, grist mill, saw mill and kiln. As justice of the peace, it is said he officiated over local marriages for nearly 30 years, and also served as court judge and coroner.

ATLANTIC SALMON MUSEUM is at 263 Main St. on the Miramichi River. Paintings, prints, publications, sculptures, exotic salmon flies and an audiovisual presentation preserve the history of the area's premier game fish. The museum is dedicated to Atlantic salmon conservation, preservation and promotion. The museum also features a visitor information center. Daily 9-5, June-Sept. Admission $5; over 59, $4; students with ID $3; family rate (four people) $12. Phone (506) 365-7787 or (866) 725-6662.

DOAK HISTORIC SITE is at 386 Main St. A house, barn and milk house on the site were built by Squire Robert Doak, who came to New Brunswick from Scotland in 1815. The house remained in the family until 1979. Original furnishings as well as kitchen and farm tools reflect pioneer life 1830-90. Costumed interpreters carry out such daily chores as cooking, quilting, rug hooking and spinning; visitors may participate in weaving. One-day training in spinning is available by appointment.

Guided tours are available. Picnicking is permitted. Allow 1 hour minimum. Mon.-Sat. 9:30-4:30, Sun. 1-4:30, late June to mid-Sept. Donations. Weaving $5. Phone (506) 365-2026.

DORCHESTER (D-5) pop. 954

Restored to its 1811 appearance, Dorchester's Bell Inn is perhaps the oldest stone building in New Brunswick. Between mid-July and early September, some 2.5 million semipalmated sandpipers—up to 90 percent of the world's population—flock to the nutrient-rich shores of Johnson's Mills, 8 kilometres (5 mi.) south on Hwy. 935.

KEILLOR HOUSE AND ST. JAMES TEXTILE MUSEUM is on Hwy. 106. The 1813 house exhibits 19th-century furnishings, domestic items and a three-story spiral staircase. Displays include shipbuilding, farming and trade tools, costumes and materials for genealogical research. The St. James Textile Museum is an 1884 structure housing antique tools, textile equipment, spinning wheels and pedal lathes. A penitentiary collection is displayed in the coach house.

Guided tours are available. Mon.-Sat. 10-5, Sun. 1-5, early June to mid-Sept; by appointment rest of year. Keillor House $3; under 12, $2. St. James Textile Museum $2; under 12, $1. Phone (506) 379-6633.

EDMUNDSTON (B-1) pop. 17,373

Edmundston serves as the honorary capital of the Republic of Madawaska, a mythical region evolved from 60 years of disputes over the location of the New Brunswick-Maine boundary. Though the boundary was settled by the Webster-Ashburton Treaty in 1842, residents adopted the unofficial territory, complete with dialect and flag.

Bilingual Edmundston dominates the province's pulp and paper industry. The city also is noted for its hand-loomed fabrics and wood sculpture. Nearby De la République Provincial Park *(see Recreation Chart and the AAA/CAA Eastern Canada Camp-Book)* is a cultural and recreational center. On the outskirts of Edmundston, Mont Farlagne provides skiing in winter and spring.

Edmundston Chamber of Commerce: 1 Canada Rd., Edmundston, NB, Canada E3V 1T6; phone (506) 737-1866.

MADAWASKA HISTORICAL MUSEUM is at jct. Hwy. 2 and Hébert Blvd. (exit 18). The museum depicts the cultural life of the Madawaska region since its settlement. A historical display and the Gallerie Colline Art Gallery are featured. Allow 30 minutes minimum. Daily 9-8, mid-June through Labour Day; Wed.-Thurs. 7-10 p.m., Sun. 1-5, rest of year. Admission $3.50; over 64 and ages 6-18, $2; family rate $7. Phone (506) 737-5282.

FORT BEAUSÉJOUR NATIONAL HISTORIC SITE OF CANADA (E-6)

Fort Beauséjour National Historic Site is 8 kilometres (5 mi.) east of Sackville on Hwy. 2 exit 513A, and 1.5 kilometres (.9 mi.) west of the Nova Scotia border, at 111 Fort Beauséjour Rd.

Built in 1751 in response to the construction of an English fort at Beaubassin a year earlier, Fort Beauséjour defended French interests in the Isthmus of Chignecto. In 1755 a force of New England militia under British command took it after a 2-week siege. That same year, the British initiated the mass deportation of the Acadians at this site.

Renamed Fort Cumberland, the fort withstood an attack by American revolutionaries in 1776. It was manned during the War of 1812 but saw no action, and its military role ceased in 1833.

The visitor center museum contains exhibits of early military and civilian life. Restored stone ruins and grassy ramparts of the star-shaped fort, a cannon exhibit, picnic facilities and outdoor interpretive paintings are on the grounds. Allow 1 hour minimum. Daily 9-5, June 1-Oct. 15. Admission $3.95;

over 65, $3.45; ages 6-16, $1.95; family rate $9.90. AX, MC, VI. Phone (506) 364-5080.

FREDERICTON (D-3) pop. 47,560

See map page 42.

One of North America's oldest settlements, Fredericton straddles the broad Saint John River. The area was inhabited by Maliseet Indians thousands of years before European settlement.

Named St. Anne by its French fur-trading founders, the settlement was burned in 1760 by the British in their struggle with the French for control of the continent. Loyalists fleeing the American Revolution revived the settlement in 1783 and renamed it Frederick's Town for the second son of King George III.

New Brunswick became a province in 1784 and Gov. Thomas Carleton made Fredericton the provincial capital in 1785. Today the city is known for its beauty, architecture, heritage and culture.

The former barracks and parade ground of the original military compound on Queen Street now contain a variety of establishments. One is the New Brunswick College of Craft and Design at 457 Queen St.; established in 1938, the school's alumni form the basis of Fredericton's crafts community. The city often is regarded as the pewter capital of Canada because of its many pewtersmiths. Quilters, potters and weavers also are well represented in the area's shops.

In addition to the shops and Saturday morning's Farmers' Market, several downtown landmarks command interest. Historically significant are two cemeteries: The Loyalist Cemetery, near the Saint John River off Waterloo Row, has interesting old tombstones; the Old Burial Ground, along Brunswick Street between York and Regent streets, contains the final resting places of many Loyalists.

A statue of Scottish poet Robert Burns stands on The Green, a grassy promenade along the Saint John River. The Playhouse on Queen Street is the home of Theatre New Brunswick, a touring theatrical company.

Fredericton is at one end of the scenic portion of Hwy. 2, which runs northwest 167 kilometres (104 mi.) along the Saint John River to Woodstock *(see place listing p. 58).*

Fredericton Chamber of Commerce: 20 Woodstock Rd., P.O. Box 275, Fredericton, NB, Canada E3B 4Y9; phone (506) 458-8006.

Self-guiding tours: The Fredericton Visitor Guide outlines a walking tour of the city's historic areas and is available at the Visitors Information Centre, 11 Carleton St.; phone (506) 460-2041.

Shopping areas: Regent Mall, at the top of Regent Street on the south side of Hwy. 8 at exit 6, counts Sears among its 95 stores. Craft shops are sprinkled throughout the city.

THE BEAVERBROOK ART GALLERY is opposite the Legislative Assembly Building at 703 Queen St. A permanent collection of artwork by noted British and Canadian artists includes paintings by 19th-century artist Cornelius Krieghoff and Canadian impressionist James Wilson Morrice. Given to the people of New Brunswick by Lord Beaverbrook in 1959, the gallery displays paintings, sculpture, furniture, porcelain and *objets d'art* dating from the 14th century to the present.

Highlights include late Renaissance paintings, Aubusson tapestries and New Brunswick landscape paintings. Salvador Dalí's *Santiago el Grande* is on display. Allow 1 hour minimum. Daily 9-5:30 (also Thurs. 5:30-9); closed Jan. 1 and Dec. 25. Admission $5; over 64, $4; students with ID $2; family rate (two adults and two children) $10; by donation Tues. AX, MC, VI. Phone (506) 458-2028.

CHRIST CHURCH CATHEDRAL is at 168 Church St. between King and Brunswick sts. Consecrated in 1853, this Anglican cathedral is a replica of St. Mary's Church in Snettisham, Norfolk, England, and exemplifies decorated Gothic architecture. Noon recitals are presented every Friday in July and August. Guided tours are offered daily 9-5, July-Aug. The cathedral is open for viewing Mon.-Fri. 9-6, Sat. 9-5, Sun. 1-5, rest of year. Donations. Phone (506) 450-8500.

FREDERICTON BOTANIC GARDEN is w. of Odell Park with entrances on Prospect St. and Cameron Ct. Established in 1990, this evolving garden will eventually have 12 themed areas. Currently 6 kilometres (4 mi.) of trails wander through a wooded hillside and along a creek past a wide variety of plants and trees, including a collection of azaleas and rhododendrons. Daily dawn-dusk. Free. Phone (506) 452-9269.

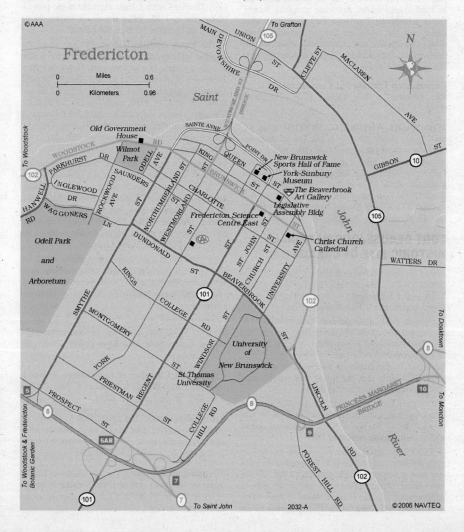

FREDERICTON SCIENCE CENTRE EAST is at 668 Brunswick St., adjacent to the City Market. "Play, discover and learn" is the motto of this science playground, where visitors may go inside a giant kaleidoscope, create tornadoes and participate in more than 100 hands-on exhibits. The center is housed in a former jail built in 1842; the cells display jail artifacts. Allow 1 hour, 30 minutes minimum. Mon.-Sat. 10-5, Sun. 1-4, June-Aug.; Tues.-Fri. noon-5, Sat. 10-5, rest of year. Admission $5, children $3, family rate $14. VI. Phone (506) 457-2340.

 KINGS LANDING HISTORICAL SETTLEMENT—see Kings Landing p. 46.

LEGISLATIVE ASSEMBLY BUILDING is at Queen and St. John sts. The seat of New Brunswick government since 1882, the building features an impressive crystal chandelier and a self-supporting grand spiral staircase. On permanent display are replicas of Joshua Reynolds' portraits of King George III and Queen Charlotte and 435 original copper engravings by John J. Audubon.

Guided tours are available. Allow 30 minutes minimum. Daily 9-7, late May to mid-Aug.; Mon.-Fri. 9-4, rest of year. Last tour departs 30 minutes before closing. Free. Phone (506) 453-2527.

NEW BRUNSWICK SPORTS HALL OF FAME is at 503 Queen St. in the Clark Building. Provincial sports heroes and teams are honored through displays of portraits, photographs and memorabilia, including Olympic medals. Mon.-Sat. 9:30-5, June-Aug.; Mon.-Fri. noon-4, rest of year. Closed major holidays. Donations. Phone (506) 453-3747.

ODELL PARK AND ARBORETUM is bounded by Smythe and Prospect sts., Hanwell Rd. and Waggoners Ln. Walking trails, playgrounds and a picnic area are part of the park, which covers more than 157 hectares (388 acres). The arboretum contains native New Brunswick plants and trees; guided tours are available by request. Local wildlife is protected in the park's game refuge. Daily 8 a.m.-10 p.m. Free. Phone (506) 460-2230.

OLD GOVERNMENT HOUSE is at 51 Woodstock Rd. Constructed 1826-28, the restored house is the residence and office of New Brunswick's present lieutenant governor and has been the home of its past governors and lieutenant governors. Antique furnishings from the early 1800s can be seen. Highlights include the reception area, dining and breakfast rooms, library, music room and two conservatories as well as rotating arts and crafts exhibits.

Allow 1 hour minimum. Guided tours daily 10-5, June 1-Sept. 1; Mon.-Fri. 10-5, rest of year. Last tour begins 1 hour before closing. Free. Phone (506) 453-2505.

UNIVERSITY OF NEW BRUNSWICK is on a hill overlooking the city and the Saint John River. Founded in 1785, the university's historic buildings include the 1829 Sir Howard Douglas Hall and the 1851 Brydone Jack Observatory. The Harriet Irving Library preserves rare manuscripts and books, including first editions by Charles Dickens, George Eliot and H.G. Wells. Photographs, films and local documents are displayed at the Provincial Archives.

Campus guided tours are available by appointment. Allow 1 hour minimum. Archives open Mon.-Fri. 10-5, Sat. 8:30-5; closed major holidays. Free. Phone (506) 458-7855 for campus tour reservations, or (506) 453-2122 for the archives.

YORK-SUNBURY MUSEUM is on Officers' Square at 571 Queen St. Exhibits portray the community from the early First Nations period. Displays illustrate both the province's military and domestic sides of life, ranging from a replica of a World War I trench to a 19-kilogram (42-lb.) Coleman frog. The changing of the guard and sentry change ceremonies can be seen on Officers' Square in summer.

Daily 10-5, July-Aug.; Tues.-Sat. 1-5, Apr.-June and Sept.-Oct; by appointment rest of year. Changing of the guard Tues.-Sat. at 11 and 7, July-Aug. Sentry changes Tues.-Sat. on the hour 11-7, July-Aug. Admission $3; over 59, $2; students with ID $1; under 6 free; family rate $6. Phone (506) 455-6041.

 FUNDY NATIONAL PARK OF CANADA (E-5)

> Elevations in the park range from sea level at the Bay of Fundy to 365 metres (1,200 ft.) at Rte. 114 near the Caribou Plains Trail. Refer to CAA/AAA maps for additional elevation information.

Between Moncton and Saint John on Rte. 114, Fundy National Park overlooks the Bay of Fundy and encompasses 206 square kilometres (80 sq. mi.) of wooded hills and valleys.

When the bay's giant tide recedes, visitors can walk on the sea floor and then climb to higher ground for a panoramic view of the water's return. Cliffs rising steeply from the bay vary from the red and khaki of layered sandstone to the gray-green remains of lava flows and granite intrusions. Occasional stream valleys make deep gashes in the cliff walls.

Meadows of wildflowers, rushing waterfalls and placid lakes characterize this wildlife sanctuary and recreation area, which includes more than 100 kilometres (62 mi.) of hiking trails.

General Information and Activities

Fundy National Park is accessible from the Trans-Canada Hwy. at Penobsquis via Rte. 114, and from Moncton south and then west via Rte. 114. The park is open all year; the visitor reception center and most services operate from the last week in May to mid-October. Some 25 hiking trails offer summer diversion while snowshoeing and cross-country skiing are popular December through March. Park headquarters is at Alma, near the mouth of the Upper Salmon River.

Park interpreters conduct a regular program of nature hikes and illustrated talks. Self-guiding trails are open all year.

Beaches on the bay include Alma, Cannontown, Herring Cove and Point Wolfe. The park contains a heated salt-water pool, golf course, bowling green and tennis courts. Trout fishing is popular at Bennett Lake, with a daily limit of five fish. The park requires a national park fishing license, which can be obtained at Bennett Lake.

Fundy's Acadian forests are home to Northern flying squirrels, American martens, Atlantic salmon, peregrine falcons and whitetail deer as well as numerous species of birds. *See Recreation Chart and the AAA/CAA Eastern Canada CampBook.*

Note: Although accustomed to people, animals should be viewed and photographed with utmost care.

ADMISSION: One-day pass $6.90; over 65, $5.90; ages 6-16, $3.45; family rate $17.30. Phone (877) 737-3783 for campsite reservations.

PETS are permitted in the park but must be kept on leashes.

ADDRESS inquiries to the Park Superintendent, Fundy National Park of Canada, P.O. Box 1001, Alma, NB, Canada E4H 1B4; phone (506) 887-6000.

GAGETOWN (E-4) pop. 682

Gagetown's Loomcrofters demonstrate weaving in a former fur-trading post, one of the oldest buildings on the Saint John River. Built in 1761, it is known as the Blockhouse because rifles and ammunition were stored in its cellar. The Loomcrofters produce tartans, draperies and upholstery materials.

QUEENS COUNTY MUSEUM is at 69 Front St. The museum encompasses two historic sites. Tilley House was the 1818 birthplace of Sir Samuel Leonard Tilley, a father of the Canadian Confederation. Furnishings of the Loyalist and Victorian periods are displayed, many salvaged from older houses in the area. The 1836 Queens County Courthouse, 16 Court House Rd., displays permanent and changing historical exhibits.

Allow 1 hour minimum. Daily 10-5, mid-June to mid-Sept. Admission (includes both sites) $3. Phone (506) 488-2966 or (506) 488-2483.

GRANDE-ANSE (A-5) pop. 853

Fishing has always been the mainstay of this French-speaking village, which was settled on the Bay of Chaleur in 1808. Two fish-processing plants handle catches of crab and lobster in the spring and herring and mackerel in the fall. Grande-Anse is also home to a 560-acre peat bog from which sphagnum peat moss is harvested and shipped to garden nurseries in the United States.

MUSÉE DES PAPES (POPES' MUSEUM) is on Hwy. 11 at 184 Acadie St. Displays about papal history include a portrait gallery and a finely detailed model of St. Peter's Basilica. Guided tours with an audiovisual presentation are available. Daily 10-6, June 11-Sept. 2. Last tour begins 1 hour before closing. Admission $9; over 65, $4.50; ages 6-16, $3; family rate $14. MC, VI. Phone (506) 732-3003.

GRAND FALLS (B-2) pop. 6,133

Grand Falls was a French settlement that became a British military post in 1790. More than 80 percent of its citizens are bilingual, and this is the only town in the Atlantic Provinces with an official name in both languages: the French version is Grand-Sault.

The great horseshoe falls of the Saint John River are considered the largest east of Niagara Falls; the Grand Falls hydroelectric plant provides power to the provincial distribution system. The town is a major shipping point for New Brunswick's seed potato-growing industry, and area farmers supply potatoes to the McCain frozen food plant in Grand Falls, which produces 10 tons of French fries per hour.

Grand Falls District Chamber of Commerce: 144 Court St., Suite 102, P.O. Box 7242, Grand Falls, NB, Canada E3Z 2R2; phone (506) 473-1905.

GRAND FALLS AND GORGE is best viewed from the Malabeam Reception Centre on the bridge that extends e. from Broadway, crossing the Saint John River gorge. A 23-metre (75-ft.) cataract gives Grand Falls its name. On either side of the river, the Malabeam and La Rochelle reception centers offer information about the area's natural and human history. A stairway at La Rochelle leads to Wells-in-Rocks, a series of deep potholes. A boat ride is offered (weather and water conditions permitting).

Guided tours are available by appointment. La Rochelle center open daily 9-9, mid-June through Labour Day. Malabeam center open daily 9-9, Victoria Day-Labour Day; 9-6, day after Labour Day to mid-Oct. Park admission and reception centers free. Wells-in-Rocks admission $3; under 12, $1; family rate $7. Phone (506) 475-7769 or (877) 475-7769.

GRAND FALLS MUSEUM is at 142 Court St. Artifacts, tools, photographs and memorabilia depict the history of the area. An exhibit chronicles Van Morrell's tightrope walk over the falls. Mon.-Fri. 9-5, late June-late Aug.; by appointment rest of year. Donations. Phone (506) 473-5265, or (506) 473-5940 in the off-season.

GRAND MANAN ISLAND (F-3) pop. 2,600

Grand Manan lies 15 kilometres (9 mi.) off the coast of Maine in the Bay of Fundy. It is known for its lobster and herring catches and for the preparation of dulse, an edible seaweed. A 1.5-hour boat trip connects the island with Black's Harbour.

Humpback, finback and North Atlantic right whales visit the waters off Grand Manan from mid-July to mid-September; the rare right whales also use the area as a mating ground. Deep-sea excursions and whale-watching trips can be scheduled locally.

Some of the 19 hiking trails that explore the coastline of this island offer visitors the chance to sight seals as well. John J. Audubon made many of his sketches here; more than 275 species of birds have been sighted.

Grand Manan Anchorage Park: 136 Anchorage Rd., Grand Manan, NB, Canada E5G 2H4; phone (506) 662-7022.

SEA WATCH TOURS leaves from the Seal Cove Pier. Passengers embark on 5-hour whale-watching trips in the Bay of Fundy. Bird-watching tours and excursions to the Machias Seal Island, noted for its puffin colony, also are available. Departures daily at 8 and 1, early July-late Sept. Fare $50; ages 12-18, $38; under 12, $30. Reservations are required. MC, VI. Phone (506) 662-8552 or (877) 662-8552.

HAMPTON (E-4) pop. 3,997

The parish of Hampton was established in Kings County in 1795 by Loyalist settlers. By the early 19th century the village on the Kennebecasis River had become a shipbuilding center. The Kings County Courthouse was built on the town square in 1870, and the county jail was moved, block by block, from the former county seat of Kingston. The province's first telephone is thought to have been installed at Hampton.

The 2,000-hectare (4,900-acre) Hampton Marsh, one of the most fertile and productive wetland systems in New Brunswick, is home to waterfowl, marsh birds, eagles, cranes, beavers, otters and moose.

Hampton Tourist Bureau: 657 Main St., Hampton, NB, Canada E5N 6C6; phone (506) 832-5671.

KINGS COUNTY MUSEUM is behind the courthouse in the Centennial Building at 27 Centennial Rd. Photographs, documents, clothing, early furniture and pioneer household and farm items are displayed. Of interest is the set of standard weights and measures sent from the government of England in 1854. A genealogical library is available. The old jail next door houses additional exhibits. Mon.-Sat. 8:30-4:30, June 15-Sept. 30. Tours by appointment rest of year. Admission (includes guided tour) $2; ages 6-12, $1. Phone (506) 832-6009.

HARTLAND (D-2) pop. 902

The 391-metre (1,282-ft.) Hartland Covered Bridge, reputedly the world's longest, carries Hwy. 103 across the Saint John River. Bridges were originally covered for protection from the weather. The life expectancy of a regular bridge was perhaps 10 years, while a covered bridge might last a century. There was one drawback in the winter—snow had to be hauled and spread across the floor so that sleds could cross.

With its barn-like roof, a covered bridge eased farm animals' fears of crossing the river. And, of course, the cover of darkness provided an opportunity for young suitors to steal a kiss. Ministers opposed construction of Hartland's "kissing bridge" as a corrupting influence, but they were outvoted. The bridge was completed in 1922.

HILLSBOROUGH (D-5) pop. 1,288

Pennsylvania Germans were the first to immigrate to the west bank of the Petitcodiac River, arriving in 1766 and naming the community Dutch Village. Two decades later the town was renamed to honor an early administrator, Lord Hillsborough.

Clapboard houses along the waterfront road to Moncton *(see place listing p. 48)* evoke images of the 19th century, when wives would pace widow's walks waiting for husbands to sail their ships home to Hillsborough. Mining, primarily of the area's vast gypsum quarries, and farming dominate Hillsborough's economy.

Hillsborough is at the eastern end of the scenic portion of Hwy. 114, which runs 205 kilometres (127 mi.) from Penobsquis, through Fundy National Park and up Chignecto Bay.

HON. WILLIAM HENRY STEEVES HOUSE is at 40 Mill St. The birthplace and home of one of the fathers of Canadian Confederation has been restored and furnished in the style of the late 19th century. Steeves family artifacts are displayed in the 1812 structure. Allow 1 hour minimum. Mon.-Sat. 9-5, Sun. 1-5, July 1-Labour Day; by appointment rest of year. Admission $2; under 12, $1; family rate $5 (two adults and two children). Phone (506) 734-3102.

NEW BRUNSWICK RAILWAY MUSEUM is on Hwy. 114. The museum houses such train-related memorabilia as lanterns, photographs, antique caboose stoves, velocipedes and motor cars. The rail yard and shop contain two diesel-electric locomotives, a steam crane, a steam engine, coaches, cabooses and maintenance equipment.

Museum daily 10-6, late June-Labour Day. Admission $5; over 65, $4; ages 6-16, $3, family rate (two adults and all children) $10. Phone (506) 734-3195.

HOPEWELL CAPE (E-5)

Richard B. Bennett, the only New Brunswick politician to become prime minister of Canada, was born at Hopewell Hill in 1870. He took office in 1930 as the country's economy faltered and, perhaps unfairly, he shouldered most of the blame for the hardships of the Great Depression. After a landslide defeat for reelection and subsequent conflicts with his fellow Conservatives, Bennett left the country for England, where he served in the House of Lords. He died in 1947 and was buried at his estate in Mickleham, Surrey. He remains the only Canadian prime minister not to be buried on Canadian soil.

ALBERT COUNTY MUSEUM is off Hwy. 114 at 12 Hopewell Cross Rd. Housed in a complex of buildings that includes an 1845 jail and a 1904 courthouse, the museum tells the stories of Albert County residents, a diverse group that includes pioneers, shipbuilders, farmers, an ax murderer and Canada's 11th prime minister, R.B. Bennett. Among the other displays are handmade dolls, wooden shipbuilder's models and a late 19th-century nickelodeon. Daily 9:30-5:30, mid-June to mid-Sept. Admission $4, over 65 and students with ID $3, under 12 free. Phone (506) 734-2003.

HOPEWELL ROCKS OCEAN TIDAL EXPLORATION SITE is near the mouth of the Petitcodiac River on Hwy. 114. Ocean tides have carved the Flower Pot Rocks, pillars of sandstone and conglomerate rock with balsam fir and dwarf spruce growing on top. Visitors may walk the beach below the rocks from 3 hours before low tide until 3 hours after low tide. At high tide, the rocks resemble islands. An interpretive center provides viewing decks and multimedia exhibits about the Bay of Fundy. A shuttle runs from the parking area to the cliff.

Daily 8-8, June 24-Aug. 18; 8-7, June 10-23 and Aug. 19-Sept. 4; 9-5, May 19-June 9 and Sept. 5-Oct. 9. Admission $9.50; over 65 and students with ID $7.25; ages 5-18, $6.25; family rate (two adults and all children under 18) $23. Shuttle $1.25; round trip $2.50. Hours and rates may vary; phone ahead. MC, VI. Phone (506) 734-3534 or (877) 734-3429 for information and daily tide tables.

RECREATIONAL ACTIVITIES

Kayaking

• **Baymount Outdoor Adventures Inc.** departs from the kayak building at the lower site of Hopewell Rocks Ocean Tidal Exploration Site. Write 17 Elvin Jay Dr., Hillsborough, NB, Canada E4H 2S9. Other activities are offered. Daily 7:30-dusk, late June-Labour Day (weather permitting). Phone (506) 734-2660 or (877) 601-2660.

KINGS LANDING (E-3)

When the Mactaquac Dam Project was proposed in the 1960s, historians sought a way to save architecturally significant buildings along the Saint John River. The best examples from the Loyalist period were dismantled and relocated from the flood plain to Kings Landing Historical Settlement. Some 70 buildings have been restored.

KINGS LANDING HISTORICAL SETTLEMENT is off Hwy. 2 exit 253. The 121-hectare (299-acre) site is a meticulous restoration of a typical village in the Saint John River Valley 1820-90. The settlement includes farms, historic houses, mills, a forge, an inn, a printing office, a school, a store and a theater. Staff members in period dress conduct tours and free wagon rides.

Special events include historical reenactments, a fall auction and harvest and Christmas candlelight dinners. A program allows children to spend 5 days in the village and dress and live as youngsters did in the 19th century. Allow 3 hours minimum. Daily 10-5, first Sat. in June-Thanksgiving. Admission $15; over 65, $13; students over 16 with ID $12; ages 6-16, $10; family rate (two adults and all children under 16) $36. AX, MC, VI. Phone (506) 363-4999.

KOUCHIBOUGUAC NATIONAL PARK OF CANADA (C-5)

Elevations in the park range from sea level at Northumberland Strait to 30 metres (100 ft.). Refer to CAA/AAA maps for additional elevation information.

Kouchibouguac National Park is entered from Hwys. 11 or 134, just south of the village of Kouchibouguac. The park consists of 238 square kilometres (92 sq. mi.) on the central eastern shore. Molded by a whimsical sea, this section of the Maritime Plain is an intricate blend of coastal and inland habitats including rivers, sand dunes, salt marshes, bogs, lagoons, fields and forests and the characteristic flora and fauna of each.

General Information and Activities

The park is open year-round for walking, hiking and winter recreation; the main gate and visitor center are open mid-May to mid-Oct. The Information Centre, 1 kilometre (.6 mi.) east inside the gate, offers a multimedia presentation about the diverse habitats of the park. Information about facilities and such activities as nature walks, evening programs and outdoor presentations also is available. The center is open daily 8-8, mid-June through Labour Day; 9-5, mid-May to mid-June and day after Labour Day-second Mon. in Oct. If the entrance gate kiosk is closed, entry passes may be purchased at the Information Centre.

The St. Louis, Black and Kouchibouguac rivers give the area its Mi'kmaq name—Kouchibouguac (KOOSH-e-boo-gwack), "river of the long tides." These waterways provide a variety of canoe routes to the park's interior. There are beach and woodlands trails, as well as hiking and interpretive self-guiding nature trails that provide access to the park's many habitats. Bicycle, boat, canoe and kayak rentals are available.

Canoes and especially tour boats are a good way to see the waterways and get a close-up view of the park's birdlife and resident seals. Visitors can find grey seals lounging on off-shore sandbars from May through October; bird-watching is best in spring and fall, when shorebirds and waterfowl stop over during their migration.

Primitive campsites are accessible by hiking, canoeing or bicycling. Those intending to use the off-road campgrounds must register at the information center when arriving and leaving.

Anglers need a national park fishing permit ($7 daily, $20 annually). Kellys Beach provides supervised swimming, a canteen and showers. A 60-kilometre (37-mi.) bicycle trail is said to be one of the best in Atlantic Canada. Cross-country skiing, snowshoeing and tobogganing also are popular.

Trail shelters contain wood stoves and picnic tables; favorite picnic areas within the park are Callanders, La Source and Kellys Beach. *See Recreation Chart and the AAA/CAA Eastern Canada CampBook.*

ADMISSION to the park is $5; over 64, $4.25; ages 6-16, $2.50; family rate $12.50. Campsites can be reserved in advance.

PETS, where permitted, must be on a leash at all times and may not be left unattended. Domestic animals are prohibited in certain posted areas.

ADDRESS correspondence to the Park Superintendent, 186 Rte. 117, Kouchibouguac National Park of Canada, NB, Canada E4X 2P1; phone (506) 876-2443, or TTY (506) 876-4205.

LAMÈQUE (A-5)

Lamèque Island, off the northeastern coast of the Acadian Peninsula, is reached by drawbridge from Route 313. Each summer, the island hosts the Lamèque International Baroque Music Festival, with performances by top vocalists and instrumentalists. Concerts take place in the 1913 Sainte-Cécile Church of Petite-Rivière-de-l'Île, which is noted for its colorful interior and flawless acoustics; for information phone (506) 344-5846, or (800) 320-2276 in Canada.

ECOLOGICAL PARK OF THE ACADIAN PENINSULA is 1 km (.6 mi.) e. on Rte. 313 to 28 rue de l'Hôpital. Interactive computer kiosks in the nature center educate guests about the Acadian Peninsula's ecological habitats. A boardwalk meanders through an estuary and leads to a 2-kilometre (1.2 mi.) interpretive nature trail. The trail crosses an arboretum with some 30 native species of conifers and deciduous trees. An observation tower provides views of the area.

Allow 2 hours minimum. Daily 9-9, mid-Apr. through late Oct. Admission $7; over 65, $6; ages 6-17, $3; family rate (two adults and two children) $15. MC, VI. Phone (506) 344-3223.

MACTAQUAC (D-3)

Completed in 1968, the Mactaquac Dam Project displaced several thousand residents along the Saint John River. Historically significant buildings were relocated from the flood plain to Kings Landing Historical Settlement (*see place listing p. 46*). Farms, towns, roads and a railroad line lie submerged beneath the Mactaquac headpond, which extends some 97 kilometres (60 mi.) upriver from the dam.

MACTAQUAC HYDROELECTRIC DAM is off the Trans-Canada Hwy. at 451 Hwy. 105. Guided 1-hour tours of the generating station demonstrate how the dam was built and how it operates. Tours daily 9-4, June 1-Labour Day; by appointment rest of year. Free. Phone (506) 462-3800.

MEMRAMCOOK (D-5) pop. 4,719

As Acadians returned to Memramcook in the years following deportation, this region came to be known as *Berceau de l'Acadie*, or "the Cradle of Acadia." The first Acadian college was built here in 1864; Memramcook hosted the first Acadian National Convention in 1881. Most locals (known as "Cookers") speak Chiac, a dialect mixture of Acadian French and English. Early Acadian settlers built dikes to drain the salt marshes; many of these *aboiteaux* are still visible.

MONUMENT LEFEBVRE NATIONAL HISTORIC SITE OF CANADA is off Hwy. 106, next to Memramcook Institute. A monument to the 19th-century renaissance of Acadian culture, this site commemorates the first French-language, degree-granting institution in Atlantic Canada, founded by Father Camille Lefebvre in 1864. A permanent exhibit explores the past, present and future of the Acadian community. A restored period theater, noted for its architecture and acoustics, is on the second floor.

Guided tours are available. Allow 1 hour minimum. Daily 9-5, June 1-Oct. 15; by appointment rest of year. Admission $3.95; over 64, $3.45; ages 6-16, $1.95; family rate $9.90. Phone (506) 758-9808 or (877) 765-1896.

MINTO (D-4) pop. 2,776

The arrival of the railroad in 1904 spurred the growth of Minto, a town originally settled by Loyalists and Irish immigrants. By the early 1910s, Minto was inhabited by Europeans from such countries as Belgium, Italy, Germany and Russia; the immigrants found work in the town's many coal mines. Coal mining is still Minto's main industry.

The Minto Museum and Information Centre, 187 Main St., contains railway and coal-mining artifacts in a renovated train station. A caboose is on the museum grounds; phone (506) 327-1114.

Recreational pursuits revolve around nearby Grand Lake's beaches and harbors and include boating, swimming, camping and fishing. In town, a golf course, parks and a nature trail are available.

THE NEW BRUNSWICK INTERNMENT CAMP MUSEUM is at 420 Pleasant Dr. at jct. Union St. in the Municipal Building. The museum pays tribute to prisoners of war interned at the Fredericton Internment Camp during World War II. Prisoners included German and Italian merchant marines, Jewish refugees and Canadian Nazi sympathizers. More than 600 artifacts are on display in the 186-square-metre (2,000-square-ft.) museum as well as a portion of a reconstructed prisoner's hut and a model of the camp.

Guided tours are available. Allow 30 minutes minimum. Mon.-Fri. 10-5, Sat.-Sun. noon-5, July-Aug.; by appointment rest of year. Admission $1.50, under 13 free, family rate $4. Phone (506) 327-3573 or (506) 450-9666.

MIRAMICHI (B-5) pop. 18,508

Miramichi was named for its original inhabitants, a Mi'kmaq Indian tribe that prized the river valley for its salmon fishing. Acadian settlers arrived from Nova Scotia in 1757. As immigrants from Ireland, Scotland and New England followed, Miramichi gained a reputation for its commercial fisheries and shipyards, which produced some of the best square-rigged ships in Canada.

Forestry replaced shipbuilding as the area's dominant industry in the late 19th century, and the last commercial cannery closed in 1972, but salmon fishing continues to draw thousands of anglers each year. The modern city of Miramichi was formed in 1995 by the merging of Newcastle, Chatham and eight other villages and districts. The area is home to Canada's Irish Festival on the Miramichi in mid-July.

BEAUBEAR'S ISLAND NATIONAL HISTORIC SITE is reached via boat from the interpretation centre at 35 St. Patrick's Dr. The island, uninhabited for more than 100 years, was home to impoverished Acadians expelled from Canada. Remains of slips, wharves and foundations are visible. Costumed guides take visitors on history and nature walks, offering details about Peter Mitchell, one of the Fathers of Confederation and the owner of Beaubear's Island 1871-93.

The interpretation center features displays about shipbuilding, the Acadians and the Mi'kmaq Indians who lived along the Miramichi River. Allow 1 hour, 30 minutes minimum. Interpretation centre open Mon.-Fri. noon-8, Sat.-Sun. noon-5. Boats to the island depart Mon.-Fri. at 6:30, Sat.-Sun. at 1:30. Island tours $10; ages 5-13, $7. Interpretation center free. Phone (506) 622-8526.

HISTORIC BEAVERBROOK HOUSE is at 518 King George Hwy. Visitors may take a guided tour of the childhood home of William Maxwell Aitken, Lord Beaverbrook. The Victorian-style home was built in 1877. Allow 30 minutes minimum. Mon.-Fri. 9-5, Sat. 10-5, Sun. noon-5, mid-June to mid-Sept. Donations. Phone (506) 622-5572.

MacDONALD FARM HISTORIC SITE is 13 km (8 mi.) n.e. on Hwy. 11, on the n. side of the Miramichi River at Bartibog Bridge. The 1815 farmhouse overlooking Miramichi Bay was built by Alexander MacDonald, a Scottish immigrant. Though typical of Georgian stone houses in rural Scotland, it is unusual for New Brunswick. Various outbuildings reflect the ways in which the MacDonald family earned a living. Costumed guides interpret the restored house and working farm and self-guiding nature trails traverse the site.

Daily 9:30-4:30, June 21-day before Labour Day. Admission $2.50; over 54 and ages 6-18, $1.50; family rate $7. Phone (506) 778-6085.

MIRAMICHI NATURAL HISTORY MUSEUM is at 149 Wellington St. Exhibits include bird, animal and marine life specimens as well as local historic artifacts and documents of the Cunard family. Allow 1 hour minimum. Mon.-Sat. 10-6, Sun. noon-5, July-Aug. Free. Phone (506) 773-7305.

RANKIN HOUSE is 2.5 km (1.5 mi.) w. of Centennial Bridge on Hwy. 8. The restored 19th-century Georgian mansion is furnished in period. Maritime artwork and local historical artifacts are displayed. Guided 30-minute tours are available. Allow 30 minutes minimum. Daily 9-5, June-late Aug. Donations. Phone (506) 773-3448.

ST. MICHAEL'S MUSEUM AND GENEALOGY CENTRE is at 10 Howard St. This museum contains historical and religious records and artifacts. The Old St. Michael's rectory, a wooden structure, contains an extensive genealogical collection. Allow 30 minutes minimum. Mon.-Fri. 9:30-5, Sat. 10-4. Museum free. Daily fee for genealogical searches $20. Phone (506) 778-5152.

W.S. LOGGIE CULTURAL CENTRE is at 222 Wellington St. Furnished with antiques, the restored 1879 Victorian Second Empire house is characterized by a mansard roof and bay windows. The former residence of William Stewart Loggie now serves as a museum, a meeting center for local organizations and an arts and crafts facility. Allow 30 minutes minimum. Daily 10-6, July-Aug. Donations. Phone (506) 773-7645.

MISCOU ISLAND (A-6)

Off the northern tip of Lamèque *(see place listing p. 47)*, Miscou Island is a place to relax and watch sea gulls, migratory birds and ships go by. Beaming its warning light since 1856, the Miscou Point Lighthouse is said to be the oldest in New Brunswick and is one of the few manned lighthouses in Canada.

MONCTON (D-5) pop. 61,046

Moncton began as a settlement of Acadian farmers near the French Fort Beauséjour *(see Fort Beauséjour National Historic Site p. 41)*. The British, under Lt. Col. Robert Monckton, captured the fort in 1755 and expelled the French. American Loyalists, Scots and Irish incorporated the town in 1855, naming it after Monckton. A clerical error accounts for its present spelling. Shipbuilding and railroads made Moncton the transportation hub of the Maritime Provinces.

Two natural phenomena, Magnetic Hill *(see attraction listing)* and the Tidal Bore, are highlights among city attractions. The Tidal Bore runs up the Petitcodiac River twice daily, causing a small tidal wave ranging in height from 20 to 45 centimetres (8 to 18 in.). The incoming tide moves upstream against the regular flow of water, causing a single river-wide wave. After the bore, the almost empty Petitcodiac River basin rapidly fills with water and, within an hour, the bore passes 28.3 million gallons of water and the water level rises more than 7.5 metres (25 ft.). A good place to observe the bore is at Bore Park, downtown.

Greater Moncton Chamber of Commerce: 910 Main St., Suite 100, Moncton, NB, Canada E1C 1G6; phone (506) 857-2883.

Self-guiding tours: A walking tour of the historic area begins at City Hall, 655 Main St. Brochures outlining the tour are available on the first floor of the Tourist Information Centre, 10 Bendview Ct.; phone (506) 853-3540.

Shopping areas: Highfield Square, at Highfield and Main, has more than 60 shops.

CENTENNIAL PARK is at 811 St. George Blvd. The 121-hectare (299-acre) park features woodland trails and a lake beach. Hiking and boating are popular; recreation areas include a football field and courts for tennis, lawn bowling and bocce ball. Canoes and paddleboats can be rented. A Sherman tank and a CF-100 jet fighter pay tribute to Canada's armed forces; a steam locomotive recalls the railroad's impact on Moncton.

Picnicking and swimming are permitted. Daily 8 a.m.-midnight. Park free. Beach $3; over 59 and ages 13-19, $2; ages 4-12, $1.50. Phone (506) 853-3516.

LUTZ MOUNTAIN HERITAGE MUSEUM is 1 km (.6 mi.) n. of Magnetic Hill at 3030 Mountain Rd. Built in 1883, the Second Moncton Baptist Church received worshippers until 1974. The building contains pioneer artifacts, cemetery records dating to 1766 and genealogical materials about families who settled the area. Guided tours are offered. Mon.-Sat. 10-6, July-Aug.; by appointment rest of year. Donations. Phone (506) 384-7719, or (506) 384-4967 in the off-season.

MAGIC MOUNTAIN WATER PARK is in Magnetic Hill Park, just off Trans-Canada Hwy. exit 450. The park contains six waterslides, a wave pool, a children's area with four smaller slides, a lazy river, a splash pad, a whirlpool, two miniature golf courses and an arcade. Entrance is via a three-level steamboat.

Food and picnic facilities are available. Daily 10-8, June 25-Aug. 21; 10-6, June 11-24 and Aug. 22-Labour Day. Admission $21; under 48 inches tall $16; over age 60, $6; under age 4 free; family rate (four people) $68 ($17 each additional person; $15 under 48 inches tall). Reduced price after 3:30 when closing at 8, after 2:30 when closing at 6, $15; under 48 inches tall $12. MC, VI. Phone (506) 857-9283, or (800) 331-9283 in Canada.

MAGNETIC HILL is on a side road next to Magic Mountain Water Park. For an unusual experience, visitors drive "downhill" to a spot indicated by a white post and then, with gears in neutral and brakes released, the car moves backward, coasting "up" the hill. This phenomenon is attributed to an optical illusion from the surrounding hillside sloping away from the road. Attendants are on duty during the main season only.

Parking is available for all vehicle types. Food is available. Daily 8-8, Victoria Day weekend-Labour Day; 10-6, day after Labour Day-Thanksgiving. Admission $5 per private vehicle. Admission free for buses and motorcycles. Phone (506) 853-3516.

MAGNETIC HILL ZOO is part of Magnetic Hill Park, just off Trans-Canada Hwy. exit 450. Visitors drive under a covered bridge to enter this 16-hectare (40-acre) zoo, which is home to 400 animals representing more than 90 species from around the world—tigers, jaguars, wolves, zebras, camels, lemurs, monkeys, hawks and pythons. At Old McDonald's Barnyard, children can feed white-tailed deer and goats.

Picnicking is permitted. Food is available. Daily 9-8, mid-June through Labour Day; daily 9-7, mid-May to mid-June; Mon.-Fri. 10-6, Sat.-Sun. 9-7, day after Labour Day-Oct. 31; Mon.-Fri. 10-4, Sat.-Sun. 9-5, Apr. 1 to mid-May. Admission mid-June through Labour Day $8.50; over 59 and ages 12-17, $7.50; ages 4-11, $5.50; family rate (two adults and two children) $24 (each additional child $4). Reduced rates offered rest of season. AX, MC, VI. Phone (506) 877-7720.

MONCTON MUSEUM is at 20 Mountain Rd. The two-story museum blends the stonework of the old City Hall with a stark, bold modern structure. Displays pertain to the history of Moncton as well as national and international traveling exhibits. The Free Meeting House, a national historic site entered through the museum, is the city's oldest building. Architecturally plain, the 1821 New England meetinghouse has no steeple or bell; its cemetery dates to 1816. Allow 1 hour minimum. Mon.-Sat. 9-4:30, Sun. 1-5. Donations. Phone (506) 856-4383.

NDSC HERITAGE ROOM is at 125 King St. in the NDSC Convent. This museum relates the contributions of the Sisters of Notre-Dame-du-Sacrè-Coeur to Acadian society in such areas as language, culture, fine arts and religion. Guided tours are offered in English. Allow 30 minutes minimum. Mon.-Fri. 9:30-noon and 2-4, Sat. 2-4; closed Jan. 1, Good Friday, Easter and Dec. 25. Donations. Phone (506) 857-9414.

THOMAS WILLIAMS HOUSE is at 103 Park St. Built in 1883 by Thomas Williams, an Intercolonial Railroad treasurer, the Victorian-style 12-room house features antiques, three fireplaces and memorabilia. Gardens cover the grounds. A tea room is open daily. Food is available. Allow 1 hour minimum. Mon.-Sat. 10-4:30, Sun. 1-4:30, July-Aug. Donations. Phone (506) 857-0590 or (506) 856-4383.

UNIVERSITÉ DE MONCTON is at 165 Massey Ave. Approximately 6,000 students are enrolled at the university, which was founded in 1963 and has campuses in Moncton, Edmundston and Shippagan.

With French as its study language, the university provides the province's Acadian community with its own academic institution. Phone (506) 858-4000.

Galerie d'Art Louise-et-Reuben-Cohen is in the Clément-Cormier Bldg. Changing monthly exhibits honor Acadian, Canadian and international artists. The permanent collection consists of contemporary works by artists mainly from the Maritime Provinces and Québec. Mon.-Fri. 10-5, Sat.-Sun. 1-5, June-Sept.; Tues.-Fri. 1-4:30, Sat.-Sun. 1-4, rest of year. Donations. Phone (506) 858-4088.

SAVE **Musée Acadien de l'Université de Moncton** is in the Clément-Cormier Bldg. The Acadian Museum specializes in the history and culture of the Acadians of the Maritime Provinces. Permanent and changing displays depict Acadian history from 1604 to the early 20th century.

Guided tours are offered by appointment. Allow 30 minutes minimum. Mon.-Fri. 10-5, Sat.-Sun. 1-5, June-Sept.; Tues.-Fri. 1-4:30, Sat.-Sun. 1-4, rest of year. Admission $4; over 59, students with ID and ages 12-18, $2. Phone (506) 858-4088.

NEW DENMARK (C-2) pop. 100

The little town of New Denmark claims to be North America's largest Danish colony. Settlers arrived in 1872, lured by promises of 100 acres of "good farming land" from the New Brunswick government. Pamphlets offered weather statistics to dispel the myth of harsh winters, noting that Canadians enjoyed healthier and longer lives than citizens of warmer climates.

NEW DENMARK MEMORIAL MUSEUM is 14 km (8 mi.) s. on Hwy. 2, then 6 km (4 mi.) to Lake Edward, following signs. Founded in 1872, New Denmark was the first Danish settlement in Canada. The museum displays farming and domestic artifacts pertaining to the lives of the settlers. Mon.-Sat. 9-5, Sun. 2-5, mid-June through Labour Day. Donations. Phone (506) 553-6724 or (506) 553-6464, or (506) 553-6764 in the off-season.

OROMOCTO (D-3) pop. 8,843

The home of Canadian Forces Base Gagetown, one of the largest military training areas in the British Commonwealth, Oromocto is on the south bank of the Saint John River. Of Maliseet origin, the town's name means "deep water" or "good river for canoes."

Oromocto Area Chamber of Commerce: Pioneer Plaza, 261 Restigouche Rd., Unit 16, Oromocto, NB, Canada E2V 2H1; phone (506) 446-6043.

CANADIAN FORCES BASE GAGETOWN MILITARY MUSEUM is on the military base in Bldg. A-5. Exhibits include uniforms, weapons and other artifacts of the 1800s, the South African War, World Wars I and II, the Korean War, United Nations missions and the present. Military vehicles are in an outdoor display area. Allow 1 hour minimum. Mon.-Fri. 8-4, Sat.-Sun. and holidays 10-4, June-Aug.;

Mon.-Fri. 8-4, rest of year. Closed legal holidays Sept.-May. Free. Phone (506) 422-1304.

PETIT-ROCHER (A-4) pop. 2,100

NEW BRUNSWICK MINING AND MINERALS INTERPRETATION CENTRE is on Hwy. 134 at 397 Rue Principale. The province's mining heritage is honored with exhibitions, educational games and visual projections. Highlights include a simulation of a mine-shaft descent to 975 metres (3,200 ft.). An amusement park is on the grounds. Picnicking is permitted. Daily 10-6, June-Aug. Admission $5.25; over 64, $4.25; ages 5-18, $3.25; under 5, $1; family rate $12. VI. Phone (506) 542-2672.

REXTON (C-5) pop. 810

Known in 1825 as The Yard, Rexton prospered as a shipyard until cargo-hauling barges, called timber droghers, were replaced by steam-powered ships later that century. The town is the birthplace of Andrew Bonar Law, the only prime minister of Great Britain born outside the British Isles.

BONAR LAW HISTORIC SITE is at jct. hwys. 134 and 116. The 1858 birthplace of Andrew Bonar Law, the only British prime minister born outside Great Britain, is preserved. This former farm has barns and other outbuildings as well as the main house, which is furnished with antiques. Also on the grounds is the Richibucto Museum. Picnic tables are provided along the scenic Richibucto River. Special events are scheduled throughout the summer. Daily 10-5, mid-June to early Sept. Donations. Phone (506) 523-7615.

RIVERSIDE-ALBERT (E-5)

Once known as Hopewell Corner, this village on the Shepody River at the upper reaches of the Bay of Fundy was a 19th-century shipbuilding center. Many homes and buildings from the period survive. The 1904 Riverside Consolidated School is the oldest of its kind still in use in New Brunswick.

CAPE ENRAGE LIGHTHOUSE is 17 km (11 mi.) s.e. on Hwy. 915, then 6.5 km (4 mi.) e. on Cape Enrage Rd. Built in 1848, this lighthouse on Chignecto Bay is fully automated and operates year-round. University and high-school students from the area live and work at the site. Fossil deposits can be seen along the coastline, where rock-climbing and rappelling are popular. Food is available and picnicking is permitted. Allow 1 hour minimum. Daily dawn-dusk. Admission $3. Phone (506) 887-2273.

SACKVILLE (D-6) pop. 5,361

Pioneer Acadians reclaimed from the sea much of the Sackville area by creating an extensive system of dikes known as *aboiteaux*. During the 18th century Sackville was called Tintamarre, derived from the French name referring to the thundering noise made by geese nesting in the surrounding marshes on a migratory bird route.

A town of firsts, Sackville claims Canada's first Baptist church as well as the first degree conferred upon a woman in the British Empire—the diploma was granted in 1875 at Mount Allison University. The liberal arts college was founded in 1839.

Sackville United Church, an 1876 white-steepled building that features woodwork, curved pews and rose stained-glass windows, houses a collection of photographs and historical items; phone (506) 536-0498. Lillas Fawcett Park on Main Street features a small beach and picnic area.

Greater Sackville Chamber of Commerce: 87 Main St., Unit 8, Sackville, NB, Canada E4L 4A8; phone (506) 364-8911.

OWENS ART GALLERY is on the campus of Mount Allison University at 61 York St. With more than 3,000 pieces in its permanent collection, the gallery specializes in contemporary Canadian art and 18th- and 19th-century European paintings, watercolors and prints. Allow 1 hour minimum. Mon.-Fri. 10-5, Sat.-Sun. 1-5; closed holidays. Donations. Phone (506) 364-2574.

SACKVILLE HARNESS SHOP is at 39 Main St. Open since 1920, the shop preserves the art of handcrafting horse collars and harnesses. Allow 30 minutes minimum. Mon.-Fri. 8-5, Sat. 8-noon; closed holidays. Free. Phone (506) 536-0642.

SACKVILLE WATERFOWL PARK is on Main St., adjacent to Mount Allison University. The 22-hectare (55-acre) park is in one of North America's major migratory bird routes. A 3.5-kilometre (2.2-mi.) boardwalk offers viewing platforms, an observation tower and interpretive signs. The visitor center provides a self-guiding tour pamphlet; guided 1.5-hour tours of the park depart from the Sackville Visitor Information Centre, which houses a wetlands display.

Park open daily dawn-dusk. Guided tours offered daily 9-4, June-Aug. Tours by appointment Sept.-Oct. Wetlands display open daily 9-8, June-Oct. Park admission free. Guided tour $5; over 49, $3.50; ages 6-16, $3; family rate (four people) $10. Reservations are recommended. Phone (506) 364-4967, or (800) 249-2020 in Canada and New England.

ST. ANDREWS (F-3) pop. 1,869

St. Andrews is on Passamaquoddy Bay; the tidal variation here is about 8 metres (26 ft.). St. Andrews was settled by United Empire Loyalists in 1783 following the American Revolution. Many of their white clapboard houses were dismantled, barged from Castine, Maine, and reassembled; the houses can still be seen today.

Around the turn of the 20th century St. Andrews-by-the-Sea flourished as Canada's first seaside resort town; the Algonquin, a renowned hotel built in 1889, still stands as testament to that era. More than 250 homes in the historic district are 100 to more than 200 years old. The heart of the town still looks much as it did in early photographs.

St. Andrews Chamber of Commerce: 46 Reed Ave., St. Andrews, NB, Canada E5B 1A1; phone (506) 529-3555 or (506) 529-3556.

ATLANTIC SALMON INTERPRETIVE CENTRE is off Hwy. 127E at 24 Chamcook Lake Rd. This complex of post-and-beam buildings features an exhibit hall and an in-stream aquarium with adult Atlantic salmon. Visitors can see the salmon up close through windows. Exhibits include a hall of fame for individuals who have contributed to the conservation of Atlantic salmon. Lectures and guided walks are available. Nature trails along Chamcook Creek are featured.

Picnic facilities are available. Daily 9-5, mid-May to late Sept. Admission $5; senior citizens $4.50; ages 13-18, $3.50; ages 5-12, $2.50; family rate $15. Phone (506) 529-4581 or (506) 529-1384.

CHARLOTTE COUNTY ARCHIVES is in the center of town at 123 Frederick St. Housed in the 1832 county jail, the archives present historical documents recounting local history. Allow 30 minutes minimum. Mon.-Fri. 9-5, July-Aug.; Mon.-Fri. 9-noon and 1-5 in June and Sept.; Mon.-Fri. 1-4, Oct.-Nov. Free. Phone (506) 529-4248.

FUNDY TIDE RUNNERS WHALE WATCHING AND NATURE TOURS departs from Market Wharf at 16 King St. Two-hour whale-watching trips are offered aboard a 7-metre (24-ft.), rigid-hull Zodiac Hurricane. Finback, humpback and minke whales may be seen, and bald eagles, marine birds, porpoises and seals are regularly sighted.

Allow 2 hours, 30 minutes minimum. Trips depart daily at 10, 1, 4 and 6:30, June-Aug.; at 10, 1 and 4, in Sept.; at 2 in May and Oct. Visitors should arrive 45 minutes prior to departure. Fare $48; ages 5-12, $35. Under 5 are not permitted. Reservations are recommended. MC, VI. Phone (506) 529-4481.

GREENOCK PRESBYTERIAN CHURCH is at Montague and Edward sts. Capt. Christopher Scott erected the church in 1824. A design of nearly perfect proportions enabled the pulpit and the minister's and precentor's platforms to be constructed entirely without nails. On the steeple is a hand-carved green oak tree with bright green foliage, the emblem of the town of Greenock (Green Oak), Scotland, Scott's birthplace.

Open Mon.-Sat. 9-noon and 1-4:30, July-Aug. Church service Sun. at 11:15, May-Oct.; at 9, rest of year. Phone (506) 529-3058.

THE HUNTSMAN AQUARIUM/MUSEUM is 3.2 km (2 mi.) n.w. on Lower Campus Rd., next to the St. Andrews Biological Station. A museum and aquarium feature the diverse marine life found in the Gulf of Maine and the Bay of Fundy, including a family of harbor seals. Displays include native fish, marine invertebrates, amphibians, reptiles and marine plants as well as fishing, research and geology exhibits, videotapes and a touch pool.

Daily 10-5, Sat. before Victoria Day-Labour Day; Thurs.-Sun. 10-5, day after Labour Day-last Sun. in

Sept. Admission $7.50; over 64, $6.50; ages 4-17, $5. MC, VI. Phone (506) 529-1202.

JOLLY BREEZE OF ST. ANDREWS is at Market Wharf near the corner of Water and King sts. Passengers board the *Jolly Breeze*—a 70-foot-long, steel-hull, square-rigged cutter—for whale watch excursions into the Bay of Fundy and Passamaquoddy Bay. Built in 1989, the ship is a replica of a tall ship from the early 1900s complete with teak decks. During the cruise, knowledgeable crew members answer questions about local history and wildlife. If weather conditions permit, passengers may assist with the sails or take the helm.

Food is available. Warm clothing is recommended. Allow 3 hours, 30 minutes minimum. Cruises depart daily at 8, noon and 4, July-Aug.; at 9:30, 1:30 and 5:30, in June and Sept. Fare $45; over 65, $41; ages 4-15, $33; family rate (four people) $132. AX, MC, VI. Phone (506) 529-8116.

KINGSBRAE GARDEN is at 220 King St. Overlooking Passamaquoddy Bay, the 11-hectare (27-acre) horticultural garden features some 50,000 flowers, shrubs and trees. Themed displays include cottage, rose, perennial, knot, ornamental grass, bird and butterfly, fantasy, gravel, culinary herb, edible and wildflower gardens. The Scents and Sensitivity Garden is notable for its raised garden and special flora chosen for the enjoyment of the visually impaired; all signs are in Braille.

Classical music is played throughout the 26 gardens of the .8-hectare (2-acre) Perennial Garden, which is enclosed by century-old cedar hedges. A woodland trail winds through an old-growth Acadian forest, and a cedar maze leads into a labyrinth. A plant center features unusual plants and shrubs; an art gallery features the works of local artists. The gates open during the winter holiday season for the Garden of Lights Festival.

Food is available. Allow 1 hour, 30 minutes minimum. Daily 9-6, mid-May through second Sat. in Oct. Admission $9; over 60 and ages 7-18, $7; family rate $23. Plant center free. Phone (506) 529-3335, ext. 1, or (866) 566-8687.

MINISTERS ISLAND HISTORIC SITE is 2 km (1.2 mi.) n. on Hwy. 127 to Bar Rd. Named for an Anglican minister who settled here in 1786, the island is the site of Covenhoven, the baronial summer home of Sir William Van Horne, first president of the Canadian Pacific Railway. Guided 2-hour tours begin with a drive across a sand bar to the island and continue through the 50-room villa, a spacious livestock barn and a bath house with a tidal swimming pool.

Visitors must provide their own transportation to the island. Tours depart twice daily, June-Oct. Tour times depend on the tides and are available from the St. Andrews Welcome Centre, 46 Reed Ave. Admission $5; ages 13-18, $2.50. Phone (506) 529-5081.

ROSS MEMORIAL MUSEUM is at 188 Montague St. at King St. Exhibits in the 1824 Georgian brick house include fine examples of 19th-century New Brunswick and American furniture as well as clocks, Canadian and American paintings, Oriental rugs and other treasures from the benefactors' world travels. Allow 30 minutes minimum. Mon.-Sat. 10-4:30, early June through day before Thanksgiving. Donations. Phone (506) 529-5124.

ST. ANDREWS BLOCKHOUSE NATIONAL HISTORIC SITE OF CANADA is at 23 Joe's Point Rd. on the waterfront. The fortification was built during the War of 1812 to protect the town from American privateers. Damaged by fire in 1993, the blockhouse has been restored and contains accurate reproductions of artifacts from the 1800s. The beachfront is popular for picnicking. Daily 10-6, June-Aug. Admission $1, students with ID 50c. Phone (506) 529-4270, or (506) 636-4011 in the off-season.

SHERIFF ANDREWS HOUSE HISTORIC SITE is at 63 King St. at Queen St. Guides dressed in period costumes offer 20-minute tours of the two-story brick home of Elijah Andrews, sheriff of Charlotte County in 1820. Mon.-Sat. 9:30-4:30, Sun. 1-4:30, late June-late Sept. Donations. Phone (506) 529-5080.

SUNBURY SHORES ARTS AND NATURE CENTRE INC. is at 139 Water St. The center offers exhibits, courses and workshops about natural history, arts and crafts. Daily 9-4:30, June 15-Sept. 1; Mon.-Fri. 9-4:30, rest of year. Donations. Phone (506) 529-3386.

WHALES & WILDLIFE CATAMARAN STYLE departs from the Public Wharf at 6 King St. Narrated 2.5- to 3-hour sightseeing trips aboard the catamaran M/V *Quoddy Link* frequently offer sightings of humpback, finback and minke whales, seals, porpoises, sea bird colonies, bald eagles, an aquaculture site and a herring weir on the Bay of Fundy.

Warm clothing is advised. Food is available. Cruises depart daily (weather permitting) at 10, 2 and 5:30, late June-early Oct. Fare $45; over 60, $42; under 14, $25. Reservations are required. MC, VI. Phone (506) 529-2600 or (877) 688-2600.

ST. GEORGE (F-3) pop. 1,509

In 1872 St. George became the site of a granite industry, supplying red granite for such important buildings as a cathedral in Boston and the Parliament buildings in Ottawa.

The town is now known for deer hunting as well as trout and salmon fishing. At St. George the Magaguadavic River flows through a scenic narrow gorge, where a fish ladder helps salmon and other fish navigate the falls. Lake Utopia, a few minutes' drive from St. George, boasts smooth sand beaches as well as plentiful fishing.

Eastern Charlotte Chamber of Commerce: 21 Main St., Unit 1, St. George, NB, Canada E5C 3H9; phone (506) 755-3202.

RECREATIONAL ACTIVITIES
Summer Activities

• **The Outdoor Adventure Company** is in Granite Town Hotel, 79 Main St., St. George, NB, Canada E5C 3J4. Daily 10-6, May 15-Oct. 15. Phone (506) 755-6415 or (800) 667-2010.

ST-JACQUES (B-1) pop. 1,715

Settled by Irish immigrants in 1834, St-Jacques later became a haven for Acadian deportees. The town on the banks of the Madawaska River is a gateway to the Upper Saint John River Valley.

St-Jacques Visitor Information Centre: 17412 Trans-Canada Hwy. 2, St-Jacques, NB, Canada E7B 2J8; phone (506) 735-2747.

ANTIQUE AUTOMOBILE MUSEUM is off Hwy. 2 exit 8 at entrance to de la République Provincial Park. Vintage cars dating 1905-30 as well as a 1974 Bricklin are displayed. Daily 9-8, early June-early Sept. Admission $3.75; over 64 and ages 6-18, $3; family rate $9. Phone (506) 735-2525.

NEW BRUNSWICK BOTANICAL GARDEN is off Hwy. 2 exit 8 at 15 Principale St. More than 80,000 annual, perennial and alpine plants are displayed in a 7-hectare (17-acre) setting. Classical music accompanies visitors as they walk through eight thematic gardens and two arboretums. Guided tours are offered by reservation. Food is available. Allow 1 hour minimum. Daily 9-8, July-Aug.; 9-6 in June and Sept. Admission $5.25; over 64 and students with ID $4.75; ages 7-12, $2.50; family rate $12. MC, VI. Phone (506) 737-5383.

SAINT JOHN (E-4) pop. 69,661
See map page 54.

Saint John, at the mouth of the Saint John River on the Bay of Fundy, is one of the most active seaports on the Atlantic coast. Its deepwater oil terminals handle some of the world's largest ships.

When Samuel de Champlain entered the estuary of the Saint John River on June 24, 1604, he named the river in honor of the saint whose feast day it was. After the American Revolutionary War several thousand United Empire Loyalists settled in Saint John. In 1785 it became the first incorporated city in Canada.

Restoration of the city's waterfront has blended the area's historic flavor with such modern fixtures as a climate-controlled skywalk, linking the central business district with the waterfront; a convention and trade center; two hotels; commercial offices; Brunswick and Market squares shopping complexes; the Mercantile Centre; Harbour Station; and the Saint John City Market. The Harbour Passage, a series of walking and bicycling trails, links heritage sites along the waterfront.

The Saint John Firefighters Museum, 24 Sydney St., is housed in an 1840 firehouse and features area artifacts, photographs and fire-related memorabilia from the Great Saint John Fire of 1877; phone (506) 633-1840.

The Grand Ole Atlantic National Exhibition commences the last weekend of August and features a large midway and horticultural and livestock exhibits.

Tourism Saint John: P.O. Box 1971, Saint John, NB, Canada E2L 4L1; phone (506) 658-2990. *See Self-guiding tours section for locations.*

Self-guiding tours: The Loyalist Trail, a 90-minute walking tour through downtown Saint John, retraces the footsteps of the city's Loyalist founders. Prince William's Walk, also about 90 minutes, is through the old commercial district along Prince William, Princess and Germain streets. The Victorian Stroll, a 2-hour tour of the downtown residential area, includes the post-1877 architecture found on King Street E. and Orange and Germain streets. The West Side Walk & Drive explores the historic Conway area.

Brochures outlining these tours are available at the following Visitor Information Centres: on the 11th floor of City Hall; on the first floor of Market Square; at the foot of King Street on Market Square; and at both seasonal city tourist information centers, located at Reversing Falls and Hwy. 1; phone (866) 463-8639.

Shopping areas: Near the waterfront are Brunswick Square and Market Square, where stores offer such items as china, crafts and antiques. Saint John's largest shopping complex, McAllister Place, is in the eastern part of the city at the corner of McAllister Drive and Westmoreland Road; the 110 stores include Sears, Sobey's and Zellers.

BARBOUR'S GENERAL STORE is at Loyalist Plaza opposite Market Square. The restored 19th-century country store contains some 2,000 artifacts, including grocery items, china, farm tools and kitchen utensils. At the back is a barbershop and dental office; a pharmacy stocks 300 remedies. Costumed interpreters provide historical information. Daily 9-6, mid-June to Labour Day. Donations. Phone (506) 658-2939, (506) 658-2855 or (866) 463-8639.

CARLETON MARTELLO TOWER NATIONAL HISTORIC SITE OF CANADA is off Hwy. 1 exit 120 (Digby Ferry) to 454 Whipple St. Completed in 1815, the circular stone fort served a crucial role in the defense of Saint John and its harbor until 1944. The tower offers a panorama of Canada's oldest incorporated city, including the harbor and the Bay of Fundy. The site includes restored 1866 barracks, a restored 1845 powder magazine, an audiovisual presentation about the defense of the city during World War II and a visitor reception center with exhibits.

Allow 30 minutes minimum. Daily 10-5:30, June 1-first weekend in Oct. Admission $3.95; over 65, $3.45; ages 6-16, $1.95; family rate $9.90. Phone (506) 636-4011.

CHERRY BROOK ZOO is at 901 Foster Thurston Dr. in Rockwood Park. The wooded setting is home to 38 species, including jaguars, lions, tigers and zebras. In a walk through the Vanished Kingdom Park, visitors can see replicas of animals that have become extinct in the past 200 years. Zoo open daily 10-dusk (weather permitting); closed Dec. 25. Last admission 1 hour before closing. Vanished Kingdom open May-Oct. Admission $6.50; over 54, $5.50; ages 13-17, $5; ages 2-12, $3.50; family rate (two adults and two children) $16.50. Rates may vary; phone ahead. AX, MC, VI. Phone (506) 634-1440.

FORT HOWE LOOKOUT is on Magazine St. First built in Halifax, Nova Scotia, in 1777, the fort was then disassembled, shipped to Fort Howe and reassembled to protect the Saint John harbor. A reconstructed blockhouse overlooks the city, and lookouts provide panoramic views of Saint John. Daily 24 hours. Free.

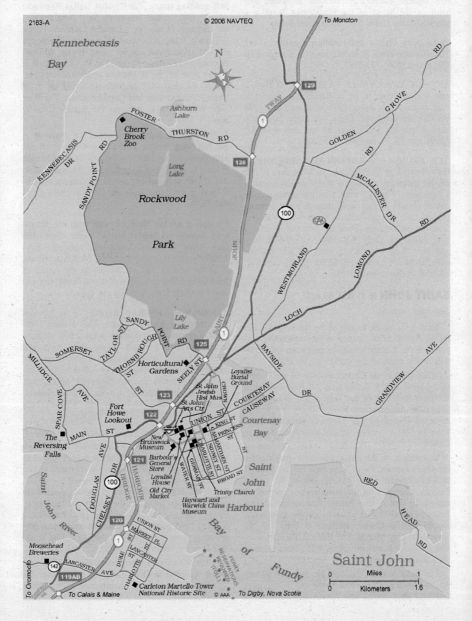

HAYWARD AND WARWICK CHINA MUSEUM is at jct. Princess and Germain sts. at 85 Princess St. Fine china, earthenware and souvenir china manufactured from 1785 to the present are on display. Also featured are exhibits about shipping methods and Foley pottery. Allow 30 minutes minimum. Mon.-Sat. 10-5; closed major holidays. Free. Phone (506) 653-9066 or (888) 653-9066.

HORTICULTURAL GARDENS is at 48 Seely St. and Crown St. Established in 1893, the 1.5-hectare (4-acre) gardens are noted for their floral displays. A monument commemorates local men who fought in World War I. Greenhouses contain a variety of annuals and perennials. Allow 30 minutes minimum. Daily dawn-dusk. Free. Phone (506) 657-1773.

IRVING NATURE PARK is off Hwy. 1 exit 119B (Catherwood), .5 km (.3 mi.) s., then 3 km (1.9 mi.) e. on Sand Cove Rd. On a peninsula in the Bay of Fundy, this protected ecosystem includes an Acadian forest, tidal pools, a salt marsh estuary, mud flats and a barrier beach. Some 250 species of migratory birds have been seen in the area.

A road encircles the park, and eight trails enable visitors to explore on foot or bicycle. An information kiosk is beyond Saints Rest Beach. Free guided tours are available. Picnicking is permitted. Trails open daily 8-dusk; road open May 1-Nov. 15 (weather permitting). Free. Phone (506) 653-7367.

LOYALIST BURIAL GROUND is at Sydney St. and King St. E. Established in 1784, the cemetery once was used as a burial site by United Empire Loyalists. Daily dawn-dusk. Free.

LOYALIST HOUSE is at 120 Union St. at Germain St. The Georgian edifice was built 1810-17 and has been restored in period. Occupied by the same family for nearly 150 years, the house—the city's oldest

unaltered building—survived the Great Fire of 1877. Costumed guides provide historical information about the house and its artifacts. Mon.-Sat. 10-5, Sun. noon-5, mid-May through Aug. 31. Admission $3; students with ID and ages 4-18, $1; family rate $7. Phone (506) 652-3590.

MOOSEHEAD BREWERIES is at 89 Main St. W. Founded in 1867, Canada's oldest independently owned brewery offers guided 1-hour tours that explain the brewing process and culminate in a free tasting. Allow 1 hour minimum. Tours depart from 49 Main St. Mon.-Fri. at 10, 1 and 3, June-Aug. Schedule may vary; phone ahead. Free. Reservations are recommended. Phone (506) 635-7020, (506) 635-7000 or (800) 793-0011.

NEW BRUNSWICK MUSEUM is downtown at 1 Market Sq. The museum describes New Brunswick history, the natural sciences and fine and decorative arts. Imposing whale models and skeletons are suspended from the ceiling in the Hall of the Great Whales. Visitors can also learn about New Brunswick's shipbuilding heritage and the Bay of Fundy high tides or see evidence of the area's geological history. Historical records are available in the archives and research library at 277 Douglas Ave.

Guided tours are offered; reservations are suggested. Museum open Mon.-Fri. 9-5 (also Thurs. 5-9), Sat. 10-5, Sun. and holidays noon-5, May-Oct.; Tues.-Fri. 9-5 (also Thurs. 5-9), Sat. 10-5, Sun. and holidays noon-5, rest of year. Closed Jan. 1, Good Friday and Dec. 25-26. Admission $6; over 59, $4.75; students with ID and ages 4-18, $3.25; family rate $13. AX, MC, VI. Phone (506) 643-2300.

THE REVERSING FALLS are at the mouth of the Saint John River near the foot of Chesley Dr. (Hwy.

Oceanfront
Accommodations
& Dining

Saint John's Only
Accommodation by the Sea.

Next to the
Irving Nature Park

INN ON THE COVE
& S P A

1371 Sand Cove Road • Toll Free: 877-257-8080 • Tel.: 506-672-7799 • Web: www.InnontheCove.com

100). The reversing "falls" are created when, at low tide, the river descends into the ocean at the bottom of a 137-metre-wide (449-ft.) gorge. At slack tide the waters are quiet. Then, with the incoming tide, the ocean rises upstream through the chasm. Several bridges span the falls, and a visitor center at 200 Bridge St. offers an excellent view. The phenomenon should be seen at high and low tides to be appreciated fully.

Food is available. Tide tables are available at CAA Maritimes and tourist bureau offices in Saint John. Visitor center open daily 8-8, June 9-Sept. 7; 8-7, Sept. 8-Oct. 13; 9-6, May 16-June 8. Visitor center free. Phone (506) 658-2937.

[SAVE] **REVERSING FALLS JET BOAT TOURS & RIDES** offers sightseeing tours departing from 1 Market Sq. and thrill rides departing from 55 Fallsview Park. A 1-hour narrated jet boat tour allows passengers to view the Reversing Falls and whirlpools as well as seals, historic sites, Fort La Tour and Partridge Island. Guides relate the legend of Glooscap, an Indian god who is the guardian of the falls.

Also available is a 20-minute thrill ride that takes participants on an accelerated trip through the rapids of the Reversing Falls. Thrill ride passengers are advised to bring a change of clothing and a towel. This trip is not recommended for pregnant women or those with back problems or other physical impairments.

Tours depart daily 10-dusk, early June to early Oct. Fare for either sightseeing tour or thrill ride $37.95; ages 3-12, $29.95. Under 42 inches tall are not permitted on the thrill ride; under age 12 must be with an adult. Reservations are recommended. MC, VI. Phone (506) 634-8987 or (888) 634-8987.

ROCKWOOD PARK is 2 km (1.2 mi.) n. overlooking Saint John on Mount Pleasant Ave. N. The 870-hectare (2,150-acre) recreational area offers a wide range of year-round outdoor recreation facilities. One of Canada's largest municipal parks, Rockwood contains gardens, nature and riding trails, a large playground, an 18-hole golf course, an arboretum, an aquatic driving range, a camping area and 13 lakes.

Canoeing, kayaking, sleigh rides, cross-country skiing and ice skating are available. Picnicking is permitted. Daily dawn-dusk. Free. Phone (506) 658-2883. *See Recreation Chart and the AAA/CAA Eastern Canada CampBook.*

SAINT JOHN ARTS CENTRE is at 20 Hazen Ave. The multi-disciplinary venue serves the community through arts, educational and cultural programming. The building was donated to the community by Andrew Carnegie in 1904. A stained-glass skylight, oak wainscoting and mosaic tile foyer floor have been restored to their original grandeur. Tues.-Wed. 10-4, Thurs.-Fri. 10-7, Sat. noon-4. Donations. Phone (506) 633-4870.

SAINT JOHN BUS TOURS depart from Barbour's General Store, Reversing Falls or Rockwood Park.

Narrated 2-hour bus tours highlight the landmarks of historic Saint John. Trips depart daily at 10 and 1, mid-June to early Oct. Fare $17; ages 6-14, $5. Phone (506) 658-4701.

SAINT JOHN CITY MARKET is at 47 Charlotte St. opposite the n.w. corner of King Sq. The interior of this 1876 building, modeled after an inverted ship's hull, reflects the city's shipbuilding heritage. Described as Canada's oldest charter market, it offers fresh seafood, meat and produce and houses a variety of working artisans, gift shops and eateries. Allow 30 minutes minimum. Mon.-Thurs. 7:30-6, Fri. 7:30-7, Sat. 7:30-5; closed holidays. Free. Phone (506) 658-2820.

SAINT JOHN JEWISH HISTORICAL MUSEUM is at 29 Wellington Row. Considered the only Jewish museum in the Atlantic Provinces, the center features seven display areas telling the story of the Jewish community. Exhibits include a Hebrew school, a chapel, an art gallery, a religious room, Jewish artifacts and memorabilia. An archive, library and guided tours are available. Allow 30 minutes minimum. Mon.-Fri. 10-4 (also Sun. 1-4, July-Aug.), late May-late Oct. Donations. Phone (506) 633-1833.

TRINITY CHURCH is at 115 Charlotte St. Built in 1791, the church was destroyed by fire in 1877 and rebuilt in 1880. It contains the Royal Coat of Arms of King George III, which was smuggled out of the Boston State House by Loyalists during the American Revolution. Guided tours are available in the summer. Mon.-Fri. 9-5, July-Aug.; 9-3, rest of year. Donations. Phone (506) 693-8558.

ST. MARTINS (E-4) pop. 374

Settled around 1783, Quaco, as St. Martins first was known, became one of the most prosperous shipbuilding centers in eastern Canada. More than 500 ships were built in a dozen family boatyards during the next 100 years. The era of great sailing ships left its imprint on the town's homes as ship's carpenters decorated them with elaborate architectural details.

Complementing these historic houses are a lighthouse and twin covered bridges. These as well as the rugged setting have made St. Martins a popular scene for photographers and painters.

[GEM] **FUNDY TRAIL** is e. off Hwy. 111. This multi-use parkway follows the northern coast of the Bay of Fundy between St. Martins and Fundy National Park, offering spectacular views of the Quaco Head Lighthouse, Melvin and Pangburn beaches, Fuller Falls and coastal wildlife. An 11-kilometre (7-mi.) low-speed roadway features scenic lookouts; 16 kilometres (10 mi.) of walking and bicycling trails include footpaths to beaches and river estuaries.

At the Big Salmon River Interpretive Centre visitors may cross a suspension foot bridge and see old wharfs and sluices, remnants of the river's lumbering days. The center features a videotape presentation and artifacts related to local history.

Food is available, and picnicking is permitted. Allow 2 hours minimum. Trail open daily 6 a.m.-8 p.m., mid-May to mid-Oct. Interpretive center daily 8-8, mid-May to mid-Oct. Fee $3 per person; under 13, $2; family rate (two adults and two children) $10; multi-day pass $12. AX, MC, VI. Phone (506) 833-2019 or (866) 386-3987.

QUACO MUSEUM AND LIBRARY is at 236 Main St. The history and heritage of the St. Martins area is preserved. The museum's main exhibits, which change annually, often deal with shipbuilding—the most important economic and social aspect of the region. Photographs trace the village's growth and show the area's more prominent topographical and geologic features. The archives contain genealogical research material.

Mon.-Sat. 10-5, Sun. 1-5, June-Oct.; by appointment rest of year. Admission $2, over 54 and students with ID $1, under 12 free with adult. Phone (506) 833-4740.

ST. STEPHEN (F-2) pop. 4,667

St. Stephen is on the banks of the tidal St. Croix River, which is the boundary between Canada and the United States; the 7-metre (24-ft.) tides rise and fall twice daily. The International Ferry Point Bridge leads to Calais, Maine, the town's nearest neighbor and closest friend. That friendship hit its acme during the War of 1812, when St. Stephen lent a supply of gunpowder to Calais so that both communities could enjoy Independence Day celebrations rather than engaging in war.

The friendship continues to be obvious during the International Festival in early August, which includes a cross-border parade, entertainment, sporting events and fireworks, typifying the St. Stephen-Calais cooperation.

Chocolate sweetens the spirit of collaboration during the Chocolate Festival in early August. This event, with its chocolate dinners, contests and demonstrations, commemorates the introduction of the chocolate bar, which is reputed to have been created locally at the Ganong Bros. candy factory in 1906; the factory also created the first heart-shaped Valentine's Day candy box.

St. Stephen Provincial Visitor Information Centre: 5 King St., St. Stephen, NB, Canada E3L 2C1; phone (506) 466-7390.

CHARLOTTE COUNTY MUSEUM is at 443 Milltown Blvd. Housed in the 1864 mansion of the lumber baron James Murchie, the museum displays artifacts depicting the county's Loyalist origins and other aspects of its history. Allow 30 minutes minimum. Mon.-Sat. 9:30-4:30, June-Aug.; by appointment in Sept. Donations. Phone (506) 466-3295.

SAVE **THE CHOCOLATE MUSEUM** is at 73 Milltown Blvd. Highlights include hands-on exhibits, interactive computer displays, a candy-making video, games, and collections of historic chocolate boxes and antique equipment from the candy-making company founded by the Ganong brothers in 1873. Chocolate samples are available. The Heritage Chocolate Walk is a guided 2- to 3-hour walking tour of the museum and St. Stephen's historic buildings.

Comfortable walking shoes are recommended. Museum open Mon.-Sat. 9-6:30, Sun. 1-5, June 15-Aug. 31; Mon.-Sat. 9-5, in Sept.; Mon.-Fri. 9-5, rest of year. Closed holidays Oct.-May. Heritage Chocolate Walk offered mid-June to mid-Sept. Museum admission $5; over 54 and ages 6-17, $4; ages 3-5, $3; family rate $15. Heritage Chocolate Walk $10; over 54 and ages 6-17, $8; ages 3-5, $6; family rate $25. Reservations are recommended for the walking tour. VI. Phone (506) 466-7848.

SHEDIAC (D-5) pop. 4,892

Known for its excellent beaches and the warmest water north of Virginia, Shediac claims to be the lobster capital of the world. The weeklong Shediac Lobster Festival takes place in early July and includes a sand sculpture contest at nearby Parlee Beach Provincial Park *(see Recreation Chart).*

Shediac Visitor Information Bureau: 229 Main St., Shediac, NB, Canada E4P 2A5; phone (506) 532-7788.

SHIPPAGAN (A-5) pop. 2,872

Of Mi'kmaq origin, the word Shippagan means "passage of ducks." The town, at the northeastern tip of the Acadian Peninsula, was the site of a Jesuit settlement 1634-62. During that period Nicholas Denys established a trading post that drew Acadian fishermen to the area. Commercial fishing now leads the town's economic concerns. Vast bogs provide major harvests of peat moss.

Municipality of Shippagan: 200 Ave. Hotel De Ville, Shippagan, NB, Canada E8S 1M1; phone (506) 336-3900.

GEM **NEW BRUNSWICK AQUARIUM AND MARINE CENTRE** is on Hwy. 113 off Hwy. 11. A modern building sits amid spacious grounds overlooking the Bay of Chaleur. The center depicts the effect of the sea on life along New Brunswick's northeast coast since the 1500s. Exhibits relate to fishermen, ships and boats; aquariums display more than 100 species of marine life.

A 20-minute audiovisual presentation explains the fishing history of the Gulf of St. Lawrence. The cabin of a reconstructed modern trawler allows visitors to see the array of electronic devices now used in the fishing industry. Educational feeding sessions are held twice daily for the aquarium's harbor seals.

Food is available. Allow 2 hours minimum. Daily 10-6, mid-May to late Sept. Admission $8; over 64, $6; ages 6-18, $5; family rate $20. MC, VI. Phone (506) 336-3013.

SUSSEX (E-4) pop. 4,182

Sussex is a traditional town at the juncture of Fundy Coastal Scenic Drive and the River Valley Scenic Drive in the heart of Kings County, known for its covered bridges. Covered to protect the flooring and timbers from the effects of sun and rain, the 16 bridges stand throughout the county; more than half are within a 12-kilometre (7-mi.) radius of Sussex. Oldfield, a 30-metre-long (98-ft.) bridge that spans Smiths Creek, was featured on a commemorative 25-cent coin in 1992.

The "kissing bridges," still romantic spots for courting couples, also are popular with the wishful. Local lore says riders' wishes come true if they can hold their breath and lift their feet from the car's floorboards until the car has traveled the span. Maps detailing bridge sites can be obtained from the Sussex and Area Tourist Interpretive Centre off Hwy. 1 exit 195.

The Atlantic Balloon Fiesta and the Giant Flea Market and Antique Car Covered Bridge Tour both take place in September.

Kings County Tourism Association: 57 Wheeler Rd., Site 1, Four Corners, NB, Canada E4G 2W3; phone (506) 433-2214.

WOODSTOCK (D-2) pop. 5,198

Woodstock is a major border-crossing point with the United States and the oldest incorporated town in New Brunswick. Largely settled by Loyalists after the American Revolution, it is now nestled between the Trans-Canada Hwy. and the Saint John River. The river affords much recreational activity, as do the Trans Canada Trail System and the N.B. Snowmobile Federation Trail.

Woodstock Provincial Visitor Information Centre: 109 Tourist Bureau Rd., Woodstock, NB, Canada E7M 4W8; phone (506) 325-4427.

OLD CARLETON COUNTY COURT HOUSE is 2 km (1.2 mi.) n. on Hwy. 560 via Hwy. 103 at 19 Court St. The court house is restored to its mid-1800s appearance. Highlights include the old jury and prisoner's rooms as well as the main courtroom and the judge's chamber. Daily 9-noon and 1-6, July-Aug. Donations. Phone (506) 328-9706.

Newfoundland and Labrador

Mighty Moose
Reaching nearly 7 feet tall, some 125,000 of these huge creatures wander the island

Immense Icebergs
Ancient mountains of fresh water silently drift past rugged coastlines

Playful Whales
Majestic humpbacks dance in the chilling waters

Visiting Vikings
Norse artifacts are unearthed at North America's first European settlement—L'Anse aux Meadows

Colliding Continents
Powerful glacial erosion and continental drift left behind dramatic landscapes in Gros Morne National Park of Canada

Point Amour Lighthouse, L'Anse-Amour
Michael Hockney
Canadian Tourism Commission

a feast for
the eyes

Cape St. Mary's Ecological Reserve, St. Bride's
Newfoundland and Labrador Tourism

C are for some cod cheeks or seal flipper
pie? These admittedly unusual dishes are
quite common fare at Newfoundland's
dinner tables.

But if such delicacies aren't your cup of tea, try
something less exotic: Bakeapple pie, made with
wild berries plucked from coastal bogs, is one
savory local treat. Walk off the extra calories with
a stroll along St. John's harbor. The east end,
guarded by windswept headlands, shelters a jumble
of brightly painted clapboard houses clinging to
rocks above the shoreline—a lovely scene repeated
all along the Newfoundland and Labrador coasts.

Explore the historic narrow streets behind the
bustling harborfront and you'll find a few
restaurants still serving traditional fare, including
Jigg's dinner (vegetables boiled with salted meat),
fish and brewis (boiled fish and boiled hard bread
chopped together) and figgy duff (steamed pudding
with raisins)—evidence of Newfoundland's British,
Irish and seafaring roots.

Trek up to Cabot Tower, high atop Signal Hill,
for breathtaking views of the city and its harbor. In
summer, you'll get another taste of the province's
heritage: the Signal Hill Tattoo, a reenactment of
military exercises performed by cadets in scarlet
and blue colonial-era uniforms.

Whether you sample local flavor with your
tongue or your eyes, Newfoundland serves up
ingredients to satisfy any appetite.

Journey to Newfoundland and Labrador, and a friendly native may ask, "What brings you here?"

Surprisingly, your best response might be "other visitors," for despite its remoteness, Newfoundland and Labrador has long been a crossroads for all sorts of fascinating travelers.

Islands of Ice

Take icebergs, for example. In spring and early summer, these arctic voyagers parade down "Iceberg Alley" courtesy of the southerly flowing Labrador Current. No casual daytrippers, the alley's mobile mountains have been on the move for thousands of years: first as compacted snow trapped in Greenland's slowly flowing glaciers, then up to 3 years more as seaborne bergs.

By the time they reach Newfoundland and Labrador, most have melted down to house- or car-sized "growlers" and smaller chunks called "bergy bits." Many, however, glide offshore as awesome blue-and-white giants sculpted by wind and waves into fantastic shapes replete with spires, domes and arches—invariably evoking images of castles and cathedrals.

With its myriad promontories jutting into the North Atlantic, Newfoundland and Labrador's east coast offers countless spots from which to observe this seasonal procession: Try Long Point, near Twillingate; Notre Dame Bay or St. Anthony.

For an even closer encounter, take a boat tour out to the ice. Excursions depart from numerous ports, including Newman Sound Wharf in Terra Nova National Park of Canada. From here your chances of spying an itinerant berg are great April through July, but even if you arrive during Iceberg Alley's slack time, the park's scenery will not disappoint.

Breakers pummel Terra Nova's imposing headlands, and once subdued, lap softly against tranquil beaches. Dense forests blanket a rugged terrain providing sanctuary for black bears, red foxes, lynx and moose. To help you take it all in, lookout towers offer panoramas at Ochre Hill and Blue Hill.

And icebergs aren't the only behemoths to watch for: Humpback whales tarry along the shoreline from May through August. Keep your camera handy; with luck, you may see one of these mighty creatures breach, dramatically thrusting its massive body out of the water and falling back again with a thunderous

---

Vikings settle along the rugged coastline at L'Anse aux Meadows.

1000

Venetian navigator John Cabot, sailing under the British flag, claims Newfoundland for the Tudor monarchs of England.

© Bettmann/Corbis

1497

British Parliament recognizes Newfoundland as a British colony.

1824

Newfoundland and Labrador Historical Timeline

1855
Newfoundland becomes completely self-governing after being managed by a seasonal British governor who remained only for the summer fishing season.

splash. A more common but still photogenic sight is a fluke or fin salute.

Using binoculars you can see these migrating mammals from good ol' terra firma, but a nautical jaunt is by far the better choice. What's more, several tour operators double your pleasure by offering combination whale- and bird-watching trips. Newfoundland and Labrador is home to some of the world's largest seabird colonies.

At Cape St. Mary's Ecological Reserve, thousands of gannets crowd atop vertigo-inducing cliffs high above the Atlantic, filling the air with their cries. Baccalieu Island teems with millions of storm petrels, and Labrador's Gannet Island, named after the HMS *Gannet* that sunk near there in the 1800s, supports a multitude of razorbills.

The Atlantic puffin—the provincial bird—is the one most closely identified with Newfoundland and Labrador. Also called sea parrots because of their vibrantly flame-colored beaks, the plump little birds are a comical sight as they wriggle underwater with surprising speed, and then, gorged with fish, struggle to fly back to their nests. Board a sightseeing boat at Bay Bulls or Witless Bay, just south of St. John's, for a tour of the Witless Bay Islands, home to thousands of the stout avians.

Doorstep to the New World

Perched at the easternmost edge of North America, Newfoundland and Labrador thrusts into the Atlantic like an outstretched hand welcoming visitors. Evidence at L'Anse aux Meadows National Historic Site of Canada shows that the first Europeans to accept this geographical invitation were 11th-century Norsemen.

Discovered in 1960, eight grassy ridges at the site yielded iron boat nails, proving a Viking settlement had existed there. Today you can step inside one of three re-created Scandinavian-style sod houses like those built at L'Anse aux Meadows a thousand years ago.

The early Norse explorers who lived here also may have been the first Europeans to see Gros Morne National Park of Canada's starkly beautiful landscape. Western Brook Pond, a narrow landlocked fjord dominated by steep rock walls, twinkles sapphirelike among Gros Morne's glacier-carved highlands.

Experts believe Newfoundland and Labrador's abundant timber lured Vikings to its shores. No matter what entices you to add your name to the province's lengthy list of visitors, rest assured you'll be in excellent company.

Guglielmo Marconi receives the first transatlantic wireless message in a hospital near Cabot Tower on Signal Hill.
1901

Newfoundland and Labrador celebrates 50 years as a province of Canada with year-long festivities.
1999

The once-abundant cod stocks reach an unprecedented low due to decades of overfishing; more than 30,000 fishermen are out of work.
1992

1927
The boundaries of Labrador are defined, granting Newfoundland rights to all of Labrador.

1949
Newfoundland and Labrador becomes Canada's 10th province.

2000
A year-long celebration is held in conjunction with the governments of Iceland and Norway to commemorate the Vikings' first landing in North America.

1866
The first successful transatlantic cable is laid at the tiny town of Heart's Content; the cable spans the ocean floor to Valentia, Ireland.

Recreation

Newfoundland and Labrador is a great place to explore the outdoors. Meadows teeming with colorful wildflowers, waves rolling onto sandy shores or crashing against tall cliffs, cool lakes and rivers—nature presents beautiful backdrops for adventure.

What would you like to do first? How about dropping a line in one of many salmon rivers or trout streams? The Gander and Humber rivers are known for record-size Atlantic salmon; **fishing** there or in any of the cold waters of nearly 200 salmon rivers requires a license. On Newfoundland and much of Labrador, licensed fishing guides must accompany non-residents on salmon fishing trips. There are hundreds of other rivers, ponds and lakes where a license is not required that are full of brook trout and Arctic char. Northern pike are often found in many of Labrador's lakes. **Ice fishing** on various frozen lakes and **hunting** by bow or rifle for moose, caribou and black bears also are popular pastimes. The Department of Tourism, Culture and Recreation publishes the handy *Guide to Hunting and Fishing Outfitters,* which contains hunting and fishing regulations and detailed lists of outfitters.

For the Birds

Each year about 40 million sea birds visit Newfoundland and Labrador. Pack a good pair of binoculars and sneak a peek at some of these feathered friends at Cape St. Mary's Ecological Reserve, arguably the largest gannet nesting area in North America. Follow a trail to Bird Rock, where gannets, thick-billed murres and numerous other species of sea birds flock (and squawk). In July, you can see humpback and minke whales feeding off the coast.

At Witless Bay Ecological Reserve, on the east coast of the Avalon Peninsula, catch a glimpse of hundreds of thousands of birds, including adorable orange-beaked puffins, the provincial bird. **Bird-watching** and **whale-watching** tours can be arranged out of Bay Bulls and Mobile. If you're there in late spring or early summer, icebergs bob in the waters.

Don't pass up a trip to beautiful Gros Morne National Park of Canada. With more than 105 kilometres (65 mi.) of trails to choose from, you may opt for **hiking** on Baker's Brook Falls Trail, which terminates in front of the large, multilevel waterfall for which it's named. Or take to the Trout River Pond Trail—it follows the north shore of Trout River Small Pond through a boreal forest into a lush valley, where it meets Trout River Big Pond. The narrows area, where the ponds converge, is quite a sight.

Break out the paddles and go **kayaking** in the aforementioned ponds. For saltwater adventures, put in along the park's coastline at Trout River and travel north to Bonne Bay—caves and 350-metre-high (1,000-ft.) cliffs accent the shore. A **boat tour** through Western Brook Pond, a freshwater fjord, or Trout River Pond also offers splendid views of the countryside.

There's so much water here that it's not surprising to learn that the provincial dog, a furry Newfoundland, has webbed feet. And you'll wish you did too, when you see all the bays, coves, lakes and ponds perfect for **sailing, scuba diving, swimming** or **windsurfing.** Get your feet wet at Quidi Vidi Lake in St. John's, site of an annual regatta since the 1820s. Most provincial parks have beaches, so don't forget your bathing suit.

Shoot the waves while **white-water rafting** or **canoeing** on the many rivers extending across the province—the Pinware, Eagle and Churchill rivers are good places to get started, while rapid-rich Kenamou River is a little rougher. In Terra Nova National Park of Canada, rent a canoe or pedal boat for a leisurely float on Sandy Pond.

Snow-carved Sports

When the snow falls, bundle up and head to Terra Nova and Gros Morne national parks of Canada. Each has an extensive system of groomed trails for **cross-country skiing** and **snowshoeing.** Trails can also be found within two provincial parks: A heated ski chalet at Notre Dame Provincial Park keeps skiers toasty in between treks, and you can ski around a frozen pond at Butter Pot Provincial Park.

For **downhill skiing,** your best bet is Marble Mountain near Corner Brook, said to receive the most snowfall in all of Canada. Snow Goose Mountain and Smokey Mountain (in Labrador) also have slopes.

Recreational Activities

Throughout the TourBook, you may notice a Recreational Activities heading with bulleted listings of recreation-oriented establishments listed underneath. Similar operations also may be mentioned in Destination City recreation sections. Since normal AAA inspection criteria cannot be applied, these establishments are presented only for information. Age, height and weight restrictions may apply. Reservations often are recommended and sometimes are required. Addresses and/or phone numbers are provided so visitors can contact the attraction for additional information.

Fast Facts

POPULATION: 512,930.

AREA: 405,212 sq km (156,452 sq mi); ranks 10th.

CAPITAL: St. John's.

HIGHEST POINT: 1,652 m/5,420 ft., Mount Caubvick, Labrador.

LOWEST POINT: Sea level, Atlantic Ocean.

TIME ZONE(S): Newfoundland is on Newfoundland Standard Time. Labrador is on Atlantic time, except for the south coast (Black Tickle and south), which is on Newfoundland Standard Time.

MINIMUM AGE FOR UNRESTRICTED DRIVER'S LICENSE: 17 years, 8 months.

SEAT BELT/CHILD RESTRAINT LAWS: Seat belts required for driver and all passengers. Child restraints required for children under 6 yrs. or under 18 kg (40 lbs.).

HELMETS FOR MOTORCYCLISTS: Required for all riders.

RADAR DETECTORS: Not permitted.

FIREARMS LAWS: By federal law, all nonresidents entering Canada with a firearm must declare their weapon in writing and pay a fee of $25 (Canadian). Contact the Canadian Firearms Centre at (800) 731-4000 to receive a declaration form or additional information.

HOLIDAYS: Jan. 1; Good Friday; Victoria Day, May 24 (or closest prior Mon.); Memorial Day, July 1; Labour Day, Sept. (1st Mon.); Thanksgiving, Oct. (2nd Mon.); Remembrance Day, Nov. 11; Christmas, Dec. 25; Dec. 26.

TAXES: Newfoundland and Labrador has a harmonized sales tax comprised of an 8 percent provincial tax and a 6 percent federal goods and services tax (for a total of 14 percent) which is applied to most goods and services.

INFORMATION CENTERS: Provincial visitor centers are operated daily from mid-May to mid-Oct. at North Sydney, Nova Scotia, 7 a.m.-11 p.m.; Channel-Port-aux-Basques, 6 a.m.-10 p.m.; Argentia, 9-7 (also Mon., Wed. and Sat. 7-11 p.m.); Deer Lake, Notre Dame Junction near Lewisporte, Clarenville and Whitbourne, 8:30-8. The visitor center at St. John's International Airport is open all year, 9:30 a.m.-midnight.

FURTHER INFORMATION FOR VISITORS:
Department of Tourism, Culture and
  Recreation
P.O. Box 8730
St. John's, NL, Canada A1B 4K2
(800) 563-6353

INTERPROVINCE FERRY INFORMATION:
Marine Atlantic Inc.
355 Purves St.
North Sydney, NS, Canada B2A 3V2
(800) 341-7981

FERRY SCHEDULES: The Department of Tourism, Culture and Recreation provides schedules for and information about ferry service.

ALCOHOL CONSUMPTION: Legal age 19.

Newfoundland and Labrador Temperature Averages Maximum/Minimum
From the records of the Canadian Government Travel Bureau
Temperatures in Celsius.

	JAN	FEB	MAR	APR	MAY	JUN	JUL	AUG	SEP	OCT	NOV	DEC
St. John's	1	0	1	6	10	15	21	20	16	11	7	2
	-6	-7	-5	-2	2	6	11	12	7	3	0	-5

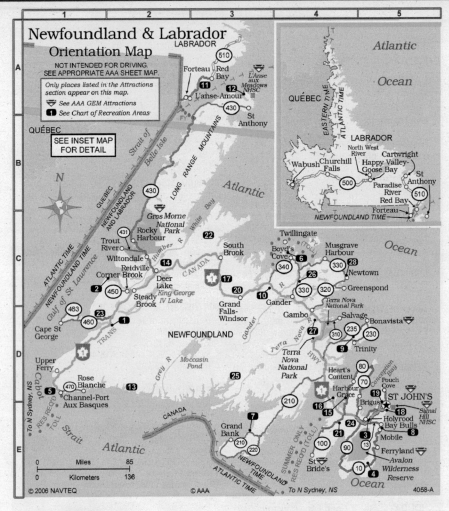

Newfoundland & Labrador
Orientation Map

NOT INTENDED FOR DRIVING.
SEE APPROPRIATE AAA SHEET MAP.

Only places listed in the Attractions section appear on this map.

⬩ *See AAA GEM Attractions*
1 *See Chart of Recreation Areas*

SEE INSET MAP
FOR DETAIL

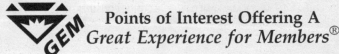

Points of Interest Offering A
Great Experience for Members®

Bonavista (D-5)

RYAN PREMISES NATIONAL HISTORIC SITE OF CANADA—The waterfront complex of restored fishery buildings commemorates Newfoundland's centuries-old fishing industry. See p. 69.

Ferryland (E-5)

COLONY OF AVALON—Visitors can peer into Newfoundland's past at this archeological site where in 1621 Sir George Calvert established a permanent English settlement. See p. 71.

Gros Morne National Park of Canada

GROS MORNE NATIONAL PARK OF CANADA—Located in the Long Range Mountains on Newfoundland's western coast, this national park is home to many lakes, fjords, cliffs, mountains, peatlands and sand dunes. Beavers, moose, squirrels, snowshoe hare and more than 230 species of birds inhabit the area. See p. 73.

L'Anse aux Meadows National Historic Site of Canada (A-3)

L'ANSE AUX MEADOWS NATIONAL HISTORIC SITE OF CANADA—Located by archeologists in 1960, the 1,000-year-old remnants of a Norse settlement proved that Vikings had visited the New World nearly 500 years before Columbus. See p. 75.

St. Bride's (E-4)

CAPE ST. MARY'S ECOLOGICAL RESERVE—Discover thousands of seabirds in this majestic setting. Each season brings different visitors to the area, including whales, ducks and migrating shorebirds. See p. 78.

St. John's (E-5)

BASILICA CATHEDRAL CHURCH AND MUSEUM—Consecrated in 1855, this church still serves its parishioners. The adjoining museum holds an extensive collection of Catholic artifacts. See p. 79.

JOHNSON GEO CENTRE—Geologic history is showcased at this state-of-the-art science center, most of which is housed underground. See p. 80.

RAILWAY-COASTAL MUSEUM—The museum tells the story of how Newfoundland's isolated fishing communities once depended on the Newfoundland Railway and Coastal Boat Services for news, mail and transportation. See p. 80.

THE ROOMS—Provincial history and culture are featured in a museum and archives as well as an art gallery with more than 7,000 works of art. See p. 80.

Signal Hill National Historic Site of Canada (E-5)

SIGNAL HILL NATIONAL HISTORIC SITE OF CANADA—The view of St. John's and the ocean belies Signal Hill's military past. Once the scene of many battles between the English and the French, the site includes a commemorative tower, several batteries built during the 18th and 19th centuries, a signal mast and barracks. See p. 80.

RECREATION AREAS

	MAP LOCATION	CAMPING	PICNICKING	HIKING TRAILS	BOATING	BOAT RAMP	BOAT RENTAL	FISHING	SWIMMING	PETS ON LEASH	BICYCLE TRAILS	WINTER SPORTS	VISITOR CENTER	LODGE/CABINS	FOOD SERVICE
NATIONAL PARKS *(See place listings)*															
Gros Morne (C-2) About 1,805 square kilometres.		•	•	•	•	•		•	•	•		•	•		
Terra Nova (D-4) About 400 square kilometres. Golf.		•	•	•	•	•		•	•	•		•	•		•
PROVINCIAL															
Barachois Pond (D-2) 3,456 hectares 74 km s. of Corner Brook on Hwy. 1. Nature programs.	❶	•	•	•	•			•	•	•			•		
Blow Me Down (C-1) 224 hectares at Lark Harbour via Hwy. 450. Lookout tower.	❷	•	•	•				•		•					
Butter Pot (E-5) 1,732 hectares 29 km s.w. of St. John's on Hwy. 1. Nature programs.	❸	•	•	•				•	•	•		•	•		
Chance Cove (E-5) 2,068 hectares 43 km s. of Ferryland off Hwy. 10.	❹	•	•					•	•	•					
Cheeseman (D-1) 182 hectares 11.3 km n.w. of Port aux Basques on Hwy. 1.	❺	•	•	•				•	•	•					
Dildo Run (C-4) 182 hectares 17.7 km n.w. of Boyd's Cove on Hwy. 340 on New World Island.	❻	•	•					•	•	•		•			
Frenchman's Cove (E-3) 50 hectares 24.2 km w. of Marystown on Hwy. 210. Bird-watching, golf.	❼	•	•					•	•	•					
La Manche (E-5) 1,378 hectares 56.2 km s. of St. John's on Hwy. 10. Bird-watching.	❽	•	•	•				•	•	•					
Lockston Path (D-4) 202 hectares 6.5 km n. of Port Rexton on Hwy. 236.	❾	•	•	•	•	•									
Notre Dame (C-3) 111 hectares 48.2 km w. of Gander via Hwy. 1. Nature programs.	❿	•	•		•			•	•	•		•	•	•	
Pinware River (A-3) 68 hectares about 10 km n. of L'Anse-au-Loup on Hwy. 510.	⓫	•	•	•				•		•					
Pistolet Bay (A-3) 880 hectares 25.7 km n. of St. Anthony on Hwy. 437. Canoeing.	⓬	•	•					•	•	•					

RECREATION AREAS

	MAP LOCATION	CAMPING	PICNICKING	HIKING TRAILS	BOATING	BOAT RAMP	BOAT RENTAL	FISHING	SWIMMING	PETS ON LEASH	BICYCLE TRAILS	WINTER SPORTS	VISITOR CENTER	LODGE/CABINS	FOOD SERVICE
Sandbanks (D-2) 230 hectares 4 km w. of Burgeo on Rte. 480. Bird-watching.	13	•	•	•					•	•					
Squires Memorial (C-2) 1,556 hectares 41.7 km n.e. of Deer Lake on Hwy. 422. Nature programs.	14	•	•	•		•	•		•					•	
OTHER															
Backside Pond (E-4) 556 hectares 3 km e. of Hopeall on Hwy. 80.	15	•	•	•				•	•	•					
Bellevue Beach (E-4) 75 hectares 11.2 km w. of Bellevue on Hwy. 201. Bird-watching.	16	•	•		•	•		•	•	•					
Beothuck (C-3) 74 hectares 3.2 km w. of Grand Falls-Windsor on Hwy. 1. Logging exhibit.	17	•	•		•	•			•	•			•		
Bowring (E-6) 80 hectares at Waterford Bridge Rd. and Cowan Ave. Tennis. *(See St. John's p. 79)*	18		•						•	•	•				•
C.A. Pippy (D-5) 1,343 hectares 1 km n. of St. John's off Hwy. 1. Canoeing, golf. *(See St. John's p. 79)*	19	•	•	•			•		•	•	•		•		
Catamaran (C-3) 44 hectares 9.7 km n. of Badger on Hwy. 1. Sailing.	20	•	•		•	•		•	•	•					•
Fitzgerald's Pond (E-4) 920 hectares 19.2 km n.e. of Dunville on Hwy. 100.	21	•	•		•	•		•	•	•					
Flatwater Pond (C-3) 98 hectares 24.2 km s. of Baie Verte on Hwy. 410.	22	•	•	•				•	•	•					
Grand Codroy (D-1) 2 hectares 11.2 km n. of Doyles at O'Regans on Hwy. 406. Canoeing.	23	•	•	•				•	•						
Gushue's Pond (E-4) 177 hectares 19.2 km w. of Holyrood on Hwy. 1.	24	•	•					•	•	•			•		
Jipujijkuei Kuespem (D-3) 882 hectares 12 km s. from Head of Bay d'Espoir on Rte. 360.	25	•	•					•	•	•					
Jonathan's Pond (C-4) 440 hectares 19.2 km n. of Gander on Hwy. 330. Butterfly habitat.	26	•	•					•	•	•			•		
Square Pond (D-4) 38 hectares 40.2 km s.e. of Gander on Hwy. 1.	27	•	•					•	•	•			•		
Windmill Bight (C-4) 73 hectares 111 km n.e. of Gambo on Hwy. 330. Beach.	28	•	•					•	•	•					

Points of Interest

BAY BULLS (E-5) pop. 1,100

Bay Bulls derives its name from the French "baie boules," a reference to the dovekie, or bull bird, which winters in Newfoundland and Labrador.

GATHERALL'S PUFFIN AND WHALE WATCH is just off Hwy. 10, following signs to Northside Rd. The 1.5-hour tour ventures to Witless Bay Ecological Reserve, home to the largest sea bird colony in North America, afford opportunities to view native wildlife, including Atlantic puffins, murres and kittiwakes. Humpback and minke whales are frequently spotted mid-June to mid-August.

Up to six departures are offered daily May-Oct.; phone for schedule. Fare $50, children $25. Reservations are recommended. MC, VI. Phone (709) 334-2887 or (800) 419-4253.

MULLOWNEY'S PUFFIN & WHALE TOURS is off Hwy. 10 on Lower Rd. Passengers can view icebergs, whales and birds from two observation decks aboard the *Mary Vincent*. Fin, humpback and minke whales are some of the species common in the area. Bird species often spotted include guillemots, murres, razorbills, black-legged kittiwakes and Atlantic puffins.

Food is available. Allow 2 hours, 30 minutes minimum. Tours depart daily at 9:30, noon, 3 and 5:30, May 1-Sept. 27. Fare $55, senior citizens $45, children $30. AX, MC, VI. Phone (709) 745-5061, or (709) 334-3666 or (877) 783-3467 May 1-Sept. 27.

O'BRIEN'S BIRD AND WHALE TOURS, on Hwy. 10, offers 2.5-hour boat tours to the Bird Islands, home to the Witless Bay Ecological Reserve and one of the largest puffin colonies on North America's east coast. Boat tours cover several islands, where kittiwakes, razorbills, storm petrels and cormorants can be seen. Tours from mid-June to mid-August provide opportunities to view humpback and minke whales. Other cruises also are available.

Food is available. Departures daily at 9:30, 11, 12:30, 2, 3:30 and 5, mid-June to mid-Aug. (weather permitting); at 11 and 2, May 1 to mid-June (weather permitting). Schedule may vary; phone ahead. Fare $46.50; over 64, $40.35; ages 10-16, $23.25; ages 4-9, $19.30. Reservations are recommended. VI. Phone (709) 753-4850 or (877) 639-4253.

BELL ISLAND (E-5)

Located in Conception Bay, just a short ferry ride from Portugal Cove, Bell Island is a photographer's dream with picturesque cliffs, a quaint village and a 1939 lighthouse still in operation.

At Bell Island Community Museum and Mine Tour visitors can take a guided tour 500 feet down to a submarine iron ore mine. From 1895 to 1966 more than 78 million tons of ore were shipped out of the mine; the area has an estimated 3.5 billion tons of ore. The museum contains artifacts from the mine's early days and town photos. Tours depart daily 11-7, June through September and by appointment the rest of the year; phone (709) 488-2880.

Visitors can bring their automobile aboard the ferry. Picnic areas are available. The ferry departs from Portugal Cove off Hwy. 40; phone (709) 895-3541 or (709) 488-2842.

BONAVISTA (D-5) pop. 4,021

John Cabot is thought to have first sighted the New World at Cape Bonavista on June 24, 1497. However, the cape was unoccupied until the 1600s when it became a French fishing station and later a permanent English settlement. Although the British fortified the point in 1696 to deter French aggression, Bonavista was the site of a notable battle in the 18th century. Outfitted with only a few armed ships, a British fishing master and local residents defended the coast from French raiders.

CAPE BONAVISTA LIGHTHOUSE PROVINCIAL HISTORIC SITE is 6 km (3.5 mi.) n. on Hwy. 230. Built in 1843 to guide mariners bound for Labrador, the lighthouse has been restored to appear as it did during the time of its first keeper, Jeremiah White. Interpretive displays on the second floor describe the history of the lighthouse and its keepers. Guides in period costume show visitors through the site. A statue of explorer John Cabot stands nearby.

Allow 1 hour minimum. Mon.-Fri. 10-5:30, June 15-Aug. 31; Mon.-Fri. 10-1 and 2-5:30, Sept. 1-Oct. 15. Admission $3, under 12 free. Phone (709) 468-7444 or (709) 729-0592.

THE MOCKBEGGAR PLANTATION PROVINCIAL HISTORIC SITE, in the center of town on Mockbeggar Rd., is the former home of F. Gordon Bradley, who served in Parliament and in the federal cabinet in the 1950s. Originally built during the 1870s, the house has been restored to its 1940s appearance. Antiques throughout the house portray the traditional Newfoundland and Labrador lifestyle.

Several outbuildings, including a carpenter's shop and fish store/factory, also have been restored. House daily 10-5:30, mid-June to early Oct. Admission $3, under 12 free. Phone (709) 468-7300 or (709) 729-0592.

 RYAN PREMISES NATIONAL HISTORIC SITE OF CANADA is at jct. Ryan's Hill and Old Catalina Rd. This five-building complex served as a major salt fish exporting business in the 19th and 20th centuries.

The site conserves and commemorates four aspects of the East Coast fishery—the inshore, international, Labrador and seal fisheries. Highlights include various interactive and multimedia displays describing the 500-year-old Atlantic fishery heritage. The Bonavista Community Museum houses memorabilia from the local community. An art gallery, interpretive programs and demonstrations of traditional fishing skills also are featured.

Guided tours are available. Allow 2 hours minimum. Daily 10-6, May 15-Oct. 15. Admission $3.50; over 65, $3; ages 6-16, $1.75; family rate $8.75. MC, VI. Phone (709) 468-1600, (709) 468-1601 or (888) 773-8888.

BOYD'S COVE (C-4) pop. 258

BOYD'S COVE BEOTHUK INTERPRETATION CENTRE, off Hwy. 340, following signs, is the former site of a 17th-century Beothuk community. Visitors can view a videotape presentation, dioramas and artifacts detailing the life of the Beothuk Indians. A 1-kilometre (.6-mi.) hiking trail leads to the archeological site where the remains of the community can be viewed; interpretative signs along the way describe the natural area. Allow 2 hours minimum. Daily 10-5:30, early June-Oct. 31. Admission $3. Phone (709) 656-3114 or (709) 729-0592.

BRIGUS (D-5) pop. 1,000

HAWTHORNE COTTAGE NATIONAL HISTORIC SITE OF CANADA, off Hwy. 70 at the corner of Irishtown Rd., was the home of Capt. Robert A. Bartlett, who commanded Adm. Robert Peary's ship, *The Roosevelt*, during the first expedition to the North Pole in 1908. The cottage contains period furnishings and photographs from Bartlett's various journeys. More local history is housed nearby in Ye Olde Stone Barn, where photographs and artifacts spanning almost 200 years are displayed.

Allow 1 hour minimum. Cottage open daily 10-6, mid-May to mid-Oct. Admission for cottage $3.75; over 64, $3.25; ages 6-16, $2.50; family rate $8.50. Admission for barn $1; under 13, 50c. Phone (709) 528-3391, or (709) 528-4004 for the cottage.

CAPE RAY (E-1) pop. 745

CAPE RAY HERITAGE SITE & LIGHTHOUSE MUSEUM is off Hwy. 1 Cape Ray exit, then 4 km (2.5 mi.) n.w. on Hwy. 408. Some 1,800 years ago Dorset Paleoeskimos camped here during their nomadic hunting trip, and artifacts are housed in the museum. In 1856 the first telegraph cable connecting Newfoundland to North America was laid here; the event is commemorated with a plaque. In addition, a lighthouse has been on this site since 1870; the current one was built in 1959. Picnicking is permitted. Allow 1 hour minimum. Daily 10-9, July-Aug. Donations. Phone (709) 695-2567.

CAPE SPEAR NATIONAL HISTORIC SITE OF CANADA (E-6)

On the easternmost point of North America, Cape Spear National Historic Site of Canada is known for its lighthouse on a rocky cliff 75 metres (245 ft.)

above sea level. The 1835 structure is one of Newfoundland and Labrador's oldest surviving lighthouses. For more than a century it has served as an important approach light to St. John's, 11 kilometres (7 mi.) to the north. During World War II a coastal defense battery at Cape Spear protected St. John's from Nazi submarines.

The lighthouse has been restored and furnished to demonstrate the tradition of lighthouse keepers' work in the province. The site contains World War II gun emplacements and a visitor center with exhibits about lighthouses. The site's scenery attracts hikers, photographers and whale watchers.

Grounds daily 24 hours. Lighthouse and visitor center daily 10-6, May 15-Oct. 15. Site free. Lighthouse $3.50; over 64, $3; ages 6-16, $1.75; family rate $8.75. For further information contact the Superintendent, Cape Spear National Historic Site of Canada, P.O. Box 1268, St. John's, NL, Canada A1C 5M9. Phone (709) 772-5367.

CASTLE HILL NATIONAL HISTORIC SITE OF CANADA (E-5)

At Placentia off Hwy. 100, Castle Hill dates from the 17th century when the French selected the small fishing village of Plaisance as the base of operations for their Newfoundland and Labrador fishing fleet. The first official French colony was founded at this site in 1662 during the reign of Louis XIV. Fort Royal, a massive fortification, was built atop a prominent hill overlooking the port and the surrounding countryside.

Under the Treaty of Utrecht the area was ceded to the British in 1713. The town was renamed Placentia, and the hill on which the fort stood became known as Castle Hill.

The stabilized ruins of Fort Royal include the remains of the barracks, a powder magazine, guard rooms and a blockhouse. Displays at the visitor center depict the French and English influence at Placentia.

Allow 30 minutes minimum. Grounds open daily 24 hours. Visitor center open daily 10-6, May 15-Oct. 15. Site free. Exhibit areas $3.50; over 64, $3; ages 6-16, $1.75; family rate $8.75. For further information contact the Superintendent, Castle Hill National Historic Site of Canada, P.O. Box 10, Jerseyside, Placentia, NL, Canada A0B 2G0. Phone (709) 227-2401.

CHANNEL-PORT-AUX-BASQUES (D-1) pop. 5,200

GULF MUSEUM, on Main St. opposite City Hall, focuses on the maritime history of this coastal town. The museum includes one of the oldest navigational tools in Canada, a 1628 astrolabe found in a shipwreck off the coast of Newfoundland. There is an exhibit about the SS *Caribou*, torpedoed in 1942 while crossing from Nova Scotia; a display of early diving equipment; and French coins dating from 1638. Excavated items from a Dorset Eskimo camp also are included. Daily 9-9, June 1-Sept. 1. Admission $5, family rate $7. Phone (709) 695-7560.

CHURCHILL FALLS (B-4)

CHURCHILL FALLS DAM UNDERGROUND POWERHOUSE is on Rte. 500. The site contains the world's largest underground powerhouse, which resides 305 metres (1,000 ft.) below the ground. Tour guides provide a history of the area, explain the reasons for the dam and take visitors to the intake ducts and tunnels. Visitors also will see the administration and control room; from here an elevator provides access to the generating station, a very large room with a constant hum from the massive turbines.

Note: Photo ID is required. Hard hats and ear plugs are provided. Allow 3 hours minimum. Tours depart daily at 9, 1:30 and 7; closed major holidays. Free. Under 8 are not permitted. Reservations are required. Phone (709) 925-3335 for the town office.

CORNER BROOK (C-2) pop. 20,103

Newfoundland and Labrador's second largest city, Corner Brook is at the mouth of the Humber River, one of the greatest salmon rivers in the world. The Humber was first charted in 1767 by Capt. James Cook, who traveled 24 kilometres (15 mi.) up the river on his expedition to survey the Newfoundland and Labrador coast.

One of Newfoundland and Labrador's first industrial sawmills was built in Corner Brook in 1894, and the city boasts one of the world's largest integrated pulp and paper mills.

The 10-story Government Centre cuts a striking silhouette against Corner Brook's skyline. Also noteworthy is the Arts and Cultural Centre, which contains a theater and art exhibition areas. Margaret Bowater Park, in the heart of town, offers swimming, picnicking and a children's playground.

Northwest from Corner Brook, hwys. 440 and 450 offer scenic drives along the north and south shores of Humber Arm, respectively. On the tip of the southern shore extending into the Bay of Islands, a tower at Blow Me Down Provincial Park *(see Recreation Chart)* offers a view of Guernsey, Tweed and Pearl islands.

Barachois Pond Provincial Park *(see Recreation Chart and AAA/CAA Eastern Canada CampBook)* also is in the area and is near Stephenville on Hwy. 1.

Tourist Chalet: 11 Confederation Drive, P.O. Box 475, Corner Brook, NL, Canada A2H 6E6; phone (709) 639-9792.

CORNER BROOK MUSEUM & ARCHIVES is at 2 West St. The 1925 building was previously used as a courthouse, customs office, post office and telegraph building. Exhibits feature the city's cultural, natural and social history. Local industries showcased include paper, fishing and forestry. Historical photos also are displayed. Allow 1 hour minimum.

Daily 10-8, June-Aug.; Mon.-Fri. 10-4:30, rest of year. Closed major holidays. Admission $4; ages 13-16, $2. Phone (709) 634-2518.

DANIELS HARBOUR (C-2) pop. 350

NURSE BENNETT HERITAGE HOUSE is just w. off Hwy. 430 on Circular Rd. British nurse Myra Grimsley came to Daniel's Harbour in 1921. When she married Angus Bennett in 1922, he built this house, out of which she administered medical care. She was the only person to do so along the nearly 200 kilometres (124 mi.) of coastline. She worked mainly out of her kitchen until a medical clinic was added onto the room in the early 1940s.

The house includes period furniture and her medical instruments. Allow 30 minutes minimum. Daily 10-6, mid-June to early Sept. Admission $3; under 14, $2. Phone (709) 243-2601.

DEER LAKE (C-2) pop. 4,769

ROY WHALEN HERITAGE MUSEUM, on Hwy. 1, contains scale models of a logging camp and a hydropower system, early lumberjack tools, photographs, household items, china, cameras, typewriters and local historic newspaper headlines. Daily 9-9, July-Aug.; 10-5, May-June and Sept.-Dec. Free. Phone (709) 635-4440.

FERRYLAND (E-5) pop. 607

Ferryland is one of the oldest fishing villages in the province. From this area pirate Peter Easton and his crews plundered Spanish treasure fleets and accumulated a fortune during the early 17th century.

In 1621 Sir George Calvert, later Lord Baltimore, attempted a settlement in Ferryland, but because of the harsh climate and frequent attacks by the Dutch and French, the venture failed. Lord Baltimore and his family abandoned the site in 1629 and founded a colony in what is now Maryland.

After Easton's time, the colonial wars continued the area's tradition of turbulence. Plaques at the Isle of Bois, a strategic point of defense at the mouth of Ferryland's harbor, mark the sites of two defensive gun batteries used in the mid-18th century against sea attacks.

COLONY OF AVALON is on Hwy. 10, following signs. In the early 1500s this part of the Avalon Peninsula was visited seasonally by Beothuk Indians and migratory fishermen from Portugal, Spain, France and England. In 1621 Sir George Calvert, later Lord Baltimore, established the Colony of Avalon at this site.

An interpretation center features recovered artifacts including arrow points, cannonballs, gold rings, iron spurs, keys and pottery shards. At Avalon's several dig sites, visitors can watch archeologists as they carefully unearth remnants of Calvert's 1621 colony. Conservators can be viewed piecing together artifacts within the Conservation Laboratory. A reproduction of a 17th-century kitchen features daily demonstrations of period domestic life.

Guided tours are available. Allow 2 hours minimum. Daily 9-7, mid-June through Aug. 31; 10-5, mid-May to mid-June and Sept. 1 to mid-Oct. Admission $5; over 65 and under 18, $3; family rate $10. MC, VI. Phone (709) 432-3200 or (877) 326-5669.

FOGO ISLAND (C-4) pop. 564

Fogo Island, 25 kilometres (15.5 mi.) long by 14 kilometres (8.7 mi.) wide, is off the north central coast and is home to several villages, each with features such as beaches, hiking trails, small museums and historic cemeteries. Fishing has played an important role in the island's history and is evident in the various wharves and fish plants. Fish stages, which are used to house fishing equipment and to process fish, also can be found. A nearly 1-hour ferry ride departing from the town of Farewell on the mainland transports passengers to Man O' War Cove near Stag Harbour; from there, Tilting is approximately 40 kilometres (24.9 mi.) on Hwy. 334, following signs. Phone (709) 627-3492 for ferry information.

The town of Tilting has the majority of the island's attractions and has been named a National Historic Site. Tilting saw the first Irish settlers in the middle of the 18th century, and eventually that nationality represented the majority of the town's population. Many of today's residents have a strong Irish heritage and speak with a brogue. The old Irish Catholic cemetery contains the graves of early immigrants. For more information about the town, phone (709) 658-7236.

Fogo Island Tourism: P.O. Box 7, Site 5, Joe Batt's Arm, NL, Canada A0G 2X0; phone (709) 266-2794.

FORTEAU (A-2) pop. 477

On the southern Labrador coast, Forteau can be reached by Hwy. 510 from Blanc Sablon, Québec, where a ferry arrives daily in the summer from St. Barbe. The Labrador Straits Museum, west off the L'Anse Amour branch road between Forteau and L'Anse-au-Loup, contains regional artifacts.

GAMBO (D-4) pop. 2,084

The name Gambo is said to derive from the Spanish or Portuguese "Baie de las Gamas" (Bay of the Does), seen on early maps. Gambo was the birthplace of Joseph R. Smallwood, the last father of Canadian Confederation. The Smallwood Sculpture, a 3-metre (10-ft.) bronze statue, stands on the village green.

SMALLWOOD INTERPRETATION CENTRE is downtown on Hwy. 320. Bordering the Gambo River, the center depicts the life and times of Newfoundland and Labrador political leader Joseph R. Smallwood. Displays include Smallwood's personal effects and items relating to the town's history. Daily 10-10, July-Aug.; 11-7, rest of year. Closed major holidays. Admission $3; over 65, $2.50; under 12 free. VI. Phone (709) 674-4342.

GANDER (C-4) pop. 9,651

Because of its low incidence of fog, Gander was chosen as the site of an English air base in the mid-1930s. During World War II Gander became an important base for convoy escort and coastal patrol aircraft as well as a refueling stop for military aircraft crossing the Atlantic.

In Peacekeeper Park, 4 kilometres (2.5 mi.) east on Hwy. 1, stands the Silent Witness Memorial. This statue of an unarmed soldier is a tribute to the 259 members of the 101st U.S. Airborne Division, killed when their plane crashed after refueling at Gander in December 1985. They were on their way home from peacekeeping duties in the Middle East.

Gander International Airport is an important link in transatlantic flying routes; it also is the site of the striking 22-metre (72-ft.) mural "Flight and Its Allegories" by artist Kenneth Lochhead.

Gander enjoys a central spot in one of the finest big-game hunting and salmon-fishing areas of the province. West of Gander across Hwy. 1 is Gander Lake, home of a large number of moose.

The Road to the Shore—Hwys. 330, 320 and 1—is a scenic loop drive through coastal communities north and east of Gander.

Cobb's Pond Rotary Park features a 3-kilometre (1.9-mi.) boardwalk that encircles the pond, allowing visitors a closer look at local plants and wildlife. Other nearby parks include Square Pond, Jonathan's Pond, and Notre Dame *(see Recreation Chart and the AAA/CAA Eastern Canada CampBook)*.

Gander Tourism Chalet: 109 Trans-Canada Hwy., Gander, NL, Canada A1V 1P6; phone (709) 256-7110.

AVIATION DISPLAY, at Gander International Airport, features exhibits about the history of aviation, including plane models and photos of such transatlantic flight pioneers as Charles A. Lindbergh, Amelia Earhart and Capt. Eddie Rickenbacker. Daily 24 hours. Free. Phone (709) 256-6677.

[SAVE] **NORTH ATLANTIC AVIATION MUSEUM** is at 135 Hwy. 1 near the tourism chalet. Newfoundland and Labrador aviation history is showcased. Many displays pertain to World War II, including Ferry Command and the Newfoundland Airmen's Memorial, a tribute to local aviators who died in that conflict. Visitors can enter a reconstructed DC-3 cockpit and inspect other fighter and bomber aircraft. A Lockheed Hudson Mk II is displayed. More than 2,900 were built, and only eight remain.

Guided tours are available by request. Allow 1 hour, 30 minutes minimum. Daily 9-9, late June-Sept. 5; Mon.-Fri. 9-5, rest of year. Admission $4; over 65 and ages 5-15, $3. Phone (709) 256-2923.

GRAND BANK (E-3) pop. 2,841

The fishing community of Grand Bank was named for the renowned Grand Banks, Newfoundland and Labrador's continental shelf that attracted

European fishermen to the island as early as the 15th century. These coastal waters still support commercial fishing fleets.

Walking trails around Grand Bank offer a variety of sights. The Marine Hike is about 5 kilometres (3 mi.) and follows the Admiral's Beach shoreline. Nature lovers will enjoy the Nature Trail on Bennett's Hill. Both trails offer a view of the town as well as opportunities to view the native plant and animal life.

Self-guiding tours: Maps of the Heritage Walk, which illustrates the cultural heritage and architecture of Grand Bank, are available at local museums and the Grand Bank Town Hall.

PROVINCIAL SEAMEN'S MUSEUM, 54 Marine Dr., presents Newfoundland and Labrador's seafaring heritage through displays of ship models, photographs and documents relating to the south coast fishing industry. The 1,115-square-metre (12,000-sq.-ft.) building resembles the sails of a schooner and is a memorial to Newfoundlanders who have died at sea; it was originally the Yugoslavian Pavilion for Montréal Expo '67.

Allow 1 hour minimum. Daily 9-4:45, May 1-late Oct.; closed major holidays. Admission $2.50, over 65 and students with ID $2, under 17 free. Phone (709) 832-1484.

GRAND FALLS-WINDSOR (C-3)
pop. 14,200

Since the Harmsworth brothers began producing newsprint for British tabloids in 1909, Grand Falls-Windsor has tapped the pulp and paper industry to become one of Newfoundland and Labrador's largest urban centers. Abitibi Consolidated, off Hwy. 1 on Mill Road, continues the brothers' business on a scale beyond its founders' wildest dreams.

Beothuk Park contains a reconstructed turn-of-the-20th-century logging camp furnished with tools of the trade; phone (709) 486-0492. *See Recreation. Chart.*

GRAND FALLS FISHWAY—SALMONID INTERPRETATION CENTRE is s. off Hwy. 1 exit 18, following signs. Exhibits depict the history and life cycle of the Atlantic salmon. A lower-level observatory allows visitors to watch the "King of Fish" fight the current on its way upstream to spawn. Allow 1 hour minimum. Daily 8-dusk, June 15-Sept. 15. Admission $5; under 12, $3. Phone (709) 489-7350.

LOGGERS' LIFE PROVINCIAL MUSEUM, off Hwy. 1, showcases the life of a logger in a recreated 1930s logging camp. Displays about food, tools and social life in the camp can be seen. Allow 30 minutes minimum. Daily 9-4:45, late May-Oct. 1. Admission $2.50, senior citizens and students with ID $2, under 19 free. Phone (709) 292-4522 or (709) 292-4523.

GREENSPOND (C-4) pop. 400

GREENSPOND COURTHOUSE, off Hwy. 320 on Center St., was built in 1899. Museum displays include the original courtroom, jail cells and attendant's quarters. Artifacts reflect the history of the Bonavista North area and include items relating to the fishing and seal-hunting industries. Mon.-Fri. 10-6, July-Sept.; by appointment rest of year. Free. Phone (709) 536-3220.

GROS MORNE NATIONAL PARK OF CANADA (C-2)

> Elevations in the park range from 230 metres (755 ft.) at Bonne Bay to 806 metres (2,644 ft.) at Gros Morne Mountain. Refer to CAA/AAA maps for additional elevation information.

Seventy kilometres (43 mi.) northwest of Deer Lake on Hwy. 430, Gros Morne National Park of Canada covers some 1,805 square kilometres (695 sq. mi.) in the Long Range Mountains on Newfoundland's western coast. Continental drift created the park's landscape and glacial erosion sculpted it to its present condition. Of the many lakes and fjords, Western Brook Pond is the most striking, with cliffs rising to 686 metres (2,250 ft.).

Baker's Brook Falls, St. Paul's Inlet, Gros Morne Mountain and the Tablelands on the south side of Bonne Bay also are impressive. Due to its outstanding geology, the park was proclaimed a UNESCO (United Nations Educational, Scientific and Cultural Organization) World Heritage Site in 1987. Other remnants of the area's turbulent geologic past include the volcanic cliffs at Green Gardens, the limestone breccia of Cow Head, bogs and sand dunes.

Though now mostly wilderness, the park area was home to two pre-European cultures, the Maritime Archaic Indians and the Dorset Eskimos, at various times from 2500 B.C. to A.D. 700. Vikings may have visited the park area around A.D. 1000; however, the first confirmed visit by a European was that of Jacques Cartier in 1534.

Typical wildlife includes moose, beavers, snowshoe hare and squirrels. Less frequently sighted are woodland caribou, black bears, foxes and lynx. Whales also are seen in nearby waters. The park boasts 239 species of birds, including gulls, terns, ducks, eagles, warblers and rock ptarmigan. More than half a million pairs of blackpoll warblers breed in the park, making this species the park's most abundant bird.

The area's varied bedrock, soil and elevation have created an environment where diverse plant communities, from seaweeds on the seashore to tundralike vegetation on the mountain plateau, can exist. Facing the sea along the coast are wind-shaped and stunted balsam fir and white spruce, called tuckamore for their dense, compact form. Peatlands cover most of the coastal plain, while spruce, fir and birch trees cloak the mountain slopes.

General Information and Activities

The park is open all year. The visitor center is open daily 9-9, June 15-Labour Day; 9-5, Victoria Day-June 14 and day after Labour Day-second Mon. in Oct.; 9-4, rest of year. Lobster Cove Lighthouse daily 10-6, June 1-late Sept. Broom Point interpretation center daily 10-6, late June-Labour Day. Park information also is available at the Wiltondale Pioneer Village *(see Wiltondale p. 83).*

Hwy. 430, the major west coast highway known as the Viking Trail, traverses the park. Hwy. 431 branches off Hwy. 430 to the communities of Woody Point and Trout River.

There are more than 20 hiking trails within the park, ranging from a half-hour stroll down Old Mail Road, 3 kilometres (1.9 mi.) north of Cow Head, to a strenuous 3-day traverse through the Long Range Mountains. Well traveled is the Green Gardens Trail, a walking trail along the coast, 10 kilometres (6 mi.) southwest of Woody Point off Hwy. 431.

In addition to hiking, park activities include camping, picnicking, fishing and cross-country skiing. Overnight back-country camping requires a permit, and fishing is subject to national park regulations; contact the park visitor center or local merchants for details. Boat tours of Western Brook Pond, Trout River Pond and Bonne Bay are available from mid-June to mid-September *(see Rocky Harbour p. 77).*

The visitor center near Rocky Harbour features a videotape theater, nature exhibits and information about park facilities. Park interpreters conduct hikes and campfire and evening programs from late June through Labour Day. The newsletter *Tuckamore* contains a current schedule of events. *See Recreation Chart.*

ADMISSION to the park mid-May to mid-Oct. is $8; over 64, $7; ages 6-16, $4; family rate $16. Seasonal pass $40; over 64, $35; ages 6-16, $20; family rate $80. Admission free rest of year.

PETS are allowed in the park but must be restrained at all times.

ADDRESS inquiries to the Superintendent, Gros Morne National Park of Canada, P.O. Box 130, Rocky Harbour, NL, Canada A0K 4N0. Phone (709) 458-2417, (905) 426-4648, (877) 737-3783 for camping, TTY (709) 772-4564, or TTY (866) 787-6221 in Canada for camping in season.

THE DISCOVERY CENTRE is 4 km (2.5 mi.) w. on Hwy. 431 in Woody Point. Displays in the center educate visitors about the geology, plants, animals and marine mammals of Gros Morne National Park of Canada. Interactive exhibits include models, video programs, local artwork, fossils, an interpretive garden and a 120-seat theater. A giant 3-D map of the park also is featured.

Allow 1 hour minimum. Daily 9-6 (also Sun. and Wed. 6-9 p.m.), late June-early Sept.; 9-5, mid-May to late June and early Sept. to mid-Oct. Free with park admission. Phone (709) 458-2417 or (709) 458-2490.

HAPPY VALLEY-GOOSE BAY (B-5)
pop. 8,700

On Lake Melville in south-central Labrador, Happy Valley-Goose Bay occupies an area known for some of the best fishing in the province. It is accessible by air or boat from Newfoundland.

HARBOUR GRACE (D-4) pop. 3,380

One of Newfoundland and Labrador's oldest and most historic towns, Harbour Grace evolved from the French settlement of Havre de Grace, founded in 1550. English pirate Peter Easton fortified the town in the early 17th century, using it as a base for his renegade band. Harbour Grace steadily developed into Newfoundland and Labrador's second largest town until a series of fires 1814-1944 reversed much of its progress.

With such setbacks on the ground, Harbour Grace turned to the skies to mark its place in history. Beginning in 1919, its runway accommodated such early transatlantic aviators as Wiley Post, who began a flight around the world in 1931, and Amelia Earhart, who took off the following year to become the first woman to make a solo flight across the Atlantic.

Among several historic structures in town spared by the seven crippling fires are one of the oldest jails in Canada, one of the oldest Canadian courthouses still in service and St. Paul's Anglican Church, built in 1835.

Harbour Grace Tourist Chalet: P.O. Box 310, Harbour Grace, NL, Canada A0A 2M0; phone (709) 596-3042.

CONCEPTION BAY MUSEUM, on Water St. in the historic district, is in the 1870 Customs House; the first recorded structure on this site was the 1610 pirate fort of Peter Easton. The museum uses artifacts and period rooms to recount local history, including early transatlantic flight. Allow 1 hour minimum. Daily 10-5, June-Sept. Admission $3; students with ID and children $2; over 65, $1. Phone (709) 596-5465, or (709) 596-0506 Oct.-May.

HEART'S CONTENT (D-4) pop. 495

In 1866 Heart's Content was the focus of one of the greatest technological achievements of the age: the landing of the first successful transatlantic cable. On July 27 the town became the western terminus of the cable that spanned the ocean floor to Valentia, Ireland. Recruited to do the job was the mammoth *Great Eastern,* five times the size of the largest ship afloat at the time.

Other cables were landed in the following decades, and Heart's Content served as a base of Western Union's international cable system until transoceanic telephone cable and satellite communication rendered submarine cable obsolete in the 1960s.

HEART'S CONTENT CABLE STATION PROVINCIAL HISTORIC SITE, 1 km (.6 mi.) n.e. on Hwy. 80 from jct. Hwy 74, consists of the original telegraph buildings and equipment used for the early transatlantic cables to Europe. Interpretive displays explain the station's role in cable history through the 19th and 20th centuries. The station received its first message in 1866 and was officially open 1876-1965. Daily 10:30-5:30, late May-late Sept.; by appointment rest of year. Admission $3, under 12 free. Phone (709) 583-2160 or (709) 729-0592.

HOLYROOD (E-5) pop. 1,906

Holyrood is a popular summer resort area with coastal scenery and excellent fishing. Nearby streams contain salmon and trout.

SALMONIER NATURE PARK, 12 km (7 mi.) s. of jct. hwys. 1 and 90, is a nature and wildlife preserve. About 40 hectares (100 acres) of the 1,200-hectare (2,965-acre) preserve have been developed for public exhibitions. A boardwalk nature trail links many large enclosures where native mammals and birds can be seen.

Trained staff members provide programs that include movies, puppet shows and interpretive theater presentations relating to the province's natural history. Picnicking is permitted. Daily 10-6, early June-Labour Day; Mon.-Fri. 10-4, day after Labour Day-second Mon. in Oct. Admission $3.45. Phone (709) 229-7189 or (709) 229-7888.

L'ANSE-AMOUR (A-3)

Situated at the southern tip of Labrador, L'Anse-Amour is the site of an ancient burial mound containing artifacts detailing the lives of the Maritime Archaic people some 7,000 years ago. Visitors to the area can view this historic site in addition to exploring the rocky coastline.

Taken from the old French name of L'Anse aux Morts, "Cove of Deaths," L'Anse-Amour has been the site of many shipwrecks, including two Royal Navy vessels. The remnants of the HMS *Raleigh*, which ran aground in 1922, can be seen along the beach.

POINT AMOUR LIGHTHOUSE, off Hwy. 510 on L'Anse Amour Rd., is the tallest in Atlantic Canada. Visitors can climb 120 steps to witness a panoramic view of the coastline and the Strait of Belle Isle; icebergs and whales occasionally are seen. A collection of artifacts traces 4 centuries of maritime history. Picnicking is permitted. Allow 1 hour minimum. Daily 10-5:30, May 19-Sept. 30. Admission $3, under 13 free. Phone (709) 927-5825 or (709) 729-0592.

L'ANSE AUX MEADOWS (A-4) pop. 1,012

NORSTEAD—A VIKING VILLAGE AND PORT OF TRADE is about 1.5 km (.9 mi.) e. off Hwy. 436, following signs. The site's features have been designed to represent the Viking era (790-1066). A church, blacksmith shop, chieftain's hall

and barns are included. Guides in period costume give interactive demonstrations, allowing visitors to get an idea of what life was like some 1,000 years ago. *Snorri,* a replica of a Viking ship, also is on the premises.

Picnicking is permitted. Allow 1 hour, 30 minutes minimum. Daily 9-9, early June-late Sept. Admission $8; over 65, $7; ages 6-15, $5; family rate $20. MC, VI. Phone (709) 623-2828 or (877) 620-2828.

GEM L'ANSE AUX MEADOWS NATIONAL HISTORIC SITE OF CANADA (A-3)

At the tip of Newfoundland's Great Northern Peninsula about 25 kilometres (16 mi.) off Hwy. 430 on Hwy. 436, L'Anse aux Meadows National Historic Site of Canada is the first authenticated Norse site in North America. In 1960 archeologists first uncovered artifacts that indicated a Norse settlement was in this area about A.D. 1000.

According to sagas, the Vikings defended this outpost against North American Indians until perils became too great and they withdrew to Greenland. Excavations have disclosed the size and location of the buildings that formed the settlement. Discoveries include houses, a cooking pit, a small forge for smelting iron, several workshops and a spindle whorl believed to have been used by Viking women.

The visitor reception center has an exhibit detailing the Norse presence in North America. Replicas of their Scandinavian-type sod houses have been constructed. Costumed interpreters explain the function of each building. The Viking site at L'Anse aux Meadows has been declared a World Heritage Site by UNESCO (United Nations Educational, Scientific and Cultural Organization). A walking trail follows the shoreline.

Picnicking is permitted. Guided tours are available. Allow 2 hours minimum. Daily 9-5, June 1-Oct. 8 (also 5-6, June 10-Sept. 3). Admission $7; over 65, $5.50; ages 6-16, $3.50; family rate (up to seven people) $17.50. MC, VI. For information write the Superintendent, L'Anse aux Meadows National Historic Site of Canada, P.O. Box 70, St. Lunaire-Griquet, NL, Canada A0K 2X0. Phone (709) 623-2608.

MOBILE (E-5) pop. 132

MOLLY BAWN WHALE AND PUFFIN TOURS is on Hwy. 10. Seabirds and whales can be seen on this 1-hour tour of Witless Bay Ecological Reserve aboard *Molly Bawn II.* Black guillemots, kittiwakes, murres, northern fulmars, puffins and razorbills are frequently sighted. Occasionally dolphins, eagles and icebergs can be seen. Tours depart daily every 90 minutes 10-7, May 15-Sept. 15. Fare $20; ages 6-16, $15. Phone (709) 334-2621.

MUSGRAVE HARBOUR (C-4) pop. 1,294

Musgrave Harbour lies on the coast of scenic Hamilton Sound where giant icebergs carried south by the Labrador Current are frequently sighted from Hwy. 320. Representative of the region's many maritime associations is the Musgrave Harbour Fisherman's Museum at 4 Marine Dr. It is in a building designed by Sir William Coaker. In 1908 Coaker founded the Fisherman's Protective Union, a political and economic power during World War I.

Sir Frederick Banting Memorial Park, 10 kilometres (6 mi.) east on Hwy. 330, has a playground, miniature golf course, picnic area and hiking trails.

NEWTOWN (C-4) pop. 1,000

BARBOUR LIVING HERITAGE VILLAGE on Hwy. 330, contains eight restored buildings that once belonged to prosperous merchants and sailors of the Barbour family. The buildings, which date to the late 1800s, are furnished with antiques and contain items brought back from the family's worldwide travels. Evening plays are presented in a restored building once used by the family to salt fish. One-hour guided tours are given daily 10-6, June-Sept. Admission $5, under 18 free. Phone (709) 536-3220 or (709) 536-2441.

NORTH WEST RIVER (B-4) pop. 551

Labrador Heritage Society Museum, on Portage Road, preserves the history of the Labrador people through photographs, manuscripts, book collections and displays; phone (709) 497-8858 or (709) 497-8566.

LABRADOR INTERPRETATION CENTRE is at 2-6 Portage Rd. Exhibits feature 9,000 years of Labrador's history and cultures. Artifacts include tools and modes of transportation. A theater shows brief films about Labrador and its people. Other highlights are life-size dioramas and a view of the mountain ranges. Allow 1 hour minimum. Wed.-Fri. 10-4, Mon.-Tues. 7-4, Sat.-Sun. 1:30-4:30, June-Sept. Donations. Phone (709) 497-8566.

PORT AU CHOIX NATIONAL HISTORIC SITE OF CANADA (B-2)

Port au Choix National Historic Site of Canada is 15 kilometres (9 mi.) west of the Port Saunders-Port au Choix turnoff from Hwy. 430. In 1967 residents excavating for the construction of a new building discovered human bones, tools and weapons. The discovery led to archeological work that uncovered four ancient burial grounds in the area. Scientific testing of the bones and artifacts disclosed that the burial ground was in use for 700 years, beginning well before 2000 B.C.; it is said to be one of the largest hunter-gatherer cemeteries in North America. A new dig in 1997 uncovered what archeologists believe is the Maritime Archaic Indian village that accompanied the burial grounds.

A visitor center has displays and artifacts from the site's resident Maritime Archaic Indians as well as from the Dorset and Groswater Eskimos, other prehistoric groups that lived along the coast. The Point Riche Lighthouse is a popular spot for picnicking and photography.

Site open daily 24 hours. Visitor center open daily 9-8, mid-June through Labour Day; 9-6, in early June; 9-5, day after Labour Day-second Mon. in Oct. Admission $7.25; over 64, $6; ages 6-16, $3.50; family rate $18. For information contact the Superintendent, P.O. Box 140, Port au Choix, NL, Canada A0K 4C0. Phone (709) 861-3522, or (709) 458-2417 off-season.

PORT AU PORT WEST–AGUATHUNA–FELIX COVE (D-1) pop. 525

OUR LADY OF MERCY CHURCH is on Hwy. 460. After 11 years of construction, the church was consecrated in 1925. The largest wooden structure in the province, its steeple reaches 30 metres (100 ft.). Statues, ornate woodwork and 14 hand-carved stations of the cross made in Italy of Carrara and travertine marble are some of the religious treasures inside. The rectory now houses a museum with such items as religious articles from the church's earlier days and local artifacts.

Picnicking is permitted. Allow 1 hour minimum. Daily 9-7, July 1-late Aug.; 9-5 in June and Sept. 1-7. Admission $1, children 50c. Phone (709) 648-2632 or (709) 648-2745.

POUCH COVE (D-5) pop. 1,669

One of the oldest communities on the Avalon Peninsula, Pouch (POOCH) Cove attracted settlers as early as 1611. Those who settled in the town did so outside the law, since permanent residence in Newfoundland and Labrador was illegal in the 17th and 18th centuries. Pouch Cove's dangerous harbor, however, kept away most ships that threatened discovery.

RED BAY (A-3) pop. 264

Red Bay is considered to be the site of the first industrial enterprise in North America—production of whale oil for European markets in the 16th century.

RED BAY NATIONAL HISTORIC SITE OF CANADA, at the end of Hwy. 510, displays artifacts from a 16th-century Basque whaling station. A short ferry ride to Saddle Island allows visitors to tour the remnants of the station's structures and a whaler's cemetery. Museum daily 9-6, June 15-Oct. 8. Saddle Island tours Mon.-Sat. 9-4, June 15-Oct. 8. Museum $7; over 65, $6.50; ages 6-16, $3.50; family rate $17.50. Ferry $2, under 12 free. Phone (709) 920-2051 or (709) 920-2142.

REIDVILLE (C-2) pop. 500

[SAVE] **NEWFOUNDLAND INSECTARIUM,** Hwy. 1 exit 16, then .5 km (.3 mi.) n. on Hwy. 430, is on 10 hectares (25 acres) bordering the Humber River. Featured are more than 100 live and mounted displays, including spiders, butterflies, beetles and scorpions.

Picnic facilities are available. Allow 1 hour minimum. Daily 9-8, July-Aug; Mon.-Fri. 9-5, Sat.-Sun.

10-5, May-June and in Sept. Admission $10; senior citizens $8.50; ages 5-14, $6.50. Phone (709) 635-4545 or (866) 635-5454.

ROCKY HARBOUR (C-2) pop. 1,002

BONTOURS boat tours depart from Norris Point Dock; the ticket office is in the Ocean View Motel. The Bonne Bay Discovery Tour cruises through the bay's deepest water, 756 metres (2,480 ft.). The 2-hour guided tour includes Gros Morne, Killdevil, The Tablelands and the Long Range Mountains. Occasionally whales can be seen. The I'se Da B'ye Tour interprets the bay's natural and cultural history. Other cruises also are available from St. Pauls and Western Brook Pond dock, both within Gros Morne National Park.

Bonne Bay Discovery Tour departs Tues., Thurs. and Sat. at 10, June 1-early Sept. I'se Da B'ye Tour departs Sun.-Mon., Wed. and Fri. at 10 and 2, Tues., Thurs. and Sat. at 2, July-Aug.; daily at 2 in June and Sept. Phone ahead to verify schedule. Bonne Bay fare $30; ages 12-16, $12; under 12, $8. I'se Da B'ye fare $32; ages 12-16, $12; under 12, $8. Rates may vary; phone ahead. Reservations are required. MC, VI. Phone (709) 458-2016 during season, (709) 458-2730, or (800) 563-9887 in Canada.

ROSE BLANCHE (D-1) pop. 668

ROSE BLANCHE LIGHTHOUSE is on Hwy. 470. Local workers built the lighthouse 1871-73 using granite from a nearby quarry. D & T Stevenson, a Scottish company named after the father and uncle of author Robert Louis Stevenson, assisted in the project. The structure was reconstructed in 1999 using most of the original materials. The house is furnished with antiques and some reproduced pieces representative of the 19th century.

Note: The lighthouse is reached via a 10-minute walk along a winding gravel path. The area sometimes is foggy. Guided tours are available. Picnicking is permitted. Allow 1 hour minimum. Daily 9-9, May 1-Oct. 13. Admission $3; ages 6-18, $2; family rate $7. MC, VI. Phone (709) 956-2052 or (709) 956-2903.

ST. ANTHONY (A-3) pop. 2,730

St. Anthony is the main service center for the northern portion of the Great Northern Peninsula. The Jordi Bonet murals, in the Charles S. Curtis Memorial Hospital, depict scenes from Sir Wilfred Grenfell's life.

GRENFELL INTERPRETATION CENTRE & HISTORIC PROPERTIES is in the center of town on Hwy. 430. The center has displays that highlight the life of Sir Wilfred Grenfell, founder of the Grenfell Hospital Mission to Newfoundland and Labrador. He established the hospital in response to the needs of destitute fishermen in the area and was knighted for his work in 1928. Exhibits at the Dockhouse Museum detail the impact of fishing on the area; displays show how boats were built and repaired. Allow 2 hours minimum. Daily 9-6, June-Sept. Admission $6; ages 6-15, $2.75. MC, VI. Phone (709) 454-4010.

St. Pierre and Miquelon Islands

Lying about 25 kilometres (16 mi.) off the southern coast of Newfoundland, the St. Pierre and Miquelon Islands constitute France's last holdings in North America. The combined land areas of St. Pierre and Miquelon total about 242 square kilometres (93 sq. mi.). Yet these small granite islands were fought over by England and France 1660-1763, until the Treaty of Paris granted France possession.

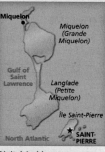

Digital Archives

The islands can be reached by plane from Halifax or Sydney, Nova Scotia; and St. John's; or by boat from Fortune. Bus service on the islands and boat transportation run from late June through Thanksgiving. Information and reservations are available from St. Pierre Tours Ltd., 5 Bayview St., Fortune; phone (800) 563-2006.

St. Pierre retains the bistros, bars, cafes, wrought-iron balconies and waterfronts that recall its French heritage. Folk dances are performed in local town squares from mid-July to late August. The St. Pierre Museum traces the history and traditions of the archipelago. Tours by taxi, rented bicycle or motorcycle can be arranged through the St. Pierre Tourist Bureau on Place du General de Gaulle.

St. Pierre is known for its low duty rates, which make it possible to buy French goods and wines at attractive prices. Those who purchase items in St. Pierre and travel through Canada must pay regular duty on these items. Visitors are required to clear customs when entering the islands; it also is necessary to clear customs upon re-entry to Canada or the United States. *For information about customs regulations see Border Information.*

Grenfell House Museum is in the center of town on Hwy. 430. The museum was the home of Dr. Grenfell. Built in the early 1900s, the building now houses artifacts, antiques and exhibits about his life and work. Allow 1 hour minimum. Guided tours are available daily 9-8, June-Sept. Phone (709) 454-4010.

NORTHLAND DISCOVERY BOAT TOURS depart from behind the Grenfell Interpretation Centre off Hwy. 430. Offering excursions aboard a 15-metre (50-ft.) vessel, this tour company takes visitors into Iceberg Alley, where passengers may view seals, whales and a variety of birds in addition to icebergs. Allow 3 hours minimum. Tours depart daily at 9, 1 and 4, late May-early Oct. Fare $42; ages 13-17, $25; under 12, $20. MC, VI. Phone (709) 454-3092 or (877) 632-3747.

ST. BRIDE'S (E-4) pop. 500

CAPE ST. MARY'S ECOLOGICAL RE-SERVE, 5 km (3 mi.) s. on Hwy. 100, then 16 km (10 mi.) s. on a paved road to the cape, features a wide variety of birds, including gannets, common murres, thick-billed murres, black-legged kittiwakes, razorbills and black guillemots. A 1.4-kilometre (.9 mi.) trail meanders along the coast and leads to Bird Rock, a 100-metre-tall (328-ft.) sandstone bank where the birds congregate; photographic opportunities abound. An interpretive center contains exhibits about seabirds and a scale model of the reserve.

Whales, dolphins, porpoises and seals can be seen during the summer. In spring and fall shorebirds and raptors migrate to the area. Winter brings sea ducks, including harlequins and common eiders.

Note: Stay on the trail and avoid steep slopes and cliff edges. Check with staff about trail conditions before beginning. The area sometimes is windy and foggy. The trail contains areas of loose rock and sometimes is slippery. Guided tours are available. Picnicking is permitted. Allow 2 hours, 30 minutes minimum. Reserve daily 24 hours. Interpretive center daily 8-7, June 1-Sept. 21; 9-5 in May and Oct.

Reserve free. Center admission $3, students with ID and children $1, family rate $7. Season pass $10, children $4. Off-season pass $5, children $2. Phone (709) 277-1666 or (800) 563-6353, or (709) 635-4520 off-season.

ST. JOHN'S (E-5) pop. 99,182

One of the oldest cities in North America, St. John's is the capital, principal port and commercial center of the island. It is believed to be named for the feast day of St. John the Baptist, since it was on that day in 1497 that John Cabot discovered Newfoundland and Labrador. The city's perfectly sheltered harbor drew many European explorers and fishermen during the 1500s, until Sir Humphrey Gilbert sailed into the harbor on Aug. 5, 1583, and reaffirmed possession of Newfoundland and Labrador by claiming the land for the British.

St. John's achieved much of its importance because of its geographic position. It is closer to Europe than any other city in North America. From Lester's Field within the city boundaries, Capt. John Alcock and Lt. Arthur Brown flew to Clifden, Ireland, in 1919, completing the first nonstop flight across the Atlantic Ocean in 16 hours.

History is commemorated with several memorials. The Sir Humphrey Gilbert Plaque on Water Street marks the area where Sir Humphrey planted the Royal Standard of Elizabeth I in 1583. Above the plaque is the Provincial War Memorial, honoring Newfoundland and Labrador's war dead. A statue of Gaspar Côrte-Real, on Prince Philip Drive in the city's north end, recognizes the significance of the explorer and his country, Portugal, in Newfoundland and Labrador history.

On King's Bridge Road is the Commissariat House, the Georgian home of the assistant commissary general who was responsible for outfitting the British garrison in town. The 1818-21 house, furnished in period, is most accessible through a walking tour of the city because parking is limited; phone (709) 729-6730 or (709) 729-0592.

The Colonial Building on Military Road was the seat of government 1850-1960. Memorial University of Newfoundland was founded in 1925 as a memorial to the province's World War I dead and has achieved a world reputation for cold-ocean research.

Of historical interest northeast of St. John's is Torbay, the 1762 landing site of Col. Jeffrey Amherst and his troops. From Torbay, Amherst marched to defeat the French at Signal Hill *(see Signal Hill National Historic Site of Canada p. 80)*. Fort Amherst, the first lighthouse in the province, was built by the British Military Garrison in 1810. It is located at the base of the Southside Hills, opposite Signal Hill.

A popular reminder of the city's past is the St. John's Regatta, held on Quidi Vidi Lake the first Wednesday in August; if the weather is unfavorable for rowing, the regatta occurs the next favorable day. Dating from 1825, the regatta is considered one of the oldest continuing sports events in North America; music and games of chance supplement the racing fun.

The East Coast Trail runs south of St. John's along the Avalon Peninsula to Cappahayden, offering hikers an unparalleled view of the Newfoundland and Labrador coast, its historic sites and settlements. When completed, the route will extend 400 kilometres (250 mi.) to Trepassey Bay. Trail segments range in difficulty and walking distance, from 1.5 to 10 hours. Phone (709) 738-4453 for trail guides and information.

The City of St. John's Economic Development and Tourism Division: P.O. Box 908, St. John's, NL, Canada A1C 5M2; phone (709) 576-8106 or (709) 576-8455.

Self-guiding tours: Walking and driving tour information is provided in the St. John's Visitor Guide, available at 348 Water St. and at the airport.

The Grand Concourse Walkways comprise a 125-kilometre (78-mi.) system of trails traversing the city as well as nearby Mount Pearl and Paradise. Phone (709) 737-1077 for more information.

Shopping areas: Water Street, one of the oldest thoroughfares in North America, has been the commercial center of St. John's for more than 400 years. The street is lined with a variety of stores, restaurants and pubs, including the Murray Premises, a restored mercantile complex along the harbor originally built in 1846. The complex currently houses specialty boutiques and restaurants.

ANGLICAN CATHEDRAL OF ST. JOHN THE BAPTIST, Gower St. at Church Hill, is said to be one of the finest examples of ecclesiastical Gothic architecture in North America. Construction began in 1847 and the cornerstone was laid in 1849. After the Great Fire of 1892, restoration efforts continued for 13 years. Sculptured arches and carved furnishings are of interest. Tours are available daily 10-5, June-Sept.; by appointment rest of year. Free. Phone (709) 726-5677.

ARTS AND CULTURE CENTRE, on Prince Philip Dr. at Allendale Rd., opened in 1967 for Canada's centennial celebration. Composed of five wings joined by a central lobby, the center contains an expansive contemporary theater. Tues.-Sun. noon-5; closed major holidays. Free. Phone (709) 729-3904.

AVALON WILDERNESS RESERVE is about 100 km (62 mi.) s. off Hwy. 10 on Horse Chops Rd. The 1,070-square-kilometre (413-sq.-mi.) reserve is home to nearly 300 Avalon caribou (the southernmost woodland caribou herd in the world), numerous moose and many smaller animals. Fishing, canoeing, hiking and hunting are popular activities. **Note:** An entry permit, available at any provincial park office and by mail, must be obtained before visiting. Picnicking is permitted. Daily 24 hours. Free. Phone (709) 635-4520 for entry permits, or (800) 563-6353.

◤ BASILICA CATHEDRAL CHURCH AND MUSEUM is at 200 Military Rd. at Harvey and Bonaventure sts. The cornerstone for the Basilica Cathedral of St. John the Baptist was laid in 1841 and construction was far enough along in 1850 to allow masses to take place; in 1855 the cathedral was completed and consecrated. Built in the shape of a Latin cross, the church is noted for its statuary, ornate ceiling design and stained glass windows. Standing some thirty feet above the intersection of the nave and transepts are marble statues of saints Matthew, Mark, Luke and John.

Attached to the church is the Basilica Cathedral Museum, which contains an extensive collection of artifacts, including books, furniture, liturgical garments, paintings and sacred vessels. Allow 1 hour minimum. Church Mon.-Fri. 8:30-8, Sat. 8:30-6, Sun. 8:30-noon. Museum Mon.-Sat. 10-4, Sun. 11:30-4, June 15-Sept. 15; by appointment rest of year. Church free. Museum $2, under 19 free. Phone

(709) 754-2170 for the church or (709) 726-3660 for the museum.

BOWRING PARK, at Waterford Bridge Rd. and Cowan Ave. on the w. end of town, is a traditional English botanical garden with several bronze statues. Many foreign dignitaries have planted trees in the park to mark their visits to the city. Summer activities include swimming, tennis and picnicking, while winter activities include cross-country skiing and tobogganing. An amphitheater plays host to events during the summer. Park open daily 8 a.m.-10 p.m. Free. Phone (709) 364-1531. *See Recreation Chart.*

C.A. PIPPY PARK is on the n. end of town via Hwy. 1 off Allandale Rd., following signs. Designed to integrate the city's modern architecture with surrounding woodlands, steep hillsides, waterways and ponds, the 1,343-hectare (3,317-acre) park contains a 158-site vehicle campground; nine- and 18-hole golf courses overlooking the city; a driving range and a miniature golf course; grand concourse and wilderness trails; and opportunities for fishing and other recreational and cultural pursuits.

Picnicking is permitted. Food is available. Allow 4 hours minimum. Grounds daily dawn-dusk. Grounds free. Phone (709) 737-3655, (877) 477-3655, or (709) 737-3669 for the campground. *See Recreation Chart.*

The Fluvarium, in C.A. Pippy Park off Prince Philip Dr., is the only facility in North America with underwater viewing windows that allow visitors to look directly into a stream, Nagles Hill Brook. There also are exhibits and interpretive programs that focus on freshwater ecology. Allow 1 hour, 30 minutes minimum. Daily 9-5, late Apr.-Oct. 31; Mon.-Fri. 9-4:30, rest of year. Admission $5.50; over 60 and students with ID $4.50; ages 3-13, $3.50; family rate (2 adults and 3 children) $15. MC, VI. Phone (709) 754-3474 or (709) 722-3825.

Memorial University of Newfoundland Botanical Garden, at 306 Mount Scio Rd. in C.A. Pippy Park, encompasses 44 hectares (110 acres) with a semiformal area and a much larger natural area. The cultivated section features rock, cottage, heritage, wildlife and wildflower gardens.

The natural area includes most of the major natural habitat types of the Canadian boreal forest biome and features a network of trails. Visitors must stay on trails and not pick or collect plants and flowers. Allow 1 hour, 30 minutes minimum. Daily 10-5, May-Nov. Guided tours are available on request. Admission $5, senior citizens $3, children $1.15. Under 10 must be accompanied by an adult. Phone (709) 737-8590.

JAMES J. O'MARA PHARMACY MUSEUM, 488 Water St. at Apothecary Hall, is a restored late 1800s drugstore. Displays include late 19th-century pharmacy equipment, scales, medicine bottles, oak store fixtures and an ornate tin ceiling. Daily 10-4:30, late June-Aug. 30; by appointment rest of year. Closed major holidays. Free. Phone (709) 753-5877.

JOHNSON GEO CENTRE is at 175 Signal Hill Rd. next to Signal Hill National Historic Site of Canada. The center houses interactive exhibits that describe the earth's geologic history with special attention paid to local rock formations, which are some of the oldest in the world. A theater presentation portrays the immense forces that have shaped the planet. The mostly underground center is an exhibit itself; constructed in a basin to take advantage of natural rock walls, it is heated by six 152-metre-deep (500-ft.) geothermal wells.

Allow 2 hours minimum. Mon.-Sat. 9:30-5, Sun. 1-5, June 1 to mid-Oct.; Tues.-Sat. 9:30-5, Sun. 1-5, rest of year. Admission $6; senior citizens and students with ID $5; ages 5-17, $3; family rate (two adults and two children) $15. AX, MC, VI. Phone (709) 737-7880, or (866) 868-7625 in Canada.

OLD GARRISON CHURCH (ST. THOMAS'), on Military Rd., was built in 1836. It is one of the oldest wooden churches in St. John's. First used by the military, the church still displays the Hanoverian coat of arms that was the royal symbol for British troops stationed in St. John's until 1870. Allow 30 minutes minimum. Tours are given Mon.-Sat. 9:30-5:30, early July-Aug. 31; by appointment rest of year. Free. Phone (709) 576-6632.

QUIDI VIDI BATTERY PROVINCIAL HISTORIC SITE is off Quidi Vidi Rd. (KIDDIE VIDI) on Cuckhold's Cove Rd., overlooking Quidi Vidi Village. The site was originally constructed by the French following their capture of St. John's in 1762. British forces rebuilt this small fortification in 1780 and held it until their withdrawal from Newfoundland and Labrador in 1870.

The battery is restored to its 1812 appearance and manned by guides in period uniform. Daily 10-5:30, May-Sept.; by appointment rest of year. Admission $3, under 13 free. Phone (709) 729-2977 or (709) 729-0592.

RAILWAY-COASTAL MUSEUM is at 495 Water St. Housed in the restored 1903 Newfoundland Railway Station building, the museum features exhibits that describe the history and importance of the Coastal Boats and the Newfoundland Railway to the province's isolated fishing communities for news, mail and transportation.

Within two converted railcars are replica interiors of a Pullman sleeper car, dining car, kitchen, smoker, coach and mail car. An automated model train passes through detailed reproductions of many of the island's scenic points. A mini-theater shows footage filmed from railways and Coastal Boats servicing Newfoundland's "outports." A 15-metre-wide (50-ft.) mural shows St. John's as it looked in the 1940s.

Allow 1 hour, 30 minutes minimum. Mon.-Sat. 10-5, Sun. 1-5, May 15 to mid-Oct.; Tues.-Sat. 10-5, Sun. 1-5, rest of year. Admission $5; over 65 and ages 13-17, $4; under 13, $3; family rate $12. MC,

VI. Phone (709) 724-5924, or (866) 600-7245 in Canada.

THE ROOMS is at 9 Bonaventure Ave. A museum, art gallery and archives make up this attraction dedicated to the history of the province. Along with the permanent collection, temporary and traveling exhibits are featured.

One of the museum exhibits is dedicated to the province's early landscape and its human and animal inhabitants. Another describes Fort Townsend, the original structure on this site. This 18th-century British fort protected Britain's fishing interests.

The art gallery consists of more than 7,000 works, most of which are contemporary pieces by Newfoundland and Labrador artists. Canadian and international artists are represented as well. The archives consists of such topics as architecture, cartography, government and sports and can be researched through a variety of mediums, including manuscripts, film and still images.

Allow 2 hours minimum. Mon.-Sat. 10-5 (also Wed.-Thurs. 5-9), Sun. noon-5, June 1-Oct. 15; Tues.-Sat. 10-5 (also Wed.-Thurs. 5-9), Sun. noon-5, rest of year. Closed Jan. 1, Good Friday and Dec. 25-26. Admission $5; over 64 and students with ID $4; ages 6-16, $3; family rate $15; free to all Wed. 6-9 p.m. and first Sat. of the month. MC, VI. Phone (709) 757-8000.

SIGNAL HILL NATIONAL HISTORIC SITE OF CANADA—*see place listing.*

SALVAGE (D-4) pop. 203

Salvage, at the tip of Eastport Peninsula on Hwy. 310, was first settled in the mid-1600s; it is one of the oldest continuously inhabited fishing communities in the province. The village has only been accessible by car since the 1940s when the first road was completed.

SALVAGE FISHERMAN'S MUSEUM, in town, is a two-story house dating from 1866. On the first floor are exhibits depicting life in the community since the late 19th century. Included are household items, fishing gear, ships' logs, and antique radios and phonographs. The upper floor is furnished as it appeared in the late 1800s. Allow 1 hour, 30 minutes minimum. Daily 10-6, June 15-Sept. 5; by appointment rest of year. Admission $2; under 13, 50c. Phone (709) 677-2414.

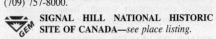

SIGNAL HILL NATIONAL HISTORIC SITE OF CANADA (E-5)

Reached from Duckworth Street, Signal Hill rises 160 metres (525 ft.) above the narrow approach to St. John's harbor. Because of its strategic location, the area was the site of many battles between the English and the French for control of Newfoundland and Labrador and its fisheries. The British defeated the French in 1762 in the last battle between the two countries in North America.

Within the site is Cabot Tower, built to commemorate the Diamond Jubilee of Queen Victoria and the 400th anniversary of John Cabot's voyage to Newfoundland and Labrador. A city landmark, the tower contains an exhibit about the history of communications and signaling. In 1901 Guglielmo Marconi received the first transatlantic wireless message in a hospital near Cabot Tower.

Other points of interest are several batteries built during the 18th and 19th centuries, a reconstructed signal mast and 1830s barracks. A visitor center houses an exhibit about the history of Newfoundland and Labrador. A summer tradition since it was first performed as a centennial celebration in 1967, the Signal Hill Tattoo re-enacts military exercises performed by the Royal Newfoundland Regiment of Foot. Picnicking is permitted on the grounds.

Allow 1 hour minimum. Visitor center open daily 8:30-8, June 15-day after Labour Day; 8:30-4:30, rest of year. Cabot Tower open daily 8:30 a.m.-9 p.m., May 15-Labour Day; 9-5, Apr. 1-May 14 and day after Labour Day-Dec. 31. Signal Hill Tattoo performances Wed.-Thurs. and Sat.-Sun. at 11 and 3, early July to mid-Aug. (weather permitting). Site closed Jan. 1 and Dec. 25-26.

Site free. Exhibits $3.95; over 64, $3.45; ages 6-16, $1.95; family rate $9.90. Tattoo $2.50; over 64, $2; ages 6-16, $1; family rate $6. For more information contact the Area Superintendent, Historic Parks & Sites/Newfoundland, P.O. Box 1268, St. John's, NL, Canada A1C 5M9; phone (709) 772-5367.

STEADY BROOK (C-2) pop. 400

RECREATIONAL ACTIVITIES
Skiing

- **Marble Mountain Ski Resort** is 10 km (6 mi.) e. on Hwy. 1. Write P.O. Box 947, Corner Brook, NL, Canada A2H 6J2. Daily Dec.-Apr. Phone (709) 637-7600.

TERRA NOVA NATIONAL PARK OF CANADA (D-5)

Elevations in the park range from sea level at Bonavista Bay to 229 metres (750 ft.) at Blue Hill. Refer to CAA/AAA maps for additional elevation information.

Seventy kilometres (45 mi.) south of Gander and 240 kilometres (150 mi.) north of St. John's on Hwy. 1, Terra Nova National Park of Canada is characterized by bold headlands extending from a rocky, mostly forested interior. Covering more than 400 square kilometres (155 sq. mi.) of the island of Newfoundland's eastern shore, the park is bounded on the south by Clode Sound, bisected by Newman Sound and touched on its northern edge by Alexander Bay.

Numerous lakes, ponds and streams in the park contain eastern brook trout, salmon and Arctic char.

Saltwater fishing offers cod, mackerel and herring. Moose, black bears, red foxes, beavers, lynx and various smaller species inhabit the area, which serves as a wildlife refuge.

Such migrating birds as the Arctic tern can be sighted off the coast during the spring and fall. Permanent feathered residents include willow ptarmigan, boreal and black-capped chickadees, bald eagles, ospreys and Canada jays.

General Information and Activities

Terra Nova National Park of Canada is open all year. A visitor center with a marine interpretation center is at Saltons in the middle of the park. Information kiosks are at the campgrounds at Malady Head and Newman Sound.

The visitor center is open daily 10-8, late June-Labour Day. Brochure boxes and the park administration building at Newman Sound provide information October through May.

Roads within the park are open all year. Hwy. 1 traverses the area; the Eastport Hwy. in the north end of the park reaches the Eastport Peninsula. Trails provide approximately 100 kilometres (62 mi.) for hiking. Some of the popular routes include the Shady Hollow Trail, which begins at the Southwest Arm Picnic Area, and the 18-kilometre (11-mi.) Coastal Trail. Trails become cross-country skiing routes December through March or April.

Back-country camping, picnicking, boating, fishing, swimming and scuba diving are among other activities available. The park contains an 18-hole golf course bordering a river filled with salmon. A restaurant, pro shop, practice green and range operate May 1 to mid-October. Docks along the park's shoreline provide mooring; a national park permit is needed for freshwater fishing.

Lodging, dining and supplies are available in such nearby communities as Musgravetown, Bunyan's Cove, Port Blandford, Terra Nova, Charlottetown, Glovertown, Traytown and communities on the Eastport Peninsula.

At the Newman Sound Day Use Area there are telescopes for viewing the nearby bird sanctuary; lookout towers are at Ochre Hill and Blue Hill. Guided hikes, outdoor theater presentations and beaver-watching expeditions are conducted by park interpreters late June through Labour Day.

The Saltons Day Use Area features a marine interpretation center, with a touch tank and other displays about marine life. The center is open daily 9-9, late May-Labour Day; 9-5, day after Labour Day to mid-Oct. The Day Use Area also features tour boat and sea-kayaking operators. *See Recreation Chart.*

ADMISSION to the park mid-May to mid-Oct. is $5.45; over 64, $4.70; ages 6-16, $2.70; family rate $13.60. Seasonal pass $27.20; over 64, $23.50; ages 6-16, $13.60; family rate $68.35. Admission free rest of year.

PETS are allowed in the park but must be on a leash or otherwise physically restricted at all times.

ADDRESS inquiries to Superintendent, Terra Nova National Park of Canada, Glovertown, NL, Canada A0G 2L0; phone (709) 533-2801, (905) 426-4648, (877) 737-3783 for camping, TTY (709) 772-4564, or TTY (866) 787-6221 in Canada for camping in season.

TRINITY (D-4) pop. 500

Portuguese explorer Gaspar Côrte-Real, the first recorded visitor to Trinity, sailed into its harbor on Trinity Sunday in 1501. The area's first settlers, under the command of Capt. Robert Ward, reportedly arrived in 1558, almost 30 years before Sir Humphrey Gilbert landed at St. John's and claimed Newfoundland for England in 1583.

In the early 1700s Trinity was frequently raided by pirates and captured twice by the French. To defend themselves, the settlers built fortifications, remains of which can be seen along the coast. Another historic structure in town is St. Paul's Church, built in 1892. During the late 1700s Dr. John Clinch, also a pastor, administered the first Jenner smallpox vaccination in North America.

Because its appearance has changed little since the late 19th century, Trinity also has a lively tourist trade. In the summer popular local activities include fishing, boating and whale watching.

GREEN FAMILY FORGE is on West St. The Green family worked as blacksmiths in town from the mid-18th- to the mid-20th century. The current building, built 1895-1900, now serves as a museum with more than 1,500 artifacts representing several hundred years of blacksmith work. Visitors can watch demonstrations by the blacksmith.

Guided tours are available. Allow 30 minutes minimum. Daily 10-5:30, May 30-Sept. 30. Admission (includes Lester-Garland House and Trinity Historical Society Museum) $4.50. Combination ticket with Hiscock House Provincial Historic Site, Lester-Garland House, Lester-Garland Premises/Ryan's Shop, Trinity Historical Society Museum and Trinity Interpretation Centre $7.50, under 13 free with adult. Phone (709) 464-3599.

HISCOCK HOUSE PROVINCIAL HISTORIC SITE, on Church St., has been restored to its 1910 appearance. The two-and-a-half-story gable-roofed house represents a typical local merchant's dwelling in rural Newfoundland during the early 20th century. Guides in period costumes conduct tours.

Allow 30 minutes minimum. Daily 10-5:30, late May-late Sept.; by appointment rest of year. Admission (includes Lester-Garland Premises/Ryan's Shop and Trinity Interpretation Centre) $3. Combination ticket with Green Family Forge, Lester-Garland House, Lester-Garland Premises/Ryan's Shop, Trinity Historical Society Museum and Trinity Interpretation Centre $7.50, under 13 free with adult. Phone (709) 464-2042 or (709) 729-0592.

LESTER-GARLAND HOUSE, on West St., is a 1997 reconstruction of the brick Georgian house that was built on this site in the 1760s for Benjamin Lester, a fish merchant from Poole, England. Lester's grandson, John Bingley Garland, was a later resident and extended the house. The original stone foundations and some of the bricks have been incorporated. Visitors can see some original furnishings as well as the Trinity Historical Society Archives.

Guided tours are available. Allow 30 minutes minimum. Daily 10-5:30, May 30-Sept. 30. Admission (includes Green Family Forge and Trinity Historical Society Museum) $4.50. Combination ticket with Green Family Forge, Hiscock House Provincial Historic Site, Lester-Garland Premises/Ryan's Shop, Trinity Historical Society Museum and Trinity Interpretation Centre $7.50, under 13 free with adult. Phone (709) 464-3599.

LESTER-GARLAND PREMISES/RYAN'S SHOP, on West St., overlooks the harbor and is perhaps the oldest wooden structure in the province. It used to serve as a counting house and merchant shop; the office area was built in the 1750s and Benjamin Lester built the shop in 1764. Artifacts from the fishing town are displayed throughout the building.

Guided tours are available. Allow 30 minutes minimum. Daily 10-5:30, May 30-Sept. 30. Admission (includes Hiscock House Provincial Historic Site and Trinity Interpretation Centre) $3. Combination ticket with Green Family Forge, Hiscock House Provincial Historic Site, Lester-Garland House, Trinity Historical Society Museum and Trinity Interpretation Centre $7.50, under 13 free with adult. Phone (709) 464-2042 or (800) 563-6353.

TRINITY HISTORICAL SOCIETY MUSEUM, off Hwy. 239 on Church St., displays more than 2,000 items of local and provincial interest in a saltbox house dating from 1880. Exhibits include 1890s medical supplies, an early 1900s shoemaker's kit and a demonstration about fish barrel construction.

Daily 10-5:30, May 30-Sept. 30; by appointment rest of year. Admission (includes Green Family Forge and Lester-Garland House) $4.50. Combination ticket with Green Family Forge, Hiscock House Provincial Historic Site, Lester-Garland House, Lester-Garland Premises/Ryan's Shop and Trinity Interpretation Centre $7.50, under 13 free with adult. Phone (709) 464-3599 or (709) 464-3706.

TRINITY INTERPRETATION CENTRE is on West St. The history of Trinity is presented through displays of illustrations, maps and photographs. Guided tours are available. Allow 30 minutes minimum.

Daily 10-5:30, May 18-Sept. 25. Admission (includes Hiscock House Provincial Historic Site and Lester-Garland Premises/Ryan's Shop) $3. Combination ticket with Green Family Forge, Hiscock House Provincial Historic Site, Lester-Garland House, Lester-Garland Premises/Ryan's Shop and Trinity Historical Society Museum $7.50, under 13 free with adult. Phone (709) 464-2042 or (709) 729-0592.

TROUT RIVER (C-2) pop. 616

TROUT RIVER POND BOAT TOURS, in the western section of Gros Morne National Park of Canada *(see place listing p. 73)*, offers 2.5-hour sightseeing cruises aboard the *Lady Catherine*. Departures daily at 10, 1 and 4, July-Aug.; at 1, May 15-June 30 and Sept. 1-Oct. 15. Fare $35; ages 8-17, $18; family rate $75. Phone (709) 451-3236, or (877) 951-3236 in Canada.

TWILLINGATE (C-4) pop. 2,611

Settled about 1700, Twillingate shares the name of the island on which it is built. Named Toulinguet by French fishermen who thought it resembled Point Toulinguet near Brest, France, the island supports a fishing community. Twillingate celebrates its seafaring heritage with the Fish, Fun and Folk Festival, which features fish dinners, dancing, music and craft displays in late July.

The Long Point Lighthouse, just north of Twillingate on Hwy. 340, offers views of the North Atlantic. The vista is especially beautiful at sunset. In June and July icebergs can be seen drifting south from the Arctic.

TWILLINGATE MUSEUM, off Hwy. 340, contains typical furnishings and household items of an average Newfoundland family during the late 19th and early 20th centuries. Displays feature local handicrafts and maritime artifacts, including reproductions of Maritime Archaic Indian artifacts. Allow 2 hours minimum. Daily 9-6, early May to mid-Oct. Hours may vary; phone ahead. Admission $1, children 50c. Phone (709) 884-2825.

WINERIES

- **Weil Winery** is 2 km (1.2 mi.) n. at 29 Durrell St. following signs. Mon.-Sat. 9-5, Sun. 1-5. Phone (709) 884-2707.

UPPER FERRY (E-1) pop. 1,708

GRAND CODROY WILDLIFE MUSEUM is off Hwy. 1 Doyles exit, then 3.5 km (2 mi.) w. on Hwy. 406. Bears, birds, caribous, fish and moose are among the more than 300 mounted animals featured in exhibits throughout the museum. A wildlife trail allows visitors to see native wild animals, including a fox and coyote. A petting zoo lets visitors get close to such animals as a llama, mule and goat.

Picnicking is permitted. Food is available. Allow 1 hour, 30 minutes minimum. Daily 10-7, early June-Sept. 30 Admission $7; under 19, $5; family rate $20. MC, VI. Phone (709) 955-2555.

WILTONDALE (C-2)

At the junction of hwys. 430 and 431, Wiltondale is midway along the road circling Bonne Bay, noted for its dramatic fjords and the Long Range Mountains. Lomond River, off the east arm of Bonne Bay, rewards anglers with Atlantic salmon. Large schools of mackerel inhabit the bay. Just north of town is the boundary of Gros Morne National Park of Canada *(see place listing p. 73)*.

PIONEER VILLAGE, on Hwy. 430 just s. of Hwy. 431, consists of a general store, country church, an animal barn, a schoolhouse and a house depicting rural life in Newfoundland during the late 1800s. The house displays artifacts and clothing from communities in the Bonne Bay area. Food is available. Daily 9-9, May-Oct. Admission $3; under 16, $1.50; family rate $8. Phone (709) 453-2470.

Funny how so much **water** can help re-ignite **flames.**

To begin your Nova Scotia vacation, visit
novascotia.com /tourbook
or call 1-800-565-0000 op 413
Visit our neighbours at novascotia.com/neighbours

This is
NOVA SCOTIA
Canada's Seacoast

Canada

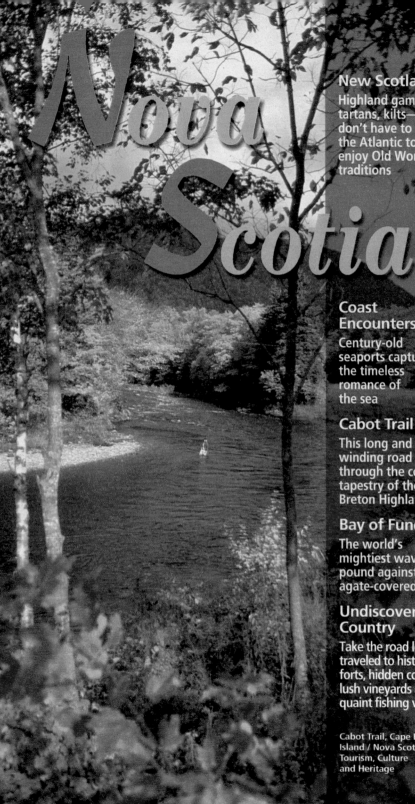

Nova

Scotia

New Scotland

Highland games,
tartans, kilts—you
don't have to cross
the Atlantic to
enjoy Old World
traditions

Coast Encounters

Century-old
seaports capture
the timeless
romance of
the sea

Cabot Trail

This long and
winding road leads
through the colorful
tapestry of the Cape
Breton Highlands

Bay of Fundy

The world's
mightiest waves
pound against the
agate-covered coast

Undiscovered Country

Take the road less
traveled to historic
forts, hidden coves,
lush vineyards and
quaint fishing villages

Cabot Trail, Cape Breton
Island / Nova Scotia
Tourism, Culture
and Heritage

Lunenburg / Nova Scotia Tourism, Culture and Heritage

established tradition

Keep your eyes and ears open in breathtaking Nova Scotia—it has plenty of treats for both.

The bounty and beauty of nature run unchecked in provincial sights. Watch the spectacular landscape unfurl along meandering back roads. Lengthy stretches of rugged coastline harbor scores of history-rich anchorages. Striking shades of crimson, orange and gold kiss leaves during autumn.

The Bay of Fundy is characterized by dramatic tides, which normally exceed 9 metres (30 feet) and have been recorded to rise 16 metres (52 feet) at Minas Basin.

Hiking trails lead to hidden surprises: waterfalls, promontories and cliffs. Many coves and islands in Kejimkujik National Park and National Historic

Site of Canada can be reached only by canoe.

And what of the province's sounds?

Crashing waves on broad, sandy beaches lure surfers and serenity seekers alike to Lawrencetown. The clap of lobster traps being stacked rings out in placid Pictou. Moose calls break the almost haunting quiet of still marshes. Fall migration is signaled by friendly squawks from thousands of visiting shorebirds.

And an established musical tradition means natives variously express themselves through Scottish strathspeys, Acadian jigs and Celtic rock, harmoniously melding the old and new.

A lively melody screams from a fiddle. Girls clad in pleated tartan skirts, waistcoats and colorful argyle kneesocks are stepping and kicking to the quick rhythm of a Scottish drum. Spectators can't help but clap along, their feet tapping to the beat. Bagpipe music echoes across lush green valleys toward the sea.

King James VI of Scotland would be proud. It was he who granted territory to Sir William Alexander in order to establish Nova Scotia, Latin for "New Scotland," in 1621. Many Scottish families later immigrated to Nova Scotia, and residents have remained loyal to their roots.

Great Scot!

"Yet still the blood is strong, the heart is Highland"—this lyric from the "Canadian Boat Song," published in 1829, aptly describes the pride that Scottish Nova Scotians have in their heritage.

And they celebrate on a grand scale: Just about every summer Saturday residents are bound to be tearing it up at a *ceilidh* (pronounced kay-lee), Gaelic for party or gathering. Sometimes spontaneous, these get-togethers have been known to spring up in kitchens or on front porches—wherever there's a fiddle. Exhibiting a distinctive Celtic sense, they're sure to include traditional singing, step dancing, fiddling concerts or storytelling.

At the annual Antigonish Highland Games, expect to see burly men dressed in kilts throwing weights and cabers (tall spruce logs), the latter of which must flip end over end before landing. Pipers decked in full Scottish finery—kilts, Prince Charlie jackets, sporrans (change purses), hose and brogues (lace-up shoes)—delight guests with tunes, just as they did at the first games in the 1860s. And no celebration would be complete without an old-fashioned pipe band competition or a Highland dance performance to fast-paced fiddle and piano music.

In the same fashion that residents don family tartans, Nova Scotia has its own plaid, the colors of which are found in nature. The green of this provincial tartan depicts approximately three-fourths of the landscape covered in forest, while blue and white represent the rugged, sapphire sea surrounding Nova Scotia, especially the staggering Bay of Fundy. But look out—when locals say "high tide," they mean it. Fundy's waves are gigantic.

Nova Scotia Historical Timeline

Jacque Cartier claims the region for France.
1534

French colonization of Acadia begins with the settlement of Port Royal.
1605

Nova Scotia becomes the first colony to win responsible government.
1848

1497
Explorer John Cabot claims Cape Breton Island for England.

© Bettmann/Corbis

1755
After France cedes the territory, Acadians who refuse to pledge British loyalty are deported.

1621
King James I grants "New Scotland" (Nova Scotia) to Sir William Alexander.

Cape Breton Highlands National Park of Canada blends the colors: Green-carpeted highlands rise steeply along a rocky coastline veiled in mist, and wooded valleys envelop a powder-blue sky.

A French Flair

The Scots weren't the only immigrants to call Nova Scotia home. Prior to their arrival, French settlers had claimed the region, naming it Acadia, French for "peaceful land." But it wouldn't stay tranquil for long, due to a prolonged conflict between Britain and France for control of the territory.

Numerous sites throughout the province remind visitors of its time as Acadia. The founding of Port-Royal in 1605 marked the beginning of French colonization in North America. Imagine fur-trading days at the reconstructed Port-Royal National Historic Site of Canada, where steeply pitched roofs and fieldstone chimneys exemplify Norman-style architecture. While you're there, take in a panorama of the beautiful Annapolis River.

Grand-Pré National Historic Site of Canada, once an Acadian village, contains an exhibit detailing the 1755 deportation of Acadians from the area by the British. Henry Wadsworth Longfellow memorialized the event with his now-famous epic poem "Evangeline." Based on a true story, the poem, which tells of a woman who becomes separated from her beloved during the exile, evolved into an Acadian myth. A statue dedicated to the poet and a wishing well named for the heroine are on the grounds.

Topping the site is the Acadian flag, similar to the tricolor French banner, yet with the addition of a yellow papal star in the blue section. The flag also decorates homes along St. Mary's Bay—the "French Shore"—where many French-speaking Acadian villages remain.

Coastal towns like Digby, Yarmouth and Pubnico in this southern corner of Nova Scotia evoke an Acadian milieu. Nearby Point de l'Eglise (Church Point) is home to the Université Ste-Anne, a French language institute focusing on Acadian cultural studies.

Whether the mood is Scottish or Acadian, visit Nova Scotia and you'll receive *ciad mile failte!*—one hundred thousand welcomes—from residents of this truly Canadian province.

Guglielmo Marconi sends the first west-east transatlantic wireless message from Glace Bay to Cornwall, England.
1901

Library of Congress

North America's first tidal power plant opens at Annapolis Royal on the Bay of Fundy.
1984

Library of Congress

1917
Some 2,000 people die when a World War I munitions ship explodes in Halifax harbor.

1912
Halifax, the closest seaport, becomes the final resting place for many *Titanic* victims.

2003
Hurricane Juan, the most damaging storm in a century, makes landfall at Shad Bay.

Recreation

Wherever you go in Nova Scotia, you are near water. With the Atlantic Ocean never more than 60 kilometres (37 mi.) away and an interior speckled with lakes, rivers and streams, water sports make a splash in this Maritime Province.

Countless waterways invite paddlers with all levels of experience. Seasoned **whitewater rafters** might want to conquer the powerful Bay of Fundy, the only place in the world where you paddle up river. Sheltered ocean inlets are perfect for adventurous **sea kayakers**, while inland waters attract the tame at heart.

Excellent harbors at Halifax and Sydney welcome world-class sailors. Numerous outfitters provide rentals and lessons. If underwater exploration is more your style, check out the more than 3,000 shipwrecks along Nova Scotia's rocky shores; June through October is the best time for **scuba diving.**

Happy Trails

Trailblazers can hit the dirt in numerous locations. The 27 trails at Cape Breton Highlands National Park of Canada will accommodate both short strolls and overnight adventures. The Trans Canada Trail, which traverses Sydney, New Glasgow and Halifax, provides opportunities for **hiking, bicycling, horseback riding, cross-country skiing** and **snowmobiling.**

When you can walk no more, hop in your car and head down one of the marked routes found throughout the province. Scenic Cabot Trail is a 300-kilometre (186-mi.) drive through the Margaree Valley and Cape Breton Highlands National Park of Canada with views of both the headlands and the sea. The trail is considered one of North America's most scenic marine drives.

A trip along the Evangeline Trail is particularly memorable in early June, when miles of blossoming apple orchards in the Annapolis Valley provide a breathtaking scene. The Lighthouse Route follows the rugged contours of the province's southern shore.

Whether you opt for a campsite or a tent in one of 22 provincial parks, Nova Scotia fits the bill as a **camping** paradise. Cape Breton Highlands National Park of Canada, on the rugged section of Cape Breton Island, offers hiking, bicycling and **swimming**. **Canoeing** a series of connected waterways is one of the best ways to explore Kejimkujik National Park and National Historic Site of Canada. Both parks have tenting facilities.

When the flurries start falling, hit one of Nova Scotia's downhill ski slopes. **Snowboarding** and **snowtubing** are popular at Ski Wentworth. Keppoch Mountain near Antigonish offers night skiing. Powder enthusiasts can camp in Cape Breton Highlands National Park's overnight ski cabins after a day of blazing cross-country trails or **downhill skiing** at Mount Cape Smokey. Kejimkujik National Park and National Historic Site of Canada beckons cross-country skiers and snowshoers. Snowmobiling also is a favorite wintertime activity.

Wildlife Wonders

Such big game as bears and deer can be snared while **hunting** in Liscomb and Chignecto sanctuaries. Small game catches yield pheasants, ruffed grouse and waterfowl. Nonresident hunters require a license in addition to a guide.

Anglers are lured to the province's rich **fishing** grounds. Saltwater enthusiasts can hook up with charter boats and head to sea, where bluefin tuna, shark, cod, halibut and mackerel can be reeled in. Striped bass lurk in the tidal estuaries and along the beaches of the Bay of Fundy. Freshwater lakes and rivers produce speckled trout, Atlantic salmon, brown trout, American shad, smallmouth bass and yellow perch. Many of the province's rivers are posted for fly fishing only. Check for specifics when obtaining your license.

Due to Nova Scotia's position on the Atlantic flyway, **bird-watching** is prime. Cruise along the coast of Cape Dauphin, where a watchful eye can spot the rare Atlantic puffin nesting on the cliffs. And keep your eyes peeled for humpback, pilot and minke whales; summer is the best time to view these migrating creatures. Outfitters can arrange wildlife-viewing charters.

Recreational Activities

Throughout the TourBook, you may notice a Recreational Activities heading with bulleted listings of recreation-oriented establishments listed underneath. Similar operations also may be mentioned in Destination City recreation sections. Since normal AAA inspection criteria cannot be applied, these establishments are presented only for information. Age, height and weight restrictions may apply. Reservations often are recommended and sometimes are required. Addresses and/or phone numbers are provided so visitors can contact the attraction for additional information.

Fast Facts

POPULATION: 908,007.

AREA: 55,284 sq km (21,345 sq mi); ranks 12th.

CAPITAL: Halifax.

HIGHEST POINT: 532 m/1,745 ft., North Barren Mountain, Cape Breton Island.

LOWEST POINT: Sea level, Atlantic Ocean.

TIME ZONE(S): Atlantic. DST.

MINIMUM AGE FOR UNRESTRICTED DRIVER'S LICENSE: 18 years, 3 months.

MINIMUM AGE FOR GAMBLING: 19.

SEAT BELT/CHILD RESTRAINT LAWS: Seat belts required for driver and all passengers age 16 and older. Children under age 16 and at least 27 kg (60 lbs.) are required to be in a child restraint or seat belt. Child restraints are required for less than 27 kg (60 lbs.).

HELMETS FOR MOTORCYCLISTS: Required for all riders.

RADAR DETECTORS: Not permitted.

FIREARMS LAWS: By federal law, all nonresidents entering Canada with a firearm must declare their weapon in writing and pay a fee of $25 (Canadian). Contact the Canadian Firearms Centre at (800) 731-4000 to receive a declaration form or for additional information.

HOLIDAYS: Jan. 1; Good Friday; Easter Monday; Victoria Day, May 24 or the closest prior Mon.; Canada Day, July 1; Labour Day, Sept. (1st Mon.); Thanksgiving, Oct. (2nd Mon.); Remembrance Day, Nov. 11; Dec. 25-26.

TAXES: Nova Scotia has a harmonized sales tax composed of an 8 percent provincial tax and a 6 percent federal goods and services tax (for a total of 14 percent), which is applied to most goods and services. Sales-tax rebate forms for non-Canadians are available at provincial visitor centers.

INFORMATION CENTERS: Provincial visitor centers open year-round are in Halifax at the Halifax International Airport, off Hwy. 102 exit 6; the International Visitors Centre at 1595 Barrington St.; and on the Halifax Waterfront at the boardwalk. The Amherst Visitor Center, on Hwy. 104 at the New Brunswick border, is open Mar.-Dec. The center in Pictou, at jct. Hwy. 106 and Rte. 6, is open May-Dec.

Other centers, generally open May-Oct., are found in Yarmouth at 228 Main St.; in Portland, Maine, at the International Ferry Terminal; in Digby on Shore Road; in Peggy's Cove; in Port Hastings off the causeway; and aboard ferries traveling from Agentia and Port aux Basques, Newfoundland, to North Sydney. Most centers are open 8:30-4:30, with longer hours at some locations during tourist season.

FURTHER INFORMATION FOR VISITORS:

Nova Scotia Dept. of Tourism and Culture
Information and Reservations
P.O. Box 456
Halifax, NS, Canada B3J 2R5
(800) 565-0000
See color ad p. 84.

FISHING AND HUNTING REGULATIONS:

Service Nova Scotia
c/o Department of Natural Resources
1707 Hollis St., 3rd Floor
Founders Square
Halifax, NS, Canada B3J 2T9
(902) 424-5935

INTERPROVINCE FERRY INFORMATION:

Marine Atlantic Inc.
355 Purves St.
North Sydney, NS, Canada B2A 3V2
(800) 341-7981
Northumberland Ferries, Ltd.
94 Water St.
P.O. Box 634
Charlottetown, PE, Canada C1A 7L3
(902) 566-3838
(888) 249-7245 for reservations
Bay Ferries, Ltd.
58 Water St.
Yarmouth, NS, Canada B5A IK9
(902) 566-3838
(888) 249-7245 for reservations

ALCOHOL CONSUMPTION: Legal age 19.

Nova Scotia
Orientation

Miles
0 — 71

Kilometers
0 — 114.2

NOT INTENDED FOR DRIVING.
SEE APPROPRIATE AAA SHEET MAP.

Only places listed in the Attractions
section appear on this map.

⩔ See AAA GEM Attractions
❶ See Chart of Recreation Areas

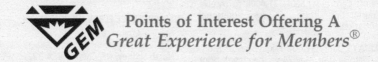

Points of Interest Offering A
Great Experience for Members®

Annapolis Royal (D-1)

ANNAPOLIS ROYAL HISTORIC GARDENS—This beautiful site illustrates the history of gardening and horticulture from early Acadian methods to today's innovative techniques. See p. 96.

FORT ANNE NATIONAL HISTORIC SITE OF CANADA—Once the center of the struggle between France and England for control of North America, the fort's ruins offer a romantic view of the Annapolis Basin. See p. 96.

UPPER CLEMENTS PARK—More than 60 themed buildings showcase Nova Scotia's history and culture while rides and live entertainment offer old-fashioned fun. See p. 96.

Baddeck (B-5)

ALEXANDER GRAHAM BELL NATIONAL HISTORIC SITE OF CANADA— Photographs and replicas convey the story of the renowned teacher and inventor at this 25-acre site near Bell's beloved summer retreat. See p. 98.

Cape Breton Highlands National Park of Canada (A-5)

CAPE BRETON HIGHLANDS NATIONAL PARK OF CANADA—Reminiscent of the Scottish settlers' homeland, these rugged slopes are home to moose, eagles and one of the world's most scenic drives—the historic Cabot Trail. See p. 100.

Fortress of Louisbourg National Historic Site of Canada (B-6)

FORTRESS OF LOUISBOURG NATIONAL HISTORIC SITE OF CANADA—The largest historic reconstruction in North America, Louisbourg boasts impressive fortifications, gardens, wharves and more than 50 restored buildings. See p. 104.

Glace Bay (B-6)

THE MINERS' MUSEUM—This museum sheds light on the history of coal mining as well as the lifestyles of miners in the 1850s and early 1900s. See p. 105.

Grand-Pré (C-2)

GRAND-PRÉ NATIONAL HISTORIC SITE OF CANADA—This site commemorates Acadian history and culture while offering stirring vistas of the Annapolis Valley, the land immortalized in Henry Wadsworth Longfellow's epic poem, "Evangeline." See p. 105.

Granville Ferry (D-1)

NORTH HILLS MUSEUM—One of the oldest houses in Nova Scotia, this 1764 farmhouse displays antiques, 18th-century paintings and glassware collections. See p. 106.

Halifax (B-5)

HALIFAX CITADEL NATIONAL HISTORIC SITE OF CANADA—Walk in the footsteps of British soldiers as you tour this massive star-shaped fort overlooking downtown Halifax. See p. 108.

MARITIME MUSEUM OF THE ATLANTIC—Nova Scotia's rich seafaring heritage is depicted through ships, artifacts and presentations. Don't miss the *Titanic* and Halifax explosion exhibits. See p. 108.

PIER 21 NATIONAL HISTORIC SITE OF CANADA—Some 1 million immigrants from around the world passed through here 1928-71. Interactive exhibits depict stories of hardship and triumph. See p. 109.

Iona (B-5)

HIGHLAND VILLAGE MUSEUM—Experience the culture of Nova Scotia's early Scottish settlers in this living-history village. See p. 110.

Lunenburg (D-2)

FISHERIES MUSEUM OF THE ATLANTIC—Housed in brightly painted red buildings against the backdrop of a picturesque waterfront, this museum commemorates the fishing heritage of Canada's Atlantic Coast. See p. 114.

New Ross (D-2)

ROSS FARM MUSEUM—Visitors go back in time to the early 19th century at this heritage farm, where daily crafts and chores reflect a bygone era. See p. 116.

Peggy's Cove (D-3)

PEGGY'S COVE—Boulders left behind by the last retreating glaciers are scattered randomly at this tiny fishing village. The local lighthouse is anchored in rock and houses the town's post office in summer. See p. 117.

Port-Royal National Historic Site of Canada (C-1)

PORT-ROYAL NATIONAL HISTORIC SITE OF CANADA—Costumed interpreters and period demonstrations re-create the original settlement of Port-Royal, a 17th-century trading post. See p. 118.

Sherbrooke (C-4)

SHERBROOKE VILLAGE—A 1860s lumber and mining town comes alive with colorful characters and realistic depictions of daily life. See p. 120.

Shubenacadie (C-3)

SHUBENACADIE PROVINCIAL WILDLIFE PARK—Shaded walkways wind through the park, offering views of stunning scenery and abundant wildlife. See p. 120.

Stellarton (C-4)

NOVA SCOTIA MUSEUM OF INDUSTRY—Hook a rug or work on an automobile assembly line at this hands-on museum. See p. 120.

Wolfville (C-2)

K.C. IRVING ENVIRONMENTAL SCIENCE CENTRE & HARRIET IRVING BOTANICAL GARDENS—Wander through nine different natural environments, all native to the region, at this botanical garden and science center. See p. 123.

Yarmouth (E-1)

YARMOUTH COUNTY MUSEUM AND ARCHIVES—Yarmouth's historic past is represented with period rooms, lighthouse equipment, various  types of vehicles and a mysterious runic stone. See p. 124.

RECREATION AREAS

RECREATION AREAS	MAP LOCATION	CAMPING	PICNICKING	HIKING TRAILS	BOATING	BOAT RAMP	BOAT RENTAL	FISHING	SWIMMING	PETS ON LEASH	BICYCLE TRAILS	WINTER SPORTS	VISITOR CENTER	LODGE/CABINS	FOOD SERVICE
NATIONAL PARKS *(See place listings)*															
Cape Breton Highlands (A-5) 950 square kilometres 5 km n.e. of Chéticamp on Cabot Tr.		•	•	•				•	•	•		•	•	•	•
Kejimkujik (D-1) 381 square kilometres in southwestern Nova Scotia off Hwy. 8 at Maitland Bridge.		•	•	•	•	•	•	•	•	•		•	•		•
PROVINCIAL															
Amherst Shore (B-3) 328 hectares 6 km e. of Lorneville off Hwy. 366.	❶	•	•	•					•						
Battery (C-5) 46 hectares 1.5 km e. of St. Peter's on Hwy. 4. *(See St. Peter's p. 119)*	❷	•	•	•				•	•	•					
Boylston (C-5) 90 hectares 6.5 km n. of Guysborough on Hwy. 16.	❸	•	•	•				•	•	•					
Caribou (B-4) 31 hectares 8 km n. of Pictou off Hwy. 106.	❹	•	•	•				•	•	•					
Clam Harbour (C-4) 180 hectares off Hwy. 7 at Lake Charlotte.	❺		•	•					•	•					•
Dollar Lake (C-3) 1,193 hectares 23 km e. of Halifax via Hwy. 212.	❻	•	•	•		•	•		•						•
Ellenwood Lake (E-1) 112 hectares 19.25 km n.e. of Yarmouth on Hwy. 340.	❼	•	•	•	•			•	•	•					
Five Islands (C-2) 408 hectares 24.25 km e. of Parrsboro off Hwy. 2.	❽	•	•	•				•	•	•					
Graves Island (D-3) 49 hectares 3.25 km e. of Chester on Hwy. 3.	❾	•	•		•	•			•						
Islands (E-2) 25 hectares 4.75 km w. of Shelburne off Hwy. 3.	❿	•	•	•	•	•		•	•	•					
Laurie (C-3) 28 hectares 40.25 km n. of Halifax on Hwy. 2 on Grand Lake.	⓫	•	•		•	•		•	•	•					
Mira (B-6) 86 hectares 22.5 km s.e. of Sydney on Hwy. 22.	⓬	•	•	•	•			•	•	•					
Porter's Lake (D-3) 86 hectares 19.25 km e. of Dartmouth off Hwy. 7.	⓭	•	•	•	•	•		•	•	•	•				
Risser's (D-2) 92 hectares 24 km s. of Bridgewater on Hwy. 331.	⓮	•	•	•				•	•	•					
Smiley's (D-3) 40 hectares 12.75 km e. of Windsor on Hwy. 14.	⓯	•	•	•				•	•	•					
Thomas Raddall (E-2) 667 hectares near Liverpool off Hwy. 103.	⓰	•	•					•							•
Whycocomagh (B-5) 205 hectares 151 km e. of Whycocomagh on Hwy. 105.	⓱	•	•	•	•	•		•	•	•					

Nova Scotia Temperature Averages
Maximum/Minimum
From the records of The Weather Channel Interactive, Inc.
Temperatures in Celsius.

	JAN	FEB	MAR	APR	MAY	JUN	JUL	AUG	SEP	OCT	NOV	DEC
Halifax	0 / -8	-1 / -9	3 / -4	8 / 0	15 / 5	20 / 10	24 / 13	23 / 14	20 / 11	14 / 6	8 / 1	2 / -5
Yarmouth	1 / -6	1 / -6	4 / -3	8 / 1	14 / 6	18 / 10	21 / 12	21 / 13	18 / 10	14 / 6	9 / 2	3 / -3

Points of Interest

ALEXANDER GRAHAM BELL NATIONAL HISTORIC SITE OF CANADA—*see Baddeck p. 98.*

AMHERST (B-2) pop. 9,470

As the geographical midpoint of the Atlantic Provinces, Amherst is known for its stately Victorian homes and for its role as Cumberland County's commercial center. Covering some 207 square kilometres (80 sq. mi.), the city is built on high ground above the fertile Tantramar marshes.

CUMBERLAND COUNTY MUSEUM is at 150 Church St. This was the home of Sen. Robert Barry Dickey, a father of confederation. Succeeding generations who resided in the 1838 house include James Dickey, a mayor of Amherst, and Arthur Dickey, a minister of defense for Canada. Exhibits interpret the natural, social and industrial history of Cumberland County. Extensive genealogy archives and gardens also are offered.

Mon.-Sat. 9-5, May-Sept.; Tues.-Sat. 9-5, rest of year. Admission $3, under 16 free, family rate $5. Phone (902) 667-2561.

ANNAPOLIS ROYAL (D-1) pop. 550

In the 1630s the French built Fort Anne on the south shore of the Annapolis Basin. When Great Britain took control in 1710, the name was changed to Annapolis Royal in honor of Queen Anne. Enlarged and altered by the British, the fort successfully withstood repeated French and Indian attacks and sieges in the 1740s. Annapolis Royal was the capital of Nova Scotia from 1710 until Halifax was founded in 1749.

Along the Annapolis Basin shore, the original French dikes hold back the Bay of Fundy tides, which rise from 6 to 9 metres (20 to 30 ft.). The best place for walking along the dikes is at the Annapolis Royal Historic Gardens *(see attraction listing)*. An explanation of the tides' effects on the local environment is provided at the Annapolis Tidal Power Generating Station *(see attraction listing)*.

St. George Street provides several examples of the town's antiquity. Among the restorations are the 1784 Robertson-McNamara House, the 1817 Runciman House and the 1922 King's Theatre. Paralleling Lower St. George Street, a waterfront walkway offers a fine view of North Mountain and the Annapolis Basin.

Annapolis Royal and District Board of Trade:
P.O. Box 2, Annapolis Royal, NS, Canada B0S 1A0;
phone (902) 532-5454.

 **ANNAPOLIS ROYAL HISTORIC GAR-
DENS** is at 441 St. George St. The
4-hectare (10-acre) park features themed
gardens representing different periods in Port Royal's history. Highlights include the Governor's Garden, the Knot Garden, the Rock Garden, the
Victorian Garden and a rose collection that includes
more than 2,000 bushes representing some 230
varieties.

The Acadian section includes a replicated 1671
thatched-roof house, which provides a glimpse into
early settlers' lives. New trends in plant materials
and gardening techniques are demonstrated in The
Innovative Garden. More than 2 kilometres (1.2 mi.)
of paths wind among the gardens and displays.

Allow 30 minutes minimum. Daily 8-dusk, mid-
May to mid-Oct. Admission $7, over 60 and stu-
dents with ID $6, under 6 free, family rate $18.
Phone (902) 532-7018.

ANNAPOLIS TIDAL GENERATING STATION is
on the causeway 1 km (.6 mi.) e. on Hwy. 1. The
station, which opened in 1984, is the first and only
modern tidal power plant in North America. It produces electricity by harnessing the tidal waters of
the Bay of Fundy. An interpretive center features
audiovisual presentations, a miniature model and
two enclosed observation decks. Allow 30 minutes
minimum. Daily 10-6, mid-May to mid-Oct. Hours
may vary; phone ahead. Donations. Phone (902)
532-5454.

**FORT ANNE NATIONAL HISTORIC SITE
OF CANADA** is 1 blk. n. of jct. hwys. 8
and 1. In the 1700s both France and England viewed this as an important site for maintaining
control of eastern Canada. The French built four
forts on the site before it was seized by the British

in 1710. Fort Anne was Nova Scotia's capital until
1749; the last regiment was withdrawn in 1854.

Surviving structures include well-preserved ramparts and bastions, a powder magazine and a store-
house. The Fort Anne Museum features exhibits
about the Mi'kmaq, Acadians, planters and Loyalists. The Fort Anne Heritage Tapestry illustrates four
centuries of area history. Monuments honor various
figures from the fort's history.

Guided tours are available. Allow 1 hour minimum. Museum daily 9-6, July-Aug.; 9-5:30, May
15-June 30 and Sept. 1-Oct. 15. Admission $3.95;
over 65, $3.45; ages 6-16, $1.95; family rate $9.90.
Phone (902) 532-2397 or (902) 532-2321.

LOWER SAINT GEORGE STREET runs along the
waterfront. The oldest section of Annapolis Royal features many historic buildings, including the SAVE O'Dell
House Museum, a restored Victorian hostelry. The
museum has shipbuilding tools, schoolroom artifacts, a tavern, a Victorian mourning room, a
kitchen and parlor, a toy room and a genealogical
research center. Museum Mon.-Sat. 9-5, Sun. 1-5,
June-Sept.; Mon.-Fri. 9-5, Sat. 1-4, rest of year. Admission $3; ages 6-17, $2. Research fee $3. Phone
(902) 532-7754.

**PORT-ROYAL   NATIONAL   HISTORIC
SITE OF CANADA—**
see place listing p. 118.

UPPER CLEMENTS PARK is 6 km (4 mi.)
w. at 2931 Hwy. 1. This family park offers
more than 20 amusement rides and attractions, including a carousel, a roller coaster and a
water slide. Miniature golf, gardens and live entertainment also are featured.

The Upper Clements Wildlife Park is home to
200 animals representing 30 species, including rein-
deer, black bears, moose, lynx and bald eagles.
Twelve hectares (30 acres) of walk-through exhibits
are open mid-May to mid-October. A tunnel and
train connect the two parks.

Picnicking is permitted. Food is available. Allow
3 hours minimum. Amusement park open daily 11-7,
mid-June through Labour Day. Admission with unlimited rides and activities $20.50. Park only (in-
cludes entertainment and wildlife park) $6.95, under
2 free with adult. Single ride tickets $2.60. MC, VI.
Phone (902) 532-7557 or (888) 248-4567 for the
amusement park, or (902) 532-5924 for the wildlife
park.

ANTIGONISH (B-4) pop. 4,754

An abundance of beech nuts—and foraging
bears—is thought to have given this area its name,
derived from a Mi'kmaq word meaning "the place
of broken branches." A group of officers from the
Nova Scotia Volunteers received a land grant at Antigonish Harbour in 1784.

ST. NINIAN'S CATHEDRAL is at 120 St. Ninian St.
Completed in 1874, the cathedral is constructed of
local limestone and sandstone in Roman Basilica
style. Highlights include impressive hand-painted

DID YOU KNOW

**The oldest
highland games
in North America
are held
in Antigonish.**

frescoes, high Gothic ceilings, handsome woodwork and two square towers that rise 38 metres (125 ft.). A painting of St. Ninian, completed in the 1850s, is in the rear of the cathedral. Sun.-Wed. 7 a.m.-8 p.m., Thurs.-Fri. 8-8, July-Aug.; daily 7-7, rest of year. Free. Phone (902) 863-2338.

AYLESFORD (C-2) pop. 807

Aylesford was settled in 1784 by United Empire Loyalists, who named the community for the Fourth Earl of Aylesford, Lord of the Bedchamber to King George III. Here, at the highest point in the Annapolis Valley, the waters of the Annapolis River wind through fertile meadows and fruit orchards.

OAKLAWN FARM ZOO is off Hwy. 101 exit 16, following signs. The zoo has one of the largest displays of cats and primates in Atlantic Canada, including a white tiger and Rutledge, who at 807 pounds is considered to be the world's heaviest lion. Hoofed animals such as deer and goats can be fed by hand. Picnicking is permitted. Food is available. Allow 1 hour, 30 minutes minimum. Daily 10-dusk, Easter to mid-Nov. Admission $6.50; over 64, $4; students with ID $3.50; ages 3-12, $2.50. Phone (902) 847-9790.

BADDECK (B-5) pop. 907

Baddeck, on the shore of the Bras d'Or Lakes on Cape Breton Island, derives its name from the Mi'kmaq word *abadak*, which means "place with an island near." The nearby island is Kidston's in Baddeck Harbour.

During the era of wooden ships Baddeck's boatyards helped sustain the economy. Today its harbor bustles with yachts and commercial boating traffic. Early on, the town was popularized by American editor and writer Charles Dudley Warner in his "Baddeck and That Sort of Thing." The village attracted many well-known persons who built summer houses in the area. Among those who came was Alexander Graham Bell, drawn because the scenery reminded him of Scotland. The resemblance does not end with the scenery; Gaelic is spoken, and old Highland Scottish customs persist in the local culture.

About 4 kilometres (2.5 mi.) from town is Bell's former summer home, Beinn Bhreagh, Gaelic for "beautiful mountain." His descendants continue to occupy the estate, which is closed to the public. On the property are the graves of Dr. and Mrs. Bell.

A number of scenic routes originate in Baddeck. The Cabot Trail, a road around northern Cape Breton, loops through here and runs through Ingonish *(see place listing p. 110)*, Cape North *(see place listing p. 101)* and Chéticamp *(see place listing p. 101)*. Other routes lead through the Margaree Valley and to Whycocomagh and Lake Ainslie. Nearby waters are renowned for trout fishing and yachting.

 ALEXANDER GRAHAM BELL NATIONAL HISTORIC SITE OF CANADA, at the e. end of town on Rte. 205, features a large collection of artifacts, photographs and personal mementos commemorating the life and work of inventor Alexander Graham Bell. Displays cover his extraordinary range of interests, including aeronautics, agriculture, genetics, marine engineering, medical science and his work with the hearing impaired.

The main building's striking architectural style is based on the tetrahedron, the geometric form Bell used in designing his passenger-carrying kites. The landscaped grounds offer a view of the Bell estate across Baddeck Bay on the Bras d'Or Lakes.

During July and August the site offers special programs, including kite-building workshops and experiments that Bell and his grandchildren performed with everyday materials, as well as presentations about Bell's life and work.

Picnicking is permitted. Allow 1 hour minimum. Daily 8:30-6, July 1-Oct. 15; 9-6, in June; 9-5, in May and Oct. 16-31; by appointment rest of year. Admission $7.15; over 64, $5.90; ages 6-16 and students with ID $3.45; family rate $17.80. Phone (902) 295-2069.

BRAS D'OR LAKES & WATERSHED INTERPRETIVE CENTRE is off Hwy. 105 exit 9, then s. to 532 Chebucto St. Housed in an 1885 stone post office, the museum features exhibits about the history, geology and wildlife of the Bras d'Or Lakes. The center offers brochures and maps of the area, including the best sites for viewing bald eagles. Allow 30 minutes minimum. Daily 9-7, June-Aug.; 1-4, in Sept. Donations. Phone (902) 295-1675.

BARRINGTON (E-1) pop. 7,648

Following the 1755 expulsion of the Acadians, French habitations in the area of what is now Barrington were destroyed. The New Englanders who replaced the Acadians re-established the site in the 1760s.

Reached by causeway from Barrington Passage, nearby Cape Sable Island is a major seafood harvesting center in southern Nova Scotia. The Cape Sable Island boat, renowned for its stability and good handling in shallow water and rough seas, was invented at Clark's Harbour in the early 1900s. Modern motorized adaptations of the boat are used in most seafood-harvesting operations.

The Cape Sable Historical Society Centre and Community Museum, 2402 Hwy. 3, contains local artifacts and genealogical material.

BARRINGTON WOOLEN MILL MUSEUM is at 2368 Hwy. 3 on the Barrington River. This was the last water-powered woolen mill to operate in eastern Canada. Built in 1882, it was in use until 1962. Displays follow the stages in the manufacture of yarn and cloth from raw wool. A mural illustrates the history of farming in Nova Scotia and contains the first tartan created in the province. Allow 30 minutes minimum. Mon.-Sat. 9:30-5:30, Sun. 1-5:30, June-Sept. Admission $3; ages 6-17, $2; family rate $9. Rates may vary; phone ahead. Phone (902) 637-2185.

OLD MEETING HOUSE MUSEUM is at 2408 Hwy. 3. The 1765 New England-style meetinghouse is said to be Canada's oldest nonconformist house of worship still in existence. Guides in period costume explain the history of the community. Many early townspeople are buried in the adjacent graveyard. Allow 30 minutes minimum. Mon.-Sat. 9:30-5:30, Sun. 1-5:30, June-Sept. Admission $3; ages 6-17, $2; family rate $9. Rates may vary; phone ahead. Phone (902) 637-2185.

SEAL ISLAND LIGHT MUSEUM is at 2410 Hwy. 3 overlooking the bay. This is a three-story replica of the original Seal Island lighthouse that was built in the early 1800s. The museum houses memorabilia including a lantern and lens used 1907-79. Allow 30 minutes minimum. Mon.-Sat. 9:30-5:30, Sun. 1-5:30, June-Sept. Admission $2, under 6 free, family rate $7. Rates may vary; phone ahead. Phone (902) 637-2185.

WEST NOVA SCOTIA MILITARY MUSEUM is at 2401 Hwy. 3 in the old courthouse building. Military artifacts from World Wars I and II include medals, uniforms and weapons as well as photographs. Allow 30 minutes minimum. Mon.-Sat. 9:30-5:30, Sun. 1-5:30, July-Aug.; Mon.-Fri. 10-5, in June. Donations. Phone (902) 637-2161 or (902) 768-2292.

BARSS CORNER (D-2)

PARKDALE-MAPLEWOOD COMMUNITY MUSEUM is at 3005 Barss Corner Rd. The museum contains agricultural implements, tools, domestic utensils, personal articles and other items from the late 1800s and early 1900s. A research center and heritage garden also are part of the museum. Mon.-Sat. 9-5, Sun. 1-5, July-Aug.; Mon.-Fri. 9-5, May-June and Sept. 1-Oct. 27. Donations. Phone (902) 644-2893.

BEAR RIVER (D-1) pop. 900

An important shipbuilding and milling center at the end of the 19th century, Bear River has retained its pioneer flavor. The village has come to be known as the "Switzerland of Nova Scotia." The Dutch Windmill serves as a tourist bureau and contains a collection of photographs and logging and shipbuilding tools.

Bear River Board of Trade: P.O. Box 235, Bear River, NS, Canada B0S 1B0; phone (902) 467-3200.

BIG BRAS D'OR (A-6) pop. 300

Big Bras d'Or, meaning "Arm of Gold" in French, is on Boularderie Island, which is separated from the rest of Cape Breton Island by two narrow channels that connect the virtually tideless Bras d'Or Lake to the Atlantic Ocean.

SAVE **BIRD ISLAND BOAT TOURS** departs from Mountain Vista Seaside Cottages and Campground, off Hwy. 105 exit 14, then 6.5 km (4 mi.) w. to 1672 Old Rte. 5. This 2.75-hour boat ride to the Bird Islands, Ciboux and Hertford, offers a look at seals, eagles and seabirds such as the Atlantic puffin, razorbill auk, great cormorant, double-crested cormorant and kittiwake gull.

Departures require a minimum of four passengers. Tours depart daily at 10, 1:30 and 5:30, July-Aug.; at 10 and 1:30, in June; at 10 and 2:30 in May and Sept. 1-15 (sea conditions permitting). Fare $33. AX, MC, VI. Phone (902) 674-2384 or (800) 661-6680.

BRIDGETOWN (C-1) pop. 1,035

At the head of navigation on the Annapolis River, Bridgetown was once an important shipbuilding center during the "age of sail." Stately Victorian-era houses are a reminder of its seafaring past.

Bridgetown & Area Board of Trade: Box 453, Bridgetown, NS, Canada B0S 1C0; phone (902) 665-4403.

Self-guiding tours: A brochure outlining walking tours of historic areas is available at Jubilee Park Visitor Information Centre, 232 W. Granville St., or at the Bridgetown Town Hall, 271 W. Granville St.; phone (902) 665-4637.

THE JAMES HOUSE MUSEUM is 1 blk. s. of Hwy. 1 at 12 Queen St. Displays in the 1835 house include a 150th anniversary quilt, period costumes, the Legion Memorial Museum and a museum collection that changes every summer. Mon.-Fri. 10-4, May-Oct. Donations. Phone (902) 665-4530.

BRIDGEWATER (D-2) pop. 7,621

A farming and manufacturing community in the heart of the LaHave River Valley, the town was founded in the early 1800s and was named for the bridge spanning the river. Picturesque drives follow both banks. As an active waterway for commercial and pleasure craft, the river contributes to Bridgewater's importance as a regional economic center.

Shipyards Landing Park offers boat ramps and scenic vistas. The Bridgewater Woodland Gardens contain winding trails punctuated by azaleas and rhododendrons. The gardens also contain a large pond and picnic tables. The town's Centennial Trail is a hiking and bicycling path that meanders through woods and along the LaHave River.

Bridgewater & Area Chamber of Commerce: P.O. Box 100, Bridgewater, NS, Canada B4V 2W8; phone (902) 543-4263.

DesBRISAY MUSEUM is .75 km (.5 mi.) s. to 130 Jubilee Rd. on the w. side of the LaHave River. One of Canada's oldest museum collections was started by Judge Mather Byles DesBrisay and opened to the public in 1902. Exhibits focus on the natural, cultural and industrial history of Bridgewater and Lunenburg County. Changing exhibits also are presented.

Picnicking is permitted. Allow 1 hour minimum. Mon.-Sat. 9-5, Sun. 1-5, June 1-Labour Day; Wed.-Sun. 1-5, rest of year. Hours may vary; phone ahead. Admission $3; over 64 and ages 5-16, $2; family rate $7. Rates may vary; phone ahead. Phone (902) 543-4033.

WILE CARDING MILL MUSEUM is at 242 Victoria Rd. (Hwy. 325). An 1860 carding mill features original machinery and an operating waterwheel. Costumed staff demonstrate how to use the machinery. Visitors may hand card wool, use a drop spindle and make a sample of yarn. Children's programs are offered. Allow 30 minutes minimum. Mon.-Sat. 9:30-5:30, Sun. 1-5:30, June-Sept. Hours may vary; phone ahead. Admission $3; over 64 and ages 6-17, $2; family rate $7. Rates may vary; phone ahead. Phone (902) 543-8233.

CANSO (C-5) pop. 992

Canso is one of the oldest fishing communities in the Maritimes. French fishermen came to Canso in the early 1600s because of the abundance of codfish. The town now offers sightseeing and sport fishing.

Town of Canso Tourism and Trade: P.O. Box 189, Canso, NS, Canada B0H 1H0; phone (902) 366-2525.

CANSO ISLANDS NATIONAL HISTORIC SITE OF CANADA lies .5km (.3 mi.) off the waterfront. A visitor center on Union Street offers views of Grassy Island Fort National Historic Site. The fort became the object of bitter feuding between the French and British until it was destroyed and abandoned abruptly in 1744. The visitor center features artifacts, dioramas and an audiovisual presentation. A boat ferries visitors to Grassy Island.

Allow 30 minutes minimum. Daily 10-6, June 1-Sept. 15. Boats depart according to demand (weather permitting). Admission (includes ferry) $2.50; over 64, $2; ages 6-16, $1.25. Phone (902) 366-3136 or (902) 295-2069.

WHITMAN HOUSE MUSEUM is at 1297 Union St. Memorabilia from the C.H. Whitman family is displayed in the 1885 house, which features extensive woodwork, solid brass hardware, antiques and two fireplaces. The house also contains exhibits reflecting Canso's days as an important Western Union communications center. Guided tours are available. Allow 1 hour minimum. Daily 9-5, June-Sept.; by appointment rest of year. Donations. Phone (902) 366-2170 or (902) 366-2525.

CAPE BRETON HIGHLANDS NATIONAL PARK OF CANADA (A-5)

Elevations in the park range from sea level to 532 metres (1,745 ft.) at White Hill. Refer to CAA/AAA maps for additional elevation information.

Cape Breton Highlands National Park of Canada (see color ad p. 95) has entrances on the Cabot Trail 5 kilometres (3 mi.) northeast of Chéticamp on the west side of the island and at Ingonish Beach on the east. The park is in the northern part of Cape Breton Island. Bounded on the west by the Gulf of St. Lawrence and on the east by the Atlantic Ocean, the park protects 950 square kilometres (366 sq. mi.) of highlands and coastal wilderness. The first national park in the Atlantic provinces, it bears a striking resemblance to coastal regions of Scotland.

Along the western shore, steep hills reaching a height of more than 335 metres (1,100 ft.) rise sharply to a broad plateau covering most of the park area. The eastern shore also is rocky, indented with numerous coves and sandy beaches at the mouths of valleys.

Less frequented by visitors, the interior high plateau of the park is similar to subarctic regions, containing heath bogs, stunted spruce forest and dry, rocky barrens. Along the seacoast headlands the trees are stunted and twisted into grotesque shapes. The rest of the park is covered with a typical Acadian mixed forest of conifers and hardwoods.

The park, a wildlife sanctuary, protects a variety of animals, including black bears, foxes and snowshoe hares. Motorists are advised to drive with care. Moose often are seen along the highways. Among the 200 species of birds are the bald eagle and redtailed hawk. Whale-watching is popular both from land and by boat tours offered in nearby communities.

The Cabot Trail, a circle tour of the eastern and western shores of Cape Breton Island and the picturesque Margaree Valley, winds along the edge of the park's rugged, forested slopes, providing a scenic 300-kilometre (186-mi.) drive.

General Information and Activities

The park is open all year, with full facilities offered mid-May to early October. Information centers are maintained at the park's entrances at Chéticamp (see place listing p. 101) and Ingonish (see place listing p. 110). The Chéticamp Visitor Centre has a 10-minute slide show about the park and a children's corner. Interpretive events are presented during July and August. An entry permit is required for park use, including Cabot Trail sightseeing.

The park offers a wide range of activities, including camping at its six campgrounds, hiking, swimming, wildlife and bird-watching, tennis, bicycling and fishing. Highland Links, within the park, is a world-class 18-hole golf course. Changing facilities, tennis courts and a picnic area are provided at the Ingonish Beach Day Use Area. The main beach is the only land separating the surf from a quiet freshwater lake; supervised swimming takes place during July and August. Picnic facilities and unsupervised swimming are available at Black Brook, La Bloc, North Bay Beach and Warren Lake.

Pilot whales are a fairly common sight offshore, while minke, finback and humpback whales can be seen periodically as well. Whale-watching and deep sea fishing excursions depart from port towns near the park.

Hiking trails lead from the Cabot Trail to the interior or along the shore. The 25 trails, ranging from short, easy strolls to challenging mountain hikes with panoramic views, are described on the park map. Bicycling is permitted on designated trails only. Fall foliage is at its best from late September to mid-October. Certain park trails are groomed for cross-country skiing in the winter. *See Recreation Chart and the AAA/CAA Eastern Canada Camp-Book.*

ADMISSION to the park is $7 per day; over 65, $6; ages 6-16, $3.50; family rate $17.50. Annual passes are available.

PETS are permitted in the park except on beaches and the Skyline Trail. They must be on a leash at all times.

ADDRESS inquiries to Cape Breton Highlands National Park of Canada, Ingonish Beach, NS, Canada B0C 1L0. Phone (902) 224-2306 or (888) 773-8888 for an information packet.

CAPE NORTH (A-5) pop. 200

Cape North, a Cape Breton Island district on Aspy Bay, is the northernmost point on the scenic Cabot Trail. The 19-kilometre (12-mi.) road, connecting Cape North with Capstick on St. Lawrence Bay, offers ocean and mountain scenery. Cabot Landing, a provincial park with a picnic area and beach on Aspy Bay, is believed to have been the landing site of John Cabot and his son Sebastian. A trail leads to the top of 442-metre (1,450-ft.) Sugar Loaf Mountain.

NORTH HIGHLANDS COMMUNITY MUSEUM is n. of Bay Saint Lawrence Rd. at 29243 Cabot Tr. Pioneer life and northern Cape Breton traditions are depicted through exhibits, artifacts and photographs. Events such as the *Titanic* and *Auguste* shipwrecks, construction of the Cabot Trail and Canso Causeway, and the development of gypsum mining also are explored. Archive and genealogy research is available by appointment. Visitor information also is available.

Allow 30 minutes minimum. Daily 9-5, early June to mid-Oct. Admission $2; family rate $5. Phone (902) 383-2579.

CENTREVILLE (E-1) pop. 700

Many residents of Cape Sable Island, on which Centreville is found, are descendants of Archelaus Smith, who was among the tide of New Englanders, mainly from Cape Cod, Mass., who settled Nova Scotia's South Shore in the 1760s. For the next half-century their livelihoods of fishing and shipping were subject to attacks by Yankee privateers.

ARCHELAUS SMITH MUSEUM is 4 km (2.5 mi.) s. to 915 Hwy. 330. The collection includes marine exhibits, local art, artifacts from shipwrecks and displays of handicrafts and household items. Genealogical information is available. Mon.-Sat. 9:30-5:30, Sun. 1:30-5:30, mid-June to late Sept.

Donations. Phone (902) 745-2411 or (902) 745-3361.

CHÉTICAMP (A-5) pop. 1,000

This thriving shore community is sheltered from the Gulf of St. Lawrence by Chéticamp Island. Farming, rug hooking and fishing for lobster and crab are the basis of the area's economy. Saint-Pierre Church dominates the waterfront. The stone church, the third on the site, was built in 1892.

Chéticamp lies on an especially scenic section of the Cabot Trail, which circles the northern tip of Cape Breton Island and passes the western entrance of Cape Breton Highlands National Park of Canada (*see place listing p. 100*), 5 kilometres (3 mi.) northeast of town.

ACADIAN MUSEUM is at 15067 Main St. near Saint-Pierre Church. Spinning, weaving and rug hooking are demonstrated at this museum, part of the Coopérative Artisanale. Displays include French-Canadian antiques, glassware and rugs dating to the 1900s. Guided tours explain how wool is carded and spun, and visitors are invited to hook their own rug strips. Food is available. Daily 8 a.m.-9 p.m., June-Aug.; 9-5 in May and Sept.-Oct. Donations. Phone (902) 224-2170.

CAPTAIN ZODIAC WHALE CRUISE departs from the town center at 14925 Cabot Tr. Whale sightings are guaranteed aboard these fast-moving Zodiak vessels, which travel close to shore for views of pilot and minke whales and farther out to sea for glimpses of humpbacks, dolphins and fin whales.

Passengers are provided with all-weather suits. Zodiak trips are not advised for pregnant women and people with back or neck problems. Allow 2 hours minimum. Cruises depart daily at 9, 11, 1, 3 and 5, May 1-Oct. 15 (weather permitting). Reservations are required. Fare $36; under 17, $18. MC, VI. Phone (902) 224-1088.

ELIZABETH LEFORT GALLERY is at 15584 Cabot Tr. in Les Trois Pignons building. A collection of tapestries by Acadian artist Dr. Elizabeth Le-Fort features more than 20 hooked rugs with historic themes. Tapestries of other local artists are displayed as well. Allow 30 minutes minimum. Daily 8-7, July-Aug.; 9-5, May-June and Sept.-Oct. Admission $3.50; over 64, $3; under 12 free. Phone (902) 224-2642.

[SAVE] **SEASIDE WHALE & NATURE CRUISES** departs from the town center at 15456 Laurie Rd. Narrated cruises offer more than a 95% chance of whale sightings as well as glimpses of eagles, seabirds and wildlife along the coast of Cape Breton Highlands National Park of Canada (*see place listing p. 100*). Hydrophones on board enable passengers to hear whale calls. Allow 3 hours minimum. Three cruises depart daily May-Sept. (weather permitting). Reservations are required. Fare $30; ages 13-18, $20; ages 6-12, $18. MC, VI. Phone (902) 224-2400.

SAVE **WHALE CRUISERS LTD.** departs from Chéti-camp Harbour opposite Saint-Pierre Church. On narrated 3-hour cruises, the *Whale Cruiser* and *Bonnie Maureen III* travel the Gulf of St. Lawrence in search of pilot, finback and minke whales. Passengers have the opportunity to view spectacular scenery, interesting geology and a variety of birds and wildlife found along the shores of Cape Breton Highlands National Park of Canada *(see place listing p. 100).*

Tours are offered daily at 9, 1 and 6, June-July; at 9, 1 and 5, Aug. 1-Sept. 15; at 9 and 5, May 15-May 31; at 10 and 4, Sept. 16 to mid-Oct. Fare $25; ages 6-12, $10. MC, VI. Phone (902) 224-3376 or (800) 813-3376.

CHURCH POINT (D-1)

When exiled Acadians returned to Nova Scotia to find their homelands occupied, many accepted the British government's offer of 40-acre lots along St. Mary's Bay, which became known as the "French Shore." In 1891, the Université Sainte-Anne was founded at Pointe de l'Eglise (Church Point) to preserve Acadian culture; it remains the only French-language university in the province.

SAINTE-MARIE (ST. MARY'S) CHURCH MUSEUM is on Hwy. 1. This 1905 Roman Catholic Church is one of the largest wooden churches in North America. The museum features a collection of vestments, religious articles, church furnishings, documents and photographs. Guided tours are available. Daily 9-5, late May to mid-Oct.; by appointment rest of year. Admission $2, family rate $5. Phone (902) 769-2832 or (902) 837-5408.

COLE HARBOUR (D-3) elev. 40 m/130'

COLE HARBOUR HERITAGE FARM MUSEUM is at 471 Poplar Dr. The museum, which consists of several historic buildings, is on a site that has been farmed since the early 1780s. Exhibits include photographs, historic documents, gardens, farm and household equipment, and livestock. The property connects with a walkway that winds through the neighboring parkland. The 1785 Giles House is a farm house filled with late 18th- to early 20th-century household items.

Picnicking is permitted. Food is available. Allow 1 hour minimum. Mon.-Sat. 10-4, Sun. and holidays noon-4, May 15-Oct. 15; by appointment rest of year. Admission $2. Phone (902) 434-0222 or (902) 462-0154.

DARTMOUTH (D-3) pop. 65,600

On the eastern shore of Halifax Harbour, Dartmouth is connected to the city of Halifax by two suspension bridges and by ferry. The Angus L. MacDonald Bridge, spanning the harbor, is the fourth longest bridge in the British Commonwealth.

The city is a popular visitor destination and offers many fine restaurants, historic houses, a waterfront boardwalk and interesting attractions. Bedford Institute of Oceanography on Bedford Basin is reputed to be the largest Canadian center for marine research. South of Dartmouth, at Cow Bay and Eastern Passage, is the Canadian Forces Base Shearwater, first built for American seaplanes during World War I.

Dartmouth's 23 lakes once provided the area with ice for summer refrigeration. Today they are the centers of year-round recreation. Lake Banook is the site of a world-class canoe paddling course where international paddling events are staged each year. Lake Micmac often is the setting of water-skiing competitions. In winter, skating and ice hockey are popular pursuits. Scenic beaches include Clam Harbour, Lawrencetown, Martinique and Rainbow Haven.

Self-guiding tours: Brochures outlining self-guiding walking tours of the Halifax-Dartmouth area are available at the visitor information centers in Halifax *(see place listing p. 106).*

BLACK CULTURAL CENTRE FOR NOVA SCOTIA is at 1149 Main St. Exhibit galleries and a library preserve the art, history and culture of the province's citizens of African descent. Permanent exhibits focus on such themes as settlement by African-American Loyalists and the African-Nova Scotian community. Mon.-Fri. 9-5, Sat. 10-3, June-Sept.; Mon.-Fri. 9-5, rest of year. Admission $6, over 54 and students with ID $4, under 5 free, family rate (maximum of five people) $15. Phone (902) 434-6223.

DARTMOUTH HERITAGE MUSEUM, EVERGREEN HISTORIC HOUSE is at 26 Newcastle St. Panoramic views of Halifax Harbour and a collection of Victorian furnishings are features of this 1867 residence. One of Dartmouth's grand estates, it was built for a prominent local judge and was also the home of Dr. Helen Creighton, noted Nova Scotian folklorist. Children's activities and special events include an annual Strawberry Tea, Folklore Program and Halloween at Helen's House.

Tues.-Sun. 10-1 and 2-5, June-Aug.; Tues.-Sat. 10-1 and 2-5, rest of year. Admission $2, under 13 free. Phone (902) 464-2301 or (902) 464-2300.

ROYAL CANADIAN LEGION MILITARY MUSEUM is at 52 King St. The collection includes military uniforms from World Wars I and II as well as the Korean and Boer wars. Separate rooms feature exhibits about the Army, Navy, Air Force, Merchant Navy and Army Medical Corps. Photographs, weapons and a collection of shoulder badges also are on display.

Mon., Wed. and Fri. 1-4, June 1-Nov. 11; by appointment rest of year. Admission $2; under 12 free. Reservations are required 1 week in advance for guided tours. Phone (902) 463-1050.

SHEARWATER AVIATION MUSEUM is off Hwy. 111, following Hwy. 322 (Pleasant St.) toward Eastern Passage, continuing to the entrance of the Canadian Forces Base Shearwater. The museum, within the grounds of a military base, displays aircraft, photographs, uniforms and memorabilia related to the history of the Canadian air defense forces.

Guided 1-hour tours are available by reservation. Tues.-Fri. 10-5, Sat.-Sun. noon-4, June-Aug.; Tues.-Fri. 10-5, Sat. noon-4, Apr.-May and in Nov.; by appointment rest of year. Closed holidays. Donations. Phone (902) 720-1083.

QUAKER HOUSE is at 57 Ochterloney St. One of the oldest houses in Dartmouth, the 1785 house is representative of the type of prefabricated structures built by the Nantucket Quaker whalers who lived in Dartmouth in the late 1700s. A trunk contains period dress-up clothes for children. A beautiful historic garden is on view. Costumed guides provide tours. Guided tours are offered Tues.-Sun. 10-1 and 2-5, June-Aug. Admission $2, under 13 free. Phone (902) 464-2253 or (902) 464-2300.

DENMARK (C-3) pop. 100

SUTHERLAND STEAM MILL is off Hwy. 6 on Hwy. 326. The site includes a restored 1894 sash and door factory, sawmill and carriage shop. Throughout its 64 years of operation, the two-story steam mill also manufactured sleighs, sleds and gingerbread trim, examples of which are displayed on the second floor.

Allow 30 minutes minimum. Mon.-Sat. 9:30-5:30, Sun. 1-5:30, June 1-Oct. 15. Admission $3; over 64 and ages 6-17, $2; family rate $7. Phone (902) 657-3365.

DIGBY (D-1) pop. 2,111

Digby overlooks the scenic Annapolis Basin and Digby Gut. Some of the highest tides on the planet occur nearby; Fisherman's Wharf is a good spot for viewing the fluctuations that can vary as much as 9.7 metres (32 feet) within 6 hours. The highest tides occur a day or two after the full moon.

The city is named for Sir Robert Digby, a British admiral whose command transported 1,500 Loyalists from New England in 1783. The Admiral's Well, dug in the 19th century, is on the admiral's original property near the entrance to Fisherman's Wharf. John Edison, great-grandfather of Thomas Alva Edison, was among the early settlers, many of whom are buried in the Old Loyalist Graveyard and Trinity Anglican Church Cemetery.

One of the most popular areas in the Atlantic Provinces, Digby is home to one of the largest scallop fleets in the world. It also is gateway to a region of spectacular beauty, Digby Neck and Islands. This narrow ribbon of land juts far out into the Bay of Fundy, providing breathtaking views and one of North America's best whale-watching areas.

Side trips lead to the village of Bear River *(see place listing p. 99)*, Point Prim on the Bay of Fundy, St. Mary's Bay and Westport *(see place listing p. 122)*. Digby is the northern terminus of scenic Hwy. 101, which follows St. Mary's Bay south to Yarmouth *(see place listing p. 124)*.

Nearby, south on Digby Neck along scenic Rte. 217, is Sandy Cove, a popular spot for painters, photographers, and whale- and bird-watchers.

Bay Ferries provides year-round car and passenger service from Digby to Saint John, New Brunswick, aboard the *Princess of Acadia*. Reservations for the 3-hour crossing are highly recommended and must be picked up 1 hour prior to sailing time; phone (902) 245-2116 or (888) 249-7245.

Digby Tourism: P.O. Box 579, Digby, NS, Canada B0V 1A0; phone (902) 245-5714 or (888) 463-4429.

ADMIRAL DIGBY MUSEUM is at 95 Montague Row. The history of Digby County is recounted through a collection of pioneer furnishings, photographs, maps and marine artifacts. Allow 30 minutes minimum. Tues.-Sat. 9-5, Sun. 1-5, mid-June to Aug. 31; Tues.-Fri. 9-5, Sept. 1 to mid-Oct.; Wed. and Fri. 9-5, rest of year. Donations. Research fee $5. Phone (902) 245-6322.

LADY VANESSA FISHERIES EXHIBIT is at the Fundy Complex on the waterfront boardwalk. Purchase tickets at the Haynes Gift Shop next to the museum. The exhibit, which provides a look at the local area's history of fishing, is aboard a former scallop dragger.

The 30-metre (98-ft.) vessel is open to visitors, with the helm, galley and sleeping quarters accessible via self-guiding tours. A 35-minute video shows underwater scenes detailing how lobsters, scallops and fish are caught. Allow 30 minutes minimum. Daily 9-6, June 15-Oct. 15 (also 6-9 p.m., July-Aug.). Admission $2, under 6 free. MC, VI. Phone (902) 245-4950.

EASTERN PASSAGE (D-3) pop. 8,872

Named for the channel of water running into Halifax Harbour between the mainland and Lawlor's and McNab's islands, Eastern Passage was first mentioned on a nautical chart in 1759.

FISHERMAN'S COVE is off Hwy. 322 at 200 Government Wharf Rd. A 1.5 mile boardwalk meanders past a complex of shops, restaurants and a tourist information center. Nature tours, harbor tours and fishing excursions are available. The Marine Interpretive Centre includes aquariums, bird exhibits, photographs and interactive exhibits.

Daily 24 hours, May-Oct.; Fri.-Sun. 24 hours, Nov. 1-Dec. 23. Information center daily 9-6, May 15-Oct. 15. Marine Interpretive Centre daily 11-6, June 1-Sept. 1; by appointment rest of year. Shop and restaurant hours vary. Complex free. Marine Interpretive Centre $2. Phone (902) 465-6093.

ENGLISHTOWN (B-6)

The French settlement of Port Dauphin was to have been the capital of Cape Breton Island (Île Royale), but instead, Louisbourg was selected as the seat of government in 1718. After the fall of Louisburg 40 years later, many British soldiers settled in the area, and Port Dauphin was renamed Englishtown.

SAVE **DONELDA'S PUFFIN BOAT TOURS** departs from the Englishtown Wharf. Puffins, eagles, razorbill auks, kittiwake gulls, cormorants and grey seals are among the species that may be viewed on these 2.5-hour narrated excursions. Bird checklists are provided. Dogs are allowed aboard with the permission of other passengers. Food is available. Tours are offered daily at 10, 1:30 and 5:15, July-Aug.; at 10:30 and 1:30, June 11-30; at 11, May 6-June 10 and in Sept. Fare $34.50; over 60, $32; ages 6-12, $15. AX, MC, VI. Phone (902) 929-2563 or (877) 278-3346.

FALMOUTH (C-2) pop. 1,143

Falmouth was one of 14 townships created by Gov. Charles Lawrence in 1759. The land left vacant after the Acadian expulsion was offered free to any New Englander who would relocate to Nova Scotia. Thousands of farmers from Connecticut, Rhode Island and Massachusetts accepted the offer; they became known in Canada as the New England Planters.

WINERIES

• **Sainte Famille Wines Ltd.** is at the corner of Dyke Rd. and Dudley Park Ln. Mon.-Sat. 9-5, Sun. noon-5, Apr.-Dec. Tours depart Mon.-Sat. at 11 and 2, Sun. at 2, May-Oct. Phone (902) 798-8311 or (800) 565-0993.

 FORT ANNE NATIONAL HISTORIC SITE OF CANADA—*see Annapolis Royal p. 96.*

 FORTRESS OF LOUISBOURG NATIONAL HISTORIC SITE OF CANADA (B-6)

On Cape Breton Island, 35 kilometres (22 mi.) south of Sydney on Hwy. 22 beyond the modern town of Louisbourg, the 6,700-hectare (14,820-acre) Fortress of Louisbourg National Historic Site includes a reconstruction of the massive fortress erected by the French 1720-45 to defend their colonies.

Under the terms of the 1713 Treaty of Utrecht, France was permitted to keep Cape Breton Island (Île Royale) and Prince Edward Island (Isle St. Jean). English Harbour, renamed Louisbourg, was then selected by the French as the most suitable point for an Atlantic stronghold. It served as headquarters for the French Fleet and became an important fishing and trading center. Later it was used as the base for French privateers preying on New England shipping.

In 1745, after a 47-day siege, Louisbourg was captured by a volunteer force from New England led by Col. William Pepperell and an English fleet under Commodore Peter Warren. Three years later the colony was returned to France by the Treaty of Aix-la-Chapelle. After being twice blockaded by

British fleets during the Seven Years' War, Louisbourg was once again captured in 1758. In 1760 the fortifications were demolished on orders from British prime minister William Pitt.

About one-quarter of colonial Louisbourg has been reconstructed to its 1744 appearance, resulting in one of Canada's largest national historic sites. Costumed guides depicting musicians, fishermen, soldiers, servants and the upper class are on hand to interpret the site. Period stories, dance, music, cooking and gardening are demonstrated. Buildings open include the house of the king's engineer; a fisherman's house; soldiers' barracks; the military bakery; a merchant's house; a civil administrator's house; and the king's bastion, one of the largest buildings in North America at the time. The king's bastion includes the lavishly furnished governor's apartments.

Visitors can sample food in the manner of the 18th century at period restaurants. Picnic areas are located on the park grounds. The park also offers saltwater beaches and fishing. Kennington Cove is within the park and has ocean beaches, picnic areas and scenic views. Lighthouse Point, the location of Canada's first lighthouse, is at the eastern end of the park.

The visitor reception center has an audiovisual presentation, models and exhibits; buses depart from the center at frequent intervals for the 5-minute drive to the reconstructed site.

A Mi'kmaq interpretive trail beginning behind the visitor reception center offers nature, history and culture exhibits as well as a panoramic view of the fortress and coastline along its 5-minute trek. Other trails include a ruins walk at the reconstructed site and an interpretive walk at the Royal Battery.

Comfortable shoes and a sweater are advised. Pets are not permitted. Guided tours are available. Allow a full day minimum.

Visitor center daily 9-6, July-Aug.; 9:30-5, May-June and Sept. 1-Oct. 15. Guided tours are offered daily at 10 (in English) and at 2 (in French), June-Sept. Grounds open year-round. Admission June-Sept. $13.50; over 65, $11.50; ages 6-16, $6.75; family rate $33.75. Admission in May and Oct. $5.50; over 65, $4.75; ages 6-16, $2.75; family rate $12.50. MC, VI. Phone (902) 733-2280.

FRASER MILLS (C-4) pop. 100

FRASER MILLS FISH HATCHERY is on Hwy. 316 following signs. Nearly half a million trout are raised here annually. Situated on the banks of the South River, the hatchery displays brook, rainbow and brown trout and landlocked Atlantic salmon in several large tanks. A separate building houses immature trout in various stages of development from fry to fingerling. Early equipment and photographs are displayed in the visitor center. Allow 30 minutes minimum. Daily 9-4. Free. Phone (902) 783-2926.

GILBERT COVE (D-1)

GILBERT COVE LIGHTHOUSE is off Hwy. 1 on Lighthouse Rd. Situated at the end of a prominent point of land, the restored lighthouse offers an excellent view of the sea as well as the village and surrounding countryside. Old photographs of the area are displayed inside. Picnicking is permitted. Allow 30 minutes minimum. Lighthouse daily 10-6, July-Aug.; hours vary in June and Sept. Grounds daily 24 hours. Free. Phone (902) 837-5584.

GLACE BAY (B-6) pop. 21,187

Since 1720, when French troops dug coal from the cliffs of the town to supply the garrison at Louisbourg, the name Glace Bay has been synonymous with coal. It shares this identity with several other communities along the northeastern corner of Cape Breton Island, where rich seams of bituminous coal extend miles into the Atlantic Ocean.

From Table Head on the outskirts of Glace Bay, Italian inventor Guglielmo Marconi sent the first west-to-east trans-Atlantic wireless message to Cornwall, England, on Dec. 15, 1902. Marconi conducted many radio experiments at his transoceanic wireless station at Table Head, the first on the North American continent.

MARCONI NATIONAL HISTORIC SITE OF CANADA is at 1 Timmerman St. Surrounded by 18-metre-high (60-ft.) cliffs that overlook the Atlantic Ocean, the site depicts the history of Guglielmo Marconi and his invention of wireless radio communication. Photographs, artifacts and models of Marconi's accomplishments are on display. Also featured is a local amateur radio station. Allow 30 minutes minimum. Daily 10-6, June 1-Sept. 15. Free. Phone (902) 295-2069.

THE MINERS' MUSEUM is 1.6 km (1 mi.) w. via Commercial and South sts. to 17 Museum St. Museum exhibits focus on the geology of coal; mining methods, techniques and equipment; and the development of the coal industry. Interactive kiosks provide information about the communities and history of Cape Breton's mining industry.

Retired miners lead guided tours of the underground mine Ocean Deeps Colliery beneath the museum as well as a miners' village with a reconstructed miner's house and company store. Visitors must don hard hats and slickers on the mine tour. During summer months, The Men of the Deeps, a choir of working and retired miners, perform at the theater. Videos about mining, an underground garden and art by Jack Lily MacLellan complete the experience.

Food is available. Daily 10-6 (also Tues. 6-7 p.m.), June 1-Labour Day; daily 9-4, day after Labour Day-Oct. 31; Mon.-Fri. 9-4, rest of year. Admission $5; under 12, $4. Museum and mine tour $10; under 12, $8; family rate $25 (two adults and two children). VI. Phone (902) 849-4522.

GLENVILLE

GLENORA DISTILLERY TOURS is 9 km (6 mi.) n. of Mabou on Rte. 19 on Ceilidh Trail. Some 66,000

gallons of whiskey are produced annually at the 121-hectare (300-acre) facility, which includes malt, kiln, milling, warehouse, bottling, and hospitality buildings. The only single malt distillery in North America, Glenora also blends and bottles Smuggler's Cove dark, white and amber rums. Guided tours and free tastings are offered.

Food is available. Allow 1 hour minimum. Guided tours depart daily on the hour 9-5, May 13-Oct. 31. Admission $7, under 17 free. AX, MC, VI. Phone (902) 258-2662 or (800) 839-0491.

GRAND-PRÉ (C-2) pop. 300

The name Grand-Pré, which means "great meadow," refers to the extensive diked lands in the area. Settlers from Port-Royal moved to Grand-Pré in the late 17th century and, copying the successful dike and floodgate system used in Port-Royal, reclaimed the rich marine sediment from the Minas Basin. Soon Grand-Pré became the largest and most important community in Acadia.

During France's attempt to retake Acadia following the British conquest, French troops made a surprise attack upon British troops in Grand-Pré on Feb. 11, 1747. The incident, which claimed nearly 100 lives, helped convince the British administration that the native Acadians should be deported. Grand-Pré was the principal scene of the Acadian expulsion in 1755, which was immortalized by Henry Wadsworth Longfellow's poem "Evangeline."

CHURCH OF THE COVENANTER is off Hwy. 101 exit 10 to 1989 Grand-Pre Rd. New England planters used hand-hewn boards held by square handmade nails to build this church, which was completed in 1811. It features box pews, sounding boards and a pulpit that reaches halfway to the ceiling. Allow 30 minutes minimum. Daily 9-dusk, May-Oct. Free. Phone (902) 542-3796.

GRAND-PRÉ NATIONAL HISTORIC SITE OF CANADA is inland from Minas Basin at 2241 Grand-Pre Rd. This site commemorates the town's Acadian settlers who were deported 1755-63 to British colonies throughout North America. The Acadian village that once stood here inspired Henry Wadsworth Longfellow's epic poem, "Evangeline."

An interpretation center celebrates 400 years of Acadian culture, beginning with the first French settlement at Port Royal in 1604. A multimedia theater re-creates the difficult conditions of the Acadian expulsion. Other highlights include a memorial church and museum, Evangeline's Well, a statue of the fictional heroine and a bust of Longfellow. As visitors walk clockwise around the statue of Evangeline, her face seems to age.

Allow 30 minutes minimum. Daily 9-6, May 1-Oct. 30. Admission $6.50; over 65, $5; ages 6-16, $3.25; family rate (maximum of seven people) $16.25. MC, VI. Phone (902) 542-3631.

GRANVILLE FERRY (D-1) pop. 182

A small village on the north side of the Annapolis River, Granville Ferry has many Victorian-style houses and a few that were built in the late 1700s. Iron door hinges in the shape of H's and L's, known as Holy Lord hinges, were brought from New England by settlers to fend off the powers of witchcraft.

 NORTH HILLS MUSEUM is off Hwy. 1 on the north shore of the Annapolis River at 5065 Granville Rd. This saltbox-style house, once part of an 18th-century farm, was renovated by R.P. Patterson in the 1960s. It contains a fine Georgian collection of English mahogany, oak and walnut furnishings, ceramics, glass, silver, 18th-century porcelain and paintings. Guided tours highlight the collection and Acadian history.

Allow 30 minutes minimum. Mon.-Sat. 9:30-5:30, Sun. 1-5:30, June 1 to mid-Oct. Admission $3; senior citizens and ages 6-17, $2; family rate $7. Phone (902) 532-2168.

GREENWOOD (C-1)

Settled by British Loyalists who fled America after the Revolutionary War, Greenwood became a market hub for farmers in the Annapolis Valley. In 1940, the Royal Air Force chose Greenwood as the site of its East Coast base, where aviators trained during World War II. Today, 14 Wing Greenwood is home to four Air Force squadrons.

GREENWOOD MILITARY AVIATION MUSEUM is at 20 Ward Rd., Bldg. 151. Exhibits trace the history of various Canadian Air Force units based at 14 Wing Greenwood from World War II to the present. Argus, Lancaster Neptune and Anson aircraft are displayed. An audiovisual presentation features flight footage. Food is available. Allow 1 hour minimum. Daily 9-5, June-Aug.; Tues.-Sat. 10-4, rest of year. Donations. Phone (902) 765-1494, ext. 5955.

GUYSBOROUGH (C-5) pop. 5,165

At the head of Chedabucto Bay, the Shiretown of Guysborough was founded in 1636 when French trader Nicholas Denys established a fishing station here. Guysborough is named in honor of Sir Guys Carleton, commander in chief of the British forces in North America and governor general of Canada during the 1780s.

Because of its seaside location, Guysborough provides many choices for water-based recreational activities; possibilities include boating and canoeing. A tourist complex and golf course overlook Mussel Cove and the harbor. Just southeast is a section of the Trans Canada Trail, which has been constructed on an abandoned railroad bed.

Guysborough Regional Development Authority: 46 Main St., P.O. Box 49, Guysborough, NS, Canada B0H 1N0; phone (902) 533-3731 or (800) 355-3731.

THE OLD COURTHOUSE MUSEUM is 34 km (21 mi.) s. of Hwy. 104 exit 37 on Hwy. 16. This restored 1843 courthouse accommodated county and supreme court sessions for 130 years. Its Gothic-style windows and cedar shingles exemplify mid-19th-century architecture. Exhibits depict an early

French fort and the timber industry. Domestic tools, handcrafts and early photographs also are featured. Genealogy information is available. Allow 30 minutes minimum. Daily 9-5, June-Oct. Donations. Phone (902) 533-4008.

HALIFAX (D-3) pop. 359,111

Because of the harbor that extends inland 26 kilometres (16 mi.), Halifax, the capital of Nova Scotia, was one of the first English settlements in Canada. It was founded in 1749 by Edward Cornwallis, who recognized the site's potential as a naval and military depot. After the British attained supremacy throughout Canada in 1763, Halifax served as the Atlantic headquarters for the Royal Army and Navy.

Until World War I, Halifax's military character was moderated by a civilian shipbuilding industry, which brought considerable wealth to the port economy. During World War I and World War II the city was part of the North American lifeline to war-torn Europe. Halifax still remains the principal naval outpost on Canada's east coast.

This commercial, administrative and military center of Atlantic Canada is distinguished by a blend of modern office towers and restored buildings. Museums, shops and galleries lure locals and visitors to the city's waterfront boardwalk. Theater, symphony performances, cinemas, pubs and cafés combine to create a lively downtown entertainment scene.

Many of the city's historic buildings were constructed by order of Prince Edward, Duke of Kent, Halifax's commander in chief 1794-1800. Princess Lodge, on Bedford Basin, was his primary residence. The prince commissioned the Town Clock on Citadel Hill to discourage tardiness, designing the four-sided tower so that it could be seen anywhere in town.

Halifax Citadel National Historic Site *(see attraction listing)* is one of Canada's most visited attractions. The massive star-shaped fortification, among the best preserved in the country, offers historic re-enactments, museums, a noon gun firing and lofty views of the harbor.

Halifax is fortunate to have anything left to preserve, considering the awesome maritime disaster that shook the city at 9:05 a.m., Dec. 6, 1917. The French munitions ship *Mont Blanc* collided with the steamer *Imo* in Halifax Harbour, causing a fire that ignited the volatile cargo of the munitions ship. The ensuing explosion literally blew the *Mont Blanc* to pieces, heaved the *Imo* onto the Dartmouth shore and leveled the north end of the city, killing more than 2,000 people. Reminders of the event still mark the city, which commemorates the "Halifax Explosion" every year. Boston, the first city to come to Halifax's aid, receives a Nova Scotian Christmas tree each year.

The Nova Scotia International Tattoo, held in early July, is an extravaganza featuring military music, pageantry and precision drills as well as dance and athletic competitions. Crack military units from around the world perform, and the traditional Naval

Gun Run Competition pits Canadian naval teams against one another in a contest that involves dismantling, transporting and reassembling a cannon.

McNabs Islands, in outer Halifax Harbour, lures hikers and picnickers during warm weather. Of historical interest is Fort McNab National Historic Site, which preserves an 1892 fort built to defend the harbor. Nearby Lawlors Island is popular with bird-watchers, and stories persist that another harbor island, named Devils Island, is haunted. Ferry service to the islands is available from McNabs Island Ferry; phone (902) 465-4563 or (800) 326-4563.

A variety of tours, including sailing, whale-watching, fishing, golfing, walking and bus excursions, are offered throughout Halifax and the surrounding area; phone Nova Scotia Department of Tourism and Culture at (800) 565-0000. Dartmouth Ferry, the oldest continually running saltwater ferry in North America, crosses the harbor year-round.

International Visitor Centre: 1595 Barrington St., Halifax, NS, Canada B3J 1Z7; phone (902) 490-5946.

Self-guiding tours: Brochures detailing tours of the historic and downtown areas of Halifax are available at the Nova Scotia Tourist Information

Centre, 1655 Lower Water St., or at the International Visitor Centre.

Shopping areas: Halifax Shopping Centre, 7001 Mumford Rd., features some 170 retailers, including Coast Mountain, Pier 1 and Sears. Spring Garden Road, between Barrington and Robbie streets, is home to a variety of specialty shops, boutiques and restaurants.

ALEXANDER KEITH'S NOVA SCOTIA BREWERY TOURS is at 1496 Lower Water St. Costumed interpreters depict the history of this restored 19th-century working brewery. Tours include demonstrations of early and modern brewing techniques as well as tastings presented in a tavern setting.

Food is available. Allow 1 hour minimum. Daily 11-9, mid-May to Oct. 31; Fri. 5-9, Sat. noon-9, Sun. noon-4, rest of year. Tours depart every 30 minutes. Admission $10.95; over 64, $8.95; ages 5-18, $6.95. AX, MC, VI. Phone (902) 455-1474, ext. 222 or (877) 612-1820.

ART GALLERY OF NOVA SCOTIA–HALIFAX is in the Old Dominion Building at 1723 Hollis St. The gallery showcases historical and contemporary

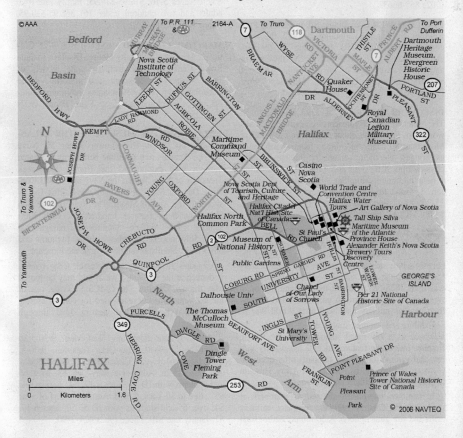

works by international, national and Nova Scotia artists. Of note is an internationally recognized collection of regional folk art. Gallery talks and tours are offered regularly. Food is available. Allow 30 minutes minimum. Daily 10-5 (also Thurs. 5-9); closed Jan. 1 and Dec. 25. Admission $10; over 64, $8; college students with ID, $4; ages 6-17, $2. Phone (902) 424-5280.

ATLANTIC CANADA AVIATION MUSEUM is at 20 Bell Blvd. at the Halifax International Airport. A comprehensive collection depicts Atlantic Canada's aviation history, beginning with the first powered flight in 1909. Artifacts include photographs, uniforms, medals, aircraft engines and weapons. A hangar displays flight simulators and restored vintage aircraft, including fighter planes, crop dusters and rescue aircraft. Allow 1 hour minimum. Daily 9-5, mid-May to mid-Oct. Admission $4, children free. VI. Phone (902) 873-3773.

CHAPEL OF OUR LADY OF SORROWS is in Holy Cross Cemetery at South and S. Park sts. This small chapel was built in one day—Aug. 31, 1843—by some 2,000 men. A stained-glass window dates from 1661, and the altar carvings are replicas of works made in 1550. Mon.-Fri. 8-4, June-Sept. Free. Phone (902) 865-6663.

DINGLE TOWER is on Dingle Rd. in Fleming Park. Built by Sir Sandford Fleming in 1912, the tower commemorates the 1758 convening of the first elected assembly. It overlooks the Northwest Arm and the western slope of the peninsula. Allow 30 minutes minimum. Daily 8-4, May-Sept. Free. Phone (902) 490-4885 or (902) 490-4886.

DISCOVERY CENTRE is at 1593 Barrington St. The science center presents changing displays, workshops and shows about science and technology. More than 80 hands-on exhibits feature such topics as bridges, electricity, chemistry, bubbles, health, physics, optical illusions and light and sound. Allow 1 hour minimum. Mon.-Sat. 10-5, Sun. 1-5; closed Jan. 1, Good Friday, Remembrance Day and Dec. 25-26. Admission $6.90; over 60 and ages 2-18, $4.60. MC, VI. Phone (902) 492-4422.

HALIFAX CITADEL NATIONAL HISTORIC SITE OF CANADA is on a hill overlooking downtown Halifax. One of the country's best surviving examples of a 19th-century fortification, the large star-shaped masonry structure was built 1828-56 to defend the city and harbor. It was occupied by the British until 1906, and then by the Canadian military until well after World War II.

Exhibits and restored rooms depict the fort's significance as a key naval station within the British Empire. Interesting features include a musketry gallery and vaulted rooms. The ramparts offer excellent views of Halifax and its harbor. The Army Museum displays military artifacts and uniforms.

In summer, interpreters dressed as members of the 78th Highlanders regiment re-enact military drills and fire guns at noon. A 50-minute audiovisual

presentation, "The Tides of History," also is featured.

Guided tours in French and English are offered in summer. Allow 2 hours minimum. Fort and exhibits daily 9-6, July-Aug.; 9-5, May-June and Sept.-Oct. Grounds daily 9-5, Nov.-Apr. Admission June 1-Sept. 15, $11; over 64, $9.25; ages 6-16, $5.50; family rate (two adults and two children) $27.50. Admission May 7-31 and Sept. 16-Oct. 31, $7.25; over 64, $6; ages 6-16, $3.50; family rate $18. Free rest of year. Parking $2.75. MC, VI. Phone (902) 426-5080.

HALIFAX WATER TOURS departs from Cable Wharf. Conducted by Murphy's on the Water, these 2-hour sightseeing tours of Halifax Harbour are offered aboard the stern-wheeler *Harbour Queen*. A narrator points out prominent sights and offers a historical commentary. Also available are amphibious Harbour Hopper tours, deep-sea fishing, tall ship excursions, and moonlight and whale-watching cruises. A ferry service to Fort McNab National Historic Site also is available.

Harbor tours depart daily 10-9:30, mid-May to Sept. 30. Fare $19.95-$33.95; over 65, $18.95-$32.95; ages 5-16, $14.95-$19.95; family rate (two adults and two children under 16) $65.95-$99.95. Phone (902) 420-1015.

MARITIME COMMAND MUSEUM is at 2725 Gottingen St. in the Admiralty House. Displays include Royal Canadian navy artifacts, scale models of ships, weapons, photographs and uniforms of the Canadian Navy. Allow 30 minutes minimum. Mon.-Fri. 10-3:30; closed holidays. Free. Phone (902) 721-8250.

MARITIME MUSEUM OF THE ATLANTIC is at 1675 Lower Water St. Nova Scotia's rich maritime heritage is presented through such exhibits as the *Titanic*, Shipwreck Treasures of Nova Scotia, the Navy and WWII Convoys, Days of Sail, Sable Island, the Halifax Explosion and the Age of Steam. The Robertson & Son Ship Chandlery features hundreds of early-20th-century marine artifacts, supplies and navigational tools. Ship models, figureheads, bells, foghorns and other items are displayed throughout the museum.

Canada's first hydrographic vessel, CSS *Acadia*, is docked at the museum's wharf and may be toured May through October. The HMCS *Sackville*, one of the last remaining corvettes used for convoy escorts during WWII, is docked nearby June through September.

Allow 1 hour minimum. Wed.-Mon. 9:30-5:30 (also Tues. 5:30-8), May-Oct.; Tues.-Sat. 9:30-5, Sun. 1-5, rest of year. Closed Jan. 1, Good Friday and Dec. 25-26. Admission May-Oct. $8; over 65 and students with ID $7; ages 6-17, $4; family rate $21; free to all Tues. 5:30-8. Admission rest of year $4; over 65 and students with ID $3.50; ages 6-17, $2; family rate $10. Phone (902) 424-7490.

MOUNT ST. VINCENT UNIVERSITY ART GALLERY is 5 km (3 mi.) w. at 166 Bedford Hwy. on the first floor of the Seton Academic Centre. The gallery offers changing artwork of local, regional, national and international origin; crafts and fine arts; and a permanent collection of paintings, sculptures and ceramics. Allow 30 minutes minimum. Tues.-Fri. 11-5, Sat.-Sun. 1-5. Free. Phone (902) 457-6160.

SAVE **MUSEUM OF NATURAL HISTORY** is off Bell Rd. at 1747 Summer St. n. of the Public Gardens. The province's natural history is presented through exhibits about marine life, geology, fossils, minerals, dinosaurs, birds and mushrooms. The Nature Centre features a bee colony; in summer, a butterfly house is filled with exotic winged wonders. The archeology display depicts nearly 11,000 years of human history, while other galleries feature a variety of natural and cultural history exhibits.

Allow 1 hour minimum. Mon.-Sat. 9:30-5:30 (also Wed. 5:30-8), Sun. 1-5:30, June 1-Oct. 15; Tues.-Sat. 9:30-5 (also Wed. 5-8), Sun. 1-5, rest of year. Closed Jan. 1, Good Friday and Dec. 25-26. Admission $5; over 65, $4.50; ages 6-17, $3; family rate $10.50-$15. Phone (902) 424-7353.

◣◥ **PIER 21 NATIONAL HISTORIC SITE OF** GEM **CANADA** is at 1055 Marginal Rd. Overlooking Halifax Harbour, this restored National Historic Site tells the stories of more than 1 million immigrants, including war brides, displaced children, and Canadian military troops, who gained entry to Canada through this port of entry from 1928-71. Pier 21 explores the immigration experience from homeland departures to assimilation in a new nation through interactive exhibits, multimedia presentations and activities for all ages.

Food is available. Allow 2 hours minimum. Daily 9:30-5:30, May-Nov.; Mon.-Fri. 10-5:30, Sat. noon-5 in April; Tues.-Fri. 10-5, Sat. noon-5, rest of year. Closed Jan. 1, Dec. 25-26 and Dec. 29. Admission $8; over 60, $7; students with ID $5.50; ages 6-16, $4.50; family rate $20. Phone (902) 425-7770.

POINT PLEASANT PARK is at the s. end of the city on Point Pleasant Dr. Commanding a view of the harbor and the Northwest Arm, Point Pleasant contains batteries and forts that served as part of Halifax's defense network until the end of World War II. The 74-hectare (183-acre) park, which was heavily damaged by a hurricane in 2003, features nature trails and walks, picnic areas and a supervised beach. Motorized vehicles are not permitted on the park grounds. Daily dawn-dusk. Free. Phone (902) 490 4700.

Prince of Wales Tower National Historic Site of Canada is in Point Pleasant Park. The 1796 tower was built under the direction of the Duke of Kent, father of Queen Victoria. The round stone structure, almost three times as wide as it is high, was the prototype of a new system of coastal defense intended to fend off possible attacks by Napoleon

Bonaparte's forces. Exhibits portray the tower's history, architectural features and significance as a defensive structure. Allow 30 minutes minimum. Daily 10-6, July 1-Labour Day. Free. Phone (902) 426-5080.

PROVINCE HOUSE is at 1726 Hollis St. This example of Georgian architecture is considered the oldest legislative building in Canada. The 1818 house contains portraits and historical relics. Nova Scotia's legislative assembly has met in the building since 1819. Legislative sessions are held in the spring and fall and are open to the public. Guided tours are available. Allow 30 minutes minimum. Mon.-Fri. 9-5, Sat.-Sun. and holidays 10-4, July-Aug.; Mon.-Fri. 9-4, rest of year. Free. Phone (902) 424-4661.

PUBLIC GARDENS are bounded by South Park St., Sackville St., Spring Garden Rd. and Summer St. Covering 7 hectares (17 acres), the gardens were designed in 1874. They are considered to be among the finest examples of Victorian gardens in North America. Tree-shaded gravel walks wind among the flower beds, fountains, ponds and shrubs. Concerts are given Sunday at 2, June through September. Allow 30 minutes minimum. Daily 8-dusk, May 1-Nov. 11. Free. Phone (902) 490-6509.

ST. PAUL'S CHURCH is at 1749 Argyle St. The 1750 church is said to be the oldest Protestant church in Canada. The walls are covered with interesting tablets depicting men and women from the city's past. The Old Burying Ground, 3 blocks south, contains the graves of some town founders and what is reputed to be the only Crimean War memorial in Canada. Allow 30 minutes minimum. Mon.-Fri. 9-5, June-Aug.; 9-4:30, rest of year. Donations. Phone (902) 429-2240.

SAVE **TALL SHIP** *SILVA* departs from Queen's Wharf at Prince and Lower Water sts. This three-mast schooner offers sailing tours of Halifax and Bedford harbors as well as McNabs Island. Marine animals, including whales, seals and birds, are frequently spotted during the cruises. Food is available. Allow 2 hours minimum. Trips depart daily at noon, 2 and 4, May-Oct. Boarding begins 15 minutes before departure. Fare $19.95; over 59, $18.95; ages 6-12, $13.95; family rate $58.95. AX, MC, VI. Phone (902) 429-9463.

THE THOMAS McCULLOCH MUSEUM is in the Life Science Centre of Dalhousie University at 1355 Oxford St. In addition to an 1833 collection of mounted native birds, the museum displays ceramic mushrooms, marine exhibits and specimens of beetles and butterflies. Guided tours are available. Mon.-Fri. 8:30-4:30; closed major holidays. Free. Phone (902) 494-3515.

YORK REDOUBT NATIONAL HISTORIC SITE OF CANADA is 13 km (8 mi.) s. on Hwy. 253 (Purcell's Cove Rd.). Established in 1793 on a bluff overlooking Halifax Harbour, this fortification was a key element in the city's defense. York Redoubt served as a training ground for Canadian troops during World War I and as the site of the Plotting Room and Fire Command Post for Halifax defenses during World War II. Exhibits include a collection of muzzle-loading guns and photographs.

Allow 1 hour minimum. Grounds and exhibits daily 9-dusk, mid-May through Oct. 31. Grounds only 9-5, rest of year. Free. Phone (902) 426-5080.

CASINOS

• **Casino Nova Scotia** is at 1983 Upper Water St. Daily 24 hours; closed major holidays. Phone (902) 425-7777 or (888) 642-6376.

HANTSPORT (C-2) pop. 1,202

Although one of Canada's smallest towns when it was incorporated in 1895, Hantsport became an important shipbuilding port. The prosperity of that era is evident today in the town's many stately Victorian homes. The mighty Bay of Fundy tides can be seen at Hantsport's wharf or at nearby Fundy Centennial Park.

Hantsport Visitor Information Centre: 2 Willow St., Hantsport, NS, Canada B0P 1P0; phone (902) 684-9302.

CHURCHILL HOUSE AND THE MARINE MEMORIAL ROOM is on Main St. This 1860 Victorian house belonged to a prominent shipbuilding family. Restored rooms feature hand-painted wallcoverings, imported crystal chandeliers and original woodwork. Shipyard artifacts and models of locally built ships are displayed throughout the house. Allow 30 minutes minimum. Daily 9-5, June-Aug. Donations. Phone (902) 684-9302 or (902) 684-3461.

INGONISH (A-6) pop. 500

The Portuguese settled around Ingonish in the 1520s, followed by the French. During most of the 17th century, Port d'Orleans, as Ingonish was known, was the leading French center, second only to Louisbourg. It was abandoned after Louisbourg was destroyed by the British.

Ingonish is a year-round resort town offering coastal scenery. Rocky parapets punctuate the shore between numerous coves. A scenic stretch of the Cabot Trail circles the northern peninsula of Cape Breton Island. Just south at Ingonish Beach is the eastern entrance to Cape Breton Highlands National Park of Canada *(see place listing p. 100).*

INVERNESS (B-5) pop. 1,702

Settled by immigrants from Invernesshire, Scotland, Inverness has been a coal-mining center since 1865. Most of the residents trace their lineage to the town's original Scottish Highlanders. Several scenic drives, including Hwy. 19 along Cape Breton Island's western shore, are accessible.

INVERNESS MINERS MUSEUM is at 62 Lower Railway St. Exhibits and artifacts in eight rooms focus on the city's pioneering, coal mining and railroad history. An arts and crafts gallery also is featured. Allow 30 minutes minimum. Mon.-Fri. 9-5, Sat.-Sun. noon-5, mid-June to early Sept.; by appointment rest of year. Donations. Phone (902) 258-3822 or (902) 258-3291.

IONA (B-5) pop. 100

HIGHLAND VILLAGE MUSEUM is at 4119 Hwy. 223. This 43-acre living-history center depicts Nova Scotia's Scottish Gaelic heritage from the late 18th through early 20th centuries. Gaelic-speaking costumed interpreters give demonstrations and staff 12 buildings, including an 1830s log house and barn, an 1874 church, a 1900s blacksmith shop, a one-room schoolhouse and a general store stocked with goods. Barnyard animals roam the grounds. A visitor center contains history exhibits and a genealogy room.

The museum's hillside location provides a beautiful view of the Bras d'Or Lakes. Living history programs for children allow them to dress in pioneer clothes and ride in a buggy. Gaelic singers accompanied by fiddlers and piano players entertain visitors. Workshops and holiday programs are presented throughout the year.

Note: The tour includes walking up a hill, on stairs and on gravel paths. Comfortable walking shoes are recommended. Picnicking is permitted. Food is available. Allow 1 hour minimum. Village daily 9:30-5:30, June 1-Oct. 14. Visitor center Mon.-Fri. 9-5, year-round. Admission $9; over 65, $7; ages 5-17, $4; family rate $22. AX, MC, VI. Phone (902) 725-2272 or (866) 442-3542.

ISLE MADAME (C-6)

Lying off the southern coast of Cape Breton Island, Isle Madame is across the Lennox Passage Bridge at the junction of hwys. 104 and 320. Named after the queen of France by Acadian settlers after the fall of Louisbourg in 1758, this 44-square-kilometre (17-sq.-mi.) island has beaches, rocky coves, picnic areas and picturesque fishing villages.

The island village of Arichat is one of the oldest communities in Nova Scotia. Highlights in Arichat include the LeNoir Forge Museum, a restored French stone blacksmith shop; phone (902) 226-9364.

JEDDORE OYSTER POND (D-4) pop. 200

Jeddore Oyster Pond is part of a community of quiet hamlets on Nova Scotia's eastern shore. A large lumber industry, based chiefly on pulpwood, once supported the Jeddore district.

FISHERMAN'S LIFE MUSEUM is at 58 Navy Pool Loop Rd. The coastal life of the early 1900s is re-created in the house where Ervin and Ethelda Myers and their 13 daughters once lived. The museum includes a vegetable garden, a barn with livestock, a chicken coop, a woodshed, a dairy, and fish shed at the wharf. Cooking and other domestic chores of the era are demonstrated. Guided tours are available. Allow 30 minutes minimum. Mon.-Sat. 9:30-5:30, Sun. 1-5:30, June 1-Oct. 15.

Admission $3; over 64 and ages 6-17, $2; family rate $7. Phone (902) 889-2053.

JOGGINS (C-2) pop. 500

Joggins is known for its fossil fields and 30-metre-high (100-ft.) cliffs where fossilized trees and plants are visible. Coal may have been mined in the area as early as 1650. Commercial mining began in 1854 with construction of a loading wharf and a narrow gauge railway. The Joggins Mine closed in 1927, and the once thriving town would never recover from a catastrophic fire a year later.

JOGGINS FOSSIL CENTRE is at 30 Main St. A sizable collection of 300-million-year-old regional fossils includes native plants, fish and insects as well as reptile and amphibian footprints. Allow 30 minutes minimum. Daily 9-5:30, June-Sept. Admission $5; over 60, $4; ages 6-18, $3. Phone (902) 251-2727 or (902) 251-2618.

KEJIMKUJIK NATIONAL PARK AND NATIONAL HISTORIC SITE OF CANADA (D-1)

Elevations in the park range from 91 metres (300 ft.) at Lake George to 168 metres (550 ft.) near Fire Tower. Refer to CAA/AAA maps for additional elevation information.

Off Hwy. 8 at Maitland Bridge, Kejimkujik (ke-jim-KOO-jik) National Park and National Historic Site encompasses 381 square kilometres (147 sq. mi.) in the southwestern region of Nova Scotia. The park's gently rolling landscape is broken by numerous lakes connected by rivers. Kejimkujik Lake, the park's namesake and largest lake, has many hidden coves and islands. Hundreds of years before the arrival of the first Europeans in Canada, this lake and its surroundings were the home of nomadic Mi'kmaq people.

For more than 1,000 years the Kejimkujik Drive (Hwy. 8), which follows a series of rivers and lakes, was used as a "highway" by the Mi'kmaq traveling in canoes. Kejimkujik National Park is at the center of the drive, with Annapolis Royal and Liverpool at opposite ends. The route meanders past forested hills, sawmills and Christmas tree plantations.

A mixture of hardwoods and conifers covers low oval-shaped hills that were carved long ago by glaciers. Wildlife includes black bears, white-tailed deer, barred owls, pileated woodpeckers, beavers, bobcats and such water birds as the common loon. A few rare bird species, such as the scarlet tanager and great crested flycatcher, also live in the park's woods. Its wetlands have the largest population of reptiles and amphibians in the Atlantic Provinces.

Canoeing along the connected waterways of the park is one of the best ways to explore its natural beauty. Self-guiding hiking trails are another means for exploration; interpretive signs along the way explain the trail's features. Fall is an especially good time to explore, as the woodlands transform into their autumn colors.

The Seaside Adjunct at Kejimkujik National Park is a wild and isolated stretch of coastline along Nova Scotia's Atlantic shore. Off Hwy. 103, 25 kilometres (16 mi.) southwest of Liverpool, this part of the park features glacier-carved headlands, expansive white beaches and rocky coves. The area also is known for its abundant wildlife. Picnicking is available at the St. Catherines River entrance, an area that also features viewing platforms and two nature trails with interpretive signs. Seals and shore birds are plentiful. Separate admission fees apply.

General Information and Activities

The park is open all year. Full services are available late June through Labour Day. A summer interpretive program includes exhibits, demonstrations, outdoor theater presentations and guided nature hikes. Back-country campsites are available along the park's canoe routes and hiking trails; for detailed camping information contact the park headquarters.

Summer brings a wide range of programs and activities. A supervised swimming beach is at Merrymakedge. Canoes, kayaks, rowboats, paddleboats and bicycles can be rented daily at Jakes Landing mid-May through mid-October. Winter activities include cross-country skiing, winter camping and snowshoeing. Picnic lunches can be enjoyed within the comfort of one of the park's warm-up shelters.

The visitor reception center is open daily 8:30 a.m.-9 p.m., mid-June through Labour Day; 8:30-4:30, rest of year. The visitor center may be closed some weekends in late fall and winter. Service areas are outside the park boundaries. *See Recreation Chart and the AAA/CAA Eastern Canada Camp-Book.*

ADMISSION to the park mid-May to mid-Oct. is $5.50; over 64, $4.75; ages 6-16, $2.75; family rate $13.75. Free rest of year. Admission to the Seaside Adjunct mid-May to mid-Oct. is $4; over 64, $3.50; ages 6-16, $2; family rate $10. Free rest of year. AX, MC, VI.

PETS are permitted in the park, but they must remain on a leash at all times and are not permitted on the beaches.

ADDRESS inquiries to the Superintendent, Kejimkujik National Park and National Historic Site of Canada, P.O. Box 236, Maitland Bridge, NS, Canada B0T 1B0. Phone (902) 682-2772.

KENTVILLE (C-2) pop. 5,610

Kentville elected its first female mayor in 1946 at a time when not all women in Canada had the right to vote. Gladys Porter would go on to become the first woman elected to the Nova Scotia Legislative Assembly.

BLAIR HOUSE MUSEUM is off Hwy. 1 on the grounds of the Kentville Agricultural Centre. Focusing on the history of the apple industry in Nova

Scotia, the museum displays apple barrel-making tools, baskets, peelers, sprayers and cider jugs. Photographs and scientific instruments illustrate the research being performed at the center. Orchards are on the grounds. Allow 1 hour minimum. Daily 8:30-4, June-Aug. Guided 30-minute tours are available Mon.-Fri. upon request. Free. Phone (902) 678-1093.

KINGS COUNTY MUSEUM is at 37 Cornwallis St. The 1903-80 Kings County courthouse now serves as a resource center for the cultural and natural history of Kings County. The museum, which features a national commemorative exhibit about the New England planters, also contains county genealogical information. Mon.-Sat. 9-4, July-Aug.; Mon.-Fri. 9-4, rest of year. Donations. Archives $3. Phone (902) 678-6237.

LaHAVE (D-2)

Artists have long been drawn to the romantic coastal scenery around LaHave, one of the oldest settlements in Canada. Arriving in 1604, Pierre de Monts named the site Cap de la Havre, meaning "the harbor."

FORT POINT MUSEUM is at 100 Fort Point Rd. (Hwy. 331). The lighthouse keeper's house serves as a museum for Fort Sainte-Marie-de-Grâce National Historic Site, which commemorates the first landing of permanent settlers under the leadership of Isaac DeRazilly, lieutenant general of Acadia, in 1632. Historical material and artifacts document DeRazilly's attempt to settle the area. The lighthouse station was built in 1855. Picnicking is permitted. Allow 1 hour minimum. Daily 10-5, June 1-Labour Day; by appointment rest of year. Free. Phone (902) 688-1632.

LaHAVE ISLANDS HERITAGE MARINE MUSEUM is off Hwy. 331 at Crescent Beach to 100 LaHave Islands Rd. The former LaHave Islands United Church displays fishing memorabilia and relics illustrating local history back to the first settlers' arrival in the 1780s. Allow 1 hour minimum. Daily 10-5, June 1-Labour Day; by appointment rest of year. Donations. Phone (902) 688-2973 or (902) 688-3192.

LAKE AINSLIE, EAST SIDE (B-5)

The largest natural freshwater lake in Nova Scotia, Lake Ainslie is a popular destination for anglers—and marathon runners who race 42 kilometres (26 mi.) around its shores every September.

THE MacDONALD HOUSE is on Hwy. 395. Overlooking Lake Ainslie, this pioneer farmhouse is furnished with antiques and items that reflect life in rural 1800s Cape Breton. Nearby are two barns with several wagons, buggies and wheeled farm implements. The property also contains hiking trails and a one-room schoolhouse that operated 1926-54. Picnicking is permitted. Daily 10-5, July-Aug. Admission $3; under 16, 50c; family rate $6. Phone (902) 258-3317.

LAKE CHARLOTTE (D-4)

(SAVE) **MEMORY LANE HERITAGE VILLAGE** is off Hwy. 7 following signs to 5435 Clam Harbour Rd. Costumed interpreters offer guided tours of this village, re-creating the sights and sounds of a typical Eastern Shore community from the 1940-50s era. Buildings include a restored store, church, school, icehouse, Esso garage and homestead, which are furnished in period detail.

Food is available. Allow 2 hours minimum. Daily 11-4, June 15-Sept. 15; by appointment rest of year. Admission $6; over 59, students with ID and ages 7-17, $4; family rate $16 (two adults and three children). MC, VI. Phone (902) 845-1937 or (877) 287-0697.

LIVERPOOL (E-2) pop. 2,888

Like its English namesake, Liverpool is at the mouth of the Mersey River. Samuel de Champlain landed at the site in 1604, but it was not until 1759 that 70 families from Connecticut established a town.

Fort Point, at Fort Point Lighthouse Park, was built in the 1700s. One of its cairns commemorates the arrival of Champlain while another honors Liverpool's privateers. Visitors can climb the stairs of the park's 1855 lighthouse, which also houses an interpretive center.

Region of Queens Department of Economic Development and Tourism: P.O. Box 1264, Liverpool, NS, Canada B0T 1K0; phone (902) 354-5741 or (800) 655-5741.

(SAVE) **HANK SNOW COUNTRY MUSIC CENTRE** is off Hwy. 103 exit 19 to 148 Bristol Ave. A large collection of personal memorabilia belonged to country music legend Hank Snow, who was born in nearby Brooklyn. Items on display include awards, photographs, clothing and Snow's 1947 Cadillac convertible. The center also is home to the Nova Scotia Country Music Hall of Fame. A country music library and archives are available. Allow 1 hour minimum. Mon.-Sat. 9-5, mid-May to mid-Oct.; Sun. noon-5 or by appointment, rest of year. Admission $3, under 13 free. MC, VI. Phone (902) 354-4675.

(SAVE) **PERKINS HOUSE MUSEUM** is at 105 Main St. This 1766 Connecticut-style house was built by Col. Simeon Perkins, noted Nova Scotian merchant, colonel, judge, legislator and diarist. Allow 30 minutes minimum. Mon.-Sat. 9:30-5:30, Sun. 1-5:30, June 1-Oct. 15. Admission $2; family rate (two adults and two children) $5. Phone (902) 354-4058.

QUEENS COUNTY MUSEUM AND EXHIBIT CENTRE is next to the Perkins House Museum at 109 Main St. Artifacts, photographs and documents relate the history of Queens County. Exhibits highlight the Mi'kmaq Indians, privateers and area forests. Col. Simeon Perkins' original diary gives an account of the colonial town between 1766 and the War of

1812. The Thomas Raddall Research Centre contains a library and genealogical data.

Allow 30 minutes minimum. Mon.-Sat. 9:30-5:30, Sun. 1-5:30, June 1-Oct. 15; Mon.-Sat. 9-5, rest of year. Admission $2; family rate (two adults and two children) $5. Phone (902) 354-4058.

ROSSIGNOL CULTURAL CENTRE is at 205 Church St. This 24,000-square-foot center features a variety of museums, art galleries, libraries and wildlife exhibits. Far-ranging collections include folk art, antique apothecary items, outhouses, hunting and fishing artifacts, scrimshaw, bronzes, historic photographs and mounted animals from around the world.

Allow 1 hour minimum. Mon.-Sat. 10-5:30, May 15-Oct. 15 (also Sun. noon-5:30, July-Aug.). Admission $4; over 65 and ages 6-18, $3. MC, VI. Phone (902) 354-3067.

SHERMAN HINES MUSEUM OF PHOTOGRAPHY is at 219 Main St. The 1902 town hall houses an extensive collection of antique stereoscopes, tripods, picture albums, cameras and other vintage paraphernalia. The museum also features galleries of contemporary photography, photographic prints and holograms. A photography research library is available. Allow 1 hour minimum. Mon.-Sat. 10-5:30, May 15-Oct. 15. (also Sun. noon-5:30, July-Aug.). Admission $4, over 64 and students with ID $3, under 6 free. Phone (902) 354-2667.

LOUISBOURG (B-6) pop. 1,071

The first French settlers arrived in Louisbourg Harbour in 1713. Seventeen years later the most formidable French military establishment on the Atlantic was under construction on the southwestern arm of the harbor. The fortress town, surrounded by a masonry and packed-earth wall almost 3.2 kilometres (2 mi.) long, served until 1758 as the governmental, commercial and military center of the French colony that included Cape Breton and Prince Edward islands.

With the development of the coal-mining industry on Cape Breton Island during the 19th century, Louisbourg took on a new role as a shipping center, connected to numerous coal mines by a network of small railroads. Fishing and tourism fuel Louisbourg's economy. The picturesque Havenside district and the town's many wharves, sailing vessels and shore facilities provide an excellent perspective of Louisbourg's fishing industry.

Near the harbor are the ruins of one of the oldest lighthouses in North America. Built 1730-33 by order of Louis XV, the Louisbourg Lighthouse was damaged by fire during the British siege of Louisbourg in 1758. A small exhibit pavilion marks the site. Nightly performances of Cape Breton music, drama, dance and comedy are presented mid-June through October at the Louisbourg Playhouse; phone (902) 733-2996 or (888) 733-2787.

 FORTRESS OF LOUISBOURG NATIONAL HISTORIC SITE OF CANADA— *see place listing p. 104.*

SYDNEY AND LOUISBURG RAILWAY MUSEUM is at 7330 Main St. This restored 1895 railway station contains the stationmaster's office and an exhibit room with displays and models devoted to the history of railway technology and marine shipping. Period coach cars, a freight car, a tanker and a caboose are behind the museum. A working model of the S & L Railway main line also is displayed. A tourist information office is on the premises.

Daily 9-7, July-Aug.; 9-5 in June and Sept. Donations. Phone (902) 733-2720.

LUNENBURG (D-2) pop. 2,568

Once the site of an Indian encampment and later a French fishing harbor, the Lunenburg area was granted by Oliver Cromwell to Charles de La Tour in 1656. Families from Hanover, as well as French, German and Swiss immigrants, founded the town and cleared farmland 1751-53.

Old Town Lunenburg—now a UNESCO World Heritage Site—has been called "the best surviving example of a planned British colonial settlement in North America." On the spit of land between front and back bays, the town was laid out in a rectangular grid with narrow streets and garden plots.

Among Old Town's many preserved 18th-century buildings are some of the earliest churches in Canada. St. John's Church, established in 1754 by royal charter, ministered to the Hanoverians, Indians, French and English. The 1776 Zion Evangelical Lutheran Church holds the St. Antoine Marie bell from Louisbourg. Also of historical interest is a monument that commemorates the sacking of the town on July 1, 1782, when a fleet from Boston plundered stores, shops and houses.

Lunenburg is one of the greatest fishing ports on the continent and was home to the *Bluenose*, the undefeated champion of the North Atlantic Fishing Fleet and the winner of four international schooner races from 1921 to 1931; her likeness is on the Canadian dime.

Tours of Lunenburg's harbor depart from the wharf behind the dory shop. Summer deep-sea fishing, whale-watching and lobster cruises depart daily from the Fisheries Museum of the Atlantic *(see attraction listing)*; reservations are advised. Guided 1-hour walking tours provided by Lunenburg Town Walking Tours include the waterfront, the fishermen's memorial, historic houses and churches, the Lunenburg Academy and the back harbor; phone (902) 634-3848.

A few kilometres south of Hwy. 3 is the village of Blue Rocks, named for the bluish hue of the surrounding rocks and ledges.

Lunenburg Visitor Information Centre: 11 Blockhouse Hill Rd., Lunenburg, NS, Canada B0J 2C0; phone (902) 634-8100.

Self-guiding tours: A walking tour map of Old Town Lunenburg is available from the visitor information center.

CAPT. ANGUS J. WALTERS HOUSE MUSEUM is at 37 Tannery Rd. The skipper of the schooner *Bluenose* lived here until his death in 1968. The simple four-square house, built in 1915, is representative of early 20th century architecture. Allow 30 minutes minimum. Mon.-Sat. 10-4, July-Aug. Admission $2, under 13 free. Phone (902) 634-2010 July-Aug. or (902) 634-4410 rest of year.

FISHERIES MUSEUM OF THE ATLANTIC is at 68 Bluenose Dr. The complex includes two historic ships and five waterfront buildings. The fishing schooner *Theresa E. Connor* is outfitted as a working ship, and visitors can inspect her decks and gear. Adjacent is the dragger *Cape Sable*, a steel-hulled trawler. Visitors are welcome below deck on both ships.

The buildings contain an aquarium with native freshwater and saltwater fish, a boat room, displays of ship models and sea artifacts, exhibits depicting the story of rumrunning and the history of the *Bluenose*, and a theater presenting 30-minute films about fishing and local history. The Fishermen's Memorial Room honors local fishermen and vessels lost at sea.

There also are three floors of exhibits, including the Banks Fishery Age of Sail Gallery and a boat-building shop. Food is available. Allow 2 hours minimum. Daily 9:30-5:30, mid-May to mid-Oct.; Mon.-Fri. 8:30-4:30, rest of year. Hours may vary; phone ahead. Admission $9; over 64, $7; ages 6-17, $3; family rate $22. MC, VI. Phone (902) 634-4794 or (866) 579-4909.

MAHONE BAY (D-2) pop. 991

The quaint seacoast village of Mahone Bay offers art, craft and antiques shops and a picturesque shoreline consisting of stones and boulders. Captain Ephraim Cook, who came to the area to start a ship-building industry, settled the town in 1754.

The Three Churches, which have stood on the bay since the mid-1800s, are renowned landmarks that greet visitors as they enter the community. Cape Cod, Georgian and Victorian-style houses also still stand. Bayview Cemetery contains the tombs of many of Mahone Bay's original settlers.

Mahone Bay Business Association: P.O. Box 59, Mahone Bay, NS, Canada B0J 2E0; phone (902) 624-6151 or (888) 624-6151.

MAHONE BAY SETTLERS MUSEUM & CULTURAL CENTRE is at 578 Main St. The 1850 house has a decoratively painted ceiling and faux marble fireplace. The museum features displays about the Protestants who settled the area in the mid-1700s. Other exhibits include architectural depictions, ceramics, rooms furnished with antiques dating 1790-1890, and seasonal and shipbuilding displays. Tues.-Sat. 10-5, Sun. 1-5, June-Sept. Donations. Phone (902) 624-6263.

MAITLAND (C-3) pop. 200

Originally called *Menesatung*, an Indian word meaning "healing waters," the area was renamed in 1828 for Sir Peregrine Maitland, lieutenant governor of Nova Scotia. Settlers were attracted to the area by the proximity of forests with trees large enough for ship timbers.

LAWRENCE HOUSE MUSEUM is at 8660 Hwy. 215. This was the home of shipbuilder William Lawrence, who built the largest three-masted ship in Canada. The 1870 Victorian house contains furnishings and memorabilia of the Lawrence family and has two formal Victorian parlors overlooking the shipyard. The marine room depicts shipbuilding in the Cobequid Bay area. Allow 30 minutes minimum. Mon.-Sat. 9:30-5:30, Sun. 1-5:30, June 1-Oct. 15. Admission $3; over 64 and ages 6-17, $2; family rate $7. Phone (902) 261-2628.

MAPLEWOOD (D-2) pop. 100

Maplewood is near Lake Sherbrooke, or Nine Mile Lake, which provides fishing waters for speckled and lake gray trout.

MARGAREE HARBOUR (A-5) pop. 100

Margaree Harbour is the northern terminus for the Ceilidh (kay-lee) Trail, Hwy. 19. Beginning at the Canso Causeway at Port Hastings *(see place listing p. 117)*, the Ceilidh Trail skirts the western shore of Cape Breton Island and provides access to many beaches before joining the Cabot Trail at Margaree Harbour, which also has a beach.

MARION BRIDGE (B-6) pop. 300

TWO RIVERS WILDLIFE PARK is 10 km (6 mi.) w. of Rte. 327. Moose, red deer, cougars, barred owls, American bald eagles, beavers and arctic foxes are among the North American wildlife on display. A pond offers refuge to waterfowl, including swans, geese and ducks. Miniature donkeys, a Shetland pony, goats, rabbits and a llama are presented in a petting zoo. Hiking, swimming and wagon rides are available.

Picnicking is permitted. Allow 1 hour, 30 minutes minimum. Daily 10-7, mid-June to Labour Day weekend; 10-4, rest of year. Admission $4.50; over 55, $3.75; ages 5-17, $3.25; family rate $15.50. Phone (902) 727-2483.

MIDDLETON (C-2) pop. 1,744

Middleton, in the heart of the Annapolis Valley, is a prosperous pastoral town. Holy Trinity Church, at the west end of town, is one of five 200-year-old Loyalist churches remaining in Nova Scotia. Keeping time at the town hall is an unusual water clock, which is powered by water flowing through carefully calibrated tubes.

Middleton Tourist Bureau: P.O. Box 907, Middleton, NS, Canada B0S 1P0; phone (902) 825-4100.

ANNAPOLIS VALLEY MACDONALD MUSEUM is at 21 School St. Devoted to the culture and natural history of the Annapolis Valley, the museum displays antique clocks and watches, local historical artifacts, a re-created classroom and general store, an art gallery, a genealogical research library, and a greenhouse with a natural history exhibit. Allow 30 minutes minimum. Mon.-Sat. 9-5, Sun. 1-5, June 15-Sept. 30; Mon.-Fri. 10:30-5, rest of year. Admission $3, family rate $6. Phone (902) 825-6116.

MILTON (E-2) pop. 1,004

MILTON BLACKSMITH SHOP MUSEUM is off Hwy. 103 exit 19, then 2 km (1.2 mi.) n. on Hwy. 8 to 351 West St. The current building dates to 1903, although the site has long been used as a blacksmith shop. Antique tools, anvils, forges and a collection of historic town photographs are displayed. Picnicking is permitted. Allow 1 hour minimum. Mon.-Fri. 10-4, Sun. 1-5, in June; Mon.-Fri. 10-5, July-Aug.; Mon.-Fri. 10-4, in Sept. Admission $1, under 18 free. Phone (902) 350-0268.

MINUDIE (B-2)

J.F.W. DesBarres received the land grant to Minudie in 1764. The DesBarres estate, which included a grindstone quarry, was later purchased by Amos Seaman, wealthy owner of a shipping and trading company. For his shrewd development of the quarry, Seaman became known as the "grindstone king." His grand mansion fell into ruin after his death, but the 1863 Universalist Church he commissioned is still in use.

AMOS SEAMAN SCHOOL MUSEUM is in the center of town at 5554 Barronsfield Rd. The museum features one of the province's oldest one-room schoolhouses as well as local artifacts. Daily 10-6, July 1-early Sept. Free. Phone (902) 251-2289.

MOUNT UNIACKE (C-3) pop. 1,100

Mount Uniacke was named by Richard John Uniacke, an aristocratic Irish adventurer who became attorney general of Nova Scotia in 1797. Serving in the post for the remainder of his life, Uniacke was responsible for a revision of the laws of the province. He chose to build his estate in this area because of the land's resemblance to his ancestral home in Ireland.

UNIACKE ESTATE MUSEUM PARK is off Hwy. 101 at exit 3 to Rte. 1. Built 1813-15 for Richard John Uniacke, this Georgian-style mansion contains original furnishings. The house is set among rows of cedar and oak trees on a 2,300-acre estate, which features seven trails. Allow 30 minutes minimum. Mon.-Sat. 9:30-5:30, Sun. 11-5:30, June 1-Oct. 15. Trails daily dawn-dusk. Admission $3; over 64 and ages 6-17, $1; family rate $7. Phone (902) 866-2560 or (902) 866-0032.

MUSQUODOBOIT HARBOUR (C-3)
pop. 900

An Indian word for "rolling out in foam," Musquodoboit is known appropriately as a sport fishing center. The Musquodoboit River offers salmon and trout fishing. In the fall, hunting is popular in the Musquodoboit Valley. Lumbering further supplements the town's economy.

Antigonish-Eastern Shore Tourist Association: 9042 Hwy. 7, Musquodoboit Harbour, NS, Canada B0J 2L0; phone (902) 889-2362.

MUSQUODOBOIT RAILWAY MUSEUM is on Hwy. 7 in the center of town. A restored 1916 station of the Canadian National Railway houses a large collection of Nova Scotian railway memorabilia and photographs. Equipment and rolling stock, including a rail snowplow, diesel engine, flat car, caboose and smoker/baggage car, are on the grounds. A tourist information bureau also is on the site. Daily 9-6, June-Aug.; Thurs.-Sun. 10-4 in May and Sept. Free. Phone (902) 889-2689.

NAPPAN (B-2)

NAPPAN RESEARCH FARM is 6 km (4 mi.) s. on Hwy. 2, then 5 km (3 mi.) w. on Hwy. 302. The 223-hectare (551-acre) farm was established in 1887 for specialized agricultural and livestock research. Cattle are raised on the farm. Plants grown include forage crops and cereal grains. The farm also has a 2-hectare (5-acre) wetland demonstration site with nature trails. Picnicking is permitted. Allow 1 hour minimum. Mon.-Fri. 8:30-4:30; closed holidays. Free. Phone (902) 667-3826.

NEW GLASGOW (C-4) pop. 9,432

On the banks of the East River, New Glasgow is at a site marked as a large Indian village on a map by French traveler and historian Pierre François Xavier de Charlevoix. The discovery of coal in 1798 in Pictou County led to the town's founding in 1875. New Glasgow was named for the Scottish hometown of the area's first settler, James Carmichael.

The Samson Trail, 2.5 kilometres (1.5 mi.) along the New Glasgow Riverfront, is named for the "Samson" locomotive. Considered to be the oldest steam locomotive in Canada, it once worked the Foord Coal Seam near Stellarton (*see place listing p. 120*).

A legend lingers of three Scottish bachelors who made a trip to Halifax to seek out and marry lassies who had recently arrived by boat. Today many in the county claim to be descendants of the trio.

Pictou County Tourist Association-New Glasgow: 40 Water St., P.O. Box 1839, Pictou, NS, Canada B0K 1H0; phone (902) 485-6151 or (877) 816-2326.

CARMICHAEL-STEWART HOUSE MUSEUM is .5 km (.3 mi.) e. at 86 Temperance St. Displays include china, pioneer artifacts, an extensive period clothing collection and glass items from three glass factories that once operated nearby. Mon.-Sat. 9:30-4:30, early June to mid-Sept. Donations. Phone (902) 752-5583.

NEW ROSS (D-2) pop. 400

At the request of the Earl of Dalhousie, governor of Nova Scotia, the lumbering center of New Ross was established in 1816 by Capt. William Ross and 172 former soldiers of the Nova Scotia Fencibles. Anxious to settle the interior uplands of the province, the governor rewarded one enterprising settler with a piano that four soldiers delivered from Chester, 24 kilometres (15 mi.) away.

ROSS FARM MUSEUM is at 4568 Hwy. 12. This living-history museum depicts Nova Scotia's agricultural heritage through the story of the Ross family, who farmed the land 1816-1970. Costumed interpreters demonstrate such daily activities as open-hearth cooking, barrel making, wool spinning and planting with oxen teams.

The farm is home to heritage breeds of cattle, horses, sheep, pigs and chickens that were common in the early 19th century. Visitors are invited to participate in feeding the animals, candle making, butter churning and other farm chores.

Buildings on the 24-hectare (60-acre) site include the family cottage, peddler's shop, country store, schoolhouse, barn, cooperage and blacksmith shop. Horse-drawn wagon rides and winter sleigh rides also are available in season.

Picnicking is permitted. Allow 2 hours minimum. Daily 9:30-5:30, May-Oct.; Wed.-Sun. 9:30-4:30, rest of year. Closed Dec. 22-Jan. 2. Admission $6; over 64, $5; ages 6-17, $2; family rate (two adults with school-age children) $15. MC, VI. Phone (902) 689-2210.

NOEL (C-3)

BURNTCOAT HEAD PARK AND INTERPRETIVE CENTRE is 5 km (3 mi.) n. of jct. hwys. 215 and 354 at 611 Burntcoat Rd. The 3-acre park overlooks the Bay of Fundy. What is thought to be the world's highest recorded tide—16 metres (52.6 feet)—was observed here in 1960. A wooden lighthouse containing history displays is open in summer. Walking trails lead to the rocky shore and offer scenic views of Cobequid Bay.

Picnicking is permitted. Allow 1 hour minimum. Daily 9-7, July-Aug.; Thurs.-Mon. 9-5, May 15-June 30 and Sept. 1-Oct. 15. Donations. Phone (902) 369-2669.

NORTH EAST MARGAREE (B-5) pop. 300

North East Margaree lies within the pastoral Margaree Valley on Cape Breton Island. Some of Canada's best salmon waters are found at the Forks, Brook, Seal and Hatchery pools along the Margaree River.

MARGAREE SALMON MUSEUM is just off the Cabot Tr. following signs. Displays include fishing and poaching equipment and an aquarium as well as books, pictures and articles relating to angling. One exhibit depicts the life cycle of the Atlantic salmon. Allow 30 minutes minimum. Daily 9-5, mid-June to

mid-Oct. Admission $2; under 12, $1. Phone (902) 248-2848.

PARRSBORO (C-2) pop. 1,529

On the north shore of Minas Basin, Parrsboro has a history rich in Indian and pirate legends. Glooscap, a Mi'kmaq man-god, mighty warrior and magician, reputedly once roamed the area. Deno, an Italian pirate, is said to have entombed the daughter of a British naval captain in a cave at Black Point.

In 1776 a settlement took root on Partridge Island around a ferry terminus. Ferry service between Partridge Island and the Annapolis Valley proved to be a valuable transportation link and continued until World War II. The fertile land around the harbor at the mouth of the Parrsboro River prompted the island's population to eventually shift to the mainland community of Mill Village, renamed Parrsboro in 1784 after John Parr, Nova Scotia's governor general.

Twice daily the Bay of Fundy tides rise and fall between 12 and 15 metres (39 and 49 ft.) in the harbor. Good areas for viewing this phenomenon are Glooscap Park, Partridge Island and Parrsboro Wharf at First Beach. Among the area's other attractions are amethysts, agates, other semiprecious stones and rare fossils. A scenic drive winds along the shore of Minas Basin between Parrsboro and Advocate.

On the waterfront an old ferry that once traversed the bay to Kingsport is now the home of Parrsboro's resident theater company. The Ship's Company Theatre offers productions in summer.

Town of Parrsboro: 4030 Eastern Ave., P.O. Box 400, Parrsboro, NS, Canada B0M 1S0; phone (902) 254-2036.

FUNDY GEOLOGICAL MUSEUM is in the center of town, following signs to 162 Two Islands Rd. The museum examines the planet's origins and early life through a 10-minute videotape and displays of Triassic and Jurassic fossils excavated from nearby Minas Basin. Other exhibits highlight minerals, rockhounding and a collection of Nova Scotian amethyst.

Allow 1 hour minimum. Daily 9:30-5:30, June 1-Oct. 15; Tues.-Sat. 9-5, rest of year. Admission $6.25; ages 6-17, $3.50; family rate $12. Rates may vary; phone ahead. Phone (902) 254-3814 or (866) 856-3466.

OTTAWA HOUSE BY-THE-SEA is 6 km (4 mi.) s.e. via Main St. at 1155 Whitehall Rd. This sole remnant of the original Partridge Island settlement was built as an inn in the late 1700s by James Ratchford, a prominent trader. Sir Charles Tupper, prime minister of Canada in 1896, bought Ottawa House as his summer retreat and hosted many visiting dignitaries here. Museum exhibits include maritime artifacts, a collection of shipbuilding tools, and photographs of vessels launched from local shipyards. Daily 10-6, June 1-Sept. 15. Admission $2; under 12 free. Phone

(902) 254-2376 June 1-Sept. 15 or (902) 254-3534 rest of year.

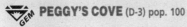 **PEGGY'S COVE** (D-3) pop. 100

Peggy's Cove is one of several fishing villages built around the snug harbors of the craggy south coast. Huge granite boulders are scattered throughout the village. An old lighthouse standing on a massive granite ledge and fishing boats moored along weatherworn wharves are a part of the atmosphere that makes this cove well-known among artists and photographers. The lighthouse also serves as the post office during the summer. The Marine Studio, built about 1875 as a fish shed, displays works by local artists.

William E. Garth Memorial Park, off Hwy. 333, features a monument dedicated to Canadian fishermen. Carved on the face of a granite outcropping, it depicts fishermen, their families and a guardian angel with outstretched wings.

PICTOU (B-4) pop. 3,875

Sent by the Philadelphia Co. in 1767, six families from Pennsylvania and Maryland settled Pictou, formerly the site of an ancient Indian village. The Dutch cargo ship *Hector* arrived in 1773 bearing 179 passengers from the Scottish Highlands, the first of thousands to emigrate from Scotland to Canada in the next century. As the main port of entry, Pictou became known as "the birthplace of New Scotland."

Three rivers empty into the harbor, making Pictou one of Nova Scotia's largest lobster fisheries as well as an active shipbuilding center.

Pictou County Tourist Association-Pictou: P.O. Box 1839, Pictou, NS, Canada B0K 1H0; phone (902) 485-6151 or (877) 816-2326.

GROHMANN KNIVES LIMITED is at 116 Water St. Guided tours of its knife production factory are offered. Allow 30 minutes minimum. Mon.-Fri. 9-5. Tours are given Mon.-Fri. 9-3:30. Weekend and evening hours may vary; phone ahead. Free. Minimum of four adults required for the tour. Phone (902) 485-4224 or (888) 756-4837.

HECTOR CENTRE is off Hwy. 106 at 86 Old Haliburton Rd. Changing exhibits reflect the history, heritage, culture and art of the people of Pictou County. Genealogy information also is available. Allow 30 minutes minimum. Tues.-Sat. 9:30-4:30. Admission $2, under 12 free. Research fee $5. Phone (902) 485-4563.

HECTOR HERITAGE QUAY is downtown on the waterfront. Anchored in the harbor is a full-scale replica of the *Hector*, the three-masted Dutch sailing ship that brought the first Scottish immigrants to Nova Scotia in 1773. An interpretation center, a working carpenter's shop and a restored blacksmith shop are on the site. Costumed interpreters depict the history.

Guided tours are available. Picnicking is permitted. Mon.-Sat. 9-5 (also Tues.-Thurs. 5-7, July-Aug.), Sun. noon-9, Victoria Day weekend to mid-Oct. Guided tours are offered daily at 10 and 2, July-Aug. Admission $5; over 60, students with ID and ages 13-18, $4; ages 6-12, $2; family rate $12 (two adults and two children). Phone (902) 485-6057.

LOCH BROOM LOG CHURCH is off Hwy. 104 exit 20 to Rte. 376 following signs. This simple country log church is a replica of Pictou County's first house of worship, built in 1787. Like the original, the interior features rough wooden benches and a candle chandelier. The church is in a placid setting overlooking the river. Picnicking is permitted. Allow 30 minutes minimum. Tues.-Sat. 11-6, Sun. 1-6, early June-early Sept. Hours may vary; phone ahead. Donations. Phone (902) 485-4725.

SAVE **NORTHUMBERLAND FISHERIES MUSEUM AND HERITAGE ASSOCIATION** is off Hwy. 106 to 71 Front St. A restored railroad station contains some 2,000 artifacts related to the fishing industry of Northumberland Strait. The collection includes an original fisherman's bunkhouse, fishing gear, restored boat engines, a cannery display, model boats, live rare lobsters and a gallery of vintage photographs. A lobster hatchery, a replica of a gulf-style lighthouse and interpretive panels about the Pictou waterfront may be seen.

Guided tours are available. Allow 30 minutes minimum. Mon.-Sat. 9-6, Sun. noon-6, mid-May to Sept. 1; Mon.-Sat. 9-5, Sun. noon-5, Sept. 2 to mid-Oct. Admission $5; over 55, $4; ages 7-16, $3; family rate $9. Phone (902) 485-4972.

PLEASANT BAY (A-5)

This fishing community on the west coast of Cape Breton Island was settled by Scottish immigrants in 1828. The town often marked its history by extraordinary events, such as the "Year of the Flour," when flour barrels washed ashore from a floundering ship in 1874. Two other years were marked by similar good fortune—fresh butter tins and barrels of rum.

WHALE INTERPRETIVE CENTRE is off Cabot Trail at 104 Harbour Rd. Displays describe 16 whale species found off Cape Breton, with life-size and scale models, recorded whale calls and interactive exhibits. A 10-minute videotape presentation chronicles the history of whaling, and a touch tank contains saltwater creatures in a landscaped marine environment. The center also serves as an outlet for dozens of whale-watch and eco-tour companies that operate along the Cabot Trail coastline.

Allow 30 minutes minimum. Daily 9-5, June 1-Oct. 15. Admission $4.50; over 54 and ages 6-18, $3.50; family rate $14. MC, VI. Phone (902) 224-1411.

PORT HASTINGS (B-5) pop. 300

Opened in 1955, the 1,370-metre (4,500-ft.) Canso Causeway (*see attraction listing*) at Port

Hastings prevents ice from entering the Strait of Canso from the north, thus providing a navigable harbor 16 kilometres (10 mi.) long year-round. Overlooking the strait and St. Georges Bay is 260-metre (850-ft.) Creignish Mountain.

Highlights of local history are the focus of the Port Hastings Historical Museum and Archives on Church Street in the village of Hastings.

CANSO CAUSEWAY crosses the Strait of Canso and links Cape Breton Island with the mainland. Said to be the world's deepest causeway, it reaches a depth of 65 metres (213 ft.) and is 244 metres (800 ft.) wide at the base. An estimated 10 million tons of rock were used in its construction. The causeway prevents ice from entering the Strait of Canso. A navigation lock allows the passage of oceangoing traffic.

☆ PORT-ROYAL NATIONAL HISTORIC SITE OF CANADA (C-1)

Off Hwy. 1 on the north shore of the Annapolis River opposite Goat Island, the historic site is a reconstruction of Port-Royal, one of the oldest European settlements in Canada and one of the first French settlements in North America.

In 1604 French explorer Samuel de Champlain named the harbor. The next year the colonists who survived the terrible winter of 1604 on Dochet's Island (St. Croix Island), where 35 out of 79 people died of scurvy, founded the Port-Royal colony.

In 1613 English captain Samuel Argall led an expedition from Virginia and captured the Port-Royal Habitation. The attackers pillaged and burned the buildings and destroyed all French markings.

The Port-Royal settlement spawned several significant accomplishments before it was destroyed, however. The colonists grew one of the first cereal crops in Canada and built one of the country's earliest water mills.

Canada's first European play, "Le Théâtre de Neptune," was written and produced in Port-Royal by Marc Lescarbot, and Champlain established North America's first recorded social club, "L'Ordre de Bon Temps" (Order of the Good Time) in 1606. Visitors to Nova Scotia can join this historic order free at Nova Scotia provincial tourist information centers by pledging to "have a good time, remember us pleasantly, think of us kindly and come back again."

Port-Royal Habitation has been rebuilt near what is believed to have been the original site, using Champlain's plan and studies of early 17th-century French architecture. The settlement, protected by a palisade and a cannon platform, centers on a courtyard in the style of a 17th-century French farm. The buildings include a governor's residence, gentleman's quarters, chapel, guardroom, kitchen, bakery, blacksmith shop, living quarters, an artisan's workshop and a common room.

All timber framing has been joined together without spikes or nails. The buildings are furnished with early 17th-century reproductions, and guides are dressed in period costume. Allow 30 minutes minimum. Daily 9-6, July-Aug; 9-5:30, May 15-June 30 and Sept. 1-Oct. 15. Admission $3.95; over 64, $3.45; ages 6-16, $1.95; family rate $9.90. Phone (902) 532-2898.

RIVERPORT (D-2) pop. 300

Settled by German immigrants in 1754, this harbor community at the mouth of the LaHave River was first known as Ritcey's Cove. In 1861, the town supported a thousand miners searching for gold in the local sea caves. Fire destroyed the town in 1920.

THE OVENS NATURAL PARK is on Hwy. 332. A cliffside nature trail leads to the sea caves or "ovens," and guided tours are available aboard inflatable boats. A museum contains pictures, tools and memorabilia from the area's 1861 gold rush. Gold panning is offered. Live music is provided nightly in July and August by Steve Chapin, the brother of singer Harry Chapin.

Picnicking is permitted. Food is available. Allow 1 hour minimum. Daily 9-9, July-Aug.; 9-5, May 15-30; 9-6 in June and Sept. Boat tours depart daily, mid-June to mid-Sept. Reservations are recommended for boat tours. Park $8; over 65 and ages 6-12, $4. Boat tours $23; ages 5-11, $20. Park admission is free to campers. Phone (902) 766-4621.

ST. ANN'S (A-5)

A large portion of New Zealand's Scottish population can trace its roots to St. Ann's, the departure point for a steady migration of about 900 residents. The exodus, which lasted 8 years, began in 1851 when the Rev. Norman MacLeod and 130 residents sailed from St. Ann's Harbour for Australia. Disappointed with conditions in Australia, the party moved in 1854 to New Zealand, where they found their promised land at Waipu.

Despite the loss of almost half its population during the 1850s, St. Ann's remains the heart of Cape Breton's Gaelic community. The lore of the clans was embodied in the figure of Angus McAskill, the Scottish giant who lived and died at St. Ann's. Residents of St. Ann's still recount tales of McAskill's great strength and appetite.

THE GAELIC COLLEGE OF CELTIC ARTS AND CRAFTS is off Hwy. 105 exit 111.5 km (.9 mi.) n. from to 51779 Cabot Tr. The only institution of its kind in North America, the Gaelic College was founded in 1938. On Wednesday nights in July and August, a traditional *ceilidh* (kay-lee) features Gaelic singing, piping, fiddle music and dancing. Phone (902) 295-3411.

Gaelic College Craft Center, on campus, displays clan tartans and other handcrafted Celtic items. Daily 8:30-8, July to mid-Sept.; daily 8:30-5, in June and late Sept.-Oct. 31; Mon.-Fri. 8:30-5, mid-to late May; Mon.-Fri. 9-4:30, Nov. 1 to mid-Dec. Free. Phone (902) 295-3441.

Great Hall of the Clans Museum, on campus, depicts the history and culture of Scotland from early days to the present and includes a brief account of the Great Migration from the Highlands. A heritage display of oil paintings and ink drawings also is presented. Daily 9-5, June-Aug.; by appointment in May and Sept.-Oct. Admission $3, under 12 free. Phone (902) 295-3441.

ST. PETER'S (B-5) pop. 700

St. Peter's, named San Pedro by its Portuguese founders, was a fishing base 1521-27. In the next century Nicholas Denys developed the area's fishing grounds and timber resources and established a fur-trading post protected by a fort. Successively renamed St. Pierre and Port Toulouse, the port remained a French stronghold until 1745, when the British plundered the community and burned four schooners at anchor.

The French returned and undertook the enormous task of building a road from the post to Louisbourg. This connection proved fatal, however, and Port Toulouse tumbled with the final fall of Louisbourg in 1758. Renamed St. Peter's, the town boasted Fort Granville, built in 1793 under the leadership of Lieutenant Colonel Moore. The remains of Fort Granville's ramparts still are visible at Battery Provincial Park *(see Recreation Chart and the AAA/ CAA Eastern Canada CampBook).*

The Mi'kmaq Indians once carried their canoes across the St. Peter's Canal on Hwy. 4. An interpretive exhibit explains the operation of the tidal lock system. The canal area, now a national historic site, is a popular spot for picnicking, fishing and watching vessels pass between the Atlantic Ocean and Bras d'Or Lake.

The Acadian Pioneers' Museum, 8 kilometres (5 mi.) west in River Bourgeois, presents exhibits that depict Acadian customs and shipbuilding 1870-1930.

NICOLAS DENYS MUSEUM is .75 km (.5 mi.) e. off Hwy. 4. Articles pertain to the man who built St. Peter's in the 1650s. Allow 1 hour minimum. Daily 9-5, June-Sept. Admission $1; under 12, 50c. Phone (902) 535-2379.

SHELBURNE (E-2) pop. 2,013

The shipbuilding center of Shelburne was founded in 1783 by Loyalists who fled the United States at the close of the Revolutionary War. By 1784 the number of refugees had grown to such an extent that Shelburne's population exceeded that of both Montréal and Québec. Eventually adverse economic conditions and the government's inability to supply free land and provisions to all the refugees caused thousands of Loyalists to seek homes elsewhere.

A number of trophy-winning yachts have been built in Shelburne. Shelburne native Donald MacKay, an American shipbuilder noted for the remarkably sleek clippers he produced in Boston, learned his trade in Shelburne shipyards early in the 19th century. Just outside town, Islands Provincial

Park affords picnicking and camping opportunities *(see Recreation Chart and the AAA/CAA Eastern Canada CampBook).*

J.C. WILLIAMS DORY SHOP MUSEUM is at 11 Dock St. Built and operated as a two-story waterside dory factory 1880-1970, this museum features interpretive displays about the processes involved in building these small fishing boats. Allow 1 hour minimum. Daily 9:30-5:30, June-Sept. Admission $3, under 16 free. Combination admission with the Muir-Cox Shipbuilding Interpretive Centre, Ross-Thomson House Museum and Shelburne County Museum $8. Phone (902) 875-3141.

MUIR-COX SHIPBUILDING INTERPRETIVE CENTRE is at the s. end of Dock St. along the waterfront. Exhibits depict the history and tradition of one of the oldest boat-building operations in Atlantic Canada. The shipyard, which operated 1820-1984, produced barques, fishing boats, schooners and yachts. The center is housed in a restored yacht shed and features boatbuilding demonstrations, photographs and artifacts.

Allow 30 minutes minimum. Daily 9-5:30, June-Sept. Admission $3, under 16 free. Combination admission with the J.C. Williams Dory Shop Museum, Ross-Thomson House Museum and the Shelburne County Museum $8. Phone (902) 875-1114.

ROSS-THOMSON HOUSE MUSEUM is at 9 Charlotte Ln. Thought to be the only surviving 18th-century store in Nova Scotia, the 1785 building features vintage merchandise and is furnished in the sparsely elegant style of the period. A militia room is upstairs. A Loyalist garden is planted with heirloom varieties of herbs, vegetables and flowers.

Daily 9:30-5:30, June 1 to mid-Oct. Admission $3, under 16 free. Combination admission with the Muir-Cox Shipbuilding Interpretive Centre, J.C. Williams Dory Shop Museum and Shelburne County Museum $8. Phone (902) 875-3141.

SHELBURNE COUNTY MUSEUM is at Dock St. and Maiden Ln. The museum houses a 1740 fire engine, said to be the oldest in Canada. Maritime and shipbuilding artifacts also are displayed. Permanent and changing exhibits depict the history of the county.

Allow 30 minutes minimum. Daily 9:30-5:30, June 1 to mid-Oct.; Mon.-Fri. 9:30-noon and 2-5, rest of year. Admission $3, under 16 free. Combination admission with the Muir-Cox Shipbuilding Interpretive Centre, J.C. Williams Dory Shop Museum and Ross-Thomson House Museum $8. Phone (902) 875-3219.

SHERBROOKE (C-4) pop. 400

Charles de Sainte-Etienne La Giraudiere, a French fur trader, built a post on the St. Mary's River at what became the village of Sherbrooke in 1655. Access to the area was by water, and a flourishing trade took advantage of the local natural resources. In 1861 gold was discovered, and the town boomed for 20 years. The village is a center for hunters and anglers.

 SHERBROOKE VILLAGE is on Hwy. 7 (Nova Scotia's Marine Drive). Costumed interpreters demonstrate skills, crafts and household chores at this restoration of an 1860s lumbering and mining town. Street performers present vignettes about colorful characters and daily life, and the McDonald Brothers' Sawmill operates daily. Other highlights include horse-drawn wagon rides, a nature center and evening concerts.

Thirty-two buildings comprise the village, including a blacksmith shop, general store, tearoom, craft workshops, boat-building shop and ambrotype photography studio. Food is available. Allow 2 hours minimum. Daily 9:30-5:30, June 1-Oct. 15. Admission $9; over 64, $7.25; ages 6-16, $3.75; family rate $25. AX, MC, VI. Phone (902) 522-2400 or (888) 743-7845.

SHUBENACADIE (C-3) pop. 906

Meaning "place where wild potatoes grow," Shubenacadie (shoo-ben-ack-a-dee) is in a district that has always been the home of the Mi'kmaq Indians of central Nova Scotia. In 1737 Abbé le Loutre, sent by the Society of Foreign Missions, established their headquarters and built an Indian mass house; the cemetery still is visible.

Pottery crafted by Mi'kmaq Indians from Shubenacadie clay has been discovered throughout the province. A local industry still uses the clay. Dairying and lumbering also are associated with the area historically.

SHUBENACADIE PROVINCIAL WILDLIFE PARK is off Hwy. 102 exit 11, then s. on Hwy. 2 to 149 Creighton Rd. The park consists of 20 hectares (49 acres) of natural woodland with a large variety of animals and birds, most native to Nova Scotia or North America. More than three dozen species of ducks and geese live in the park, while hundreds of others come to nest or rest while migrating. Of particular interest is a small herd of Sable Island horses.

The Creighton Environmental Centre, housed in three buildings, contains photographs and interactive exhibits describing wildlife and their habitat. Displays enhanced by sound effects portray environments as a forest community. The DUC Greenwing Legacy Interpretive Centre provides displays about waterfowl and wetlands and their importance in the environment. A playground is on the premises. Guided tours of two wetland trails are available.

Picnicking is permitted. Allow 1 hour minimum. Park and environmental center daily 9-7, May 15-Oct. 19; Sat.-Sun. 9-3, rest of year. Admission $4; ages 6-17, $1.50. Children must be with an adult. Phone (902) 758-2040.

SPRINGHILL (C-3) pop. 4,091

A 6-metre (20-ft.) monument topped by a statue of a miner stands on Main Street as a memorial to the hundreds of workers who have died in mishaps since mining began in Springhill in 1872. Despite the great promise manifested in the Number 2 mine, said to be the deepest in Canada, Springhill's mining industry was plagued with a series of tragic accidents that finally prompted the closure of the mines in 1958.

Even after two fires completely devastated its business district, the indomitable town refused to die. Springhill was awarded a gold medal from the Carnegie Hero Fund Commission for its courage in the face of disaster. Recovery has followed development of a diversified industrial base.

Springhill Chamber of Commerce: P.O. Box 1030, Springhill, NS, Canada B0M 1X0; phone (902) 597-4012.

ANNE MURRAY CENTRE is at 36 Main St. This museum chronicles the life and career of singer Anne Murray, Springhill's favorite daughter. Awards, costumes, memorabilia and photographs are featured. Allow 1 hour minimum. Daily 10-6, mid-May to mid-Oct. Admission $6; over 55 and ages 7-17, $5; family rate (maximum of three adults) $18. AX, MC, VI. Phone (902) 597-8614.

SPRINGHILL MINERS' MUSEUM is 1 km (.6 mi.) s.w. off Hwy. 2 at 145 Black River Rd. The museum offers exhibits about the history of coal mining in Springhill. Protective wear and plastic bags are provided for those wishing to dig coal. Experienced miners conduct tours of the mine. Picnicking is permitted. Allow 30 minutes minimum. Daily 9-5, mid-May to mid-Oct. Admission $5.20; over 60, $4.60; ages 7-18, $4.30; ages 3-6, $2.85; family rate (maximum of two adults) $17.55. Phone (902) 597-3449.

STELLARTON (C-4) pop. 4,809

While coal fueled the growth of Stellarton, the Sobeys put food on miners' tables. J.W. Sobey started a meat delivery service in 1907, and his son persuaded him to open a small grocery store in 1924. Their family business would expand to more than 1,300 supermarkets across the country. Sobeys, now one of Canada's largest food distributors, is still headquartered in Stellarton.

NOVA SCOTIA MUSEUM OF INDUSTRY is at 147 N. Foord St. The museum is, appropriately enough, on the site where industrialization first took place in Nova Scotia: In the 1820s the General Mining Co. began mining coal here using newly developed methods, such as steam engines, brought from Great Britain. Canada's oldest locomotive, "Samson," is among the more than 30,000 artifacts displayed at the museum.

Hands-on exhibits demonstrate bottle making, loom mills and steam and water power. Early household appliances and a collection of Nova Scotia glass also are displayed. Retired coal miners, steelworkers and printers serve as gallery guides, adding personal insights into their fields. Modern industries such as forestry, hairstyling, munitions and tourism are explored and the Shaping the Future Gallery takes a look at what lies ahead.

Mon.-Sat. 9-5, Sun. 10-5, July-Oct.; Mon.-Sat. 9-5, Sun. 1-5, May-June; Mon.-Fri. 9-5, rest of year. Closed Jan. 1, Good Friday, Thanksgiving and Dec. 25-26. Admission $7; over 64, $4; ages 6-17, $3; family rate $15. MC, VI. Phone (902) 755-5425.

SYDNEY (B-6) pop. 26,100

Colonists from New York and New Hampshire settled Sydney, Nova Scotia's third-largest city, beginning in 1785. Known as Spanish Bay, Sydney was renamed in honor of England's colonial secretary, Lord Sydney. The city was the capital of the Cape Breton colony 1785-1820, before the island was annexed by Nova Scotia. The area attracted a large number of Scottish settlers in the early 1800s, and with the opening of the coal mines and a steel plant at the turn of the 20th century, a large number of Eastern European settlers arrived, helping to account for the city's diverse ethnic population.

Sydney, on scenic Sydney Harbour, is an important seaport and the commercial capital of picturesque Cape Breton Island. The University College of Cape Breton also is in the city.

Industrial Cape Breton Board of Trade: P.O. Box 131, Sydney, NS, Canada B1P 6G9; phone (902) 564-6453.

CAPE BRETON CENTRE FOR HERITAGE AND SCIENCE is in the Lyceum Building at 225 George St. Permanent and changing historical exhibits focus on the Cape Breton area. Discovery Corner offers displays for children. Local exhibits are presented in the summer. Allow 30 minutes minimum. Mon.-Sat. 9-5, June-Aug.; Tues.-Fri. 10-4, Mon. 1-4, rest of year. Donations. Phone (902) 539-1572.

COSSIT HOUSE MUSEUM is at 75 Charlotte St. This is one of the oldest houses in Sydney. Built in 1787 by the Rev. Ranna Cossit, the first Anglican minister assigned to permanent duty in Cape Breton, the house is restored to its late 18th-century appearance and has period furnishings. Allow 30 minutes minimum. Mon.-Sat. 9-5, Sun. 1-5, June 1-Oct. 15. Admission $2; over 64 and ages 6-17, $1; family rate $5. Phone (902) 539-7973.

THE JOST HOUSE is at 54 Charlotte St. The 1786 two-story dwelling depicts 2 centuries of regional history. Highlights include an 18th-century kitchen, Victorian antiques, an apothecary display and a maritime exhibit. Guided tours are available. Allow 1 hour minimum. Mon.-Sat. 9-5, June-Aug.; Mon.-Sat. 10-4, Sept.-Oct. Admission $2; over 64 and under 12, $1; family rate $5. Phone (902) 539-0366.

SAINT PATRICK'S MUSEUM is at the n. end of the Government Wharf at 89 Esplanade. Built in 1828, this is said to be the oldest Roman Catholic church on Cape Breton Island. It contains exhibits about the history of Sydney and the surrounding area. Daily 9-5, June-Aug.; by appointment rest of year. Admission $2, family rate $5. Phone (902) 562-8237 or (902) 539-1572.

CASINOS

- **Casino Nova Scotia** is at 525 George St. Mon.-Thurs. 11 a.m.-4 a.m., Fri.-Sun. 24 hours; closed Good Friday, Easter, Nov. 11 and Dec. 25. Phone (902) 563-7777.

TATAMAGOUCHE (B-3) pop. 738

At the mouth of the French and Waugh rivers, Tatamagouche is named for an Indian word meaning "meeting place of the waters." The original French settlement came to an abrupt end in 1755, when a detachment of New Englanders destroyed Tatamagouche and two schooners bound for the Louisbourg fortress with supplies.

Following the close of the Seven Years' War, a second attempt at settlement was directed by Col. Joseph Frederick Walsh Desbarres, a French Huguenot who received a land grant along the French and Waugh rivers. Nothing remains of the village he built, although many residents of Tatamagouche trace their lineage to these first Huguenot settlers.

One notable resident was Anna Swan, born in 1846. The 240-centimetre-tall (8-ft.) woman toured with P.T. Barnum's "Greatest Show on Earth" for several years.

The Fraser Culture Centre on Main Street contains maritime art, North Shore archives, a tourist office and a room devoted to Anna Swan and her husband; phone (902) 657-3285.

Northumberland Chamber of Commerce: 225 Main St., P.O. Box 152, Tatamagouche, NS, Canada B0K 1V0; phone (902) 657-3811.

BALMORAL GRIST MILL MUSEUM is 5 km (3 mi.) s. off Hwy. 311 on Hwy. 256. Built in 1874, this is thought to be the oldest operational gristmill in Nova Scotia. Visitors can see flour being ground and examine the mill's unique Scottish oat-drying kiln. Allow 30 minutes minimum. Mon.-Sat. 9:30-5:30, Sun. 1-5:30, June 1-Oct. 15. Admission $3; over 64 and ages 6-17, $2; family rate $7. Phone (902) 657-3016.

SUNRISE TRAIL MUSEUM is on Hwy. 6. Permanent exhibits pertain to North Shore Indians, shipbuilding, Acadians at Tatamagouche and early agriculture. Daily 9-5, July 1-Labour Day; Sat.-Sun. 1-5, day after Labour Day-Sept. 30. Admission $2; under 13, 50c; family rate $3. Phone (902) 657-2689.

TIVERTON (D-1) pop. 300

On a column of land known as Digby Neck that extends beyond Digby (see place listing p. 103) into the Bay of Fundy, Tiverton's main industry is fishing. Lobsters are caught during the winter season. A variety of seabirds and whales frequently can be seen from boat charters and whale cruises, which are available during the summer.

Balancing Rock, located on the eastern shore is a natural landmark situated along a scenic trail. The

Island Museum and Visitor Information Centre, houses historical memorabilia and exhibits depicting the area's heritage; phone (902) 839-2853.

TRURO (C-3) pop. 11,457

Once a large community of Acadian farmers, Truro was later settled by the Scottish and English. Their descendants operate extensive dairy farms in the vicinity. The Nova Scotia Agricultural College, across the Salmon River at Bible Hill, opened in 1905.

Bible Hill also is the site of harness racing on Sundays year-round at Nova Scotia Provincial Exhibition Raceway; phone (902) 895-7893.

Note: Policies concerning admittance of children to pari-mutuel betting facilities vary. Phone for information.

Victoria Park, 400 hectares (1,000 acres) of woodlands interspersed with numerous springs and two waterfalls, has hiking trails, picnic facilities, a swimming pool, tennis courts and other recreational facilities.

The tidal bore is a natural phenomenon of the Salmon River's changing flow. Unlike typical tides that advance gradually, here the water rushes into the river in strong currents or even waves. A viewing area is just off Hwy. 102 exit 14 at the end of Tidal Bore Road. A timetable for the bore is available from the chamber of commerce.

Truro and District Chamber of Commerce: 574 Prince St., Truro, NS, Canada B2N 1G3; phone (902) 895-6328.

COLCHESTER HISTORICAL MUSEUM is at 29 Young St. Changing exhibits and displays pertain to the human and natural history of Colchester County. Permanent exhibits include maps, photographs, cemetery records and historical documents. The museum also has a research library specializing in genealogy and community histories. Allow 1 hour minimum. Mon.-Fri. 10-5, Sat. 2-5, July-Aug.; Tues.-Fri. 10-noon and 1-4, Sat. 1-4, rest of year. Admission $2, students with ID $1. Phone (902) 895-6284.

LITTLE WHITE SCHOOLHOUSE MUSEUM is on the campus of Nova Scotia Community College at 20 Arthur St. The 1871 one-room schoolhouse contains antique school desks, books and various artifacts. An archive includes old textbooks, educational publications, school records and photographs of former students. Allow 30 minutes minimum. Mon.-Fri. 10-5, July-Aug.; by appointment rest of year. Donations. Phone (902) 895-5170, (902) 895-7703 or (902) 897-0804.

TUPPERVILLE (D-2) pop. 100

Tupperville is in the fertile orchard country of the Annapolis Valley, farmed by the Acadians as early as 1630. At nearby Bloody Creek, British soldiers from Annapolis Royal were massacred by the French and Indians in 1711 and 1757. Despite the area's violent history, Col. James Delancy, leader of

the pro-British raids around New York during the American Revolution, settled at this site after being banished from the United States in 1783. It was also home to Sir Charles Tupper, a 19th-century provincial prime minister.

TUPPERVILLE SCHOOL MUSEUM is at 2663 Hwy. 201. This 1858 one-room schoolhouse contains century-old desks, books, a potbellied stove, a school bell and other furnishings. The museum also contains photographs of former students and community members as well as the works of wood-carver Louis Jeremy. Picnicking is permitted. Allow 30 minutes minimum. Daily 10-5, mid-May through Labour Day. Donations. Phone (902) 665-2427.

WESTPORT (D-1) pop. 274

[SAVE] **BRIER ISLAND WHALE AND SEABIRD CRUISES** depart from Brier Island, which is reached by two car ferries from Digby Neck. The ferry connections must be timed to avoid a delay in crossing. The cruises into the Bay of Fundy offer sightings and behavioral observations of various species of whales, dolphins, porpoises and seabirds.

Warm clothing is necessary. Allow 4 hours minimum. Cruises are offered daily at 8:30, 10:30, 1:30, 3:30 and 5:30, mid-May to mid-Oct. (weather permitting). Additional cruises may be added during peak season; phone ahead. Fare $45; over 60, $36; ages 6-12, $24; under 6, $18. Reservations are advised. MC, VI. Phone (902) 839-2995 or (800) 656-3660.

[SAVE] **MARINER CRUISES WHALE & SEABIRD TOURS** departs from Brier Island, reached via Hwy. 217 and car ferries from Digby Neck. Two-and-a-half to 5-hour whale-watching tours in the Bay of Fundy are conducted by a naturalist. Visitors may spot several species of whales, including humpbacks, fin and minke as well as porpoises, dolphins, seals and various seabirds.

Warm clothing is advised. Food is available. Daily 8-8, June 12-Oct. 15. Fare $46; over 64 and students with ID $39; ages 5-12, $25; under 5, $19. AX, MC, VI. Phone (902) 839-2346 or (800) 239-2189.

WESTVILLE (C-4) pop. 3,879

[SAVE] **MAGIC VALLEY** is 9 km (6 mi.) w. off Hwy. 104 exit 20. The park includes Storybook Village and Old MacDonald's Farm. Pedal and bumper boats, miniature golf, go-carts, park rides, train rides, a pool and waterslide complex also are featured. Food is available. Daily 11-6, July 1-Labour Day (weather permitting). Park rides (includes all rides except go-carts, miniature golf and water activities) $14.95, under 3 free; family rate (two adults and two children) $53.95. Park only $7. Go-carts $4.25. Phone (902) 396-4467.

WINDSOR (C-2) pop. 3,778

A popular base for exploring the Annapolis Valley, Windsor is at the confluence of the Avon and St. Croix rivers. The town's original Acadian settlers reclaimed thousands of hectares from the sea by building several kilometres of dikes. During the mid-18th century the area was resettled by Loyalists and planters from New England and Imperial troops garrisoned at Fort Edward.

The phenomenal tidal fluctuations at Windsor average about 12 metres (40 ft.) each day. For the best times and viewing locations, contact the Windsor-West Hants Visitor Information Centre, off Hwy. 1 exit 6; phone (902) 798-2690.

Of historic interest is King's-Edgehill School, one of the oldest educational institutions in the British Commonwealth. Home to a respected touring company of puppeteers, the Mermaid Theatre of Nova Scotia, 132 Gerrish St., allows visitors to view puppets and stages from previous shows or watch new ones being created. Windsor also claims the title of "Birthplace of Hockey" thanks to 19th-century author Thomas Chandler Haliburton, who described an early form of the game being played at Long Pond.

On Sundays in summer, the Evangeline Express offers 3-hour train excursions to Wolfville in open-air cars or enclosed coaches; phone (902) 798-0798.

Town of Windsor: P.O. Box 158, Windsor, NS, Canada B0N 2T0; phone (902) 798-2275.

FORT EDWARD NATIONAL HISTORIC SITE OF CANADA is off King St. on Fort Edward Rd. The blockhouse and earthworks are all that remain of Fort Edward, built in 1750 by British Maj. Charles Lawrence. Many Acadian families were detained here after the 1755 deportation. Garrisoned by Imperial troops for more than a century, Fort Edward was an important base during the Seven Years' War, the American Revolution and the War of 1812. Canadian and American forces trained at the fort during World War I.

Allow 30 minutes minimum. Fort daily 10-5, mid-June through Labour Day. Grounds daily dawn-dusk, year-round. Free. Phone (902) 532-2321 or (902) 798-4706.

HALIBURTON HOUSE MUSEUM is .75 km (.5 mi.) w. on Clifton Ave. This was the estate of Judge Thomas C. Haliburton, who created the fictional Yankee clock peddler Sam Slick in his mid-1800s books "The Clockmaker" and "The Attaché." The 1836 villa features Victorian furnishings as well as Haliburton's desk. Allow 1 hour minimum. Mon.-Sat. 9:30-5:30, Sun. 1-5:30, June 1-Oct. 15. Admission $3; over 64 and ages 6-17, $2; family rate $7. Phone (902) 798-2915.

SHAND HOUSE MUSEUM is off Hwy. 101, .75 km (.5 mi.) s. on Avon St. The 1890 Victorian house with gingerbread trim contains original period furniture as well as all the conveniences of 1890, including central heating, closets, electric lighting and indoor plumbing. Allow 30 minutes minimum. Mon.-Sat. 9:30-5:30, Sun. 1-5:30, June 1-Oct. 15. Admission $3; over 64 and ages 6-17, $2; family rate $7. Phone (902) 798-8213.

WEST HANTS HISTORICAL SOCIETY MUSEUM is at 281 King St. Home furnishings, housewares, clothing, toys, maritime objects, books and musical instruments reflect daily provincial life. A genealogy research library is available. Allow 1 hour minimum. Tues.-Sat. 9-5, mid-June through Aug. 31; Tues.-Fri. 10-4, in Sept. Donations. Research fee $2. Phone (902) 798-4706.

WINDSOR HOCKEY HERITAGE CENTRE is at 128 Gerrish St. Exhibits trace the development of the sport of ice hockey from its origins around 1800 to the present. Displays include hockey sticks carved by Mi'kmaq Indians, wooden pucks cut from tree branches, early hockey nets and Acme Club Spring Skates that clamped to boot or shoe bottoms. Allow 30 minutes minimum. Daily 9-7, July-Aug.; 9-5, rest of year. Donations. Phone (902) 798-1800.

WOLFVILLE (C-2) pop. 3,658

Wolfville was resettled by New Englanders following the expulsion of the Acadians in 1755. It is the home of Acadia University, founded in 1838 by the Nova Scotia Baptist Educational Society.

The closest town to Grand-Pré *(see place listing p. 105)*, Wolfville is a popular base for exploring the historic region associated with the Acadian deportation. Several old Acadian settlements lie along the Gaspereau River and are accessible from Gaspereau Avenue in town.

K.C. IRVING ENVIRONMENTAL SCIENCE CENTRE & HARRIET IRVING BOTANICAL GARDENS is off University Ave. on the campus of Acadia University. The 2-hectare (6-acre) botanical gardens contain nine habitats from the Acadia Forest Region, including a sand barrens, a coniferous woodland and a marsh. Interpretive signs provide details about more than 1,000 native plants and endangered species. A glassed-in winter garden and a medicinal and food garden also are on the grounds.

The science center features greenhouses, a conservatory and botanical laboratories. Nature trails and picnic areas are available. Allow 1 hour, 30 minutes minimum. Gardens daily 7:30 a.m.-dusk. Science center daily 8 a.m.-10 p.m. Free. Phone (902) 585-5242.

PRESCOTT HOUSE MUSEUM is off Hwy. 101 exit 11, is 1.5 km (.9 mi.) n. of Greenwich on Hwy. 358, then 4 km (2.5 mi.) e. to 1633 Starrs Point Rd. Built by Charles Ramage Prescott, merchant, legislator and pioneer horticulturist, the 1800s Georgian house features gardens and is known for its collections of oriental rugs and samplers. Allow 30 minutes minimum. Mon.-Sat. 9:30-5:30, Sun. 1-5:30, June 1-Oct. 15. Admission $3; over 65 and ages 6-17, $2; family rate $7. Phone (902) 542-3984.

RANDALL HOUSE MUSEUM is at 259 Main St. The museum displays historical artifacts from the New England planters who settled in the area after the expulsion of the Acadians. Other exhibits chronicle regional history up to present times. Food is available. Mon.-Sat. 10-5, Sun. 2-5, mid-June to mid-Sept. Donations. Phone (902) 542-9775.

WINERIES

- **Domaine de Grand Pré** is 3 km (1.9 mi.) e. on Rte. 1. Tours depart daily at 11, 3 and 5. Phone (902) 542-1753 or (866) 479-4637.

YARMOUTH (E-1) pop. 7,561

Yarmouth was founded in 1651 by French colonists, who subsequently were expelled by the British in 1755. The area was settled by New Englanders in 1761 and later by returning Acadians and Loyalists. An important shipbuilding and shipping town during the days of sail, Yarmouth prospered during the 19th century. Figuring prominently in the city's economy was the Killam Brothers Shipping Office, 90 Water St., which managed sailing fleets for more than 200 years. Now a museum, its 19th-century furnishings and ledgers tell the story of the era; phone (902) 742-5536.

Bay Ferries operates a high-speed catamaran providing car and passenger service from Bar Harbor and Portland, Maine, to Yarmouth. Reservations are recommended for the 3-hour ferry trip. Service is available late May through mid-October; for schedules, fares or reservations phone (877) 283-7240.

Yarmouth lies at the end of two scenic routes: Hwy. 1, which follows St. Mary's Bay north to Digby (*see place listing p. 103*), and Hwy. 3, which heads east to Shelburne (*see place listing p. 119*).

Yarmouth Chamber of Commerce: P.O. Box 532, Yarmouth, NS, Canada B5A 4B4; phone (902) 742-3074.

Self-guiding tours: A tourist information center on Forest Street in front of the ferry terminal provides brochures outlining a self-guiding walking tour of various points of interest, including the city's Georgian and Italianate houses. The center also provides additional information about ferry service; phone (902) 742-6639.

DID YOU KNOW

Paul Revere earned his degree in freemasonry near Yarmouth around 1772.

ARGYLE TOWNSHIP COURT HOUSE & GAOL is 15 km (9 mi.) s. on Rte. 3 (Lighthouse Rte.) in Tusket. Built 1803-05, the court house remained in use until 1945. Guided tours of the old jail, courtroom, judge's chamber and jail keeper's quarters are available. Genealogical archives contain Argyle and Yarmouth County records and provincial census data from 1770-1891. Allow 30 minutes minimum. Daily 9-5, July-Aug.; Mon.-Fri. 9-noon and 1-4, May-June and Sept.-Oct. Admission $2, family rate $4. Research fee $5, half-day $3. Phone (902) 648-2493.

ART GALLERY OF NOVA SCOTIA–YARMOUTH is at 341 Main St. A permanent collection of Nova Scotia art is on display. Temporary exhibits from Canada and around the world also may be seen. Allow 1 hour minimum. Daily noon-8. Admission $6.50; over 59, $5; students with ID $2.50; ages 6-17, $1.50; family rate (two adults and three children) $12.50. MC, VI. Phone (902) 749-2248.

FIREFIGHTERS MUSEUM OF NOVA SCOTIA is at 451 Main St. Vintage firefighting equipment includes horse-drawn steamers and hand-drawn, hand-operated pumpers. Photographs, leather hoses, lanterns and buckets also are on display. A library is available on site.

Allow 1 hour minimum. Mon.-Sat. 9-9, Sun. 10-5, July-Aug.; Mon.-Sat. 9-5 in June and Sept.; Mon.-Fri. 9-4, Sat. 1-4, rest of year. Admission $3; over 60, $2.50; under 18, $1.50; family rate $6. Phone (902) 742-5525.

YARMOUTH COUNTY MUSEUM AND ARCHIVES is at 22 Collins St. Housed in a granite church, the museum contains one of Canada's largest collections of ships portraits. Also featured are ships models, a lens from the Yarmouth lighthouse, costumes, a 1921 electric car, and a collection of tools, glass, china, toys and household items.

Another highlight is a stone bearing a mysterious runic inscription that is linked to Norse explorations of around A.D. 1000. Five period rooms are offered. Archives contain historical documents, photographs and genealogical records.

Allow 30 minutes minimum. Mon.-Sat. 9-5, Sun. 2-5, June 1 to mid-Oct.; Tues.-Sat. 2-5, rest of year. Archive hours vary; phone ahead. Admission $3; ages 14-18, $1; ages 6-13, 50c; family rate $6. Combination ticket with Pelton-Fuller House $5; ages 14-18, $2; ages 6-13, $1; family rate $10. Phone (902) 742-5539.

Pelton-Fuller House is at 20 Collins St. This 1895 Victorian house served as the summer retreat for businessman Alfred Fuller, the original Fuller Brush man. Antiques and collections as well as some of Mr. Fuller's brushes are displayed; visitors also may stroll through the gardens. Guided tours are offered on request. Allow 30 minutes minimum. Mon.-Sat. 10-4, July 1-Sept. 14. Admission $3. Combination ticket with the Yarmouth County Museum and Archives $5; ages 14-18, $2; ages 6-13, $1; family rate $10. Phone (902) 742-5539.

Prince Edward Island

The Island Life
Careful—the relaxed pace and laid-back atmosphere of this isle can be contagious

Land of Anne
Visit places of pastoral beauty immortalized in the novel "Anne of Green Gables"

Shaped by the Sea
Golden beaches and red sandstone cliffs adorn the crescent coastline

Just Picture It
Fertile farmlands, captivating coastal scenery and cozy inlets—perfect postcard settings

Charlottetown
This modern capital is still tied to its colonial seaport past

Greenwich, Prince Edward Island National Park
Ron Watts / Getty Images

unhurried
exploration

Green Gables House, Cavendish / Tourism Prince Edward Island

A visit to laid-back Prince Edward Island is like slipping into a sea of blissful nostalgia.

Tiny fishing ports do a booming business in catches of flounder, mackerel and bluefin tuna, as well as in such shellfish as lobsters, mussels and scallops.

Humble farmers cultivate crops of potatoes, turnips, grains and hay while raising cattle, pigs, sheep, poultry and horses.

Quiet communities—such as Cavendish, described in Lucy Maud Montgomery's "Anne of Green Gables"—move at a leisurely pace that reflects an earlier time.

The island not only recalls memories, but also creates them.

Vivid natural tapestries are woven from the vibrant greens of pasture, rich rusts of sandstone cliffs and deep, glistening blues of rolling ocean. In autumn, shades of apricot-orange, scarlet red and brilliant gold illuminate the landscape.

Waves crash on the sands of secluded, relaxing beaches.

From charming Charlottetown, "Canada's birthplace"—to lively Orwell, where Celtic traditions thrive—to the shops in which Mi'kmaq Indians still display their crafted wares, Prince Edward Island presents a character so deeply steeped in a precious past.

When Anne, the quirky, red-headed orphan in the classic novel "Anne of Green Gables," first gazed upon Prince Edward Island on a dewy June morning, she believed it to be "as lovely as anything she ever dreamed..."

What did she gaze upon? Country lanes protected by the shade of moss-draped trees. Surf-carved rocks. The sea, cobalt blue and sparkling in the sun. Apple and cherry trees sprinkled with blossoms. Lofty, red sandstone cliffs fronting the coast. Dandelions dotting grassy fields. And lilac trees, limbs heavy with aromatic purple flowers.

It's easy to see why author Lucy Maud Montgomery used Cavendish, her childhood hometown, as a model for this story, numerous sequels and other novels. The island's fairy-tale setting proves just as magical in real life as on the page.

Memories of Home, Sweet Home

The author's love of nature and this unspoiled maritime island was apparent in her tribute to the pastoral area she called home and the easygoing lifestyle of its residents.

The story's fictional hamlet Avonlea was based upon Cavendish, on the island's northern shore. Fans of the novel flock to the town, where the restored Green Gables House calls to mind scenes from the book. Originally a cottage belonging to the author's cousins, it's more popularly recognized as Anne's home base for dreaming up shenanigans.

Behind the house, couples stroll along Lover's Lane and explore Haunted Wood in much the same manner as the character did. Folks even choose to say "I do" in a nearby farmhouse, the locale of the author's wedding in 1911.

Two museums in Park Corner are dedicated to Montgomery and her fictional characters, and a musical version of the story packs Charlottetown's Confederation Centre, which also contains original manuscripts and displays.

Bordering Cavendish, Prince Edward Island National Park is a veritable delight. Beaches, freshwater ponds, saltwater marshes, woodlands and historical landmarks appeal to nature lovers. A leisurely drive on Gulf Shore Highway, which cuddles the northern coast, offers stunning vistas.

Jacques Cartier is the first European to land on the island, later named Île Saint-Jean.

1534

© Bettmann/Corbis

The French establish a capital at Port La Joye near present-day Charlottetown.

1720

The island is renamed for Queen Victoria's father, Prince Edward, Duke of Kent.

1799

1758
Britain gains control of the island and deports Acadian settlers.

© Bettmann/Corbis

Prince Edward Island Historical Timeline

1803
Lord Selkirk establishes a colony of 800 Scottish Highlanders at Belfast.

Taking it Easy

Other areas on the island that aren't specifically featured in Montgomery's stories nevertheless exhibit a similar unhurried, relaxed mood.

Make yourself at home in one of numerous cottages, country inns or bed and breakfasts; the island boasts a wide variety of graceful properties in idyllic settings, where unwinding is the most important thing on the "to do" list.

Set out for a stroll along the coast—with so many public beaches, you won't have to go far to squish white (or red) sand between your toes. Watch as Irish moss is gathered off the beaches after a storm. It's then hauled away in carts, dried in the sun and used in creating products as diverse as ice cream, tea and hand lotion.

Acquaint yourself with the countryside on a lighthouse hunt—more than 50 dot the coast. En route amid rolling hills are roadside stands offering home-grown fruits, and cafes filled with the aroma of just-baked scones. For lunch, feast on seafood chowder at a wharfside restaurant.

In Charlottetown, brick government buildings, Victorian houses and shingled taverns on Great George, King and Water streets have been restored to preserve the past. Tour Province House, site of meetings in 1864 that led to Canada's confederation 3 years later. Visit Founders' Hall, which traces the nation's history from its birth to the present day. Or peruse quaint shops selling works created by local artists and craftspeople in Olde Charlottetown and Peake's Wharf.

Bagpipe and fiddle music celebrates Summerside's Celtic heritage, while museums depict Acadian culture, fox breeding and shipbuilding. Watch sailboats dock from the waterfront boardwalk or fill a basket with yummy jams and jellies at the town's farmer's market.

Then snuggle under a blanket woven at an island woolen mill and crack the spine on one of Lucy Maud Montgomery's popular tales.

The author was so fond of Prince Edward Island that she made her childhood memories indelible. A visit may just have you creating a few stories of your own.

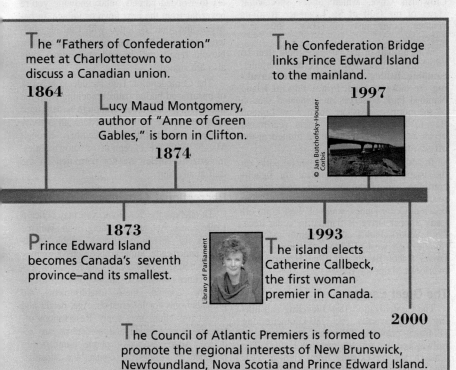

The "Fathers of Confederation" meet at Charlottetown to discuss a Canadian union.
1864

The Confederation Bridge links Prince Edward Island to the mainland.
1997

© Jan Butchofsky-Houser Corbis

Lucy Maud Montgomery, author of "Anne of Green Gables," is born in Clifton.
1874

1873
Prince Edward Island becomes Canada's seventh province–and its smallest.

Library of Parliament

1993
The island elects Catherine Callbeck, the first woman premier in Canada.

2000
The Council of Atlantic Premiers is formed to promote the regional interests of New Brunswick, Newfoundland, Nova Scotia and Prince Edward Island.

Recreation

Fields with colorful crops. Carpets of bright green grass. White sandy beaches and red sandstone cliffs. Surrounded by the deep blue sea, they create a patchwork of cheery hues and pleasing textures that defines picturesque Prince Edward Island.

Landscapes and Seascapes

The island makes up for its lack of deep-wilderness recreation areas with a variety of well-maintained outdoor playgrounds. You can enjoy **golf** May through October on the rolling greens of more than 30 parklike courses tucked about, most within an hour's drive of Charlottetown. Eighteen-hole venues include championship Brudenell River, which also has a golf academy; Dundarave, Brudenell's companion course; and the course at Summerside, challenging to any skill level.

Renovated Belvedere, just a putt or two away from downtown Charlottetown, is one of Canada's oldest courses. Also steeped in tradition is Green Gables, off Hwy. 6 on the northern shore; this redesigned venerable has been an oceanside favorite since 1939. Tournament-caliber greens include Mill River, north of O'Leary, and the celebrated Links at Crowbush Cove, which offers spectacular views of the Gulf of St. Lawrence from its vantage point just off Hwy. 350 near Lakeside.

With no part of the province more than 16 kilometres (10 mi.) from the ocean or an inlet, **camping, fishing, swimming** and **sea kayaking** are close at hand. Prince Edward Island National Park preserves an elongated section of the northern seashore from New London Bay to Tracadie Bay and offers year-round ocean access; park services are limited in the off-season.

In addition to camping, provincial parks on the island's perimeter are ideal for **beachcombing** and **clamming**. And most can be reached from one of three scenic routes. The beach at Cedar Dunes, south of West Point off Lady Slipper Drive, is flanked by cedar trees. Lord Selkirk Park's activity center caters to families; it's west of Eldon off Kings Byway Drive. Cabot Beach, off Blue Heron Drive, overlooks Malpeque Bay.

The Great Escape

The Confederation Trail **bicycling** and **hiking** path traverses the 280-kilometre-long (174-mi.) province, following an abandoned railway bed that roughly parallels Hwy. 2. The western section extends from Tignish, near land's end at North Cape, to Kensington.

Diversions along the way might include a visit to historic railway stations in Alberton and Kensington, the sighting of Canada geese while crossing the isthmus between Malpeque and Bedeque bays (It's a flyway!), and the smell of freshly turned earth in this fertile agricultural region. A potato museum in O'Leary pays homage to the province's prime product.

The central trail begins at Kensington and travels across Queens County, branching off on a side route to Charlottetown. From Mount Stewart, the eastern section runs to Elmira, near the island's northeastern tip. The trail comes closest to the northern shore near St. Peters Bay, where several estuaries are bridged. This is an ideal place to spot shorebirds—or a bald eagle, if you're lucky. At Harmony Junction a spur road winds south to Souris, on the coast, while the main road continues northward through wetlands and farming communities.

Whether you pedal your own wheels, rent a mountain bike from a local outfitter or indulge in a customized, guided tour with van support, you'll find this an easy ride. As the route shifts from pastoral fields to scenic rivers to wooded parcels, relax knowing you're never far from the next town or village; in between, the route is dotted with trailside shelters. Interpretive sites, observation points, bicycle repair stations and connecting trails also are signed.

The Confederation Trail includes a network of unsurfaced hiking paths branching from the interior to coastal areas. Although widely used in summer, the trail is closed to all activity except **snowmobiling** December through March. With the exception of snowmobiles, motorized vehicles are not permitted on the trail at any time.

Recreational Activities

Throughout the TourBook, you may notice a Recreational Activities heading with bulleted listings of recreation-oriented establishments listed underneath. Similar operations also may be mentioned in Destination City recreation sections. Since normal AAA inspection criteria cannot be applied, these establishments are presented only for information. Age, height and weight restrictions may apply. Reservations often are recommended and sometimes are required. Addresses and/or phone numbers are provided so visitors can contact the attraction for additional information.

Fast Facts

POPULATION: 135,294.

AREA: 5,656 sq km (2,184 sq mi); ranks 12th.

CAPITAL: Charlottetown.

HIGHEST POINT: 152 m/499 ft., Queens County.

LOWEST POINT: Sea level, Atlantic Ocean.

TIME ZONE(S): Atlantic. DST.

MINIMUM AGE FOR UNRESTRICTED DRIVER'S LICENSE: 17.

SEAT BELT/CHILD RESTRAINT LAWS: Seat belts required for driver and all passengers over 15. Children under 16 and at least 18 kg (40 pounds) are required to be in a child restraint or seat belt; child restraints required for under 18 kg (40 pounds).

HELMETS FOR MOTORCYCLISTS: Required for all riders.

RADAR DETECTORS: Not permitted.

FIREARMS LAWS: By federal law, all nonresidents entering Canada with a firearm must declare their weapon in writing and pay a fee of $25 (Canadian). Contact the Canadian Firearms Centre at (800) 731-4000 to receive a declaration form and additional information.

HOLIDAYS: Jan. 1; Good Friday; Easter; Easter Monday; Victoria Day, May 24 or closest prior Mon.; Canada Day, July 1; Labour Day, Sept. (1st Mon.); Thanksgiving, Oct. (2nd Mon.); Remembrance Day, Nov. 11; Christmas, Dec. 25; Boxing Day, Dec. 26.

TAXES: The Federal general sales tax is 6 percent on goods and services. Prince Edward Island's provincial sales tax is 10 percent.

INFORMATION CENTERS: Prince Edward Island has one provincial information center on the mainland at Caribou, Nova Scotia. The island has visitor information centers at Gateway Village in Borden-Carleton, Brackley Beach, Cavendish, Charlottetown, Mount Pleasant, Pooles Corner, Souris, Summerside and Wood Islands. The Charlottetown center is open year-round. The Borden-Carleton location is open March through November; the others are open mid-May to mid-October.

FURTHER INFORMATION FOR VISITORS:
Charlottetown Visitor Center
6 Prince St.
Charlottetown, PE, Canada C1A 4P5
(902) 368-4444
(888) 734-7529

FISHING AND HUNTING REGULATIONS:
Dept. of Environment, Energy and Forestry
P.O. Box 2000
Charlottetown, PE, Canada C1A 7N8
(902) 368-6080

INTERPROVINCE FERRY INFORMATION:
Northumberland Ferries & Bay Ferries Ltd.
94 Water St.
P.O. Box 634
Charlottetown, PE, Canada C1A 7L3
(902) 566-3838
(888) 249-7245 (reservations)

Traversier C.T.M.A. Ferry
P.O. Box 245, Cap-aux-Meules
Îles de la Madeleine, QC, Canada G0B 1B0
(902) 687-2181
(888) 986-3278 (reservations)

ALCOHOL CONSUMPTION: Legal age 19.

Prince Edward Island Temperature Averages Maximum/Minimum

From the records of The Weather Channel Interacitve, Inc.
Temperatures in Celsius.

	JAN	FEB	MAR	APR	MAY	JUN	JUL	AUG	SEP	OCT	NOV	DEC
Charlottetown	-3	-4	1	7	14	20	24	24	19	13	6	-1
	-12	-12	-7	-1	4	10	15	15	11	6	0	-7

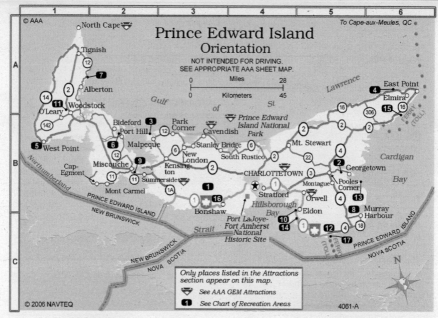

© AAA

North Cape ▽

Prince Edward Island
Orientation

NOT INTENDED FOR DRIVING.
SEE APPROPRIATE AAA SHEET MAP.

To Cape-aux-Meules, QC

Miles   0 ———— 28
Kilometers 0 ———— 45

Tignish (12)
(7)
Alberton (2)
O'Leary (14) (11) Woodstock
(142)
West Point (5)
Cap-Egmont
Mont Carmel
Bideford (3)
Port Hill (12)
Park Corner
Malpeque (6)
Miscouche (12) (9)
(11) Summerside ▽
(1A)
Bonshaw (1)
Cavendish
Stanley Bridge
New London (6)
Kensington
Prince Edward Island National Park ▽
South Rustico (2)
CHARLOTTETOWN (3)
Stratford
Hillsborough Bay
Port LaJoye-Fort Amherst National Historic Site
Mt. Stewart
Montague
Pooles Corner
Orwell (4)
Eldon
Murray Harbour
East Point (4)
Elmira (16)
(15)
(306)
(16)
(2) (2)
Georgetown
Cardigan Bay
(8)
(13)
(10)
(14)
(12)
(18)
(17)

Gulf of St. Lawrence
Northumberland
PRINCE EDWARD ISLAND
NEW BRUNSWICK
Strait
NEW BRUNSWICK
NOVA SCOTIA
NOVA SCOTIA
PRINCE EDWARD ISLAND

N

Only places listed in the Attractions
section appear on this map.
▽　See AAA GEM Attractions
❶　See Chart of Recreation Areas

© 2006 NAVTEQ

4061-A

Points of Interest Offering A
Great Experience for Members®

Cavendish (B-3)

AVONLEA VILLAGE OF ANNE OF GREEN GABLES—The schoolhouse where Lucy Maud Montgomery taught and a church she attended are highlights of this village based on the "Anne of Green Gables" novels. See p. 134.

GREEN GABLES HOUSE—Visited by Lucy Maud Montgomery during her childhood, this late 19th-century farmhouse provided the author with the inspiration for the setting of "Anne of Green Gables." See p. 135.

Charlottetown (B-4)

CONFEDERATION CENTRE OF THE ARTS—Home of the renowned Charlotte-town Festival, this national arts center reflects Canadian culture through its art gallery, museum and theater productions. See p. 136.

FOUNDERS' HALL—History comes to life at this multimedia museum, which commemorates the nation's birth. See p. 136.

PROVINCE HOUSE NATIONAL HISTORIC SITE—The Fathers of Confederation held meetings here that led to Canada's confederation in 1867. See p. 137.

North Cape (A-1)

NORTH CAPE, NATURE & TECHNOLOGY IN PERFECT HARMONY—Dedicated to the research of how wind can be harnessed as a power source, this coastal site features a wind test facility and wind farm, a lighthouse, an interpretive center and aquarium. Displays along the nature trail explain the area's history and ecology. See p. 139.

Orwell (C-5)

ORWELL CORNER HISTORIC VILLAGE—This recreation of an 1890s rural community includes a blacksmith shop, church, general store, working farm, schoolhouse and an agriculture museum. The shopkeeper's home features furnishings of the period. See p. 140.

Prince Edward Island
National Park (B-4)

PRINCE EDWARD ISLAND NATIONAL PARK—Red foxes, waterfowl and shore birds populate this 26-square-kilometre (10-sq.-mi.) park replete with sandy beaches, sweeping sand dunes, ponds, woodlands and salt marshes. See p. 141.

Summerside (C-2)

WYATT HERITAGE PROPERTIES—Three beautifully restored properties preserve and reveal the city's history. See p. 143.

RECREATION AREAS

	MAP LOCATION	CAMPING	PICNICKING	HIKING TRAILS	BOATING	BOAT RAMP	BOAT RENTAL	FISHING	SWIMMING	PETS ON LEASH	BICYCLE TRAILS	WINTER SPORTS	VISITOR CENTER	LODGE/CABINS	FOOD SERVICE
NATIONAL PARKS *(See place listings)*															
Prince Edward Island (B-4) 26 square kilometres. Windsurfing.		•	•	•	•	•		•	•	•	•	•	•	•	•
PROVINCIAL															
Brookvale Ski Park (B-3) 175 hectares 9 km n.e. of Crapaud on Hwy. 13. Cross-country skiing, snowboarding, tubing; ski rental, toboggan rental.	❶		•							•	•	•	•		•
Brudenell River (B-5) 563 hectares 3 mi. w. of Georgetown on Hwy. 3. Golf (36 holes), horseback riding, horseshoes, lawn bowling, tennis, windsurfing; boat tours, canoe rental, interpretive programs, playground, sea kayak rental.	❷	•	•	•	•	•	•	•	•	•	•		•	•	•
Cabot Beach (B-2) 138 hectares 16 km n.w. of Kensington off Hwy. 20. Supervised swimming, windsurfing; interpretive and recreation programs, playground.	❸	•	•						•	•			•		
Campbell's Cove (A-6) 10 hectares 4.75 km w. of Elmira on Hwy. 16. Windsurfing; playground.	❹	•	•						•	•					
Cedar Dunes (B-1) 57 hectares 24.25 km s.w. of O'Leary on Hwy. 14 at West Point. Supervised swimming, windsurfing; interpretive programs, lighthouse museum, playground.	❺	•	•						•	•			•		
Green (B-2) 94 hectares on Hwy. 12. Windsurfing; playground, river beach. *(See Port Hill p. 141)*	❻	•	•		•	•			•	•			•	•	
Jacques Cartier (A-2) 11 hectares 6.5 km n. of Alberton on Cape Kildare. Supervised swimming, windsurfing; children's programs, full-time naturalist, playground.	❼	•	•						•	•					
King's Castle (B-5) 8 hectares 3.25 km e. of Murray River on Hwy. 348. Playground, riverfront.	❽		•						•	•	•				
Linkletter (B-2) 29 hectares 6.5 km w. of Summerside via Hwy. 11. Windsurfing; playground.	❾	•	•						•	•					
Lord Selkirk (C-4) 60 hectares 1.6 km e. of Eldon on Hwy. 1. Clamming, golf (nine holes), windsurfing; playground.	❿								•	•					
Mill River (B-1) 183 hectares at St. Anthony on Hwy. 136 off Hwy. 2. Cross-country skiing, golf (18 holes), tennis, windsurfing; canoe rental, interpretive programs, playground.	⓫	•	•	•	•	•	•	•	•	•	•		•	•	•
Northumberland (C-5) 30 hectares 3.25 km e. of Wood Islands Ferry Terminal on Hwy. 4. Clamming, windsurfing; playground, recreation program.	⓬	•	•						•	•					
Panmure Island (B-5) 35 hectares n. of Gaspereaux on Hwy. 347 off Hwy. 17. Supervised swimming; lighthouse tours, playground.	⓭	•	•		•				•	•					•
Pinette (C-4) 3 hectares 4.25 km s. of Eldon on Hwy. 1. Playground.	⓮		•						•	•	•				
Red Point (A-6) 7 hectares 12.75 km n.e. of Souris on Hwy. 16. Supervised swimming; playground, recreation program.	⓯	•	•						•	•					
Strathgartney (B-3) 16 hectares 21 km w. of Charlottetown on Hwy. 1. Playground.	⓰	•	•	•					•	•					
Wood Islands (C-5) 12 hectares at the Wood Islands Ferry Terminal.	⓱		•		•	•			•	•					•

Points of Interest

ALBERTON (A-1) pop. 1,115

Alberton's name was changed from Cascumpec in honor of Albert Edward, Prince of Wales, who visited the island in 1860. Just outside the community a plaque commemorates the founding of the silver fox fur industry in Alberton.

ALBERTON MUSEUM is on Hwy. 12 at 457 Church St. Furnished rooms in this restored 1878 courthouse include exhibits about harness racer Joe O'Brien, Indian relics, farm implements, photographs, a military display and items relating to the silver fox fur industry. Island genealogical research material is available. Mon.-Sat. 10-5:30, Sun. 1-5, mid-June through September 30; by appointment rest of year. Donations. Phone (902) 853-4048, or (902) 853-3372 in the off-season.

BIDEFORD (B-2) pop. 898

[SAVE] **BIDEFORD PARSONAGE MUSEUM** is at 784 Bideford Rd., Rte. 166. Originally built as a private residence for Thomas H. Pope, an accountant and a telegraph operator, this 1878 house later became a parsonage and a manse for the Methodist Church and United Church, respectively. From 1894 to 1895 it was the home of Canadian author Lucy Maud Montgomery. The restored house still has its original flooring. Guided tours are offered. Allow 30 minutes minimum. Daily 9-6, July-Aug.; 9-5, June and Sept. Admission $4; ages 7-18, $2; a family rate is available. Phone (902) 831-3133.

BONSHAW (B-3)

W.W. Irving named this settlement after Bonshaw Tower in his native Dumfries, Scotland. The scenic drive between Borden and Churchill on Hwy. 1 runs through Bonshaw, providing exceptional sightseeing by car.

CAR LIFE MUSEUM is on Hwy. 1. The museum features a collection of restored antique cars dating from 1898, farm machinery from the early 1800s and farm tractors of the early 1900s. Highlights include a 1959 Cadillac owned by Elvis Presley. Daily 9-7, July-Aug.; 10-5, May-June and Sept. 1 through mid-Sept. Admission $5; senior citizens $4.50; ages 6-14, $2. Phone (902) 675-3555 or (902) 892-1754.

CAP-EGMONT (B-1)

The Egmont Bay coastline features red sandstone cliffs with such rock formations as The Horse. Although rumors suggest that pirates' treasure might be buried nearby, fresh fish and lobsters are the cape's most commonly found riches.

[SAVE] **BOTTLE HOUSES** are at 6891 Hwy. 11 (North Cape Coastal Drive). Three fanciful buildings are made of more than 25,000 glass bottles of various shapes and sizes. Visitors can walk through a chapel, a six-gabled house and another structure—all built with bottles. The surrounding grounds feature rock gardens and more than 70 varieties of flowers. Bilingual service is available.

Allow 30 minutes minimum. Daily 9-8, July-Aug.; 10-6 in June and Sept. Admission $5; senior citizens and students with ID $4.50; ages 6-16, $2; family rate $14. Phone (902) 854-2987, or (902) 854-2254 in the off-season.

CAVENDISH (B-3) pop. 200

Cavendish was affectionately described in Lucy Maud Montgomery's popular works "Anne of Green Gables" and "Anne of Avonlea." Maud, as she preferred to be called, came to Cavendish when she was 21 months old to live with her maternal grandparents after her mother died. The author, who died in Toronto in 1942, is buried in Cavendish Cemetery.

In the waters off Cavendish rest the remains of the *Marco Polo,* a wooden sailing ship that established a world speed record in 1852 when it sailed from Liverpool, England, to Melbourne, Australia. The vessel ran aground and broke up in an 1883 gale.

The north shore is noted for its scenic beaches, many of which are operated by Prince Edward Island National Park *(see place listing p. 141).* A long-established tradition of community lobster dinners distinguishes this part of the province. The feasts pack throngs of people into community halls, particularly around New Glasgow and St. Ann.

[GEM] **AVONLEA VILLAGE OF ANNE OF GREEN GABLES** is 1.6 km (1 mi.) w. of Hwy. 13 on Hwy. 6. The schoolhouse where Lucy Maud Montgomery taught in 1896 and the church she attended are preserved on the site, which features costumed interpreters, live theater with characters from "Anne of Green Gables," musical shows, puppet shows and a chocolate factory. Visitors can attend a period county fair complete with games, a pie-eating contest and a pig race; attend four concerts; take island dance lessons; and play period children's games.

Also on the grounds are the Clifton Manse, a fishing shanty and gardens. Horse, pony and wagon rides are available. Some bilingual service is available. Allow 2 hours minimum. The 2007 schedule is daily 9-5, June 23-Aug. 31; 10-4, June 1-22 and Sept. 1-16. Admission (good for 2 days) $18.95; over 65, $16.95; ages 6-18, $12.95; family rate (two adults and all dependent children under 18) $59.95. AX, MC, VI. Phone (902) 963-3050.

GREEN GABLES HOUSE is w. of Hwy. 13 on Hwy. 6 at 8618 Cavendish Rd. Immortalized in Lucy Maud Montgomery's "Anne of Green Gables," the site is affiliated with Prince Edward Island National Park (see place listing p. 141).

The farm was the home of David Jr. and Margaret Macneill, cousins of Montgomery's grandfather. The house is furnished in late 19th-century style, and outbuildings have been restored to the Victorian period. Two walking trails are on the grounds. A visitor center features an audiovisual presentation and exhibits about Montgomery's life; bilingual guide services are available.

Daily 9-8, June 21-Aug. 25; daily 9-5, May 1-June 20 and Aug. 26-Oct. 31; by appointment rest of year. Admission $5.75; over 65, $4.75; ages 6-16, $2.75; family rate $14.50. MC, VI. Phone (902) 963-7874.

RIPLEY'S BELIEVE IT OR NOT! MUSEUM is 1.4 km (.9 mi.) w. on Hwy. 6 at Cranberry Village. Fourteen galleries with collections of unusual objects provide visitors with experiences such as standing next to a 10-foot-tall robot, seeing a shrunken head or touching a piece of the Berlin Wall. Optical illusions and videotape presentations round off the experience.

Allow 1 hour minimum. Daily 9 a.m.-10 p.m., July-Aug.; 9:30-5:30 in June and Sept. 1-16. Last admission 1 hour before closing. Admission $9.95; ages 7-15, $6.95; family rate $28.95. MC, VI. Phone (902) 963-2242, or (902) 962-2022 in the off-season.

SANDSPIT is 2 km (1.2 mi.) w. of Hwy. 13 on Hwy. 6. This amusement park offers rides and old-fashioned carnival games. Visitors can try the Cyclone roller coaster, Can-Am race cars, bumper boats, miniature golf and an antique-style carousel. Picnic facilities and a children's play area also are available. Daily 10 a.m.-11 p.m., mid-June through Labour Day. Admission is free. Rides $2-$8. Daily pass $16.95, under 48 inches tall $12.75. MC, VI. Phone (902) 963-2626.

SHINING WATERS FAMILY FUN PARK is 1.6 km (1 mi.) w. on Hwy. 6 from jct. Hwy. 13. This 30-acre amusement park has a petting farm, walking trails through a streamside forest, a Storybook Land, paddleboat rides, an inner tube slide, two waterslides and a wading pool. Food is available and picnicking is permitted. Allow 4 hours minimum. The 2007 schedule is daily 10-7, June 30-Aug. 19; 10-5, June 16-29 and Aug. 20-Sept. 3. The 2006 prices were 48 inches and taller $16, under 48 inches $14, under age 3 free. MC, VI. Phone (902) 963-3939 or (877) 963-3939.

SITE OF LUCY MAUD MONTGOMERY'S CAVENDISH HOME is on Hwy. 6, .4 km (.2 mi.) e. of jct. hwys. 6 and 13. This is the homestead where the author wrote "Anne of Green Gables" and lived for half of her life. The site captures the essence of the Cavendish Montgomery knew and loved. Although the old farmhouse and buildings no longer exist, signs on the property containing quotes from Montgomery's journal help visitors understand her life on this farm. Daily 9-7, July-Aug.; 10-5 in June and Sept. 1 through mid-Oct. Admission $3; under 16, $1. Phone (902) 963-2231.

WAX WORLD OF THE STARS is 1.4 km (.9 mi.) w. on Hwy. 6. Wax displays of the famous feature such film, TV and music personalities as Julia Roberts, Jim Carey and Stompin' Tom, as well as royal personages. Exhibits include memorabilia, sound effects and videotapes. Visitors are permitted to take photographs. Allow 1 hour minimum.

The 2007 schedule is daily 9 a.m.-9:30 p.m., July-Aug.; 9:30-5, June 9-30 and Sept. 1-16. Last admission 1 hour before closing. Phone to verify schedule. Admission $9.95; ages 7-15, $6.95; family rate $28.95. MC, VI. Phone (902) 963-3444, or (902) 962-2022 in the off season.

CHARLOTTETOWN (B-4) pop. 32,245

Settled as a French fortified post called Port La Joye in 1720, Charlottetown was named after Queen Charlotte, consort to George III, after Prince Edward Island was ceded to Britain. In 1764 it became the capital of the province, a position it retains. In 1864 the Fathers of Confederation convened in the town to consider a political-economic union that resulted in the formation of Canada 3 years later.

Presently Charlottetown is a commercial and educational center. Despite its 20th-century character, the city still evokes the feeling of a colonial seaport. Quaint sections include Great George Street and Peake's Wharf, a restored waterfront area now housing craft shops, boutiques, restaurants, a hotel and convention center. Tours of the capital and its coastline are offered daily in double-decker London buses.

Charlottetown owes much of its charm to William and Robert Harris, brothers who were major creative forces both on the island and in Canada during the late 1800s and early 1900s. Robert, the painter, is noted for his portrayal of the 1864 Confederation meetings; William, the architect, is known for his Gothic-style churches, public buildings and houses. The combined efforts of the brothers can be seen in the All Souls Chapel of St. Peter's Cathedral.

The Charlottetown Festival (see color ads starting on p. 361) is held at the Confederation Centre of the Arts (see attraction listing) from late June to early October. The festival features such original Canadian musical productions as "Anne of Green Gables—The Musical." Other productions also are performed on the Mainstage and in other theaters. Festival of the Fathers, held in early September on the waterfront, celebrates the 1864 Confederation meetings during which provincial delegates met and debated the creation of a union of all the provinces.

Harness racing at the Charlottetown Driving Park takes place seasonally; the busiest times are May through August. Phone (902) 620-4222 or (877) 620-4222.

Note: Policies concerning admittance of children to pari-mutuel betting facilities vary. Phone for information.

Greater Charlottetown Area Chamber of Commerce: 127 Kent St., P.O. Box 67, Charlottetown, PE, Canada C1A 7K2; phone (902) 628-2000.

Self-guiding tours: Walking tours with an historical focus, including waterfront and Victoria park walks, are described in a brochure called "Historic Charlottetown." Brochures cost $1 and are available at The Charlottetown Visitor Information Centre, 178 Water St.; phone (902) 368-4444. A more ambitious tour is the 177-kilometre (110-mi.) Blue Heron Scenic Drive, which begins and ends in Charlottetown and encircles all of Queens County.

Shopping areas: The Charlottetown Mall on University Avenue features numerous shops. The Confederation Court Mall, downtown on Queen Street, offers shopping opportunities in its more than 75 stores. Craft, gift and specialty shops at Peake's Wharf on the waterfront are open May through October.

ABEGWEIT SIGHTSEEING TOURS departs from various locations. Narrated trips are offered aboard double-decker London buses. The 1-hour Charlottetown Tour retraces the steps of the Fathers of Confederation. Seven-hour tours of the North Shore, the South Shore and sites from "Anne of Green Gables" include stops at several attractions along the way.

One-hour tour departs from the Confederation Centre of the Arts daily at 10:30, 11:45, 1:15, 2:30, 3:45 and 5, June-Sept. Seven-hour tours leave the Charlottetown Hotel daily at 10:30, June-Sept.; by appointment rest of year. One-hour tour $9.50; under 12, $1. Seven-hour tours $65; under 12, $32.50; prices include admission fees to visited attractions. Phone (902) 894-9966.

ARDGOWAN NATIONAL HISTORIC SITE is at jct. Mt. Edward Rd. and Palmers Ln. Ardgowan was the home of W.H. Pope, one of Prince Edward Island's Fathers of Confederation. The restored gardens illustrate the Victorian style of the 19th century. Visitors can stroll through the orchard, past the croquet lawn and along paths winding by foliage trees. Daily dawn-dusk. Free. Phone (902) 566-7050.

[SAVE] **BEACONSFIELD HISTORIC HOUSE** is at 2 Kent St. This 25-room residence was designed in 1877 for James Peake, a wealthy shipbuilder. Restored and furnished in Victorian style, the house features imported chandeliers, marble fireplaces, gas lights and central heating. The verandah and gardens offer a fine view of the harbor. Daily 10-5, June-Aug.; Mon.-Fri. noon-4, rest of year. Admission $4.25, senior citizens $3.25, under 12 free except for special events, family rate $11.75. Phone (902) 368-6603.

[GEM] [SAVE] **CONFEDERATION CENTRE OF THE ARTS** is downtown at Grafton and Queen sts. Canada's national memorial to the Fathers of Confederation, this arts and culture center is recognized for its musical theater and choral productions, art exhibitions and heritage programs. The center houses the Mainstage and several theaters, a major art gallery, a public library and an outdoor amphitheater. The MacKenzie Theatre, part of the complex, is on the corner of University Avenue and Grafton Street.

The permanent collection of the gallery includes more than 15,000 works of Canadian historical and contemporary art. Featured are works by Canada's foremost portrait artist, Robert Harris, and the original manuscript for Lucy Maud Montgomery's "Anne of Green Gables." The center also hosts the Charlottetown Festival; musical productions may be seen from late June to early October.

Art gallery open daily 9-5, mid-June through Aug. 31; daily 9-5, Sept. 1 through mid-Oct.; Wed.-Sat. 11-5, Sun. 1-5, rest of year. Musical productions are offered at the outdoor amphitheater Mon.-Sat. at noon, July-Aug. Gallery admission $4; over 65, $3; family rate $5; under 17 and students with ID free. Outdoor musical productions free. Mainstage ticket prices for the Charlottetown Festival range from $20-$58. Reservations are recommended for all ticketed events. Phone (902) 628-1864, or (800) 565-0278 for the box office. *See color ad starting on p. 361.*

[GEM] [SAVE] **FOUNDERS' HALL** is at 6 Prince St. at Confederation Landing. Built to commemorate Canada's birthplace, Founders' Hall focuses on the historic meetings of the Fathers of Confederation in 1864. Visitors don audio headsets as they move through the Time Travel Tunnel, where multimedia displays and interactive exhibits depict Canada's evolution as a country.

The Hall of Delegates includes life-size statues and holovisual portrayals of the founding fathers. The Road of the Provinces reflects each new part of the country at the time it joined Confederation.

Allow 1 hour, 30 minutes minimum. Mon.-Sat. 8-8, Sun. 8-5, late June through mid-Aug.; Mon.-Tues. 8-6, Wed. 8-5, Thurs.-Sat. 8-6, Sun. 8-5, late Aug.-early Sept.; daily 8-5, mid-Sept. through early Oct.; Mon.-Fri. 9-3:30, mid-Oct. through Oct. 31; Mon.-Fri. 10-3, in Nov. and Feb.-Apr.; daily 9-5, May-June. Phone to verify schedule. Admission $7; over 60, $6; under 13, $3.75; family rate (two adults and two children) $17, extra child $2. A combined Confederation Players Walking Tour ticket is available. MC, VI. Phone (902) 368-1864 or (800) 955-1864. *See color ad starting on p. 361.*

Confederation Players Walking Tour departs from Founders' Hall. Costumed interpreters take visitors on a guided walking tour through the streets of Charlottetown. Trips include the 1-hour Historic District of Great George Street tour, the 1-hour The Settlers tour and the 90-minute The Ghostly Realm tour.

Allow 1 hour minimum. Historic District of Great George Street tour departs daily at 11 and 1, late June through mid-Sept. (the 1 p.m. is in English and French July-Aug.). The Settlers tour departs daily at 3:30, July 1-late Aug. The Ghostly Realm tour departs Tues.-Sat. at 7:30 p.m., July 1-late Aug. Phone to verify schedules. Tours $10; under 13, $5. A $2 discount is offered when combined with admission to Founders' Hall. AX, DS, MC, VI. Phone (902) 368-1864 or (800) 955-1864.

GOVERNMENT HOUSE is at 1 Government Dr. Built in 1834, the Georgian-style house comprises two stories. On the main floor, highlights include an impressive stairway, eight Doric columns that support the gallery and, in the dining room, a mahogany table that seats 24. The second floor contains the apartments for official visitors such as the British royal family as well as the private living quarters of the Lieutenant Governor.

Guided tours are offered. Allow 30 minutes minimum. Grounds Mon.-Fri. dawn-dusk. House Mon.-Fri. 8-4, July-Aug.; closed July 1-2. Tours of house are given every 15 minutes. Donations. Phone (902) 368-5480.

PRINCE EDWARD TOURS leaves Founders' Hall at 6 Prince St. A variety of tours ranging from 3 to 7 hours is offered, using buses, vans and limousines. Seaplane tours also are offered. Several tours daily May-Oct.; phone for schedule. Driving tour fares range from $35-$60 for adults, with discounted rates for children and families; under age 4 free. All tours include admission fees. Reservations are required. AX, MC, VI. Phone (902) 566-5259 or (877) 286-6532.

PROVINCE HOUSE NATIONAL HISTORIC SITE is at Richmond and Great George sts. next to the Confederation Centre of the Arts. This was the site of meetings that led to Canada's confederation in 1867; the Provincial Legislature still meets in the building. The Confederation Chamber is a national memorial with original furnishings; restored and refurnished rooms reflect the 1860s period.

Self-guiding tours are offered, with bilingual guides on hand. The 17-minute film "A Great Dream" is shown. Open daily 8:30-6, July-Aug.; daily 8:30-5 in June and Sept. 1-second Mon. in Oct.; Mon.-Fri. 9-5, rest of year. Donations. Phone (902) 566-7626.

ST. DUNSTAN'S BASILICA is on Great George St. The basilica is the fourth Roman Catholic church to occupy this site. Built in the form of a Gothic cross, its triple spires are a Charlottetown landmark. A rose window from Germany is above the main altar. Fan vaulting and marble details highlight the church's interior. Allow 30 minutes minimum. Daily 8-4. Donations. Phone (902) 894-3486.

EAST POINT (A-6)

EAST POINT LIGHTHOUSE is off Hwy. 16 following signs, at the n.e. tip of the island. The 20-metre

(67-ft.) octagonal tower was constructed in 1867 at the point where the Gulf of St. Lawrence and Northumberland Strait meet. Interpretive displays and scenic views from the top of the tower can be seen on guided tours of the structure.

Picnicking is permitted. Allow 1 hour, 30 minutes minimum. Guided tours are offered daily 10-7:30, mid-July to mid-Aug.; 10-6, June 1 through mid-July and mid-Aug. through Aug. 31. Last tour departs 30 minutes before closing. Admission $3; senior citizens and ages 7-16, $2; family rate $8. Phone (902) 357-2106, or (902) 687-3489 in the off-season.

ELDON (B-5)

Led by Lord Selkirk, 800 Highlanders settled the area around Eldon and Belfast in 1803. Lord Selkirk Provincial Park (see Recreation Chart), on the opposite side of Hwy. 1, overlooks Orwell Bay. Skirting the coastline, the Trans-Canada Highway continues southeast to Wood Islands, where Northumberland Ferries Ltd. regularly departs for a 75-minute trip to Caribou, Nova Scotia; phone (888) 249-7245 for information. For further information about the park phone (902) 659-7221.

ELMIRA (A-6)

At its peak, the railway system linking Prince Edward Island to the mainland included 121 stations along 400 kilometres (250 mi.) of track. The circuitous route connected almost every village on the island, ending at the Elmira station. Today, the depot marks the eastern terminus of the Confederation Trail.

[SAVE] **ELMIRA RAILWAY STATION** is e. on Hwy. 16A. Containing one of the largest model railway collections in Canada, the station features exhibits that recount the history of railroading on Prince Edward Island. Photographs and maps highlight the island's rail stations with their varied architecture. Artifacts displayed include the station's telegraph equipment, fare books and schedules. Visitors can ride the PEI Miniature Railway.

Picnicking is permitted. Allow 30 minutes minimum. Daily 9-5, mid-June through Labour Day. Admission $4, students with ID $3, family rate $11. Miniature train ride $5, children $3.50, family rate $13.50. Phone (902) 357-7234, or (902) 368-6600 in the off-season.

GEORGETOWN (B-5) pop. 721

The first town built near what is now Georgetown did not survive its infancy. Soon after French immigrant Jean-Pierre de Roma and his followers built dwellings, storehouses, wharves and bridges at nearby Brudenell Point in the early 1740s, some of the settlers defected and field mice ruined the crops. In 1745 a group of New Englanders burned the settlement, causing de Roma and his family to flee to Québec.

The town, re-established across the Brudenell River from the point, has since become a primary harbor and deepwater port. The principal local industry is shipbuilding. A rock causeway links the Georgetown shore with Brudenell Island, a former 1750s Scottish cemetery.

KING'S PLAYHOUSE is on Hwy. 3 at 65 Kent St. The summer theater presents professional repertory productions in a 300-seat 1983 playhouse which is a reproduction of the town hall. The box office opens daily at 1 p.m. Play tickets $15, senior citizens and students with ID $12.50. Ticket prices and schedule vary by performance; phone ahead. Phone (902) 652-2053.

KENSINGTON (B-3) pop. 1,385

Prior to the opening of the Prince Edward Island Railway in 1870, Kensington was called Barrett's Cross after a Mrs. Barrett who ran an inn at the crossroads of what are now highways 2, 6, 20 and 101.

Kensington and Area Chamber of Commerce: P.O. Box 234, Kensington, PE, Canada C0B 1M0; phone (902) 836-3209.

DO DUCK INN PETTING FARM is on Hwy. 102. The 4-hectare (10-acre) farm is home to a large variety of baby farm animals and exotic birds. The wildlife trail affords visitors an opportunity to view the wildlife and wildflowers. Pony rides are offered for an additional fee. Allow 1 hour minimum. Daily 11-7, June 1-Labour Day. Admission $4.40; ages 4-15, $3.85. Phone (902) 836-5219.

[SAVE] **KENSINGTON WATER GARDENS** is on Hwy. 2 opposite the Royal Canadian Legion Home. Waterfalls, fountains, streams and pools adorn the flowering gardens, which include a children's area, an aerial tree-walk and small-scale reproductions of such landmarks as the Eiffel Tower and King Ludwig's Castle. A Tudor-style building houses the sound-and-light Illuminations, King Arthur's Camelot, the Tipsy-Turvey Gallery and a walk-through medieval street.

Allow 1 hour minimum. Daily 9-8, July-Aug.; 9-5 in June and Sept. Admission $7; senior citizens $6; ages 6-12, $4. Phone (902) 836-3336.

VETERANS MEMORIAL MILITARY MUSEUM is at 86 Victoria St. W., next to the Kensington Royal Canadian Legion. Dedicated to those who served during wartime, the two-story museum displays dioramas and artifacts such as diaries, arms, uniforms, medals and photographs from Prince Edward Island military personnel. Allow 30 minutes minimum. Mon.-Sat. 9:30-4:30, July 15-Sept. 15. Donations. Phone (902) 836-5400.

WOODLEIGH REPLICAS & GARDENS is 5.2 km (3 mi.) n. on Hwy. 101, then 2 km (1.2 mi.) e. on Hwy. 234. This 18-hectare (45-acre) site features 30 large-scale models of castles and cathedrals from the British Isles, set amid English country gardens. Several of the buildings contain antique furnishings, paintings and carvings, and are big enough to enter.

Paved walkways, fountains and water gardens adorn the grounds.

Picnicking is permitted. Food is available. Allow 1 hour, 30 minutes minimum. Daily 9-7, July-Aug.; 9-5 in June and Sept. Last admission 1 hour before closing. Admission $8.50; over 65, $8; ages 13-17, $7; ages 6-12, $4.50. Phone (902) 836-3401.

MALPEQUE (B-3)

Malpeque is known for the remarkable Malpeque oyster. Deemed "the tastiest oyster in the world" at a 1900 Paris exhibition, the species almost completely died out in 1917 from cancer. Miraculously, the hardy oyster overcame the disease and proliferated. One of few creatures known to have conquered cancer on its own, the Malpeque oyster has been the subject of medical research and testing for many years.

At the Malpeque wharf, visitors can arrange deep-sea and tuna fishing expeditions. Fine beach and recreation facilities are available at nearby Cabot Beach Provincial Park (see Recreation Chart).

KEIR MEMORIAL MUSEUM is on Hwy. 20 at Malpeque Corner. Housed in a 1927 Presbyterian church, the museum chronicles the Malpeque oyster harvest, early farming, fishing, shipbuilding and the community's cultural and religious life. Displays include a Victorian kitchen, a weaving room and an 1887 horse-drawn hearse. Guided tours are available. Allow 30 minutes minimum. Mon.-Fri. 9-5, Sat.-Sun. 1-5, mid-June to mid-Sept. Admission $2, under 12 free, family rate $5. Phone (902) 836-3054, or (902) 836-5613 in the off-season.

MISCOUCHE (B-2) pop. 766, elev. 18 m/59′

[SAVE] **ACADIAN MUSEUM OF PRINCE EDWARD ISLAND** is 8 km (5 mi.) w. on Hwy. 2. The museum collection includes farming, woodworking, shoemaking and blacksmith tools and many other items of Acadian life and culture. An audiovisual presentation is shown at the start of the tour. Acadian genealogical research materials are available. Allow 1 hour minimum. Daily 9:30-7, July-Aug.; Mon.-Fri. 9:30-5, Sun. 1-4, rest of year. Admission $4.50; ages 6-18, $3.50; family rate $12.50; under 6 free except during special events. Phone (902) 432-2880.

MONTAGUE (B-5) pop. 1,945

One of the largest towns on Prince Edward Island, Montague was named in the 1760s for George Brudenell, the Earl of Cardigan and Duke of Montague. Montague serves as a port and commercial center. Nearby on Hwy. 4 is Buffaloland Provincial Park, where herds of North American bison and white deer can be seen.

[SAVE] **CRUISE** *MANADA* departs from the Montague marina. Two-hour sightseeing cruises are offered aboard the *Manada* and *Manada II*. The restored fishing vessels cruise the harbor and the picturesque Montague River. Harbor seals, native sea birds and other wildlife can be seen. The tour includes sailing through working mussel farms.

Departures daily at 10, 1, 3:30 and 6:30, July-Aug.; at 2, mid-May through June 30 and in Sept. Fare $21; over 65 and students with ID $19; ages 5-13, $10.50. Reservations are recommended. Phone (902) 838-3444 or (800) 986-3444.

GARDEN OF THE GULF MUSEUM is at 564 Main St. Exhibits include 19th-century farm and cooking implements, a pictorial history exhibit and a themed display, which changes every year. Mon.-Sat. 9-5, July-Aug.; Mon.-Fri. 9-5 in June and Sept. Admission $3, under 12 free. Phone (902) 838-2467.

MONT-CARMEL (B-2) pop. 200

A handful of Acadian families who left Malpeque in 1812 founded the parish of Mont-Carmel. These settlers had to clear new land to create their village, as their ancestors were forced to do during the Acadian deportations of 1758. Many years later, in the mid-1960s, Mont-Carmel's residents used their Acadian heritage to promote tourism as a replacement for their faltering fishing trade.

LE VILLAGE DE L'ACADIE is on Hwy. 11. This reproduction of the local Acadian pioneer settlement includes a blacksmith shop, schoolhouse, church and other buildings as they appeared in 1820. Daily 9-7, early June-late Sept. Admission $4, students with ID $2, under 12 free. MC, VI. Phone (902) 854-2227.

OUR LADY OF MONT-CARMEL ACADIAN CHURCH is on Hwy. 11 just e. of jct. Hwy. 124. Overlooking the Northumberland Strait, the brick church features a Gothic interior and two steeples. The symmetrical facade and rounded vaults of the 1898 church suggest the homeland of the island's Acadian settlers. An old graveyard is next to the church. Allow 30 minutes minimum. Daily 9-6. Donations. Phone (902) 854-2789.

MOUNT STEWART (B-4) pop. 312

HILLSBOROUGH RIVER ECO-CENTRE is at 104 Main St. This center features interpretive displays about the river's importance in terms of its history, the variety of bird species and plant life it supports and its use as a transportation route. Picnicking is permitted. Food is available. Allow 30 minutes minimum. Daily 10-6, July 1-early Sept.; by appointment rest of year. Donations. Phone (902) 676-2811.

MURRAY HARBOUR (C-6) pop. 357

Murray Harbour, once known as Eskwader, or "the fishing place," by the Mi'kmaq Indians, is one of several busy seaports that line the harbor of the same name. A number of fresh seafood outlets occupy the area. Deep-sea or tuna fishing expeditions depart daily from the wharf in nearby Murray River.

CAPE BEAR LIGHTHOUSE & MARCONI MUSEUM is 6 km (4 mi.) e. on Hwy. 18. Overlooking the Northumberland Strait, the lighthouse has guided vessels since 1881. Visitors are permitted to climb to the top of the lighthouse. A replica of the Marconi station that once stood beside the lighthouse 1905-22 also is on site. The museum features maritime artifacts, audiovisual displays, archival photographs and artwork. Guided tours are available. Allow 30 minutes minimum. Daily 10-6, June-Sept. Admission $2.75; over 65, $2.50; ages 6-15, $1.50; family rate $8. VI. Phone (902) 962-2917.

LOG CABIN MUSEUM is 1 km (.6 mi.) s. on Hwy. 18A. The museum contains antiques from the late 18th century. Household items and furnishings, farm equipment and dolls dating from 1850 are displayed. An attached kitchen is outfitted with period hardware. Daily 9-6, July 1-Labour Day. Admission $2.50; ages 6-12, 50c. Phone (902) 962-2201.

NEW GLASGOW (B-3) pop. 9,432

NEW GLASGOW COUNTRY GARDENS & BUTTERFLY HOUSE is at on Hwy. 224 just e. of Hwy. 13. Twelve acres of landscaped water and flower gardens overlook the Clyde River. Nearly 2 kilometres (1.2 mi.) of trails wend past gardens, sculptures and the butterfly house. Sunday afternoons concerts are given. Allow 2 hours minimum. Daily 9-8, July 1-Labour Day; reduced hours daily Mother's Day-June 30 and day after Labour Day-second Mon. in Oct. Admission $6.50; ages 5-17, $4. AX, MC, VI. Phone (902) 964-3340.

NEW LONDON (B-3)

Lobster suppers began in 1964 when the parish of St. Ann sponsored the dinners to raise money. They have since become immensely popular and are held in several area communities. St. Ann's Church and the New London Lions Club sponsor lobster suppers from late June to late September.

SAVE **LUCY MAUD MONTGOMERY BIRTHPLACE** is off Hwy. 6 on Hwy. 20 at New London Corner. Memorabilia of the author, whose works include "Anne of Green Gables," includes the author's personal scrapbooks and her wedding dress, shoes and veil. Daily 9-5, mid-May through mid-Oct. Admission $3; ages 6-12, 50c. Phone (902) 886-2099, or (902) 836-5502 in the off-season.

NORTH CAPE (A-1)

The northernmost point on Prince Edward Island, North Cape was originally called Cap du Sauvage by explorer Jacques Cartier. In 1534 his vessel was beckoned by an Indian standing on the shore, but when it arrived the Indian was gone. Also gone are the hundreds of walrus that inhabited nearby Sea Cow Pond before they were killed by early inhabitants.

GEM **NORTH CAPE, NATURE & TECHNOLOGY IN PERFECT HARMONY** is on Hwy. 12 at the n.w. tip of the island. The site includes the 1866 North Cape Lighthouse, an interpretive center, a wind test facility and a commercial wind farm. At low tide, visitors can walk out to the longest natural rock reef in North America to view sea life and the harvesting of Irish moss. The Black Marsh Nature Trail leads through an open bog area, interpreting the area's history, local fishing and coastal ecology.

Towering windmills and turbines generate energy at the Atlantic Wind Test Site, Canada's only research center devoted to studying how wind can be harnessed as a power supply. The North Cape Interpretive Centre features an aquarium as well as displays and a videotape presentation about the Atlantic Wind Test Site. Exhibits about North Cape history and Atlantic Canada's first wind farm also are showcased.

Picnicking is permitted. Food is available. Allow 1 hour; 30 minutes minimum. Daily 9-8, July-Aug.; 10-6 in June and Sept. 1-second Mon. in Oct. Admission $5; over 55, $4; students with ID $3; family rate $13. MC, VI. Phone (902) 882-2991.

O'LEARY (A-1) pop. 860

O'Leary was named for an Irish settler who arrived on Prince Edward Island in 1837. The town's location on the island railway line made it a center for trade and industry. Fishing and agriculture—particularly potato production—are mainstays of the local economy.

PRINCE EDWARD ISLAND POTATO MUSEUM is off Hwy. 142 at Parkview Dr. and Dewar Ln. The Potato Hall of Fame is a highlight of the museum, where visitors are greeted by a 4-metre (14-ft.) sculptured spud. The importance of the potato is depicted through industry displays and a collection of farm equipment. The complex includes a community museum, a historic schoolhouse, a chapel and a log barn. Picnicking is permitted. Allow 1 hour minimum. Mon.-Sat. 9-5, Sun. 1-5, May 15-Oct. 15. Admission $5, family rate $12. Phone (902) 859-2039.

ORWELL (B-5)

Founded in the late 1700s by Scottish, Irish and British Loyalist settlers, Orwell was named for Sir Francis Orwell, England's Minister of Plantations.

A notable Orwellian was Sir Andrew Macphail, a talented man whose occupations included medicine, education, journalism and agriculture. Macphail, a physician and medical professor at McGill University in Montréal, wrote "The Master's Wife," the story of local Scottish immigrants. He also was the first editor of the *Canadian Medical Journal*. His agricultural research led him to develop new strains of potato plants, a boost for one of the province's most important crops.

Besides potatoes, strawberries are an important local crop. Also held periodically are ceilidhs (KAYlees), Old World community music festivals.

ORWELL CORNER HISTORIC VILLAGE is off Hwy. 1 following signs. Visitors to this restored small rural crossroads village of the late 1890s can tour a period home, general store, church, community hall, post office,

smithy, shingle mill and barns. The shopkeeper's home is outfitted with such items as a cast-iron stove, horsehair sofa, pump organ, 1820s loom and spinning wheels. The barns house chickens, goats, Belgian draft horses, pigs and sheep. Carts, wagons, farm machinery and tools from the late 19th century are displayed. The vintage farm equipment in the PEI Agricultural Heritage Museum helps tell the story of European agriculture on the island from the 17th century to 1950.

Food is available. Allow 1 hour minimum. Daily 9-5, mid-June to early Sept.; Sun.-Thurs. 9-5, early Sept.-early Oct.; Mon.-Fri. 9-5, mid-May to mid-June. Admission $7.50, student with ID $5; family rate (two adults and two children) $20. Phone (902) 651-8515, or (902) 368-6600 in the off season.

SIR ANDREW MACPHAIL HOMESTEAD is off Hwy. 1, behind the Orwell Corner Historic Village. Built in 1850, the 65-hectare (160-acre) homestead features the restored Macphail home, antiques, gardens, a carriage house and barn, a playhouse and many nature trails. Guided tours are available. Food is available. Allow 1 hour minimum. Wed. 11-7:30, Thurs.-Sat. 11-4:30, Sun. 11-7:30, late June-Sept. 30. Donations. Phone (902) 651-2789.

PARK CORNER (B-3)

Park Corner was settled in 1775 by James Townsend and his family. Townsend, whose descendants include Lucy Maud Montgomery, named the town after his former home in Berkshire, England.

The shore north of Park Corner is graced by gently sloping sand dunes. Sprouting from the dunes is marram grass, whose long roots mesh beneath the dunes and anchor them. While the grass can withstand the salty breezes, it cannot withstand being walked on. Once the grass has been trampled, the sand dunes shift and large holes called blowouts form, stifling the marram grass and disrupting the otherwise stable shoreline.

ANNE OF GREEN GABLES MUSEUM AT SILVER BUSH HOME is on Hwy. 20 (Blue Heron Dr.). Lucy Maud Montgomery, who wrote "Anne of Green Gables," spent some of her childhood here. The house, which was fondly described in several of her books, contains autographed first editions and other personal items. Visitors may take a carriage ride around the "lake of shining waters."

Allow 30 minutes minimum. Daily 9-5, July-Aug.; 9-4, mid-May through June 30 and Sept. 1 to mid-Oct. Admission $3; ages 6-18, $1. Carriage ride $4, children $1. Phone (902) 836-5502, (902) 886-2884 or (800) 665-2663.

LUCY MAUD MONTGOMERY HERITAGE MUSEUM is on Hwy. 20. This was the home of Senator Donald Montgomery, Lucy Maud Montgomery's grandfather. Built in 1879 and still owned by the Montgomery family, the home features many family antiques, memorabilia from the author's nine novels, parlors and sleeping rooms. Guided tours are offered. Daily 10-6, June-Sept. Admission $2.50, under 13 free. Phone (902) 886-2807.

POOLES CORNER (B-5)

POOLES CORNER VISITOR INFORMATION CENTRE is at jct. hwys. 3 and 4. The museum describes the area's cultural history through displays, photomurals and artifacts. Daily 8-7, June 22-Aug. 23; 9-4:30, June 1-21 and Aug. 24-Oct. 10. Free. Phone (902) 838-0670, or (902) 368-4444 in the off-season.

PORT HILL (B-2)

Port Hill and Bideford are neighboring towns named by English settlers for two similarly situated towns in Devonshire, England.

[SAVE] **GREEN PARK SHIPBUILDING MUSEUM AND YEO HOUSE** are on Hwy. 12 at Port Hill near Tyne Valley. The museum traces the history of shipbuilding on Prince Edward Island, where some 4,500 vessels set sail in the 19th century. Costumed guides conduct tours of the 1865 Yeo House, once home to the island's wealthiest shipbuilder. An interpretive center features historical displays about the Yeo family business. Nature trails lead to a restored shipyard.

Picnicking is permitted. Allow 2 hours minimum. Daily 9:30-5:30, July-Aug.; reduced hours in June and Sept. Admission $5, senior citizens and children $4, under 13 free except for special events, family rate $13.50. MC, VI. Phone (902) 831-7947.

PORT LA JOYE—FORT AMHERST NATIONAL HISTORIC SITE (C-4)

Port La Joye—Fort Amherst National Historic Site of Canada is west of Charlottetown on Hwy. 1, then southeast on Hwy. 19 to Rocky Point. The site consists of 89 hectares (220 acres) of woods and rolling grasslands overlooking Hillsborough Bay and Charlottetown Harbour where the French built the first European settlement in 1720.

The English took the area in 1758 and constructed Fort Amherst, which quickly fell into disrepair after 1768 when the official military presence was withdrawn; only the earthworks remain. A visitor center offers an interpretive display. Guide service and picnic facilities are available. Grounds open daily dawn-dusk. Visitor center open daily 9-5, mid-June through Aug. 31. Admission $3.50; over 65, $3; ages 6-16, $1.75; family rate $8.75. Phone (902) 675-2220, (902) 566-7050 or (902) 566-7626.

▽GEM PRINCE EDWARD ISLAND NATIONAL PARK (B-4)

Elevations in the park range from sea level to 49 metres (160 ft.). Refer to CAA/AAA maps for additional elevation information.

Prince Edward Island National Park of Canada can be reached from six entrances along hwys. 6, 13, 15 and 25. With an area of about 26 square kilometres (10 sq. mi.), the park extends 40 kilometres (25 mi.) along the island's northern shore along the Gulf of St. Lawrence. It offers long stretches of sandy beaches, sweeping sand dunes, ponds and woodlands, and salt marshes that abound with waterfowl and shore birds, including the great blue heron.

Many years of wind and wave erosion have carved the park's sand dunes, beaches and red sandstone cliffs. Greenwich, east on Hwy. 2 to Hwy. 313 at St. Peters, shelters a rare and relatively undisturbed parabolic dune, a migrating wave of sand that has swept through forests, leaving skeletal trees in its wake. Sharp-eyed hikers may glimpse a variety of wildlife throughout the park, including the red fox.

General Information and Activities

The park is open daily. Camping is available at Cavendish mid-May to mid-September, or at Stanhope or Robinsons Island mid-June through Labour Day; there is a camping fee. Hiking trails traverse the park. Vehicles (including motorcycles and minibikes) must stay on designated roadways and are not allowed on the sand dunes, beaches or trails.

Prince Edward Island's north shore offers ample opportunities for water sports in July and August. Lifeguards supervise beaches at Brackley, Cavendish, Greenwich, North Rustico, Ross' Lane and Stanhope Lane. Anglers can charter boats at nearby harbors for deep-sea fishing. A national park fishing license is required to fish in the ponds and streams within the park. A number of small lakes and ponds have brook trout, but motorboats are not permitted on these ponds.

The park also has facilities for golf and tennis. A 1-metre-wide (3-ft.) paved shoulder along the Gulf Shore Parkway is a scenic route for bicyclists; an 8-kilometre (5-mi.) bicycling and hiking trail is located near the Cavendish campground; and a 5-kilometre (3-mi.) cycling trail is near the Dalvay entrance gate. A regular schedule of interpretive activities is offered daily July through August.

Two visitor centers offer park information daily mid-June to mid-October—one at the intersection of hwys. 6 and 13, the second at the intersection of hwys. 15 and 6. The Greenwich Interpretive Centre, at the intersection of hwys. 2 and 313, includes displays about the peninsula's fragile ecosystem and archeological significance. *See Recreation Chart and the AAA/CAA Eastern Canada CampBook.*

ADMISSION early June-Labour Day $5; senior citizens $4.25; ages 6-16, $2.50; family rate $12.50. Admission is free, rest of year.

PETS are allowed in most areas except as posted. Animals must be leashed or otherwise physically restrained at all times and are not permitted at beaches or in public buildings.

ADDRESS inquiries to Parks Canada, 2 Palmers Ln., Charlottetown, PE, Canada C1A 5V6. Phone (902) 566-7050.

RUSTICO (B-3)

Trail rides through the fields and woods bordering scenic Rustico Bay are offered by area outfitters mid-June through Labour Day.

FARMERS' BANK OF RUSTICO MUSEUM AND DOUCET HOUSE is Hwy. 243 next to St. Augustine's Church. Opened in 1864 and operated until 1894, the bank was important in the establishment of credit unions in Canada. The small museum traces the history of Acadians in this area. The Doucet House was built about 1764 and may be the oldest dwelling in the province. Allow 1 hour minimum. Mon.-Fri. 9:30-5:30, Sun. 1-5:30. Admission $4; over 65 $3; ages 12-17, $2; ages 5-11, $1. Phone (902) 963-3168.

SOURIS (B-6) pop. 1,248

Ships bringing provisions to Prince Edward Island during its early settlement also brought mice, which proliferated at such an amazing rate that the French settlers named their town after them. Souris also gained recognition through American playwright Elmer Harris, who used the town as the setting for his play "Johnny Belinda," which ran for 320 consecutive performances in New York.

Some of the island's finest white sand beaches lie between Souris and Bothwell. In town, the beach is accessible from a small park off Hwy. 2. Red Point Provincial Park *(see Recreation Chart)* also has an excellent beach and developed recreational facilities.

Local waters support industry as well as recreation. Souris has a large fishing and lobster industry. Ferry service to Québec's Magdalen Islands in the Gulf of St. Lawrence is available April through January; phone Traversier C.T.M.A. Ferry at (902) 687-2181, or (888) 986-3278 in Canada.

[SAVE] **BASIN HEAD FISHERIES MUSEUM** is 12 km (8 mi.) e. on Hwy. 16. On a bluff overlooking the Northumberland Straight, the museum tells the story of Prince Edward Island's historic inshore fishery. The ways of inshore fishing are reflected in boat gear, photographs and dioramas. A boardwalk offers access to a white "singing" sands beach and playground.

Food and picnic areas are available. Allow 1 hour minimum. Museum open daily 9-5, June 1-late Sept. Admission $4, students with ID $3.50, family rate $11.50. Phone (902) 357-7233, or (902) 368-6600 in the off-season.

STANLEY BRIDGE (B-3)

Stanley Bridge, a resort community southwest of Cavendish, is noted for its picturesque inlets and fine inland fishing on the Stanley and Trout rivers. Tuna boat charters can be arranged at the Stanley Bridge wharf.

STANLEY BRIDGE MARINE AQUARIUM AND MANOR OF BIRDS is off Hwy. 6 at 32 Campbellton Rd. The facility features an aquarium with native fish; Irish moss and interpretive shellfish exhibits; and mounted fur-bearing animals, butterflies and more than 700 birds. Food is available. Allow 30 minutes minimum. Daily 9:30-8, June-Oct. The 2006 admission was $5.10; ages 6-14, $3.40. Phone to verify prices. MC, VI. Phone (902) 886-3355.

SUMMERSIDE (B-2) pop. 14,654

Often referred to as Prince Edward Island's western capital, Summerside lies on the narrow strip of land that connects Prince and Queens counties. Supposedly warmer than its neighboring towns on the north shore, the city is considered to be on the "summer side" of the island.

Summerside boasts neat residential streets lined with stately wood-frame houses that resemble chateaus. The town is dependent on fishing, agriculture and tourism. Its public wharf serves the large oceangoing vessels that carry Prince Edward Island potatoes to ports worldwide.

Lady Slipper Drive, the scenic 288-kilometre (179-mi.) coastal drive of Prince County, officially begins in Summerside. The Lady Slipper Visitor Information Centre in Wilmot, 2 kilometres (1.2 mi.) east of Summerside on Hwy. 1A, has interpretive displays highlighting the region's Acadian culture.

Greater Summerside Chamber of Commerce: 263 Harbour Dr., Suite 10, Summerside, PE, Canada C1N 5P1; phone (902) 436-9651.

Shopping areas: Spinnakers Landing, on the waterfront, features several shops, boutiques, entertainment and eateries. Also on the waterfront are Waterfront Place and Summerside Mall. County Fair Mall is nearby.

[SAVE] **EPTEK ART & CULTURE CENTRE** is at 130 Harbour Dr. on the waterfront. History and the fine arts are the focus of changing exhibits originating in local and other Canadian communities. Allow 30 minutes minimum. Mon.-Sat. 9-6, Sun. noon-6, July-Aug; Tues.-Fri. 10-4, Sun. noon-4, rest of year. Admission $4, students with ID $3, family rate $11. Phone (902) 888-8373.

INTERNATIONAL FOX MUSEUM & HALL OF FAME is at 286 Fitzroy St. In the Holman Homestead, once the residence of a Summerside mercantile magnate, the museum traces the attempts to breed foxes in captivity. Photographs, traps and trophies of champion foxes are displayed. The Hall of Fame honors the pioneers of fox farming, once the island's main industry. The gardens and grounds surrounding the museum also are noteworthy. Mon.-Fri. 10-5, May-Sept. Donations. Phone (902) 436-2400.

PRINCE EDWARD ISLAND SPORTS HALL OF FAME AND MUSEUM is at 124 Harbour Dr. The facility features displays and information about the accomplishments of the many men and women who have been inducted into the Hall of Fame. Allow 30 minutes minimum. Daily 10-6, June 1 through mid-Sept.; by appointment rest of year. Donations. Phone (902) 436-0423.

WYATT HERITAGE PROPERTIES, at 75-85 Spring St., and 205 Prince St., is comprised of three buildings. The Mac-Naught History Centre and Archives (75 Spring St.) is a genealogical resource that also features changing historical exhibits. The 1867 Wyatt House Museum (85 Spring St.), residence of the late Wanda Lefurgey Wyatt, has been restored and displays many historically significant artifacts. The Lefurgey Cultural Centre (205 Prince St.), an 1867 shipbuilder's house, now serves as an arts and crafts center. Guided and self-guiding tours give visitors a glimpse into the life of the Lefurgey and Wyatt families.

Allow 1 hour minimum. History center and archives open Tues. 10-9, Wed.-Sat. 10-5, all year. Wyatt house open Mon.-Sat. 10-5, June 1-late Sept.; by appointment rest of year. Cultural center open year-round; phone for schedule. Admission $5.50; under 18, $4.50. MC, VI. Phone (902) 432-1327.

TIGNISH (A-1) pop. 831

Tignish was founded in 1799 by eight Acadian families who came by open boat from Malpeque. Twelve years later they were joined by Irish settlers. The community's first priest noted that the blending of French and English language and culture did not go easily at first, though the two groups eventually forged a peaceful coexistence.

A convent was built in 1868 for the sisters of the Congregation de Notre Dame, who came from Montréal to teach. The private girls' school was opened to the public 50 years later and continued to serve as an educational facility until 1966. Scholars debate about the origin of the town's name, attributing it to both Mi'kmaq and Irish sources.

ST. SIMON AND ST. JUDE CATHOLIC CHURCH is at Church and Maple sts. The red brick church houses the Tignish Pipe Organ, built in 1882 by Louis Mitchell. The 1,118-pipe organ has been used to help celebrate many of Tignish's historical events, including its bicentennial in 1999. Daily 8-7. Free. Phone (902) 882-2049 for organ recital times.

WEST POINT (B-1)

WEST POINT LIGHTHOUSE MUSEUM is off Hwy. 14 at 364 Cedar Dunes Park Rd. Built in 1875, the light was manned continuously until 1963. The beacon and its attached dwelling have been restored, and a museum includes exhibits and memorabilia documenting the history of the island's lighthouses. One room on the second floor is an overnight rental. Food is available. Museum open daily 8-8, late May-late Sept. Admission $2.50; senior citizens $2; under 12, $1.50; family rate $7. Phone (902) 859-3605 or (800) 764-6854.

WOODSTOCK (B-1) pop. 500

MILL RIVER FUN PARK is 1 km (.6 mi.) w. of Hwy. 136 on Hwy. 2. The park offers adult and children's waterslides, other water rides, bumper boats and miniature golf. Picnicking is permitted. Daily 11-7, late June-late Aug. Admission $9, under 6 free. MC, VI. Phone (902) 859-3915.

 **Choose Well.
AAA/CAA Approved.**

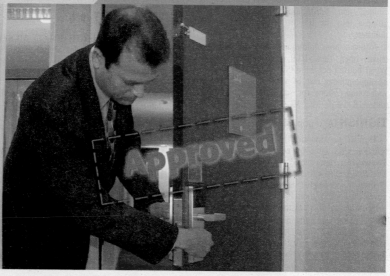

Discover the secret to choosing well, every time …
AAA/CAA Approved. After all, AAA's high standards are based
on member input and feedback.

From simple motels to luxury resorts, rest assured. AAA/CAA's
professional evaluators have checked for cleanliness, service,
and value — qualities most important to members.

Use the ratings of one to five Diamonds to choose your
AAA/CAA Approved accommodations from the TourBook®,
in print and on aaa.com.

For more information on **AAA/CAA
Diamond Ratings,** turn to page 20-21
or visit <u>aaa.com/Diamonds</u>.

Québec

Whale Watching
Pods of graceful whales cruise the bountiful waters of the St. Lawrence estuary

Gallantly Guarding Old Québec
Venerable walls protect North America's only fortified city

Secluded Gaspé Peninsula
Rugged shoreline gives way to quaint fishing villages nestled beneath coastal cliffs

Île de Montréal
Framed by towering Mont-Royal, Québec's largest city lies at the confluence of the St. Lawrence and Outaouais rivers

Head for the Mountains
Grab your skis and swoosh down the powder-covered hills of Québec's vast Laurentian Mountains

Île-aux-Coudres / © MTOQ
Marc Archambault

beautiful in any language

Jacques Cartier National Park, Québec / © Ministère du Tourisme du Québec / Heiko Wittenborn

"Parlez-vous français?"

In Québec, the answer will most likely be a resounding "Oui!" But even if your French is limited to menu items, don't worry. Many Québécers can converse in English, especially in Montréal and Québec City. Besides, visitors don't need to speak a word of French to enjoy what Canada's largest province has to offer.

For instance, even if you don't know that *château* means castle, one look at medieval-style Château Frontenac's turrets soaring above Québec City's historic Lower Town will give you an idea. Adjacent to the imposing 19th-century hotel is Dufferin Terrace, which commands a view of the St. Lawrence River that's *magnifique*.

Being bilingual isn't necessary to appreciate the brightly colored *fleurs* blossoming at the Botanical Garden of Montréal, or to be impressed by the sleek, ultramodern stadium and tower at that city's *Parc Olympique*, site of the 1976 Summer Olympics.

Skiers enjoy the *neige* of the Laurentian Highlands whether or not they know the Gallic word for snow, and a crunchy *pomme* from an orchard in the rustic Eastern Townships region tastes delicious no matter what it's named.

Can't recall an appropriate French adjective to describe the majestic headlands rising from the sea at Forillon National Park? A simple "wow" will suffice. All you really need to remember is that Québec means beautiful in any language.

Je me souviens. The provincial motto is a statement of pride: "I remember who I am."

And just "who" is Québec? Four centuries after Samuel de Champlain established la Nouvelle France, "the New France," near the present-day city of Québec, Canada's largest province remains warm and friendly to visitors despite its separatist ideology, evolved from a rich and storied French heritage.

Reflecting on folklore and traditions—from the days of the Indians and Inuits, who migrated from Asia thousands of years ago, to the modern era—are such revered institutions as Gatineau's Canadian Museum of Civilization and Montréal's McCord Museum of Canadian History. Exhibits trace successive periods of migration, native settlement, exploration, fur trading and immigration.

Of these influences, Québec remains most true to its French roots and stands today as a separate province that regulates its own social structures, collects its own taxes and staunchly defends its culture.

As a result, an interesting chemistry brews in the province. Although a French perspective clearly predominates, native traditions blend with other European and North American conventions, resulting in a bubbling cauldron of creative energy.

Strikingly Constructed

To see firsthand what are arguably the province's most stunning examples, look to its churches and sanctuaries. An awe-inspiring, neo-Gothic edifice, Montréal's Basilica of Notre-Dame took 5 years to build and houses a 10-bell carillon, massive pipe organ and 11,240-kilogram (12-ton) bell. Romanesque and Gothic features at the striking Basilica of Ste-Anne-de-Beaupré in Ste-Anne-de-Beaupré include five naves, splendid mosaics and hundreds of stained-glass panels. An octagonal design lends to the appeal of the Shrine of Notre-Dame-du-Cap in Cap-de-la-Madeleine.

Also remarkable is Québec's main Parliament Building. Nearly 2 dozen bronze statues of figures who had a profound impact on provincial history look out from cozy niches in the facade of the 1886 Second Empire-style building, which has four wings and an impressive fountain at its main entrance.

Jacques Cartier claims the area around the Gulf of St. Lawrence for King François I of France.
1534

© Bettmann/Corbis

Sir Wilfrid Laurier becomes Canada's first French-Canadian prime minister.
1896

Library of Congress

Samuel de Champlain establishes the first European settlement near present-day Québec City.
1608

Library of Congress

1759
Great Britain gains control of New France; formalized under the 1763 Treaty of Paris.

1936
Canada's French-language broadcasting network, Société Radio-Canada, is founded.

Québec Historical Timeline

As landscape architecture goes, Mont-Royal Park—designed by Frederick Law Olmsted, the mind behind New York's Central Park—skillfully blends form and function. The use of exaggerated vegetation emphasizes the mountainous topography and completes the illusion of greater height.

Colorful visions inspire horticulturists who tend beautiful gardens. More than 21,000 plant varieties flourish in the breathtaking Botanical Garden of Montréal. At the confluence of the Mitis and St. Lawrence rivers in Grand-Métis, Reford Gardens is known for its artfully arranged primroses and blue poppies. During summer, National Battlefields Park maintains the multiflorous Jeanne-d'Arc Garden.

Aesthetically Fruitful

On a considerably smaller scale, painters, sketchers and sculptors unleash their flights of fancy in various media. Many splendid works by Canadian artists are among those at the Montréal Museum of Contemporary Art. An important collection of Canadian painting resides at the Montréal Museum of Fine Arts. To appreciate Québécois art from the French Colonial period to the present, meander amid the extensive collections at National Museum of Fine Arts of Québec in the capital city.

Native crafts are the focus not only of the Québec Handicraft Show in Montréal, but also of such facilities as Museum of the Early Canadians in St-Jean-Port-Joli.

Music, too, is central to the lives of many Québécers. Born in Charlemagne, pop superstar Céline Dion has lined scores of mantels with GRAMMYs and other prestigious awards. Melodic sounds fill the air at such Montréal events as the International Music Competition, the Francofolies de Montréal Song Festival and the Montréal Jazz Festival, which welcomes some of the world's most renowned performers to showcase their talent.

From the fertile imaginations of its residents throughout the years, Québec metaphorically remembers who it is: a lovely land of people with a contagious *joie de vivre* you'd do well to catch.

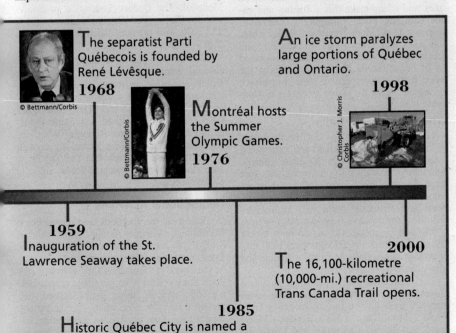

The separatist Parti Québecois is founded by René Lévêsque.
1968
© Bettmann/Corbis

© Bettmann/Corbis

Montréal hosts the Summer Olympic Games.
1976

An ice storm paralyzes large portions of Québec and Ontario.
1998

© Christopher J. Morris Corbis

1959
Inauguration of the St. Lawrence Seaway takes place.

2000
The 16,100-kilometre (10,000-mi.) recreational Trans Canada Trail opens.

1985
Historic Québec City is named a UNESCO World Heritage Treasure.

Recreation

Whatever recreational favorite or new pastime you wish to pursue, it's possible in Québec—from wildlife viewing to high-energy athletic activities.

Montréal and Québec City offer large parks where you can **hike, bicycle, swim, toboggan** or **cross-country ski.** Montréal's Parc du Mont-Royal has a network of bike paths, and in the winter Parc des Îles is perfect for cross-country skiing and **ice skating.** *Route Verte* is an accessible, extensive and expanding provincial network of bike paths. Québec City's Plains of Abraham (Battlefields Park) offers excellent cross-country skiing and **snowshoeing.**

More than 75 percent of Québec is still wild and unspoiled, and the 38 plus parks and wildlife reserves within the province conserve this heritage. Their terrain varies from craggy peaks at Mont-Tremblant to nearly impenetrable forests in La Mauricie National Park of Canada. Some 6,000 kilometres (3,750 mi.) of coastline allow you to explore such treasures as the Gaspé Peninsula, Saguenay Fjord's marine park and the innumerable lakes and rivers of Réserve faunique la Vérendrye.

At 13,615 square kilometres (5,257 sq. mi.), Réserve faunique la Vérendrye is the province's largest preserve. More than 4,000 lakes and rivers make this a **fishing** and **canoe camping** Eden. **Camping** is marvelous year-round in Mont-Tremblant Park, where 500 lakes and seven rivers lure anglers, and scenic valleys, waterfalls and the pine-scented air of dense forests help to restore even the most frazzled perspective. And **horseback riding** on one of the stable mounts is a whinnying idea.

When Jack Frost Calls

Huts and relay stations dot the thousands of kilometres of well-marked and maintained cross-country ski trails in 30 major centers. And there's no excuse for not trying your foot at it, because many areas offer equipment rental and instruction. Gatineau, Mont-Sainte-Anne and Gaspésie parks and Laurentides Wildlife Reserve have networks ranging from 150 to 300 kilometres (95 to 185 mi.). Linear Park is a network of 200 kilometres (130 mi.) of well-groomed trails between St-Jérôme and Mont-Laurier.

The Laurentian and Appalachian mountain ranges beckon **downhill skiers** with more than 800 trails and 80 resorts, including Gray Rocks, Mont-Blanc, Mont-Gabriel, Mont-Saint-Sauveur, Ski Chantecler and Tremblant. Only minutes from Québec City are the 50 trails of Mont-Sainte-Anne and the night-skiing facilities of Stoneham. The Charlevoix region and Appalachian range also offer plenty of opportunities for both downhill and cross-country ski adventures.

Thinking of **snowboarding?** Remember to call ahead, as snowboards still are not allowed at some ski areas. For those with the sure footing of a mountain goat, there's **ice climbing** on the Sugarloaf of Montmorency Falls in Québec city. Or, if you're more of a traditionalist, hop on a **dog sled** at such places as the Laurentides and on the floes off Îles-de-la-Madeleine.

The Mobile Society

Joseph-Armand Bombardier of Québec invented the **snowmobile** in 1922 and marketed the single-passenger Ski-Doo in 1960—and mobile mania has been riding rampant over the province ever since. Each winter visitors and residents hit 33,500 kilometres (20,800 mi.) of natural and man-made routes—old logging roads, abandoned railway tracks, frozen rivers and lakes. Along the marked and maintained trails are service and food areas, lodgings and heated huts. Popular access points for snowmobiling along portions of the 16,100-kilometre (1,005-mi.) Trans Canada Trail include Gatineau, Mont-Laurier and Montréal. The Québec Federation of Snowmobile Clubs (FCMQ) in Montréal, (514) 252-3076, will provide materials to help you plan your trip.

Want to stay put for a spell? Each winter colorful temporary villages of **ice fishing** shacks spring up on frozen lakes and rivers, and some of these are available for rent. Spots include Saint-Pierre and Deux-Montagnes lakes, the Saguenay Fjord and Sainte-Anne-de-la-Pérade, near Trois-Rivières. What are you going to catch? Have a creel big enough for redfish, cod and turbot in the Saguenay, and rainbow and speckled trout in the Laurentians.

Recreational Activities

Throughout the TourBook, you may notice a Recreational Activities heading with bulleted listings of recreation-oriented establishments listed underneath. Similar operations also may be mentioned in Destination City recreation sections. Since normal AAA inspection criteria cannot be applied, these establishments are presented only for information. Age, height and weight restrictions may apply. Reservations often are recommended and sometimes are required. Addresses and/or phone numbers are provided so visitors can contact the attraction for additional information.

Fast Facts

POPULATION: 7,237,479.

AREA: 1,667,926 sq km (643,986 sq mi); ranks 2nd.

CAPITAL: Québec.

HIGHEST POINT: 1,622 m/5,321 ft., Mont-d'Iberville.

LOWEST POINT: Sea level, Gulf of St Lawrence.

TIME ZONE(S): Eastern. DST in Canada begins in the early morning of the first Sunday in April and ends in the early morning of the last Sunday in October.

MINIMUM AGE FOR UNRESTRICTED DRIVER'S LICENSE: 18 years and 8 months.

MINIMUM AGE FOR GAMBLING: 18.

SEAT BELT/CHILD RESTRAINT LAWS: Seat belts are required for driver and all passengers. Children whose seated height is under 63 centimeters (25 inches) are required to be in a child restraint.

HELMETS FOR MOTORCYCLISTS: Required.

RADAR DETECTORS: Not permitted.

FIREARMS LAWS: By federal law, all nonresidents entering Canada with a firearm must declare their weapon in writing and pay a fee of $25 (Canadian). Contact the Canadian Firearms Centre at (800) 731-4000 to receive a declaration form or for additional information.

HOLIDAYS: Jan. 1; Good Friday; Easter Mon.; Victoria Day, May 24 (if a Mon.) or the closest prior Mon.; St-Jean Baptiste Day, June 24; Canada Day, July 1; Labour Day, Sept. (1st Mon.); Thanksgiving, Oct. (2nd Mon.); Christmas, Dec. 25.

TAXES: The Federal general sales tax is 6 percent. Québec's provincial sales tax is 7.5 percent on goods and services.

INFORMATION CENTERS: Travel information is distributed free daily at provincial information centers in Dégelis, Lacolle, Montréal, Québec, Rigaud, Rivière-Beaudette and Stanstead. The Montréal and Québec offices, which are open year-round, are closed Jan. 1 and Dec. 25. **Note:** Schedules are subject to change; phone Tourisme Québec at (877) 266-5687 to confirm schedules.

The Montréal office is open 8:30-7:30, June 1-Labour Day; 9-6, rest of year. The Québec offices are open daily 8:30-7:30, June 24 or the closest prior Monday-Labour Day; 9-5, rest of year. The Lacolle, Rigaud, and Rivière-Beaudette offices are open 9-7, June 24 or the closest prior Monday-Labour Day; 9-5, day after Labour Day-Oct. 31 and Apr. 1 to June 24 or the closest prior Monday. Dégelis is open 8-7, June 24 or the closest prior Monday-Labour Day; 8-4, day after Labour Day to second Mon. in Oct., and May 24 or the closest prior Monday to June 24 or the closest prior Monday. Stanstead is open daily 9-7, June 24 or the closest prior Monday-Labour Day; 9-5, day after Labour Day to second Mon. in Oct., and May 24 or the closest prior Monday, to June 24 or the closest prior Monday.

FURTHER INFORMATION FOR VISITORS:
Tourisme Québec
900 Renee Levesque
Montréal, QC, Canada G1R 2B5
(800) 482-2433

RECREATION INFORMATION:
SÉPAQ
Place de la Cite
Tour Cominar
2640 Boulevard Laurier, Suite 250
Québec, QC, Canada G1V 5C2
(418) 890-6527
(800) 665-6527

ALCOHOL CONSUMPTION: Legal age 18.

Québec Temperature Averages Maximum/Minimum

From the records of The Weather Channel Interactive, Inc. Temperatures in Celsius.

	JAN	FEB	MAR	APR	MAY	JUN	JUL	AUG	SEP	OCT	NOV	DEC
Gaspé	-7 / -17	-6 / -17	-1 / -11	5 / -3	12 / 2	20 / 8	25 / 12	23 / 10	19 / 6	12 / 1	3 / -5	-4 / -13
Montréal	-5 / -15	-4 / -13	2 / -6	10 / 1	18 / 8	24 / 14	26 / 17	25 / 16	20 / 11	13 / 5	5 / -1	-4 / -10
Québec	-7 / -15	-6 / -14	0 / -8	7 / -1	16 / 6	22 / 12	25 / 15	24 / 14	18 / 10	11 / 4	3 / -3	-4 / -11

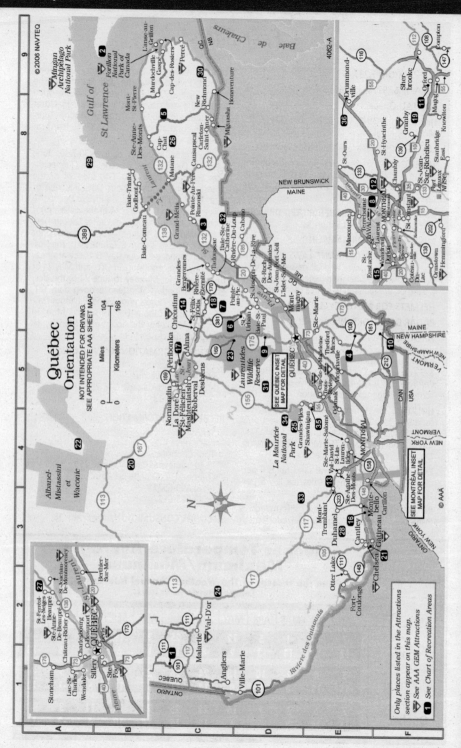

© 2006 NAVTEQ

4062-A

Québec
Orientation

NOT INTENDED FOR DRIVING.
SEE APPROPRIATE AAA SHEET MAP.

Miles   104
Kilometers   166

Only places listed in the Attractions
section appear on this map.

● See AAA GEM Attractions

1 See Chart of Recreation Areas

© AAA

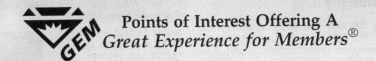

Points of Interest Offering A
Great Experience for Members®

Beauport (D-5)

MONTMORENCY FALLS PARK—The promontory offers a spectacular view of Niagara Falls' big brother. See p. 221.

Cap-de-la-Madeleine (D-4)

SHRINE OF NOTRE-DAME-DU-CAP—Modern architecture inspires traditional pilgrimages. See p. 161.

Chambly (E-8)

FORT CHAMBLY NATIONAL HISTORIC SITE OF CANADA—Visitors can walk the grounds and hallways where French and British troops have held post since 1655. See p. 195.

Chelsea (E-3)

GATINEAU PARK—The summer and winter outdoor opportunities make this extensive and scenic park a must-see for visitors to the Gatineau area. See p. 162.

Chicoutimi (C-6)

SAGUENAY CRUISES—The diesel-powered *Bagotville* and *Marjolaine II* explore the Saguenay River and fjord. See p. 163.

Forillon National Park of Canada (B-9)

FORILLON NATIONAL PARK OF CANADA—Spectacular scenery, wildlife from moose to mink, and abundant recreational opportunities make this a "must-visit." See p. 165.

Fort Lennox National Historic Site of Canada (F-8)

FORT LENNOX NATIONAL HISTORIC SITE OF CANADA—There have been fortifications on this site since 1759. See p. 165.

Gatineau (E-3)

CANADIAN MUSEUM OF CIVILIZATION—Located directly across the river from the Parliament Buildings in Ottawa, this museum focuses on Canada's history from the continent's prehistoric beginnings to present day. See p. 166.

Granby (E-8)

GRANBY ZOO—More than 800 animals representing some 175 species from five continents call this zoo home. See p. 167.

Grand-Métis (B-7)

REFORD GARDENS—Paths lead through formal and natural gardens that display some 3,000 species of trees, shrubs and flowers. See p. 167.

Hemmingford (F-7)

PARK SAFARI—A zoo, water rides and shows can all be found at this family-oriented park. See p. 168.

La Mauricie National Park of Canada (D-4)

LA MAURICIE NATIONAL PARK OF CANADA—This scenic park's chains of narrow lakes, pristine forests, trails and plentiful wildlife offer year-round recreational opportunities. See p. 169.

Laval (C-5)

COSMODÔME—The fun interactive exhibits exploring space science and technology will allow your imagination to go where it has never gone before. See p. 196.

Lévis (B-6)

LÉVIS FORTS NATIONAL HISTORIC SITE OF CANADA—The beautifully restored Fort No. 1 was built to protect Québec City from invasion by the United States. See p. 221.

Miguasha (C-8)

MIGUASHA NATIONAL PARK—You'll "dig" the fossils displayed at this a UNESCO World Heritage Site. See p. 171.

Mingan Archipelago National Park Reserve of Canada (A-9)

MINGAN ARCHIPELAGO NATIONAL PARK RESERVE OF CANADA—View spectacular rock formations while you kayak or dive. See p. 171.

Montmagny (D-6)

GROSSE ÎLE AND THE IRISH MEMORIAL NATIONAL HISTORIC SITE OF CANADA—For 105 years immigrants passed through this port of entry. See p. 172.

Montréal (B-6)

BASILICA OF NOTRE-DAME—One of the largest in North America, this church is home to various stained-glass windows depicting religious scenes. See p. 185.

BOTANICAL GARDEN OF MONTRÉAL—This 75-hectare (180-acre) garden contains more than 22, 000 varieties of plants. See p. 181.

CHÂTEAU RAMEZAY MUSEUM—Travel through time in the oldest private museum in Québec. See p. 185.

LACHINE RAPIDS JET BOAT TOURS—Flatbottom boats negotiate whirlpools and high waves as visitors get a chance to travel up the St. Lawrence River through the historic Lachine Rapids, the once-unnavigable waterway that accounted for Montréal's strategic location. See p. 188.

McCORD MUSEUM OF CANADIAN HISTORY—This museum offers exhibits pertaining to Canada's history from the 18th century to the present. See p. 184.

MONTRÉAL BIODÔME—Travel from the Poles to the Equator without jet lag. See p. 186.

MONT-ROYAL PARK—This park was designed by American landscape architect Frederick Law Olmsted and contains trails for walking and skiing. See p. 184.

MONTRÉAL MUSEUM OF FINE ARTS—Founded in 1860, this is Canada's oldest art museum. See p. 184.

THE OLD FORT AND STEWART MUSEUM—The fort was erected 1820-24 by the order of the Duke of Wellington to protect the city and defend the St. Lawrence against possible U.S. aggression. See p. 184.

OLD MONTRÉAL—A walking tour along the cobblestone streets of this 18th-century slice of Nouveau France is a must-do. See p. 185.

OLYMPIC PARK—The ancient Greeks would envy this facility. See p. 186.

POINTE-À-CALLIÈRE, MONTRÉAL MUSEUM OF ARCHAEOLOGY AND HISTORY—Take a trip through the history of Montréal. See p. 186.

ST. JOSEPH'S ORATORY—The dimensions are impressive: 105 metres (355 feet) long, 65 metres (213 feet) wide, and 60 metres (197 feet) high. See p. 187.

Percé (B-9)

ÎLE BONAVENTURE AND PERCÉ ROCK NATIONAL PARK—This wildfowl sanctuary shelters a colony of 120,000 gannets and other species, including puffins, guillemots and cormorants. See p. 200.

Pointe-au-Père (C-7)

RIMOUSKI MARINE MUSEUM—The view from the lighthouse is superb. See p. 200.

Québec (D-5)

ARTILLERY PARK NATIONAL HISTORIC SITE OF CANADA—Strategically built within Porte Saint-Jean, the park has been used for an array of military purposes since the city's settlement. See p. 208.

THE CITADEL—This is the official residence of the governor-general of Canada and remains the largest fortification in North America garrisoned regularly by troops. See p. 209.

DUFFERIN TERRACE—The terrace is linked to Battlefield Park by the Promenade des Gouverneurs, a 670-metre (2,198-ft.) walk anchored by cliffs overlooking the St. Lawrence River. See p. 209.

HOTEL-DIEU AUGUSTINES MUSEUM—This is the site of North America's oldest hospital. See p. 210.

LAURENTIDES WILDLIFE RESERVE—Wooded uplands, rivers, streams and mountains make up this vast reserve where moose, beavers and bears can be seen. See p. 211.

MUSEUM OF CIVILIZATION—Explore the human experience here. See p. 210.

MUSEUM OF FRENCH AMERICA—Housed in an old university boarding school, the museum's collections include items acquired by priests during their travels throughout Europe and Canada in the 19th century. See p. 210.

NATIONAL BATTLEFIELDS PARK—The park encompasses the Plains of Abraham, where the armies of Gen. James Wolf and the Marquis de Montcalm fought in 1759. An interpretative center with a multimedia presentation, exhibits and tablets explain the area's history. See p. 212.

NATIONAL MUSEUM OF FINE ARTS OF QUÉBEC—Highlights of this museum chronicle the province's art from the French Colonial period to the present. See p. 212.

OUR LADY OF VICTORY CHURCH—This 1688 church, built on the foundation of Samuel de Champlain's trading post, houses commemorative paintings and tablets. See p. 213.

PARLIAMENT BUILDINGS—Monuments of historical figures can be seen throughout the grounds of the buildings. See p. 212.

PLACE-ROYALE—This area in lower town was the 1608 site of Samuel de Champlain's French colonization of North America. See p. 212.

QUÉBEC CITY CRUISES—Ninety-minute harbor cruises offer sightseeing tours of the historic city. See p. 214.

Rivière-Éternité (C-6)

SAGUENAY-ST. LAWRENCE MARINE PARK—Spectacular scenery and native whales await visitors. See p. 224.

Roberval (C-4)

VAL-JALBERT HISTORIC VILLAGE—This historic area preserves the remains of Val-Jalbert, a once thriving early 20th-century industrial village. See p. 225.

St-Constant (E-7)

EXPORAIL, THE CANADIAN RAILWAY MUSEUM—You won't go off the tracks visiting here. See p. 196.

St-Félicien (C-4)

ST-FÉLICIEN WILD ANIMAL ZOO—Some 1,000 specimens of more than 75 species of birds, reptiles and other animals call this 162-hectare (400-acre) park home. See p. 225.

St-Joachim (D-5)

CAP TOURMENTE NATIONAL WILDLIFE AREA—Situated along the marshy plains of the St.

Lawrence River, the reserve is host to some 325,000 geese in April and late September. See p. 227.

Ste-Anne-de-Beaupré (A-6)

BASILICA OF STE-ANNE-DE-BEAUPRÉ—The Gothic and Romanesque basilica was built in 1923 and is dedicated to Ste. Anne. See p. 222.

CANYON OF STE-ANNE—While this breathtaking sight is much more accessible than when Henry David Thoreau viewed it in 1850, it is just as impressive. See p. 222.

Ste-Anne-des-Monts (E-3)

GASPÉSIE NATIONAL PARK—This caribou refuge offers a recreational respite for the world-weary. See p. 229.

Ste-Foy (B-5)

QUÉBEC AQUARIUM PARK—Meet the denizens of the deep at this modern facility which opened in 2003. See p. 223.

Shawinigan (E-4)

CITY OF ENERGY—Here's your chance to visit a science and technology theme park. See p. 229.

Trois-Rivières (E-4)

THE FORGES OF SAINT MAURICE NATIONAL HISTORIC SITE OF CANADA—This 50-hectare (124-acre) site marks the spot where Canada's first ironmaking operation took place 1729-1883. See p. 232.

Val-d'Or (C-2)

THE CITY OF GOLD—Explore an early-20th-century gold mine and the company town. See p. 232.

RECREATION AREAS

	MAP LOCATION	CAMPING	PICNICKING	HIKING TRAILS	BOATING	BOAT RAMP	BOAT RENTAL	FISHING	SWIMMING	PETS ON LEASH	BICYCLE TRAILS	WINTER SPORTS	VISITOR CENTER	LODGE/CABINS	FOOD SERVICE
NATIONAL PARKS (See place listings)															
Forillon (B-9) 244 sq. km 20 km n.e. of Gaspé via Hwy. 132.		•	•	•	•	•		•	•	•	•	•	•		•
La Mauricie (D-4) 536 sq. km n. of Trois-Rivières via Hwy. 55 Exit 226.		•	•	•	•	•	•	•	•	•	•	•	•	•	•
Mingan Archipelago National Park Reserve of Canada (A-9) 112 sq. km 858 km e. of Québec via Hwy. 138.		•	•	•	•								•		
PROVINCIAL															
Aiguebelle National (C-1) 243 sq. km 50 km n.e. of Rouyn-Noranda via Hwy. 101. Nature programs. Snowshoeing; equipment rentals.	❶	•	•	•	•			•	•	•		•	•	•	•
Anticosti National (B-9) 572 sq. km. 35 km from Longue-Pointe-de-Mingan. Horseback riding; bicycle and kayak rentals.	❷	•	•	•				•	•				•	•	•
Bic National (C-7) s. of Bic via Hwy. 132. Kayaking; yurts. (See Bic p. 160)	❸	•	•	•	•	•		•	•						
Frontenac National (E-5) 155 sq. km 120 km s. of Québec via Hwys. 73 and 112. Nature programs. Canoe camping, kayaking.	❹	•	•	•	•	•	•	•	•		•	•	•	•	
Gaspésie National (B-8) 802 sq. km 20 km s. of Ste-Anne-des-Monts via Hwy. 299. Nature programs. Canoeing, cross-country and telemark skiing, fishing.	❺	•	•	•	•	•		•	•		•	•	•	•	
Grands-Jardins National (C-6) 310 sq. km 20 km n. of St-Urbain via Hwy. 381. Canoeing and kayaking, cross-country skiing. (See St-Urbain p. 228)	❻	•	•	•	•			•	•		•	•	•	•	
Hautes-Gorges-de-la-Rivière-Malbaie National (C-6) 224 sq. km 30 min. from the Village of Saint-Aimé-des-Lacs	❼	•	•	•	•	•		•	•		•		•	•	
Îles de Boucherville National (E-7) 10 km e. of Montréal Hwy. 25 via the Louis-Hyppolite Lafontaine Tunnel-Bridge. Nature programs. Canoeing, kayaking.	❽		•	•		•		•		•	•		•		•
Jacques-Cartier National (D-5) 670 sq. km 40 km n.w. of Québec via Hwy. 175. Canoeing, rafting. (See Québec p. 211)	❾	•	•	•	•	•	•		•	•	•		•		
Mont-Mégantic National (F-5) 10 km from Notre-Dame-des-Bois.	❿	•	•								•	•	•		
Mont-Orford National (F-8) 58.4 sq. km n. on Hwy. 10. Canoeing, cross-country skiing; huts. (See Orford p. 199)	⓫	•	•	•	•	•		•	•			•	•		
Mont-Saint-Bruno National (E-7) 20 km e. of Montreal via Hwys. 20 and 30.	⓬		•	•								•	•	•	•
Mont-Tremblant National (E-4) 1,510 sq. km 23 km e. of Hwy. 117N. Nature programs. Back country hiking, canoeing, cross-country skiing with huts, snowshoeing. (See Mont-Tremblant p. 198)	⓭	•	•	•	•	•	•	•	•		•	•	•	•	
Monts-Valin National (C-6) 17 km n.e. of Chicoutimi. Food Service in winter only.	⓮	•	•	•	•			•				•	•	•	•
Oka National (E-6) 23.7 sq. km 1.5 km e. of Oka on Hwy. 344. Nature programs. Canoeing, cross-country skiing, snowshoeing, windsurfing.	⓯	•	•	•	•	•	•	•		•	•	•	•	•	
Plaisance National (E-3) 55 km e. of Gatineau via Hwy. 148E. Canoeing.	⓰	•	•	•	•	•	•	•	•		•		•		
Pointe-Taillon National (C-5) s. of Péribonka off Hwy. 169.	⓱	•	•	•	•	•		•	•		•	•	•		•
Saguenay-St. Lawrence Marine Park and Saguenay National Park (C-6) 300 sq. km on Hwy. 170. (See Rivière-Éternité p. 224)	⓲	•	•	•	•	•		•	•	•		•	•		•
Yamaska National (F-8) 12.9 sq. km 15 km n.e. of Granby via Hwy. 112. Cross-country skiing, snowshoeing, windsurfing. Food Service in summer only.	⓳	•	•	•	•	•	•		•	•		•	•		
OTHER															
Ashuapmushuan (B-4) 11,025 sq. km n.w. of St.-Félicien on Hwy. 167. Canoeing, fishing, hunting. (See St-Félicien p. 225)	⓴	•	•	•	•	•		•	•				•	•	•

RECREATION AREAS

RECREATION AREAS	MAP LOCATION	CAMPING	PICNICKING	HIKING TRAILS	BOATING	BOAT RAMP	BOAT RENTAL	FISHING	SWIMMING	PETS ON LEASH	BICYCLE TRAILS	WINTER SPORTS	VISITOR CENTER	LODGE/CABINS	FOOD SERVICE
Gatineau (F-3) 36,300 hectares n. of Gatineau between the Gatineau and Ottawa rivers via hwys. 5, 105, 148 and 366. *(See Chelsea p. 162)*	21	•	•	•	•	•		•	•	•	•	•	•	•	•
Lac la Pêche Sector C Canoeing.		•	•		•	•	•	•	•						
Lac Philippe Cross-country skiing, snowshoeing.		•	•	•	•	•	•	•	•	•		•	•	•	
Parkway Sector Alpine and cross-country skiing, snowshoeing.			•	•	•	•		•	•	•	•	•	•		•
Lacs Albanel Mistassini Waconichi (A-4) 25,285 sq. km 32 km n. of Chibougamau. Canoeing.	22	•			•	•	•	•						•	•
Laurentides Wildlife Reserve (C-5) 7,861 sq. km in the Laurentian Mountains, n.w. of Québec via Hwy. 175. Canoeing, cross-country skiing, snowmobiling, snowshoeing; nature trails. *(See Québec p. 211)*	23	•	•		•	•	•	•	•			•	•	•	•
La Vérendrye (C-2) 13,615 sq. km 60 km n.w. of Mont-Laurier on Hwy. 117. Canoeing, hunting, snowmobile trails. *(See Mont-Laurier p. 172)*	24	•	•		•	•	•	•	•				•	•	•
Mastigouche (D-4) 1,534 sq. km 100 km n.w. of Trois-Rivières off Hwy. 349. Canoeing, snowmobiling.	25	•	•		•	•	•	•	•				•	•	•
Matane (C-8) 1,282 sq. km 40 km s.e. of Matane.	26	•	•	•	•	•	•	•	•			•	•	•	•
Mont-Ste-Anne (A-2) 64 sq. km n.w. of Beaupré on Hwy. 360E. Golf. *(See Beaupré p. 221)*	27	•	•	•					•	•	•	•	•	•	•
Papineau-Labelle (E-3) 1 628 sq. km 82 km n. of Gatineau via Hwys. 50 and 309. Cross-country skiing, snowmobiling.	28	•	•		•	•	•	•	•			•	•		
Port-Cartier Sept-Îles Animal Reserve (A-8) 6,423 sq. km n. of Port Cartier. Canoeing.	29	•	•		•	•	•	•				•		•	
Port-Daniel Reserve (C-9) 64 sq. km 8 km n. of Port Daniel.	30	•	•		•	•	•	•	•				•	•	
Réserve faunique de Portneuf (D-5) 775 sq. km 5 km n. of Rivière-à-Pierre. Canoeing, cross-country skiing, mountain climbing, snowmobiling, snowshoeing.	31	•	•		•	•	•	•	•	•		•	•		
Rimouski (C-7) 774 sq. km 48 km s.e. of Rimouski.	32	•	•												
Rouge-Matawin (D-3) w. of Saint-Michel-des-Saints via Hwy. 131. Canoeing, hunting, snowmobiling. Food Service in winter only.	33	•	•		•	•	•	•	•			•	•	•	•
St-Maurice (D-4) 784 sq. km 48.25 km n. of Grand-Mère. Canoeing.	34	•	•		•	•	•	•	•				•	•	
Shawinigan-Falls (E-4) between Shawinigan and Shawinigan-Sud on Hwy. 157. Cross-country skiing.	35	•	•		•	•		•	•			•			
Voltigeurs (E-8) 3 sq. km 2 km e. of Drummondville off Autoroute 20 exit 181 following signs. Cross-country skiing, snowshoeing. *(See Drummondville p. 164)*	36	•	•					•	•	•		•	•		•

Québec Tourist Regions

For the purposes of providing tourism information, the province of Québec divides itself into 20 regions. The **northern regions** are Abitibi-Témiscamingue, Saguenay—Lac-Saint-Jean, Côte-Nord (Manicouagan and Duplessis). The **southern regions** are Eastern townships, Montréal, Laval, Montérégie. The **eastern regions** are Québec, Charlevoix, Gaspésie, Îles-de-la-Madeleine, Chaudière-Appalaches (South shore of Québec), Bas-Saint-Laurent. The **western regions** are Laurentides and Outaouais. The **central regions** are Lanaudière, Mauricie, Centre-du-Québec.

Driving in Québec

International driving symbols are in use throughout Québec; see the CAA/AAA Atlantic Provinces and Québec Map. Prohibitory information is presented in signs with a white-centered red circle with a red diagonal slash. Mandatory information, such as seat belt usage, is presented in signs with a white-centered green circle. Radar detectors are not permitted. Québec uses the 24-hour clock, e.g., 1730 is 5:30 p.m.

Below are French/English equivalents of some of the more common driving directions and information appearing on signs.

GENERAL INFORMATION

Nord	North	Mer.	Wed.
Sud	South	Jeu.	Thurs.
Est	East	Ven.	Fri.
Ouest	West	Sam.	Sat.
Lun.	Mon.	Dim.	Sun.
Mar.	Tues.		

SIGNS

ARRÊT	STOP	Pas de Virage à Gauche	No Left Turn
Accottement Mou	Soft Shoulder	Pas de Virage à Droite	No Right Turn
Arrét Interdit	No Stopping	Passage à Niveau	Railroad Crossing
Cul-de-sac	Dead End	Reculez	Back Up
Débarcadére	Loading Zone	Rétrécissement	Road Narrows
Demi-tour Interdit	No U Turn	Route à Chaussées Séparées	Divided Highway
Dépassement Interdit	No Passing	Sens Unique	One Way
Déviation	Bypass	Stationnement	Parking
École	School	Stationnement Interdit	No Parking
Fin	End	Vitesse	Speed
Glissant	Slippery	Voie Réservée	Reserved Lane
Lentement	Slow		

Points of Interest

ALMA (C-5) pop. 25,918

Alma is on the Saguenay River, which connects lac St-Jean with the St. Lawrence River. Called Piekouagami, meaning "flat lake," by the Montagnais Indians, lac St-Jean was discovered by Jesuit missionary Father Jean de Quen in 1647. This vast lake, 49 kilometres (31 mi.) long and 29 kilometres (18 mi.) wide, is surrounded by agricultural land known for its blueberries.

Two-hour cruises on lac St-Jean are offered by Complexe touristique de la Dam-en-Terre aboard the NV *La Tournée*, which departs from 1385 chemin de la Marina Dam-en-Terre. The Dam-en-Terre tourist complex offers a marina, beach, cottages, summer theater and camping; phone (418) 668-3016 or (888) 289-3016.

Alma Tourist Information Bureau: 1682 av. du Pont Nord, Alma, QC, Canada G8B 5G3; phone (418) 668-3611 or (877) 668-3611.

SAVE **THE ODYSSEY OF THE BUILDERS THEME PARK** (L'Odyssée des Bâtisseurs Parc Thématique is off Hwy. 169, at 1671 av. du Pont Nord. This site explores the importance of water in the economic and social development of the region. Explored in depth is the construction of the Isle-Maligne hydroelectric plant and its dam. Bicyclists and hikers can take a ferry to the island in the summer.

Allow 2 hours minimum. Daily 9-5, mid-June through Sept. 30; Mon.-Fri. 9-4, rest of year. Admission $14; over 59, $13; under 15 free with adult. MC, VI. Phone (418) 668-2606 or (866) 668-2606.

ANGLIERS (C-1) pop. 331

T.E. DRAPER, 11 rue T.E. Draper at the waterfront, plied the river floating wood 1929-72 for Canadian International Paper. A video presentation, guided warehouse tour, visit aboard the towboat, provide insights into mid-20th-century logging techniques. The warehouse contains displays about logging camps and machinery.

Tour narration is available in English. Allow 1 hour minimum. Guided tours are given daily 10-6, June 24-Labour Day. Last tour begins 1 hour before closing. Admission $5; over 65, $4; ages 6-11, $1.50. Phone (819) 949-4431.

GEM **ARTILLERY PARK NATIONAL HISTORIC SITE OF CANADA**—*see Québec p. 208.*

BAIE-COMEAU (B-7) pop. 23,079

Baie-Comeau began as a pulp and newsprint milling town. Publisher Robert R. McCormick, who needed paper for his Chicago and New York newspapers, established the mill in 1936. McCormick is memorialized in a downtown statue that depicts him exploring the area by canoe.

A ferry service operates from 14 rte. Maritime in Baie-Comeau to Matane; advance reservations are required. Phone (418) 294-8593 for information, or (877) 562-6560 for reservations.

Association Touristique Manicouagan: 337 boul. La Salle, Bureau 304, Baie-Comeau, QC, Canada G4Z 2Z1; phone (418) 294-2876.

MANICOUAGAN 2 AND MANICOUAGAN 5 HYDROELECTRIC DAMS AND INSTALLATIONS (Installations de Production d'Électricité de Manicouagan 2 et de Manicouagan 5), 22 km (14 mi.) and 214 km (133 mi.) n. on Hwy. 389, respectively, are among the world's largest hydroelectric power dams, each capable of producing more than 1 million kilowatts.

Manic 2 has a 70-metre (230-ft.) waterfall and a 518-square-kilometre (200-sq.-mi.) reservoir. The Manic 5, Barrage Daniel-Johnson, which has a 2,000-square-kilometre (772-sq.-mi.) reservoir and a 150-metre (490-ft.) waterfall, is the largest arch and buttress type dam in the world.

Narration is available in English. Both separate guided 90-minute tours of each installation are offered daily at 9, 11, 1:30 and 3:30, June 24-Labour Day. Free. Reservations are required for guided tours and may be made at the information center, 135 boul. Comeau jct. hwys. 138 and 389. Phone (418) 294-3923 or (866) 526-2642.

BAIE-ST-PAUL (D-5) pop. 7,290

In a narrow river valley that opens on the St. Lawrence River, Baie-St-Paul has been a source of inspiration for generations of Canadian painters. Houses built in the early 1800s line the narrow streets of the town, which has numerous art galleries. The Centre d'art de Baie-St-Paul displays the works of noted Charlevoix painters.

In the surrounding mountains a number of outlooks, such as the Cap-aux-Corbeaux and rang Ste-Catherine, provide a panorama of the bay and Île-aux-Coudres (*see place listing p. 168*), which lie opposite the village in the St. Lawrence River.

Maison du tourisme de Baie-St-Paul: 444 boul. Mgr-De Laval, Baie-St-Paul, QC, Canada G3Z 2V3; phone (418) 435-4160 or (800) 667-2276.

DOMAINE CHARLEVOIX, 7 km (4.4 mi.) e. of town at 340 Rte. 362, offers hiking, mountain bicycling and sightseeing in 700 acres of wilderness. Terraces and trails afford beautiful views of waterfalls, mountains and the St. Lawrence River. Picnicking is permitted. Food is available.

Allow 2 hours minimum. Daily 10-6, June-Oct. Hours may vary; phone ahead. Admission $10; ages 6-12, $5. MC, VI. Phone (418) 435-2626.

GRANDS-JARDINS NATIONAL PARK— see St-Urbain p. 228.

BAIE-STE-CATHERINE (C-6) pop. 273

At the confluence of the Saguenay and St. Lawrence rivers, this small town is the home base for several whale-watching cruise companies. From May through early October, Croisières AML, offers daily 3-hour and 6.5-hour cruises (weather permitting); phone (800) 563-4643. There is no guarantee that whales will be sighted, though often several are. A free ferry service connects Baie-Ste-Catherine to Tadoussac (see place listing p. 230); phone (418) 235-4395 for schedule.

POINTE-NOIRE INTERPRETATION AND OBSER-VATION CENTRE—see Tadoussac p. 231.

BAIE-TRINITÉ (B-7) pop. 600

POINTE-DES-MONTS HISTORIC LIGHTHOUSE (Phare de Pointe-des-Monts) is 5 km (3 mi.) w. on Hwy. 138, then 11 km (7 mi.) s. following signs. Two iron cannons, fired to warn ships during times of heavy fog, are near the 1830 lighthouse. A staircase leads to the top of the lighthouse, which affords an excellent view.

The Pointe-des-Monts Historic Lighthouse Corporation has displays pertaining to a lighthouse keeper's lifestyle, navigation and shipwrecks off Pointe-des-Monts. Whales and many species of waterfowl can be seen. Allow 30 minutes minimum. Daily 9-5, mid-June to mid-Sept. Admission $6. Phone (418) 939-2400.

BEAUPORT—see Québec p. 221.

BEAUPRÉ—see Québec p. 221.

BERTHIER-SUR-MER (B-2)
pop. 1,307, elev. 11 m/35′

LACHANCE CRUISES, (Croisières Lachance), 110 de la Marina offers narrated cruises to Grosse Île and the Irish Memorial National Historic Site with guided tours of the site. Also available are cruises on the archipelago that include a stop and a guided tour on l'Isle-aux-Grues.

Bilingual cruises and guided tours are available May-Oct. Departure times vary; phone for times. Cruises board 30 minutes before departure. Five- to 6-hour tour $41; ages 6-16, $22. Reservations are recommended. Phone (418) 259-2140 or (888) 476-7734.

BIC (C-7)

BIC NATIONAL PARK (Parc national du Bic), s. via Hwy. 132, preserves some of the tidal coastline along the St. Lawrence River. The park's inlets, marshes and wooded hills are home to a variety of marine life and thousands of eider ducks and seals.

Hiking and bicycle trails traverse the park; cross-country skiing and camping are popular activities. Interpretation center open daily 9-5, late May-early Oct. (weather permitting). Admission $3.50; ages 6-17, $1.50; family rate (two adults and children ages 6-17) $7. Phone (418) 736-5035 or (800) 665-6527 for park information and reservations. See Recreation Chart and the AAA/CAA Eastern Canada CampBook.

BONAVENTURE (C-8) pop. 2,756

A seaside resort, Bonaventure was founded in 1760 by 12 Acadian families who were among those expelled from Nova Scotia by the British in 1755. The climate and conditions of the region are favorable for agriculture.

Bonaventure Tourist Information Bureau: 93 av. Port-Royal, Bonaventure, QC, Canada G0C 1E0; phone (418) 534-4014.

ACADIAN HISTORICAL MUSEUM OF QUÉBEC (Musée acadien du Québec), on Hwy. 132 at 95 av. Port-Royal, has handicrafts, antiques and artifacts depicting the region's Acadian legacy. Guided tours are available. English narration is available.

Allow 1 hour minimum. Daily 9-6, June 24-Labour Day; Mon.-Fri. 9-noon and 1-5, Sat.-Sun. 1-4:30, rest of year. Admission $7, over 65 and students with ID $5, family rate (one parent and 2 children) $15. VI. Phone (418) 534-4000.

CABANO (C-7) pop. 3,213

FORT INGALL is 2 km (1.2 mi.) n. of Hwy. 185 at 81 Chemin Caldwell (Hwy. 232). The original of this reconstructed fort on the shores of lac Témiscouata, built in 1839 to protect the vital portage between Québec and Halifax, Nova Scotia, was occupied during the border conflict between Maine and Canada. Guided tours and picnic facilities are available. English narration is available.

Allow 1 hour, 30 minutes minimum. Daily 9:30-5, June-Sept.; 10-4, in May and Oct. Admission $7; over 65 and students with ID $6; ages 5-12, $5; family rate $17. VI. Phone (418) 854-2375.

Roseraie du Témiscouata, 81 Chemin Caldwell, features some 1,500 rose bushes representing more than 400 varieties of roses. Flowers bloom June through September. Daily 9:30-5, June-Sept.; 10-4 in May and Oct. Admission included with fort entry. Phone (418) 854-2375.

CANTLEY (E-3)

MONT CASCADES, 7 km (4.3 mi.) w. on Hwy. 307 to 448 Mont Cascades Rd., is a downhill ski area in the winter and a water park in the summer. Water-park highlights include a speed slide, raft rides, activity pools and children's rides. Food is available. Allow one full day.

Waterpark open daily 10-6, mid-June through Labour Day. Fee for 48 inches tall and over $21.95, under 48 inches and non-sliders $14.95. After 2 p.m. $18.95, under 48 inches and non-sliders $12.95. MC, VI. Phone (819) 827-0301 or (888) 282-2722.

CAP-CHAT (B-8) pop. 2,913

The Cap-Chat takes its name from a rock 1 km (.6 mi.) west of town that resembles a crouching cat *(chat)*. Safari Anticosti Pourvoirie offers 2-day/1 night ecotours June 24 through Aug. 31. Write Safari Anticosti Pourvoirie, 208B, Notre-Dame, C.P. 398, Cap Chat, QC G0J 1E0; phone (418) 786-5788.

THE AEOLIAN OF CAP-CHAT (Éole Cap-Chat) is 2 km (1.2 mi.) w. on Hwy. 132, following signs. The Aeolian of Cap-Chat, said to be the tallest (110 m, 360 ft.) and most powerful (4 megawatts) vertical axis windmill in the world, is named for Aeolus, the Greek god of the winds. Like the Aeolian harp, a box with strings that sound when wind passes over them, the Aeolian of Cap-Chat makes a resonant sound when the wind strikes it.

Guided tours of the Nordais wind park are offered. Allow 30 minutes minimum. Daily 9-5, June-Sept. Admission $10; over 65, $9; ages 6-18, $7; family rate $25. Phone (418) 786-5719 or (418) 763-9935.

CAP-DE-LA-MADELEINE (E-5) pop. 32,534

On the St. Lawrence River at the mouth of the St. Maurice River, Cap-de-la-Madeleine has been a shipping and trading center since it was settled in 1651. The city has more than 30 industries manufacturing such products as aluminum foil, clothing and newsprint. The scenic portion of Hwy. 138 follows the St. Lawrence River between Cap-de-la-Madeleine and Neuville.

Trois-Rivières Chamber of Commerce—Cap-de-la-Madeleine: 168 rue Bonaventure, C.P. 1045, Trois-Rivières, QC, Canada G9A 5K4; phone (819) 375-9628.

▼ SHRINE OF NOTRE-DAME-DU-CAP (Sanctuaire Notre-Dame-du-Cap) is .7 km (.5 mi.) s. of Hwy. 138 at 626 rue Notre-Dame Est. Thousands of believers make their pilgrimages to the shrine each year, Canada's national shrine to Mary. The 1659 wooden chapel was replaced by a stone building inaugurated in 1720. The Basilica of Notre-Dame-du-Cap, inaugurated in 1964, is a modernistic octagonal structure that seats 1,660.

The Madonna of Notre-Dame-du Cap within the chapel has been considered miraculous since 1888, when her eyes allegedly became momentarily animated. Daily 8 a.m.-9 p.m., May 1 through mid-Oct.; 9-5, rest of year. Free. Phone (819) 374-2441.

CAP-DES-ROSIERS (C-9)

CAP-DES-ROSIERS LIGHTHOUSE NATIONAL HISTORIC SITE (Lieu historique national du Phare de Cap-des-Rosiers) is on Rte. 132 at the n.e. tip of the Gaspé Peninsula. The 1858 lighthouse, fog signal and radio beacon are still in operation. The structure is 34 metres (112 ft.) tall and the light is 41 metres (135 ft.) above the high-water line. From this point a messenger was dispatched in 1759, in one of the decisive battles of the French and Indian War, to warn Québec of the impending arrival of British general James Wolfe's fleet.

Guided tours are available. Daily 10-7, mid-June through Sept. 30. Admission free. Guided tour $2.50, family rate $5. Phone (418) 892-5577.

CAP-TOURMENTE—

see St-Joachim p. 227.

CARILLON (F-4) pop. 266

On the banks of the Ottawa River some 85 kilometres (53 miles) from Montréal, Carillon was the site of the Battle of Long Sault in May 1660, when 17 men saved New France from an Indian invasion. In 1833 British Army engineers built the first Carillon Canal as part of the inland waterway system designed to link Montréal and Kingston as a defensive measure against invasion by the United States.

Plaques at the entry lock, which is intact, detail the history of the canal. The Carillon Canal National Historic Site of Canada lock and dam, (450) 447-4888, are part of a 654,500-kilowatt power project. With a gradient of 24 metres (79 feet), this is highest conventional lock in Canada; small craft pass through in 40 minutes. The collector's house presents an exhibit about the first two canal systems. The Carillon Barracks National Historic Site of Canada, an early 19th-century stone military building, now houses the Argenteuil County Historical Museum *(see attraction listing).*

ARGENTEUIL COUNTY HISTORICAL MUSEUM (Musée Régional d'Argenteuil) is at the Carillon Ferry, 44 rte. Long Sault; from Hwy. 40 follow signs for Pointe-Fortune à Carillon Ferry, which operates April through November. The museum is in a four-story stone barracks built 1834-37 to house soldiers guarding the first Carillon Canal. The barracks housed 108 men during the Rebellion of 1837.

Displays include local history items, military artifacts and natural history specimens. Tues.-Sun. 10:30-5, late Mar.-early Dec. Admission $3; over 65 and ages 7-12, $2.50. Phone (450) 537-3861.

CARLETON-ST-OMER (C-8) pop. 4,010

A popular seaside resort community, Carleton was settled by Acadians who eluded exile to Louisiana. The town's name was originally Tracadièche, a Micmac Indian word meaning "place of many herons." It was changed to Carleton in honor of Guy Carleton, governor general of Canada during the late 18th century.

The arts have a secure role in Carleton-St-Omer. Galleries display the work of area artists. A work of art itself, the St-Joseph-de-Carleton Church, on Boulevard Perron, contains paintings, silverware and vestments acquired in 1800. Productions by the Moluque Theatre are offered Tuesday through Saturday evenings from mid-July to late August.

Preserved fossils are found at Miguasha National Park (see Miguasha p. 171), southwest via Hwy. 132. The park contains the Escuminac Geological Formation, which represents a paleoecosystem of the Devonian period, 370 million years ago. These fossils illustrate the transition from aquatic vertebrates to land vertebrates, making the park an important paleontological site.

Carleton Tourist Information Bureau: 629 boul. Perron, Carleton-St-Omer, QC, Canada G0C 1J0; phone (418) 364-3544.

NOTRE-DAME ORATORY OF MOUNT SAINT-JOSEPH (Oratoire Notre-Dame-du-Mont-Saint-Joseph), reached by car or bus, is a chapel on the summit of Mont St-Joseph. At 555 metres (1,820 ft.), it offers one of the best views on Baie-des-Chaleurs. Daily 9-7, June 23-Labour Day; 8-5, day after Labour Day-second Mon. in Oct. Admission $4, senior citizens and students with ID $3, family rate $10. Phone (418) 364-3723 or (418) 364-2256.

CAUSAPSCAL (C-7) pop. 2,634

At the confluence of the salmon-filled Causapscal and Matapédia rivers, Causapscal serves as a lumber and fishing center on the Gaspé Peninsula. On the edge of town, tall conical chimneys mark the sawing complexes where wood processing residues are burned.

Scenic points of interest in the Causapscal area include a covered bridge over the Matapédia River just south of town, and the Chutes à Philomène, a 40-metre-high (131-ft.) waterfall 16 kilometres (10 mi.) north off Hwy. 132. Even though the last 10 kilometres (6 miles) of road to the river at Chutes à Philomène is not very good, the spot is a favorite of fly fishermen.

Causapscal Tourist Information Bureau: 53C rue St-Jacques Sud, Causapscal, QC, Canada G0J 1J0; phone (418) 756-6048.

MATAMAJAW HISTORICAL SITE (Site historique Matamajaw), 48 rue St-Jacques, is the restored former facility of the Matamajaw Salmon Fishing Club, founded in the early 1900s by a group of businessmen who bought the 1870 estate of a British lord. The club operated for more than 60 years. Exhibits include a man-made salmon pool.

Allow 30 minutes minimum. Daily 9-5, early June through mid-Sept.; phone to verify schedule. Admission in 2006 was $5; over 65, $4.25. Phone to verify prices. VI. Phone (418) 756-5999.

CHAMBLY—see Montréal p. 195.

CHÂTEAU-RICHER—see Québec p. 221.

CHELSEA (E-2) pop. 6,036

 GATINEAU PARK (Parc de la Gatineau) is just n. between the Gatineau and Ottawa rivers. Hwys. 5, 105, 148 and 366 provide access from Gatineau to the park's recreation areas. The park encompasses about 36,300 hectares (89,661 acres) of the rocky, wooded Laurentian Mountains.

In the southern section the scenic Gatineau Parkway links the lac des Fées and lac Meech areas. Along with a bicycle path, the route provides access to picnic grounds and lookouts. In the northwestern section, the lac La Pêche area provides more wilderness, a beach and canoe-camping facilities.

Meech, Philippe and La Pêche lakes provide bass fishing. Alpine skiing is available at Camp Fortune. There are 200 kilometres (125 mi.) of cross-country ski trails with day-use and overnight shelters. In summer ski trails are hiking trails.

Anglers must have a valid Québec fishing license. Park open daily 24 hours. Camping is permitted year-round

Park free. Access fee to the beach, boat ramp areas and picnic areas at lakes Meech, La Pêche and Philippe is $8 per private vehicle, mid-June through Labour Day. Access fee to the cross-country ski network is $10 per person over age 18 per day. AX, MC, VI. Phone (819) 827-2020 for information or (800) 465-1867. See Recreation Chart.

Moorside Tearoom—Mackenzie King Estate, Scott Rd. to Old Chelsea Rd. to Gatineau Pkwy. following signs, was a summer residence of three-time prime minister Mackenzie King. The first floor is now a tearoom. Historical interpreters and audio-visual presentations give an overview of the 1921-48 era during Canada's longest-governing prime minister. Presentations are available in English. The formal gardens are restored and gardener-historians describe King's gardening techniques.

Guided tours are available. Food is available. Allow 1 hour, 30 minutes minimum. Mon.-Fri. 11-5, Sat.-Sun. 10-6, mid-May to mid-Oct. Admission $8 per private vehicle. Phone (819) 827-2020.

CHICOUTIMI (C-6) pop. 60,008

Chicoutimi, at the farthest point of deepwater navigation on the Saguenay River, is a regional trade center. Many galleries in town contain local arts and crafts. St-François-Xavier Cathedral, at rues Bégin and Racine, is known for its stained-glass windows. Nearby lakes and forests provide hunting and fishing opportunities.

Chicoutimi lies along the scenic Saguenay River, which flows 160 kilometres (100 mi.) east from lac St-Jean to the St. Lawrence River.

The Saguenay begins as a series of rapids tumbling out of the lake. The river then passes Chicoutimi's aluminum smelters, slices through the sheer,

400-metre-high (1,312-ft.) cliffs of Saguenay Provincial Park (see Recreation Chart and Rivière Éternité in the AAA/CAA Eastern Canada CampBook) and finally empties into a section of the St. Lawrence River, where various species of whales feed. Sightseeing cruises are available during the summer months.

Chicoutimi Tourisme Bureau: 295 rue Racine est., Chicoutimi, QC, Canada G7H 5G4; phone (418) 698-3167 or (800) 463-6565.

Self-guiding tours: Maps detailing self-guiding tours of the downtown area are in the guidebooks available at the tourist information center.

Shopping areas: Place du Royaume and Place Saguenay on Boulevard Talbot together have 330 stores. The Bay and Place du Royaume are among the centers' department stores.

[SAVE] **THE PULPMILL OF CHICOUTIMI HISTORICAL SITE AND MUSEUM** (La Pulperie de Chicoutimi lieu historique et musée), 300 rue Dubuc, is 1 km (.6 mi.) s.w. of Pont Dubuc, following signs. On the grounds are the remains of the Chicoutimi Pulp Co., founded in 1896, a regional museum and two restored stone buildings of architectural distinction. Also here is the former home of noted folk artist Arthur Villeneuve, who began his career by painting his house with scenes of his life and regional history. The interpretive center offers interactive displays dealing with history.

Bilingual tours are available by reservation. Picnicking is permitted. Allow 2 hours minimum. Site and museum open daily 9-6, June 24-Labour Day (last admission 1 hour before closing); museum only Wed.-Sun. 9-5, day after Labour Day-second Mon. in Oct. and first Wed. in June-June 23; museum only Wed.-Sun. 10-4, rest of year. Closed Jan. 1 and Dec. 24-25 and 31. Phone to verify schedule.

Grounds free. Museum admission $10.25; over 65, $8.50; students with ID $5.50; ages 5-17, $4; family rate (two adults and two ages 5-17) $26; family rate (two adults and one age 5-17) $23; family rate each additional child ages 5-17 is $2. Phone to confirm prices and to schedule tours in English. MC, VI. Phone (418) 698-3100 or (877) 998-3100.

SAFETY VILLAGE (Village de la Sécurité) is 200 rue Pinel, is 5 km (3 mi.) n. via Pont Dubuc, following signs. This miniature village allows visitors to experience a simulated automobile collision and house fire, a train ride and a 30-metre (98-ft.) lookout tower. Allow 1 hour minimum. Daily 10-5, June 24-Aug. 31; otherwise by appointment. Admission $9. VI. Phone (418) 545-6925 or (888) 595-6925.

[GEM] [SAVE] **SAGUENAY CRUISES** (Croisières Marjolaine Inc.) depart the Chicoutimi wharf and the wharf at Ste-Rose-du-Nord. The diesel-powered, 400-passenger *Marjolaine* explores the Saguenay River and fjord from Chicoutimi to Cap Trinité.

Cruise No. 1 is to caps Éternité and Trinité and ends at Ste-Rose where food is available; passengers return to town by bus. Cruise No. 2 leaves Chicoutimi via bus to Ste-Rose, where the ship is boarded. Cruise No. 3 is 3 hours round-trip from Ste-Rose. Evening cruises also are available. Inquire about weather policies.

Departures require a minimum of 20 passengers. Cruise No. 1 departs daily at 8:30, July-Aug.; Cruise No. 2 departs July-Aug, phone for times. Cruise No. 3 leaves at 10:15 and 1:15, June-Sept. Fare $40-$45; ages 5-14, $20-$22.50. Reservations are required. AX, MC, VI. Phone (418) 543-7630 or (800) 363-7248.

COATICOOK (F-9) pop. 8,988

The banks of the Coaticook River were first settled about 1750 by the Abenaki Indians, who named the site Koakitchou, or "river of the land of pines." The town of Coaticook, incorporated in 1888, is a center of light manufacturing and industry.

Coaticook Tourist Information Bureau: 137 rue Michaud, Coaticook, QC, Canada J1A 1A9; phone (819) 849-6669 or (866) 665-6669.

COATICOOK RIVER GORGE PARK (Parc de la Gorge de Coaticook) is 10 km (6 mi.) n. at 135 rue Michaud. A 3.5-kilometre (2 mi.) trail with wooden steps and a suspension bridge parallels the preglacial gorge with cliffs rising to 50 metres (164 ft.). Tour narration is available in English.

The steep terrain may be difficult for some to negotiate. Nonslip walking shoes are required. Picnic facilities and a playground are available. Guided tours are given daily 10-7, June 24-day before Labour Day; 10-5, first weekend in May-June 23 and Labour Day-last week in Oct. Phone to confirm schedule. Fee $7; ages 6-15, $4. Reservations are required for guided tours. VI. Phone (819) 849-2331.

COMPTON (F-9) pop. 3,047

LOUIS S. SAINT-LAURENT NATIONAL HISTORIC SITE OF CANADA (Lieu historique national du Canada Louis-S.-Saint-Laurent) is at 6790 rte. Louis-S.-Saint-Laurent (Hwy. 147). The site consists of the house in which Louis S. Saint-Laurent, prime minister of Canada 1948-57, was born, and his father's general store, where audiotapes re-create the passionate political discussions that often took place. Visitors glimpse the atmosphere of the rural way of life in the early 20th century. A sound and light show recalls Saint-Laurent's career as a lawyer and politician.

Allow 1 hour, 30 minutes minimum. Daily 10-5, mid-May through second Mon. in Oct. Admission $3.95; over 65, $3.45; ages 6-16, $1.95; family rate $9.90. Phone (819) 835-5448 or (888) 773-8888.

COTEAU-DU-LAC (F-6) pop. 5,573

A resort community on the St. Lawrence River, Coteau-du-Lac is in an agricultural region known for its dairy and pig farms. Not far from the river is a small hill (coteau) on which a church was built—hence the town's name.

COTEAU-DU-LAC NATIONAL HISTORIC SITE OF CANADA (Lieu historique national du Canada de Coteau-du-Lac) is 1.5 km (.9 mi.) s. off Hwy. 20 exit 17, then 2 km (1.2 mi.) s. on rue Principale to 308 A Chemin du fleuve, following signs. This was the 1779 location of the first lock canal in Canada. A British military post built during the War of 1812 defended the strategic site until the mid-19th century. Of interest are the remaining canal and fortifications foundations, as well as a reconstructed octagonal blockhouse that contains historical items.

Guided tours are available; English narration is available. Wed.-Sun. 10-5, Mother's Day through day before Labour Day; Sat.-Sun. 10-5, day after Labour Day-second Sun. in Oct. Admission $3.95; over 65 and students with ID $3.45; ages 6-16, $1.95; family rate $10. Phone (450) 763-5631 or (888) 773-8888.

DESBIENS (C-5) pop. 1,128

CENTER FOR THE HISTORY AND OF ARCHEOLOGY OF THE MÉTABETCHOUANE (Centre d'histoire et d'archéologie de la Métabetchouane), 234 rue Hébert along the Métabetchouane River, relates the story of the first meetings between the indigenous peoples and the French explorers and trappers. On the grounds are replicas of a 17th-century fur trading post and a Jesuit chapel, a historic stone powder keg and former archeological dig sites.

Guided tours in English are available with advance reservation. Picnicking is permitted. Allow 1 hour minimum. Open daily 10-5, mid-June through Aug. 31; by appointment rest of year. Admission $7; ages 4-12, $3. AX, MC, VI. Phone (418) 346-5341.

THE HOLE OF THE FAIRY CAVE (Caverne Trou de la fée) is 5.5 km (3.5 mi.) w. on 7ieme av. Visitors can take a guided tour of an impressive underground cavern and/or enjoy gravel walking trails to view two impressive sets of waterfalls and the ruins of a 1922 concrete river dam. Visitors to the cavern must be physically agile and not inhibited by claustrophobia, as the cavern has narrow and rocky passages, and 101 steep steps that descend 68 metres (228 ft.). Bats and mice live in the cave and may be encountered during the tour.

The underground temperature remains a stable and damp 4-6 degrees C (39-43 F), so a warm sweater, long pants and appropriate walking shoes are suggested. English tours may be available by advance booking only. Allow 2 hours minimum. Daily 9-5, mid-June to mid-Aug.; 10-4, mid-Aug. through Labour Day. Fee $11; ages 4-11, $6. Phone (418) 346-1242.

DRUMMONDVILLE (E-9) pop. 46,559

Founded in 1815, Drummondville took the name of Sir Gordon Drummond, then governor of Canada. Electric power dams on the St-François River and the Hemming Rapids spurred the town's industrial growth.

Drummondville Tourism Bureau: 1350 rue Michaud, Drummondville, QC, Canada J2C 2Z5; phone (819) 477-5529 or (877) 235-9569.

PIONEER VILLAGE (Village Québécois d'Antan), 1425 rue Montplaisir, is 5 km (3 mi.) e. off Autoroute 20 exit 181 following signs. The living-history village contains 70 buildings dating 1810-1910. The buildings are furnished in period; costumed interpreters demonstrate the trades and crafts of colonial Québec.

Note: All descriptions and interpretations are in French. Village open daily 10-6, June-Aug.; Fri.-Sun. 10-5:30 in Sept. Village admission $17.95; over 65, $15.95; students with ID $11.95; under 12, $7.95; family rate $39.95. MC, VI. Phone (877) 710-0267.

VOLTIGEURS CAMPING (Camping des Voltigeurs) is 2 km (1.2 mi.) e. off Autoroute 20 exit 181 following signs to 575 rue Montplaisir Drummondville. Named after the Québec regiment that defeated an invading American army in the War of 1812, Voltigeurs Park overlooks the St-François River. The recreation complex includes 291 campsites.

Park daily dawn-dusk. Reception desk and campground 8 a.m.-11 p.m., late May-early Sept. A camping fee is charged. Phone (819) 477-1360. *See Recreation Chart and the AAA/CAA Eastern Canada CampBook.*

DUHAMEL (E-3) pop. 361

FORT TÉMISCAMINGUE NATIONAL HISTORIC SITE OF CANADA (Lieu historique national du Canada du Fort-Témiscamingue), 6 km (4 mi.) s. via Hwy. 101 at 830 ch. du Vieux-Fort, occupies the site of a fur-trading post built about 1720; only the fort's chimneys and cemeteries remain. The post operated for nearly 200 years. The interpretation center depicts the history of the fort and the fur trade. The Enchanted Forest is composed of strangely shaped eastern cedars. Picnic and camping facilities are available at Lake Témiscamingue.

Guided tours and English narration are available. Allow 1 hour, 30 minute minimum. Open daily 9-5, first Sun.-third Fri. in June; 9:30-5:30, third Sat. in June-first Fri. in Sept. Admission $4.95; over 65 and students with ID $4.20; ages 6-16, $2.95; family rate $11.85. Season passes are available. Reservations are recommended for guided tours. Phone (819) 629-3222 or (888) 773-8888.

EATON (F-5) pop. 2,766

[SAVE] **COMPTON COUNTY HISTORICAL SOCIETY MUSEUM** (Musée de la Société d'histoire du Comté de Compton), at 374 RR 253, is housed in a former 1841 congregational church and the Eaton Academy. The church displays local artifacts and period furniture; the schoolhouse contains agricultural equipment and utensils. An archive stores books about the history of the Eastern Townships.

Allow 1 hour, 30 minutes minimum. Wed.-Fri. 1-5 June-Aug.; Wed-Sun. 1-5 in Sept. Admission $5; over 65, $4; ages 6-17, $3. Phone (819) 875-5256.

FORILLON NATIONAL PARK OF CANADA (B-9)

Elevations in the park range from sea level at the Gulf of St. Lawrence to 553 metres (1,750 ft.) in the center of the park at a series of four lakes. Refer to CAA/AAA maps for additional elevation information.

Forillon National Park of Canada encompasses 244 square kilometres (95 sq. mi.) on the northeast tip of the Gaspé Peninsula and is accessible from Gaspé via Hwy. 132 E. Jagged seaside cliffs, capes, pebbled beach coves, fir covered highlands and ocean terraced lowlands typify park scenery. Of sedimentary origin, geologic formations contain rocks ranging in age from the Ordovician to the Devonian periods.

White-tailed deer, moose, black bears, foxes, beavers, minks and coyotes can be seen from the many hiking trails. The cliffs and headlands are home to colonies of seabirds, including double-crested cormorants, black-legged kittiwakes, black guillemots and other marine bird species; during spring and fall migrating birds rest there. Grey and harbor seals bask on offshore rocks, and seven species of whales cavort in the park's bays.

The Interpretation Centre on Highway 132 near Cap-des-Rosiers offers exhibits and films daily. Evening talks and naturalist-guided walks also are offered. Guided walks are available in English. Three campgrounds are available. The park is open year-round. Reception and information centers near Penouille and L'Anse-au-Griffon are open daily, mid-June through Labour Day. Cap-des-Rosiers Interpretation Centre is open daily 10-5, June 1 through mid-Oct. *See Recreation Chart and the AAA/CAA Eastern Canada CampBook.*

ADMISSION to the park is $6.90; over 65, $5.90; ages 6-16, $3.45; family rate $17.30. Reduced rates are offered off season. The daily camping fee is $22.75, or $24.75 for a site with electricity.

ADDRESS inquiries to the Park Superintendent, Forillon National Park of Canada, 122 boul. Gaspé, Gaspé, QC, Canada G4X 1A9; phone (418) 638-5505 mid-May through early Aug. or (888) 773-8888, or (877) 737-3783 for campsite reservations.

FORT-COULONGE (E-2) pop. 1,661

SAVE **WATERFALLS OF COULONGE** (Chutes Coulonge), via Hwy. 148 following signs to 100 Promenade du Parc des Chutes, are in a small park that includes a 48-metre (157-ft.) waterfall, a 762-metre (2,500-ft.) canyon and a 1-kilometre (0.6-mi.) walking trail. A museum displays sawmill artifacts and presents a videotape about the history of logging in the area.

Allow 1 hour, 30 minutes minimum. Open daily 9-5, mid-Apr. to mid-Oct., with extended summer hours. Admission $6; senior citizens and students with ID $5; ages 7-17, $2. Phone to verify prices. Phone (819) 683-2770.

FORT LENNOX NATIONAL HISTORIC SITE OF CANADA (F-8)

Fort Lennox National Historic Site of Canada (Lieu historique national du Canada du Fort-Lennox) is in Saint-Paul-de-l'île-aux-Noix on the Richelieu River about 19 km (12 mi.) s. of Saint-Jean-sur-Richelieu. The 81-hectare (200-acre) park is accessible by ferry, which departs from the visitor center on the mainland every 30 minutes on the quarter-hour. At the south end of the island are the well-preserved buildings of Fort Lennox, one of the largest forts built in Canada.

The first fortifications were begun by the French in 1759 during the Seven Years' War to resist the advance of the British, who captured and destroyed the fort the following year. In 1775 the island was captured and occupied by American troops under generals Richard Montgomery and Philip Schuyler. After the Americans evacuated the island in 1776, the British built stronger fortifications. During the War of 1812, the British established a shipyard and the island became a naval base.

Between 1819 and 1829 a new building was constructed; the complex was named for Charles Lennox, Duke of Richmond. The fort was garrisoned during the revolution of 1837-38 and during the American Civil War, but the British finally abandoned it in 1870. Among the massive stone buildings are the officers' quarters, guardhouse, powder magazine, barracks and commissary. Narrated tours are available. Picnicking is permitted.

Daily 10-6, June 24-Labour Day; daily 10-5, mid-May through June 23; Sat.-Sun. 10-6, day after Labour Day through mid-Oct. Admission $7.50; over 65, $6.50; ages 6-16, $3.50; family rate $18. Phone (450) 291-5700 or (888) 773-8888.

GASPÉ (B-9) pop. 14,932

At the eastern extremity of the Gaspé Peninsula, the town of Gaspé adjoins the mouth of the York River and overlooks an immense natural harbor. Explorer Jacques Cartier sailed into this bay in 1534 with two ships, and upon landing erected a cross claiming Canada for France. The word Gaspé is derived from the Micmac Indian word *gespeg*, meaning "land's end."

Commemorating the French explorer's landing is the Jacques Cartier Monument, 2 kilometres (1.2 mi.) north on Hwy. 132. Six slabs shaped like dolmens recall Cartier's Breton heritage and depict the events of his landing. For further information phone (418) 368-1534.

Gaspé lies along the scenic portion of Hwy. 132, which follows the tip of the Gaspé Peninsula from Ste-Anne-des-Monts on the northern coast to Grand-Rivière on the southern coast.

Gaspé Tourist Information Bureau: 27 York Est, Gaspé, QC, Canada G4X 2K9; phone (418) 368-6335.

GASPÉSIE MUSEUM (Musée de la Gaspésie) is at 80 boul. Gaspé. This museum presents exhibits about the history of the region and of works by local artists. A library has works about Gaspésian history and people. On the grounds are the Jacques Cartier Monument, an amphitheater in which concerts are presented July and August evenings, and a historic interpretation trail. Guided tours are available if requested a minimum of three days in advance.

Allow 30 minutes minimum. Daily 9-5, June 24-Labour Day; Tues.-Fri. 9-5, Sat.-Sun. 1-5, rest of year. Admission $7; over 65 and ages 12-18, $5; family rate $11-$15. MC, VI. Phone (418) 368-1534.

GASPÉ PENINSULA (B, C-8)

Approaching the Gaspé Peninsula on his 1534 first voyage to North America, Jacques Cartier enjoyed one of the most spectacular views on the continent: sheer cliffs battered by the sea, clouds of seabirds and craggy mountains covered with forests.

Bounded by the Gulf of St. Lawrence to the northeast, the St. Lawrence River and Cap-Chat to the north and Matapédia and the Baie des Chaleurs to the south, the Gaspé is circled by an 885-kilometre (553-mi.) section of Hwy. 132.

French-Canadian fishermen have molded the history of the peninsula's rugged north shore; villages shelter in the coves and display their catches drying on *vigneau* racks. Acadian, Basque, Loyalist and Micmac Indian communities as well as fashionable resorts give the south shore a cosmopolitan flavor.

Forming a 1,268-metre-high (4,160-ft.) backdrop, the Chic-Chocs Mountains of the peninsula's interior shelter herds of moose and rare woodland caribou inside Gaspésie National Park *(see Ste-Anne-des-Monts p. 228)*. At the northeastern tip of the peninsula, the Chic-Chocs meet the sea in Forillon National Park of Canada *(see place listing p. 165)*.

Towns listed individually on the Gaspé Peninsula are Bonaventure, Cap-Chat, Causapscal, Gaspé, Grand-Métis, Murdochville, Percé, Pointe-à-la-Croix and Ste-Anne-des-Monts. Another town worth visiting is New-Carlisle, a picturesque Loyalist village.

GATINEAU (F-3) pop. 234,679

Part of the National Capital Region, Gatineau is one of the oldest settlements in the area. In 1800 Philemon Wright arrived from Woburn, Mass., with his family and a number of townspeople and soon established the timber trade that sustained the region for more than a century. The E.B. Eddy Co., a pulp and paper products factory that is the city's main industry, was built then.

Several parks offer recreational facilities and picnic areas *(see the AAA/CAA Eastern Canada Camp-Book)*. Ski centers abound in the region. Of historical interest are a monument to Saint-Jean de Brébeuf, a Jesuit missionary and martyr, and an original timber slide that cuts through a wall of solid rock.

Outaouais Tourism Association: 103 rue Laurier, Gatineau, QC, Canada J8X 3V8; phone (819) 778-2222 or (800) 265-7822. *See color ad card insert.*

Shopping areas: Three shopping malls serve the Gatineau area: Les Galeries de Hull, 320 St. Joseph Blvd.; Les Promenades de l'Outaouais, 1100 W. Maloney Blvd.; and Place du Centre, 200 Promenade du Portage. Les Galeries de Hull has 70 stores. Les Promenades de l'Outaouais' has 200 stores. Place du Centre has 60 stores.

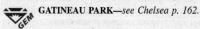 **CANADIAN MUSEUM OF CIVILIZATION** (Musée canadien des civilisations) at 100 Laurier St., directly across the Ottawa River from the Parliament Buildings, illustrates Canada's history from the continent's prehistoric beginnings through successive periods of migration, native settlement, exploration, fur trading, immigration and the modern era.

Life-size reconstructions such as a West Coast native village and other historic sites present a dramatic interpretation of the country's past. Other highlights include the Canadian Children's Museum, the Canadian Postal Museum and an IMAX theater. Food is available.

Sat.-Wed. 9-6, Thurs.-Fri. 9-9, July 1-Labour Day; Fri.-Wed. 9-6, Thurs. 9-9, May-June and day after Labour Day-second Mon. in Oct.; Tues.-Wed. and Fri.-Sun. (also Easter Mon.) 9-5, Thurs. 9-9, rest of year. Extended evening hours do not apply to the children's museum. The IMAX schedule does not always correspond with museum schedule; phone ahead for show times. Closed Dec. 25.

Museum admission $10; over 65 and ages 13-17, $8; ages 3-12, $6; family rate (four persons with maximum of two adults) $25. IMAX film $9.50; over 65 and ages 13-17, $8; ages 3-12, $7. Ask about reduced rates for a second CinéPlus film. Combination museum admission and one film $17; over 65, $14; ages 13-17, $13; ages 3-12, $10. Free to all Thurs. 4-9 and Heritage Day (third Mon. in Feb.), Museums Day (early May), July 1, and Nov. 11. Phone to verify prices. AX, MC, VI. Phone (819) 776-7000, (800) 555-5621, TTY (819) 776-7003, or (819) 776-7010 for show times.

GATINEAU PARK—*see Chelsea p. 162.*

HULL-CHELSEA-WAKEFIELD STEAM TRAIN (Train à vapeur de Hull-Chelsea-Wakefield) departs Gare Station at 165 rue Deveault for a 5-hour, 64-kilometre (40-mi.) steam-powered round-trip rail excursion through the scenic Gatineau Valley. A 2-hour stay in the picturesque village of Wakefield is included. A sunset dinner train and Sunday brunch trains also are available. Food is available.

The 2007 schedule is departures at 10, May 5-6, 8-9, 12-13, 15-16, 19-21, 26-27, 29-30; Tues.-Wed. and Fri.-Sun. at 10, June 1-29; daily at 10, June 30-Labour Day; at 10, Sept. 8-16, 18-19 and 22-28; Mon.-Fri. at 10, Sat.-Sun. at 8:30 and 2, Sept. 29-Oct. 14; departures at 10, Oct. 15-17, 20, and 28.

Phone to confirm all schedules. Arrive 30 minutes prior to departure. **Note:** Reservations are required.

Fare May 5-Sept. 20, 2007, $41; over 60, $39; students with ID $38; ages 3-12, $20; family rate (two adults and two children) $105. Fare Sept. 22-Oct. 28, $47; over 60, $43; students with ID $42; ages 3-12, $25; family rate (two adults and two children) $119. Brunch trains $69; ages 3-12, $35. Reservations are required. AX, JC, MC, VI. Phone (819) 778-7246 or (800) 871-7246.

CASINOS

- **Casino du Lac-Leamy**, 1 boul. du Casino. Daily 9 a.m.-4 a.m. Phone (819) 772-2100 or (800) 665-2274.

GODBOUT (B-7) pop. 327

A fishing village on the North Shore of the Gulf of St. Lawrence, Godbout was the site of an early Hudson's Bay fur-trading post. It is now known among anglers for the salmon fishing opportunities it affords. A ferry service runs between Godbout and Matane; phone (418) 568-7575 for schedules and fares.

AMERINDIAN AND INUIT MUSEUM OF GODBOUT (Musée Amerindian et Inuit de Godbout), 134 rue Pascal-Comeau, presents a collection of recent Indian and Inuit sculpture, small pottery and other artifacts. Visitors can observe artists at work. Schedule may vary; phone ahead. Daily 9-9, mid-June to late Sept. Admission $4; ages 5-15, $2.50. Phone (418) 568-7306.

GRANBY (F-8) pop. 44,121

Granby is an industrial city known for its fountains, which include a 3,200-year-old Greek fountain on Boulevard Laval, a first-century Roman fountain in Pelletier Park and a fountain sculpted and dug in rock on Boulevard Leclerc.

Tourism Granby: 111 rue Denison, Granby, QC, Canada J2G 8L4; phone (450) 372-7056 or (800) 567-7273.

GEM GRANBY ZOO (Zoo de Granby), Eastern Townships Hwy. 10 exit 68 or 74 following signs to 525 rue St-Hubert, contains more than 1,000 animals representing 200 exotic species, including African elephants, Amur tigers, lowland gorillas, snow leopards and spectacled bears. The animals live in enclosures that resemble their natural habitats. Of interest to the younger set is the petting zoo and the pony, camel, and monorail rides. Twenty daily presentations allow visitors to learn more about animal life. A miniature train is in the amusement park.

Food is available. Picnic facilities are available, but alcoholic beverages and glass containers are not permitted. Pets are not permitted. Allow 3 hours minimum. Opens daily at 10, late June-Aug.; phone for fall schedule and closing times. Combined admission to zoo and water park $26.49; over 65, $20.49; ages 3-12, $16.49; family rate (two adults

and two ages 3-12) $79.49. Two-day passes are available. AX, MC, VI. Phone (877) 472-6299.

AmaZoo Aquatic Park is off Hwy. 10 exit 68 or 74 following signs to 525 rue St-Hubert. This water park contains a large wave pool, an adventurous river ride and water games; the water is heated. Food is available and picnicking is permitted.

Alcoholic beverages and glass containers are not permitted. Pets are not permitted. Open daily 10-7, late June to late Aug.; daily 10-5, Memorial Day weekend to late June. Phone to confirm schedule Combined admission to zoo and water park $24.99; over 65, $19.99; ages 3-12, $15.99. Phone to confirm prices. MC, VI. Phone (877) 472-6299.

NATURE INTERPRETATION CENTRE OF LAC BOIVIN (Centre d'interprétation de la nature du lac Boivin), 700 rue Drummond, is a park offering more than 13 kilometres (8 mi.) of hiking trails and an observation tower overlooking marsh and swamp. Explanatory signs s in French identify different flora and fauna along the trails. Allow 1 hour, 30 minutes minimum. Mon.-Fri. 8:30-4:30, Sat.-Sun. 9-5; closed Jan. 1, Dec. 25-26. Free. Phone (450) 375-3861.

GRAND-MÉTIS (C-7) pop. 281

Until the construction in 1929 of Boulevard Perron (Hwy. 132) around the land's perimeter, Grand-Métis was an isolated village on the Gaspé Peninsula. At the turn of the 20th century, Grand-Métis was the favorite salmon and summer vacation spot of the wealthy Sir George Stephen (Lord Mount Stephen), the first president of the Canadian Pacific Railway.

GEM REFORD GARDENS (Jardins de Métis) are n.e. on Hwy. 132, following signs. Once the summer fishing camp of Lord Mount Stephen, the estate was given in 1918 to Stephen's niece, Elsie Reford, who transformed the property into one of eastern Canada's most beautiful gardens.

Paths lead through formal and natural beds that display more than 3,000 species of trees, flowers and shrubs. Colorful rhododendrons and crab apples highlight the gardens in early summer and give way to thousands of lilies, roses and blue poppies in mid- and late summer. Estevan Lodge houses a museum with exhibitions about the history of the gardens and summer life at Métis. The International Garden Festival is a showcase for innovation and avant-garde design

Allow 2 hours minimum. Daily 8:30-6, July-Aug.; 8:30-5, in June and Sept.-Oct. Admission $14; over 65 and students with ID $12; under 14 free. AX, MC, VI. Phone (418) 775-2222.

GRANDES-BERGERONNES—
see Les Bergeronnes p. 170.

GRANDES-PILES (D-4)
pop. 374, elev. 122 m/400'

LUMBERJACK'S MUSEUM (Le Musée du Bûcheron), 780 5th av., is a restored lumberjack village chronicling the timber trade 1850-1950. Pit saws, fire towers, charcoal kilns and wood shops are on the grounds. Guided tours are available. English narration is available. Allow 1 hour minimum. Daily 10-6, May 15-Oct. 15. Admission $11.30; over 65 and students with ID $10; ages 6-12, $5; family rate $34. MC, VI. Phone (819) 538-7895.

HEMMINGFORD (F-7) pop. 1,703

Like many other villages across the Québec countryside, Hemmingford's origins were as a mission and parish. With the extension of the Canadian National Railway through town, it became a trading site for the surrounding rural region. Today, 1 million apple trees, a cider mill and wine makers characterize the region.

 PARK SAFARI (Parc Safari), 5 km (3 mi.) e. on Hwy. 202, is a 200-acre family oriented park with a zoological park, rides, shows and a water park.

The drive-through wildlife park has more than 800 animals from five continents. There are seven themed areas, including the Safari Drive-thru; the Deer Trail; the animal Observatory and the Insectarium. Arctic wolves, bears, chimpanzees, lions, macaques and tigers.

Mechanical rides and Parc Nairobi, a soft play area for children, picnic facilities, tubes rides and lake and beach areas for swimming and sunbathing are available. The Magic Creek provides tube rides. Four stages present live musical and trained animal shows.

Food is available. Allow 4 hours minimum. Daily 10-dusk, Sat. before third Mon. in May-Labour Day; Fri.-Sun. and second Mon. in Oct. 10-dusk, day after Labour Day-second Mon. in Oct. Admission $29; over 65, $21, ages 11-17, $19; ages 2-10, $13. Family rate (two adults and two children under 11) $78. AX, MC, VI. Phone (450) 247-2727.

ÎLE-AUX-COUDRES (D-6)

Île-aux-Coudres can be reached by a ferry that departs daily from the village of St-Joseph-de-la-Rive, which is just off Hwy. 362; phone (418) 438-2743 for schedule and fare information. The scenic island, in Charlevoix County on the north shore of the St. Lawrence River, was first visited in 1535 by Jacques Cartier, who named it for the abundance of hazelnut trees found there.

Now visited for its rugged, tree-shrouded beauty and tranquil charm, the island is a center for artisans who make textiles, including Québec rag rugs (*catalognes*), table mats and bed covers.

THE MILLS OF ISLE-AUX-COUDRES (Les Moulins de Île-aux-Coudres Économusée de la Meunerie), on the Rouge River, following signs to 36 chemin du Moulin, consist of a restored 1825 watermill and 1836 windmill that took turns grinding flour, depending on which source of energy was more abundant. Today the buildings as well as the miller's house and forge contain displays about 19th-century rural life; guides conduct milling demonstrations. Tour narration is available in English.

Allow 30 minutes minimum. Daily 9:30-5:30, mid-May through mid-Oct. Admission $8; ages 6-18, $5. Phone to verify prices. Phone (418) 438-2184.

ÎLES DE LA MADELEINE

The îles de la Madeleine (Magdalen Islands) are 215 kilometres (134 mi.) east of the Gaspé Peninsula in the Gulf of St. Lawrence. The 96-kilometre-long (60-mi.) archipelago encompasses about a dozen islands and several islets. First visited by Jacques Cartier in 1534, the islands were settled in 1755 by Acadians expelled from Nova Scotia.

Most Madelinots are fishermen who live in small port communities that dot the islands. The culture and heritage of the people are captured in the exhibits at the Museum of the Sea (Musée de la Mer) in Havre-Aubert; phone (418) 937-5711.

Colonies of birds, representing more than 50 species, inhabit the islands during migration periods. A large bird sanctuary, île Rocher-aux-Oiseaux, can be visited by boat through arrangements with local fishermen in Grande-Entrée; phone (418) 986-2245.

The islands are accessible by boat from Montréal as well as Souris, Prince Edward Island. Daily air service is available from Charlottetown, Prince Edward Island; Moncton, New Brunswick; and Montréal and Gaspé.

Îles de la Madeleine Tourist Information Bureau: 128 ch. Principal, Cap-aux-Meules, QC, Canada G4T 1C5; phone (418) 986-2245 or (877) 624-4437.

JONQUIÈRE (C-5) pop. 54,842

Two modernistic churches in Jonquière reflect the province's revival of religious architecture during the 1960s. The St-Raphaël Church, 2381 St-Jean-Baptiste, has no walls; instead, the copper roof rises 19.4 metres (64 ft.) from the ground, supporting itself and enclosing the space. The Notre-Dame-de-Fatima Church, 3635 Notre-Dame, is shaped like an Indian tepee.

Jonquière Tourist Information Office: Convention Center, 2665 boul. du Royaume, Jonquière, QC, Canada G7S 5B8; phone (418) 548-4004 or (800) 561-9196.

KAHNAWAKE—*see Montréal p. 195.*

LAC-BROME (KNOWLTON) (F-8)
pop. 5,100

At the foot of Mont Brome and on the shores of lac Brome, the country resort of Lac-Brome is known for its Victorian Swiss chalet-style villas along the lake. Recreational activities include tennis, golf, fishing and water sports. The area also is noted for its duck breeding.

SAVE **BROME COUNTY HISTORICAL MUSEUM** (Musée de la Société d'histoire du comté de Brome), 130 rue Lakeside in Knowlton, comprises five buildings, including a general store and the old Knowlton Academy, built in 1854. The buildings contain displays of Victorian and Indian items, military memorabilia, farm tools, embroidery and weaving.

The World War I Fokker biplane, part of German war reparations to Canada, is the only one known with the original camouflage-fabric covering intact. Allow 1 hour, 30 minutes minimum. Mon.-Sat. 10-4:30, Sun. 11-4:30, mid-May to mid-Sept. Admission $5; over 65, $3; under 16, $2.50. Phone (450) 243-6782.

LACHINE—see Montréal p. 195.

LA DORÉ (C-4) pop. 1,553

[SAVE] **THE PIONEERS MILL** (Moulin des Pionniers), 4201 rue des Peupliers, is the site of an 1889 sawmill. Other highlights include a landlocked salmon pond, an exhibit about forest fires, a 1904 farm house and mountain bicycle and hiking trails past the site's 21 species of trees. Visitors can fish for trout. Daily 9-5, early June through mid-Oct. Admission $12; over 65 and students with ID $10; under 12, $8; family rate (parents and dependent children under 15) $25. MC, VI. Phone (418) 256-8242 or (886) 272-8242.

LA MALBAIE (C-6) pop. 4,000

La Malbaie is a popular summer resort along the St. Lawrence River. Samuel de Champlain chose the name, meaning "bad bay," because of its rugged, perilous shoreline. An artists' colony, the town has several small galleries and craft shops open during the summer.

Charlevoix Tourist Information Bureau: 495 boul. de Comporté, La Malbaie, QC, Canada G5A 3G3; phone (418) 665-4454 or (800) 667-2276. *See color ad p. 385.*

CASINOS

• **Casino de Charlevoix**, 183 rue Richelieu. Sun.-Thurs. 10 a.m.-2 a.m., Fri.-Sat. 10 a.m.-3 a.m., late June-Labour Day; Sun.-Thurs. 11 a.m.-1 a.m., Fri.-Sat. 11 a.m.-3 a.m., mid-May through mid-June and day after Labour Day-last Sun. in Oct.; Sun.-Thurs. 11 a.m.-midnight, Fri.-Sat. 11 a.m.-3 a.m., rest of year. Phone (418) 665-5300 or (800) 665-2274.

◥GEM LA MAURICIE NATIONAL PARK OF CANADA (D-4)

Elevations in the park range from 98 metres (320 ft.) along the St-Maurice River to 457 metres (1,500 ft.) at an area near Lake Houle. Refer to CAA/AAA maps for additional elevation information.

North of Trois-Rivières, halfway between Montréal and Québec and accessible from Hwy. 55, La Mauricie National Park of Canada (Parc national du Canada de la Mauricie) is an unspoiled area in the Laurentian Mountains that occupies 536 square kilometres (206 sq. mi.) in the St-Maurice Valley. The park overlies bedrock dating from the Precambrian era, which began about 980 million years ago.

During the last ice age, glaciers scored the land and left rolling hills. Terraces along the St-Maurice River once formed the beaches of the postglacial Champlain Sea. Two main valleys are marked by chains of narrow lakes.

Of the more than 193 bird species that have been observed, 116 nest in the park. Mammals include moose, black bears, coyotes, and lynxes.

Picnicking, camping, canoeing, swimming and fishing are popular pastimes in summer; winter brings cross-country skiing, snowshoeing and winter camping. The park is open all year. *See Recreation Chart and the AAA/CAA Eastern Canada Camp-Book.*

ADMISSION to the park is $6.90; over 65, $5.90; ages 6-16, $3.45; family rate $17.30.

ADDRESS inquiries to the Park Superintendent, La Mauricie National Park of Canada, 702 5th St., P.O. Box 160, Main Station, Shawinigan, QC, Canada G9N 6T9; phone (819) 538-3232 or (888) 773-8888, or (877) 737-3783 for camping reservations.

L'ANSE-AU-GRIFFON (B-9)

LeBOUTILLIER MANOR (Manoir LeBoutillier), on Hwy. 132 at 578 boul. Griffon, was the home of merchant and legislator John LeBoutillier during the mid-19th century. The house faces the harbor, where LeBoutillier could oversee his fishing fleets. Exhibits depict the commercial development of the region's fishing industry. Daily 9-5, June 18-Oct. 8, 2007. Admission $7, over 65 and students with ID $5, family rate $16. Phone (418) 892-5150.

LAURENTIAN HIGHLANDS (E-3,4)

The Laurentian Mountain region, *Laurentides* in French, is part of Québec's vast wilderness of dense forests, glacial lakes and rivers stretching northwest of the populous St. Lawrence Valley. The land's inhospitableness caused many settlers to leave Québec in the 19th century, but not Father Antoine Labelle.

As proof of his faith, Father Labelle created 20 new parishes in the Laurentian wilderness just northwest of Montréal, promising his parishioners that one day strangers would flock to the area and scatter gold by the handful. When Father Labelle began his efforts, there were barely a dozen communities north of St-Jérôme, and gold was nowhere apparent.

If he returned today, Labelle would find his prophecy fulfilled in the 19 ski resorts that line Hwy. 117 from St-Jérôme to Mont-Tremblant. The mountains and lakes that once provided foresters and farmers with their livelihoods are now the backbone of a resort area devoted principally to skiing.

Herman "Jack Rabbit" Johannssen loved touring the region and created the Maple Leaf Trail, which linked Prévost with Mont-Tremblant; only part of the trail remains today.

Improvising with lines, tackles and an automobile engine, Alex Foster laid the cornerstone for alpine skiing by building Canada's first ski tow and laying out a slalom run in Prévost in the 1930s.

From a simple rope tow and slalom run have come the more than 350 ski runs that now dot the mountainsides as well as the many trails connecting various communities.

The Laurentians are more than a ski resort; they also are a retreat from the nearby urban centers. The tranquility of the area has encouraged painters, musicians, artisans and writers to settle in Ste-Adèle, Val-David and other such villages.

During the summer, works are displayed in numerous theaters, craft fairs and folklore festivals. The region also is known for its spectacular fall foliage from mid-September to mid-October.

Mont-Tremblant Park *(see Mont-Tremblant p. 198)* has hundreds of trails from which to view the park's many lakes, waterfalls and wildlife.

Towns in the Laurentian Highlands listed individually are Mont-Tremblant, Ste-Adèle, Ste-Agathe-des-Monts and Val-David. Other towns of interest include St-Jérôme and St-Sauveur-des-Monts, known for its crafts, waterslides and ski slopes.

LAVAL—*see Montréal p. 195.*

LES BERGERONNES (C-6)
pop. 600, elev. 32 m/105′

CAP DE BON-DÉSIR INTERPRETATION AND OBSERVATION CENTRE (Centre d'interprétation et d'observation du Cap-de-Bon-Désir), 166 Rte. 138 in the Saguenay-St Lawrence Marine Park *(see listing p. 224)*, allows visitors to view the marine wildlife in the St. Lawrence estuary, including whales, seals and birds. On-site naturalists answer questions and conduct various interpretation activities. English narration is available.

Picnicking is permitted. Daily 8-8, mid-June-Labour Day; 9-6, June 1-early June and day after Labour Day to mid-Oct. Admission $6.90; over 65, $5.90; ages 6-16, $3.45; family rate $17.30. MC, VI. Phone (418) 232-6756 or (888) 773-8888.

LES ESCOUMINS

MARINE ENVIRONMENT DISCOVERY CENTRE is at 41 Rue des Pilotes, .6 km (.4 mi) s. of Rte. 138, following signs. This riverfront center features displays about the marine life of the St-Lawrence River and explores its underwater mysteries. An optional live interactive show allow visitors to watch scuba-diving guides explore the coastline in front of the center.

Rental scuba gear is available to certified divers. Allow 1 hour, 30 minutes minimum. Open daily 9-6 (interactive shows Wed.-Sun.), mid-June through Labour Day; Sat.-Sun. 9-6, day after Labour Day-second Mon. in Oct. Admission $6.90; over 65,

$5.90; ages 4-17, $3.45. An additional fee is charged for the show. AX, MC, VI. Phone (418) 233-4414, or (418) 235-4703 in the off season.

LÉVIS—*see Québec p. 221.*

L'ISLET-SUR-MER (D-6) pop. 643

For more than 3 centuries L'Islet-sur-Mer has produced seafarers; as a result, it is known locally as *la patrie des marins*, "the sailor's homeland." Native Capt. Joseph Elzéar Bernier took possession of the Arctic islands in the name of Canada on July 1, 1909. A plaque on Melleville Island commemorates the event.

Of interest is the 1768 Notre-Dame-de-Bon-Secours Church in the center of the village. The church has a wealth of decorative objects, including artwork by Ranvoyzé and sculptor Médard Bourgault.

L'Islet lies just north of the northern terminus of the scenic portion of Hwy. 132, which runs along the St. Lawrence from Sorel-Tracy to L'Islet.

SAVE **MARITIME MUSEUM OF QUÉBEC** (Musée Maritime du Québec), on Hwy. 132 at 55 chemin des Pionniers Est in a former 1877 convent, contains memorabilia describing the history of navigation on the St. Lawrence River. Models, sailing ships and exhibits about Capt. J.E. Bernier's Arctic exploration are displayed. Behind the museum are several ships, including the ice breaker *Ernest Lapointe* and the hydrofoil *Bras d'Or 400*; the ships are not open after Labour Day. Picnic facilities are available.

Daily 9-6, mid-June through Labour Day; 10-5, late May-early June and day after Labour Day-second Mon. in Oct.; 10-noon and 1:30-4, rest of year. Phone to confirm schedule. Admission $9; senior citizens $8; under 16, $4.50; family rate $22. VI. Phone (418) 247-5001.

MAGOG (F-8) pop. 14,283

Magog was founded in 1799 by British Loyalists who left America after the Revolutionary War. It is named for nearby lac Memphrémagog, which is the Abenaki Indian word for "vast expanse of water." The lake as well as the area's rivers, streams and mountains has made Magog a popular vacation resort, offering fishing, hiking, and water and winter sports.

In Ste-Catherine-de-Hatley the Île-du-Marais Nature Trail is reached by a causeway into lac Magog. The trail offers a self-guiding hike around the island April through October. More than 226 species of birds use the island as a nesting ground.

Magog Tourist Information Bureau: 55 rue Cabana, Magog, QC, Canada J1X 2C4; phone (819) 843-2744 or (800) 267-2744.

MONT ORFORD PARK—*see Orford p. 199.*

MALARTIC (C-1) pop. 3,704

MALARTIC MINERALOGICAL MUSEUM (Musée minéralogique de Malartic), 1 blk. s. of Hwy. 117 at

650 rue de la Paix, offers exhibits about mining operations and geology, and a multimedia presentation about geological landscape conversion. Guided tours last 1 hour; narration is available in English. Allow 1 hour minimum. Daily 9-5, June 1-Sept. 15; Mon.-Fri. 9-5, Sat.-Sun by appointment, rest of year. Admission $8; over 55 and students with ID $6; ages 5-12, $4; family rate (two adults and two children) $20. VI. Phone (819) 757-4677.

MASCOUCHE—see Montréal p. 196.

MASHTEUIATSH (C-4) elev. 107 m/350'

AMERINDIAN MUSEUM OF MASHTEUIATSH (Musée Amérindien de Mashteuiatsh), 1787 rue Amishk, is dedicated to preserving the history and culture of the First Nations peoples who first inhabited the Saguenay-Lac-Saint-Jean region. The Ilnuatsh, as they are known, are depicted through archeology, art and hand crafts. Educational films show the traditional Montagnais lifestyle.

Allow 1 hour minimum. Daily 10-6, May 15-Oct. 15; Mon.-Thurs. 9-noon and 1-4, Fri. 9-noon and 1-3, rest of year. Closed holidays. Admission $8; over 65, $7; students with ID $6; under 6 free; family rate (four persons) $18. Phone (418) 275-4842 or (888) 275-4842.

MATANE (B-7) pop. 11,635

A fishing community at the confluence of the Matane and St. Lawrence rivers, Matane is the outfitting point for salmon fishing in the Matane Animal Reserve *(see Recreation Chart)*. Matane fishermen also harvest halibut, cod and shrimp from the St. Lawrence River. Visitors can observe salmon fishing downtown along the Matane River; in season migrating salmon leap across the Mathieu-D'Amours Dam.

A ferry service from Matane runs to Baie-Comeau and Godbout in Québec's northlands; phone (418) 562-2500 for schedules and fares; reservations are required.

Matane Tourist Office: 968 av. du Phare Ouest, Matane, QC, Canada G4W 1V7; phone (418) 562-1065 or (877) 762-8263.

MELOCHEVILLE—see Montréal p. 196.

MIGUASHA (C-8)

MIGUASHA NATIONAL PARK (Parc national de Miguasha), 231 Rte. Miguasha Ouest, 6 km (4 mi.) s. jct. Hwy. 132, is a UNESCO World Heritage Site. This fossil site was discovered and many well-preserved fossils removed until the late 20th century. A preservation park was created in 1985 to protect and enhance the Escuminac Formation—a paleoecosystem of the Devonian period dating 378 million years ago. These fossils illustrate a very important event in the course of evolution—the transition from aquatic vertebrates to land vertebrates.

Today a visitor to the park is likely to find fossils only in the exhibits in the Museum of Natural History because digging is strictly forbidden. Food and picnic facilities are available. Museum open daily 9-6, June-Aug; daily 9-5, Sept. 1-second Mon. in Oct.; Mon.-Fri. 8:30-4:30, rest of year. Admission $11; ages 6-17, $5.50; family rate (one adult and dependent children ages 6-17) $15, family rate (two adults and children ages 6-17) $22.50. Phone (418) 794-2475 or (800) 665-6527 in Québec.

MINGAN ARCHIPELAGO NATIONAL PARK RESERVE OF CANADA (A-9)

Elevations in the park range from sea level at the Gulf of St. Lawrence to 46 metres (150 ft.) on some of the islands within the reserve. Refer to CAA/AAA maps for additional elevation information.

Mingan Archipelago National Park Reserve of Canada (Réserve de parc national du Canada de l'Archipel-de-Mingan), approximately 870 kilometres (540 miles) from Québec via Route 138 East, consists of a group of 1,000 islands off the n. shore of the St. Lawrence Gulf and is accessible by boat from Longue Pointe, Mingan and from Havre-St-Pierre. The archipelago, directly north of île Anticosti in the Jacques Cartier Strait, stretches about 150 kilometres (93 mi.) and was formed mostly from sedimentary rock. Erosion by the sea has resulted in spectacular rock formations.

The islands support a variety of arctic and subarctic plant life and an abundant waterfowl population. Around the chain the sea harbors clams, crabs, fish, whales and other marine animals. Coniferous boreal forests cover most of the islands.

The cold waters surrounding the islands are suitable for such recreational activities as boating, sea kayaking, scuba diving and fishing. Boating season lasts from June to September. In addition, the islands' interesting topography and other features make for excellent wilderness camping.

Note: Campers are advised to take extra provisions and water, and to allow extra time to return, because the unpredictable sea can cause delays. Visitor centers offer information about park interpretation programs; phone Longue-Pointe-de-Mingan at (418) 949-2126, and Havre-St-Pierre at (418) 538-3285.

The park can be reached either by air or by Hwy. 138 from the city of Québec. The highway goes as far as Havre-St-Pierre, where boats depart for the islands from June to September; reservations are required. Take extra provisions and water, and allow extra time to return, as the unpredictable sea can cause delays.

ADMISSION to the park is $5.45; over 65, $4.70; ages 6-16, $2.70; family rate (seven persons, two adults maximum) $13.60. A permit is required for wilderness camping; the fee is $13.85-$15.85. Fees are charged by private transporters authorized by Parks Canada to offer boat service to the islands. These fees vary depending on the destination and the type of service provided. Reservations are required for boat trips. The park web site has a list of transportation providers with phone numbers and links.

ADDRESS inquiries to the Superintendent, Mingan Archipelago National Park Reserve, 13040 rue de la Digue, Havre-St-Pierre, QC, Canada G0G 1P0; phone (888) 773-8888. *See Recreation Chart.*

MONTEBELLO (E-3) pop. 1,039

MANOIR PAPINEAU NATIONAL HISTORIC SITE OF CANADA (Lieu historique national du Canada du Manoir Papineau), 500 Notre-Dame next to the Château Montebello on Hwy. 148, was built by prominent political figure Louis-Joseph Papineau about 1850. The three-story manor house on the wooded north bank of the Ottawa River is restored and furnished in period. A small stone chapel on the grounds contains the tombs of Papineau and other family members. Two other historical buildings are open to the public.

Guided tours are given regularly; English narration is available. Allow 1 hour minimum. The 2007 schedule is daily 10-5, mid-June through Aug. 26; Wed.-Sun. 10-5, mid-May through early June and Aug. 27-Oct. 7. Admission $7.15; over 65, $5.90; ages 6-16, $3.45; family rate $17.80. Phone (819) 423-6965 or (888) 773-8888.

MONT-LAURIER (D-3) pop. 7,365

Named after Sir Wilfrid Laurier (prime minister 1896-1911), Mont-Laurier is at the foot of Mont Sir Wilfrid. The town is a shipping and trading center for the surrounding dairy and lumber industries and is popular with fishing and hunting enthusiasts. The Benedictine nuns at the Abbaye des Moniales operate a large goat-breeding farm where they sell homemade goat cheese, chocolate and caramel; phone (819) 623-3780.

Mont-Laurier Chamber of Commerce: 436 de la Madone, Bureau 2, Mont-Laurier, QC, Canada J9L 1S3; phone (819) 623-4544 or (888) 560-9988.

LA VÉRENDRYE WILDLIFE RESERVE (Réserve faunique la Vérendrye), 60 km (37 mi.) n.w. on Hwy. 117, covers 13,615 square kilometres (5,257 sq. mi.), with approximately 2,200 square kilometres (849 sq. mi.) suitable for canoe trips and wilderness camping. Fishing is excellent. The reserve is a game sanctuary; motorists should be alert for animals crossing the roadway.

Sat.-Wed. 7-7, Thurs. 7 a.m.-9 p.m., Fri. 7 a.m.-10 p.m., mid-May mid-September. Admission

free. Phone (819) 438-2017 or (819) 736-7431. *See Recreation Chart.*

MONTMAGNY (D-6) pop. 11,654

One of the earliest towns along the south shore of the St. Lawrence River, Montmagny is the commercial center for a fertile valley region. Wheat fields and 18th-century villages dot the landscape south of Montmagny before giving way to hilly country crossed by rivers and snowmobile and cross-country skiing trails.

The coastal town is known for its arts and crafts, and the spring and fall arrival of thousands of snow geese. Montmagny also is a point of debarkation for cruises of the archipelago of Île aux Grues.

The Manoir Couillard-Dupuis, at 301 boul. Taché Est, is a 1789 stone manor house containing the Musée de l'Accordéon; phone (418) 248-7927.

Montmagny Tourism Information Bureau: 45 av. du Quai, C.P. 71, Montmagny, QC, Canada G5V 3S3; phone (418) 248-9196 or (800) 463-5643.

 GROSSE ÎLE AND THE IRISH MEMORIAL NATIONAL HISTORIC SITE OF CANADA, in the St. Lawrence River, is reached by cruises from Berthier-sur-Mer, Québec and Ste-Anne de Beaupré. Private watercraft are not permitted to dock on the island. The island was once known as Quarantine Island because of the great number of European immigrants who were quarantined here during the period 1832-1937.

A Celtic cross on the summit of the island's western section commemorates the Great Irish Famine and the tragic events of 1847 on Grosse Île, when 100,000 mostly Irish immigrants arrived—thousands of them died of typhoid and are buried in Grosse Île's Irish cemetery. Today more than 100 historic buildings are on the island; many are being restored. Guided tours are available mid-May to mid-Oct. (weather permitting). The tours include a visit to the disinfection building, a 60-minute walking tour and a 60-minute tram tour.

Narration is available in English. Food is available. Allow 4 hours minimum on site. Site open May-Oct. Durations of trips and length of stay on the island vary. Carriers depart daily, mid-June through Aug. 31; by appointment early May-early June and Sept.-Oct. The park tour fee is included in the carriers' packages. Package cruise rates $42-$60. Some departures require a minimum number of persons; phone ahead. MC, VI. Phone (888) 773-8888.

ÎLE AUX GRUES, reached by a free automobile and passenger ferry from Montmagny, is the largest of the 21 islands in the archipelago and the only one inhabited throughout the year. Bicycling and guided tours of historical buildings are available; narration in English is available. Ferry runs daily Apr.-Dec. Free. Phone (418) 248-6869 for ferry information.

Montréal

City Population: 1,039,534   Elevation: 15 m/49 ft.

Editor's Picks:

Botanical Garden of Montréal.....*(see p. 181)*
Mont-Royal Park...................*(see p. 184)*
Old Montréal.......................*(see p. 185)*

You are invited to a party. The hostess is French and the *hors-d'oeuvres* and decor have a decidedly European flair. A five-course meal enhanced with fine French wine soon will grace the elegantly appointed dining table. Hushed *tête-à-têtes* on one side of the room, however, are likely to be in English. On the coffee table are the *Times* of New York and the *Times* of London, and through the windows the rows of prim Victorian homes are evidence of an architectural legacy of British inspiration.

The neighborhood is probably in Montréal—Canada's bilingual, multicultural city. Two distinct, homogenous societies, each lending its distinctions to the other but the two rarely melding, have emerged peacefully side-by-side. However, this tolerant coexistence also is defined by linguistic tensions that spark endless political battles.

Faced with the task of finding gold for the reigning King Francis I, French sailor Jacques Cartier set out in 1535 in search of a shortcut to the Orient. His geography a tad off, the explorer came instead upon the north shore of an island. He took the opportunity to climb the mountain in the middle of the island and called it Mont Royal. Upon his descent he noticed a village on the side of the mountain, home to some 1,500 Iroquois. Cartier called the native settlement Hochelaga, meaning "at the place of the beaver dam," and returned to France the following year without gold. He wasn't empty-handed, however; his treasure was a valuable Canadian beaver's pelt.

In 1556 the Italian Giovanni Battista Ramusio reviewed Cartier's discoveries and attempted to translate his log. Mount Royal in Italian became *Monte Réal*, which is believed to be the origin of Montréal.

Some 70 years after Cartier's visit, Samuel de Champlain traveled to the island interested in fur. In 1611 he arrived at the St. Lawrence River island, dubbed Mont-Royal, and established a fur-trading post at Place Royale. His fancy for a small island led him to spend his wife's dowry to purchase it; he named the island—Île Ste-Hélène—in her honor.

The Old Port, Old Montréal
© Ministère du Tourisme du Québec / Linda Turgeon

While the fur trade was the key reason for France's interest in colonizing Canada, Montréal's foundation rested on a more pious base. Tales began to circulate of errant Indians and the tortured Jesuit priests who tried to convert them. Under the leadership of Paul de Chomedey, Sieur de Maisonneuve, a mission of 50 colonists set off for Champlain's Place Royale. Their fervent passion for converting heathen Indians led to the founding of Ville-Marie in 1642.

It is worthwhile to mention the geographical advantages afforded by the area that encouraged the founding of what would come to be known as Montréal. The city resides on an island in the St. Lawrence River, the main route into northeastern North America. The Lachine rapids made it difficult to negotiate the river at this point, and the site provided an opportunity for respite and easy access to other waterways.

Thus was laid the groundwork on which Montréal soon would flourish as a French outpost for the fur trade. Quick wealth brought people, and the growing population necessitated the need for more services.

Getting There — starting on p. 180

Getting Around — starting on p. 180

What To See — starting on p. 181

What To Do — starting on p. 188

Where To Stay — starting on p. 428

Where To Dine — starting on p. 458

The settlement's first chapel, Notre-Dame-de-Bon-Secours, led to the founding of the first native Canadian order. Most of Montréal's impressive architecture resulted from such religious influence. Montréal quickly became North America's principal Roman Catholic city and remained so nearly 2 centuries.

Following an intense period of fighting with the Iroquois in 1716, the French built a wall that roughly followed the boundaries of today's Old Montréal. It served not only to secure the city from attack but also to shield the pious from the drunken antics of hardy woodsmen who had "gone native" and joined the Indians in their lucrative fur-trading endeavors.

Five decades of prosperity behind the walls ended when the English began seeking a foothold in North America. In 1763, the Treaty of Paris ceded all of Canada to the British, ending the era of French control in Montréal. Surprisingly, British governors were accepting of the culture and guaranteed use of the French language and Roman Catholic religion under the Québec Act of 1774. Nevertheless, local demographics underwent a radical change.

When the British mandated import taxes on American colonists, infuriated colonists openly rebelled against the crown. Feeling certain the French would support their rejection of Colonial rule, American troops marched to Montréal in 1775. Though little love was lost between French Canadians and the English, staunch Montréal Royalists had no patience for the revolutionists either. Their failure to back the American cause led to a short-lived occupation.

The 19th century saw, among other things, the expansion of Montréal's city limits. Walls around

Mont-Royal Park / © Tourisme Montréal

the old city were demolished, the first mayor was elected, and Montréal emerged as a progressive city, making the subsequent clamor for representative government understandable. Montréalers rejoiced when, in 1867, the British North America Act joined Nova Scotia, New Brunswick, Ontario and Québec, creating modern Canada.

By the turn of the 20th century, the Canadian Pacific Railway boom had fueled a building frenzy. Fabulous mansions bloomed throughout the "Golden Square Mile"—bordered by boulevard René-Lévesque, rue Guy, avenue des Pins and rue University. The harbor became another architectural showpiece.

As Montréal basked in the glow of its Golden Age, wealthy residents moved away from the town center, inching up Mont-Royal. Pockets of ethnic neighborhoods began to appear as newcomers made their way from the harbor and the train station. The city's population exploded with emigrants from Ireland, China, Greece, Italy and Portugal. Today, the

Destination Montréal

*M*ontréal works hard: It is the world's largest inland port; a hub of light and heavy manufacturing; a web of information technology; and a center of international finance and commerce.

*B*ut Montréal also knows how to relax. Its parks and gardens are beautiful. The museums, galleries and entertainments are excellent. And its shopping is first-rate.

© Andre Jenny

Pointe-à-Callière, Montréal Museum of Archaeology and History. This unusual structure relates 1,000 years of Montréal's history. (See listing page 186)

© MTOQ / Paul Villecourt

The Old Fort and Stewart Museum, Montréal. In the summer, a piper plays perfectly pitched period parade pieces. (See listing page 184)

Montréal

St-Eustache

Ste-Anne-de-Bellevue

Vaudreuil-Dorion

Melocheville

*P*laces included in this AAA Destination City:

© Tourisme Montréal
Stéphan Poulin

Old Montréal.
A horse-drawn carriage ride along
these cobblestone streets is the perfect
way to begin an exploration of this
slice of 18th-century Nouveau France.
(See listing page 185)

© Buddy Mays Travel Stock Photography

Biosphere, Montréal.
This Buckminster Fuller
geodesic dome graced
Expo '67 World's Fair.

Mascouche

Terrebonne

Laval

**See Downtown
map page 182**

St-
Laurent

Westmount

See Vicinity map page 182

Lachine

Chambly

Kahnawake

St-Constant

© Alt-6 / Alamy

*McCord Museum of Canadian
History, Montréal.*
Visitors explore 3 centuries
of Canadian history in this
venerable building. (See
listing page 184)

The Informed Traveler

Sales Tax: Canada levies a 6 percent sales tax. Québec's provincial sales tax is 7.5 percent on goods and services. The Montréal area hotel room occupancy tax is 3 percent per night.

WHOM TO CALL

Emergency: 911
Police (non-emergency): (514) 280-2222
Temperature: (514) 283-4006
Hospitals: Montréal General Hospital, (514) 934-1934; Royal Victoria Hospital of the McGill University Health Centre, (514) 934-1934; Sir Mortimer B. Davis-Jewish General Hospital, (514) 340-8222.

WHERE TO LOOK

Newspapers

Four major papers, printed daily except Sunday, serve the city. The *Gazette* is printed in English; *La Presse, Le Devoir* and *Journal de Montréal* are in French. All the papers carry daily events columns. The weekly *Montréal Mirror* tabloid and *Montréal Scope* magazine also carry events columns. The Sunday newspapers are *La Presse* and *Le Journal de Montréal*, (French) and *The Gazette*, (English).

Radio

Montréal radio stations CBC (940 FM) and CBM-FM (93.5 FM) are programmed by the Canadian Broadcasting Corp. Broadcasts are in English.

Visitor Information

Tourism Montréal Centre Infotouriste: 1255 Peel St., Suite 400, Montréal, QC, Canada H3B 4V4; phone (514) 873-2015 or (800) 363-7777.

Walk-in centers are at 1001 rue du Square-Dorchester, between Peel and Metcalfe streets; and in Old Montréal at Place Jacques-Cartier, 174 Notre-Dame St. E.

WHAT TO PACK

Montréal's invigorating weather ranges from cool to frigid most of the year. Temperatures dip below freezing as early as November, and on rare occasion snow may fall as late as May; a warm coat, hat and gloves are essential, and sunglasses and protective footwear also are recommended.

Although the onset of spring in mid-March brings periodic rain, the weather normally remains chilly; pack a raincoat and warm jacket. Sunshine and pleasant temperatures characterize June, July and August. Even after warm summer days, however, nighttime temperatures may fall, so carry a sweater.

Lasting from late September through mid-November, autumn generally is short. But what it lacks in longevity, it makes up for in brilliance as Canadian maples blaze with color. Days border on warm, and nights are comfortably cool. *For additional information see temperature chart p. 151.*

Hungarian bakeries, Portuguese gift shops and mixed bag of commercial activity along culturally diverse *"La Main"* (Boulevard St-Laurent) echo this influx.

It was during this time that Montréal filled its résumé with colorful goings-on. While Prohibition kept the United States and much of Canada sober, a very "wet" Montréal handed out stiff drinks to bootleggers, prostitutes and hordes of hucksters, who mingled with the rowdy set down at the port.

With economic inequality increasing, the gap between the French and English widened. Canada's economic focus began to shift away from the St. Lawrence River ports and toward Toronto and the Great Lakes. The result: Following World War II, Québec was left an isolated province where the church dictated public policy. The "Quiet Revolution" reawakened the masses and unveiled the face of Montréal that visitors see today.

The prevailing feeling was that a culturally French Québec should not have to endure a federalist government that failed to protect its uniqueness. Talk turned to separatism, and the liberated Québécois acted to effect religious, political and social reform.

Expo '67, a memorable World's Fair, was a turning point. Montréal proved it could serve as host for an international gathering, and 50 million people were introduced to the city's cultural charms. The impressive pavilions created for the event survived for 14 years.

After René Lévesque's Parti Québécois came into power in 1976, French was voted the province's official language. Over the next decade, Québec continued to fight, at various times and in various ways, for sovereignty. Voters repeatedly have turned down the proposal, however.

Today the "two solitudes," as Canadian novelist Hugh McLennan described them, have created two parallel communities within one modern city. While most residents are bilingual, the Francophone and Anglophone communities rarely interact. Perhaps the greatest tension is that each group is aware of being a vulnerable minority: The French are a distinct minority within Canada, and Anglophones are a distinct minority within Montréal. Squabbling persists primarily among politicians, and Montréalers, for the most part, are content to leave it that way.

Although Montréal is bilingual, it is a *multi*cultural city with a throng of visible ethnic communities. The two largest—Italian and Jewish—have been present in Montréal since the 19th century and have more successfully retained their identities than other groups that gradually merged into one of the great "solitudes." Recent immigration again has changed the face of the city as newcomers from Asia, Africa, the Antilles and the Near East make homes in Montréal.

Deep loyalty to its Gallic roots gives Montréal its individuality as a Canadian city. But it is not merely sidewalk cafes and croissants that have made the city *très* cosmopolitan. Montréal is a colorful canvas

Place Jacques-Cartier, Old Montréal / © Ministère du Tourisme du Québec / Linda Turgeon

of grand boulevards and twisting alleys, of Gothic cathedrals and cavernous beer halls, of Bohemian artists and *haute couture*. It is these broad strokes that set Montréal apart and attract millions of visitors each year to the city's considerable *joie de vivre*.

Getting There
By Car

The major highway route from the United States is I-87, which becomes Autoroute 15; I-87 enters Canada from northeastern New York. Autoroute 10 enters the city from the Eastern Townships and Vermont. From the east across the Champlain Bridge, Autoroute 20 allows controlled access to the downtown areas, and Autoroute 40 proceeds along the north shore of the St. Lawrence River. The Montréal Laurentian Autoroute, Hwy. 15, arrives from the north, while Autoroute 40 enters Montréal from the west.

Air Travel

Dorval's Pierre Elliott Trudeau International Airport (formerly Dorval Airport), 22 kilometres (14 mi.) west, handles commercial flights. Terminal exit signs direct travelers to Hwy. 20, which becomes Hwy. 720 (Autoroute Ville-Marie). From here, the exits to rues Guy, Atwater and de la Montagne provide access to downtown and Old Montréal.

Taxis to downtown average $28 from Pierre Elliott Trudeau International Airport. Station Aérobus, (800) 465-1213, serves the airport.

Nearly all major rental-car companies serve Montréal, and desks are inside airline terminals at the Pierre Elliott Trudeau International Airport. Be prepared for a high provincial tax on car rentals and an extra charge for insurance coverage. For the best prices, reservations should be made several weeks in advance, especially during peak seasons. Local AAA/CAA clubs can provide this assistance or additional information. Hertz, (514) 842-8537, (800) 263-0600 in Canada for English speakers, (800) 263-0678 in Canada for French speakers, or (800) 654-3131 outside Canada, offers discounts to CAA/AAA members.

Rail Service

Amtrak, (800) 872-7245, and VIA Rail Canada, (514) 989-2626, operate from Central Station, 895 de la Gauchetière beneath Queen Elizabeth Hotel. As part of the underground city, Central Station is connected to the Métro subway and to Windsor Station, at rues Peel and de la Gauchetière.

Buses

Greyhound Lines Inc. and Adirondacks Trailways run to New York City. Orléans Montréal operates within Québec. Terminus Voyageur station serves Canada and the United States. Vermont Transit serves major New England cities. Voyageur buses link Ontario cities.

Boats

Large vessels put in at Montréal's docks. Port d'escale du Vieux-Port de Montréal (Bassin Jacques Cartier), 333 de la Commune Ouest, charges $1.75 per 3 metre (1 ft.) or $6 per hour; phone (514) 283-5414.

Getting Around
Street System

Montréal can be a tricky place to navigate until you fully understand its odd layout. The city is on an island in the St. Lawrence River, which generally flows west to east from the Great Lakes to the Atlantic Ocean. The banks of the St. Lawrence are known as the north shore and south shore, even though the river flows almost due north where it meets Montréal. Consequently, the streets that run parallel to the river are labeled from Boulevard Saint-Laurent east-west, even though they actually run north-south; those perpendicular to the water, though nearly east-west, are labeled north-south.

Though it makes for an odd sensation at sunrise, it is easiest to orient yourself as if the harbor were to your south. Accordingly, the principal east-west streets downtown include Boulevard René-Lévesque, rue Ste-Catherine, Boulevard de Maisonneuve and rue Sherbrooke. The main downtown arteries running north-south include rue Crescent, rue McGill, rue St-Denis and Boulevard St-Laurent.

In Old Montréal, rues St-Jacques, Notre-Dame, St-Paul and de la Commune are the main thoroughfares running parallel to the south shore. Avenues du Mont-Royal and Laurier are the major streets north of the downtown area, near Mount Royal Park.

Boulevard St-Laurent is the dividing point between east and west (*est* and *ouest*) in Montréal. North-south streets do not have an equivalent dividing line, but numbers start at the south shore and climb with the topography. Even-numbered addresses are on the south and west sides of streets, odd-numbered addresses on the north and east sides.

Expressways in Québec are called autoroutes, and two such highways provide quick routes around the city. Canada's premier highway, the Trans-Canada, forks when it reaches Montréal, with Autoroute 40 crossing the northern side east to west and Autoroute 20 traveling along the south side. Though always well-patrolled, neither route is well-maintained. Both may have limited access.

Avenues De Lorimier and Papineau merge south of rue Ontario as the Jacques-Cartier Bridge, which crosses the St. Lawrence River to the islands of Ste-Hélène and Notre-Dame.

Drivers should be aware that right turns on red lights are illegal in Montréal.

Note: In the *What To See* section attraction listings will often include the nearest Métro (M) station or stations. Consult a Métro map to determine which train line is nearest and most direct.

Parking

Most major downtown office buildings, shopping centers and hotels have underground parking; Place d'Youville, the World Trade Center, Place Jacques-Cartier and Quai de l'Horloge all have lots. There is metered street parking in most commercial areas though parking generally is prohibited on main arteries during rush hours, 7-9 a.m. and 4-6 p.m. Regulations are posted on white signs throughout the city. Rates vary from lot to lot, but normally range $3-$5 per hour or $8-$15 per day.

Taxis

You should have no problem hailing a cab in Montréal; they are metered. Taxis are metered and fares generally are fixed at $3.15 to start, plus $1.45 for each kilometre traveled. Major companies are Diamond, (514) 273-6331; Taxi Co-op, (514) 725-9885; and Taxi Veteran, (514) 273-6351.

Public Transportation

Montréal Urban Community Transit Corp. (STM) provides clean, safe and comfortable bus, Métro (subway) and commuter train service throughout greater Montréal. Tickets are good for both bus and Métro. Transfer tickets are valid in any direction for the next 90 minutes; request one when you pay your fare. Buses on major routes operate through the night, but the Métro closes at 12:58 a.m. except Saturday night/Sunday morning, when it closes at 1 a.m.; service resumes at 5:30 a.m.

Tickets are sold at subway stations for $2.50 each or in strips of six for $10. For short visits, the best deal is a 1-day tourist pass for $7 or a 3-day pass for $16. A monthly pass, CAM (carte d'abonnement mensuel), can be purchased for $54 up to 10 days before the month for which it is valid. CAM hebdo, a 7-day pass, is $16. Métro tickets are good on buses, but if you don't have a ticket, you must have exact change.

Murals, sculpture, stained-glass windows, enameled frescoes and ceramics adorn the 65 Métro stations. Artistic themes range from city history to the abstract. Pick up a free transit guide and commuter train schedule at ticket booths, or phone (514) 288-6287.

What To See

ANGRIGNON PARK (Parc Angrignon), 3400 boul. des Trinitaires (M: Angrignon), covers 107 hectares (264 acres). Cross-country skiing and ice-skating are popular activities in winter. Picnic facilities are available. Free.

BOTANICAL GARDEN OF MONTRÉAL (Jardin botanique de Montréal) is opposite Olympic Stadium on rue Sherbrooke Est, next to Parc Maisonneuve (M: Pie-IX). Founded in 1931 by botanist Frère Marie-Victorin, the 75-hectare (180-acre) garden contains more than 22,000 varieties of plants within 30 gardens, 10 exhibition greenhouses and a 40-hectare (96-acre) arboretum. The garden is internationally recognized.

The Courtyard of the Senses was designed for the visually impaired, but others enjoy its aromas, sounds and textures. The Rose Garden contains more than 10,000 plants. The First Nations Garden spotlights the bond between the Amerindian and Inuit peoples and the plant world. Changing exhibits are highlighted throughout the year. Food is available.

Allow 2 hours, 30 minutes minimum. Daily 9-6, mid-June through Labour Day; daily 9-9, day after Labour Day-Oct. 31; Tues.-Sun. 9-5, rest of year. Admission May 15-Oct. 31, $13.75; over 65 and students with ID $10.25; ages 5-17, $7. Admission rest of year $10; over 65 and students with ID $8; ages 5-17, $5.50. Phone to verify prices and schedule. MC, VI. Phone (514) 872-1400.

Chinese Garden (Jardin de Chine), 4101 rue Sherbrooke E., is a 2.5-hectare (6-acre) Ming Dynasty style garden that features plants and trees native to Canada and southern China, including a pavilion with penjings (miniature trees). Other highlights in-

Old Montréal / © Andre Jenny

clude a 9-metre (30-ft.) waterfall and an ornamental pond. Changing art exhibits are displayed. The garden celebrates The Magic of Lanterns, a show featuring Chinese silk lanterns, mid-September through October. Open May-Oct.

Japanese Garden and Pavilion (Jardin et Pavillon Japonais), 4101 rue Sherbrooke E., comprises 2.5 hectares (6 acres) of native Canadian plants arranged in traditional Japanese style, with koi ponds, streams and bridges. Among the designs are a stone garden, bonsai courtyard and the tea garden, which leads to the tea ceremony room. The contemporary

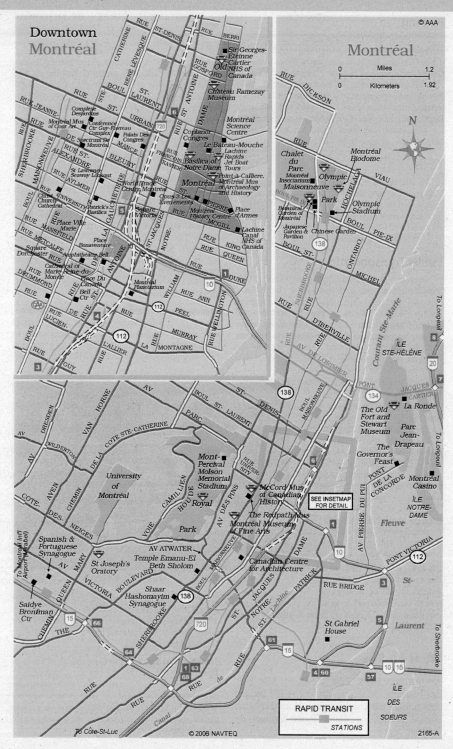

Downtown Montréal

RUE ST-DENIS
RUE BERRI
RUE CATHERINE
RUE ST-DENIS
RUE RENE LEVESQUE
BOUL ST-LAURENT
STE
ST
RUE JEANNE-
RUE
URBAIN
Complexe Desjardins
Montréal Mus of Cont Art
Conference Ctr Guy-Favreau Complex
Palais Des Congres
DE Spectrum De Montréal
RUE ST. MANCE
BLEURY
ALEXANDRE
RUE ST. FRANCOIS XAVIER
SHERBROOKE
MAISONNEUVE
RUE AYLMER
St Lawrence Seaway Lookout
World Trade Center Montréal
BOUL UNIVERSITY
Christ Church Cathedral
St Patrick's Basilica
Place Ville Marie
RUE MANSFIELD
RUE METCALFE
Place Bonaventure
Square Dorchester
Amphitheatre Bell
RUE PEEL
Cathedral of Marie-Reine-du-Monde
RUE DRUMMOND
Place Du Canada
Bell Ctr
RUE DE LA
RUE LUCIEN.
BOUL
RUE GUY
RUE L'ALLIER
112
Montréal Planetarium
112

Sir Georges-Etienne Cartier NHS of Canada
Old
RUE GOSFORD
RUE ST. ANTOINE
Château Ramezay Museum
Montréal Science Centre
Coplanor-Congres
Le Bateau-Mouche
Lachine Rapids Jet Boat Tours
Basilica of Notre Dame
Montréal
Pointe-à-Callière, Montréal Mus of Archaeology and History
RUE ST. JACQUES
Opus 3 Les Evenements
Square Victoria
Montréal History Centre
Place d'Armes
McGILL
Lachine Canal NHS of Canada
RUE NOTRE
RUE KING
RUE QUEEN
RUE
DUKE
RUE WILLIAM
RUE ANN
PEEL
RUE
MURRAY
LA MONTAGNE
10

Montréal

© AAA

RUE DICKSON

0 Miles 1.2
0 Kilometers 1.92

N

RUE
Chalet du Parc Maisonneuve
Montréal Biodome
Montréal Insectarium
Olympic
Park
Botanical Garden of Montréal
Japanese Garden & Pavilion
Chinese Garden
Olympic Stadium
BOUL PIE-IX
138
BOUL ST.
ONTARIO
RUE MICHEL
BOUL
RUE D'IBERVILLE
RUE SHERBROOKE
AV DE LORIMIER
138
AV
BOUL ST-LAURENT
RUE ST. DENIS
RUE UNIVER.
BOUL MAISONNEUVE
6
PONT
134
JACQUES CARTIER
20
ÎLE STE-HÉLÈNE
8
7
To Longueuil
To Longueuil
La Ronde
The Old Fort and Stewart Museum
Parc Jean-Drapeau
The Governor's Feast
Montréal Casino
ÎLE NOTRE-DAME
Fleuve
PONT DE LA CONCORDE
AV PIERRE DU PUI

DRESDEN
AV
WILDERTON
COTE.
AVEN
AV
VAN HORNE
BOUL ST- LAURENT
PARC
DE LA COTE STE-CATHERINE
CHEMIN
DES.
NEIGES
University of Montréal
CAMILLIEN HOU DE
VOIE
Mont-Royal
Park
Mont-Percival Molson Memorial Stadium
RUE UNIVER.
AV DES PINS
McCord Mus of Canadian History
The Redpath Mus
Montréal Museum of Fine Arts
SEE INSETMAP FOR DETAIL
1
10
AV PIERRE DU PUI

Spanish & Portuguese Synagogue
St Joseph's Oratory
AV ATWATER
Temple Emanu-El Beth Sholom
Shaar Hashomayim Synagogue
138
Saidye Bronfman Ctr
QUEEN MARY
VICTORIA
BOULEVARD
THE
CHEMIN
15
66
64
Canadian Centre for Architecture
BOUL MAISONNEUVE
RUE ST- JACQUES
NOTRE
RUE
720
61
15
RUE BRIDGE
3
St Gabriel House
5
112
PONT VICTORIA
St- Laurent
To Sherbrooke
63
68
4
60
57
10
15
ÎLE DES SOEURS

To Montréal Int'l Airport (Mirabel)
To Montréal Int'l Airport (Mirabel)
To Côte-St-Luc
Canal

RAPID TRANSIT
STATIONS

2165-A

style Japanese pavilion provides a glimpse into the culture of Japan. Open May-Oct.

Montréal Insectarium (Insectarium de Montréal), 4581 rue Sherbrooke E., has collections of butterflies and other exotic insects and arthropods from more than 100 countries. Terrariums display the insects in their native habitats. Interactive exhibits allow visitors to learn about insects and their impact on human culture.

CANADIAN CENTRE FOR ARCHITECTURE (Centre Canadien d'Architecture), 1920 rue Baile (M: Guy-Concordia) is an international research center and museum. Its extensive collections advance knowledge, promote public understanding, and widen thought and debate on the art of architecture, its history, theory, practice and role in society. The sculpture garden evokes the history of architecture as well as the city that surrounds the site.

Open Wed. 10-5, Thurs. 10-9, Fri.-Sun. 10-5. Admission $10; over 65, $7; students with ID $5; ages 6-12, $3; free to all Thurs. 5:30-9 p.m. MC, VI. Phone (514) 939-7026.

CATHEDRAL OF MARIE-REINE-DU-MONDE (Cathédrale Marie-Reine-du-Monde), bounded by Cathédrale and Mansfield sts. on boul. René-Lévesque (M: Bonaventure or Peel), was built 1870-94. The Roman Catholic cathedral, a one-third scale replica of St. Peter's in Rome, contains a collection of paintings by Québec artist George Delfosse.

Allow 30 minutes minimum. Mon.-Fri. 7-6, Sat. 7:30-6, Sun. 8:30-6. Free. Phone (514) 866-1661.

CHRIST CHURCH CATHEDRAL (Anglican), 635 rue Ste-Catherine Ouest, between Union and University (M: McGill), is Gothic in style. Completed in 1859, it is a copy of a 14th-century English church. In partnership with local property developers, an underground shopping mall and meeting and activity rooms for the church were constructed beneath the cathedral. Concerts are offered periodically throughout the year. Allow 30 minutes minimum. Daily 8-6. Free. Phone (514) 843-6577.

ÎLE NOTRE-DAME (Notre Dame Island) is next to île Ste-Hélène in the St. Lawrence River (M: Jean-Drapeau). Summer facilities include a floral park, a beach and an in-line skating and bicycling path on Gilles Villeneuve circuit. Winter offerings are a long ice-skating path and cross-country ski trails. From the last week of January to the middle of February, the more than 125 activities and exhibits of the Fête des Neiges Festival (Snow Festival) include snow and ice sculptures, dogsledding and a tube slide.

Allow 4 hours minimum. Open daily 6 a.m.-midnight. Admission free. Parking $10. Phone (514) 872-6120.

ÎLE STE-HÉLÈNE (St. Helen's Island), in the middle of the St. Lawrence River, can be reached via the Jacques-Cartier Bridge or the Cité du Havre (M: Jean-Drapeau). Parc Jean Drapeau enables visitors to walk or bike (rentals are available at the

© Ministère du Tourisme du Québec / Linda Turgeon

Métro station) past sculptures and buildings from Expo '67, a rose garden and historic sites such as an 1822 powder magazine and a military cemetery. In the center of the island is Parc Hélène-de-Champlain, a landscaped area with picnic facilities; on the east end is the amusement park La Ronde.

Allow 4 hours minimum. Open daily 6 a.m.-midnight. Admission free. Parking $10 Phone (514) 872-6120.

The Governor's Feast (Le Festin du Gouverneur) is in the barracks building of the Old Fort (M: Jean-Drapeau). Visitors are the nobles to whom maidens and vassals serve meals, while other minions entertain during the 2-hour, 17th-century bilingual feast in New France. Daily at 6 p.m. and 8 p.m., Apr.-Oct.; daily at 6 p.m., rest of year. Admission $40.37; under 12, $19.75. Reservations are suggested. AX, CB, DS, MC, VI. Phone (514) 879-1141, or (800) 713-0111 in the U.S.

La Ronde, at the e. end of the Île Ste-Hélène (M: Jean-Drapeau), is an amusement park with more than 40 rides. It includes the Vampire, a suspended looping roller coaster, and a section of children's rides. Stage and diving shows as well as fireworks also are presented.

Daily 10-9, mid-May to mid-June; daily 10 a.m.-11:30 p.m., mid-June through Labour Day; Sat-Sun 10-8, day after Labour Day-late Sept.; Fri. 5-10, Sat.-Sun. noon-9, Oct. 1-Oct. 23. Phone to confirm schedule. All-inclusive admission $30.42; 36 to 52 inches tall $19.99. AX, MC, VI. Phone (514) 397-2000.

The Old Fort and Stewart Museum (Le Vieux Fort et Musée Stewart) are on île Ste-Hélène in Parc Jean-Drapeau (M: Jean-Drapeau). The Old Fort was erected 1820-24 by order of the Duke of Wellington to protect Montréal and defend the St. Lawrence against possible U.S. aggression. The fort comprises barracks, an armory, arsenal, blockhouse, powder magazine and the Stewart Museum.

The museum exhibits domestic utensils and decorative arts, military artifacts, maps and models relating the history of Montréal and Canada. Of particular interest is a bronze cannon lost by British general Jeffrey Amherst at the Pointe-des-Cascades rapids in 1760 and recovered in 1957.

Military parades by La Compagnie franche de la Marine and the Olde 78th Fraser Highlanders are conducted at the fort. Other activities are offered during the summer. During the winter curling and snowshoeing are popular activities at the site.

Allow 1 hour, 30 minutes minimum. Daily 10-5, mid-May through second Mon. in Oct.; Wed.-Mon. 10-5, rest of year. Closed Jan. 1 and Dec. 25. Parades and special activities take place daily at 1, 3 and 4:30, late June-late Aug. Admission (includes fort and museum) $10; over 65 and ages 7-25, $7; family rate (two adults and two children or one adult and three children) $20. Parking fee late May-Labour Day $10. AX, MC, VI. Phone (514) 861-6701.

McCORD MUSEUM OF CANADIAN HISTORY (Musée McCord d'histoire canadienne), across from McGill University at 690 rue Sherbrooke W. (M: McGill), has exhibits about the history of Canada dating from the 18th century to the present. In addition to a library and archives, collections dealing with costumes and textiles, decorative arts, archeology and ethnology, paintings, prints and drawings, and photographs by noted photographer William Notman are presented. Changing exhibits also are offered.

Sat.-Mon. 10-5, Tues.-Fri. 10-6, in summer; Tues.-Fri. 10-6, Sat.-Sun. and Mon. holidays 10-5, rest of year. Closed Jan. 1 and Dec. 25. Admission $12; over 65, $9; students with ID $6; ages 6-12 $4; family rate $22. MC, VI. Phone (514) 398-7100.

MONTRÉAL HISTORY CENTRE (Centre d'histoire de Montréal), 335 Place d'Youville (M: Square-Victoria), is in a late 19th-century fire hall. Exhibits depict the events behind the history and development of Montréal, and audiovisual presentations recreate the sound- and landscapes of various periods in the city's long and rich history.

Allow 1 hour minimum. Open Tues.-Sun. 10-5, late Jan.-early Dec.; closed holidays. Phone to verify schedule. Admission $4.50, over 54 and students with ID $3, family rate $13. Phone (514) 872-3207.

MONTRÉAL MUSEUM OF CONTEMPORARY ART (Musée d'Art Contemporain de Montréal), next to the Place des Arts at 185 rue Ste-Catherine Ouest (M: Place-des-Arts), displays more than 7,000 works by Canadian and foreign contemporary artists. Works date from 1940 to the present; a sculpture garden is on the premises. Food is available.

Allow 1 hour minimum. Tues 11-6, Wed. 11-9, Thurs.-Sun and Mon. holidays 11-6. Admission $8; over 65, $6; students with ID $4; under 12 free; family rate $16; free to all Wed. 6-9 p.m. Schedule may vary; phone ahead. MC, VI. Phone (514) 847-6226.

MONTRÉAL MUSEUM OF FINE ARTS (Musée des beaux-arts de Montréal) is at 1380 rue Sherbrooke W. (M: Guy-Concordia or Peel) Founded in 1860, this was one of the first public art galleries in Canada. The museum offers exhibitions from extensive holding, some 33 000 objects representing the main trends in art from antiquity to the present day, and impressive temporary exhibitions.

Tues. 11-5, Wed.-Fri. 11-9, Sat.-Sun. 10-5. Permanent collection free. Special exhibits $15; over 65 and students with ID $7.50; ages 3-12, $3; family rate (two adults and two children or one adult and 3 children) $30. Half-price Wed. 5-9. AX, MC, VI. Phone (514) 285-2000 or (800) 899-6873.

MONTRÉAL PLANETARIUM (Planétarium de Montréal) is at 1000 rue St-Jacques Ouest in Square Chaboillez (M: Bonaventure). Lectures in French and English, combined with audiovisual presentations, explore various aspects of astronomy.

Allow 2 hours minimum. Ticket counter open Mon. 12:30-5, Tues.-Thurs. 9:30-5, Fri. 9:30-4:30 and 7-9, Sat.-Sun. 12:30-4:30 and 7-9, mid-June through Labour Day; Tues.-Thurs. 9:30-5, Fri. 9:30-5 and 6:45-9 p.m., Sat.-Sun. 10-5 and 6:45-9 p.m., rest of year. Phone for show times. Admission $8.25; over 65 and students with ID $6.25; under 17, $4.25. MC, VI. Phone (514) 872-4530.

MONT-ROYAL PARK (Parc du Mont-Royal) is on the summit of Mont-Royal (M: Mont-Royal), with an entrance at 1260 chemin Remembrance. The lighted cross at the top commemorates Maisonneuve's promise to erect a cross if the colony was spared during the flood of Dec. 25, 1642. The first cross was erected in 1643. A lookout near a 1932 chalet offers a panorama of Montréal and the St. Lawrence River.

The park is traversed by trails used by summer joggers and winter skiers. Beaver Lake is a haven for skaters in the winter. The Beaver Lake Pavilion offers seasonal rental of bicycles, pedal-boats, snowtubes, cross-country skis, snowshoes and skates.

The 1858 Smith House, at the park entrance, is a reception and exhibition center offering visitor services year-round, including maps for self-guiding tours and several guided walking tours. Mon.-Fri. 9-5, Sat.-Sun. 9-8. Free. Phone (514) 843-8240.

THE MUSEUM OF QUÉBEC MASTERS AND ARTISANS—
see St-Laurent in the Vicinity section p. 196.

NOTRE DAME ISLAND—
see Île Notre-Dame p. 183.

OLD MONTRÉAL (Vieux Montréal), bounded by the river and rues McGill, Notre-Dame and Berri (M: Place-d'Armes or Champ-de-Mars), is a 38-hectare (94-acre) historic area with some buildings dating the 18th century. Government offices, courthouses, shipping interests and the financial district occupy the site of Ville-Marie, the original settlement. In the Maison de mère d'Youville, residence and headquarters of the Sisters of Charity of Montréal ("Grey Nuns of Montréal), visitors can view artifacts of Montréal's early history and tour rooms in which Marguerite d'Youville lived and died; phone (514) 842-9411 to make the required reservation.

The Old City is best seen by walking along Notre-Dame, Bon-Secours and St-Paul. A brochure with a map outlining a self-guiding tour of the area is available from the Tourisme Montréal *(see The Informed Traveler)*. The Old Montréal office at 174 Notre-Dame Est offers tourism information and is open daily 9-7, first Fri. in June-Labour Day; 9-5, rest of year. Closed Jan. 1 and Dec. 25.

Basilica of Notre Dame (Basilique Notre-Dame), on the Place d'Armes at 110 rue Notre-Dame Ouest, is among the most magnificent of French-Canadian churches and is one of the largest churches in North America. Stained-glass windows depict religious scenes and the history of the original parish. Guided 20-minute tours are offered. An evening sound and light show "And Then There was Light" is offered; phone for schedule.

Daily 8-4:30. Admission, including guided tour, $4 ($5 in 2008); ages 7-17, $2 ($4 in 2008). Sound and light show $10; over 60, $9; ages 1-17, $5. Phone (514) 842-2925.

SAVE **Chapel of Notre Dame de Bon-Secours and Marguerite Bourgeoys Museum** (Chapelle Notre-Dame-de-Bon-Secours et Musée Marguerite-Bourgeoys) is at 400 rue St-Paul Est (M: Champs-de-Mars). The remains of Marguerite Bourgeoys are under the left side altar. Exhibits in the museum relate the accomplishments of the founders of Montréal using artifacts, some as old as 2,000 years. The museum has the highest lookout point accessible to the public in Old Montreal and provides views of the river and the harbor.

Allow 30 minutes minimum. Tues.-Sun. 10-5:30, May-Oct.; Tues.-Sun. 11-3:30, Nov. 1 to mid-Jan. and Mar.-Apr. Admission $6; over 65 and students with ID $4; ages 6-12, $3. Phone (514) 282-8670.

Château Ramezay Museum (Musée du Château Ramezay), 280 rue Notre-Dame Est (M: Champ-de-Mars), is in a structure built for Claude de Ramezay, French governor of Montréal 1703-24. The property has been meticulously restored, even to a small, 18th-century rear garden with flowers, fruits and vegetables and medicinal plants. The museum traces the history of the area from before European settlement through the beginning of the 20th-century.

Basilica of Notre Dame / © Tourisme Montréal

The exhibition *"Hochelaga, Ville-Marie and Montréal: The past pervades the present!"* uses pieces from the museum's 30,000 pieces to relate the history of the city and the province from precontact Amerindian times through the early 20th century. The museum's five collections are not open to the general public, but are drawn upon for permanent and rotating exhibitions.

Daily 10-6, June-Sept; Tues.-Sun. 10-4:30, rest of year. Closed Jan. 1 and Dec. 23-25 and 31. Admission $8; over 60, $6; students with ID $5; ages 5-17, $4; family rate $16.50. MC, VI. Phone (514) 861-3708.

Montréal Science Centre (Centre des sciences de Montréal) is at jct. Saint-Laurent Blvd. and de la Commune St. W. (M: Place d'Armes) This hands-on, learning center presents science and technology in such a way as to make learning fun. Eye-catching, high-tech interactive displays cover such topics as robotics, health and communications. The IMAX-TELUS Theatre also is in the center.

Allow 3 hours minimum. Museum open Mon. 10-3:40; Tues.-Sun., 10-8:20, mid-May through Labour Day; Mon.-Fri. 9-4, Sat.-Sun. 10-5, rest of year. IMAX shows generally begin every 50 minutes Tues.-Sun. 10-8:30, Mon. 10-3:50. Phone for exact IMAX schedule. Closed Jan. 1 (also Jan. 8-11, 2007) and Dec. 25.

Admission to exhibits or to one IMAX 2-D film $10; over 60 and ages 13-17, $9; ages 4-12, $7; family rate (two adults and two ages 4-17, or one adult and three ages 4-17; additional ages 4-17, $5) $30. IMAX 3-D film $12; over 60 and ages 13-17,

$11; ages 4-12, $9; family rate (two adults and two ages 4-17, or one adult and three ages 4-17; additional ages 4-17, $8) $38. Exhibits and one IMAX 2-D film $17; over 60 and ages 13-17, $15; ages 4-12, $13; family rate $55 (two adults and two ages 4-17, or one adult and three ages 4-17; additional ages 4-17, $10). Other packages are available. MC, VI. Phone (514) 496-4724 or (877) 496-4724.

The Old Port (Vieux Port) is in the old Montréal Harbour, and has entrances at the foot of place Jacques-Cartier and south of Saint-Laurent Blvd. This outdoor urban recreation, entertainment and cultural site is a federal park. The Old Port offers events, shows and recreational activities. Facilities include restaurants, boutiques and a free observation deck atop the Clock Tower.

Park open daily 10 a.m.-1 a.m.; most activities take place May 15-Sept. 30. Admission free. Phone (514) 496-7678 or (800) 971-7678.

Place d'Armes, adjoining rue St-Jacques, is the old financial center of Montréal. Here stands the monument to Paul de Chomedey, founder of the city in 1642.

Place Jacques-Cartier, on the slope from Champs-de-Mars to the waterfront, contains the Nelson monument, erected in 1809 to honor Lord Horatio Nelson's victory at Trafalgar. Artists, musicians, jugglers, and acrobats perform in the square during the summer. Flower markets, cafes and historic buildings also highlight the area.

Place Royale, bounded by rues St-Paul and de la Commune West, is the city's oldest public square. Dating back to 1657, it was originally the marketing center of the settlement.

Sir Georges-Étienne Cartier National Historic Site of Canada (Le lieu historique national du Canada de Sir-Georges-Étienne-Cartier), 458 rue Notre-Dame Est, consists of two 1837 buildings, each a former residence of Sir Georges-Étienne Cartier. Cartier, a 19th-century lawyer, businessman and political leader, who helped shape many of Québec's and Canada's institutions.

The west house has been carefully restored to its Victorian style and illustrates the lifestyle of the upper-middle class to which Cartier belonged. The east house presents modern exhibits that highlight Cartier's achievements in a period of major changes.

Daily 10-6, June-Aug.; Wed.-Sun. 10-noon and 1-5, Apr.-May and first Wed. in Sept.-Dec. 23. Phone to verify schedule. Admission $3.95; over 65, $3.45; ages 6-16, $1.95; family rate $9.90. Phone (800) 463-6769 or (888) 773-8888.

OLYMPIC PARK (Parc Olympique), 46 hectares (114 acres) in the eastern part of the city (M: Pie-IX or Viau), was host to the 1976 Summer Olympics.

A major highlight of the park is the 175-metre-high (575-ft.) Montréal Tower. An observatory at the top of the tower offers 80-kilometre (50-mi.) views

of the Montréal environs. It is reached by a funicular that takes visitors to the top via a cable system along the side of the building. Guided tours of the stadium also offered daily. All activities begin at the Tourist Hall located at the base of the Montréal Tower.

Cable car rides to the tower daily 9-7, mid-June through early Sept.; 9-5, mid-Feb. to mid-June and mid-Sept. to early Jan. Closed early Jan.-early Feb. for annual maintenance. Phone for stadium tour schedule. Stadium tours $8; senior citizens $7.25; ages 5-17, $6.25. Cable car $14; senior citizens and students with ID $10.50; ages 5-17, $7. Stadium tour, Montréal Biodôme and Botanical Garden of Montréal combination packages are available. AX, MC, VI. Phone (514) 252-4737 or (877) 997-0919.

Montréal Biodôme (Biodôme de Montréal) is at 4777 Pierre-de-Coubertin in Olympic Park (M: Viau). Four ecosystems are explored through re-creations of their natural habitats: a tropical forest, a Laurentian forest, the St. Lawrence marine environment and the polar regions. Interpreters are stationed at various points in the habitats to provide explanations.

The Tropical Forest contains more than 1,000 fish, amphibians, reptiles, birds and mammals. In the Laurentian Forest a conifer forest and impressive rock formations surround a beaver lake. Scarce vegetation, a rich variety of wildlife and a granite basin holding 2.5 million liters (660,500 U.S. gallons) of saltwater are the hallmarks of the Marine Environment of the St. Lawrence River. The Polar World illustrates the dramatic—and distinct—landscapes and fauna of the Arctic and Antarctic.

Allow 2 hours minimum. Daily 9-6, mid-June through Labour Day; Tues.-Sun. 9-5, rest of year. Open statutory holidays. Admission $13.75; over 65 and students with ID $10.25; ages 5-17, $7. Parking $8. MC, VI. Phone (514) 868-3000.

POINTE-À-CALLIÈRE, MONTRÉAL MUSEUM OF ARCHAEOLOGY AND HISTORY (Pointe-à-Callière, Musée d'archéologie et d'histoire de Montréal), 350 Place Royale, is built atop actual remains of the original European settlement. A multimedia show unfolds the history of Montréal, followed by self guiding, interactive tours where interpreters are stationed at various points to answer questions. Highlights include visits to an excavated cemetery, an early Montréal sewer system and fortifications, as well as displays of artifacts that date back 1,000 years.

Food is available. Mon.-Fri. 10-6, Sat.-Sun. 11-6, June 24-Labour Day; Tues.-Fri. 10-5, Sat.-Sun. 11-5, rest of year. Admission $13; over 55, $10; students with ID $7.50; ages 6-12, $6.50; family rate $27. Phone to verify prices. AX, MC, VI. Phone (514) 872-9150.

THE REDPATH MUSEUM (Le Musée Redpath) is at 859 rue Sherbrooke W., between McTavish and University on the McGill University campus (M: Peel or McGill). When erected in 1882, this was Canada's first building designed to be a museum.

The themes of the permanent exhibits include ethnology and archeology, minerals and gems, invertebrates, vertebrates, Québec fauna, and paleontology.

Mon.-Fri. 9-5, Sun. 1-5; closed holidays. Free. Phone (514) 398-4086, ext. 4092.

SAIDYE BRONFMAN CENTRE (Centre des arts Saidye Bronfman), 5170 ch. de la Côte Ste-Catherine (M: Côte Ste-Catherine), presents changing exhibits of Canadian and international contemporary art. Mon.-Thurs. 8:30-6, Fri. 8:30-4:30, Sun. 10-5, July-Aug.; Mon.-Thurs. 8:30 a.m.-10 p.m., Fri. 8:30-4:30, Sun. 10-5, rest of year. Free. Phone (514) 739-2301.

ST. GABRIEL HOUSE (Maison St-Gabriel), 2146 Place Dublin (M: Charlevoix and bus 57), was purchased by Marguerite Bourgeoys in 1668 and is a fine example of traditional Québec architecture. Converted into a museum in 1966, it showcases aspects of rural life in the 17th century and the experience of the King's Wards. Its garden has been re-created in the spirit of New France.

Guided tours are given Tues.-Sun. 11-6, June 25-Labour Day; Tues.-Sun. 1-5, mid-Apr. through June 24 and day after Labour Day-early Dec.; by reservation, rest of year. Fee $8; over 65, $5; students with ID $4; ages 6-12, $2; family rate $16. Phone (514) 935-8136.

ST. HELEN'S ISLAND—*see Île Ste-Hélène p. 183.*

▲▲▲ **ST. JOSEPH'S ORATORY** (Oratoire Saint-Joseph), 3800 ch. Queen Mary (M: Côte-des-Neiges), is one of the world's largest basilicas and one of the city's most important religious shrines. It was begun in 1904 and the basilica was completed in 1967. The oratory was the dream of Holy Cross Brother André, who had a simple wooden chapel on the site. During his service there from 1870 (when he was 25 years old) until his death in 1937, Brother André was known as a healer, invoking cures for hundreds through prayer to his patron saint, St. Joseph.

Blessed André was beatified in 1982; his tomb is behind the crypt. Other highlights include the original chapel, built 1904-1910, and a French-made, 56-bell carillon. Daily 7 a.m.-10 p.m. The carillon plays Wed.-Fri. at noon and 3, Sat.-Sun at noon and 2:30. Donations. Phone (514) 733-8211.

ST. LAWRENCE SEAWAY LOOKOUT (Observatoire extérieur de la Voie Maritime du Saint-Laurent), s. end of Pont Victoria (M: Longueuil), is at St.-Lambert Lock and accessible by visitor's parking. The Seaway is open late March through December. Daily 6:30 a.m.-10 p.m., late Mar.-late Dec. Phone to verify schedule and accessibility. Free. Phone (450) 672-4115, ext. 2237.

ST. PATRICK'S BASILICA (Basilique St-Patrick), 460 boul. René-Lévesque Ouest (M: Square-Victoria), is a religious center for English-speaking Catholics. Gothic panels, paintings and stations of

Pointe-á-Callière, Montréal Museum of Archaeology and History / © MTOQ / Marc Renaud

the cross decorate the interior. Daily 8:30-6. Free. Phone (514) 866-7379.

SHAAR HASHOMAYIM SYNAGOGUE—*see Westmount in the Vicinity section p. 197.*

SPANISH AND PORTUGUESE SYNAGOGUE (Synagogue Espagnole et Portugaise), 4894 av. St-Kevin (M: Côte-Ste-Catherine), is the oldest Orthodox Jewish congregation in Canada. The 1958 synagogue is the third site the congregation has occupied since it was founded in 1768. By appointment Mon.-Thurs. 9-5, Fri. 9-1, Sun. 9-noon. Free. Phone (514) 737-3695.

TEMPLE EMANU-EL BETH SHOLOM—*see Westmount in the Vicinity section p. 197.*

CASINOS

• **Montréal Casino**, 1 rue du Casino. Daily 24 hours. A dress code is enforced. Phone (514) 392-2746 or (800) 665-2274.

RECREATIONAL ACTIVITIES

White-water Rafting

• **Rafting and Jet Boating the Lachine Rapids** (Les Descentes sur le St-Laurent), 8912 boul. La-Salle. Write C.P. 3222, Succursale Lapierre, La-Salle, QC, Canada H8N 3H3. Trips depart several times daily, early May-Sept. 30. Reservations are required. Phone (514) 767-2230 or (800) 324-7238.

What To Do

Sightseeing

Boat Tours

[SAVE] *LE BATEAU-MOUCHE* departs from the Jacques-Cartier Pier at the foot of Place Jacques-Cartier (M: Champs-de-Mars). The glass-roofed, Paris-style riverboat offers four 1-hour and one 90-minute French and English narrated tours on the St. Lawrence River and around the Expo '67 islands. The tours provide good views of the waterfront and skyline. A 3.5-hour dinner cruise also is offered.

One-hour cruises depart daily at 10, 1:30, 3 and 4:30, 90-minute cruise at 11:30, mid-May to mid-Oct. Boarding is 30 minutes before departure. One-hour fare $17.95; over 65 and students with ID $16.95; ages 2-12, $10; family rate $42.95. Ninety-minute cruise fare $23.95; over 65 and students with ID $21.95; ages 2-12 $10. Reservations are required for the dinner cruise. Phone to verify prices. MC, VI. Phone (514) 849-9952 or (800) 361-9952.

[GEM] **LACHINE RAPIDS JET BOAT TOURS** (Le voyage Saute-Moutons sur les Rapides de Lachine) depart the s. end of rue Berri at the Clock Tower Basin in Montréal's Old Port (M: Champ-de-Mars). The 1-hour trip travels upstream on the St. Lawrence through the historic Lachine Rapids. These once unnavigable waterways accounted for Montréal's strategic location.

Fête des Neiges / © Tourisme Montréal

The 1,350-horsepower, flat-bottom boats negotiate whirlpools as well as waves up to 3 metres (10 ft.) high. Although rain ponchos, hats and plastic footwear are provided, a change of clothes is recommended. For more information contact Lachine Rapids Tours, 47 rue de la Commune West, Montréal, QC, Canada H2Y 2C6.

Trips depart daily at 10, noon, 2, 4, and 6, May 1 through mid-Oct. Fare $60; over 65, $55; ages 13-18, $50; ages 6-12, $40. Under 6 are not permitted. Reservations are required. AX, MC, VI. Phone (514) 284-9607 daily.

[SAVE] **MONTRÉAL HARBOUR CRUISES** (Croisières AML), departing from the Quai King-Edward Pier in Montréal's Old Port (M: Champ-de-Mars), offer 90-minute sightseeing, 4-hour fireworks and 4-hour dinner-dance cruises. The tours traverse Montréal Harbour and the St. Lawrence River and circle the Boucherville Islands. Food is available.

Sightseeing cruises depart daily at 11:30, 2 and 4, May 1 through mid-Oct. Fireworks cruises are offered June-July; phone for schedule. Sightseeing cruises $22.95; over 65 and students with ID $20; ages 6-16, $10. Phone for fireworks and dinner-dance cruise fares. Parking $15. Reservations are required. Phone to verify schedule and prices. AX, MC, VI. Phone (514) 842-3871 or (800) 563-4643.

Bus, Carriage and Limousine Tours

Visitors to Montréal have a wide choice of tour itineraries and prices. Gray Line de Montréal, (514) 934-1222, offers local tours. Also, calèches, or horse-drawn carriages, circulate around the city.

A flexible way to see the city is by taxi. Guides who ride in your automobile also are available. The competency and fees of all guides are regulated by law. They must hold a certificate from the School of Tourism of Montréal, wear an official city badge and produce a valid tourist guide license.

GRAY LINE DOUBLE DECKER TOURS departs from the Infotouriste Centre at 1001 rue du Sq. Dorchester and takes visitors on a narrated sightseeing tour of the downtown area. Bilingual drivers detail Montréal's history in English and French. From early May through the second Mon. in Oct., the fare is good for unlimited daily round trips.

Tours depart on the hour daily 11-3, mid-June through early Sept. Other tours are available year-round. Phone to verify schedule and fares. Fare $35; over 59 and students with ID $32; ages 5-12, $20. MC, VI. Phone (514) 871-4733.

Driving Tours

Although multilane divided highways provide fast transit between Montréal and the rest of Québec, older roads that follow the same route—Hwy. 132 on the south shore of the river and Hwy. 138 on the north—offer scenic alternatives. These roads, which follow the courses of original 18th-century roads, wind through small villages and towns with the best examples of Québec's domestic and ecclesiastical architecture.

Beyond the towns, the roads pass through farmland divided in parallel strips, each with its own access to the river—remnants of a system laid out under seigneurial ownership during French colonial times.

In summer the farms beckon motorists to stop and pick raspberries; roadside stands offer *frites* (french fries), vegetables and baked goods, and shops sell hand-carved whirligigs or homemade *catalognes* (rag rugs). In short, these old highways offer an introduction to a resilient and singular culture.

Walking Tours

Brochures outlining self-guiding walking tours of Old Montréal with explanations of its architecture can be obtained at the information bureau at 174 Notre-Dame Est and at the information kiosk at Infotouriste, 1001 rue du Square-Dorchester.

Spectator Sports

Few would argue with the assertion that Canadians are perhaps the best hockey players in the world and that Canadian hockey fans are the most loyal and discriminating sports fans anywhere. Indeed, hockey *belongs* to Canada. And although no sport is likely to match hockey on Montréal's popularity scale, a handful of other professional sports ably compete to fill gaps on the entertainment bill.

Football

The **Montréal Alouettes** (Larks) play in the Canadian Football League from June to October at Percival Molson Stadium; phone (514) 871-2255.

Hockey

Near the end of the 19th century two enterprising students at McGill University are said to have invented not only the puck but the general rules of the game of hockey as it is known today. By the time the National Hockey League (NHL) was formed in 1917, the 6-year-old **Montréal Canadiens** already were the pride of Montréal. An epic 5-year winning streak in the late 1950s even was dramatized as a metaphor for Québécois pride in Rick Salutin's play, "Les Canadiens."

The Canadiens have taken possession of the Stanley Cup a record 25 times. The team has garnered enough NHL title banners to intimidate even the most formidable opponent, and has achieved an impressive presence in the Hockey Hall of Fame. Among the former players honored there are such legends as Maurice "Rocket," Henri Richard, Jean Beliveau and Guy Lafleur. Home games during the regular season are played at **Centre Bell** from October through March, with playoffs starting in April and ending in June; phone (514) 932-2582.

Horse Racing

Harness racing is the ticket at **Hippodrome de Montréal**, 7440 Boulevard Décarie. International events in the trotting circuit are held at the track. Races are scheduled year-round; phone (514) 739-2741. Public transportation is recommended, as traffic is heavy.

Note: Policies vary concerning admittance of children to pari-mutuel betting facilities. Phone for information.

Soccer

Soccer is the **Montréal Impact's** game. The North American Soccer League team plays in **Centre Claude-Robillard**, 1000 Émile-Journault, from late May to mid-September; phone (514) 328-3668.

Recreation

Winter sports predominate in a city where the weather swings between cool and frigid most of the year. However, sunshine and rising temperatures in the summer months permit a wide range of activities.

Bicycling

Montréal's extensive network of bicycle paths covers nearly 140 miles of the island. Bicycling maps are available at most sporting goods stores and *Infotouriste* centers; phone (514) 873-2015.

The 11-kilometre (7.5-mi.) **Lachine Canal** path runs along the old canal and offers a view of the Lachine Rapids between René-Lévesque and St-Louis parks. This path is illuminated at night. **Old Port's** waterfront views, though more placid, also make it popular; the 2.4-kilometre (1.5-mi.) path is perfect for a quick trip. **Parc Maisonneuve** offers a well-maintained track that winds past the Botanical Garden of Montréal and a golf course. For those with more time and energy, the **St. Lawrence Seaway** route, 16 kilometres (10 miles) long, lets bicyclists follow the narrow part of the seaway.

Though there are no designated paths, **Île Notre-Dame** and **Île Ste-Hélène** also are prime spots for exploring on two wheels. Bicyclists should keep in mind that the islands often are slightly cooler and more windy than downtown.

One caveat about pedaling around the city: Montréal residents are notorious for wild driving, so it is highly recommended that bicyclists wear helmets and pay close attention to road signs. Vélo-Québec, 1251 rue Rachel est (Maison des Cyclistes), provides brochures, guidebooks and path information; phone (514) 521-8356.

For those without their own wheels, La Cordée, 2159 rue Ste-Catherine est, and Vélo Adventures in Old Port have rentals.

Fishing

Its abundance of lakes and rivers makes Montréal a popular place with those who enjoy fishing. Anglers must obtain a provincial license, which is available at most sporting goods stores. The Ministry of Environment and Société de la Faune et des Parcs du Québec provides information about fishing areas: phone (800) 561-1616 in Canada.

Hardier souls may prefer the challenge of ice fishing, in which groups huddle around a hole in the ice inside a traditional Québécois ice-fishing shack. Muskie, perch and pike are typical catches.

Golf

Several golf courses are easily accessible from downtown Montréal. The following courses are among the many in the city that offer at least 18 holes and are open to the public, weather permitting, from late April to mid-October: Club de Golf Atlantide Inc., (514) 425-2000, 2201 Don Quichotte in Île Perrot; Club de Golf Chantecler, (450) 229-3742, 2520 ch. Du Club in Ste-Adèle; Club de Golf Vaudreuil Inc., (450) 455-2731, 1126 St-Antoine in

Vaudreuil-Dorion; and Golf Dorval, (514) 631-6624, 2000 Reverchon in Dorval.

For information about courses and tournaments contact the Association de golf du Québec, 2500 boul. Casavant, Suite 103, Saint-Hyacinthe, QC, Canada J2S 7R8; phone (450) 773-2847.

Hiking

With a landmark like **Mont Royal**, the city obviously has a preferred site for scenic hikes. Beginning at the Mont-Royal Métro stop, well-marked trails ascend to two lookout points and provide views from the main chalet at **Mont-Royal Park**. The adventurous may want to bypass the heavily traveled trails and make their way through the woods for a more rugged hike.

Jogging and Walking

Montréal's myriad parks prove popular with joggers and walkers alike. Those who prefer level and forgiving terrain should follow Lachine Canal or negotiate a park, such as **Lafontaine** or Maisonneuve. Mont-Royal Park, with its uphill climbs and natural terrain, is more challenging, but the view makes the extra effort worthwhile.

Tennis

Most of Montréal's 200-plus municipal courts are open to the public at no charge or for a small fee. **Centre Claude-Robillard**, **Jeanne-Mance**, **Kent**, Lafontaine and **Somerled** are community parks with courts. Area clubs include **Mirabel Racquet Club** in Pointe-Claire, 355 boul. Brunswick, (514) 697-5610; **Stade Uniprix** in Montréal, 285 rue Faillon Ouest, (514) 273-1234; **Tennis Île-des-Soeurs** in Île-des-Soeurs, 300 ch. du Golf, (514) 766-1208; and **Tennis Longueuil** in Longueuil, 550 Curé-Poirier Ouest, (450) 679-6131.

Water Sports

Although most of the water around Montréal is too polluted for swimming, taking a dip is popular at pools scattered around the city. The indoor Olympic-size pool at **Olympic Park** is open to the public for a small admission fee; phone (514) 252-8687. Two other public indoor pools are the **Cégep du Vieux Montréal**, 255 rue Ontario est, and the Centre Claude-Robillard, 1000 rue Émile-Journault. Both locations charge a nominal fee. Several large outdoor pools are near the Métro stop on Île Ste-Hélène; phone (514) 872-7708. A fee is charged.

Island hop to Île Notre-Dame for the city's only beach. Artificial **Plage de l'Île Notre-Dame** is the former **Regatta Lake** from Expo '67. The water comes from the Lachine Rapids and is treated to make it safe for swimming. Locals flock here in the summer months to picnic and bask in the sun before winter strikes again.

Winter Sports

A city fanatical about hockey is certain to have a wealth of places for ice-skating. Montréal offers nearly 200 outdoor rinks. The most popular is at the Old Port of Montreal **Bassin Bon Secours**.

Speed demons will be interested in tobogganing and ice sliding when the city freezes over. The best toboggan runs are in Mont-Royal Park and on the hills around **Beaver Lake**.

The thick blanket of snow that covers Montréal makes the city and its environs prime skiing venues. Mont-Royal has excellent trails for cross-country enthusiasts, and it's possible to ski in several other city parks when the powder gets deep. Cross-country skiers and snowshoers frequent the ecology trail at Parc Maisonneuve next to the Botanical Garden of Montréal *(see attraction listing p. 181)*.

Cross-country trails and rental equipment are available at Détour Nature, (514) 271-6046, and La poubelle du ski, (514) 384-1315.

For downhill skiers, city runs are strictly for beginners. Mont-Royal, Cabrini, Ignace-Bourget and des Hirondelles parks are popular with families and usually are crowded after a good snowfall. Serious skiers need only make a short road trip to the nearby **Laurentians** and **Eastern Townships** for the fabulous runs at Bromont, Owl's Head, Orford, Sutton or Mont-Tremblant.

Some of these areas have dog sledding, sleigh rides and snowmobiling available. In fact, the inventor of the snowmobile—Joseph Bombardier—was born in the Eastern Townships in the town of Valcourt, which markets itself as the "snowmobile capital of the world." For more information, phone Ski East (Association Touristique des Cantons-de-l'Est) at (819) 564-8989 or the Association Touristique des Laurentides (ATL) at (450) 436-8532.

Shopping

Montréal's stores reflect the city's cosmopolitan nature and its French heritage. The city is considered Canada's *haute couture* capital, not only for the number of stores but also for their variety. Wares range from imported designer labels to local handicrafts.

Antiques

The best concentrations of antique dealers are along **rue Notre-Dame ouest**, between rue Guy and avenue Atwater, and on **St-Paul** in Old Montréal. A cluster of restored graystones scattered up and down both sides of the street houses a dozen or more shops with various quaint treasures. Discriminating collectors may want to venture to the west end of **rue Sherbrooke**, where exquisite mahogany, Royal Crown Derby china and popular old china and silver patterns can be had for a price. Antique dealers in **Westmount** also cater to a more discriminating clientele. Bargain-hunters should visit rue Notre-Dame shops, where the prices often are negotiable.

Malls

What began in 1962 as a simple shopping center beneath Place Ville-Marie is now an underground maze of walkways stretching 18 miles and embracing 1,600 shops, a department store, 200 restaurants and 30 theaters. Subterranean promenades and the Métro connect the clusters of buildings. Most of

Montréal's spectacular shopping malls have found a home in **Underground Montréal**. Many malls begin underground and reach upward to several floors above ground.

Shops in the underground are open 10-6 except for Sunday, when they are open noon-5 p.m. Most are closed holidays.

Place Ville-Marie, with its shop-lined corridors centered on a sculpted fountain, was the first of these subterranean centers to be built. Known to locals as PVM (pronounced "pay-vay-em"), the complex teems with trendy boutiques.

Other shopping clusters have since been added, including **Centre Eaton**, **Les Cours Mont-Royal**, **Place Bonaventure**, **Place Montréal Trust** and **Les Promenades de la Cathédrale**.

In Place Montréal Trust, underground at the corner of rue Ste-Catherine and avenue McGill College, bright atria and cascading fountains link innovative architecture and glass walls. Directly beneath Christ Church Cathedral at 625 rue Ste-Catherine ouest, Les Promenades de la Cathédrale has shops on two levels. Place Bonaventure, at rues de la Gauchetière and University, links some 100 shops with the Bonaventure Hilton International.

A modern restoration of the Hôtel Mont-Royal resulted in Les Cours Mont-Royal, a three-story mall at 1455 rue Peel. Centre Eaton, 705 rue Ste-Catherine, is anchored by Les Ailes de la Mode department store.

Complexe Desjardins, a partially underground marvel of waterfalls, fountains, trees and hanging vines, comprises lanes of shops connected to four tall office towers and the Hotel Wyndham.

These underground marketplaces present an almost endless array of merchandise, from everyday items to luxury articles. Just browsing can be as pleasurable as shopping, for the window displays are interesting.

Markets

On rue Ste-Catherine the fruit, vegetable and import stands at **Faubourg Ste-Catherine** are reminiscent of New York's Fulton Market and Boston's Quincy Market. Oriental and Mexican crafts are abundant.

Outlets

Hordes of Montréalers shop right off the factory rack in the **Chabanel Fashion District**, on rue Chabanel, west of rue St-Laurent. A solid row of towering garment factories and fashion wholesalers provides everything a bargain hunter could want. Most showrooms are open to the public only on Saturday, when serious shoppers storm the place for deals on jeans, lingerie, sweaters, bathing suits and the like. On Sunday morning, head for **Old Montréal**, where a similar scene takes place at numerous clothes discounters that congregate along rue Notre-Dame east of rue McGill.

Specialty Districts

Most of Montréal's big department stores were founded when Scottish, Irish and English families

Old Montréal
© MTOQ / Linda Turgeon

dominated the city's commerce, so the names remain noticeably Anglophone—Holt Renfrew, Ogilvy and The Bay. The main branches of Ogilvy and The Bay, dazzling emporiums, stretch along **rue Ste-Catherine**, where the city's traditional downtown shopping street comprises myriad shops in the blocks between rues Guy and Carré Phillips.

Rue Sherbrooke, 2 blocks north of rue Ste-Catherine, is the center of high fashion, represented by the venerable Holt Renfrew, exclusive art galleries and such haute couture boutiques as Ralph Lauren and Yves St-Laurent. Holt Renfrew also has a small branch across the street from the Ritz-Carlton Montréal on rue Sherbrooke. For local creations there are a number of boutiques along rues Laurier, St-Denis, St-Hubert and St-Laurent.

Running south off Sherbrooke, the businesses housed in quaint Victorian-style townhouses along **rue Crescent** and **rue de la Montagne** are popular for shopping. Those looking for the best in exotic coffees and avant-garde bookstores won't want to miss **rue St-Denis**, where cafes and restaurants spill out into the streets to accommodate shoppers taking a break for pasta or pastries. Other shops along this street offer an array of items for the home. *La Main* (Boulevard St-Laurent) is a hodgepodge of ethnic eateries and gift shops. Begin at the intersection of avenue Viger and head north.

Near the intersection of **rue de la Gauchetière**, the Chinese community offers its wares. The smells of deli meats and sausages mingle where the Hungarians and Polish Jews congregate several blocks up near rue Sherbrooke. Still farther north, clothing

Montréal World Film Festival
© Tourisme Montréal

and ceramics stores operated by Portuguese emigrants occupy the area that the Greek community once embraced. The ice cream parlors and pastry shops in **Little Italy**, near rue Jean-Talon, offer shoppers a place to refuel before making their way back along the street. Mah-jongg sets, jade carvings, silk saris and delicate brocades are among the items that can be found along the way.

Shops along rue Laurier, in the posh French neighborhood of **Outremont**, have built a reputation for staying on the cutting edge of European trends, whether it be in clothes, food or home furnishings. A selection of boutiques and local stores similar in quality to those on Laurier can be found along **avenue Greene**. This smaller area is less frequented by tourists, so it is usually easier to find parking.

Outside the downtown area are a number of suburban shopping malls offering many of the same attractions as their urban counterparts. They include **Carrefour Laval**, hwys. 15 and 440, in Laval; **Centre Fairview Pointe-Claire**, Hwy. 40 and Boulevard St-John, in Pointe-Claire; **Centre Rockland**, Hwy. 40 and Boulevard L'Acadie, in Mount Royal; and **Les Galleries d'Anjou**, Hwys. 40 and 25, in Ville d'Anjou.

Performing Arts

With its distinctly European tastes and modern air, Montréal would seem a hotbed of innovative performing arts. But the cultural scene here actually is new. It wasn't until the 1960s that cinema and dance hit the city with full force. Today French-language productions are presented at about a dozen theaters around town, and the city is hailed within the province for its provocative avant-garde cinema.

Dance

The **Grand Canadian Ballet of Montréal**, performing both classical and modern repertory at **Place des Arts**, has attracted enthusiastic audiences for more than 35 years. The troupe has toured internationally and has featured the works of many new Canadian composers and choreographers. Its December production of "The Nutcracker" is a big seasonal event in Montréal. Phone the box office at (514) 842-2112.

Another longtime company is the **Ensemble National de Folklore Les Sortilèges**. The group of 20 dancers has performed Québécois and other folk dances in colorful costumes for more than 25 years. They entertain in various halls around the city; check the local papers or phone (514) 522-5955.

Film

Montréal is host to many film festivals *(see event listings p. 193)*. **Cinéma du Parc**, 3575 avenue du Parc, shows specialized and offbeat fare.

Music

The world-renowned **Montréal Symphony Orchestra** performs during its regular season at the **Salle Wilfrid-Pelletier** at the Place des Arts, but locals recommend attending one of the performances at the **Notre-Dame Basilica**, 116 rue Notre-Dame. Performances usually begin at 8 p.m.; phone (514) 842-2925. The **Orchestre Métropolitain** promotes classical music while preparing new generations of musicians. The orchestra's regular season performances are at the **Maisonneuve Theatre** in Place des Arts, but it also performs in **St-Jean-Baptiste Church** and tours regionally; phone (514) 842-2112.

Opera

Founded in 1980, **L'Opéra de Montréal** is a young assemblage that stages six productions, both traditional and lesser-known, annually at Place des Arts. All operas are presented with English and French subtitles. The company's season runs from September through June. Phone the box office at (514) 842-2112.

Theater

Cirque du Soleil is perhaps Montréal's most extraordinary theatrical event. The modern, extravagant affair, which was founded in the city in 1984, is a circus without animals. The performers' kaleidoscopic shows—which include a mix of theatrical gymnastics, vertical pole-walking, music and fantastic special effects—captivate audiences of all ages. Having already achieved cult status on its American tours, the troupe stunned European audiences during its debut visit in 1996. Phone (514) 522-2324 for performance dates and admission costs.

The Old Stock Exchange building at 453 rue St-François-Xavier now is home to the **Centaur Theatre**, (514) 288-3161, Montréal's primary venue for English-language drama and musicals. Centaur's seven-play lineup has included contemporary Canadian dramas and Broadway hits. The **Yiddish Theater**, founded in 1937, stages two plays a year in Yiddish. Each runs for 4 weeks or longer, usually in June and November, at the **Saidye Bronfman Centre for the Arts**, 5170 chemin de la Côte-Ste-Catherine; phone (514) 739-2301 for schedule information.

At least 10 major French theater companies in the city stage productions stretching from classics to farce. **Théâtre de Quat'Sous**, 100 avenue des Pins est; **Théâtre du Nouveau Monde**, 84 rue Ste-Catherine ouest; and **Théâtre d'Aujourd'hui**, 3900 rue St-Denis, offer eclectic French fare from September through May. **Théâtre du Rideau Vert**, 4664 rue St-Denis, unveils mostly French classics and modern works by Québec playwrights year-round. The **Compagnie Jean Duceppe**, at 175 rue Sainte-Catherine Ouest in the Métro Place des Arts, presents contemporary works examining society and mores; phone (514) 842-2112 or (866) 842-2112.

Open-air theater draws crowds during the summer to Lafontaine Park and Île Ste-Hélène. The **Repercussion Theatre** puts on Shakespearean productions at various Montréal parks; phone (514) 931-2644.

Special Events

A hub on the international film festival circuit, Montréal welcomes a remarkable variety of programs each year.

The granddaddy is the **Montréal World Film Festival**, a competition similar to those held at Cannes and Venice. Staged from late August to early September, the event occupies various theaters throughout the area. Other significant festivals include the **International Film Festival on Art** in March; and the 9-day **Montréal Fringe Festival** in June.

Premier sporting events include the 65-kilometre (40-mi.) **Tour de l'Île de Montréal**, which brings 45,000 cyclists to the city in early June; the July **Valleyfield International Regatta**, said to be the largest speedboat event in North America; Canada's international tennis championships, and **Le Masters de tennis du Canada**, from late July to mid-August.

The city's other events cover a broad spectrum. Each new year gets off to a frosty start with the ice sculptures and competitive winter sports of the week-long **Fête des Neiges** at the end of January. The Snow Festival keeps the city entertained with costume balls, giant ice slides and all varieties of winter fun.

The **International Music Competition**, held at the Place des Arts, begins in mid-May and runs into the first week of June. This competition is divided into strings, piano and voice categories. June marks the beginning of the **Mondial SAQ International Fireworks Competition**, which ends in late July.

The **St-Jean-Baptiste Celebration** on June 24 is an official holiday honoring the patron saint of French Canadians. Bonfires, fireworks, dancing and

Montréal Museums Pass

The Montréal Museum Pass provides admission-free access to 32 major Montréal museums and attractions in the city for a period of 3 consecutive days, with public transportation services included.

Included in the pass are Canadian Centre for Architecture, Centre d'histoire de Montréal, Château Dufresne Museum, Château Ramezay Museum, Cinémathèque québécoise, Écomusée du fier monde, Environment Canada's Biosphère, Galerie d'art Stewart Hall Art Gallery, Just For Laughs Museum, Leonard & Bina Ellen Art Gallery, Maison Saint-Gabriel—Museum and Historical Site, Marguerite-Bourgeoys Museum, McCord Museum of Canadian History, Montréal Biodôme, Montréal Botanical Garden, Montréal Holocaust Memorial Centre Museum, Montréal Insectarium, Montréal Planétarium, Musée d'art contemporain de Montréal, Musée de Lachine, Musée des Hospitalières de l'Hôtel-Dieu de Montréal, Musée des maîtres et artisans du Québec, Musée Marc-Aurèle Fortin, Pointe-à-Callière—Montréal Museum of Archaeology and History, Redpath Museum—McGill University, Sir George-Étienne Cartier National Historic Site of Canada, Stewart Museum at the Fort—Île Sainte-Hélène, The Fur Trade at Lachine National Historic Site of Canada, The Montreal Museum of Fine Arts, The Montréal Science Centre.

The pass is valid for 3 consecutive days, as is the STM (public transportations service) visitors pass, and sells for $45 (taxes included). There is no senior citizen or student/child discount. The pass can be purchased from the 30 member institutions; downtown at the Tourism Information Bureau of Montréal Infotouriste Centre at the Travelprice agency counter, 1255 Peel St., Suite 100; in the Village of Montreal at the Travelprice agency office, 576 Sainte-Catherine East Suite 202; in Old Montréal at Infotouriste Centre at 174 Notre-Dame St. E.; and from some major hotels. For more information phone (514) 873-2015 or (877) 266-5687.

music are among the day's events and activities. Bridging late June and early July is the **Montréal International Jazz Festival**, during which the world's foremost jazz artists participate in concerts; the 2007 festival is June 28-July 8.

The **Just for Laughs (Juste pour Rire) Festival**, running the entire month of July, is a program of comedy acts from around the world. Performers are both established comedians and newcomers. Many acts perform in the Latin Quarter on St-Denis St.

and are free; admission is charged for others taking place in theatres. Some acts are in French and some in English. The schedule for English presentations is July 12-22, 2007; July 10-20, 2008; July 9-19, 2009. Phone (514) 845-2322 or (888) 244-3155.

The **Francofolies de Montréal Song Festival** is held in late July. December ushers in the **Québec Handicraft Show** and scores of Christmas festivities.

The Montréal Vicinity

CHAMBLY (F-7) pop. 20,342

FORT CHAMBLY NATIONAL HISTORIC SITE OF CANADA (Lieu historique national du Canada du Fort-Chambly) is off Hwy. 10 exit 22 at 2 rue De Richelieu at jct. Bourgogne and Langevin, at the foot of the Richelieu River Rapids. This 1-hectare (2.5-acre) park contains one of several forts built here by the French. In 1665, Jacques de Chambly constructed a wooden fort on this site to subdue the Iroquois. Two other wooden forts followed before the French built a stone fort on the site to prevent a British invasion.

Taken by English troops in 1760, the fort was invaded by American troops in 1775 during the American Revolution and again in 1812 during the war with the United States. A British garrison occupied the fort sporadically during the 19th century until its final abandonment in 1860.

The restored fort has appears as it did in 1750 when the Compagnie franche de la Marine was garrisoned here. Interpretive center displays explain the living conditions of the French garrison.

Picnic facilities are available; barbeques and campfires are not permitted. Allow 1 hour, 30 minutes minimum. Daily 10-6, June-Aug.; Wed.-Sun. 10-5, Apr.-May and Sept.-Oct. Admission $5.70; over 65, $4.95; students with ID $2.95; ages 6-16, $3; family rate $14.50. Phone (450) 658-1585 or (888) 773-8888.

KAHNAWAKE (F-7)

In 1670-71 a French and Indian village was founded at La Prairie by French Jesuits. The native population moved farther up the St. Lawrence beginning in 1676 and finally established a settlement in Kahnawake, meaning "by the rapids," in 1716. The village served as a refuge for Iroquois converts to Christianity. The reservation has no street names or numbers.

ST. FRANCIS XAVIER MISSION AND SHRINE OF KATERI TEKAKWITHA (Mission St-François-Xavier et Sanctuaire de Kateri Tekakwitha) is at the center of the village on Route de l'Église. The church houses the tomb of Iroquois maiden Kateri Tekakwitha, who has been beatified by the Vatican and is expected to become the first North American Indian saint. A small museum contains material relating to Blessed Kateri as well as paintings and other artifacts. Allow 30 minutes minimum. Mon.-Fri. 10-noon and 1-4; Sat.-Sun. 10-4. Donations. Phone (450) 632-6030.

LACHINE (E-7) pop. 40,222

THE FUR TRADE AT LACHINE NATIONAL HISTORIC SITE OF CANADA (Lieu historique national du Canada du Commerce-de-la-Fourrure-à-Lachine), 1255 boul. Saint-Joseph at av. 12, centers on a stone shed built in 1803 for the storage of pelts owned by the North West Co. After the Hudson's Bay Co. merged with the North West Co., the firm established its headquarters in Lachine in 1833. Displays portray Lachine's and Montréal's roles in the fur trade during the 18th and 19th centuries. Events are held Saturday and Sunday afternoons during the summer.

Mon.-Fri. 10-12:30 and 1-5:30, Sat.-Sun. 10-12:30 and 1-6, Apr. 1-second Mon. in Oct.; Wed.-Sun. 9:30-12:30 and 1-5, late Oct.-first Sun. in Dec. Admission $3.95; over 65, $3.45; ages 6-16, $1.95; family rate $9.90 (maximum 8 persons). Phone (514) 637-7433 or (888) 773-8888.

LACHINE CANAL NATIONAL HISTORIC SITE OF CANADA (Lieu historique national du Canada Canal-de-Lachine) runs 13.4 km (8 mi.) s.w. from the Old Port in Montréal, through Lachine and LaSalle to lac Saint-Louis (M: Lionel-Groulx). The canal was conceived in 1680 but completed in 1825. Recreational uses replaced shipping in 1970. A 12-kilometre (7.5-mi.) bicycle and skate path, hiking trails and picnic areas line the canal; cross-country skiing is permitted on a trail lighted from dawn to midnight. The visitor center has free exhibits about the canal's history.

Food is available. Canal grounds daily dawn-midnight. Canal open to pleasure boats daily mid-May through second Mon. in Oct. Visitor center open Mon.-Fri. 9-5, mid-May through Sept. 30. Admission free. Fees may be charged for services. Phone (514) 364-4490 or (888) 773-8888.

LACHINE MUSEUM (Musée de la ville de Lachine), 1 ch. Musée Lachine (M: Angrignon), is a complex of buildings that includes the French Colonial Jacques LeBer-Charles LeMoyne House, built 1670-85. Once used as a trading post, it is considered the oldest house in the area.

The museum complex displays 19th-century furniture, costumes and paintings. Changing exhibitions display the works of contemporary Canadian artists. Guided tours are available; narration in English is available. Allow 30 minutes minimum. Wed.-Sun. 11:30-4:30, Apr. 1 through mid-Dec. Free. Phone (514) 634-3471, ext. 346.

LAVAL (B-6) pop. 343,005

In the heart of the Saint-Laurent Valley, Laval is surrounded by three bodies of water: the Mille Îles River, des Prairies River and the Deux-Montagnes Lake. Named after the Archbishop de Laval, Laval is one of the largest cities in the province of Québec.

Laval Tourism: 2900 boul. St-Martin Ouest, Laval, QC, Canada H7T 2J2; phone (450) 682-5522 or (877) 465-2825.

COSMODÔME is off Hwy. 15 exit 9, .5 km (.3 mi.) w. on boul. St-Martin, .8 km (.5 mi.) n. on boul. Pierre Péladeau, and .2 km (.1 mi.) on av. du Cosmodôme. The Cosmodôme is a science center devoted to the science and technologies of space flight. Visitors can explore the laws of space science by activating more than 50 hands-on displays. A space camp also is offered.

Allow 2 hours, 30 minutes minimum. Daily 10-5, last Tues. in June-Labour Day; Tues.-Sun. 10-5, rest of year. Closed holidays except Easter, Victoria Day, Labour Day and Thanksgiving. Hours may vary; phone ahead. Admission $11.50; over 65, $8.50; students ages 6-22 with ID $7.50; family rate $29.50. AX, MC, VI. Phone (450) 978-3600 or (800) 565-2267.

MASCOUCHE (E-7) pop. 29,556

MOORE GARDENS (Les Jardins Moore) is off Hwy. 25 at exit 28, then 3.8 km (2.3 mi.) w. on chemin Ste-Marie to 1455 chemin Pincourt. This 2.2-hectare (5.5-acre) display garden of what grows in Québec gardens easily and well is a riot of color provided by 120 species of perennials, and masses of annuals the banks of the Mascouche River. The garden planning area emphasizes ecology-friendly methods. A small museum honors the founder, W.D. Moore.

Allow 2 hours minimum. Daily 9:30-8, June 24-Labour Day. Admission $5; ages 9-17, $2. Phone (450) 474-0588.

MELOCHEVILLE (F-6)

BEAUHARNOIS GENERATING STATION, (Centrale Hydroelectrique de Beauharnois), take Rte. 132 w. 10 km (6.5 mi.) from Beauharnois to 80 rue Edgar-Hebert in Melocheville, is one of the world's largest hydroelectric power stations. The 90-minute guided tour includes exhibits in the interpretation center and a chance to view the 36 turbine-alternator units in the 1-km (.6-mi.) building.

Guided tours daily at 9:30, 11:15, 1 and 2:45, mid-May through Labour Day. Free. Phone (800) 365-5229.

ST-CONSTANT (F-7) pop. 22,577

EXPORAIL, THE CANADIAN RAILWAY MUSEUM (Exporail, le Musée ferroviaire canadien), at 110 rue Saint-Pierre, opened a new pavilion in 2003. The museum contains a collection of 250,000 railway objects and documents, including 162 pieces of rolling stock, an exhibit pavilion showcasing 44 of its best vehicles, a turntable and two train stations. Visitors can take a ride aboard a vintage streetcar and miniature railroad.

Picnicking is permitted. Allow 30 minutes minimum. Daily 10-6, May 1-Labour Day; Wed.-Sun. 10-5, day after Labour Day-Oct. 31; Sat.-Sun. 10-5, rest of year. Admission $12; over 59, $9.50; students with ID ages 13-17, $7; ages 4-12, $6; family rate (two adults and two children) $30. Phone (450) 632-2410.

ST-EUSTACHE (E-6) pop. 40,378

EXOTARIUM: REPTILE FARM (Exotarium: Ferme de Reptiles) is off Autoroute 640 exit 11, w. on Hwy. 148 to boul. Industriel, s. 2 km (1.2 mi.) to ch. Fresnière, then w. 7 km (4 mi.) to 846 ch. Fresnière. This breeding farm and mini-zoo for reptiles displays 135 species, including boa constrictors, crocodiles, iguanas, pythons, turtles and insects.

Allow 1 hour minimum. Daily noon-5, June-Aug.; Fri.-Sun. noon-5, Feb.-May and Sept. 1-Dec. 15. Animal shows at 1, 2:30 and 4. Admission $9.50; ages 3-15, $6; family rate $30. VI. Phone (450) 472-1827.

ST-LAURENT (E-7) pop. 77,391

THE MUSEUM OF QUÉBEC MASTERS AND ARTISANS (Le Musée des maîtres et artisans du Québec) is in an 1867 neo-Gothic church at 615 Ave. Ste-Croix, on the grounds of the College St-Laurent. The permanent exhibition, From Masters' Hands, displays furniture and other objects dating from 1650 to the present, and details old crafts honed by centuries of use and carefully transmitted from generation to generation.

Allow 30 minutes minimum. Wed.-Sun. noon-5. Admission $5; over 65, $4; students with ID $3; under 6 free; family rate (two adults and children) $10; free to all Wed. AX, VI. Phone (514) 747-7367.

STE-ANNE-DE-BELLEVUE (F-7) pop. 5,062

Sainte-Anne-de-Bellevue Canal National Historic Site of Canada, 170 rue Ste-Anne, links Saint-Louis Lake and the Des Deux-Montagnes Lake. When the canal opened in 1843 it was a crucial link in the Montréal-Ottawa-Kingston shipping route. Today, the canal primarily is used by pleasure craft. From mid-May to mid-October, visitors can take advantage of the site's park area and enjoy watching boat traffic. Phone (450) 447-4888 or (888) 773-8888.

TERREBONNE (E-7) pop. 43,149

ÎLE DES MOULINS (Mill Island) is an island in the Mille Îles River off Hwy. 25N exit 22E, then 2 km (1.6 mi.) following signs. An 1803 bakery, an 1804 wood mill, an 1846 flour mill, an 1850 office and an 1850 carding mill built about 1850 grace the island, which is a popular recreation center. A guided tour recounts the development of the site.

Picnicking is permitted. Island accessible daily 7 a.m.-11 p.m. Interpretation center open daily. 1-8, June 24-Labour Day. Exhibits free. Fee for tour. Phone (450) 471-0619.

VAUDREUIL-DORION (F-6) pop. 18,500

Vaudreuil-Dorion, a country resort on the Ottawa River, dates back to the 1773 founding of the Parish of Vaudreuil. Established in 1850, the village changed from a predominantly farming and dairying center to a popular vacation spot with the construction of bridges connecting it to the île Perrot and Montréal.

VAUDREUIL-SOULANGES REGIONAL MUSEUM (Musée Régional de Vaudreuil-Soulanges), 431 av. St-Charles, is in a 19th-century stone schoolhouse. The museum offers changing exhibits about the traditional and domestic arts of Québec.

Allow 1 hour minimum. Tues.-Fri. 9:30-noon and 1-4:30 (also Tues. 7-9:30 p.m.); Sat.-Sun. 1-4:30; closed during Christmas holidays. Admission $5; free to all Tues. 7-9:30 p.m. Phone to verify holiday closures. MC, VI. Phone (450) 455-2092.

WESTMOUNT (F-7) pop. 19,727

SHAAR HASHOMAYIM SYNAGOGUE (Synagogue de Shaar Hashomayim), 450 rue Kensington (M: Atwater), dates from 1846 and is the second oldest synagogue in Canada. The size of the congregation, more than 1,600 families, and the 2,000-person seating capacity of the sanctuary make this among the largest synagogues in the country.

Guided tours are available in English. Tours are given Mon.-Thurs. 9:30-4. Donations. Reservations are required for guided tours. Phone (514) 937-9471.

TEMPLE EMANU-EL BETH SHOLOM, 4100 rue Sherbrooke Ouest (M: Atwater), dates from 1882 and is known as the country's oldest Reform Jewish congregation. Mon.-Thurs. 8:30-5, Fri. 8:30-3. Donations. Phone (514) 937-3575.

Fête des Neiges / © Tourisme Montréal

This ends listings for the Montréal Vicinity.
The following page resumes the alphabetical listings of cities in Québec.

MONT-ST-PIERRE (B-8)
pop. 239, elev. 8 m/25′

Because of its high altitude, Mont-St-Pierre is among the few southern Canada locales with a tundra region and a herd of caribou. At the edge of town is 411-metre (1,555-ft.) Mont St-Pierre, one of the most challenging hang-gliding sites in eastern North America. A road travels to its summit, which offers outstanding views.

The town provides access to the Chic-Choc's 1,268-metre (4,797-ft.) Mont Jacques-Cartier, the tallest mountain in southeast Canada.

The scenic portion of Hwy. 132 passes through Mont-St-Pierre on its tour of the Gaspé Peninsula. East of town, Hwy. 132 joins Hwy. 299, which enters Gaspésie National Park (see Ste-Anne-des-Monts p. 228).

MONT-TREMBLANT (E-4) pop. 8,352

Overshadowed by the 931-metre-high (3,055-ft.) peak of Mont Tremblant, the highest peak in the Laurentians, the town of Mont-Tremblant is surrounded by the Laurentians' greatest concentration of resort areas. Just a little more than an hour's drive from Montréal and less than 2 hours from Ottawa, scenic Mont-Tremblant is a year-round recreation destination where visitors can indulge in favorite pastimes or learn new ones from professionals.

Spring through fall, hiking and bicycling opportunities are many and the settings are varied—flat or steep, open or wooded, inland or waterside. The 200-kilometre (120-mi.) Parc linéaire Le P'tit train du Nord is Canada's longest linear park, and a favorite with bicyclists. Park du Mont-Tremblant (see attraction listing) is forest wilderness with ample wildlife viewing opportunities. The more adventurous can climb rock faces. Five golf courses and numerous tennis courts round out the venue.

The area's streams, rivers and waterfalls as well as hundreds of lakes offer myriad chances for swimming, boating, sailing, kayaking, water skiing, canoeing and viewing experiences. Fishing aficionados can count among their catch speckled and brown trout and northern pike.

Winter recreation facilities include 92 alpine ski runs, tubing slopes and groomed trails for cross-country skiers. For snowmobilers, thousands of kilometres of trails lead to and through small towns and through wilderness areas. Morning and noontime dogsledding trips are available. For the truly hardy, ice climbing lessons are available—along with the rental gear.

Special events, large and small, are held throughout the year. In the summer the Championnat national du Canada racetrack holds international automobile races from mid-June through September 30; phone (819) 425-6363. Thursday through Sunday of the last weekend in July, Festival international du blues de Tremblant attracts thousands—bands from across North and South America perform on outdoor stages and in bars and restaurants.

Mont-Tremblant Chamber of Commerce and Tourism Bureau: 5080 Montée Ryan, Mont-Tremblant, QC, Canada J8E 1S4; phone (819) 425-2434.

MONT-TREMBLANT NATIONAL PARK (Parc national du Mont-Tremblant), 23 km (14 mi.) e. of Hwy. 117N, is a year-round favorite for outdoor recreational activities in the Laurentian Mountains. Rounded hilltops alternating with high peaks, trees as far as you can see, some 400 lakes, a network of rivers and streams, 196 species of birds and facilities for summer and winter activities make the park one of Québec's more popular vacation areas. Open daily; hours vary with the season. Admission $3.50; ages 6-17, $1.50. Phone (819) 688-2281. See Recreation Chart.

MURDOCHVILLE (B-9) pop. 1,171

Since the early 1950s Murdochville has been the site of a prosperous copper mining industry. Local companies are known for their use of the room and pillar method of mining: thick pillars of rock are left to support the ceilings of dugout chambers.

Murdochville Tourist Bureau: 573 av. Miller, Murdochville, QC, Canada G0E 1W0; phone (418) 784-2444.

COPPER INTERPRETATION CENTRE (Centre d'interprétation du cuivre), 345 Rte. 198, offers displays and interactive exhibits about the history of copper mining, as well as a 1-hour tour of a copper mine. Allow 1 hour minimum. Daily 9-5, early June 5 through mid-Sept. Admission $10; over 65 and students with ID $8; under 14, $6; family rate $35. Phone to verify prices. VI. Phone (418) 784-3335 or (800) 487-8601.

NEW RICHMOND (C-8) pop. 7,760

GASPÉSIAN BRITISH HERITAGE CENTRE (Village Gaspésien de l'Héritage Britannique) is 1.6 km (1 mi.) s. on ch. Campbell, then 1.7 km (1.1 mi.) w. to 351 boul. Perron Ouest. This living-history village recreates periods from 1800 to 1900. Visitors can take a horse and wagon ride or wooded paths running down to the sea and visit 24 buildings celebrating the heritage of the Loyalist, Scottish, Irish and Channel Island settlers.

Allow 2 hours minimum. Daily 9-5, mid-June through mid-Sept. Admission $10, over 65 and students with ID $7, family rate $25. MC, VI. Phone (418) 392-4487.

NORMANDIN (C-5) pop. 3,524

LES GRANDS JARDINS DE NORMANDIN, 1515 av. du Rocher, are 17 hectares (42 acres) of lush gardens illustrating the evolution of the gardening art. Guided tours are conducted through such areas as an herb garden, an English garden, a flower path and an Oriental flower tapestry.

Allow 1 hour, 30 minutes minimum. Daily 9-6, June 23-Labour Day. Fee $12; over 65, $10; ages 7-22, $6; family rate (parents and their dependent children under age 12) $25. MC, VI. Phone (418) 274-1993 or (800) 920-1993.

NORTH HATLEY (F-9) pop. 746

SAVE CAPELTON MINES (des mines Capelton), 8 km (5 mi.) e. to Rte. 108, is a journey through time. First visitors travel by wagon up the mountain to the copper mine's entry, then they explore the shafts and galleries on foot for 2 hours, accompanied by a guide who is passionate about the mines as they were in 1863. Also on the 263-hectare (650-acre) site are nature trails, a physical fitness course and a mining museum.

English tours are available by advance reservation. The temperature in the mine is 9 C (48 F) so dress warmly. Bicycle rentals and food are available. Picnicking is permitted. Tours on the hour daily 10-3, June-Aug. Phone to verify schedule. Fee $20.50; students with ID $17; ages 6-15, $13; ages 3-5, $4; family rate (two adults and two ages 6-15) $45. AX, MC, VI Phone (819) 346-9545 for reservations.

ODANAK (E-5)

In the 17th century the French-allied Abenaki Indians moved to Odanak from New England. To convert and educate them, Jesuits established a mission in 1700.

ABÉNAKIS MUSEUM (Musée des Abénakis), 108 rue Waban-Aki on Rte. 226, is reached from Hwy. 132 at the n. end of the Pierreville Bridge following signs. The museum's displays relate the history of the Abenaki Tribe of Odanak. Mon.-Fri. 10-5, Sat.-Sun. 1-5, May-Oct.; Sat.-Sun. by appointment, rest of year. Admission $6.50; over 65, $5.50; students ages 13-24 with ID $4.50; ages 5-12, $3.50. Phone (450) 568-2600.

ORFORD (F-9) pop. 1,987

MONT ORFORD PARK (Parc du Mont Orford), in the Eastern Townships, is n. on Hwy. 10. Mont Chauve is 600 metres (1,968 ft.) high. The park offers a visitor center, 80 kilometres (500 miles) of cross country skiing, hiking trails, 470 camping sites, swimming and huts. The park's Centre d'Arts Orford offers summer music courses, plays, performances by well-known artists and art exhibits.

Park open daily 8 a.m.-9 p.m., June-Aug.; 8-4, rest of year. Centre d'Arts Orford daily 8 a.m.-8:30 p.m., July-Aug.; Mon.-Fri. 9-5, May-June and Sept.-Oct. Park admission $3.50; ages 6-17, $1.50. Park parking $6.25. MC, VI. Phone (819) 843-9855 for the park, or (800) 567-6155 for the arts center. *See Recreation Chart and the AAA/CAA Eastern Canada CampBook.*

ORMSTOWN (F-6) pop. 3,647

Ormstown began as a small settlement of farms in the late 1790s and early 1800s. Around 1810 the area's population began to shrink as speculators finagled local farmers out of their land, and American settlers left for the United States under the growing threat of war.

Ormstown was the site of the Battle of Châteauguay, an important clash in the War of 1812. After the war the town settled into quiet prosperity as a farming and cattle raising center.

BATTLE OF THE CHÂTEAUGUAY NATIONAL HISTORIC SITE OF CANADA (Lieu historique national du Canada de la Bataille-de-la-Châteauguay), 6 km (4 mi.) e. on Hwy. 138 at 2371 Rivière Châteauguay, commemorates the battle of Oct. 26, 1813, when Lt. Col. Charles-Michel de Salaberry and his force of 300 Canadians stopped 3,000 United States. Interpretation center exhibits analyze the background of the battle and the living conditions of its participants. A 30-minute documentary film in French and English precedes a presentation of the strategies used in the battle.

Allow 1 hour, 30 minutes minimum. Wed.-Sun. 10-5, second Sat. in May-day before Labour Day; Sat.-Sun. 10-5, Labour Day-second Mon. in Oct. Admission $3.95; over 65 and students with ID $3.45; ages 6-16, $1.95; family rate $9.90. Phone (450) 829-2003 or (888) 773-8888.

PERCÉ (C-9) pop. 3,614

Percé lies at the eastern extremity of the Gaspé Peninsula on the Gulf of St. Lawrence. During the 17th century the town was a favored port for ships traveling to Québec from France. Percé was later destroyed by British frigates in a 1690 attack on Québec.

Although dormant for a half-century, the site's sheltered location eventually drew enough fishermen to make Percé an important fishing port. While the wharves are still busy with lobster boats, the town also has become a popular destination for visitors to the Gaspé Peninsula.

Available in French and in English, Taxi Percé offers a 2-hour narrated tour of the mountains and towns aboard a four-wheel-drive vehicle; phone (418) 782-2102. Starting from behind the Church of St-Michel, the hiking trails of Mont Ste-Anne, the grotto and the crevice allow walkers to explore the mountains of Percé and discover spectacular landscapes. A detailed map is available at the tourism bureau office.

The scenic drive around the mountains starts at the west end of the village, by turning north on Route des Failles. At the intersection where St. Paul's Anglican Church is located keep north and follow the very steep hill. You will then drive on a sinuous mountain road for about 5 km (3 mi.) until you reach Route 132. You turn east to go back to Percé village. Along the 5 km (3 mi.) drive back to Percé the road passes the Mont-Blanc, the Overlook, the Big Bowl, the Pic of Dawn, the Three Sisters Cliffs and a spectacular view of the natural Amphitheater of Percé.

For scuba-diving enthusiasts, the nautical center of Percé offers equipment rentals, a diving school and snorkeling and scuba sites. Rental sea kayaks and mountain bikes also are available. For information about whale-watching tours contact the Percé Tourism Bureau.

Percé Tourism Bureau: 142 Rte. 132, Percé, QC, Canada G0C 2L0; phone (418) 782-5448.

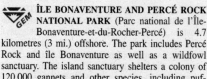 **ÎLE BONAVENTURE AND PERCÉ ROCK NATIONAL PARK** (Parc national de l'Île-Bonaventure-et-du-Rocher-Percé) is 4.7 kilometres (3 mi.) offshore. The park includes Percé Rock and île Bonaventure as well as a wildfowl sanctuary. The island sanctuary shelters a colony of 120,000 gannets and other species, including puffins, guillemots and cormorants. A trail leads to the cliffs overlooking the bird ledges. An interpretation center is in downtown Percé. Guide service is available; English narration is available.

Park open daily 9-5, June 1 to mid-Oct. From Percé, a sightseeing cruise around the island is available daily on the hour 8-5, July 1 to mid-Sept.; every 2 hours 9-3, May-June and mid-Sept. to mid-Oct.

Park $3.50; ages 6-17, $1.50. Family rate, one adult and dependent children ages 6-17, $5; two adults and dependent children ages 6-17, $7. Boat fare for 9 a.m. trip to île Bonaventure $20; under 13, $6-$8. MC, VI. Phone (418) 782-2240, (418) 890-6527 or (800) 665-6527.

Interpretation Centre is in Le Chafaud, at 4 rue du Quai. The center, within sight of île Bonaventure, uses films and wildlife displays to explain the interaction of land and ocean. Daily 9-7, June 1 to mid-Oct. Center admission included in park admission. A fee is charged for parking. Phone (418) 782-2240.

Percé Rock (Rocher Percé) is off shore. Percé Rock is one of the most recognized natural attractions in Canada. Visitors can walk to the rock at low tide on an exposed pebble ridge; information about low tides is available from the Tourist Office. At low tide naturalists hold talks about marine life. Phone (418) 782-2240.

LE CHAFAUD is at 145 Hwy. 132. This museum is devoted to the cultural heritage of the Gaspé Peninsula. Housed in one of the oldest preserved structures in the region, it includes an art gallery. Daily 10-8, mid-June through late Sept. Admission $5; over 65 and students with ID $3.50; under 13, $2; family rate $13. Phone (418) 782-5100.

PÉRIBONKA (B-5) pop. 600

French author Louis Hémon brought fame to Péribonka in 1912 when he used the remote agricultural locale on the north shore of lac St-Jean as the setting for his romantic novel *Maria Chapdelaine*. The Musée Louis-Hémon at 700 Maria Chapdelaine honors the novelist; phone (418) 374-2177.

Péribonka marks the departure point of the Traversée Internationale du lac St-Jean, held the last Sunday in July. This swimming competition dates from 1955, when Jacques Amyot swam across lac St-Jean from Péribonka to Roberval in 11 hours and 32 minutes. Contestants must swim the same passage, a distance of 40 kilometres (64 mi.). Phone (418) 275-2851 for information.

POINTE À-LA-CROIX (C-8) pop. 1,513

BATTLE OF RESTIGOUCHE NATIONAL HISTORIC SITE OF CANADA (Lieu historique national du Canada de la Bataille-de-la-Restigouche), w. on Hwy. 132, was the location of last naval battle fought in North America during the Seven Years War, 1756-63. The interpretation center exhibits include sections of an 18th-century French frigate recovered during underwater excavation of the site. A documentary explains the battle and life aboard ships of that period. Guided tours are available; English narration is available.

Daily 9-5, early June-second Mon. in Oct.; other times by appointment. Admission $3.95; over 65, $3.45; ages 6-16, $1.95; family rate $9.90. Phone (418) 788-5676 or (888) 773-8888.

POINTE-AU-PÈRE (C-7) pop. 4,171

RIMOUSKI MARINE MUSEUM (Musée de la Mer), Hwy. 132 to rue Père Nouvel to 1034 rue du Phare Ouest, houses exhibits about regional history, marine life and the shipwreck of the *Empress of Ireland*, a cruise ship which sank off Rimouski on May 29, 1914, with a loss of 1,012 lives. A 3D projection recreates the final moments of the ship's journey. Guided tours of the 33-metre-high (108-ft.) lighthouse are conducted; English narration is available.

Allow 1 hour, 30 minutes minimum. Daily 9-6, June-Aug.; 9-5, Sept.-Oct. Admission $10.50; over 60, $9.50; students with ID $8.50; ages 6-12, $5; family rate $28. VI. Phone (418) 724-6214.

Pointe-au-Père Lighthouse (Le phare de Pointe-au-Père) is at 1034 rue du Phare Ouest. This 33-metre-high (108 feet) rare octagonal structure was completed in 1909. Allow 1 hour minimum. Daily 9-6, mid-June through Labour day; 9-5, early to mid-June and day after Labour Day-second Mon. in Oct. Tour included in price of Rimouski Marine Museum admission. VI. Phone (418) 724-6214.

POINTE-AU-PIC (C-6)

La Malbaie-Pointe-au-Pic, a summer resort established in the 19th century, is noted for its cottage architecture and the stunning views across the St. Lawrence River afforded by its high cliffs.

CHARLEVOIX MUSEUM Musée de Charlevoix, 10 ch. du Havre, presents changing exhibitions about the culture, history and arts of Charlevoix County. Allow 30 minutes minimum. Daily 9-5, June 24-Labour Day; Mon.-Fri. 10-5, Sat.-Sun. 1-5, rest of year. Admission $5, over 60 and students with ID $4, under 11 free. Phone (418) 665-4411.

Québec

City Population: 169,076   **Elevation:** 59 m/194'

Editor's Picks:

The Citadel ....(see p. 209)

Dufferin Terrace ....(see p. 209)

Place-Royale ....(see p. 212)

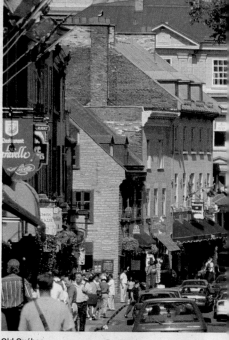

Old Québec
© Ministère du Tourisme du Québec
Jean-Guy Lavoie

Québec, carved into the bluffs overlooking the St. Lawrence River by the forces of time and history, is a complex city. Capital of the province, it is the only walled city north of Mexico. It can almost be divided by a line into the old and the new. Twentieth-century Québec, extending up the hill beyond the Parliament Buildings, is shut off from the winding streets and 17th-century buildings of Upper and Lower Town by aging walls. A European bastion, it also is a profoundly French city.

In 1608 Samuel de Champlain, realizing the strategic importance of the site—not only would the cliffs provide an impregnable fortress for a settlement, but they also would protect ships anchored in the deep waters of the St. Lawrence River—built an *abitation*, or trading post, by the river at the foot of Cap Diamant. The city of Québec was established.

A growing base for trade and exploration of the interior continent, Québec expanded in the only direction possible—up the cliff. Lower Town, or Basse-Ville, the city's mercantile district, was to be protected by Haute-Ville, the Upper Town, built on the cliff above it.

The French colony prospered in the 1600s, becoming the center of New France and enjoying a brisk trade with its mother country, which was at peace with rival England 1629-32. The tranquility ended in 1690 with a British attack on the city; it was the first of several to come.

Québec was successfully defended for 6 decades due to its natural defenses as well as the protective wall and fortifications built by Chassegros de Léry around Upper Town in 1720. In 1759, however, Québec fell to Britain.

The siege of the city culminated early on Sept. 13, when British general James Wolfe and his troops scaled sheer cliffs to reach the Plains of Abraham (known today as National Battlefield Park or Parc national des Champs-de-Bataille) above fortified Québec. They surprised and defeated the Marquis de Montcalm and his troops in about 20 minutes. With the peace treaty in 1763, France lost the province to Great Britain.

The French city became English, but in name only; in culture and tradition Québec remained French. Acceding to this fact, Britain passed the Québec Act in 1774, which allowed the French to worship in their native Roman Catholic Church rather than forcing them to attend the English Anglican Church.

A year later an American invasion challenged British troops to defend the city. The British were successful in defeating the attackers, whose New Year's Eve assault was spearheaded by generals Richard Montgomery and Benedict Arnold.

During the last of the 18th and most of the 19th centuries, Québec was a shipbuilding and wheat and lumber trading center. City walls and other defenses were refortified. By 1880 most English-speaking settlers had moved to Montréal, the United States or elsewhere, leaving Québec the predominantly French-speaking city it is today.

Getting There — starting on p. 203

Getting Around — starting on p. 203

What To See — starting on p. 207

What To Do — starting on p. 213

Where To Stay — starting on p. 521

Where To Dine — starting on p. 537

Getting There

By Car

From points south the city's major entrance is via Pont Pierre-Laporte (Autoroute 73), which brings traffic across the river from Autoroute 20, the area's principal artery traversing the south side of the St. Lawrence River. Autoroute 73, extending southward along the Chaudière River, also collects traffic from portions of the province's southern extremity as well as arrivals from Maine, New Hampshire and parts of Vermont.

North of the St. Lawrence, Hwy. 138 and Autoroute 40 closely parallel the river and form through routes. However, either Autoroute 440 or Hwy. 175 offers shorter, more convenient travel directly through the city. Hwy. 175 brings traffic from the north, joining Autoroute 73 before entering the city.

Autoroutes 40 and 73 combine to form a bypass north of the heart of the city, interchanging with all major highways en route.

Getting Around

Street System

The city can be divided into two major sections— Old and New Québec. Old Québec itself is divided into two areas: Lower Town, centering on Place-Royale at the foot of Cap Diamant, and Upper Town, which extends up the hill from Place d'Armes and Dufferin Terrace to just past rue d'Auteuil.

New, or modern, Québec spreads northward, westward and southwestward from the walls of Old Québec to the outlying suburbs of Ste-Foy, Sillery, L'Ancienne-Lorette, Charlesbourg and Beauport.

Winter Carnival / © Rubens Abboud / Alamy

The street system actually has no system; it is a haphazard arrangement of narrow streets, especially in the older sections of the city. In Old Québec it is advisable to park in one of the several public lots and walk.

Most of the street names are in French; directional signs are usually accompanied by international symbols. The use of seat belts is mandatory. Any driver's license is valid, but visitors should obtain a Canadian Nonresident Interprovince Motor Vehicle Liability Insurance card from an insurance agent before leaving the United States *(see Border Information)*.

If you must drive in the city, it is best to have a map handy and to beware of one-way streets and sightseeing pedestrians.

Parking

It is much easier to park in Québec than to drive. Public lots in the older section are at Place de l'Hôtel-de-Ville, Le Château Frontenac, 47 rue St-Louis, rue d'Auteuil and Marché-Finlay. There are

Destination Québec

© Bill Brooks / Alamy

Q uébec City is a mélange of French and English cultures in a North American setting.

T he designs of the historic buildings reflect little adaptation to the new continent. The cuisine is definitely French, but sometimes adapted to ingredients undreamed of in France. But the residents are unabashedly *French* Canadian, in their hearts as well as their language.

Le Château Frontenac and the Royal Battery, Québec.
The *splendide* Château Frontenac overlooks the restored Battery Park and walls of the fortification. (See listing page 208 and page 213)

© Glenn van der Knijff / Lonely Planet Images

Museum of French America (Musée de l'Amérique Française), Québec.
The collections in this traditional building trace the history of French culture and influence on this continent. (See listing page 210)

Stoneham-et-Tewkesbury •

Wendake •
73

St-Gabriel-de-Valcartier •

St-Catherine-de-la-Jacques-Cartier •
307

40

40

P laces included in this AAA Destination City:

The drill hall at the National Battlefields Park, Québec.
Fear of an invasion from the United States prompted the beginning of the fortress in 1820. (See listing page 212)

© Wolfgang Kaehler

St-Ferréol-les-Neiges
Ste-Anne-de-Beaupré
Beaupré
Château-Richer

138

Charlesbourg
Beauport
See Downtown map page 208

410

Lévis

20

Ste-Foy
Sillery

Québec

73

© Francis Lépine / Alamy

Québec Aquarium Park, Ste-Foy.
Visitors watch visitors watching denizens of the deep. (See listing page 223)

© Wolfgang Kaehler

Buggy ride on Grande Allée, Québec.
Buggy rides lead past the Parliament Buildings and National Battlefields Park.

The Informed Traveler

Sales Tax: Canada levies a 6 percent sales tax. Québec's provincial sales tax is 7.5 percent on good and services. The Québec City area has a 3 percent lodging surcharge.

WHOM TO CALL

Emergency: 911

Police (non-emergency): (418) 641-6292 or (900) 561-2002.

Time and Temperature: (418) 648-7766

Hospitals: Hôpital du Saint-Sacrement, (418) 682-7511.

WHERE TO LOOK

Newspapers

Both daily newspapers published in Québec, *Le Journal de Québec* and *Le Soleil*, are in French. An English daily, *The Gazette*, is printed in Montréal. *Québec Magazine* is a quarterly, bilingual guide to restaurants and entertainment.

Radio

Québec radio station CBU (980 AM) is programmed by Radio Canada; CBVE-FM (104.7 FM) is programmed by the Canadian Broadcasting Corp.

Visitor Information

Québec City and Area Tourism: 399 Saint-Joseph Est, Québec, QC, Canada G1K 8E2; phone (418) 641-6654.

Information kiosks at 835 av. Wilfrid-Laurier, (418) 641-6290, and at 3300 av. des Hôtels in Ste-Foy, (418) 641-6290, are open daily 8:30-7:30, June 24-Labour Day; daily 8:30-6:30, day after Labour Day-second Mon. in Oct.; Mon.-Thurs. 9-5, Fri. 9-6, Sat. 9-5, Sun. 10-4, rest of year.

TRANSPORTATION

Air Travel

Québec International Airport Jean-Lesage is 16 kilometres (10 mi.) west in Ste-Foy. A taxi to the center of the city averages $24.20, limousine service $50-$80.

Rental Cars

Hertz, offering discounts to CAA/AAA members, is downtown, (418) 647-4949; in Old Québec, (418) 694-1224; in Québec, (418) 681-1698; in Lévis, (418) 835-6855; in Ste-Foy, (418) 658-6795 and at the Québec airport, (418) 871-1571. Phone (800) 263-0600 in Canada, or (800) 654-3131 outside Canada. See the telephone directory for other companies.

Rail Service

Québec City area terminals of Via Rail Canada, serving U.S. and Canadian cities, are the Gare du Palais, 450 rue de la Gare-du-Palais; and Gare-Ste.-Foy, 3255 ch. de la Gare in Ste-Foy. Phone (888) 842-7245.

Buses

The bus terminal, Gare du Palais, is at 320 rue Abraham-Martin; phone (418) 525-3000. The Ste-Foy terminal is at 3001 ch. des Quatre Bourgeois; phone (418) 650-0087.

Taxis

You must get a taxi at a cab stand or order by phone. Base fare is $3.15, plus $1.45 per kilometre (.6 mi.). Major companies are Taxis Coop Québec, (418) 525-5191, Taxis Québec, (418) 525-8123, and Taxi Coop Ste-Foy and Sillery, (418) 653-7777.

Public Transport

Québec Transit System (RTC) buses run 5:30 a.m.-1 a.m. The fare is $2.50 (a ticket is $2.25); exact change is required. A daily pass is $5.80. Phone (418) 627-2511.

Boats

Québec's harbor accommodates pleasure craft, ferries, sightseeing cruises and oceangoing vessels. The Port of Québec (Société du Port de Québec) is at 150 rue Dalhousie, C.P. 2268, Québec City, QC, Canada G1K 7P7; phone (418) 648-3640 or (418) 648-4956. The ferry from Lévis docks at 10 rue des Traversiers; phone (418) 644-3704 or (418) 837-2408.

numerous parking lots in the newer sections of the city as well.

What To See

Within the Fortifications

Most of the historic section of Old Québec is within the walls of Upper Town. Totaling 4.6 kilometres (3 mi.) in length, the well-preserved walls were either built or reconstructed by the British during the 1820s to protect the city from invasion by the United States. The British followed the course of the original structures erected by the French throughout the 18th century.

Initially seven gates, or *portes,* penetrated the massive walls. Because of high maintenance costs and the need for improved traffic flow, three gates were torn down in the 1880s.

Had it not been for Lord Frederick Dufferin, who was appointed governor general of Canada in 1873, Québec might have lost its walls. Struck by the city's unique fortifications and influenced by the trend toward historic romanticism then popular in Europe, Lord Dufferin introduced a campaign to preserve the walls and rebuild the destroyed gates.

Wider and more medieval gates, such as Porte St-Louis, were constructed, and Porte Kent was added to create a new opening. Dufferin also enlarged the terrace overlooking the St. Lawrence River and Lower Town, which was then named after him. Dufferin's concepts prevailed and were adopted by 20th-century leaders.

Although destroyed in 1897, Porte St-Jean was rebuilt in 1939 in the same medieval style. In 1957 the fortifications were declared to be of national historical importance: Artillery Park National Historic Site of Canada *(see attraction listing p. 208)* was created to protect the buildings as well as to present and interpret their history.

The best way to explore this area of narrow streets, lined with a mixture of military, religious and residential buildings from the 17th through the 19th centuries, is on foot, wearing a pair of sturdy shoes. The city's administrative, military, religious and cultural history unfolds in this compact area.

The Fortifications Promenade begins at 100 rue St-Louis skirts the top of the ramparts and features interpretive panels describing the walls. The rue du Trésor is lined with artists demonstrating their crafts during an open-air festival in the summer, and restaurants serving cuisine québécoise occupy some of the older buildings.

To pass through the city gates is to enter a world unique on the North American continent: It is the 17th-century heart of an essentially European city.

The interpretation center for the Fortifications of Québec National Historic Site of Canada is in an addition to the British powder magazine (Poudrière de l'Esplanade), built around 1810, near the St-Louis Gate at 100 rue St-Louis. The center has a scale model that describes the evolution of Québec's defense system. Guided 2-kilometre (1.3 mi.) tours interpret the history of the walls and gates. The center is open the second Sun. in May through the second

Carnaval de Québec / © Glenn van der Knijff / Lonely Planet Images

Sunday in October. The center admission fee is $3.95; over 65, $3.45; ages 6-16, $1.95; family rate $9.90. Phone (418) 648-7016 or (888) 773-8888.

ARTILLERY PARK NATIONAL HISTORIC SITE OF CANADA (Lieu historique national du Parc de l'Artillerie) was built strategically just within the walls at Porte St-Jean. To protect the vulnerable St-Charles River area, the French established the Dauphine Redoubt here by 1712. After the conquest in 1759, the British utilized the facilities to garrison their army. Numerous ancillary military installations were built during the 19th century. By 1871 the barracks were no longer needed and were converted into a munitions factory that was active until the end of World War II.

The interpretation center describes the evolution of the site over 3 centuries and displays a relief map of Québec City in 1808. The richly furnished Officers' Quarters have an 1830s atmosphere. The Dauphine Redoubt depicts scenes from the lives of the soldiers, officers and arsenal superintendent who once occupied it.

Guided tours and English narration are available. Daily 10-5, early Apr.-second Sun. in Oct. Admission $4; over 65, $3.45; ages 6-16, $1.95; family rate $9.90. Phone (418) 648-4205 or (888) 773-8888.

LE CHÂTEAU FRONTENAC, 1 rue des Carrières opposite Place d'Armes, was built in 1893 in the medieval French style, with numerous turrets and verdigris copper roofs, and is an example of 19th-century Canadian Railway architecture. The Château Frontenac was the meeting place for Winston Churchill, Franklin Roosevelt and leaders of other Allied Nations during World War II. The painted

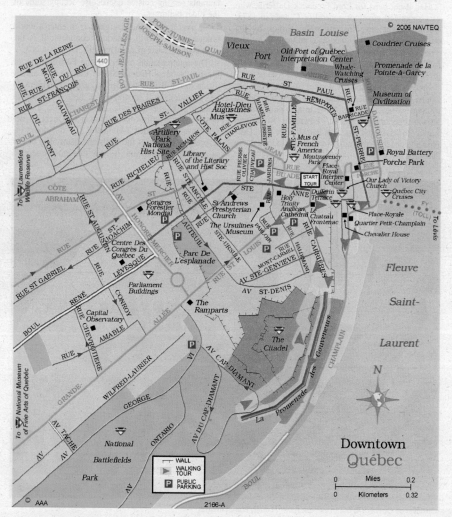

Downtown Québec

ceilings and handsome metalwork of the banisters in the lobby recall its lavish past.

Guided 50-minute tours are available in French or English by reservation only. Daily 10-6, May 1 to mid-Oct.; noon-5, rest of year. Admission $8.50; over 65, $7.75; ages 6-16, $6. Reservations are required. Phone (418) 691-2166.

THE CITADEL (La Citadelle) is on the Cap Diamant promontory; the entrance is off St-Louis St. at Porte St-Louis at Côte de la Citadelle. Constructed 1820-52 on the site of 17th-century French defenses, the fortification is one of the two official residences of the Governor-General of Canada. It remains the largest fortification in North America garrisoned by regular troops. A museum contains military items and documents.

One-hour guided tours are given alternately in French and English daily 9-6, July 1-Labour Day; 9-4, day after Labour Day-Oct. 31; 10-4 in Apr.; 9-5, May-June. A bilingual guided tour is given at 1:30, Nov.-late Mar. Ceremonial guard changes daily at 10 a.m., June 24-Labour Day (weather permitting).

Tour, including changing of the guard, $8; over 65 and students with ID $7; ages 7-17, $4.50; physically impaired free; family rate $18. Phone (418) 694-2815.

DUFFERIN TERRACE, next to le Château Frontenac, offers a spectacular view of Old Lower Town and the St. Lawrence. An 1898 monument to Samuel de Champlain is at the north end of the terrace. From here one can descend the 55 metres (180 ft.) to Place-Royale, the center of Old Lower Town, via a stairway of 61 steps. A funicular links upper and lower Québec.

The terrace is linked to Battlefield Park by the Promenade des Gouverneurs, a 670-metre-long (2,198-ft.-long) walk anchored to a cliff overlooking the St. Lawrence. Terrace and promenade daily; promenade is not maintained Dec.-Mar. A funicular is available daily 7:30 a.m.-11:30 (to midnight in summer). Terrace and promenade free. Funicular $1.50, under 5 free. Phone (418) 692-1132.

THE FORT MUSEUM (Musée du Fort), opposite le Château Frontenac at 10 rue Ste-Anne, presents a diorama depicting the six sieges of Québec with a 400-square-foot model of the city in 1750.1 Narrations are given alternately in French and English. Daily 10-5, Apr.-Oct.; Thurs.-Sun. 11-4, in Nov. and Feb.-Mar.; daily 11-4 during Christmas holidays. Admission $7.50; over 65, $5.50; students with ID $4.50. MC, VI. Phone (418) 692-1759 or (418) 692-2175.

HOLY TRINITY ANGLICAN CATHEDRAL (Cathédrale Anglicane de la Ste-Trinité), 31 rue des Jardins, was completed in 1804 on the former site of the Récollet friars' chapel. The original church was the first Anglican cathedral built outside the British Isles. It was built to resemble London's St. Martin-in-the-Fields Cathedral. Guided tours are given during the summer months, with narration in English

Québec City at 400

On July 3, 2008, Québec City turns 400, and the year-long events celebrating *la belle Grande Dame* of the continent will be spectacular.

The Old Port of Québec Interpretation Centre/*Espace 400e* (Centre d'interprétation du Vieux-Port-de-Québec/*Espace 400e*) in Lower Town on the Bassin Louise at 100 rue St-André, has exhibits and information about the celebration; phone (800) 463-6769.

Québec City and Area Tourism, 399 Saint-Joseph Est, Québec, QC, Canada G1K 8E2, also is an excellent source of celebration information; phone (418) 641-6654.

Information kiosks at 835 av. Wilfrid-Laurier, (418) 641-6290, and at 3300 av. des Hôtels in Ste-Foy, (418) 641-6290, are open daily 8:30-7:30, June 24-Labour Day; daily 8:30-6:30, day after Labour Day-second Mon. in Oct.; Mon.-Thurs. 9-5, Fri. 9-6, Sat. 9-5, Sun. 10-4, rest of year.

available. Daily 9-8, July-Aug.; 9-5, May-June and Sept.-Oct. Free. Phone (418) 692-2193.

HOTEL-DIEU AUGUSTINES MUSEUM (Musée des Augustines de l'Hôtel-Dieu), 32 rue Charlevoix, is behind Hôtel-Dieu Hospital. The museum marks the site of North America's first hospital, which was founded in 1639 by three French nuns of the order of les Augustines Hospitalières.

The museum has collections of silver from France and New France, portraits of persons associated with the hospital during its three centuries of existence, furnishings and a display of early medical tools from France and England. Tour narration is available in English. Guided tours are given Tues.-Sat. 9:30-noon and 1:30-5, Sun. 1:30-5. Donations. Phone (418) 692-2492.

LIBRARY OF THE LITERARY AND HISTORICAL SOCIETY OF QUÉBEC (Bibliothèque de la Société Historique et Littéraire de Québec), 44 rue chaussée des Ecossais, was founded in 1824 by British Governor General Lord Dalhousie. The library has evolved into the only English library in the city and its environs, becoming a repository for Canadiana and classic works. The library's collection of memorabilia includes a wooden statue of Gen. James Wolfe and Georges-Étienne Cartier's desk.

Open Tues. noon-9, Wed.-Fri. noon-4; Sat. 10-4; Sun. 1-4; closed major holidays. Free. Phone (418) 694-9147.

MONTMARTRE CANADIEN—
see Sillery in the Vicinity section p. 223.

MONTMORENCY PARK (Parc Montmorency), bounded by Côte de la Montagne and rues Port-Dauphin and des Remparts, occupies the site of the first Canadian Parliament building and affords a view of the St. Lawrence River. The park has monuments to Sir Georges-Étienne Cartier, one of the Fathers of Confederation, and Louis Hébert, one of Canada's earliest farmers. Daily 24 hours. Free.

MUSEUM OF CIVILIZATION (Musée de la civilisation), 85 rue Dalhousie across from the St. Lawrence River, is a landmark of architecture. A series of separate galleries presents permanent and temporary thematic exhibitions that illustrate the history and culture of Québec and other civilizations through ideas and inventions. Seminars, lectures and exhibits are scheduled daily.

Presentations are in French and English. Bilingual guides are available for tours. Daily 9:30-6:30, June 24-Labour Day; Tues.-Sun. 10-5, rest of year. Closed Dec. 25. Admission $10; over 65, $9; students with ID $7; ages 12-16, $4; free to all Tues., Nov.-May. MC, VI. Phone (418) 643-2158.

Chevalier House (Maison Chevalier), 50 rue du Marché-Champlain, next to Place-Royale, was built for ship owner Jean-Baptiste Chevalier in 1752. The house, together with the adjoining Maisons Frérot and Chenay, is now a gallery that recreates the feel and atmosphere of bygone days. Daily 9:30-5, June

24-Labour Day; Tues.-Sun. 10-5, day after Labour Day through mid-Oct., winter holiday season and May 1-June 23; Sat.-Sun. 10-5, rest of year. Closed Dec. 25. Free. Phone (418) 646-3167.

MUSEUM OF FRENCH AMERICA (Musée de l'Amérique Française), 2 Côte de la Fabrique, is housed in an old boarding school. The museum relates the establishment of French culture in the New World. Many of the museum's items were acquired by priests during their travels in Canada and Europe in the 19th century. Collections include secular and religious paintings from the 17th to the early 20th century, 19th-century scientific instruments and fine silver of the Ancien Regime and New France.

Open daily 9:30-5, June 24-Labour Day; Tues.-Sun. 10-5, rest of year. Guided 1-hour tours are available Sat.-Sun.; register at the reception pavilion. The language used (French or English) during the guided tour is determined by the preference of the first person to register for the tour. Closed Dec. 25. Admission $6; over 65, $5; students with ID $3.50; ages 12-16, $2; free to all Tues., Nov.-May. AX, MC, VI. Phone (418) 692-2843.

THE RAMPARTS (Les Remparts), along rue des Remparts, are studded with iron cannons, reminders of the heavy fortifications in the area during the battle for Canada in 1759.

ST. ANDREW'S PRESBYTERIAN CHURCH (Église Presbytérienne de St-Andrew), 106 rue Ste-Anne, was built in 1810. The church has a high sidewall pulpit and an interesting arrangement of the pews and balcony. Marble tablets commemorating past ministers and benefactors adorn the walls, and documents and historic church-related objects are displayed in the vestry. Guide service and narration in English are available. Open daily 10-4, July-Aug. Free. Phone (418) 694-1347.

THE URSULINES MUSEUM (Musée des Ursulines), 12 rue Donnacona, displays art objects, liturgical embroideries, documents and furniture detailing the daily life and the educational work of the Ursulines in the 17th century. The Ursuline Chapel was built in 1902 on the site of a chapel built in 1723.

Museum Tues.-Sat. 10-noon and 1-5, Sun. 1-5, May-Sept.; Tues.-Sun. 1-4:30, Mar.-Apr. and Oct.-Nov. Closed holidays. Phone to confirm schedule. Admission $6; over 65, $5; students with ID $4; under 11 free. Phone (418) 694-0694.

WOLFE-MONTCALM MONUMENT (Monument Wolfe-Montcalm), in the Governor's Garden (Parc des Gouverneurs) behind le Château Frontenac at 1 rue des Carrières, is an 1827 obelisk honoring the generals who fought on the Plains of Abraham in 1759. Garden open all year. Free.

Outside the Fortifications

CAPITAL OBSERVATORY (Observatoire de la capitale), in the Marie Guyart Building at 1037 rue de la Chevrotière at jct. boul. René-Lévesque, is on the 31st floor and affords excellent views of the city and its surroundings. On clear days the Appalachian Mountains are visible.

Open daily 10-5, June 24-second Sun. in Oct.; Tues.-Sun. 10-5, rest of year. Admission $5, over 65 and students with ID $4, under 13 free. VI. Phone (418) 644-9841 or (888) 497-4322.

CARTIER-BRÉBEUF NATIONAL HISTORIC SITE OF CANADA (Lieu historique national du Canada Cartier-Brébeuf), 3.5 km (2 mi.) n. via Côte d'Abraham and rue Dorchester, is at 175 rue de L'Espinay. The landscaped park on the St-Charles River commemorates the site where Jacques Cartier and his crew wintered during his second voyage to Canada in 1535. Highlights include the interpretation center and an Amerindian longhouse. Guide service and narration in English are available.

Daily 10-5, first Mon. in May-day before Labour Day; 1-4, Labour Day-first Sun. in Oct.; by appointment rest of year. Admission $3.95; over 65 and students with ID $3.45; ages 6-16, $1.95; family rate $9.90. Phone (418) 648-4038 or (888) 773-8888.

CHEVALIER HOUSE—
see Museum of Civilization p. 210.

ÎLE D'ORLÉANS, in the St. Lawrence River, is reached by bridge from Hwy. 138. The island contains churches built by the French. The 1717-19 St-Pierre and the 1743-48 Ste-Famille retain much of their original decor. The restored Norman-style Mauvide-Genest Manor, in the village of St-Jean at 1451 ch. Royal, was built 1734-52 by Jean Mauvide, surgeon to Louis XV; it can be toured by appointment late August through early December.

JACQUES CARTIER NATIONAL PARK (Parc national de la Jacques-Cartier) is 40 km (25 mi.) n.w. via Hwy. 175. Encompassing 670 square kilometres (259 sq. mi.), this conservation area, surrounded by Laurentides Wildlife Reserve, centers on the Jacques-Cartier River and the surrounding wooded uplands and mountains. Atlantic salmon spawn in late September. The visitor center, 10 kilometres (6 mi.) from Hwy. 175, has exhibits and audiovisual presentations describing the park and its habitat.

Park open daily mid-May through late Oct. and mid-Dec.-early Mar. Admission $3.50; ages 6-17, $1.50; family rate $7. Phone (418) 848-3169 in summer, or (800) 665-6527 in Québec. *See Recreation Chart and the AAA/CAA Eastern Canada CampBook.*

THE JESUIT HOUSE—
see Sillery in the Vicinity section p. 223.

LAURENTIDES WILDLIFE RESERVE (Réserve faunique des Laurentides), 60 km (37 mi.) n.w. via Hwy. 175, is in the Laurentian Mountains. The reserve covers 7,861 square kilometres (3,035 sq. mi.) of wooded uplands and

contains more than 1,500 lakes and many rivers. Mountain peaks rise to elevations of 1,219 metres (4,000 ft.). Parts of the vast reserve are still unexplored. Its solitude offers refuge to various game, all protected by strict regulations.

The paved Québec-Chicoutimi Highway (Hwy. 175) traverses the reserve, shortening the distance between the two cities to 212 kilometres (132 mi.). Hwy. 169 (paved) branches north through the reserve to Hébertville. The road from Baie-St-Paul to Chicoutimi, which passes through St-Urbain, skirts the eastern boundary where the Laurentians are highest.

Bait fishing, except with minnows, and fly fishing are permitted. Guides always should be employed for trips into remote areas. Daily fishing permits can be obtained at the reserve entrance. The reserve is open year-round for outdoor activities, including seasonal hunting and fishing. Free.

For further information contact the Société des établissements de plein air du Québec (SÉPAQ), Reservations Office, 2640 boul. Laurier, bureau 1300, Sainte-Foy, QC, Canada G1V 5C2; phone (800) 665-6527. *See Recreation Chart and the AAA/ CAA Eastern Canada CampBook.*

NATIONAL BATTLEFIELDS PARK (Parc des Champs-de-Bataille nationaux) is between rue Bougainville and the St-Louis Gate, with entrances on Grande Allée. It encompasses the Plains of Abraham, where the armies of Gen. James Wolfe and the Marquis de Montcalm fought in 1759. The information and reception center is in the Discovery Pavilion of the Plains of Abraham. The park celebrates its centennial in 2008.

The Louis S. St-Laurent Heritage House details his careers as lawyer and politician, as well as his family life. Two restored Martello Towers, vestiges of the 19th-century, offer an exhibit about the architectural importance of the fortifications, and an 1814-style mystery dinner production called "Council of War at Martello Tower." The "Odyssey" is a multimedia exhibition, a virtual journey covering 400 years of history on the Plains of Abraham; more than 20 regimental uniforms complete this exhibition.

Guided bus tours are available; narration in English is available. Tower 1 daily 10-5, June 24-Labour Day. Odyssey daily 10-5:30, June 24-Labour Day; 10-5, rest of year. Heritage house daily 1-5, June 24-Labour Day. Bandstand concerts Thurs.-Sun. at 8, mid-June to mid-Aug. Dinner Mystery presented in Feb., July-Aug., Halloween season and Christmas season; phone for times and dates. Bus tour daily 10:30-4.15, June 25-Labour Day.

June 24-Labour Day combination admission (includes bus, heritage house, tower, "Odyssey") $10; over 54 and ages 13-17, $8. "Odyssey" $8; over 65 and ages 13-17, $7. Dinner mystery $35; over 65 and under 18, $32. Garden and bandstand free. Phone (418) 648-4071.

NATIONAL MUSEUM OF FINE ARTS OF QUÉBEC (Musée national des beaux-arts du Québec), in National Battlefields Park, has three distinctive pavilions. The Grand Hall, which features large expanses of glass, connects the original 1933 Gérard Morisset building and the 1871 Baillairgé building, a former prison that now contains an interpretive center for National Battlefields Park.

The museum, which chronicles Québec's art from the French Colonial period to the present, contains a large collection of fine arts, including paintings, sculpture and ceramics as well as articles fashioned of gold and silver. Features include traveling exhibitions, music recitals and films.

Food is available. Thurs.-Tues. 10-6, Wed. 10-9, June 1-Labour Day; Tues. 10-5, Wed. 10-9, Thurs.-Sun. 10-5, rest of year. Closed Dec. 25. Admission $12; over 65, $10; students under 25 with ID $5; ages 12-16, $3. Permanent collection free to all. AX, MC, VI. Phone (418) 643-2150 or (866) 220-2150.

OLD PORT OF QUÉBEC INTERPRETATION CENTRE/ESPACE 400E (Centre d'interprétation du Vieux-Port-de-Québec/Espace 400e) is in Lower Town on the Bassin Louise at 100 rue St-André. As a part of Quebec City's 400th anniversary celebrations in 2008, Parks Canada is expanding the Old Port of Quebec Interpretation Centre. *Espace 400e* took over this space in the fall of 2006. Parks Canada will resume normal activities in spring 2009. Phone for information about exhibits and schedules.

Daily 10-5, early May-day before Labour Day; daily noon-4, Labour Day-second Sun. in Oct.; by appointment rest of year. Admission $3.50; over 65 and students with ID $3; ages 6-16, $2; family rate $8.75. Phone (800) 463-6769.

PARLIAMENT BUILDINGS (Hôtel du Parlement), on Grande Allée, are surrounded by monument-studded grounds. The 1886 main building, constructed in French Renaissance style, has niches in the facade containing statues of historical figures. Free guided tours are available in French, English, Spanish and, upon request, Italian. Mon.-Fri. 9-4:30, Sat.-Sun. and holidays 10-4:30, June 24-Labour Day; Mon.-Fri. 9-4:30, rest of year. Closed holidays and during some parliament sessions. Free. Phone (418) 643-7239 or (866) 337-8837.

PLACE-ROYALE (Vieux-Québec), center of Lower Town, was the 1608 site of Samuel de Champlain's *abitation*, the beginning of French colonization in America. Despite a ruinous fire in 1682 and numerous attacks by the British, who finally captured the city in 1759, the area has been preserved virtually as it was during the 18th century.

Along the St. Lawrence are the docks for the Québec-Lévis ferry on rue des Traversiers and for the sightseeing boat MV *Louis Jolliet*, Quai Chouinard at 10 rue Dalhousie *(see What To Do, Sightseeing)*.

Events and entertainment take place in the summer. Using a multimedia show, exhibitions and guided tours, the interpretation center at 27 rue Notre-Dame relates the story of this cradle of French culture in the New World.

Guided tours of Place-Royale in both French and English depart from the interpretation center daily 10-5, early May-late Sept.; by appointment rest of year. Place-Royale admission free. Phone (418) 646-3167.

Our Lady of Victory Church (Église Notre-Dame-des-Victoires), jct. Notre-Dame and rue Sous-le-Fort, was restored after being destroyed by fire during the siege of Québec. The 1688 church, built on the foundations of Samuel de Champlain's trading post, has commemorative paintings and tablets. Daily 9-5, May 1 through mid-Oct.; 10-4, rest of year. Free. Phone (418) 692-1650.

Place-Royale Interpretation Centre (Centre d'interprétation de Place Royale) is at 27 rue Notre-Dame. Using a multimedia show, exhibitions and a costume workshop, this center relates the story of Place Royale, cradle of French culture in the New World. Allow 1 hour minimum. Daily 9:30-5, June 24-Labour Day; Tues.-Sun. 10-5, rest of year. Closed Dec. 25.

Admission $5; over 65, $4.50; students with ID $3.50; ages 12-16, $2; free to all Tues., Nov.-May. MC, VI. Phone (418) 646-3167.

Porche Park, at rues St-Pierre and du Porche, is a historical and maritime playground for children.

Quartier Petit-Champlain is in Lower town and Dufferin Terrace, and is bounded by boul. Champlain, rue Petit-Champlain and rue Sous-le Fort. This area features many boutiques and restaurants on different street levels. The Louis Jolliet House is the lower station of the *funiculaire* that links Lower Town with Dufferin Terrace. The Théâtre Petit-Champlain, Maison de la Chanson at 68 rue Petit-Champlain regularly presents song recitals. Phone (418) 692-2631.

Royal Battery (La Batterie Royale), rues St-Pierre and Sous-le-Fort, is part of the military defense system built in 1691. The battery was used to defend the city during the siege of 1759. It was completely rebuilt in 1977. Daily 10-5, mid-June through Labour Day. Free.

PROMENADE DES GOUVERNEURS—
see Dufferin Terrace p. 209.

VILLA BAGATELLE—
see Sillery in the Vicinity section p. 223.

What To Do

Sightseeing

Boat Tours

COUDRIER CRUISES (Les Croisières le Coudrier), departing Dock 19 (close to the

La Cuisine Québécoise

Gourmets consider the cuisine of Québec, which incorporates the best of Old and New World France, to be among the finest in North America. Though wine and cheese, espresso coffee, croissants and other Continental staples appear on the menu, a Québécois meal typically consists of hearty, traditional *du terroir* dishes.

Originally created to sustain the colonial habitant farmers through long winters, these energy-rich meals use such native North American ingredients as corn, blueberries, potatoes, pork, molasses, maple sugar and Gaspé salmon and cod. The omnipresent apple- or cider-based foods are adapted from 17th-century Norman recipes.

Ministère du Tourisme du Québec

On special occasions French-Canadian homes serve *cipaille,* a deep-dish pie filled with partridge, hare, quail, bacon and potatoes flavored with cloves. Other *specialités de la maison* include *tourtière,* chopped veal or pork pies; *ragoût de boulettes,* a pork hock and meatball stew; *soupe aux pois à la canadienne,* pea soup made with dried yellow peas; *fèves au lard,* baked beans; and *tarte au sucre,* a maple sugar pie favored by children. Many country-inn-style restaurants, which are often decorated with Canadian pine and antiques, serve these dishes.

In contrast, Québécers often boast that their province provides the best fast food in Canada. *Casse-croûtes* snack bars along the highways specialize in *steamé,* hot dogs on steamed buns, and *poutines,* french fries with a cheddar-cheese sauce.

Most eating establishments post their prices outside. *Bon appétit!*

lock) in the Old Port of Québec, at 180 Dalhousie St. at jct. St-André, are bilingual narrated sightseeing cruises around Québec City aboard a 65-foot vessel. Sightseeing cruises last 90 minutes. Also offered are day-long trips to Grosse Île, Île aux Grues, Île d'Orléans and Ste-Anne-de-Beaupré, as well as dinner cruises.

Daily at 11, 1, 3:30 and 7:30, June 24-Labour Day; daily at 1, early May-June 23 and day after Labour Day-Oct. 15. Fare for 90-minute trip $27.50; over 65 and students with ID $25.50; ages 6-16, $13.75; family rate (two adults and one child) $55. Parking $6-$12. Phone to confirm prices and schedule. MC, VI. Phone (418) 692-0107 or (888) 600-5554.

QUÉBEC CITY CRUISES (Croisières AML Inc.), Quai Chouinard at 10 rue Dalhousie, offers sightseeing cruises of the Québec area aboard the MV *Louis Jolliet*. Dinner cruises, Sunday brunch cruises and fireworks cruises also are available. Food is available. Sightseeing cruises depart daily at 11:30, 2 and 4, May 1 through mid-Oct. Boarding begins 30 minutes before departure.

Harbor cruise $24.95; over 65, $22.95; ages 6-16, $10. Phone for fares for other cruises. AX, MC, VI. Phone (418) 692-1159 or (800) 563-4643.

Bus and Carriage Tours

The major sightseeing bus company is Autocar Dupont; (418) 649-9226. Buses regularly depart from the Place d'Armes, opposite Le Château Frontenac (*see attraction listing p. 208*), and from major hotels.

Calèches, or horse-drawn carriages, are stationed at the Parc de l'Esplanade beside the tourist kiosk at rues Ste-Anne and D'Auteuil, porte St-Louis and Château Frontenac. A 45-minute tour costs $60 per ride (maximum four passengers).

Driving Tours

Alternatives to the multilane divided highways connecting Québec with Montréal are Hwy. 132 and Hwy. 138, which follow the southern and northern banks of the St. Lawrence River, respectively. These roads wind through picturesque small towns and villages, offering an unspoiled look at Gallic culture and domestic and ecclesiastical architecture.

Walking Tours

Walking Tour: Vieux-Québec

Refer to the Québec downtown map. This tour should take about 2 hours to complete, depending on your pace and the number of listed sites you visit along the way. Those that appear in bold type have detailed listings in the *What to See* section. Even if you decide not to visit a listed site, reading the listing when you reach that point should make the tour more interesting.

A walk along the hilly, cobbled lanes of Vieux-Québec (Old Québec) might fool you into thinking that you're in France. Perhaps it's the dominating French architecture; residents and shopkeepers calling "Bonjour!"; ancient fortifications; or the

many bakeries and outdoor cafés. There's no better way to get to know upper Québec, poised 92 metres (300 feet) above the St. Lawrence River and surrounded by ramparts. Pull on some walking shoes, grab your camera and prepare to explore.

Begin your tour in front of the Visitors Information building at the corner of rue Ste-Anne and rue du Fort, across from the Musée du Fort (**Fort Museum**). In front of you is place d'Armes, once a military parade ground facing a governor's mansion that has since been replaced by the **Château Frontenac** hotel, which looms over the square's opposite side. A grassy plot surrounds the Monument de la Foi (Monument to the Faith), which honors Récollets (Franciscan monks from France) who arrived in 1615 to assist Québec City founder Samuel de Champlain in colonization; they were later granted a plot of land by the king of France to build a church and monastery.

Topped with mint green copper roofs and embellished with Scottish brick, gables, crenellations, parapets and stone turrets, the Château Frontenac seems stolen from the pages of a fairy tale. Perched atop Cap Diamant (Cape Diamond), it is the highlight of Old Québec's skyline and can be seen from various points along the St. Lawrence River.

On this site in 1620, Champlain built Fort St-Louis, which housed the headquarters of New France and served as the governor's mansion. After the original building burned, the land was graced with this opulent hotel in 1892-93, built by the Canadian Pacific Railway Company to reflect French medieval influences. Designed by New York architect Bruce Price, the structure was named for Louis de Buade, Comte de Frontenac, who served as governor-general 1672-98 and defended the city against British attack in 1690. The count's coat of arms is displayed throughout the hotel.

Originally designed with 170 rooms, the castle now boasts 613 rooms (the central tower was added in 1925). Costumed guides offer tours. Famous guests have included King George VI and Princess Elizabeth in 1939, and in 1943-44, the château was the site of the Québec Conferences of World War II, at which Franklin D. Roosevelt, Winston Churchill and William Lyon Mackenzie King were in attendance.

Turn west to face rue du Trésor, which is usually lined with calèches (horse-drawn carriages). To your left, the Ancien Palais de Justice, a striking French Renaissance-style building at rue du Trésor and rue St-Louis, was once the site of the Récollets monks' monastery (it is now a government building). To the right of the Palais de Justice is the rear of the Palladian-style Cathédrale de la Sainte-Trinité (Holy Trinity Anglican Cathedral). (The tour will intersect with the front of the church at a later point.)

Peer to the right down rue du Trésor, a tight, crowded alley where paintings, watercolors and prints by talented local artists are displayed under beaming spotlights. "Treasure Street" once was where colonists paid taxes to the Royal Treasury. Since the 1960s artists have been displaying their

Québec
City and Area

Your *EuroStyle* Destination

We're celebrating 400 years—and you're invited!

Four centuries ago, Samuel de Champlain chose Québec as the site of the first permanent French settlement in North America. A meeting ground and place of trade from the beginning, Québec has remained a diverse and welcoming city rich in color and contrasts. In 2008, we'll be celebrating our first 400 years in style! Won't you join us?

For information, visit **www.quebecregion.com/AAA-w7**

Québec   Canada

Québec
City and Area
A Québec City Tourism advertisement.

treasures here, and caricature artists take the place of tax collectors at the alley's entrance.

Now walk toward the large green "funiculaire" sign. Surrounded by any number of guitarists, flute players and jugglers is a large statue of Samuel de Champlain, who founded Québec in 1608. Created by French artists, it is rumored that the statue is not an accurate depiction of the explorer—in fact, it is said it does not even resemble the man—because the artists had never seen Champlain. In any event, the impressive effigy has stood here since 1898.

You are now standing above appropriately named Basse-Ville (Lower Town), which is divided from Haute-Ville (Upper Town) by both natural and man-made impediments. Warehouses and port facilities were housed in Basse-Ville, while the governor and military and religious orders called Haute-Ville home. While the city's position on rocky, steep cap Diamant functioned as a natural defense, New France wanted to further protect the city and its lucrative fur trade from British invaders. Beginning in 1745, a giant wall—les Ramparts (the Ramparts)—was built surrounding what is now known as Vieux-Québec.

To the left of the Champlain figure is a diamond-shaped monument informing visitors that Vieux-Québec is a UNESCO World Heritage Site; the city was honored in 1985 with this designation due to its prominence as the only city in North America to have preserved its fortifications. The city owes its thanks to Frederick Dufferin, the governor-general of Canada 1872-78, who insisted they be saved.

Behind the statue is a spectacular view of the Fleuve Saint-Laurent (St. Lawrence River). Directly below is Basse-Ville, sitting on a ribbon of land between the river and the ridges of Cap Diamant. The funicular, an elevator of sorts, descends the bluff to the Maison Louis-Jolliet (Louis-Jolliet House) in Basse-Ville. Across the river is the city of Lévis; to the left is the Île d'Orléans; and beyond that you can see the Laurentian Mountains to the north, where the river opens up to the Gulf of St. Lawrence. In spring, the sunlight sparkles off the water; in winter, the river—frozen up to 3.7 metres (12 feet) thick—is heavy with snow. So memorable is the panorama that the city is named for it: Québec is derived from the Algonquian Indian word "Kebek" meaning "where the river narrows."

Meander along Terrasse Dufferin (Dufferin Terrace), the wide boardwalk on which you are standing. Established in the 1870s, the promenade was named for Lord Dufferin, who commissioned its construction. Situated between your choice of lovely views—the Château Frontenac or the St. Lawrence River—it's a great place to stroll or rest under one of the green gazebos. Entertainers, market stands and a book fair add to the charm. In winter, the boardwalk bustles with the events of Festival d'hiver (Winter Carnival), during which it is transformed into a winter sports mecca, complete with ice-skating and hockey rinks as well as a toboggan run (note the slide just past the park on your right).

Stroll to the "Dufferin" gazebo. Then, if you're ready for some exercise, continue up 310 steps along La Promenade des Gouverneurs. The path skirts the cliff wall past the Citadelle (Citadel).

Backtrack along the terrace until you reach a row of cannons, brought from England in the 19th century. Ascend the stairs between the cannons to the Jardin des Gouverneurs, once a backyard garden to Fort St-Louis. Laid out in 1647, it now houses a memorial to the city's disputing suitors. The large obelisk, otherwise known as the Monument Wolfe-Montcalm (Wolfe-Montcalm Monument), honors the two generals who fought for the ownership of Québec in 1759. At the Battle of the Plains of Abraham, the British, under Gen. James Wolfe, defeated the French, under Gen. Marquis de Montcalm. But it wasn't until the Treaty of Paris in 1763 that Great Britain assumed ownership of Canada. Interestingly, the memorial honors both men.

The brick building with the copper roof to the left of the monument is the American consulate. Houses overlooking the west side of the garden once belonged to lumber barons; they were built 1818-65 using brick as a display of wealth. Head north on rue du Trésor, walking through the courtyard of the Château Frontenac to rue St-Louis. Note the plaques denoting historical meetings that have taken place at the hotel. Wander through the lobby if time permits.

Once on rue St-Louis, you should be facing place d'Armes. Turn left and continue along rue St-Louis to Maison Kent (Kent House), on the left at the corner of rue Haldimond. The 1648 house, said to be the oldest building in Québec City, features English sash windows and a low-pitched roof. It was the 1791-94 home of Prince Edward, Duke of Kent, who lived here with his mistress before returning to England to marry Victoria Maria Louisa of Saxe-Coburg and later father Queen Victoria. The French officially surrendered to the British at this site. Colors over the door signify that the French consulate occupies the house.

You can't miss the adorable white house with a steeply-pitched, cranberry-colored tin roof on the right at the corner of rue St-Louis and rue des Jardins. This is Maison Jacquet (Jacquet House), built 1675-76 on land donated from nuns at the nearby Ursulines Convent. It was home to Philippe-Aubert de Gaspé, author of the novel "Les Anciens Canadiens," after which the present occupant—a popular restaurant—is named. The exterior looks similar to how it appeared in the 17th century—the plain white front wall, inset door, roof and dormer windows are typical of French Canadian architectural features. The interior contains wainscoting and recessed cupboards, also found in homes of that period.

Continue on rue St-Louis, one of the oldest roads in town and once a popular spot to "see and be seen." Just past the Inuit Museum, turn right on rue du Parloir. The road intersects with rue Donnacona at the Couvent des Ursulines (Ursulines Convent), a little stone building with a tin roof. In front of the convent, a statue represents Marie de l'Incarnation, the Ursuline nun who arrived in Québec in 1639, founded the school and devoted herself to the education of girls. The school and convent have occupied this site since 1642. Check out the date on her statue: Monuments for non-Canadians depict the date the person arrived in Canada, while monuments for native Canadians show their date of birth.

Also on the property are the Musée des Ursulines (**Ursulines Museum**) and the Chapelle des Ursulines (Ursulines Chapel), which is a few steps farther on rue Donnacona. The tomb of Marie de l'Incarnation is in the chapel, which dates from the 1730s: Some of the finest architectural elements existing in Canada from this time period, including the 17th-century wooden staircase in the monastery.

Follow rue Donnacona to where it intersects with rue des Jardins. The small, hand-shaped monument in the middle of this street honors religious women dedicated to education. Veer left onto rue des Jardins. The Cathédrale Anglicane de la Ste-Trinité (**Holy Trinity Anglican Cathedral**) is on your right. The stone neoclassical church, with its Palladian-style windows and attached Ionic columns, occupies a portion of the original land decreed to the Récollets monks. The church was built in 1804 under the order of King George III, who supplied the funds as well as a prayer book, Bible and communion silverware. He asked that there be a pew reserved for the royal family—it is carved of oak from Britain's Royal Windsor Forest. The church contains a booming organ with more than 2,500 pipes and offers services in French and English.

Continue a few steps to rue Ste-Anne. On the corner of rue Ste-Anne and rue des Jardins is the 1870 Hotel Clarendon, considered the oldest hotel in the city. Dark woodwork in the dining room is reminiscent of its Victorian style. Continue along rue Ste-Anne. Next you'll notice the Édifice Price (Price Building), Old Québec's first and only skyscraper, on the left at 65 rue Ste-Anne. The 15-story, Art Deco building features two maple elevators and bronze bas-reliefs depicting scenes of the Price Pulp and Paper Company. The building caused quite a raucous when it was built in 1929; residents did not take well to how it cast a shadow over their gardens. A city ordinance was later instituted that no building may be taller than 60 metres (197 feet).

The immense building taking up the opposite side of the street is the left side of Hôtel-de-Ville (City Hall). Topped with turrets and a patina roof, the stone building was built 1895-96 on the site of the Jesuits' college and church. The style is difficult to determine, though Victorian, neo-Gothic Château, American Romanesque Revival and Classic elements can be seen. The result rivals the Château Frontenac for center stage in the skyline.

Continue along rue Ste-Anne. Where rue Ste-Anne meets rue Cook is a gray stone building with a green cupola and steeple—Église Presbytérienne de St-Andrew (**St. Andrew's Presbyterian Church**). Said to be the oldest English-speaking Scottish congregation in Canada, worship began in 1759, and in 1802 King George III granted the land

for the present church building, completed in 1810. The petition that encouraged the king to donate the land can be seen in the church vestry.

Backtrack along rue Ste-Anne to rue des Jardins and turn left. Continue for one block to rue de Buade. City Hall will be on your left. At rue de Buade, turn right. Bordered by rue de Buade, rue Ste-Famille, rue des Jardins and Côte de la Fabrique is the Plaza des Jardins, which features a statue of Elzéar Alexandre Taschereau, who served as archbishop of Québec and was the first Canadian cardinal. The bronze and gold statue illustrates his devotion to God and assistance to Irish victims of typhus. Surrounding the plaza are stores that have operated in this location since the early 1800s—specifically Simons department store (with a green awning) and the J.E. Giguère tobacco shop.

Turn left onto rue Ste-Famille. You should be standing in front of the Basilique Notre-Dame-de-Québec (Notre-Dame Basilica). On this site in 1633, Samuel de Champlain built a modest church; it was destroyed and rebuilt three times—this magnificent structure dates from 1922. Inside, the Baroque-style cathedral is filled with treasures: a massive organ; colorful stained-glass windows; a governor's bench, church-warden's bench and bishop's throne; Old Masters paintings; and a sanctuary lamp and chalice, both given to the first bishop of Québec, François de Laval, by Louis XIV. A crypt holds the remains of most of Québec's bishops.

To the left of the cathedral, entered through giant iron gates topped with a coat of arms, is the Séminaire de Québec (Québec Seminary). This school, founded in 1663 by Bishop Laval, educated boys and trained priests. It later evolved into Laval University, which operated in Old Québec from 1852 until 1952, when it was relocated to Ste-Foy.

Follow narrow rue Ste-Famille along the walls of the seminary, past charming stone houses with tin roofs and paned glass windows. Most old-world dwellings were modeled after French architecture; note the large chimneys and raised gabled-end roofs, which were enforced in the city by the mid-1700s because they helped prevent the spread of fire. Windowpanes were shipped across the Atlantic in molasses barrels, hence their small size.

The street ends at rue des Ramparts, which runs along the fortification walls circling Old Québec. The walls you see are original, although they were much wider when first constructed and contained various enhancements to aid in defense, such as outworks (a defensive position outside the walls), a ditch and a covered path. An underground room, built by the French in the 1750s, housed an additional battery to double the firepower installed on the wall. You might see openings in the wall at places; these were entryways used by soldiers to sneak to the outworks when the gates were closed.

After the British takeover, the Citadel was constructed for fear of American attacks, yet the fortifications were eventually abandoned and military gates were demolished; however, in 1874 Governor-general Dufferin set forth plans to preserve the walls. Four gates remain: Portes St-Louis and Kent were rebuilt 1878-81; Porte St-Jean was reconstructed in 1938-39; and Porte Prescott Gate is the newest, rebuilt in 1983.

After admiring the view of Basse-Ville, turn right. Opposite the wall at 45-51 rue des Ramparts is Maison Montcalm, a gray and maroon house with dormer windows, where the French general resided during the Battle of Plains of Abraham.

Continue along rue des Ramparts, which turns into rue Port-Dauphin. On the right opposite the seminary is Parc Montmorency **(Montmorency Park)**, site of the city's bishop's house and its first cemetery. Meander through the shady park, created in 1875 by Lord Dufferin so citizens could enjoy the view of the lower harbor—you might choose to do the same by peeking through one of the coin-operated telescopes along the wall. A monument opposite the seminary honors the first family to colonize in New France: At the request of Samuel de Champlain, Louis Hébert and Marie Rollet, husband and wife, settled in 1617 with their three children. Hébert was a farmer as well as a physician and surgeon; here he is shown offering a sheaf of wheat to God. Guillaume Couillard, the third figure on the monument, married their daughter Guillemette and worked the family land. Another statue of Georges-Étienne Cartier, a Canadian prime minister, is near Porte Prescott.

Across Côte de la Montagne near Porte Prescott is a large monument honoring François de Laval, the first bishop of Québec. Figures representing his religious and educational achievements adorn the statue's base. From the park, ascend the stairs and cross over Porte Prescott, then descend onto Côte de la Montagne, following the street as it curves downhill. You are officially in Basse-Ville. On the left is the city's first cemetery; Marie Rollet is buried there. Continue to and descend the Escalier Casse-Cou (Breakneck Stairs), which will be on your right. These stairs have existed since the beginning of the settlement; due to the steep grade, an order issued in 1698 forbade residents from transporting their livestock on the stairway. The flight of stairs leads you to rue Petit-Champlain, said to be the oldest street in North America and the heart of **Quartier Petit-Champlain**. The pedestrians-only lane is lined with boutiques, galleries and outdoor cafés. Merry tunes from street musicians invite visitors to linger.

Directly at the bottom of the stairs at rue Sous-le-Fort is the 1683 Maison Louis Jolliet. It houses the funicular that climbs the promontory to Haute-Ville. Jolliet, a native of Québec, was the first European to explore the Mississippi River, accompanied by his comrade Jacques Marquette. A plaque to the left of the house points out these details (in French).

Follow rue Sous-le-Fort—at 2.69 metres (8 feet, 10 inches) wide, it is rumored to be the narrowest road in North America—one block to rue Notre-Dame and turn left, which will bring you to **Place Royale**, a cobblestone plaza that is the nucleus of Basse-Ville. It was here in 1608 that Samuel de Champlain established the first trading post in New France, called "Abitation." The square, which hosted markets and military parades, is surrounded by Norman-style merchants' homes restored from the 17th through 19th centuries. Note the thick stone walls, dormer windows, low entryways with wooden doors, colorful tin roofs and partition firewalls separating the rooftops. A bust of Louis XIV, a gift from the city of Paris in 1928, graces the square.

Also on the square is the small, 1688 Église Notre-Dame-des-Victoires **(Our Lady of Victories Church)**, which has experienced three renovations and name changes. Originally called Enfant Jésus, its most recent renovation was completed in 1969. Inside you can't miss the boat suspended from the ceiling; it arrived in Canada in 1664.

After exploring the quaint lanes of Basse-Ville, take the funicular over the ramparts to Terrasse Dufferin and the place d'Armes, where you began the tour.

Self-guiding Walking Tours

Visitors may obtain the booklet "Official Tourist Guide of Québec City" at the information kiosks at 835 av. Wilfrid-Laurier and 3300 av. des Hôtels. The booklet outlines a walking tour.

Sports and Recreation

Québec offers as much to the sports enthusiast as to the history buff. Provincial and city parks and resorts as well as mountains, forests, lakes and rivers offer a wide variety of activities, from golf and tennis to skiing and sledding.

The sports-minded spectator has several choices for entertainment, depending upon the season. **Harness racing** takes place at the Québec Hippodrome on the Exposition Grounds (Parc d'Expo-Cité); phone (418) 524-5283.

Note: Policies vary concerning admittance of children to pari-mutuel betting facilities. Phone for information.

For the sports enthusiast who likes to participate, many activities are available. With all the snow that falls on Québec, **skiing** is naturally a popular pastime. Forty kilometres (25 mi.) east on Hwy. 138 near Beaupré (see place listing p. 221) is Mont Ste-Anne, one of the most noted spots for alpine and cross-country skiing in eastern Canada; for further information phone (418) 827-4561. Another popular spot is Camp Mercier (Réserve faunique des Laurentides); for additional information phone (418) 848-2422.

Le Relais at Lac Beauport, (418) 849-1851, is popular for alpine skiing. Mont-Ste-Anne, (418) 827-4561, is known for both alpine and cross-country skiing. Stoneham, (418) 848-2411 or (800) 463-6888, is another popular ski slope, while Lac Delage, (418) 848-2551, and the Plains of Abraham, (418) 648-4212, offer excellent cross-country skiing and snowshoeing.

Other winter sports include **skating** at Place d'Youville, (418) 641-6256; the Parc de l'Esplanade off rue d'Auteuil, (418) 641-6001; and the Village

Vacances Valcartier, (418) 844-2200. **Curling** also is popular, especially during the Québec International Bonspiel in January; phone (418) 681-1221.

In the summer, **swimming** is available at the 36,100-student Laval University pool, (418) 656-7377. Public beaches are found in such nearby suburbs as Lac St-Joseph northwest of the city, Lac Beauport and Ste-Foy.

More than 20 **golf** courses are in the area. Popular clubs include Golf Métropolitain, (418) 872-9292, 4135 boul. Chauveau in Ste-Foy; Lorette, (418) 842-8441, 12986 rue Monseigneur-Cooke in Loretteville; and the Grand Vallon, (418) 827-4653.

Tennis enthusiasts can find indoor and outdoor courts at Club de Tennis Avantage Inc., (418) 627-3343, 1080 rue Bouvier; Club de Tennis Montcalm, (418) 687-1250, 901 boul. Champlain; and Nautilus Plus, (418) 872-0111, 6280 boul. Hamel in L'Ancienne-Lorette. For information about recreation and parks in Québec, phone (418) 641-6224, in Ste-Foy phone (418) 641-6043.

Shopping

For specialty and handicraft boutiques and neighborhood groceries, Old Town is the place to go. Items such as antiques, books, clothing, Eskimo and Indian art, handicrafts, leather goods and rare wines are for sale.

In spring rue du Trésor becomes an outdoor art gallery where local artists display their works. Adrien Racine, 30 Côte de la Fabrique at Place de l'Hôtel-de-Ville, is a popular shop known for its hand-knitted scarves and sweaters decorated with caribou designs.

Straight down from the Château Frontenac and in the oldest part of the city is a group of renovated businesses known as the Quartier Petit-Champlain. These restored houses contain cafes, art galleries and boutiques. Handcrafted jewelry, pottery, clothing, leather and woodwork are among the items

DID YOU KNOW

?

More than 80 percent of Québec's inhabitants speak French.

found in the shops. The main shopping street in the district is rue Petit-Champlain.

The main downtown shopping district is along **St-Joseph**, which has been transformed into an indoor shopping complex called **Mail Centre-Ville**. Downtown's shopping centers are **Les Galeries de la Capitale**, at 5401 boul. des Galeries, with 250 stores; **Place Fleur de Lys**, with more than 250 stores at 552 boul. Wilfrid-Hamel; and **Place Québec**, next to the Québec Hilton.

Shopping malls in Québec's suburbs include **Les Galeries Chagnon**, at 1200 boul. Alphonse-des-Jardins. **Place Laurier**, with 350 stores, and **Place Ste-Foy**, with 118 stores, are both on Boulevard Laurier in Ste-Foy. Major department stores include The Bay, Holt Renfrew, Sears and Simons. Malls generally are open Mon.-Tues. 9:30-5:30, Wed.-Fri. 9:30-9, Sat. 9-5 and Sun. noon-5.

Performing Arts

The Grand Théâtre de Québec, 269 boul. René-Lévesque Est, is home to the Québec Symphony Orchestra and major theatrical productions, including those staged by the theatrical group Le Théâtre du Trident; phone (418) 643-8131.

Other major theaters in the city include Le Capitole, (418) 694-4444, Place d'Youville; Palais Montcalm, (418) 641-6181, 995 Place d'Youville. Most theater productions are in French.

Student and summer theater productions are presented on small stages throughout the city, in churches and at the university.

Fans of the silver screen won't want to miss the films at the Théâtre IMAX, where the offerings include 3D productions; phone (418) 624-4629.

Special Events

Of Québec's three major events, the Carnaval de Québec is the most popular. The 17-day celebration of winter, with the 2-metre (7-ft.) snowman Bonhomme as master of ceremonies, begins the last Friday in January and attracts more than 500,000 people each year.

Highlights of the event include parades, snow sculpture contests, ice-skating shows, races, games and fireworks displays. Most of the activities are free. For further information contact the Carnaval de Québec Inc., 290 rue Joly, C.P. 8, Québec, QC, Canada G1L 4T8; phone (418) 626-3716.

The second Thursday in July, a ten-day celebration of Québec's cultural heritage commences with the Québec International Summer Festival. The event features concerts, songfests, theater presentations, dances, fireworks and horse and puppet shows.

The city's third major event is Expo City, which lasts 10 days in late August. Held at Exhibition Park, the expo is an agricultural, industrial and commercial fair; for further information phone (418) 691-7110.

The Québec Vicinity

BEAUPORT (D-5) pop. 72,813

MONTMORENCY FALLS PARK (Parc de la Chute-Montmorency), 11.2 km (7 mi.) e. via Autoroute 440, is at the confluence of the Montmorency and St. Lawrence rivers. On the promontory, the park is reached via Hwy. 360 (avenue Royale), and offers a spectacular view of the 83-metre-high (270-ft.) falls, the St. Lawrence and the south shore of Québec. The falls are 30 metres (98 ft.) higher than Niagara Falls. A gondola lift provides rides to the promontory and offers a view of the falls.

A fortification built by Gen. James Wolfe's army in July 1759 is in the park, as is Le Manoir Montmorency (Kent House), which was the 1791-94 home of Prince Edward, Duke of Kent, father of Queen Victoria. Picnicking is permitted.

Park daily 9-9. Gondola daily 8:30-7, mid-Apr. through early Oct.; daily 8:30-6, mid- through late Oct.; daily 9-4, Dec. 26-first Sun. in Jan.; Sat.-Sun. 9-4, late Jan. to mid-Apr. Interpretive center daily 9-9, May-Oct.; 9-5, rest of year. Phone to verify schedules. Park free. One-way gondola ride $8; ages 6-16, $4. Parking $8.75 maximum. AX, MC, VI. Phone (418) 663-3330.

BEAUPRÉ (A-2) pop. 2,761

MONT-SAINTE-ANNE (Mont-Ste-Anne), on Hwy. 360E, is a popular year-round recreation area. Alpine and cross-country skiing and snowboarding are available on the park's many slopes and 63 trails, with a vertical drop of 625 metres (2,050 ft.). An extensive snowmaking system covers the trails with snow all winter. In the summer the gondola lift provides a panorama of mountains, valleys, and rivers. Mountain biking, hiking, camping and golfing facilities are available.

Park open daily dawn-dusk, year-round. Gondola daily 10-4:30, June-Oct. Phone for Nov.-May schedule. Parking free. Gondola $13; over 65, $11; students with ID $10; family rate (four persons) $32. AX, MC, VI. Phone (418) 827-4561 or (888) 827-4579. *See Recreation Chart and the AAA/CAA Eastern Canada CampBook.*

CHÂTEAU-RICHER (A-1) pop. 3,442

Settled in 1640, Château-Richer was established as a parish in 1678 by Bishop de Laval, the first bishop of New France. De Laval reportedly named the village after the priory of Château-Richer in France. There also is a legend that one of the town's settlers named Richer established a shelter in a huge tree trunk. The townspeople ridiculed him by calling his habitat Château Richer, a name later assumed by the parish.

Primarily an agricultural community, the town has a number of area roadside stands selling summer vegetables and maple syrup as well as bread baked in two old stone ovens that stand near the highway.

The Albert Gilles Copper Art Museum and the Christorama are at 7450 boul. Ste-Anne; phone (418) 824-4224. The series of 50 cast copper and silver-plated panels depicting the life of Christ was executed by French sculptor Albert Gilles.

BEE MUSEUM (Musée de l'Abeille), 4 km (2.5 mi.) w. on Hwy. 138, 8862 boul. Ste-Anne, Château-Richer, features interpretive exhibits about bees and humans. Visitors observe the bees at work in a glass beehive and watch the production of honey wine. In the summer, the Bee Safari takes visitors outside for a humorous presentation with a beekeeper. Honey and honey wine tastings are offered.

Allow 30 minutes minimum. Daily 9-6, June 24-Labour Day; daily 9-5, day after Labour Day-Dec. 31 and Mar. 1-June 23; Mon.-Fri. 9-5, Sat.-Sun. 9-5; rest of year. Closed Jan. 1-2 and Dec. 25-26. Museum free. Phone (418) 824-4411.

CÔTE-DE-BEAUPRÉ INTERPRETATION CENTRE (Centre d'interprétation de la Côte-de-Beaupré) is at 7976 av. Royale. The center provides information about the geography, heritage and socioeconomic development of the Côte-de-Beaupré region, where 170 pioneer families settled in the 17th century. Displays include documents, maps, sketches and photographs. On the grounds are the ruins of 1694 and 1829 convents.

Allow 30 minutes minimum. Daily 9:30-4:30, mid-May to mid-Oct.; Mon.-Fri. 9:30-4:30, rest of year. Admission $6; over 65 and students with ID $5; under 17 free; free to all Mon. Phone (418) 824-3677.

ÎLE D'ORLÉANS—see attraction listing p. 211.

LÉVIS (B-2)

LÉVIS FORTS NATIONAL HISTORIC SITE OF CANADA (Lieu historique national du Canada des Forts-de-Lévis), on the s. shore of the St. Lawrence River, .5 km (.3 mi.) n. of jct. rue Mgr Ignace Bourget and Hwy. 132. One of three British military forts built 1865-72 on the heights of Pointe-Lévy, the first fort was to protect the city of Québec from anticipated hostility by the United States, but none of the forts housed a garrison.

The Treaty of Washington between the United States and England, signed in 1871, settled the disagreements between the two countries. The last British soldiers left the city that year.

The restored fort offers both guided and self-guiding tours available in English. Tours highlight the structure's 19th-century military architecture, which includes grooved cannons, armored compartments for artillery, protected trenches and the massive surrounding earthworks.

Allow 2 hours minimum. Daily 10-5, early May-day before Labour Day; Sat.-Sun. 1-4, day after Labour Day-last Sun. in Sept. Admission $3.95; over 65 and students with ID $3.45; ages 6-16, $1.95; family rate $9.90. Phone (418) 835-5182 or (888) 773-8888.

ST-FERRÉOL-LES-NEIGES (D-5)
pop. 2,014

THE SEVEN WATERFALLS (Les Sept-Chutes), on the Ste-Anne River, were once tapped for hydroelectric power. Five kilometres (3 mi.) of hiking trails link the waterfalls with a dam, power generating station, historic village and several overlooks. On the grounds are an interpretation center, water play area and a playground.

Picnicking is permitted. Allow 30 minutes minimum. The 2007 schedule is daily 9-5:45, June 23-Aug. 19; daily 10-4:30, May 19-June 22 and Aug. 20-Oct. 8. Phone to verify schedule. Admission $8.75; over 65 and ages 18-21, $7.75; ages 6-17, $5.75; family rate $22.25. VI. Phone (418) 826-3139 or (877) 724-8837.

ST-GABRIEL-DE-VALCARTIER (D-5)

VALCARTIER VACATION VILLAGE (Village Vacances Valcartier), 1860 boul. Valcartier, is a summer and winter recreation complex 20 minutes from downtown Québec City. In the summer, the waterpark offers more than 35 water slides, two theme rivers, a wave pool, acrobatic diving shows, whitewater rafting and hydrospeed. Winter fare includes 42 inner-tube and carpet slides, snow rafting, 17 mechanical lifts, skating paths and karting on ice.

Food is available. Opens daily at 10, mid-Dec. through late Mar. and early June-late Aug. The 2006 summer admission was $26.33, over age 65 and children under 52 inches $20.18. The 2006-07 winter season rate was $19.31-$24.57; ages 5-11, $15.80-$21.06; ages 3-4, $7.02. Phone or check their web site for both the 2007 summer and winter rates, as well as to confirm both schedules. MC, VI. Phone (418) 844-2200 or (888) 384-5524.

STE-ANNE-DE-BEAUPRÉ (A-2) pop. 2,752

On the north shore of the St. Lawrence River, Ste-Anne-de-Beaupré is the site of a shrine that annually attracts more than a million pilgrims and visitors. Soon after the first chapel was built in 1658, those who visited the shrine reported miraculous cures.

BASILICA OF STE-ANNE-DE-BEAUPRÉ (Basilique de Ste-Anne-de-Beaupré), between av. Royale and boul. Ste-Anne (Hwy. 138), was erected in 1923. It contains the Miraculous Statue of Saint Anne and relics of the saint. The basilica's architecture has Neo-Romanesque features. On Avenue Royale near the site of the first chapel, is the Memorial Chapel, remodeled in 1878.

Next to the chapel is the Scala Santa, a replica of the 28 steps Jesus ascended to meet Pontius Pilate. Life-size bronze figures depicting the stations of the cross are on the hillside. Basilica open daily 6:30 a.m.-10 p.m., June-Sept.; 7-6, rest of year. Free. Phone (418) 827-3781.

Museum of Saint Anne (Musée de Saint-Anne), 9803 boul. Ste-Anne, features interactive exhibits relating to Saint Anne, the history of the Basilica and the 300 years of pilgrimage at Ste-Anne-de-Beaupré. Guided tours are available on request. Daily 9-5, June-Sept. Free. Phone (418) 827-3781, ext. 754.

CANYON OF STE-ANNE (Canyon Ste-Anne) is 6 km (4 mi.) e. to 206 Hwy. 138.
The Ste-Anne River cuts through narrow chasms and tumbles 74 metres (245 ft.) in a series of falls and whirlpools to the riverbed. East of the basilica 6 kilometres (3.7 mi.), a path through the woods leads to a network of trails, bridges and lookouts that follows the river's course. The falls can be crossed at three places by cable suspension bridges. On sunny days, rainbows can be seen from the scenic overlooks.

The majesty of the canyon has long been admired. In September 1850, transcendental author and naturalist Henry David Thoreau wrote of the canyon "Take it altogether, it was a most wild and rugged and stupendous chasm, so deep and narrow where a river had worn itself a passage through a mountain of rock, and all around was the comparatively untrodden wilderness."

A sightseeing shuttle is available. Food is available, and picnicking is permitted. Allow 1 hour, 30 minutes minimum. Daily 9-5:45, June 24-Labour Day; 9-5, day after Labour Day-third Sun. in Oct. and May 1-June 23. Admission $9.50; ages 6-12, $4. AX, MC, VI. Phone (418) 827-4057.

CYCLORAMA OF JERUSALEM (Cyclorama de Jérusalem), Hwy. 138 at 8 rue Régina, is a cylindrical painting, 14 metres (46 ft.) in height and 110 metres (361 ft.) in circumference. Painted in Munich, this work depicts events in Jerusalem, on Calvary and in the surrounding countryside at the time of Jesus' crucifixion. The panorama, exhibited since 1895, is viewed from a raised platform in the center of the painting; a bilingual narration is provided.

Daily 9-6, May 1-late Oct. Admission $8; ages 6-16, $5. MC, VI. Phone (418) 827-3101.

(SAVE) MUSÉE EDISON DU PHONOGRAPHE, from Hwy. 138 go .4 km (.2 mi.) n. on rue Regina St., then w. to 9812 rue Royale, offers bilingual guided tours explaining the history of Thomas Alva Edison's invention of the phonograph. More than 200 gramophones and phonographs are displayed, including some of the rarest. Of particular interest is a display of talking dolls, the earliest commercial application of phonographic technology.

Daily 10-6. Admission $5; over 59 and students with ID $4; ages 7-12, $2.50. Phone (418) 827-5957.

STE-CATHERINE-DE-LA-JACQUES-CARTIER (D-5)

ICE HOTEL QUÉBEC-CANADA (Hôtel de Glace Québec-Canada) is at 143 Rte. Duchesnay; from

Hwy. 40 take exit 295 then n. 18 km (11 mi.) Rte. 367 following signs. The structure is made of ice and snow and has artwork and furniture carved from blocks of ice. Common areas include a wedding chapel, nightclub, two hot tubs and a sauna. Overnight guests sleep in sleeping bags in room made of ice and snow.

Allow 1 hour minimum. Self-guiding tours daily 10-9, Jan.-Apr. Admission $15; over 65 and students with ID $13; ages 6-15, $7.50; family rate $42. AX. Phone (418) 875-4522 or (877) 505-0423.

STE-FOY (B-1) pop. 72,547

GEM **SAVE** **QUÉBEC AQUARIUM PARK** (Parc Aquarium du Québec) is at 1675 av. des Hôtels; from Hwy. 73S take exit 132 (last exit before accessing Pierre-Laporte Bridge), then just s.e. (loop around to av. des Hôtels, following signs). The 16-hectare (40-acre) outdoor park and the main pavilion enable visitors to explore marine life in carefully re-created indoor and outdoor environments.

Outdoors visitors can see mammals such as polar bears, walruses and seals. The main pavilion houses 10,000 fish, 3,000 of which surround visitors as they walk in an acrylic tunnel surrounded by 350,000 litres (92,470 gallons) of saltwater. Animal shows and feedings are scheduled throughout the day.

Food is available. Allow 3 hours minimum. Daily 10-5, May-Oct; 10-4, rest of year. Closed Dec. 25. Admission $15.50; over 65, $14.50; ages 13-17, $12.75; ages 6-12, $10.50; ages 3-5, $5.50. Family rates are available. AX, DC, MC, VI. Phone (866) 659-5264.

SILLERY (A-1) pop. 11,909

THE JESUIT HOUSE (La Maison des Jésuites), is along the St. Lawrence River at 2320 ch. du Foulon. Built about 1637, the house contains an archeological and historical museum, along with arts and crafts exhibits. Daily 11-5, June-Sept; Wed.-Sun. 1-5, Apr.-May and Oct.-Dec.; Sun. 1-5, Feb.-Mar. Free. Phone (418) 654-0259.

MONTMARTRE CANADIEN, 1679 ch. St-Louis, is a replica of the Paray-le-Monial in Paris, France. The sanctuary and grounds contain chapel stations, the Grotto of Lourdes and a monument to Our Lady of the Assumption. Grounds open daily. Phone for hours. Admission free. Guided tours are available for a fee. Phone (418) 681-7357.

VILLA BAGATELLE, 1563 ch. St-Louis with access by James LeMoine St., is a restored neo-Gothic villa surrounded by a formal garden. Sillery—now a suburb of Québec—was wooded wilderness when an English upper-class family built the villa as a country house in the 19th century. Impressive gardens display more than 350 varieties of native and exotic flowers. Art and history exhibits also are presented.

Daily 11-5, June-Sept; Tues.-Sun. 11-5, Apr.-May and Oct.-Dec.; Sun. 1-5, Feb.-Mar. Free. Phone (418) 654-0259.

STONEHAM-ET-TEWKESBURY (A-5) pop. 5,266

THE MARSHES OF THE NORTH (Les Marais Du Nord) is at 1100 chemin de la Grand-Ligne. Visitors to these marshes at the confluence of three waterways can walk through a natural environment rich in flora and fauna, or explore it on a narrated 90-minute canoe trip. Canoe departures require a minimum of six persons.

Open daily. Admission $3.50; ages 6-17, $2. Canoe trip $12; ages 6-17, $6; under 6, $4. Reservations are required for canoe trips. Phone (418) 841-4629.

RECREATIONAL ACTIVITIES

Skiing and Snowboarding

• **Stoneham Mountain Resort,** 1420 Hibou Rd., Stoneham-et-Tewkesbury, QC, Canada G0A 4P0. Daily 6-6 (also some nights), mid-Nov. through early Apr. Other activities are available rest of year. Phone (418) 848-2411 or (800) 463-6888.

WENDAKE (A-1)

The contemporary re-creation of the old Huron Village *(Village des Hurons)* established during the 18th century is built around the 1730 Huron Chapel, which was partially destroyed by fire in 1862. Displayed in the chapel are some of the French ecclesiastical silver, vestments and treasures brought to New France by missionaries. The key must be obtained from the nearby Maison Tsawenhohi; phone (418) 845-0700. Huron Village is open May 1 to early September. The tourism office offers guided tours of the village.

In nearby Lac-St-Charles, one can drift back in time aboard a canoe traversing the same ecologically rich passages the Amerindians paddled before European settlement: phone Les Marais du Nord at (418) 841-4629.

This ends listings for the Québec Vicinity.
The following page resumes the alphabetical listings of cities in Québec.

RIMOUSKI (C-7) pop. 31,305

Rimouski is the administrative capital of eastern Québec, and an important educational and cultural center halfway between Québec City and Gaspé.

Rimouski Tourism & Information Bureau: 50 rue St-Germain Ouest, Rimouski, QC, Canada G5L 4B5; phone (418) 723-2322 or (800) 746-6875.

LAMONTAGNE HOUSE (Maison Lamontagne), 1.5 km (.9 mi.) e. of Rimouski Port via Hwy. 132 to 707 boul. du Rivage, is a restored 18th-century half-timbered house furnished in period. The house has antique furniture, archeology exhibits and a slide show about the restoration process. Guided tours and English narration are available.

Allow 1 hour minimum. Daily 10-6, June 24-Labour Day. Admission $4; over 65, $3; students with ID $2; under 13 free. Phone (418) 722-4038.

RIMOUSKI REGIONAL MUSEUM (Musée régional de Rimouski), 35 rue St-Germain Ouest, is in an 1824 stone church built that has a modern interior. Exhibitions deal with local history, science and technology in the Bas St-Laurent and contemporary Canadian art.

Allow 30 minutes minimum. Wed.-Fri. 9:30-8, Sat.-Tues. 9:30-6, late June-early Sept.; Wed.-Sun. noon-5 (also Thurs. 5-9), rest of year. Admission $4, over 50 and students with ID $3, family rate $10. MC, VI. Phone (418) 724-2272.

RIVIÈRE-DU-LOUP (C-6) pop. 17,772

According to local legend, Rivière-du-Loup owes its name to the sea lions, or *loups marins,* that once frequented the mouth of the river. Other tales suggest that it was named after the French ship *Le Loup,* which was stranded at the mouth of the river around 1660.

The area is noted for its eight beautiful waterfalls; the largest, at 30 metres (100 ft.), and most picturesque, is reached via rues de la Chute and Frontenac and highlights the center of the city. The Park of the Illuminated Cross (Parc de la Croix Lumineuse) affords an excellent view of the region and contains a large illuminated cross.

From June to mid-October large numbers of whales migrate through nearby waters. Up to seven different species, ranging from the relatively small beluga to the enormous blue whale, can be sighted. Whale-watching cruises are offered in late summer.

Rivière-du-Loup Tourism & Information Bureau: 189 boul. de l'Hôtel-de-Ville, Rivière-du-Loup, QC, Canada G5R 5C4; phone (418) 862-1981 or (888) 825-1981.

SAVE **LOWER ST. LAWRENCE ISLAND CRUISES** (Croisières dans les Îles du Bas-St-Laurent) depart from the Rivière-du-Loup ferry service dock. La Société Duvetnor Ltd. offers a variety of naturalist guided sightseeing cruises of the lower St. Lawrence islands, ranging from 90 minutes to 4 hours. Tour narration in English is available. Inquire about weather policies and minimum number of passengers for departure.

Cruise to Île aux Lièvres departs at varying times daily, late May through mid-Sept. Cruise to Île du Pot à l'Eau-de-Vie departs daily at 2, early July to mid-Sept. Two-hour, 30-minute cruise to Île du Pot à l'Eau-de-Vie, $40; ages 2-15, $20. Cruise to Île aux Lièvres $40; ages 2-15, $20. Overnight cruise to lighthouse at Île du Pot à l'Eau-de-Vie $200. Reservations are required for all cruises. AX, MC, VI. Phone (418) 867-1660.

LOWER ST. LAWRENCE MUSEUM (Musée du Bas-St-Laurent), 300 rue St-Pierre, includes contemporary artworks, including photographs. Daily 10-6, June 24 to mid-Oct.; daily 1-5, rest of year. Admission $5; over 65 and students with ID $3; family rate $12. Phone (418) 862-7547.

WHALE-WATCHING CRUISES (Croisières d'observation aux Baleines-Croisières AML) depart from the yacht club near the St-Siméon/Rivière-du-Loup ferry service. Bilingual naturalists help passengers discover the whales, birds and lighthouses of the St. Lawrence River. Inquire about weather policies and minimum number of passengers required for departure.

Cruises depart daily at 9, 1 and 5, mid-June through late Sept. Fare $52; senior citizens and students with ID $47; ages 6-16, $22; family rate $135. Reservations are required. AX, MC, VI. Phone (800) 563-4643.

RIVIÈRE-ÉTERNITÉ (C-6) pop. 553

GEM **SAGUENAY-ST. LAWRENCE MARINE PARK AND SAGUENAY NATIONAL PARK** (Parc marin Saguenay-St-Laurent), Hwy. 170, consists of most of the river bed of Saguenay Fjord and a part of the northern half of the St Lawrence estuary, managed by both the provincial and the federal government, and 300 square kilometres (116 sq. mi.) of the long, rugged and heavily forested valley on each side of the Saguenay River are managed by the provincial government and designated as Saguenay National Park.

Although the Saguenay Fjord is its major feature, there are hiking trails along the river, and a short hike ascends cap Trinité to a statue of the Virgin Mary. At the Saguenay Fjord Interpretation Centre naturalists explain how the fjord was formed. A 1-hour guided cruise is available; English narration is available. Primitive camping is permitted throughout the park; developed facilities are available at Baie Éternité.

Daily 9-5, May 20-second Mon. in Oct. Admission $3.50, students with ID $1.50, family rate $5. MC, VI.

Phone Parks Canada for Saguenay-St. Lawrence Marine Park, at (418) 235-4703 or (888) 773-8888; phone Parks Québec for Saguenay National Park information, at (418) 272-1556; or phone (877) 272-5229 for campground information. *See also Pointe-Noire Interpretation and Observation Centre p. 231, Cap De Bon-Désir Interpretation and Observation Centre p. 170, and Recreation Chart.*

ROBERVAL (C-5) pop. 10,906

Settled in 1855, Roberval was named for Jean François de la Roque, who served as the first lieutenant general of the king in New France. The town developed into a commercial center for the western portion of lac St-Jean County.

In late July the Traversée Internationale du lac St-Jean, a 40-kilometre (25-mi.) swimming marathon, takes place between Péribonka (*see place listing p. 200*) and Roberval. Swimmers from around the world compete in the event. Phone (418) 275-2851 for information.

VAL-JALBERT HISTORIC VILLAGE (Village Historique de Val-Jalbert), 10 km (6 mi.) s. on Hwy. 169, preserves the remains of Val-Jalbert, a once thriving early 20th-century industrial village. Built to exploit the churning waters and 72-metre (235 ft.) falls of the Ouiatchouane River, the village was abandoned in 1927. Features include a school, hotel, bank and rows of workers' houses.

The Ouiatchouane falls can be seen from a scenic overlook, or belvedere, above the park. There are campsites, picnic facilities and a hiking trail. Allow 3 hours minimum. The 2007 schedule is daily 9:30-5:30, June 17-Aug. 20; 10-5, June 3-June 16 and Aug. 21-Oct. 8. Phone to verify schedule. Admission June 17-Aug. 20, $17; ages 6-13, $8. Admission rest of season $13; ages 6-13, $7. Phone to verify prices. MC, VI. Phone (418) 275-3132. *See the AAA/CAA Eastern Canada CampBook.*

STANSTEAD (F-9)

In some homes in Stanstead meals prepared in the United States are eaten in Canada because slightly fewer than 60 buildings were constructed before the international boundary was established through the community in 1961. Referred to as "line houses," the structures include houses, factories, a hotel and cocktail lounge and the historic Haskell Free Library and Opera House.

HASKELL FREE LIBRARY AND OPERA HOUSE (Bibliothèque et la Salle d'Opéra Haskell) 1 Church St. is on the international boundary. The stage is in Canada; half the 400 seats are in the United States. Many performances are staged in the Opera House during the summer. Library Tues.-Sat. 10-5, (also Thurs. 5-8). Library free. Fees for performances vary. Phone (819) 876-2471, or (802) 873-3022 in Vt.

SAGUENAY—*see Chicoutimi p. 162.*

ST-CONSTANT—*see Montréal p. 196.*

ST-EUSTACHE—*see Montréal p. 196.*

ST-FAUSTIN-LAC-CARRÉ (E-3)

Settled in 1817 and incorporated in 1878, St-Faustin is a farming and lumber center on the Canadian Pacific Railway. The town is a country resort in the Laurentides, offering both winter and water sports as well as camping, fishing and hunting.

ST-FÉLICIEN (C-5) pop. 10,622

St-Félicien, on the Ashuapmushuan River, is an important spawning area for ouananiche (landlocked salmon) as well as home to a paper mill.

Communication Québec: 1209 boul. Sacré Coeur, St-Félicien, QC, Canada G8K 2P8; phone (418) 679-9888.

ASHUAPMUSHUAN WILDLIFE RESERVE (Réserve Faunique Ashuapmushuan), n.w. of town on Hwy. 167, contains approximately 4,487 square kilometres (1,732 sq. mi.) of virgin country, traversed by Hwy. 167. Hunting and fishing are permitted seasonally. Reservations are required for cottages. A special fishing permit is necessary in addition to a provincial fishing license.

For further information contact the Société des établissements de plein air du Québec (SÉPAQ), Reservations Office, 2640 boul. Laurier, bureau 1300, Sainte-Foy, QC, Canada G1V 5C2. Open daily 24 hours. Admission free. Phone (418) 890-6527 to reserve a cottage, or (800) 665-6527. *See Recreation Chart.*

ST-FÉLICIEN WILD ANIMAL ZOO (Zoo Sauvage de St-Félicien) is 5 km (3 mi.) n.w. on Hwy. 167 toward Chibougamau, at 2230 boul. du Jardin. A river winds through 162 hectares (400 acres) of wooded and landscaped areas. Exhibits include about 1,000 specimens of more than 75 species of birds, reptiles and other animals. Fauna roam freely in natural settings.

The visitor center contains an interactive nature museum and two large movie theaters, one with a giant screen. A train ride takes visitors through the North American Habitat where there are re-creations of a lumberjack camp, a trading post, an Indian village and a 19th-century farmhouse. Other highlights include children's zoo, picnic areas and a nature trail.

Allow 3 hours, 30 minutes minimum. Daily 9-6, June-Aug.; daily 9-5 May 15-May 31 and Sept.-Oct.; by reservation May 1-May 14. Last departure of nature trails train is at 3:30. Admission $29; over 65 and students with ID $25; ages 6-14, $19; ages 4-5, $12. Family rates are available. Phone to verify prices and schedule. MC, VI. Phone (418) 679-0543 or (800) 667-5687.

ST-FÉLIX-D'OTIS (C-6) pop. 790

SITE DE LA NOUVELLE-FRANCE is at 370 du Vieux Chemin. Bilingual guides lead visitors through a faithfully re-created 17th-century Québec settlement for 90 minutes, providing insight into the customs of a typical Montagnais family and details of the traditions of early French and Amerindian villagers. Boat tours recall the route taken by the early explorer Samuel de Champlain. An equestrian show features trick riding and acrobatics.

Daily 9-4:30, mid-June through early Sept. Admission $15; senior citizens $14; ages 6-13, $7. Phone to verify prices. VI. Phone (418) 544-8027 or (888) 666-8027.

ST-FERRÉOL-LES-NEIGES—
see Québec p. 222.

ST-GABRIEL-DE-VALCARTIER—
see Québec p. 222.

ST-HYACINTHE (E-8) pop. 38,739

Colonists arrived in Saint-Hyacinthe in 1757 and began clearing land for crops. Shortly after, a waterfall was discovered on the Yamaska River and a sawmill, a flour mill and a carding mill were built. Today, it ranks among the 30 largest cities in the province and its rich soil and bountiful harvests have made the area the agribusiness capital of Québec. This bounty is celebrated the third Friday in July through the last Sunday of the month when more than 175,000 visitors attend the Saint-Hyacinthe Agriculture and Food Exposition, a celebration held annually since 1837; phone (450) 773-9307. Many other special events are offered throughout the year.

Saint-Hyacinthe has been the seat of a Roman Catholic diocese since 1852, and therefore has many churches and chapels worth a visit. The Saint-Hyacinthe Cathedral, 1900 rue Girouard Ouest, was built in 1878 and is noted for its chandeliers. The Sanctuaire Notre-Dame de Fatima, 650 rue Girouard Ouest, is an eight-sided chapel. Église Notre-Dame-du-Rosaire, 2200 rue Girouard Ouest, is richly decorated.

May through September the domesticated animals and 300 species of perennial plants of Ferme la Rabouillère, (514) 345-8521, delight visitors. Birds of prey are the subject of presentations given in French late June through early October at the Chouette à Voir—The Owl Sees site in nearby St-Jude; phone (450) 773-8521, ext. 18545.

In nearby St-Pie, Ferme Du Coq à l'Âne offers French narrated tours of a working farm by reservation; phone (450) 772-6512 For a hands-on agricultural experience, there are farms where you can pick your own blueberries, strawberries, tomatoes and apples—or you cans always just purchase these fruits from the roadside stands.

Bureau de tourisme et des congrès de Saint-Hyacinthe: 2090 Cherrier Street, St-Hyacinthe, QC, Canada J2S 8R3; phone (450) 774-7276 or (800) 849-7276.

Shopping Areas: A public market built more than 100 years ago, le vieux marché de Saint-Hyacinthe at 1555 rue Des Cascades Ouest dominates the old part of the town and continues to offer foodstuffs; it

is open Mon.-Wed. 9-6, Thurs.-Fri. 8:30-9, Sat. 8:30-5 and Sunday 10-5. Galeries St-Hyacinthe, 3200 boul. Laframboise, houses more than 100 stores and restaurants and fast-food establishments.

DANIEL A. SÉGUIN GARDEN (Le jardin de Daniel A. Séguin) is off Hwy. 20 exit 130, then s. on rue Laframboise .4 km (.25 mi.), w. on rue Casavant, then 1 km (.6 mi.) s. on rue Choquette, then .8 km (.5 mi.) w. to 3215 rue Sicotte.

Founded by a retired professor and affiliated with a school of agriculture, the 16 gardens and their landscaping and integration in this 4.5-hectare (11.25-acre) site are impressive. Visitors can stroll through an herb garden, a French garden, a Zen garden, a Japanese garden, a Québec garden of yesteryear and through a rockery and past a waterfall. Picnicking is permitted.

Allow 1 hour, 30 minutes minimum. Daily 10-5, mid-June through Labour Day. Admission $8.50; students with ID $5, family rate (two adults and two students) $17. Phone to confirm prices. Phone (450) 778-0372 or (450) 778-6504, ext. 215 in the off season.

ST-JEAN-PORT-JOLI (D-6) pop. 3,372

Founded in 1721, St-Jean-Port-Joli is a handicraft center known as the wood carving capital of Québec. It is noted for Bourgault woodcarvings and Leclerc miniature boats as well as for weavings and paintings. Most of the church of St-Jean-Baptiste on Hwy. 132 dates from 1779. The interior, designed by the Baillairgé brothers, remains intact, and a manger scene of 22 figures is displayed.

SAVE **MUSEUM OF THE EARLY CANADIANS** (Musée des Anciens Canadiens), 4 km (2.5 mi.) s. on Hwy. 132 at 332 av. de Gaspé Ouest, displays carvings and handicrafts by local artisans, including sculptures by the Bourgault brothers. Allow 30 minutes minimum. Daily 8:30 a.m.-9 p.m., July-Aug.; 9-5:30, May-June and Sept.-Oct.; by appointment rest of year. Admission $6; students with ID $5; ages 7-12, $2.50; family rate $14. MC, VI. Phone (418) 598-3392.

ST-JEAN-SUR-RICHELIEU (F-7)
pop. 37,386

St-Jean-sur-Richelieu, once a terminus of the first railway in Canada, opened traffic between St-Jean and La Prairie in 1836. A boulder on rue Champlain marks the site of Fort St-Jean, which was built 1666-68 and reconstructed in 1775.

The town has interesting examples of early 19th-century domestic and public architecture. The Chambly Canal was built alongside the Richelieu River in 1843 to bypass the river's rapids. No longer a waterway for forest products, the 20-kilometre-long (12-mi.-long) canal connecting to Chambly now accommodates pleasure craft, and the towpath accommodates hikers and bikers. Most of the locks and bridges still work, and are operated daily from mid-May through mid-October; phone (450) 447-4888.

Haut-Richelieu Tourism Bureau: 31 rue Frontenac, St-Jean-sur-Richelieu, QC, Canada J3B 7X2; phone (450) 542-9090 or (888) 781-9999.

MUSEUM OF HAUT-RICHELIEU, (Musée du Haut-Richelieu), 182 rue Jacques-Cartier Nord, contains exhibits about regional and military history, the first Canadian railroad in 1836, the opening of the Chambly Canal, the history of local ceramics and hot-air balloons. Allow 1 hour minimum. Tues.-Sat. 11-5, Sun. 1-5. Admission $4; over 65, $3; ages 6-12, $2; family rate (two adults and two ages 6-12) $10. Phone (450) 347-0649.

ST-JOACHIM (A-2)

◥◣ **CAP TOURMENTE NATIONAL WILD-**
GEM **LIFE AREA** (Réserve nationale de faune du cap Tourmente), 10 km (6 mi.) n.e. of Beaupré off Hwy. 360, is a major habitat for migrating snow geese on their way from the Arctic to a winter home in the Carolinas. The 2,399 hectares (5,930 acres) of marshy plains along the St. Lawrence accommodate thousands of geese in April and May, and from the last week of September to late October.

The changing foliage provides a vivid backdrop for viewing many bird species as well as other wildlife. Twenty kilometres (12 mi.) of nature trails wind through marsh, plain and forest. Nature activities and guided tours are available by reservation; narration is available in English. Daily 8:30-5, mid-Apr. to late Oct.; 8:30-4, early Jan. through mid-Mar.; limited access rest of year. Admission $6, students with ID $5, under 12 free. Phone (418) 827-4591.

WINERIES

- **Domaine Royarnois Vignoble (Vineyard)** is off Hwy. 138; briefly go s. on rue Prévost, then 5.2 km (3.3 mi.) s.e. on ave. Royale, then follow signs to 146, chemin du Cap-Tourmente. Guided and self-guiding tours are available, as well as tastings. Food is available. Daily 9-5; closed Jan. 1, Dec. 25-26 and 31. Phone (418) 827-4465.

ST-JOSEPH-DE-LA-RIVE (D-6) pop. 222

On the St. Lawrence River, St-Joseph-de-la-Rive is the departure point for ferries to Île-aux-Coudres (*see place listing p. 168*). A popular beach is near the ferry dock. Île-aux-Coudres can be reached by a ferry that departs daily from 3 rue du Port; phone (418) 438-2743 for schedule and fare information.

The St-Joseph-de-la-Rive Church contains unusual decorations, including a giant seashell baptismal font.

CHARLEVOIX MARITIME MUSEUM (Le Musée Maritime de Charlevoix), in the village center at 305 rue de l'Église, depicts the traditional trading boat of the St. Lawrence River at a shipyard where generations of boatbuilders have worked. A small museum demonstrates the development of the schooner and displays three original boats and a restored carpentry shop.

Allow 30 minutes minimum. Daily 9-5, June 24-Labour Day; Mon.-Fri. 9-4, Sat.-Sun. 11-4, mid-May through June 23 and day after Labour Day-second Mon. in Oct.; Mon.-Fri. 9-4:15, rest of year. Admission $5; ages 12-17, $2. Phone (418) 635-1131.

THE SAINT-GILLES PAPER FACTORY (Papeterie Saint-Gilles ÉCONOMUSÉE), 304 Félix-Antoine-Savard, offers tours of its small mill, which uses 17th-century methods to produce a cotton and acid free handmade paper. Comparable to the chiné papers of France, this high quality paper contains image of Saint-Gilles in its watermark.

Daily 8-11:30 and 1-5. Schedule may vary; phone for hours. Free. Phone (418) 635-2430 or (866) 635-2430.

ST-LAURENT—see Montréal p. 196.

ST-LIN-LAURENTIDES (E-7)

St-Lin-Laurentides, originally called the Parish of Saint-Lin, was founded in 1828. Twenty-seven years later the village elected as its first mayor Carolus Laurier, father of Sir Wilfrid Laurier, Canada's prime minister 1896-1911. In 1883 the village of Saint-Lin was incorporated, and the name was changed to "Ville des Laurentides." Near the Achigan River, it is in a tobacco farming and dairying region.

At the heart of the village stands a magnificent Byzantine-style church, many historic ancestral houses and a national historic site. This mix of 19th- and early 20th-century architecture can be explored on the Heritage Walking Tour.

SIR WILFRID LAURIER NATIONAL HISTORIC SITE OF CANADA (Lieu historique national de Sir-Wilfrid-Laurier) is at the jct. of hwys. 158 and 337 at 945 12th Ave. Born in Saint-Lin in 1841, Sir Wilfrid Laurier was the first French Canadian to head the federal government (1896-1911). The 1870 house is furnished in period, vividly re-creating the interior of a mid-19th-century rural home. Guided tours offer visitors a look at Sir Wilfrid Laurier's lifestyle when he was a child. Adjoining the house is an interpretation center with displays detailing Laurier's life.

Daily 10-6, mid-June through Sun. before Labour Day weekend; Mon.-Fri. 9-5, May 1 to mid-June. Admission $3.95; over 65, $3.45; ages 6-16, $1.95; family rate, $9.90. Phone (450) 439-3702 or (888) 773-8888.

ST-OURS (E-7) pop. 1,624

ST-OURS CANAL NATIONAL HISTORIC SITE OF CANADA (Lieu historique national du Canada du canal de St-Ours) is on Rte. 133, 2 km (1.2 mi.) s. at 2930 Chemin des Patriotes. Visitors may view the operations of a functioning canal lock, used primarily by pleasure craft navigating the Richelieu River. Boats are raised and lowered in the locks most days between 8:30 a.m. and 8 p.m. in season.

The former superintendent's house on this 1849 canal contains exhibitions about the development of the Richelieu River Canal System.

Canal open daily 10-6, mid-May through mid-Oct. Site free. House admission $2.95; over 65, $2.45; ages 6-16, $1.45; family rate $7.40. Phone (450) 785-2212 or (888) 773-8888.

ST-ROCH-DES-AULNAIES (D-6)
pop. 1,003

SAVE **AULNAIES MANOR** (Seigneurie des Aulnaies), 525 de la Seigneurie, dates from a 1656 seigneurial grant. The manor house was built by Québec architect Charles Baillairgé in 1850. Also on the property are a 19th-century mill and ornamental, rose and kitchen gardens and woods. A 90-minute tour, in French or English, by a costumed guide describes the work of the mill and the social and historical background of the manor.

Food is available. Daily 9-6, mid-June through Labour Day; Sat.-Sun. 10-4, in early June and day after Labour Day-second Mon. in Oct. Admission $8.75; over 65 and students with ID $8; ages 6-12, $5.50; family rate $21. MC, VI. Phone (418) 354-2800 or (877) 354-2800.

ST-URBAIN (D-6) pop. 1,430

GRANDS-JARDINS NATIONAL PARK (Parc national des Grands-Jardins), 20 km (12 mi.) n. via Hwy. 381, conserves 310 square kilometres (120 sq. mi.) of subarctic vegetation—black spruce, lichen and peat bogs known collectively as taiga. This vegetative cloak overlies a landscape of rivers, lakes and mountains that can be seen from the 2.6-kilometre (1.6 mi.) hiking trail that ascends Mont du lac des Cygnes. Wildlife includes black bears, moose, reintroduced caribou and trout.

Daily 8 a.m.-10 p.m., late June to mid-Aug.; 9-5, late May through mid-June and late Aug. through mid-Oct. Admission $3.50; ages 6-17, $1.50; family rate (two adults and children ages 6-17) $7. Phone (800) 665-6527 or (418) 890-6527. *See Recreation Chart.*

STE-ADÈLE (E-3)

On the slopes of Mont Chantecler and the shores of lac Ste-Adèle, Ste-Adèle is a writers' and artists' colony and a popular ski resort.

Tourism Bureau: 1490 rue St-Joseph, Ste-Adèle, QC, Canada J8B 1G4; phone (450) 229-3729 or (800) 898-2127.

THE WONDERLAND (Au Pays des Merveilles), at 3795 ch. de la Savane, presents settings inspired by fairy tales; costumed characters; playgrounds with inflatable structures, slides and a wading pool; a maze; amusements-park rides; a petting zoo; miniature golf; and a train ride.

Allow 2 hours minimum. The 2007 schedule is daily 10-6, June 16-Aug. 26; Sat.-Sun. 10-6, June 9-10 and Sept. 1-2. Admission $15, under 2 free. MC, VI. Phone (450) 229-3141.

STE-AGATHE-DES-MONTS (E-3)
pop. 7,116

Capital of the Laurentians, Ste-Agathe-des-Monts is a year-round recreation center. The town's centerpiece is Lac des Sables, which creates three municipal beaches: Plage Major, Plage Sainte-Lucie and Plage Tessier. In addition to providing the beaches, the lake is popular for a variety of water sports, including swimming, canoeing and sailing.

The surrounding Canadian Shield, covered with trees and laced with nature trails, is ideal for hiking. Bicyclists, fishing enthusiasts and golfers will find plenty to do in the town and its environs. Winter sports include ice-skating, snowmobiling and cross-country skiing.

A nature preserve with hiking trails is about 20 miles north of the lake. Ste-Agathe-des-Monts also boasts a summer stock theater, Le Patriote. Village du Mont-Castor, about 1 km (.6 mi.) north, is a recreation of a turn-of-the-20th-century village of Québécois influence. The houses are private, but visitors are welcome to drive through and admire this unique community.

Ste-Agathe-des-Monts Tourist Information Bureau: 24 rue Saint-Paul Est, C.P. 323, Ste-Agathe-des-Monts, QC, Canada J8C 3C6; phone (819) 326-0457 or (888) 326-0457.

ALOUETTE CRUISES (Les Bateaux Alouette) departs from the main street pier; take exit 86 off Autoroute 15N to the n. end of rue Principale and Centre-Ville. The narration on these 50-minute cruises on lac des Sables is in both French and English. Cruises depart daily at 10:30, 11:30, 1:30, 2:30 and 3:30, mid-May through early Oct. (also at 5 and 7:30 late June-late Aug.) Fare $12; over 60 and students with ID $10; physically impaired $8.75; ages 5-14, $5. MC, VI. Phone (819) 326-3656 to verify fares.

STE-ANNE-DE-BELLEVUE—
see Montréal p. 196.

STE-ANNE-DE-BEAUPRÉ—
see Québec p. 222.

STE-ANNE-DES-MONTS (B-8) pop. 5,511

EXPLORAMER, DISCOVERING THE SEA (Centre de découverte Exploramer), 1 rue du Quai, offers three innovative exhibits dedicated to exploring the wonders of the marine world: A Garden Under the Sea introduces species of the St-Lawrence River in aquariums and touch-pools. The *Exploramer* offers an ecological sea excursion.

Picnicking is permitted. Allow 1 hour, 30 minutes minimum. Daily 9-6, mid-June to mid-Oct. Admission $12; over 65 and students with ID $9.50; ages 7-17, $7; family rate (two adults and two children) is available. MC, VI. Phone (418) 763-2500.

GASPÉSIE NATIONAL PARK (Parc de la Gaspésie) covering 802 square kilometres (310 sq. mi.) on the Gaspé Peninsula, is 20 km s. on Hwy. 299. It includes the Chic-Chocs Mountains, with peaks rising to 1,268 metres (4,160 ft.). Lush flora enhances the view that extends from 1,083-metre (3,553-ft.) Mont Albert. Both are sanctuaries for the caribou that frequent the area in the spring and fall.

Park open daily dawn-dusk (weather permitting). Visitor Center daily 8 a.m.-10 p.m., June 24-early Sept.; daily 8-8, mid-May through June 23 and mid-Sept. through mid-Oct. Admission $3.50; ages 6-17, $1.50 Family rate, one adult and dependent children ages 6-17, $5; two adults and dependent children ages 6-17, $7.

For additional information contact the park at 1981 route du Parc, Ste-Anne-des-Monts, QC, Canada G4V 2E4; phone (866) 727-2427. *See Recreation Chart.*

STE-CATHERINE-DE-LA-JACQUES-CARTIER—*see Québec p. 222.*

STE-FOY—*see Québec p. 223.*

STE-MARIE (E-6) pop. 11,320

The first Canadian cardinal, Elzéar Alexandre Cardinal Taschereau, was born in Ste-Marie in the early 1800s. The shrine of Ste-Anne-de-Beauce is next to the 1809 neo-Classical Maison Taschereau, the cardinal's boyhood home on rue Notre-Dame. The town is known for its food industries. The Maison J.A. Vachon offers tours of its baking facilities; phone (418) 387-4052.

STE-MARIE CHURCH (Église Ste-Marie), 62 rue Notre-Dame, is an 1856 neo-Gothic structure with a vaulted ceiling and 14 monochrome paintings on glass. Mon.-Sat. 8-8, Sun. 8-noon. Phone (418) 387-5467.

SEPT-ÎLES (A-8) pop. 25,200

Sept-Îles is named for the seven islands that protect the mouth of its almost circular bay. Tucked into the northwest corner of the Gulf of St. Lawrence, the bay has long been a refuge from the storms of the Atlantic and the Gulf of St. Lawrence.

Sept-Îles' location and nearness to the iron mines of northern Québec have made the city a major shipping port. Old Wharf Urban Park offers fresh seafood and crafts along a boardwalk.

Sept-Îles Tourism Bureau: 1401 boul. Laure Ouest, Sept-Îles, QC, Canada G4R 4K1; phone (418) 962-1238 or (888) 880-1238.

MUSEUM OF THE NORTH SHORE REGION (Musée Régional de la Côte-Nord), 500 boul. Laure, presents a permanent exhibition devoted to the area's history. Also displayed are changing exhibits of works by regional and well known artists, as well as

expositions about the natural sciences, archeology and ethnology of the north shore and its history.

Allow 1 hour minimum. Daily 9-5, June 25-Labour Day; Tues.-Fri. 10-noon and 1-5, Sat.-Sun. 1-5, rest of year. Closed Jan. 1-2 and Dec. 25-26. Admission $5, over 65 and students with ID $4. Phone (418) 968-2070.

OLD TRADING POST (Vieux Poste de Traite), at end of Shimun Street, replicates a 17th-century Hudson Bay French trading post. Exhibits include collections of archeological artifacts, handicrafts and fauna of the North Shore region. Allow 1 hour, 30 minutes minimum. Daily 9-5, June 25-third week in Aug. Admission $3. Phone (418) 968-2070.

SHAWINIGAN (E-4) pop. 17,535

CITY OF ENERGY (La Cité de l'Énergie), 1000 av. Melville, is a science and technology theme park located near Shawinigan Falls, source of vast quantities of hydroelectric power. The history of the city of Shawinigan and its significant roles in the fields of hydroelectricity and the pulp, paper, aluminum and electrochemical industries are explained.

The bilingual exhibits include interactive modules and state-of-the-art multimedia presentations. Visitors can visit the Shawinigan-2 hydroelectric power station, take a ride on a ferryboat, and enjoy the view from the 38-floor observation tower.

Food is available. The 2007 schedule is daily 10-6, June 26-Sept. 3; Tues.-Sun. 10-5, June 9-June 25 and Sept. 4-30. Last admission 2 hours before closing. Admission $16; over 65, $15; students with ID $14; ages 6-12, $9. Family rate, two adults and one child, $36; two adults and two children (additional children $5 each) $38. City tours or river cruises $10. Phone to verify prices. MC, VI. Phone (819) 536-8516 or (866) 900-2483

"ECLYPS" is presented in the City of Energy at 1000 av. Melville. This unusual evening stage performance incorporates drama, dance, music, acrobatics and pyrotechnics in a round open-air theater with a roof but no walls. Scenery revolves around the audience and a rotating platform rotates the entire audience. The play discusses the mythology of the Earth's moon.

Note: The show is in French, but a printed plot summary in English may be available. Guests must remain in the theater for the entire show. Food is available. Allow 2 hours minimum. Performances Tues.-Sat. at dusk, July 10-Aug. 25. Phone to verify schedule. Admission $48; under 13, $18. MC, VI. Phone (819) 536-8516 or (866) 900-2483.

SHERBROOKE (E-9) pop. 75,916

Once a hunting and fishing ground of the Abenaki Indians, Sherbrooke is now a center for both transportation and industry. In 1796 Gilbert

Hyatt chose this site at the confluence of the Magog and St. Francis rivers for his mill. The settlement was named after Hyatt, but in 1818 the name was changed to honor Sir John Coape Sherbrooke, then governor of Canada.

Adding color to the city are more than 50,000 plants arranged in decorative mosaics at several sites downtown, including the area near the courthouse on rue Grandes Fourches and along rue King Ouest and rue Portland. Enrollment at the University of Sherbrooke is 22,000.

Sherbrooke Tourism Bureau: 2964 rue King Ouest, Sherbrooke, QC, Canada J1L 1Y7; phone (819) 821-1919 or (800) 561-8331.

Shopping areas: Two malls serve the Sherbrooke area: Carrefour de l'Estrie, 3050 boul. Portland, and Galerie 4 Saisons, 930 13ème av. Nord. Among Carrefour de l'Estrie's 190 stores are Sears and Zellers; Galerie 4 Saisons also has a Zellers among its 80 stores.

BEAUVOIR SHRINE (Sanctuaire de Beauvoir), Hwy. 10 exit 143 via boul. St-François to 169 ch. Beauvoir, provides a panorama from 366 metres (1,201 ft.) above the St. Francis Valley. Daily 8 a.m.-8:30 p.m., early May-late Oct. Donations. Phone (819) 569-2535.

MUSEUM OF NATURE AND SCIENCES (Musée de la nature et des sciences), 225 rue Frontenac, allows visitors to explore nature and the life sciences through varied exhibits and hands-on activities.

Wed.-Sun. 10-5. Admission $7.50; over 55 and students with ID $6.75; ages 4-17, $5; family rate (two adults and two children, extra children $1 each) $20. VI. Phone (819) 564-3200.

THE SHERBROOKE UNIVERSITY CULTURAL CENTRE'S ART GALLERY (Galerie d'Art du Centre Culturel de l'Université), at 2500 boul. de l'Université, is next to the Maurice O'Bready Concert Hall. This contemporary art gallery is dedicated to the presentation of regional, national and international exhibitions of works in various media by professional artists.

Food is available. Open Mon.-Fri. 12:30-5, Sat.-Sun. 1-5 during the school year; Thurs.-Sat. 1-10, Sun. 1-5, during summer session. Closed between exhibitions. Phone to verify schedule. Admission free. Parking $4.25-$6.50. Phone (819) 821-8000, ext. 63748.

SILLERY—*see Québec p. 223.*

STANBRIDGE-EAST (F-8) pop. 908

Stanbridge-East, in the fertile farming and dairying region of the Eastern Townships (Cantons-del'Est), was settled in the early 1800s by British sympathizers, also known as United Empire Loyalists, who had fled the United States after the Revolutionary War.

MISSISQUOI MUSEUM (Musée de Missisquoi), 2 rue River (Hwy. 2), is a rural complex of three buildings. The three-story main building, historic Cornell Mill, dates from 1830 and has displays of 19th-century domestic arts, artifacts, local historic memorabilia and a model village. Near the mill is Hodge's General Store, furnished with the inventory of a typical country store of the late 19th and early 20th centuries. Bill's Barn contains old farm equipment.

Allow 1 hour, 30 minutes minimum. Daily 10-5, last Sun. in May-second Sun. in Oct. Admission $5; over 65, $4; students with ID $1. MC, VI. Phone (450) 248-3153.

STANSTEAD—*see Rock Island p. 225.*

STONEHAM-ET-TEWKESBURY—
see Québec p. 223.

TADOUSSAC (C-6) pop. 870

At the confluence of the St. Lawrence and Saguenay rivers, Tadoussac reigned as capital of the territory allotted to Pierre Chauvin for his trade with the Indians. A reconstruction of the Chauvin dwelling contains artifacts recovered from the area. A cross near the village church commemorates the visit of Jacques Cartier in 1535.

Dominating the town's horizon is the red-roofed colonial-style Hôtel Tadoussac, a popular summer resort. Free ferry service is available between Tadoussac and Baie-Ste-Catherine; phone (418) 235-4395 for schedules.

Expeditions to watch whales that travel the St. Lawrence to the mouth of the Saguenay to feed from June to October, can be arranged in Tadoussac and Les Bergeronnes *(see place listing p. 170),* 25 kilometres (16 mi.) northeast. It is often very cold in the middle of the St. Lawrence, which is 10 miles wide at this point, so warm clothing and dressing in layers is advisable. Although whales usually are sighted on trips, there is no guarantee they will be. Calm weather increases the probability of sighting whales. Tours may require a minimum number of passengers. Inquire about weather policies.

Vessels range from luxurious triple-deck boats to dinghies. Some companies make pickups at the north end of the Saguenay at Baie-Ste-Catherine *(see place listing p. 160)* as well as at Tadoussac. Companies providing whale-watching cruises are Compagnie de la Baie Tadoussac, (418) 235-4642 or (800) 563-4643; Croisières AML, (800) 563-4643; Croisières Groupe Dufour, (418) 855-1384 or (800) 463-5250; Cruises 2001 Inc., (418) 235-3333 or (800) 694-5489; Express Cruise, (418) 235-4642 or (800) 563-4643.

DUNES INTERPRETATION CENTER (La Maison des Dunes) is 5 km (3 mi.) e. of Hwy. 138 at 750 ch. du Moulin à Baude in Saguenay-St. Lawrence Marine Park. The center, in a restored 1922 stone house at the summit of the dunes, provides scenic views of the St. Lawrence and Saguenay rivers. Exhibits interpret the history of the region and the sand dunes formed by glacial action in the last ice age.

Allow 30 minutes minimum. Daily 7-7, mid-June through early Oct. Admission $3.50; family rate (two adults and children under age 18) $7. Phone (418) 235-4238. See Saguenay-St. Lawrence Marine Park p. 224.

THE MARINE MAMMAL INTERPRETATION CENTRE (Centre d'interprétation des mammifères marins), 108 de la Cale-Sèche, educates visitors about the world's largest mammal—the whale. Visitors can compare a whale's breathing patterns to their own, listen to the singing of the whales and see a model of the world's second largest whale. There are several hands-on exhibits, and bilingual guides are available to answer questions.

Allow 1 hour minimum. Daily 9-8, mid-June through late Sept.; noon-5, mid-May through early June and in Oct. Admission $6.25; over 65, $4; ages 6-12, $3; family rate $14. MC, VI. Phone (418) 235-4701.

THE OLD CHAPEL (Petite Chapelle), on the St. Lawrence riverfront off Hwy. 138, rue Bord de l'Eau, is on the site of the oldest Indian mission in Canada. The original Jesuit chapel, built in 1642, was burned in 1665; the present structure dates from 1747. Daily 9-6, mid-June through early Sept. Admission $2; ages 7-14, 50c. Phone (418) 235-4324.

POINTE-NOIRE INTERPRETATION AND OBSERVATION CENTRE (Centre d'interprétation et d'observation de Pointe-Noire), on Rte. 138, 1.6 km (1 mi.) s. of the Tadoussac ferry dock, is part of the Saguenay-St. Lawrence Marine Park (see listing p. 224). Visitors can observe marine mammals, especially beluga whales. Stairways descend from the interpretation center to a platform, perched on rocks above the water, offering a view of the fjord and the St. Lawrence River.

Daily 9-6, mid-June through Labour Day; Fri.-Sun. 9-5, day after Labour Day-second Mon. in Oct. Admission $5.45; senior citizens $4.70; ages 6-16, $2.70; family rate $13.60. Phone (800) 237-4460 or (888) 773-8888.

TERREBONNE—see Montréal p. 196.

THETFORD MINES (E-5) pop. 16,628

[SAVE] **THETFORD MINES MINING AND MINER-ALOGICAL MUSEUM** (Musée Minéralogique et Minier de la Thetford Mines), 711 boul. Frontenac Ouest, focuses on asbestos, mineralogy, geology and mining operations. Collections include more than 8,000 mineral specimens from around the world, including one 3.8 billion years old. Five different exhibitions are presented each year. A 2-hour guided tour of an asbestos mine departs the museum. English narration is available.

Daily 9-6, mid-June through early Aug.; 9-5, mid-Aug. through Labour Day; 1-5, rest of year. Phone to verify schedule. Museum admission $8, senior citizens $7, students with ID $3.50, under 7 free. Museum and mine tour (no discount) $18; ages 6-17, $10. Phone to verify prices. MC, VI. Phone (418) 335-2123.

TROIS-RIVIÈRES (E-5) pop. 46,264

Founded in 1634, Trois-Rivières is the second oldest French city in the province. As a frontier post, it served as a rampart against Iroquois invasion and as a center for trade with the enemies of the Iroquois, the Huron, who brought furs down the St. Maurice River from the Great Lakes region.

Trois-Rivières also was a departure point for a number of legendary explorers: Pierre Gaultier de Varennes was one of the first to see the Rocky Mountains; Pierre Esprit Radisson and Médard Chouart Des Groseilliers traveled to Lake Superior and Hudson Bay; and Father Jacques Marquette explored the Mississippi River and the Midwest.

Trois-Rivières' early importance stemmed from its location. At the junction of the St. Lawrence and the three channels—hence its name—of the St. Maurice River, and halfway between Montréal and Québec, the settlement became a major crossroads for New France in the 1700s.

Location continues to play a vital role, ensuring the city's status as one of the world's largest paper-manufacturing centers. Harbourfront Park (Parc portuaire) is a riverfront park on the site of the old port.

The Pulp and Papers Industry Exhibition Center (Centre d'Exposition sur l'Industrie des Pâtes et Papiers), at 800 parc Portuaire, has an exhibit detailing the processes required in this important local industry; phone (819) 372-4633.

The Laviolette Bridge is one of Canada's longest at 3,490 metres (11,450 ft.) and the only bridge between Québec and Montréal to span the St. Lawrence River.

Trois-Rivières' old section, the rue des Ursulines and its adjoining side streets, is characterized by 18th-century-style structures. The renovated 1794 Manoir de Tonnancour, 864 rue des Ursulines, houses a gallery of contemporary art. Phone (819) 374-2355.

The Manoir Boucher-de-Niverville, 168 rue Bonaventure, is an 18th-century manor house that contains the chamber of commerce. The first floor contains Québec memorabilia. Phone (819) 375-9628.

Nearby Sainte-Anne-de-la-Pérade, is well-known for its tom cod. From Christmas to early February a village of shacks is built on the Rivière Sainte-Anne to accommodate thousands of sport fishers.

Trois-Rivières Chamber of Commerce—Trois-Rivières: 168 rue Bonaventure, C.P. 1045, Trois-Rivières, QC, Canada G9A 5K4; phone (819) 375-9628.

Shopping areas: Two major shopping malls serve the Trois-Rivières area: Le Centre Commercial Les Rivières, with 117 stores at 4125 boul. des Forges, and Carrefour Trois-Rivières Ouest, with 123 stores at 4520 boul. Royal Trois-Rivières Ouest.

THE FLAMBEAU is in Place Pierre Boucher. This shaft of granite commemorates the city's tercentenary in 1934. Financed by the contributions of local schoolchildren, it is dedicated to those who contributed to the city's growth.

THE FORGES OF SAINT MAURICE NATIONAL HISTORIC SITE OF CANADA (Lieu historique national du Canada des Forges-du-Saint-Maurice), 13 km (8 mi.) n. at 10000 boul. des Forges, is the 50-hectare (124-acre) site of Canada's first industrial community. From 1730 to 1883 the industrial village of Trois-Rivières influenced the economic, political and social climate of Canada. The forge mainly produced iron bars for shipbuilding, stoves, pots and pans, kettles, horseshoes, wagon wheels, axes and ammunition.

The two main interpretation centers, the Ironmaster's House and the Blast Furnace present the story of cast-iron making, charcoal making and the processes of treating such raw materials as iron ore. A sound and light show presents a scale model of the village of the period. A variety of interpretation activities is offered.

English narration and picnic facilities are available Allow 1 hour, 30 minutes minimum for guided tours. Daily 9:30-5:30, mid-May through Labour Day; 9:30-4:30, day after Labour Day-second Mon. in Oct. Admission $3.95; over 65, $3.45; ages 6-16, $1.95; family rate $9.90. Phone (819) 378-5116 or (888) 773-8888.

PIERRE BOUCHER MUSEUM (Musée Pierre Boucher) is at 858 rue Laviolette. This living heritage museum presents changing displays of artifacts, furnishings and tools, and exhibits regional art. Tues.-Sun. 1:30-4:30 and 7-9. Free. Phone (819) 376-4459.

SAVE **THE QUÉBEC MUSEUM OF FOLK CULTURE** (Musée québécois de culture populaire) is at 200 rue Laviolette. This facility offers visitors a chance to explore six exhibit rooms detailing Québec's society and folk art. The decommissioned historic Trois-Rivières Prison features the interactive "Go to Jail!" exhibit in which guides are ex-convicts who explain prison life in the 1960s and '70s.

Guided tours in English and French are offered. Allow 1 hour, 30 minutes minimum. Daily 10-6, June 24-Labour Day; Tues.-Sun. 10-5, rest of year. Closed Jan. 1 and Dec. 24-25 and 31. Museum admission $8; senior citizens $7; students with ID $6; ages 5-17, $5; family rate (two adults and two children) $20. Separate individual admission to the prison is available. Phone to verify prices. MC, VI. Phone (819) 372-0406.

TROIS-RIVIÈRES CATHEDRAL (Cathédrale de Trois-Rivières) is at 363 rue Bonaventure. This beautiful example of Westminster Gothic architecture was begun in 1858. The stained-glass windows by Guido Nincheri are some of the finest in North America. Mon.-Fri. 7-11:30 and 1:30-5:45, Sat. 9-11 and 1:30-5:15, Sun. 9:30-noon and 2-6. Free. Phone (819) 374-2409.

URSULINE MONASTERY (Couvent des Ursulines), 734 rue des Ursulines near St. James' Anglican Church, dates from 1697 and houses a museum and an art collection. The architecture is typical of convents in Normandy, France. A sundial dating from 1860 is on the exterior wall of the monastery.

Ursuline Museum (Musée des Ursulines), 734 rue des Ursulines, has a large collection of textiles, books, silverware and decorative arts collected by the Ursuline nuns of Trois-Rivières since the late 17th century. Across the street, Ursulines Gardens (Jardin des Ursulines) provides scenic views of the St. Lawrence River. Guided tours of the Ursuline chapel are available; English narration is available.

Tues.-Sun.10-5, May-Nov.; Wed.-Sun. 1-5, Mar.-Apr.; other times by appointment. Admission $3.50, over 65 and students with ID $2.50. Phone (819) 375-7922.

VAL-DAVID (E-4) pop. 3,819

Val-David is a Laurentian village of artists and artisans. For physical recreation the 22-metre-high (70-ft.) Mont Condor and the 23-metre-high (75-ft.) Condor Needle offer challenging climbs.

Québec Federation for Climbing and Mountaineering: 4545, av. Pierre-de-Coubertin, Succursale M, Montréal, QC, Canada H1V 3R2; phone (514) 252-3004 or (866) 204-3763.

SANTA CLAUS' VILLAGE (Village du Père Noël) is at 987 rue Morin, 2 km (1.2 mi.) n. from Autoroute 15 exit 76; take Hwy. 117 n., then e. at the first traffic light. This summer residence of Father Christmas offers 40 recreational facilities such as slides, an electric train, pedal boats, climbing nets and a 10 metre (32 ft.) high decorated Christmas tree which spouts jets of water onto visitors frolicking in a wading pool. A petting zoo houses goats, pot-bellied pigs, small sheep, lamas and fallow deer.

Picnicking is permitted. Allow 2 hours minimum. Daily 10-6, June-Aug.; Sat.-Sun. 10-6, Labour Day weekend. Phone for winter holiday schedule. Admission $10.50; over 65, $8; under 2 free. MC, VI. Phone (819) 322-2146 or (800) 287-6635.

VAL-D'OR (C-2) pop. 22,748

THE CITY OF GOLD (La Cité de l'Or) is at 90 Perreault av. Visitors don overalls and mining hats to descend 91 metres (298 ft.) into a gold mine where a bilingual guide details how gold is mined during the 2.5-hour tour. Surface exhibits include a museum, a laboratory where the guide explains gold-extraction methods, the workers' locker room and the massive hoist used to haul ore to the surface. A tour of the 1935 mining village also is available. **Note:** The temperature in the mine is 7 C (45 F), so dress warmly; closed shoes are required.

Food is available. Allow 3 hours minimum. Guided tours daily 8-1:30, late June-Labour Day; by reservation rest of year. Phone to verify tour times. **Note:** If you reserve a tour time, specify French or English tour preference.

Combined mine tour and surface exhibits $32.60; over 60 and students with ID $26.08; ages 6-11, $15.65; family rate $87.37. Mine tour only $21.73; over 60 and students with ID $17.39; ages 6-11, $10.43; family rate $58.25. Surface exhibits only $15.65; over 60 and students with ID $13.04; ages 6-11, $10.43; family rate $41.73. Under age 6 are not permitted on the mine tour. Reservations are requested. MC, VI. Phone (819) 825-7616.

VAUDREUIL-DORION—*see Montréal p. 197.*

VICTORIAVILLE (E-5) pop. 38,841

Victoriaville grew rapidly as its wood and metal industries developed. Now an economic center of the Bois-Francs region, the town is known for its Victorian houses.

LAURIER MUSEUM (Musée Laurier), 16 rue Laurier Ouest, was once the home of Sir Wilfrid Laurier, the first French-Canadian prime minister—he held office 1896-1911. Built in 1876, the Victorian mansion houses a collection of Laurier memorabilia and furniture, and temporary historical and political exhibits. The Pavillon Hôtel des Postes, a striking 1910 Second-Empire style post office, presents fine arts exhibits.

Allow 30 minutes minimum. Mon.-Fri. 10-5, Sat.-Sun. 1-5, July-Aug.; Tues.-Fri. 10-noon and 1-5, Sat.-Sun. 1-5, rest of year. Admission $5; over 65, $4; students with ID and ages 13-18, $3; ages 7-12, $2. Phone (819) 357-8655.

VILLE-MARIE (D-1) pop. 2,770

BROTHER MOFFET'S HOUSE (Maison du Frère Moffet), 2 blks. w. of Hwy. 101 at 7 rue Notre-Dame-de-Lourdes, was built in 1881 of interlocked logs, and features period furniture and clothing. An herb garden and tool shed also are on the grounds. Guided tours of the house are available; English narration is available. Allow 1 hour minimum. Daily 10-6, June 21-Labour Day; by appointment early May to mid-June. Admission $2.50, under 12 free. Phone (819) 629-3533.

VILLE DE MONT-TREMBLANT—
Mont-Tremblant p. 198.

WENDAKE—*see Québec p. 223.*

WESTMOUNT—*see Montréal p. 197.*

Where a boy's home is his castle,

no matter what his age.

AAA/CAA Travel offers Disney vacations

with all the special benefits you could wish for.

Only Disney vacations offer the magic and memories that dreams are made of. And only *Walt Disney World*® Resort packages offered by *AAA Vacations*® offer such special benefits and great values. So call or stop by your AAA/CAA Travel Office today.

Walt Disney World®

Because the voyage of your dreams
just happens to be theirs, too.

AAA/CAA Travel adds special
benefits to your Disney dreams.

On a *Disney Cruise Line*®
vacation, you'll find something
enchanting for everyone of
every age—it's the kind of
magic only Disney can create.
And when you book through
AAA/CAA Travel, you'll enjoy
many special benefits! So call
or stop by your AAA/CAA
Travel Office today.

New Brunswick

Riverside-Albert
© Walter Bibikow
Danita Delimont Agency

ALMA pop. 290

——— **WHERE TO STAY** ———

PARKLAND VILLAGE INN

CAA SAVE

Small-scale Hotel

5/25-10/1   1P: $85-$135   2P: $95-$145   Phone: (506)887-2313
5/1-5/24 & 10/2-11/14   1P: $75-$95   2P: $85-$125   XP: $10   XP: $5
Location: On Rt 114; centre. 8601 Main St E4H 1N6. **Fax:** 506/887-2315. **Facility:** Smoke free premises. 15 units. 10 one- and 3 two-bedroom standard units. 2 one-bedroom suites ($85-$135). 3 stories (no elevator), interior/exterior corridors. *Bath:* combo or shower only. **Parking:** on-site. **Terms:** open 5/1-11/14, cancellation fee imposed. **Amenities:** hair dryers. **Dining:** Tides Restaurant, see separate listing. **Leisure Activities:** limited beach access. **Guest Services:** wireless Internet. **Business Services:** meeting rooms. **Cards:** MC, VI. **Free Special Amenities:** local telephone calls and newspaper. *(See color ad below)*

——— *The following lodging was either not evaluated or did not* ———
meet AAA rating requirements but is listed for your information only.

CAPTAINS INN

fyi

Phone: 506/887-2017

Not evaluated. **Location:** On Rt 114; centre. 8602 Main St E4H 1N5. Facilities, services, and decor characterize a mid-range property.

——— **WHERE TO DINE** ———

TIDES RESTAURANT

CAA

Canadian

Lunch: $7-$14   **Dinner:** $9-$22   **Phone:** 506/887-2313
Location: On Rt 114; centre; in Parkland Village Inn. 8601 Main St E4H 1N6. **Hours:** Open 5/15-10/31; 8 am-9 pm; hours vary off season. **Reservations:** accepted. **Features:** This harbourfront restaurant offers both indoor and outdoor patio dining overlooking the wonderful Bay of Fundy. Specializing in fresh seafood including lobster, they also serve a fine variety of steak, ribs, chicken and pasta entrees. Casual dress; cocktails. **Parking:** on-site. **Cards:** MC, VI. *(See color ad below)*

BAS-CARAQUET pop. 1,689

——— **WHERE TO STAY** ———

LES CHALETS DE LA PLAGE

Cottage

5/28-4/30   1P: $125   2P: $125   Phone: (506)726-8920
5/1-5/27   1P: $99   2P: $99   XP: $20   F
    XP: $20   F
Location: Oceanfront. Jct Rt 11 and 145, 5 mi (8 km) e on Rt 145. 2 rue du Phare E1W 1M9. **Fax:** 506/726-8921. **Facility:** These lovely one- and two-story cottages are fully equipped and offer nice decks with barbecues. 17 cottages. 1 story, exterior corridors. **Parking:** on-site. **Terms:** office hours 7 am-11 pm, package plans. **Amenities:** DVD players, irons, hair dryers. **Leisure Activities:** beach access, playground. **Guest Services:** coin laundry. **Business Services:** meeting rooms. **Cards:** AX, MC, VI.

BATHURST pop. 12,924

——— **WHERE TO STAY** ———

ATLANTIC HOST HOTEL   *Book at AAA.com*

Small-scale Hotel

All Year   1P: $88-$98   2P: $94-$120   Phone: (506)548-3335
    XP: $5   F12
Location: Rt 11, exit 310 (Vanier Blvd). 1450 Vanier Blvd E2A 4H7 (PO Box 910). **Fax:** 506/548-9769. **Facility:** 100 one-bedroom standard units. 2 stories (no elevator), interior corridors. **Parking:** on-site, winter plug-ins. **Terms:** package plans, small pets only. **Amenities:** video library (fee), voice mail, hair dryers. *Some:* honor bars, irons. **Dining:** Atlantic Host Restaurant, see separate listing. **Pool(s):** heated indoor. **Leisure Activities:** sauna, whirlpool, racquetball court, cross country skiing, bicycles, hiking trails, exercise room. **Guest Services:** wireless Internet. **Business Services:** meeting rooms, PC. **Cards:** AX, MC, VI.

SOME UNITS

Moments
that
Matter

COMFORT INN
Phone: (506)547-8000

6/16-9/15 [CP]	1P: $88-$90	2P: $88-$100	XP: $10 F17
5/1-6/15 & 9/16-10/15 [CP]	1P: $79-$81	2P: $89-$91	XP: $10 F17
10/16-4/30 [CP]	1P: $71-$73	2P: $81-$83	XP: $10 F17

Small-scale Hotel   **Location:** 2.1 mi (3.4 km) n on Rt 134 (St Peter's Ave). Located in a commercial area. 1170 St Peter's Ave E2A 2Z9.
Fax: 506/548-2477. **Facility:** 78 one-bedroom standard units, some with whirlpools. 2 stories (no elevator), interior corridors.
Parking: on-site. **Terms:** small pets only (on ground floor). **Amenities:** video library (fee), irons, hair dryers. *Some:* high-speed
Internet, dual phone lines. **Guest Services:** wireless Internet. **Business Services:** PC. **Cards:** AX, DC, DS, MC, VI.
(See color ad card insert)

SOME UNITS

(A$K) (S•D) (⚑) (Ⅱ→) (📷) (▣) / (✕) (VCR) (📶) (📠) /
FEE

DANNY'S INN & CONFERENCE CENTRE
Phone: (506)546-6621

6/16-8/31	1P: $80-$90	2P: $90-$100	XP: $8 F18
5/1-6/15 & 9/1-4/30	1P: $72-$82	2P: $72-$82	XP: $8 F18

Small-scale Hotel   **Location:** Rt 11, exit 310 (Vanier Blvd) northbound to Rt 134 (St Peter's Ave), 2.5 mi (4 km) n; exit 318 southbound to
Rt 134 (St Peter's Ave), 2.3 mi (3.8 km) s. Located in a rural area. (PO Box 180, E2A 3Z2). Fax: 506/548-3266.
Facility: 37 units. 36 one-bedroom standard units, some with efficiencies, kitchens and/or whirlpools. 1 one-bedroom suite
($134-$149) with whirlpool. 1 story, interior/exterior corridors. **Parking:** on-site, winter plug-ins. **Terms:** package plans, small
pets only. **Amenities:** video library, voice mail, hair dryers. *Some:* high-speed Internet, dual phone lines, honor bars, irons.
Dining: Danny's, see separate listing. **Pool(s):** heated outdoor. **Leisure Activities:** tennis court, playground, game room.
Guest Services: valet laundry, wireless Internet. **Business Services:** conference facilities. **Cards:** AX, DC, DS, MC, VI.

SOME UNITS

(S•D) (✈→) (⚑) (Ⅱ) (Y) (🏊) (🏄) (✕) (VCR) (▣) / (✕) (📶) /

LAKEVIEW INNS & SUITES
Phone: (506)548-4949

1/1-4/30 [ECP]	1P: $96-$106	2P: $96-$106	XP: $10 F18
5/1-12/31 [ECP]	1P: $94-$104	2P: $94-$104	XP: $10 F18

Small-scale Hotel   **Location:** 1.8 mi (3 km) n on Rt 134 (St Peter's Ave). Located in a residential area. 777 St Peter's Ave E2A 2Y9.
Fax: 506/548-8595. **Facility:** 78 units. 40 one-bedroom standard units. 38 one-bedroom suites, some with
whirlpools. 3 stories, interior corridors. **Parking:** on-site. **Terms:** $2 service charge, small pets only ($5 extra charge, on ground
floor). **Amenities:** video library, irons, hair dryers. **Guest Services:** coin laundry, wireless Internet. **Business Services:** meeting
rooms. **Cards:** AX, DC, DS, MC, VI. *(See color ad on TourBookMark)*

SOME UNITS

(A$K) (S•D) (⚑) (Ⅱ→) (♿M) (VCR) (📶) (▣) / (✕) (📠) /
FEE

--------- **WHERE TO DINE** ---------

ATLANTIC HOST RESTAURANT   **Lunch:** $7-$11   **Dinner:** $9-$18   **Phone:** 506/548-3335

Canadian   **Location:** Rt 11, exit 310 (Vanier Blvd); in Atlantic Host Hotel. **Hours:** 6:30 am-10 pm. Closed: 12/25.
Reservations: accepted. **Features:** The pleasant, family restaurant features a good variety of seafood,
beef, pasta and chicken dishes, as well as fresh sandwiches, salads and soups. The delicious array of rich
desserts created by the in-house pastry chef is sure to satisfy the sweet tooth. Casual dress; cocktails.
Parking: on-site. **Cards:** AX, CB, DC, MC, VI.   (Y)

DANNY'S   **Lunch:** $8-$12   **Dinner:** $14-$24   **Phone:** 506/546-6621

Canadian   **Location:** Rt 11, exit 310 (Vanier Blvd) northbound to Rt 134 (St Peter's Ave), 2.5 mi (4 km) n; exit 318 southbound to
Rt 134 (St Peter's Ave), 2.3 mi (3.8 km) s; in Danny's Inn & Conference Centre. **Hours:** 7 am-10 pm. Closed: 1/1,
12/25. **Reservations:** suggested. **Features:** This attractive dining room and coffee shop with two fireplaces
and a patio that's perfect for outdoor dining, is the comfortable setting for an overall good meal. Excellent
home-style desserts, tasty seafood, steak, ribs and chicken, are sure to please most any palate. Casual dress; cocktails.
Parking: on-site. **Cards:** AX, CB, DC, DS, MC, VI.   (Y)

HOUSE OF LEE   **Lunch:** $7-$12   **Dinner:** $10-$18   **Phone:** 506/548-3019

Chinese   **Location:** Centre. 315 Main St E2A 1B1. **Hours:** 11 am-10 pm, Fri & Sat-11 pm, Sun 3 pm-10 pm. Closed:
12/25. **Reservations:** accepted. **Features:** The spacious restaurant has several dining areas, including a
back section that affords a fine view of the harbor. On the menu is a wide variety of Chinese and Canadian
cuisine. Another choice is the daily buffet. Casual dress; cocktails. **Parking:** on-site. **Cards:** AX, MC, VI.

THE MEGALODON PUB   **Lunch:** $6-$12   **Dinner:** $8-$16   **Phone:** 506/547-8384

Canadian   **Location:** At St Peter's Ave. 100 Main St E2A 1A3. **Hours:** 10 am-midnight. Closed: 12/25. **Features:** In the
heart of town, the upbeat sports bar has pool tables and TVs. In addition to classic pub foods, the menu lists
popular brick-oven pizzas. Several draft beers are among beverage choices. Casual dress; cocktails.
Parking: street. **Cards:** MC, VI.   (Y)

ST-HUBERT BBQ   **Lunch:** $6-$11   **Dinner:** $8-$16   **Phone:** 506/548-4413

Barbecue   **Location:** 2 mi (3.5 km) n on Rt 134 (St Peter's Ave). 1244 St Peter's Ave E2A 2Z9. **Hours:** 11 am-9 pm, Fri & Sat-
10 pm. Closed: 12/25. **Reservations:** accepted. **Features:** The pleasantly decorated family-friendly
restaurant serves affordable chicken dinners, ribs, club sandwiches, chicken wings, salads, soups and hot
chicken sandwiches. The children's menu includes animal nuggets. Casual dress; cocktails. **Parking:** on-
site. **Cards:** AX, DC, MC, VI.

BLOOMFIELD

--------- **WHERE TO STAY** ---------

EVELYN'S BED & BREAKFAST
Phone: (506)832-7788

All Year	1P: $70	2P: $90	XP: $20 F

Bed & Breakfast   **Location:** Hwy 1, exit 166, follow signs. Located in a rural area. 374 Rt 121 E5N 4T4. Fax: 506/832-4450.
Facility: Smoke free premises. 4 one-bedroom standard units. 2 stories (no elevator), interior corridors.
Bath: combo or shower only. **Parking:** on-site. **Terms:** office hours 7 am-10:30 pm, check-in 4 pm, 7 day
cancellation notice-fee imposed, weekly rates available, package plans. **Amenities:** video library, hair dryers. **Pool(s):** heated
outdoor. **Leisure Activities:** playground. **Cards:** AX, JC, MC, VI.

(A$K) (🏄) (✕) (🎿) (VCR) (Ⓩ)

BOUCTOUCHE pop. 2,426

———— **WHERE TO STAY** ————

AUBERGE BOUCTOUCHE INN & SUITES
▼▼ ▼▼
Phone: 506/743-5003

| | 6/16-9/5 | 2P: $119 | XP: $10 | F16 |
| | 5/1-6/15 & 9/6-4/30 | 2P: $79 | XP: $10 | F16 |

Small-scale Hotel   **Location:** Rt 11, exit 32A/B. 50 Industrielle St E4S 3H9. Fax: 506/743-8005. **Facility:** 38 one-bedroom standard units, some with whirlpools. 2 stories (no elevator), interior corridors. *Bath:* combo or shower only. **Parking:** on-site. **Terms:** pets ($10 extra charge). **Amenities:** high-speed Internet, hair dryers. **Leisure Activities:** exercise room. **Business Services:** meeting rooms. **Cards:** AX, MC, VI.

ASK ▣ ▣ ▣ ▣ ▣ ▣ ▣ ▣ ▣
FEE

———— *The following lodging was either not evaluated or did not* ————
meet AAA rating requirements but is listed for your information only.

LE GITE DE LA SAGOUINE
(fyi)
Phone: 506/743-5554
Not evaluated. **Location:** On Rt 515; centre. 43 Irving Blvd E4S 3J5. Facilities, services, and decor characterize a mid-range property.

———— **WHERE TO DINE** ————

RESTAURANT LA SAGOUINE
▼▼ ▼▼
Lunch: $7-$12   **Dinner:** $9-$19   **Phone: 506/743-6606**
Location: On Rt 515; centre; in Le Gite de la Sagouine. 43 Irving Blvd E4S 3J5. **Hours:** 6 am-10 pm; hours vary off
Canadian   season. Closed: 12/25. **Features:** Pleasant dining in the heart of town, this country-style restaurant offers a selection of Acadian dishes and seafood cuisine. Nice patio dining is available in season. Casual dress; cocktails. **Parking:** on-site. **Cards:** AX, MC, VI.

CAMPBELLTON pop. 7,798

———— **WHERE TO STAY** ————

COMFORT INN
▼▼ ▼▼
Phone: (506)753-4121

| | 5/1-10/31 | 1P: $105-$120 | 2P: $115-$130 | XP: $10 | F18 |
| | 11/1-4/30 | 1P: $109-$110 | 2P: $110-$120 | XP: $10 | F18 |

Small-scale Hotel   **Location:** Hwy 11, exit 415, 0.6 mi (1 km) e on Sugarloaf St W. 111 chemin Val D'Amour E3N 5B9. Fax: 506/753-2238. **Facility:** 60 one-bedroom standard units. 2 stories (no elevator), interior/exterior corridors. **Parking:** on-site, winter plug-ins. **Terms:** pets (on ground floor). **Amenities:** irons, hair dryers. **Guest Services:** wireless Internet. **Cards:** AX, DC, DS, JC, MC, VI. *(See color ad card insert)*

ASK ▣ ▣ ▣ ▣ ▣ ▣ ▣/▣ ▣ ▣/   SOME UNITS
FEE   FEE

HOWARD JOHNSON   *Book great rates at AAA.com*
(CAA) (SAVE)
Phone: (506)753-4133
All Year   1P: $98-$117   2P: $98-$117   XP: $17   F17
▼▼ ▼▼   **Location:** Hwy 134; in City Centre Complex. 157 Water St E3N 3H2. Fax: 506/753-6386. **Facility:** 66 one-bedroom standard units. 5 stories, interior corridors. **Parking:** on-site. **Terms:** small pets only. **Amenities:** high-speed Internet, voice mail. *Some:* irons, hair dryers. **Dining:** 1026 Bar & Grill, see
Small-scale Hotel   separate listing. **Business Services:** meeting rooms. **Cards:** AX, DC, MC, VI. **Free Special Amenities:** continental breakfast and high-speed Internet.

▣ ▣ ▣ ▣ ▣/▣ ▣/   SOME UNITS

———— **WHERE TO DINE** ————

1026 BAR & GRILL
▼▼ ▼▼
Lunch: $6-$10   **Dinner:** $8-$16   **Phone: 506/753-3640**
Location: Hwy 134; in City Centre Complex; in Howard Johnson. 157 Water St E3N 3H2. **Hours:** 7 am-9 pm.
Canadian   **Features:** A casual mood pervades the popular sports bar. Guests can choose from daily specials, as well as items on the full menu, which lists steaks, seafood and a variety of finger foods. Casual dress; cocktails. **Parking:** on-site. **Cards:** AX, DC, MC, VI.
▣

CHEZ NIC DINER
▼▼
Lunch: $5-$11   **Dinner:** $7-$16   **Phone: 506/753-7897**
Location: Hwy 11, exit 415, 0.6 mi (1 km) e on Sugarloaf St; in Sugarloaf Mall. 312 chemin Val D'Amour E3N 4E2.
Canadian   **Hours:** 10 am-10 pm. Closed: 1/1, 12/25, 12/26; also Sun. **Features:** A '50s rock 'n' roll theme lends character to the spacious restaurant, which offers booth, table or soda bar seating. Widely ranging comfort foods are served in ample portions. Casual dress; cocktails. **Parking:** on-site. **Cards:** AX, MC, VI.

CHINA COAST RESTAURANT
▼▼ ▼▼
Lunch: $7-$12   **Dinner:** $9-$16   **Phone: 506/759-9660**
Location: Hwy 11, exit 415, 0.6 mi (1 km) e. 127 chemin Val D'Amour E3N 3S6. **Hours:** 11 am-11 pm, Fri-1 am, Sat
Chinese   3 pm-1 am, Sun 3 pm-11 pm. **Features:** Minimal Oriental decorations color the quiet dining room, where families gather to sample Chinese and Canadian food. Buffets lay out a good variety Wednesday through
MC, VI.   Friday for lunch and on the weekends for dinner. Casual dress; cocktails. **Parking:** on-site. **Cards:** AX,

SOMETHING ELSE RESTAURANT
▼▼ ▼▼
Dinner: $12-$25   **Phone: 506/753-7744**
Location: Centre; opposite City Hall. 65 Water St E3N 1A9. **Hours:** 5 pm-10 pm. Closed major holidays; also Sun
Regional   9/1-6/30. **Reservations:** suggested. **Features:** Homemade pasta, fresh seafood and locally grown produce
Canadian   are all featured on this menu of creative, well-prepared entrees. Enjoy a quiet, candlelit evening over a quality meal, topped off by the "Something Else" dessert of rich Belgium chocolate and almonds. Casual dress; cocktails. **Parking:** on-site. **Cards:** AX, DC, MC, VI.

UPPER DECK STEAKHOUSE **Lunch:** $8-$13 **Dinner:** $16-$26 **Phone:** 506/753-2225
♥♥ ♥♥ **Location:** Centre; adjacent to City Centre Complex. 15 Water St E3N 1A6. **Hours:** 11 am-9 pm, Sun from 10 am.
Steak & Seafood Closed: 12/25; also Mon. **Reservations:** suggested. **Features:** The atmosphere is casual and friendly in the steakhouse, which specializes in fine cuts of Alberta beef but also offers a good selection of seafood and Sunday brunch choices. Casual dress; cocktails. **Parking:** on-site. **Cards:** AX, MC, VI. ▼

CAMPOBELLO ISLAND pop. 1,300

———— **WHERE TO STAY** ————

———— *The following lodging was either not evaluated or did not* ————
meet AAA rating requirements but is listed for your information only.

THE LUPINE LODGE **Phone:** 506/752-2555
[fyi] Not evaluated. **Location:** Centre. 610 Rt 774 E5E 1A5. Facilities, services, and decor characterize a basic property.

———— **WHERE TO DINE** ————

THE LUPINE LODGE RESTAURANT **Lunch:** $6-$11 **Dinner:** $9-$20 **Phone:** 506/752-2555
♥♥ ♥♥ **Location:** Centre; in The Lupine Lodge. 610 Rt 774 E5E 1A4. **Hours:** Open 5/27-10/31; 8 am-9 pm.
Canadian **Reservations:** accepted. **Features:** With its massive central stone fireplace, log walls and fine ocean views, the lodge is a great stop for lunch or dinner. Varied meat entrees complement specialties of seafood. Casual dress; cocktails. **Parking:** on-site. **Cards:** MC, VI. ▼

CAP-PELE pop. 2,200

———— **WHERE TO STAY** ————

———— *The following lodging was either not evaluated or did not* ————
meet AAA rating requirements but is listed for your information only.

CHALETS DE L'ABOITEAU **Phone:** 506/577-2005
[fyi] Not evaluated. **Location:** Hwy 15, exit 53, 0.6 mi (1 km) n on Rt 950; in Aboiteau Park. 55 Chalets Ln. Facilities, services, and decor characterize a mid-range property.

———— **WHERE TO DINE** ————

FRED'S SEAFOOD RESTAURANT **Lunch:** $5-$15 **Dinner:** $5-$15 **Phone:** 506/577-4269
♥♥ ♥♥ **Location:** Hwy 15, exit 53, 0.6 mi (1 km) n on Rt 950. 2270 Acadie Rd E4N 2A5. **Hours:** 7 am-11 pm. Closed:
Canadian 12/25. **Reservations:** accepted. **Features:** Popular with the locals, the spacious restaurant serves a wide variety of Acadian and Canadian cuisine. The take-out bar opens seasonally. Casual dress; cocktails. **Parking:** on-site. **Cards:** AX, MC, VI.

CARAQUET pop. 4,442

———— **WHERE TO STAY** ————

GITE "LE POIRIER" BED & BREAKFAST **Phone:** (506)727-4359
♥♥♥ 6/24-9/1 1P: $89 2P: $98 XP: $25 F6
5/1-6/23 & 9/2-4/30 1P: $79 2P: $89 XP: $25 F6
Historic Bed **Location:** On Rt 11; centre. 98 St Pierre Blvd W E1W 1B6. Fax: 506/726-6084. **Facility:** This heart-of-town 1927
& Breakfast house, formerly a judge's residence, is now a tastefully decorated, service-oriented B&B. Smoke free premises. 5 one-bedroom standard units. 2 stories (no elevator), interior corridors. *Bath:* combo or shower only. **Parking:** on-site. **Terms:** office hours 7 am-11 pm, 2-3 night minimum stay - seasonal and/or weekends, age restrictions may apply, [BP] meal plan available, package plans. **Amenities:** DVD players, hair dryers. **Guest Services:** wireless Internet. **Cards:** AX, MC, VI. [icons]

GITE L'ISLE-DU-RANDONNEUR B & B

Phone: (506)727-3877

(CAA) (SAVE)

▽▽▽▽

Bed & Breakfast

All Year [BP]   1P: $69-$99   2P: $89-$109   XP: $20
Location: 3 mi (5 km) n on Rt 11. 539 St Pierre Blvd W E1W 1A3. Fax: 506/727-4109. **Facility:** Offering a pleasant view of Caraquet Bay, this home dating from 1850 borders on the New Brunswick bike trail and is walking distance from the beach. Smoke free premises. 4 units. 2 one-bedroom standard units. 1 one- and 1 two-bedroom suites. 2 stories (no elevator), interior corridors. **Bath:** combo or shower only. **Parking:** on-site. **Terms:** office hours 7 am-midnight, package plans. **Amenities:** hair dryers. *Some:* DVD players. **Leisure Activities:** sauna, whirlpool, hiking trails. **Guest Services:** complimentary evening beverages. **Cards:** VI. **Free Special Amenities: full breakfast and preferred room (subject to availability with advance reservations).**

SOME UNITS

[✕] [✕] / [🅰🅲] [VCR] [📶] /

HOTEL PAULIN

Phone: 506/727-9981

▽▽▽

**Historic
Country Inn**

7/1-9/15   1P: $105-$210   2P: $115-$235   XP: $25
5/1-6/30 & 9/16-4/30   1P: $89-$150   2P: $105-$180   XP: $25
Location: On Rt 11; centre. 143 St Pierre Blvd E1W 1B6. Fax: 506/727-4808. **Facility:** A handsome hotel built in 1891, the property offers a variety of tastefully decorated guest rooms and deluxe suites with exceptional views of the bay. Smoke free premises. 12 units. 8 one-bedroom standard units, some with whirlpools. 4 one-bedroom suites. 3 stories (no elevator), interior corridors. **Parking:** on-site. **Terms:** office hours 7 am-10 pm, 14 day cancellation notice-fee imposed, weekly rates available, package plans. **Amenities:** high-speed Internet, hair dryers. *Some:* DVD players, CD players, irons. **Dining:** restaurant, see separate listing. **Leisure Activities:** recreation programs, rental bicycles. *Fee:* spa services. **Business Services:** meeting rooms. **Cards:** MC, VI.

SOME UNITS

[ASK] [🍴] [✕] / [VCR] /

SUPER 8 MOTEL   *Book at AAA.com*

Phone: 506/727-0888

▽▽▽

Small-scale Hotel

Property failed to provide current rates
Location: Just e of jct Rt 11 and St Pierre Blvd E. 9 Carrefour Ave E1W 1B6. Fax: 506/727-4888. **Facility:** 50 units. 32 one-bedroom standard units, some with whirlpools. 18 one-bedroom suites. 3 stories, interior corridors. **Bath:** combo or shower only. **Parking:** on-site. **Terms:** small pets only ($10 fee). **Amenities:** high-speed Internet, irons, hair dryers. **Pool(s):** heated indoor. **Leisure Activities:** whirlpool, waterslide, playground. *Fee:* miniature golf. **Guest Services:** coin laundry. **Business Services:** meeting rooms.

SOME UNITS

[🛏] [🍴+] [♿M] [♿] [≋] [✕] [📶] [📷] [💻] / [✕] /
FEE

──── WHERE TO DINE ────

CARAQUETTE FAMILY RESTAURANT

Lunch: $5-$12   **Dinner:** $9-$20   **Phone:** 506/727-6009

▽▽ ▽▽

Canadian

Location: From jct Rt 11, 1 mi (1.6 km) e on Rt 145. 89 St Pierre Blvd E E1W 1B6. **Hours:** 5 am-10 pm, Fri & Sat-11 pm; to 9 pm 1/1-5/31 & 10/1-10/31. Closed major holidays. **Features:** Bordering the harbor and offering fine views of the Baie des Chaleurs, the family-style restaurant offers a menu of home-style cooking. Included are preparations of fresh seafood, steak, burgers and sandwiches. Casual dress; cocktails.
Parking: on-site. **Cards:** DS, MC, VI.

[🍸]

HOTEL PAULIN DINING ROOM

Dinner: $25-$40   **Phone:** 506/727-9981

▽▽▽

Canadian

Location: On Rt 11; centre; in Hotel Paulin. 143 St Pierre Blvd W E1W 1B6. **Hours:** 6 pm-9 pm. **Reservations:** required. **Features:** In a historic boutique hotel, the restaurant presents a daily changing menu of creative fresh local seafood, meats and produce. Reservations are required. Casual dress; cocktails. **Parking:** on-site. **Cards:** MC, VI. **Historic**

[🅰🅲]

MITCHAN SUSHI RESTAURANT

Dinner: $12-$18   **Phone:** 506/726-1103

▽▽▽

Japanese

Location: On Rt 11; centre. 114 St Pierre Blvd W E1W 1B6. **Hours:** 5 pm-10 pm. Closed: 12/25, 12/26; also Mon & Tues. **Reservations:** accepted. **Features:** Several pleasant dining sections fill two levels in the converted home. Fresh local seafood and curry dishes factor heavily on the menu of well-prepared Japanese cuisine. Casual dress; cocktails. **Parking:** on-site. **Cards:** MC, VI.

CHANCE HARBOUR

──── WHERE TO STAY ────

THE MARINER'S INN

Phone: (506)659-2619

(CAA) (SAVE)

▽▽▽▽

Country Inn

All Year [ECP]   1P: $110-$135   2P: $119-$139   XP: $15
Location: Hwy 1, exit 96, 5.6 mi (9 km) s on Rt 790; 18.7 mi (30 km) w of Saint John. Located in a quiet rural area. 32 Mawhinney Cove Rd E5J 2B8. Fax: 506/659-1890. **Facility:** An elevated view of the waterfront is offered from this tucked-away inn; some rooms feature patios, decks and seating areas. Smoke free premises. 11 one-bedroom standard units, some with efficiencies. 2 stories (no elevator), interior corridors. **Parking:** on-site. **Terms:** office hours 7 am-10 pm, 3 day cancellation notice-fee imposed, [MAP] meal plan available, package plans, pets ($10 fee, in designated unit). **Amenities:** video library, DVD players, hair dryers. **Dining:** 5 pm-9:30 pm, cocktails. **Leisure Activities:** whirlpool, rental bicycles. **Guest Services:** gift shop. **Business Services:** meeting rooms. **Cards:** AX, DC, DS, MC, VI. **Free Special Amenities: expanded continental breakfast and local telephone calls.**
(See color ad p 268)

SOME UNITS

[🛏] [🍴] [✕] [📺] / [📶] [📷] [💻] /
FEE

CHARLO pop. 1,449

──── WHERE TO STAY ────

The following lodging was either not evaluated or did not meet AAA rating requirements but is listed for your information only.

HERON'S NEST COTTAGES

Phone: 506/684-3766

[fyi]

Not evaluated. **Location:** 6 Heron's Nest Rd E8E 2L1. Facilities, services, and decor characterize a mid-range property.

COCAGNE pop. 2,659

──────── WHERE TO STAY ────────

COCAGNE MOTEL   **Phone:** 506/576-6657

Motel

Property failed to provide current rates
Location: Rt 11, exit 15, 0.6 mi (1 km) n on Rt 535. (PO Box 1043, E4R 1N6). Fax: 506/576-8227. **Facility:** 20 one-bedroom standard units, some with efficiencies. 2 stories (no elevator), exterior corridors. **Parking:** on-site. **Terms:** open 5/1-9/30, office hours 8 am-midnight, small pets only.

SOME UNITS

DALHOUSIE pop. 3,975

──────── WHERE TO STAY ────────

BEST WESTERN MANOIR ADELAIDE   *Book great rates at AAA.com*   **Phone:** (506)684-5681

Small-scale Hotel

All Year   1P: $109   2P: $119   XP: $7   F12
Location: Centre. 385 Adelaide St E8C 1B4. Fax: 506/684-3433. **Facility:** 52 one-bedroom standard units, some with efficiencies and/or whirlpools. 4 stories, interior corridors. **Parking:** on-site. **Terms:** [BP] & [CP] meal plans available, package plans, small pets only (must be attended). **Amenities:** irons, hair dryers. *Some:* high-speed Internet. **Dining:** Le Menuet, see separate listing. **Leisure Activities:** exercise room. **Guest Services:** coin laundry, wireless Internet. **Business Services:** meeting rooms, PC. **Cards:** AX, DC, DS, MC, VI.

SOME UNITS

──────── WHERE TO DINE ────────

CANTON PALACE   **Lunch:** $6-$10   **Dinner:** $9-$16   **Phone:** 506/684-3389

Chinese

Location: Centre. 436 William St E8C 2X6. **Hours:** 11:30 am-9 pm, Fri & Sat-10 pm. Closed: 12/25, 12/26; also Mon. **Reservations:** accepted. **Features:** In the heart of town, the cozy cafe serves a good selection of fresh seafood and other traditional cuisine. Some Canadian dishes also are available. Casual dress; cocktails. **Parking:** street. **Cards:** MC, VI.

LE MENUET   **Lunch:** $5-$15   **Dinner:** $9-$26   **Phone:** 506/684-5681

Canadian

DC, MC, VI.

Location: Centre; in Best Western Manoir Adelaide. 385 Adelaide St E8C 1B4. **Hours:** 7 am-10 pm. **Reservations:** accepted. **Features:** The candlelit dining room affords a view of Chaleur Bay and an active mill. The menu lists a variety of meat and seafood dishes, including steak, salmon, shrimp and trout. Among the delectable desserts is a tempting cheesecake. Casual dress; cocktails. **Parking:** on-site. **Cards:** AX,

DIEPPE pop. 14,951

──────── WHERE TO DINE ────────

JUNGLE JIM'S RESTAURANT   **Lunch:** $7-$11   **Dinner:** $8-$20   **Phone:** 506/854-5467

Canadian

Location: Adjacent to Champlain Mall. 451 Paul St E1A 6W8. **Hours:** 11 am-10 pm, Fri & Sat-midnight. Closed: 12/25. **Features:** Guests can step into a tropical theme at the casual eatery, which employs a friendly staff and nurtures a bustling atmosphere. The menu lines up a wide variety of comfort foods, salads, chicken, beef, seafood and hot wings, all served in ample, flavorful portions. Casual dress; cocktails. **Parking:** on-site. **Cards:** AX, DC, MC, VI.

SWISS CHALET   **Lunch:** $6-$11   **Dinner:** $8-$16   **Phone:** 506/859-8608

Canadian

Location: At Champlain Mall. 9 Champlain St E1A 1N4. **Hours:** 11 am-10:30 pm, Fri-11 pm, Sun-10 pm. Closed: 12/25. **Reservations:** accepted. **Features:** The popular restaurant is known for its rotisserie chicken and ribs and the tangy Chalet sauce that gives food its special zip. Diners munch on a half or quarter chicken with sides such as steamed vegetables, fries, baked potatoes and salads. Lunch guests often go for the great soup and sandwich combination. Take-out and delivery service are popular options. Casual dress; cocktails. **Parking:** on-site. **Cards:** AX, DC, MC, VI.

DOAKTOWN pop. 955

──────── WHERE TO STAY ────────

THE LEDGES INN   **Phone:** 506/365-1820

Country Inn

Property failed to provide current rates
Location: On Rt 8; centre. Located in a rural area. 30 Ledges Inn Ln E9C 1A7. Fax: 506/365-7138. **Facility:** Most of the well-appointed guest rooms in this comfortable, modern log home overlook a natural setting along the Miramichi River. Smoke free premises. 11 one-bedroom standard units. 2 stories (no elevator), interior corridors. **Parking:** on-site. **Terms:** office hours 7 am-10 pm. **Amenities:** hair dryers. **Leisure Activities:** canoeing, fishing. **Business Services:** meeting rooms.

SOME UNITS

DORCHESTER pop. 954

──────── WHERE TO DINE ────────

THE BELL INN RESTAURANT   **Lunch:** $7-$15   **Dinner:** $7-$15   **Phone:** 506/379-2580

Canadian

Location: On Hwy 106; centre. 3515 Cape Rd E4K 2X2. **Hours:** Open 5/1-11/30 & 3/20-4/30; 9 am-7 pm. Closed: Mon & Tues. **Reservations:** suggested. **Features:** Established in New Brunswick's oldest stone structure, a Provincial historic site built in 1811, this pleasant eatery offers home-style cooking that includes savory chowder and luscious dessert. Historic memorabilia lends an air of authenticity. Casual dress. **Parking:** on-site. **Cards:** MC, VI. **Historic**

EDMUNDSTON pop. 17,373

——— WHERE TO STAY ———

CHATEAU EDMUNDSTON HOTEL & SUITES
Phone: (506)739-7321

(CAA) (SAVE)

Small-scale Hotel

| | All Year | 1P: $85-$130 | 2P: $95-$140 | XP: $10 | F18 |

Location: Trans-Canada Hwy 2, exit 18 (Hebert Blvd), 1 mi (1.6 km) sw, then just w on Church Rd. 100 rue Rice E3V 1T4. Fax: 506/735-9101. **Facility:** 102 units. 100 one-bedroom standard units, some with whirlpools. 2 one-bedroom suites with whirlpools. 5 stories, interior corridors. **Parking:** on-site. **Terms:** package plans, small pets only (in smoking units). **Amenities:** voice mail, irons, hair dryers. *Some:* high-speed Internet, dual phone lines, safes. **Dining:** Restaurant La Terrasse, see separate listing. **Pool(s):** heated indoor. **Leisure Activities:** sauna, whirlpool. **Guest Services:** wireless Internet. **Business Services:** conference facilities, PC. **Cards:** AX, DC, DS, MC, VI. **Free Special Amenities:** room upgrade (subject to availability with advance reservations) and high-speed Internet.

SOME UNITS

COMFORT INN   *Book great rates at AAA.com*
Phone: (506)739-8361

Small-scale Hotel

| | All Year [CP] | 1P: $82-$155 | 2P: $92-$165 | XP: $10 | F18 |

Location: Trans-Canada Hwy 2, exit 18 (Hebert Blvd). 5 Bateman Ave E3V 3L1. Fax: 506/737-8183. **Facility:** 121 units. 118 one-bedroom standard units. 3 one-bedroom suites. 2 stories (no elevator), interior corridors. **Parking:** on-site, winter plug-ins. **Terms:** pets (on ground floor). **Amenities:** irons, hair dryers. *Some:* high-speed Internet. **Leisure Activities:** limited exercise equipment. **Guest Services:** coin laundry, wireless Internet. **Cards:** AX, CB, DC, DS, JC, MC, VI. *(See color ad card insert)*

SOME UNITS

DOMAINE DU PRESIDENT B & B
Phone: 506/735-0003

Bed & Breakfast

| | 5/1-9/30 | 1P: $85-$115 | 2P: $115-$125 | XP: $10 | F8 |
| | 10/1-4/30 | 1P: $75-$105 | 2P: $85-$115 | XP: $10 | F8 |

Location: Trans-Canada Hwy 2, exit 18 (Hebert Blvd), 1 mi (1.6 km) sw, then just w on Church Rd; downtown. 100 Fraser Ave E3V 1Z8. Fax: 506/739-6913. **Facility:** Located in a residential area, the lovely inn offers spacious, well appointed guestrooms, each individually decorated. Smoke free premises. 4 units. 3 one-bedroom standard units. 1 one-bedroom suite with whirlpool. 2 stories (no elevator), interior corridors. **Parking:** on-site. **Terms:** office hours 7 am-10 pm, check-in 4 pm. **Amenities:** video library, hair dryers. *Some:* irons. **Pool(s):** heated outdoor. **Cards:** MC, VI.

QUALITY INN   *Book great rates at AAA.com*
Phone: (506)735-5525

Small-scale Hotel

| | 7/1-8/31 | 1P: $108-$135 | 2P: $117-$144 | XP: $10 | F18 |
| | 5/1-6/30 & 9/1-4/30 | 1P: $72-$108 | 2P: $81-$117 | XP: $10 | F18 |

Location: Trans-Canada Hwy 2, exit 13B eastbound; exit 13BA westbound. 919 Canada Rd E3V 3X2. Fax: 506/739-6243. **Facility:** 133 one-bedroom standard units. 3 stories (no elevator), interior/exterior corridors. *Bath:* combo or shower only. **Parking:** on-site. **Terms:** [AP], [BP], [CP], [ECP] & [MAP] meal plans available, pets (in smoking units). **Amenities:** irons, hair dryers. **Pool(s):** heated indoor. **Leisure Activities:** sauna, whirlpool. **Business Services:** meeting rooms. **Cards:** AX, DC, MC, VI. *(See color ad card insert)*

SOME UNITS

——— WHERE TO DINE ———

BEL-AIR FAMILY RESTAURANT
Lunch: $5-$11   **Dinner:** $6-$17   **Phone:** 506/735-3329

Canadian

Location: Trans-Canada Hwy 2, exit 18 (Hebert Blvd), 0.8 mi (1.2 km) s. 174 Victoria St E3V 2H8. **Hours:** 24 hours. **Features:** Open 24 hours, the great family restaurant has a modern theme with a selection of comfortable booths and tables. The menu incorporates several cuisine styles, and portions are ample. Casual dress; cocktails. **Parking:** on-site. **Cards:** AX, DC, MC, VI.

RESTAURANT LA TERRASSE
Lunch: $6-$14   **Dinner:** $14-$31   **Phone:** 506/739-7321

Canadian

Location: Trans-Canada Hwy 2, exit 18 (Hebert Blvd), 1 mi (1.6 km) sw, then just w on Church Rd; in Chateau Edmundston Hotel & Suites. 100 rue Rice E3V 1T4. **Hours:** 7 am-2 & 5-9:30 pm. **Reservations:** accepted. **Features:** Just off the main lobby of the hotel, the pleasant restaurant serves well-prepared steaks and seafood in a relaxing environment. The daily lunch buffet is popular. Casual dress; cocktails. **Parking:** on-site. **Cards:** AX, CB, DC, DS, MC, VI.

SEAFOOD PARADISE & STEAK RESTAURANT
Lunch: $7-$12   **Dinner:** $14-$23   **Phone:** 506/739-7822

(CAA)

Steak & Seafood

Location: Trans-Canada Hwy 2, exit 18 (Hebert Blvd), 0.8 mi (1.2 km) s. 174 Victoria St E3V 2H8. **Hours:** 11 am-10 pm, Thurs-Sat to 11 pm, Sun 10 am-10 pm. **Reservations:** suggested. **Features:** Serving patrons since 1970, the popular, family-run restaurant lets diners relax in a casual, riverfront setting. Large bay windows afford a postcard-perfect view. The menu lists Oriental entrees, fine steaks and fresh seafood. Casual dress; cocktails. **Parking:** on-site. **Cards:** AX, DC, MC, VI.

TAM'S CHINESE RESTAURANT
Lunch: $5-$8   **Dinner:** $7-$14   **Phone:** 506/735-3349

Chinese

Location: Trans-Canada Hwy 2, exit 18 (Hebert Blvd), 0.8 mi (1.2 km) s. 261 Victoria St E3V 2H8. **Hours:** 11 am-11 pm. Closed: 12/25. **Features:** Reasonably priced meals and a casual atmosphere mark the small, popular restaurant. A take-out menu is available. Casual dress. **Parking:** on-site. **Cards:** MC, VI.

FLORENCEVILLE pop. 762

——— WHERE TO STAY ———

FLORENCEVILLE MOTOR INN   **Phone: 506/392-6053**

5/15-9/14	1P: $79-$99	2P: $84-$104	XP: $5
5/1-5/14 & 9/15-4/30	1P: $75-$92	2P: $80-$97	XP: $5

Small-scale Hotel **Location:** 0.3 mi (0.5 km) s on Trans-Canada Hwy 2. Located in a quiet rural area. 239 Burnham Rd E7L 1Z1 (PO Box 741). Fax: 506/392-6363. **Facility:** 39 one-bedroom standard units, some with whirlpools. 2 stories (no elevator), interior/exterior corridors. **Parking:** on-site. **Amenities:** irons, hair dryers. **Dining:** Thomas's Table, see separate listing. **Pool(s):** heated indoor. **Leisure Activities:** sauna, whirlpool. **Business Services:** meeting rooms, PC. **Cards:** AX, DC, MC, VI.

——— WHERE TO DINE ———

BOOTJACKS RESTAURANT   **Lunch:** $6-$9   **Dinner:** $9-$15   **Phone: 506/392-6006**

Canadian **Location:** Trans-Canada Hwy 2, exit 153; centre. 331 Main St E7L 3G8. **Hours:** 11 am-9 pm, Fri & Sat-10 pm. **Closed:** 12/26. **Reservations:** accepted. **Features:** On the second level of a converted store, the restaurant offers a pleasant country theme with a choice of booth or table seating. The menu offers a selection of burgers, sandwiches, chicken and fish & chips. Casual dress; cocktails. **Parking:** on-site and street. **Cards:** AX, DC, MC, VI.

THOMAS'S TABLE   **Lunch:** $5-$9   **Dinner:** $11-$16   **Phone: 506/392-6053**

Canadian **Location:** 0.3 mi (0.5 km) s on Trans-Canada Hwy 2; in Florenceville Motor Inn. 239 Burnham Rd E7L 1Z1. **Hours:** 7 am-10 pm. **Closed:** 12/23-12/28. **Reservations:** accepted. **Features:** The large restaurant overlooks hills and farm fields. The menu selection is ample, with selections ranging from burgers and sandwiches to fresh seafood and steaks as well as good seafood chowder. Outdoor seating can be requested in season. Casual dress; cocktails. **Parking:** on-site. **Cards:** AX, DC, MC, VI.

FREDERICTON pop. 47,560

——— WHERE TO STAY ———

AMSTERDAM INN   *Book at AAA.com*   **Phone: (506)474-5050**

7/1-9/15	1P: $120	2P: $130	XP: $10	F
5/16-6/30	1P: $90	2P: $100	XP: $10	F
5/1-5/15	1P: $85	2P: $95	XP: $10	F
9/16-4/30	1P: $79	2P: $89	XP: $10	F

Small-scale Hotel
Location: Rt 8, exit 6A eastbound; exit 6B westbound, just w of Regent Mall. 559 Bishop Dr E3C 2M6. Fax: 506/474-5054. **Facility:** Smoke free premises. 50 one-bedroom standard units. 3 stories, interior corridors. **Parking:** on-site. **Amenities:** video library, DVD players, high-speed Internet, voice mail, irons, hair dryers. **Leisure Activities:** exercise room. **Business Services:** meeting rooms. **Cards:** AX, MC, VI.

AUBERGE WANDLYN INN   *Book at AAA.com*   **Phone: (506)462-4444**

6/1-12/31	1P: $95-$110	2P: $95-$110	XP: $10	F16
5/1-5/31 & 1/1-4/30	1P: $90-$110	2P: $90-$110	XP: $10	F16

Small-scale Hotel **Location:** Rt 8, exit 3 (Hanwell Rd) eastbound; exit 5 (Smythe St) westbound. 958 Prospect St E3B 2T8. Fax: 506/452-7658. **Facility:** 101 units. 97 one-bedroom standard units. 1 one- and 3 two-bedroom suites ($110-$140), some with kitchens and/or whirlpools. 2 stories (no elevator), interior/exterior corridors. **Parking:** on-site, winter plug-ins. **Terms:** package plans, pets (in selected units). **Amenities:** voice mail. *Some:* hair dryers. **Dining:** Oscar's Bar & Grill, see separate listing. **Pool(s):** heated outdoor, heated indoor. **Leisure Activities:** sauna, whirlpool. **Guest Services:** coin laundry. **Business Services:** meeting rooms, PC. **Cards:** AX, DC, MC, VI.

CARRIAGE HOUSE INN   **Phone: 506/452-9924**

5/1-9/30 [BP]	1P: $115-$125	2P: $115-$125	XP: $15
10/1-4/30 [BP]	1P: $95-$110	2P: $99-$115	XP: $15

Historic Bed & Breakfast **Location:** Centre. 230 University Ave E3B 4H7. Fax: 506/452-2770. **Facility:** Handsome woodwork and other fine details lend a warm ambience to this 1875 Victorian inn. Smoke free premises. 10 one-bedroom standard units. 3 stories (no elevator), interior corridors. *Bath:* some combo or shower only. **Parking:** on-site. **Terms:** office hours 7:30 am-10 pm, age restrictions may apply. **Amenities:** hair dryers. **Guest Services:** wireless Internet. **Business Services:** PC. **Cards:** AX, MC, VI.

CITY MOTEL   **Phone: 506/450-9900**

All Year	1P: $85-$105	2P: $95-$115	XP: $10	F16

Small-scale Hotel **Location:** Trans-Canada Hwy 2, exit 285A and B eastbound; exit 285B westbound, 2 mi (3.3 km) n on Rt 101 (Regent St). 1216 Regent St E3B 3Z4. Fax: 506/452-1915. **Facility:** 55 units. 52 one-bedroom standard units. 3 one-bedroom suites. 3 stories (no elevator), interior corridors. **Parking:** on-site. **Terms:** small pets only (in limited units). **Amenities:** hair dryers. **Guest Services:** wireless Internet. **Business Services:** meeting rooms, PC. **Cards:** AX, MC, VI. **Free Special Amenities:** early check-in/late check-out and high-speed Internet.

THE COLONEL'S IN BED AND BREAKFAST
Phone: 506-452-2802

6/2-10/31 [BP]	1P: $99-$125	2P: $110-$150	XP: $20 F10
5/1-6/1 [BP]	1P: $95-$119	2P: $110-$129	XP: $20 F10
11/1-4/30 [BP]	1P: $95-$119	2P: $99-$129	XP: $20 F10

Bed & Breakfast **Location:** On Rt 105, 1.8 mi (3 km) nw of Prince Margaret Bridge. 843 Union St E3A 3P6. Fax: 506/457-2939. **Facility:** The charming B&B is located on the east side of the Saint John River close to a walking bridge; guest rooms are well appointed and vary in size. Smoke free premises. 3 one-bedroom standard units, some with whirlpools. 3 stories (no elevator), interior/exterior corridors. **Parking:** on-site. **Terms:** office hours 6:30 am-10:30 pm, package plans. **Amenities:** video library, hair dryers. *Some:* DVD players, irons. **Guest Services:** wireless Internet. **Cards:** MC, VI.

SOME UNITS

COMFORT INN
Book great rates at AAA.com
Phone: (506)453-0800

7/1-9/30	1P: $99-$124	2P: $109-$134	XP: $10 F18
5/1-6/30 & 10/1-4/30	1P: $89-$104	2P: $99-$114	XP: $10 F18

Small-scale Hotel **Location:** Rt 8, exit 3 (Hanwell Rd) eastbound; exit 5 (Smythe St) westbound. Located in a commercial area. 797 Prospect St E3B 5Y4. Fax: 506/457-0328. **Facility:** 100 units. 98 one-bedroom standard units. 2 one-bedroom suites. 2 stories (no elevator), interior corridors. **Parking:** on-site. **Terms:** pets (on ground floor). **Amenities:** coin laundry, irons, hair dryers. *Some:* high-speed Internet. **Leisure Activities:** exercise room. **Guest Services:** coin laundry, wireless Internet. **Business Services:** PC. **Cards:** AX, CB, DC, DS, JC, MC, VI.
(See color ad card insert)

SOME UNITS

CROWNE PLAZA FREDERICTON LORD BEAVERBROOK
Book great rates at AAA.com
Phone: (506)455-3371

5/1-10/31	1P: $139-$169	2P: $149-$179	XP: $10 F19
11/1-4/30	1P: $139-$159	2P: $149-$169	XP: $10 F19

Large-scale Hotel **Location:** Corner of Regent St. 659 Queen St E3B 5A6. Fax: 506/455-1441. **Facility:** 168 units. 158 one-bedroom standard units. 10 one-bedroom suites, some with whirlpools. 7 stories, interior corridors. **Parking:** on-site. **Terms:** cancellation fee imposed, [AP], [BP], [CP] & [ECP] meal plans available, package plans, pets ($15 extra charge, 1st floor units). **Amenities:** voice mail, irons, hair dryers. **Dining:** 7 am-11 pm, cocktails, also, Governor's Dining Room, James Joyce Irish Pub, see separate listings. **Pool(s):** heated indoor. **Leisure Activities:** sauna, whirlpool, exercise room. *Fee:* massage. **Guest Services:** gift shop, valet laundry, wireless Internet. **Business Services:** conference facilities, business center. **Cards:** AX, CB, DC, DS, JC, MC, VI. **Free Special Amenities: local telephone calls and high-speed Internet.**

SOME UNITS
FEE

DELTA FREDERICTON
Book great rates at AAA.com
Phone: (506)457-7000

All Year	1P: $160-$235	2P: $160-$235	XP: $15 F18

Large-scale Hotel **Location:** 1 mi (1.6 km) n on Rt 102; downtown. 225 Woodstock Rd E3B 2H8. Fax: 506/457-4000. **Facility:** 222 units. 208 one-bedroom standard units. 14 one-bedroom suites, some with whirlpools. 7 stories, interior corridors. **Parking:** on-site. **Terms:** check-in 4 pm, package plans, small pets only ($35 fee, limit 2). **Amenities:** video games (fee), high-speed Internet, dual phone lines, voice mail, irons, hair dryers. *Some:* honor bars. **Dining:** Bruno's, see separate listing. **Pool(s):** heated outdoor, heated indoor. **Leisure Activities:** sauna, whirlpool, exercise room. *Fee:* massage. **Guest Services:** gift shop, valet laundry, beauty salon. **Business Services:** conference facilities, business center. **Cards:** AX, DC, MC, VI. **Free Special Amenities: high-speed Internet.**

SOME UNITS
FEE

HOLIDAY INN FREDERICTON
Book great rates at AAA.com
Phone: (506)363-5111

6/1-9/30	1P: $129-$169	2P: $129-$169	XP: $10 F18
5/1-5/31 & 10/1-4/30	1P: $109-$169	2P: $109-$169	XP: $10 F18

Small-scale Hotel **Location:** Trans-Canada Hwy 2, exit 258 eastbound, 7 mi (11 km) e; exit 294 westbound, 19 mi (30 km) w. Located in a rural area. 35 Mactaquac Rd (Hwy 102) E3E 1L2. Fax: 506/363-3000. **Facility:** 82 units. 76 one-bedroom standard units, some with whirlpools. 6 cottages ($159-$259). 3 stories, interior/exterior corridors. **Parking:** on-site. **Terms:** cancellation fee imposed, [AP] & [BP] meal plans available, package plans, small pets only. **Amenities:** video games (fee), high-speed Internet, voice mail, irons, hair dryers. **Dining:** Parkview Restaurant, see separate listing. **Pool(s):** heated indoor. **Leisure Activities:** whirlpool, boat dock, tennis court, playground, exercise room, basketball, horseshoes, shuffleboard. **Guest Services:** coin laundry, wireless Internet. **Business Services:** meeting rooms, PC. **Cards:** AX, DC, DS, MC, VI.

SOME UNITS

LAKEVIEW INNS & SUITES-FREDERICTON
Book great rates at AAA.com
Phone: (506)459-0035

All Year	1P: $99-$114	2P: $109-$124	XP: $10 F18

Small-scale Hotel **Location:** Rt 8, exit 3 (Hanwell Rd) eastbound; exit 5 (Smythe St) westbound. Located in a commercial area. 665 Prospect St E3B 6B8. Fax: 506/458-1011. **Facility:** 98 units. 53 one-bedroom standard units. 45 one-bedroom suites. 4 stories, interior corridors. **Parking:** on-site. **Terms:** [CP] meal plan available, small pets only ($50 deposit, $4 extra charge, in smoking units). **Amenities:** video library, DVD players, irons, hair dryers. **Leisure Activities:** exercise room. **Guest Services:** coin laundry, wireless Internet. **Business Services:** meeting rooms. **Cards:** AX, DC, DS, JC, MC, VI. *(See color ad on TourBookMark)*

SOME UNITS
FEE

RAMADA HOTEL FREDERICTON

Book great rates at AAA.com

Phone: (506)460-5500

CAA SAVE

6/16-9/15	1P: $129-$139	2P: $149-$169	XP: $10	F18
9/16-4/30	1P: $99-$129	2P: $119-$139	XP: $10	F18
5/1-6/15	1P: $99-$109	2P: $119-$129	XP: $10	F18

Small-scale Hotel

Location: On Rt 105 at the north end of Princess Margaret Bridge. 480 Riverside Dr E3B 5E3 (PO Box 1414). Fax: 506/472-0170. **Facility:** 114 one-bedroom standard units. 2 stories (no elevator), interior corridors. **Parking:** on-site. **Terms:** [AP] & [BP] meal plans available, package plans, small pets only. **Amenities:** voice mail, irons, hair dryers. *Some:* high-speed Internet, honor bars. **Dining:** The Courtyard Restaurant, see separate listing. **Pool(s):** heated indoor. **Leisure Activities:** whirlpool, driving range, exercise room. *Fee:* golf-9 holes, miniature golf, volleyball, game room. **Guest Services:** valet and coin laundry, wireless Internet. **Business Services:** meeting rooms, business center. **Cards:** AX, DC, DS, MC, VI. **Free Special Amenities:** newspaper and high-speed Internet.

SOME UNITS

THE VERY BEST-A VICTORIAN B&B

Phone: 506/451-1499

All Year	1P: $119-$129	2P: $119-$129	XP: $15	F10

Historic Bed & Breakfast

Location: At Church St. 806 George St E3B 1K7. Fax: 506/454-1454. **Facility:** This B&B is in the center of town and offers well-decorated accommodations with modern amenities. Smoke free premises. 3 one-bedroom standard units, some with whirlpools. 2 stories (no elevator), interior corridors. **Parking:** on-site. **Terms:** office hours 7 am-11 pm, age restrictions may apply, cancellation fee imposed, [BP] meal plan available, no pets allowed (owner's dog on premises). **Amenities:** video library, DVD players, hair dryers. **Pool(s):** heated outdoor. **Leisure Activities:** sauna, game room. **Guest Services:** wireless Internet. **Business Services:** PC. **Cards:** AX, MC, VI.

--------- **WHERE TO DINE** ---------

THE BLUE DOOR RESTAURANT & BAR

Lunch: $6-$10 **Dinner:** $6-$19 **Phone:** 506/455-2583

California

Location: Corner of King and Regent sts. 100 Regent St E3B 3W4. **Hours:** 11:30 am-10 pm, Fri & Sat-11 pm. Closed: 4/9, 10/8, 12/25. **Reservations:** suggested. **Features:** One way to classify the cuisine is as offering a combination of West Coast flavors. Among the varied choices are pasta, curry, pizza, lobster, ribs, burgers, fish and chips and a tasty seafood medley over rice. Casual dress; cocktails. **Parking:** street. **Cards:** AX, DC, MC, VI.

BOSTON PIZZA

Lunch: $7-$12 **Dinner:** $9-$16 **Phone:** 506/454-3344

Italian

Location: At Regent St; adjacent to Fredericton Mall. 1230 Prospect St E3B 3C2. **Hours:** 11 am-midnight, Fri & Sat-2 am. Closed: 12/25. **Reservations:** accepted. **Features:** The popular chain features an atmosphere that's comfortable for group and family dining. In addition to the gourmet pizzas that gave this place its name, the tasty offerings include pasta dishes, hearty burgers, sandwiches, ribs and chicken and fish. Casual dress; cocktails. **Parking:** on-site. **Cards:** AX, DC, MC, VI.

BREWBAKERS RESTAURANT

Lunch: $7-$11 **Dinner:** $11-$25 **Phone:** 506/459-0067

Canadian

Location: Centre. 546 King St E3B 1E6. **Hours:** 11:30 am-10 pm, Fri & Sat-11 pm, Sun 4 pm-10 pm. Closed: 12/25, 12/26. **Reservations:** accepted. **Features:** The popular restaurant has the feel of an upbeat pub. The menu is extensive, with offerings ranging from pasta and brick-oven pizzas to fresh seafood and meat entrees. Spacious patio dining is available in season. Casual dress; cocktails. **Parking:** on-site (fee). **Cards:** AX, MC, VI.

BRUNO'S

Lunch: $8-$14 **Dinner:** $14-$23 **Phone:** 506/457-7000

Canadian

Location: 1 mi (1.6 km) n on Rt 102; centre; in Delta Fredericton. 225 Woodstock Rd E3B 2H8. **Hours:** 6 am-2 & 5-10 pm, Sat & Sun from 7 am. **Reservations:** accepted. **Features:** The restaurant has several dining sections with a bistro decor, and a large patio borders the Saint John River. The seafood-focused menu lists planked salmon, halibut and excellent chowder. Various meat entrees also are available. Casual dress; cocktails. **Parking:** on-site. **Cards:** AX, DC, DS, JC, MC, VI.

CHEZ RIZ INDIAN & PAKISTANI CUISINE

Lunch: $8-$14 **Dinner:** $10-$19 **Phone:** 506/454-9996

Indian

Location: Downtown. 366 Queen St E3B 1B2. **Hours:** 11:30 am-2:30 & 5-9 pm. Closed: 12/25, 12/26; also Sun. **Reservations:** accepted. **Features:** The cozy restaurant features rich dark wood accents and pressed-tin walls and ceilings. The buffet lines up well-prepared Indian and Pakistani dishes. Casual dress; cocktails. **Parking:** street. **Cards:** AX, MC, VI.

CORA'S BREAKFAST & LUNCH

Lunch: $6-$10 **Phone:** 506/472-2672

Canadian

Location: At Carleton St; centre. 476 Queen St E3B 1B6. **Hours:** 6 am-3 pm, Sun from 7 am. Closed: 12/25. **Reservations:** accepted. **Features:** Although this place specializes in breakfast, it offers a varied daytime menu that includes bacon, eggs, sausages, crepes, grilled cheese, sandwiches, freshly prepared quiches, salads, fruit platters and freshly squeezed juices. The family-friendly dining room is casual and modern. Casual dress. **Parking:** on-site (fee). **Cards:** AX, DC, MC, VI.

THE COURTYARD RESTAURANT

Lunch: $6-$11 **Dinner:** $9-$20 **Phone:** 506/460-5511

Canadian

Location: On Rt 105 at the north end of Princess Margaret Bridge; in Ramada Hotel Fredericton. 480 Riverside Dr E3B 5E3. **Hours:** 7 am-10 pm; to 9 pm 11/1-4/30. Closed: 12/25. **Reservations:** accepted. **Features:** Decorated with beautiful, hand-painted murals and ceilings depicting Venetian scenes, the spacious restaurant offers booth and table seating. The vast menu is sure to offer something for everyone. Daily specials are prepared for lunch and dinner. Casual dress; cocktails. **Parking:** on-site. **Cards:** AX, DC, MC, VI.

DIMITRI'S SOUVLAKI RESTAURANT

Lunch: $7-$11 **Dinner:** $9-$18 **Phone:** 506/452-8882

Greek

Location: Centre; in Pipers Lane area. 349 King St E3B 1E4. **Hours:** 11 am-10 pm, Thurs-Sat to 10:30 pm. Closed: Sun. **Reservations:** accepted. **Features:** The popular restaurant serves distinctive Greek cuisine in a casual atmosphere. Try the classic lamb kebab, chicken brochette or jumbo shrimp. Outdoor seating is a seasonal option. Casual dress; cocktails. **Parking:** on-site (fee). **Cards:** AX, DC, MC, VI.

DIPLOMAT RESTAURANT Lunch: $6-$12 Dinner: $12-$20 Phone: 506/454-2400
Chinese

Location: 1 mi (1.6 km) n on Rt 102. 253 Woodstock Rd E3B 2H8. **Hours:** 24 hours. Closed: 12/25. **Features:** The popular restaurant surprisingly combines Canadian and Chinese cuisines. Portions are ample and nicely presented. Superb desserts are made in house. Casual dress; cocktails. **Parking:** on-site. **Cards:** AX, DS, MC, VI.

EL BURRITO LOCO Lunch: $8-$14 Dinner: $12-$21 Phone: 506/459-5626
Mexican

Location: Corner of Westmorland Ave. 304 King St E3B 1E3. **Hours:** 11 am-midnight; hours vary off season. Closed: 12/25, 12/26; also Sun 10/1-6/15. **Reservations:** accepted. **Features:** A touch of Puerto Vallarta in the heart of town, this colorfully decorated restaurant prepares Mexican cuisine that patrons can savor on the seasonal patio. Among items on the full menu are quesadillas, chimichangas, burritos and fajitas, in addition to some steak and seafood options. Casual dress; cocktails. **Parking:** on-site. **Cards:** AX, DC, MC, VI.

GOVERNOR'S DINING ROOM Dinner: $16-$22 Phone: 506/451-1804
Canadian

Location: Corner of Regent St; in Crowne Plaza Fredericton Lord Beaverbrook. 659 Queen St E3B 5A6. **Hours:** 5:30 pm-11 pm. Closed: Sun & Mon. **Reservations:** suggested. **Features:** Intimate with a cozy ambience, this eatery offers creative entrees that range from fresh seafood to well-prepared, traditional beef and chicken dishes. Choose one of the many delectable homemade desserts to bring your meal to a sweet and satisfying close. Casual dress; cocktails. **Parking:** on-site. **Cards:** AX, DC, DS, MC, VI.

HILLTOP GRILL & BEVERAGE CO Lunch: $6-$10 Dinner: $8-$15 Phone: 506/458-9057
Canadian

Location: Rt 8, exit 3 (Hanwell Rd) eastbound; exit 5 (Smythe St) westbound. 1034 Prospect St E3B 3C1. **Hours:** 11 am-11 pm, Fri-midnight, Sat 8 am-midnight, Sun 11 am-9 pm. Closed: 12/25. **Reservations:** accepted. **Features:** A popular spot for an upbeat gathering, the spacious, sports bar-style restaurant offers mainly booth seating. On the menu is a wide variety of satisfying comfort foods, as well as seafood and steaks. Casual dress; cocktails. **Parking:** on-site. **Cards:** AX, DC, MC, VI.

JAMES JOYCE IRISH PUB Lunch: $7-$11 Dinner: $8-$16 Phone: 506/450-9820
Irish

Location: Corner of Regent St; in Crowne Plaza Fredericton Lord Beaverbrook. 659 Queen St E3B 5A6. **Hours:** 11 am-10 pm, Thurs-Sat to 11 pm, Sun noon-10 pm. **Reservations:** accepted. **Features:** Guests can relax in a laid-back pub that has a spacious seasonal patio. On tap is a fine selection of local and imported beers. Examples of splendid Irish-style pub fare include steak and mushroom pie, soda bread with seafood chowder, fish and chips and plenty of finger foods. Casual dress; cocktails. **Parking:** on-site. **Cards:** AX, MC, VI.

THE JESTER'S COURT Lunch: $6-$13 Dinner: $9-$21 Phone: 506/450-9385
Canadian

Location: Centre. 426 Queen St E3B 5A6. **Hours:** 11 am-1 am, Thurs-Sat to 2 am. Closed: 12/25. **Reservations:** accepted. **Features:** The staff of the spacious English-style pub is friendly and upbeat. On the menu is a nice selection of traditional British pub grub, as well as steaks, chicken and seafood. A splendid selection of beers on tap is on hand to wash it all down. Casual dress; cocktails. **Parking:** street. **Cards:** AX, DC, MC, VI.

JUBILEE SUPER BUFFET Lunch: $7-$10 Dinner: $10-$16 Phone: 506/452-8888
Chinese

Location: At Greenfields St. 837 Prospect St E3B 5Y4. **Hours:** 11:30 am-9 pm. Closed: 12/25. **Reservations:** accepted. **Features:** More than 100 items line up on the spacious restaurant's all-you-can-eat buffet. This place also offers take-out service. Casual dress; cocktails. **Parking:** on-site. **Cards:** AX, DC, MC, VI.

KEYSTONE KELLY'S Lunch: $8-$11 Dinner: $12-$20 Phone: 506/459-3003
Canadian

Location: In Smythe Street Plaza. 1188 Smythe St E3B 3H5. **Hours:** 11 am-10 pm, Fri & Sat-midnight, Sun noon-10 pm. Closed: 12/25, 12/26. **Reservations:** accepted. **Features:** The menu selection is varied, with seafood, steak, pasta and chicken dishes all making appearances, along with homemade soups, sandwiches and desserts. The upbeat decor blends both Mexican and Italian traditions. Casual dress; cocktails. **Parking:** on-site. **Cards:** AX, DC, MC, VI.

THE LUNAR ROGUE PUB Lunch: $6-$14 Dinner: $10-$19 Phone: 506/450-2065
Canadian

Location: At Regent St. 625 King St E3B 4Y2. **Hours:** 11 am-1 am, Sat from 10 am, Sun 11 am-10 pm. Closed: 1/1, 12/25. **Reservations:** accepted. **Features:** The popular landmark nurtures a relaxed atmosphere. Guests can dine inside or out on the patio. Good pub grub, served in ample portions, couples with a fine selection of whistle-whetting beers and single malts. Casual dress; cocktails. **Parking:** street. **Cards:** AX, DC, MC, VI.

MCGINNIS LANDING RESTAURANT Lunch: $8-$14 Dinner: $14-$22 Phone: 506/458-1212
Canadian

Location: At Westmorland St. 280 King St E3B 1E2. **Hours:** 11 am-10 pm, Tues-Thurs to 11 pm, Fri & Sat-midnight. Closed: 12/25. **Reservations:** accepted. **Features:** Decked out with hardwood floors and hand-painted murals, the roomy, colorful dining room sustains an upbeat atmosphere. On the menu, which boasts an Oriental flair, are fresh seafood and varied meat dishes. Casual dress; cocktails. **Parking:** on-site. **Cards:** AX, DC, MC, VI.

MEXICALI ROSA'S Lunch: $7-$11 Dinner: $12-$16 Phone: 506/451-0686
Mexican

Location: At Regent St. 546 King St E3B 1E6. **Hours:** 11:30 am-11:30 pm, Fri-12:30 am, Sat noon-12:30 am, Sun noon-11 pm. Closed: 12/25. **Features:** The Mexican cantina makes an excellent choice for family-friendly fun. Old West paintings and murals add color to stucco walls and wooden beams, while a Tex-Mex menu provides a feast of favorites such as fajitas, burritos and some seafood items. Fried ice cream is a sweet treat. Casual dress; cocktails. **Parking:** street. **Cards:** AX, DC, MC, VI.

MIKE'S RESTAURANT   **Lunch:** $6-$10   **Dinner:** $8-$16   **Phone:** 506/454-6453

Canadian

Location: Centre; adjacent to Fredericton Mall. 1040 Prospect St E3B 3C1. **Hours:** 7 am-10 pm, Fri-11 pm, Sat 8 am-11 pm, Sun 8 am-10 pm. Closed: 12/25. **Reservations:** accepted. **Features:** This popular family-friendly restaurant specializes in pizza and hot submarine sandwiches, along with fries, burgers, soup, salads, pasta, grilled meats and seafood. An excellent variety of colorful desserts rounds out the offerings. Casual dress; cocktails. **Parking:** on-site. **Cards:** AX, DC, MC, VI.

OSCAR'S BAR & GRILL   **Lunch:** $7-$13   **Dinner:** $10-$18   **Phone:** 506/455-6014

Canadian

Location: Rt 8, exit 3 (Hanwell Rd) eastbound; exit 5 (Smythe St) westbound; in Auberge Wandlyn Inn. 958 Prospect St E3B 2T8. **Hours:** 7 am-10 pm, Fri & Sat-11 pm. **Reservations:** accepted. **Features:** Aquariums and waterfall accents enhance the relaxed, upscale and colorful bistro. Well-prepared meat and seafood dishes are presented with an eye for detail. The staff is youthful and friendly. Casual dress; cocktails. **Parking:** on-site. **Cards:** AX, DC, MC, VI.

THE PALATE RESTAURANT & CAFE   **Lunch:** $8-$12   **Dinner:** $14-$22   **Phone:** 506/450-7911

Canadian

Location: Corner of Queen St and Wilmon Alley; centre. 462 Queen St E3B 5A6. **Hours:** 11 am-9 pm, Sat from 10 am. Closed major holidays. **Reservations:** accepted. **Features:** The restaurant's menu offers a wide variety of items including fresh seafood and various meats including duck, chicken and lamb. A nice mix of salads and pasta is also available. Casual dress; cocktails. **Parking:** street. **Cards:** AX, DC, MC, VI.

PARKVIEW RESTAURANT   **Lunch:** $8-$16   **Dinner:** $12-$24   **Phone:** 506/363-5111

Canadian

Location: Trans-Canada Hwy 2, exit 258 eastbound, 7 mi (11 km) e; exit 294 westbound, 19 mi (30 km) w; in Holiday Inn Fredericton. 35 Mactaquac Rd E3E 1L2. **Hours:** 7 am-2 & 5-10 pm. Closed: 12/25. **Reservations:** accepted. **Features:** Served in a pleasant, resort-style atmosphere overlooking the Saint John River, well-prepared menu offerings of seafood and meat blend French and Canadian influences. Also satisfying are tasty soups and homemade desserts. Outdoor dining is a nice seasonal diversion. Casual dress; cocktails. **Parking:** on-site. **Cards:** AX, DC, DS, MC, VI.

SMITTY'S FAMILY RESTAURANT   **Lunch:** $6-$11   **Dinner:** $8-$16   **Phone:** 506/454-0022

Canadian

Location: Centre; at Regent Mall. 1381 Regent St E3C 1A2. **Hours:** 6:30 am-10 pm, Sun 8 am-8 pm. Closed: 12/25. **Reservations:** accepted. **Features:** The family-oriented restaurant satisfies patrons with its ever-popular all-day breakfast items, as well as tasty and wholesome soups and salads at lunchtime. A relaxed mood characterizes the dining space. Casual dress; cocktails. **Parking:** on-site. **Cards:** AX, DC, MC, VI.

SWISS CHALET   **Lunch:** $6-$11   **Dinner:** $8-$16   **Phone:** 506/458-8278

Canadian

Location: At Smythe St. 961 Prospect St E3B 2T7. **Hours:** 11 am-10 pm, Fri & Sat-11 pm. Closed: 12/25. **Reservations:** accepted. **Features:** The popular restaurant is known for its rotisserie chicken and ribs and the tangy Chalet sauce that gives food its special zip. Diners munch on a half or quarter chicken with sides such as steamed vegetables, fries, baked potatoes and salads. Lunch guests often go for the great soup and sandwich combination. Take-out and delivery service are popular options. Casual dress; cocktails. **Parking:** on-site. **Cards:** AX, DC, MC, VI.

GAGETOWN pop. 682

——— WHERE TO DINE ———

THE CREEK VIEW RESTAURANT   **Lunch:** $6-$10   **Dinner:** $8-$15   **Phone:** 506/488-9806

Canadian

Location: Centre. 38 Tilley Rd E5N 1A8. **Hours:** 8 am-9 pm; hours may vary off season. Closed: 12/25, 12/26. **Reservations:** accepted. **Features:** The quaint restaurant overlooks the village and river and offers pleasant outdoor seating in season. The former 1900s automobile dealership displays turn-of-the-20th-century memorabilia. Tasty country cuisine makes up the full menu. Casual dress; cocktails. **Parking:** on-site. **Cards:** AX, MC, VI.

GRAND FALLS pop. 6,133

——— WHERE TO STAY ———

AUBERGE PRES-DU-LAC INN   **Phone:** (506)473-1300

6/15-9/3	1P: $105-$115	2P: $115-$125	XP: $10	F18
5/1-6/14 & 9/4-4/30	1P: $85-$95	2P: $90-$100	XP: $10	F18

Small-scale Hotel

Location: Trans-Canada Hwy 2, exit 75, just w. 10039 Rt 144 E3Y 3H5 (PO Box 7300, E3Z 1G5). Fax: 506/473-5501. **Facility:** 100 units. 83 one-bedroom standard units. 17 cabins. 2 stories (no elevator), interior/exterior corridors. **Parking:** on-site, winter plug-ins. **Terms:** small pets only (in designated cabins). **Amenities:** hair dryers. Some: irons. **Dining:** Pres-du-Lac Restaurant, see separate listing. **Pool(s):** heated indoor. **Leisure Activities:** sauna, whirlpool, paddleboats, fishing, putting green, playground, exercise room, basketball. **Guest Services:** coin laundry, wireless Internet. **Business Services:** meeting rooms, PC, fax. **Cards:** AX, MC, VI.   SOME UNITS

BEST WESTERN GRAND-SAULT HOTEL & SUITES   *Book great rates at AAA.com*   **Phone:** 506/473-6200

	1P	2P	XP	
6/16-9/30 [CP]	1P: $120-$189	2P: $130-$199	XP: $5	F
5/1-6/15 & 10/1-12/31 [CP]	1P: $113-$189	2P: $123-$199	XP: $5	F
1/1-4/30 [CP]	1P: $111-$189	2P: $121-$199	XP: $5	F

Small-scale Hotel

Location: Trans-Canada Hwy 2, exit 79. 187 Ouellette St E3Z 3E8 (PO Box 7755). Fax: 506/473-3564. **Facility:** 62 units. 50 one-bedroom standard units, some with whirlpools. 12 one-bedroom suites ($189-$199). 3 stories, interior corridors. **Bath:** combo or shower only. **Parking:** on-site. **Terms:** cancellation fee imposed, pets ($25 extra charge, in designated units). **Amenities:** high-speed Internet, dual phone lines, voice mail, irons, hair dryers. **Pool(s):** heated indoor. **Leisure Activities:** whirlpool, exercise room. **Guest Services:** coin laundry. **Business Services:** meeting rooms, PC. **Cards:** AX, DC, DS, MC, VI.   SOME UNITS

COTE'S BED & BREAKFAST
▼▼▼▼▼ **Phone: (506)473-1415**

All Year [BP]   1P: $75-$119   2P: $95-$175   XP: $20   D12

Bed & Breakfast **Location:** Trans-Canada Hwy 2, exit 79, follow signs to Main St. 575 Broadway Blvd W E3Z 2L2. **Facility:** A quiet residential area on the edge of town. The guest rooms are tastefully decorated and two suites have a shared deck and hot tub. Smoke free premises. 5 units. 3 one-bedroom standard units, some with whirlpools. 2 one-bedroom suites, some with whirlpools. 2 stories (no elevator), interior corridors. **Parking:** on-site. **Terms:** age restrictions may apply, 3 day cancellation notice, package plans, no pets allowed (owner's pets on premises). **Amenities:** video library, DVD players, CD players, irons, hair dryers. **Guest Services:** wireless Internet. **Cards:** MC, VI.

⊠ ▣

HILL TOP MOTEL & RESTAURANT
▼▼▼ **Phone: 506/473-2684**

All Year   1P: $65-$94   2P: $77-$106   XP: $8   F12

Small-scale Hotel **Location:** Centre; adjacent to The Gorge. 131 Madawaska Rd E3Y 1A7. Fax: 506/473-4567. **Facility:** 37 one-bedroom standard units, some with efficiencies. 2 stories (no elevator), exterior corridors. **Parking:** on-site. **Terms:** office hours 6 am-11 pm. **Dining:** restaurant, see separate listing. **Guest Services:** wireless Internet. **Business Services:** meeting rooms. **Cards:** AX, MC, VI.

SOME UNITS

🍴 ☕ 🛏 ▣ / ⊠ 📺 /

RIVER TRAIL BED & BREAKFAST
▼▼ **Phone: (506)475-8818**

All Year [BP]   1P: $50-$75   2P: $65-$90   XP: $15   D7

Bed & Breakfast **Location:** 1.2 km nw on (Madawaska Rd) just s on Carrier St; Centre. 34 Dominique St E3Y 1A2. Fax: 506/473-4654. **Facility:** Smoke free premises. 4 one-bedroom standard units. 1 story, interior corridors. *Bath:* combo or shower only. **Parking:** on-site. **Terms:** office hours 7 am-10 pm, weekly rates available. **Amenities:** video library, hair dryers. *Some:* DVD players.

⊠ 🄰 🆅🄲🆁 🕿

The following lodging was either not evaluated or did not meet AAA rating requirements but is listed for your information only.

MOTEL LEO
[fyi] **Phone: 506/473-2090**

Not evaluated. Location: 2.5 mi (4 km) w on Trans-Canada Hwy 2. (PO Box 2784, E0J 1M0). Facilities, services, and decor characterize a mid-range property.

--- **WHERE TO DINE** ---

CHINESE VILLAGE RESTAURANT
◆◆ **Lunch:** $7-$11   **Dinner:** $12-$17   **Phone:** 506/473-1884

Chinese **Location:** 0.6 mi (1 km) nw of jct Rt 108; centre. 238 Madawaska Rd E3G 1C1. **Hours:** 11 am-10 pm, Fri & Sat-11 pm. Closed: 12/25. **Reservations:** accepted. **Features:** The popular restaurant's menu delivers generous portions of such traditional foods as sweet and sour pork, lomein, egg rolls and beef with broccoli. Casual dress; cocktails. **Parking:** on-site. **Cards:** AX, DC, MC, VI.

HILL TOP RESTAURANT/PIZZA SHACK
▼▼ **Lunch:** $5-$12   **Dinner:** $6-$20   **Phone:** 506/473-2684

Canadian **Location:** Centre, adjacent to The Gorge; in Hilltop Motel. 131 Madawaska Rd E3Y 1A7. **Hours:** 6 am-10 pm. **Reservations:** accepted. **Features:** Guests can request seating in any of several dining sections or on the seasonal patio. Many tables afford a splendid view of the gorge and falls. All items on the extensive menu are homemade, and deep-frying is a "no-no" here. Casual dress; cocktails. **Parking:** on-site. **Cards:** AX, DC, MC, VI.

☕

LE GRAND 'SAUT RISTORANTE
▼▼ **Lunch:** $6-$12   **Dinner:** $8-$22   **Phone:** 506/473-3876

Italian **Location:** Centre. 155 Broadway Blvd E3Z 2J8. **Hours:** 10:30 am-11 pm, Fri & Sat-midnight. Closed: 12/25. **Reservations:** accepted. **Features:** In the heart of town, the spacious two-level lodge-style restaurant has a central stone fireplace and booth and table seating. Specializing in excellent pizza, this place also serves a good range of pasta, meat and seafood items. Casual dress; cocktails. **Parking:** on-site. **Cards:** AX, MC, VI.

☕

PRES-DU-LAC RESTAURANT
▼▼ **Lunch:** $7-$11   **Dinner:** $15-$21   **Phone:** 506/473-1300

Canadian **Location:** Trans-Canada Hwy 2, exit 75, just w; in Auberge Pres-du-Lac Inn. 10039 Rt 144 E3Y 3H5. **Hours:** 7 am-10 pm. Closed: 12/25. **Features:** Meat and seafood selections fill the menu, which also includes homemade soups and pies and a tasty quiche. Patrons can request seating in one of several pleasant dining sections. Casual dress; cocktails. **Parking:** on-site. **Cards:** AX, CB, DC, DS, MC, VI.

☕

HAMPTON pop. 3,997

--- **WHERE TO DINE** ---

HOLLY'S RESTAURANT
▼▼ **Lunch:** $6-$15   **Dinner:** $9-$19   **Phone:** 506/832-5520

Canadian **Location:** Centre; in Hampton Mall. 454 Main St E5N 6C1. **Hours:** 8 am-10 pm, Sun 9 am-9 pm. Closed: 12/25. **Features:** The selection of country-style cuisine is ample. Patio seating can be requested in season. Casual dress; cocktails. **Parking:** on-site. **Cards:** AX, MC, VI.

☕

HARTLAND pop. 902

———— WHERE TO STAY ————

REBECCA FARM BED & BREAKFAST   Phone: 506/375-1699
 All Year [BP]   1P: $100-$130   XP: $20   D16
Location: 3 mi (5 km) ne. Located in a quiet area. 656 Rockland Rd E7P 1J7. Fax: 506/375-1698.
Bed & Breakfast **Facility:** Farmlands surround this restored 1828 house offering a variety of tastefully decorated
accommodations. Smoke free premises. 7 one-bedroom standard units, some with whirlpools. 2 stories (no
elevator), interior corridors. *Bath:* combo or shower only. **Parking:** on-site. **Terms:** office hours 7 am-9 pm, check-in 5 pm, age
restrictions may apply, cancellation fee imposed. **Amenities:** hair dryers. **Guest Services:** wireless Internet. **Business
Services:** PC. **Cards:** AX, DC, MC, VI.   ⊠ ☎

HARVEY pop. 349

———— WHERE TO DINE ————

THE LOUGHEED PUB & EATERY   **Lunch:** $6-$11   **Dinner:** $8-$15   Phone: 506/366-9197
Location: Centre. 3 Hanselpacker Rd E6K 1A6. **Hours:** 11:30 am-9:30 pm, Fri & Sat-10 pm. Closed: 12/25,
12/26. **Features:** In the heart of the village, this neighborhood pub-style restaurant has two dining sections
Canadian   and an outdoor deck. The menu lists typical pub fare, including fish and chips, burgers, sandwiches and
snack foods. Live entertainment enhances weekend visits. Casual dress; cocktails. **Parking:** on-site.
Cards: MC, VI.   ♈

HAWKSHAW

———— WHERE TO STAY ————

———— *The following lodging was either not evaluated or did not* ————
meet AAA rating requirements but is listed for your information only.

SUNSET VIEW COTTAGES   Phone: 506/575-2592
[fyi]   Did not meet all AAA rating requirements for some guest rooms at time of last evaluation. **Location:** Trans-
Canada Hwy 2, exit 231, 1.2 mi (2 km) e on Rt 102. 45 Hawkshaw Rd E6G 1N8. Facilities, services, and decor
Cottage   characterize a mid-range property.

HOPEWELL CAPE

———— WHERE TO STAY ————

FAMILY TREASURES INN B & B   Phone: 506/882-2077
 All Year [BP]   1P: $95-$120   2P: $95-$120   XP: $20   D12
Location: On Rt 114, 4.8 mi (8 km) w. 4941 Hwy 114 E0A 1Y0. Fax: 506/882-2784. **Facility:** This pleasant
property overlooking the bay has modern guest rooms, some with gas fireplaces and small decks. 10 one-
Bed & Breakfast bedroom standard units, some with whirlpools. 2 stories (no elevator), interior corridors. **Parking:** on-site.
Terms: office hours 7 am-10 pm, 7 day cancellation notice-fee imposed, package plans. **Amenities:** video library, DVD players,
hair dryers. **Guest Services:** coin laundry. **Cards:** AX, MC, VI.
                                                            SOME UNITS
                                                         ⊠ / VCR 🖳 /

INNISFREE BED & BREAKFAST   Phone: 506/734-3510
All Year [BP]   1P: $75-$130   2P: $75-$130   XP: $30
Location: 1 mi (1.6 km) w on Rt 114. Located in a rural area. 4270 Rt 114 E4H 3P4. **Facility:** Gardens enrich this
well-appointed B&B within walking distance of Hopewell Rocks Ocean Tidal Exploration Site; a few rooms
Bed & Breakfast have a view of the bay. Smoke free premises. 4 one-bedroom standard units. 2 stories (no elevator), interior
corridors. **Parking:** on-site. **Terms:** office hours 7 am-10 pm, age restrictions may apply, 7 day cancellation notice-fee imposed,
package plans. **Amenities:** video library, hair dryers. **Leisure Activities:** hiking trails. **Guest Services:** coin laundry, wireless
Internet. **Business Services:** PC. **Cards:** DC, MC, VI.   A$K S🖳 ⊠ 🅰️ VCR 📷 🖳

———— WHERE TO DINE ————

BROADLEAF GUEST RANCH   *Menu on AAA.com*   **Lunch:** $5-$10   **Dinner:** $8-$20   Phone: 506/882-2349
(AAA)   **Location:** On Rt 114, 7.2 mi (12 km) sw. 5526 Rt 114 E4H 3N5. **Hours:** 8 am-10 pm; Sunday brunch; hours vary
off season. **Reservations:** suggested. **Features:** At a guest ranch, the Broadleaf—or ranch kitchen, as they
like to call it—offers a fine selection of reasonably priced home-style entrees. Portions are ample. Casual
Canadian   dress; cocktails. **Parking:** on-site. **Cards:** AX, MC, VI.   ♈ 🅰️

THE OLD SHEPODY MILL RESTAURANT   **Dinner:** $15-$22   Phone: 506/882-2211
Location: 9.6 km w. 5095 Hopewell Cape, Hwy 114 E4H 4K5. **Hours:** Open 5/1-10/15; 4:30 pm-9 pm. Closed:
Mon & Tues. **Reservations:** suggested. **Features:** Fresh Bay of Fundy seafood and European cuisine are
Seafood   the claim to fame for the pleasant restaurant, which offers 100 percent gluten-free meals. Several dining
sections overlook farm fields and the distant bay. Casual dress; cocktails. **Parking:** on-site. **Cards:** AX, DC,
MC, VI.   🅰️

IRISHTOWN

———— **WHERE TO STAY** ————

IRISHTOWN BED & BREAKFAST
Phone: 506/383-5083

5/1-9/30   1P: $85   2P: $95   XP: $25   F6

Bed & Breakfast
Location: Trans-Canada Hwy 2, exit 459 A-B, 8 mi (13.5 km) n on Rt 115; 9.6 mi (16 km) n of Moncton. Located in a rural area. 2924 Rt 115 E1H 2N4. **Fax:** 506/863-6244. **Facility:** This country-style home is just a short drive from Moncton and offers individually decorated guestrooms with modern amenities. Smoke free premises. 3 one-bedroom standard units, some with whirlpools. 2 stories (no elevator), interior corridors. **Parking:** on-site. **Terms:** open 5/1-9/30, office hours 7 am-9 pm, weekly rates available. **Amenities:** video library, DVD players, hair dryers. **Leisure Activities:** whirlpool. **Cards:** VI.

KINGSTON pop. 2,817

———— **WHERE TO STAY** ————

THE OSPREY INN
Phone: (506)832-2525

5/1-12/31 [BP]   1P: $99-$149   2P: $99-$149

Country Inn
Location: From Gondola Point Ferry, 3 mi (5 km) e on Rt 845, then 2.5 mi (4 km) e. 191 Rt 850 E5N 1W3. **Fax:** 506/832-0304. **Facility:** A charming secluded inn, perched on the banks of the Kingston Peninsula. Rooms are spacious and individually decorated, some with a fine water view. Smoke free premises. 5 units. 4 one-bedroom standard units, some with whirlpools. 1 cottage ($100). 2 stories (no elevator), interior/exterior corridors. *Bath:* combo or shower only. **Parking:** on-site. **Terms:** open 5/1-12/31, office hours 7 am-11 pm, age restrictions may apply, 7 day cancellation notice-fee imposed, weekly rates available. **Amenities:** CD players, hair dryers. **Leisure Activities:** whirlpool, limited beach access, canoeing, boat dock. **Cards:** DC, DS, MC, VI.

SOME UNITS

MACTAQUAC

———— **WHERE TO STAY** ————

ON THE POND COUNTRY RETREAT & SPA
Phone: 506/363-3420

5/1-11/1   1P: $125   2P: $145   XP: $20
11/2-4/30   1P: $100   2P: $125   XP: $20

Country Inn
Location: From Mactaquac Bridge, 4 mi (6 km) w via Rt 105 and 106. Located in a quiet secluded area. 20 Rt 615 E6L 1M2. **Fax:** 506/363-3479. **Facility:** This lodge on secluded, river-view grounds offers on-site spa service by advance reservation; rooms are well appointed and comfortably sized. Smoke free premises. 8 one-bedroom standard units. 2 stories (no elevator), interior corridors. **Parking:** on-site. **Terms:** age restrictions may apply, [BP] meal plan available, package plans. **Amenities:** video library, hair dryers. **Leisure Activities:** sauna, beach access, rental canoes, rental bicycles, exercise room. *Fee:* massage. **Cards:** AX, MC, VI.

MIRAMICHI pop. 18,508

———— **WHERE TO STAY** ————

COMFORT INN   *Book great rates at AAA.com*
Phone: (506)622-1215

6/1-9/30   1P: $89-$115   2P: $97-$135   XP: $8   F18
1/1-4/30   1P: $82-$102   2P: $89-$118   XP: $8   F18
5/1-5/31 & 10/1-12/31   1P: $79-$99   2P: $87-$115   XP: $8   F18

Small-scale Hotel
Location: 0.6 mi (1 km) w on Rt 8. Located in a commercial area. 201 Edward St E1V 2Y7. **Fax:** 506/622-0633. **Facility:** 69 one-bedroom standard units. 2 stories (no elevator), interior corridors. **Parking:** on-site. **Terms:** [ECP] meal plan available, pets (on ground floor). **Amenities:** irons, hair dryers. **Guest Services:** wireless Internet. **Business Services:** PC. **Cards:** AX, DC, DS, MC, VI. *(See color ad card insert)*

SOME UNITS

LAKEVIEW INNS & SUITES *Book great rates at AAA.com* **Phone:** (506)627-1999

5/1-9/30 [ECP]	1P: $89-$99	2P: $99-$109	XP: $10 F18
10/1-4/30 [ECP]	1P: $80-$90	2P: $90-$100	XP: $10 F18

Small-scale Hotel **Location:** 1.1 mi (1.8 km) w on Rt 8. Located in a commercial area. 333 King George Hwy E1V 1L2. **Fax:** 506/627-1907. **Facility:** 60 units. 32 one-bedroom standard units. 28 one-bedroom suites ($110-$150). 3 stories, interior corridors. **Parking:** on-site. **Terms:** 7 day cancellation notice, small pets only ($50 deposit, in smoking units). **Amenities:** video library, irons, hair dryers. **Guest Services:** coin laundry, wireless Internet. **Cards:** AX, DC, DS, JC, MC, VI. *(See color ad on TourBookMark)*

SOME UNITS
(ASK) (SD) (🛏) (VCR) (FEE) (🖥) (📺) / (✕) (🖨) /

RODD MIRAMICHI RIVER-A RODD SIGNATURE HOTEL *Book great rates at AAA.com* **Phone:** (506)773-3111

6/1-9/30	1P: $135-$204	2P: $135-$204	XP: $10 F16
5/1-5/31 & 10/1-4/30	1P: $109-$186	2P: $109-$186	XP: $10 F16

Small-scale Hotel **Location:** Hwy 11, exit 120, 0.4 mi (0.6 km) e. 1809 Water St E1N 1B2. 76 one-bedroom standard units. 4 one-bedroom suites ($142-$233) with whirlpools. 3 stories, interior corridors. *Bath:* combo or shower only. **Parking:** on-site. **Terms:** cancellation fee imposed, package plans, pets ($10 extra charge, in smoking units). **Amenities:** high-speed Internet, voice mail, irons, hair dryers. *Some:* dual phone lines. **Dining:** The Angler's Reel, see separate listing. **Pool(s):** heated indoor. **Leisure Activities:** whirlpool, exercise room. **Guest Services:** valet laundry. **Business Services:** meeting rooms. **Cards:** AX, DC, DS, MC, VI. *(See color ad p 359 & p 252)*

SOME UNITS
(ASK) (SD) (🛏) (🍴) (📶) (♿M) (🚬) (🏊) (💼) (🖥) / (✕) (🖨) /
FEE

──── *The following lodging was either not evaluated or did not meet AAA rating requirements but is listed for your information only.* ────

ALL NIGHT ALL DAY COTTAGES AND B & B **Phone:** 506/773-6252

(fyi) **Not evaluated. Location:** 6 mi (10 km) s on Hwy 11, 0.6 mi (1 km) e. 116 N Black River Rd E1N 5S4. Facilities, services, and decor characterize a mid-range property.

──── **WHERE TO DINE** ────

THE ANGLER'S REEL **Lunch:** $7-$17 **Dinner:** $14-$27 **Phone:** 506/773-3111

Canadian **Location:** Hwy 11, exit 120, 0.4 mi (0.6 km) e; in Rodd Miramichi River-A Rodd Signature Hotel. 1809 Water St E1N 1B2. **Hours:** 6:30 am-11 pm, Fri & Sat-midnight, Sun-10 pm. **Closed:** 12/25. **Reservations:** accepted. **Features:** Couples settled at tables for two can see the sights of the Miramichi River while sampling fresh seafood, steak and palate-pleasing homemade desserts. The specialty salmon is prepared more than 20 ways. Fresh treats are made in the on-site bakery. The atmosphere is warm and friendly. Casual dress; cocktails. **Parking:** on-site. **Cards:** AX, DC, MC, VI.

(♿M) (🍸)

JUNGLE JIM'S RESTAURANT **Lunch:** $7-$11 **Dinner:** $8-$20 **Phone:** 506/623-5467

Canadian **Location:** Centre; in Northumberland Square Mall. 2441 King George Hwy E1V 6W2. **Hours:** 11 am-9 pm, Wed & Thurs-10 pm, Fri & Sat-11 pm. **Closed:** 12/25. **Reservations:** accepted. **Features:** Guests can step into a tropical theme at the casual eatery, which employs a friendly staff and nurtures a bustling atmosphere. The menu lines up a wide variety of comfort foods, salads, chicken, beef, seafood and hot wings, all served in ample, flavorful portions. Casual dress; cocktails. **Parking:** on-site. **Cards:** AX, DC, MC, VI.

KINGSWAY RESTAURANT **Lunch:** $5-$10 **Dinner:** $8-$15 **Phone:** 506/622-1138

Canadian **Location:** Opposite Miramichi Mall. 367 King George Hwy E1V 1L5. **Hours:** 7 am-10 pm, Sun from 8 am. **Closed:** 1/1, 12/25, 12/26. **Features:** Serving patrons since 1960, the popular family restaurant presents a menu that lists everything from burgers and hot and cold sandwiches to steaks and seafood. Portions are ample, and parking is plentiful. Casual dress; cocktails. **Parking:** on-site. **Cards:** MC, VI.

PORTAGE RESTAURANT **Lunch:** $6-$11 **Dinner:** $9-$16 **Phone:** 506/773-6447

Canadian **Location:** From Centennial Bridge, 1.8 mi (3 km) s on Rt 11. 191 King St E1N 2P1. **Hours:** 6 am-10 pm, Sun 7 am-9 pm. **Closed:** 12/25. **Reservations:** accepted. **Features:** A local favorite, the large restaurant has a country feel and hospitable staffers. The menu lists everything from steaks to seafood to various comfort foods. Casual dress; cocktails. **Parking:** on-site. **Cards:** AX, DC, MC, VI.

TRAN'S PALACE **Lunch:** $5-$11 **Dinner:** $8-$15 **Phone:** 506/622-0653

Chinese **Location:** Centre. 226 Pleasant St E1V 1Y5. **Hours:** 11 am-9 pm, Fri & Sat-10 pm. **Closed:** 12/25. **Features:** Basic decor, good food and ample portions are what diners find at the popular restaurant. On the menu is a selection of Chinese, Vietnamese and some Canadian dishes. Casual dress; cocktails. **Parking:** on-site. **Cards:** AX, MC, VI.

MONCTON pop. 61,046

──── **WHERE TO STAY** ────

AMSTERDAM INN **Phone:** (506)383-5050

7/1-9/18	1P: $120	2P: $120	XP: $10 F
5/16-6/30	1P: $90	2P: $100	XP: $10 F
5/1-5/15	1P: $85	2P: $95	XP: $10 F
9/19-4/30	1P: $79	2P: $89	XP: $10 F

Small-scale Hotel **Location:** Trans-Canada Hwy 2, exit 450. 2550 Mountain Rd E1G 1B4. **Fax:** 506/383-1438. **Facility:** Smoke free premises. 48 one-bedroom standard units. 2 stories (no elevator), interior corridors. **Parking:** on-site. **Amenities:** video library, high-speed Internet, irons, hair dryers. *Some:* video games. **Business Services:** meeting rooms. **Cards:** AX, MC, VI.

SOME UNITS
(ASK) (SD) (📶) (✕) (VCR) / (🖥) (📺) (🖨) /

ARCHIBALD BED & BREAKFAST
Phone: (506)382-0123

Bed & Breakfast

| | 6/1-9/30 [BP] | 1P: $65-$85 | 2P: $75-$95 | XP: $12 |
| | 5/1-5/31 & 10/1-4/30 [BP] | 1P: $55-$75 | 2P: $65-$85 | XP: $12 |

Location: 2 blks s of jct Mountain Rd and Archibald St; centre. Located in a residential area. 194 Archibald St E1C 5J9. Fax: 506/857-9188. **Facility:** Smoke free premises. 6 one-bedroom standard units. 2 stories (no elevator), interior corridors. *Bath:* some shared or private, combo or shower only. **Parking:** on-site. **Terms:** office hours 7 am-10 pm, check-in 4 pm. **Amenities:** hair dryers. **Guest Services:** wireless Internet. **Cards:** MC, VI.

🍴 ✕ 💻

AUBERGE WILD ROSE INN
Phone: (506)383-9751

Country Inn

| | All Year | 1P: $99-$229 | 2P: $105-$239 | XP: $16 |

Location: Trans-Canada Hwy 2, exit 465, 0.6 mi (1 km) n on Rt 134 (Lewisville Rd). Located in a quiet rural area. 17 Baseline Rd E1H 1N5. Fax: 506/383-9751. **Facility:** Bordering a golf course in a rural area, the inn offers well-appointed rooms, many with gas fireplaces and double whirlpool baths. Smoke free premises. 16 one-bedroom standard units, some with whirlpools. 2 stories (no elevator), interior corridors. **Parking:** on-site. **Terms:** office hours 7 am-10 pm, cancellation fee imposed, package plans. **Amenities:** video library, irons, hair dryers. **Dining:** Le Flair Restaurant, see separate listing. **Leisure Activities:** game room. **Guest Services:** wireless Internet. **Business Services:** meeting rooms. **Cards:** AX, MC, VI.

🍴 ✕ 📼 💻

BEACON LIGHT MOTEL
Phone: 506/384-1734

(CAA) (SAVE)

Motel

| | All Year | 1P: $75-$120 | 2P: $75-$120 | F18 |

Location: Trans-Canada Hwy 2, exit 454 (Mapleton Rd), 1.7 mi (2.8 km) to Rt 126 (Mountain Rd), then just s. Located in a commercial area. 1062 Mountain Rd E1C 2T1. Fax: 506/384-1718. **Facility:** 48 one-bedroom standard units, some with efficiencies, kitchens and/or whirlpools. 2 stories (no elevator), interior/exterior corridors. **Parking:** on-site. **Terms:** office hours 7 am-midnight, small pets only. **Amenities:** *Some:* irons, hair dryers. **Dining:** 7-11 am. **Pool(s):** heated indoor. **Leisure Activities:** whirlpool. **Guest Services:** wireless Internet. **Free Special Amenities:** local telephone calls and high-speed Internet. **Cards:** AX, CB, DC, DS, JC, MC, VI.

SOME UNITS

🛏 🍴 🐾 🔒 / ✕ 💻 /

BEST WESTERN MONCTON
Book great rates at AAA.com
Phone: (506)388-0888

Small-scale Hotel

	6/16-9/30	1P: $119-$220	2P: $129-$230	XP: $10	F
	5/1-6/15	1P: $112-$220	2P: $122-$230	XP: $10	F
	10/1-4/30	1P: $105-$220	2P: $115-$230	XP: $10	F

Location: Trans-Canada Hwy 2, exit 459A eastbound, s on Rt 115 to Lewisville Rd, then left; exit 467A westbound, 5 mi (8 km) w on Hwy 15, exit 10. 300 Lewisville Rd E1A 5Y4. Fax: 506/388-0883. **Facility:** 80 units. 58 one-bedroom standard units. 22 one-bedroom suites ($155-$240), some with whirlpools. 3 stories, interior corridors. *Bath:* combo or shower only. **Parking:** on-site. **Terms:** [ECP] meal plan available, small pets only (in smoking units). **Amenities:** video games (fee), high-speed Internet, voice mail, irons, hair dryers. *Some:* dual phone lines. **Pool(s):** heated indoor. **Leisure Activities:** exercise room. **Guest Services:** coin laundry. **Business Services:** meeting rooms, PC. **Cards:** AX, CB, DC, DS, MC, VI.

SOME UNITS

(ASK) 🆂 🐾 🛏 🅼 📶 🐾 📹 💻 / ✕ 🔒 📶 /

CHATEAU MONCTON HOTEL & SUITES
Book great rates at AAA.com
Phone: (506)870-4444

(CAA) (SAVE)

Large-scale Hotel

| | All Year | 1P: $129 | 2P: $129 | XP: $10 | F12 |

Location: Opposite of Champlain Mall. Located in a commercial area. 100 Main St E1C 1B9. Fax: 506/870-4445. **Facility:** 106 units. 100 one-bedroom standard units. 6 one-bedroom suites with whirlpools. 5 stories, interior corridors. **Parking:** on-site. **Amenities:** high-speed Internet, voice mail, honor bars, irons, hair dryers. **Leisure Activities:** exercise room. **Guest Services:** valet laundry, wireless Internet. **Business Services:** meeting rooms. **Cards:** AX, MC, VI. **Free Special Amenities:** expanded continental breakfast and high-speed Internet.

SOME UNITS

🆂 🍸 🅼 📹 💻 / ✕ /

COASTAL INN CHAMPLAIN
Book great rates at AAA.com
Phone: (506)857-9686

(CAA) (SAVE)

Small-scale Hotel

| | 7/20-9/30 [ECP] | 1P: $109-$129 | 2P: $109-$129 | XP: $12 | F18 |
| | 5/1-7/19 & 10/1-4/30 [ECP] | 1P: $99-$119 | 2P: $99-$119 | XP: $12 | F18 |

Location: At Paul St; opposite Champlain Place Shopping Centre. 502 Kennedy St E1A 5Y7. Fax: 506/857-1791. **Facility:** 105 one-bedroom standard units, some with efficiencies. 2 stories (no elevator), interior/exterior corridors. **Parking:** on-site. **Terms:** [AP] & [BP] meal plans available, pets (in designated smoking units). **Amenities:** video library (fee). *Some:* high-speed Internet, hair dryers. **Dining:** 7 am-10 pm; to 9 pm off season, cocktails. **Pool(s):** heated indoor. **Leisure Activities:** sauna. **Guest Services:** coin laundry. **Business Services:** meeting rooms. **Cards:** AX, DC, MC, VI. **Free Special Amenities:** expanded continental breakfast and newspaper.

SOME UNITS

🆂 🐾 🍴 🍸 🐾 💻 / ✕ 📼 🔒 📶 /
FEE

COLONIAL INNS
Phone: (506)382-3395

Small-scale Hotel

| | All Year | 1P: $89 | 2P: $97 | XP: $8 | F16 |

Location: 1 blk n of Main St; centre. Located in a commercial area. 42 Highfield St E1C 8T6. Fax: 506/858-8991. **Facility:** 61 one-bedroom standard units. 2 stories (no elevator), interior/exterior corridors. **Parking:** on-site. **Terms:** [BP] meal plan available, 15% service charge, small pets only (in designated units). **Amenities:** hair dryers. **Pool(s):** heated outdoor. **Leisure Activities:** sauna, whirlpool, game room. **Guest Services:** wireless Internet. **Business Services:** meeting rooms, PC. **Cards:** AX, DC, MC, VI.

SOME UNITS

(ASK) 🆂 🐾 🍴 🍸 🐾 ✕ / ✕ 🔒 📶 /

COMFORT INN
Book great rates at AAA.com
Phone: (506)859-6868

(CAA) (SAVE)

Small-scale Hotel

| | 7/1-10/31 [CP] | 1P: $125-$155 | 2P: $125-$295 | XP: $10 | F17 |
| | 5/1-6/30 & 11/1-4/30 [CP] | 1P: $85-$135 | 2P: $85-$195 | XP: $10 | F17 |

Location: Trans-Canada Hwy 2, exit 459A onto Hwy 115 S, left on Rt 134 E (Lewisville Rd). Located in a residential area. 20 Maplewood Dr E1A 6P9. Fax: 506/854-3575. **Facility:** 79 one-bedroom standard units. 2 stories (no elevator), interior corridors. **Parking:** on-site, winter plug-ins. **Terms:** pets (on ground floor). **Amenities:** high-speed Internet, irons, hair dryers. *Some:* CD players. **Cards:** AX, CB, DC, DS, JC, MC, VI. *(See color ad card insert)*

SOME UNITS

🆂 🐾 📹 🔒 📶 💻 / ✕ /

COMFORT INN · *Book great rates at AAA.com*   Phone: (506)384-3175

7/1-10/31 [CP]	1P: $105-$195	2P: $105-$295	XP: $10	F17
5/1-6/30 & 11/1-4/30 [CP]	1P: $85-$125	2P: $105-$175	XP: $10	F17

Small-scale Hotel **Location:** Trans-Canada Hwy 2, exit 450. 2495 Mountain Rd E1G 2W4. Fax: 506/853-7307. **Facility:** 59 one-bedroom standard units. 2 stories (no elevator), interior corridors. **Parking:** on-site. **Amenities:** high-speed Internet, irons, hair dryers. *Some:* CD players. **Cards:** AX, CB, DC, DS, JC, MC, VI. *(See color ad card insert)*

SOME UNITS

(ASK) (SD) 🐾 (🍴) 🎥 🖥 / ✕ 🔌 🖼 /

COUNTRY INN & SUITES BY CARLSON · *Book great rates at AAA.com*   Phone: (506)852-7000

5/1-10/1	1P: $104-$117	2P: $119-$132	XP: $15	F18
10/2-4/30	1P: $90-$99	2P: $90-$100	XP: $15	F18

Small-scale Hotel **Location:** Trans-Canada Hwy 2, exit 450. Located in a rural area. 2475 Mountain Rd E1G 2J5. Fax: 506/852-7008. **Facility:** 76 units. 38 one-bedroom standard units. 38 one-bedroom suites ($105-$145). 3 stories, interior corridors. **Parking:** on-site. **Terms:** cancellation fee imposed, [ECP] meal plan available, small pets only ($5 extra charge, in smoking units). **Amenities:** video library, DVD players, irons, hair dryers. **Leisure Activities:** exercise room. **Guest Services:** coin laundry, wireless Internet. **Cards:** AX, DC, DS, MC, VI. *(See color ad on TourBookMark)*

SOME UNITS

(ASK) (SD) 🐾 🔌 🖥 / ✕ 🖼 /
FEE

CROWNE PLAZA MONCTON DOWNTOWN · *Book great rates at AAA.com*   Phone: (506)854-6340

(CAA) (SAVE)   All Year   1P: $149-$179   2P: $149-$179   XP: $10   F17

Large-scale Hotel **Location:** Highfield and Main sts; downtown. 1005 Main St E1C 1G9. Fax: 506/857-4176. **Facility:** 191 units. 186 one-bedroom standard units. 5 one-bedroom suites ($199-$299) with whirlpools. 9 stories, interior corridors. **Parking:** on-site. **Terms:** cancellation fee imposed, pets ($10 extra charge, in smoking units). **Amenities:** video games (fee), dual phone lines, voice mail, irons, hair dryers. **Dining:** 6:30 am-11 pm. **Pool(s):** heated indoor. **Leisure Activities:** whirlpool, steamroom, exercise room. **Guest Services:** gift shop, valet and coin laundry, wireless Internet. **Business Services:** conference facilities, business center. **Cards:** AX, CB, DC, DS, JC, MC, VI. **Free Special Amenities: local telephone calls and high-speed Internet.**

SOME UNITS

(SD) 🐾 🍴 (24) 🍽 🏊 ✕ 🎥 🖥 / ✕ 🔌 /
FEE

DELTA BEAUSEJOUR · *Book great rates at AAA.com*   Phone: (506)854-4344

All Year   1P: $129-$199   2P: $129-$199

Large-scale Hotel **Location:** Main and Bacon sts; centre of downtown. 750 Main St E1C 1E6. Fax: 506/858-0957. **Facility:** Smoke free premises. 310 units. 301 one-bedroom standard units. 9 one-bedroom suites. 10 stories, interior corridors. **Parking:** on-site (fee). **Terms:** check-in 4 pm, cancellation fee imposed, pets ($38 fee). **Amenities:** voice mail, honor bars, irons, hair dryers. *Fee:* video games, high-speed Internet. **Dining:** Windjammer Dining Room, see separate listing. **Pool(s):** heated indoor. **Leisure Activities:** whirlpool, exercise room. **Guest Services:** gift shop, valet laundry. **Business Services:** conference facilities, PC. **Cards:** AX, CB, DC, DS, JC, MC, VI. *(See color ad below)*

(ASK) 🐾 🍴 (24) 🍽 🏊 ✕ 🎥 🖥
FEE

FUTURE INNS MONCTON   Phone: (506)852-9600

5/1-10/31	1P: $169-$199	2P: $169-$199	XP: $10	F18
11/1-4/30	1P: $159-$189	2P: $159-$189	XP: $10	F18

Small-scale Hotel **Location:** Trans-Canada Hwy 2, exit 454. 40 Lady Ada Blvd E1C 8P2. Fax: 506/852-9692. **Facility:** Smoke free premises. 130 units. 120 one-bedroom standard units. 10 one-bedroom suites ($189-$229). 5 stories, interior corridors. *Bath:* combo or shower only. **Parking:** on-site. **Terms:** cancellation fee imposed, package plans available, package plans. **Amenities:** high-speed Internet, voice mail, irons, hair dryers. *Some:* CD players. **Dining:** Maverick's Steakhouse, see separate listing. **Guest Services:** valet and coin laundry, wireless Internet. **Business Services:** conference facilities, business center. **Cards:** AX, MC, VI.

(ASK) (SD) 🍴 🍽 (GM) ♿ 🐾 ✕ 🎥 🖥

HOLIDAY INN EXPRESS HOTEL & SUITES MONCTON
Book great rates at AAA.com
Phone: (506)384-1050

CAA SAVE

7/1-8/31	1P: $139-$199	2P: $139-$199	XP: $10 F18
9/1-4/30	1P: $119-$159	2P: $119-$159	XP: $10 F18
5/1-6/30	1P: $119-$149	2P: $119-$149	XP: $10 F18

Small-scale Hotel
Location: Trans-Canada Hwy 2, exit 450. 2515 Mountain Rd E1C 8R7 (PO Box 5005). Fax: 506/859-6070. **Facility:** 152 units. 97 one-bedroom standard units. 55 one-bedroom suites, some with whirlpools. 1-3 stories, interior/exterior corridors. **Parking:** on-site. **Terms:** check-in 4 pm, [ECP] meal plan available, pets (ground floor units). **Amenities:** video games (fee), high-speed Internet, voice mail, irons, hair dryers. *Some:* dual phone lines, honor bars. **Dining:** Pastificio Pub & Eatery, see separate listing. **Pool(s):** heated indoor. **Leisure Activities:** sauna, whirlpools, exercise room. **Guest Services:** valet and coin laundry. **Business Services:** meeting rooms. **Cards:** AX, DC, DS, MC, VI.
Free Special Amenities: expanded continental breakfast and high-speed Internet. *(See color ad card insert)*

SOME UNITS

RAMADA PLAZA HOTEL CRYSTAL PALACE
Book at AAA.com
Phone: (506)858-8584

All Year	1P: $109-$169	2P: $109-$169	XP: $10 F18

Small-scale Hotel
Location: Trans-Canada Hwy 2, exit 459A eastbound, s on Rt 115 to Lewisville Rd, then left; exit 467A westbound, 4.8 mi (8 km) w on Rt 15 to rotary. Located in Crystal Palace Amusement Park. 499 Paul St E1A 6S5. Fax: 506/858-5486. **Facility:** 115 one-bedroom standard units, some with whirlpools. 3 stories, interior corridors. **Parking:** on-site. **Terms:** cancellation fee imposed. **Amenities:** voice mail, honor bars, irons, hair dryers. *Some:* CD players. **Pool(s):** heated indoor. **Leisure Activities:** sauna, whirlpool, exercise room. **Guest Services:** valet laundry, wireless Internet. **Business Services:** meeting rooms, business center. **Cards:** AX, DC, MC, VI.

SOME UNITS

RODD PARK HOUSE INN
Book great rates at AAA.com
Phone: (506)382-1664

6/1-9/30	1P: $92-$182	2P: $102-$182	XP: $10 F16
5/1-5/31 & 10/1-4/30	1P: $73-$160	2P: $83-$160	XP: $10 F16

Small-scale Hotel
Location: On Rt 106 (Main St) at King St. 434 Main St E1C 1B9. Fax: 506/855-9494. **Facility:** 97 units. 96 one-bedroom standard units. 1 one-bedroom suite ($158-$218). 4 stories, interior/exterior corridors. *Bath:* combo or shower only. **Parking:** on-site, winter plug-ins. **Terms:** cancellation fee imposed, package plans, pets (in smoking units). **Amenities:** hair dryers. *Some:* honor bars. **Pool(s):** heated outdoor. **Guest Services:** valet laundry, wireless Internet. **Business Services:** meeting rooms. **Cards:** AX, DC, DS, MC, VI. *(See color ad p 359)*

SOME UNITS

SAUNDERS COUNTRY INN & ESTATE Phone: (506)861-9091
All Year   1P: $100-$200   2P: $100-$200
Location: Trans-Canada Hwy 2, exit 450, 6 mi (10 km) n. 4113 Rt 126 (Mountain Rd) E1G 2Z4. Fax: 506/388-9062.
Country Inn **Facility:** Set back from the road on 250-acres, this lovely cedar home has cathedral ceilings and tastefully decorated guestrooms. Smoke free premises. 4 one-bedroom standard units, some with whirlpools. 2 stories (no elevator), interior corridors. **Parking:** on-site. **Terms:** office hours 7 am-10 pm, 7 day cancellation notice-fee imposed, weekly rates available. **Amenities:** hair dryers. **Leisure Activities:** whirlpool. **Guest Services:** complimentary laundry. **Cards:** MC, VI.

SUPER 8 MOTEL MONCTON/DIEPPE *Book at AAA.com*   Phone: 506-858-8880
Property failed to provide current rates
Location: Hwy 15, exit 16, 0.6 mi (1 km) s. 370 Dieppe Blvd E1A 8H4. Fax: 506/343-8808. **Facility:** Smoke free premises. 86 units. 56 one-bedroom standard units, some with whirlpools. 30 one-bedroom suites. 3 stories, Small-scale Hotel interior corridors. **Bath:** combo or shower only. **Parking:** on-site. **Terms:** small pets only ($10 extra charge, in limited units). **Amenities:** high-speed Internet, voice mail, irons, hair dryers. **Pool(s):** heated indoor. **Leisure Activities:** whirlpool, waterslide. **Guest Services:** coin laundry, wireless Internet. **Business Services:** meeting rooms.

FEE

─────── WHERE TO DINE ───────

THE BAMBOO GARDEN RESTAURANT Lunch: $7-$11   Dinner: $9-$16   Phone: 506-857-8801
Location: Just n of Main St; centre. 37 Highfield St E1C 5N2. **Hours:** 11 am-9 pm, Fri-10 pm, Sat & Sun 4 pm-9 pm. Closed: 12/25; also Tues. **Reservations:** accepted. **Features:** Steak, lobster and tasty Chinese Chinese selections make up the popular restaurant's diverse menu. The daily buffet lines up a good variety of flavorful dishes. Casual dress; cocktails. **Parking:** on-site. **Cards:** AX, DC, MC, VI.

THE BARNYARD BBQ Lunch: $6-$12   Dinner: $10-$22   Phone: 506-389-9042
Location: 0.4 mi (0.7 km) e of Elmwood Dr. 131 Mill Rd E1A 6R1. **Hours:** 11 am-10 pm. Closed: 1/1, 12/25, 12/26. **Reservations:** accepted. **Features:** Pardners can grab their cowboy hat and boots and head on over to the Barbecue eatery for a feed of ribs, steaks and chicken wings. The on-site microbrewery offers several tasty thirst quenchers. Casual dress; cocktails. **Parking:** on-site. **Cards:** AX, DS, MC, VI.

BOGART'S BAR & GRILL Lunch: $7-$12   Dinner: $14-$20   Phone: 506-855-5335
Location: Corner of Lester Ave. 589 Main St E1C 1C6. **Hours:** 11:30 am-9 pm, Fri & Sat-10 pm, Sun 5 pm-9 pm. Closed major holidays. **Reservations:** accepted. **Features:** Tables at the delightful, jazzy bistro are set with Canadian fresh flowers and oil lamps that offer subdued lighting. A varied menu is anchored by fresh, creative seafood dishes such as salmon tornado. Casual dress; cocktails. **Parking:** street. **Cards:** AX, DC, MC, VI.

BOOMERANG'S STEAKHOUSE Lunch: $7-$12   Dinner: $14-$21   Phone: 506-857-8325
Location: Centre. 130 Westmorland St E1C 2T9. **Hours:** 11:30 am-2 & 4-10 pm, Fri-11 pm, Sat 4 pm-11 pm, Sun 4 pm-9 pm. Closed: 12/24-12/26. **Features:** Have a g'day and a good meal at this upbeat and raucous Aussie-style eatery. Huge helpings of steak, chicken and burgers are sure to satisfy even the heartiest of Steak House appetites; and nachos, coconut shrimp and a "boomerang blossom" add touches of outback fun. Casual dress; cocktails. **Parking:** on-site. **Cards:** AX, DC, MC, VI.

BOSTON PIZZA Lunch: $6-$12   Dinner: $7-$17   Phone: 506-860-7777
Location: Trans-Canada Hwy 2, exit 450, 3 mi (5 km) se on Rt 126 (Mountain Rd). 1380 Mountain Rd E1C 2T8. **Hours:** 11 am-1 am, Fri & Sat-2 am. Closed: 12/25. **Reservations:** accepted. **Features:** The popular chain Italian features an atmosphere that's comfortable for group and family dining. In addition to the gourmet pizzas that gave this place its name, the tasty offerings include pasta dishes, hearty burgers, sandwiches, ribs and chicken and fish. Casual dress; cocktails. **Parking:** on-site. **Cards:** AX, DC, MC, VI.

CAFE ARCHIBALD Lunch: $5-$11   Dinner: $8-$13   Phone: 506-853-8819
Location: Corner of Archibald St and Mountain Rd. 221 Mountain Rd E1C 2L5. **Hours:** 10:30 am-11 pm, Fri & Sat-midnight. Closed: 1/1, 12/25. **Reservations:** not accepted. **Features:** The casual, upbeat cafe specializes in Canadian fine crepes, pizza, bruschetta and great salads prepared in an open kitchen. The spot is particularly popular with students and artists, who enjoy seasonal dining on the small patio. Casual dress; beer & wine only. **Parking:** on-site. **Cards:** AX, DC, MC, VI.

CHAN'S HOUSE RESTAURANT & TAKE-OUT Lunch: $6-$10   Dinner: $9-$16   Phone: 506-858-0112
Location: Centre; opposite Champlain Mall. 80 Champlain St E1C 1B9. **Hours:** 11 am-midnight, Fri & Sat-1 am, Sun-11 pm. Closed: 12/25. **Reservations:** accepted. **Features:** The convenient location is opposite a large Chinese shopping center. In addition to a vast menu that includes some Canadian dishes, the restaurant offers daily buffets. Casual dress; cocktails. **Parking:** on-site. **Cards:** AX, MC, VI.

CHEZ LUC FINE DINING Dinner: $20-$28   Phone: 506-386-7271
Location: At Weldon St. 329 St George St E1C 1W8. **Hours:** 5 pm-10 pm. Closed: 12/25. **Reservations:** accepted. **Features:** This pleasant dining room nurtures a charming Old World feel, which is French enhanced by candles, chandeliers, antique furnishings and classic paintings. The specialty is rack of lamb, but patrons also will find a nice selection of seafood, steaks and chicken. Dressy casual; cocktails. **Parking:** on-site. **Cards:** AX, DC, MC, VI.

CORA'S BREAKFAST & LUNCH Lunch: $6-$10   Phone: 506-382-2672
Location: Centre; adjacent to Delta Beausejour. 730 Main St E1C 1E4. **Hours:** 6 am-3 pm, Sun from 7 am. Closed: 12/25. **Reservations:** accepted. **Features:** Although this place specializes in breakfast, it offers a varied daytime menu that includes bacon, eggs, sausages, crepes, grilled cheese, sandwiches, freshly Canadian prepared quiches, salads, fruit platters and freshly squeezed juices. The family-friendly dining room is casual and modern. Casual dress. **Parking:** on-site (fee). **Cards:** AX, DC, MC, VI.

DON CHERRY'S SPORTS GRILL   **Lunch:** $7-$11   **Dinner:** $9-$16   **Phone:** 506/852-3363

Canadian

Location: Centre at Acadie St; adjacent to Dieppe City Hall. 200 Champlain St E1A 1P1. **Hours:** 11 am-10 pm, Thurs & Fri-11 pm, Sat 8 am-11 pm, Sun 8 am-9 pm. Closed: 12/25. **Reservations:** accepted. **Features:** In a convenient location in a large mall, the hockey-oriented restaurant presents a menu that is sure to score. Guests can "crosscheck" the selection, which ranges from cocktails to entrees, but shouldn't penalize themselves by skipping dessert. Casual dress; cocktails. **Parking:** on-site. **Cards:** AX, DC, MC, VI.

EAST SIDE MARIO'S   **Lunch:** $6-$12   **Dinner:** $9-$15   **Phone:** 506/857-3204

Italian

Location: Trans-Canada Hwy 2, exit 450, 2.5 mi (4 km) s on Rt 126 (Mountain Rd), then just e. 99 Trinity Dr E1C 2J7. **Hours:** 11 am-11 pm, Fri & Sat-midnight. Closed: 10/8, 12/25. **Reservations:** accepted. **Features:** Pizza, steak, sandwiches, salads, burgers, hot dogs, chicken, fish, calamari and pasta are among offerings at the chain of family restaurants, which also has a children's menu. The lively dining room is decorated to resemble a European market, with shop facades and vintage signage. Casual dress; cocktails. **Parking:** on-site. **Cards:** AX, DC, MC, VI.

FISHERMAN'S PARADISE SEAFOOD &
STEAK RESTAURANT   *Menu on AAA.com*   **Lunch:** $7-$16   **Dinner:** $10-$30   **Phone:** 506/859-4388

Seafood

Location: Rt 15, exit 11, just s; corner of Dieppe Blvd and Champlain St. 330 Dieppe Blvd E1A 6S4. **Hours:** 11 am-11 pm; closing hours may vary. Closed: 12/24, 12/25. **Reservations:** suggested. **Features:** Spacious dining rooms feature a nautical theme and a friendly staff dressed in early Acadian attire. Specialties include fresh seafood dishes like halibut and hearty chowder, as well as a selection of meat entrees, fresh salad and home-style dessert. Casual dress; cocktails. **Parking:** on-site. **Cards:** AX, DC, MC, VI.

GOLDEN EAGLE RESTAURANT   **Lunch:** $5-$10   **Dinner:** $9-$15   **Phone:** 506/858-8508

Chinese

Location: Trans-Canada Hwy 2, exit 450, 2.4 mi (4.2 km) se on Rt 126 (Mountain Rd). 1590 Mountain Rd E1G 1A4. **Hours:** 11 am-9:30 pm, Sun noon-8:30 pm. Closed: 12/25; also Mon. **Reservations:** accepted. **Features:** A popular spot for a good meal, the restaurant specializes in reasonably priced combination plates. Canadian dishes also are available. Casual dress. **Parking:** on-site. **Cards:** AX, DC, MC, VI.

GRAFFITI   **Lunch:** $7-$14   **Dinner:** $9-$17   **Phone:** 506/382-4299

Mediterranean

Location: Centre. 879 Main St E1C 5J9. **Hours:** 11 am-11 pm, Sat-midnight. Closed: 1/1, 12/25. **Reservations:** suggested. **Features:** The popular spot sustains a bustling atmosphere and offers seating on two levels. Food is prepared to order and is nicely presented. Casual dress; cocktails. **Parking:** on-site (fee) and street. **Cards:** AX, DC, MC, VI.

THE HOMESTEAD RESTAURANT   **Lunch:** $5-$12   **Dinner:** $6-$15   **Phone:** 506/386-1907

Canadian

Location: On Rt 114; in Riverview Village. 358 Coverdale Rd E1B 3J5. **Hours:** 6:45 am-8:30 pm. Closed: 1/1, 9/3, 12/25; also 7/1. **Features:** The popular family restaurant is across the river from town and serves a wide variety of home-style items. Ample portions and great desserts keep folks coming back. Casual dress. **Parking:** on-site. **Cards:** AX, MC, VI.

HOUSE OF LAM   **Lunch:** $8-$15   **Dinner:** $14-$21   **Phone:** 506/384-1101

Chinese

Location: 2.2 mi (3.6 km) nw on Rt 126 (Mountain Rd). 957 Mountain Rd E1C 2S4. **Hours:** 11 am-11 pm, Sun-10 pm. Closed: 12/25, 12/26. **Reservations:** accepted. **Features:** Szechuan dinners are the focus of the restaurant's menu. Sample a variety of dishes from the lunch buffet, served weekdays, and the Sunday dinner buffet. A water fountain at the entrance, as well as red, gold and bamboo accents, decorate the interior. Casual dress; cocktails. **Parking:** on-site. **Cards:** AX, DC, MC, VI.

JEAN'S RESTAURANT   **Lunch:** $4-$10   **Dinner:** $7-$14   **Phone:** 506/856-8988

Canadian

Location: Trans-Canada Hwy 2, exit 452, 1 mi (1.6 km) s on George Rd. 1999 Mountain Rd E1G 1B1. **Hours:** 5:45 am-10 pm. Closed: 12/25. **Features:** The conveniently located spot employs casual, friendly servers who wend through the country-themed setting. Ample choices line the breakfast and lunch menu. Casual dress; cocktails. **Parking:** on-site. **Cards:** MC, VI.

JUNGLE JIM'S RESTAURANT   **Lunch:** $5-$11   **Dinner:** $8-$20   **Phone:** 506/386-5467

Canadian

Location: In Rogers Mini Mall. 1134 Mountain Rd E1C 2T3. **Hours:** 11 am-10 pm, Thurs & Fri-11 pm, Sat 10 am-11 pm, Sun 10 am-10 pm. Closed: 12/25. **Features:** Guests can step into a tropical theme at the casual eatery, which employs a friendly staff and nurtures a bustling atmosphere. The menu lines up a wide variety of comfort foods, salads, chicken, beef, seafood and hot wings, all served in ample, flavorful portions. Casual dress; cocktails. **Parking:** on-site. **Cards:** AX, DC, MC, VI.

LE CHATEAU A PAPE   **Dinner:** $16-$28   **Phone:** 506/855-7273

Canadian

Location: Centre. 2 Steadman St E1C 4N9. **Hours:** 4 pm-10 pm, Fri & Sat-midnight. Closed: 12/25, 12/26. **Reservations:** suggested. **Features:** This attractive converted home overlooks the ebb and flow of an Atlantic tidal bore which can be viewed from several dining sections. Tastefully prepared seafood and meat entrees are served by a cordial staff who offer the added flair of tableside flambe. Dressy casual; cocktails. **Parking:** on-site. **Cards:** AX, CB, DC, DS, MC, VI.

LE FLAIR RESTAURANT   **Dinner:** $24-$37   **Phone:** 506/383-9751

Canadian

Location: Trans-Canada Hwy 2, exit 465, 0.6 mi (1 km) n on Rt 134 (Lewisville Rd). 17 Baseline Rd E1H 1N5. **Hours:** 5:30 pm-8:30 pm. Closed: 12/25. **Reservations:** suggested. **Features:** Prix fixe three- and four-course meals incorporate a fine selection of creatively prepared dishes, such as pork tenderloin, shrimp and scallop provencale and the always-popular captain's plate. The heavenly desserts are prepared daily. Dressy casual; cocktails. **Parking:** on-site. **Cards:** AX, DC, MC, VI.

LONE STAR CAFE   **Lunch:** $7-$11   **Dinner:** $10-$20   **Phone:** 506/384-7772

Tex-Mex

Location: Centre; at Blue Cross Centre. 644 Main St E1C 1E2. **Hours:** 11:30 am-10 pm, Fri-11 pm, Sat noon-11 pm, Sun noon-10 pm. Closed: 1/1, 12/25. **Features:** The spacious restaurant serves a vast selection of Tex-Mex entrees in ample portions. The atmosphere is upbeat and lively. Casual dress; cocktails. **Parking:** on-site. **Cards:** AX, MC, VI.

MAVERICK'S STEAKHOUSE   **Lunch: $9-$15**   **Dinner: $18-$27**   **Phone: 506/855-3346**
Steak House

Location: Trans-Canada Hwy 2, exit 454; in Future Inns Moncton. 40 Lady Ada Blvd E1C 8P2. **Hours:** 7 am-10 pm, Fri & Sat-11 pm. **Reservations:** accepted. **Features:** The restaurant offers thoughtful preparations of dry-aged prime beef, veal and such seafood as lobster, salmon and jumbo shrimp. The wine list is extensive. The staff provides knowledgeable, friendly service. Casual dress; cocktails. **Parking:** on-site.

MCGINNIS LANDING RESTAURANT   **Lunch: $6-$11**   **Dinner: $9-$21**   **Phone: 506/856-6995**
Canadian

Location: Trans-Canada Hwy 2, exit 459A eastbound, s on Rt 115 to Lewisville Rd, then just e; exit 467A westbound, 5 mi (8 km) w on Rt 15 to rotary; in Crystal Palace Amusement Park. 499 Paul St E1A 6S5. **Hours:** 7 am-midnight, Fri & Sat-1 am. Closed: 12/25. **Reservations:** accepted. **Features:** This restaurant prepares menu options ranging from burgers and fish and chips to steaks, seafood, stir-fry and various salads. Casual dress; cocktails. **Parking:** on-site. **Cards:** AX, MC, VI.

MEXICALI ROSA'S   **Lunch: $7-$11**   **Dinner: $9-$16**   **Phone: 506/855-7672**
Mexican

Location: Centre. 683 Main St E1C 1E3. **Hours:** 11:30 am-11 pm, Fri & Sat-midnight, Sun 4 pm-10 pm. Closed: 12/25. **Reservations:** accepted. **Features:** The Mexican cantina makes an excellent choice for family-friendly fun. Old West paintings and murals add color to stucco walls and wooden beams, while a Tex-Mex menu provides a feast of favorites such as fajitas, burritos and some seafood items. Fried ice cream is a sweet treat. Casual dress; cocktails. **Parking:** on-site (fee). **Cards:** AX, MC, VI.

MIKES RESTAURANT   **Lunch: $6-$10**   **Dinner: $8-$16**   **Phone: 506/855-6464**
Canadian

Location: At Mountain Rd. 30 Mapleton Rd E1C 2T1. **Hours:** 7 am-11 pm, Fri & Sat-midnight. Closed: 12/25. **Reservations:** accepted. **Features:** This popular family-friendly restaurant specializes in pizza and hot submarine sandwiches, along with fries, burgers, soup, salads, pasta, grilled meats and seafood. An excellent variety of colorful desserts rounds out the offerings. Casual dress; cocktails. **Parking:** on-site. **Cards:** AX, DC, MC, VI.

MIKES RESTAURANT   **Lunch: $6-$10**   **Dinner: $8-$16**   **Phone: 506/855-6461**
Canadian

Location: At Champlain Mall. 9 Champlain St E1A 6S5. **Hours:** 7 am-11 pm, Fri & Sat-midnight. Closed: 12/25. **Reservations:** accepted. **Features:** This popular family-friendly restaurant specializes in pizza and hot submarine sandwiches, along with fries, burgers, soup, salads, pasta, grilled meats and seafood. An excellent variety of colorful desserts rounds out the offerings. Casual dress; cocktails. **Parking:** on-site. **Cards:** AX, DC, MC, VI.

MONTANA'S COOKHOUSE   **Lunch: $6-$10**   **Dinner: $8-$20**   **Phone: 506/384-7427**
Steak House

Location: Adjacent to Trinity Shopping Area. 225 Mapleton Rd E1C 2T9. **Hours:** 11 am-11 pm. Closed: 12/25. **Reservations:** accepted. **Features:** Pine boards, exposed beams, a fireplace and Western gear displayed about the dining room give the feeling of a back-country setting. The menu lists hearty portions of comfort fare, such as Yankee pot roast. While the focus is on steaks, ribs and chicken, some seafood entrees also are among offerings. Service is efficient and friendly. Casual dress; cocktails. **Parking:** on-site. **Cards:** AX, DC, MC, VI.

PASTALLI PASTA HOUSE   **Lunch: $8-$14**   **Dinner: $13-$22**   **Phone: 506/383-1050**
Italian

Location: Centre. 611 Main St E1C 2T1. **Hours:** 11 am-11 pm, Fri & Sat-midnight, Sun 4 pm-11 pm. Closed: 1/1, 12/24-12/26. **Reservations:** accepted. **Features:** Several cozy dining sections provide an intimate bistro setting in which a pleasant, knowledgeable staff dishes up selections from a creative menu. Patrons can choose from fresh seafood or traditional meats. The homemade desserts are excellent. Casual dress; cocktails. **Parking:** on-site (fee). **Cards:** AX, DC, MC, VI.

PASTIFICIO PUB & EATERY   **Dinner: $11-$22**   **Phone: 506/384-1050**
Italian

Location: Trans-Canada Hwy 2, exit 450; in Holiday Inn Express Hotel & Suites Moncton. 2515 Mountain Rd E1C 8R7. **Hours:** 4 pm-11 pm. Closed: 12/25; also Sun. **Reservations:** accepted. **Features:** A friendly atmosphere emanates from the pub-style bistro. The menu features a variety of pizza and pasta dishes, as well as burgers and fish and chips. Portions are ample. Casual dress; cocktails. **Parking:** on-site. **Cards:** AX, DC, DS, JC, MC, VI.

PUMP HOUSE BREWERY   **Lunch: $7-$16**   **Dinner: $7-$16**   **Phone: 506/855-2337**
Canadian

Location: Jct Main St. 5 Orange Ln E1C 4L6. **Hours:** 11 am-11 pm, Fri & Sat-2 am, Sun noon-midnight. Closed: 1/1, 12/25. **Reservations:** accepted. **Features:** Diners seeking an upbeat, casual place that serves basic, pub-style food and excellent microbrewed beers need look no further. Fine pizzas are baked in a wood-fired oven. Casual dress; cocktails. **Parking:** on-site (fee). **Cards:** AX, DC, MC.

ROCKWELZ RESTAURANT   **Lunch: $7-$14**   **Dinner: $16-$30**   **Phone: 506/854-0444**
Canadian

Location: Centre; adjacent to Chateau Moncton Hotel. 300 Main St E1C 1B9. **Hours:** 11:30 am-10 pm, Sat & Sun from 4 pm. Closed: 12/25, 12/26. **Reservations:** accepted. **Features:** This colorful restaurant with a jazz theme is located on the boardwalk overlooking the tidal bore. The menu offers a selection of fresh seafood and meat entrees, with some hints of Italian, Greek and Spanish cuisine styles. Casual dress; cocktails. **Parking:** on-site. **Cards:** AX, DC, MC, VI.

ST-HUBERT BBQ   **Lunch: $6-$11**   **Dinner: $8-$16**   **Phone: 506/858-0053**
Barbecue

Location: Trans-Canada Hwy 2, exit 454, 2.8 km s. 1049 Mountain Rd E1C 2S9. **Hours:** 11 am-10 pm, Fri & Sat-11 pm. Closed: 12/24-12/26. **Reservations:** accepted. **Features:** The pleasantly decorated family-friendly restaurant serves affordable chicken dinners, ribs, club sandwiches, chicken wings, salads, soups and hot chicken sandwiches. The children's menu includes animal nuggets. Casual dress; cocktails. **Parking:** on-site. **Cards:** AX, DC, MC, VI.

ST. JAMES GATE   Lunch: $7-$12   Dinner: $12-$20   Phone: 506/388-4283

▼▼ ▼▼

Canadian

MC, VI.

Location: Corner of Main and Church sts; centre. 14 Church St E1C 4Y9. **Hours:** 11 am-11 pm, Sun 4 pm-10 pm. Closed: 12/25. **Reservations:** accepted. **Features:** The appealing pub-style restaurant has a distinctive cellar decor with comfortable booths and tables. Classic pub fare is served in ample portions and coupled with a good selection of wines and beers on tap. Casual dress; cocktails. **Parking:** street. **Cards:** AX, DC,

SASHA'S MARTINIS, TAPAS & LOUNGE   Lunch: $7-$13   Dinner: $10-$18   Phone: 506/854-8748

▼▼ ▼▼

Canadian

cocktails. **Parking:** street. **Cards:** AX, DC, MC, VI.

Location: At Main St. 196 Robinson Ct E1C 5C4. **Hours:** 11:30 am-2 am, Sun 4 pm-midnight. Closed: 12/25. **Reservations:** accepted. **Features:** The lounge is a great spot to mingle and listen to soft jazz while sampling a delightful martini or cocktail from the extensive list. More than 30 tapas items and a full lunch and dinner menu are among choices to satisfy most any taste. The patio opens seasonally. Casual dress;

TAJMAHAL FLAVOUR OF INDIA   Lunch: $6-$10   Dinner: $12-$20   Phone: 506/854-5557

▼▼ ▼▼

Indian

Location: At Robinson St. 882 Main St E1C 1G4. **Hours:** 11:30 am-10 pm, Sat from 4 pm. Closed: 12/25; also Sun. **Reservations:** accepted. **Features:** In the heart of town, the cozy, tastefully decorated restaurant serves dishes that the chef prepares to order and spices to the diner's preference. Casual dress; cocktails. **Parking:** street. **Cards:** MC, VI.

VINA THAI RESTAURANT   Lunch: $9-$14   Dinner: $14-$20   Phone: 506/869-9996

▼▼ ▼▼

Thai

street. **Cards:** AX, DC, MC, VI.

Location: Jct Main St. 7 Orange Ln E1C 4L6. **Hours:** 11:30 am-9:30 pm, Sat & Sun from noon. **Reservations:** accepted. **Features:** The pleasant dining room has a casual, friendly atmosphere. Representative of authentic Thai cuisine are preparations of fresh seafood, chicken, beef and curry dishes, in addition to some vegetarian and combination plates. Casual dress; cocktails. **Parking:** on-site (fee) and

VITO'S RESTAURANT   Lunch: $7-$14   Dinner: $11-$18   Phone: 506/858-5000

▼▼ ▼▼

Italian

tempting pizzas. Casual dress; cocktails. **Parking:** on-site. **Cards:** AX, MC, VI.

Location: Corner of Mountain Rd and Vaughn Harvey Hwy. 726 Mountain Rd E1C 2P9. **Hours:** 11 am-11 pm, Fri & Sat-midnight, Sun 4 pm-11 pm. Closed: 12/25. **Reservations:** accepted. **Features:** Bordering a bustling street, this spacious restaurant has dining rooms decorated with stonework and mirrors. On the menu are such Italian specialties as fettuccine Alfredo, seafood lasagna, tortellini au gratin and various palate-

WINDJAMMER DINING ROOM   Dinner: $26-$39   Phone: 506/854-4344

▼▼▼ ▼▼▼

Continental

Location: Main and Bacon sts; centre of downtown; in Delta Beausejour. 750 Main St E1C 1E6. **Hours:** 5:30 pm-11 pm. Closed major holidays; also Sun. **Reservations:** suggested. **Features:** The elegant dining room carries out a nautical theme set off by tall ship models and brass porthole aquariums. Formally attired and professional in demeanor, the staff impresses even the most discerning traveler with tableside preparations and presentations of many fresh and creative dishes. The Caesar salad should not be missed. Dressy casual; cocktails. **Parking:** on-site (fee). **Cards:** AX, DC, DS, JC, MC, VI.

NIGADOO pop. 983

——— WHERE TO DINE ———

LA FINE GROBE SUR-MER   Dinner: $17-$26   Phone: 506/783-3138

(AAA)

▼▼ ▼▼

French

Location: Hwy 11, exit 321 to Rt 134, 0.5 mi (0.8 km) n; watch for road sign to ocean; from Bathurst, 6.9 mi (11 km) n on Rt 134. 289 Main St E8K 3Y5. **Hours:** 4:30 pm-10 pm. Closed: 12/25; also Sun 9/15-6/15. **Reservations:** suggested. **Features:** A charming oceanside hideaway, it overlooks picturesque Nepisiguit Bay. Enjoy such savory dishes as crab claws, salmon with sorrel and sauteed scallops either on the outdoor terrace cafe, or in the dining room surrounded by the paintings of local artists. Casual dress; cocktails. **Parking:** on-site. **Cards:** AX, DC, MC, VI.

OROMOCTO pop. 8,843

——— WHERE TO STAY ———

DAYS INN OROMOCTO   *Book great rates at AAA.com*   Phone: (506)357-5657

	1P:	2P:	XP:	
5/1-9/30	1P: $112	2P: $122	XP: $10	F
10/1-4/30	1P: $104	2P: $114	XP: $10	F

▼▼▼

Small-scale Hotel

MC, VI.

Location: Trans-Canada Hwy 2, exit 301 eastbound; exit 303 westbound, just s to Pioneer Ave, then 1 mi (1.6 km) w. 60 Brayson Blvd E2V 4T9. Fax: 506/357-5459. **Facility:** 81 units. 71 one-bedroom standard units. 10 one-bedroom suites ($209-$230), some with whirlpools. 3 stories, interior corridors. *Bath:* combo or shower only. **Parking:** on-site. **Terms:** pets ($15 extra charge). **Amenities:** voice mail, irons, hair dryers. **Pool(s):** heated indoor. **Leisure Activities:** whirlpool, exercise room. **Guest Services:** valet laundry, wireless Internet. **Business Services:** meeting rooms, PC. **Cards:** AX, DC, DS,

SOME UNITS

ASK 🅂🄳 🛏 🍴 ▼ 🄼 🖥/☒ 🗄 🖼/
FEE

——— *The following lodging was either not evaluated or did not meet AAA rating requirements but is listed for your information only.* ———

ROBIN'S INN   Phone: 506/446-9077

(fyi)

Motel

Did not meet all AAA rating requirements for locking devices in some guest rooms at time of last evaluation on 10/13/2005. **Location:** Trans-Canada Hwy 2, exit 297. 42 Chaperral Rd E3B 9Z4. Facilities, services, and decor characterize a basic property.

─── WHERE TO DINE ───

DREAMCATCHER DINING ROOM **Lunch:** $6-$12 **Dinner:** $10-$22 **Phone:** 506/357-5657
▼▼▼
Canadian
Location: Trans-Canada Hwy 2, exit 301 eastbound; exit 303 westbound, just s to Pioneer Ave, then 1 mi (1.6 km) w; in Days Inn Oromocto. 60 Brayson Blvd E2V 4T9. **Hours:** 7 am-11 pm. **Reservations:** accepted. **Features:** The pleasant restaurant turns out basic comfort foods, such as pizza, burgers and fish and chips, as well as fresh local seafood, prime steaks and chicken. Casual dress; cocktails. **Parking:** on-site. **Cards:** AX, DS, MC, VI.

JUNGLE JIM'S RESTAURANT **Lunch:** $7-$11 **Dinner:** $8-$20 **Phone:** 506/357-0831
▼▼▼
Canadian
Location: Trans-Canada Hwy 2, exit 303; in Parkview Garden Mall. 2 Gateway Dr E2V 4R3. **Hours:** 11:30 am-9 pm, Wed-Fri to 10 pm, Sat 10 am-10 pm, Sun 10 am-9 pm. Closed: 12/25, 12/26. **Reservations:** accepted. **Features:** Guests can step into a tropical theme at the casual eatery, which employs a friendly staff and nurtures a bustling atmosphere. The menu lines up a wide variety of comfort foods, salads, chicken, beef, seafood and hot wings, all served in ample, flavorful portions. Casual dress; cocktails. **Parking:** on-site. **Cards:** AX, DC, MC, VI.

PENNFIELD pop. 2,417

─── WHERE TO DINE ───

COMEAU'S SEAFOOD RESTAURANT **Lunch:** $5-$11 **Dinner:** $5-$12 **Phone:** 506/755-3011
▼
Seafood
Location: Centre. 5025 Hwy 1 E5H 1Y4. **Hours:** 11 am-9 pm. Closed: 10/8, 12/25, 12/26. **Features:** Fresh seafood is served in ample portions. The atmosphere is casual in the two dining sections. Takeout service is available. Casual dress. **Parking:** on-site. **Cards:** AX, MC, VI.

PERTH-ANDOVER pop. 1,908

─── WHERE TO STAY ───

THE CASTLE INN **Phone:** (506)273-9495
▼▼▼
Country Inn
All Year [BP] 1P: $100-$290 2P: $100-$290
Location: Trans-Canada Hwy 2, exit 115, follow signs over St John River Bridge. 21 Brentwood Dr E7H 1P1. **Fax:** 506/273-3663. **Facility:** A delightful, 200-acre wooded estate with well-appointed rooms and suites, the inn is perched on a hillside overlooking St. John River and township. Smoke free premises. 6 one-bedroom standard units, some with whirlpools. 3 stories (no elevator), interior corridors. **Bath:** combo or shower only. **Parking:** on-site. **Terms:** office hours 7 am-11 pm, cancellation fee imposed, weekly rates available, [AP] & [MAP] meal plans available, package plans, 15% service charge. **Amenities:** video library, DVD players, irons, hair dryers. **Leisure Activities:** whirlpool, hiking trails. **Guest Services:** wireless Internet. **Cards:** AX, MC, VI.

─── WHERE TO DINE ───

YORK'S DINING ROOM **Lunch:** $7-$13 **Dinner:** $18-$38 **Phone:** 506/273-2847
▼▼
Canadian
Location: Trans-Canada Hwy 2, exit 115, follow signs. 1333 Aroostook Rd E7H 1A7. **Hours:** Open 5/1-9/25; noon-9 pm, Sat 4:30 pm-9:30 pm. Closed: Mon. **Reservations:** suggested. **Features:** In business for more than 70 years, the casual country restaurant overlooks the Saint John River. Patrons can sample hearty five-course prix fixe dinners and a la carte lunch items. Arriving with an appetite is a good idea. Casual dress; cocktails. **Parking:** on-site. **Cards:** MC, VI.

POCOLOGAN

─── WHERE TO DINE ───

BAY BREEZE RESTAURANT **Lunch:** $5-$10 **Dinner:** $7-$15 **Phone:** 506/755-3850
▼
Seafood
Location: On Hwy 1; centre. 6410 Hwy 1 E5J 1E1. **Hours:** Open 5/1-10/31; 7 am-9 pm. **Features:** This casual diner offers an array of comfort foods for you to enjoy while taking in the splendid ocean vista. Casual dress; cocktails. **Parking:** on-site. **Cards:** AX, DS, MC, VI.

POINTE-VERTE pop. 1,041

─── WHERE TO STAY ───

GITE TOUTES SAISONS BED & BREAKFAST **Phone:** (506)783-3122
▼▼▼
Bed & Breakfast

	1P	2P	XP	
5/1-8/18 [BP]	1P: $98-$138	2P: $118-$148	XP: $30	D14
12/31-4/30 [BP]	1P: $104-$134	2P: $114-$144	XP: $28	D14
8/19-12/30 [BP]	1P: $98-$124	2P: $124-$138	XP: $25	D14

Location: Rt 11, exit 333 to Rt 134, 0.8 mi (1.3 km) nw. 10 rue des Oiseaux E8J 2V6. **Facility:** Each individually decorated guest room in this log home on the Bay des Chaleur offers an ocean view, and two rooms have private balconies. Smoke free premises. 4 one-bedroom standard units, some with whirlpools. 2 stories (no elevator), interior corridors. **Bath:** combo or shower only. **Parking:** on-site. **Terms:** office hours 7 am-10 pm, 7 day cancellation notice-fee imposed, [AP] & [MAP] meal plans available, package plans. **Amenities:** hair dryers. Some: irons. **Leisure Activities:** game room. **Guest Services:** TV in common area, complimentary laundry, wireless Internet. **Cards:** MC, VI.

REXTON pop. 810

—— WHERE TO STAY ——

JARDINE'S INN

(CAA) (SAVE)

◊◊◊ ◊◊◊

Historic Bed
& Breakfast

Phone: 506/523-7070

All Year [BP]   1P: $99   2P: $99   XP: $25
Location: On Rt 134; centre. 104 Main St E4W 2B3. Fax: 506/523-7072. **Facility:** A quaint property offering comfortable guestrooms with modern amenities. Spacious farm fields can be viewed while enjoying breakfast in the sun porch. Smoke free premises. 5 one-bedroom standard units. 2 stories (no elevator), interior corridors. **Parking:** on-site. **Terms:** office hours 8 am-11 pm. **Amenities:** hair dryers. *Some:* irons. **Leisure Activities:** horseshoes. **Guest Services:** wireless Internet. **Cards:** MC, VI. **Free Special Amenities:** full breakfast and high-speed Internet.

✖ ☎

—— WHERE TO DINE ——

REXTON VILLAGE CAFE   Lunch: $5-$9   Dinner: $9-$16   Phone: 506/523-6680

◊◊◊ ◊◊◊

Canadian

Location: On Rt 134; centre. 114 Main St E4W 2P3. **Hours:** 7 am-9 pm, Sat & Sun from 8 am; hours vary off season. Closed: 12/25, 12/26. **Features:** In the heart of town, the popular family restaurant specializes in seafood but also prepares a wide variety of comfort foods. Portions are ample, and desserts are baked fresh daily. Casual dress; cocktails. **Parking:** on-site. **Cards:** MC, VI.

RICHIBUCTO pop. 1,341

—— WHERE TO STAY ——

HABITANT MOTEL & RESTAURANT   Phone: (506)523-4421

◊◊◊ ◊◊◊

Small-scale Hotel

5/1-9/30   1P: $89-$139
10/1-4/30   1P: $64-$99
Location: 1.2 mi (2 km) n on Rt 134; Hwy 11, exit 57, 3 mi (5 km) n on Rt 134. 9600 Main St E4W 4E6. Fax: 506/523-9155. **Facility:** 29 units. 28 one-bedroom standard units. 1 one-bedroom suite. 2 stories (no elevator), interior corridors. **Parking:** on-site, winter plug-ins. **Terms:** 5 day cancellation notice. **Amenities:** high-speed Internet. **Dining:** restaurant, see separate listing. **Pool(s):** heated indoor. **Leisure Activities:** sauna, whirlpool, steamroom, playground. **Business Services:** meeting rooms. **Cards:** AX, CB, DC, DS, JC, MC, VI.

SOME UNITS

(ASK) (S/D) (¶¶) (Y) (◢) (✦) (✖) / (✖) (VCR) (▣) /
FEE

—— *The following lodging was either not evaluated or did not* ——
meet AAA rating requirements but is listed for your information only.

LES CHALETS DU HAVRE   Phone: 506/523-1570

(fyi)

Cottage

Did not meet all AAA rating requirements for locking devices in some guest rooms at time of last evaluation on 07/06/2006. **Location:** Centre. 79 York St E4W 4K1. Facilities, services, and decor characterize a mid-range property.

—— WHERE TO DINE ——

HABITANT RESTAURANT   Lunch: $7-$12   Dinner: $13-$17   Phone: 506/523-4421

◊◊◊ ◊◊◊

Canadian

Location: 1.2 mi (2 km) n Rt 134; Hwy 11, exit 57, 3 mi (5 km) n on Rt 134; in Habitant Motel & Restaurant. 9600 Main St E4W 4E6. **Hours:** 7 am-11 pm. Closed: 12/25. **Reservations:** accepted. **Features:** A rustic fireplace enhances a cozy country decor. Fresh seafood dishes, Canadian specialties, homemade pastries and reliable burgers and fries, are all served by a very personable staff. Soup and sandwich topped off with a slice of pie makes a fine lunch. Casual dress; cocktails. **Parking:** on-site. **Cards:** AX, DC, DS, MC, VI.

(Y)

MORGAN PUB & EATERY   Lunch: $5-$10   Dinner: $7-$14   Phone: 506/523-6063

◊◊◊

Canadian

Location: 0.6 mi (1 km) n on Rt 134. 9501 Main St E4W 4C1. **Hours:** 11 am-8 pm, Fri & Sat-9 pm. Closed: 12/25, 12/26. **Features:** A good spot for an upbeat gathering, the sports bar prepares a wide variety of comfort foods, as well as steaks. The reasonably priced fare is served in ample portions. Casual dress; cocktails. **Parking:** on-site. **Cards:** MC.

(Y)

RIVERSIDE-ALBERT pop. 393

—— WHERE TO STAY ——

LAKEVIEW INN   Phone: (506)882-2245

◊◊◊ ◊◊◊

Bed & Breakfast

7/1-9/15 [BP]   1P: $100   2P: $110   XP: $10   F10
5/1-6/30 & 9/16-10/31 [BP]   1P: $90   2P: $100   XP: $10   F10
Location: On Rt 915, 6 mi (10 km) w. 794 Rt 915 E4H 3T4. Fax: 506/882-1994. **Facility:** A Colonial-style exterior dresses this modern inn; in a secluded area bordering a lake, it offers well-appointed rooms with allergen-free features. Smoke free premises. 5 one-bedroom standard units. 2 stories (no elevator), interior corridors. **Parking:** on-site. **Terms:** open 5/1-10/31, office hours 7 am-10 pm, 3 day cancellation notice. **Amenities:** video library, DVD players, hair dryers. **Leisure Activities:** canoeing, paddleboats, hiking trails, game room. **Cards:** MC, VI.

✖ ✖ (A/C) (CTV) (VCR)

—— *The following lodging was either not evaluated or did not* ——
meet AAA rating requirements but is listed for your information only.

FLORENTINE MANOR BED & BREAKFAST   Phone: 506/882-2271

(fyi)

Not evaluated. **Location:** On Rt 915, 3 mi (5 km) w. 356 Rt 915 E4H 2M2. Facilities, services, and decor characterize a mid-range property.

WHERE TO DINE

THE KEEPER'S LUNCHROOM   *Menu on AAA.com*   **Lunch:** $6-$11   **Dinner:** $6-$11   **Phone:** 506/887-2273

⊂AA

▽▽▽

Canadian

Location: 10.6 mi (17 km) w on Rt 114 and 915, 4 mi (6.5 km) e; at Cape Enrage Lighthouse. 650 Cape Enrage Rd E4H 4Z4. **Hours:** Open 5/22-9/7; 8:30 am-6 pm. **Features:** Seating on the outdoor deck and in the dining room of the wonderful location at Cape Enrage Lighthouse looks out over the Bay of Fundy. Patrons peruse a limited menu for breakfast, lunch or early dinners. Casual dress. **Parking:** on-site. **Cards:** AX, DC, MC, VI.

ROTHESAY pop. 11,505

WHERE TO STAY

SHADOW LAWN INN   **Phone:** (506)847-7539

▽▽▽▽

Historic
Country Inn

5/1-10/31	2P: $125-$195	XP: $15	F
11/1-4/30	2P: $119-$175	XP: $15	F

Location: Hwy 1, exit 137B eastbound; exit 137A westbound, follow signs for Rothesay Rd and Rt 100, 1 mi (1.6 km) left on Old Hampton Rd (Rt 100), then left on Rt 100. Located in a semi-residential area. 3180 Rothesay Rd E2E 5V7. **Fax:** 506/849-9238. **Facility:** Manicured grounds surround this stately Victorian manor house, which offers handsome common areas and varied, well-decorated rooms. Designated smoking area. 11 units. 9 one-bedroom standard units, some with whirlpools. 2 one-bedroom suites ($175). 2 stories (no elevator); interior corridors. **Bath:** combo or shower only. **Parking:** on-site. **Terms:** office hours 7 am-11 pm, 3 day cancellation notice-fee imposed, weekly rates available, [ECP] meal plan available, small pets only ($30 fee). **Amenities:** hair dryers. **Dining:** The Summer House, see separate listing. **Guest Services:** wireless Internet. **Business Services:** meeting rooms. **Cards:** AX, CB, DC, MC, VI.

WHERE TO DINE

THE SUMMER HOUSE   **Lunch:** $12-$17   **Dinner:** $23-$32   **Phone:** 506/847-7539

▽▽▽

Continental

Location: Hwy 1, exit 137B eastbound; exit 137A westbound, follow signs for Rothesay Rd and Rt 100, 1 mi (1.6 km) left on Old Hampton Rd (Rt 100), then left on Rt 100; in Shadow Lawn Inn. 3180 Rothesay Rd E2E 5V7. **Hours:** 7-9:30 am, 11:30-2 & 5-8 pm, Sat & Sun 7-10 am, 11:30-2 & 5-8 pm. Closed: 1/1, 12/25. **Reservations:** required. **Features:** Located in a lovely historic mansion, the restaurant's dining room is the perfect setting for a romantic candlelit dinner. The creative cuisine is predominantly continental with some French accents. Dressy casual; cocktails. **Parking:** on-site. **Cards:** MC, VI.

VITO'S PIZZA & SPAGHETTI HOUSE   **Lunch:** $6-$11   **Dinner:** $10-$17   **Phone:** 506/847-4400

▽▽▽

Italian

Location: Just e of Marr St; centre. 111 Old Hampton Rd E2E 5V7. **Hours:** 11 am-11 pm, Fri & Sat-midnight. Closed: 12/25. **Reservations:** accepted. **Features:** The modern restaurant has ample parking. Although this place specializes in pizza and spaghetti, it also prepares chicken, seafood and steaks, as well as fine salads. Casual dress; cocktails. **Parking:** on-site. **Cards:** AX, DS, MC, VI.

SACKVILLE pop. 5,361

WHERE TO STAY

COASTAL INN SACKVILLE   *Book at AAA.com*   **Phone:** 506/536-0000

▽▽ ▽▽

Small-scale Hotel

5/1-9/30 [ECP]	1P: $99-$115	2P: $99-$115	XP: $12	F18
10/1-4/30 [ECP]	1P: $89-$99	2P: $89-$99	XP: $12	F18

Location: Trans-Canada Hwy 2, exit 504. 15 Wright St E4L 4P8. **Fax:** 506/536-0009. **Facility:** 50 one-bedroom standard units. 2 stories (no elevator); interior corridors. **Parking:** on-site. **Terms:** package plans, small pets only (in smoking units). **Amenities:** video library (fee), hair dryers. *Some:* DVD players (fee). **Guest Services:** coin laundry, wireless Internet. **Business Services:** meeting rooms. **Cards:** AX, DC, MC, VI.

MARSHLANDS INN   **Phone:** 506/536-0170

⊂AA SAVE

▽▽▽▽

Historic
Country Inn

5/1-10/31	1P: $84-$190	2P: $89-$190	XP: $10
11/1-4/30	1P: $74-$170	2P: $84-$170	XP: $10

Location: On Hwy 106; centre. Located in a residential area. 55 Bridge St E4L 3N8. **Fax:** 506/536-0721. **Facility:** This pleasant inn is made up of a main building and a newer carriage house; rooms vary in size and shape. Smoke free premises. 17 one-bedroom standard units, some with whirlpools. 3 stories (no elevator); interior corridors. **Bath:** combo or shower only. **Parking:** on-site. **Terms:** office hours 7 am-midnight, [BP] meal plan available, package plans, small pets only (in carriage house). **Dining:** restaurant, see separate listing. **Cards:** MC, VI. **Free Special Amenities:** newspaper and high-speed Internet.

WHERE TO DINE

MARSHLANDS INN DINING ROOM   **Lunch:** $7-$12   **Dinner:** $14-$26   **Phone:** 506/536-0170

▽▽▽

Canadian

Location: On Hwy 106; centre; in Marshlands Inn. 55 Bridge St E4L 3N8. **Hours:** 7-9:30 am, 11:30-2 & 5:30-8:30 pm. Closed: 12/25, 12/26. **Reservations:** suggested. **Features:** Quartered in a historic inn, the eatery houses two large dining sections. A menu of regional favorites includes a fine variety of fresh seafood and meat entrees for both lunch and dinner. Also offered are daily specials and fine homemade desserts. Dressy casual; cocktails. **Parking:** on-site. **Cards:** MC, VI.

MEL'S TEA ROOM   **Lunch:** $4-$7   **Dinner:** $6-$11   **Phone:** 506/536-1251

▽▽

Canadian

Location: At Bridge and Main sts. 17 Bridge St E4L 3N6. **Hours:** 7:30 am-midnight, Sun 10 am-11 pm. Closed: 12/25, 12/26. **Features:** A distinctive spot in which to mingle with the locals, the '50s-style diner/store has been serving folks for more than 50 years. Offerings include home-style burgers, fries, sandwiches and items from the old-fashioned dairy bar. Casual dress; beer only. **Parking:** on-site.

THE OLIVE BRANCH CASUAL DINING   **Lunch:** $6-$11   **Dinner:** $9-$16   **Phone:** 506/536-0409

▽▽

Canadian

Location: At Main; opposite university. 28 A York St E4L 4R4. **Hours:** 11 am-8:30 pm, Sat & Sun from 4:30 pm. Closed: 12/25, 12/26. **Features:** Opposite the university and a gathering place for teachers and students, the quaint little cafe prepares fresh soups, quiche, sandwiches and pita wraps. Casual dress; cocktails. **Parking:** street. **Cards:** AX, MC, VI.

PATTERSON'S FAMILY RESTAURANT　　　**Lunch:** $5-$9　　　**Dinner:** $8-$15　　　**Phone:** 506/364-0822

▼▼▼
Canadian

Location: Trans-Canada Hwy 2, exit 504. 16 Mallard Ln E0A 3C0. **Hours:** 7 am-10 pm. Closed: 12/25.
Features: This simple, diner-style operation serves everything from an all-day breakfast to burger favorites to hearty dinners. Homemade desserts are sure to please, as will the take-out dairy bar. A game room keeps the kids busy while the adults relax over coffee. Casual dress; beer & wine only. **Parking:** on-site.
Cards: AX, DC, DS, MC, VI.

ST. ANDREWS pop. 1,869

—— WHERE TO STAY ——

THE FAIRMONT ALGONQUIN　　*Book great rates at AAA.com*　　　　　　**Phone:** (506)529-8823

(CAA) (SAVE)

▼▼▼▼

Historic
Large-scale Hotel

6/1-10/31	1P: $189-$299	2P: $189-$299	XP: $25　　F18
5/1-5/31 & 11/1-4/30	1P: $129-$189	2P: $129-$189	XP: $25　　F18

Location: Off Hwy 127. 184 Adolphus St E5B 1T7. Fax: 506/529-7162. **Facility:** On picturesque landscaped grounds, this is a striking historic hotel with a newer annex section; some rooms offer water views. 234 one-bedroom standard units, some with whirlpools. 3-4 stories, interior corridors. **Parking:** on-site. **Terms:** check-in 4 pm, 3 day cancellation notice-fee imposed, small pets only ($25 extra charge). **Amenities:** video games (fee), voice mail, irons, hair dryers. *Some:* CD players, high-speed Internet (fee), honor bars. **Dining:** 2 restaurants, 6:30 am-10 pm, cocktails, also, Passamaquoddy Dining Room, see separate listing, entertainment. **Pool(s):** heated outdoor. **Leisure Activities:** saunas, whirlpool, 2 tennis courts, racquetball court, recreation programs, squash courts, rental bicycles, playground, exercise room, shuffleboard, volleyball. *Fee:* golf-18 holes, golf & tennis equipment. **Guest Services:** gift shop, coin laundry. **Business Services:** conference facilities, business center. **Cards:** AX, CB, DC, DS, JC, MC, VI. **Free Special Amenities:** local telephone calls and newspaper. *(See color ad below)*

SOME UNITS
🛏 🍴 🍸 ☆ ✕ 🎥 ▦ / ✕ 🕪 🔋 ▦ /
FEE

HARRIS HATCH INN　　　　　　　　　　　　　　　　　　　**Phone:** 506/529-4995

▼▼▼
Historic Bed
& Breakfast

5/15-10/15 [BP]	1P: $85-$125	2P: $85-$125

Location: Centre. Located in a residential area. 142 Queen St E5B 1E2. Fax: 506/529-4713. **Facility:** Built in 1840 of bricks baked on site, this stately home offers spacious, tastefully decorated guest rooms, two with wood-burning fireplaces. Smoke free premises. 3 one-bedroom standard units. 3 stories (no elevator), interior corridors. **Parking:** on-site. **Terms:** open 5/15-10/15, office hours 9 am-11 pm, 7 day cancellation notice, package plans. **Amenities:** irons, hair dryers. **Cards:** MC, VI.

✕ 🔋 ▦

THE PANSY PATCH　　　　　　　　　　　　　　　　　　　**Phone:** (506)529-3834

(CAA) (SAVE)

▼▼▼▼

Historic Bed
& Breakfast

7/1-8/31 [BP]	1P: $148-$218	2P: $156-$225	XP: $12　　F12
6/1-6/30 & 9/1-9/30 [BP]	1P: $112-$163	2P: $117-$169	XP: $12　　F12

Location: Centre. Located in a residential area. 59 Carleton St E5B 1M8 (PO Box 1210, E5B 1N8). Fax: 506/529-9042. **Facility:** This attractive 1912 French Normandy home and an adjacent cottage offer individually appointed guest rooms and well-tended gardens. Smoke free premises. 9 units. 7 one-bedroom standard units. 2 one-bedroom suites ($210-$220). 3 stories (no elevator), interior/exterior corridors. *Bath:* combo, shower or tub only. **Parking:** street. **Terms:** open 6/1-9/30, office hours 9 am-9 pm, 10 day cancellation notice-fee imposed, [CP] meal plan available, package plans. **Amenities:** video library, hair dryers. **Guest Services:** gift shop, complimentary evening beverages, valet laundry. **Cards:** AX, MC, VI. **Free Special Amenities:** full breakfast and local telephone calls.

SOME UNITS
🆂 🍴 ✕ 🄰 / VCR 🔋 🖥 ▦ /

ST. ANDREWS COTTAGES
Phone: 506/529-8555

6/25-8/31	1P: $139	2P: $139	XP: $15 F
5/1-6/24 & 9/1-4/30	1P: $95	2P: $95	XP: $15 F

Cottage
◈◈◈◈

Location: On Rt 127, 1.5 mi (2.5 km) n. 3907 Rt 127 E5B 2T3. **Facility:** These pleasant cottages with covered porches are located in a private wooded setting on the outskirts of town. 6 cottages. 1 story, exterior corridors. **Parking:** on-site. **Terms:** office hours 9 am-8 pm, 2-4 night minimum stay - seasonal, 14 day cancellation notice, weekly rates available, small pets only. **Amenities:** hair dryers. **Pool(s):** heated outdoor. **Leisure Activities:** hiking trails, playground. **Guest Services:** coin laundry. **Cards:** MC, VI.

TARA MANOR INN
Phone: (506)529-3304

(CAA) (SAVE)

7/1-8/26	1P: $129-$179		XP: $15 F12
5/15-6/30 & 8/27-10/15	1P: $99-$149		XP: $15 F12

Historic Bed & Breakfast
◈◈◈◈

Location: 1.7 mi (2.8 km) n on Hwy 127. Located in a quiet secluded area. 559 Mowat Dr E5B 2P2. Fax: 506/529-4755. **Facility:** From the groomed gardens to the well-coordinated decor of guest rooms, attention to detail is evident at this quiet and secluded estate. 28 units. 23 one-bedroom standard units. 2 one- and 3 two-bedroom suites ($149-$179). 1-3 stories (no elevator), exterior corridors. **Parking:** on-site. **Terms:** open 5/15-10/15, office hours 7:30 am-10 pm, 7 day cancellation notice-fee imposed, package plans. **Amenities:** video library, irons, hair dryers. **Pool(s):** heated outdoor. **Leisure Activities:** whirlpool, tennis court. **Guest Services:** wireless Internet. **Business Services:** meeting rooms. **Cards:** AX, DC, DS, MC, VI. **Free Special Amenities:** continental breakfast and local telephone calls. *(See color ad below)*

SOME UNITS

TREADWELL INN
Phone: (506)529-1011

◈◈◈

All Year [BP]	1P: $125-$250	2P: $145-$250	XP: $15 F12

Country Inn

Location: Centre. Located in a commercial area. 129 Water St E5B 1A7. Fax: 506/529-4826. **Facility:** The lawn of this 1820s inn extends to Passamaquoddy Bay, and many of the inn's pleasant rooms offer views of the water. Smoke free premises. 7 units. 5 one-bedroom standard units. 2 one-bedroom suites with whirlpools. 3 stories (no elevator), interior corridors. *Bath:* combo or shower only. **Parking:** on-site. **Terms:** office hours 7:30 am-10 pm, age restrictions may apply, 7 day cancellation notice-fee imposed, weekly rates available, package plans. **Amenities:** video library, hair dryers. **Dining:** The Treadwell Snug & Oyster Bar, see separate listing. **Leisure Activities:** bicycles. **Guest Services:** gift shop. **Cards:** AX, MC, VI.

SOME UNITS

THE WINDSOR HOUSE OF ST. ANDREWS
Phone: (506)529-3330

▼▼▼▼
| | 7/1-9/30 | 1P: $225-$300 | 2P: $225-$300 |
| | 5/1-6/30 & 10/1-4/30 | 1P: $125-$200 | 2P: $125-$200 |

Historic
Country Inn
Location: Centre. Located in a commercial area. 132 Water St E5B 1A8. **Fax:** 506/529-4063. **Facility:** This restored historic inn in the center of town offers gracious public areas and guest rooms furnished with fine antiques. Smoke free premises. 6 one-bedroom standard units. 3 stories (no elevator), interior corridors. **Parking:** on-site. **Terms:** office hours 8 am-10 pm, age restrictions may apply, 14 day cancellation notice-fee imposed, package plans, small pets only (with prior approval). **Amenities:** hair dryers. **Dining:** The Windsor House Dining Room, see separate listing. **Cards:** AX, CB, DC, MC, VI.

SOME UNITS
(ASK) (S/D) (🛏) (🍽) (Y) (✕) (VCR) / (AC) /

─────── *The following lodgings were either not evaluated or did not* ───────
meet AAA rating requirements but are listed for your information only.

KINGSBRAE ARMS
Phone: 506/529-1897
(fyi)
Not evaluated. **Location:** Centre. 219 King St E5B 1Y1. Facilities, services, and decor characterize an upscale property.

ROSSMOUNT INN
Phone: 506/529-3351
(fyi)
Not evaluated. **Location:** On Hwy 127, 3.8 mi (6.3 km) ne. 4599 Rt 127 E5B 2Z3. Facilities, services, and decor characterize a mid-range property.

─────── **WHERE TO DINE** ───────

THE GABLES RESTAURANT
Lunch: $6-$12   **Dinner:** $9-$24   Phone: 506/529-3440
▼▼ ▼▼
Canadian
Location: Centre. 143 Water St E5B 1A7. **Hours:** Open 5/1-10/31 & 4/1-4/30; 11 am-11 pm; hours vary off season. **Reservations:** accepted. **Features:** In the relaxed atmosphere, guests can sit indoors or outdoors on the spacious treed deck bordering the harbor. A variety of tasty comfort foods and fresh seafood complete the menu. Casual dress; cocktails. **Parking:** street. **Cards:** AX, MC, VI.
(AC)

HARBOUR FRONT RESTAURANT
Lunch: $8-$14   **Dinner:** $13-$22   Phone: 506/529-4887
(AAA)
▼▼ ▼▼
Canadian
Location: Centre. 225 Water St E5B 1B3. **Hours:** Open 5/1-10/24; 11 am-9:30 pm. **Reservations:** accepted. **Features:** Befitting its name, the spacious restaurant is in town on the harborfront. The menu lists a fine selection of fresh seafood and meat dishes. Guests can enjoy sea breezes on the outdoor deck. Casual dress; cocktails. **Parking:** street. **Cards:** AX, MC, VI.
(Y) (AC)

PASSAMAQUODDY DINING ROOM
Dinner: $20-$35   Phone: 506/529-8823
(AAA)
▼▼ ▼▼
Canadian
Location: Off Hwy 127; in The Fairmont Algonquin. 184 Adolphus St E0G 2X0. **Hours:** 6:30 am-10:30 & 6-10 pm. Closed: 12/25. **Reservations:** suggested. **Features:** The landmark establishment presents fine, creative cuisine with artful presentations and preparations. From fresh local lobster to perfectly cooked steak, every meal is a flavorful event. Dressy casual; cocktails. **Parking:** on-site. **Cards:** AX, DS, MC, VI. **Historic**
(Y) (AC)

ROSSMOUNT INN DINING ROOM
Dinner: $16-$29   Phone: 506/529-3351
▼▼ ▼▼
Canadian
Location: On Hwy 127, 4 mi (6.3 km) ne; in Rossmount Inn. 4599 Rt 127 E5B 2Z3. **Hours:** 6 pm-9:30 pm. Closed: 12/25. **Reservations:** suggested. **Features:** The Rossmount offers fine dining with a European flair. The menu changes daily and offers a variety of fresh local seafood, meat and produce selections. Finish with a delightful dessert. Casual dress; cocktails. **Parking:** on-site. **Cards:** AX, MC, VI.
(Y) (AC)

THE TREADWELL SNUG & OYSTER BAR
Lunch: $7-$15   **Dinner:** $11-$21   Phone: 506/529-8005
▼▼ ▼▼
Canadian
Location: Centre; in Treadwell Inn. 129 Water St E5B 1A7. **Hours:** Open 5/15-10/31; 11:30 am-9 pm, Sun-3 pm. **Reservations:** accepted. **Features:** The waterfront restaurant nurtures a laid-back atmosphere in which guests can unwind. Seating can be requested in the small dining area or on outdoor decks overlooking the harbor. Well-prepared entrees range from gourmet pizza to fresh local seafood. Casual dress; cocktails. **Parking:** on-site. **Cards:** MC, VI.
(Y) (AC)

THE WINDSOR HOUSE DINING ROOM
Dinner: $20-$28   Phone: 506/529-3330
▼▼▼▼
Continental
Location: Centre; in The Windsor House of St. Andrews. 132 Water St E0G 2X0. **Hours:** Open 5/1-12/31 & 3/1-4/30; 5:30 pm-9:30 pm; hours vary in winter. **Reservations:** suggested. **Features:** The historic former loyalist home has several elegant dining locations, one in front overlooking the street and a quieter room in the back, plus a lovely covered patio for outdoor dining. The menu highlights classic French cuisine. Excellent presentation is equally matched to the exceptional flavors the professional chefs create. Service is relaxed and friendly. Dressy casual; cocktails. **Parking:** on-site. **Cards:** AX, DS, MC, VI. **Historic**
(Y)

ST. BASILE

─────── **WHERE TO STAY** ───────

DAYS INN EDMUNDSTON   *Book great rates at AAA.com*
Phone: (506)263-0000
▼▼▼▼
| | 6/16-9/15 [ECP] | 1P: $107-$153 | 2P: $113-$162 | XP: $10 | F17 |
| | 5/1-6/15 & 9/16-4/30 [ECP] | 1P: $75-$93 | 2P: $80-$98 | XP: $10 | F17 |

Small-scale Hotel
Location: Trans-Canada Hwy 2, exit 26. 10 rue Mathieu E7C 3E1. **Fax:** 506/263-2952. **Facility:** 78 one-bedroom standard units. 2 stories (no elevator), interior corridors. **Parking:** on-site. **Amenities:** video library (fee), DVD players, high-speed Internet, irons, hair dryers. **Guest Services:** wireless Internet. **Business Services:** meeting rooms, PC. **Cards:** AX, CB, DC, DS, JC, MC, VI.

SOME UNITS
(ASK) (S/D) (🛏) (📶) / (✕) (🔒) /

ST. GEORGE pop. 1,509

------ WHERE TO STAY ------

GRANITE TOWN HOTEL & COUNTRY INN　　　　　　　　　　　**Phone:** (506)755-6415

CAA SAVE

Small-scale Hotel

5/1-10/1	1P: $98-$108	2P: $108-$118	XP: $10	F12
10/2-4/30	1P: $88-$98	2P: $98-$108	XP: $10	F12

Location: Hwy 1, exit 56, 1.8 mi (3 km) w. Located next to a playing field. 79 Main St E5C 3J4. **Fax:** 506/755-6009. **Facility:** 33 one-bedroom standard units, some with efficiencies and/or whirlpools. 2 stories (no elevator), interior corridors. **Parking:** on-site. **Terms:** package plans. **Amenities:** video library (fee), irons, hair dryers. **Dining:** 7 am-10 & 5-10 pm, cocktails. **Business Services:** meeting rooms. **Cards:** AX, MC, VI.
Free Special Amenities: local telephone calls and high-speed Internet.

SOME UNITS

------ WHERE TO DINE ------

DANNY'S RESTAURANT　　　　**Lunch:** $5-$11　　　　**Dinner:** $9-$16　　　　**Phone:** 506/755-2665

Canadian

Location: Centre. 14 Main St E5C 3J1. **Hours:** 11:30 am-8 pm. Closed major holidays; also Mon. **Reservations:** accepted. **Features:** Many of the fresh seafood items are deep-fried, but chefs will pan-fry them for diners who prefer that style. Among other choices are beef, chicken, burgers and sandwiches. Casual dress. **Parking:** on-site.

ST-JACQUES pop. 1,715

------ WHERE TO STAY ------

AUBERGE LES JARDINS INN　　　　　　　　　　　　　**Phone:** (506)739-5514

Small-scale Hotel

All Year	1P: $79-$169	2P: $89-$169	XP: $10	

Location: Trans-Canada Hwy 2, exit 8; 6 mi (10 km) w of Edmundston. 60 Principale St E7B 1V7. **Fax:** 506/739-5518. **Facility:** 37 units. 26 one-bedroom standard units. 4 one-bedroom suites with whirlpools. 7 cabins, some with whirlpools. 2 stories, interior/exterior corridors. **Bath:** combo or shower only. **Parking:** on-site. **Terms:** package plans. **Amenities:** hair dryers. *Some:* DVD players, irons. **Dining:** restaurant, see separate listing. **Pool(s):** outdoor. **Leisure Activities:** playground, exercise room. **Guest Services:** coin laundry, wireless Internet. **Business Services:** meeting rooms. **Cards:** AX, DC, DS, MC, VI.

SOME UNITS

------ WHERE TO DINE ------

AUBERGE LES JARDINS INN DINING ROOM　　　　**Dinner:** $16-$28　　　　　　　　　　**Phone:** 506/739-5514

CAA

Traditional Canadian

Location: Trans-Canada Hwy 2, exit 8; 6 mi (10 km) w of Edmundston; in Auberge Les Jardins Inn. 60 Principale St E7B 1V7. **Hours:** 7 am-11 & 6-10 pm; to 9 pm off season. Closed: 12/25. **Reservations:** required. **Features:** Country-cottage decor lends to a pleasant, homey atmosphere. The chef offers a fine selection of creative appetizers and entrees, including fresh Atlantic salmon and various fine cuts of meat. Seafood chowder and fine homemade desserts should not be missed. Casual dress; cocktails. **Parking:** on-site. **Cards:** AX, DC, DS, MC, VI.

SAINT JOHN pop. 69,661

------ WHERE TO STAY ------

COLONIAL INNS　　　　　　　　　　　　　　　　**Phone:** (506)652-3000

Small-scale Hotel

All Year	1P: $92-$100	2P: $102-$110	XP: $10	F16

Location: Adjacent to Hwy 1, exit 123. 175 City Rd E2L 3T5 (PO Box 2149). **Fax:** 506/658-1664. **Facility:** 96 one-bedroom standard units. 2 stories (no elevator), interior/exterior corridors. **Parking:** on-site. **Terms:** small pets only. **Amenities:** voice mail. **Pool(s):** heated indoor. **Leisure Activities:** sauna, whirlpool. **Guest Services:** wireless Internet. **Business Services:** meeting rooms. **Cards:** AX, MC, VI.

SOME UNITS

COMFORT INN　　*Book great rates at AAA.com*　　　　　　**Phone:** (506)674-1873

CAA SAVE

Small-scale Hotel

1/1-4/30	1P: $115-$135	2P: $125-$145	XP: $10	F18
5/1-10/15	1P: $111-$131	2P: $121-$141	XP: $10	F18
10/16-12/31	1P: $110-$130	2P: $120-$140	XP: $10	F18

Location: Hwy 1, exit 117 westbound; exit 119 eastbound, turn left. Located in a commercial area. 1155 Fairville Blvd E2M 5T9. **Fax:** 506/674-1343. **Facility:** 59 one-bedroom standard units. 2 stories (no elevator), interior corridors. **Parking:** on-site. **Terms:** [CP] meal plan available, package plans, pets only. **Amenities:** high-speed Internet. *Some:* irons, hair dryers. **Cards:** AX, DC, DS, JC, MC, VI. *(See color ad card insert)*

SOME UNITS

COUNTRY INN & SUITES　　*Book great rates at AAA.com*　　　**Phone:** (506)635-0400

Small-scale Hotel

7/1-9/30	1P: $98-$128	2P: $108-$138	XP: $10	F18
5/1-6/30 & 10/1-4/30	1P: $89-$119	2P: $99-$129	XP: $10	F18

Location: Hwy 1, exit 119B eastbound, left on Catherwood Dr, left at lights; exit 119A westbound. Located in a commercial area. 1011 Fairville Blvd E2M 5T9. **Fax:** 506/635-3818. **Facility:** 60 units. 29 one-bedroom standard units. 31 one-bedroom suites ($117-$147). 3 stories, interior corridors. **Parking:** on-site. **Terms:** [CP] meal plan available, small pets only ($15 extra charge). **Amenities:** video library, DVD players, irons, hair dryers. **Guest Services:** coin laundry, wireless Internet. **Business Services:** meeting rooms. **Cards:** AX, DC, DS, MC, VI. *(See color ad on TourBookMark)*

SOME UNITS

FEE

DELTA BRUNSWICK   *Book great rates at AAA.com*   Phone: (506)648-1981

All Year   1P: $109-$169   2P: $109-$169   XP: $20   F18

Large-scale Hotel   **Location:** Centre of downtown; in Brunswick Square Mall. 39 King St E2L 4W3. Fax: 506/658-0914. **Facility:** 254 units. 249 one-bedroom standard units. 5 one-bedroom suites ($159-$299), some with whirlpools. 8 stories, interior corridors. *Bath:* combo or shower only. **Parking:** on-site (fee). **Terms:** cancellation fee imposed, package plans, small pets only ($50 deposit). **Amenities:** video games (fee), voice mail, irons, hair dryers. *Some:* CD players, high-speed Internet, dual phone lines, honor bars. **Pool(s):** heated indoor. **Leisure Activities:** sauna, whirlpool, playground, exercise room. **Guest Services:** gift shop, valet and coin laundry, wireless Internet. **Business Services:** conference facilities, business center. **Cards:** AX, DC, DS, MC, VI. *(See color ad below)*

SOME UNITS

(ASK) (S/D) [icons] / (X) (□) /

ECONO LODGE & SUITES   *Book great rates at AAA.com*   Phone: (506)635-8700

5/1-10/31 [ECP]   1P: $99-$149   2P: $114-$165   XP: $15   F17

11/1-4/30 [ECP]   1P: $79-$99   2P: $89-$115   XP: $15   F17

Motel   **Location:** Hwy 1, exit 119 eastbound, 1.8 mi (3 km) w on Rt 100; exit 117 westbound, 0.3 mi (0.6 km) w on Rt 100. 1441 Manawagonish Rd E2M 3X8. Fax: 506/672-8853. **Facility:** 31 units. 30 one-bedroom standard units. 1 two-bedroom suite. 2 stories (no elevator), interior/exterior corridors. **Parking:** on-site. **Amenities:** high-speed Internet, hair dryers. *Some:* irons. **Guest Services:** coin laundry. **Business Services:** PC. **Cards:** AX, CB, DC, DS, MC, VI. *(See color ad card insert)*

SOME UNITS

(ASK) (S/D) (X) (□) / (■) (□) /

FORT HOWE HOTEL & CONVENTION CENTRE

Book at AAA.com

Phone: (506)657-7320

	1P: $109-$175	2P: $109-$175	XP: $10	F18
6/1-9/30				
5/1-5/31 & 10/1-4/30	1P: $99-$145	2P: $99-$145	XP: $10	F18

Small-scale Hotel **Location:** Hwy 1, exit 121 eastbound off Harbour Bridge; exit 123 westbound. 10 Portland St E2K 4H8. Fax: 506/693-1146. **Facility:** 135 one-bedroom standard units, some with whirlpools. 9 stories, interior corridors. **Parking:** on-site. **Terms:** small pets only (1st floor units). **Amenities:** video library (fee), hair dryers. **Pool(s):** heated indoor. **Leisure Activities:** whirlpool. **Guest Services:** valet laundry. **Business Services:** conference facilities. **Cards:** AX, MC, VI.

SOME UNITS

(ASK) (SD) (🐾) (🍴) (🍸) (🍽) (📖) / (☒) (VCR) (🔌) (📷) /
FEE

HILTON SAINT JOHN

Book great rates at AAA.com

Phone: (506)693-8484

| All Year | 1P: $99-$199 | 2P: $119-$219 | XP: $20 | F18 |

Large-scale Hotel **Location:** Hwy 1, exit 122 at Market Square. Located in a commercial area. One Market Square E2L 4Z6. Fax: 506/657-6610. **Facility:** 197 units. 182 one-bedroom standard units. 15 one-bedroom suites, some with whirlpools. 10 stories, interior corridors. **Parking:** on-site (fee). **Amenities:** video games (fee), dual phone lines, voice mail, honor bars, irons, hair dryers. *Some:* high-speed Internet (fee), safes. **Dining:** Turn of the Tide Dining Room, see separate listing. **Pool(s):** heated indoor. **Leisure Activities:** saunas, whirlpool, exercise room. **Guest Services:** valet laundry. **Business Services:** conference facilities, business center. **Cards:** AX, CB, DC, DS, MC, VI.

SOME UNITS

(🐾) (🍴) (🍸) (🍽) (☒) (🎮) (📖) / (☒) /

HOLIDAY INN EXPRESS HOTEL & SUITES

(CAA) (SAVE)

Book great rates at AAA.com

Phone: (506)642-2622

| 5/1-9/30 [ECP] | 1P: $109-$179 | 2P: $109-$179 | XP: $10 | F18 |
| 10/1-4/30 [ECP] | 1P: $99-$169 | 2P: $99-$169 | XP: $10 | F18 |

Small-scale Hotel **Location:** 0.6 mi (1 km) w on Hwy 1; north end Chesley Dr, exit 121; off Harbour Bridge. 400 Main St/Chesley Dr E2K 4N5. Fax: 506/658-1529. **Facility:** Smoke free premises. 94 units. 92 one-bedroom standard units. 2 one-bedroom suites ($159-$279), some with whirlpools. 7 stories, interior corridors. **Parking:** on-site. **Amenities:** high-speed Internet, dual phone lines, voice mail, irons, hair dryers. **Pool(s):** heated indoor. **Leisure Activities:** whirlpool, exercise room. **Guest Services:** valet and coin laundry, wireless internet. **Business Services:** meeting rooms, PC. **Cards:** AX, DC, DS, MC, VI. **Free Special Amenities: expanded continental breakfast and local telephone calls.** *(See color ad card insert)*

SOME UNITS

(SD) (🐾) (🍽) (☒) (🎮) (📖) / (🔌) (📷) /

HOMEPORT HISTORIC INN CIRCA 1858

Phone: (506)672-7255

| All Year | 1P: $90-$175 | 2P: $95-$175 | XP: $15 |

Historic Bed & Breakfast **Location:** Hwy 1, exit 121 eastbound; exit 123 westbound. 80 Douglas Ave E1E 1E4. Fax: 506/672-7250. **Facility:** This appealing inn offers a variety of tastefully decorated guest rooms and suites with whirlpool baths; some rooms have water views. Smoke free premises. 10 units. 6 one-bedroom standard units. 4 one-bedroom suites ($140-$175), some with efficiencies and/or whirlpools. 2 stories (no elevator), interior corridors. **Parking:** on-site. **Terms:** office hours 7 am-10 pm, 3 day cancellation notice, package plans, no pets allowed (owner's dog on premises). **Amenities:** video library, hair dryers. **Guest Services:** wireless Internet. **Cards:** AX, MC, VI.

SOME UNITS

(🍸) (☒) / (VCR) (🔌) (📷) /

INN ON THE COVE AND SPA

(CAA) (SAVE)

Phone: (506)672-7799

6/22-10/13 [BP]	1P: $155-$225	2P: $155-$225
5/18-6/21 [BP]	1P: $125-$195	2P: $125-$195
5/1-5/17 [BP]	1P: $119-$175	2P: $119-$175
10/14-4/30 [BP]	1P: $109-$165	2P: $109-$165

Country Inn **Location:** Hwy 1, exit 119, right to Sand Cove Rd, then 3.2 mi (2 km) w. 1371 Sand Cove Rd E2M 4Z9. **Facility:** Near the Irving Nature Park, this lovely oceanside inn offers tastefully appointed guest rooms with exceptional sea views, some with private balconies. Smoke free premises. 8 one-bedroom standard units with whirlpools. 2 stories (no elevator), interior corridors. **Parking:** on-site. **Terms:** office hours 7 am-10 pm, age restrictions may apply, 7 day cancellation notice-fee imposed, package plans, small pets only (in designated units). **Amenities:** video library, hair dryers. *Some:* DVD players, CD players, high-speed Internet. **Dining:** dinner by reservation; 7 pm seating, cocktails. **Leisure Activities:** recreation programs, lawn games, spa. **Cards:** AX, DC, DS, JC, MC, VI. **Free Special Amenities: full breakfast and high-speed Internet.** *(See color ad below & p 55)*

SOME UNITS

(SD) (🐾) (🍴) (🔊M) (☒) (☒) (🎮) / (🎮) (📖) /

ISLAND VIEW MOTEL

Motel

All Year   1P: $55-$85   2P: $60-$85   XP: $10

Phone: (506)672-1381   F12

Location: 1.1 mi (1.8 km) w on Rt 100. 1726 Manawagonish Rd E2M 3Y5. **Fax:** 506/674-1089. **Facility:** 22 units. 20 one- and 2 two-bedroom standard units, some with efficiencies. 1-2 stories (no elevator), exterior corridors. **Parking:** on-site. **Terms:** office hours 7 am-10 pm, cancellation fee imposed, weekly rates available. **Pool(s):** outdoor. **Guest Services:** wireless Internet. **Cards:** AX, MC, VI.

SOME UNITS

The following lodging was either not evaluated or did not meet AAA rating requirements but is listed for your information only.

CHIPMAN HILL SUITES

[fyi]

Condominium

Phone: 506/693-1171

Did not meet all AAA rating requirements for locking devices in some guest rooms at time of last evaluation on 09/05/2006. **Location:** At Union St. 9 Chipman Hill E2L 2A7. Facilities, services, and decor characterize a mid-range property.

WHERE TO DINE

3 MILE STEAKHOUSE & PUB

Steak House

Lunch: $5-$10   **Dinner:** $8-$17   **Phone:** 506/657-8325

Location: At Rothesay Ave. 5 Golden Grove Rd E2L 3X1. **Hours:** 11 am-8 pm, Wed-Sat to 9 pm. **Features:** Popular with sports fans, the steakhouse has numerous TVs and presents a hefty menu with all of the favorite finger foods, as well as steaks, chicken and some seafood entrees, including fish and chips. Casual dress; cocktails. **Parking:** on-site. **Cards:** AX, DC, MC, VI.

ASIAN PALACE

Indian

Lunch: $8-$14   **Dinner:** $11-$20   **Phone:** 506/642-4909

Location: Centre; in Market Square. 1 Market Square E2L 4Z6. **Hours:** 11 am-2 & 5-9 pm, Fri & Sat-10 pm. **Closed:** 10/8, 12/25, 12/26. **Reservations:** accepted. **Features:** Located on the lower level of Brunswick Square, the restaurant offers a fine selection of authentic Indian cuisine spiced to your liking. Pleasant patio dining is available in season. Casual dress; cocktails. **Parking:** on-site (fee). **Cards:** AX, DC, MC, VI.

BILLY'S SEAFOOD RESTAURANT

Seafood

Lunch: $6-$10   **Dinner:** $12-$18   **Phone:** 506/672-3474

Location: Centre; in City Market. 51 Charlotte St E2L 2H8. **Hours:** 11 am-10 pm, Fri & Sat-11 pm, Sun 4 pm-10 pm. **Closed:** 12/25, 12/26; also Sun 1/1-4/15. **Features:** In the heart of uptown Saint John, the casually upscale restaurant offers a good selection of fresh seafood dishes and an on-site fish market. Patio dining and jazz music set a relaxing scene in which to feast on lobster, oysters and scallops. Casual dress; cocktails. **Parking:** on-site (fee). **Cards:** AX, DC, MC, VI.

CHURCH STREET STEAKHOUSE

Steak & Seafood

Lunch: $8-$13   **Dinner:** $16-$28   **Phone:** 506/648-2374

Location: Corner of Prince William and Church sts; centre. 10 Grannan's Ln E2L 4S5. **Hours:** 11:30 am-11 pm, Fri & Sat-midnight, Sun noon-10 pm. **Closed:** 12/25. **Reservations:** accepted. **Features:** In the town's old quarter, the restaurant is a fine spot for informal dining in a warm atmosphere. The specialty is prime cuts of meat, but a selection of well-prepared fresh seafood and a few pasta dishes is also presented. Casual dress; cocktails. **Parking:** street. **Cards:** AX, DC, MC, VI.

CORA'S BREAKFAST & LUNCH

Canadian

Lunch: $6-$10   **Phone:** 506/634-2672

Location: Centre of downtown; in Brunswick Square Mall. 39 King St E2L 4W3. **Hours:** 6 am-3 pm, Sun from 7 am. **Closed:** 12/25. **Reservations:** accepted. **Features:** Although this place specializes in breakfast, it offers a varied daytime menu that includes bacon, eggs, sausages, crepes, grilled cheese, sandwiches, freshly prepared quiches, salads, fruit platters and freshly squeezed juices. The family-friendly dining room is casual and modern. Casual dress. **Parking:** street. **Cards:** AX, DC, MC, VI.

EAST SIDE MARIO'S

Italian

Lunch: $6-$11   **Dinner:** $9-$16   **Phone:** 506/633-8899

Location: In Westmorland Mall. 75 Consumers Dr E2J 4Z6. **Hours:** 11 am-10 pm, Wed & Thurs-11 pm, Fri & Sat-midnight. **Closed:** 12/25, 12/26. **Reservations:** accepted. **Features:** Pizza, steak, sandwiches, salads, burgers, hot dogs, chicken, fish, calamari and pasta are among offerings at the chain of family restaurants, which also has a children's menu. The lively dining room is decorated to resemble a European market, with shop facades and vintage signage. Casual dress; cocktails. **Parking:** on-site. **Cards:** AX, DC, MC, VI.

THE FALLS RESTAURANT

Canadian

Lunch: $6-$14   **Dinner:** $11-$25   **Phone:** 506/635-1999

Location: Hwy 1A, 2.5 mi (4 km) sw; at Reversing Falls. 200 Bridge Rd E2M 7Y9. **Hours:** 8 am-10 pm; hours vary in winter. **Closed:** 12/24, 12/25. **Reservations:** suggested. **Features:** Large windows overlook the river and Reversing Falls at the cozy restaurant. Aged photographs of the falls and environs decorate the walls of the octagon shaped chandelier room. Atlantic salmon and roast beef are among well prepared selections. Casual dress; cocktails. **Parking:** on-site. **Cards:** AX, DC, MC, VI.

GRANNAN'S SEAFOOD RESTAURANT

Seafood

Lunch: $8-$12   **Dinner:** $13-$24   **Phone:** 506/634-1555

Location: Centre; in Market Square. 1 Market Square E2L 4Z6. **Hours:** 11:30 am-11 pm, Thurs-Sat to midnight, Sun noon-10 pm. **Closed:** 12/25. **Reservations:** accepted. **Features:** The pleasant, harborside eatery features a casual atmosphere and a bilevel dining room with seasonal patio seating. Including fresh regional seafood, lobsters from a tank and oyster bar preparations, the menu also tempts with pasta and prime rib. Casual dress; cocktails. **Parking:** on-site. **Cards:** AX, DC, MC, VI.

JADE CITY RESTAURANT

Chinese

Lunch: $8-$12   **Dinner:** $10-$18   **Phone:** 506/652-1688

Location: Centre; in Parkway Mall. 212 McAllister Dr E2J 2S5. **Hours:** 11 am-10 pm, Fri & Sat-11 pm. **Closed:** 12/25. **Features:** In a convenient mall location, the casual restaurant offers patrons a choice of either booth or table seating. They can choose from the daily buffet, dim sum or selections on the wide menu. Casual dress; cocktails. **Parking:** on-site. **Cards:** MC, VI.

JUNGLE JIM'S EATERY **Lunch:** $7-$8 **Dinner:** $9-$22 **Phone:** 506/652-5467

Canadian

Location: Centre. 87 Prince William St E2L 2B2. **Hours:** 11 am-11 pm, Sat-midnight, Sun-10 pm. Closed: 12/25. **Reservations:** accepted. **Features:** Guests can step into a tropical theme at the casual eatery, which employs a friendly staff and nurtures a bustling atmosphere. The menu lines up a wide variety of comfort foods, salads, chicken, beef, seafood and hot wings, all served in ample, flavorful portions. Casual dress; cocktails. **Parking:** on-site (fee) and street. **Cards:** AX, DC, MC, VI.

LEMONGRASS THAI FARE **Lunch:** $7-$11 **Dinner:** $10-$20 **Phone:** 506/657-8424

Thai

Location: At Prince William St; centre. 42 Princess St E2L 1K2. **Hours:** 11:30 am-9 pm, Thurs-10 pm, Fri & Sat-11 pm. Closed: 12/25, 12/26; also Sun. **Reservations:** accepted. **Features:** This quaint restaurant offers several dining sections, as well as a lower lounge and seasonal courtyard. The menu lists a wide variety of well-prepared traditional and creative Thai dishes. Casual dress; cocktails. **Parking:** street. **Cards:** DC, MC, VI.

MEDITERRANEAN RESTAURANT **Lunch:** $6-$11 **Dinner:** $9-$17 **Phone:** 506/634-3183

Canadian

Location: Rt 100, 2.5 mi (4 km) ne. 419 Rothesay Rd E2J 2C3. **Hours:** 11:30 am-10:30 pm, Sun-8 pm. Closed: 12/25, 12/26. **Reservations:** accepted. **Features:** Sirloin tips, tenderloin steak, lasagna and salmon are representative of dishes on the laid-back restaurant's menu. Family-owned and operated since 1971, the popular spot radiates warmth and friendly charm. The service staff is pleasant and prompt. Casual dress; cocktails. **Parking:** on-site. **Cards:** AX, DC, MC, VI.

MEXICALI ROSA'S **Lunch:** $6-$11 **Dinner:** $10-$18 **Phone:** 506/652-5252

Mexican

Location: Centre. 88 Prince William St E2L 2B3. **Hours:** 11:30 am-1 am, Sun-midnight. Closed: 12/25. **Reservations:** accepted. **Features:** The Mexican cantina makes an excellent choice for family-friendly fun. Old West paintings and murals add color to stucco walls and wooden beams, while a Tex-Mex menu provides a feast of favorites such as fajitas, burritos and some seafood items. Fried ice cream is a sweet treat. Casual dress; cocktails. **Parking:** on-site (fee). **Cards:** AX, DC, MC, VI.

MIKES RESTAURANT **Lunch:** $7-$14 **Dinner:** $9-$18 **Phone:** 506/652-6453

Canadian

Location: Centre; in McAllister Place Mall. 519 Westmorland Rd E2J 3W9. **Hours:** 7:30 am-10 pm, Fri & Sat-11 pm, Sun-9 pm. Closed: 12/25. **Reservations:** accepted. **Features:** This popular family-friendly restaurant specializes in pizza and hot submarine sandwiches, along with fries, burgers, soup, salads, pasta, grilled meats and seafood. An excellent variety of colorful desserts rounds out the offerings. Casual dress; cocktails. **Parking:** on-site. **Cards:** AX, MC, VI.

REGGIE'S RESTAURANT **Lunch:** $5-$10 **Dinner:** $5-$10 **Phone:** 506/657-6270

Canadian

Location: Centre; adjacent to Brunswick Square Mall. 26 Germain St E2M 5T9. **Hours:** 6 am-5:30 pm, Sat-5 pm, Sun 7 am-5 pm. Closed: 3/24, 12/25. **Features:** Since 1969, the town landmark has been serving great custom-made sandwiches, soups and all-day breakfast items. Casual dress; beer & wine only. **Parking:** street. **Cards:** AX, MC, VI.

STEAMERS LOBSTER COMPANY **Lunch:** $8-$14 **Dinner:** $12-$20 **Phone:** 506/648-2325

Seafood

Location: Centre; across from the cruise ship terminal. 110 Water St E2L 4S6. **Hours:** 11 am-11 pm, Sun 4 pm-10 pm; 4 pm-10 pm 11/1-3/31. Closed: 12/25; also Sun-Wed 1/1-3/31. **Reservations:** accepted. **Features:** The restaurant lives up to its name with lobster, clams and mussels fresh from the tank and into the pots. The atmosphere is upbeat and friendly, with a large patio for seasonal dining. A dinner theater goes on upstairs on Thursday, Friday and Saturday. Casual dress; cocktails. **Parking:** street. **Cards:** AX, DC, MC, VI.

SUWANNA RESTAURANT **Dinner:** $15-$22 **Phone:** 506/637-9015

Thai

Location: Just s of Bridge Rd (Reversing Falls). 325 Lancaster Ave E2M 2L3. **Hours:** 5 pm-10:30 pm. Closed: 12/25, 12/26; also Mon. **Reservations:** suggested. **Features:** Pleasant dining rooms are staged throughout the circa 1851 former lumber baron's home. Authentic Thai cuisine is creatively prepared to suit any spice tolerance. Fresh local meat and seafood are at the heart of the menu. The atmosphere is relaxed and unhurried. Dressy casual; cocktails. **Parking:** on-site. **Cards:** MC, VI.

SWISS CHALET **Lunch:** $6-$11 **Dinner:** $8-$16 **Phone:** 506/657-9477

Canadian

Location: At Westmorland Ave. 86 Consumer Dr E2J 4Z3. **Hours:** 11 am-10 pm, Fri & Sat-11 pm, Sun-9 pm. Closed: 12/25. **Reservations:** accepted. **Features:** The popular restaurant is known for its rotisserie chicken and ribs and the tangy Chalet sauce that gives food its special zip. Diners munch on a half or quarter chicken with sides such as steamed vegetables, fries, baked potatoes and salads. Lunch guests often go for the great soup and sandwich combination. Take-out and delivery service are popular options. Casual dress; cocktails. **Parking:** on-site. **Cards:** AX, DC, MC, VI.

TACO PICA **Lunch:** $6-$10 **Dinner:** $9-$17 **Phone:** 506/633-8492

Mexican

Location: Centre. 96 Germain St E2L 4W3. **Hours:** 10 am-10 pm. Closed: 12/25; also Sun. **Reservations:** accepted. **Features:** A colorful decor and upbeat Latin music infuse this place with energy. The menu offers wonderful authentic Guatemalan, Mexican and Spanish entrees, including such specialties as soft-shell tacos, fajitas and chimichangas. Service is relaxed and friendly. Casual dress; cocktails. **Parking:** street. **Cards:** AX, MC, VI.

TURN OF THE TIDE DINING ROOM **Lunch:** $11-$16 **Dinner:** $22-$32 **Phone:** 506/632-8564

Continental

Location: Hwy 1, exit 122 at Market Square; in Hilton Saint John. 1 Market Square E2L 4Z6. **Hours:** 6:30 am-2 & 5:30-10 pm, Sat & Sun from 6 pm; from 6 am 6/1-9/30. **Reservations:** suggested. **Features:** Along with a lovely location overlooking the harbor, the dining room offers a sophisticated yet relaxed atmosphere. Panels of dark wood and etched glass divide the room into more intimate sections. Specialties include seafood and farm-raised game. Dressy casual; cocktails. **Parking:** on-site (fee). **Cards:** AX, CB, DC, DS, JC, MC, VI.

VITO'S RESTAURANT

▼▼▼ ▼▼▼
Italian

Lunch: $6-$13   **Dinner:** $8-$18   **Phone:** 506/634-1300
Location: Hwy 1, exit 129, 1.6 mi (2 km) w on Rt 100. 324 Rothesay Ave E2H 2C2. **Hours:** 7 am-10:30 pm, Fri & Sat-1 am. Closed: 12/25. **Reservations:** accepted. **Features:** The popular, spacious restaurant displays a pleasant, modern decor. On the menu is a wide variety of Italian dishes, including pizza. Take-out orders are accepted. Casual dress; cocktails. **Parking:** on-site. **Cards:** AX, DC, MC, VI.

VITO'S RESTAURANT

▼▼▼ ▼▼▼
Italian

Lunch: $6-$11   **Dinner:** $10-$19   **Phone:** 506/634-3900
Location: Centre. 1 Hazen Ave E2L 3G6. **Hours:** 11 am-11:30 pm, Fri & Sat-12:30 am, Sun-10 pm. Closed: 12/25. **Reservations:** accepted. **Features:** This popular, conveniently located restaurant offers two levels of seating with the upper floor exclusively non-smoking. An interesting mix of Italian, Greek and Canadian cuisines, the menu includes pizza, lasagna, chicken souvlaki and baklava. Casual dress; cocktails. **Parking:** on-site. **Cards:** AX, DC, MC, VI.

VIVALDI'S RESTAURANT

▼▼▼ ▼▼▼
Italian

Lunch: $7-$14   **Dinner:** $10-$23   **Phone:** 506/633-1414
Location: Hwy 1, exit 129, 2 mi (3.3 km) sw on Rt 100. 337 Rothesay Ave E2J 2C3. **Hours:** 11:30 am-9:30 pm, Fri-10 pm, Sat & Sun 4 pm-10 pm. Closed: 12/25, 12/26. **Reservations:** accepted. **Features:** Those who crave Italian food should add this casually upscale restaurant to their list. On the menu are fine-quality pasta dishes, Italian specialties, homemade soups, breads and desserts. Casual dress; cocktails. **Parking:** on-site. **Cards:** AX, MC, VI.

ST-LEONARD pop. 1,500

———— **WHERE TO STAY** ————

DAIGLE'S MOTEL

(CAA) (SAVE)
▼▼ ▼▼
Small-scale Hotel

Phone: (506)423-6351

	1P: $81-$89	2P: $89-$99	XP: $7	F16
6/1-9/30	1P: $72-$78	2P: $78-$86	XP: $7	F16
5/1-5/31 & 10/1-4/30				

Location: Hwy 17, 0.6 mi (1 km) s of Trans-Canada Hwy 2, exit 58. 68 rue DuPont E7E 1Y1. **Fax:** 506/423-7821. **Facility:** 50 one-bedroom standard units. 2 stories (no elevator), exterior corridors. **Parking:** on-site, winter plug-ins. **Terms:** office hours 7 am-midnight, small pets only ($7 extra charge, in designated units). **Dining:** restaurant, see separate listing. **Pool(s):** heated outdoor, wading. **Business Services:** meeting rooms. **Cards:** AX, DC, MC, VI. **Free Special Amenities:** local telephone calls and high-speed Internet.

SOME UNITS

———— **WHERE TO DINE** ————

DAIGLE'S DINING ROOM & LOUNGE

▼▼ ▼▼
Canadian

Lunch: $6-$10   **Dinner:** $9-$18   **Phone:** 506/423-6351
Location: Hwy 17, 0.6 mi (1 km) s of Trans-Canada Hwy 2, exit 58; in Daigle's Motel. 68 rue DuPont E7E 1Y1. **Hours:** 6 am-10 pm, Sat & Sun from 7 am; to 9 pm in winter. Closed: 12/24, 12/25. **Reservations:** accepted. **Features:** Floral arrangements add splashes of color to the casual, family eatery. A widely varied menu offers something for all tastes, from prime rib to scallops to fish 'n' chips. Casual dress; cocktails. **Parking:** on-site. **Cards:** AX, DC, MC, VI.

ST. MARTINS pop. 374

———— **WHERE TO STAY** ————

QUACO INN

▼▼▼▼
Country Inn

Phone: (506)833-4772

| 5/1-10/31 | 1P: $99-$175 | 2P: $99-$175 | XP: $15 | F10 |

Location: Centre. 16 Beach St E5R 1C7. **Facility:** Well-appointed rooms are featured in both the main inn and a newer annex; many rooms have electric fireplaces. Smoke free premises. 12 units. 10 one-bedroom standard units, some with whirlpools. 2 one-bedroom suites. 2 stories (no elevator), interior/exterior corridors. **Parking:** on-site. **Terms:** open 5/1-10/31, office hours 8 am-10 pm, 7 day cancellation notice, package plans. **Amenities:** hair dryers. Some: CD players. **Cards:** MC, VI.

SOME UNITS

ST. MARTINS COUNTRY INN

▼▼▼▼
Country Inn

Phone: (506)833-4534

| 5/15-10/31 | 1P: $95-$165 | 2P: $95-$165 | XP: $15 | F10 |

Location: Centre. 303 Main St E5R 1C1. **Fax:** 506/833-4725. **Facility:** Dating from 1857, this Queen Anne mansion and a newer annex offer varied rooms, some with bay views and some with balconies. Designated smoking area. 16 units. 14 one-bedroom standard units, some with whirlpools. 2 one-bedroom suites ($165), some with whirlpools. 3 stories (no elevator), interior corridors. **Parking:** on-site. **Terms:** open 5/15-10/31, office hours 7 am-11 pm, age restrictions may apply, 7 day cancellation notice, weekly rates available, [BP] & [MAP] meal plans available, package plans. **Amenities:** video library, hair dryers. **Leisure Activities:** whirlpool. **Cards:** MC, VI.

WESLAN INN

▼▼▼▼
Country Inn

Phone: 506/833-2351

Property failed to provide current rates

Location: Just e off Rt 111. 45 Main St E5R 1B4. **Fax:** 506/833-2351. **Facility:** The lovely 1844 former sea captain's home features individually decorated rooms, most equipped with fireplace and whirlpool bath and a few with decks. Smoke free premises. 3 one-bedroom standard units with whirlpools. 2 stories (no elevator), interior corridors. **Parking:** on-site. **Terms:** open 5/1-12/15 & 4/1-4/30, office hours 8 am-11 pm. **Amenities:** irons, hair dryers.

———— **WHERE TO DINE** ————

CAVE VIEW FAMILY RESTAURANT

▼▼
Seafood

Lunch: $4-$12   **Dinner:** $5-$20   **Phone:** 506/833-4698
Location: Off Rt 111. 82 Bayview Rd E5R 1C2. **Hours:** Open 5/1-10/31; 11 am-9 pm; hours vary off season. **Reservations:** accepted. **Features:** The casual restaurant affords great views of the ocean and caves from the dining room and deck alike. Guests order at the service counter, and then items are brought to the table. This place is noted for its chowder. Casual dress. **Parking:** on-site. **Cards:** AX, MC, VI.

ST. STEPHEN pop. 4,667

——— WHERE TO STAY ———

BLAIR HOUSE HERITAGE INN
Phone: (506)466-2233

6/22-9/3 [BP]	1P: $89-$99	2P: $99-$109	XP: $20	D10
9/4-10/8 [BP]	1P: $85-$89	2P: $89-$99	XP: $20	D10
5/1-6/21 [BP]	1P: $79-$89	2P: $89-$99	XP: $20	D10
10/9-4/30 [BP]	1P: $79-$89	2P: $85-$99	XP: $20	D10

Historic Bed & Breakfast

Location: Centre. Located in a residential area. 38 Prince William St E3L 1S3. Fax: 506/466-1699. **Facility:** First- and second-floor rooms with a view of the river are featured at this pleasant 1850s-era home. Smoke free premises. 5 one-bedroom standard units. 2 stories (no elevator), interior corridors. *Bath:* combo or shower only. **Parking:** on-site. **Terms:** check-in 4 pm, 7 day cancellation notice. **Amenities:** hair dryers. *Some:* CD players. **Guest Services:** complimentary evening beverages, wireless Internet. **Cards:** AX, MC, VI.

(ASK) (X)

ST. STEPHEN INN
Phone: (506)466-1814

7/1-9/3 [CP]	1P: $69-$89	2P: $69-$89	XP: $5	F12
5/1-6/30 & 9/4-12/31 [CP]	1P: $59-$69	2P: $64-$74	XP: $5	F12
1/1-4/30 [CP]	1P: $59-$64	2P: $59-$69	XP: $5	F12

Small-scale Hotel

Location: On Hwy 1; centre. 99 King St E3L 2C6. Fax: 506/466-6148. **Facility:** 51 one-bedroom standard units. 2 stories (no elevator), interior/exterior corridors. *Bath:* combo or shower only. **Parking:** on-site, winter plug-ins. **Terms:** pets ($10 extra charge). **Business Services:** meeting rooms. **Cards:** AX, DC, JC, MC, VI.

SOME UNITS

(ASK) (S/D) (🛏) (🍴) / (X) /
FEE

WINSOME INN
Phone: (506)466-2130

(CAA) (SAVE)

6/25-9/1 [ECP]	1P: $92-$105	2P: $99-$119	XP: $10	F6
9/2-11/10 [ECP]	1P: $86-$96	2P: $94-$108	XP: $8	F6
5/1-6/24 [ECP]	1P: $84-$95	2P: $86-$99	XP: $8	F6
11/11-4/30 [ECP]	1P: $73-$83	2P: $78-$88	XP: $5	F6

Motel

Location: Centre. 198 King St E3L 2E2. Fax: 506/466-4651. **Facility:** 39 one-bedroom standard units. 1 story, exterior corridors. **Parking:** on-site. **Pool(s):** heated outdoor. **Leisure Activities:** playground, horseshoes, volleyball. **Guest Services:** wireless Internet. **Business Services:** meeting rooms. **Cards:** AX, DC, MC, VI. **Free Special Amenities:** expanded continental breakfast and local telephone calls.

SOME UNITS

(S/D) (🏊) (X) (🎛) (🛏) (📷) / (X) /

——— WHERE TO DINE ———

CARMAN'S DINER
Lunch: $5-$14   **Dinner:** $5-$14   Phone: 506/466-3528

Canadian

Location: On Hwy 1; centre. 164 King St E3L 2W9. **Hours:** 7 am-10 pm, Sun from 8 am. Closed: 12/25, 12/26. **Features:** Popular for basic fare at reasonable prices, the restaurant has been around forever. Choices range from sandwiches, burgers and fish and chips to steak and seafood. Parking is plentiful. Casual dress. **Parking:** on-site. **Cards:** MC, VI.

RED ROOSTER COUNTRY RESTAURANT
Lunch: $5-$10   **Dinner:** $7-$14   Phone: 506/466-0018

Canadian

Location: 1.6 (2.5 km) e on Hwy 1. 5 Old Bay Rd E3L 3W7. **Hours:** 6 am-10 pm, Fri & Sat-11 pm; Fri & Sat-10 pm 9/6-5/30. **Features:** Painted murals on the walls contribute to the casual restaurant's early country and Western theme. Home-style cooking includes everything from sandwiches and burgers to steak and seafood. Homemade pies and pastries are a special treat. Service is friendly and relaxed. Casual dress; cocktails. **Parking:** on-site. **Cards:** AX, DC, MC, VI.

ST. JEROME'S FAMILY GRILL
Lunch: $6-$16   **Dinner:** $9-$19   Phone: 506/466-3027

Canadian

Location: Centre; adjacent to Ganong Building. 73 Milltown Blvd E3L 2X5. **Hours:** 8 am-8 pm. Closed: 12/25, 12/26; also 4/14. **Reservations:** accepted. **Features:** Wide variety on menu, specializing in chicken and ribs. Casual dress; cocktails. **Parking:** on-site. **Cards:** AX, DC, MC, VI.

SHEDIAC pop. 4,892

——— WHERE TO STAY ———

AUBERGE BELCOURT INN
Phone: 506/532-6098

6/22-9/5 [BP]	1P: $85-$110	2P: $85-$110
5/1-6/21, 9/6-11/30 & 3/1-4/30 [BP]	1P: $75-$95	2P: $75-$95

Historic Bed & Breakfast

Location: Centre. 310 Main St E4P 2E3. Fax: 506/533-9398. **Facility:** Each guest room is tastefully decorated at this elegant 1912 Victorian mansion; the property has a maximum two person per room policy. Smoke free premises. 7 one-bedroom standard units. 2 stories (no elevator), interior corridors. *Bath:* combo or shower only. **Parking:** on-site. **Terms:** open 5/1-11/30 & 3/1-4/30, office hours 9 am-9 pm, 3 day cancellation notice-fee imposed. **Amenities:** hair dryers. **Guest Services:** TV in common area. **Cards:** AX, CB, DC, DS, MC, VI.

(📶) (X) (W) (🐾)

GAUDET CHALETS & MOTEL
Phone: 506/533-8877
Property failed to provide current rates

Motel

Location: On Rt 133, 1.4 mi (2.4 km) w of Rt 15, exit 37. 14 Belleview Heights E4P 8C7. Fax: 506/533-8498. **Facility:** 46 units. 24 one-bedroom standard units. 6 one-bedroom suites with kitchens. 16 cottages, some with whirlpools. 1 story, exterior corridors. *Bath:* combo or shower only. **Parking:** on-site. **Terms:** open 5/1-10/31, office hours 8 am-10 pm, check-in 4 pm, small pets only. **Amenities:** *Some:* hair dryers. **Leisure Activities:** playground. **Guest Services:** wireless Internet.

SOME UNITS

(🛏) (📶) / (X) (🎛) (🛏) (📷) (📺) /

SEELY'S MOTEL

CAA SAVE

Motel

	7/15-9/5	1P: $69-$75	2P: $90-$125	XP: $10	F12
	9/6-4/30	1P: $55-$65	2P: $65-$85	XP: $7	F12
	5/1-7/14	1P: $60-$65	2P: $65-$80	XP: $7	F12

Phone: (506)532-6193

Location: On Rt 133; 1.5 mi (2.4 km) w of Rt 15, exit 37. 21 Bellevue Heights E4P 1G9. Fax: 506/533-8089. **Facility:** 34 one-bedroom standard units, some with efficiencies and/or whirlpools. 2 stories (no elevator), exterior corridors. **Parking:** on-site. **Terms:** 3 day cancellation notice, weekly rates available. **Cards:** AX, DC, MC, VI. **Free Special Amenities:** local telephone calls and high-speed Internet.

SOME UNITS

------- WHERE TO DINE -------

BAYOU PUB & EATERY

Canadian

Lunch: $5-$12 **Dinner:** $8-$16 **Phone:** 506/533-9008

Location: Rt 15, exit 37; 1.4 mi (2.4 km) w of Rt 15 on Rt 133. 607 Main St E4P 8C7. **Hours:** 6 am-9 pm, Fri & Sat-10 pm. Closed: 12/25, 12/26. **Features:** Offerings at the casual pub include quick-serve appetizers, as well as preparations from the full menu. Patio seating is a seasonal option. Casual dress; cocktails. **Parking:** on-site. **Cards:** AX, DC, MC, VI.

THE GREEN HOUSE ON MAIN

Canadian

Lunch: $9-$14 **Dinner:** $13-$28 **Phone:** 506/533-7097

Location: Centre. 406 A Main St E4P 2G1. **Hours:** Open 5/1-11/30 & 2/14-4/30; 11:30 am-10:30 pm; hours vary off season. Closed: 1/1, 10/8, 12/25. **Reservations:** accepted. **Features:** The converted home has several cozy dining sections and a pleasant sundeck for seasonal outdoor dining. The menu features a variety of fresh seafood and pasta dishes. Save room for one of the sumptuous desserts. Casual dress; cocktails. **Parking:** on-site. **Cards:** MC, VI.

THE LOBSTER DECK RESTAURANT & SANDBAR
LOUNGE

Seafood

Lunch: $8-$13 **Dinner:** $14-$26 **Phone:** 506/532-8737

Location: Hwy 11, exit 1 northbound, 1.1 mi (1.8 km) e; exit 2A southbound, follow signs to Shediac; centre. 312 Main St E4P 2E3. **Hours:** Open 5/1-10/1 & 11/1-4/30; 11 am-9 pm; to 8 pm off season. **Reservations:** suggested. **Features:** This popular restaurant offers relaxed dining with a nautical theme or one can enjoy the evening breeze and dine outside on the terrace. An extensive selection of fresh seafood includes such favourites as the shrimp plate and delicious boiled or stuffed lobster. Casual dress; cocktails. **Parking:** on-site. **Cards:** AX, DC, MC, VI.

SUSSEX pop. 4,182

------- WHERE TO STAY -------

ALL SEASONS INN

Motel

| | 6/21-10/20 | 1P: $65-$90 | 2P: $85-$125 | XP: $10 | F17 |
| | 5/1-6/20 & 10/21-4/30 | 1P: $55-$65 | 2P: $65-$100 | XP: $10 | F17 |

Phone: (506)433-2220

Location: Hwy 1, exit 192 eastbound; exit 198 westbound, left towards Sussex Corner; centre. Located in a quiet rural area. 1015 Main St E4E 2M6. Fax: 506/433-2224. **Facility:** 24 one-bedroom standard units, some with efficiencies and/or whirlpools. 1 story, exterior corridors. **Parking:** on-site, winter plug-ins. **Terms:** pets ($10 extra charge). **Dining:** restaurant, see separate listing. **Business Services:** meeting rooms. **Cards:** AX, DC, DS, MC, VI.

SOME UNITS

FEE

AMSTERDAM INN *Book at AAA.com*

Small-scale Hotel

	7/1-9/15	1P: $106	2P: $116	XP: $10	F12
	5/16-6/30	1P: $77	2P: $87	XP: $10	F12
	5/1-5/15 & 9/16-4/30	1P: $74	2P: $84	XP: $10	F12

Phone: (506)432-5050

Location: Hwy 1, exit 192. Located opposite Gateway Mall. 143 Main St E4E 1S8. Fax: 506/432-5069. **Facility:** Smoke free premises. 31 one-bedroom standard units. 2 stories (no elevator), interior/exterior corridors. **Parking:** on-site. **Amenities:** video library, DVD players, irons, hair dryers. **Guest Services:** wireless Internet. **Business Services:** meeting rooms. **Cards:** AX, MC, VI.

SOME UNITS

FAIRWAY INN *Book at AAA.com*

Small-scale Hotel

	6/15-10/15 [CP]	1P: $98-$125	2P: $108-$155	XP: $10	F16
	10/16-4/30 [CP]	1P: $78-$115	2P: $92-$125	XP: $10	F16
	5/1-6/14 [CP]	1P: $78-$98	2P: $92-$102	XP: $10	F16

Phone: (506)433-3470

Location: Hwy 1, exit 193. 216 Roachville Rd E4E 5L6 (PO Box 4437). Fax: 506/433-2676. **Facility:** 54 one-bedroom standard units, some with efficiencies. 2 stories (no elevator), interior/exterior corridors. **Parking:** on-site. **Terms:** pets ($10 extra charge). **Amenities:** *Some:* hair dryers. **Dining:** J J's Diner, see separate listing. **Pool(s):** heated indoor. **Leisure Activities:** sauna, whirlpool. **Guest Services:** coin laundry, wireless Internet. **Business Services:** meeting rooms. **Cards:** AX, DC, DS, MC, VI.

SOME UNITS

FEE

PINE CONE MOTEL

Motel

| | 5/1-10/15 | 1P: $55-$60 | 2P: $65-$75 | XP: $8 | F12 |

Phone: (506)433-3958

Location: Hwy 1, exit 198, 1.2 mi (2 km) e on Hwy 114 towards Penobsquis. 12808 Rt 114 E4E 5L9 (Box 4752). Fax: 506/433-5037. **Facility:** 20 one-bedroom standard units. 1 story, exterior corridors. **Bath:** combo or shower only. **Parking:** on-site. **Terms:** open 5/1-10/15, small pets only (in smoking units). **Cards:** AX, MC, VI.

SOME UNITS

——— WHERE TO DINE ———

ALL SEASONS RESTAURANT   Lunch: $6-$10   Dinner: $9-$16   Phone: 506/433-2220
◆◆ ◆◆   **Location:** Hwy 1, exit 192 eastbound; exit 198 westbound, left towards Sussex Corner; in All Seasons Inn. 1015 Main St E4E 2M6. **Hours:** 7 am-10 pm. **Closed:** 12/25, 12/26. **Reservations:** accepted. **Features:** In a log
Canadian   building with fireplaces, the relaxed, family-oriented restaurant delivers a wide range of favorites. Selections include chicken cordon bleu, ribs, lasagna and lobster rolls. Nice music plays in the background. Casual dress; cocktails. **Parking:** on-site. **Cards:** AX, DC, DS, MC, VI.

BROADWAY CAFE   Lunch: $6-$10   Dinner: $12-$25   Phone: 506/433-5414
◆◆ ◆◆   **Location:** Centre; opposite The Old Train Station. 73 Broad St E0E 1P1. **Hours:** 10 am-9 pm, Mon & Tues-3 pm.
Closed: Sun. **Reservations:** suggested. **Features:** In a cozy setting of wrought iron and antique mirrors, a
Canadian   menu of creative meat and seafood entrees, excellent homemade bread and rich dessert, awaits your delight. Enjoy a steaming cup of cappuccino or espresso with a slice of white chocolate pecan pie. Casual dress; cocktails. **Parking:** on-site. **Cards:** MC, VI.   [AC]

CATHY'S CHINESE RESTAURANT   Lunch: $6-$10   Dinner: $8-$15   Phone: 506/433-4007
◆◆ ◆◆   **Location:** Centre. 612 Main St E4E 7H8. **Hours:** 11 am-10 pm, Fri & Sat-midnight, Sun noon-9 pm. **Closed:**
12/25, 12/26. **Features:** In the heart of town, the cozy restaurant presents a menu of varied Oriental dishes,
Chinese   as well as some Canadian items. Casual dress. **Parking:** street. **Cards:** AX, MC, VI.

J J'S DINER   Lunch: $5-$9   Dinner: $7-$21   Phone: 506/433-3470
◆◆ ◆◆   **Location:** Hwy 1, exit 193; in Fairway Inn. 216 Roachville Rd E4E 5L6. **Hours:** 6 am-11 pm. **Features:** In a handy
location bordering the highway, the restaurant has an upbeat atmosphere, thanks in part to its 1950s theme.
Canadian   Patrons can choose either booth or table seating. Menu offerings range from burgers, fries and sandwiches to fresh seafood and steak. Casual dress; cocktails. **Parking:** on-site. **Cards:** AX, DC, DS, MC, VI.

TRACADIE-SHEILA

——— WHERE TO STAY ———

LE CHATEAU D'ACADIE   Phone: 506/395-7565
◆◆◆◆   All Year [BP]   1P: $99-$135   XP: $15   F18
Location: Centre. 3559 rue Principale E1X 1C9. Fax: 506/395-1721. **Facility:** In the heart of town, the attractive
Bed & Breakfast   1939 home offers tastefully decorated guest rooms with modern amenities. Smoke free premises. 5 units. 4 one-bedroom standard units. 2 stories (no elevator), interior corridors. *Bath:* combo or shower only. **Parking:** on-site. **Terms:** office hours 8 am-11 pm, package plans. **Amenities:** video library, high-speed Internet, hair dryers. **Guest Services:** complimentary laundry. **Cards:** AX, DC, MC, VI.   [⊓+] [⊠] [VCR]

——— WHERE TO DINE ———

LE BON VIVANT RESTAURANT   Lunch: $7-$13   Dinner: $10-$21   Phone: 506/394-9990
◆◆ ◆◆   **Location:** Centre. 352 rue du Quai E1X 1C9. **Hours:** 7 am-10 pm, Fri & Sat-midnight. **Closed:** 12/25, 12/26.
Reservations: accepted. **Features:** In the heart of downtown, the restaurant offers patrons a comfortable
Canadian   and relaxing dining experience. The menu includes selections such as fresh seafood, steaks, burgers, fries and sandwiches. Casual dress; cocktails. **Parking:** on-site. **Cards:** MC, VI.

WOODSTOCK pop. 5,198

——— WHERE TO STAY ———

BEST WESTERN WOODSTOCK INN & SUITES   *Book great rates at AAA.com*   Phone: (506)328-2378
(CAA) [SAVE]   7/1-9/6 [ECP]   1P: $119-$189   2P: $119-$189   XP: $10   F12
9/7-4/30 [ECP]   1P: $109-$189   2P: $109-$189   XP: $10   F12
◆◆◆◆   5/1-6/30 [ECP]   1P: $109-$169   2P: $109-$169   XP: $10   F12
Small-scale Hotel   **Location:** Trans-Canada Hwy 2, exit 185. 123 Gallop Ct E7M 3P7. Fax: 506/328-9195. **Facility:** Smoke free
premises. 50 units. 38 one-bedroom standard units. 12 one-bedroom suites ($129-$199). 3 stories, interior corridors. *Bath:* combo or shower only. **Parking:** on-site. **Terms:** cancellation fee imposed, package plans.
Amenities: video library, DVD players, high-speed Internet, dual phone lines, voice mail, irons, hair dryers. **Pool(s):** heated indoor. **Leisure Activities:** exercise room. **Guest Services:** coin laundry, wireless Internet. **Business Services:** meeting rooms. **Cards:** AX, CB, DC, DS, MC, VI. **Free Special Amenities:** expanded continental breakfast and newspaper.
SOME UNITS
[S/D] [⊓+] [Y] [&] [⇆] [⊠] [▣] /[⊟] [⊡] /

ECONO LODGE   *Book great rates at AAA.com*   Phone: 506/328-8876
◆◆ ◆◆   6/15-9/15   1P: $110-$130   2P: $110-$130   XP: $10   F12
5/1-6/14 & 9/16-4/30   1P: $85-$90   2P: $85-$90   XP: $10   F12
Small-scale Hotel   **Location:** Trans-Canada Hwy 2, exit 188 (Houlton Rd). 168 Rt 555 E7M 6B5 (PO Box 9051). Fax: 506/328-4828.
Facility: 50 one-bedroom standard units. 3 stories (no elevator), interior/exterior corridors. **Parking:** on-site,
winter plug-ins. **Terms:** pets ($10 fee, in smoking units). **Amenities:** voice mail, hair dryers. *Some:* high-speed Internet, dual phone lines, irons. **Dining:** O'Riley's Restaurant, see separate listing. **Pool(s):** heated outdoor. **Business Services:** meeting rooms. **Cards:** AX, MC, VI. *(See color ad card insert)*
SOME UNITS
[ASK] [S/D] [⊭] [⊓] [Y] [⇆] [▣] /[⊠]/
FEE

HOWARD JOHNSON INN   *Book at AAA.com*   Phone: (506)328-3315
◆◆ ◆◆   6/16-9/15   1P: $100   2P: $110   XP: $10   F16
5/1-6/15   1P: $80   2P: $90   XP: $10   F16
9/16-4/30   1P: $70   2P: $80   XP: $10   F16
Small-scale Hotel   **Location:** Trans-Canada Hwy 2, exit 188 (Houlton Rd). 159 Rt 555, exit 188 TCH E7M 6B5 (PO Box 9002).
Fax: 506/328-4562. **Facility:** 50 one-bedroom standard units. 1-2 stories (no elevator), interior/exterior corridors. **Parking:** on-site, winter plug-ins. **Terms:** cancellation fee imposed, package plans. **Amenities:** hair dryers. *Some:* irons. **Pool(s):** heated indoor. **Leisure Activities:** sauna, whirlpool, playground. **Business Services:** meeting rooms. **Cards:** AX, DC, MC, VI.
SOME UNITS
[ASK] [S/D] [⊭] [⊓] [Y] [⇆] [⊠] [▣] /[⊠]/

STILES MOTEL HILL VIEW

Phone: 506/328-6671

Property failed to provide current rates

Small-scale Hotel

Location: Trans-Canada Hwy 2, exit 185 eastbound, 1.6 mi (2.5 km) e; exit 188 (Houlton Rd) westbound, 3.4 mi (5.5 km) via Rt 555 and 103 (Main St). Located in a semi-residential area. 827 Main St E7M 2E9. Fax: 506/328-3737. **Facility:** 32 one-bedroom standard units. 1 story, exterior corridors. **Parking:** on-site, winter plug-ins. **Terms:** small pets only. **Amenities:** *Some:* dual phone lines. **Dining:** Home Town Restaurant, see separate listing.

SOME UNITS

———— WHERE TO DINE ————

HOME TOWN RESTAURANT

Canadian

Lunch: $5-$12   **Dinner:** $10-$19   Phone: 506/328-6671

Location: Trans-Canada Hwy 2, exit 185 eastbound, 1.6 mi (2.5 km) e; exit 188 (Houlton Rd) westbound, 3.4 mi (5.5 km) via Rt 555 and 103 (Main St). 827 Main St E7M 2E9. **Hours:** 7 am-10, noon-2 & 5-9 pm. **Reservations:** accepted. **Features:** The menu of the popular local restaurant offers a wide variety of selections: from burgers and sandwiches to steak and seafood. Casual, friendly service is one aspect of the homey, unpretentious atmosphere. Casual dress; cocktails. **Parking:** on-site. **Cards:** DC, MC, VI.

O'RILEY'S RESTAURANT

Canadian

Lunch: $5-$10   **Dinner:** $10-$18   Phone: 506/328-8876

Location: Trans-Canada Hwy 2, exit 188 (Houlton Rd). 168 Rt 555 E7M 6B5. **Hours:** 7 am-10 & 4-10 pm. Closed: 12/25, 12/26. **Reservations:** accepted. **Features:** The pleasant, family-friendly restaurant offers a splendid view of the valley and surrounding hills. Casual dress; cocktails. **Parking:** on-site. **Cards:** AX, DC, MC, VI.

SMITTY'S FAMILY RESTAURANT

Canadian

Lunch: $6-$11   **Dinner:** $8-$16   Phone: 506/325-1132

Location: Jct Houlton Rd. 365 Connell St E7M 6B5. **Hours:** 6:30 am-9 pm, Sun from 8 am. Closed: 12/25. **Reservations:** accepted. **Features:** The family-oriented restaurant satisfies patrons with its ever-popular all-day breakfast items, as well as tasty and wholesome soups and salads at lunchtime. A relaxed mood characterizes the dining space. Casual dress; cocktails. **Parking:** on-site. **Cards:** AX, DC, MC, VI.

YOUNGS COVE ROAD

———— WHERE TO STAY ————

MCCREADY'S MOTEL

Motel

Phone: 506/362-2916

| All Year | 1P: $44-$52 | 2P: $56-$65 | XP: $4 |

Location: Trans-Canada Hwy 2, exit 365, just w. Located in a quiet rural area. 10995 Rt 10 E4C 2G5. **Facility:** 10 one-bedroom standard units. 1 story, exterior corridors. **Parking:** on-site, winter plug-ins. **Terms:** office hours 6 am-11 pm, small pets only. **Dining:** 7 am-10 pm. **Cards:** AX, CB, DC, DS, MC, VI.

Newfoundland and Labrador

BADGER pop. 906

——— WHERE TO DINE ———

KELLIE'S RESTAURANT & TAKE-OUT | **Lunch:** $5-$10 | **Dinner:** $7-$14 | **Phone:** 709/539-2539

◆◆
Location: On Trans-Canada Hwy 1; centre. 1 Badger Dr A0H 1A0. **Hours:** 8 am-11 pm; hours vary off season. Closed: 12/25, 12/26. **Features:** In a convenient location just off the highway, the restaurant sustains a casual atmosphere. Home-style cooking is served in ample portions. Casual dress. **Parking:** on-site. **Cards:** AX, JC, MC, VI.

Canadian

BADGER'S QUAY

——— WHERE TO STAY ———

——— *The following lodging was either not evaluated or did not* ———
meet AAA rating requirements but is listed for your information only.

BLUE MIST MOTEL | **Phone:** 709/536-5690

[fyi]
Not evaluated. **Location:** On Rt 320 (Main St). Rt 320 A0G 1B0 (Box 56). Facilities, services, and decor characterize a basic property.

BAY ROBERTS pop. 5,237

——— WHERE TO DINE ———

JUNGLE JIM'S RESTAURANT | **Lunch:** $7-$11 | **Dinner:** $8-$20 | **Phone:** 709/786-4888

◆◆ ◆◆
Location: Jct Conception Bay Hwy; centre. Water St A0A 1G0. **Hours:** 11 am-11 pm, Fri & Sat-midnight. Closed: 1/1, 12/25. **Reservations:** accepted. **Features:** Guests can step into a tropical theme at the casual eatery, which employs a friendly staff and nurtures a bustling atmosphere. The menu lines up a wide variety of comfort foods, salads, chicken, beef, seafood and hot wings, all served in ample, flavorful portions. Casual dress; cocktails. **Parking:** on-site. **Cards:** AX, DC, MC, VI.

Canadian

BIRCHY LAKE

——— WHERE TO DINE ———

FORT BIRCHY PARK RESTAURANT | **Lunch:** $6-$9 | **Dinner:** $6-$9 | **Phone:** 709/636-3678

◆◆
Location: Trans-Canada Hwy 1, between Deer Lake and Badger; in Fort Birchy Park. **Hours:** Open 6/15-9/30; 8 am-8 pm. **Features:** This family owned and operated country cafe serves a variety of down-home comfort foods. No frills, just good, home-style cooking served in a friendly atmosphere. Casual dress. **Parking:** on-site. **Cards:** VI.

Canadian

[AC]

BROOKLYN

——— WHERE TO STAY ———

——— *The following lodging was either not evaluated or did not* ———
meet AAA rating requirements but is listed for your information only.

ASPEN BY-THE-SEA | **Phone:** 709/467-5219

[fyi]
Not evaluated. **Location:** Rt 234, just off Rt 230; centre. Main Rd (PO Box 1587, CLARENVILLE, A0E 1J0). Facilities, services, and decor characterize a mid-range property.

CARBONEAR pop. 4,759

——— WHERE TO STAY ———

——— *The following lodging was either not evaluated or did not* ———
meet AAA rating requirements but is listed for your information only.

FONG'S MOTEL | **Phone:** 709/596-5114

[fyi]
Not evaluated. **Location:** On Hwy 70; centre. 143 Columbus Dr A1Y 1A6. Facilities, services, and decor characterize a basic property.

CHANNEL-PORT-AUX-BASQUES pop. 5,200

——— WHERE TO STAY ———

ST. CHRISTOPHER'S HOTEL | | | **Phone:** (709)695-7034

◆◆ ◆◆

7/1-9/30	1P: $99-$109	2P: $103-$113
6/1-6/30	1P: $89-$99	2P: $94-$104
10/1-4/30	1P: $79-$89	2P: $83-$93
5/1-5/31	1P: $76-$86	2P: $80-$90

Small-scale Hotel

Location: Trans-Canada Hwy 1, exit Port Aux Basques (downtown), follow signs 1.2 mi (2 km). 146 Caribou Rd A0M 1C0 (PO Box 2049, PORT AUX BASQUES). Fax: 709/695-9841. **Facility:** 83 units. 79 one-bedroom standard units. 4 one-bedroom suites, some with kitchens. 3 stories, interior corridors. **Parking:** on-site, winter plug-ins. **Terms:** weekly rates available. **Amenities:** high-speed Internet, hair dryers. *Some:* irons. **Dining:** The Captain's Room, see separate listing. **Leisure Activities:** exercise room. **Guest Services:** coin laundry. **Business Services:** meeting rooms, PC, fax (fee). **Cards:** AX, MC, VI.

SOME UNITS

[ASK] [SD] [🛏] [🍴] [Y] [▦] / [⊠] [🛏] [🖥] /

CAA & Choice Hotels.
No one knows Canada better.

When travelling within Canada, CAA members always save at participating Choice Hotels.°

With 229 locations across Canada, Choice Hotels® fits your travel plans and your budget. Plus earn nights or flights when you take advantage of our rewards program, *Choice Privileges*.° To book now and save, call today and ask for CAA preferred rates,° and for hotel information visit us online.

800.228.1222
choicehotels.ca

We'll see you there.
CHOICE HOTELS CANADA™

──────── *The following lodging was either not evaluated or did not* ────────
meet AAA rating requirements but is listed for your information only.

HOTEL PORT AUX BASQUES   Phone: 709/695-2171

[fyi]   Not evaluated. **Location:** Jct Trans-Canada Hwy 1. 1 Grand Bay Rd A0M 1C0 (PO Box 400, PORT AUX BASQUES). Facilities, services, and decor characterize a mid-range property.

──────── **WHERE TO DINE** ────────

THE CAPTAIN'S ROOM   **Lunch:** $5-$10   **Dinner:** $8-$17   Phone: 709/695-7034

▽▽▽ ▽▽▽   **Location:** Trans-Canada Hwy 1, exit Port Aux Basques (downtown), follow signs 1.2 mi (2 km); in St. Christopher's Hotel. 146 Caribou Rd A0M 1C0. **Hours:** 6 am-2 & 5-10 pm; hours vary off season. Closed: 12/25.
Canadian   **Reservations:** accepted. **Features:** A friendly crew is on deck in the restaurant, which specializes in seafood. Also on the menu is a decent selection of steaks, poultry and salads. Casual dress; cocktails.
Parking: on-site. **Cards:** AX, DC, MC, VI.

CHURCHILL FALLS

──────── **WHERE TO STAY** ────────

──────── *The following lodging was either not evaluated or did not* ────────
meet AAA rating requirements but is listed for your information only.

CHURCHILL FALLS INN   Phone: 709/925-3211

[fyi]   Did not meet all AAA rating requirements for locking devices in some guest rooms at time of last evaluation on 04/29/2006. **Location:** Centre; in town complex. Ressigieu Dr A0R 1A0. Facilities, services, and decor characterize
Small-scale Hotel   a mid-range property.

──────── **WHERE TO DINE** ────────

BANNIKEN'S FOOD & BEVERAGE EMPORIUM   **Lunch:** $6-$11   **Dinner:** $8-$17   Phone: 709/925-3211

▽▽▽   **Location:** Centre; in town complex; in Churchill Falls Inn. Ressigieu Dr A0R 1A0. **Hours:** 7 am-9 pm. Closed: 12/25, 12/26. **Reservations:** accepted. **Features:** The modern eatery offers a choice of booth or table seating.
California   Seafood and steaks share menu space with a good selection of comfort foods. Casual dress; cocktails.
Parking: on-site. **Cards:** DC, MC, VI.

CLARENVILLE pop. 5,104

──────── **WHERE TO STAY** ────────

RESTLAND MOTEL   Phone: (709)466-7636

▽▽▽   All Year   1P: $85-$95   2P: $95-$105   XP: $10   F
Small-scale Hotel   **Location:** Centre. Located adjacent to Town Hall. 262 Memorial Dr A5A 1N9. Fax: 709/466-2743. **Facility:** 25 units. 23 one- and 2 two-bedroom standard units, some with efficiencies, kitchens and/or whirlpools. 2 stories (no elevator), interior/exterior corridors. **Parking:** on-site. **Terms:** weekly rates available, package plans, small pets only. **Guest Services:** wireless Internet. **Business Services:** meeting rooms. **Cards:** AX, DC, MC, VI.

SOME UNITS
(ASK) (S🛏) (🛏) (🍽) (ⓨ) (🅰️C) / (✖️) (📵) (📠) /

ST. JUDE HOTEL   Phone: 709/466-1717

▽▽▽ ▽▽▽   All Year   1P: $90-$98   2P: $92-$110   XP: $8
   Location: On Trans-Canada Hwy 1; centre. 247 Trans-Canada Hwy A5A 1Y4 (PO Box 2500, A0E 1J0).
Small-scale Hotel   Fax: 709/466-1714. **Facility:** 63 units. 62 one-bedroom standard units, some with whirlpools. 1 one-bedroom suite ($125-$250) with whirlpool. 3 stories, interior corridors. **Parking:** on-site. **Terms:** cancellation fee imposed, weekly rates available, small pets only (ground floor units). **Amenities:** video library (fee), irons, hair dryers. *Some:* high-speed Internet. **Dining:** Dustabella's Restaurant, see separate listing. **Business Services:** meeting rooms, PC. **Cards:** AX, DC, MC, VI.

SOME UNITS
(🛏) (🍽) (ⓨ) (📵) / (✖️) (VCR) (📠) /
FEE

──────── *The following lodging was either not evaluated or did not* ────────
meet AAA rating requirements but is listed for your information only.

CLARENVILLE INN   Phone: 709/466-7911

[fyi]   Not evaluated. **Location:** On Trans-Canada Hwy 1; centre. 134 Trans Canada Hwy A5A 1Y3. Facilities, services, and decor characterize a mid-range property.

──────── **WHERE TO DINE** ────────

DUSTABELLA'S RESTAURANT   **Lunch:** $6-$12   **Dinner:** $9-$21   Phone: 709/466-1717

▽▽▽ ▽▽▽   **Location:** On Trans-Canada Hwy 1; in St. Jude Hotel. 247 Trans-Canada Hwy A5A 1Y4. **Hours:** 7 am-10 pm; hours
   vary off season. Closed: 12/25. **Reservations:** accepted. **Features:** Upscale decor characterizes the
Canadian   pleasant dining room, where diners savor fresh seafood, various meat dishes and some comfort foods in a casual setting. Casual dress; cocktails. **Parking:** on-site. **Cards:** AX, DC, MC, VI.

RANDOM SOUND RESTAURANT   **Lunch:** $6-$12   **Dinner:** $9-$20   **Phone:** 709/466-7911

🔺🔺🔺 🔺🔺🔺
Canadian

Location: On Trans-Canada Hwy 1; centre; in Clarenville Inn. 134 Trans-Canada Hwy A5A 1Y3. **Hours:** 7 am-10 pm. **Reservations:** accepted. **Features:** On a hilltop overlooking the harbor, bay and township, the relaxed restaurant offers not only great views but also a bounty in seafood, steaks and comfort foods. Casual dress; cocktails. **Parking:** on-site. **Cards:** AX, DC, MC, VI.

COLINET

——— **WHERE TO STAY** ———

——— *The following lodging was either not evaluated or did not meet AAA rating requirements but is listed for your information only.* ———

TRELAWNEY BED & BREAKFAST   **Phone:** 709/521-2498

[fyi]

Not evaluated. **Location:** Jct Rt 93 and 91. Rt 91 A0B 1M0 (PO Box 51). Facilities, services, and decor characterize a basic property.

CORNER BROOK pop. 20,103

——— **WHERE TO STAY** ———

COMFORT INN   *Book great rates at AAA.com*   **Phone:** (709)639-1980

🔺🔺🔺 🔺🔺🔺
Small-scale Hotel

6/17-9/16	1P: $110-$120	2P: $120-$130
5/1-6/16 & 9/17-4/30	1P: $100-$110	2P: $110-$120

Location: Trans-Canada Hwy 1, exit 5 eastbound; exit 6 westbound, via Confederation Ave. 41 Maple Valley Rd A2H 6T2. Fax: 709/639-1549. **Facility:** 78 one-bedroom standard units. 2 stories (no elevator), interior corridors. **Parking:** on-site. **Amenities:** irons, hair dryers. **Dining:** Jungle Jim's Restaurant, see separate listing. **Guest Services:** wireless Internet. **Business Services:** meeting rooms, PC. **Cards:** AX, DC, DS, JC, MC, VI. *(See color ad card insert)*

SOME UNITS
(ASK) (S/D) 🛏 (TI) (✿) (▣) / (✕)

GLYNMILL INN   *Book at AAA.com*   **Phone:** (709)634-5181

🔺🔺🔺 🔺🔺🔺
Small-scale Hotel

All Year	1P: $101	2P: $111	XP: $10	F18

Location: Centre. 1B Cobb Ln A2H 6E6 (PO Box 550). Fax: 709/634-5106. **Facility:** 91 units. 70 one-bedroom standard units. 21 one-bedroom suites ($125-$135), some with whirlpools. 4 stories, interior corridors. **Parking:** on-site. **Terms:** package plans, pets (must be attended). **Amenities:** video library (fee). *Some:* high-speed Internet, voice mail, irons, hair dryers. **Dining:** The Wine Cellar, see separate listing. **Leisure Activities:** hiking trails, exercise room. **Guest Services:** valet laundry, wireless Internet. **Business Services:** meeting rooms, business center. **Cards:** AX, MC, VI.

SOME UNITS
🛏 (TI) (Y) / (✕) (AC) (PW) (VCR) (✆) 🖥 (▣)
FEE

GREENWOOD INN & SUITES-CORNER BROOK   *Book at AAA.com*   **Phone:** 709/634-5381

🔷🔷🔷🔷
Large-scale Hotel

6/1-9/30	1P: $119	2P: $119
5/1-5/31 & 10/1-4/30	1P: $109	2P: $109

Location: Centre. 48 West St A2H 2Z2. Fax: 709/634-1723. **Facility:** 102 units. 97 one-bedroom standard units. 5 one-bedroom suites, some with whirlpools. 5 stories, interior corridors. **Parking:** on-site. **Amenities:** video games (fee), high-speed Internet, voice mail, irons, hair dryers. **Pool(s):** heated indoor. **Leisure Activities:** whirlpool, exercise room. **Guest Services:** valet and coin laundry. **Business Services:** meeting rooms. **Cards:** AX, DC, DS, MC, VI.

SOME UNITS
🛏 (TI) (Y) (✿) (✿) (▣) / (✕) 🖥 /

MAMATEEK INN   **Phone:** 709/639-8901

🔺🔺🔺 🔺🔺🔺
Small-scale Hotel

Property failed to provide current rates

Location: Trans-Canada Hwy 1, exit 5 eastbound; exit 6 westbound via Confederation Ave. Maple Valley Rd A2H 6G7 (PO Box 787). Fax: 709/639-7567. **Facility:** 55 one-bedroom standard units. 2 stories (no elevator), interior corridors. **Parking:** on-site. **Terms:** small pets only. **Amenities:** video library (fee), irons, hair dryers. *Some:* honor bars. **Dining:** My Brother's Place, see separate listing. **Leisure Activities:** exercise room. **Guest Services:** wireless Internet. **Business Services:** meeting rooms.

SOME UNITS
🛏 (TI) (Y) / (✕) (VCR) /
FEE

——— *The following lodging was either not evaluated or did not meet AAA rating requirements but is listed for your information only.* ———

BELL'S INN   **Phone:** 709/634-5736

[fyi]

Not evaluated. **Location:** Corner of St. Marks Ave and Ford's Rd; centre. 2 Ford's Rd A2H 1S6. Facilities, services, and decor characterize a mid-range property.

——— **WHERE TO DINE** ———

JADE GARDEN RESTAURANT   **Lunch:** $6-$9   **Dinner:** $8-$13   **Phone:** 709/639-7003

🔺🔺🔺
Chinese
Cards: MC, VI.

Location: Centre. 82 West St A2H 2Z2. **Hours:** 11 am-midnight. Closed: 12/25. **Reservations:** accepted. **Features:** With a convenient downtown location, simple decor and casual tone, this eatery offers guests a pleasant experience and a tasty meal. Chinese lanterns light the way as you savor a variety of Cantonese and Szechuan entrees, as well as some Canadian dishes. Casual dress; cocktails. **Parking:** street.

JENNIFERS-THE UPPER LEVEL RESTAURANT   **Lunch:** $7-$10   **Dinner:** $10-$16   **Phone:** 709/632-7979

Steak & Seafood

Location: Jct Caribou. 48-50 Broadway A2H 2Z2. **Hours:** 11:30 am-9:30 pm. Closed: 12/25. **Reservations:** accepted. **Features:** Old English-style decor characterizes the restaurant, which is above a large gift shop in a commercial area. A good variety is available on the full luncheon buffet and on the daily a la carte menu. Dinners include a selection of fresh seafood, beef, poultry and ribs, with many value-priced specials. Food is fresh. The large, open dining room has comfortable seating and good table spacing. The staff provides friendly, casual service. Casual dress; cocktails. **Parking:** on-site. **Cards:** AX, DC, MC, VI.

JUNGLE JIM'S RESTAURANT   **Lunch:** $6-$10   **Dinner:** $9-$20   **Phone:** 709/639-2222

Canadian

Location: Trans-Canada Hwy 1, exit 5 eastbound; exit 6 westbound, via Confederation Ave; in Comfort Inn. 41 Maple Valley Rd A2H 6T2. **Hours:** 7 am-11 pm. Closed: 12/25. **Reservations:** accepted. **Features:** Guests can step into a tropical theme at the casual eatery, which employs a friendly staff and nurtures a bustling atmosphere. The menu lines up a wide variety of comfort foods, salads, chicken, beef, seafood and hot wings, all served in ample, flavorful portions. Casual dress; cocktails. **Parking:** on-site. **Cards:** AX, DC, MC, VI.

MY BROTHER'S PLACE   **Lunch:** $7-$12   **Dinner:** $9-$20   **Phone:** 709/639-2767

Canadian

MC, VI.

Location: Trans-Canada Hwy 1, exit 5 eastbound; exit 6 westbound via Confederation Ave; in Mamateek Inn. 64 Maple Valley Rd A2H 6G7. **Hours:** 7 am-10 pm. **Reservations:** accepted. **Features:** A fantastic view of the city, ocean and mountains awaits guests at the casual, upbeat eatery. Included in the vast selection on the menu are daily specials and all-day breakfast items. Casual dress; cocktails. **Parking:** on-site. **Cards:** AX,

THIRTEEN WEST RESTAURANT   **Lunch:** $10-$15   **Dinner:** $17-$32   **Phone:** 709/634-1300

Canadian

Parking: street. **Cards:** AX, MC, VI.

Location: Centre; opposite Holiday Inn. 13 West St A2H 2Y6. **Hours:** 11:30 am-2:30 & 5:30-10 pm. Closed major holidays. **Reservations:** suggested. **Features:** Innovative preparations—such as stuffed pork tenderloin with apricots and cream cheese and hickory-grilled beef strip loin with tiger shrimp—burst with exceptional flavor. The renovated old mill house is decorated with the paintings of local artists. Casual dress; cocktails.

THE WINE CELLAR   **Dinner:** $15-$26   **Phone:** 709/634-5181

Steak & Seafood

Location: Centre; in Glynmill Inn. 18 Cobb Ln A2H 6E6. **Hours:** 6 pm-10 pm. Closed: 12/25, 12/26; also Sun. **Reservations:** suggested. **Features:** As the name might imply, the delightful restaurant is in the basement of a fine hotel. The specialty is beef steaks, but the menu also lists some pork, chicken and a few seafood dishes. A decent wine list is on hand. Dressy casual; cocktails. **Parking:** on-site. **Cards:** AX, DC, MC, VI.

COW HEAD pop. 511

——— **WHERE TO STAY** ———

SHALLOW BAY MOTEL & CABINS   **Phone:** 709/243-2471

5/1-9/30	1P: $95	2P: $105	XP: $10	F12
10/1-4/30	1P: $77	2P: $85	XP: $10	F12

Small-scale Hotel

Location: Hwy 430, 2.5 mi (4 km) w towards the ocean, follow signs. (PO Box 44). Fax: 709/243-2816. **Facility:** 76 units. 59 one-bedroom standard units, some with whirlpools. 17 cottages, some with whirlpools. 1-2 stories (no elevator), interior/exterior corridors. **Parking:** on-site. **Terms:** package plans. **Amenities:** voice mail, irons, hair dryers. **Dining:** restaurant, see separate listing. **Pool(s):** heated outdoor. **Leisure Activities:** sauna. **Fee:** miniature golf. **Guest Services:** gift shop, coin laundry, wireless Internet. **Business Services:** meeting rooms, PC. **Cards:** AX, DC, MC, VI.

SOME UNITS

——— **WHERE TO DINE** ———

SHALLOW BAY RESTAURANT   **Lunch:** $7-$11   **Dinner:** $10-$20   **Phone:** 709/243-2471

Canadian

Location: Hwy 430, 2.4 mi (4 km) w towards the ocean, follow signs; in Shallow Bay Motel & Cabins. **Hours:** 7 am-10 pm. Closed: 12/25, 12/26. **Reservations:** accepted. **Features:** On the waterfront, the spacious family restaurant presents a menu of comfort foods and fresh local seafood. Casual dress; cocktails. **Parking:** on-site. **Cards:** AX, MC, VI.

DEER LAKE pop. 4,769

——— **WHERE TO STAY** ———

DEER LAKE MOTEL   **Phone:** (709)635-2108

6/1-9/30 & 1/1-4/30	1P: $89-$134	2P: $95-$140	XP: $6	F18
5/1-5/31 & 10/1-12/31	1P: $60-$80	2P: $66-$86	XP: $6	F18

Small-scale Hotel

Location: 1 mi (1.6 km) e on Trans-Canada Hwy 1, jct Hwy 430. 15 Trans-Canada Hwy 1 A8A 2E5. Fax: 709/635-3842. **Facility:** 56 one-bedroom standard units. 2 stories (no elevator), interior/exterior corridors. **Parking:** on-site. **Amenities:** voice mail, irons, hair dryers. *Some:* high-speed Internet. **Dining:** Cormack Dining Room & Coffee Shop, see separate listing. **Business Services:** meeting rooms. **Cards:** AX, MC, VI.

SOME UNITS

FEE

——— *The following lodging was either not evaluated or did not* ——— *meet AAA rating requirements but is listed for your information only.*

THE DRIFTWOOD INN   **Phone:** 709-635-5115

[fyi]

Not evaluated. **Location:** Off Trans-Canada Hwy 1; centre. 3 Nicholsville Rd A0K 2E0. Facilities, services, and decor characterize a basic property.

——— WHERE TO DINE ———

CORMACK DINING ROOM & COFFEE SHOP   **Lunch:** $8-$15 · **Dinner:** $15-$25   **Phone:** 709/635-2108
▽▽ ▽▽ **Location:** 1 mi (1.6 km) e on Trans-Canada Hwy 1, jct Hwy 430; in Deer Lake Motel. 15 Trans-Canada Hwy 1 A8A 2E5.
Canadian **Hours:** 7 am-8 pm; to 10 pm 6/1-10/31. **Closed:** 12/25. **Reservations:** accepted. **Features:** This eatery offers three seating areas. In front, a coffee shop serves tasty soup, salad and sandwiches. In the back is a finer dining room in which to enjoy steak, seafood and favorite Canadian meals. A small deck offers seasonal dining in the open air. Casual dress; cocktails. **Parking:** on-site. **Cards:** AX, DC, MC, VI.

JUNGLE JIM'S RESTAURANT   **Lunch:** $6-$11   **Dinner:** $8-$20   **Phone:** 709/635-5054
▽▽ ▽▽ **Location:** Off Trans-Canada Hwy 1; centre; in The Driftwood Inn. 3 Upper Nicholsville Rd A8A 2E8. **Hours:** 11 am-11
Canadian pm, Sun-10 pm. **Reservations:** accepted. **Features:** Guests can step into a tropical theme at the casual eatery, which employs a friendly staff and nurtures a bustling atmosphere. The menu lines up a wide variety of comfort foods, salads, chicken, beef, seafood and hot wings, all served in ample, flavorful portions. Casual dress; cocktails. **Parking:** on-site. **Cards:** AX, MC, VI.

DILDO pop. 1,299

——— WHERE TO STAY ———

INN BY THE BAY   **Phone:** (709)582-3170
▽▽ ▽▽ ▽ 6/2-9/1 [BP]   1P: $99-$149   2P: $99-$149   XP: $20   F10
Country Inn 5/1-6/1 & 9/2-10/30 [BP]   1P: $79-$149   2P: $79-$149   XP: $20   F10
Location: Hwy 1, exit 28, 7.6 mi (13.5 km) on Rt 80. 78 Front St A0B 1P0. Fax: 709/582-3175. **Facility:** Located on a hillside overlooking the harbour and village, the quaint B&B offers pleasant guest rooms in two homes. Smoke free premises. 8 one-bedroom standard units. 2 stories (no elevator), interior corridors. **Parking:** on-site. **Terms:** open 5/1-10/30, office hours 7 am-10 pm, 3 day cancellation notice-fee imposed, 15% service charge. **Amenities:** video library, DVD players, hair dryers. **Cards:** AX, DC, DS, MC, VI.

SOME UNITS
(ASK) ⊠ / (AC) (VCR) /

EASTPORT pop. 509

——— WHERE TO STAY ———

——— *The following lodging was either not evaluated or did not* ———
meet AAA rating requirements but is listed for your information only.

SANDY COVE BEACH HOUSEKEEPING CABINS   **Phone:** 709/677-3158
[fyi] Not evaluated. **Location:** On Rt 310; on Sandy Cove Beach. Barbour Ave (Box 10, Site 16). Facilities, services, and decor characterize a basic property.

GANDER pop. 9,651

——— WHERE TO STAY ———

ALBATROSS HOTEL   *Book at AAA.com*   **Phone:** (709)256-3956
▽▽ ▽▽ All Year   1P: $81-$82   2P: $91-$92
Small-scale Hotel **Location:** On Trans-Canada Hwy 1. (PO Box 450, A1V 1W8). Fax: 709/651-2692. **Facility:** 96 units. 90 one-bedroom standard units. 6 one-bedroom suites, some with whirlpools. 3 stories, interior/exterior corridors. **Parking:** on-site. **Terms:** pets (in designated units). **Amenities:** voice mail, irons, hair dryers. *Some:* high-speed Internet. **Dining:** restaurant, see separate listing. **Guest Services:** valet laundry, wireless Internet. **Business Services:** meeting rooms, business center. **Cards:** AX, DC, MC, VI.

SOME UNITS
(ASK) 🐾 🍴 🍽 💻 / ⊠ (AC) /

COMFORT INN ·   *Book great rates at AAA.com*   **Phone:** (709)256-3535
▽▽ ▽▽ All Year [CP]   1P: $90-$119   2P: $100-$129
·Small-scale Hotel **Location:** Centre. 112 Trans-Canada Hwy 1 A1V 1P8. Fax: 709/256-9302. **Facility:** 63 one-bedroom standard units, some with efficiencies. 2 stories, interior/exterior corridors. **Parking:** on-site. **Terms:** package plans, pets (must be attended). **Amenities:** irons, hair dryers. **Dining:** Jungle Jim's Restaurant, see separate listing. **Leisure Activities:** exercise room. **Guest Services:** complimentary laundry, wireless Internet. **Business Services:** meeting rooms, PC. **Cards:** AX, MC, VI. *(See color ad card insert)*

SOME UNITS
(ASK) (S📠) 🐾 🍴 💻 / ⊠ 🛄 🖨 /

HOTEL GANDER ·   *Book at AAA.com*   **Phone:** 709/256-3931
▽▽ ▽▽ Property failed to provide current rates
Small-scale Hotel **Location:** Centre. 100 Trans-Canada Hwy 1 A1V 1P5. Fax: 709/651-2641. **Facility:** 152 units. 148 one-bedroom standard units. 4 one-bedroom suites, some with whirlpools. 4 stories, interior corridors. *Bath:* combo or shower only. **Parking:** on-site. **Terms:** small pets only (ground floor units). **Amenities:** voice mail, irons, hair dryers. *Some:* high-speed Internet. **Dining:** Alcock & Brown's Eatery, see separate listing. **Pool(s):** heated indoor. **Guest Services:** coin laundry. **Business Services:** meeting rooms, PC.

SOME UNITS
🐾 🍴 🍽 ⚓ 🎣 💻 / ⊠ (AC) 🛄 /

SINBAD'S HOTEL & SUITES   *Book at AAA.com*   **Phone:** 709/651-2678
▽▽ ▽▽ All Year   1P: $80   2P: $90
Small-scale Hotel **Location:** Centre; opposite Gander Mall. Bennett Dr A1V 1W8 (PO Box 450). Fax: 709/651-3123. **Facility:** 112 units. 102 one-bedroom standard units, some with efficiencies. 10 one-bedroom suites ($170-$220). 3 stories, exterior corridors. **Parking:** on-site. **Terms:** weekly rates available, pets (in designated units, must be attended). **Amenities:** voice mail, irons, hair dryers. **Leisure Activities:** exercise room. **Guest Services:** coin laundry, wireless Internet. **Business Services:** meeting rooms, business center. **Cards:** AX, MC, VI.

SOME UNITS
(ASK) (S📠) 🐾 🍴 🍽 💻 / ⊠ 🛄 /

——— WHERE TO DINE ———

ALBATROSS DINING ROOM   **Lunch:** $7-$12   **Dinner:** $12-$20   **Phone:** 709/256-3956

Location: On Trans-Canada Hwy 1; in Albatross Hotel. **Hours:** 7 am-2 & 5-10 pm. Closed: 12/25.
Reservations: accepted. **Features:** This dining room overlooks the lobby through smoked glass windows.
Canadian   They serve a variety of fresh seafood, steak and Newfoundland specialties, home-style cooking with limited
flair. The atmosphere is relaxed and the staff provides friendly casual service. Casual dress; cocktails.
Parking: on-site. **Cards:** AX, DC, MC, VI.

ALCOCK & BROWN'S EATERY   **Lunch:** $7-$11   **Dinner:** $10-$19   **Phone:** 709/651-3756

Location: Centre; in Hotel Gander. 100 Trans-Canada Hwy 1 A1V 1P5. **Hours:** 7 am-2 & 5-10 pm, Sun-9 pm.
Reservations: accepted. **Features:** The family restaurant's menu dabbles in a little bit of lots of things:
Canadian   pasta, stir-fry, surf and turf, poultry and plenty of children's dishes. Off the hotel's main lobby, the large,
colorful dining space has several sections. Pleasant, thoughtful servers lend to the upbeat, casual
atmosphere. Casual dress; cocktails. **Parking:** on-site. **Cards:** AX, DC, MC, VI.

JUNGLE JIM'S RESTAURANT   **Lunch:** $6-$11   **Dinner:** $8-$15   **Phone:** 709/651-3444

Location: Centre; in Comfort Inn. 112 Trans-Canada Hwy 1 A1V 1W6. **Hours:** 11 am-11 pm. Closed: 12/24, 12/25.
Reservations: accepted. **Features:** Guests can step into a tropical theme at the casual eatery, which
Canadian   employs a friendly staff and nurtures a bustling atmosphere. The menu lines up a wide variety of comfort
foods, salads, chicken, beef, seafood and hot wings, all served in ample, flavorful portions. Casual dress;
cocktails. **Parking:** on-site. **Cards:** AX, DC, MC, VI.

GRAND BANK pop. 2,841

——— WHERE TO STAY ———

The following lodging was either not evaluated or did not
meet AAA rating requirements but is listed for your information only.

THORNDYKE BED & BREAKFAST   **Phone:** 709/832-0820

[fyi]   Not evaluated. **Location:** Centre. 33 Water St A0E 1W0 (PO Box 39). Facilities, services, and decor characterize a
mid-range property.

GRAND FALLS-WINDSOR pop. 12,738

——— WHERE TO STAY ———

MOUNT PEYTON HOTEL   **Phone:** 709/489-2251

1/1-4/30	1P: $106	2P: $112	XP: $6	F12
5/1-12/31	1P: $103	2P: $109	XP: $6	F12

Small-scale Hotel   **Location:** 0.6 mi (1 km) ne on Trans-Canada Hwy 1. 214 Lincoln Rd A2A 1P8. Fax: 709/489-6365. **Facility:** 150
units. 146 one-bedroom standard units, some with efficiencies. 4 one-bedroom suites ($180), some with
whirlpools. 2 stories, interior/exterior corridors. **Parking:** on-site. **Terms:** weekly rates available, [BP], [CP] & [ECP] meal plans
available, package plans. **Amenities:** voice mail, irons, hair dryers. *Some:* video games (fee). **Dining:** Peyton Corral
Steakhouse, see separate listing. **Guest Services:** valet and coin laundry, wireless Internet. **Business Services:** meeting
rooms, PC. **Cards:** AX, DC, DS, MC, VI.

SOME UNITS

ASK 🛇 🐾 🍽 🍸 📹 💻 / ✉ 🛗 🖥 🖨 /

——— WHERE TO DINE ———

JUNGLE JIM'S RESTAURANT   **Lunch:** $7-$11   **Dinner:** $8-$20   **Phone:** 709/489-2939

Location: Centre; in Exploits Valley Mall. 19 Cromer Ave A2A 2K5. **Hours:** 11 am-9 pm, Wed, Fri & Sat-11 pm.
Closed: 9/3, 12/25, 12/26. **Reservations:** accepted. **Features:** Guests can step into a tropical theme at the
Canadian   casual eatery, which employs a friendly staff and nurtures a bustling atmosphere. The menu lines up a wide
variety of comfort foods, salads, chicken, beef, seafood and hot wings, all served in ample, flavorful
portions. Casual dress; cocktails. **Parking:** on-site. **Cards:** AX, DC, MC, VI.

PEYTON CORRAL STEAKHOUSE   **Dinner:** $15-$25   **Phone:** 709/489-2251

Location: 0.6 mi (1 km) ne on Trans-Canada Hwy 1; in Mount Peyton Hotel. 214 Lincoln Rd A2A 1P8. **Hours:** 5 pm-
11 pm. Closed major holidays; also Sun. **Reservations:** accepted. **Features:** The restaurant specializes in
Steak & Seafood   prime cuts of meat but also prepares a few seafood entrees. The dining room has a Western theme, with a
full-size antique carriage at the entrance. Casual dress; cocktails. **Parking:** on-site. **Cards:** AX, DC,
MC, VI.

TAI WAN RESTAURANT   **Lunch:** $6-$11   **Dinner:** $8-$15   **Phone:** 709/489-4222

Location: Centre. High St A2A 1P8. **Hours:** 11 am-10 pm, Fri & Sat-11 pm, Sun noon-10 pm. Closed: 12/25.
Reservations: accepted. **Features:** Serving its guests for four decades, the eatery is a local landmark. On
Chinese   the menu are combination plates, as well as an ample array of individual dishes and some Canadian
cuisine. Casual dress; cocktails. **Parking:** street. **Cards:** AX, MC, VI.

HAPPY VALLEY-GOOSE BAY pop. 8,700

——— WHERE TO STAY ———

CHERRYWOOD CORPORATE SUITES   **Phone:** 709/896-4000

Property failed to provide current rates
Location: At Loring Dr. 5 Cherrywood Dr A0P 1C0. Fax: 709/896-8899. **Facility:** 6 units. 4 one- and 2 two-
Small-scale Hotel   bedroom suites with kitchens. 1 story, interior corridors. **Parking:** on-site. **Terms:** off-site registration.
Amenities: irons, hair dryers. **Guest Services:** coin laundry.

🍽 ✉ VCR 🛗 🖥 💻

HOTEL NORTH
♦♦ ♦♦
Small-scale Hotel

All Year   1P: $99-$159
Location: Just w of Hamilton River Rd. 25 Loring Dr A0P 1C0. Fax: 709/896-9302. **Facility:** 54 units. 50 one-bedroom standard units, some with efficiencies and/or whirlpools. 4 one-bedroom suites ($159) with whirlpools. 1-2 stories (no elevator), interior corridors. **Parking:** on-site. **Terms:** package plans.
Amenities: video library, irons, hair dryers. **Dining:** Mariners Galley, see separate listing. **Leisure Activities:** exercise room.
Guest Services: wireless Internet. **Business Services:** meeting rooms. **Cards:** AX, DC, MC, VI.

Phone: 709/896-9301
XP: $10   F10

SOME UNITS

[Y1] [VCR] [icons] / [X] /

ROYAL INN & SUITES
♦♦ ♦♦
Motel

All Year   1P: $77-$89   2P: $87-$99
Location: Corner of Tenth St. 5 Royal Ave A0P 1E0. Fax: 709/896-5501. **Facility:** 29 units. 19 one-bedroom standard units, some with efficiencies. 8 one- and 2 two-bedroom suites ($100-$135), some with efficiencies, kitchens and/or whirlpools. 2 stories (no elevator), exterior corridors. **Parking:** on-site.
Terms: office hours 7 am-11:50 pm, cancellation fee imposed. **Amenities:** irons, hair dryers. *Some:* DVD players, high-speed Internet. **Guest Services:** coin laundry, wireless Internet. **Business Services:** meeting rooms. **Cards:** AX, DC, MC, VI.

Phone: 709/896-2456

SOME UNITS

[S/D] [icons] / [X] [VCR] [icons] /

──────── The following lodging was either not evaluated or did not ────────
meet AAA rating requirements but is listed for your information only.

DAVIS' BED & BREAKFAST
(fyi)
Bed & Breakfast

Did not meet all AAA rating requirements for locking devices in some guest rooms at time of last evaluation on 04/29/2006. **Location:** Corner of Cook St. 14 Cabot Crescent A0P 1E0. Facilities, services, and decor characterize a basic property.

Phone: 709/896-5077

──────── **WHERE TO DINE** ────────

HONG KONG RESTAURANT
♦♦
Chinese

Lunch: $6-$13   **Dinner:** $10-$19   **Phone:** 709/896-2558
Location: Just s of Loring Dr. 345 Hamilton River Rd A0P 1E0. **Hours:** 11 am-midnight, Fri & Sat-1 am. Closed: 12/25. **Reservations:** accepted. **Features:** The spacious restaurant carries out a pleasant Chinese theme. The menu lists a wide range of traditional dishes and some Canadian items. Casual dress; cocktails. **Parking:** on-site. **Cards:** MC, VI.

[Y]

LAVENIA'S COUNTRY KITCHEN
♦♦
Canadian

Lunch: $4-$11   **Dinner:** $4-$11   **Phone:** 709/896-7330
Location: Centre. 6 Grand St A0P 1E0. **Hours:** 11 am-8 pm, Sun-7 pm. Closed: 12/25, 12/26. **Features:** On the menu are home-style preparations and some traditional dishes, including caribou burgers, cod tongues and cod cheeks. Among other choices are daily specials and selections from the all-day breakfast menu. Casual dress; cocktails. **Parking:** on-site. **Cards:** MC, VI.

[Y]

MARINERS GALLEY
♦♦ ♦♦
Canadian

Lunch: $6-$11   **Dinner:** $8-$16   **Phone:** 709/896-9301
Location: Just w of Hamilton River Rd; in Hotel North. 25 Loring Dr A0P 1C0. **Hours:** 7 am-9 pm; hours vary off season. Closed: 12/25. **Reservations:** accepted. **Features:** The pleasant nautical decor includes model ships and a large galleon divider. The menu includes a fine selection of fresh seafood and some steak and chicken selections, as well as basic comfort foods. Servers are friendly and accommodating. Casual dress; cocktails. **Parking:** on-site. **Cards:** AX, DC, MC, VI.

TRICIA DEE'S RESTAURANT & LOUNGE
♦♦ ♦♦
Canadian

Dinner: $14-$26   **Phone:** 709/896-4441
Location: Centre. 96 Hamilton River Rd A0P 1E0. **Hours:** 4:30 pm-10:30 pm. Closed: 12/25, 12/26. **Reservations:** accepted. **Features:** A popular spot for steaks, chicken, ribs and seafood, the restaurant gives guests their choice of a lounge or dining room setting. Casual dress; cocktails. **Parking:** on-site. **Cards:** MC, VI.

[Y]

LABRADOR CITY pop. 8,500

──────── **WHERE TO STAY** ────────

CAROL INN
♦♦ ♦♦
Small-scale Hotel

Property failed to provide current rates
Location: Centre. 215 Drake Ave A2V 2B6. Fax: 709/944-7110. **Facility:** 22 one-bedroom standard units with efficiencies. 2 stories (no elevator), interior corridors. **Parking:** on-site. **Terms:** small pets only. **Amenities:** honor bars, irons, hair dryers. **Dining:** Samantha's Fine Dining, see separate listing. **Business Services:** meeting rooms.

Phone: 709/944-7736

SOME UNITS

[icons] [Y1] [Y] [icons] / [X] /

──────── The following lodging was either not evaluated or did not ────────
meet AAA rating requirements but is listed for your information only.

TWO SEASONS INN
(fyi)
Small-scale Hotel

Did not meet all AAA rating requirements for locking devices in some guest rooms at time of last evaluation on 04/29/2006. **Location:** At Drake Ave; centre. Avalon Dr A2V 2L3 (PO Box 572). Facilities, services, and decor characterize a mid-range property.

Phone: 709/944-2661

———— **WHERE TO DINE** ————

SAMANTHA'S FINE DINING
▼▼▼▼▼
Canadian

Dinner: $16-$29

Phone: 709/944-7736

Location: Centre; in Carol Inn. 215 Drake Ave A2V 2B6. **Hours:** 6 pm-10 pm. Closed: 12/25, 12/26; also Sun & Mon. **Reservations:** accepted. **Features:** Soft lighting and classical music contribute to a more formal atmosphere. In addition to fresh seafood and fine cuts of meat, the menu incorporates some local game dishes. The knowledgeable staff prepares some items tableside. Casual dress; cocktails. **Parking:** on-site.
Cards: AX, DC, MC, VI.

⅄

TERRACE DINING ROOM
▼▼ ▼▼
Canadian

Lunch: $6-$11

Dinner: $8-$18

Phone: 709/944-3334

Location: At Drake Ave; centre; in Two Seasons Inn. Avalon Dr A2V 2L3. **Hours:** 6:30 am-10 pm. Closed: 12/25. **Reservations:** accepted. **Features:** In a convenient location, the restaurant has two dining sections: the more casual front section and the more upscale spot in the back. Food is served fresh and in ample portions. Casual dress; cocktails. **Parking:** on-site. **Cards:** AX, DC, MC, VI.

⅄

L'ANSE AU CLAIR pop. 241

———— **WHERE TO STAY** ————

NORTHERN LIGHT INN
▼▼ ▼▼
Small-scale Hotel

6/1-10/15	1P: $90	2P: $110
5/1-5/31 & 10/16-4/30	1P: $75	2P: $90

Phone: (709)931-2332

Location: On Rt 510; centre. Rt 510 A0K 3K0 (PO Box 92). **Fax:** 709/931-2708. **Facility:** 54 units. 49 one-bedroom standard units, some with whirlpools. 5 cottages. 2 stories (no elevator), interior corridors. **Parking:** on-site. **Terms:** 21 day cancellation notice, pets (in designated units). **Amenities:** hair dryers. *Some:* high-speed Internet. **Dining:** Basque Dining Room, see separate listing. **Guest Services:** gift shop, coin laundry, wireless Internet. **Business Services:** meeting rooms, PC. **Cards:** AX, DC, MC, VI.

SOME UNITS
(ASK) (SD) 🐕 🍴 ⅄ / ✕ 🖥 🖨 /

———— **WHERE TO DINE** ————

BASQUE DINING ROOM
▼▼ ▼▼
Canadian

Lunch: $6-$12

Dinner: $9-$20

Phone: 709/931-2332

Location: On Rt 510; centre; in Northern Light Inn. Rt 510 A0K 3K0. **Hours:** 7 am-10 pm. Closed: 12/25. **Reservations:** accepted. **Features:** Home-style cooking is what guests expect at the family restaurant. Representative of fresh seafood and meat entrees are some local favorites, including cod tongues and cheeks. Portions are hearty, but it's worth saving room for one of the homemade desserts. Casual dress; cocktails. **Parking:** on-site. **Cards:** AX, MC, VI.

⅄

LITTLE RAPIDS

———— **WHERE TO STAY** ————

ADAMS HOUSE BED & BREAKFAST
▼▼▼▼▼
Bed & Breakfast

Property failed to provide current rates

Phone: 709/634-0064

Location: Trans-Canada Hwy 1, exit 10, just s, follow signs. 4 Roberts Dr A2H 6C9. **Facility:** The inn is located in a residential area with pleasant landscaped grounds and a large deck with a hot tub. The guestrooms are individually decorated and offer modern amenities. Smoke free premises. 4 one-bedroom standard units. 2 stories (no elevator), interior corridors. **Parking:** on-site. **Terms:** office hours 8 am-11 pm. **Amenities:** video library, DVD players, irons, hair dryers. **Leisure Activities:** whirlpool. *Fee:* snowmobiling. **Business Services:** PC.

✕ 🎥

———— *The following lodging was either not evaluated or did not* ————
meet AAA rating requirements but is listed for your information only.

STRAWBERRY HILL RESORT
[fyi]

Phone: 709/634-0066

Not evaluated. **Location:** Trans-Canada Hwy 1, exit 10, follow signs. (PO Box 2200, A2H 2N2). Facilities, services, and decor characterize a mid-range property.

MARYSTOWN pop. 5,908

———— **WHERE TO STAY** ————

———— *The following lodging was either not evaluated or did not* ————
meet AAA rating requirements but is listed for your information only.

MARYSTOWN HOTEL & CONVENTION CENTRE
[fyi]

Phone: 709/279-1600

Not evaluated. **Location:** Centre. 76 Ville Marie Dr A0E 2M0. Facilities, services, and decor characterize a mid-range property.

———— **WHERE TO DINE** ————

JUNGLE JIM'S RESTAURANT
▼▼ ▼▼
Canadian

Lunch: $7-$11

Dinner: $8-$20

Phone: 709/279-5467

Location: Centre; in Marystown Mall. Ville Marie Dr A0E 2M0. **Hours:** 11 am-10 pm, Fri & Sat-11 pm. Closed: 1/1, 12/25. **Reservations:** accepted. **Features:** Guests can step into a tropical theme at the casual eatery, which employs a friendly staff and nurtures a bustling atmosphere. The menu lines up a wide variety of comfort foods, salads, chicken, beef, seafood and hot wings, all served in ample, flavorful portions. Casual dress; cocktails. **Parking:** on-site. **Cards:** AX, DC, MC, VI.

MOBILE pop. 132

———— WHERE TO DINE ————

THE CAPTAIN'S TABLE RESTAURANT | Lunch: $7-$12 | Dinner: $9-$18 | Phone: 709/334-2278
♦♦♦ ♦♦♦
Seafood

Location: On Rt 10; centre. **Hours:** Open 5/1-9/21 & 4/15-4/30; 11:30 am-8:30 pm. **Reservations:** accepted. **Features:** The restaurant is a delightful spot to sample great seafood in a relaxing atmosphere. The fish and chips dish is made with fresh cod, and the chowders are a must. Homemade desserts include bumbleberry pie and warm apple dumplings. Casual dress; cocktails. **Parking:** on-site. **Cards:** MC, VI.

MOUNT CARMEL

———— WHERE TO STAY ————

———— *The following lodging was either not evaluated or did not* ————
meet AAA rating requirements but is listed for your information only.

SALMONIER COUNTRY MANOR "THE CONVENT
INN"   **Phone:** 709/521-2778
[fyi]   Not evaluated. **Location:** Centre. Rt 93 A0B 2M0. Facilities, services, and decor characterize a mid-range property.

MOUNT PEARL

———— WHERE TO DINE ————

SMITTY'S FAMILY RESTAURANT | Lunch: $6-$11 | Dinner: $8-$16 | Phone: 709/368-8690
♦♦♦ ♦♦♦
Canadian

Location: Corner of Old Placentia Rd. 26 Gibson Dr A1N 5K8. **Hours:** 7 am-9 pm, Fri & Sat-10 pm. Closed: 12/25. **Reservations:** accepted. **Features:** The family-oriented restaurant satisfies patrons with its ever-popular all-day breakfast items, as well as tasty and wholesome soups and salads at lunchtime. A relaxed mood characterizes the dining space. Casual dress; cocktails. **Parking:** on-site. **Cards:** AX, DC, MC, VI.

MUSGRAVE HARBOUR pop. 1,294

———— WHERE TO STAY ————

———— *The following lodging was either not evaluated or did not* ————
meet AAA rating requirements but is listed for your information only.

SPINDRIFT-BY-THE-SEA   **Phone:** 709/655-2175
[fyi]   Not evaluated. **Location:** Rt 330, on oceanfront. 87 Main St A0G 3J0. Facilities, services, and decor characterize a mid-range property.

NORRIS POINT pop. 900

———— WHERE TO STAY ————

———— *The following lodging was either not evaluated or did not* ————
meet AAA rating requirements but is listed for your information only.

SUGAR HILL INN   **Phone:** 709/458-2147
[fyi]   Not evaluated. **Location:** Rt 430, 2.5 mi (4 km) s, follow signs. (PO Box 100, A0K 3V0). Facilities, services, and decor characterize a mid-range property.

PARADISE pop. 9,598

———— WHERE TO DINE ————

WOODSTOCK COLONIAL INN | Lunch: $8-$15 | Dinner: $17-$25 | Phone: 709/722-6933
♦♦♦ ♦♦♦ ♦♦♦
Canadian

Location: Trans-Canada Hwy 1, exit 43, 3 mi (5 km) n. Rt 60 A1B 1R7. **Hours:** Open 5/1-10/15; 11:30 am-2:30 & 5-9:30 pm. **Reservations:** suggested. **Features:** For 70 years, this spacious restaurant has featured a colonial country decor with several dining sections available. Home-style cooking includes a fine variety of fresh seafood and Newfoundland game meat including flipper pie, wild rabbit and venison. Casual dress; cocktails. **Parking:** on-site. **Cards:** AX, DC, MC, VI.

PLACENTIA pop. 4,426

———— WHERE TO DINE ————

———— *The following restaurant has not been evaluated by AAA* ————
but is listed for your information only.

HAROLD HOTEL RESTAURANT   **Phone:** 709/227-2107
[fyi]   Not evaluated. **Location:** On Rt 100; centre. Main St A0B 2Y0. **Features:** Serving the area for 30 years, the casual diner serves reliable, wholesome food.

PORT AU CHOIX pop. 1,010

———— WHERE TO DINE ————

THE ANCHOR CAFE   **Lunch:** $6-$10   **Dinner:** $9-$17   **Phone:** 709/861-3665
▼▼ ▼▼▼▼   **Location:** Centre. Fisher St A0K 4C0. **Hours:** Open 5/1-9/30 & 4/15-4/30; 11 am-9 pm, Fri & Sat-10 pm.
Canadian   **Reservations:** accepted. **Features:** Although the nautically themed family restaurant doesn't offer ocean views, it does serve the freshest made-to-order seafood and comfort foods, which come in ample portions. Casual dress; cocktails. **Parking:** on-site. **Cards:** MC, VI.

PORT AU PORT EAST

———— WHERE TO STAY ————

SPRUCE PINE ACRES COUNTRY INN   **Phone:** (709)648-9600
▼▼▼ ▼▼▼   All Year   1P: $125-$135   2P: $125-$135   XP: $20   F12
Country Inn   **Location:** On Rt 460, 9.4 mi (15 km) w of Stephenville. Located in a rural area. Rt 460 A0N 1T0 (PO Box 219, PORT AU PORT WEST). Fax: 709/648-9600. **Facility:** Large decks overlook the inn's scenic, oceanfront setting; rooms and chalets are tastefully decorated and some offer views of the water. Smoke free premises. 6 units. 5 one-bedroom standard units. 1 two-bedroom suite ($125-$145) with kitchen and whirlpool. 1 story, interior/exterior corridors. **Parking:** on-site. **Terms:** office hours 8 am-11 pm, 7 day cancellation notice. **Amenities:** video library, irons, hair dryers. *Some:* DVD players. **Leisure Activities:** sauna, whirlpool, hiking trails. **Guest Services:** wireless Internet. **Business Services:** meeting rooms, PC. **Cards:** AX, JC, MC, VI.

SOME UNITS
(ASK) (S⊡) (†1) (⊠) (✕) (⊀) (🖥) / (VCR) (🖥) /

PORT BLANDFORD pop. 580

———— WHERE TO STAY ————

TERRA NOVA GOLF RESORT   **Phone:** 709/543-2525
▼▼▼ ▼▼▼   Property failed to provide current rates
Small-scale Hotel   **Location:** Centre. Trans-Canada Hwy 1 A0C 2G0 (PO Box 160). Fax: 709/543-2201. **Facility:** 83 one-bedroom standard units, some with efficiencies. 4 stories, interior corridors. **Parking:** on-site. **Terms:** open 5/18-10/25. **Amenities:** video library, irons, hair dryers. **Pool(s):** heated outdoor. **Leisure Activities:** 2 tennis courts, hiking trails, game room. *Fee:* golf-27 holes. **Guest Services:** coin laundry. **Business Services:** meeting rooms.

SOME UNITS
(†1) (⊻) (🌊) (⊠) (☕) / (✕) (VCR) (🖥) (🖥) /
FEE

———— *The following lodging was either not evaluated or did not meet AAA rating requirements but is listed for your information only.* ————

TERRA NOVA HOSPITALITY HOME & COTTAGES   **Phone:** 709/543-2260
(fyi)   Not evaluated. **Location:** On Trans-Canada Hwy 1; centre. (General Delivery, Rt 1, A0C 2G0). Facilities, services, and decor characterize a mid-range property.

PORTLAND CREEK pop. 98

———— WHERE TO STAY ————

———— *The following lodging was either not evaluated or did not meet AAA rating requirements but is listed for your information only.* ————

MOUNTAIN WATERS RESORT   **Phone:** 709/898-2490
(fyi)   Not evaluated. **Location:** On Rt 430, 3 mi (5 km) n, 1 mi (1.6 km) on gravel entry road. (General Delivery, A0K 4G0). Facilities, services, and decor characterize a mid-range property.

PORT REXTON pop. 432

———— WHERE TO STAY ————

FISHER'S LOFT INN   **Phone:** (709)464-3240
▼▼▼ ▼▼▼   6/6-9/15   1P: $112-$176   2P: $112-$176   XP: $25   F12
          5/1-6/5 & 9/16-10/31   1P: $99-$150   2P: $99-$150   XP: $25   F12
Country Inn   **Location:** On Rt 230; centre. Mill Rd A0C 2H0 (PO Box 36). Fax: 709/464-3852. **Facility:** Wonderful location nestled on a hill overlooking Trinity Bay. Three buildings house spacious guest rooms, some with water view. Smoke free premises. 21 one-bedroom standard units. 2 stories (no elevator), interior corridors. **Parking:** on-site. **Terms:** open 5/1-10/31, 14 day cancellation notice, package plans. **Amenities:** hair dryers. **Leisure Activities:** hiking trails. **Cards:** MC, VI.

(†1) (⊻) (⊠) (⊀)

RATTLING BROOK

———— WHERE TO STAY ————

———— *The following lodging was either not evaluated or did not meet AAA rating requirements but is listed for your information only.* ————

WINDERMERE CABINS   **Phone:** 709/268-3863
(fyi)   Not evaluated. **Location:** 0.6 mi (1 km) s. Rt 391 A0J 1H0 (PO Box 154). Facilities, services, and decor characterize a basic property.

ROCKY HARBOUR pop. 1,002

──────── WHERE TO STAY ────────

FISHERMAN'S LANDING INN   Phone: (709)458-2711

◈◈ ◈◈   6/1-9/30   1P: $129-$189   2P: $139-$189   XP: $12   F16

            5/1-5/31 & 10/1-4/30   1P: $89-$129   2P: $89-$129   XP: $12   F16

Small-scale Hotel **Location:** Rt 430; first entrance to Rocky Harbour. W Link Rd A0K 4N0 (PO Box 124). Fax: 709/458-2168. **Facility:** Smoke free premises. 40 one-bedroom standard units, some with whirlpools. 1 story, interior/exterior corridors. **Parking:** on-site. **Amenities:** irons, hair dryers. **Leisure Activities:** whirlpool, exercise room. **Guest Services:** coin laundry. **Cards:** AX, DC, MC, VI.

SOME UNITS

(ASK) (S☎) (❒❒) (Y) (☒) (▣) / (▤) /

────── *The following lodgings were either not evaluated or did not* ──────
meet AAA rating requirements but are listed for your information only.

A-1 WILDFLOWERS BED & BREAKFAST   Phone: 709/458-3000

(fyi)   Not evaluated. **Location:** Rt 430, just s on West Link Rd, just w on Pond Rd, then 0.6 mi (1 km) n. Main St N A0K 4N0 (Box 291). Facilities, services, and decor characterize a basic property.

BAYSIDE HOUSEKEEPING UNITS   Phone: 709/458-2749

(fyi)   Not evaluated. **Location:** Rt 430, just s on West Link Rd, just w on Pond Rd, then just s. Main St S A0K 4N0 (PO Box 116). Facilities, services, and decor characterize a basic property.

GROS MORNE CABINS   Phone: 709/458-2020

(fyi)   Not evaluated. **Location:** Rt 430, just s on West Link Rd, just w on Pond Rd, then just s. Main St S A0K 4N0 (PO Box 151). Facilities, services, and decor characterize a mid-range property.

OCEAN VIEW MOTEL   Phone: 709/458-2730

(fyi)   Not evaluated. **Location:** Rt 430, just s on West Link Rd, just w on Pond Rd, then just n. Main St N A0K 4N0 (Box 129). Facilities, services, and decor characterize a basic property.

ST. ALBANS pop. 1,600

──────── WHERE TO STAY ────────

────── *The following lodging was either not evaluated or did not* ──────
meet AAA rating requirements but is listed for your information only.

ST. ALBAN'S INN   Phone: 709/538-3885

(fyi)   Not evaluated. **Location:** Centre. 140 Main St A0H 2E0 (PO Box 449). Facilities, services, and decor characterize a basic property.

ST. ANTHONY pop. 2,730

──────── WHERE TO STAY ────────

────── *The following lodging was either not evaluated or did not* ──────
meet AAA rating requirements but is listed for your information only.

VINLAND MOTEL   Phone: 709/454-8843

(fyi)   Not evaluated. **Location:** Off Rt 430; centre. West St A0K 4S0 (PO Box 400). Facilities, services, and decor characterize a mid-range property.

ST. BRIDE'S pop. 473

──────── WHERE TO STAY ────────

────── *The following lodging was either not evaluated or did not* ──────
meet AAA rating requirements but is listed for your information only.

MANNINGS BIRD ISLAND RESORT   Phone: 709/337-2450

(fyi)   Not evaluated. **Location:** Centre. Rt 100 A0B 2Z0. Facilities, services, and decor characterize a basic property.

──────── WHERE TO DINE ────────

────── *The following restaurant has not been evaluated by AAA* ──────
but is listed for your information only.

ATLANTICA INN RESTAURANT   Phone: 709/337-2860

(fyi)   Not evaluated. **Location:** Centre. General Delivery A0B 2Z0. **Features:** Basic favorite dishes are on the menu of the modest restaurant.

ST. JOHN'S pop. 99,182

——— WHERE TO STAY ———

ABBA INN (DOWNTOWN)   *Book at AAA.com*   **Phone:** 709/754-0058

5/1-8/31   1P: $69-$269   2P: $79-$279
9/1-4/30   1P: $59-$159   2P: $69-$250

Bed & Breakfast   **Location:** Centre. 36 Queens Rd A1C 2A5. Fax: 709/729-2092. **Facility:** Smoke free premises. 4 one-bedroom standard units. 3 stories (no elevator), interior corridors. **Parking:** street. **Terms:** office hours 8 am-11 pm. **Amenities:** hair dryers. *Some:* DVD players. **Guest Services:** wireless Internet. **Cards:** AX, MC, VI.

SOME UNITS
⊠ / VCR /

A GOWER STREET HOUSE (DOWNTOWN)   *Book at AAA.com*   **Phone:** (709)754-0058

5/1-10/1 [BP]   1P: $59-$199   2P: $69-$209
10/2-4/30 [BP]   1P: $39-$89   2P: $49-$99

Bed & Breakfast   **Location:** Centre. Located in a residential area. 180 Gower St A1C 1P9. **Facility:** Smoke free premises. 5 one-bedroom standard units. 3 stories (no elevator), interior corridors. **Bath:** some shared or private, combo or shower only. **Parking:** on-site. **Terms:** office hours 8 am-11 pm, 3 day cancellation notice-fee imposed. **Amenities:** hair dryers. **Cards:** AX, MC, VI.

SOME UNITS
ASK SO Ɓ▸ ⊠ / VCR /

THE BATTERY HOTEL & SUITES   *Book great rates at AAA.com*   **Phone:** (709)576-0040

5/1-9/30   1P: $109-$169   2P: $109-$169
10/1-11/15   1P: $99-$139   2P: $99-$139
11/16-4/30   1P: $89-$129   2P: $89-$129

Large-scale Hotel   **Location:** 1 mi (1.6 km) e; on historic Signal Hill. 100 Signal Hill Rd A1A 1B3. Fax: 709/576-6943. **Facility:** 125 units. 124 one-bedroom standard units, some with whirlpools. 1 one-bedroom suite ($129-$199) with whirlpool. 6 stories, interior corridors. **Parking:** on-site. **Terms:** cancellation fee imposed. **Amenities:** *Some:* hair dryers. **Pool(s):** heated indoor. **Leisure Activities:** sauna, whirlpool. **Guest Services:** valet and coin laundry, wireless Internet. **Business Services:** meeting rooms, business center. **Cards:** AX, DC, MC, VI.

SOME UNITS
ASK SO Ɓ Ψ ⌘ K ✻ ▣ / ⊠ ▤ ⌷ /

BEST WESTERN TRAVELLERS INN   *Book great rates at AAA.com*   **Phone:** (709)722-5540

5/1-9/15   1P: $92-$149   2P: $99-$159   XP: $10   F18
9/16-4/30   1P: $79-$119   2P: $89-$139   XP: $10   F18

Small-scale Hotel   **Location:** Just w of Pippy Place Rd. Located in a commercial area. 199 Kenmount Rd A1B 3P9. Fax: 709/722-1025. **Facility:** 88 one-bedroom standard units. 2 stories (no elevator), interior/exterior corridors. **Parking:** on-site. **Terms:** cancellation fee imposed, [AP] & [BP] meal plans available. **Amenities:** video games (fee), voice mail, irons, hair dryers. *Some:* high-speed Internet. **Dining:** 7 am-10 pm, Sun from 8 am, cocktails. **Pool(s):** heated outdoor. **Guest Services:** wireless Internet. **Business Services:** meeting rooms, PC. **Cards:** AX, CB, DC, DS, JC, MC, VI. **Free Special Amenities:** early check-in/late check-out and room upgrade (subject to availability with advance reservations).

SOME UNITS
SO Ɓ Ψ ⌘ ✻ ▣ / ⊠ K ▤ ⌷ /

CAPITAL HOTEL   *Book at AAA.com*   **Phone:** (709)738-4480

All Year   1P: $118   2P: $118

Small-scale Hotel   **Location:** Just w of Pippy Place Rd. 208 Kenmount Rd A1B 3P9. Fax: 709/738-4481. **Facility:** 88 one-bedroom standard units, some with whirlpools. 4 stories, interior corridors. **Parking:** on-site. **Terms:** cancellation fee imposed, small pets only. **Amenities:** high-speed Internet, voice mail, irons, hair dryers. **Leisure Activities:** exercise room. **Business Services:** meeting rooms, business center. **Cards:** AX, MC, VI.

SOME UNITS
ASK SO Ɓ Ψ ⌘ ▣ / ⊠ ▤ /

COMFORT INN AIRPORT   *Book great rates at AAA.com*   **Phone:** (709)753-3500

All Year   1P: $99-$149   2P: $99-$149   XP: $10   F17

Small-scale Hotel   **Location:** Trans-Canada Hwy 1, exit 47A, 0.6 mi (1 km) n on Rt 40 (Portugal Cove Rd). 106 Airport Rd A1A 4Y3. Fax: 709/753-3711. **Facility:** 101 one-bedroom standard units. 2 stories (no elevator), interior corridors. **Parking:** on-site. **Amenities:** voice mail, irons, hair dryers. **Dining:** 7 am-10 pm, cocktails. **Leisure Activities:** exercise room. **Guest Services:** complimentary and valet laundry, wireless Internet. **Business Services:** meeting rooms, PC. **Cards:** AX, DC, DS, MC, VI. **Free Special Amenities:** full breakfast and high-speed Internet.

SOME UNITS
SO ⊞ Ɓ Ψ ⌘ ✻ ▣ / ⊠ ▤ /

COURTYARD BY MARRIOTT ST. JOHN'S   *Book great rates at AAA.com*   **Phone:** 709/722-3892

Property failed to provide current rates

Location: At Ordnance St. 131 Duckworth St A1C 1E9. Fax: 709/738-3775. **Facility:** Smoke free premises. 87 units. 83 one-bedroom standard units, some with whirlpools. 4 one-bedroom suites. 4 stories, interior corridors. **Bath:** combo or shower only. **Parking:** on-site. **Amenities:** video games (fee), high-speed Internet, voice mail, irons, hair dryers. **Leisure Activities:** exercise room. **Guest Services:** valet and coin laundry. **Business Services:** meeting rooms, business center.

SOME UNITS
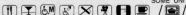
Ψ ⌘ ⌖M ✑ ⊠ ✻ ▤ ⌷ ▣ / ▤ /

DELTA ST. JOHN'S HOTEL AND CONFERENCE CENTRE *Book at AAA.com*

Phone: (709)739-6404

5/1-10/31	1P: $155	2P: $155	XP: $15	F18
11/1-4/30	1P: $135	2P: $135	XP: $15	F18

Large-scale Hotel **Location:** At Barter's Hill Rd; centre. 120 New Gower St A1C 6K4. Fax: 709/570-1622. **Facility:** 403 units. 393 one-bedroom standard units. 10 one-bedroom suites with whirlpools. 11 stories, interior corridors. *Bath:* combo or shower only. **Parking:** on-site (fee). **Terms:** 30 day cancellation notice-fee imposed, [AP], [BP], [CP] & [MAP] meal plans available, small pets only. **Amenities:** video games (fee), high-speed Internet, voice mail, honor bars, irons, hair dryers. *Some:* CD players. **Dining:** Mickey Quinn's Pub, see separate listing. **Pool(s):** heated indoor. **Leisure Activities:** sauna, whirlpool, exercise room. **Guest Services:** gift shop, valet laundry. **Business Services:** conference facilities, business center. **Cards:** AX, DC, DS, MC, VI.

SOME UNITS

THE FAIRMONT NEWFOUNDLAND *Book at AAA.com*

Phone: (709)726-4980

5/14-10/14	1P: $189-$332	2P: $189-$332	XP: $20	F17
10/15-4/30	1P: $180-$303	2P: $180-$303	XP: $20	F17
5/1-5/13	1P: $161-$284	2P: $161-$284	XP: $20	F17

Large-scale Hotel **Location:** Centre. Cavendish Square A1C 5W8. Fax: 709/726-2025. **Facility:** 301 one-bedroom standard units. 9 stories, interior corridors. **Parking:** on-site. **Terms:** package plans, small pets only ($25 fee). **Amenities:** video games (fee), voice mail, honor bars, irons, hair dryers. *Some:* high-speed Internet (fee). **Dining:** The Cabot Club Fine Dining, see separate listing. **Pool(s):** heated indoor. **Leisure Activities:** saunas, whirlpool, racquetball court, exercise room. **Guest Services:** gift shop, valet laundry, wireless Internet. **Business Services:** conference facilities, business center. **Cards:** AX, CB, DC, DS, JC, MC, VI.

SOME UNITS

FEE

HOLIDAY INN ST. JOHN'S-GOVT CENTRE *Book great rates at AAA.com*

Phone: 709/722-0506

6/1-6/30	1P: $135	2P: $135	XP: $10	F
5/1-5/31	1P: $130	2P: $130	XP: $10	F
1/1-4/30	1P: $124	2P: $124	XP: $10	F
7/1-12/31	1P: $120	2P: $120	XP: $10	F

Large-scale Hotel **Location:** Trans-Canada Hwy 1, exit 47A, 0.9 mi (1.4 km) s. 180 Portugal Cove Rd A1B 2N2. Fax: 709/722-9756. **Facility:** 252 units. 248 one-bedroom standard units. 4 one-bedroom suites. 5 stories, interior/exterior corridors. **Parking:** on-site. **Terms:** small pets only. **Amenities:** voice mail, irons, hair dryers. *Fee:* video games, high-speed Internet. **Pool(s):** heated outdoor. **Leisure Activities:** playground, exercise room. **Guest Services:** gift shop, valet and coin laundry, beauty salon. **Business Services:** meeting rooms, business center. **Cards:** AX, CB, DC, DS, JC, MC, VI. *(See color ad card insert)*

SOME UNITS

LEASIDE MANOR HERITAGE INN

Phone: (709)722-0387

5/1-10/15 [BP]	2P: $109-$325	XP: $15	F12
10/16-4/30 [BP]	2P: $109-$325	XP: $15	F12

Historic Bed & Breakfast **Location:** Centre. Located in a residential area. 39 Topsail Rd A1E 2A6. Fax: 709/739-1835. **Facility:** A stylized roof, Colonial columns and leaded windows add interest to this 1922 Tudor mansion surrounded by a sweeping expanse of manicured grounds. Smoke free premises. 11 one-bedroom standard units, some with kitchens and/or whirlpools. 2 stories (no elevator), interior/exterior corridors. *Bath:* combo or shower only. **Parking:** on-site. **Terms:** office hours 6:30 am-8 pm, age restrictions may apply, cancellation fee imposed. **Amenities:** video library, DVD players, CD players, irons, hair dryers. **Guest Services:** coin laundry, wireless Internet. **Business Services:** meeting rooms, PC. **Cards:** AX, CB, DC, DS, JC, MC, VI.

SOME UNITS

MCCOUBREY MANOR B & B

Phone: 709/722-7577

5/1-10/15	1P: $89-$249	2P: $89-$249	XP: $10	F3
10/16-4/30	1P: $89-$179	2P: $89-$179	XP: $10	F3

Historic Bed & Breakfast **Location:** Centre. Located in a commercial area. 6-8 Ordnance St A1C 3K7. Fax: 709/579-7577. **Facility:** This lovely, 1904 Queen Anne-style heritage home in the heart of town offers tastefully decorated rooms and two kitchen suites. Smoke free premises. 6 units. 4 one-bedroom standard units, some with whirlpools. 2 one-bedroom suites with kitchens, some with whirlpools. 2 stories, interior/exterior corridors. *Bath:* combo or shower only. **Parking:** on-site. **Terms:** office hours 8 am-11 pm, age restrictions may apply, cancellation fee imposed, [BP] meal plan available. **Amenities:** video library, DVD players, CD players, hair dryers. *Some:* irons. **Guest Services:** complimentary laundry, wireless Internet. **Business Services:** PC. **Cards:** AX, DC, MC, VI. **Free Special Amenities: full breakfast and high-speed Internet.**

SOME UNITS

MURRAY PREMISES HOTEL

Phone: (709)738-7773

All Year	1P: $139-$249	2P: $139-$249	XP: $10	D12

Small-scale Hotel **Location:** At Harbour Dr; centre. Located opposite city wharf. 5 Becks Cove A1C 6H1. Fax: 709/738-7775. **Facility:** Smoke free premises. 47 units. 45 one-bedroom standard units, some with whirlpools. 2 one-bedroom suites with whirlpools. 4 stories, interior corridors. **Parking:** on-site. **Terms:** [CP] meal plan available. **Amenities:** high-speed Internet, voice mail, irons, hair dryers. **Guest Services:** gift shop, valet laundry, wireless Internet. **Business Services:** meeting rooms, PC. **Cards:** AX, DC, MC, VI.

SOME UNITS

QUALITY HOTEL-HARBOURVIEW *Book great rates at AAA.com*

Phone: (709)754-7788

All Year	1P: $125-$165	2P: $140-$180	XP: $15	F

Large-scale Hotel **Location:** At Cavendish Square; centre. 2 Hill-O-Chips A1C 6B1. Fax: 709/754-5209. **Facility:** 160 one-bedroom standard units. 5 stories, interior corridors. **Parking:** on-site. **Terms:** [AP], [BP], [CP], [ECP] & [MAP] meal plans available, package plans. **Amenities:** voice mail, irons, hair dryers. *Some:* high-speed Internet, dual phone lines. **Dining:** Rumpelstiltskin's, see separate listing. **Guest Services:** valet laundry, wireless Internet. **Business Services:** meeting rooms, PC. **Cards:** AX, DC, DS, JC, MC, VI.

SOME UNITS

RAMADA ST. JOHN'S   *Book great rates at AAA.com*   **Phone:** (709)722-9330

(CAA) (SAVE)

	6/16-9/15	1P: $129-$179	2P: $129-$179	XP: $10	F12
	5/1-6/15 & 1/1-4/30	1P: $119-$169	2P: $119-$169	XP: $10	F12
	9/16-12/31	1P: $109-$159	2P: $109-$159	XP: $10	F12

Location: Corner of Pippy Place Rd. 102 Kenmount Rd A1B 3R2. Fax: 709/722-9231. **Facility:** 80 units. 76 one-
Small-scale Hotel   bedroom standard units, some with kitchens. 4 one-bedroom suites ($169-$189) with kitchens. 4 stories,
interior corridors. **Parking:** on-site. **Terms:** package plans. **Amenities:** voice mail, irons, hair dryers.
Dining: 7 am-10 pm, cocktails. **Leisure Activities:** exercise room. **Guest Services:** valet and coin laundry, wireless Internet.
Business Services: meeting rooms, PC. **Cards:** AX, DC, DS, MC, VI. **Free Special Amenities: local telephone calls and
high-speed Internet.**

SOME UNITS

SUPER 8 MOTEL   *Book at AAA.com*   **Phone:** (709)739-8888

| | 6/16-9/15 [CP] | 1P: $119-$139 | 2P: $119-$139 | XP: $10 | F19 |
| | 5/1-6/15 & 9/16-4/30 [CP] | 1P: $109-$129 | 2P: $109-$129 | XP: $10 | F19 |

Location: Trans-Canada Hwy 1, exit 47A, just s on Rt 40 (Portugal Cove Rd). 175 Higgins Line Rd A1B 4N4.
Small-scale Hotel   Fax: 709/739-8811. **Facility:** 82 units. 67 one-bedroom standard units, some with whirlpools. 15 one-
bedroom suites. 4 stories, interior corridors. **Bath:** combo or shower only. **Parking:** on-site. **Terms:** cancellation fee imposed,
package plans, pets ($10 extra charge). **Amenities:** high-speed Internet, voice mail, irons, hair dryers. **Pool(s):** heated indoor.
Leisure Activities: whirlpool, waterslide. **Guest Services:** coin laundry. **Business Services:** meeting rooms, PC. **Cards:** AX,
CB, DC, DS, JC, MC, VI.

SOME UNITS

FEE

———— *The following lodgings were either not evaluated or did not* ————
meet AAA rating requirements but are listed for your information only.

BANBERRY HOUSE B & B   **Phone:** 709/579-8006

(fyi)   Not evaluated. **Location:** Centre. 116 Military Rd A1C 2C9. Facilities, services, and decor characterize a mid-range
property.

COMPTON HOUSE HERITAGE INN   **Phone:** 709/739-5789

(fyi)   Not evaluated. **Location:** Just s of jct Water St. 26 Waterford Bridge Rd A1E 1C6. Facilities, services, and decor
characterize a mid-range property.

MONROE HOUSE B&B   **Phone:** 709/754-0610

(fyi)   Not evaluated. **Location:** Centre. 8 A Forest Rd A1C 2B9. Facilities, services, and decor characterize a mid-range
property.

WATERFORD MANOR   **Phone:** 709/754-4139

(fyi)   Not evaluated. **Location:** 2 mi s of jct Water St. 185 Waterford Bridge Rd A1E 1C7. Facilities, services, and decor
characterize a mid-range property.

WINTERHOLME HERITAGE INN   **Phone:** 709/739-7979

(fyi)   Not evaluated. **Location:** Centre. 79 Rennies Mill Rd A1C 3R1. Facilities, services, and decor characterize a mid-
range property.

———— **WHERE TO DINE** ————

BIANCA'S RESTAURANT   **Lunch:** $10-$17   **Dinner:** $18-$32   **Phone:** 709/726-9016

Location: Centre. 171 Water St A1C 6J9. **Hours:** noon-2:30 & 5:30-10 pm, Sat & Sun from 5:30 pm. Closed
major holidays. **Reservations:** suggested. **Features:** This colourful upscale bistro is located in the heart of
Regional   the city and through the large plate glass windows you can watch the bustling street scene. The menu
Canadian   features creatively presented fresh seafood, steak, and some game meat prepared in the open style
kitchen. To complement the fine cuisine they offer a superb selection of wine. Dressy casual; cocktails.
Parking: street. **Cards:** AX, DC, DS, MC, VI.

THE CABOT CLUB FINE DINING   **Dinner:** $30-$40   **Phone:** 709/726-4980

(CAA)   **Location:** Centre; in The Fairmont Newfoundland. Cavendish Square A1C 5W8. **Hours:** 6 pm-10 pm.
Reservations: suggested. **Features:** Picture windows showcase a spectacular view of Signal Hill and the
harbor while strains of Mozart play softly in the background. A skillful, professional wait staff presents fine
local seafood, traditional Newfoundland cuisine, and exquisite desserts. Dressy casual; cocktails. **Parking:**
Continental   on-site. **Cards:** AX, CB, DC, DS, JC, MC, VI.

THE CELLAR RESTAURANT   **Lunch:** $10-$18   **Dinner:** $18-$34   **Phone:** 709/579-8900

Location: Centre. 152 Water St A1C 5M5. **Hours:** 11:30 am-2:30 & 5:30-9:30 pm, Sun 5:30 pm-9 pm. Closed
major holidays. **Reservations:** suggested. **Features:** This is an elegant dining room with very nice paintings
Regional   from local artists on display. The menu features a fine array of meat and fresh seafood items. The entrees
Canadian   show creative preparation and artful presentation. They also offer a fine selection of wine with many by-the-
glass choices. The splendid desserts add the finishing touch to a fine experience. Dressy casual; cocktails.
Parking: street. **Cards:** AX, MC, VI.

CORA'S BREAKFAST & LUNCH   **Lunch:** $6-$10   **Phone:** 709/722-6720

Location: Downtown; in Atlantic Place. 215 Water St A1C 6K3. **Hours:** 6 am-3 pm. Closed: 12/25.
Reservations: accepted. **Features:** Although this place specializes in breakfast, it offers a varied daytime
Canadian   menu that includes bacon, eggs, sausages, crepes, grilled cheese, sandwiches, freshly prepared quiches,
salads, fruit platters and freshly squeezed juices. The family-friendly dining room is casual and modern.
Casual dress. **Parking:** on-site (fee). **Cards:** AX, DC, MC, VI.

INDIA GATE RESTAURANT   Lunch: $8-$14   Dinner: $11-$16   Phone: 709/753-6006

Indian
cocktails.

Location: Centre. 286 Duckworth St A1C 5W8. **Hours:** 11 am-2 & 5-10:30 pm, Sat & Sun from 5 pm. Closed major holidays. **Reservations:** accepted. **Features:** An extensive menu offers a wide range of traditional Indian favorites, spiced to order from mild to fiery hot. Exotic Indian music and soft lighting create a serene mood as you sample items from the very good lunch buffet available Monday through Friday. Casual dress; cocktails. **Parking:** on-site (fee). **Cards:** DS, MC, VI.

JUNGLE JIM'S RESTAURANT   Lunch: $7-$11   Dinner: $8-$20   Phone: 709/722-0261

Canadian
Casual dress; cocktails.

Location: Corner of Newfoundland Dr; centre. 286 Torbay Rd A1C 6K1. **Hours:** 11 am-11 pm, Fri-Sun to midnight. Closed: 12/25. **Reservations:** accepted. **Features:** Guests can step into a tropical theme at the casual eatery, which employs a friendly staff and nurtures a bustling atmosphere. The menu lines up a wide variety of comfort foods, salads, chicken, beef, seafood and hot wings, all served in ample, flavorful portions. Casual dress; cocktails. **Parking:** on-site. **Cards:** AX, DC, MC, VI.

JUNGLE JIM'S RESTAURANT   Lunch: $7-$11   Dinner: $8-$20   Phone: 709/753-5467

Canadian

Location: Centre. 2 Holdsworth Ct, George St A1C 4J7. **Hours:** 11 am-midnight, Fri & Sat-4:30 am. Closed: 12/25. **Reservations:** accepted. **Features:** Guests can step into a tropical theme at the casual eatery, which employs a friendly staff and nurtures a bustling atmosphere. The menu lines up a wide variety of comfort foods, salads, chicken, beef, seafood and hot wings, all served in ample, flavorful portions. Casual dress; cocktails. **Parking:** on-site (fee). **Cards:** AX, DC, MC, VI.

JUNGLE JIM'S RESTAURANT   Lunch: $7-$11   Dinner: $8-$20   Phone: 709/745-6060

Canadian
dress; cocktails.

Location: Just e of Burgeo St. 657 Topsail Rd A1E 2E3. **Hours:** 11 am-11 pm, Wed, Fri & Sat-midnight. Closed: 12/25. **Reservations:** accepted. **Features:** Guests can step into a tropical theme at the casual eatery, which employs a friendly staff and nurtures a bustling atmosphere. The menu lines up a wide variety of comfort foods, salads, chicken, beef, seafood and hot wings, all served in ample, flavorful portions. Casual dress; cocktails. **Parking:** on-site. **Cards:** AX, DC, MC, VI.

MAGIC WOK EATERY   Lunch: $7-$12   Dinner: $9-$16   Phone: 709/753-6907

Chinese

Location: At Princess St; centre. 402-408 Water St A1C 1C9. **Hours:** noon-midnight, Sat & Sun from 4 pm. Closed: 1/1, 12/25, 12/26; also Mon. **Reservations:** accepted. **Features:** The spacious modern restaurant presents a menu of traditional Chinese cuisine, prepared Hong Kong style, and some Canadian dishes. Casual dress; cocktails. **Parking:** on-site. **Cards:** AX, DC, MC, VI.

MEXICALI ROSA'S   Lunch: $7-$11   Dinner: $9-$16   Phone: 709/739-6394

Mexican
sweet treat.

Location: At Adelaide St. 36 George St A1C 1M5. **Hours:** 11:30 am-midnight, Sat & Sun from noon. Closed: 1/1, 12/25. **Reservations:** accepted. **Features:** The Mexican cantina makes an excellent choice for family-friendly fun. Old West paintings and murals add color to stucco walls and wooden beams, while a Tex-Mex menu provides a feast of favorites such as fajitas, burritos and some seafood items. Fried ice cream is a sweet treat. Casual dress; cocktails. **Parking:** on-site (fee). **Cards:** AX, DC, MC, VI.

MICKEY QUINN'S PUB   Lunch: $6-$18   Dinner: $11-$28   Phone: 709/570-1333

Canadian
Parking: on-site (fee).

Location: At Barter's Hill Rd; centre; in Delta St. John's Hotel and Conference Centre. 120 New Gower St A1C 6K4. **Hours:** 6:30 am-11 pm. **Reservations:** accepted. **Features:** Guests find a full pub menu, as well as a splendid selection of single malts and 16 fine beers on tap. Shepherd's pie, bangers and mash and fish and chips are but a few of the tempting, well-prepared dishes. Portions are ample. Casual dress; cocktails. **Parking:** on-site (fee). **Cards:** AX, DC, MC, VI.

PETER BELBIN'S STEAK HOUSE & SALAD BAR   Lunch: $8-$15   Dinner: $12-$28   Phone: 709/753-8530

Steak House
homemade desserts.

Location: Centre; at Haymarket Square. 223 Duckworth St A1C 6N1. **Hours:** 11:30 am-9:30 pm, Fri & Sat-10 pm. Closed: 7/1, 12/25, 12/26. **Reservations:** accepted. **Features:** The focus of the diverse menu is on top-quality aged beef, which is hand cut on the premises. Also offered are chicken, pork, seafood and some pasta dishes. Guests can couple the entrees with the excellent salad bar and a delightful array of homemade desserts. Servers are friendly and competent. Casual dress; cocktails. **Parking:** street. **Cards:** AX, DC, MC, VI.

RUMPELSTILTSKIN'S   Lunch: $8-$12   Dinner: $11-$17   Phone: 709/579-6000

Canadian
dress; cocktails.

Location: At Cavendish Square; centre; in Quality Hotel-Harbourview. 2 Hill-O-Chips A1C 6B1. **Hours:** 7 am-10 pm, Fri-11 pm, Sat 8 am-11 pm. Closed: 12/25, 12/26. **Features:** The atmosphere is warm and upbeat in the pleasant restaurant, which offers a great view of the harbor from several tables. Among the varied entrees are preparations of steak and seafood. Tempting desserts include the cheesecake and custard. Casual dress; cocktails. **Parking:** on-site. **Cards:** AX, MC, VI.

STAGEHEAD RESTAURANT   Lunch: $8-$15   Dinner: $13-$29   Phone: 709/739-8668

Canadian

Location: 1.3 mi (2 km) e on Quidi Vidi Rd. 16 Barrows Rd A1K 1A2. **Hours:** noon-2 & 5:30-9:30 pm, Sat & Sun 5:30 pm-9 pm. Closed: 10/8, 12/25, 12/26. **Reservations:** accepted. **Features:** Nestled in the historic fishing village of Quidi Vidi, the restaurant offers a pleasant view of the harbour. The menu features fresh seafood, steaks and pasta dishes. Casual dress; cocktails. **Parking:** on-site. **Cards:** AX, MC, VI.

SUN SUSHI JAPANESE RESTAURANT   Lunch: $6-$11   Dinner: $9-$15   Phone: 709/726-8688

Japanese

Location: Centre. 186 Duckworth St A1C 1G5. **Hours:** noon-9:30 pm, Thurs-Sat to 10:30 pm. Closed: 12/25, 12/26. **Reservations:** accepted. **Features:** Located in the heart of town, this open-style dining room offers a vast array of tasty Japanese entrees and sushi bar combinations. Casual dress; beer & wine only. **Parking:** street. **Cards:** MC, VI.

SWISS CHALET
▼▼ ▼▼
Canadian

Lunch: $6-$11 **Dinner:** $8-$16 **Phone:** 709/726-6849
Location: At Piggy Pl. 193 Kenmount Rd A1B 3P9. **Hours:** 11 am-10 pm, Fri & Sat-11 pm. Closed: 12/25.
Reservations: accepted. **Features:** The popular restaurant is known for its rotisserie chicken and ribs and the tangy Chalet sauce that gives food its special zip. Diners munch on a half or quarter chicken with sides such as steamed vegetables, fries, baked potatoes and salads. Lunch guests often go for the great soup and sandwich combination. Take-out and delivery service are popular options. Casual dress; cocktails. **Parking:** on-site.
Cards: AX, DC, MC, VI.

SWISS CHALET
▼▼ ▼▼
Canadian

Lunch: $6-$11 **Dinner:** $8-$16 **Phone:** 709/753-6030
Location: At Stavenger Dr; centre. 70 Aberdeen Ave A1A 5N6. **Hours:** 11 am-10 pm, Fri & Sat-11 pm. Closed: 12/25. **Reservations:** accepted. **Features:** The popular restaurant is known for its rotisserie chicken and ribs and the tangy Chalet sauce that gives food its special zip. Diners munch on a half or quarter chicken with sides such as steamed vegetables, fries, baked potatoes and salads. Lunch guests often go for the great soup and sandwich combination. Take-out and delivery service are popular options. Casual dress; cocktails. **Parking:** on-site. **Cards:** AX, DC, MC, VI.

TAJ MAHAL RESTAURANT
▼▼ ▼▼
Indian

Lunch: $6-$11 **Dinner:** $12-$17 **Phone:** 709/576-5500
Location: Centre. 203 Water St A1A 5G6. **Hours:** 11:30 am-2 & 4:30-10 pm. Closed: 1/1, 12/25. **Reservations:** accepted. **Features:** Although the Taj Mahal doesn't factor much into the decor, the food is hard to beat. Through the kitchen window, guests can view traditional Indian dishes being carefully prepared to patrons' spice comfort zones. Casual dress; cocktails. **Parking:** street. **Cards:** AX, DC, MC, VI.

ZACHARY'S RESTAURANT
▼▼ ▼▼
Canadian

Lunch: $6-$12 **Dinner:** $10-$19 **Phone:** 709/579-8050
Location: At Kings Bridge Rd. 71 Duckworth St A1C 1E6. **Hours:** 7 am-10 pm. Closed: 12/25. **Reservations:** accepted. **Features:** Conveniently open for all meals, the casual restaurant offers a nice selection on menu, ranging from burgers and sandwiches to fresh seafood, steaks and homemade desserts. Casual dress; cocktails. **Parking:** street. **Cards:** AX, MC, VI.

———— *The following restaurant has not been evaluated by AAA* ————
but is listed for your information only.

NAUTICAL NELLIES
[fyi]

Phone: 709/738-1120
Not evaluated. **Location:** Centre. 201 Water St A1A 1A1. **Features:** On the menu of the upbeat, cozy eatery is traditional, tried-and-true pub fare. Ⓨ

ST. PAULS pop. 330

———— **WHERE TO STAY** ————

———— *The following lodging was either not evaluated or did not* ————
meet AAA rating requirements but is listed for your information only.

GROS MORNE RESORT
[fyi]

Phone: 709/243-2606
Not evaluated. **Location:** On Rt 430 at north end of park; centre. (PO Box 100, A0K 4Y0). Facilities, services, and decor characterize a mid-range property.

———— **WHERE TO DINE** ————

GROS MORNE RESORT RESTAURANT
▼▼ ▼▼
Canadian

Lunch: $7-$14 **Dinner:** $8-$20 **Phone:** 709/243-2606
Location: On Rt 430 at north end of park; centre; in Gros Morne Resort. **Hours:** 7 am-10 pm; from 8 am 10/1-3/31. **Reservations:** accepted. **Features:** A welcome port in a storm, the large dining room overlooks the Gros Morne Mountains. The vast menu selection is likely to have something for everyone, from full dinners to lighter fare. Portions are good, and the cooking is home-style. Casual dress; cocktails. **Parking:** on-site. **Cards:** AX, DC, DS, MC, VI. Ⓨ

SPRINGDALE pop. 3,045

———— **WHERE TO STAY** ————

———— *The following lodging was either not evaluated or did not* ————
meet AAA rating requirements but is listed for your information only.

BURNT BERRY LODGE
[fyi]

Phone: 709/673-3926
Not evaluated. **Location:** 1.2 mi (2 km) e of Springdale jct, on Trans-Canada Hwy 1. (PO Box 1449, A0J 1T0). Facilities, services, and decor characterize a basic property.

STEADY BROOK

———— **WHERE TO STAY** ————

———— *The following lodgings were either not evaluated or did not* ————
meet AAA rating requirements but are listed for your information only.

THE LODGES AT GEORGE'S MOUNTAIN VILLAGE
[fyi]

Phone: 709/639-8168
Not evaluated. **Location:** Trans-Canada Hwy 1, exit Marble Mountain, follow signs. (Box 211, A2H 2N2). Facilities, services, and decor characterize a mid-range property.

MARBLEWOOD VILLAGE RESORT   **Phone:** 709/632-7900
(fyi)   Not evaluated. **Location:** Off Trans-Canada Hwy 1; centre. 8 Thistle Dr A2H 6G1 (PO Box 623, CORNER BROOK).
Facilities, services, and decor characterize a mid-range property.

STEPHENVILLE pop. 7,109

──────── WHERE TO STAY ────────

HOLIDAY INN STEPHENVILLE   *Book great rates at AAA.com*   **Phone:** (709)643-6666
▼▼ ▼▼   All Year   1P: $110   2P: $140   XP: $8   F19
Location: Centre. Adjoins a shopping mall. 44 Queen St A2N 2M5. Fax: 709/643-3900. **Facility:** 47 one-bedroom
Small-scale Hotel   standard units. 2 stories, interior corridors. **Parking:** on-site. **Terms:** [BP] & [CP] meal plans available.
Amenities: video library (fee), voice mail, irons, hair dryers. *Some:* high-speed Internet, honor bars.
Dining: Emile's Pub & Eatery, see separate listing. **Guest Services:** valet laundry, wireless Internet. **Business Services:**
meeting rooms, PC. **Cards:** AX, DC, DS, MC, VI.

SOME UNITS

(ASK) [S🔌] [🛏] [🍴] [🍽] [💻] / [⊠] [VCR] /
FEE

──────── WHERE TO DINE ────────

CASTAWAYS GRUB AND PUB   **Lunch:** $6-$14   **Dinner:** $9-$17   **Phone:** 709/643-7725
▼▼ ▼▼   **Location:** Jct Main. 75 West St A2N 3B5. **Hours:** 11 am-10 pm, Fri & Sat-11 pm. Closed: 12/25, 12/26.
Reservations: accepted. **Features:** A rustic Caribbean theme creates a fun, relaxed atmosphere where
Canadian   seasonal outdoor dining is a treat. Extensive menu options feature hearty portions of casual fare, including
burgers, pasta, salad, sandwiches and old-time favorites such as fish and chips. Casual dress; cocktails.
Parking: on-site. **Cards:** AX, DC, MC, VI.

[🍽] [🍴]

EMILE'S PUB & EATERY   **Lunch:** $6-$9   **Dinner:** $12-$19   **Phone:** 709/643-6666
▼▼ ▼▼   **Location:** Centre; in Holiday Inn Stephenville. 44 Queen St A2N 2M5. **Hours:** 7 am-10 pm, Sat & Sun from 8 am.
Closed: 12/25. **Reservations:** suggested. **Features:** Named in honor of the famous local fiddler Emile
Canadian   Benoit, the pleasant restaurant prepares a fine selection of fresh seafood, steaks, ribs, chicken and pasta
dishes. A bowl of the wonderful chowder should not be missed. Casual dress; cocktails. **Parking:** on-site.
Cards: AX, DC, DS, MC, VI.

[🍽]

SWIFT CURRENT

──────── WHERE TO STAY ────────

──────── *The following lodging was either not evaluated or did not* ────────
meet AAA rating requirements but is listed for your information only.

KILMORY RESORT   **Phone:** 709/549-2410
(fyi)   Not evaluated. **Location:** On Rt 210; centre. (PO Box 130, A0E 2W0). Facilities, services, and decor characterize a
mid-range property.

TRAYTOWN pop. 272

──────── WHERE TO STAY ────────

──────── *The following lodgings were either not evaluated or did not* ────────
meet AAA rating requirements but are listed for your information only.

PINETREE LODGE & TRAYTOWN CABINS   **Phone:** 709/533-6601
(fyi)   Not evaluated. **Location:** On Rt 310. Main St A0G 4K0. Facilities, services, and decor characterize a mid-range
property.

SPLASH 'N' PUTT RESORT   **Phone:** 709/533-2753
(fyi)   Not evaluated. **Location:** Rt 1, western entrance to Terra Nova National Park. (PO Box 42, GLOVERTOWN, A0G
2L0). Facilities, services, and decor characterize a mid-range property.

TRINITY pop. 500

──────── WHERE TO STAY ────────

──────── *The following lodgings were either not evaluated or did not* ────────
meet AAA rating requirements but are listed for your information only.

ARTISAN INN AND CAMPBELL HOUSE   **Phone:** 709/464-3377
(fyi)   Not evaluated. **Location:** Centre. High St A0C 2S0. Facilities, services, and decor characterize a mid-range property.

ERIKSEN PREMISES   **Phone:** 709/464-3698
(fyi)   Not evaluated. **Location:** Centre. West St A0C 2S0 (PO Box 58). Facilities, services, and decor characterize a mid-
range property.

------ **WHERE TO DINE** ------

HERITAGE TEA ROOM **Lunch:** $7-$13 **Dinner:** $12-$21 **Phone:** 709/464-3698
♦♦ ♦♦ **Location:** Centre: in Eriksen Premises. West St A0C 2S0. **Hours:** Open 5/1-10/31; 10 am-10 pm.
Features: Hearty portions of down-home cooking mean no diner leaves hungry from the quaint village
Canadian restaurant. Casual dress; cocktails. **Parking:** on-site. **Cards:** AX, MC, VI. **Historic**

TWILLINGATE pop. 2,611

------ **WHERE TO STAY** ------

------ *The following lodgings were either not evaluated or did not* ------
meet AAA rating requirements but are listed for your information only.

ANCHOR INN MOTEL **Phone:** 709/884-2777
[fyi] Not evaluated. **Location:** On Main St, on oceanfront. (PO Box 550, A0G 4M0). Facilities, services, and decor
characterize a basic property.

HARBOUR LIGHTS INN **Phone:** 709/884-2763
[fyi] Not evaluated. **Location:** Overlooking the harbour. 189 Main St A0G 4M0 (PO Box 729). Facilities, services, and
decor characterize a mid-range property.

WABUSH

------ **WHERE TO STAY** ------

------ *The following lodging was either not evaluated or did not* ------
meet AAA rating requirements but is listed for your information only.

WASBUSH HOTEL **Phone:** 709/282-3221
[fyi] Did not meet all AAA rating requirements for locking devices in some guest rooms at time of last evaluation
on 05/02/2006. **Location:** Centre. 9 Grenfell St A0R 1B0. Facilities, services, and decor characterize a mid-range
Small-scale Hotel property.

------ **WHERE TO DINE** ------

GREAT WALL RESTAURANT **Lunch:** $6-$11 **Dinner:** $8-$17 **Phone:** 709/282-3261
♦♦ ♦♦ **Location:** Centre; in Wabush Hotel. 9 Grenfell St A0R 1B0. **Hours:** 6:30 am-midnight. **Reservations:** accepted.
Features: Guests are seated in either of two dining sections, one of which is more casual. Those not in the
Chinese mood for the daily buffet can peruse the full menu of Chinese and Canadian entrees. Casual dress;
cocktails. **Parking:** on-site. **Cards:** MC, VI. ⊻

WILTONDALE

------ **WHERE TO STAY** ------

------ *The following lodging was either not evaluated or did not* ------
meet AAA rating requirements but is listed for your information only.

FRONTIER COTTAGES **Phone:** 709/453-2520
[fyi] Not evaluated. **Location:** Jct Hwy 430 and 431; entrance to Gros Morne National Park. (PO Box 172, ROCKY
HARBOUR, A0K 4N0). Facilities, services, and decor characterize a mid-range property.

Nova Scotia

Cabot Trail, Cape Breton
Island / Nova Scotia
Tourism, Culture
and Heritage

AMHERST pop. 9,470

―――― WHERE TO STAY ――――

AUBERGE WANDLYN INN   *Book at AAA.com*   Phone: 902/667-3331

▼▼ ▼▼   All Year   1P: $115-$149   2P: $115-$149   XP: $10   F18
Location: Trans-Canada Hwy 104, exit 3, 0.6 mi (1 km) w. W Victoria St B4H 3Z2 (PO Box 275). Fax: 902/667-0475.
Small-scale Hotel   **Facility:** 88 units. 84 one-bedroom standard units, some with whirlpools. 4 one-bedroom suites ($149-$200). 3 stories (no elevator), interior/exterior corridors. **Parking:** on-site, winter plug-ins. **Terms:** [AP] meal plan available, pets (in smoking units). **Amenities:** voice mail, hair dryers. *Some:* irons. **Dining:** Field & Marsh Dining Room, see separate listing. **Pool(s):** heated indoor. **Leisure Activities:** whirlpool. **Guest Services:** coin laundry. **Business Services:** meeting rooms. **Cards:** AX, DC, DS, MC, VI.

SOME UNITS

[A$K] 🐕 🍴 🍸 🚤 🖥 / ✕ 🔋 🖸 /

COMFORT INN   *Book great rates at AAA.com*   Phone: (902)667-0404

▼▼ ▼▼   7/1-9/30   1P: $95-$156   2P: $106-$167   XP: $10   F18
         5/1-6/30   1P: $100-$145   2P: $112-$156   XP: $10   F18
Small-scale Hotel   1/1-4/30   1P: $107-$135   2P: $118-$146   XP: $10   F18
         10/1-12/31   1P: $100-$125   2P: $111-$136   XP: $10   F18
Location: Trans-Canada Hwy 104, exit 4, 1 mi (1.5 km) n on Rt 2. Located in a commercial area. 143 Albion St S B4H 2X2.
Fax: 902/667-2522. **Facility:** 61 one-bedroom standard units. 2 stories (no elevator), interior corridors. **Parking:** on-site.
Terms: 14 day cancellation notice. **Amenities:** voice mail, irons, hair dryers. **Guest Services:** wireless Internet. **Business Services:** meeting rooms, PC. **Cards:** AX, DC, DS, JC, MC, VI. *(See color ad card insert)*

SOME UNITS

[A$K] [S🔊] 🐕 🍴 📺 🖥 / ✕ 🔋 🖸 /

SUPER 8 MOTEL   *Book at AAA.com*   Phone: (902)660-8888

▼▼▼▼   7/1-9/5   1P: $139   2P: $139   XP: $10   F18
         9/6-4/30   1P: $125   2P: $125   XP: $10   F18
Small-scale Hotel   5/1-6/30   1P: $115   2P: $115   XP: $10   F18
Location: Trans-Canada Hwy 104, exit 4. 40 Lord Amherst Dr B4H 4W6. Fax: 902/660-8000. **Facility:** Smoke free premises. 50 units. 32 one-bedroom standard units. 18 one-bedroom suites, some with whirlpools. 3 stories, interior corridors.
Parking: on-site. **Terms:** package plans, small pets only ($10 extra charge, in limited units). **Amenities:** high-speed Internet, irons, hair dryers. **Pool(s):** heated indoor. **Leisure Activities:** whirlpool, waterslide. **Guest Services:** coin laundry. **Business Services:** meeting rooms. **Cards:** AX, DC, DS, MC, VI.

[A$K] [S🔊] 🐕 [🅼] 🚤 ✕ 🔋 🖸 🖥

FEE

―――― WHERE TO DINE ――――

FIELD & MARSH DINING ROOM   Lunch: $6-$13   Dinner: $9-$23   Phone: 902/667-3331

▼▼ ▼▼   **Location:** Trans-Canada Hwy 104, exit 3, 0.6 mi (1 km) w; in Auberge Wandlyn Inn. W Victoria St B4H 3Z2. **Hours:** 7
Canadian   am-9 pm. Closed: 12/24-12/26. **Reservations:** accepted. **Features:** Windows wrapping around the dining room overlook lovely Tantramar Marsh. The casual decor reflects a marsh theme, with a duck border tracing the edge of the dining room. The seasonal menu lays out a fine selection of fresh seafood and meat entrees. Casual dress; cocktails. **Parking:** on-site. **Cards:** AX, DC, DS, MC, VI.

🍸

JUNGLE JIM'S BAR & EATERY   Lunch: $5-$12   Dinner: $8-$18   Phone: 902/661-4414

▼▼ ▼▼   **Location:** Trans-Canada Hwy 104, exit 4, 0.8 mi (1.3 km) n on Rt 2; in Town Square Mall.
Canadian   **Hours:** 11 am-10 pm, Fri & Sat-11 pm. Closed: 12/25, 12/26. **Features:** Guests can step into a tropical theme at the casual eatery, which employs a friendly staff and nurtures a bustling atmosphere. The menu lines up a wide variety of comfort foods, salads, chicken, beef, seafood and hot wings, all served in ample, flavorful portions. Casual dress; cocktails. **Parking:** on-site. **Cards:** AX, DC, MC, VI.

🍸

LOON ONN RESTAURANT   Lunch: $6-$9   Dinner: $11-$14   Phone: 902/667-1333

▼▼   **Location:** Trans-Canada Hwy 104, exit 4, 1 mi (1.6 km) n on Rt 2. 107 Albion St S B4H 2X2. **Hours:** 11 am-11 pm,
Chinese   Fri & Sat-midnight, Sun noon-11 pm. Closed: 12/25, 12/26. **Features:** Popular with families, business travelers and young professionals, the restaurant is convenient to major shopping malls. Among the dishes, all of which are prepared to order, are delightful house specialties including moo goo gai pan, seafood wor bar and Cantonese chow mein. Vibrant red and natural pine walls decorate the large, open dining room. Service level is casual and friendly. Casual dress; cocktails. **Parking:** on-site. **Cards:** AX, MC, VI.

🍸

SMITTY'S FAMILY RESTAURANT **Lunch:** $6-$11 **Dinner:** $8-$16 **Phone:** 902/667-1288
▼▼▼ **Location:** At Winston Ave. 138 S Albion St B4H 2X3. **Hours:** 7 am-9 pm. Closed: 12/25.
Reservations: accepted. **Features:** The family-oriented restaurant satisfies patrons with its ever-popular
Canadian all-day breakfast items, as well as tasty and wholesome soups and salads at lunchtime. A relaxed mood
characterizes the dining space. Casual dress; cocktails. **Parking:** on-site. **Cards:** AX, DC, MC, VI.

ANNAPOLIS ROYAL pop. 550

——— WHERE TO STAY ———

ANNAPOLIS ROYAL INN **Phone:** (902)532-2323
▼▼ ▼▼ 6/16-10/15 1P: $120-$148 2P: $120-$148 XP: $10 F18
5/1-6/15 & 10/16-4/30 1P: $89-$109 2P: $89-$109 XP: $10 F18
Motel **Location:** 0.6 mi (1 km) w on Hwy 1. Located in a rural area. (PO Box 551, B0S 1A0). **Fax:** 902/532-7277.
Facility: 30 one-bedroom standard units. 1 story, exterior corridors. **Parking:** on-site. **Terms:** office hours 7
am-11 pm, 30 day cancellation notice, small pets only (in designated units). **Amenities:** *Some:* high-speed Internet, hair dryers.
Leisure Activities: sauna, whirlpool. **Guest Services:** gift shop, coin laundry. **Cards:** AX, DC, MC, VI.

SOME UNITS

(ASK) (S☐) (🛏) (💻) / (✕) (VCR) /

CHAMPLAIN MOTEL **Phone:** (902)532-5473
▼▼ ▼▼ 5/15-10/15 1P: $105-$125 2P: $105-$125 XP: $10 F18
Location: 2.5 mi (4.2 km) w on Hwy 1. RR 2 B0S 1A0. **Facility:** 23 units. 21 one-bedroom standard units, some
Motel with efficiencies and/or whirlpools. 2 one-bedroom suites ($99-$207) with whirlpools. 1 story, exterior
corridors. **Parking:** on-site. **Terms:** open 5/15-10/15, office hours 7 am-11 pm, 30 day cancellation notice,
small pets only (in designated units). **Pool(s):** heated outdoor. **Cards:** AX, DC, MC, VI.

SOME UNITS

(ASK) (S☐) (🛏) (🍽) (💻) / (✕) (📶) (📠) /

GARRISON HOUSE INN **Phone:** (902)532-5750
▼▼▼ 7/22-9/30 1P: $75-$99 2P: $79-$199 XP: $15 D12
7/1-7/21 1P: $69-$89 2P: $79-$139 XP: $10 D12
Country Inn 5/1-6/30 & 10/1-11/15 1P: $59-$79 2P: $65-$119 XP: $10 D12
Location: Jct Rt 8 and Hwy 1. Located across from Fort Anne National Historic Park. 350 St George St B0S 1A0 (PO
Box 108). **Fax:** 902/532-5501. **Facility:** In the heart of town, the inn dates from 1854 and is within walking distance of several
attractions. Smoke free premises. 7 one-bedroom standard units, some with whirlpools. 3 stories (no elevator), interior corridors.
Bath: combo or shower only. **Parking:** on-site. **Terms:** open 5/1-11/15, office hours 7 am-11 pm, cancellation fee imposed,
package plans. **Amenities:** DVD players, hair dryers. **Dining:** restaurant, see separate listing. **Cards:** AX, MC, VI.

(🍴) (✕) (☎)

HILLSDALE HOUSE INN **Phone:** (902)532-2345
(CAA) (SAVE) 7/1-9/30 [BP] 1P: $109-$139 2P: $109-$139 XP: $15
5/1-6/30 [BP] 1P: $99-$119 2P: $99-$119 XP: $15
▼▼▼▼ 10/1-10/31 [BP] 1P: $79-$119 2P: $79-$119 XP: $15
Bed & Breakfast 4/1-4/30 [BP] 1P: $79-$99 2P: $79-$99 XP: $15
Location: Just e of Rt 1; centre. 519 St George St B0S 1A0. **Fax:** 902/532-0752. **Facility:** The circa 1856
Hillsdale House is a fine mansion with lovely grounds and tastefully decorated rooms on three levels as well
as in a carriage house. Smoke free premises. 13 one-bedroom standard units. 3 stories (no elevator), interior corridors. *Bath:*
combo or shower only. **Parking:** on-site. **Terms:** open 5/1-10/31 & 4/1-4/30, office hours 7 am-10 pm, cancellation fee imposed,
pets (with prior approval). **Amenities:** DVD players, CD players, hair dryers. **Leisure Activities:** lawn games, horseshoes.
Guest Services: wireless Internet. **Business Services:** PC. **Cards:** AX, MC, VI. **Free Special Amenities: full breakfast and
high-speed Internet.**

SOME UNITS

(🛏) (🍴) (✕) / (🐾) /

THE KING GEORGE INN **Phone:** (902)532-5286
▼▼▼ 5/1-11/15 1P: $79-$99 2P: $89-$159
Location: Centre. Located in a commercial area. 548 Upper St George St B0S 1A0 (PO Box 734).
Historic Bed **Fax:** 902/532-0144. **Facility:** Once a sea captain's home, this inn dating from 1868 offers some rooms with
& Breakfast private decks; guests should note the property's "scent-free" policy. Smoke free premises. 8 one-bedroom
standard units, some with whirlpools. 2 stories (no elevator), interior corridors. *Bath:* combo or shower only.
Parking: on-site. **Terms:** open 5/1-11/15, office hours 7 am-11 pm, weekly rates available, [BP] meal plan available, package
plans, small pets only (in designated units). **Amenities:** hair dryers. **Cards:** MC, VI.

(ASK) (S☐) (🛏) (🍴) (✕) (☎)

——— WHERE TO DINE ———

CHARLIE'S PLACE RESTAURANT **Lunch:** $5-$10 **Dinner:** $9-$18 **Phone:** 902/532-2111
▼▼ ▼▼ **Location:** On Hwy 1, 0.3 mi (0.5 km) w. Hwy 1 B0S 1A0. **Hours:** Open 5/1-12/15; 11 am-9 pm; to 8 pm off
season. Closed: Mon. **Reservations:** accepted. **Features:** Some of the restaurant's dining sections
Chinese overlook historic Fort Anne. On the menu are a variety of combination plates, an ample selection of Chinese
food and some Canadian dishes. Casual dress; cocktails. **Parking:** on-site. **Cards:** AX, MC, VI.

THE GARRISON HOUSE DINING ROOM **Dinner:** $15-$30 **Phone:** 902/532-5750
▼▼▼ **Location:** Jct Rt 8 and Hwy 1; in Garrison House Inn. 350 St George St B0S 1A0. **Hours:** Open 5/1-12/15; 8 am-
9:30 & 5:30-8:30 pm. **Reservations:** suggested. **Features:** The charming country inn specializes in lobsters
Canadian and fresh seafood from the Bay of Fundy and produce from the Annapolis Valley. Eclectic folk art,
particularly of fish, and antique mirrors enhance the intimate feel. Homemade pie, cake and torte are
delicious. Casual dress; cocktails. **Parking:** on-site. **Cards:** AX, MC, VI. **Country Inn**

(&M)

LEO'S CAFE   **Lunch:** $7-$13   **Phone:** 902/532-7424
▽▽ ▽▽
Canadian   **Location:** Centre. 222 St George St B0S 1A0. **Hours:** 9 am-3 pm. Closed: 1/1, 12/25, 12/26. **Features:** The popular cafe enables guests to relish the flavors of creative sandwiches, pita wraps, fresh salads and tasty soups and chowders. Homemade desserts quiet a sweet tooth. Casual dress. **Parking:** street. **Cards:** AX, MC, VI.

YE OLDE TOWNE PUB   **Lunch:** $7-$12   **Dinner:** $8-$16   **Phone:** 902/532-2244
▽▽ ▽▽
Canadian   **Location:** Across from town wharf; centre. 9-11 Church St B0S 1A0. **Hours:** 11 am-11 pm, Sat from 10 am, Sun noon-8 pm. Closed: 12/25. **Reservations:** accepted. **Features:** Traditional pub fare—such as fish and chips, steak and kidney pie and steak and eggs—is hearty and flavorful. The upbeat, friendly atmosphere attracts a bustling tourist trade. An interesting selection of draft beer is offered in the 1884 building. Smoking is permitted after 9 pm. Casual dress; cocktails. **Parking:** on-site. **Cards:** MC, VI.

ANTIGONISH pop. 4,754

—————— **WHERE TO STAY** ——————

ANTIGONISH VICTORIAN INN   **Phone:** 902/863-1103
▽▽ ▽▽▽   5/1-10/15 [BP]   1P: $125-$170   2P: $125-$170   XP: $15   F12
Historic Bed   10/16-4/30 [BP]   1P: $105-$170   2P: $110-$150   XP: $15   F12
& Breakfast   **Location:** Centre. Located in a commercial area. 149 Main St B2G 2B6. **Facility:** Located in the heart of town on 5 landscaped acres, this Queen Anne-style mansion offers a variety of tastefully decorated guest rooms and suites. Smoke free premises. 12 one-bedroom standard units. 2 stories (no elevator), interior/exterior corridors. *Bath:* combo or shower only. **Parking:** on-site. **Terms:** office hours 9 am-9 pm, age restrictions may apply, package plans. **Amenities:** irons, hair dryers. **Cards:** AX, MC, VI.

SOME UNITS

(ASK) (S₀) (◉↑→) (⊠) / (VCR) ▤ ▤ ▢ /

MARITIME INN ANTIGONISH   **Phone:** (902)863-4001
(CAA) (SAVE)   7/1-9/30   1P: $125-$145   2P: $125-$145   XP: $15   F12
▽▽ ▽▽   5/1-6/30 & 10/1-4/30   1P: $105-$125   2P: $105-$125   XP: $15   F12
Small-scale Hotel   **Location:** Centre. Located in residential area. 158 Main St B2G 2B7. Fax: 902/863-2672. **Facility:** 32 units. 31 one-bedroom standard units. 1 one-bedroom suite ($159-$175) with whirlpool. 2 stories (no elevator), interior/exterior corridors. **Parking:** on-site. **Terms:** [BP] & [MAP] meal plans available, package plans. **Amenities:** hair dryers. *Some:* irons. **Dining:** Main Street Cafe, see separate listing. **Guest Services:** wireless Internet. **Business Services:** meeting rooms. **Cards:** AX, DC, DS, MC, VI. **Free Special Amenities:** newspaper and high-speed Internet.

SOME UNITS

(🛏) (🍴) (💪) (▢) / (⊠) (VCR) /

—————— **WHERE TO DINE** ——————

GABRIEAU'S BISTRO   **Lunch:** $8-$14   **Dinner:** $14-$25   **Phone:** 902/863-1925
(CAA)   **Location:** Corner of Hawthorne St. 350 Main St B2G 2C5. **Hours:** 8 am-9:30 pm, Fri & Sat-10 pm. Closed: Sun.
▽▽▽ ▽▽▽   **Reservations:** accepted. **Features:** The cozy bistro is open for all meals. Evening dining is more sophisticated but still reflects a casual atmosphere. The diverse menu offers a fine selection of seafood and
Canadian   meat entrees and an array of excellent homemade desserts. Casual dress; cocktails. **Parking:** on-site. **Cards:** AX, MC, VI.

LOBSTER TREAT RESTAURANT   **Lunch:** $6-$14   **Dinner:** $9-$23   **Phone:** 902/863-5465
▽▽ ▽▽▽   **Location:** 1 mi (1.6 km) w on Trans-Canada Hwy 104. 241 Post Rd B2G 2K6. **Hours:** Open 5/1-10/31 & 4/15-4/30;
Steak & Seafood   11 am-10 pm. **Reservations:** suggested. **Features:** The quiet dining room finished in pine and tastefully decorated with local art is a cozy spot in which to unwind. Fresh seafood—with limited selections of steak, chicken and pasta—shares top billing with such sinful desserts as German apple cake. Casual dress; cocktails. **Parking:** on-site. **Cards:** AX, DC, MC, VI.

MAIN STREET CAFE   **Lunch:** $7-$13   **Dinner:** $11-$25   **Phone:** 902/863-4001
▽▽ ▽▽   **Location:** Centre; in Maritime Inn Antigonish. 158 Main St B2G 2B7. **Hours:** 7 am-10 pm. Closed: 12/25.
Canadian   **Reservations:** suggested. **Features:** Overlooking the main street, the friendly, family-focused cafe features fresh regional seafood, steaks and pasta dishes. Casual dress; cocktails. **Parking:** on-site. **Cards:** AX, CB, DC, DS, MC, VI.

(Y)

SUNSHINE ON MAIN CAFE & BISTRO   **Lunch:** $7-$13   **Dinner:** $10-$25   **Phone:** 902/863-5851
(CAA)   **Location:** Centre. 332 Main St B2G 2C4. **Hours:** 7 am-9:30 pm, Fri & Sat-10 pm. Closed: 1/1, 12/25.
▽▽ ▽▽   **Features:** The informal restaurant provides a menu that focuses on health-conscious cuisine, fresh local
Canadian   produce, seafood, meat and cheese. Excellent homemade desserts includes bumbleberry pie and cheesecake. Casual dress; cocktails. **Parking:** street. **Cards:** DC, MC, VI.

AULD'S COVE pop. 200

—————— **WHERE TO STAY** ——————

THE COVE MOTEL & RESTAURANT/GIFT SHOP   **Phone:** (902)747-2700
(CAA) (SAVE)   5/1-10/31   1P: $98-$118   2P: $118   XP: $10   F12
▽▽ ▽▽   **Location:** 0.6 mi (1 km) n off Trans-Canada Hwy 104; 1.9 mi (3 km) w of Canso Cswy. 227 Auld B0H 1P0 (PO Box
Motel   9680, PORT HASTINGS, B9A 3R7). Fax: 902/747-2010. **Facility:** 30 one-bedroom standard units. 1 story, exterior corridors. *Bath:* combo or shower only. **Parking:** on-site. **Terms:** open 5/1-10/31, office hours 7 am-11 pm, small pets only (in chalets, must remain caged). **Amenities:** hair dryers. **Dining:** restaurant, see separate listing. **Leisure Activities:** boating, canoeing, boat dock, fishing, gazebo. **Guest Services:** gift shop, coin laundry. **Cards:** AX, DC, MC, VI.

SOME UNITS

(🛏) (🍴) (⊠) (🎣) (▢) / (⊠) ▢ /

─── **WHERE TO DINE** ───

THE COVE MOTEL RESTAURANT Lunch: $6-$15 Dinner: $10-$30 Phone: 902/747-2700
Location: 0.6 mi (1 km) n off Trans-Canada Hwy 104; 1.9 mi (3 km) w of Canso Cswy; in The Cove Motel &
Restaurant/Gift Shop. 227 Auld B9A 3R7. **Hours:** Open 5/1-10/31; 7 am-10 pm. **Reservations:** accepted.
Features: An impressive waterfront location offers a fine view of Canso Strait. Enjoy a pleasant nautical
decor as you peruse a menu of fresh Nova Scotia seafood like lobster, scallops, mussels and a good
selection of fish. Steak, ribs, chicken and pasta entrees are also offered. Casual dress; cocktails. **Parking:**
on-site. **Cards:** AX, DC, MC, VI.

Seafood

BADDECK pop. 907

─── **WHERE TO STAY** ───

AUBERGE GISELE'S COUNTRY INN Phone: (902)295-2849
| | 7/1-10/12 | 1P: $135-$150 | 2P: $140-$180 | XP: $15 | F10 |
| | 5/10-6/30 & 10/13-10/20 | 1P: $125-$150 | 2P: $135-$175 | XP: $15 | F10 |

Small-scale Hotel **Location:** Trans-Canada Hwy 105, exit 8, 1 mi (1.6 km) e. 387 Shore Rd B0E 1B0 (PO Box 132). Fax: 902/295-2033.
Facility: Designated smoking area. 75 units. 72 one- and 3 two-bedroom standard units, some with
whirlpools. 3 stories, exterior corridors. **Parking:** on-site. **Terms:** open 5/10-10/20, office hours 7 am-11 pm, 3 day cancellation
notice, [BP], [CP] & [MAP] meal plans available, package plans. **Amenities:** irons, hair dryers. **Dining:** Gisele's Dining Room,
see separate listing. **Leisure Activities:** sauna, whirlpool. **Guest Services:** coin laundry. **Business Services:** meeting rooms,
PC. **Cards:** AX, DS, MC, VI.

SOME UNITS
ASK SD (T) X ▣ / 🛏 🖼 /

THE CEILIDH COUNTRY LODGE Phone: 902/295-3500
Property failed to provide current rates
Location: Trans-Canada Hwy 105, exit 8, 1 mi (1.6 km) e on Rt 205 (Shore Rd). 357 Shore Rd B0E 1B0 (PO Box 190).
Motel Fax: 902/295-3527. **Facility:** Smoke free premises. 52 units. 51 one-bedroom standard units. 1 two-
bedroom suite with whirlpool. 2-3 stories (no elevator), interior/exterior corridors. **Parking:** on-site.
Terms: open 5/1-10/15, office hours 7 am-11 pm, small pets only. **Amenities:** voice mail, hair dryers. *Some:* CD players.
(See color ad below)

SOME UNITS
🐾 (T+) X ▣ / 🛏 /

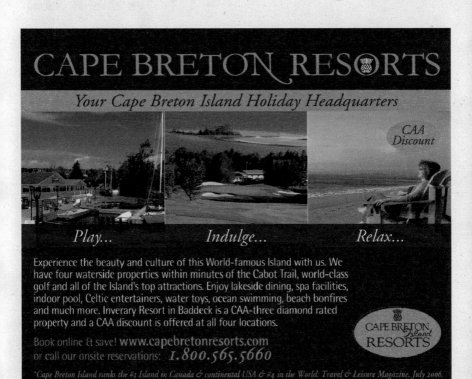

CHANTERELLE COUNTRY INN & COTTAGES

Phone: (902)929-2263

▼▼✕✕▼   5/1-10/31   1P: $125-$215   2P: $135-$225   XP: $25   F
Country Inn   **Location:** Trans-Canada Hwy 105, exit 11, 10.6 mi (17 km) ne. 48678 Cabot Trail B0E 1B0. Fax: 902/929-2039. **Facility:** Smoke free premises. 12 units. 8 one-bedroom standard units. 1 one-bedroom suite. 3 cottages ($850-$1000), some with whirlpools. 2 stories (no elevator), interior/exterior corridors. **Parking:** on-site, winter plug-ins. **Terms:** open 5/1-10/31, office hours 7:30 am-10 pm, check-in 4 pm, 14 day cancellation notice, 28 day for cottages-fee imposed, weekly rates available, [MAP] meal plan available, package plans. **Amenities:** irons, hair dryers. Some: DVD players. **Leisure Activities:** paddleboats, hiking trails. **Cards:** AX, MC, VI.

SOME UNITS

(ASK) (S☐) (†1) (Y) (✕) (✕) (CTV) (✇) / (VCR) (▤) (▤) /

HUNTER'S MOUNTAIN CHALETS

Phone: (902)295-3392

(CAA) (SAVE)   6/22-9/8   1P: $108-$138   2P: $108-$138   XP: $18   D11
▼▼✕✕▼   5/1-6/21 & 9/9-10/20   1P: $78-$118   2P: $78-$118   XP: $18   D11
Cottage   **Location:** Trans-Canada Hwy 105, exit 7, 1.6 mi (2.6 km) n. Located in a quiet area. 562 Cabot Tr B0E 1B0 (RR 3). Fax: 902/295-3392. **Facility:** In a peaceful setting overlooking fields and hills, the property offers spacious, comfortable, fully equipped units in duplex and fourplex buildings. 12 units. 8 two-bedroom standard units with efficiencies. 4 one-bedroom suites with efficiencies. 1 story, exterior corridors. **Parking:** on-site. **Terms:** open 5/1-10/20, office hours 8:30 am-9 pm, check-in 4 pm, 4 day cancellation notice-fee imposed, weekly rates available, small pets only ($10 extra charge, with prior approval). **Amenities:** hair dryers. **Leisure Activities:** hiking trails, playground. **Cards:** MC, VI. **Free Special Amenities:** local telephone calls and high-speed Internet.

(🛏) (✕) (✕) (📹) (✇) (▤) (▤)
FEE

INVERARY RESORT

Phone: (902)295-3500

(CAA) (SAVE)   6/16-10/31   1P: $159-$189   2P: $159-$189
▼▼✕✕▼   5/1-6/15   1P: $109-$139   2P: $159-$189
Small-scale Hotel   11/1-11/30   1P: $109-$139   2P: $109-$139
Location: Trans-Canada Hwy 105, exit 8, 1 mi (1.6 km) e on Rt 205 (Shore Rd). 368 Shore Rd B0E 1B0 (PO Box 190). Fax: 902/295-3527. **Facility:** Smoke free premises. 138 units. 123 one-bedroom standard units. 6 one-bedroom suites, some with whirlpools. 9 cottages. 1-3 stories (no elevator), interior/exterior corridors. **Bath:** combo or shower only. **Parking:** on-site. **Terms:** open 5/1-11/30, 3 day cancellation notice, [MAP] meal plan available, package plans, small pets only ($10 extra charge). **Amenities:** voice mail, irons, hair dryers. Some: CD players. **Dining:** 7 am-10 & 11-9 pm; hours vary off season, cocktails, also, Flora's Dining Room, see separate listing. **Pool(s):** heated indoor. **Leisure Activities:** sauna, whirlpool, rental boats, rental canoes, rental paddleboats, boat dock, 2 tennis courts, rental bicycles, playground, exercise room, spa. **Fee:** inflatable power boats, kayaks. **Guest Services:** gift shop, wireless Internet. **Business Services:** conference facilities, PC. **Cards:** AX, DC, DS, MC, VI. **Free Special Amenities:** high-speed Internet.
(See color ad p 301)

SOME UNITS

(🛏) (†1) (Y) (🖾) (🛶) (✕) (✕) (▣) / (▤) (▤) /
FEE

MCINTYRE'S HOUSEKEEPING COTTAGES

Phone: (902)295-1133

(CAA) (SAVE)   5/1-6/15   1P: $88-$115   2P: $88-$250   XP: $10
▼▼✕✕▼   6/16-10/20   1P: $120-$165   2P: $120-$165   XP: $10
Cottage   10/21-11/11   1P: $88-$115   2P: $88-$115   XP: $10
    11/12-4/30   1P: $68-$95   2P: $68-$95   XP: $10
Location: Trans-Canada Hwy 105, 3 mi (5 km) w. 8908 Hwy 105 B0E 1B0. Fax: 902/295-1790. **Facility:** Cozy duplex cottages with decks are set back from the highway, and all offer fireplaces and lovely lake views; a three-bedroom home also is available. Smoke free premises. 7 units. 1 vacation home ($200-$350) and 6 cottages, some with whirlpools. 1 story, exterior corridors. **Parking:** on-site. **Terms:** office hours 8 am-10 pm, 4 day cancellation notice-fee imposed, pets ($7.50 extra charge). **Amenities:** irons, hair dryers. Some: DVD players. **Leisure Activities:** cross country skiing, playground, basketball. **Guest Services:** wireless Internet. **Cards:** MC, VI. **Free Special Amenities:** local telephone calls and high-speed Internet.

SOME UNITS

(S☐) (🛏) (✕) (✕) (▤) (▤) / (✕) (✇) /
FEE

SILVER DART LODGE & MACNEIL HOUSE

Phone: (902)295-2340

(CAA) (SAVE)	7/1-8/26	1P: $129-$249	2P: $129-$249	XP: $15	F12
	8/27-10/15	1P: $116-$249	2P: $116-$249	XP: $15	F12
◆◆◆	6/15-6/30	1P: $116-$224	2P: $116-$224	XP: $15	F12
	5/15-6/14	1P: $97-$199	2P: $97-$199	XP: $15	F12

Small-scale Hotel **Location:** Trans-Canada Hwy 105, exit 8, 0.6 mi (1 km) e on Rt 205 (Shore Rd). 257 Hwy 205 B0E 1B0 (PO Box 399). Fax: 902/295-2484. **Facility:** Smoke free premises. 90 units. 85 one-bedroom standard units, some with efficiencies. 4 one- and 1 two-bedroom suites ($199-$249) with kitchens and whirlpools. 1-3 stories (no elevator), interior/exterior corridors. **Parking:** on-site. **Terms:** open 5/15-10/15, 3 day cancellation notice, [BP], [CP] & [MAP] meal plans available, package plans, small pets only ($15 fee, in designated units). **Amenities:** video library, hair dryers. *Some:* DVD players, irons. **Dining:** 7 am-10 & 5:30-9 pm, cocktails, entertainment. **Pool(s):** heated outdoor. **Leisure Activities:** bicycles, hiking trails, playground, exercise room, basketball, horseshoes. **Guest Services:** gift shop, coin laundry. **Business Services:** PC. **Cards:** AX, DC, DS, MC, VI. **Free Special Amenities:** high-speed Internet.

SOME UNITS

🛏️ 🍴 🍸 🛋️ ⊗ ⊗ 🖥️ / (VCR) 🔌 📠 /
FEE   FEE

The following lodging was either not evaluated or did not meet AAA rating requirements but is listed for your information only.

THE LYNWOOD INN

Phone: 902/295-1995

[fyi]   Not evaluated. **Location:** Centre. 23 Shore Rd B0E 1B0. Facilities, services, and decor characterize a mid-range property.

--------- WHERE TO DINE ---------

BADDECK LOBSTER SUPPERS

Lunch: $6-$9   **Dinner:** $17-$28   Phone: 902/295-3307

◆◆◆ ◆◆◆
Seafood

Location: Centre. 17 Ross St B0E 1B0. **Hours:** Open 6/8-10/31; 11:30 am-1:30 & 4-9 pm. **Features:** A very informal, basic decor and a pleasant staff make this a relaxing all-you-can-eat dinner experience. Fresh mussels, a tasty chowder, homemade bread and dessert are included with the purchase of any main entree, such as lobster. Casual dress; cocktails. **Parking:** on-site. **Cards:** MC, VI.

BELL BUOY RESTAURANT & SUPPER

HOUSE *Menu on AAA.com*   **Lunch:** $7-$15   **Dinner:** $12-$33   Phone: 902/295-2581

(CAA)
◆◆◆
Seafood

Location: On Rt 205; centre. 536 Chebucto St B0E 1B0. **Hours:** Open 5/22-10/24; 4 pm-9 pm; from 11:30 am 7/1-10/24. **Reservations:** accepted. **Features:** A good selection of wine complements selections of seafood, steak and poultry. If you are a land and sea lover, the combination platters will satisfy any appetite. Most tables have a view of Baddeck Bay. Casual dress; cocktails. **Parking:** on-site. **Cards:** AX, DC, DS, MC, VI.

FLORA'S DINING ROOM

Dinner: $14-$28   Phone: 902/295-3500

◆◆◆
Canadian

Location: Trans-Canada Hwy 105, exit 8, 1 mi (1.6 km) e on Rt 205 (Shore Rd); in Inverary Resort. 368 Shore Rd B0E 1B0. **Hours:** Open 5/1-10/31; 6:30 am-10:30 & 5:30-9 pm. **Reservations:** suggested. **Features:** A delightful restaurant situated on the waterfront overlooking the harbour, they offer indoor and outdoor covered patio dining. The menu features fresh seafood, some meat entrees and great homemade desserts. Casual dress; cocktails. **Parking:** on-site. **Cards:** AX, DC, DS, MC, VI.

🍸

GISELE'S DINING ROOM

Dinner: $20-$28   Phone: 902/295-2849

◆◆◆
Canadian

Location: Trans-Canada Hwy 105, exit 8, 1 mi (1.6 km) e; in Auberge Gisele's Country Inn. 387 Shore Rd B0E 1B0. **Hours:** Open 5/15-10/31; 7:30 am-9:30 & 6-9 pm. **Reservations:** accepted. **Features:** Fine dining in a relaxed atmosphere is what guests can expect. The menu features fresh local seafood, prime cuts of meat and a nice selection of homemade desserts. Casual dress; cocktails. **Parking:** on-site. **Cards:** AX, DC, MC, VI.

YELLOW CELLO CAFE

Lunch: $7-$12   **Dinner:** $9-$18   Phone: 902/295-2303

◆◆
Italian

Location: Centre. 525 Chebucto St B0E 1B0. **Hours:** Open 5/1-10/31; 8 am-11 pm. **Features:** A very popular gathering spot for locals and tourists alike. Fine selection of tasty homemade pizza, pasta and seafood entrees. Casual dress; cocktails. **Parking:** on-site. **Cards:** AX, MC, VI.

🎷

BAYFIELD

--------- WHERE TO STAY ---------

SEA'SCAPE COTTAGES

Phone: (902)386-2825

◆◆ ◆◆◆	6/21-10/31	1P: $90-$115	2P: $90-$115	XP: $10	D16
	5/1-6/20	1P: $85-$100	2P: $85-$100	XP: $10	D16

Cottage   **Location:** Trans-Canada Hwy 104, exit 36, 3.1 mi (5.1 km) n on Sunrise Trail, then 1 mi (1.6 km) w. Located in a quiet secluded area. Bayfield Antigonish Civil 6 B0H 1R0 (PO Box 94, HEATHERTON). **Facility:** 8 units. 1 cabin and 7 cottages. 1 story, exterior corridors. *Bath:* shower only. **Parking:** on-site. **Terms:** open 5/1-10/31, office hours 7 am-9 pm, 21 day cancellation notice-fee imposed, small pets only (with prior approval). **Amenities:** *Some:* DVD players. **Leisure Activities:** fishing, hiking trails. *Fee:* boats, canoes. **Guest Services:** coin laundry. **Cards:** MC, VI.

SOME UNITS

(ASK) 🛏️ ⊗ 🎷 📺 🔔 🔌 📠 🖥️ / ⊗ (VCR) /

BELLE COTE

--------- WHERE TO STAY ---------

The following lodging was either not evaluated or did not meet AAA rating requirements but is listed for your information only.

ISLAND SUNSET RESORT & SPA

Phone: 902/235-2669

[fyi]   Not evaluated. **Location:** Centre; on Cabot Trail. 19 Beach Cove Ln B0E 1C0 (PO Box 27, MARGAREE HARBOUR, B0E 2B0). Facilities, services, and decor characterize a mid-range property.

BIG POND

———— WHERE TO DINE ————

RITA'S TEA ROOM
▼▼▼▼
Canadian
Lunch: $6-$11　　**Dinner:** $9-$16　　**Phone:** 902/828-2667
Location: Centre. Rt 4 B1J 1Z3. **Hours:** Open 6/15-10/31; 10 am-6 pm. **Features:** Run by singer/songwriter Rita MacNeil, the spacious tea room occupies a former one-room schoolhouse. Casual dress; beer & wine only. **Parking:** on-site. **Cards:** AX, CB, DC, DS, MC, VI.

BLACK POINT

———— WHERE TO STAY ————

GRAND VIEW MOTEL AND COTTAGES
▼
Motel
Phone: 902/857-9776
Property failed to provide current rates
Location: Hwy 103, exit 5 westbound, 1.2 mi (2 km) s to Rt 3, then 9 mi (15 km) w; exit 6 eastbound to Rt 3, then 5.4 mi (9 km) e. 8414 Hwy 3 B0J 1B0. Fax: 902/857-9776. **Facility:** 13 units. 10 one-bedroom standard units, some with efficiencies. 3 cottages. 1 story, exterior corridors. *Bath:* combo or shower only. **Parking:** on-site.
Terms: open 5/1-11/1, office hours 9 am-10 pm, pets (with prior approval).
SOME UNITS

BRIDGETOWN pop. 1,035

———— WHERE TO STAY ————

BRIDGETOWN MOTOR INN
▼▼▼▼ ▼▼▼▼
Small-scale Hotel
Phone: 902/665-4403

7/1-9/18	1P: $75	2P: $82	XP: $7　F16
9/19-4/30	1P: $69	2P: $75	XP: $5　F16
9/15-6/30	1P: $67	2P: $72	XP: $5　F16

Location: Hwy 101, exit 20, 0.6 mi (1 km) w on Rt 1. 396 Granville St B0S 1C0 (PO Box 453). Fax: 902/665-4091.
Facility: 28 one-bedroom standard units. 2 stories (no elevator), exterior corridors. **Parking:** on-site, winter plug-ins. **Terms:** small pets only. **Pool(s):** heated outdoor. **Leisure Activities:** playground. **Guest Services:** coin laundry. **Business Services:** meeting rooms. **Cards:** AX, MC, VI.
SOME UNITS

BRIDGEWATER pop. 7,621

———— WHERE TO STAY ————

AUBERGE WANDLYN INN　*Book at AAA.com*
▼▼▼▼ ▼▼▼▼
Small-scale Hotel
Phone: (902)543-7131

5/1-9/14 & 1/1-4/30	1P: $100-$120	2P: $110-$130	XP: $10　F18
9/15-12/31	1P: $83-$96	2P: $93-$100	XP: $10　F18

Location: Hwy 103, exit 12, 1.1 mi (1.7 km) s on Rt 10. 50 North St B4V 2V6. Fax: 902/543-7170. **Facility:** 70 units. 68 one-bedroom standard units. 2 one-bedroom suites ($185-$200), some with whirlpools. 2 stories (no elevator), interior corridors. **Parking:** on-site. **Terms:** [BP] & [CP] meal plans available, package plans, pets (in designated units). **Amenities:** voice mail, hair dryers. *Some:* high-speed Internet. **Dining:** The Lighthouse Dining Room, see separate listing. **Pool(s):** heated indoor. **Guest Services:** coin laundry, wireless Internet. **Business Services:** conference facilities, PC. **Cards:** AX, DC, MC, VI.
SOME UNITS

BRIDGEWATER BOGAN VILLA INN
▼▼▼▼ ▼▼▼▼
Small-scale Hotel
Phone: (902)543-8171

6/1-9/30	1P: $85-$109	2P: $95-$119	XP: $10　F16
10/1-4/30	1P: $65-$85	2P: $75-$95	XP: $10　F16
5/1-5/31	1P: $65-$75	2P: $75-$85	XP: $10　F16

Location: Hwy 103, exit 13, just e. 35 High St B4V 1V8. Fax: 902/543-7113. **Facility:** 42 one-bedroom standard units. 2 stories (no elevator), interior corridors. **Parking:** on-site. **Terms:** weekly rates available, package plans. **Amenities:** voice mail. **Dining:** High Street Cafe, see separate listing. **Pool(s):** heated indoor. **Leisure Activities:** sauna, whirlpool. **Business Services:** meeting rooms. **Cards:** AX, DS, MC, VI.
SOME UNITS

COMFORT INN　*Book great rates at AAA.com*
▼▼▼▼ ▼▼
Small-scale Hotel
Phone: (902)543-1498

7/1-10/31 [ECP]	1P: $120-$145	2P: $130-$155	XP: $10　F18
5/1-6/30 & 11/1-4/30 [ECP]	1P: $80-$100	2P: $90-$110	XP: $10　F18

Location: Hwy 103, exit 12, 1.1 mi (1.7 km) s on Rt 10. 49 North St B4V 2V7. Fax: 902/543-9257. **Facility:** 60 one-bedroom standard units. 2 stories (no elevator), interior corridors. **Parking:** on-site. **Terms:** pets (ground floor units). **Amenities:** irons, hair dryers. **Guest Services:** wireless Internet. **Business Services:** meeting rooms, PC. **Cards:** AX, DC, DS, JC, MC, VI. *(See color ad card insert)*
SOME UNITS

———— WHERE TO DINE ————

HIGH STREET CAFE
▼▼▼▼ ▼▼
Canadian
Lunch: $6-$11　　**Dinner:** $9-$18　　**Phone:** 902/543-8171
Location: Hwy 103, exit 13, just e; in Bridgewater Bogan Villa Inn. 35 High St B4V 1V8. **Hours:** 7 am-9 pm. **Reservations:** accepted. **Features:** The family-run restaurant's full menu focuses on fresh seafood and steak. Diners have a choice of either booth or table seating in the casual pub-style dining space. Smoking is permitted after 9 pm. Casual dress; cocktails. **Parking:** on-site. **Cards:** AX, DC, MC, VI.

KO'S RESTAURANT **Lunch:** $6-$12 **Dinner:** $8-$15 **Phone:** 902/543-6080

Chinese

Location: Corner of King and Dufferin sts; centre. 434 King St B4V 1B2. **Hours:** 11:30 am-10 pm, Thurs-11 pm, Fri & Sat-midnight, Sun 11 am-10 pm. **Closed:** 12/25. **Reservations:** accepted. **Features:** A popular spot for a casual meal, the restaurant presents a menu of widely varied traditional entrees, including combination plates. Canadian dishes are another option. Casual dress; cocktails. **Parking:** street. **Cards:** AX, MC, VI.

THE LIGHTHOUSE DINING ROOM **Lunch:** $6-$10 **Dinner:** $10-$19 **Phone:** 902/543-7131

Canadian

Location: Hwy 103, exit 12, 1.1 mi (1.7 km) s on Rt 10; in Auberge Wandlyn Inn. 50 North St B4V 2V6. **Hours:** 7 am-2 & 5-9 pm. **Closed:** 12/25. **Reservations:** accepted. **Features:** No water views are available from the landlocked restaurant, but guests will find friendly, casual service and a nice selection of fresh seafood, steaks and comfort foods. Casual dress; cocktails. **Parking:** on-site. **Cards:** AX, DC, MC, VI.

TWO CHEF'S **Lunch:** $6-$11 **Dinner:** $8-$16 **Phone:** 902/543-9661

Canadian

Location: Centre; in Eastside Plaza. 28 Davison Dr B4V 3A2. **Hours:** 11 am-9 pm. **Closed:** 1/1, 12/25, 12/26. **Reservations:** suggested. **Features:** The restaurant entices guests with its informal atmosphere, friendly service and diverse menu, which includes several East Indian dishes. Casual dress; cocktails. **Parking:** on-site. **Cards:** AX, DC, MC, VI.

BUCKLAW

———— **WHERE TO STAY** ————

CASTLE MOFFETT **Phone:** (902)756-9070

CAA SAVE

5/15-10/15 1P: $250-$1000 2P: $250-$1000

Country Inn

Location: On Trans-Canada Hwy 105; 11.8 mi (19 km) w of Baddeck. 11980 Trans-Canada Hwy 105 B0E 1B0 (PO Box 678, WHYCOCOMAGH, B0E 3M0). Fax: 902/756-3399. **Facility:** A new world castle, the property spans a brook and overlooks Bras d'Or Lakes; spacious rooms have gas fireplaces, four-poster beds and lovely views. Smoke free premises. 10 units. 7 one-bedroom standard units with whirlpools. 3 one-bedroom suites ($400-$1000) with whirlpools. 3 stories (no elevator), interior corridors. **Parking:** on-site. **Terms:** open 5/15-10/15, office hours 6:30 am-11:30 pm, 14 day cancellation notice-fee imposed, package plans. **Amenities:** video library, CD players, irons, hair dryers. *Some:* DVD players. **Dining:** 7 pm seating; by reservation for guests, cocktails. **Leisure Activities:** sauna, hiking trails, exercise room. *Fee:* massage. **Guest Services:** valet laundry, wireless Internet. **Business Services:** PC. **Cards:** MC, VI. **Free Special Amenities:** newspaper and preferred room (subject to availability with advance reservations).** (See color ad p 302)**

SOME UNITS

CALEDONIA

———— **WHERE TO STAY** ————

———— *The following lodging was either not evaluated or did not meet AAA rating requirements but is listed for your information only.* ————

MERSEY RIVER CHALETS **Phone:** 902/682-2443

fyi

Not evaluated. **Location:** 1.2 mi (1.8 km) e on gravel entry road, 0.3 mi (0.5 km) n of Kejimkujik National Park; centre on Rt 8. (General Delivery, B0T 1B0). Facilities, services, and decor characterize a mid-range property.

CANNING pop. 811

———— **WHERE TO STAY** ————

THE FARMHOUSE INN **Phone:** 902/582-7900

5/1-10/31 1P: $110-$160 2P: $110-$160 XP: $15

11/1-4/30 1P: $79-$150 2P: $79-$150 XP: $15

Historic Bed & Breakfast

Location: Hwy 101, exit 11, follow Canning signs, then 5 mi (8 km) n on Rt 358. 9757 Main St B0P 1H0 (PO Box 38). **Facility:** With a history that dates to the 1850s, this converted house combines a rich heritage with modern amenities such as whirlpool tubs. Smoke free premises. 6 one-bedroom standard units, some with whirlpools. 2 stories (no elevator), interior/exterior corridors. *Bath:* combo or shower only. **Parking:** on-site. **Terms:** office hours 8 am-11 pm, cancellation fee imposed, package plans. **Amenities:** hair dryers. *Some:* DVD players. **Cards:** AX, MC, VI.

SOME UNITS

CENTREVILLE

———— **WHERE TO DINE** ————

BETWEEN THE BUSHES **Lunch:** $7-$14 **Dinner:** $14-$25 **Phone:** 902/582-3648

Canadian

Location: Hwy 101, exit 12, 6 mi (10 km) n on Middle Dyke Rd, follow signs. 1225 Middle Dyke Rd B0P 1J0. **Hours:** Open 5/1-12/18 & 4/15-4/30; 11:30 am-2:30 & 5-8 pm. **Closed:** Mon. **Reservations:** accepted. **Features:** In the middle of a pick-your-own blueberry field, the restaurant is casual at lunch and more of a fine-dining spot in the evening. The chefs focus on farm-fresh produce, meats and seafood in nicely presented entrees. Desserts and breads are homemade. Casual dress; cocktails. **Parking:** on-site. **Cards:** AX, DC, MC, VI.

CHARLOS COVE

——— WHERE TO STAY ———

SEAWIND LANDING COUNTRY INN   **Phone:** (902)525-2108
▼▼▼▼▼   6/1-10/15   1P: $85-$179   2P: $95-$189   XP: $20
Country Inn   **Location:** Rt 316, 0.5 mi (0.8 km) se on gravel road. Located in a quiet rural setting. 157 Wharf Rd B0H 1T0 (RR 2, LARRYS RIVER). Fax: 902/525-2108. **Facility:** In a rural area overlooking the Atlantic Ocean, the inn offers pleasant guest rooms in a main inn and a seaside annex. 14 one-bedroom standard units, some with whirlpools. 2 stories (no elevator), interior/exterior corridors. **Parking:** on-site. **Terms:** open 6/1-10/15, office hours 7 am-10 pm, 7 day cancellation notice-fee imposed, [AP] & [MAP] meal plans available. **Amenities:** video library (fee), hair dryers. *Some:* DVD players, CD players. **Dining:** restaurant, see separate listing. **Leisure Activities:** boating, canoeing, bicycles. **Guest Services:** coin laundry. **Cards:** AX, MC, VI.

SOME UNITS
[ASK] [S🍴] [†1] [Y] [⊠] [⊠] [🏃] / [🏋] [📺] /

——— WHERE TO DINE ———

SEAWIND LANDING COUNTRY INN DINING ROOM   **Dinner:** $22-$29   **Phone:** 902/525-2108
▼▼▼▼▼   **Location:** Rt 316, 0.5 mi (0.8 km) se on gravel road; in Seawind Landing Country Inn. 157 Wharf Rd B0H 1T0.
Regional   **Hours:** Open 5/15-10/15; 8 am-9:30 & 6:30-8 pm. **Reservations:** required. **Features:** Reservations are
Canadian   required at the elegant country inn, which features a good selection of "country gourmet" food. The menu changes nightly, and guests are asked to make their dinner selection when they reserve. The chef relies heavily on regional ingredients and infuses dishes with a French flair. Choices might include scallops drenched in vermouth and wild blueberry cake for dessert. Whatever the menu, the food is delicious and lovely, and the service is fine. Casual dress; cocktails. **Parking:** on-site. **Cards:** AX, MC, VI.

[Y] [🏋]

CHESTER pop. 10,781

——— WHERE TO STAY ———

MECKLENBURGH INN   **Phone:** 902-275-4638
▼▼▼   5/1-1/1 [BP]   1P: $85-$135   2P: $85-$135   XP: $20
Historic Bed   **Location:** Centre. 78 Queen St B0J 1J0 (PO Box 350). **Facility:** This converted house, built in 1890, is in the
& Breakfast   heart of town. Smoke free premises. 4 one-bedroom standard units. 2 stories (no elevator), interior corridors. *Bath:* combo or shower only. **Parking:** on-site. **Terms:** open 5/1-1/1, office hours 8 am-10 pm, 7 day cancellation notice. **Amenities:** hair dryers. **Guest Services:** TV in common area, wireless Internet.
Cards: AX, MC, VI.

[††] [⊠] [🏋] [📺] [☎]

WINDJAMMER MOTEL   **Phone:** 902-275-3567
▼▼   7/1-9/15   1P: $60-$75   2P: $65-$85   XP: $10   F12
5/1-6/30 & 9/16-4/30   1P: $55-$65   2P: $65-$75   XP: $10   F12
Motel   **Location:** 0.6 mi (1 km) w. 4070 Rt 3 B0J 1J0 (PO Box 240). **Facility:** 18 one-bedroom standard units. 2 stories, exterior corridors. **Parking:** on-site, winter plug-ins. **Terms:** office hours 7 am-10 pm, small pets only.
Amenities: video library, DVD players. **Dining:** restaurant, see separate listing. **Cards:** CB, DC, DS, MC, VI.

SOME UNITS
[ASK] [S🍴] [🛏] [†1] / [⊠] [🏋] [VCR] [🔌] [🖥] /

——— WHERE TO DINE ———

ROPE LOFT DINING ROOM   **Lunch:** $7-$15   **Dinner:** $15-$20   **Phone:** 902-275-3430
▼▼▼ ▼▼▼   **Location:** Off Rt 3; on Front Harbour. 36 Water St B0J 1J0. **Hours:** Open 5/1-10/31; 11:30 am-10 pm, Sat & Sun
Seafood   from 11 am; Saturday & Sunday brunch. **Reservations:** accepted. **Features:** This rustic sea shanty has enjoyed the same splendid location overlooking Chester Harbor since 1816. Offering a fine selection of fresh local seafood with an emphasis on regional creations, the menu includes such favorites as chowder and fish cakes. Casual dress; cocktails. **Parking:** street. **Cards:** AX, DC, MC, VI. **Historic**

[Y] [🏋]

WINDJAMMER RESTAURANT   **Lunch:** $7-$11   **Dinner:** $8-$16   **Phone:** 902-275-3714
▼▼▼ ▼▼▼   **Location:** 0.6 mi (1 km) w; adjacent to Windjammer Motel. Rt 3 B0J 1J0. **Hours:** Open 5/1-12/23 & 3/1-4/30; 11
Seafood   am-9 pm; hours vary off season. **Reservations:** accepted. **Features:** Daily fresh catches and grill specials are popular at the friendly restaurant, which is a local favorite for tasty seafood. Many windows bring light into the dining room, which is decorated with flowers, candles and the work of local artists. A must try is the fish chowder. Casual dress; cocktails. **Parking:** on-site. **Cards:** AX, DC, MC, VI.

CHESTER BASIN

——— WHERE TO STAY ———

THE SWORD & ANCHOR BED & BREAKFAST   **Phone:** 902-275-2478
▼▼ ▼▼   5/1-10/31   1P: $95-$250   2P: $95-$250   XP: $10   F4
Historic Bed   **Location:** Centre. 5306 Hwy 3 B0J 1K0. Fax: 902/275-5116. **Facility:** The large front porch at this former sea
& Breakfast   captain's home overlooks the bay. 9 units. 8 one-bedroom standard units. 1 one-bedroom suite with kitchen and whirlpool. 2 stories (no elevator), interior corridors. **Parking:** on-site. **Terms:** open 5/1-10/31, 7 day cancellation notice. **Guest Services:** TV in common area. **Cards:** MC, VI.

SOME UNITS
[⊠] [🏋] [📺] [☎] / [🔌] [🖥] /

——— WHERE TO DINE ———

SEASIDE SHANTY RESTAURANT   **Lunch:** $6-$12   **Dinner:** $11-$20   **Phone:** 902/275-2246
◆◆◆ ◆◆◆   **Location:** Centre; at Marina. 5317 Rt 3 B0J 1J0. **Hours:** Open 5/1-10/28; 11:30 am-10 pm; to 9 pm off season.
Canadian   **Features:** Its wise to make a reservation to dine at this restaurant in peak season. The popular spot offers
fine dining with a relaxed atmosphere. Entrees are creatively presented and prepared to order, from fine
cuts of meat to salmon, scallops and lobster, there is likely something to tempt anyone's palate. Casual
dress; cocktails. **Parking:** on-site. **Cards:** MC, VI.   🅺

CHETICAMP pop. 1,000

——— WHERE TO STAY ———

CABOT TRAIL SEA & GOLF CHALETS   **Phone:** (902)224-1777
◆◆◆ ◆◆◆   6/16-10/20   1P: $139-$159   2P: $149-$169   XP: $15   F6
5/18-6/15   1P: $119-$139   2P: $129-$149   XP: $15   F6
Cottage   **Location:** Centre. 71 Fraser Doucet Ln B0E 1H0 (PO Box 324). Fax: 902/224-1999. **Facility:** Smoke free
premises. 13 cottages, some with whirlpools. 1 story, exterior corridors. **Parking:** on-site. **Terms:** open 5/18-
10/20, office hours 8:30 am-9 pm, 7 day cancellation notice-fee imposed, small pets only ($15 extra charge). **Leisure
Activities:** basketball, horseshoes, volleyball. **Cards:** AX, DC, MC, VI.
                                                                                      SOME UNITS
(ASK) 🐕 ⊠ ⊠ 🅩 🖥 🖳 🖵 / 🅺 /
                                                            FEE

LAURIE'S MOTOR INN   **Phone:** (902)224-2400
(CAA) (SAVE)   6/16-10/12   1P: $95-$129   2P: $99-$149   XP: $10   F12
5/1-6/15, 10/13-10/31 & 4/1-4/30   1P: $75-$95   2P: $80-$115   XP: $10   F12
◆◆◆ ◆◆◆   **Location:** Centre. 15456 Laurie Rd B0E 1H0 (PO Box 1). Fax: 902/224-2069. **Facility:** 53 one-bedroom
standard units, some with whirlpools. 6 one-bedroom suites ($159-$299), some with kitchens and/or
Small-scale Hotel   whirlpools. 2 vacation homes ($160-$190). 2 stories (no elevator), interior/exterior corridors. **Parking:** on-
site. **Terms:** open 5/1-10/31 & 4/1-4/30, office hours 6:30 am-11 pm, package plans. **Amenities:** hair
dryers. **Dining:** Laurie's Dining Room, see separate listing. **Leisure Activities:** playground. **Fee:** whale & nature cruises. **Guest
Services:** coin laundry. **Business Services:** meeting rooms. **Cards:** MC, VI.
                                                                            SOME UNITS
🆂🅳 🐕 🍽 🛋 🎥 / ⊠ 🅺 (VCR) 🖥 🖳 /

PARKVIEW MOTEL, DINING ROOM & LOUNGE   **Phone:** 902/224-3232
(CAA) (SAVE)   6/16-9/15   1P: $85-$109   2P: $89-$109   XP: $10   F10
9/16-10/15   1P: $75-$109   2P: $79-$109   XP: $10   F10
◆◆◆   5/1-6/15   1P: $75-$99   2P: $79-$109   XP: $10   F10
Motel   **Location:** 4.5 mi (7.2 km) n at West Gate Cape Breton Highlands National Park. Located in a quiet secluded area.
16546 Cabot Tr B0E 1H0 (PO Box 117). Fax: 902/224-2596. **Facility:** Smoke free premises. 17 one-bedroom
standard units. 1 story, exterior corridors. **Parking:** on-site. **Terms:** open 5/1-10/25, office hours 7:30 am-
midnight, package plans, small pets only (in designated units, with prior approval). **Dining:** 7:30 am-10:30 & 5-10 pm, cocktails.
Leisure Activities: Fee: fly fishing guide. **Cards:** AX, MC, VI.
                                                                            SOME UNITS
🐕 🍽 🛋 ⊠ 🎥 🅩 / 🖥 🖳 🖵 /

——— WHERE TO DINE ———

LAURIE'S DINING ROOM   **Dinner:** $13-$25   **Phone:** 902/224-2400
◆◆◆ ◆◆◆   **Location:** Centre; in Laurie's Motor Inn. 15456 Laurie Rd B0E 1H0. **Hours:** Open 6/1-10/26; 7 am-10 & 5:30-8 pm.
Canadian   **Reservations:** accepted. **Features:** In business since 1938, the restaurant focuses on fresh seafood,
particularly lobster and chowder. The menu also lists meat entrees, baked bread and fresh pastry. The
pleasant, spacious dining room and outdoor patio are comfortable. Casual dress; cocktails. **Parking:** on-
site. **Cards:** MC, VI.   🛋

LE GABRIEL RESTAURANT   **Lunch:** $6-$12   **Dinner:** $10-$25   **Phone:** 902/224-3685
(CAA)   **Location:** Centre. 15424 Cabot Tr B0E 1H0. **Hours:** Open 5/1-10/26; 11 am-10 pm; to 9 pm off season.
Reservations: accepted. **Features:** The relaxing restaurant favors traditional preparations of primarily
◆◆◆ ◆◆◆   seafood—such as shellfish noodle bake and seafood kabobs. An interesting lighthouse facade adds to the
nautical charm. Set aside room for a delicious slice of butterscotch pie. Casual dress; cocktails. **Parking:**
Canadian   on-site. **Cards:** AX, DC, MC, VI.

CHURCH POINT

——— WHERE TO STAY ———

MANOIR SAMSON   **Phone:** (902)769-2526
◆◆◆ ◆◆◆   5/1-8/31 [CP]   1P: $85-$125   2P: $85-$125   XP: $10   F
Location: On Hwy 1; centre. 1768 Rt 1 B0W 1M0 (Box 89). Fax: 902/769-2560. **Facility:** 13 units. 12 one-
Motel   bedroom standard units. 1 one-bedroom suite with kitchen. 2 stories (no elevator), exterior corridors.
Parking: on-site. **Terms:** open 5/1-8/31, cancellation fee imposed, small pets only. **Amenities:** hair dryers.
Cards: AX, MC, VI.
(ASK) 🆂🅳 🐕 ⊠ 🅺 🖥 🖳

——— *The following lodging was either not evaluated or did not* ———
meet AAA rating requirements but is listed for your information only.

BAIE STE-MARIE OCEAN FRONT COTTAGES   **Phone:** 902/769-0797
[fyi]   Did not meet all AAA rating requirements for locking devices in some guest rooms at time of last evaluation
on 02/02/2006. **Location:** Oceanfront. Hwy 101, exit 28, follow signs; 19 mi (30 km) sw of Digby. Riverside Rd B0W
Cottage   1M0 (PO Box 142). Facilities, services, and decor characterize a mid-range property.

DARTMOUTH pop. 65,600 (See map and index starting on p. 313)

------ WHERE TO STAY ------

COMFORT INN
Book great rates at AAA.com

Phone: (902)463-9900 30

CAA SAVE

Small-scale Hotel

6/16-10/31	1P: $145-$155	2P: $155-$165	XP: $10	F18
5/1-6/15 & 11/1-4/30	1P: $114-$119	2P: $129-$134	XP: $10	F18

Location: Hwy 111, exit Shannon Park. Located in a commercial area, quieter units in back. 456 Windmill Rd B3A 1J7. Fax: 902/466-2080. **Facility:** 80 one-bedroom standard units. 2 stories (no elevator), interior corridors. **Parking:** on-site. **Terms:** small pets only (in smoking units). **Amenities:** high-speed Internet, voice mail, irons, hair dryers. **Cards:** AX, CB, DC, DS, JC, MC, VI. *(See color ad card insert)*

SOME UNITS

COUNTRY INN & SUITES BY CARLSON
Book great rates at AAA.com

Phone: (902)465-4000 29

Small-scale Hotel

7/1-10/13 [CP]	1P: $115-$160	2P: $115-$170	XP: $10	F18
3/16-4/30 [CP]	1P: $110-$155	2P: $110-$165	XP: $10	F18
5/1-6/30 & 10/14-3/15 [CP]	1P: $105-$150	2P: $105-$160	XP: $10	F18

Location: Hwy 111, exit Princess Margaret Blvd. 101 Yorkshire Ave Ext B2Y 3Y2. Fax: 902/465-6006. **Facility:** 77 units. 38 one-bedroom standard units. 39 one-bedroom suites. 3 stories, interior corridors. **Parking:** on-site. **Terms:** 2-5 night minimum stay - seasonal and/or weekends, package plans, pets ($50 deposit, $5 extra charge, in smoking units). **Amenities:** video library, voice mail, irons, hair dryers. **Guest Services:** valet and coin laundry, wireless Internet. **Cards:** AX, DC, DS, JC, MC, VI. *(See color ad on TourBookMark)*

SOME UNITS

FEE

FUTURE INNS DARTMOUTH
Book at AAA.com

Phone: (902)465-6555 28

Small-scale Hotel

5/1-10/31	1P: $139-$179	2P: $139-$179	XP: $10	F16
11/1-4/30	1P: $129-$169	2P: $129-$169	XP: $10	F16

Location: From Murray Mackay Bridge, 0.8 mi (1.2 km) n on Hwy 111, exit 3 (Burnside Dr). Located in a commercial area, quieter rooms in back. 20 Highfield Park Dr B3A 4S8. Fax: 902/469-0868. **Facility:** 144 units. 141 one-bedroom standard units. 3 one-bedroom suites ($169-$179), some with whirlpools. 2 stories, interior/exterior corridors. **Bath:** combo or shower only. **Parking:** on-site. **Terms:** cancellation fee imposed. **Amenities:** high-speed Internet, irons, hair dryers. **Dining:** Favorites Cuisine, see separate listing. **Leisure Activities:** limited exercise equipment. **Guest Services:** coin laundry. **Business Services:** meeting rooms, PC, fax. **Cards:** AX, DC, MC, VI.

SOME UNITS

HOLIDAY INN HALIFAX-HARBOURVIEW
Book great rates at AAA.com

Phone: (902)463-1100 32

CAA SAVE

Large-scale Hotel

5/1-10/31	1P: $129-$169	2P: $139-$179	XP: $20	F18
11/1-4/30	1P: $119-$149	2P: $129-$159	XP: $20	F18

Location: Adjacent to Angus L MacDonald Bridge. 99 Wyse Rd B3A 1L9. Fax: 902/464-1227. **Facility:** 196 units. 192 one-bedroom standard units. 4 one-bedroom suites, some with whirlpools. 7 stories, interior corridors. **Parking:** on-site. **Terms:** [BP] & [CP] meal plans available, package plans, pets ($25 fee, 1st floor units). **Amenities:** video games (fee), voice mail, irons, hair dryers. *Some:* high-speed Internet. **Dining:** 7 am-10 pm, cocktails. **Pool(s):** heated outdoor. **Leisure Activities:** sportsplex privileges, exercise room. **Guest Services:** gift shop, valet and coin laundry. **Business Services:** conference facilities, fax. **Cards:** AX, CB, DC, DS, JC, MC, VI.. *(See color ad card insert)*

SOME UNITS

FEE

PARK PLACE HOTEL & CONFERENCE CENTRE
RAMADA PLAZA
Book great rates at AAA.com

Phone: (902)468-8888 27

CAA SAVE

Large-scale Hotel

7/1-10/31	1P: $152	2P: $152	XP: $20	F18
5/1-6/30	1P: $137	2P: $137	XP: $20	F18
1/1-4/30	1P: $123	2P: $123	XP: $20	F18
11/1-12/31	1P: $115	2P: $115	XP: $20	F18

Location: From Murray Mackay Bridge, 0.7 mi (1.2 km) n on Hwy 111, exit 3 (Burnside Dr). Located in Park Place Centre. 240 Brownlow Ave B3B 1X6. Fax: 902/468-8765. **Facility:** 178 units. 153 one-bedroom standard units. 25 one-bedroom suites ($179-$500), some with whirlpools. 5 stories, interior corridors. **Parking:** on-site. **Terms:** package plans, small pets only ($50 deposit, 1st floor units). **Amenities:** video games (fee), voice mail, irons, hair dryers. *Some:* high-speed Internet, dual phone lines. **Dining:** The Peppermill Restaurant, see separate listing. **Pool(s):** heated indoor, wading. **Leisure Activities:** sauna, whirlpool, waterslide, exercise room. **Guest Services:** gift shop, valet laundry, area transportation-downtown, wireless Internet. **Business Services:** conference facilities, business center. **Cards:** AX, DS, MC, VI. **Free Special Amenities:** local telephone calls and high-speed Internet.

SOME UNITS

FEE

QUALITY INN HALIFAX/DARTMOUTH
Book great rates at AAA.com

Phone: (902)469-5850 31

CAA SAVE

Small-scale Hotel

6/16-10/31	1P: $80-$180	2P: $80-$180	XP: $10	F17
5/1-6/15	1P: $80-$150	2P: $80-$150	XP: $10	F17
11/1-4/30	1P: $80-$100	2P: $80-$100	XP: $10	F17

Location: Hwy 111, exit 6A, 1 blk s. 313 Prince Albert Rd B2Y 1N3. Fax: 902/469-5859. **Facility:** 54 one-bedroom standard units. 4 stories, interior corridors. **Parking:** on-site. **Terms:** small pets only (in smoking units). **Amenities:** video library (fee), DVD players, voice mail, irons, hair dryers. *Some:* dual phone lines. **Dining:** Roccos Italian Restaurant, see separate listing. **Leisure Activities:** exercise room. **Guest Services:** valet laundry, wireless Internet. **Business Services:** meeting rooms. **Cards:** AX, DC, DS, MC, VI. **Free Special Amenities:** newspaper and high-speed Internet. *(See color ad card insert)*

SOME UNITS

FEE

(See map and index starting on p. 313)

──────── *The following lodging was either not evaluated or did not* ────────
meet AAA rating requirements but is listed for your information only.

HOWARD JOHNSON MARANOVA HOTEL & SUITES   Phone: 902/463-9520

[fyi]   Did not meet all AAA rating requirements for locking devices in some guest rooms at time of last evaluation
on 02/21/2006. **Location:** Corner of King and Queen sts; centre of downtown. 65 King St B2Y 1N3. Facilities,
Small-scale Hotel services, and decor characterize a mid-range property.

──────── **WHERE TO DINE** ────────

CORA'S BREAKFAST & LUNCH   **Lunch:** $6-$10   Phone: 902/433-0079
Location: Just w of Carver St. 644 Portland Centre B2W 6C4. **Hours:** 6 am-3 pm, Sun from 7 am. Closed: 12/25.
Reservations: accepted. **Features:** Although this place specializes in breakfast, it offers a varied daytime
menu that includes bacon, eggs, sausages, crepes, grilled cheese, sandwiches, freshly prepared quiches,
Canadian   salads, fruit platters and freshly squeezed juices. The family-friendly dining room is casual and modern.
Casual dress. **Parking:** on-site. **Cards:** AX, DC, MC, VI.

FAN'S RESTAURANT   **Lunch:** $6-$11   **Dinner:** $9-$15   Phone: 902/469-9165   33
Location: Hwy 111, exit Shannon Park; across from Comfort Inn. 451 Windmill Rd B3A 1J9. **Hours:** 11 am-2 & 5-10
pm, Sat & Sun from 4:30 pm. Closed: 12/25. **Features:** Well-prepared Northern Chinese cuisine includes
Chinese   such dishes as ginger beef, salt and pepper squid and sweet and sour chicken. The dessert menu offers
candied bananas or apples and flavorful mango pudding. Casual dress; cocktails. **Parking:** on-site.
Cards: AX, DC, MC, VI.

FAVORITES CUISINE   **Lunch:** $7-$15   **Dinner:** $9-$17   Phone: 902/466-4001   32
Location: From Murray Mackay Bridge, 0.8 mi (1.2 km) n on Hwy 111, exit 3 (Burnside Dr); in Future Inns Dartmouth.
20 Highfield Dr B3A 4S8. **Hours:** 6:30 am-10:30 pm, Sat & Sun from 7:30 am. Closed: 12/25, 12/26.
Canadian   **Features:** The atmosphere is casual and upbeat in the open, airy restaurant, a favorite gathering spot for
families. Large-sized portions of such entrees as fajitas and filet mignon are tasty and filling. Chocolate
lovers' mouths water for the brownie-bottom pie. Casual dress; cocktails. **Parking:** on-site. **Cards:** AX, DC, MC, VI.   Ⓨ

JUNGLE JIM'S RESTAURANT   **Lunch:** $7-$11   **Dinner:** $8-$20   Phone: 902/435-4414
Location: At Portland St; in Staples Plaza. 114 Woodlawn Rd B2W 2S7. **Hours:** 11 am-10 pm, Thurs-Sat to 11 pm.
Closed: 12/25, 12/26. **Reservations:** accepted. **Features:** Guests can step into a tropical theme at the
Canadian   casual eatery, which employs a friendly staff and nurtures a bustling atmosphere. The menu lines up a wide
variety of comfort foods, salads, chicken, beef, seafood and hot wings, all served in ample, flavorful
portions. Casual dress; cocktails. **Parking:** on-site. **Cards:** AX, DC, MC, VI.

LA PERLA DINING ROOM   **Lunch:** $10-$15   **Dinner:** $15-$25   Phone: 902/469-3241   35
Location: Centre; opposite ferry terminal. 73 Alderney Dr B2Y 2N7. **Hours:** 11:30 am-9:30 pm, Sat from 5 pm,
Sun 5 pm-8 pm. Closed: 7/1, 8/6, 12/25. **Reservations:** accepted. **Features:** The ambience is cozy is the
Italian   sophisticated dining room, where opera music plays in the background and elegant table settings are
spaced amid subtle illumination. The menu centers on well-prepared Northern Italian selections of pasta,
veal and seafood. Casual dress; cocktails. **Parking:** on-site (fee). **Cards:** AX, MC, VI.   Ⓨ

MACASKILL'S   **Lunch:** $11-$16   **Dinner:** $17-$25   Phone: 902/466-3100   36
Location: In ferry terminal; Alderney Dr at Portland St. 88 Alderney Dr B2Y 4J2. **Hours:** 11:30 am-2 & 5-10 pm, Sat
& Sun from 5 pm. Closed: 1/1, 12/25, 12/26; also Sun 10/11-5/9. **Reservations:** accepted.
Canadian   **Features:** Several dining areas, as well as the breezy patio, overlook the lovely harbor and city. Menu
selections include thoughtful preparations of local seafood and meat. Servers are knowledgeable and
friendly. Casual dress; cocktails. **Parking:** on-site (fee). **Cards:** AX, DC, MC, VI.   Ⓨ

THE PEPPERMILL RESTAURANT   *Menu on AAA.com*   **Lunch:** $7-$13 **Dinner:** $10-$20 **Phone:** 902/468-8888   31
Location: From Murray Mackay Bridge, 0.7 mi (1.2 km) n on Hwy 111, exit 3 (Burnside Dr); in Park Place Hotel &
Conference Centre Ramada Plaza. 240 Brownlow Ave B3B 1X6. **Hours:** 6:30 am-10 pm.
Reservations: accepted. **Features:** The attractive, spacious restaurant prepares a wide variety of entrees,
Canadian   including steaks, seafood and pasta dishes. The splendid lunch buffet is set up weekdays. A "Pizza Hut
Express" menu is available. Casual dress; cocktails. **Parking:** on-site. **Cards:** AX, DC, MC, VI.   Ⓨ

ROCCOS ITALIAN RESTAURANT   **Lunch:** $8-$15   **Dinner:** $14-$21   Phone: 902/461-0211   34
Location: Hwy 111, exit 6A, 1 blk s; in Quality Inn Halifax/Dartmouth. 313 Prince Albert Rd B2Y 1N3. **Hours:** 7-11 am,
11:30-2:30 & 5-10 pm, Sat 8 am-11 & 5-10 pm, Sun 8 am-11 & 5-9 pm. Closed: 1/1, 12/25.
Italian   **Reservations:** suggested. **Features:** Nicely decorated in Southern Italian accents, the restaurant is a
relaxing spot for fine dining. Creative specialties include fresh pan-fried haddock with lemon juice and
tortellini in a creamy tomato-pesto sauce. Dressy casual; cocktails. **Parking:** on-site. **Cards:** AX, DC, MC, VI.   Ⓨ

SWISS CHALET   **Lunch:** $6-$11   **Dinner:** $8-$16   Phone: 902/462-0906
Location: At Tacoma St. 100 Main St B2X 1R5. **Hours:** 11 am-10 pm, Fri & Sat-11 pm. Closed: 12/25.
Reservations: accepted. **Features:** The popular restaurant is known for its rotisserie chicken and ribs and
Canadian   the tangy Chalet sauce that gives food its special zip. Diners munch on a half or quarter chicken with sides
such as steamed vegetables, fries, baked potatoes and salads. Lunch guests often go for the great soup
and sandwich combination. Take-out and delivery service are popular options. Casual dress; cocktails. **Parking:** on-site.
Cards: AX, DC, MC, VI.

DIGBY pop. 2,111

―――― **WHERE TO STAY** ――――

ADMIRAL DIGBY INN
Phone: (902)245-2531

(CAA) (SAVE)

7/1-9/15 [ECP]	1P: $119-$129	2P: $119-$129	XP: $10	F10
5/13-6/30 & 9/16-10/15 [ECP]	1P: $75-$85	2P: $75-$85	XP: $10	F10

Location: Hwy 101, exit 26, 1.5 mi (2.5 km) n, follow St John Ferry signs, 3 mi (5 km) w on Victoria Rd, just e of ferry terminal. 441 Shore Rd B0V 1A0 (PO Box 608). Fax: 902/245-2533. **Facility:** 47 units. 46 one-bedroom standard **Small-scale Hotel** units, some with kitchens. 1 cottage ($175-$250). 2 stories (no elevator), exterior corridors. **Parking:** on-site. **Terms:** open 5/13-10/15, small pets only (in smoking units). **Amenities:** hair dryers. **Dining:** The Admiralty Room, see separate listing. **Pool(s):** heated indoor. **Guest Services:** gift shop, coin laundry, wireless Internet. **Cards:** AX, CB, DC, DS, MC, VI. **Free Special Amenities:** expanded continental breakfast and high-speed Internet.

SOME UNITS

🔊 🐾 🍴 🍸 🏊 💻 / ✕ 🖥 🖼 /

BAYSIDE INN B & B
Phone: 902/245-2247

6/15-10/15 [BP]	1P: $58-$98	2P: $58-$98	XP: $15	F3
5/1-6/14 & 4/1-4/30 [BP]	1P: $55-$85	2P: $55-$85	XP: $15	F3
10/16-3/31 [BP]	1P: $55-$75	2P: $55-$75	XP: $15	F3

Bed & Breakfast **Location:** Centre of downtown. 115 Montague Row B0V 1A0 (PO Box 459). **Facility:** Smoke free premises. 11 one-bedroom standard units. 3 stories (no elevator), interior corridors. *Bath:* some shared or private, combo or shower only. **Parking:** on-site and street. **Terms:** office hours 8 am-11 pm. **Guest Services:** gift shop, wireless Internet. **Cards:** AX, CB, DC, DS, MC, VI.

✕ 🎴 📠

DIGBY PINES GOLF RESORT AND SPA   *Book at AAA.com*
Phone: (902)245-2511

5/18-10/7 [BP]	1P: $150-$249	2P: $177-$328	XP: $41	F17

Location: Hwy 101, exit 26, 1.5 mi (2.5 km) n, follow St John Ferry signs, 1.5 mi (2.5 km) w on Victoria Rd, follow signs; **Large-scale Hotel** 1.2 mi (2 km) e of ferry terminal. 103 Shore Rd B0V 1A0 (PO Box 70). Fax: 902/245-6133. **Facility:** Designated smoking area. 147 units. 82 one-bedroom standard units, some with whirlpools. 64 cabins and 1 cottage. 1-3 stories, interior/exterior corridors. **Parking:** on-site. **Terms:** open 5/18-10/7, 3 day cancellation notice, [MAP] meal plan available. **Amenities:** voice mail, irons, hair dryers. **Dining:** The Annapolis Dining Room, see separate listing. **Pool(s):** heated outdoor. **Leisure Activities:** sauna, 2 lighted tennis courts, recreation programs, rental bicycles, playground, exercise room, spa, shuffleboard. *Fee:* golf-18 holes. **Guest Services:** gift shop. **Business Services:** conference facilities. **Cards:** AX, CB, DC, DS, MC, VI.

SOME UNITS

A$K 🍴 🍸 🏊 ✕ ✕ 💻 / 🎴 🖥 🖼 /

DOCKSIDE SUITES
Phone: (902)245-4950

7/1-8/31		2P: $129-$169	XP: $10	F12
5/1-6/30 & 9/1-4/30		2P: $89-$139	XP: $10	F12

Location: Centre; in Fundy Complex. 34 Water St B0V 1A0. Fax: 902/245-6680. **Facility:** 6 units. 3 one-bedroom **Small-scale Hotel** standard units with whirlpools, some with efficiencies. 3 one-bedroom suites with kitchens, some with whirlpools. 2 stories, interior/exterior corridors. **Amenities:** DVD players, high-speed Internet, voice mail, irons, hair dryers. **Dining:** Fundy Restaurant & Dockside Bar, see separate listing. **Leisure Activities:** *Fee:* charter fishing. **Guest Services:** gift shop, wireless Internet. **Business Services:** meeting rooms. **Cards:** AX, DC, DS, MC, VI.

A$K 🔊 🍴 🍸 ✕ 📼 🖥 🖼 💻

HARMONY SUITES AND BED & BREAKFAST
Phone: (902)245-2817

6/12-9/30	1P: $90-$125	2P: $90-$125	XP: $15
5/1-6/11 & 10/1-10/31	1P: $80-$115	2P: $80-$115	XP: $15
11/1-4/30	1P: $69-$99	2P: $69-$99	XP: $15

Bed & Breakfast **Location:** Centre of downtown. Located overlooking the harbour. 111 Montague Row B0V 1A0. Fax: 902/245-2152. **Facility:** Smoke free premises. 10 one-bedroom standard units. 2 stories (no elevator), exterior corridors. *Bath:* combo or shower only. **Parking:** on-site. **Terms:** cancellation fee imposed. **Amenities:** video library, high-speed Internet, hair dryers. *Some:* irons. **Cards:** AX, CB, DC, DS, JC, MC, VI.

SOME UNITS

♿M ♿ ✕ 📼 🖥 / 🖼 💻 /

L'AUBERGE AU HAVRE DU CAPITAINE

| | 5/1-9/30 | 1P: $75-$119 | 2P: $75-$119 | XP: $10 | F12 |
| | 10/1-4/30 | 1P: $60-$109 | 2P: $60-$109 | XP: $10 | F12 |

Small-scale Hotel **Location:** Hwy 101, exit 31 to Rt 1; follow signs. 9118 Rt 1 B0W 2J0. **Facility:** 18 one-bedroom standard units, some with whirlpools. 2 stories (no elevator), interior/exterior corridors. **Parking:** on-site. **Terms:** office hours 7 am-10 pm, weekly rates available, [BP] meal plan available. **Amenities:** hair dryers. **Cards:** AX, MC, VI.

Phone: 902/769-2001

(A$K) (Y1) (✕) (K)

──────── WHERE TO DINE ────────

THE ADMIRALTY ROOM

(CAA)

Canadian

Dinner: $10-$29   Phone: 902/245-2531

Location: Hwy 101, exit 26, 1.5 mi (2.5 km) n, follow St John Ferry signs, 3 mi (5 km) w on Victoria Rd, just e of ferry terminal; in Admiral Digby Inn. 441 Shore Rd B0V 1A0. **Hours:** Open 5/1-10/31; 5 pm-10 pm; hours vary off season. **Reservations:** accepted. **Features:** Home-style cooking is what the comfortable, friendly restaurant is all about. The dining room treats guests to a nice view of the Annapolis Basin. Included in the array of seafood choices are scallops and lobster from the tank. Casual dress; cocktails. **Parking:** on-site. **Cards:** AX, DC, DS, MC, VI.

(Y)

THE ANNAPOLIS DINING ROOM

(CAA)

Canadian

Lunch: $13-$22   **Dinner:** $18-$30   Phone: 902/245-2511

Location: Hwy 101, exit 26, 1.5 mi (2.5 km) n, follow St John Ferry signs, 1.5 mi (2.5 km) w on Victoria Rd, follow signs; 1.2 mi (2 km) e of ferry terminal; in Digby Pines Golf Resort and Spa. **Hours:** Open 5/11-10/31; 7 am-10, noon-2 & 6-9 pm. **Reservations:** suggested. **Features:** Pillars, elegant draperies and attractive table settings add to the sophisticated allure of the charming dining room. Well prepared entrees of local seafood, chicken, beef and veal make up most of the menu. Delicious desserts are made in-house. Dressy casual; cocktails. **Parking:** on-site. **Cards:** AX, CB, DC, DS, MC, VI.

(Y) (K)

FUNDY RESTAURANT & DOCKSIDE BAR

Canadian

Lunch: $9-$15   **Dinner:** $11-$25   Phone: 902/245-4950

Location: Centre; in Fundy Complex. 34 Water St B0V 1A0. **Hours:** 7 am-11 pm; off season 11 am-10 pm. Closed: 12/25. **Reservations:** accepted. **Features:** The spacious restaurant has several dining sections and affords splendid views of the harbor and scallop fleet. Specializing in fresh local seafood, this place also prepares some steak, chicken and pasta dishes. Large decks provide ample outdoor seating in season. Casual dress; cocktails. **Parking:** on-site and street. **Cards:** AX, DC, MC, VI.

(Y)

EASTERN PASSAGE pop. 8,872

──────── WHERE TO DINE ────────

BOONDOCKS RESTAURANT

Seafood

Lunch: $8-$13   **Dinner:** $12-$22   Phone: 902/465-3474

Location: 5.4 mi (9 km) e of Dartmouth on Rt 322; centre. 200 Government Wharf Rd B3G 1M7. **Hours:** Open 5/1-12/31 & 3/1-4/30; 11 am-10 pm; hours vary off season. Closed: 12/25. **Reservations:** accepted. **Features:** Bordering Fisherman's Cove, the pleasant location is known for its views of the busy harbour. Ample portions of seafood and other meat entrees are nicely presented and served piping hot. The large patio offers comfortable seating in season. Casual dress; cocktails. **Parking:** on-site. **Cards:** AX, DC, MC, VI.

(Y)

ECONOMY

──────── WHERE TO STAY ────────

FOUR SEASONS RETREAT

Cottage

| | All Year | | 2P: $100-$195 | XP: $10 |

Phone: 902/647-2628

Location: 3 mi (5 km) e on Rt 2. 320 Cove Rd B0M 1J0 (RR 1). Fax: 902/647-2288. **Facility:** The Four Seasons Retreat is a nice selection of private cottages nestled in the trees; most border the shore of Cobequid Bay. 13 units. 2 one-bedroom standard units. 11 cottages. 1 story, exterior corridors. *Bath:* combo or shower only. **Parking:** on-site. **Terms:** 3 day cancellation notice-fee imposed, weekly rates available. **Amenities:** video library, hair dryers. **Pool(s):** outdoor. **Leisure Activities:** whirlpool, cross country skiing, hiking trails, horseshoes. **Business Services:** meeting rooms. **Cards:** MC, VI.

SOME UNITS

(≈) (✕) (✕) (K) (VCR) (☎) (⌨) / (🖨) (📠) /

GLENVILLE

──────── WHERE TO STAY ────────

────── *The following lodging was either not evaluated or did not* ──────
meet AAA rating requirements but is listed for your information only.

GLENORA INN & DISTILLERY RESORT

(fyi)

Phone: 902/258-2662

Not evaluated. **Location:** Centre. Rt 19 B0E 1X0 (PO Box 181, MABOU). Facilities, services, and decor characterize a mid-range property.

──────── WHERE TO DINE ────────

POST-AND-BEAM DINING ROOM

Canadian

Lunch: $12-$18   **Dinner:** $15-$28   Phone: 902/258-2662

Location: Centre; in Glenora Inn & Distillery Resort. Rt 19 B0E 1X0. **Hours:** Open 5/13-10/31; 7 am-9, noon-3 & 5-9 pm. **Reservations:** suggested. **Features:** Located in North America's only single malt distillery, this dining room is very pleasant in an open, airy concept with cathedral ceilings and large windows overlooking gardens. The chef uses fresh local ingredients and creates very appealing seafood and meat entrees from Digby scallops to rack of lamb; they also smoke their own salmon. Casual dress; cocktails. **Parking:** on-site. **Cards:** AX, DC, MC, VI.

(Y) (K)

GRANVILLE FERRY pop. 182

—— WHERE TO STAY ——

—— *The following lodging was either not evaluated or did not* ——
meet AAA rating requirements but is listed for your information only.

MOUNTAIN TOP COTTAGES | Phone: 902/532-2564
[fyi] Not evaluated. **Location:** Hwy 1, 2.7 mi (4.5 km) n. Parker Mountain Rd B0S 1H0 (PO Box 3022). Facilities, services, and decor characterize a mid-range property.

—— WHERE TO DINE ——

HOLMESTEAD FAMILY RESTAURANT | **Lunch:** $5-$16 | **Dinner:** $8-$16 | **Phone:** 902/532-2302
Location: Centre. 4733 Hwy 1 B0S 1K0. **Hours:** 7:30 am-9 pm, Fri & Sat-10 pm; to 7 pm, Fri & Sat-8 pm 9/7-5/8. Closed: 12/25, 12/26; also from 2 pm 12/24. **Features:** The spacious family restaurant, with booth and table seating, presents a menu with enough variety to include something for everyone, such as steaks, seafood, burgers and fish and chips. Patio seating and a take-out menu are available seasonally. Casual dress; cocktails. **Parking:** on-site. **Cards:** AX, MC, VI.
Canadian

GUYSBOROUGH pop. 5,165

—— WHERE TO STAY ——

DESBARRES MANOR INN | Phone: 902/533-2099
Property failed to provide current rates
Location: Centre. Located in a residential area. 90 Church St B0H 1N0 (Box 110). Fax: 902/533-2841. **Facility:** In a charming village, this circa 1837 mansion offers richly furnished living rooms and guest units, and the dining room and deck overlook a valley. Smoke free premises. 10 one-bedroom standard units. 3 stories (no elevator), interior corridors. **Parking:** on-site, winter plug-ins. **Terms:** office hours 7 am-10 pm. **Amenities:** voice mail. **Guest Services:** valet laundry, wireless Internet. **Business Services:** meeting rooms.
Country Inn

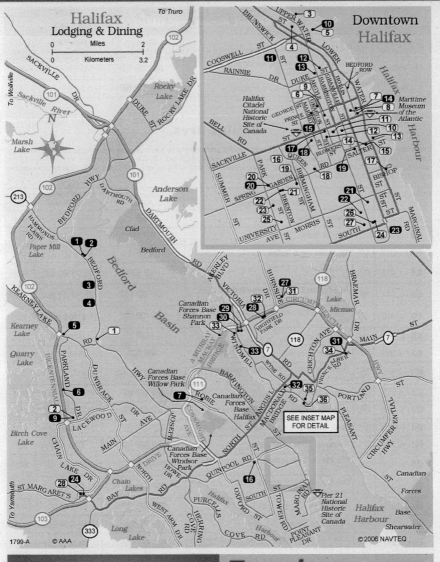

Halifax Lodging & Dining

Miles 0 — 2
Kilometers 0 — 3.2

Downtown Halifax

Halifax Citadel National Historic Site of Canada

Maritime Museum of the Atlantic

SEE INSET MAP FOR DETAIL

Pier 21 National Historic Site of Canada

1799-A © AAA

©2006 NAVTEQ

✈ Airport Accommodations

Spotter/Map Page Number	OA	HALIFAX	Diamond Rating	Rate Range High Season	Listing Page
N/A	CAA	**Hilton Garden Inn Halifax Airport, 1.8 mi (3 km) e of terminal**	◆◆◆	$139-$159 SAVE	321
N/A		Inn on the Lake, 14 km e of airport	◆◆◆	$156-$199	322

Halifax Area

This index helps you "spot" where approved accommodations and restaurants are located on the corresponding detailed maps. Lodging rate ranges are for comparison only and show the property's high season; rates are per night, unless only weekly (W) rates are available. Restaurant rate range is for dinner, unless only lunch (L) is served. Turn to the listing page for more detailed rate information and consult display ads for special promotions.

Spotter/Map Page Number	OA	HALIFAX - Lodgings	Diamond Rating	Rate Range High Season	Listing Page
1 / p. 313		Travelers Motel	◆	Failed to provide	324
2 / p. 313		Esquire Motel	◆◆	$79-$90	318
3 / p. 313	CAA	**Bluenose Inn & Suites**	◆	$52-$119 SAVE	316
4 / p. 313	CAA	**Econo Lodge & Suites** - see color ad card insert	◆◆	$109-$189 SAVE	318
5 / p. 313	CAA	**Holiday Inn Express Halifax/Bedford** - see color ad card insert	◆◆◆	$109-$129 SAVE	322
6 / p. 313		Quality Inn & Suites Halifax - see color ad card insert	◆◆◆	$108-$163	323
7 / p. 313		Chebucto Inn	◆	$105-$145	317
9 / p. 313		Future Inns Halifax	◆◆	$149-$189	319
10 / p. 313	CAA	**Halifax Marriott Harbourfront** - see color ad p 320	◆◆◆◆	$149-$299 SAVE	319
11 / p. 313	CAA	**Citadel Halifax Hotel**	◆◆◆	$124-$269 SAVE	317
12 / p. 313	CAA	**Delta Barrington** - see color ad p 317	◆◆◆	$132-$208 SAVE	317
13 / p. 313	CAA	**Delta Halifax** - see color ad p 318	◆◆◆	$132-$208 SAVE	318
14 / p. 313	CAA	**Radisson Suite Hotel Halifax**	◆◆◆	$179 SAVE	324
15 / p. 313	CAA	**The Prince George Hotel** - see color ad p 324	◆◆◆◆	$179-$209 SAVE	323
16 / p. 313	CAA	**Holiday Inn Select Halifax-Centre** - see color ad card insert	◆◆◆	$149-$189 SAVE	322
17 / p. 313		Residence Inn by Marriott	◆◆◆	$179-$199	324
18 / p. 313	CAA	**Cambridge Suites** - see color ad p 316	◆◆◆	$169-$249 SAVE	316
19 / p. 313	CAA	**Four Points Sheraton Halifax** - see color ad p 5, p 319	◆◆◆	$145-$235 SAVE	318
20 / p. 313	CAA	**The Lord Nelson Hotel & Suites** - see color ad p 322	◆◆◆	$149-$229 SAVE	323
21 / p. 313	CAA	**The Halliburton** - see color ad p 321	◆◆◆	$150-$255 SAVE	320
22 / p. 313		Halifax's Waverley Inn - see color ad p 319	◆◆◆	$125-$229	319
23 / p. 313	CAA	**The Westin Nova Scotian** - see color ad p 325, p 5 & coupon in Savings Section	◆◆◆	$129-$295 SAVE	325
24 / p. 313		Lakeview Inns & Suites - see color ad on TourBookMark	◆◆◆	$179-$399	323
		HALIFAX - Restaurants			
① / p. 313		China Town Restaurant	◆◆◆	$13-$20	326
② / p. 313		Redwood Grill	◆◆	$12-$21	328
③ / p. 313		Salty's on the Waterfront	◆◆◆	$18-$27	328

Spotter/Map Page Number	OA	HALIFAX - Restaurants (continued)	Diamond Rating	Rate Range High Season	Listing Page
④ / p. 313		Sweet Basil Bistro	◈◈◈	$16-$23	329
⑤ / p. 313		44 North Restaurant	◈◈◈	$15-$28	326
⑥ / p. 313		Five Fishermen	◈◈◈	$31-$40	327
⑦ / p. 313		McKelvie's Delishes Fishes Dishes	◈◈	$14-$25	327
⑨ / p. 313		The Press Gang Seafood Restaurant & Oyster Bar	◈◈◈	$22-$35	328
⑩ / p. 313		Pogue Fado Irish Public House	◈◈	$9-$16	328
⑪ / p. 313		Opa Greek Taverna	◈◈◈	$12-$21	328
⑫ / p. 313		Seven Wine Bar & Restaurant	◈◈◈	$21-$28	328
⑬ / p. 313		Waterfront Warehouse Restaurant & Tug's Pub	◈◈◈	$13-$21	329
⑭ / p. 313		da Maurizio Dining Room	◈◈◈◈	$27-$35	326
⑮ / p. 313		Cheelin Restaurant	◈◈	$9-$16	326
⑯ / p. 313		Fid	◈◈◈	$15-$25	327
⑰ / p. 313		Bish World Cuisine	◈◈◈◈	$18-$35	326
⑱ / p. 313		The Fireside	◈◈	$8-$20	327
⑲ / p. 313		Deco Restaurant	◈◈◈	$18-$26	327
⑳ / p. 313	CAA	**Victory Arms Pub**	◈◈	$10-$30	329
㉑ / p. 313		Ryan Duffy's	◈◈◈	$15-$28	328
㉒ / p. 313		il Mercato Ristorante	◈◈◈	$15-$23	327
㉓ / p. 313		Curry Village Indian Cuisine	◈◈	$9-$16	326
㉔ / p. 313		Cafe Chianti	◈◈◈	$15-$20	326
㉕ / p. 313		Trinity	◈◈◈	$12-$22	329
㉖ / p. 313		Taj Mahal Restaurant	◈◈	$14-$22	329
㉗ / p. 313		Henry House Restaurant and Pub	◈◈	$10-$17	327
㉘ / p. 313		Canadiana Restaurant & Lounge	◈◈	$8-$18	326
		DARTMOUTH - Lodgings			
㉗ / p. 313	CAA	**Park Place Hotel & Conference Centre Ramada Plaza**	◈◈◈	$152 SAVE	308
㉘ / p. 313		Future Inns Dartmouth	◈◈	$139-$179	308
㉙ / p. 313		Country Inn & Suites By Carlson - see color ad on TourBookMark	◈◈	$115-$170	308
㉚ / p. 313	CAA	**Comfort Inn** - see color ad card insert	◈◈	$145-$165 SAVE	308
㉛ / p. 313	CAA	**Quality Inn Halifax/Dartmouth** - see color ad card insert	◈◈	$80-$180 SAVE	308
㉜ / p. 313	CAA	**Holiday Inn Halifax-Harbourview** - see color ad card insert	◈◈◈	$129-$179 SAVE	308
		DARTMOUTH - Restaurants			
㉛ / p. 313	CAA	**The Peppermill Restaurant**	◈◈	$10-$20	309
㉜ / p. 313		Favorites Cuisine	◈◈	$9-$17	309
㉝ / p. 313		Fan's Restaurant	◈◈	$9-$15	309
㉞ / p. 313		Roccos Italian Restaurant	◈◈◈	$14-$21	309
㉟ / p. 313		La Perla Dining Room	◈◈◈	$15-$25	309
㊱ / p. 313		MacAskill's	◈◈◈	$17-$25	309

HALIFAX pop. 359,111   (See map and index starting on p. 313)

─────── **WHERE TO STAY** ───────

BLUENOSE INN & SUITES   Phone: 902/443-3171   **3**

CAA SAVE   All Year   1P: $52-$119   2P: $52-$119   XP: $10   F12
⬥⬥⬥   **Location:** Rt 2 (Bedford Hwy), 6 mi (10.4 km) nw. 636 Bedford Hwy B3M 2L8. Fax: 902/443-9368. **Facility:** 52 one-
          bedroom standard units, some with efficiencies (utensils extra charge). 3 stories (no elevator), exterior
Motel   corridors. *Bath:* combo or shower only. **Parking:** on-site. **Terms:** weekly rates available. **Amenities:** *Some:*
          high-speed Internet. **Guest Services:** coin laundry. **Business Services:** meeting rooms, PC. **Cards:** AX,
          DC, DS, MC, VI. **Free Special Amenities: local telephone calls and early check-in/late check-out.**
                                                                                                    SOME UNITS

          ⓢ ⓘ / ⊠ ⓐ /

CAMBRIDGE SUITES   *Book great rates at AAA.com*   Phone: (902)420-0555   **18**

CAA SAVE   5/1-10/31 [ECP]   1P: $169-$249   2P: $169-$249   XP: $20   F18
⬥⬥⬥ ⬥⬥   11/1-4/30 [ECP]   1P: $119-$169   2P: $119-$169   XP: $20   F18
          Location: Corner of Brunswick and Sackville sts. 1583 Brunswick St B3J 3P5. Fax: 902/420-9379. **Facility:** 200
          units. 100 one-bedroom standard units. 100 one-bedroom suites. 6 stories, interior corridors. *Bath:* combo
Large-scale Hotel or shower only. **Parking:** on-site (fee). **Amenities:** voice mail, irons, hair dryers. *Fee:* video games, high-
          speed Internet. *Some:* dual phone lines. **Dining:** 7 am-11 pm, cocktails. **Leisure Activities:** sauna,
whirlpool, pool privileges, exercise room. **Guest Services:** sundries, valet and coin laundry, wireless Internet. **Business
Services:** meeting rooms, PC. **Cards:** AX, DC, DS, MC, VI. **Free Special Amenities: expanded continental breakfast and
newspaper.** *(See color ad below)*
                                                                                                    SOME UNITS

          ⓘ ⓜ ⓒ ⊠ ⓥ ⓑ ⓣ ⓛ / ⊠ /

(See map and index starting on p. 313)

CHEBUCTO INN   **Phone: (902)453-4330**   **7**

5/1-10/31	1P: $105-$145	2P: $105-$145	XP: $10	F12
11/1-4/30	1P: $75-$105	2P: $75-$105	XP: $10	F12

Small-scale Hotel   **Location:** Jct Hwy 111 and Rt 2 (Bedford Hwy), 0.4 mi (0.7 km) e. Located in a residential area. 6151 Lady Hammond Rd B3K 2R9. Fax: 902/454-7043. **Facility:** 31 one-bedroom standard units. 2 stories (no elevator), exterior corridors. **Parking:** on-site. **Terms:** cancellation fee imposed, pets (in designated units). **Amenities:** *Some:* high-speed Internet. **Business Services:** meeting rooms. **Cards:** AX, DC, DS, MC, VI.

SOME UNITS

ASK 🐕 🍴 / ✕ /

CITADEL HALIFAX HOTEL   *Book great rates at AAA.com*   **Phone: (902)422-1391**   **11**

11/1-4/30	1P: $124-$269	2P: $124-$269	XP: $15	F17
5/1-10/31	1P: $149-$219	2P: $149-$219	XP: $15	F17

Large-scale Hotel   **Location:** Between Cogswell and Duke sts. 1960 Brunswick St B3J 2G7. Fax: 902/429-6672. **Facility:** 266 units. 262 one-bedroom standard units. 4 one-bedroom suites. 7-11 stories, interior corridors. **Parking:** on-site (fee). **Amenities:** video games (fee), voice mail, irons, hair dryers. *Some:* high-speed Internet, dual phone lines. **Dining:** 6:30 am-11 pm, cocktails. **Pool(s):** heated indoor, wading. **Leisure Activities:** sauna, whirlpool, limited exercise equipment. **Guest Services:** gift shop, valet laundry. **Business Services:** conference facilities, PC. **Cards:** AX, DC, DS, MC, VI. **Free Special Amenities:** newspaper and early check-in/late check-out.

SOME UNITS

🆂 🐕 🍴 🍸 🏊 ✕ 🎥 💻 / ✕ 🛏 /

DELTA BARRINGTON   *Book great rates at AAA.com*   **Phone: (902)429-7410**   **12**

5/16-10/30	1P: $132-$208	2P: $132-$208	XP: $15	F18
1/1-4/30	1P: $101-$175	2P: $101-$175	XP: $15	F18
5/1-5/15	1P: $99-$170	2P: $99-$170	XP: $15	F18
10/31-12/31	1P: $98-$170	2P: $98-$170	XP: $15	F18

Large-scale Hotel   **Location:** Between Cogswell and Duke sts. 1875 Barrington St B3J 3L6. Fax: 902/420-6524. **Facility:** 200 units. 199 one-bedroom standard units. 1 one-bedroom suite. 3 stories, interior corridors. **Parking:** on-site (fee) and valet. **Terms:** [AP], [BP] & [CP] meal plans available, package plans, 2% service charge. **Amenities:** voice mail, honor bars, irons, hair dryers. *Fee:* video games, high-speed Internet. *Some:* CD players, dual phone lines. **Dining:** 6:30 am-9:30 pm, cocktails. **Pool(s):** heated indoor. **Leisure Activities:** saunas, whirlpool, exercise room. *Fee:* massage. **Guest Services:** gift shop, valet laundry. **Business Services:** conference facilities, business center. **Cards:** AX, DC, DS, MC, VI.

(See color ad below)

SOME UNITS

🆂 🐕 🍴 🍸 🏊 ✕ 🎥 💻 / ✕ /

(See map and index starting on p. 313)

DELTA HALIFAX
Book great rates at AAA.com

Phone: (902)425-6700 **13**

(CAA) (SAVE)

5/16-10/30	1P: $132-$208	2P: $132-$208	XP: $15	F18
1/1-4/30	1P: $101-$175	2P: $101-$175	XP: $15	F18
5/1-5/15 & 10/31-12/31	1P: $98-$170	2P: $98-$170	XP: $15	F18

Large-scale Hotel **Location:** Corner of Cogswell and Barrington sts. Located in Scotia Square. 1990 Barrington St B3J 1P2. Fax: 902/425-6214. **Facility:** 296 units. 291 one-bedroom standard units. 4 one- and 1 two-bedroom suites. 8 stories, interior corridors. **Parking:** on-site (fee) and valet. **Terms:** package plans. **Amenities:** voice mail, irons, hair dryers. **Fee:** video games, high-speed Internet. **Some:** honor bars. **Dining:** 6:30 am-10 pm, cocktails. **Pool(s):** heated indoor. **Leisure Activities:** saunas, whirlpool, exercise room. **Fee:** massage. **Guest Services:** gift shop, valet laundry. **Business Services:** conference facilities, business center. **Cards:** AX, DC, DS, MC, VI. *(See color ad below)*

SOME UNITS

ECONO LODGE & SUITES
Book great rates at AAA.com

Phone: (902)443-0303 **4**

(CAA) (SAVE)

6/15-10/13	1P: $109-$189	2P: $109-$189	XP: $10	F18
5/1-6/14 & 3/15-4/30	1P: $79-$129	2P: $79-$129	XP: $10	F18
10/14-3/14	1P: $69-$119	2P: $69-$119	XP: $10	F18

Small-scale Hotel **Location:** On Rt 2 (Bedford Hwy), 6 mi (9.6 km) w. 560 Bedford Hwy B3M 2L8. Fax: 902/457-0663. **Facility:** 59 units. 54 one-bedroom standard units, some with efficiencies. 5 one-bedroom suites ($99-$179) with efficiencies, some with whirlpools. 3 stories, interior corridors. **Parking:** on-site. **Terms:** small pets only ($10 extra charge, in designated units). **Amenities:** video library, irons, hair dryers. **Some:** high-speed Internet. **Dining:** 7-11 am. **Pool(s):** heated indoor. **Leisure Activities:** limited exercise equipment. **Guest Services:** coin laundry. **Business Services:** meeting rooms, PC. **Cards:** AX, CB, DC, DS, JC, MC, VI. **Free Special Amenities:** local telephone calls and newspaper. *(See color ad card insert)*

SOME UNITS

FEE

ESQUIRE MOTEL

Phone: (902)835-3367 **2**

6/1-10/31	1P: $79-$90	2P: $79-$90	XP: $10	F15
5/1-5/31 & 11/1-4/30	1P: $65-$90	2P: $65-$90	XP: $10	F15

Motel **Location:** Hwy 102, exit 4A, 3.3 mi (5.3 km) e on Rt 2 (Bedford Hwy). 771 Bedford Hwy B4A 1A1. Fax: 902/835-9507. **Facility:** 28 units. 26 one-bedroom standard units. 2 one-bedroom suites ($135-$150). 1 story, exterior corridors. **Parking:** on-site, winter plug-ins. **Terms:** office hours 7 am-midnight, small pets only. **Amenities:** *Some:* hair dryers. **Pool(s):** outdoor. **Cards:** AX, DC, MC, VI.

SOME UNITS

ASK

FOUR POINTS SHERATON HALIFAX
Book great rates at AAA.com

Phone: (902)423-4444 **19**

(CAA) (SAVE)

5/1-10/31	1P: $145-$235	2P: $145-$235	XP: $20	F18
1/1-4/30	1P: $130-$220	2P: $130-$220	XP: $20	F18
11/1-12/31	1P: $120-$210	2P: $120-$210	XP: $20	F18

Large-scale Hotel **Location:** Between Salter and Bishop sts. 1496 Hollis St B3J 3Z1. Fax: 902/423-2327. **Facility:** Smoke free premises. 177 units. 159 one-bedroom standard units. 18 one-bedroom suites with whirlpools. 6 stories, interior corridors. **Bath:** combo or shower only. **Parking:** on-site (fee). **Terms:** 2% service charge. **Amenities:** video games (fee), high-speed Internet, dual phone lines, voice mail, irons, hair dryers. **Some:** CD players. **Dining:** 6:30 am-2 & 5-10 pm, Sat & Sun from 7 am, cocktails. **Pool(s):** small heated indoor. **Leisure Activities:** whirlpool, exercise room. **Guest Services:** valet laundry. **Business Services:** meeting rooms, administrative services (fee). **Cards:** AX, DC, MC, VI. **Free Special Amenities:** local telephone calls and high-speed Internet. *(See color ad p 5 & p 319)*

SOME UNITS

(See map and index starting on p. 313)

FUTURE INNS HALIFAX *Book at AAA.com* Phone: (902)443-4333 **9**

5/1-10/31   1P: $149-$189   2P: $149-$189   XP: $10   F16
11/1-4/30   1P: $139-$179   2P: $139-$179   XP: $10   F16

Small-scale Hotel **Location:** Hwy 102, exit 2A. Located adjacent to Bayers Lake Business Park. 30 Fairfax Dr B3S 1P1. Fax: 902/443-9775. **Facility:** 135 units. 127 one-bedroom standard units. 8 one-bedroom suites ($179-$189). 4 stories, interior corridors. **Parking:** on-site. **Terms:** cancellation fee imposed. **Amenities:** high-speed Internet, voice mail, irons, hair dryers. **Dining:** Redwood Grill, see separate listing. **Leisure Activities:** exercise room. **Guest Services:** valet and coin laundry. **Business Services:** meeting rooms, PC, fax. **Cards:** AX, DC, MC, VI.

SOME UNITS

ASK S⊖ ⑪ ⛊ ⓛM ⊘ / ⊠ 🖪 /

HALIFAX MARRIOTT HARBOURFRONT *Book great rates at AAA.com* Phone: (866)211-4607 **10**

(CAA) [SAVE]

All Year   1P: $149-$299   2P: $149-$299

Resort **Location:** Adjacent to historic properties and Casino Nova Scotia. Located in a commercial area. 1919 Upper Water St
Large-scale Hotel B3J 3J5. Fax: 902/422-5805. **Facility:** Views of the waterfront and city are offered from many rooms at this sophisticated hotel on the harbour. Smoke free premises. 352 units. 343 one-bedroom standard units, some with whirlpools. 5 one- and 4 two-bedroom suites ($499-$1200), some with whirlpools. 6 stories, interior corridors. *Bath:* combo or shower only. **Parking:** on-site (fee) and valet. **Terms:** cancellation fee imposed, package plans. **Amenities:** voice mail, irons, hair dryers. *Fee:* video games, high-speed Internet.
Dining: 44 North Restaurant, see separate listing. **Pool(s):** heated indoor. **Leisure Activities:** whirlpool, steamrooms, exercise room, spa. **Guest Services:** gift shop, valet laundry. **Business Services:** conference facilities, business center.
Free Special Amenities: newspaper. *(See color ad p 320)*

SOME UNITS

🎲 ⑪ ⛊ ⓛM ⊘ 🏊 ⋊ ⊠ 🎮 🖵 / 🖪 /

HALIFAX'S WAVERLEY INN *Book great rates at AAA.com* Phone: (902)423-9346 **22**

♦♦♦♦

5/1-10/31 [BP]   1P: $125-$229   2P: $125-$229   XP: $15   F16
11/1-4/30 [BP]   1P: $99-$179   2P: $99-$179   XP: $15   F16

Historic **Location:** Between Harvey and Morris sts. Located 2 blks from Via Rail Station. 1266 Barrington St B3J 1Y5.
Small-scale Hotel Fax: 902/425-0167. **Facility:** Built in 1866, the inn offers many accommodations furnished with antiques; rooms vary in size and all are individually decorated. Smoke free premises. 34 one-bedroom standard units, some with whirlpools. 3 stories (no elevator), interior corridors. *Bath:* combo or shower only. **Parking:** on-site. **Terms:** package plans. **Amenities:** hair dryers. *Some:* DVD players, irons. **Guest Services:** valet laundry, wireless Internet. **Business Services:** PC. **Cards:** AX, DC, DS, MC, VI. *(See color ad below)*

SOME UNITS

ASK S⊖ ⑪+ ⊠ / VCR 🖪 /

(See map and index starting on p. 313)

THE HALLIBURTON   *Book great rates at AAA.com*   **Phone:** (902)420-0658

CAA SAVE	5/1-10/31 [ECP]	1P: $150-$255	2P: $150-$255	XP: $25	F16
	11/1-4/30 [ECP]	1P: $120-$175	2P: $120-$175	XP: $25	F16

Small-scale Hotel **Location:** Between Barrington and Hollis sts. Located by Dalhousie Tech University. 5184 Morris St B3J 1B3. **Fax:** 902/423-2324. **Facility:** Smoke free premises. 29 units. 24 one-bedroom standard units. 5 one-bedroom suites ($350), some with whirlpools. 3 stories (no elevator), interior corridors. *Bath:* combo or shower only. **Parking:** on-site. **Terms:** cancellation fee imposed. **Amenities:** irons, hair dryers. **Dining:** 5 pm-9 pm; to 10 pm 7/1-8/31; by reservation only, cocktails. **Guest Services:** valet laundry, wireless Internet. **Business Services:** meeting rooms, PC. **Cards:** AX, DC, JC, MC, VI. **Free Special Amenities:** expanded continental breakfast and local telephone calls. *(See color ad p 321)*

(See map and index starting on p. 313)

HILTON GARDEN INN HALIFAX AIRPORT   *Book great rates at AAA.com*   Phone: (902)873-1400

CAA SAVE

Small-scale Hotel

All Year   1P: $139-$159   2P: $139-$159   XP: $10   F18

Location: Hwy 102, exit 5A, 0.8 mi (1.2 km) e, then just n. 200 Pratt Whitney Dr B2T 0A2. Fax: 902/873-1800. **Facility:** Smoke free premises. 145 one-bedroom standard units, some with whirlpools. 5 stories, interior corridors. *Bath:* combo or shower only. **Parking:** on-site. **Terms:** 2% service charge. **Amenities:** video games (fee), high-speed Internet, voice mail, irons, hair dryers. **Dining:** 7 am-10 pm, cocktails. **Pool(s):** heated indoor. **Leisure Activities:** whirlpool, exercise room. **Guest Services:** sundries, coin laundry, airport transportation-Halifax International Airport, wireless Internet. **Business Services:** meeting rooms, business center. **Cards:** AX, CB, DC, DS, JC, MC, VI. *(See color ad below)*

(See map and index starting on p. 313)

HOLIDAY INN EXPRESS HALIFAX/BEDFORD   *Book great rates at AAA.com*   Phone: (902)445-1100   **5**

(CAA) (SAVE)   All Year [CP]   1P: $109-$129
Location: Hwy 102, exit 2. Located in a residential area. 133 Kearney Lake Rd B3M 4P3. Fax: 902/445-1101. **Facility:** 99 one-bedroom standard units. 3 stories, interior corridors. *Bath:* combo or shower only. **Parking:** on-site. **Terms:** 14 day cancellation notice, small pets only ($25 extra charge, on ground floor). Small-scale Hotel **Amenities:** video games (fee), high-speed Internet, dual phone lines, voice mail, irons, hair dryers. **Pool(s):** heated indoor. **Leisure Activities:** whirlpool, exercise room. **Guest Services:** valet and coin laundry. **Business Services:** meeting rooms, PC. **Cards:** AX, CB, DC, DS, JC, MC, VI. **Free Special Amenities:** expanded continental breakfast and local telephone calls. *(See color ad card insert)*

SOME UNITS
(icons) FEE

HOLIDAY INN SELECT HALIFAX-CENTRE   *Book great rates at AAA.com*   Phone: (902)423-1161   **16**

(CAA) (SAVE)   5/1-10/31   1P: $149-$189   2P: $149-$189   XP: $20   F18
11/1-4/30   1P: $129-$169   2P: $139-$179   XP: $20   F18
Location: Jct Quinpool St. Located opposite the commons. 1980 Robie St B3H 3G5. Fax: 902/423-9069. **Facility:** 232 units. 229 one-bedroom standard units. 3 one-bedroom suites. 15 stories, interior corridors. Large-scale Hotel **Parking:** on-site (fee). **Terms:** [BP] & [CP] meal plans available, package plans, small pets only (in designated units). **Amenities:** high-speed Internet, voice mail, irons, hair dryers. *Some:* dual phone lines. **Dining:** 6:30 am-11 pm, cocktails. **Pool(s):** heated indoor, wading. **Leisure Activities:** sauna, whirlpool, sun deck, exercise room. **Guest Services:** gift shop, valet and coin laundry. **Business Services:** conference facilities, business center. **Cards:** AX, CB, DC, DS, JC, MC, VI. *(See color ad card insert)*

SOME UNITS
(icons)

INN ON THE LAKE   *Book at AAA.com*   Phone: (902)861-3480

(icons)   7/31-10/31   1P: $156-$199   2P: $156-$199   XP: $10   F16
5/1-7/30   1P: $129-$179   2P: $129-$179   XP: $10   F16
Small-scale Hotel   11/1-4/30   1P: $119-$169   2P: $119-$169   XP: $10   F16
Location: Hwy 102, exit 5. 3009 Hwy 2 B2T 1J5. Fax: 902/861-4883. **Facility:** Smoke free premises. 40 units. 36 one-bedroom standard units, some with whirlpools. 3 one- and 1 three-bedroom suites with whirlpools. 3 stories (no elevator), interior corridors. **Parking:** on-site. **Terms:** 7 day cancellation notice. **Amenities:** irons, hair dryers. *Some:* high-speed Internet. **Dining:** Encore Traditional Cuisine, see separate listing. **Pool(s):** outdoor. **Leisure Activities:** canoeing, paddleboats, 2 tennis courts. **Guest Services:** wireless Internet. **Business Services:** meeting rooms, PC. **Cards:** AX, DC, DS, MC, VI.

SOME UNITS
(icons)

(See map and index starting on p. 313)

LAKEVIEW INNS & SUITES   *Book great rates at AAA.com*   **Phone:** (902)450-3020   **24**
5/1-9/30 [CP]   1P: $179-$399   2P: $179-$399   XP: $20   F17
10/1-4/30 [CP]   1P: $159-$399   2P: $159-$399   XP: $20   F17
Small-scale Hotel **Location:** Hwy 102, exit 2A eastbound; Hwy 103, exit 2. Located in Bayers Lake Business Park. 98 Chain Lake Dr B3S 1A2. Fax: 902/450-3021. **Facility:** 65 units. 52 one-bedroom standard units. 13 one-bedroom suites, some with whirlpools. 3 stories, interior corridors. **Parking:** on-site. **Terms:** small pets only ($100 deposit). **Amenities:** video library, DVD players, voice mail, irons, hair dryers. *Some:* dual phone lines. **Pool(s):** small indoor. **Leisure Activities:** exercise room. **Guest Services:** valet and coin laundry, wireless Internet. **Business Services:** meeting rooms, PC, fax. **Cards:** AX, CB, DC, DS, JC, MC, VI. **(See color ad on TourBookMark)**

SOME UNITS

(ASK) (SD) 🐕 (T↑) (&M) 🏊 🖥 🖨 🖵 / (✕) /
FEE

THE LORD NELSON HOTEL & SUITES   *Book great rates at AAA.com*   **Phone:** (902)423-6331   **20**
(CAA) (SAVE)   5/1-10/31   1P: $149-$229   2P: $149-$229   XP: $20   F17
                              11/1-4/30   1P: $159-$399   2P: $159-$399   XP: $20   F17
🛆🛆🛆 **Location:** Corner of Park St and Spring Garden Rd; centre. 1515 S Park St B3J 2L2. Fax: 902/491-6148.
Large-scale Hotel **Facility:** 260 units. 219 one-bedroom standard units. 41 one-bedroom suites. 8 stories, interior corridors. *Bath:* combo or shower only. **Parking:** on-site (fee) and valet. **Terms:** cancellation fee imposed, package plans, pets ($50 deposit). **Amenities:** voice mail, irons, hair dryers. *Fee:* video games, high-speed Internet. *Some:* dual phone lines, fax. **Dining:** Victory Arms Pub, see separate listing. **Leisure Activities:** exercise room. **Guest Services:** valet and coin laundry. **Business Services:** meeting rooms, business center. **Cards:** AX, DC, DS, MC, VI. **Free Special Amenities:** local telephone calls and newspaper. *(See color ad p 322)*

SOME UNITS

🐕 (T↑) (Y) (&M) (&↑) 🖨 📹 🖵 / (✕) 🖥 🖨 /
FEE

THE PRINCE GEORGE HOTEL   *Book great rates at AAA.com*   **Phone:** 902/425-1986   **15**
(CAA) (SAVE)   5/1-10/31   1P: $179-$209   2P: $179-$209   XP: $20
🛆🛆🛆 🛆🛆🛆   11/1-4/30   1P: $149-$179   2P: $149-$179   XP: $20
Location: Between Prince and Carmichael sts. Located next to World Trade Centre. 1725 Market St B3J 3N9.
Large-scale Hotel **Fax:** 902/429-6048. **Facility:** This full-service downtown hotel offers rooms and suites overlooking the city or waterfront and close to the Citadel. 203 units. 189 one-bedroom standard units. 14 one-bedroom suites, some with whirlpools. 6 stories, interior corridors. **Parking:** on-site (fee) and valet. **Amenities:** video games (fee), high-speed Internet, voice mail, honor bars, irons, hair dryers. *Some:* CD players, dual phone lines, safes. **Dining:** 6:30 am-11 pm, cocktails. **Pool(s):** heated indoor. **Leisure Activities:** sauna, whirlpool, exercise room. **Guest Services:** valet laundry. **Business Services:** conference facilities, business center. **Cards:** AX, CB, DC, DS, JC, MC, VI. **Free Special Amenities:** local telephone calls and newspaper. *(See color ad p 324)*

SOME UNITS

FEE

🐕 (T↑) (Y) (&M) 🏊 (✕) 📹 🖵 / (✕) (VCR) /

QUALITY INN & SUITES HALIFAX   *Book great rates at AAA.com*   **Phone:** (902)444-6700   **6**
🛆🛆🛆   All Year [CP]   1P: $108-$163   2P: $108-$163   XP: $10   F18
Location: Hwy 102, exit 2. 980 Parkland Dr B3M 4Y7. Fax: 902/444-4410. **Facility:** Smoke free premises. 113
Small-scale Hotel units. 104 one-bedroom standard units. 9 one-bedroom suites, some with whirlpools. 5 stories, interior corridors. **Parking:** on-site. **Terms:** cancellation fee imposed, 2% service charge, small pets only. **Amenities:** high-speed Internet, voice mail, irons, hair dryers. *Some:* dual phone lines. **Pool(s):** heated indoor. **Leisure Activities:** whirlpool, waterslide, exercise room, spa. *Fee:* game room. **Guest Services:** valet and coin laundry. **Business Services:** meeting rooms, PC. **Cards:** AX, DC, DS, MC, VI. **(See color ad card insert)**

(ASK) (SD) 🐕 (T↑) (&M) 🏊 (✕) (✕) 📹 🖥 🖨 🖵

(See map and index starting on p. 313)

RADISSON SUITE HOTEL HALIFAX

Phone: (902)429-7233 **14**

(CAA) (SAVE)

| | 5/1-10/31 [CP] | 1P: $179 | XP: $20 | F18 |
| | 11/1-4/30 [CP] | 1P: $149 | XP: $10 | F18 |

Large-scale Hotel

Location: Between Sackville and Prince sts. 1649 Hollis St B3J 1V8. Fax: 902/429-9700. **Facility:** 104 one-bedroom suites, some with whirlpools. 8 stories, interior corridors. **Parking:** valet. **Amenities:** video games (fee), high-speed Internet, dual phone lines, voice mail, honor bars, irons, hair dryers. **Dining:** 11 am-11 pm, cocktails. **Pool(s):** small heated indoor. **Leisure Activities:** saunas, whirlpool, exercise room. **Guest Services:** valet and coin laundry. **Business Services:** meeting rooms, PC. **Cards:** AX, DC, DS, JC, MC, VI. **Free Special Amenities:** expanded continental breakfast and high-speed Internet.

SOME UNITS

RESIDENCE INN BY MARRIOTT

Phone: (902)422-0493 **17**

| | 5/1-10/31 [BP] | 1P: $179-$199 | 2P: $179-$199 | XP: $20 | F18 |
| | 11/1-4/30 [BP] | 1P: $149-$159 | 2P: $149-$159 | XP: $20 | F18 |

Small-scale Hotel

Location: Corner of Sackville St. 1599 Grafton St B3J 2C3. Fax: 902/422-0413. **Facility:** Smoke free premises. 92 units. 76 one-bedroom standard units. 11 one- and 5 two-bedroom suites ($159-$299). 6 stories, interior corridors. *Bath:* combo or shower only. **Parking:** on-site (fee). **Terms:** cancellation fee imposed, pets ($75 fee). **Amenities:** CD players, high-speed Internet, voice mail, irons, hair dryers. **Leisure Activities:** whirlpool, exercise room. **Guest Services:** valet and coin laundry, wireless Internet. **Business Services:** meeting rooms, PC. **Cards:** AX, DC, JC, MC, VI.

FEE

STARDUST MOTEL TIMBERLEA

Phone: (902)876-2301

| | 5/1-10/15 | 1P: $79-$99 | 2P: $89-$109 | XP: $10 | F12 |
| | 10/16-4/30 | 1P: $69-$79 | 2P: $79-$89 | XP: $10 | F12 |

Motel

Location: Hwy 103, exit 2A, 3 mi (5 km) w on Rt 3; in Timberlea. 1791 St. Margaret Rd B3T 1B8. Fax: 902/876-2261. **Facility:** 21 one-bedroom standard units. 2 stories (no elevator), exterior corridors. **Parking:** on-site. **Terms:** office hours 7 am-midnight, cancellation fee imposed. **Amenities:** hair dryers. **Cards:** AX, DC, MC, VI.

SOME UNITS

TRAVELERS MOTEL

Phone: 902/835-3394 **1**

Property failed to provide current rates

Motel

Location: Hwy 102, exit 4A, 3.3 mi (5.3 km) e on Rt 2 (Bedford Hwy). 773 Bedford Hwy B4A 1A4. Fax: 902/835-6887. **Facility:** 25 one-bedroom standard units. 1 story, exterior corridors. **Parking:** on-site, winter plug-ins. **Terms:** office hours 7 am-midnight, small pets only (in designated units).

SOME UNITS

(See map and index starting on p. 313)

THE WESTIN NOVA SCOTIAN   *Book great rates at AAA.com*   Phone: (902)421-1000   **23**

CAA SAVE   All Year   2P: $129-$295   XP: $20   F16

Classic Historic
Large-scale Hotel

Location: Between Barrington and Lower Water sts. 1181 Hollis St B3H 2P6. Fax: 902/422-9465. **Facility:** This circa 1931 grand hotel with lovely public areas overlooks the Halifax waterfront and Cornwallis Park; guest rooms vary in size and decor. Smoke free premises. 297 units. 285 one-bedroom standard units. 12 one-bedroom suites ($250-$995). 9-11 stories, interior corridors. **Parking:** on-site (fee). **Terms:** package plans. **Amenities:** high-speed Internet (fee), dual phone lines, voice mail, safes, honor bars, irons, hair dryers. *Some:* DVD players. **Dining:** 6:30 am-11 pm, cocktails. **Pool(s):** heated indoor. **Leisure Activities:** whirlpool, lighted tennis court, exercise room, spa. **Guest Services:** sundries, valet laundry, area transportation-downtown, personal trainer. **Business Services:** conference facilities, business center. **Cards:** AX, DC, DS, MC, VI. **Free Special Amenities:** newspaper and high-speed Internet. *(See color ad below, p 5 & coupon in Savings Section)*

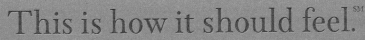

(See map and index starting on p. 313)

———— WHERE TO DINE ————

44 NORTH RESTAURANT **Lunch:** $9-$15 **Dinner:** $15-$28 **Phone:** 902/421-1700 ⑤
Canadian
Location: Adjacent to historic properties and Casino Nova Scotia; in Halifax Marriott Harbourfront. 1919 Upper Water St B3J 3J5. **Hours:** 6:30 am-10:30 pm. **Reservations:** accepted. **Features:** Affording one of the city's finest harbour views, the spacious dining room has two levels designed to focus on the sights. The menu reflects the ocean location with a splendid array of fresh seafood. For meat lovers, there is a selection of choice meats. Casual dress; cocktails. **Parking:** on-site (fee) and valet. **Cards:** AX, CB, DS, MC, VI.

BISH WORLD CUISINE **Dinner:** $18-$35 **Phone:** 902/425-7993 ⑰
International
Location: Centre; at Bishop's Landing Complex. 1475 Lower Water St B3J 3Z2. **Hours:** 5 pm-10 pm. Closed: Sun. **Reservations:** suggested. **Features:** The delightful waterfront restaurant overlooks Halifax harbor. Each of the chef's creations of global cuisine is imaginative and colorful. Patio seating opens in summer. Dressy casual; cocktails. **Parking:** on-site (fee). **Cards:** AX, DC, MC, VI.

CAFE CHIANTI **Lunch:** $7-$12 **Dinner:** $15-$20 **Phone:** 902/423-7471 ㉔
Italian
Location: Across from Westin Hotel. 5165 South St B3J 2A6. **Hours:** 11:30 am-2:30 & 5-10 pm, Sun from 5 pm. Closed: 12/25, 12/26. **Reservations:** suggested. **Features:** The extensive menu lists selections of pasta, seafood, beef and chicken, with several vegetarian choices. Goulash and stroganoff are among Eastern European specialties. Chianti bottles hang from the ceiling while hand painted murals adorn the walls. Wine list is excellent. Dressy casual; cocktails. **Parking:** street. **Cards:** AX, DC, MC, VI.

CANADIANA RESTAURANT & LOUNGE **Lunch:** $7-$18 **Dinner:** $8-$18 **Phone:** 902/450-1286 ㉘
Canadian
Location: Hwy 103, exit 2; in Bayers Lake Business Park. 15 Lakelands Blvd B0J 1Z2. **Hours:** 10 am-8:30 pm, Fri & Sat from 9 am. Closed: 1/1, 12/25, 12/26. **Reservations:** accepted. **Features:** Patrons can choose either booth or table seating at the large, family-oriented restaurant. The varied menu swings from burgers and pizza to fresh seafood, steaks and pasta. Casual dress; cocktails. **Parking:** on-site. **Cards:** AX, MC, VI.

CHEELIN RESTAURANT **Lunch:** $6-$11 **Dinner:** $9-$16 **Phone:** 902/422-2252 ⑮
Chinese
Location: Centre; in Brewery Market. 1496 Lower Water St B3J 1R9. **Hours:** 11:30 am-2:30 & 5:30-10 pm, Sat & Sun from 5:30 pm. Closed major holidays. **Reservations:** accepted. **Features:** Menu choices focus on Beijing and Szechuan cuisine—such as sweet and sour chicken and beef with broccoli. Attractive table settings add to the ambience of the comfortable dining area. Casual dress; cocktails. **Parking:** on-site (fee). **Cards:** AX, DC, DS, MC, VI.

CHINA TOWN RESTAURANT **Lunch:** $6-$12 **Dinner:** $13-$20 **Phone:** 902/443-2444 ①
Chinese
Location: 5 mi (8 km) w on Rt 2 (Bedford Hwy), exit Birch Cove-Kearney Lake from Bicentennial Dr. 381 Bedford Hwy B3M 2L3. **Hours:** 11 am-11 pm. Closed: 12/25. **Reservations:** accepted. **Features:** Diners can appreciate views of the waterfront marina on the shore of Bedford Basin from booths and tables in the spacious restaurant. The menu blends Chinese, Peking, Szechuan and Cantonese cuisine. Casual dress; cocktails. **Parking:** on-site. **Cards:** AX, DC, MC, VI.

CORA'S BREAKFAST & LUNCH **Lunch:** $6-$10 **Phone:** 902/832-5252
Canadian
Location: Just e of Union St. 107-1475 Bedford Hwy B4A 3Z5. **Hours:** 6 am-3 pm, Sun from 7 am. Closed: 12/25. **Reservations:** accepted. **Features:** Although this place specializes in breakfast, it offers a varied daytime menu that includes bacon, eggs, sausages, crepes, grilled cheese, sandwiches, freshly prepared quiches, salads, fruit platters and freshly squeezed juices. The family-friendly dining room is casual and modern. Casual dress. **Parking:** on-site. **Cards:** AX, DC, MC, VI.

CORA'S BREAKFAST & LUNCH **Lunch:** $6-$10 **Phone:** 902/457-2672
Canadian
Location: Just e of Dunbrack St. 287 Lacewood Dr B3M 3Y7. **Hours:** 6 am-3 pm, Sun from 7 am. Closed: 12/25. **Reservations:** accepted. **Features:** Although this place specializes in breakfast, it offers a varied daytime menu that includes bacon, eggs, sausages, crepes, grilled cheese, sandwiches, freshly prepared quiches, salads, fruit platters and freshly squeezed juices. The family-friendly dining room is casual and modern. Casual dress. **Parking:** on-site. **Cards:** AX, DC, MC, VI.

CORA'S BREAKFAST & LUNCH **Lunch:** $6-$10 **Phone:** 902/490-2672
Canadian
Location: Between Birmingham St and Dresden Row. 5523 Spring Garden Rd B3J 3T1. **Hours:** 6 am-3 pm, Sun from 7 am. Closed: 12/25. **Reservations:** accepted. **Features:** Although this place specializes in breakfast, it offers a varied daytime menu that includes bacon, eggs, sausages, crepes, grilled cheese, sandwiches, freshly prepared quiches, salads, fruit platters and freshly squeezed juices. The family-friendly dining room is casual and modern. Casual dress. **Parking:** on-site (fee). **Cards:** AX, DC, MC, VI.

CURRY VILLAGE INDIAN CUISINE **Lunch:** $6-$11 **Dinner:** $9-$16 **Phone:** 902/429-5010 ㉓
Indian
Location: Centre; just s of Spring Garden Rd. 5677 Brenton Pl B3J 1E4. **Hours:** 11:30 am-2 & 5-10 pm. Closed: 1/1, 12/25. **Reservations:** accepted. **Features:** Diners can choose from many favorite Indian dishes, including several combination plates. Prepared-to-order entrees are served in ample portions. Casual dress; cocktails. **Parking:** street. **Cards:** AX, MC, VI.

DA MAURIZIO DINING ROOM **Dinner:** $27-$35 **Phone:** 902/423-0859 ⑭
Italian
Location: Between Salter and Bishops sts; in the Brewery Market. 1496 Lower Water St B3J 1R9. **Hours:** 5:30 pm-10 pm. Closed major holidays; also Sun. **Reservations:** suggested. **Features:** The upscale, highly acclaimed restaurant offers elegant decor and a sophisticated atmosphere. Fresh seafood, prime meats and pasta are the basis for a menu of creative, flavorful cuisine. Dressy casual; cocktails. **Parking:** on-site (fee). **Cards:** AX, DC, DS, MC, VI.

(See map and index starting on p. 313)

DECO RESTAURANT   Lunch: $8-$15   Dinner: $18-$26   Phone: 902/423-9795   19

Location: Between Birmingham St and Dresden Row. 5518 Spring Garden Rd B3J 1G6. Hours: 11:30 am-10 pm, Fri-11 pm, Sat 9 am-11 pm, Sun 9 am-10 pm. Closed: 12/25, 12/26. Reservations: suggested. Features: A wonderful art deco design greets you as you walk through the doors, from the unique hanging lights to the posters on the walls. The menu offers items such as local chicken, halibut and salmon as well as area mussels and scallops. There is a nice, extensive wine list available and the prices are very reasonable. Casual dress; cocktails. Parking: street. Cards: AX, MC, VI.

Continental

ENCORE TRADITIONAL CUISINE   Lunch: $8-$14   Dinner: $14-$27   Phone: 902/861-3480

Location: Hwy 102, exit 5; in Inn on the Lake. 3009 Hwy 2 B2P 1J5. Hours: 7 am-10 pm, Sun-9 pm. Closed: 12/24-12/26. Reservations: suggested. Features: The attractive Victorian-style inn, appointed with antiques, looks out at scenic Lake Thomas. Couples favor the restaurant for special occasions. Planked salmon is served with smoked tomato chutney. Death by chocolate is deliciously decadent. Dressy casual; cocktails. Parking: on-site. Cards: AX, DC, DS, MC, VI.

Canadian

FID   Lunch: $10-$16   Dinner: $15-$25   Phone: 902/422-9162   16

Location: Between Artillery Place and Sackville St. 1569 Dresden Row Rd B3N 1H6. Hours: 11:30 am-2 & 5-10 pm, Sat, Sun & Tues from 5 pm. Closed major holidays; also Mon. Reservations: suggested. Features: A delightful restaurant and true to its name "fid" manages to splice a blend of Asian and French cuisine in a most colorful and creative style. A superb wine list will sure to please the most discriminating wine buff. Casual dress; cocktails. Parking: street. Cards: AX, MC, VI.

French

THE FIRESIDE   Lunch: $7-$15   Dinner: $8-$20   Phone: 902/423-5995   18

Location: Corner of Spring Garden Rd. 1500 Brunswick St B3J 3X9. Hours: 11:30 am-10 pm, Fri & Sat-midnight, Sun 4:30 pm-10 pm. Closed major holidays. Features: Examples of dishes here include tarragon chicken crepes, dilled salmon and fiery pork chops. Casual dress; cocktails. Parking: street. Cards: AX, DC, MC, VI.

Canadian

FIVE FISHERMEN   Dinner: $31-$40   Phone: 902/422-4421   6

Location: Centre. 1740 Argyle B3J 2W1. Hours: 5 pm-10 pm, Fri & Sat-11 pm. Closed: 1/1, 12/24-12/26. Reservations: suggested. Features: The all-you-can-eat salad and mussel bar is a big attraction at the moderately upscale restaurant, which is inside an 1816 building appointed in nautical decor. Delicious entrees include Cajun-blackened halibut and creative daily specials. The restaurant has been in business since 1974. Casual dress; cocktails. Parking: street. Cards: AX, DC, MC, VI.

Steak & Seafood

HENRY HOUSE RESTAURANT AND PUB   Lunch: $6-$12   Dinner: $10-$17   Phone: 902/423-5660   27

Location: Between Morris and South sts. 1222 Barrington St B3J 1Y4. Hours: 11:30 am-10:30 pm, Thurs-Sat to midnight, Sun noon-10:30 pm. Closed: 12/25, 12/26; also 4/18. Features: In the 1830s Henry House, the restaurant is decorated with granite, fireplaces and pub-style furnishings. On a menu of mostly basic fare are such specialties as fish and chips, smoked salmon fettuccine and Mediterranean meatloaf. Home-brewed ales are fitting accompaniments. Casual dress; beer & wine only. Parking: on-site. Cards: AX, DC, MC, VI. Historic

Canadian

IL MERCATO RISTORANTE   Lunch: $11-$18   Dinner: $15-$23   Phone: 902/422-2866   22

Location: At S Park St; centre. 5650 Spring Garden Rd B3J 3M7. Hours: 11 am-11 pm. Closed major holidays; also Sun & 12/24. Reservations: accepted. Features: The colorful bistro, with its bustling atmosphere, prepares a fine selection of gourmet delights: pasta, fresh seafood and meat entrees, as well as thin-crust pizza. Save room for an excellent dessert from the showcase. Casual dress; cocktails. Parking: street. Cards: AX, DC, DS, MC, VI.

Italian

JUNGLE JIM'S RESTAURANT   Lunch: $7-$11   Dinner: $8-$20   Phone: 902/450-5468

Location: In Bayers Lake Business Park. 189 Chain Lake Dr B3S 1G9. Hours: 11 am-10 pm, Thurs-Sat to 11 pm. Closed: 1/1, 12/25, 12/26. Reservations: accepted. Features: Guests can step into a tropical theme at the casual eatery, which employs a friendly staff and nurtures a bustling atmosphere. The menu lines up a wide variety of comfort foods, salads, chicken, beef, seafood and hot wings, all served in ample, flavorful portions. Casual dress; cocktails. Parking: on-site. Cards: AX, DC, MC, VI.

Canadian

THE KEG STEAKHOUSE & BAR   Dinner: $14-$27   Phone: 902/425-8355

Location: At Prince St. 1712 Market St B3J 2E3. Hours: 4:30 pm-10 pm, Fri & Sat-10:30 pm, Sun-9:30 pm. Closed: 12/25. Reservations: accepted. Features: Known for its mesquite-grilled steaks and fun, laid-back atmosphere, the steak house is a longtime favourite with the local crowd. In addition to great beef, the traditional menu lists seafood, grilled chicken, hickory ribs and pasta dishes. Casual dress; cocktails. Parking: street. Cards: AX, DC, MC, VI.

Steak House

MCKELVIE'S DELISHES FISHES DISHES   Lunch: $8-$15   Dinner: $14-$25   Phone: 902/421-6161   7

Location: Between Prince and Sackville sts. 1680 Lower Water St B3J 2Y3. Hours: 11:30 am-9 pm, Fri & Sat-10 pm. Closed: 12/25, 12/26; also Sun 9/1-6/30. Reservations: accepted. Features: Crab bisque, crunchy haddock and crispy crab cakes are representative of tastefully prepared menu choices. In a refurbished fire station, the restaurant bustles with activity. All desserts, including pleasing ice creams and sorbets, are homemade. Casual dress; cocktails. Parking: street. Cards: AX, DC, MC, VI.

Seafood

MEXICALI ROSA'S   Lunch: $7-$11   Dinner: $9-$16   Phone: 902/422-7672

Location: At Dresden Rd; centre. 5680 Spring Garden Rd B3J 1H5. Hours: 11:30 am-11 pm, Thurs-Sat to midnight. Closed: 12/25. Reservations: accepted. Features: The Mexican cantina makes an excellent choice for family-friendly fun. Old West paintings and murals add color to stucco walls and wooden beams, while a Tex-Mex menu provides a feast of favorites such as fajitas, burritos and some seafood items. Fried ice cream is a sweet treat. Casual dress; cocktails. Parking: on-site (fee). Cards: AX, DC, MC, VI.

Mexican

(See map and index starting on p. 313)

MIKES RESTAURANT
Lunch: $6-$10   Dinner: $8-$16   Phone: 902/835-2378

Canadian

Location: Centre; in Bedford Place Mall. 1658 Bedford Hwy B4A 1A4. **Hours:** 8 am-10 pm. **Closed:** 12/25. **Reservations:** accepted. **Features:** This popular family-friendly restaurant specializes in pizza and hot submarine sandwiches, along with fries, burgers, soup, salads, pasta, grilled meats and seafood. An excellent variety of colorful desserts rounds out the offerings. Casual dress; cocktails. **Parking:** on-site.
Cards: AX, DC, MC, VI.

MONTANA'S COOKHOUSE
Lunch: $5-$10   Dinner: $8-$20   Phone: 902/450-1011

Steak House

Location: Hwy 102, exit 2A; in Bayer Lake Business Park. 194 B Chain Lake Dr B3S 1C5. **Hours:** 11 am-11 pm, Fri & Sat-midnight. **Closed:** 12/25. **Reservations:** accepted. **Features:** Pine boards, exposed beams, a fireplace and Western gear displayed about the dining room give the feeling of a back-country setting. The menu lists hearty portions of comfort fare, such as Yankee pot roast. While the focus is on steaks, ribs and chicken, some seafood entrees also are among offerings. Service is efficient and friendly. Casual dress; cocktails. **Parking:** on-site. **Cards:** AX, DC, MC, VI.

OPA GREEK TAVERNA
Lunch: $7-$14   Dinner: $12-$21   Phone: 902/492-7999   (11)

Greek

Location: At Blowers St. 1565 Argyle St B3J 2B2. **Hours:** 11 am-11 pm, Sun 4 pm-10 pm. **Closed:** 10/8, 12/25, 12/26. **Reservations:** accepted. **Features:** A delightful Greek setting awaits patrons who venture into the stylish taverna. From the open-style kitchen comes an array of Greek dishes coupled with a fine wine list. Save room for one of the splendid desserts. Casual dress; cocktails. **Parking:** street. **Cards:** AX, DC, MC, VI.

POGUE FADO IRISH PUBLIC HOUSE
Lunch: $6-$11   Dinner: $9-$16   Phone: 902/429-6222   (10)

Irish

Location: At Salter St. 1581 Barrington St B3J 1Z7. **Hours:** 11 am-10 pm. **Closed:** 12/25. **Features:** Folks with a touch of the blarney in the upbeat Irish-themed pub. Traditional Irish fare and basic comfort foods pair with a good selection of imported and domestic draft beers. Casual dress; cocktails. **Parking:** street. **Cards:** AX, MC, VI.

THE PRESS GANG SEAFOOD RESTAURANT & OYSTER BAR
Dinner: $22-$35   Phone: 902/423-8816   (9)

Seafood

Location: Corner of Prince and Argyle sts; centre. 5218 Prince St B3J 3X4. **Hours:** 5:30 pm-11 pm. **Closed:** 12/25. **Reservations:** suggested. **Features:** Candlelight enhances the distinctive setting—amid 250-year-old exposed stone walls, pillars and wooden beams. Although the menu centers on fresh seafood, it also lists organic meats, fine chowders and items from the raw oyster bar. Casual dress; cocktails. **Parking:** on-site (fee). **Cards:** AX, DC, MC, VI.

REDWOOD GRILL
Lunch: $7-$14   Dinner: $12-$21   Phone: 902/446-4243   (2)

Canadian

Location: Hwy 102, exit 2A; in Future Inns Halifax. 30 Fairfax Dr B3S 1P1. **Hours:** 7 am-10 pm. **Reservations:** accepted. **Features:** Booths and tables alike contribute to the modern, contemporary decor. In addition to comfort foods, such as burgers, pizza and fish and chips, the menu lists fresh seafood, steaks and creatively prepared pasta dishes. Casual dress; cocktails. **Parking:** on-site. **Cards:** AX, DC, MC, VI.

RYAN DUFFY'S
Lunch: $9-$15   Dinner: $15-$28   Phone: 902/421-1116   (21)

Steak & Seafood

Location: In Spring Garden Place shopping promenade. 5640 Spring Garden Rd B3J 3M7. **Hours:** 11:30 am-10 pm, Fri & Sat-11 pm, Sun 5 pm-10 pm. Closed major holidays. **Reservations:** suggested, for dinner. **Features:** Corn fed Nebraska beef results in such succulent steaks as the New York strip, filet mignon and strip loin. Black velvet chairs, a cozy fireplace, subtle illumination and antique accents lend the dining room the ambience of a friendly pub. Casual dress; cocktails. **Parking:** on-site (fee). **Cards:** AX, DC, MC, VI.

SALTY'S ON THE WATERFRONT
Lunch: $8-$16   Dinner: $18-$27   Phone: 902/423-6818   (3)

Seafood

Location: On waterfront in historic properties. 1869 Upper Water St B3J 1S9. **Hours:** 11:30 am-10 pm; seasonal hours vary. **Closed:** 1/1, 12/24-12/26. **Reservations:** suggested, for upstairs. **Features:** Overlooking the harbor, the popular restaurant has a fine-dining space upstairs, a more casual, booth-filled area on the first floor and a spacious dining deck. Fresh-off-the-boat fish is prepared with quality ingredients and attractively presented. An irresistible array of homemade desserts tempts the sweet tooth. Casual dress; cocktails. **Parking:** on-site (fee). **Cards:** AX, DC, DS, MC, VI.

SEVEN WINE BAR & RESTAURANT
Dinner: $21-$28   Phone: 902/444-4777   (12)

Continental

Location: Between Blowers and Sackville sts. 1579 Grafton St B3J 2C3. **Hours:** 4 pm-10 pm, Thurs-Sat to 11 pm. **Closed:** 12/25, 12/26. **Reservations:** suggested. **Features:** The restaurant's two levels are located in an old red brick fire hall known as Fire Hall #7. For fine dining head upstairs; for casual dining choose the main level, which offers a wonderful wine bar with several wines available by the glass. Items like wood-grilled steaks as well as "main plates" of halibut and salmon. Parking is at street meters only. Dressy casual; cocktails. **Parking:** street. **Cards:** AX, DC, MC, VI.

(See map and index starting on p. 313)

SMITTY'S FAMILY RESTAURANT   **Lunch:** $6-$11   **Dinner:** $8-$16   **Phone:** 902/835-7204
Canadian — **Location:** At Sunnyside Mall. 1552 Bedford Hwy B4A 1E4. **Hours:** 7 am-9 pm, Sat & Sun from 8 am. Closed: 12/25. **Reservations:** accepted. **Features:** The family-oriented restaurant satisfies patrons with its ever-popular all-day breakfast items, as well as tasty and wholesome soups and salads at lunchtime. A relaxed mood characterizes the dining space. Casual dress; cocktails. **Parking:** on-site. **Cards:** AX, DC, MC, VI.

SMITTY'S FAMILY RESTAURANT   **Lunch:** $6-$11   **Dinner:** $8-$16   **Phone:** 902/429-1148
Canadian — **Location:** Between Spring Garden Rd and College St. 1472 Tower Rd B3H 4K8. **Hours:** 6:30 am-8 pm, Sun from 8 am. Closed: 12/25. **Reservations:** accepted. **Features:** The family-oriented restaurant satisfies patrons with its ever-popular all-day breakfast items, as well as tasty and wholesome soups and salads at lunchtime. A relaxed mood characterizes the dining space. Casual dress; cocktails. **Parking:** on-site (fee). **Cards:** AX, DC, MC, VI.

SMITTY'S FAMILY RESTAURANT   **Lunch:** $6-$11   **Dinner:** $8-$16   **Phone:** 902/435-4444
Canadian — **Location:** Corner of Gordon Ave and Main St. 107 Main St B2W 1R6. **Hours:** 7 am-8 pm. Closed: 12/25. **Reservations:** accepted. **Features:** The family-oriented restaurant satisfies patrons with its ever-popular all-day breakfast items, as well as tasty and wholesome soups and salads at lunchtime. A relaxed mood characterizes the dining space. Casual dress; cocktails. **Parking:** on-site. **Cards:** AX, DC, MC, VI.

SWEET BASIL BISTRO   **Lunch:** $8-$15   **Dinner:** $16-$23   **Phone:** 902/425-2133   [4]
Italian — **Location:** Centre. 1866 Upper Water St B3J 1S8. **Hours:** 11:30 am-10 pm; hours vary off season. Closed: 12/24, 12/25. **Reservations:** accepted. **Features:** This colourful bistro with its works of modern art is conveniently located close to historic properties. The entrees are creatively prepared and presented with the use of fresh local ingredients. Enjoy one of their tasty desserts with a cappuccino. Casual dress; cocktails. **Parking:** on-site (fee). **Cards:** AX, MC, VI.

SWISS CHALET   **Lunch:** $6-$11   **Dinner:** $8-$16   **Phone:** 902/454-4226
Canadian — **Location:** At Young St. 3462 Kempt Rd B3K 4X7. **Hours:** 11 am-10 pm, Thurs-Sat to 11 pm. Closed: 12/25. **Reservations:** accepted. **Features:** The popular restaurant is known for its rotisserie chicken and ribs and the tangy Chalet sauce that gives food its special zip. Diners munch on a half or quarter chicken with sides such as steamed vegetables, fries, baked potatoes and salads. Lunch guests often go for the great soup and sandwich combination. Take-out and delivery service are popular options. Casual dress; cocktails. **Parking:** on-site. **Cards:** AX, DC, MC, VI.

TAJ MAHAL RESTAURANT   **Lunch:** $8-$15   **Dinner:** $14-$22   **Phone:** 902/492-8251   [26]
Indian — **Location:** Corner of South and Barrington sts. 5175 South St B3J 1A2. **Hours:** 11:30 am-10:30 pm, Fri-11:30 pm, Sat noon-11 pm, Sun noon-10:30 pm. Closed: 12/25. **Reservations:** accepted. **Features:** Guests can sample fine Northern and Southern Indian cuisine in a relaxing atmosphere. The extensive menu features many fresh seafood items and vegetarian dishes, as well as some Thai entrees. Casual dress; cocktails. **Parking:** street. **Cards:** AX, MC, VI.

TRINITY   **Lunch:** $8-$14   **Dinner:** $12-$22   **Phone:** 902/423-8428   [25]
Italian — **Location:** Centre; in Park Victoria Building. 1333 S Park St B3J 2K9. **Hours:** 11 am-10 pm. Closed: 12/25. **Reservations:** accepted. **Features:** Creative bistro dishes on a varied menu of seafood, steak and fowl include seafood minestrone and curry and chicken crepe with mandarin oranges, raisins and almonds. For dessert, the lightly sweet and tart flavor of the lemon ice cream parfait pie is delightful. Casual dress; cocktails. **Parking:** street. **Cards:** AX, DC, MC, VI.

VICTORY ARMS PUB   *Menu on AAA.com*   **Lunch:** $8-$14   **Dinner:** $10-$30   **Phone:** 902/420-9781   [20]
Canadian — **Location:** Corner of Park St and Spring Garden Rd; centre; in The Lord Nelson Hotel & Suites. 1515 S Park St B3J 2L2. **Hours:** 7 am-midnight, Fri & Sat-1 am. **Reservations:** accepted. **Features:** The delightful English-style pub nurtures a relaxing atmosphere. Guests can couple well-prepared, traditional pub entrees, a quality steak or fresh seafood with a favorite beverage for a meal that won't disappoint. Casual dress; cocktails. **Parking:** on-site (fee). **Cards:** AX, DC, MC, VI.

WATERFRONT WAREHOUSE RESTAURANT & TUG'S PUB   **Lunch:** $7-$12   **Dinner:** $13-$21   **Phone:** 902/425-7610   [13]
Canadian — **Location:** Centre. 1549 Lower Water St B3J 1S2. **Hours:** 11:30 am-10 pm; from 5 pm 11/15-5/7. Closed major holidays; also Mon 11/15-5/7. **Reservations:** accepted. **Features:** A pleasant nautical theme weaves through the large, converted warehouse, boat shed and seasonal patio. Ample portions of a wide variety of foods are served with aromatic, warm bread. Casual dress; cocktails. **Parking:** on-site (fee). **Cards:** AX, DC, MC, VI.

HUBBARDS

—————— **WHERE TO STAY** ——————

DAUPHINEE INN   **Phone:** (902)857-1790
5/1-10/29 [CP]   2P: $99-$195   XP: $15
Country Inn — **Location:** Rt 103, exit 6, 1.4 mi (2.4 km) e on Rt 3, then 0.5 mi (0.8 km) s. Located in a quiet area. 167 Shore Club Rd B0J 1T0. Fax: 902/857-9555. **Facility:** Large sun decks provide outdoor lounging space for guests at this inn bordering a marina on Hubbards Cove. Smoke free premises. 6 one-bedroom standard units, some with whirlpools. 3 stories (no elevator), interior corridors. *Bath:* combo or shower only. **Parking:** on-site. **Terms:** open 5/1-10/29, office hours 8 am-10 pm, cancellation fee imposed. **Amenities:** CD players, hair dryers. **Dining:** restaurant, see separate listing. **Leisure Activities:** fishing, bicycles. *Fee:* boat dock. **Guest Services:** wireless Internet. **Cards:** AX, DC, DS, MC, VI.

——— WHERE TO DINE ———

DAUPHINEE INN DINING ROOM   Dinner: $17-$29   Phone: 902/857-1790

Location: Rt 103, exit 6, 1.4 mi (2.4 km) e on Rt 3, then 0.5 mi (0.8 km) s; in Dauphinee Inn. 167 Shore Club Rd B0J
Canadian   1T0. **Hours:** Open 6/18-10/31; 5:30 pm-9 pm. **Reservations:** accepted. **Features:** A picturesque setting
overlooking Hubbards Cove. The Dauphinee offers fine dining on upper floor with focus on fresh seafood. A
DC, DS, MC, VI.   pub with deck on lower floor for offers comfort foods. Casual dress; cocktails. **Parking:** on-site. **Cards:** AX,

SHORE CLUB LOBSTER SUPPERS   Dinner: $24-$34   Phone: 902/857-9555
Location: Rt 103, exit 6, 1.4 mi (2.4 km) e on Rt 3, then 0.6 mi (1 km) s. 250 Shore Club Rd B0J 1T0. **Hours:** Open
6/14-9/30; 4 pm-8 pm. Closed: Mon & Tues. **Features:** In a former dance hall, the spacious restaurant
Seafood   offers an all-you-can-eat self-serve salad and mussel bar, as well as a choice of lobster or beef dinner and
dessert. Casual dress; cocktails. **Parking:** on-site. **Cards:** AX, DC, DS, MC, VI.

INGONISH

——— WHERE TO STAY ———

——— *The following lodging was either not evaluated or did not* ———
meet AAA rating requirements but is listed for your information only.

GLENGHORM BEACH RESORT   Phone: 902/285-2049
[fyi]   Not evaluated. **Location:** 1 mi (1.6 km) n of Cape Breton Highlands National Park. 36743 Cabot Tr B0C 1K0 (PO Box
39). Facilities, services, and decor characterize a mid-range property. *(See color ad p 301)*

INGONISH BEACH

——— WHERE TO STAY ———

KELTIC LODGE   *Book at AAA.com*   Phone: (902)285-2880
6/8-10/8 [MAP]   1P: $254   2P: $344   XP: $96   F12
5/18-6/7 & 10/9-10/20   1P: $141   2P: $161   XP: $26   F12
Classic Historic   **Location:** Inside the Cape Breton Highlands National Park; off Cabot Trail main highway. Located in a quiet area.
Resort   Middle Head Peninsula B0C 1L0 (PO Box 70, INGONISH). Fax: 902/285-2859. **Facility:** This lovely property at
Large-Scale Hotel   the tip of a peninsula offers rooms in a main hotel, an annex wing and duplex chalets. 105 units. 92 one-
bedroom standard units. 2 two-bedroom suites. 11 cottages, some with whirlpools. 1-3 stories (no elevator),
interior/exterior corridors. **Parking:** on-site. **Terms:** open 5/18-10/20, 3 day cancellation notice-fee imposed, package plans,
small pets only (in cottages). **Amenities:** voice mail, irons, hair dryers. *Some:* CD players. **Dining:** Atlantic Restaurant, Purple
Thistle Dining Room, see separate listings. **Pool(s):** heated outdoor. **Leisure Activities:** limited beach access, fishing, bicycles,
hiking trails, exercise room, spa, game room. *Fee:* saunas, whirlpools, golf-18 holes. **Guest Services:** gift shop, valet laundry.
Business Services: conference facilities, PC. **Cards:** AX, DC, DS, MC, VI.

SOME UNITS

ASK ⬛ 🐾 🍴 🍷 🏊 ✂ ✉ 🎥 💻 / 🍳 📞

LANTERN HILL & HOLLOW   Phone: 902/285-2010
5/25-10/15   1P: $215-$235   2P: $215-$235
Location: 36845 Cabot Tr B0C 1L0 (PO Box 235). Fax: 902/285-2001. **Facility:** These lovely, large cottages (all
with decks and BBQs) and three tastefully decorated guest rooms are in a scenic setting bordering a sandy
Cottage   beach. Smoke free premises. 9 units. 3 one-bedroom standard units. 6 cottages, some with whirlpools. 1-2
stories (no elevator), interior/exterior corridors. **Parking:** on-site. **Terms:** open 5/25-10/15, office hours 8 am-9 pm, 3 day
cancellation notice. **Amenities:** irons, hair dryers. **Leisure Activities:** limited beach access. **Cards:** MC, VI.

SOME UNITS

✉ 🍳 🎥 📞 💻 / 🍽 /

——— WHERE TO DINE ———

ATLANTIC RESTAURANT   Lunch: $8-$16   Dinner: $10-$20   Phone: 902/285-2880
Location: Inside the Cape Breton Highlands National Park; off Cabot Trail main highway; in Keltic Lodge. Middle Head
Peninsula B0C 1L0. **Hours:** Open 6/4-10/31; 11 am-9 pm. **Features:** Atlantic's spacious dining room with
Canadian   cathedral ceilings and large windows offers a lovely view of the ocean and coastline. Menu items include a
wide selection of fresh local seafood as well as burgers and fries. Casual dress; cocktails. **Parking:** on-site.
Cards: AX, CB, DC, DS, JC, MC, VI.

MAIN STREET RESTAURANT & BAKERY   Lunch: $6-$13   Dinner: $6-$13   Phone: 902/285-2225
Location: 0.6 mi (1 km) s of park gate; right on Cabot Trail. 37764 Cabot Tr B0C 1L0. **Hours:** Open 5/15-10/20; 7
am-9 pm. Closed: Mon. **Features:** This bakery/restaurant is small and simple and the decor and service
Canadian   casual. However, the menu lines up a great selection of home-cooked food. Soups and sandwiches are
featured daily, as are varied baked goods, including super-soft, delicious cinnamon buns. Guests can eat in
or outside on the small patio. Casual dress; beer & wine only. **Parking:** on-site. **Cards:** AX, MC, VI.

PURPLE THISTLE DINING ROOM   Dinner: $53   Phone: 902/285-2880
Location: Inside the Cape Breton Highlands National Park; off Cabot Trail main highway; in Keltic Lodge. Middle Head
Peninsula B0C 1L0. **Hours:** Open 5/21-10/24; 7 am-10 & 6-9 pm. **Reservations:** required. **Features:** The
Continental   lovely, spacious dining room is in the main section of a hotel. The staff provides steady service amid a
relaxed atmosphere. On the menu are seafood items and some meat entrees. Dressy casual; cocktails.
Parking: on-site. **Cards:** AX, CB, DC, DS, JC, MC, VI.

INGONISH FERRY

———— WHERE TO STAY ————

———— *The following lodging was either not evaluated or did not* ————
meet AAA rating requirements but is listed for your information only.

THE CASTLE ROCK COUNTRY INN   **Phone: 902/285-2700**
[fyi]   Not evaluated. **Location:** Northern slope of Cape Smokey Mountain. 39339 Cabot Tr B0C 1L0. Facilities, services, and decor characterize a mid-range property.

IONA

———— WHERE TO STAY ————

HIGHLAND HEIGHTS INN   **Phone: (902)725-2360**

	7/1-10/15	1P: $109-$130	2P: $109-$130		F16
	5/20-6/30	1P: $80-$109	2P: $80-$109	XP: $10	
	10/16-12/20	1P: $69	2P: $69		

Small-scale Hotel **Location:** Trans-Canada Hwy 105, exit 6, short ferry ride leads to Rt 223, 13.8 mi (22 km) e, exit 4, then 20.6 mi (33 km) e. 4115 Rt 223 B2C 1A3. Fax: 902/725-2800. **Facility:** Smoke free premises. 32 one-bedroom standard units. 2 stories (no elevator), exterior corridors. **Parking:** on-site. **Terms:** open 5/20-12/20, office hours 7 am-9 pm, 3 day cancellation notice-fee imposed, weekly rates available, [BP] & [MAP] meal plans available, package plans. **Dining:** restaurant, see separate listing. **Guest Services:** wireless Internet. **Cards:** MC, VI. *(See color ad p 301)*

(ASK) (SD) (TI) (X) (AC) (DV) (⊟) (▭)

———— WHERE TO DINE ————

HIGHLAND HEIGHTS RESTAURANT   **Lunch: $8-$17   Dinner: $12-$23   Phone: 902/725-2360**
Canadian **Location:** Trans-Canada Hwy 105, exit 6, short ferry ride leads to Rt 223, 13.8 mi (22 km) e, exit 4, then 20.6 mi (33 km) e; in Highland Heights Inn. 4115 Hwy 223 B2C 1A3. **Hours:** Open 5/15-10/19; 7:30 am-9 pm. **Reservations:** accepted. **Features:** Tasty chowders, fresh seafood and well-prepared meat entrees make up much of a varied menu of home-style country cooking. The hilltop location affords lovely views of the inlet and surrounding hills. The patio is open seasonally. Casual dress; cocktails. **Parking:** on-site. **Cards:** AX, MC, VI.

(AC)

KEMPT

———— WHERE TO STAY ————

THE WHITMAN INN   **Phone: (902)682-2226**

| | 6/1-9/30 | 1P: $59-$119 | 2P: $59-$119 | XP: $10 | F |

Country Inn **Location:** On Rt 8, 2.4 mi (4 km) s of Kejimkujik National Park. Located in a quiet secluded area. 12389 Hwy 8 B0T 1B0 (RR 2, CALEDONIA). Fax: 902/682-3171. **Facility:** Smoke free premises. 9 units. 8 one-bedroom standard units, some with whirlpools. 1 two-bedroom suite ($125) with kitchen. 2 stories (no elevator), interior corridors. *Bath:* combo or shower only. **Parking:** on-site. **Terms:** open 6/1-9/30, office hours 8 am-10 pm, cancellation fee imposed, weekly rates available, package plans. **Pool(s):** heated indoor. **Leisure Activities:** sauna, game room. **Guest Services:** TV in common area. **Cards:** MC, VI.

(ASK) (TI) (⊷) (X) (AC) (PV) (Z)

KEMPTVILLE

———— WHERE TO STAY ————

TROUT POINT LODGE   **Phone: (902)482-8360**

| | | 6/22-8/31 & 10/1-11/15 | 1P: $205-$265 | 2P: $205-$265 | XP: $65 | F5 |
| | | 5/15-6/21 & 9/1-9/30 | 1P: $165-$205 | 2P: $165-$205 | XP: $65 | F5 |

Country Inn **Location:** 6.6 mi (11 km) e on Rt 203, 2.1 mi (3.5 km) n on gravel entry road. 189 Trout Point Rd B0W 1Y0. **Facility:** Built of logs and granite, the lodge is on 200-acres at Trout Point, which is adjacent to a large wilderness area, bording a scenic river system. Designated smoking area. 8 one-bedroom standard units. 3 stories (no elevator), exterior corridors. **Parking:** on-site. **Terms:** open 5/15-11/15, office hours 8 am-11 pm, 21 day cancellation notice-fee imposed, [AP] & [MAP] meal plans available, package plans, 15% service charge. **Amenities:** CD players, irons, hair dryers. **Dining:** lunch seating 1 pm, dinner seating 7:30 pm, cocktails. **Leisure Activities:** whirlpool, canoeing, kayaks, bicycles, hiking trails. **Cards:** MC, VI. **Free Special Amenities:** local telephone calls and room upgrade (subject to availability with advance reservations).

(SD) (🛏) (TI) (Y) (X) (X) (AC) (PV) (Z)

KENTVILLE pop. 5,610

———— WHERE TO STAY ————

ALLEN'S MOTEL   **Phone: 902/678-2683**

| | 5/1-12/31 & 3/21-4/30 | 1P: $66 | 2P: $66 | XP: $6 | F6 |

Motel **Location:** Hwy 101, exit 14, 1.8 mi (3 km) e on Rt 1. 384 Park St B4N 1M9. Fax: 902/678-1910. **Facility:** Designated smoking area. 12 units. 11 one-bedroom standard units, some with kitchens and/or whirlpools. 1 cottage ($85-$91). 2 stories (no elevator), exterior corridors. *Bath:* combo or shower only. **Parking:** on-site. **Terms:** open 5/1-12/31 & 3/21-4/30, office hours 7:30 am-10 pm, [BP] meal plan available. **Amenities:** high-speed Internet. *Some:* DVD players, hair dryers. **Guest Services:** coin laundry. **Cards:** MC, VI. **Free Special Amenities:** local telephone calls and high-speed Internet.

SOME UNITS
(SD) (X) / (⊟) (▣) (▭) /

AUBERGE WANDLYN INN   *Book at AAA.com*   Phone: 902/678-8311

Property failed to provide current rates

Small-scale Hotel   **Location:** Hwy 101, exit 14. 7270 Hwy 1 B4R 1B9. **Fax:** 902/679-1253. **Facility:** 70 one-bedroom standard units. 3 stories (no elevator), interior/exterior corridors. **Parking:** on-site. **Terms:** pets ($10 extra charge). **Amenities:** voice mail, hair dryers. *Some:* high-speed Internet. **Pool(s):** heated indoor. **Leisure Activities:** sauna, whirlpool. **Guest Services:** wireless Internet. **Business Services:** meeting rooms.

SOME UNITS

SUN VALLEY MOTEL   Phone: 902/678-7368

Motel

| All Year | 1P: $66-$90 | 2P: $66-$90 | XP: $7 | F5 |

Location: Hwy 101, exit 14, 0.5 mi (0.8 km) e on Rt 1. 905 Park St B4N 3V7. **Fax:** 902/678-5585. **Facility:** 13 one-bedroom standard units, some with efficiencies. 1 story, exterior corridors. **Parking:** on-site. **Terms:** office hours 7:30 am-10:30 pm, small pets only (in designated units). **Leisure Activities:** playground. **Cards:** AX, DC, MC, VI. **Free Special Amenities:** continental breakfast.

SOME UNITS

―――― **WHERE TO DINE** ――――

KAI-WING RESTAURANT   **Lunch:** $6-$10   **Dinner:** $8-$16   Phone: 902/679-6599

Chinese   **Location:** Hwy 101, exit 14, just e. 7299 Hwy 1 B4R 1B9. **Hours:** 11 am-9 pm, Fri & Sat-10 pm. Closed: 12/25; also Mon. **Reservations:** accepted. **Features:** On the edge of town, the comfortable restaurant offers a wide variety of well-prepared Oriental and Canadian entrees. All dishes are fresh and prepared to order. Casual dress; cocktails. **Parking:** on-site. **Cards:** DC, MC, VI.

PADDY'S BREWPUB & ROSIES RESTAURANT   **Lunch:** $7-$15   **Dinner:** $9-$15   Phone: 902/678-3199

Canadian   **Location:** Centre, at Webster St. 42 Aberdeen St B4N 1M9. **Hours:** 11 am-10 pm. **Reservations:** accepted. **Features:** Patrons can choose either the pub section or the restaurant for well-prepared seafood and steaks, as well as some traditional pub favorites and daily specials. Casual dress; cocktails. **Parking:** street. **Cards:** AX, DC, MC, VI.

STONEROOM LOUNGE CORNWALLIS DINING ROOM   **Lunch:** $6-$13   **Dinner:** $9-$16   Phone: 902/678-0955

Canadian   **Location:** Centre; in Cornwallis Inn Complex. 325 Main St B4N 1K5. **Hours:** 11:30 am-2:30 & 5-9 pm, Fri & Sat-10 pm; hours vary off season. Closed: 12/25, 12/26. **Reservations:** accepted. **Features:** High ceilings, stone walls and wooden beams add to the Old World feel of the pleasant, 1930s building. The menu centers on fresh seafood and meat entrees served in ample portions. Pub fare is served in the spacious lounge. The patio is open in season. Casual dress; cocktails. **Parking:** on-site. **Cards:** AX, DS, MC, VI.

LISCOMB

―――― **WHERE TO STAY** ――――

LISCOMBE LODGE   *Book at AAA.com*   Phone: (902)779-2307

| 7/1-9/30 [BP] | 1P: $155-$175 | 2P: $155-$175 | XP: $30 | F |
| 5/19-6/30 & 10/1-10/20 [BP] | 1P: $140-$155 | 2P: $140-$155 | XP: $30 | F |

Small-scale Hotel   **Location:** On Hwy 7. RR 1, 2884 Hwy 7 B0J 2A0. **Fax:** 902/779-2700. **Facility:** 68 units. 66 one-bedroom standard units. 1 one-bedroom suite with whirlpool. 1 cottage. 1-2 stories (no elevator), interior/exterior corridors. **Bath:** combo or shower only. **Parking:** on-site. **Terms:** open 5/19-10/20, 3 day cancellation notice-fee imposed, pets (in chalets). **Amenities:** video library, voice mail, irons, hair dryers. *Some:* DVD players (fee). **Dining:** restaurant, see separate listing. **Pool(s):** heated indoor. **Leisure Activities:** sauna, whirlpools, boating, canoeing, paddleboats, tennis court, recreation programs in summer, bicycles, playground, exercise room, horseshoes, shuffleboard. *Fee:* boat dock, game room. **Guest Services:** gift shop, coin laundry. **Business Services:** meeting rooms, PC. **Cards:** AX, DC, DS, MC, VI.

SOME UNITS

―――― **WHERE TO DINE** ――――

LISCOMBE LODGE RIVERSIDE ROOM   **Lunch:** $9-$16   **Dinner:** $21-$35   Phone: 902/779-2307

Canadian   **Location:** On Hwy 7; in Liscombe Lodge. Rt 7 B0J 2A0. **Hours:** Open 5/16-10/31; 7 am-9 pm. **Reservations:** not accepted. **Features:** Pleasant location bordering the Liscomb River. Charming and rustic atmosphere. Menu offers a wide range of seafood and meat options including planked salmon. Fine desserts. Casual dress; cocktails; entertainment. **Parking:** on-site. **Cards:** AX, DC, MC, VI.

LITTLE BROOK

―――― **WHERE TO STAY** ――――

CHATEAU D'LA BAIE B & B INN   Phone: (902)769-3113

| 5/1-9/30 [ECP] | 1P: $89-$129 | 2P: $89-$129 | XP: $10 | F12 |
| 10/1-4/30 [ECP] | 1P: $85-$115 | 2P: $85-$115 | XP: $10 | F12 |

Bed & Breakfast   **Location:** Oceanfront. Hwy 101, exit 29 to Rt 1. 959 Rt 1 B0W 1Z0. **Facility:** A beautiful 1920s home on the shore of St. Marys Bay, this B&B has spacious rooms and public areas that are tastefully furnished with period antiques. 7 one-bedroom standard units. 2 stories (no elevator), interior corridors. **Bath:** combo or shower only. **Parking:** on-site. **Terms:** office hours 7 am-10 pm, weekly rates available. **Amenities:** DVD players, hair dryers. **Cards:** AX, MC, VI.

SOME UNITS

LORNEVILLE

──── WHERE TO STAY ────

AMHERST SHORE COUNTRY INN

CAA SAVE

Country Inn

	6/22-9/22	1P: $89-$169	2P: $89-$169	XP: $15
	5/1-6/21 & 9/23-10/31	1P: $79-$149	2P: $79-$149	XP: $15
	12/1-4/30	1P: $79-$129	2P: $79-$129	XP: $15

Phone: (902)661-4800

Location: On Rt 366; centre. Located in a quiet rural area. (RR 2, B4H 3X9). **Facility:** Gas fireplaces warm the varied rooms and duplex suites of this country inn, which overlooks Northumberland Strait; open weekends only off season 12/1-4/30. Smoke free premises. 8 one-bedroom standard units, some with whirlpools. 2 stories (no elevator), interior/exterior corridors. **Parking:** on-site. **Terms:** open 5/1-10/31 & 12/1-4/30, office hours 9 am-10:30 pm, age restrictions may apply, 7 day cancellation notice-fee imposed, package plans. **Amenities:** irons, hair dryers. **Dining:** 7:30 pm seating; reservation required, cocktails. **Leisure Activities:** limited beach access, hiking trails. **Cards:** MC, VI. *(See color ad p 298)*

SOME UNITS

🍽 ✕ / 🛢 📷 💻 /

LOUISBOURG pop. 1,071

──── WHERE TO STAY ────

CRANBERRY COVE INN

Historic Country Inn

| | 6/16-9/15 [BP] | 1P: $105-$160 | 2P: $105-$160 | XP: $20 |
| | 5/1-6/15 & 9/16-10/30 [BP] | 1P: $94-$144 | 2P: $94-$144 | XP: $20 |

Phone: 902/733-2171

Location: Centre. Located in a residential area. 12 Wolfe St B1C 2J2. **Facility:** Each guest room at this converted turn-of-the-20th-century home has a distinctive theme; four have fireplaces. Smoke free premises. 7 one-bedroom standard units, some with whirlpools. 3 stories (no elevator), interior corridors. **Parking:** on-site. **Terms:** open 5/1-10/30, office hours 8 am-10 pm, age restrictions may apply, 3 day cancellation notice. **Amenities:** high-speed Internet, hair dryers. **Guest Services:** wireless Internet. **Business Services:** PC. **Cards:** AX, JC, MC, VI.

🍽 ✕ 🅺

POINT OF VIEW SUITES & RV PARK LTD

Condominium

| | 5/15-10/15 | 1P: $89-$125 | 2P: $89-$125 | XP: $10 |

Phone: (902)733-2080

Location: 0.6 mi (1 km) e on Rt 22. 15 Commercial St Ext B1C 2J4. Fax: 902/733-2638. **Facility:** Most of the large guest rooms have water views at this pleasant seaside property overlooking the harbour. Smoke free premises. 19 units. 16 one- and 1 two-bedroom standard units, some with kitchens and/or whirlpools. 2 one-bedroom suites ($145-$250) with kitchens. 2 stories (no elevator), exterior corridors. **Parking:** on-site. **Terms:** open 5/15-10/15, office hours 8 am-9 pm, [BP] meal plan available. **Amenities:** irons, hair dryers. **Leisure Activities:** fishing. **Guest Services:** coin laundry. **Cards:** AX, MC, VI.

🍽 ✕ 🅺 📹 🛢 📷 💻

──── WHERE TO DINE ────

THE GRUBSTAKE DINING ROOM & LOUNGE

CAA

Canadian

Lunch: $6-$18   **Dinner:** $12-$25   **Phone:** 902/733-2308

Location: On Hwy 22. 7499 Main St B1C 1H8. **Hours:** Open 6/15-10/7; noon-close. Closed: 9/3. **Reservations:** suggested. **Features:** The restaurant has the distinctive atmosphere of a turn-of-the-20th-century coastal town. Thoughtfully prepared seafood, steak and flambe selections fall into the realm of upscale country cuisine. Portion sizes are generous, and dessert is homemade. Casual dress; cocktails. **Parking:** on-site. **Cards:** AX, MC, VI.

🅺

LOBSTER KETTLE RESTAURANT

Seafood

Lunch: $6-$15   **Dinner:** $8-$22   **Phone:** 902/733-2723

Location: Just s off Main St; along waterfront. 41 Strathcona St B1C 1B5. **Hours:** Open 5/10-10/31; 11:30 am-2 & 5-9 pm. **Features:** A popular spot with tourists, the harborside restaurant prepares a wide variety of seafood, including lobster and crab in season. The serve-yourself salad bar is a great accompaniment to any meal, and servings are generous. Casual dress; cocktails. **Parking:** on-site. **Cards:** MC, VI.

🅺

LOWER SACKVILLE

──── WHERE TO DINE ────

SWISS CHALET

Canadian

Lunch: $6-$11   **Dinner:** $8-$16   **Phone:** 902/864-1886

Location: At Cross Rd; centre. 560 Sackville Dr B4C 2S2. **Hours:** 11 am-10 pm, Fri & Sat-11 pm. Closed: 12/25. **Reservations:** accepted. **Features:** The popular restaurant is known for its rotisserie chicken and ribs and the tangy Chalet sauce that gives food its special zip. Diners munch on a half or quarter chicken with sides such as steamed vegetables, fries, baked potatoes and salads. Lunch guests often go for the great soup and sandwich combination. Take-out and delivery service are popular options. Casual dress; cocktails. **Parking:** on-site. **Cards:** AX, DC, MC, VI.

LUNENBURG pop. 2,568

──── WHERE TO STAY ────

BOSCAWEN INN

CAA SAVE

Historic Bed & Breakfast

| | 5/1-12/31 | 1P: $90-$205 | 2P: $90-$205 | XP: $15 |

Phone: (902)634-3325

F5

Location: Centre. Located in a residential area. 150 Cumberland St B0J 2C0. Fax: 902/634-9293. **Facility:** Common areas are spacious and guest rooms vary in size and decor at this 1888 mansion on a hillside overlooking the harbour. Smoke free premises. 22 one-bedroom standard units, some with whirlpools. 3 stories (no elevator), interior corridors. **Bath:** combo, shower or tub only. **Parking:** on-site. **Terms:** open 5/1-12/31, office hours 7 am-11 pm, 3 day cancellation notice-fee imposed, small pets only. **Amenities:** hair dryers. **Some:** irons. **Guest Services:** valet laundry. **Cards:** AX, DC, MC, VI. **Free Special Amenities:** expanded continental breakfast and local telephone calls.

🐾 ✕ 🅺

BRIGANTINE INN & SUITES

(CAA) (SAVE)

Small-scale Hotel

Phone: (902)634-3300

	1P: $79-$179	2P: $79-$179	XP: $15	F13
6/28-9/3 [CP]	1P: $75-$149	2P: $75-$149	XP: $15	F13
5/1-6/27 & 9/4-10/15 [CP]	1P: $65-$125	2P: $65-$129	XP: $15	F13
10/16-4/30 [CP]				

Location: Centre. Located opposite the harbour. 82 Montague St B0J 2C0. **Fax:** 902/634-1907. **Facility:** Smoke free premises. 17 units. 7 one-bedroom standard units, some with whirlpools. 9 one- and 1 two-bedroom suites, some with kitchens and/or whirlpools. 3 stories (no elevator), interior corridors. *Bath:* combo or shower only. **Parking:** street. **Terms:** office hours 8 am-10 pm, package plans. **Amenities:** voice mail, irons, hair dryers. **Dining:** The Grand Banker Seafood Bar & Grill, see separate listing. **Cards:** AX, DC, DS, MC, VI. **Free Special Amenities:** local telephone calls and high-speed Internet.

SOME UNITS

⊘ ⊠ / ▤ ▣ ▦ /

THE HOMEPORT MOTEL

Motel

Phone: (902)634-8234

6/16-9/15	1P: $103	2P: $103	XP: $10	F12
9/16-12/15	1P: $85	2P: $85	XP: $10	F12
5/1-6/15 & 12/16-4/30	1P: $75	2P: $75	XP: $10	F12

Location: 0.6 mi (1 km) w on Rt 3. 167 Victoria Rd B0J 2C0. **Fax:** 902/634-7100. **Facility:** 17 units. 10 one- and 1 two-bedroom standard units, some with whirlpools. 6 one-bedroom suites ($120-$195) with kitchens and whirlpools. 1 story, exterior corridors. *Bath:* combo or shower only. **Parking:** on-site. **Terms:** office hours 7 am-11 pm. **Amenities:** *Some:* hair dryers. **Guest Services:** coin laundry. **Cards:** MC, VI.

SOME UNITS

(ASK) ⊛ ⊯ ⊠ ▤ ▦ ▣ / (VCR) /

KAULBACH HOUSE HISTORIC INN

(CAA) (SAVE)

Historic Bed & Breakfast

speed Internet.

Phone: 902/634-8818

| 6/16-9/30 | 1P: $129-$169 | 2P: $129-$169 | XP: $25 |
| 5/1-6/15 & 10/1-4/30 | 1P: $99-$133 | 2P: $99-$133 | XP: $25 |

Location: Centre. 75 Pelham St B0J 2C0. **Fax:** 902/640-3036. **Facility:** This restored, in-town home dates from around 1880; guest rooms vary in size and style, with some having compact baths. Smoke free premises. 6 one-bedroom standard units. 3 stories (no elevator), interior corridors. *Bath:* shower only. **Parking:** on-site. **Terms:** office hours 7 am-9 pm, 14 day cancellation notice-fee imposed. **Amenities:** video library, DVD players, CD players, irons, hair dryers. **Cards:** MC, VI. **Free Special Amenities:** full breakfast and high-

▥ ⊠ ⓩ ▣

LUNENBURG ARMS HOTEL & SPA

(CAA) (SAVE)

Small-scale Hotel

Phone: (902)640-4040

| 5/16-10/15 | 1P: $139-$255 | 2P: $139-$255 | XP: $15 | F16 |
| 5/1-5/15 & 10/16-4/30 | 1P: $99-$189 | 2P: $99-$189 | XP: $15 | F16 |

Location: Corner of Pelham and Duke sts; centre. 94 Pelham St B0J 2C0. **Fax:** 902/640-4041. **Facility:** Smoke free premises. 26 units. 21 one-bedroom standard units. 5 one-bedroom suites, some with whirlpools. 3 stories, interior corridors. *Bath:* combo or shower only. **Parking:** on-site. **Terms:** office hours 8 am-10 pm, 7 day cancellation notice-fee imposed, package plans. **Amenities:** high-speed Internet, hair dryers. **Dining:** Rissers Casual Dining, see separate listing. **Business Services:** meeting rooms. **Cards:** AX, DC, MC, VI. **Free Special Amenities:** local telephone calls and high-speed Internet.

⊯ ⊘ ⊤ ⓜ ⊛ ⊠ ▣

THE LUNENBURG INN

(CAA) (SAVE)

Historic Bed & Breakfast

Phone: (902)634-3963

6/1-10/15 [BP]	1P: $115-$150	2P: $120-$155	XP: $20	D12
5/1-5/31 & 10/16-10/31 [BP]	1P: $95	2P: $100	XP: $20	D12
4/1-4/30 [BP]	1P: $85	2P: $90	XP: $20	D12

Location: Centre. 26 Dufferin St B0J 2C0 (PO Box 1407). **Fax:** 902/634-9419. **Facility:** A large sun deck at this 1893 Victorian home overlooks the town; rooms are tastefully appointed and very well maintained. Smoke free premises. 7 units. 6 one-bedroom standard units, some with whirlpools. 1 one-bedroom suite ($100-$190) with whirlpool. 3 stories (no elevator), interior corridors. **Parking:** on-site. **Terms:** open 5/1-10/31 & 4/1-4/30, office hours 9 am-10 pm, cancellation fee imposed. **Amenities:** video library, hair dryers. *Some:* DVD players. **Business Services:** PC. **Cards:** AX, DC, MC, VI. **Free Special Amenities:** local telephone calls and high-speed Internet.

SOME UNITS

⊯ ⊠ / ⓚ (VCR) ▣ ▦ /

The following lodging was either not evaluated or did not meet AAA rating requirements but is listed for your information only.

THE RUMRUNNER INN

(fyi)

Phone: 902/634-9200

Not evaluated. **Location:** Centre. 66-70 Montague St B0J 2C0. Facilities, services, and decor characterize a mid-range property.

WHERE TO DINE

FLEUR DE SEL RESTAURANT

French

Lunch: $9-$17   **Dinner:** $24-$33   **Phone:** 902/640-2121

Location: Jct Lower St. 53 Montague St B0J 2C0. **Hours:** Open 5/1-12/31 & 4/1-4/30; 5 pm-10 pm, Thurs-Sat also 11:30 am-2:45 pm; hours vary off season. **Reservations:** suggested. **Features:** In the heart of the historic town, the pleasant, cozy gem sustains a casual elegance with help from a decor that incorporates butter yellow and white accents. A fair-weather option is to dine on the lovely garden patio. The chef creates wonderful dishes using fresh regional ingredients; specialties include butter-poached lobster, pan-seared Lunenburg scallops, grilled beef tenderloin and duck breast. The decadent desserts shouldn't be overlooked. Dressy casual; cocktails. **Parking:** street. **Cards:** AX, MC, VI.

THE GRAND BANKER SEAFOOD BAR & GRILL

Canadian

DS, MC, VI.

Lunch: $5-$15   **Dinner:** $9-$20   **Phone:** 902/634-3300

Location: Centre; located opposite the harbour; in Brigantine Inn & Suites. 82 Montague St B0J 2C0. **Hours:** 11 am-10 pm; from 8 am 6/1-10/31. **Closed:** 12/25, 12/26. **Reservations:** accepted. **Features:** Views of the harbor are splendid from the casual eatery. The staff is upbeat and attentive. Menu selections range from comfort foods to steak, chicken and fresh seafood dinners. Casual dress; cocktails. **Parking:** street. **Cards:** AX, DC,

⊤

MAGNOLIA'S GRILL **Lunch:** $7-$12 **Dinner:** $10-$20 **Phone:** 902/634-3287

Canadian
Location: Centre. 128 Montague St B0J 2C0. **Hours:** Open 5/1-11/30 & 3/1-4/30; 11 am-3 pm; 11:30 am-10 pm 6/1-9/20. Closed: 4/9, 12/25; also Sun. **Features:** In the heart of town lies this cozy gem. A chalkboard menu lists a selection of fine homemade comfort foods and desserts. A bustling atmosphere and staff provide friendly, casual service. Casual dress; cocktails. **Parking:** street. **Cards:** AX, MC, VI.

OLD FISH FACTORY RESTAURANT **Lunch:** $8-$16 **Dinner:** $14-$24 **Phone:** 902/634-3333

Seafood
Location: In Fisheries Museum of the Atlantic. 68 Bluenose Dr B0J 2C0. **Hours:** Open 5/1-10/31; 11 am-close, Fri-Sun to 9 pm. **Reservations:** accepted. **Features:** The nautically themed dining room affords a splendid view of Lunenburg Harbor. The pleasant, knowledgeable staff aptly explains preparations of fresh Atlantic seafood, including lobster, mussels and salmon. Outside seating is available on a wharf. Casual dress; cocktails. **Parking:** on-site and street. **Cards:** AX, CB, DC, DS, JC, MC, VI. ⓨ

RISSERS CASUAL DINING **Lunch:** $8-$14 **Dinner:** $13-$20 **Phone:** 902/640-4040

Canadian
Location: Corner of Pelham and Duke sts; centre; in Lunenburg Arms Hotel. 94 Pelham St B0J 2C0. **Hours:** 7 am-10 pm; hours vary off season. **Reservations:** accepted. **Features:** This new kid on the block doesn't offer a view, but the food is well-prepared and well-presented. Choices include seafood dishes—such as fresh salmon, halibut and lobster—as well as chicken, lamb and steaks. Casual dress; cocktails. **Parking:** on-site.
Cards: AX, DC, MC, VI. ⓨ

MABOU

──── **WHERE TO DINE** ────

THE MULL CAFE & DELI **Lunch:** $6-$13 **Dinner:** $9-$20 **Phone:** 902/945-2244

Canadian
Location: Centre. 11630 Rt 19 B0E 1X0. **Hours:** 11 am-9 pm; to 7 pm off season. Closed: 1/1, 12/25. **Reservations:** suggested. **Features:** The extensive menu includes fresh seafood, Caesar salad, pizza and homemade desserts. Casual dress; cocktails. **Parking:** on-site. **Cards:** AX, MC, VI.

MAHONE BAY pop. 991

──── **WHERE TO STAY** ────

AMBER ROSE INN **Phone:** (902)624-1060

7/1-9/30 [BP]	1P: $115-$125	2P: $125	XP: $20 F3
5/19-6/30 & 10/1-11/1 [BP]	1P: $95-$115	2P: $95-$115	XP: $20 F3

Bed & Breakfast
Location: Centre. 319 W Main St B0J 2E0. Fax: 902/624-0997. **Facility:** This quaint property, built in 1875 as a general store, now houses three tastefully decorated, spacious rooms and an on-site antiques store. Smoke free premises. 3 one-bedroom standard units with whirlpools. 2 stories (no elevator). **Parking:** no self-parking. **Terms:** open 5/19-11/1, office hours 7 am-11 pm, cancellation fee imposed, weekly rates available, package plans. **Amenities:** hair dryers. *Some:* DVD players. **Cards:** MC, VI.
SOME UNITS
(ASK) (Y1+) ⊠ 🛢 💻 / (VCR) /

BAYVIEW PINES COUNTRY INN **Phone:** 902/624-9970

5/1-10/31	1P: $80-$150	2P: $85-$150	XP: $20 F3

Historic Bed & Breakfast
Location: Hwy 103, exit 10, 1.2 mi (2 km) w on Rt 3 to Kedy's Landing, 3.6 mi (6 km) e of Mahone Bay. Located in a quiet rural area. 678 Oakland Rd B0J 2E0. Fax: 902/624-9970. **Facility:** Bay views are featured from most accommodations at this country-style inn on quiet, expansive grounds; guest rooms are in the main inn and an annex. Designated smoking area. 10 units. 9 one-bedroom standard units, some with kitchens and/or whirlpools. 1 two-bedroom suite ($120-$150) with kitchen. 2 stories (no elevator); interior/exterior corridors. **Parking:** on-site. **Terms:** open 5/1-10/31, 5 day cancellation notice, small pets only (in designated units). **Amenities:** hair dryers. **Leisure Activities:** boat ramp, hiking trails. **Guest Services:** wireless Internet. **Business Services:** PC. **Cards:** MC, VI.
SOME UNITS
🐾 ⊠ 🅺 ☎ / 🕅 🛢 🍽 💻 /

FISHERMAN'S DAUGHTER BED & BREAKFAST **Phone:** 902/624-0483

5/1-10/31 [BP]	1P: $80-$100	2P: $100-$125	XP: $25 F5
11/1-4/30 [BP]	1P: $80-$100	2P: $90-$110	XP: $25 F5

Historic Bed & Breakfast
Location: On Rt 3; centre. 97 Edgewater St B0J 2E0 (PO Box 515). **Facility:** A lovingly restored 1840 heritage property bordered by two churches and overlooking the picturesque Mahone Bay. Smoke free premises. 4 one-bedroom standard units. 2 stories (no elevator), interior corridors. *Bath:* combo or shower only.
Parking: on-site. **Terms:** cancellation fee imposed. **Amenities:** *Some:* hair dryers. **Cards:** AX, MC, VI.
(ASK) (S🔊) (Y1+) ⊠ 🅺 ☎

OCEAN TRAIL RETREAT **Phone:** 902/624-8824

Motel
Property failed to provide current rates
Location: On Rt 3, 1.4 mi (2.4 km) w. 927A RR 3 B0J 2E0 (RR 1). Fax: 902/624-8899. **Facility:** 22 units. 18 one-bedroom standard units. 1 one-bedroom suite with whirlpool. 3 cottages. 2 stories (no elevator), exterior corridors. *Bath:* combo or shower only. **Parking:** on-site. **Terms:** open 5/1-10/31, office hours 8 am-11 pm.
Pool(s): heated outdoor.
SOME UNITS
🏊 🅺 ☎ 💻 / ⊠ (VCR) 🛢 🍽 /

──── *The following lodging was either not evaluated or did not* ────
meet AAA rating requirements but is listed for your information only.

THE MANSE AT MAHONE BAY COUNTRY INN **Phone:** 902/624-1121

(fyi)
Not evaluated. **Location:** Just off harbour; centre. 88 Orchard St B0J 2E0 (PO Box 475). Facilities, services, and decor characterize a mid-range property.

──── **WHERE TO DINE** ────

THE INNLET CAFE & RESTAURANT Lunch: $8-$15 Dinner: $14-$19 Phone: 902/624-6363
Regional Seafood
Location: On Rt 3, 0.6 mi (1 km) s. 249 Edgewater St B0J 2E0. **Hours:** 11:30 am-9 pm. Closed: 12/25, 12/26. **Reservations:** accepted. **Features:** Overlooking the busy harbour, the cozy, attractive cafe serves well-prepared seafood and meat dishes, in addition to lighter fare. The breezy patio, which is popular during summer, looks out at three lovely churches. Casual dress; cocktails. **Parking:** on-site. **Cards:** MC, VI.

MUG & ANCHOR PUB Lunch: $6-$11 Dinner: $9-$16 Phone: 902/624-6378
Canadian
Location: On Rt 3; centre; in Mader's Wharf. Rt 3 B0J 2E0. **Hours:** 11:30 am-9:30 pm, Sun from noon; to 10 pm 6/15-9/15. Closed: 12/25, 12/26. **Reservations:** accepted. **Features:** The spacious, rustic pub, which has a large seasonal deck, overlooks the harbor. A fine selection of draft beers accompanies a variety of seafood, chicken and steak. Casual dress; cocktails. **Parking:** on-site. **Cards:** AX, DC, MC, VI.

SALTSPRAY CAFE Lunch: $6-$11 Dinner: $9-$15 Phone: 902/624-0457
Canadian
Location: On Rt 3; centre. 621 S Main St B0J 2E0. **Hours:** 7 am-9 pm; 8 am-8 pm 9/16-6/15. Closed: 12/25, 12/26. **Features:** Splendid views of the harbour and marina can be enjoyed from the outdoor deck. The casual eatery specializes in fresh local seafood, including great chowders and lobster rolls. Fine desserts are homemade. Casual dress; cocktails. **Parking:** on-site. **Cards:** AX, DC, MC, VI.

MAVILLETTE

──── **WHERE TO STAY** ────

CAPE VIEW MOTEL & COTTAGES Phone: 902/645-2258
Motel
Property failed to provide current rates
Location: Rt 1, 19.2 mi (32 km) ne of Yarmouth; centre. (PO Box 9, SALMON RIVER, B0W 2Y0). Fax: 902/645-3999. **Facility:** 15 units. 10 one-bedroom standard units, some with efficiencies. 5 cottages. 1 story, exterior corridors. **Parking:** on-site. **Terms:** open 6/1-10/15, office hours 7:30 am-10 pm.
SOME UNITS

──── **WHERE TO DINE** ────

CAPE VIEW RESTAURANT Lunch: $6-$12 Dinner: $11-$25 Phone: 902/645-2519
Canadian
Location: Rt 1, 19.2 mi (32 km) ne of Yarmouth; centre. 157 John Doucette Rd B0W 1L0. **Hours:** Open 5/1-10/31; 9 am-10 pm; hours vary off season. **Reservations:** accepted. **Features:** The spacious restaurant affords a splendid view of the ocean and Mavillette Beach. On the vast menu are selections of fresh seafood, steaks and various comfort foods, as well as some Acadian dishes, such as rappie pie. Guests can request seating on the patio in season. Casual dress; cocktails. **Parking:** on-site. **Cards:** AX, MC, VI.

MIDDLETON pop. 1,744

──── **WHERE TO STAY** ────

CENTURY FARM INN Phone: 902/825-6989
Historic Bed & Breakfast
6/1-9/30 [BP] 1P: $65-$90 2P: $75-$100
Location: Hwy 101, exit 18, 0.6 mi (1 km) s on Brooklyn St, then just w on Rt 1. Located in a quiet rural setting. 10 Main St B0S 1P0 (Box 1287). Fax: 902/825-6649. **Facility:** Pleasant rooms of varying size are offered in this 1886 farmhouse on 110 acres; surrounding fields border a brook and the Annapolis River. Smoke free premises. 4 one-bedroom standard units. 2 stories (no elevator), interior corridors. **Bath:** combo or shower only. **Parking:** on-site. **Terms:** open 6/1-9/30, office hours 10 am-10 pm, age restrictions may apply, 3 day cancellation notice-fee imposed, package plans. **Amenities:** video library, hair dryers. **Leisure Activities:** fishing, cross country skiing, hiking trails. **Guest Services:** coin laundry, wireless Internet. **Business Services:** meeting rooms. **Cards:** AX, CB, DC, DS, JC, MC, VI.

FALCOURT INN Phone: (902)825-3399
Historic Country Inn
All Year [ECP] 1P: $100-$110 2P: $110-$120 XP: $10
Location: Hwy 101, exit 18 or 18A to Hwy 1, take Hwy 1 to Rt 10, 1.8 mi (3 km) s to Rt 201, then 0.6 mi (1 km) e. Located in a quiet rural area. 8979 Hwy 201, RR 3 B0S 1P0. Fax: 902/825-3422. **Facility:** The well-appointed rooms and cozy two-bedroom cottage at this former fishing lodge look out onto the scenic countryside along a meandering river. 11 units. 7 one-bedroom standard units. 1 one-bedroom suite ($170). 2 vacation homes ($200) and 1 cottage. 2 stories (no elevator), interior/exterior corridors. **Bath:** combo or shower only. **Parking:** on-site. **Terms:** age restrictions may apply. **Amenities:** video library. *Some:* DVD players, hair dryers. **Dining:** restaurant, see separate listing. **Leisure Activities:** hiking trails. **Fee:** fishing. **Guest Services:** coin laundry, wireless Internet. **Cards:** AX, DC, MC, VI.
SOME UNITS

MID-VALLEY MOTEL Phone: 902/825-3433
Small-scale Hotel
Property failed to provide current rates
Location: Hwy 101, exit 18, 0.6 mi (1 km) w on Rt 1. 121 Main St B0S 1P0 (PO Box 1300). Fax: 902/825-3433. **Facility:** 57 units. 56 one-bedroom standard units, some with efficiencies. 1 one-bedroom suite with kitchen. 1 story, exterior corridors. **Parking:** on-site. **Terms:** office hours 8 am-2 am, pets ($5 extra charge, in designated units). **Dining:** restaurant, see separate listing. **Pool(s):** outdoor. **Leisure Activities:** playground. **Guest Services:** coin laundry. **Business Services:** meeting rooms.
SOME UNITS
FEE

──────── **WHERE TO DINE** ────────

EISNER'S RESTAURANT   **Lunch:** $5-$9   **Dinner:** $9-$15   **Phone:** 902/825-3582
▽▽▽   **Location:** Centre. 255 Main St B0S 1P0. **Hours:** 11 am-8 pm. Closed: 12/25, 12/26; also Tues.
      Reservations: accepted. **Features:** Family-operated since 1951, the popular restaurant is known for freshly
Canadian   baked rolls, yummy soup and scrumptious gingerbread. Mussels, scallops, haddock, fresh Atlantic salmon
      and crab flavor the seafood chowder. White lace curtains and paneling set the mood in the dining room.
Casual dress; cocktails. **Parking:** on-site. **Cards:** AX, MC, VI.

FALCOURT INN DINING ROOM   **Dinner:** $13-$29   **Phone:** 902/825-3399
▽▽▽   **Location:** Hwy 101, exit 18 or 18A to Hwy 1, take Hwy 1 to Rt 10, 1.8 mi (3 km) s to Rt 201, then 0.6 mi (1 km) e; in
      Falcourt Inn. 8979 Hwy 201 B0S 1P0. **Hours:** 5 pm-8:30 pm. Closed: 12/25. **Reservations:** accepted.
Canadian   **Features:** Sophisticated menu offerings include escargot, rack of lamb, pan-fried haddock and sirloin steak.
      A stone fireplace, beamed ceilings and oak paneling give the dining room—which overlooks the Nictaux
River—the rustic aura of a 1920s fishing lodge. Dressy casual; cocktails. **Parking:** on-site. **Cards:** AX, MC, VI.

MID-VALLEY RESTAURANT   **Lunch:** $6-$11   **Dinner:** $8-$18   **Phone:** 902/825-3433
▽▽   **Location:** Hwy 101, exit 18, 0.6 mi (1 km) w on Rt 1; in Mid-Valley Motel. 121 Main St B0S 1P0. **Hours:** 7 am-9 pm.
      Closed: 12/25. **Reservations:** accepted. **Features:** Floral decor brightens the pleasant dining room, where
Canadian   patrons sample good-size portions of seafood, steak, chicken and pasta. Casual dress; cocktails. **Parking:**
on-site. **Cards:** AX, DC, MC, VI.

MOOSE RIVER

──────── **WHERE TO STAY** ────────

──────── *The following lodging was either not evaluated or did not* ────────
meet AAA rating requirements but is listed for your information only.

TIDAL RIVER RIDGE COTTAGES   **Phone:** 902/254-3333
[fyi]   Not evaluated. **Location:** On Rt 2, 7.8 mi (13 km) e of Parrsboro; centre. Located in a rural area. Rt 2 B0M 1N0 (RR
      1). Facilities, services, and decor characterize a mid-range property.

MUSQUODOBOIT HARBOUR pop. 900

──────── **WHERE TO STAY** ────────

THE ELEPHANT'S NEST BED & BREAKFAST   **Phone:** 902/827-3891
▽▽▽   5/1-10/21   1P: $95-$115   2P: $100-$130   XP: $15   F3
      10/22-4/30   1P: $80-$100   2P: $85-$115   XP: $15   F3
      Location: From jct Hwy 107 and 7, 2.5 mi (4 km) w, follow signs. Located in a rural, residential area. 127 Pleasant Dr
Bed & Breakfast   B0J 1N0. Fax: 902/827-3891. **Facility:** This cozy, waterfront B&B offers well-appointed rooms and lovely
gardens. Smoke free premises. 3 one-bedroom standard units, some with whirlpools. 2 stories (no elevator). **Parking:** on-site.
Terms: office hours 6 am-11 pm, check-in 4 pm, 3 day cancellation notice, package plans, small pets only (in designated unit).
Amenities: video library, irons, hair dryers. *Some:* DVD players. **Leisure Activities:** whirlpool, canoeing, paddleboats. **Guest
Services:** wireless Internet. **Business Services:** PC. **Cards:** MC, VI.

(ASK) 🐾 ⊠ ✕ 𝒦 VCR 🐕

NEW GLASGOW pop. 9,432

──────── **WHERE TO STAY** ────────

COMFORT INN   *Book great rates at AAA.com*   **Phone:** (902)755-6450
▽▽ ▽▽   6/1-10/15 [ECP]   1P: $109-$155   2P: $119-$165   XP: $10   F18
      5/1-5/31 [ECP]   1P: $99-$140   2P: $109-$150   XP: $10   F18
Small-scale Hotel   10/16-4/30 [ECP]   1P: $89-$129   2P: $89-$129   XP: $10   F18
      Location: On Hwy 289, just e of jct Trans-Canada Hwy 104, exit 23. Located opposite shopping mall. 740 Westville Rd
B2H 2J8. Fax: 902/752-6680. **Facility:** 62 one-bedroom standard units. 2 stories (no elevator), interior corridors. **Parking:** on-
site. **Amenities:** voice mail, irons, hair dryers. *Some:* high-speed Internet. **Guest Services:** wireless Internet. **Cards:** AX, DC,
DS, JC, MC, VI. *(See color ad card insert)*

SOME UNITS
(ASK) 🆂🅳 🐾 🍴 🐾 ▯ / ✕ 🔒 🖥

COUNTRY INN & SUITES BY CARLSON   *Book great rates at AAA.com*   **Phone:** (902)928-1333
▽▽   5/1-10/14 [ECP]   1P: $129-$160   2P: $129-$160   XP: $15   F18
      1/1-4/30 [ECP]   1P: $105-$136   2P: $105-$136   XP: $15   F18
Small-scale Hotel   10/15-12/31 [ECP]   1P: $99-$130   2P: $99-$130   XP: $15   F18
      Location: On Hwy 289, just e of jct Trans-Canada Hwy 104, exit 23. Located opposite shopping mall. 700 Westville Rd
B2H 2J8. Fax: 902/928-1363. **Facility:** 66 units. 33 one-bedroom standard units. 33 one-bedroom suites. 3 stories, interior
corridors. **Parking:** on-site. **Terms:** small pets only ($50 deposit, $5 extra charge). **Amenities:** video library, DVD players, voice
mail, irons, hair dryers. *Some:* dual phone lines. **Guest Services:** coin laundry, wireless Internet. **Cards:** AX, DS, JC, MC, VI.
(See color ad on TourBookMark)

SOME UNITS
(ASK) 🆂🅳 🐾 🔒 🖥 / ✕ 🖥 /
FEE

──────── *The following lodging was either not evaluated or did not* ────────
meet AAA rating requirements but is listed for your information only.

HEATHER HOTEL & CONVENTION CENTRE   **Phone:** 902/752-8401
[fyi]   Did not meet all AAA rating requirements for locking devices in some guest rooms at time of last evaluation
      on 04/04/2006. **Location:** Trans-Canada Hwy 104, exit 24, just s. Foord St B0K 1S0. Facilities, services, and decor
Small-scale Hotel   characterize a mid-range property.

——— **WHERE TO DINE** ———

CROFTER'S STEAK & SEAFOOD   **Lunch:** $5-$9   **Dinner:** $9-$18   **Phone:** 902/755-3383
Location: Trans-Canada Hwy 104, exit 24, 0.6 mi (1 km) n on Rt 374. 565 Stellarton Rd B2H 1M7. **Hours:** 11 am-9
pm. **Closed:** 12/25, 12/26; also Mon. **Reservations:** accepted. **Features:** A popular spot with the locals, the
Steak & Seafood   restaurant seats patrons in two dining sections decorated with historical photographs and artifacts of early
Nova Scotia. On the menu is a good selection of seafood and meat entrees, as well as burgers, sandwiches
and homemade soups and chowders. Casual dress; cocktails. **Parking:** on-site. **Cards:** AX, MC, VI.

THE DOCK FOOD, SPIRITS, ALES   **Lunch:** $6-$11   **Dinner:** $11-$19   **Phone:** 902/752-0884
Location: River Rd and George St; centre. 130 George St B2H 2K6. **Hours:** 11:30 am-11 pm, Fri & Sat-midnight,
Sun noon-8 pm. **Closed:** 12/24-12/26. **Features:** The traditional Irish pub is in one of the oldest commercial
Canadian   buildings in Nova Scotia. A warm, friendly atmosphere prevails inside the 1845 stone building. A fine
selection of beers complements offerings from the full pub menu. Casual dress; cocktails. **Parking:** on-site.
Cards: AX, MC, VI.

HEATHER DINING ROOM   **Lunch:** $7-$14   **Dinner:** $12-$20   **Phone:** 902/752-8401
Location: Trans-Canada Hwy 104, exit 24, just s; in Heather Hotel & Convention Centre. Foord St B0K 1S0. **Hours:** 7
am-2 & 5-9 pm. **Reservations:** accepted. **Features:** Locally popular, the pleasant family-focused dining
Canadian   room serves a wide variety of well-prepared seafood and meat entrees. The staff is friendly and attentive.
Casual dress; cocktails. **Parking:** on-site. **Cards:** AX, MC, VI.

JUNGLE JIM'S RESTAURANT   **Lunch:** $6-$12   **Dinner:** $10-$18   **Phone:** 902/695-5467
Location: Trans-Canada Hwy 104, exit 24, just n. 127 N Foord St B0K 1S0. **Hours:** 11 am-10 pm, Thurs-Sat to 11
pm. **Closed:** 12/25, 12/26. **Features:** Guests can step into a tropical theme at the casual eatery, which
Canadian   employs a friendly staff and nurtures a bustling atmosphere. The menu lines up a wide variety of comfort
foods, salads, chicken, beef, seafood and hot wings, all served in ample, flavorful portions. Casual dress;
cocktails. **Parking:** on-site. **Cards:** AX, DC, MC, VI.

SWISS CHALET   **Lunch:** $6-$11   **Dinner:** $8-$16   **Phone:** 902/752-5013
Location: Jct Western Ave. 660 Westville Rd B2H 2J8. **Hours:** 11 am-10 pm, Fri & Sat-11 pm. **Closed:** 12/25,
12/26. **Reservations:** accepted. **Features:** The popular restaurant is known for its rotisserie chicken and
Canadian   ribs and the tangy Chalet sauce that gives food its special zip. Diners munch on a half or quarter chicken
with sides such as steamed vegetables, fries, baked potatoes and salads. Lunch guests often go for the
great soup and sandwich combination. Take-out and delivery service are popular options. Casual dress; cocktails. **Parking:** on-
site. **Cards:** AX, DC, MC, VI.

NEW HARBOUR

——— **WHERE TO STAY** ———

LONELY ROCK SEASIDE BUNGALOWS   All Year   **Phone:** (902)387-2668
2P: $90-$230
Location: Rt 316, 0.4 mi (0.7 km) s. Located in a rural area. 150 New Harbour Rd B0H 1T0 (RR 1).
Cottage   Fax: 902/387-2023. **Facility:** Bordered on one side by the ocean, this property enjoys a secluded setting;
offered are one-, two- and three-bedroom deluxe cottages with decks. Smoke free premises. 6 cottages. 1
story, exterior corridors. **Parking:** on-site. **Terms:** office hours 7 am-10 pm, 14 day cancellation notice-fee imposed, pets (in
designated units, no cats). **Amenities:** video library, CD players, hair dryers. **Leisure Activities:** rental canoes, bicycles, hiking
trails, playground, horseshoes. **Cards:** AX, MC, VI.

NEW MINAS pop. 4,299

——— **WHERE TO DINE** ———

JUNGLE JIM'S EATERY   **Lunch:** $6-$11   **Dinner:** $8-$16   **Phone:** 902/681-5467
Location: Centre; in New Minas Court. 9049 Commercial St B4N 5A4. **Hours:** 11 am-10 pm, Thurs-Sat to 11 pm.
Closed: 12/25. **Reservations:** accepted. **Features:** Guests can step into a tropical theme at the casual
Canadian   eatery, which employs a friendly staff and nurtures a bustling atmosphere. The menu lines up a wide variety
of comfort foods, salads, chicken, beef, seafood and hot wings, all served in ample, flavorful portions.
Casual dress; cocktails. **Parking:** on-site. **Cards:** AX, DC, MC, VI.

SMITTY'S FAMILY RESTAURANT   **Lunch:** $6-$11   **Dinner:** $8-$16   **Phone:** 902/681-1858
Location: Hwy 101, exit 12, just n. 5494 Prospect Rd B4N 3K8. **Hours:** 7 am-9 pm, Fri & Sat-10 pm, Sun-8 pm.
Closed: 12/25. **Reservations:** accepted. **Features:** The family-oriented restaurant satisfies patrons with its
Canadian   ever-popular all-day breakfast items, as well as tasty and wholesome soups and salads at lunchtime. A
relaxed mood characterizes the dining space. Casual dress; cocktails. **Parking:** on-site. **Cards:** AX, DC,
MC, VI.

SWISS CHALET   **Lunch:** $6-$11   **Dinner:** $8-$16   **Phone:** 902/681-1761
Location: Centre. 9275 Commercial St B4N 3G2. **Hours:** 11 am-10 pm, Fri & Sat-11 pm. **Closed:** 12/25.
Features: The popular restaurant is known for its rotisserie chicken and ribs and the tangy Chalet sauce
Canadian   that gives food its special zip. Diners munch on a half or quarter chicken with sides such as steamed
vegetables, fries, baked potatoes and salads. Lunch guests often go for the great soup and sandwich
combination. Take-out and delivery service are popular options. Casual dress; cocktails. **Parking:** on-site. **Cards:** AX, DC,
MC, VI.

NORTH SYDNEY —See also SYDNEY.

———— WHERE TO STAY ————

BEST WESTERN NORTH STAR INN   *Book great rates at AAA.com*   **Phone:** (902)794-8581
All Year   1P: $122   2P: $122   XP: $8   F12
Small-scale Hotel   **Location:** Trans-Canada Hwy 105, exit 21; at ferry terminal. 39 Forrest St B2A 3B1. Fax: 902/794-4628. **Facility:** 101 units. 100 one-bedroom standard units. 1 one-bedroom suite ($225) with whirlpool. 2 stories, interior corridors. *Bath:* combo or shower only. **Parking:** on-site. **Terms:** 14 day cancellation notice-fee imposed. **Amenities:** irons, hair dryers. **Pool(s):** small heated indoor. **Leisure Activities:** whirlpool. **Guest Services:** wireless Internet. **Business Services:** meeting rooms, PC. **Cards:** AX, DC, DS, MC, VI.
SOME UNITS

CLANSMAN MOTEL   **Phone:** (902)794-7226
6/15-9/15   1P: $79-$125   2P: $89-$125   XP: $10   F18
5/1-6/14 & 9/16-4/30   1P: $69-$115   2P: $79-$115   XP: $10   F18
Small-scale Hotel   **Location:** Hwy 125, exit 2, just e on King St. 9 Baird St B2A 3M3 (PO Box 216). Fax: 902/794-4157. **Facility:** 46 units. 43 one-bedroom standard units, some with whirlpools. 3 cottages ($200-$250) with whirlpools. 2 stories (no elevator), interior/exterior corridors. **Parking:** on-site, winter plug-ins. **Terms:** [AP] meal plan available. **Amenities:** hair dryers. **Dining:** restaurant, see separate listing. **Pool(s):** heated outdoor. **Leisure Activities:** playground. **Guest Services:** coin laundry. **Business Services:** meeting rooms, PC. **Cards:** AX, DC, MC, VI. **Free Special Amenities:** local telephone calls and early check-in/late check-out.
SOME UNITS

———— WHERE TO DINE ————

CLANSMAN RESTAURANT   **Lunch:** $5-$8   **Dinner:** $8-$19   **Phone:** 902/794-7226
Canadian   **Location:** Hwy 125, exit 2, just e on King St; in Clansman Motel. 9 Baird St B2A 3M3. **Hours:** 7 am-9 pm. Closed: 12/25, 12/26. **Features:** Home-style cooking is the focus of the warm, homey restaurant. Once a favorite with area miners, the delicious poor man's pudding blends cake, sauce, brown sugar and coconut and tops the mixture with ice cream or whipped topping. Casual dress; cocktails. **Parking:** on-site. **Cards:** AX, DC, MC, VI.

PARRSBORO pop. 1,529

———— WHERE TO STAY ————

GILLESPIE HOUSE INN   **Phone:** (902)254-3196
7/1-9/30   1P: $100-$110   2P: $110-$119   XP: $15   F6
5/1-6/30 & 10/1-10/31   1P: $90-$100   2P: $100-$110   XP: $15   F6
Bed & Breakfast   **Location:** On Rt 2; centre. 358 Main St B0M 1S0 (PO Box 879). Fax: 902/484-6585. **Facility:** An Old World ambience enhances guest rooms at this pleasant 1890s home, where guests may relax on the spacious sun porch or in one of the parlors. Smoke free premises. 7 units. 6 one-bedroom standard units. 1 one-bedroom suite. 2 stories (no elevator), interior corridors. **Parking:** on-site. **Terms:** open 5/1-10/31. **Amenities:** CD players, hair dryers. **Guest Services:** TV in common area. **Cards:** AX, MC, VI.

THE MAPLE INN BED & BREAKFAST   **Phone:** (902)254-3735
6/16-9/30   1P: $75-$150   2P: $90-$165   XP: $15   F5
5/1-6/15 & 10/1-4/30   1P: $65-$140   2P: $80-$155   XP: $15   F5
Historic Bed & Breakfast   **Location:** Centre. 2358 Western Ave B0M 1S0 (Box 457). Fax: 902/254-3735. **Facility:** The historic inn's parlor areas and guest rooms are tastefully decorated; on the top floor is a spacious two-bedroom suite. Smoke free premises. 8 units. 6 one-bedroom standard units. 1 one- and 1 two-bedroom suites ($150-$180) with whirlpools. 3 stories (no elevator), interior corridors. *Bath:* combo or shower only. **Parking:** on-site. **Terms:** office hours 7 am-10 pm, 5 day cancellation notice-fee imposed. **Amenities:** hair dryers. **Cards:** AX, DC, MC, VI.
SOME UNITS

THE PARRSBORO MANSION INN   **Phone:** (902)254-2585
7/1-9/14 [BP]   1P: $95-$110   2P: $110-$125   XP: $20   D15
6/16-6/30 & 9/15-10/14 [BP]   1P: $85-$95   2P: $100-$110   XP: $20   D15
Bed & Breakfast   **Location:** On Rt 2; centre. 3916 Eastern Ave B0M 1S0 (PO Box 579). Fax: 902/254-2585. **Facility:** Acreage surrounds this pleasant property offering spacious, tastefully decorated guest rooms in the main home and in an attached annex wing. Smoke free premises. 4 units. 3 one-bedroom standard units. 1 one-bedroom suite ($120-$150). 2 stories (no elevator), interior corridors. **Parking:** on-site. **Terms:** open 6/16-10/14, check-in 4 pm, 7 day cancellation notice. **Amenities:** DVD players, irons, hair dryers. **Pool(s):** heated outdoor. **Leisure Activities:** sauna, limited exercise equipment. **Guest Services:** coin laundry, wireless Internet. **Cards:** AX, MC, VI.
SOME UNITS

THE SUNSHINE INN   **Phone:** 902/254-3135
5/1-10/31   1P: $76-$150   2P: $76-$150   XP: $10
Motel   **Location:** 2 mi (3.2 km) n on Rt 2. Located in a rural area. (PO Box 353, B0M 1S0). **Facility:** 15 units. 11 one-bedroom standard units, some with whirlpools. 4 cottages ($125-$150), some with whirlpools. 1 story, exterior corridors. **Parking:** on-site. **Terms:** open 5/1-10/31, office hours 6 am-10:30 pm, weekly rates available, [BP] meal plan available, pets ($10 extra charge, in designated units). **Amenities:** hair dryers. **Leisure Activities:** fishing, hiking trails, playground. **Cards:** MC, VI.
SOME UNITS

——— **WHERE TO DINE** ———

GLOOSCAP RESTAURANT & LOUNGE **Lunch:** $5-$12   **Dinner:** $8-$16   Phone: 902-254-3488

Canadian

Location: 0.8 mi (1.2 km) n on Rt 2. 758 Upper Main St B0M 1S0. **Hours:** 11:30 am-9 pm. Closed: 1/1, 12/25, 12/26. **Reservations:** accepted. **Features:** The popular family restaurant offers a choice of seating in the main restaurant, in the lounge or on the outdoor deck. Comfort foods include some seafood and steak items, in addition to homemade desserts. Casual dress; cocktails. **Parking:** on-site. **Cards:** AX, MC, VI.

STOWAWAY RESTAURANT **Lunch:** $5-$10   **Dinner:** $7-$15   Phone: 902-254-3371

Seafood

Location: Centre. 121 Lower Main St B0M 1S0. **Hours:** Open 5/1-12/31 & 2/1-4/30; 9 am-9 pm; to 8 pm off season. Closed: 12/25. **Features:** Seafood chowder, sauteed scallops and seafood au gratin are among generously portioned specialties on the restaurant's menu. Pleasant servers are efficient and attentive. For dessert, blueberry cake is one of several delicious, homemade choices. Casual dress; cocktails. **Parking:** on-site. **Cards:** AX, MC, VI.

PICTOU pop. 3,875

——— **WHERE TO STAY** ———

AUBERGE WALKER INN   *Book at AAA.com*   Phone: 902/485-1433

Historic Bed & Breakfast

All Year   1P: $59-$149   2P: $59-$149   XP: $10   D10
Location: Between Water and Front sts; centre. 78 Coleraine St B0K 1H0 (PO Box 629). Fax: 902/485-1222. **Facility:** Views of the waterfront enhance some rooms at this inn dating from 1865. Smoke free premises. 11 units. 10 one-bedroom standard units. 1 one-bedroom suite with efficiency and whirlpool. 4 stories (no elevator), interior corridors. *Bath:* combo or shower only. **Parking:** on-site. **Amenities:** hair dryers. **Business Services:** meeting rooms. **Cards:** AX, MC, VI.

BRAESIDE INN   *Book at AAA.com*   Phone: (902)485-5046

Historic Country Inn

All Year   1P: $65-$130   2P: $80-$165   XP: $15   D12
Location: Between Chapel and Welsford sts; centre. 126 Front St B0K 1H0 (Box 159). Fax: 902/485-1701. **Facility:** Several of this 1938 inn's comfortable, individually decorated accommodations overlook the harbour; some rooms are compact, perfect for one guest. Smoke free premises. 18 one-bedroom standard units, some with whirlpools. 3 stories (no elevator), interior corridors. *Bath:* combo or shower only. **Parking:** on-site. **Terms:** office hours 7:30 am-10 pm, 3 day cancellation notice-fee imposed, package plans. **Amenities:** video library, hair dryers. **Dining:** restaurant, see separate listing. **Guest Services:** wireless Internet. **Business Services:** meeting rooms, PC. **Cards:** AX, DC, MC, VI.

SOME UNITS

CARIBOU RIVER COTTAGE LODGE   Phone: (902)485-6352

Cottage

All Year   1P: $99-$189
Location: From PEI ferry terminal, 2.7 mi (4.5 km) w on Three Brooks Rd to Shore Rd. 1308 Shore Rd B0K 1H0. Fax: 902/485-6352. **Facility:** Designated smoking area. 8 cottages, some with whirlpools. 1 story, exterior corridors. **Parking:** on-site. **Terms:** 3 day cancellation notice, 28 day 7/1-8/31-fee imposed, weekly rates available, package plans. **Leisure Activities:** sauna, whirlpool, canoeing, bicycles, hiking trails. *Fee:* massage. **Guest Services:** coin laundry. **Cards:** MC, VI.

CONSULATE INN   Phone: (902)485-4554

Bed & Breakfast

6/1-10/31 [BP]   1P: $75-$159   2P: $75-$159   XP: $15
5/1-5/31 & 4/1-4/30 [BP]   1P: $65-$149   2P: $65-$149   XP: $15
11/1-3/31 [BP]   1P: $65-$139   2P: $65-$139   XP: $15
Location: Corner of Willow and Water sts; centre. 157 Water St B0K 1H0. Fax: 902/485-1532. **Facility:** This 1810 stone home is on expansive grounds bordering the waterway and offers modern rooms, some with water view decks. Smoke free premises. 11 units. 10 one-bedroom standard units, some with whirlpools. 1 cottage ($99-$119). 2 stories (no elevator), interior/exterior corridors. **Parking:** on-site. **Terms:** age restrictions may apply, cancellation fee imposed, no pets allowed (owner's cat on premises). **Amenities:** video library, hair dryers. **Guest Services:** gift shop. **Business Services:** PC. **Cards:** AX, MC, VI.

SOME UNITS

THE CUSTOMS HOUSE INN   *Book at AAA.com*   Phone: (902)485-4546

Historic Bed & Breakfast

All Year   1P: $79-$179   2P: $79-$179
Location: Depot St at Front St, towards water; centre. 38 Depot St B0K 1H0 (PO Box 1542). Fax: 902/485-1657. **Facility:** This sturdy structure of brick and stone dates from 1870; some of the rooms offer waterfront views, plus there's a pleasant pub on the lower floor. Smoke free premises. 8 one-bedroom standard units. 2 stories (no elevator), interior corridors. **Parking:** on-site. **Terms:** cancellation fee imposed, [CP] meal plan available. **Amenities:** high-speed Internet, hair dryers. **Guest Services:** wireless Internet. **Business Services:** meeting rooms. **Cards:** AX, DC, MC, VI.

SOME UNITS

PICTOU LODGE RESORT   Phone: (902)485-4322

Small-scale Hotel

5/15-10/15   1P: $135-$289   2P: $135-$289   XP: $15   F12
Location: 4.3 mi (7 km) nw on Braeshore Rd; midway between Pictou and PEI ferry terminal at Caribou. Located in a quiet area. 172 Lodge Rd B0K 1H0 (PO Box 1539). Fax: 902/485-4945. **Facility:** 51 units. 20 one-bedroom standard units. 21 one-, 4 two- and 6 three-bedroom suites, some with efficiencies, kitchens and/or whirlpools. 1 story, exterior corridors. *Bath:* combo or shower only. **Parking:** on-site. **Terms:** open 5/15-10/15, 3 day cancellation notice-fee imposed. **Amenities:** video library, irons, hair dryers. **Dining:** restaurant, see separate listing. **Pool(s):** heated outdoor. **Leisure Activities:** canoeing, paddleboats, golf net, lawn checker board, bicycles, hiking trails, jogging, playground, limited exercise equipment, horseshoes, volleyball. *Fee:* game room. **Guest Services:** coin laundry, wireless Internet. **Business Services:** meeting rooms, PC. **Cards:** AX, DC, DS, MC, VI. **Free Special Amenities:** high-speed Internet.

SOME UNITS

WILLOW HOUSE INN

Phone: 902/485-5740

Historic Bed & Breakfast

6/16-9/15 [BP]	1P: $80	2P: $80	XP: $10	F11
5/1-6/15 [BP]	1P: $70	2P: $70	XP: $10	F11
9/16-4/30 [BP]	1P: $55	2P: $55	XP: $10	F11

Location: Corner of Willow and Church sts; centre. 11 Willow St B0K 1H0 (PO Box 1900). **Facility:** Said to have been built by the town's first mayor, this restored 1840 home offers individually styled rooms. Smoke free premises. 6 units. 4 one- and 2 two-bedroom standard units. 3 stories (no elevator), interior corridors. *Bath:* combo or shower only. **Parking:** on-site. **Terms:** cancellation fee imposed, package plans, small pets only (with prior approval, owner's dog on premises). **Cards:** AX, MC, VI.

──────── **WHERE TO DINE** ────────

BRAESIDE INN DINING ROOM

Dinner: $17-$29   **Phone:** 902/485-5046

Seafood

Location: Between Chapel and Welsford sts; centre; in Braeside Inn. 126 Front St B0K 1H0. **Hours:** 5:30 pm-8:30 pm; Sunday brunch 11:30 am-1:30 pm in summer; off season by reservation. Closed: 12/25. **Reservations:** required, off season. **Features:** Well-prepared specialties of seafood and meat include rack of lamb, prime rib of beef and fresh local seafood. Displays of china and glass, as well as carved ducks and geese, decorate the attractive dining room, which overlooks picturesque Pictou Harbour. Casual dress; cocktails. **Parking:** on-site. **Cards:** AX, DC, MC, VI.

FOUGERE'S RESTAURANT

Lunch: $7-$14   **Dinner:** $14-$22   **Phone:** 902/485-1575

Seafood

Location: Centre. 91 Water St B0K 1H0. **Hours:** Open 5/1-12/31; 11:30 am-9 pm. Closed: Mon off season. **Reservations:** accepted. **Features:** Fresh seafood dishes are a specialty at the downtown restaurant, which treats guests to a view of the harbour. Locals favor the captain's platter, which features haddock, shrimp, lobster, salmon, scallops and mussels. Also on the menu are meat entrees and such basic comfort foods as burgers and sandwiches. Homemade pie and cake are dessert favorites. Pleasant servers are attentive. Casual dress; cocktails. **Parking:** on-site. **Cards:** AX, MC, VI.

MRS. MACGREGOR'S TEA ROOM

Lunch: $6-$12   **Phone:** 902/382-1878

Canadian

Location: Between Market and Carrolls sts; centre. 59 Water St B0K 1H0. **Hours:** 11 am-6 pm; hours vary off season. Closed major holidays; also Mon 9/1-6/30. **Reservations:** accepted. **Features:** A lovely tea room located in the downtown area, the eatery serves an array of tasty lunch items as well as homemade desserts. Reservations are recommended for the afternoon tea service which, for the time being, is served only on the weekends, but this may change to weekdays; call ahead and inquire. Casual dress; beer & wine only. **Parking:** street. **Cards:** MC, VI.

PICTOU LODGE RESORT

Lunch: $8-$14   **Dinner:** $19-$30   **Phone:** 902/485-4322

Canadian

Location: 4.3 mi (7 km) nw on Braeshore Rd; midway between Pictou and PEI ferry terminal at Caribou; in Pictou Lodge Resort. 172 Lodge Rd B0K 1H0. **Hours:** Open 5/15-10/31; 7 am-11, noon-2 & 5:30-8:30 pm. **Reservations:** suggested. **Features:** The historic dining room features attractive log construction and a large stone fireplace. Guests can enjoy a pre-dinner beverage or post-dinner dessert in the comfortable lounge, which overlooks the ocean. On the menu is a bountiful selection of fresh local seafood and some fine meat dishes. Homemade baked goods are tempting. Casual dress; cocktails. **Parking:** on-site. **Cards:** AX, CB, DC, DS, MC, VI. **Historic**

PIPER'S LANDING COUNTRY DINING

Dinner: $14-$28   **Phone:** 902/485-1200

Canadian

Location: Pictou Rotary, 1.8 mi (3 km) w. Hwy 376 B0K 1H0. **Hours:** 5 pm-9 pm. Closed major holidays; also Thurs. **Reservations:** accepted. **Features:** Beautiful views of the water can be enjoyed from several sections in the charming, bayfront restaurant. A creative home-style flair flavors traditional fresh seafood and meat entrees, as well as some pasta dishes. It's hard to choose from a list of fine desserts. Casual dress; cocktails. **Parking:** on-site. **Cards:** AX, MC, VI.

PLEASANT BAY

──────── **WHERE TO DINE** ────────

RUSTY ANCHOR RESTAURANT

Lunch: $7-$13   **Dinner:** $9-$20   **Phone:** 902/224-1313

Seafood

Location: Centre. 23197 Cabot Trail Rd B0E 2P0. **Hours:** Open 5/20-10/20; 11 am-9 pm; from 8 am 7/1-8/31. **Features:** From a spot overlooking Pleasant Bay, diners can savor fresh local seafood, including boiled lobster and crab. The popular restaurant's spacious deck affords splendid views. Casual dress; cocktails. **Parking:** on-site. **Cards:** MC, VI.

PORT DUFFERIN

──────── **WHERE TO STAY** ────────

MARQUIS OF DUFFERIN SEASIDE INN

Phone: (902)654-2696

Motel

6/15-9/30	1P: $68-$86	2P: $76-$94	XP: $8	F10
5/1-6/14 & 10/1-10/31	1P: $54-$70	2P: $60-$76	XP: $6	F10

Location: On Hwy 7. Located in a quiet rural area. 25658 Hwy 7, RR 1 B0J 2R0. Fax: 902/654-2406. **Facility:** 14 units. 13 one- and 1 two-bedroom standard units, some with efficiencies. 1 story, exterior corridors. *Bath:* combo or shower only. **Parking:** on-site. **Terms:** open 5/1-10/31, office hours 7 am-9 pm. **Amenities:** video library. **Leisure Activities:** canoeing, boat dock, fishing, bicycles. **Guest Services:** gift shop. **Cards:** AX, MC, VI.

SOME UNITS

PORT HASTINGS

──── WHERE TO STAY ────

CAPE BRETON CAUSEWAY INN

(CAA) (SAVE)

Small-scale Hotel

All Year	1P: $84-$125	2P: $94-$135	XP: $10	F

Phone: (902)625-0460

Location: E of Canso Cswy on Trans-Canada Hwy 105 rotary; entrance through north side of church. (21 Old Victoria Rd, B9A 1L2). Fax: 902/625-1275. **Facility:** 69 units. 68 one-bedroom standard units. 1 one-bedroom suite ($125-$155). 2 stories (no elevator), interior/exterior corridors. **Parking:** on-site. **Terms:** cancellation fee imposed, [BP] meal plan available, small pets only. **Amenities:** voice mail, irons, hair dryers. **Dining:** 4 pm-10 pm, cocktails. **Guest Services:** coin laundry. **Business Services:** meeting rooms. **Cards:** AX, DC, DS, MC, VI. **Free Special Amenities:** local telephone calls and high-speed Internet.

SOME UNITS

🇸 🛏 🍴 🍽 💻 / ✕ 🔌 🖨 /

ECONO LODGE MACPUFFIN   *Book great rates at AAA.com*

Motel

6/13-10/16	1P: $99-$119	2P: $99-$119	XP: $10	F16
5/1-6/12 & 10/17-4/30	1P: $84-$94	2P: $84-$94	XP: $10	F16

Phone: (902)625-0621

Location: 1 mi (1.6 km) n on Hwy 4; 1 mi (1.6 km) s of Canso Cswy. 373 Hwy 4 B9A 1M8. Fax: 902/625-1525. **Facility:** 33 units. 32 one-bedroom standard units. 1 one-bedroom suite with whirlpool. 1-2 stories (no elevator), exterior corridors. **Parking:** on-site, winter plug-ins. **Terms:** small pets only (on ground floor). **Amenities:** irons, hair dryers. **Pool(s):** heated indoor. **Leisure Activities:** exercise room. **Guest Services:** gift shop, coin laundry. **Business Services:** meeting rooms. **Cards:** AX, CB, DC, DS, MC, VI. *(See color ad card insert)*

SOME UNITS

(ASK) 🇸 🛏 🍽 💻 / ✕ /

SKYE LODGE

(CAA) (SAVE)

Small-scale Hotel

6/16-10/15	1P: $84	2P: $84	XP: $10	F14
5/1-6/15 & 10/16-4/30	1P: $75	2P: $75	XP: $10	F14

Phone: (902)625-1300

Location: Jct Trans-Canada Hwy 105, Rt 104 and 19. 160 Hwy 4 B9A 1M5 (PO Box 9626). Fax: 902/625-1966. **Facility:** 49 one-bedroom standard units. 2 stories (no elevator), interior/exterior corridors. **Parking:** on-site. **Amenities:** *Some:* high-speed Internet. **Dining:** 6:30 am-10 pm. **Business Services:** PC. **Cards:** AX, DC, DS, MC, VI. **Free Special Amenities:** local telephone calls and early check-in/late check-out.

SOME UNITS

🇸 🍴 🍽 💻 / ✕ 🔌 /

──── WHERE TO DINE ────

SMITTY'S FAMILY RESTAURANT

Canadian

Lunch: $6-$11   **Dinner:** $8-$16   **Phone:** 902/625-3346

Location: Just e of Canso Cswy at Rotary. 10 Rt 19 B0E 2T0. **Hours:** 7 am-9 pm, Thurs & Fri-10 pm. **Reservations:** accepted. **Features:** The family-oriented restaurant satisfies patrons with its ever-popular all-day breakfast items, as well as tasty and wholesome soups and salads at lunchtime. A relaxed mood characterizes the dining space. Casual dress; cocktails. **Parking:** on-site. **Cards:** AX, DC, MC, VI.

PORT HAWKESBURY pop. 3,701

──── WHERE TO STAY ────

MARITIME INN PORT HAWKESBURY

(CAA) (SAVE)

Small-scale Hotel

7/1-10/15	1P: $112-$149	2P: $112-$149	XP: $15	F12
1/1-4/30	1P: $101-$142	2P: $101-$142	XP: $15	F12
5/1-6/30 & 10/16-12/31	1P: $98-$138	2P: $98-$138	XP: $15	F12

Phone: (902)625-0320

Location: 4.2 mi (6.4 km) e of Canso Cswy on Hwy 4. Located opposite shopping centre. 717 Reeves St B9A 2S2. Fax: 902/625-3876. **Facility:** 73 units. 72 one-bedroom standard units. 1 two-bedroom suite ($164-$198). 3 stories (no elevator), interior/exterior corridors. **Parking:** on-site. **Terms:** package plans, small pets only (in smoking units). **Amenities:** *Some:* irons, hair dryers. **Dining:** Miller's Cafe, Tap & Grill, see separate listing. **Pool(s):** outdoor, heated indoor. **Leisure Activities:** sauna, exercise room. **Guest Services:** valet and coin laundry, wireless Internet. **Business Services:** meeting rooms. **Cards:** AX, DS, MC, VI. **Free Special Amenities:** newspaper and high-speed Internet.

SOME UNITS

🛏 🍴 🍽 🐾 💻 / ✕ (VCR) 🔌 🖨 /
FEE FEE

──── WHERE TO DINE ────

MILLER'S CAFE, TAP & GRILL

Canadian

Lunch: $7-$12   **Dinner:** $10-$25   **Phone:** 902/625-0320

Location: 4.2 mi (6.4 km) e of Canso Cswy on Hwy 4; in Maritime Inn Port Hawkesbury. 717 Reeves St B9A 2S2. **Hours:** 6:30 am-2 & 5-10 pm, Sat & Sun 7 am-2 pm; 6:30 am-2 & 5-9 pm, Sat & Sun 7 am-2 pm 10/16-5/31. Closed: 12/25. **Reservations:** suggested. **Features:** The cozy restaurant is a quaint little spot for relaxed breakfasts and lunches, while the pub section is suitable for dinner meals. Fresh catches of such fish as haddock and halibut are well-prepared and attractively presented. Tempting dessert is made on the premises. Casual dress; cocktails. **Parking:** on-site. **Cards:** AX, CB, DC, DS, MC, VI.

🍽

ROSE GARDEN CHINESE RESTAURANT

Chinese

Lunch: $6-$11   **Dinner:** $8-$15   **Phone:** 902/625-5600

Location: Centre. 708 Reeves St B0E 2V0. **Hours:** 11 am-9 pm, Thurs-Sat to 10 pm. Closed: 12/25. **Features:** Booth and table seating are available in the basic dining rooms of the casual restaurant. Offerings include ample portions of quality food, including a large selection of combination plates. Casual dress; cocktails. **Parking:** on-site. **Cards:** DS, MC, VI.

PORT HOOD

------- **WHERE TO STAY** -------

HAUS TREUBURG COUNTRY INN & COTTAGES Phone: (902)787-2116

▼▼ ▼▼ All Year 1P: $95-$135 2P: $95-$135
Location: Centre. 175 Main St B0E 2W0. **Fax:** 902/787-3216. **Facility:** Smoke free premises. 6 units. 3 one-
Country Inn bedroom standard units. 3 cottages. 2 stories (no elevator), interior/exterior corridors. **Parking:** on-site.
Terms: office hours 7 am-11 pm, 5 day cancellation notice, weekly rates available, [MAP] meal plan
available, package plans. **Amenities:** *Some:* DVD players. **Leisure Activities:** limited beach access. **Business Services:** PC.
Cards: MC, VI.

⟦¶⟧ ⟦✕⟧ ⟦AC⟧ ⟦VCR⟧

QUEENSLAND

------- **WHERE TO STAY** -------

SURFSIDE INN Phone: (902)857-2417

▼▼▼ ▼ 6/16-10/15 1P: $94-$194 2P: $99-$199 XP: $15 F5
5/1-6/15 & 10/16-4/30 1P: $80-$170 2P: $85-$175 XP: $15 F5
Historic **Location:** Hwy 103, exit 6, follow signs on Rt 3. 9609 St Margarets Bay Rd B0J 1T0. **Fax:** 902/857-2107. **Facility:** A
Country Inn nice beach is opposite this inn, which offers a deck, a dining area, some bay view rooms and some rooms
with whirlpool tubs. Smoke free premises. 8 units. 7 one-bedroom standard units with whirlpools. 1 one-
bedroom suite with whirlpool. 2 stories (no elevator), interior corridors. **Parking:** on-site. **Terms:** office hours 8 am-9 pm,
package plans. **Amenities:** video library, hair dryers. *Some:* DVD players. **Cards:** AX, DC, DS, MC, VI.

SOME UNITS
⟦ASK⟧ ⟦S♦⟧ ⟦¶⟧ ⟦✕⟧ ⟦AC⟧ ⟦☎⟧ / ⟦VCR⟧ /

ST. ANN'S

------- **WHERE TO DINE** -------

THE LOBSTER GALLEY RESTAURANT **Lunch:** $7-$18 **Dinner:** $14-$27 **Phone:** 902/295-3100
ⓒAA **Location:** Hwy 105, exit 11, just w. 51943 Cabot Tr B0E 1B0. **Hours:** Open 5/6-10/25; 10 am-10 pm; from 8 am
▼▼ ▼▼ 7/1-8/15; to 9 pm off season. **Reservations:** suggested. **Features:** Bordering St. Ann's Harbour, the
restaurant is a lovely place to enjoy ocean scenes and a good variety of fresh local seafood. The specialty
Seafood is lobster, which diners select from large tanks. A nautical theme prevails in all three informal dining areas.
Casual dress; cocktails. **Parking:** on-site. **Cards:** AX, DC, MC, VI.

SALMON RIVER BRIDGE

------- **WHERE TO STAY** -------

SALMON RIVER HOUSE COUNTRY INN, Phone: (902)889-3353
ⓒAA ⟦SAVE⟧ All Year [CP] 1P: $78-$84 2P: $99-$144 XP: $25 F12
▼▼ ▼▼ **Location:** At Salmon River Bridge. 9931 Hwy 7 B0J 1P0. **Fax:** 902/889-3653. **Facility:** Smoke free premises. 8
one-bedroom standard units, some with whirlpools. 2 stories (no elevator), interior corridors. *Bath:* combo or
Country Inn shower only. **Parking:** on-site. **Terms:** office hours 9 am-9 pm, 3 day cancellation notice-fee imposed, [AP],
[BP], [ECP] & [MAP] meal plans available, package plans. **Amenities:** hair dryers. **Dining:** The Lobster
Shack Restaurant, see separate listing. **Leisure Activities:** canoeing, fishing. **Cards:** AX, CB, DC, DS, JC,
MC, VI. **Free Special Amenities:** expanded continental breakfast and local telephone calls.

SOME UNITS
⟦S♦⟧ ⟦¶⟧ ⟦✕⟧ ⟦AC⟧ ⟦☎⟧ / ⟦▮⟧ /

------- **WHERE TO DINE** -------

THE LOBSTER SHACK RESTAURANT **Lunch:** $8-$19 **Dinner:** $12-$35 **Phone:** 902/889-3353
▼▼ ▼▼ **Location:** At Salmon River Bridge; in Salmon River House Country Inn. 9931 Hwy 7 B0J 1P0. **Hours:** Open 5/1-
Seafood 10/15; 7 am-9 pm. **Reservations:** accepted. **Features:** Patrons can relax inside the rustic, sea-shanty-style
restaurant or on the large screened porch that overlooks the Salmon River. Boiled lobster, mussels,
chowder and some meat entrees are among choices here. Casual dress; cocktails. **Parking:** on-site.
Cards: AX, CB, DC, DS, MC, VI.

⟦&M⟧ ⟦AC⟧

SANDY COVE

------- **WHERE TO STAY** -------

OLDE VILLAGE INN Phone: (902)834-2202
▼▼ ▼▼ 7/1-9/7 1P: $100-$160 2P: $100-$160 XP: $15
5/1-6/30 & 9/8-10/30 1P: $70-$140 2P: $70-$140 XP: $15
Historic **Location:** On Rt 217 W, on Digby Neck; 19.2 mi (32 km) s of Digby; centre. Located in a secluded area. 387 Church Hill
Country Inn Rd B0V 1E0. **Fax:** 902/834-2927. **Facility:** This pleasant inn features a variety of room styles and a few older
cabins in the back. Smoke free premises. 16 units. 13 one-bedroom standard units. 3 cabins ($90-$160). 2
stories (no elevator), interior/exterior corridors. *Bath:* combo or shower only. **Parking:** on-site. **Terms:** open 5/1-10/30, office
hours 7 am-11 pm, 2 night minimum stay - weekends, 3 day cancellation notice-fee imposed, [BP] meal plan available. **Guest
Services:** gift shop. **Business Services:** meeting rooms. **Cards:** AX, MC, VI.

SOME UNITS
⟦ASK⟧ ⟦S♦⟧ ⟦¶⟧ ⟦✕⟧ ⟦AC⟧ ⟦☎⟧ / ⟦▮⟧ ⟦▭⟧ ⟦▦⟧ /

SCOTSBURN

------ **WHERE TO STAY** ------

STONEHAME LODGE & CHALETS   **Phone:** 902/485-3468
▼▼▼   7/1-8/31   2P: $105-$205   XP: $10   F16
        5/1-6/30 & 9/1-4/30   2P: $65-$195   XP: $10   F16
Cottage   **Location:** Rt 256, 7.5 mi (12 km) w of Pictou via Rt 376, last 1.2 mi (2 km) on gravel entry road. Located in a quiet secluded area. RR 3 B0K 1R0. Fax: 902/485-5928. **Facility:** Set on a scenic mountaintop, the property offers sweeping views from the cottages or the main lodge. Smoke free premises. 27 units. 17 one-bedroom standard units, some with whirlpools. 10 cottages ($135-$205), some with whirlpools. 2 stories (no elevator), exterior corridors. **Parking:** on-site, winter plug-ins. **Terms:** office hours 7 am-10 pm, weekly rates available, [CP] meal plan available, package plans, pets (in limited units). **Amenities:** video library. *Some:* DVD players, irons, hair dryers. **Pool(s):** heated outdoor. **Leisure Activities:** whirlpool, hiking trails, horseshoes. **Guest Services:** coin laundry. **Cards:** AX, DC, MC, VI.

SOME UNITS
(ASK) 🛇 🛏 ⊇ ⊠ ⊠ ▣ / 🅰 VCR ⊘ 🔌 📷 /

SHELBURNE pop. 2,013

------ **WHERE TO STAY** ------

THE COOPER'S INN   **Phone:** 902/875-4656
▼▼▼   All Year [BP]   1P: $100-$185   2P: $100-$185   XP: $12
        Location: Hwy 103, exit 26, 1.5 mi (2.5 km) e on Rt 3, follow one way Dock St. Located in the historic district. 36 Dock
Historic Bed   St B0T 1W0 (PO Box 959). **Facility:** A lovely suite on the top floor is the crowning glory of this pre-1800s
& Breakfast   converted home, which offers some rooms with water views. Smoke free premises. 8 units. 7 one-bedroom
        standard units. 1 two-bedroom suite. 3 stories (no elevator), interior/exterior corridors. *Bath:* combo or
shower only. **Parking:** on-site. **Terms:** office hours 8 am-10 pm, cancellation fee imposed. **Amenities:** video library, hair dryers.
Guest Services: wireless Internet. **Cards:** AX, JC, MC, VI.

📶 ⊠ 🅰 VCR ▣

MACKENZIE'S MOTEL, COTTAGES, AND SUITES   **Phone:** 902/875-2842
(CAA) (SAVE)   All Year   1P: $70-$135   2P: $75-$135   XP: $10
        Location: Hwy 103, exit 26, 1 mi (1.6 km) e on Rt 3. Located in a commercial area. 260 Water St B0T 1W0 (PO Box
▼▼ ▼▼   225). Fax: 902/875-2842. **Facility:** 14 units. 8 one-bedroom standard units, some with kitchens and/or
Motel   whirlpools. 6 cottages ($95-$145), some with whirlpools. 1 story, exterior corridors. *Bath:* some combo or
        shower only. **Parking:** on-site. **Terms:** office hours 8 am-11 pm, cancellation fee imposed, weekly rates
available, small pets only (with prior approval). **Amenities:** *Some:* DVD players, hair dryers. **Pool(s):** heated
outdoor. **Cards:** AX, MC, VI. **Free Special Amenities: expanded continental breakfast and high-speed Internet.**

SOME UNITS
🛏 ⊇ 🔌 📷 ▣ / ⊠ VCR /

WILDWOOD MOTEL   **Phone:** 902/875-2964
(CAA) (SAVE)   All Year   1P: $65-$75   2P: $75-$90   XP: $10   F12
▼▼ ▼▼   **Location:** Hwy 103, exit 26, 1.1 mi (1.8 km) e on Rt 3. Located in a residential area. Minto St B0T 1W0 (PO Box 358).
Motel   **Facility:** 20 one-bedroom standard units. 1 story, exterior corridors. **Parking:** on-site. **Terms:** office hours 7
        am-11 pm. **Cards:** AX, MC, VI. **Free Special Amenities: continental breakfast and high-speed Internet.**

SOME UNITS
🛇 / ⊠

------ **WHERE TO DINE** ------

CHARLOTTE LANE CAFE & CRAFTS   **Lunch:** $7-$20   **Dinner:** $12-$27   **Phone:** 902/875-3314
▼▼▼   **Location:** Between John St and Maiden Ln; centre. 13 Charlotte Ln B0T 1W0. **Hours:** Open 5/12-12/31; 11:30 am-
        2:30 & 5-8 pm. Closed major holidays; also Sun & Mon. **Reservations:** accepted, evenings only.
Continental   **Features:** Well-prepared, creative entrees, such as garlic shrimp linguine and lobster and scallop brandy
        gratin, make up a menu full of interesting choices. The mid-1800s home is loaded with character, from its
old wood floors to its wrought-iron light fixtures. Patio dining is available in season. Casual dress; cocktails. **Parking:** street.
Cards: MC, VI. **Historic**

🅰

LUONG'S RESTAURANT   **Lunch:** $6   **Dinner:** $9-$11   **Phone:** 902/875-1300
▼▼ ▼▼   **Location:** Centre. 165 Water St B0T 1W0. **Hours:** 11 am-9 pm, Fri-10 pm, Sat & Sun noon-9 pm. Closed:
        12/25, 12/26; also Mon. **Reservations:** accepted. **Features:** The popular restaurant prepares a wide
Chinese selection of Chinese and Canadian cuisine, including some Szechuan dishes and combination plates.
        Casual dress; cocktails. **Parking:** street. **Cards:** MC, VI.

SMITHS COVE

------ **WHERE TO STAY** ------

BIRCH VILLA COTTAGES   **Phone:** (902)245-4945
▼▼ ▼▼   5/1-10/1   1P: $92-$156   2P: $92-$156
        Location: Hwy 101, exit 25 eastbound; exit 24 westbound. RR 1 B0S 1S0. Fax: 902/245-4964. **Facility:** 13 units. 2
Cottage one-bedroom standard units. 11 cottages ($92-$156). 1 story, exterior corridors. **Parking:** on-site.
        Terms: open 5/1-10/1, office hours 8 am-11 pm, 2 night minimum stay - seasonal and/or weekends, 7 day
cancellation notice-fee imposed. **Pool(s):** heated outdoor. **Leisure Activities:** playground. **Guest Services:** coin laundry.
Cards: AX, DC, DS, MC, VI.

📶 ⊇ ⊠ 🅰 ⊘ 🔌 📷 ▣

HARBOURVIEW INN

Phone: (902)245-5686

▼▼ ▼▼

6/26-9/15 [BP] 1P: $99-$149 2P: $99-$149 XP: $20
5/15-6/25 & 9/16-10/15 [BP] 1P: $69-$99 2P: $69-$99 XP: $20

Bed & Breakfast **Location:** Hwy 101, exit 25 eastbound; exit 24 westbound. 25 Harbourview Rd B0S 1S0. Fax: 902/484-6520.
Facility: 12 units. 10 one-bedroom standard units, some with whirlpools. 2 two-bedroom suites. 1-2 stories (no elevator), interior/exterior corridors. **Parking:** on-site. **Terms:** open 5/15-10/15, office hours 7 am-10 pm, 7 day cancellation notice-fee imposed, package plans, small pets only (with prior approval). **Amenities:** video library, irons, hair dryers. *Some:* DVD players. **Pool(s):** outdoor. **Leisure Activities:** tennis court, playground, shuffleboard. **Cards:** MC, VI.

SOME UNITS

🐾 ➰ 🖾 ✕ ☎ 🖥 / 🖵 🗐 🖼 /

HEDLEY HOUSE INN BY THE SEA

Phone: 902/245-2500

▼▼ ▼▼

Property failed to provide current rates

Motel **Location:** Hwy 101, exit 25 eastbound; exit 24 westbound. RR 1 B0S 1S0. Fax: 902/245-1012.
Facility: Designated smoking area. 14 one-bedroom standard units, some with efficiencies. 1 story, exterior corridors. *Bath:* combo or shower only. **Parking:** on-site. **Terms:** open 5/1-10/15, office hours 8 am-8:30 pm, pets (with prior approval). **Amenities:** hair dryers.

SOME UNITS

🐾 🍴 🖾 🖎 ☎ 🗐 🖥 / 🗐 /

MOUNTAIN GAP INN   *Book great rates at AAA.com*

Phone: (902)245-5841

(CAA) (SAVE)

6/16-9/15 1P: $128-$145 2P: $128-$145 XP: $15 F18
5/17-6/15 & 9/16-9/30 1P: $79-$110 2P: $79-$110 XP: $15 F18

▼▼ ▼▼

Small-scale Hotel **Location:** Hwy 101, exit 25 eastbound; exit 24 westbound. 217 Hwy 1, Smiths Cove B0S 1S0 (PO Box 504, DIGBY, B0V 1A0). Fax: 902/245-2277. **Facility:** 105 units. 94 one-bedroom standard units. 1 one-bedroom suite ($195-$275) with whirlpool. 6 cabins and 4 cottages ($125-$153), some with whirlpools. 1 story, exterior corridors. *Bath:* combo or shower only. **Parking:** on-site. **Terms:** open 5/17-9/30, office hours 7 am-midnight, 3 day cancellation notice-fee imposed, [MAP] meal plan available, pets ($10 fee). **Amenities:** video library. **Dining:** 7:30 am-9 pm; hours vary off season, cocktails. **Pool(s):** heated outdoor. **Leisure Activities:** whirlpool, tennis court, giant chess board, lawn games, rental bicycles, hiking trails, playground, horseshoes. **Guest Services:** gift shop, coin laundry. **Business Services:** meeting rooms, PC. **Cards:** AX, DC, DS, MC, VI.

SOME UNITS

🗂D 🐾 🍴 ➰ 🖾 / ✕ 🖎 🖵 🗐 🖼 🖥 /
FEE   FEE

SUMMERVILLE

——— **WHERE TO STAY** ———

——— *The following lodging was either not evaluated or did not* ———
meet AAA rating requirements but is listed for your information only.

QUARTERDECK BEACHSIDE VILLAS

Phone: 902/683-2998

(fyi) Not evaluated. **Location:** Oceanfront. Hwy 103, exit 20, 0.3 mi (0.5 km) n. Rt 3 B0N 2K0 (PO Box 70, PORT MOUTON, B0T 1T0). Facilities, services, and decor characterize a mid-range property.

SYDNEY —*See also NORTH SYDNEY.*

——— **WHERE TO STAY** ———

CAMBRIDGE SUITES HOTEL   *Book great rates at AAA.com*

Phone: (902)562-6500

(CAA) (SAVE)

5/1-9/30 1P: $130-$180 2P: $145-$195 XP: $15 F18
1/1-4/30 1P: $119-$169 2P: $134-$184 XP: $15 F18

▼▼▼▼

10/1-12/31 1P: $109-$159 2P: $124-$174 XP: $15 F18

Large-scale Hotel **Location:** Hwy 4, 3.1 mi (5 km) e of jct Hwy 125, exit 6E; downtown. 380 Esplanade B1P 1B1. Fax: 902/564-6011. **Facility:** 148 units. 18 one-bedroom standard units. 130 one-bedroom suites, some with efficiencies. 8 stories, interior corridors. **Parking:** on-site. **Terms:** cancellation fee imposed, weekly rates available, [AP] & [BP] meal plans available, package plans, small pets only. **Amenities:** video games (fee), high-speed Internet, voice mail, irons, hair dryers. *Some:* dual phone lines, fax, safes, honor bars. **Dining:** Goody's Cafe, see separate listing. **Leisure Activities:** sauna, exercise room. **Guest Services:** coin laundry, wireless Internet. **Business Services:** meeting rooms, business center. **Cards:** AX, DC, DS, JC, MC, VI. **Free Special Amenities:** continental breakfast and local telephone calls. *(See color ad p 316 & p 346)*

SOME UNITS

🗂D 🐾 🍴 🍸 🎬 🖥 🗐 🖼 / 🖾 /

COMFORT INN   *Book great rates at AAA.com*

Phone: (902)562-0200

▼▼ ▼▼

7/1-10/15 [ECP] 1P: $122-$179 2P: $132-$189 XP: $10 F18
5/1-6/30 [ECP] 1P: $109-$139 2P: $119-$149 XP: $10 F18
10/16-4/30 [ECP] 1P: $95-$132 2P: $105-$142 XP: $10 F18

Small-scale Hotel **Location:** Hwy 4, 2.1 mi (3.5 km) e of jct Hwy 125, exit 6E. Located in a commercial area. 368 Kings Rd B1S 1A8. Fax: 902/564-6410. **Facility:** 61 one-bedroom standard units. 2 stories (no elevator), interior corridors. **Parking:** on-site. **Terms:** cancellation fee imposed, small pets only. **Amenities:** voice mail, irons, hair dryers. **Guest Services:** wireless Internet. **Cards:** AX, DC, DS, JC, MC, VI. *(See color ad card insert)*

SOME UNITS

(ASK) 🗂D 🐾 🎬 🖥 / 🖾 🗐 🖼 /

DAYS INN SYDNEY   *Book great rates at AAA.com*

Phone: (902)539-6750

(CAA) (SAVE)

5/1-10/31 1P: $119 2P: $119
11/1-4/30 1P: $89-$99 2P: $89-$99

▼▼▼▼

Small-scale Hotel **Location:** Hwy 4, 1.7 mi (2.8 km) e of jct Hwy 125, exit 6E. 480 Kings Rd B1S 1A8. Fax: 902/539-2773. **Facility:** 165 one-bedroom standard units. 3 stories (no elevator), interior corridors. **Parking:** on-site. **Terms:** [BP] meal plan available, package plans, small pets only (in smoking units). **Amenities:** voice mail, irons, hair dryers. **Pool(s):** heated indoor. **Leisure Activities:** sauna, whirlpool, exercise room. **Guest Services:** coin laundry, wireless Internet. **Business Services:** meeting rooms. **Cards:** AX, DC, DS, MC, VI. **Free Special Amenities:** room upgrade (subject to availability with advance reservations) and high-speed Internet.

SOME UNITS

🗂D 🐾 ➰ 🖾 🎬 🖥 / 🖾 🗐 🖼 /

DELTA SYDNEY *Book great rates at AAA.com*

Phone: (902)562-7500

5/1-10/31	1P: $144-$174	2P: $164-$194	XP: $20 F18
11/1-4/30	1P: $124-$154	2P: $144-$174	XP: $20 F18

CAA SAVE

Large-scale Hotel

Location: Centre at Prince St. 300 Esplanade B1P 1A7. **Fax:** 902/562-7402. **Facility:** 152 units. 150 one-bedroom standard units. 2 one-bedroom suites with whirlpools. 8 stories, interior corridors. **Parking:** on-site. **Terms:** small pets only. **Amenities:** video games (fee), voice mail, irons, hair dryers. **Dining:** Highland Mermaid Pasta & Seafood Restaurant, see separate listing. **Pool(s):** heated indoor. **Leisure Activities:** sauna, whirlpool, waterslide, exercise room. **Guest Services:** valet laundry, wireless Internet. **Business Services:** conference facilities, business center. **Cards:** AX, CB, DC, DS, JC, MC, VI. *(See color ad below)*

SOME UNITS

Here you don't just get a room. **You get much more.**

Spacious one & two-room suites •
Separate bedroom and living room areas •
COMPLIMENTARY deluxe continental breakfast •
Patio, fitness centre & sauna •
GREAT DOWNTOWN LOCATION •

380 Esplanade • Sydney, NS

1.800.565.9466 • 902.562.6500

www.cambridgesuiteshotel.com

CAMBRIDGE SUITES HOTEL

real suite.

aeroplan

Approved

• 152 harbourview guest rooms and suites
• Located downtown, on the boardwalk
• Casual relaxed dining in the Highland Mermaid Restaurant, with a panoramic waterfront view
• British-style pub, the Crown & Moose
• Complimentary wireless high-speed Internet
• Complimentary outdoor parking

DELTA
SYDNEY

Your room is ready

902-562-7500 Fax: 902-562-3023	CANADA and U.S. 1-800-268-1133 www.deltahotels.com	300 Esplanade, Sydney, NS B1P 1A7

QUALITY INN SYDNEY   *Book great rates at AAA.com*   Phone: 902/539-8101

▽▽▽

Small-scale Hotel

Property failed to provide current rates

Location: Hwy 4, 2 mi (3.3 km) e of jct Hwy 125. 560 Kings Rd B1S 1B8. Fax: 902/539-1743. **Facility:** 70 one-bedroom standard units, some with whirlpools. 3 stories (no elevator), interior corridors. *Bath:* combo or shower only. **Parking:** on-site. **Terms:** small pets only (on ground floor). **Amenities:** irons, hair dryers. **Dining:** Cape Bretoner Restaurant, see separate listing. **Pool(s):** heated indoor. **Leisure Activities:** exercise room. **Guest Services:** coin laundry, wireless Internet. **Business Services:** meeting rooms. *(See color ad card insert)*

SOME UNITS

🛏️ 🍴 ⚙️ 🏊 📼 / ⊠ /

────── **WHERE TO DINE** ──────

CAPE BRETONER RESTAURANT   Lunch: $6-$10   Dinner: $8-$17   Phone: 902/539-8101

▽▽▽

Canadian

Location: Hwy 4, 2 mi (3.3 km) e of jct Hwy 125; in Quality Inn Sydney. 560 Kings Rd B1S 1B8. **Hours:** 7 am-2 & 5-9 pm. **Reservations:** accepted. **Features:** Many guests visit for the well-known lunch buffet. Everything, including the super desserts, is homemade. The atmosphere is casual, and service is friendly. Casual dress; cocktails. **Parking:** on-site. **Cards:** AX, DC, MC, VI.

DON CHERRY'S SPORTS GRILL   Lunch: $7-$14   Dinner: $10-$19   Phone: 902/539-5343

▽▽▽

Canadian

Location: Hwy 125, exit 6; in Value Check Plaza. 1290 Kings Rd B1S 1E2. **Hours:** 11 am-10 pm, Fri & Sat-midnight. **Closed:** 12/25. **Reservations:** accepted. **Features:** This hockey-oriented restaurant presents a menu that is sure to score. Guest's can "crosscheck" the selections which ranges from light appetizers to full entrees, but shouldn't penalize themselves by skipping dessert. Casual dress; cocktails. **Parking:** on-site. **Cards:** AX, DC, MC, VI.

GOODY'S CAFE   Lunch: $9-$14   Dinner: $13-$21   Phone: 902/563-7009

▽▽▽

Canadian

Location: Hwy 4, 3.1 mi (5 km) e of jct Hwy 125, exit 6E; downtown; in Cambridge Suites Hotel. 380 Esplanade B1P 1B1. **Hours:** 11 am-10 pm, Sun & holidays from 5 pm. **Features:** Candles, linens and upbeat music give the small, waterfront restaurant the energized feel of a lively bistro. Diverse menu offerings include chicken stir-fry, stuffed haddock, tortellini, pork tenderloin and rack of lamb. The seafood chowder should not be missed. Casual dress; cocktails. **Parking:** on-site. **Cards:** AX, DC, DS, MC, VI.

GOVERNORS RESTAURANT   Lunch: $5-$11   Dinner: $12-$19   Phone: 902/562-7646

(AAA)

▽▽▽

Canadian

Location: Hwy 4, 5.5 km e of Hwy 125, exit 6E; centre. 233 Esplanade B1P 1A6. **Hours:** 11 am-11 pm. **Closed:** 1/1, 12/24-12/26. **Reservations:** suggested. **Features:** Some sections of the late-19th-century former mayor's house overlook the harbor. On the menu are seafood, beef and chicken entrees. Homemade desserts are worth saving room for. Diners can request seating on the deck or venture upstairs for lighter pub fare. Casual dress; cocktails. **Parking:** on-site. **Cards:** AX, DS, MC, VI.

HIGHLAND MERMAID PASTA & SEAFOOD RESTAURANT   Dinner: $12-$25   Phone: 902/562-7500

▽▽▽

Canadian

Location: Centre at Prince St; in Delta Sydney. 300 Esplanade B1P 1A7. **Hours:** 7 am-11 & 5-9 pm. **Reservations:** accepted. **Features:** Fish and chips stands out on a menu of traditionally prepared seafood choices. The relaxed location, decorated with draped nets and pictures of ships, overlooks Sydney Harbour. Casual dress; cocktails. **Parking:** on-site. **Cards:** AX, DC, MC, VI. *(See color ad p 346)*

JOE'S WAREHOUSE & FOOD EMPORIUM   Lunch: $8-$15   Dinner: $13-$22   Phone: 902/539-6686

▽▽▽

Steak & Seafood

Location: Off Hwy 4, 3 mi (5 km) e of jct Hwy 125, exit 6E; centre. 424 Charlotte St B1P 6R7. **Hours:** 11:30 am-11 pm, Sun from 4 pm; hours vary off season. **Closed** major holidays. **Reservations:** accepted. **Features:** The converted warehouse is decorated with antiques and rustic furnishings. An extensive selection of wines complements preparations of steak, ribs and seafood, as well as several Italian choices. Cheesecakes, apple tortes and pies are tempting desserts. Casual dress; cocktails. **Parking:** on-site. **Cards:** AX, DC, MC, VI.

PEKING RESTAURANT   Lunch: $6-$16   Dinner: $10-$18   Phone: 902/539-7775

▽▽▽

Chinese

Location: Just e of Hwy 4; centre. 355 Charlotte St B1P 1E1. **Hours:** 11 am-10 pm, Fri & Sat-11 pm, Sun 4 pm-10 pm. **Closed:** 12/25. **Reservations:** suggested. **Features:** Traditional choices—such as beef with broccoli, lo mein and sweet and sour pork—are served in plentiful portions. Illuminated photographs of China, as well as other Oriental appointments, decorate the slightly fancy, and peacefully quiet, dining rooms. Casual dress; cocktails. **Parking:** street. **Cards:** AX, DC, MC, VI.

SMITTY'S FAMILY RESTAURANT   Lunch: $6-$11   Dinner: $8-$16   Phone: 902/539-0979

▽▽▽

Canadian

Location: In Sydney Shopping Centre. 272 B Prince St B1P 5N6. **Hours:** 7 am-9 pm, Fri & Sat-10 pm, Sun-8 pm. **Closed:** 12/25. **Reservations:** accepted. **Features:** The family-oriented restaurant satisfies patrons with its ever-popular all-day breakfast items, as well as tasty and wholesome soups and salads at lunchtime. A relaxed mood characterizes the dining space. Casual dress; cocktails. **Parking:** on-site. **Cards:** AX, DC, MC, VI.

SWISS CHALET   Lunch: $6-$11   Dinner: $8-$16   Phone: 902/562-3232

▽▽▽

Canadian

Location: Jct Hwy 125. 482 Grand Lake Rd B1P 5S8. **Hours:** 11 am-10 pm, Fri & Sat-11 pm. **Closed:** 12/25, 12/26. **Reservations:** accepted. **Features:** The popular restaurant is known for its rotisserie chicken and ribs and the tangy Chalet sauce that gives food its special zip. Diners munch on a half or quarter chicken with sides such as steamed vegetables, fries, baked potatoes and salads. Lunch guests often go for the great soup and sandwich combination. Take-out and delivery service are popular options. Casual dress; cocktails. **Parking:** on-site. **Cards:** AX, DC, MC, VI.

SYDNEY MINES pop. 16,068

─────── WHERE TO STAY ───────

GOWRIE HOUSE COUNTRY INN

Historic
Country Inn

Phone: (902)544-1050

5/1-10/31 [BP]	1P: $135-$265	2P: $145-$265	XP: $20	F5
11/1-12/30 [BP]	1P: $89-$189	2P: $99-$189	XP: $20	F5

Location: Hwy 105, exit 21E, 1.9 mi (3 km) n on Rt 305. Located in a residential area. 840 Shore Rd B1V 1A6. **Fax:** 902/736-0077. **Facility:** On the property's manicured grounds are a main inn, which was built in 1830, as well as an annex building and a cottage; many rooms have fireplaces. Smoke free premises. 11 one-bedroom standard units, some with whirlpools. 2 stories (no elevator), interior/exterior corridors. **Parking:** on-site. **Terms:** open 5/1-12/30, age restrictions may apply, 3 day cancellation notice, [MAP] meal plan available, small pets only (in garden house). **Amenities:** hair dryers. *Some:* DVD players, irons. **Guest Services:** wireless Internet. **Cards:** AX, MC, VI.

SOME UNITS

🛏 🍴 ✕ / VCR 📶 📠 🖥 /

TRURO pop. 11,457

─────── WHERE TO STAY ───────

BAKER'S CHEST TEAROOM AND BED & BREAKFAST
Bed & Breakfast

Phone: (902)893-4824

All Year [BP]	1P: $90-$110	2P: $90-$110	XP: $15	D12

Location: Hwy 102, exit 14A, 3 mi (4.6 km) e to Main St. 53 Farnham Rd B2N 2X6. **Fax:** 902/893-7634. **Facility:** Tastefully decorated guest rooms and public areas comprise this delightful, century-old home on the edge of town; antique organs are on display. Smoke free premises. 4 one-bedroom standard units. 2 stories (no elevator), interior corridors. *Bath:* combo or shower only. **Parking:** on-site. **Terms:** office hours 7 am-11 pm. **Amenities:** hair dryers. **Leisure Activities:** waterskiing, tobogganing. **Guest Services:** complimentary laundry. **Business Services:** PC. **Cards:** MC, VI.

SOME UNITS

🍴 ✕ ☎ / VCR /

BEST WESTERN GLENGARRY HOTEL *Book great rates at AAA.com*
Small-scale Hotel

Phone: 902/893-4311

6/1-10/1	1P: $157	2P: $167	XP: $12	F17
5/1-5/31 & 10/2-4/30	1P: $147	2P: $157	XP: $12	F17

Location: 0.6 mi (1 km) se on Hwy 2. 150 Willow St B2N 4Z6. **Fax:** 902/893-1759. **Facility:** 92 one-bedroom standard units, some with whirlpools. 3 stories, interior/exterior corridors. **Parking:** on-site, winter plug-ins. **Amenities:** irons, hair dryers. *Some:* high-speed Internet. **Dining:** Glengarry Dining Room, see separate listing. **Pool(s):** heated outdoor, heated indoor, wading. **Leisure Activities:** whirlpool. **Business Services:** conference facilities, PC. **Cards:** AX, CB, DC, DS, MC, VI. **Free Special Amenities:** local telephone calls and high-speed Internet.

SOME UNITS

🍴 🍸 🏊 🖥 / ✕ VCR 📶 🖥 /

COMFORT INN *Book great rates at AAA.com*
Small-scale Hotel

Phone: (902)893-0330

5/16-10/15 [CP]	1P: $124-$150	2P: $142-$169	XP: $10	F16
3/16-4/30 [CP]	1P: $129-$156	2P: $138-$165	XP: $10	F16
5/1-5/15 & 10/16-3/15 [CP]	1P: $124-$151	2P: $133-$160	XP: $10	F16

Location: Hwy 102, exit 14. Located in a commercial area. 12 Meadow Dr B2N 5V4. **Fax:** 902/897-0176. **Facility:** 81 one-bedroom standard units. 2 stories (no elevator), interior corridors. **Parking:** on-site. **Terms:** pets (on ground floor). **Amenities:** irons, hair dryers. **Guest Services:** wireless Internet. **Business Services:** PC. **Cards:** AX, DC, DS, MC, VI. *(See color ad card insert)*

SOME UNITS

ASK 🖥 🛏 🍴 🎥 🖥 / ✕ 📶 🖥 /

HOWARD JOHNSON HOTEL AND CONVENTION CENTRE *Book at AAA.com*
Small-scale Hotel

Phone: (902)895-1651

5/1-9/30	1P: $88-$96	2P: $88-$96	XP: $10	F18
10/1-4/30	1P: $80-$88	2P: $80-$88	XP: $10	F18

Location: Centre. 437 Prince St B2N 1E6. **Fax:** 902/893-4427. **Facility:** 113 one-bedroom standard units, some with whirlpools. 3 stories (no elevator), interior/exterior corridors. **Parking:** on-site, winter plug-ins. **Terms:** cancellation fee imposed, [BP] & [CP] meal plans available, pets (must be attended). **Amenities:** voice mail, irons, hair dryers. **Pool(s):** heated indoor, wading. **Guest Services:** coin laundry, wireless Internet. **Business Services:** meeting rooms, PC. **Cards:** AX, DS, MC, VI.

SOME UNITS

ASK 🖥 🛏 🍴 🏊 🖥 / ✕ 📶 🖥 /

THE JOHN STANFIELD INN
Historic
Country Inn

Phone: (902)895-1505

5/1-9/15 [CP]	1P: $139-$149	2P: $139-$149	
9/16-4/30 [CP]	1P: $119-$139	2P: $119-$139	

Location: Centre; behind Howard Johnson. 437 Prince St B2N 1A6. **Fax:** 902/897-0827. **Facility:** Stylish details at this 1902 Queen Anne mansion include intricate woodwork and hand-carved fireplace mantels. Smoke free premises. 12 one-bedroom standard units, some with whirlpools. 3 stories (no elevator), interior corridors. **Parking:** on-site. **Terms:** office hours 7 am-9 pm, 3 day cancellation notice, package plans. **Amenities:** hair dryers. *Some:* DVD players. **Dining:** restaurant, see separate listing. **Business Services:** meeting rooms. **Cards:** AX, MC, VI.

ASK 🖥 🍴 ✕ 🖥

THE PALLISER MOTEL
Motel

Phone: (902)893-8951

5/1-10/20 [BP]	1P: $75	2P: $75	F15
		XP: $10	

Location: Hwy 102, exit 14. 103/104 Tidal Bore Rd B2N 5G6 (PO Box 821). **Fax:** 902/895-8475. **Facility:** 42 units. 41 one- and 1 two-bedroom standard units. 1 story, exterior corridors. *Bath:* combo or shower only. **Parking:** on-site. **Terms:** open 5/1-10/20, office hours 7 am-11 pm, [AP] meal plan available, small pets only. **Dining:** restaurant, see separate listing. **Guest Services:** gift shop. **Cards:** AX, MC, VI. **Free Special Amenities:** full breakfast and early check-in/late check-out.

SOME UNITS

SUPER 8 MOTEL **Book at AAA.com**
      Phone: (902)895-8884
▼▼▼▼ All Year [ECP]   1P: $129-$179   2P: $139-$189   XP: $15   F17
    Location: Hwy 102, exit 13A. 85 Treaty Tr B2N 5A9. **Fax:** 902/895-8801. **Facility:** 50 units. 32 one-bedroom
Small-scale Hotel standard units, some with whirlpools. 18 one-bedroom suites. 3 stories, interior corridors. *Bath:* combo or
shower only. **Parking:** on-site. **Terms:** pets ($10 fee, in designated units). **Amenities:** high-speed Internet,
safes, irons, hair dryers. **Pool(s):** heated indoor. **Leisure Activities:** whirlpool, waterslide. **Guest Services:** coin laundry.
Business Services: meeting rooms, PC. **Cards:** AX, DC, DS, JC, MC, VI.   SOME UNITS

    [ASK] [S⊘] [🛏] [🍴] [⚙M] [🐕] [➖] [🔒] [🖨] [🖥] / [✕] /
      FEE

———— *The following lodging was either not evaluated or did not* ————
meet AAA rating requirements but is listed for your information only.

IRWIN LAKE CHALETS   **Phone:** 902-673-2219
[fyi]   Not evaluated. **Location:** Hwy 102, exit 14, 3 mi (5 km) s on Rt 236, 1.8 mi (3 km) w on gravel entry road. (PO Box
    288, BROOKFIELD, B0N 1C0). Facilities, services, and decor characterize a mid-range property.

———— **WHERE TO DINE** ————

CHOW FAMILY RESTAURANT   **Lunch:** $6-$12   **Dinner:** $10-$20   **Phone:** 902-895-9256
▼▼ ▼▼   **Location:** Centre. 344 Prince St B2N 1E6. **Hours:** 10:30 am-11 pm, Fri & Sat-midnight. Closed: 12/25, 12/26.
    Reservations: accepted. **Features:** The interesting menu dabbles in Canadian, Chinese and Polynesian
Chinese   cuisine. One dining area carries out an Oriental theme, while another has a Polynesian feel. The patio is
    relaxed and cozy. Servers show good menu knowledge and follow-up skills. Casual dress; cocktails.
Parking: on-site. **Cards:** AX, MC, VI.

FRANK & GINO'S GRILL AND PASTA HOUSE   **Lunch:** $8-$14   **Dinner:** $10-$20   **Phone:** 902-895-2165
▼▼ ▼▼   **Location:** Corner of Robie and Juniper sts. 286 Robie St B2N 1L3. **Hours:** 11 am-10 pm, Fri & Sat-11 pm. Closed:
    12/25. **Reservations:** accepted. **Features:** An upbeat, bustling atmosphere is what guests will find at the
Italian   popular eatery. Diners can relax in a booth or at a table while perusing a menu of well-prepared pasta, pizza
    and meat dishes, as well as tasty focaccia. Casual dress; cocktails. **Parking:** on-site. **Cards:** AX, DC,
MC, VI.   [🍴]

GLENGARRY DINING ROOM   **Lunch:** $6-$12   **Dinner:** $9-$20   **Phone:** 902-893-4311
▼▼ ▼▼   **Location:** 0.6 mi (1 km) se on Hwy 2; in Best Western Glengarry Hotel. 150 Willow St B2N 4Z8. **Hours:** 7 am-9 pm.
    Closed: 12/24-12/26. **Features:** Patrons can relax in the bright atrium of the casual and contemporary
Canadian   dining room. The daily lunch buffet is a nice complement to a menu of seafood, beef and chicken choices.
    Homemade seafood casserole is flavorful, as are the fresh-baked biscuits and pies. Casual dress; cocktails.
Parking: on-site. **Cards:** AX, DC, DS, MC, VI.   [🍴]

THE JOHN STANFIELD DINING ROOM   **Dinner:** $16-$30   **Phone:** 902-895-1505
▼▼▼ ▼▼▼   **Location:** Centre; in The John Stanfield Inn. 437 Prince St B2N 1E6. **Hours:** 5 pm-9 pm, Fri & Sat-9:30 pm.
    Closed: 12/25. **Reservations:** suggested. **Features:** Lovely dining rooms with ornate woodwork make up
Canadian   the historic inn. The menu comprises creative selections of meat and seafood, including the signature
    fisherman's harvest, which employs salmon, halibut, sole and shrimp. Service is friendly and gracious.
Dressy casual; cocktails. **Parking:** on-site. **Cards:** AX, DC, DS, MC, VI.   [🍴]

JUNGLE JIM'S RESTAURANT   **Lunch:** $7-$11   **Dinner:** $8-$20   **Phone:** 902-895-5467
▼▼ ▼▼   **Location:** Centre; in Truro Mall. 245 Robie St B2N 5N6. **Hours:** 11 am-10 pm, Wed-Sat to 11 pm. Closed: 12/25,
    12/26. **Reservations:** accepted. **Features:** Guests can step into a tropical theme at the casual eatery,
Canadian   which employs a friendly staff and nurtures a bustling atmosphere. The menu lines up a wide variety of
    comfort foods, salads, chicken, beef, seafood and hot wings, all served in ample, flavorful portions. Casual
dress; cocktails. **Parking:** on-site. **Cards:** AX, DC, MC, VI.

KEGGER'S ALEHOUSE   **Dinner:** $11-$17   **Phone:** 902-895-5347
▼▼ ▼▼   **Location:** Centre; opposite rail station. 75-76 Inglis Pl B2N 4B4. **Hours:** 4 pm-10 pm, Fri & Sat-midnight. Closed:
    12/25, 12/26; also Sun. **Reservations:** accepted. **Features:** Unwind in this spacious British-style pub which
Canadian   offers live entertainment most nights. A good selection of seafood, chicken or steaks is available as well as
    a fine selection of beers on tap. Casual dress; cocktails. **Parking:** on-site. **Cards:** AX, MC, VI.   [🍴]

MURPHY'S FAMOUS FISH & CHIP RESTAURANT   **Lunch:** $6-$10   **Dinner:** $8-$15   **Phone:** 902-895-1275
▼▼ ▼▼   **Location:** Centre; adjacent to rail station. 88 Esplanade B2N 2K3. **Hours:** 11 am-7 pm, Fri-8 pm. Closed major
    holidays. **Features:** English style seafood, such as the signature fish and chips, is the specialty at this
Steak & Seafood   bustling, friendly restaurant. Portion sizes are ample and flavors are fresh. Homey, relaxed atmosphere.
    Casual dress. **Parking:** on-site. **Cards:** AX, MC, VI.

THE PALLISER RESTAURANT AND
    GIFTS   **Lunch:** $8-$18   **Dinner:** $14-$25   **Phone:** 902-893-8951
[Ⓐ]   **Location:** Hwy 102, exit 14; in Palliser Motel. Tidal Bore Rd B2N 5G6. **Hours:** Open 5/1-10/31; 7:30 am-8:30 pm.
    Reservations: accepted. **Features:** On spacious grounds bordering the Salmon River, the restaurant is at
▼▼ ▼▼   the site of the tidal bore. The dining room boasts a pleasant, Colonial atmosphere. Home-style menu
    selections include varied preparations of seafood and meat. Lobster is the specialty in season. Service is
Canadian   friendly. Casual dress; cocktails. **Parking:** on-site. **Cards:** AX, DC, MC, VI.

SMITTY'S FAMILY RESTAURANT
Lunch: $6-$11   **Dinner:** $8-$16   **Phone:** 902-843-0843

Canadian
MC, VI.

Location: Hwy 102, exit 14, 0.6 mi (1 km) e. 64 Robie St B2N 5C1. **Hours:** 6:30 am-9 pm, Fri & Sat-10 pm. **Closed:** 12/25. **Reservations:** accepted. **Features:** The family-oriented restaurant satisfies patrons with its ever-popular all-day breakfast items, as well as tasty and wholesome soups and salads at lunchtime. A relaxed mood characterizes the dining space. Casual dress; cocktails. **Parking:** on-site. **Cards:** AX, DC,

SWISS CHALET
Lunch: $6-$11   **Dinner:** $8-$16   **Phone:** 902-895-6699

Canadian
DC, MC, VI.

Location: Hwy 102, exit 14, 0.6 mi (1 km) e. 79 Robie St B2N 5H8. **Hours:** 11 am-10 pm, Fri & Sat-11 pm. **Closed:** 12/25. **Features:** The popular restaurant is known for its rotisserie chicken and ribs and the tangy Chalet sauce that gives food its special zip. Diners munch on a half or quarter chicken with sides such as steamed vegetables, fries, baked potatoes and salads. Lunch guests often go for the great soup and sandwich combination. Take-out and delivery service are popular options. Casual dress; cocktails. **Parking:** on-site. **Cards:** AX,

THE WOODEN HOG & RED BIRD LOUNGE
Lunch: $6-$11   **Dinner:** $9-$17   **Phone:** 902-895-0779

Canadian
cocktails. **Parking:** on-site. **Cards:** AX, MC, VI.

Location: Corner of Louise and Prince sts. 627 Prince St B2N 1G2. **Hours:** 9 am-10 pm, Sat from 11 am. Closed major holidays; also Sun 11/22. **Reservations:** accepted. **Features:** A friendly, relaxed atmosphere envelops the delightful cafe. The lighter menu lists tasty soup, salad, nachos and sandwiches, while full meals include fresh halibut, poached salmon, fettuccine primavera and chicken cordon bleu. Casual dress;

TUSKET

———— WHERE TO DINE ————

MARCO'S GRILL & PASTA HOUSE
Lunch: $6-$11   **Dinner:** $10-$18   **Phone:** 902/648-0253

Italian

Location: Hwy 103, exit 33, just w. 237 Gavel Rd B0W 3M0. **Hours:** Open 5/1-1/31 & 3/1-4/30; 11 am-8 pm, Fri & Sat-9 pm. Closed major holidays. **Reservations:** accepted. **Features:** Not far from Yarmouth, the restaurant is worth the drive for well-prepared seafood, pasta and fine chowders. Homemade desserts shouldn't be missed. Casual dress; cocktails. **Parking:** on-site. **Cards:** MC, VI.

WESTERN SHORE

———— WHERE TO STAY ————

OAK ISLAND RESORT, SPA AND CONVENTION
CENTRE   *Book great rates at AAA.com*   **Phone:** (902)627-2600

6/16-10/15	1P: $129-$159	2P: $129-$159	XP: $12	F16
5/1-6/15 & 10/16-4/30	1P: $99-$109	2P: $99-$109	XP: $12	F16

Resort
Small-scale Hotel
Internet.

Location: Hwy 103, exit 9 or 10, follow signs on Rt 3; 6 mi (10 km) e of Mahone Bay. 36 Treasure Dr B0J 3M0 (PO Box 6). **Fax:** 902/627-2020. **Facility:** Overlooking the bay and marina, the resort offers 13 deluxe, oceanfront chalets as well as rooms either with a deck or facing the parking area. Designated smoking area. 120 units. 107 one-bedroom standard units. 13 cottages ($159-$289) with whirlpools. 3 stories; interior corridors. **Parking:** on-site. **Terms:** package plans. **Amenities:** voice mail, irons, hair dryers. *Some:* high-speed Internet. **Dining:** La Vista Dining Room, see separate listing. **Pool(s):** heated outdoor, heated indoor. **Leisure Activities:** sauna, whirlpool, steamroom, fishing, boat cruises, miniature golf, tennis court, walking trail, playground, exercise room, spa, horseshoes, shuffleboard. **Fee:** marina, charter fishing. **Guest Services:** gift shop, coin laundry. **Business Services:** conference facilities, business center. **Cards:** AX, DC, MC, VI. *(See color ad p 323)*

SOME UNITS

———— WHERE TO DINE ————

LA VISTA DINING ROOM
Lunch: $9-$15   **Dinner:** $12-$25   **Phone:** 902/627-2600

Canadian

Location: Hwy 103, exit 9 or 10, follow signs on Rt 3; 6 mi (10 km) e of Mahone Bay; in Oak Island Resort, Spa and Convention Centre. 55 Vaughn Rd B0J 2G0. **Hours:** 7 am-2 & 5-9 pm; to 10 pm in season. **Reservations:** accepted. **Features:** A bounty of food awaits at the La Vista, the portions are very generous as is the superb view of the marina and bay from the spacious dining room. Evening buffet in season. Casual dress; cocktails. **Parking:** on-site. **Cards:** AX, DC, MC, VI.

WESTPORT pop. 274

———— WHERE TO STAY ————

BRIER ISLAND LODGE & RESTAURANT   **Phone:** 902/839-2300

5/1-10/31	2P: $60-$139	XP: $10	F12

Small-scale Hotel

Location: On Rt 217; centre. 557 Water St B0V 1H0 (PO Box 33). **Fax:** 902/839-2006. **Facility:** 39 one-bedroom standard units, some with whirlpools. 1-2 stories (no elevator), interior/exterior corridors. **Parking:** on-site. **Terms:** open 5/1-10/31, office hours 6 am-11 pm. **Amenities:** hair dryers. **Dining:** Brier Island Restaurant, see separate listing. **Leisure Activities:** hiking trails. **Business Services:** meeting rooms. **Cards:** AX, DC, MC, VI. *(See color ad p 310)*

——— WHERE TO DINE ———

BRIER ISLAND RESTAURANT
Dinner: $15-$24
Phone: 902/839-2300

Canadian
Location: On Rt 217; centre; in Brier Island Lodge & Restaurant. 557 Water St B0V 1H0. **Hours:** Open 5/1-10/31; 7 am-10 & 6-9:30 pm. **Reservations:** accepted. **Features:** Located on a hillside and offering a splendid view of the harbour and strait, the restaurant specializes in fresh seafood with a selection of chicken and beef entrees and daily specials. Casual dress; cocktails. **Parking:** on-site. **Cards:** AX, MC, VI.

WHITE POINT

——— WHERE TO STAY ———

WHITE POINT BEACH RESORT
Phone: (902)354-2711

6/8-9/15	1P: $140-$180	2P: $140-$180
9/16-10/20	1P: $110-$180	2P: $110-$180
10/21-4/30	1P: $100-$180	2P: $100-$180
5/1-6/7	1P: $110-$165	2P: $110-$165

Resort
Small-scale Hotel
Location: Hwy 103, exit 20A, 5.6 mi (9 km) w on Rt 3. 75 White Point Rd 2 B0T 1G0 (c/o Hunts Point Post Office). **Fax:** 902/354-7278. **Facility:** Decks adjoin many of this seaside resort's lodge rooms; porches accent its rustic cabins. 126 units. 73 one-bedroom standard units, some with whirlpools. 44 cabins and 9 cottages ($135-$310), some with whirlpools. 2 stories, interior/exterior corridors. **Parking:** on-site. **Terms:** 3 day cancellation notice-fee imposed, [AP] & [MAP] meal plans available, package plans, pets (in designated units). **Amenities:** irons, hair dryers. *Some:* DVD players. **Pool(s):** saltwater. **Leisure Activities:** whirlpool, boating, paddleboats, 2 tennis courts, recreation programs, rental bicycles, playground, limited exercise equipment, basketball, horseshoes, volleyball. *Fee:* golf-9 holes. **Guest Services:** gift shop, coin laundry. **Business Services:** meeting rooms, administrative services, PC, fax. **Cards:** DS, MC, VI. *(See color ad p 325)*

SOME UNITS
(ASK) 🐄 🍴 🍷 🛁 🏊 ⊠ ✕ 🚪 🖥 / 🍴 🖥 /

WHYCOCOMAGH

——— WHERE TO STAY ———

KELTIC QUAY BAYFRONT LODGE & COTTAGES
Phone: 902/756-1122

5/1-10/31	1P: $199-$299	
11/1-4/30	1P: $149-$249	

Cottage
Location: Just se off Trans-Canada Hwy 105; centre. 90 Main St B0E 3M0. **Facility:** Set in a quiet spot on the Bras d'Or Lakes, this property offers pleasant, spacious and well-equipped duplex cottages with splendid views of the bay. Smoke free premises. 12 cottages ($149-$299) with whirlpools. 2 stories (no elevator), exterior corridors. **Parking:** on-site. **Terms:** office hours 8 am-10 pm, check-in 4 pm, 3 day cancellation notice-fee imposed, pets (must be attended). **Amenities:** video library, DVD players, voice mail, irons, hair dryers. **Leisure Activities:** horseshoes, shuffleboard. **Business Services:** meeting rooms. **Cards:** AX, MC, VI.

🐄 🍴 🍷 ✕ 🍴 🚪 🖥 🖥

WINDSOR pop. 3,778

——— WHERE TO DINE ———

THE SPITFIRE ARMS ALEHOUSE
Lunch: $7-$12
Dinner: $9-$18
Phone: 902/792-1460

Canadian
Location: Hwy 101, exit 6, just e to King St. 29 Water St B0N 2T0. **Hours:** 11 am-9 pm, Fri & Sat-10 pm. Closed: 12/25, 12/26. **Reservations:** accepted. **Features:** The classic English-style pub is decorated in a theme recalling the famous Spitfire fighter plane. A bounty of beers is on tap to assist in washing down well-prepared pub fare, including burgers, wraps, fish and chips, meat pies, stir-fries and ploughman's lunches. Casual dress; cocktails. **Parking:** street. **Cards:** DC, MC, VI.

🍷

WOLFVILLE pop. 3,658

——— WHERE TO STAY ———

BLOMIDON INN
Book great rates at AAA.com
Phone: (902)542-2291

(CAA) (SAVE)

6/15-9/30	1P: $89-$189	2P: $99-$199	XP: $12
5/1-6/14 & 10/1-12/17	1P: $89-$179	2P: $99-$189	XP: $12
12/28-4/30	1P: $89-$159	2P: $99-$169	XP: $12

Historic
Country Inn
Location: On Rt 1. Located in a residential area. 195 Main St B4P 1C3. **Fax:** 902/542-7461. **Facility:** Meticulously landscaped gardens surround this 19th-century sea captain's mansion; guest rooms vary in size, style and furnishings. Smoke free premises. 26 units. 20 one-bedroom standard units, some with whirlpools. 5 one-bedroom suites ($139-$179) with whirlpools. 1 cottage ($249-$269) with whirlpool. 3 stories (no elevator), interior corridors. **Bath:** combo or shower only. **Parking:** on-site. **Terms:** open 5/1-12/17 & 12/28-4/30, office hours 6:30 am-1 am, cancellation fee imposed. **Amenities:** high-speed Internet, irons, hair dryers. **Dining:** restaurant, see separate listing. **Leisure Activities:** tennis court. **Guest Services:** gift shop. **Business Services:** meeting rooms, PC. **Cards:** MC, VI. *(See color ad p 298)*

SOME UNITS
🍴 ⊠ / 🚪 🖥 /

TATTINGSTONE INN
Phone: (902)542-7696

(CAA) (SAVE)

7/1-9/7 [BP]	1P: $108-$175	2P: $108-$175	XP: $15	D12
5/1-6/30 & 9/8-10/31 [BP]	1P: $98-$165	2P: $98-$165	XP: $15	D12
11/1-4/30 [BP]	1P: $88-$160	2P: $88-$160	XP: $15	D12

Historic Bed
& Breakfast
Location: 0.4 mi (0.7 km) w on Rt 1. Located in a residential area. 620 Main St B4P 1E8. **Fax:** 902/542-4427. **Facility:** Well-coordinated decor is accented with artwork and antiques to bring a charming ambience to this 1877 inn and carriage house. Smoke free premises. 10 units. 9 one-bedroom standard units, some with whirlpools. 1 one-bedroom suite ($139-$175) with whirlpool. 2 stories (no elevator), interior/exterior corridors. **Parking:** on-site. **Terms:** office hours 8 am-10 pm, age restrictions may apply, cancellation fee imposed. **Amenities:** hair dryers. **Pool(s):** heated outdoor. **Guest Services:** valet laundry. **Cards:** AX, MC, VI. **Free Special Amenities:** full breakfast and newspaper.

🍴 🍷 🏊 ✕ (VCR)

VICTORIA'S HISTORIC INN
▼▼▼▼

5/1-10/31	1P: $108-$189	2P: $108-$189	XP: $20	F6
11/1-4/30	1P: $95-$160	2P: $95-$160	XP: $20	F6

Phone: (902)542-5744

Historic Bed & Breakfast

Location: 0.4 mi (0.6 km) w on Rt 1. Located in a commercial-residential area. 600 Main St B4P 1E8. **Fax:** 902/542-7794. **Facility:** Built in 1893, the mansion offers a variety of well appointed guest rooms and suites in a main inn and a carriage house. Smoke free premises. 16 units. 15 one-bedroom standard units, some with whirlpools. 1 one-bedroom suite ($195-$245) with whirlpool. 3 stories (no elevator), interior/exterior corridors. **Parking:** on-site. **Terms:** office hours 7 am-11 pm, package plans. **Amenities:** video library, CD players, hair dryers. **Guest Services:** wireless Internet. **Cards:** AX, DC, MC, VI.

[11+] [✕] [VCR]

The following lodging was either not evaluated or did not meet AAA rating requirements but is listed for your information only.

OLD ORCHARD INN
[fyi]

Small-scale Hotel

Phone: 902/542-5751

Did not meet all AAA rating requirements for locking devices in some guest rooms at time of last evaluation on 02/02/2006. **Location:** On Hwy 101, exit 11. 153 Greenwich Rd, RR 2 B4P 2R2. Facilities, services, and decor characterize a mid-range property.

--- **WHERE TO DINE** ---

ACTON'S GRILL & CAFE
▼▼▼▼

| **Lunch:** $9-$14 | **Dinner:** $16-$24 | **Phone:** 902/542-7525 |

Canadian

Location: On Rt 1; centre. 406 Main St B4P 1C9. **Hours:** 11:30 am-2 & 5-9 pm. Closed: 12/25; also Sun 11/1-3/31. **Reservations:** suggested. **Features:** For many years, the restaurant has attracted patrons with its creative cuisine. A relaxed bistro-style atmosphere and a menu of varied fresh seafood, choice meats and pasta dishes are the main draws. Finish with a decadent dessert, cappuccino or espresso. Casual dress; cocktails. **Parking:** on-site. **Cards:** AX, MC, VI.

THE BLOMIDON INN DINING ROOM
▼▼▼▼

| **Lunch:** $9-$14 | **Dinner:** $17-$28 | **Phone:** 902/542-2291 |

Canadian

Location: On Rt 1; in Blomidon Inn. 195 Main St B4P 1C3. **Hours:** 11:30 am-2 & 5-9:30 pm. Closed: 12/23-12/29. **Reservations:** accepted. **Features:** A renowned wine list complements creative regional cuisine, including preparations of fresh seafood from the Bay of Fundy. The romantic inn restaurant, which has the ambience of a Victorian manor house, is a favorite spot for special occasions. Casual dress; cocktails. **Parking:** on-site. **Cards:** MC, VI. **Country Inn**

LE CAVEAU RESTAURANT   Lunch: $10-$25   Dinner: $16-$35   Phone: 902/542-7177

Canadian

Location: On Rt 1, 1.8 mi (3 km) e; Hwy 101, exit 10, 0.6 mi (1 km) w; in Grand-Pre Winery. 11611 Hwy 1 B0P 1M0. **Hours:** Open 5/1-12/31 & 3/15-4/30; 11:30 am-2 & 5-9 pm, Sun-8 pm. Closed: 3/24. **Reservations:** suggested. **Features:** A lovely location in a vineyard, the 1826 Georgian-style farmhouse has been converted into a fine restaurant and wine bar. The use of local and homegrown produce is evident in the creative entrees. This place offers a fine selection of its own wines and ciders, as well as imports. A nice patio dining area opens in season. Dressy casual; cocktails. **Parking:** on-site. **Cards:** AX, DC, MC, VI.

PADDY'S BREWPUB & ROSIE'S RESTAURANT   Lunch: $6-$13   Dinner: $6-$18   Phone: 902/542-0059

Canadian

Location: Centre. 460 Main St B4P 1E2. **Hours:** 11 am-10 pm; Saturday & Sunday brunch. **Reservations:** not accepted. **Features:** Guests can opt for seating in one of two sections: the casual, upbeat pub or the quieter dining room. Both offer the same menu items and friendly casual service. Food selection is good, from fresh seafood to burgers to pizza. Casual dress; cocktails. **Parking:** on-site. **Cards:** AX, DC, MC, VI.

TEMPEST RESTAURANT   Lunch: $9-$16   Dinner: $15-$25   Phone: 902/542-0588

Canadian

Location: Just down from corner of Main St and Central Ave; centre. 117 Front St B4P 1A5. **Hours:** Open 5/1-2/29 & 3/21-4/30; 11:30 am-2 & 5-9 pm, Sat & Sun 11:30 am-3 & 5-9 pm. Closed: 1/1; also Mon off season. **Reservations:** suggested. **Features:** The attractive dining room displays contemporary decor in several sections inside. Guests enjoy the additional option of dining on the patio under a lovely mature grape arbor. The menu centers on creatively prepared meats and fresh seafood. Dressy casual; cocktails. **Parking:** on-site. **Cards:** AX, DC, MC, VI. **Historic**

YARMOUTH pop. 7,561

——— WHERE TO STAY ———

BEST WESTERN MERMAID   *Book great rates at AAA.com*   Phone: (902)742-7821

Motel

7/4-10/23	1P: $99-$180	2P: $99-$180	XP: $8	F17
6/6-7/3	1P: $89-$155	2P: $89-$155	XP: $8	F17
5/1-6/5 & 10/24-4/30	1P: $79-$135	2P: $79-$135	XP: $8	F17

Location: Corner of Main St and Starrs Rd. Located near downtown. 545 Main St B5A 1J6. Fax: 902/742-2966. **Facility:** 45 one-bedroom standard units, some with efficiencies. 2 stories (no elevator), exterior corridors. **Parking:** on-site. **Terms:** small pets only. **Amenities:** high-speed Internet, irons, hair dryers. **Pool(s):** heated outdoor. **Guest Services:** gift shop, coin laundry, wireless Internet. **Business Services:** PC. **Cards:** AX, DC, DS, MC, VI. **Free Special Amenities:** room upgrade (subject to availability with advance reservations) and high-speed Internet.

SOME UNITS

CAPRI MOTEL   Phone: (902)742-7168

Motel

7/4-8/31	1P: $69-$160	2P: $69-$160	XP: $8	F17
5/15-7/3 & 9/1-10/23	1P: $59-$130	2P: $59-$130	XP: $8	F17

Location: Corner of Herbert and Main sts. 8-12 Herbert St B5A 1J6. Fax: 902/742-2966. **Facility:** 34 units. 33 one- and 1 two-bedroom standard units, some with kitchens. 2 stories (no elevator), exterior corridors. **Bath:** combo or shower only. **Parking:** on-site. **Terms:** open 5/15-10/23, office hours 7 am-11 pm, package plans, small pets only. **Amenities:** irons. *Some:* hair dryers. **Leisure Activities:** pool privileges. **Cards:** AX, DC, DS, MC, VI. **Free Special Amenities:** early check-in/late check-out.

SOME UNITS

COMFORT INN   *Book great rates at AAA.com*   Phone: (902)742-1119

Small-scale Hotel

6/1-10/31	1P: $95-$185	2P: $105-$195	XP: $10	F18
11/1-4/30	1P: $85-$105	2P: $105-$195	XP: $10	F18
5/1-5/31	1P: $85-$105	2P: $95-$125	XP: $10	F18

Location: Jct Hwy 101 E and Hwy 3. Located adjacent to mall. 96 Starrs Rd B5A 2T5. Fax: 902/742-1114. **Facility:** 79 one-bedroom standard units. 2 stories (no elevator), interior corridors. **Parking:** on-site. **Terms:** [ECP] meal plan available, pets (1st floor units). **Amenities:** irons, hair dryers. **Guest Services:** wireless Internet. **Business Services:** PC. **Cards:** AX, DC, DS, MC, VI. *(See color ad card insert)*

SOME UNITS

LAKELAWN MOTEL

Phone: (902)742-3588

| | 7/1-9/30 | 1P: $69-$89 | 2P: $79-$99 | XP: $5 | F12 |
| Motel | 5/1-6/30 & 10/1-10/30 | 1P: $64-$79 | 2P: $74-$99 | XP: $5 | F12 |

Location: 0.6 mi (1 km) n on Hwy 1. 641 Main St B5A 1K2. Fax: 902/742-3588. **Facility:** 30 one-bedroom standard units. 2 stories (no elevator), interior/exterior corridors. *Bath:* combo or shower only. **Parking:** on-site. **Terms:** open 5/1-10/30, office hours 7 am-11 pm, small pets only. **Cards:** AX, DS, MC, VI.

MANOR INN LAKESIDE RESORT

Phone: (902)742-2487

CAA SAVE

	7/1-8/31 [ECP]	1P: $93-$131	2P: $99-$136	XP: $6	F12
	5/15-6/30 & 9/1-9/30 [ECP]	1P: $73-$111	2P: $79-$116	XP: $6	F12
Small-scale Hotel	10/1-10/31 [ECP]	1P: $63-$93	2P: $69-$96	XP: $6	F12

Location: Hwy 101, exit 34, 4.8 mi (8 km) ne of ferry terminal. Rt 1 Hebron B0W 1X0 (PO Box 56, HEBRON). Fax: 902/742-8094. **Facility:** Designated smoking area. 53 units. 52 one-bedroom standard units, some with whirlpools. 1 one-bedroom suite ($120-$205) with whirlpool. 2 stories (no elevator), interior/exterior corridors. *Bath:* combo or shower only. **Parking:** on-site. **Terms:** open 5/15-10/31, cancellation fee imposed, [MAP] meal plan available. **Amenities:** video library, voice mail, hair dryers. *Some:* high-speed Internet, irons. **Dining:** The Manor Inn Dining Room, see separate listing. **Pool(s):** heated outdoor. **Leisure Activities:** whirlpool, canoeing, paddleboats, boat dock, fishing, rowboats, tennis court, bicycles, horseshoes. **Business Services:** PC. **Cards:** AX, MC, VI. **Free Special Amenities:** expanded continental breakfast and newspaper.

SOME UNITS

RODD COLONY HARBOUR INN

Book at AAA.com

Phone: (902)742-9194

| | 6/1-9/30 | 1P: $111-$139 | 2P: $121-$149 | XP: $10 | F16 |
| | 5/1-5/31 & 10/1-4/30 | 1P: $85-$119 | 2P: $95-$129 | XP: $10 | F16 |

Small-scale Hotel **Location:** At ferry terminal. 6 Forest St B5A 3K7. Fax: 902/742-6291. **Facility:** 65 units. 57 one-bedroom standard units. 8 one-bedroom suites ($105-$171). 4 stories (no elevator), interior corridors. **Parking:** on-site. **Terms:** cancellation fee imposed, package plans. **Amenities:** hair dryers. *Some:* irons. **Dining:** The Colony Restaurant, Pub & Patio, see separate listing. **Guest Services:** valet laundry, wireless Internet. **Business Services:** meeting rooms, PC. **Cards:** AX, DC, DS, MC, VI. *(See color ad p 359)*

SOME UNITS

RODD GRAND YARMOUTH-A RODD SIGNATURE HOTEL

Book great rates at AAA.com

Phone: (902)742-2446

| | 6/1-9/30 | 1P: $150-$215 | 2P: $160-$225 | XP: $10 | F16 |
| | 5/1-5/31 & 10/1-4/30 | 1P: $119-$181 | 2P: $129-$191 | XP: $10 | F16 |

Large-scale Hotel **Location:** Near centre of downtown. 417 Main St B5A 4B2. Fax: 902/742-4645. **Facility:** 138 one-bedroom standard units. 7 stories, interior corridors. **Parking:** on-site. **Terms:** cancellation fee imposed, package plans, small pets only. **Amenities:** irons, hair dryers. **Dining:** The Ship's Bell Restaurant, see separate listing. **Pool(s):** heated indoor. **Leisure Activities:** sauna, whirlpool, exercise room. **Guest Services:** gift shop, valet laundry, wireless Internet. **Business Services:** conference facilities, business center. **Cards:** AX, DC, DS, JC, MC, VI. *(See color ad p 359 & p 353)*

SOME UNITS

VOYAGEUR MOTEL

Phone: (902)742-7157

| | All Year | 1P: $69-$89 | 2P: $79-$104 | XP: $10 | F12 |
| Motel | | | | | |

Location: 3 mi (4.8 km) ne on Hwy 1. (RR 1, Box 1020, B5A 4A5). Fax: 902/742-1208. **Facility:** 33 units. 32 one-bedroom standard units, some with kitchens. 1 one-bedroom suite ($189) with whirlpool. 1 story, exterior corridors. *Bath:* combo or shower only. **Parking:** on-site. **Terms:** office hours 6:30 am-midnight, 3 day cancellation notice, weekly rates available, package plans, small pets only (in limited units). **Guest Services:** coin laundry. **Cards:** MC, VI.

SOME UNITS

———— **WHERE TO DINE** ————

THE AUSTRIAN INN

Lunch: $6-$14 **Dinner:** $9-$23 Phone: 902/742-6202

CAA

Ethnic **Location:** 2.6 mi (4.4 km) ne on Hwy 1. **Hours:** Open 5/1-12/31 & 3/1-4/30; 11 am-9 pm, Wed-Sat to 10 pm. **Reservations:** suggested. **Features:** Representative of menu choices are Wiener schnitzel, pork cordon bleu, chicken Oscar and plenty of Canadian-style steak and seafood entrees. The quiet dining room is a pleasant place for a romantic, candlelit dinner. Soft music plays in the background. Casual dress; cocktails. **Parking:** on-site. **Cards:** AX, MC, VI.

THE COLONY RESTAURANT, PUB & PATIO

Lunch: $6-$14 **Dinner:** $9-$20 Phone: 902/742-2391

Canadian **Location:** At ferry terminal; in Rodd Colony Harbour Inn. 6 Forest St B5A 3K8. **Hours:** 7 am-10 pm. Closed: 12/25, 12/26. **Features:** Overlooking the harbour and convenient to the ferry terminal, the casual restaurant constructs its menu around fresh seafood. Casual dress; cocktails. **Parking:** on-site. **Cards:** AX, DC, MC, VI.

JUNGLE JIM'S RESTAURANT

Lunch: $6-$11 **Dinner:** $8-$16 Phone: 902/742-9708

Canadian **Location:** Jct Hwy 101 E and Hwy 3; opposite mall. 95 Starrs Rd B5A 2T6. **Hours:** 11 am-10 pm, Fri & Sat-11 pm, Sun noon-10 pm. Closed: 12/25. **Reservations:** accepted. **Features:** Guests can step into a tropical theme at the casual eatery, which employs a friendly staff and nurtures a bustling atmosphere. The menu lines up a wide variety of comfort foods, salads, chicken, beef, seafood and hot wings, all served in ample, flavorful portions. Casual dress; cocktails. **Parking:** on-site. **Cards:** AX, DC, MC, VI.

KELLEY'S

Seafood

Lunch: $6-$14   **Dinner:** $14-$22   **Phone:** 902/742-9191

Location: Corner of Herbert and Main sts. 577 Main St B5A 1J6. **Hours:** 11 am-10 pm; also 7 am-11 am in season. Closed: 12/25. **Reservations:** accepted. **Features:** This restaurant offers a quiet dining experience in a relaxed atmosphere at the front of the building. If it's a more casual atmosphere you crave, visit their sports pub or lounge on the first and second levels. Their menu offers a selection of seafood, steak, pasta and pork, as well as finger foods. Casual dress; cocktails. **Parking:** on-site. **Cards:** AX, DC, DS, JC, MC, VI.

LOTUS GARDEN RESTAURANT

Chinese

Lunch: $5-$9   **Dinner:** $8-$15   **Phone:** 902/742-1688

Location: Centre. 280 Main St B5A 3K7. **Hours:** 11 am-9 pm, Fri & Sat-10 pm, Sun 11:30 am-8 pm. Closed: 12/25. **Reservations:** accepted. **Features:** A popular spot with the local crowd, the restaurant presents a vast menu that lists a good mix of combination plates. At lunch, the buffet is a draw. Evening hours are limited. Casual dress; cocktails. **Parking:** on-site. **Cards:** MC, VI.

THE MANOR INN DINING ROOM

CAA

Canadian

Lunch: $8-$15   **Dinner:** $14-$23   **Phone:** 902/742-2487

Location: Hwy 101, exit 34, 4.8 mi (8 km) ne of ferry terminal; in Manor Inn Lakeside Resort. 15 Lakeside Rd B0W 1X0. **Hours:** Open 5/1-10/31; 6 am-2 & 5-9:30 pm. **Reservations:** accepted. **Features:** Guests enjoy fine dining in a relaxed atmosphere. The staff offers friendly and attentive service. On the menu is a selection of fresh seafood, meat entrees, homemade pies and tasty desserts. Casual dress; cocktails. **Parking:** on-site. **Cards:** AX, DC, MC, VI.

THE PRINCE ARTHUR RESTAURANT

Steak & Seafood

Lunch: $6-$9   **Dinner:** $9-$16   **Phone:** 902/742-1129

Location: 0.6 mi (1 km) w of jct Hwy 3 and 101 E on Hwy 3. 73 Starrs Rd B5A 2T5. **Hours:** 11 am-9 pm, Fri & Sat-10 pm, Mon 11 am-2 pm. Closed: 12/25. **Reservations:** accepted. **Features:** The popular restaurant—which delivers reliably good steaks, seafood, pasta and sandwiches—is known locally for its wonderful Sunday brunch. A nice selection of wines is offered. Casual dress; cocktails. **Parking:** on-site. **Cards:** AX, DC, MC, VI.

RUDDER'S SEAFOOD RESTAURANT & BREW PUB

Canadian

Lunch: $7-$15   **Dinner:** $10-$23   **Phone:** 902/742-7311

Location: At Killam's Wharf, close to ferry terminal; centre. 96 Water St B5A 4P9. **Hours:** 11 am-10 pm; hours vary off season. Closed: 12/25. **Reservations:** accepted. **Features:** Overlooking Killam's Marina, the restaurant has seating on two levels, as well as a spacious deck for seasonal dining. Specializing in seafood, the menu also lists a selection of steaks, chicken and burgers. Boiled lobster suppers are another option. Casual dress; cocktails. **Parking:** on-site. **Cards:** AX, DC, MC, VI.

THE SHIP'S BELL RESTAURANT

Seafood

Lunch: $7-$13   **Dinner:** $14-$22   **Phone:** 902/742-2446

Location: Near centre of downtown; in Rodd Grand Yarmouth-A Rodd Signature Hotel. 417 Main St B5A 4B2. **Hours:** 7 am-2 & 5-9 pm, Fri & Sat-10 pm. Closed: 12/24-12/26. **Reservations:** accepted. **Features:** Off the main lobby of the Grand Hotel, the restaurant presents a menu of fresh local seafood and meat entrees. During peak season, the establishment also offers a popular dinner theater. Casual dress; cocktails. **Parking:** on-site. **Cards:** AX, DC, DS, JC, MC, VI.

Prince Edward Island

Greenwich, Prince Edward
Island National Park
Ron Watts / Getty Images

ALBERTON pop. 1,115

———— WHERE TO STAY ————

BRIARWOOD INN, COTTAGES & LODGE   **Phone:** 902/853-2518

6/16-9/15	1P: $65-$95	2P: $75-$125	XP: $10	F6
5/1-6/15 & 9/16-4/30	1P: $50-$75	2P: $60-$85	XP: $10	F6

Motel   **Location:** 1.9 mi (3 km) e on Rt 12. 253 Matthews Ln C0B 1B0 (PO Box 215). **Fax:** 902/853-2518. **Facility:** 25 units. 17 one- and 2 two-bedroom standard units, some with kitchens and/or whirlpools. 6 cottages ($85-$125). 1-2 stories (no elevator), interior/exterior corridors. **Bath:** some shared or private, combo or shower only. **Parking:** on-site. **Terms:** office hours 7 am-11 pm, 7 day cancellation notice-fee imposed, weekly rates available. **Leisure Activities:** boating, playground. **Guest Services:** coin laundry. **Business Services:** meeting rooms. **Cards:** AX, MC, VI.

SOME UNITS

(A$K) (SD) (⊠) (AC) (VCR) / (🛏) (▣) (▣) /

NORTHPORT PIER INN   **Phone:** 902/853-4520

6/16-9/15 [BP]	1P: $145	2P: $145	XP: $15	F15
9/16-10/15 [BP]	1P: $130	2P: $130	XP: $15	F15
5/1-6/15 [BP]	1P: $125	2P: $125	XP: $15	F15

Small-scale Hotel   **Location:** 1.8 mi (3 km) s on Rt 152 (Northport Rd). 298 Rt 152 C0B 1B0 (PO Box 533, NORTHPORT). **Fax:** 902/853-3990. **Facility:** 14 units. 12 one-bedroom standard units. 2 one-bedroom suites ($165-$180) with whirlpools. 2 stories (no elevator), interior/exterior corridors. **Bath:** combo or shower only. **Parking:** on-site. **Terms:** open 5/1-10/15, 7 day cancellation notice-fee imposed, weekly rates available. **Amenities:** irons, hair dryers. **Some:** DVD players. **Leisure Activities:** playground, limited exercise equipment. **Guest Services:** wireless Internet. **Business Services:** meeting rooms. **Cards:** MC, VI.

SOME UNITS

(¶→) (ⓜ) (⅍) (⊠) / (VCR) (🛏) (▣) /

———— WHERE TO DINE ————

THE PIER RESTAURANT   **Lunch:** $9-$12   **Dinner:** $11-$37   **Phone:** 902/853-4510

Seafood   **Location:** 1.8 mi (3 km) s on Rt 152 (Northport Rd); adjacent to pier; centre. 296 Harbourview Dr C0B 1B0. **Hours:** Open 6/1-9/30; 11:30 am-9 pm. **Reservations:** suggested. **Features:** A splendid ocean view awaits visitors to the converted boat building shop, on the pier overlooking Northport Harbour and Cascumpec Bay. The contemporary menu specializes in seafood dishes made from local ingredients. Patio seating is available. Casual dress; cocktails. **Parking:** on-site. **Cards:** AX, DC, MC.

(Ⓨ)

ANNANDALE

———— WHERE TO STAY ————

THE INN AT SPRY POINT   **Phone:** (902)583-2400

6/17-9/3 [BP]	1P: $185-$335	2P: $185-$335	XP: $25	D11
9/4-10/1 [BP]	1P: $155-$300	2P: $155-$300	XP: $25	D11

Bed & Breakfast   **Location:** Off Rt 310, 2.6 mi (4.3 km) e on Spry Point Rd, follow signs. Located in a quiet secluded area. (RR 4, SOURIS). **Fax:** 902/583-2176. **Facility:** On 80 acres at the tip of a peninsula, this handsome inn captures broad views of the ocean and beaches; many rooms have private balconies. Smoke free premises. 15 one-bedroom standard units, some with whirlpools. 2 stories (no elevator), interior/exterior corridors. **Bath:** combo or shower only. **Parking:** on-site. **Terms:** open 6/17-10/1, office hours 7 am-11 pm, 8 day cancellation notice-fee imposed, weekly rates available. **Amenities:** CD players, irons, hair dryers. **Leisure Activities:** hiking trails. **Guest Services:** TV in common area. **Business Services:** meeting rooms. **Cards:** AX, MC, VI.

(ⓜ) (⅍) (⊠) (Ⱳ)

BAY FORTUNE pop. 793

———— WHERE TO STAY ————

THE INN AT BAY FORTUNE   **Phone:** (902)687-3745

(CAA) (SAVE)

5/25-9/22 [BP]	1P: $135-$300	2P: $150-$335	XP: $25	D11
9/23-10/7 [BP]	1P: $135-$295	2P: $150-$300	XP: $25	D11

Country Inn   **Location:** Jct Hwy 2, 1.2 mi (2 km) s on Rt 310; 7.2 mi (12 km) w of Souris. Located in a rural quiet area. Rt 310 C0A 2B0 (RR 4, SOURIS). **Fax:** 902/687-3540. **Facility:** Overlooking Bay Fortune, the inn offers an array of tastefully decorated rooms, many featuring wood or gas fireplaces and balconies or decks. Smoke free premises. 18 one-bedroom standard units, some with whirlpools. 1-4 stories (no elevator), interior/exterior corridors. **Bath:** combo or shower only. **Parking:** on-site. **Terms:** open 5/25-10/7, office hours 6:30 am-11:30 pm, 8 day cancellation notice-fee imposed, weekly rates available, [MAP] meal plan available, package plans. **Amenities:** CD players, irons, hair dryers. **Dining:** restaurant, see separate listing. **Guest Services:** TV in common area, wireless Internet. **Business Services:** PC. **Cards:** MC, VI. **Free Special Amenities:** full breakfast and high-speed Internet.
(See color ad starting on p 361)

SOME UNITS

(¶¶) (Ⓨ) (⊠) (Ⱳ) / (AC) /

———— WHERE TO DINE ————

THE INN AT BAY FORTUNE   **Dinner:** $27-$38   **Phone:** 902/687-3745

Regional Canadian   **Location:** Jct Hwy 2, 1.2 mi (2 km) s on Rt 310, 7.2 mi (12 km) w of Souris; in The Inn at Bay Fortune. **Hours:** Open 5/26-10/31; 5:30 pm-9 pm. **Reservations:** suggested. **Features:** In a wonderful location overlooking Bay Fortune, the restaurant lets patrons sample the chef's lovingly prepared, creative, contemporary cuisine. The menu is rich in traditional dishes that use fresh local produce, meats and seafood. Much of the produce comes from the property's extensive organic gardens. Casual dress; cocktails. **Parking:** on-site. **Cards:** AX, MC, VI.

(Ⓨ)

BEDEQUE

———— WHERE TO STAY ————

HISTORIC MAPLETHORPE BED AND BREAKFAST   **Phone:** (902)887-2909

5/1-9/14   2P: $80-$160   XP: $15   F
9/15-4/30   2P: $60-$100   XP: $15   F

Bed & Breakfast   **Location:** On Rt 112; centre. 2123 Hwy 112 C0B 1C0 (PO Box 4109). **Facility:** 5 units. 3 one- and 1 two-bedroom standard units, some with whirlpools. 1 two-bedroom suite with kitchen. 2 stories (no elevator), interior corridors. *Bath:* combo or shower only. **Parking:** on-site. **Terms:** office hours 7 am-11 pm, 7 day cancellation notice. **Amenities:** video library, hair dryers. *Some:* irons. **Leisure Activities:** bicycles. **Business Services:** PC. **Cards:** MC, VI.

SOME UNITS

(A$K) ⊠ (VCR) (☎) / (AC) ▯ ▭ /

BORDEN-CARLETON

———— WHERE TO DINE ————

GATEWAY LOBSTER SHOP   *Menu on AAA.com*   **Lunch:** $6-$10   **Dinner:** $8-$18   **Phone:** 902/437-2070

(CAA)   **Location:** Trans-Canada Hwy 1, exit Gateway Village. 103A Main St C0B 1X0. **Hours:** Open 5/16-10/31; 11 am-6 pm, Sat & Sun to 7 pm. **Features:** In the Gateway Village, the casual restaurant offers a nice variety of fresh local seafood, including fish and chips, scallops and boiled lobster. Patio seating is available in season. Casual dress; beer & wine only. **Parking:** on-site. **Cards:** AX, MC, VI.

Seafood

BRACKLEY BEACH

———— WHERE TO STAY ————

BRACKLEY BEACH NORTH WINDS INN & SUITES   **Phone:** (902)672-2245

All Year [ECP]   1P: $65-$150   2P: $65-$150   XP: $7

Motel   **Location:** Jct Rt 6 and 15. 3828 Portage Rd C1E 1Z3 (RR 9, Station Main, CHARLOTTETOWN). Fax: 902/672-2046. **Facility:** Smoke free premises. 66 one-bedroom standard units, some with kitchens and/or whirlpools. 2 stories (no elevator), exterior corridors. **Parking:** on-site. **Terms:** office hours 7 am-midnight, 14 day cancellation notice-fee imposed, weekly monthly rates available. **Amenities:** irons, hair dryers. *Some:* DVD players. **Pool(s):** small heated indoor. **Leisure Activities:** playground. **Guest Services:** coin laundry, wireless Internet. **Business Services:** meeting rooms, PC. **Cards:** AX, MC, VI. *(See color ad starting on p 361)*

SOME UNITS

🎞️↦ 🛏️ ⊠ ▯ ▭ / (VCR) ▭ /

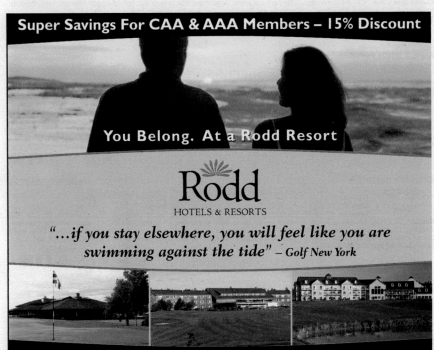

──────── **WHERE TO DINE** ────────

THE DUNES CAFE & STUDIO GALLERY   **Lunch:** $10-$16   **Dinner:** $20-$32   **Phone:** 902/672-1883
▼▼▼▼   **Location:** Jct of Rt 6 and 15, 0.6 mi (1 km) n. Rt 15 C1E 1Z3. **Hours:** Open 6/15-9/30; 11:30 am-4 & 5:30-10 pm.
Canadian   **Reservations:** suggested. **Features:** Dine in or out at this pleasant gem, which has a large art gallery
        overlooking a delightful water garden and distant sand dunes. The menu is varied, with the focus on fresh
local seafood and produce creatively presented on the Dunes own handmade pottery. Although ample
portions are likely to fill you up, try to save room to sample one of the sumptuous desserts. Dressy casual; cocktails. **Parking:**
on-site. **Cards:** AX, DC, MC, VI.   [&M] [AC]

CARDIGAN

──────── **WHERE TO DINE** ────────

CARDIGAN LOBSTER SUPPERS   **Dinner:** $18-$30   **Phone:** 902/583-2020
▼▼ ▼▼   **Location:** Centre. Rt 321 C0A 1G0. **Hours:** Open 6/15-10/31; 5 pm-9 pm. **Reservations:** accepted.
Seafood   **Features:** The spacious, casual restaurant's large deck overlooks the harbour and marina. Guests can
        linger over tasty five-course lobster suppers or sample any of several other meat and seafood dishes.
Casual dress; cocktails. **Parking:** on-site. **Cards:** MC, VI.   [Y]

THE GULNARE RESTAURANT & PUB   **Lunch:** $7-$11   **Dinner:** $10-$20   **Phone:** 902/583-3111
▼▼▼ ▼▼▼   **Location:** Jct Rt 311 and 321. 6864 Water St C0A 1G0. **Hours:** Open 5/1-11/21; 11 am-9 pm.
Canadian   **Reservations:** accepted. **Features:** Sitting on a rise overlooking the Cardigan River and Marina, the
        restaurant not only offers a splendid view, but they have darts, shuffleboard and tasty pub-style foods,
including fish and chips, wings and chowders and import beers on tap. Casual dress; cocktails. **Parking:**
on-site. **Cards:** MC, VI.   [Y] [AC]

CAVENDISH

──────── **WHERE TO STAY** ────────

ANNE SHIRLEY MOTEL & COTTAGES   **Phone:** (902)963-2224
▼▼ ▼▼   6/25-9/2   1P: $85-$110   2P: $101-$110   XP: $9   F12
        5/19-6/24 & 9/3-10/4   1P: $54-$62   2P: $57-$62   XP: $7   F12
Motel   **Location:** On Rt 13, just s of jct Rt 6. RR 1 C0A 1N0. **Facility:** 36 units. 29 one- and 4 two-bedroom standard
        units, some with efficiencies, kitchens and/or whirlpools. 3 cottages ($114-$153), some with whirlpools. 1-2
stories (no elevator), exterior corridors. **Parking:** on-site. **Terms:** open 5/19-10/4, office hours 7:30 am-10 pm, 7 day
cancellation notice, [CP] meal plan available, package plans. **Amenities:** hair dryers. *Some:* high-speed Internet, irons. **Pool(s):**
heated outdoor. **Leisure Activities:** whirlpool. **Guest Services:** coin laundry, wireless Internet. **Cards:** AX, MC, VI.
(See color ad starting on p 361)
                                                                                     SOME UNITS
                                                  [¶+] [🚲] / [✕] [🔒] [🖥] /

ANNE'S WINDY POPLARS   **Phone:** (902)963-2888
(CAA) (SAVE)   7/13-9/2   1P: $233-$320   2P: $233-$320   XP: $10   F18
        6/22-7/12   1P: $181-$279   2P: $181-$279   XP: $10   F18
▼▼▼ ▼▼▼   5/1-6/21 & 9/3-4/30   1P: $99-$195   2P: $99-$195   XP: $10   F18
Cottage   **Location:** On Rt 13, 1 mi (1.6 km) s. RR 1 C0A 1N0. Fax: 902/963-3166. **Facility:** This fine property offers a
        large variety of cottage styles, each tastefully decorated and most with decks and barbecues; some boast
        private hot tubs. 19 units. 1 one-bedroom suite with kitchen and whirlpool. 18 cottages, some with
whirlpools. 1 story, exterior corridors. **Parking:** on-site. **Terms:** office hours 7:30 am-10:30 pm, 2-3 night minimum stay, 30 day
cancellation notice-fee imposed, weekly rates available, package plans. **Amenities:** video library, DVD players, CD players,
voice mail, irons, hair dryers. **Pool(s):** heated outdoor. **Leisure Activities:** sauna, whirlpool, pool tables, playground, exercise
room, game room. **Guest Services:** coin laundry, wireless Internet. **Cards:** AX, MC, VI. **Free Special Amenities:** preferred
room (subject to availability with advance reservations) and high-speed Internet. *(See color ad starting on p 361)*
                                                  [🚲] [✕] [✕] [VCR] [🔒] [🖥]

BAY VISTA MOTOR INN   **Phone:** 902/963-2225
▼▼ ▼▼   6/25-8/23   2P: $92-$99   XP: $7
        8/24-9/9   2P: $53-$89   XP: $4
Motel   6/8-6/24   2P: $53-$69   XP: $4
        Location: Jct Rt 13, 2.8 mi (4.8 km) w on Rt 6. Located in a quiet rural area. 9517 Cavendish Rd C0A 1E0.
Facility: 31 units. 30 one-bedroom standard units, some with efficiencies. 1 cottage ($1390). 1 story, exterior corridors.
Parking: on-site. **Terms:** open 6/8-9/9, office hours 7:30 am-10:30 pm, small pets only. **Amenities:** video library (fee), high-
speed Internet. **Pool(s):** heated outdoor. **Leisure Activities:** playground. **Business Services:** PC (fee). **Cards:** AX, MC, VI.
(See color ad starting on p 361)
                                                                                     SOME UNITS
                                             [🐾] [🚲] [Ẑ] / [✕] [VCR] [🔒] [🖥] /

CAVENDISH BEACH COTTAGES   **Phone:** 902/963-2025
▼▼ ▼▼   6/16-9/2   2P: $155-$210   XP: $10
        5/11-6/15 & 9/3-10/4   2P: $85-$135   XP: $10
Cottage   **Location:** 1.1 mi (1.9 km) ne of jct Rt 6 and 13, on Gulf Shore Rd; free access to property through park. Located in PEI
        National Park. (Box 3088, CHARLOTTETOWN, C1A 7N9). Fax: 902/963-2025. **Facility:** 13 cottages. 1 story,
exterior corridors. *Bath:* combo or shower only. **Parking:** on-site. **Terms:** open 5/11-10/4, office hours 8 am-10 pm, 10 day
cancellation notice-fee imposed. **Amenities:** hair dryers. *Some:* DVD players (fee). **Leisure Activities:** limited beach access,
playground. **Guest Services:** coin laundry. **Cards:** MC, VI.
                                                                                     SOME UNITS
                                                  [✕] [Ẑ] [🔒] [🖥] / [VCR] /
                                                                                     FEE

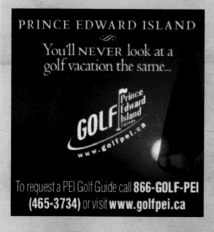

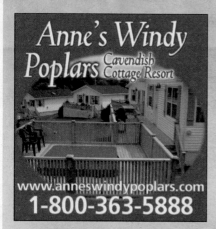

CAVENDISH BOSOM BUDDIES COTTAGES

Phone: (902)963-3449

7/6-9/2	2P: $150-$280	XP: $8
6/22-7/5	2P: $120-$215	XP: $8
Cottage	5/1-6/21 & 9/3-10/31	2P: $80-$160	XP: $8

Location: Jct Rt 6 and 13, 0.4 mi (0.7 km) e on Rt 6. RR 1 C0A 1N0 (19 Keppoch Rd, SOUTHPORT, C1B 1R8). Fax: 902/963-3110. **Facility:** 15 units. 5 one-bedroom standard units with whirlpools. 10 cottages, some with whirlpools. 1-2 stories (no elevator), exterior corridors. **Parking:** on-site. **Terms:** office hours 8 am-10 pm, 14 day cancellation notice-fee imposed, weekly rates available, package plans, small pets only. **Amenities:** video library, hair dryers. *Some:* DVD players. **Leisure Activities:** playground. **Guest Services:** coin laundry. **Cards:** MC, VI. *(See color ad starting on p 361)*

SOME UNITS
(ASK) (S) 🐾 ✕ 🅺 ☎ 🖥 🖴 💻 / (VCR) /

CAVENDISH MAPLES COTTAGES

Phone: 902/963-2818

| 6/23-9/3 | 2P: $140-$280 | XP: $8 |
| 5/15-6/22 & 9/4-10/15 | 2P: $70-$170 | XP: $8 |

Location: Jct Rt 6 and 13, 1.5 mi (2.5 km) w on Rt 6. 79 Avonlea Blvd C0A 1M0 (29 Westhaven Cres, CHARLOTTETOWN, C1E 1L6). **Facility:** Guests will find a gas grill on the deck of each of these pleasant cottages nestled among the trees. 20 cottages, some with whirlpools. 1 story, exterior corridors. **Parking:** on-site. **Terms:** open 5/15-10/15, office hours 9 am-9 pm, 30 day cancellation notice-fee imposed, package plans, small pets only (during off season). **Amenities:** video library, hair dryers. **Pool(s):** heated outdoor. **Leisure Activities:** whirlpool, playground, horseshoes, volleyball, game room. **Guest Services:** coin laundry, wireless Internet. **Cards:** AX, MC, VI. **Free Special Amenities:** newspaper and high-speed Internet.

🐾 🍴 🏊 🗙 ✕ (VCR) ☎ 🖥 🖴 💻

KINDRED SPIRITS COUNTRY INN & COTTAGES

Phone: 902/963-2434

| 6/19-7/2 [ECP] | 1P: $75-$175 | 2P: $95-$285 | XP: $20 | F3 |
| 5/13-6/18 & 7/3-10/31 [ECP] | 1P: $55-$125 | 2P: $75-$225 | XP: $20 | F3 |

Location: Jct Rt 13, 0.5 mi (0.8 km) w. Memory Ln, Rt 6 C0A 1N0. Fax: 902/963-2619. **Facility:** Tastefully decorated inn rooms are set back from the highway on spacious grounds, while six cottages offer private hot tubs on large decks. Smoke free premises. 45 units. 25 one-bedroom standard units, some with whirlpools. 20 cottages ($95-$450), some with whirlpools. 2 stories (no elevator), interior/exterior corridors. **Parking:** on-site. **Terms:** open 5/13-10/31, office hours 7 am-11 pm, cancellation fee imposed, weekly rates available, package plans. **Amenities:** video library, voice mail, hair dryers. *Some:* DVD players, irons. **Pool(s):** heated outdoor. **Leisure Activities:** whirlpool, lawn chess board, rental bicycles, playground, exercise room, game room. **Guest Services:** coin laundry, wireless Internet. **Business Services:** meeting rooms, PC. **Cards:** AX, JC, MC, VI. **Free Special Amenities:** expanded continental breakfast and high-speed Internet. *(See color ad starting on p 361)*

SOME UNITS
🍴 🏊 🗙 ✕ (VCR) / 🖥 🖴 💻 /

LAKEVIEW LODGE & COTTAGES

Phone: 902/963-2436

| 6/18-9/2 | 1P: $94-$365 | 2P: $94-$365 | XP: $12 |
| 5/25-6/17 & 9/3-10/1 | 1P: $48-$206 | 2P: $48-$206 | XP: $12 |

Location: Jct Rt 13, 0.6 mi (1 km) w. Located in a quiet area; adjacent to Green Gables Golf Course. Hwy 6 C0A 1N0 (8715 Cavendish Rd, C0A 1N0). Fax: 902/963-2493. **Facility:** 36 units. 6 one-bedroom standard units, some with efficiencies. 30 cottages. 1 story, exterior corridors. *Bath:* combo or shower only. **Parking:** on-site. **Terms:** open 5/25-10/1, office hours 7:30 am-10 pm, 14 day cancellation notice-fee imposed, package plans. **Amenities:** *Some:* DVD players, high-speed Internet, irons, hair dryers. **Pool(s):** heated outdoor. **Leisure Activities:** whirlpool, playground, horseshoes. **Guest Services:** coin laundry. **Cards:** MC, VI.

SOME UNITS
🏊 🗙 ✕ / 🅺 (VCR) ☎ 🖥 🖴 /

MARCO POLO INN

Phone: (902)963-2352

| 6/22-9/3 | 1P: $75-$80 | 2P: $100-$105 | XP: $25 | F |
| 5/28-6/21 & 9/4-9/17 | 1P: $55-$65 | 2P: $80-$90 | XP: $25 | F |

Location: 0.6 mi (1 km) s. Rt 13 C0A 1N0 (RR #3, HUNTER RIVER). Fax: 902/963-2442. **Facility:** Smoke free premises. 6 one-bedroom standard units. 2 stories (no elevator), interior/exterior corridors. *Bath:* combo or shower only. **Parking:** on-site. **Terms:** open 5/28-9/17, office hours 7 am-11 pm, 7 day cancellation notice, [BP] meal plan available. **Amenities:** hair dryers. **Cards:** MC, VI.

(S) 🍴 ✕ 🅺

THE RESORT AT CAVENDISH CORNER
Phone: (902)963-2244

(CAA) (SAVE)

Motel

6/23-9/3	1P: $115-$145	2P: $115-$145	XP: $7
5/15-6/22 & 9/4-10/15	1P: $59-$84	2P: $59-$84	XP: $7

Location: Jct Rt 6 and 13. Cavendish Rd C0A 1N0 (PO Box 2333, CHARLOTTETOWN, C1A 8C1). Fax: 902/368-1642. **Facility:** 105 units. 99 one-bedroom standard units, some with whirlpools. 6 cottages ($90-$290). 2 stories (no elevator), exterior corridors. *Bath:* combo or shower only. **Parking:** on-site. **Terms:** open 5/15-10/15, office hours 8 am-10 pm, check-in 4 pm, 30 day cancellation notice-fee imposed, [BP] meal plan available, package plans. **Amenities:** *Some:* irons, hair dryers. **Pool(s):** heated outdoor. **Leisure Activities:** playground. **Business Services:** meeting rooms, PC. **Cards:** AX, MC, VI. **Free Special Amenities: local telephone calls and high-speed Internet.** *(See color ad starting on p 361)*

SOME UNITS

SILVERWOOD MOTEL
Phone: 902/963-2439

Motel

7/1-8/26	1P: $90-$150	2P: $90-$150	XP: $10	D5
6/1-6/30 & 8/27-10/10	1P: $55-$90	2P: $55-$90	XP: $10	D5

Location: Jct Rt 6, 1 mi (1.6 km) w of jct Rt 13. (Green Gables Post Office, C0A 1N0). Fax: 902/963-2439. **Facility:** 45 units. 36 one- and 9 two-bedroom standard units, some with efficiencies. 2 stories (no elevator), interior/exterior corridors. **Parking:** on-site. **Terms:** open 6/1-10/10, office hours 8 am-11 pm, 7 day cancellation notice. **Pool(s):** heated outdoor. **Leisure Activities:** playground. **Business Services:** meeting rooms. **Cards:** MC, VI.

SOME UNITS

SUNDANCE COTTAGES
Phone: (902)963-2149

(CAA) (SAVE)

Cottage

6/20-9/3	2P: $175-$350	XP: $8
5/1-6/19 & 9/4-10/31	2P: $80-$175	XP: $8

Location: Jct Rt 13, 0.4 mi (0.6 km) e on Rt 6. 34 Mac Coubrey Ln C0A 1N0. Fax: 902/963-2100. **Facility:** On spacious grounds with distant ocean views, Sundance offers a nice selection of family cottages with decks and barbecues. 23 cottages, some with whirlpools. 1 story, exterior corridors. **Parking:** on-site. **Terms:** open 5/1-10/31, office hours 8 am-10:30 pm, 14 day cancellation notice-fee imposed, package plans. **Amenities:** video library, irons, hair dryers. *Some:* DVD players. **Pool(s):** heated outdoor. **Leisure Activities:** whirlpool, bicycles, playground. **Guest Services:** coin laundry. **Business Services:** meeting rooms. **Cards:** AX, DC, DS, MC, VI. **Free Special Amenities: newspaper and high-speed Internet.** *(See color ad starting on p 361)*

SWEPT AWAY COTTAGES
Phone: 902/963-2929

Cottage

5/1-10/31	2P: $79-$275

Location: Jct Rt 13, 2.4 mi (4 km) w on Rt 6. 40 Simpson Mill Rd C0A 1N0. **Facility:** 12 units. 1 one-bedroom suite with whirlpool. 11 cottages, some with whirlpools. 2 stories (no elevator), exterior corridors. **Parking:** on-site. **Terms:** open 5/1-10/31, office hours 8 am-10 pm, 30 day cancellation notice-fee imposed, weekly rates available. **Amenities:** video library, DVD players, hair dryers. *Some:* irons. **Pool(s):** heated outdoor. **Leisure Activities:** whirlpool, playground. **Guest Services:** coin laundry. **Business Services:** meeting rooms. **Cards:** MC, VI.

--------- WHERE TO DINE ---------

THE FRIENDLY FISHERMAN
Lunch: $6-$11   **Dinner:** $13   **Phone: 902/963-2234**

Canadian

MC, VI.

Location: Jct Rt 6 and 13, 0.3 mi (0.5 km) e. Rt 6 C0A 1X0. **Hours:** Open 6/11-9/30; 8 am-9 pm. **Features:** Picture windows in the spacious dining area show off a lovely oceanfront view, and a gift shop offers after-dinner browsing. Cafeteria-style breakfast and lunch gives way to an all-you-can-eat buffet at dinner, including chowders and fresh seafood. Casual dress; cocktails. **Parking:** on-site. **Cards:** AX, DC,

THE GALLEY RESTAURANT
Lunch: $5-$11   **Dinner:** $9-$16   **Phone: 902/963-2354**

(CAA)

Canadian

Location: 0.6 mi (1 km) s. Rt 13 C0A 1N0. **Hours:** Open 5/31-9/19; 8 am-10 pm. **Reservations:** accepted. **Features:** The hillside location affords expansive views of the countryside. The family-oriented restaurant delivers a full menu of seafood and meat selections, all served in ample portions. Pleasant music plays as the friendly staff focuses on prompt service. Casual dress; cocktails. **Parking:** on-site. **Cards:** MC, VI.

RACHEAL'S RISTORANTE
Lunch: $7-$11   **Dinner:** $9-$21   **Phone: 902/963-3227**

Italian

Location: Jct Rt 6 and 13. Rt 6 C0A 1N0. **Hours:** Open 5/21-10/31; 7:30 am-9 pm. **Reservations:** accepted. **Features:** Located in the heart of town, this spacious two-story restaurant also offers a large outdoor deck. The menu selection ranges from sandwiches to tasty brick oven pizza and pasta dishes. Casual dress; cocktails. **Parking:** on-site. **Cards:** MC, VI.

CHARLOTTETOWN pop. 32,245

--------- WHERE TO STAY ---------

BEST WESTERN CHARLOTTETOWN
Book great rates at AAA.com   **Phone: (902)892-2461**

(CAA) (SAVE)

Small-scale Hotel

All Year	1P: $199-$239	2P: $199-$239	XP: $10	D18

Location: Centre. 238 Grafton St C1A 1L5. Fax: 902/566-2979. **Facility:** 146 one-bedroom standard units, some with efficiencies. 2-4 stories, interior corridors. **Parking:** on-site, winter plug-ins. **Terms:** small pets only. **Amenities:** voice mail, irons, hair dryers. *Some:* high-speed Internet. **Dining:** 7 am-9 pm, Sun from 8 am. **Pool(s):** heated indoor. **Leisure Activities:** sauna, whirlpool, exercise room. **Business Services:** meeting rooms, PC. **Cards:** AX, DC, DS, MC, VI. **Free Special Amenities: local telephone calls and high-speed Internet.**

SOME UNITS

COMFORT INN — *Book great rates at AAA.com* — **Phone:** (902)566-4424

6/16-9/30 [CP]	1P: $155-$185	2P: $165-$195	XP: $10 — F18
5/1-6/15 [CP]	1P: $129-$159	2P: $139-$169	XP: $10 — F18
1/1-4/30 [CP]	1P: $121-$151	2P: $131-$161	XP: $10 — F18
10/1-12/31 [CP]	1P: $119-$149	2P: $129-$159	XP: $10 — F18

Small-scale Hotel

Location: Trans-Canada Hwy 1, 2.8 mi (4.5 km) w. Located in a commercial area. 112 Trans-Canada Hwy 1 C1E 1E7. Fax: 902/368-1174. **Facility:** 81 one-bedroom standard units. 2 stories (no elevator), interior corridors. **Parking:** on-site. **Terms:** package plans. **Amenities:** high-speed Internet, irons, hair dryers. **Cards:** AX, CB, DC, DS, JC, MC, VI. *(See color ad card insert)*

SOME UNITS
(ASK) (SD) (🛏) (🍽+) (🐕) (💻) / (✕) /

DELTA PRINCE EDWARD — *Book great rates at AAA.com* — **Phone:** (902)566-2222

6/29-10/17	1P: $189-$369	2P: $209-$389	XP: $20 — F18
5/1-6/28 & 10/18-4/30	1P: $119-$339	2P: $139-$359	XP: $20 — F18

Large-scale Hotel

Location: At Water and Queen sts. Located at harbourfront. 18 Queen St C1A 8B9 (PO Box 2170). Fax: 902/566-1745. **Facility:** 211 one-bedroom standard units, some with whirlpools. 10 stories, interior corridors. **Parking:** on-site (fee). **Terms:** cancellation fee imposed, pets ($25 extra charge). **Amenities:** voice mail, irons, hair dryers. *Fee:* video games, high-speed Internet. *Some:* CD players, honor bars. **Dining:** Selkirk Dining Room, see separate listing. **Pool(s):** heated indoor, wading. **Leisure Activities:** saunas, whirlpools, exercise room, spa. *Fee:* game room. **Guest Services:** gift shop, valet and coin laundry, wireless Internet. **Business Services:** conference facilities, business center. **Cards:** AX, DC, DS, JC, MC, VI. *(See color ad below)*

SOME UNITS
(ASK) (SD) (🛏) (🍽) (Y) (🏋) (🏊) (✕) (🐕) (💻) / (✕) /
FEE

DUNDEE ARMS — *Book great rates at AAA.com* — **Phone:** 902/892-2496

(CAA) (SAVE)

6/1-9/30 [CP]	1P: $145-$265	2P: $155-$275	XP: $15 — F12
5/1-5/31 & 10/1-4/30 [CP]	1P: $115-$240	2P: $125-$250	XP: $15 — F12

Country Inn

Location: At Fitzroy St; centre. 200 Pownal St C1A 3W8. Fax: 902/368-8532. **Facility:** Main inn is circa 1903 Victorian-style with pleasant, well-appointed guest units. An additional two story annex section offers comfortable motel units. 22 units. 20 one-bedroom standard units, some with whirlpools. 2 one-bedroom suites with whirlpools. 3 stories (no elevator), interior/exterior corridors. **Parking:** on-site. **Terms:** office hours 7 am-11 pm, 3 day cancellation notice. **Amenities:** irons, hair dryers. *Some:* DVD players. **Dining:** Griffon Dining Room, see separate listing. **Guest Services:** valet laundry, wireless Internet. **Business Services:** meeting rooms. **Cards:** AX, DC, JC, MC, VI. **Free Special Amenities:** high-speed Internet.

SOME UNITS
(🍽) (Y) (✕) / (VCR) (🖥) (🖨) /

ECONO LODGE — *Book great rates at AAA.com* — **Phone:** (902)368-1110

6/1-9/30 [CP]	1P: $109-$199	2P: $109-$199	XP: $10 — F18
5/1-5/31 [CP]	1P: $89-$149	2P: $89-$149	XP: $10 — F18
10/1-4/30 [CP]	1P: $79-$139	2P: $79-$139	XP: $10 — F18

Motel

Location: Jct Trans-Canada Hwy 1 and Lower Malpeque Rd, 2.8 mi (4.5 km) w. 20 Lower Malpeque Rd C1A 7J9. Fax: 902/368-1110. **Facility:** 63 one-bedroom standard units, some with efficiencies and/or whirlpools. 2 stories (no elevator), interior/exterior corridors. **Parking:** on-site. **Terms:** cancellation fee imposed, package plans. **Amenities:** video library (fee), voice mail, hair dryers. *Some:* DVD players (fee), CD players, irons. **Pool(s):** heated outdoor. **Leisure Activities:** whirlpool. **Guest Services:** coin laundry, wireless Internet. **Business Services:** meeting rooms, PC. **Cards:** AX, DC, DS, MC, VI. *(See color ad card insert)*

SOME UNITS
(ASK) (SD) (🛏) (🏊) (💻) / (✕) (🖥) (🖨) /

FAIRHOLM INN & CARRIAGE HOUSE

Phone: (902)892-5022

5/1-10/15 [BP]	1P: $165-$285	2P: $165-$285	XP: $25	F12
10/16-4/30 [BP]	1P: $125-$185	2P: $125-$185	XP: $25	F12

Historic Bed & Breakfast

Location: Corner of Prince and Fitzroy sts. 230 Prince St C1A 4S1. Fax: 902/892-5060. **Facility:** A beautifully restored 1838 mansion and a fine example of 18th-century Picturesqe architecture. Rooms are spacious and furnished with period antiques. Smoke free premises. 7 units. 6 one-bedroom standard units, some with whirlpools. 1 one-bedroom suite ($125-$285) with whirlpool. 3 stories (no elevator), interior corridors. **Parking:** on-site. **Terms:** office hours 10 am-8 pm, 14 day cancellation notice-fee imposed, package plans. **Amenities:** hair dryers. *Some:* DVD players. **Guest Services:** valet laundry. **Cards:** AX, MC, VI.

SOME UNITS

(ASK) (Yl+) (X) / (VCR) /

FITZROY HALL

Phone: 902/368-2077

(CAA) (SAVE)

5/1-10/15 [BP]	2P: $125-$275	XP: $35	F6
10/16-4/30 [BP]	2P: $95-$200	XP: $25	F6

Historic Bed & Breakfast

Location: Corner of Fitzroy and Pownal sts. Located in a historic residential area. 45 Fitzroy St C1A 1R4. Fax: 902/894-5711. **Facility:** Guest rooms at this stately 1872 Victorian mansion are large and tastefully decorated, and some are suite-style rooms with private decks. Smoke free premises. 8 units. 7 one-bedroom standard units, some with whirlpools. 1 one-bedroom suite with whirlpool. 3 stories (no elevator), interior corridors. **Parking:** on-site. **Terms:** office hours 7 am-10 pm, 30 day cancellation notice, weekly rates available, package plans. **Amenities:** irons, hair dryers. *Some:* DVD players, CD players. **Guest Services:** valet laundry. **Business Services:** PC. **Cards:** AX, MC, VI. **Free Special Amenities: full breakfast and high-speed Internet.**

SOME UNITS

(Yl+) (X) (VCR) / (E) (E) /

GARDEN GATE INN

Phone: (902)892-3411

(CAA) (SAVE)

6/25-9/3	1P: $75-$80	2P: $80-$85	XP: $10	D9
5/1-6/24 & 9/4-4/30	1P: $55-$65	2P: $60-$65	XP: $8	D9

Motel

Location: 2.1 mi (3.5 km) w on Trans-Canada Hwy 1. 639 University Ave C1E 1E5. Fax: 902/368-3697. **Facility:** 17 units. 15 one-bedroom standard units. 1 one- and 1 three-bedroom suites, some with kitchens. 1 story, interior/exterior corridors. **Bath:** combo or shower only. **Parking:** on-site. **Terms:** office hours 7:30 am-11 pm, weekly rates available. **Cards:** AX, MC, VI. **Free Special Amenities: local telephone calls and preferred room (subject to availability with advance reservations).**

SOME UNITS

(Yl+) (X) (E) / (E) /

THE GREAT GEORGE   *Book at AAA.com*

Phone: (902)892-0606

6/1-9/30 [ECP]	1P: $199-$899	2P: $199-$899	XP: $15	F3
10/1-10/31 [ECP]	1P: $166-$899	2P: $166-$899	XP: $15	F3
11/1-4/30 [ECP]	1P: $142-$899	2P: $142-$899	XP: $15	F3
5/1-5/31 [ECP]	1P: $162	2P: $162	XP: $15	F3

Small-scale Hotel

Location: Corner of Dorchester St. Located in a historic area. 58 Great George St C1A 4K3. Fax: 902/628-2079. **Facility:** Smoke free premises. 53 units. 34 one-bedroom standard units, some with whirlpools. 19 one-bedroom suites ($219-$375), some with efficiencies, kitchens and/or whirlpools. 4 stories, interior corridors. **Parking:** on-site. **Terms:** package plans. **Amenities:** high-speed Internet, irons, hair dryers. *Some:* DVD players (fee), CD players, dual phone lines. **Leisure Activities:** exercise room. **Guest Services:** valet and coin laundry, wireless Internet. **Business Services:** meeting rooms, PC. **Cards:** AX, DC, JC, MC, VI.

SOME UNITS

(ASK) (SD) (Yl+) (fork) (X) / (VCR) (E) (E) (E) /
FEE

HERITAGE HARBOUR HOUSE INN

Phone: (902)892-6633

5/31-10/15	1P: $115-$200	2P: $115-$200	XP: $20	D16
5/1-5/30 & 10/16-4/30	1P: $80-$150	2P: $80-$150	XP: $20	D16

Bed & Breakfast

Location: At Rochford St. 9 Grafton St C1A 1K3. Fax: 902/892-8420. **Facility:** This large downtown B&B features a wide variety of room styles and sizes; each guest room is tastefully decorated and many are in a recently built section. Smoke free premises. 22 units. 18 one-bedroom standard units. 4 one-bedroom suites with efficiencies and whirlpools. 3 stories (no elevator), interior corridors. **Bath:** combo or shower only. **Parking:** on-site. **Terms:** 3 day cancellation notice-fee imposed, [BP] meal plan available. **Amenities:** hair dryers. *Some:* DVD players. **Guest Services:** coin laundry, wireless Internet. **Business Services:** PC. **Cards:** AX, DC, JC, MC, VI.

SOME UNITS

(Yl+) (X) (fork) / (E) (E) /

HILLHURST INN

Phone: (902)894-8004

6/10-9/30 [BP]	2P: $135-$235	XP: $25	F3
10/1-10/16 [BP]	2P: $110-$190	XP: $25	F3
5/1-6/9 & 10/17-11/1 [BP]	2P: $99-$175	XP: $25	F3

Historic Bed & Breakfast

Location: Centre at Hillsborough St. Located in a residential area. 181 Fitzroy St C1A 1S3. Fax: 902/892-7679. **Facility:** Featuring distinctive oak and beech woodwork in common areas, the 1897 Georgian Revival home has guest rooms in varied size and decor; one is compact. Smoke free premises. 9 units. 8 one-bedroom standard units, some with whirlpools. 1 one-bedroom suite with whirlpool. 3 stories (no elevator), interior corridors. **Bath:** combo or shower only. **Parking:** on-site. **Terms:** open 5/1-11/1, office hours 7 am-10 pm, 14 day cancellation notice-fee imposed, package plans. **Amenities:** hair dryers. **Cards:** AX, DC, DS, MC, VI.

(ASK) (SD) (Yl+) (X)

HOLIDAY INN EXPRESS HOTEL & SUITES CHARLOTTETOWN   *Book great rates at AAA.com*

Phone: (902)892-1201

(CAA) (SAVE)

6/1-9/30 [BP]	1P: $159-$269	2P: $159-$269	XP: $10	F18
5/1-5/31 & 10/1-4/30 [BP]	1P: $99-$149	2P: $99-$149	XP: $10	F18

Small-scale Hotel

Location: On Trans-Canada Hwy 1, 3 mi (5 km) w. 200 Trans-Canada Hwy C1A 8L4 (PO Box 9500). Fax: 902/892-2178. **Facility:** 135 units. 134 one-bedroom standard units, some with whirlpools. 1 one-bedroom suite ($139-$289) with whirlpool. 3 stories, interior corridors. **Parking:** on-site. **Terms:** package plans. **Amenities:** video games (fee), high-speed Internet, voice mail, irons, hair dryers. **Pool(s):** heated indoor. **Leisure Activities:** whirlpool, exercise room. **Guest Services:** valet and coin laundry. **Business Services:** meeting rooms, business center. **Cards:** AX, DC, DS, MC, VI. **Free Special Amenities: expanded continental breakfast and local telephone calls.** *(See color ad card insert)*

SOME UNITS

(SD) (dog) (GM) (wheelchair) (walk) (X) (fork) (E) / (E) (E) /

QUALITY INN ON THE HILL *Book great rates at AAA.com*

| | 6/21-10/15 | 1P: $161-$271 | 2P: $171-$281 | XP: $10 | F16 |
| | 5/1-6/20 & 10/16-4/30 | 1P: $114-$214 | 2P: $124-$224 | XP: $10 | F16 |

Small-scale Hotel **Location:** Just e of University Ave. 150 Euston St C1A 1W5. Fax: 902/368-3556. **Facility:** 62 units. 54 one-bedroom standard units. 8 one-bedroom suites, some with whirlpools. 5 stories, interior corridors. **Parking:** on-site. **Terms:** cancellation fee imposed, small pets only (in designated units). **Amenities:** video library, irons, hair dryers. *Some:* honor bars. **Guest Services:** wireless Internet. **Business Services:** meeting rooms. **Cards:** AX, DC, JC, MC, VI.
(See color ad card insert)

Phone: (902)894-8572

SOME UNITS
ASK SD 🐾 🍴 🍸 💻 / ✕ VCR 🔌 🖥 /

RODD CHARLOTTETOWN-A RODD SIGNATURE HOTEL *Book great rates at AAA.com*

| | 6/1-10/15 | 1P: $170-$250 | 2P: $170-$250 | XP: $10 | F16 |
| | 5/1-5/31 & 10/16-4/30 | 1P: $109-$154 | 2P: $109-$154 | XP: $10 | F16 |

Classic Historic Small-scale Hotel **Location:** Corner of Kent and Pownal sts. 75 Kent St C1A 7K4 (PO Box 159). Fax: 902/368-2178. **Facility:** This classic hotel built in 1931 features woodwork with a coat-of-arms motif; the guest rooms reflect an older charm and vary in size. 115 units. 108 one-bedroom standard units. 7 one-bedroom suites ($185-$350), some with whirlpools. 5 stories, interior corridors. **Parking:** on-site. **Terms:** cancellation fee imposed, package plans. **Amenities:** high-speed Internet, irons, hair dryers. **Dining:** Chambers Restaurant & Bar, see separate listing. **Pool(s):** heated indoor. **Leisure Activities:** sauna, whirlpool, limited exercise equipment. **Guest Services:** valet laundry. **Business Services:** meeting rooms, business center. **Cards:** AX, DC, DS, JC, MC, VI. *(See color ad p 359 & below)*

Phone: (902)894-7371

SOME UNITS
ASK SD 🐾 🍴 🍸 🏊 ✕ 📷 💻 / ✕ 🔌 /

RODD CONFEDERATION INN & SUITES *Book at AAA.com*

| | 6/1-9/30 [CP] | 1P: $99-$158 | 2P: $99-$158 | XP: $10 | F16 |
| | 5/1-5/31 & 10/1-4/30 [CP] | 1P: $75-$123 | 2P: $75-$123 | XP: $10 | F16 |

Motel **Location:** On Trans-Canada Hwy 1, 2.5 mi (4 km) w. Trans-Canada Hwy 1 C1A 7L3 (PO Box 651). Fax: 902/368-3247. **Facility:** 62 units. 35 one-bedroom standard units. 27 one-bedroom suites. 2 stories (no elevator), interior/exterior corridors. **Parking:** on-site. **Terms:** cancellation fee imposed, package plans, small pets only. **Amenities:** *Some:* hair dryers. **Pool(s):** heated outdoor. **Guest Services:** valet laundry. **Cards:** AX, DC, DS, JC, MC, VI. *(See color ad p 359)*

Phone: (902)892-2481

SOME UNITS
ASK SD 🐾 🍴 🍸 🏊 💻 / ✕ 🔌 🖥 /

RODD ROYALTY INN *Book at AAA.com*

| | 6/1-9/30 | 1P: $145-$185 | 2P: $145-$185 | XP: $10 | F16 |
| | 5/1-5/31 & 10/1-4/30 | 1P: $96-$131 | 2P: $96-$131 | XP: $10 | F16 |

Small-scale Hotel **Location:** 2.5 mi (4 km) w on Trans-Canada Hwy 1. Located in a commercial area. Intersection Hwy 1 & 2 C1A 8C2 (PO Box 2499). Fax: 902/892-8488. **Facility:** 121 units. 104 one-bedroom standard units. 17 one-bedroom suites ($130-$255). 3 stories, interior/exterior corridors. **Parking:** on-site. **Terms:** cancellation fee imposed, package plans, pets (in smoking units). **Amenities:** voice mail, hair dryers. *Some:* irons. **Pool(s):** heated indoor. **Leisure Activities:** waterslide. **Guest Services:** valet laundry. **Business Services:** meeting rooms. **Cards:** AX, DC, DS, MC, VI. *(See color ad p 359)*

Phone: (902)894-8566

SOME UNITS
ASK SD 🐾 🍴 🍸 🏊 ✕ 📷 💻 / ✕ 🔌 🖥 /

SHIPWRIGHT INN

| | 5/15-10/14 [BP] | 1P: $149-$289 | 2P: $149-$289 | XP: $30 | D |
| | 5/1-5/14 & 10/15-4/30 [BP] | 1P: $99-$199 | 2P: $99-$199 | XP: $30 | D |

CAA SAVE

Historic Bed & Breakfast **Location:** Just e of Pownal St. Located in a residential area. 51 Fitzroy St C1A 1R4. Fax: 902/628-1905. **Facility:** Pleasant grounds surround this attractive 1860 Victorian home; seven of its well-appointed rooms feature fireplaces. Smoke free premises. 9 units. 7 one-bedroom standard units, some with whirlpools. 2 one-bedroom suites with whirlpools. 2 stories (no elevator), interior corridors. **Parking:** on-site. **Terms:** office hours 7 am-10 pm, age restrictions may apply, 14 day cancellation notice-fee imposed, package plans. **Amenities:** video library, irons, hair dryers. *Some:* DVD players, CD players. **Guest Services:** valet laundry, DVD library, wireless Internet. **Business Services:** PC. **Cards:** AX, MC, VI. **Free Special Amenities:** early check-in/late check-out and high-speed Internet.

Phone: (902)368-1905

SOME UNITS
🍴 ✕ VCR / 🔌 🖥 💻 /

─────── The following lodging was either not evaluated or did not ───────
meet AAA rating requirements but is listed for your information only.

THE ELMWOOD HERITAGE INN   Phone: 902/368-3310
[fyi]   Not evaluated. **Location:** Centre; entrance opposite Green St. Located in a residential area. 121 N River Rd C1A 3K7.
Facilities, services, and decor characterize a mid-range property.

─────── **WHERE TO DINE** ───────

ANGELS RESTAURANT   Lunch: $7-$12   Dinner: $12-$20   Phone: 902/892-9953
▼▼ ▼▼   **Location:** At Queen St. 85 Belvedere Ave C1A 6B2. **Hours:** 11 am-9 pm, Sat & Sun from 8 am. Closed: 12/25,
12/26. **Reservations:** accepted. **Features:** The spacious modern restaurant has convenient parking. Well-
Italian   prepared food is served in ample portions. Friendly servers contribute to the relaxed atmosphere. Patio
seating is available in season. Casual dress; cocktails. **Parking:** on-site. **Cards:** AX, DC, MC, VI.

BLOSSOMS RESTAURANT   Lunch: $5-$11   Dinner: $9-$16   Phone: 902/566-2567
▼▼   **Location:** Corner of University Ave and Grafton St. 32 University Ave C1A 4K6. **Hours:** 11 am-midnight, Thurs-1
am, Fri-3 am, Sat noon-3 am, Sun noon-midnight. Closed: 12/25. **Reservations:** accepted. **Features:** The
Chinese decor is simple and unpretentious in the multilevel dining room. The focus of the menu is on Szechuan,
Cantonese and some Canadian entrees. Casual dress; cocktails. **Parking:** on-site (fee) and street.
Cards: AX, MC, VI.

CANTON CAFE   Lunch: $6-$10   Dinner: $13-$18   Phone: 902/892-2527
▼▼ ▼▼   **Location:** Centre. 73 Queen St C1A 4A8. **Hours:** 11 am-2 am, Sat from noon, Sun noon-midnight. Closed:
12/25. **Features:** Popular local restaurant established in 1970. Menu features a wide variety of well-
Chinese prepared Cantonese and Szechuan dishes prepared to your own taste. Service is relaxed but competent.
Casual dress; cocktails. **Cards:** DS, MC, VI.

CHAMBERS RESTAURANT & BAR   Lunch: $8-$12   Dinner: $13-$25   Phone: 902/894-7371
▼▼▼▼   **Location:** Corner of Kent and Pownal sts; in Rodd Charlottetown-A Rodd Signature Hotel. Kent St & Pownal St C1A
7K4. **Hours:** 7 am-2 & 5-9 pm; to 9 pm off season. Closed: 12/25. **Reservations:** accepted. **Features:** The
Canadian elegant dining room is decorated in rich, floral wallpaper with wood trim and brass chandeliers. The menu
selection is ample with a focus on prime cuts of beef and fresh local seafood. Dressy casual; cocktails.
Parking: on-site. **Cards:** AX, DC, DS, JC, MC, VI.

THE CHURCHILL ARMS PUB   Lunch: $5-$9   Dinner: $8-$15   Phone: 902/367-3450
▼▼ ▼▼   **Location:** Centre. 75 Queen St C1A 4A8. **Hours:** 11:30 am-10 pm, Fri & Sat-11 pm. Closed: 12/25, 12/26; also
Sun. **Reservations:** accepted. **Features:** The delightfully cozy pub serves authentic English-style pub foods
English   with a decent selection of imported beers on tap. Casual dress; cocktails. **Parking:** street. **Cards:** MC, VI.

THE CLADDAGH ROOM   Dinner: $17-$24   Phone: 902/892-9661
▼▼▼▼   **Location:** Just off corner of Queen and Sydney sts. 131 Sydney St C1A 1G5. **Hours:** 5 pm-10 pm, Fri & Sat-10:30
pm, Sun-9 pm. **Reservations:** suggested. **Features:** The restored building is attractively decorated with
Seafood etched dividers, soft lighting and candle centerpieces. The menu lists such tempting selections as the well-
presented stuffed fish with vegetables. All of the mouthwatering desserts are made in-house. Upstairs, a
pleasant pub serves food until 11 pm. Casual dress; cocktails. **Parking:** street. **Cards:** AX, DC, MC, VI.

CORA'S BREAKFAST & LUNCH   Lunch: $6-$10   Phone: 902/892-6400
▼▼ ▼▼   **Location:** Between Richmond and Grafton sts. 123 Queen St C1A 4B3. **Hours:** 6 am-3 pm, Sun from 7 am.
Closed: 12/25. **Reservations:** accepted. **Features:** Although this place specializes in breakfast, it offers a
Canadian varied daytime menu that includes bacon, eggs, sausages, crepes, grilled cheese, sandwiches, freshly
prepared quiches, salads, fruit platters and freshly squeezed juices. The family-friendly dining room is
casual and modern. Casual dress. **Parking:** street. **Cards:** AX, DC, MC, VI.

EAST SIDE MARIO'S   Lunch: $6-$11   Dinner: $9-$16   Phone: 902/892-6100
▼▼ ▼▼   **Location:** In University Plaza. 449 University Ave C1A 8K3. **Hours:** 11 am-11 pm, Fri & Sat-midnight. Closed:
12/25. **Reservations:** accepted. **Features:** Pizza, steak, sandwiches, salads, burgers, hot dogs, chicken,
Italian   fish, calamari and pasta are among offerings at the chain of family restaurants, which also has a children's
menu. The lively dining room is decorated to resemble a European market, with shop facades and vintage
signage. Casual dress; cocktails. **Parking:** on-site. **Cards:** AX, DC, MC, VI.

THE GAHAN HOUSE BREWERY   Lunch: $7-$14   Dinner: $9-$19   Phone: 902/626-2337
▼▼ ▼▼   **Location:** Centre; in historic area. 126 Sydney St C1A 1G5. **Hours:** 11 am-close, Sun 4 pm-9 pm. Closed: 12/25.
Reservations: accepted. **Features:** The island's only brewery restaurant brews a wide variety of
Canadian handcrafted ales the old-fashioned way with no preservatives. Friendly servers contribute to the relaxing,
casual atmosphere. Guests can request patio seating in season. Casual dress; cocktails. **Parking:** street.
Cards: AX, MC, VI.

GRIFFON DINING ROOM   Lunch: $8-$14   Dinner: $15-$26   Phone: 902/892-2496
(AAA)   **Location:** At Fitzroy St; centre; in Dundee Arms. 200 Pownal St C1A 3W8. **Hours:** 7 am-10 pm; 11:30 am-9 pm off
▼▼▼▼   season. Closed: 1/1, 12/25. **Reservations:** suggested. **Features:** Enjoy fine dining in the relaxed
atmosphere of this 1903 Victorian home. Attentive servers deliver menu offerings of nicely presented fresh
Canadian seafood and varied meat entrees, including some preparations of game. Seasonal patio dining is a casual
option at the Hearth and Cricket Pub. Casual dress; cocktails. **Parking:** on-site. **Cards:** AX, DC, JC, MC, VI.
Historic

HUNTER'S ALE HOUSE

Canadian

Lunch: $7-$12   **Dinner:** $10-$20   **Phone:** 902/367-4040

Location: Corner of Prince and Kent sts. 185 Kent St C1A 8S9. **Hours:** 11 am-11 pm. **Closed:** 12/25. **Features:** This upbeat pub-style restaurant offers outdoor dining in season. The menu ranges from fresh seafood and steaks to burgers, sandwiches, fine chowders and salads. Portions are ample and desserts are made on the premises. Casual dress; cocktails. **Parking:** street. **Cards:** AX, MC, VI.

LOBSTER ON THE WHARF

Seafood

Lunch: $8-$15   **Dinner:** $13-$32   **Phone:** 902/368-2888

Location: At Confederation Landing Park; centre. 2 Prince Street Wharf C1A 8C1. **Hours:** Open 5/6-10/28; 11:30 am-9:30 pm. **Reservations:** suggested. **Features:** A casual atmosphere is the focus of the spacious harborfront restaurant, which has two levels and an outdoor deck. Although lobster is the specialty, the menu also includes clams, mussels, oysters and scallops for seafood lovers and steaks and chicken for those who prefer meat. Dressy casual; cocktails. **Parking:** on-site. **Cards:** AX, DC, JC, MC, VI.

LUCY MAUD DINING ROOM

Canadian

Lunch: $13-$19   **Dinner:** $17-$28   **Phone:** 902/894-6868

Location: Centre; in The Culinary Institute of Canada. 4 Sydney St C1A 8B9. **Hours:** 11:30 am-1:30 & 6-8 pm, Sat from 6 pm. **Closed:** major holidays; also Sun & Mon, 7/23-8/6. **Reservations:** accepted. **Features:** In the Canadian Culinary Institute, the restaurant has its services provided by students. Views of the harbour are outstanding, and table appointments are elegant. Seasonal game selections stand out on a menu of creatively presented seafood and meat preparations. Dressy casual; cocktails. **Parking:** on-site. **Cards:** AX, MC, VI.

THE MERCHANTMAN PUB

Canadian

Lunch: $9-$13   **Dinner:** $17-$25   **Phone:** 902/892-9150

Location: Corner of Queen and Water sts; centre. 23 Queen St C1A 4A2. **Hours:** 11 am-10 pm, Sat from 11:30 am. **Closed:** major holidays; also Sun. **Reservations:** suggested. **Features:** Original brick and wood-beam ceilings enhance the warm, friendly ambience of the casual, neighborhood eatery. Pub foods are available all day, while evening selections center on heartier selections, including well-seasoned Thai and Cajun specialties. Casual dress; cocktails. **Parking:** street. **Cards:** AX, DC, MC, VI.

MIKES RESTAURANT

Canadian

Lunch: $6-$10   **Dinner:** $8-$16   **Phone:** 902/367-6453

Location: 2.3 mi (3.5 km) w on Trans-Canada Hwy 1. 660 University Ave C1E 1E5. **Hours:** 6:30 am-10 pm, Sat & Sun 8 am-11 pm. **Closed:** 12/25. **Reservations:** accepted. **Features:** This popular family-friendly restaurant specializes in pizza and hot submarine sandwiches, along with fries, burgers, soup, salads, pasta, grilled meats and seafood. An excellent variety of colorful desserts rounds out the offerings. Casual dress; cocktails. **Parking:** on-site. **Cards:** AX, DC, MC, VI.

OFF BROADWAY RESTAURANT & 42 STREET LOUNGE

Canadian

Lunch: $7-$12   **Dinner:** $15-$25   **Phone:** 902/566-4620

Location: Just off corner of Queen and Sydney sts. 125 Sydney St C1A 1G5. **Hours:** 11:30 am-11 pm, Sun 11 am-10 pm; hours vary off season. **Closed:** 12/25. **Reservations:** suggested. **Features:** Cozy atmosphere, all booth seating with brick and wood-beam interior, and high pine dividers, enhances the restored 1870s building. The Saturday and Sunday brunch draws a good crowd. The menu lists appetizers, crepes, steak and seafood, plus a tempting assortment of homemade desserts. Casual dress; cocktails. **Parking:** street. **Cards:** AX, DC, MC, VI. **Historic**

PAPA JOE'S RESTAURANT & LOUNGE

Canadian

Lunch: $6-$12   **Dinner:** $8-$16   **Phone:** 902/566-5070

Location: Corner of University Ave and Pond St. 345 University Ave C1A 4M8. **Hours:** 11 am-10 pm. **Closed:** 12/25. **Reservations:** accepted. **Features:** The cheerful, family-friendly roadside restaurant presents a diverse menu that features fresh seafood and steaks, as well as sandwiches, burgers and a selection of Lebanese dishes. Casual dress; cocktails. **Parking:** on-site. **Cards:** AX, DC, MC, VI.

PIAZZA JOE'S ITALIAN EATERY & BISTRO

(AAA)

Italian

Lunch: $5-$14   **Dinner:** $11-$20   **Phone:** 902/894-4291

Location: At Prince St; centre. 189 Kent St C1A 1P1. **Hours:** 11 am-11 pm, Fri & Sat-midnight; to 10 pm, Fri & Sat-11 pm 9/5-6/30. **Closed:** 12/25. **Reservations:** accepted. **Features:** The spacious, Italian-themed bistro has an open kitchen, an aromatic bread bar and an atmosphere that is welcoming to families. Listing both Italian and Canadian cuisine, the menu centers on pizzas. Portions are ample. Casual dress; cocktails. **Parking:** on-site (fee). **Cards:** AX, DC, MC, VI.

PIECE A CAKE RESTAURANT

Canadian

Lunch: $8-$15   **Dinner:** $14-$22   **Phone:** 902/894-4585

Location: At Confederation Court Mall; centre. 119 Grafton St C1A 1K9. **Hours:** 11 am-9 pm, Fri & Sat-10 pm. **Closed:** 12/24-12/26; also Sun & for dinner Mon off season. **Reservations:** accepted. **Features:** Strip loin steaks, salmon, crusted pork loin and tasty soups and sandwiches are representative of the diverse menu. Pumpkin-orange walls, attractive art and decorative plants give the dining room a bright, cheerful ambience. Service is attentive. Casual dress; cocktails. **Parking:** on-site (fee). **Cards:** AX, DC, MC, VI.

THE PILOT HOUSE FINE FOOD & SPIRITS

Canadian

Lunch: $8-$14   **Dinner:** $13-$23   **Phone:** 902/894-4800

Location: Just w of Queen St. 70 Grafton St C1A 1K7. **Hours:** 11:30 am-10 pm. **Closed:** 12/25, 12/26; also Sun. **Reservations:** accepted. **Features:** An upbeat atmosphere and friendly service are what guests find at the popular watering hole. The menu lists a good selection of fresh seafood and meat entrees. Casual dress; cocktails. **Parking:** street. **Cards:** AX, MC, VI.

RUM RUNNERS

(AAA)

Canadian

Lunch: $7-$14   **Dinner:** $9-$19   **Phone:** 902/892-2207

Location: Corner of Queen and Water sts; centre. 73 Water St C1A 1A5. **Hours:** 11 am-10 pm. **Closed:** 12/25. **Reservations:** accepted. **Features:** A friendly, pub-style atmosphere prevails at the upbeat restaurant. Patrons can order from the full menu or the lighter pub menu. A European-style sidewalk cafe opens seasonally. Casual dress; cocktails. **Parking:** street. **Cards:** AX, DC, MC, VI.

SELKIRK DINING ROOM Lunch: $9-$15 Dinner: $22-$34 Phone: 902/894-1208
▼▼▼▼ **Location:** At Water and Queen sts; in Delta Prince Edward. 18 Queen St C1A 8B9. **Hours:** 7 am-1:30 & 5-9 pm,
Canadian Sun 11 am-2 & 5-9 pm; Sunday brunch. **Reservations:** suggested. **Features:** A pianist plays nightly in this elegant lobby dining room which features a waterfall to offset lobby noise. Soft lighting and comfortable winged-back chairs set the stage for a romantic mood. The menu offers creative fresh seafood and meats including their tasty seafood chowder or sample the delightful seafood platter for two. They also have a fine selection of steak, pork and prime rib to satisfy the meat lover. Casual dress; cocktails; entertainment. **Parking:** on-site (fee). **Cards:** AX, DC, MC, VI.

SHADDY'S MEDITERRANEAN CUISINE Lunch: $6-$11 Dinner: $8-$18 Phone: 902/368-8886
▼▼▼ ▼▼▼ **Location:** Centre. 44 University Ave C1A 4K6. **Hours:** 8 am-10 pm, Sat from 11 am, Sun 5 pm-9 pm. Closed:
Mediterranean 4/9, 12/25, 12/26. **Reservations:** accepted. **Features:** A local landmark in the heart of town, the restaurant serves a wide variety of Canadian and Lebanese entrees. Among choices are great sandwiches, burgers, fresh seafood, souvlaki, shish taouk and seasonal lobster. The patio opens seasonally. Casual dress; cocktails. **Parking:** street. **Cards:** AX, DC, MC, VI.

SIRENELLA RISTORANTE Lunch: $9-$14 Dinner: $13-$21 Phone: 902/628-2271
▼▼▼ **Location:** Centre; adjacent to Prince Edward Hotel. 83 Water St C1A 1A5. **Hours:** 11:30 am-2 & 5-10 pm, Sat from
Italian 5 pm. Closed major holidays; also Sun. **Reservations:** accepted. **Features:** The cozy restaurant is a trendy spot for comfortable dining or a cup of delicious gourmet coffee. Decorative lighting and candles soften the mood in the dining room. Outdoor dining is popular during the summer months. Casual dress; cocktails.
Parking: on-site. **Cards:** AX, DC, JC, MC, VI.

SMITTY'S FAMILY RESTAURANT Lunch: $6-$11 Dinner: $8-$16 Phone: 902/892-5752
▼▼ ▼▼ **Location:** In University Plaza. 449 Universtiy Ave C1A 8K3. **Hours:** 6:30 am-10 pm, Sun from 7:30 am. Closed:
Canadian 12/25. **Features:** The family-oriented restaurant satisfies patrons with its ever-popular all-day breakfast items, as well as tasty and wholesome soups and salads at lunchtime. A relaxed mood characterizes the dining space. Casual dress; cocktails. **Parking:** on-site. **Cards:** AX, DC, MC, VI.

SWISS CHALET Lunch: $6-$11 Dinner: $8-$16 Phone: 902/894-7440
▼▼ ▼▼ **Location:** At Summer St. 359 University Ave C1A 4M9. **Hours:** 11 am-10 pm, Fri & Sat-11 pm. Closed: 12/25.
Canadian **Reservations:** accepted. **Features:** The popular restaurant is known for its rotisserie chicken and ribs and the tangy Chalet sauce that gives food its special zip. Diners munch on a half or quarter chicken with sides such as steamed vegetables, fries, baked potatoes and salads. Lunch guests often go for the great soup and sandwich combination. Take-out and delivery service are popular options. Casual dress; cocktails. **Parking:** on-site.
Cards: AX, DC, MC, VI.

CLEAR SPRINGS

—— WHERE TO STAY ——

The following lodging was either not evaluated or did not meet AAA rating requirements but is listed for your information only.

JOHNSON SHORE INN Phone: 902/687-1340
[fyi] Not evaluated. **Location:** Jct Rt 16 and 305, 0.6 mi (1 km) w on Rt 16, 1 mi (1.5 km) n on dirt entry road. RR 3, Rt 16 C0A 2B0. Facilities, services, and decor characterize a mid-range property.

CORNWALL pop. 4,412

—— WHERE TO STAY ——

FIREDANCE COUNTRY INN B & B Phone: 902/675-3471
▼▼▼▼ All Year [BP] 1P: $125-$155 2P: $125-$155 XP: $15 F6
Location: Hwy 1, exit 9, 4 mi (6 km) s on Rt 9, follow signs. 35 Firedance Ridge C0A 1H0. Fax: 902/675-2608.
Bed & Breakfast **Facility:** The inn occupies a lovely, rural location overlooking farm fields and the Clyde River; some rooms have water views or soaker tubs. Smoke free premises. 7 units. 6 one-bedroom standard units, some with efficiencies. 1 vacation home. 2 stories (no elevator), interior/exterior corridors. **Parking:** on-site. **Terms:** office hours 7 am-10 pm, 14 day cancellation notice-fee imposed, package plans. **Amenities:** video library, irons, hair dryers. **Business Services:** PC. **Cards:** AX, JC, MC, VI.

SOME UNITS
(ASK) (&M) (&) (X) (X) (VCR) / (🛏) (🖨) /

HOWARD JOHNSON HOTEL *Book at AAA.com* Phone: (902)566-2211
▼▼ ▼▼ 6/16-10/15 [CP] 1P: $135 2P: $145 XP: $10 F16
5/1-6/15 & 10/16-4/30 [CP] 1P: $85 2P: $95 XP: $10 F16
Small-scale Hotel **Location:** On Hwy 1, 4.3 mi (7 km) w of Charlottetown. Located in a quiet rural area. 100 Trans-Canada Hwy C0A 1H0 (RR 4). Fax: 902/566-2214. **Facility:** 58 units. 55 one- and 3 two-bedroom standard units. 2 stories (no elevator), interior/exterior corridors. **Parking:** on-site. **Terms:** cancellation fee imposed, [BP] meal plan available. **Amenities:** voice mail, irons, hair dryers. *Some:* high-speed Internet. **Pool(s):** heated indoor. **Leisure Activities:** sauna, whirlpool. *Fee:* miniature golf. **Guest Services:** coin laundry. **Business Services:** meeting rooms. **Cards:** AX, DC, DS, MC, VI.

SOME UNITS
(ASK) (SD) (¶¶) (□) (🐄) (X) (✗) (🖨) / (X) (🛏) (🖨) /

SUNNY KING MOTEL Phone: 902/566-2209
▼▼ *Property failed to provide current rates*
Motel **Location:** On Hwy 1; centre. (PO Box 788, C0A 1H0). Fax: 902/566-4209. **Facility:** 34 units. 16 one-bedroom standard units, some with efficiencies. 15 one- and 3 two-bedroom suites with kitchens. 2 stories (no elevator), exterior corridors. **Parking:** on-site, winter plug-ins. **Terms:** office hours 8 am-11 pm, pets ($10 extra charge). **Pool(s):** heated outdoor. **Guest Services:** coin laundry.

SOME UNITS

FEE

SUPER 8 MOTEL

Phone: (902)892-7900

6/16-9/30 [CP]	1P: $119-$209	2P: $119-$209	XP: $10	F18
5/1-6/15 & 10/1-4/30 [CP]	1P: $89-$169	2P: $89-$169	XP: $10	F18

Small-scale Hotel

Location: On Hwy 1, 3.7 mi (6 km) w of Charlottetown. 11 York Point Rd C0A 1H0 (Box 684). Fax: 902/892-5533. **Facility:** Smoke free premises. 63 one-bedroom standard units, some with whirlpools. 2 stories (no elevator), interior corridors. **Parking:** on-site. **Terms:** check-in 4 pm. **Amenities:** hair dryers. *Some:* high-speed Internet, irons. **Dining:** Maggie's Family Restaurant, see separate listing. **Pool(s):** heated indoor. **Leisure Activities:** whirlpool. **Guest Services:** coin laundry, wireless Internet. **Business Services:** meeting rooms. **Cards:** AX. **Free Special Amenities:** continental breakfast and high-speed Internet.

SOME UNITS

------- WHERE TO DINE -------

MAGGIE'S FAMILY RESTAURANT

Lunch: $6-$28	Dinner: $6-$28	Phone: 902/892-7772

Canadian

Location: On Hwy 1, 3.7 mi (6 km) w of Charlottetown; in Royal Park Country Inn. 11 York Point Rd C0A 1H0. **Hours:** 7 am-close, Sun from 8 am. Closed: 12/25. **Reservations:** accepted. **Features:** Both tables and booths fill the spacious restaurant. Many items on the vast menu are homemade. Casual dress; cocktails. **Parking:** on-site. **Cards:** MC, VI.

DALVAY BEACH

------- WHERE TO STAY -------

DALVAY BY-THE-SEA HERITAGE INN

Phone: 902/672-2048

6/17-9/21 [MAP]	1P: $180-$200	2P: $270-$390	XP: $90	D12

Historic
Country Inn

Location: Off Rt 6; at the east end of National Park. 16 Cottage Cres National Pkwy C0A 1P0 (PO Box 8, YORK). Fax: 902/672-2741. **Facility:** A wonderful historic inn located in the park and bordering a pond. A variety of room styles and sizes and some deluxe cottages with decks. Smoke free premises. 34 units. 26 one-bedroom standard units. 8 cottages ($550-$920). 3 stories (no elevator), interior/exterior corridors. **Parking:** on-site. **Terms:** open 6/17-9/21, 2 night minimum stay - seasonal, 10 day cancellation notice-fee imposed. **Amenities:** irons, hair dryers. **Dining:** restaurant, see separate listing. **Leisure Activities:** beach access, boating, canoeing, kayaks, golf driving range, 2 tennis courts, rental bicycles, hiking trails, playground, horseshoes. **Guest Services:** gift shop, coin laundry. **Business Services:** meeting rooms, PC. **Cards:** AX, DC, MC, VI. **Free Special Amenities:** newspaper.

SOME UNITS

------- WHERE TO DINE -------

DALVAY BY-THE-SEA HERITAGE INN DINING ROOM

Menu on AAA.com

Lunch: $12-$20	Dinner: $22-$31	Phone: 902/672-2048

Canadian

Location: Off Rt 6; at east end of National Park; in Dalvay by-the-Sea Heritage Inn. **Hours:** Open 6/5-9/30; 8 am-9:30, noon-1:30 & 5:30-9 pm. **Reservations:** suggested. **Features:** The elegant dining room is in the historic 1895 Dalvay mansion. On the menu are fresh local seafood, theatrical meat selections and some specialty items, including venison and duck. Breakfast, lunch and afternoon tea are served in a more casual service style than dinner. Dressy casual; cocktails. **Parking:** on-site. **Cards:** AX, DC, MC, VI.

EAST BIDEFORD

------- WHERE TO STAY -------

------- *The following lodging was either not evaluated or did not* -------
meet AAA rating requirements but is listed for your information only.

RED SHORE COTTAGES

Phone: 902/831-2173

[fyi]
Cottage

Did not meet all AAA rating requirements for locking devices in some guest rooms at time of last evaluation on 05/11/2006. **Location:** On Rt 163; centre. 85 Red Shore Ln C0B 1J0. Facilities, services, and decor characterize a mid-range property.

FRENCH RIVER

------- WHERE TO STAY -------

THE BEACH HOUSE INN

Phone: 902/886-2145

5/1-10/31 [BP]	1P: $79-$139	2P: $79-$139	XP: $20	

Bed & Breakfast

Location: Just off Rt 20; centre. Located in rural area. Cape Rd C0B 1M0 (RR 2). Fax: 902/886-3492. **Facility:** In a secluded area a short stroll from the beach, this quaint property has an artsy style and offers individually decorated guest rooms and cottages. Smoke free premises. 9 units. 7 one-bedroom standard units, some with whirlpools. 2 cottages ($129-$169), some with whirlpools. 2 stories (no elevator), interior/exterior corridors. **Parking:** on-site. **Terms:** open 5/1-10/31, office hours 7 am-1 am, 14 day cancellation notice-fee imposed. **Amenities:** video library, CD players, hair dryers. *Some:* DVD players. **Leisure Activities:** bicycles. **Cards:** AX, MC, VI.

SOME UNITS

GEORGETOWN pop. 721

——— WHERE TO STAY ———

THE GEORGETOWN INN
▼▼▼ ▼▼▼
Historic Bed
& Breakfast

6/15-9/14 [BP] 1P: $95-$140 2P: $95-$140 XP: $15 F8
5/1-6/14 & 9/15-4/30 [BP] 1P: $77-$112 2P: $77-$112 XP: $15 F8
Phone: 902/652-2511

Location: Centre. 62 Richmond St C0A 1L0 (PO Box 192). Fax: 902/652-2544. **Facility:** Now a cozy inn, this 1840 building has formerly served as a mercantile store, a post office, a bank, a Masonic lodge and a hardware store. Smoke free premises. 8 one-bedroom standard units, some with whirlpools. 3 stories (no elevator), interior corridors. *Bath:* combo or shower only. **Parking:** on-site. **Terms:** office hours 7 am-10 pm, 5 day cancellation notice-fee imposed, package plans. **Amenities:** hair dryers. **Guest Services:** complimentary evening beverages. **Cards:** AX, MC, VI.

SOME UNITS
(ASK) (TI+) (✕) (⚙) / (🍴) /

KENSINGTON pop. 1,385

——— WHERE TO DINE ———

FROSTY TREAT DAIRY BAR
▼▼▼
Canadian

Lunch: $4-$11 **Dinner:** $4-$11 **Phone:** 902/836-3000
Location: On Rt 2; centre. 109 Victoria St W C0B 1M0. **Hours:** Open 5/21-9/30; 9:30 am-11 pm; hours vary off season. **Features:** The popular take-out spot serves fried clams, fish and chips, burgers and a bounty of ice cream flavors. Casual dress. **Parking:** on-site.

(🍴)

THE HOME PLACE RESTAURANT
▼▼▼ ▼▼▼
Canadian
Cards: MC, VI.

Dinner: $14-$21 **Phone:** 902/836-5686
Location: Just e on Rt 6; in The Home Place Inn. 21 Victoria St E C0B 1M0. **Hours:** 5 pm-9 pm. **Reservations:** accepted. **Features:** The quaint restaurant offers a choice of seating inside or on the pleasant screened porch. The menu lists a wide variety of well-prepared seafood and meat dishes, including fresh oysters and mussels, as well as tasty homemade desserts. Casual dress; cocktails. **Parking:** on-site.

MAYFIELD

——— WHERE TO STAY ———

CAVENDISH GATEWAY RESORT BY CLARION COLLECTION *Book great rates at AAA.com*
▼▼ ▼▼
Motel

Property failed to provide current rates
Phone: 902/963-2213
Location: On Rt 13, 3.6 mi (6 km) w of Cavendish; centre. Rt 13 C0A 1N0 (Box 5506, HUNTER RIVER). Fax: 902/963-3064. **Facility:** 55 units. 43 one-bedroom standard units. 6 one-bedroom suites with kitchens. 6 cottages. 3 stories (no elevator), interior/exterior corridors. **Parking:** on-site. **Terms:** open 5/1-10/15. **Amenities:** hair dryers. *Some:* irons. **Pool(s):** heated indoor. **Leisure Activities:** tennis court. *Fee:* game room. **Guest Services:** coin laundry, wireless Internet. **Business Services:** meeting rooms. *(See color ad card insert & p 364)*

SOME UNITS
(🛏) (➤) (✕) (💻) / (🍴) (⚙) (🔲) (🖥) /

MONTAGUE pop. 1,945

——— WHERE TO DINE ———

GILLIS' DRIVE-IN RESTAURANT
▼▼
Canadian

Lunch: $4-$11 **Dinner:** $4-$11 **Phone:** 902/838-2031
Location: On Rt 4, 0.6 mi (1 km) n. Rt 4 C0A 1R0. **Hours:** 11 am-11 pm; hours vary off season. **Features:** Guests can step back in time at the popular '50s-style drive-in. Leaving the lights on indicates curb service is desired, but the option to dine inside also is available. On the menu are fish, beef and chicken burgers, fish and chips and fine items from the dairy bar. Casual dress. **Parking:** on-site.

(🍴)

WINDOWS ON THE WATER CAFE
▼▼ ▼▼▼
Canadian
Parking: on-site. **Cards:** MC, VI.

Lunch: $8-$14 **Dinner:** $15-$23 **Phone:** 902/838-2080
Location: At Main St. 106 Sackville St C0A 1N0. **Hours:** Open 5/1-10/31; 11:30 am-9 pm; to 8 pm off season. **Reservations:** suggested. **Features:** Overlooking the picturesque river and marina, the casual restaurant delivers well-prepared and well-presented specialties of country-style seafood and meats. Sweet temptations beckon from the dessert tray. The summer deck is popular in season. Casual dress; cocktails.

MORELL pop. 332

——— WHERE TO STAY ———

RODD CROWBUSH GOLF & BEACH RESORT *Book great rates at AAA.com*
(CAA) (SAVE)
▼▼▼ ▼▼▼
Resort
Small-scale Hotel

6/1-9/30 1P: $202-$297 2P: $202-$297 XP: $20 F16
5/15-5/31 & 10/1-10/15 1P: $141-$227 2P: $141-$227 XP: $20 F16
Phone: (902)961-5600

Location: 3 mi (5 km) w on Rt 2, follow signs. Rt 350 Lakeside C0A 1S0 (PO Box 164). Fax: 902/961-5601. **Facility:** Located on the eastern shore, this resort offers a great opportunity for relaxation in standard hotel rooms or suites, or in townhouse-styled cottages. 81 units. 25 one-bedroom standard units. 24 one-bedroom suites ($178-$357) with whirlpools. 32 cottages ($224-$554) with whirlpools. 2-3 stories, interior/exterior corridors. **Parking:** on-site. **Terms:** open 5/15-10/15, 3 day cancellation notice-fee imposed, package plans. **Amenities:** video library (fee), DVD players, voice mail, irons, hair dryers. *Some:* dual phone lines, honor bars. **Dining:** restaurant, see separate listing. **Pool(s):** heated indoor. **Leisure Activities:** sauna, whirlpool, limited beach access, driving range, 2 lighted tennis courts, exercise room, spa. *Fee:* golf-18 holes. **Guest Services:** gift shop, valet and coin laundry, wireless Internet. **Business Services:** meeting rooms, business center. **Cards:** AX, DC, MC, VI. **Free Special Amenities:** full breakfast and high-speed Internet. *(See color ad p 359)*

SOME UNITS
(S/D) (TI) (24T) (Y) (🚶) (➤) (✕) (💻) / (✕) (🔲) (🖥) /

——— WHERE TO DINE ———

RODD CROWBUSH DINING ROOM
Dinner: $25-$38
Phone: 902/961-5600

▼▼▼▼
Canadian
MC, VI.

Location: 3 mi (5 km) w on Rt 2, follow signs; In Rodd Crowbush Golf & Beach Resort. **Hours:** Open 5/15-10/31; 6 am-11 & 6-10 pm. **Reservations:** accepted. **Features:** The pleasant dining room overlooks the fifth fairway at the Links at Crowbush Cove. In addition to specialties of fresh local island seafood, the menu lists prime cuts of meat and homemade desserts. Casual dress; cocktails. **Parking:** on-site. **Cards:** AX, DC, JC,

[Ⓨ]

MURRAY HARBOUR pop. 357

——— WHERE TO STAY ———

FOX RIVER COTTAGES
Phone: 902/962-2881

▼▼
Cottage

6/24-9/2   2P: $115-$140   XP: $10
5/18-6/23 & 9/3-10/10   2P: $75-$91   XP: $10
Location: From Rt 18, 0.6 mi (1 km) se. 239 Machon Point Rd C0A 1V0. **Facility:** 4 cottages. 1 story, exterior corridors. **Parking:** on-site. **Terms:** open 5/18-10/10, 30 day cancellation notice. **Amenities:** DVD players.
Leisure Activities: limited beach access, canoeing. **Guest Services:** coin laundry. **Cards:** MC, VI.

NEW GLASGOW pop. 9,432

——— WHERE TO STAY ———

MY MOTHER'S COUNTRY INN
Phone: 902/964-2508

▼▼▼▼
Bed & Breakfast

6/1-9/30 [BP]   2P: $90-$200   XP: $25
Location: On Rt 13, 1.5 mi (2.5 km) n. Rt 13 C0A 1N0 (PO Box 172, HUNTER RIVER). **Fax:** 902/964-2606. **Facility:** A cottage, inn and motel all offer accommodations at this pleasant property set on spacious grounds. 10 units. 7 one-bedroom standard units, some with whirlpools. 3 cottages ($125-$250), some with whirlpools. 2 stories (no elevator), interior/exterior corridors. **Parking:** on-site. **Terms:** open 6/1-9/30, office hours 8 am-10 pm, cancellation fee imposed, weekly rates available, package plans. **Amenities:** *Some:* hair dryers. **Leisure Activities:** boating. **Cards:** AX, MC, VI.

SOME UNITS
[✕] [Ⓚ] / [Ⓟ] [☎]

——— WHERE TO DINE ———

CAFE' ON THE CLYDE
Lunch: $7-$12
Dinner: $9-$16
Phone: 902/964-4300

Ⓐ
▼▼
Canadian

Location: Off Rt 13 at jct Rt 224 and 258. **Hours:** Open 6/1-10/31; 9 am-8 pm; to 4 pm 6/1-6/15 & 9/22-10/8; 8 am-9 pm 7/1-9/4. **Reservations:** suggested. **Features:** Overlooking the picturesque Clyde River, the casual restaurant prepares home-style potato pie, fish cakes, lobster sandwiches and excellent desserts. Cathedral ceilings, hardwood floors and stenciled walls enhance the appeal of the dining room. Service is pleasant and attentive. Casual dress; beer & wine only. **Parking:** on-site. **Cards:** AX, DC, MC, VI.

NEW GLASGOW LOBSTER SUPPERS
Dinner: $14-$36
Phone: 902/964-2870

Ⓐ
▼▼
Seafood

Location: Off Rt 13 at jct Rt 224 and 258; 5.8 mi (9.6 km) s of Cavendish. **Hours:** Open 5/29-10/15; 4 pm-8:30 pm. **Reservations:** accepted. **Features:** Serving guests since 1958, the restaurant is known for its lobster pound, which contains 20,000 pounds of the tasty bottom-dwellers. Fittingly, the menu features lots of delicious lobster dinners, which are served with all-you-can-eat chowder, mussels, salad and tempting homemade dessert. Casual dress; cocktails. **Parking:** on-site. **Cards:** AX, DC, MC, VI.

THE OLDE GLASGOW MILL
RESTAURANT   *Menu on AAA.com*   **Lunch:** $8-$14   **Dinner:** $15-$30   **Phone:** 902/964-3313

Ⓐ
▼▼▼
Canadian

Location: Centre. Rt 13 C0A 1N0. **Hours:** Open 5/7-10/31; 11:30 am-9:30 pm; hours vary off season. **Reservations:** accepted. **Features:** This restored 1896 feed mill is located in a charming area bordering the Tidal River Clyde and hills. You can dine on two levels and both offer a nice view. They offer creative preparations of fresh seafood, meat and pasta, finish with one of their excellent desserts over a special coffee. Casual dress; cocktails. **Parking:** on-site. **Cards:** AX, DC, MC, VI.

NORTH CAPE

——— WHERE TO DINE ———

WIND & REEF SEAFOOD RESTAURANT
Lunch: $8-$15
Dinner: $10-$21
Phone: 902/882-3535

▼▼
Seafood

Location: On Rt 12; in Interpretive Centre. **Hours:** Open 5/15-10/31; noon-9 pm. **Reservations:** accepted. **Features:** At the northern tip of the island, the restaurant overlooks the ocean, reef and wind turbines. On the menu is a fine variety of fresh seafood, including chowders and lobster. Casual dress; cocktails. **Parking:** on-site. **Cards:** MC, VI.

[Ⓨ]

NORTH MILTON

──── WHERE TO STAY ────

COUNTRY GARDEN INN B & B   **Phone:** 902/566-4344

7/1-8/31	1P: $95	2P: $119	XP: $10	D10
5/1-6/30 & 9/1-9/15	1P: $80	2P: $95	XP: $10	D10
9/16-11/30	1P: $70	2P: $85	XP: $10	D10

Bed & Breakfast **Location:** Jct Hwy 2 and Rt 7, 3 mi (5 km) n on Rt 7. Located in a quiet rural area. Winsloe RR 10 C1E 1Z4.
Facility: This modern home featuring spacious guest rooms stands in a rural farming area surrounded by fields. Smoke free premises. 4 one-bedroom standard units, some with whirlpools. 1 story, interior corridors. **Parking:** on-site. **Terms:** open 5/1-11/30, office hours 8 am-11 pm, age restrictions may apply, 10 day cancellation notice-fee imposed. **Amenities:** hair dryers.
Cards: MC, VI.

NORTH RUSTICO pop. 637

──── WHERE TO STAY ────

GULF VIEW COTTAGES   **Phone:** 902/963-2052

6/24-9/4	1P: $140	2P: $140	XP: $12
5/24-6/23 & 9/5-10/8	1P: $85	2P: $85	XP: $10

Cottage **Location:** On Gulf Shore Rd. Located in PEI National Park. (PO Box 119, C0A 1X0). Fax: 902/963-3171.
Facility: 15 cottages. 1 story, exterior corridors. **Parking:** on-site. **Terms:** open 5/24-10/8, office hours 7 am-11 pm, 14 day cancellation notice-fee imposed, weekly rates available. **Amenities:** *Some:* DVD players (fee). **Leisure Activities:** playground. **Guest Services:** coin laundry. **Cards:** MC, VI.

SOME UNITS

ST. LAWRENCE MOTEL   **Phone:** (902)963-2053

7/4-8/17	1P: $69-$159	2P: $69-$159	XP: $7
6/16-7/3 & 8/18-9/30	1P: $60-$128	2P: $60-$128	XP: $7
5/17-6/15	1P: $49-$110	2P: $49-$110	XP: $7

Motel **Location:** On RR 2. Located in PEI National Park. 351 Gulf Shore Rd C0A 1N0. Fax: 902/963-2053.
Facility: Smoke free premises. 16 units. 7 one- and 9 two-bedroom standard units, some with kitchens. 1 story, exterior corridors. *Bath:* combo or shower only. **Parking:** on-site. **Terms:** open 5/17-9/30, office hours 8 am-10 pm, 14 day cancellation notice-fee imposed, weekly rates available, small pets only (in designated units). **Leisure Activities:** chipping range, driving range, playground, game room. **Guest Services:** coin laundry. **Cards:** AX, MC, VI.
Free Special Amenities: local telephone calls and preferred room (subject to availability with advance reservations).

SOME UNITS

SAINT NICHOLAS MOTEL   **Phone:** 902/963-2898

5/1-10/15	1P: $70	2P: $75	XP: $10

Motel **Location:** Triangle, just w on Rt 6. Located in a quiet rural setting. RR 3 Hunter River C0A 1N0 (Box 165). **Facility:** 18 one-bedroom standard units. 1 story, exterior corridors. **Parking:** on-site. **Terms:** open 5/1-10/15, office hours 7 am-11 pm, cancellation fee imposed. **Cards:** MC, VI.

──── WHERE TO DINE ────

FISHERMAN'S WHARF LOBSTER
SUPPERS & RESTAURANT *Menu on AAA.com*   **Lunch:** $6-$16   **Dinner:** $18-$30   **Phone:** 902/963-2669
Location: Centre. Main St (Rt 6) C0A 1X0. **Hours:** Open 5/15-10/31; 11 am-10 pm. **Reservations:** not accepted. **Features:** This spacious restaurant is a favorite for lobster suppers, which include lobster in the shell, steamed mussels, seafood chowder and the all-you-can-eat salad bar. Steak, ham and scallops also are offered. Baked goods are fresh and tasty. Casual dress; cocktails. **Parking:** on-site. **Cards:** AX, DC, MC, VI.

Seafood

RICHMOND

──── WHERE TO STAY ────

CAERNARVON COTTAGES, B&B AND GARDENS   **Phone:** 902/854-3418

6/15-9/15	1P: $100	2P: $100	XP: $10	F12

Cottage **Location:** Jct Hwy 2 and Rt 131, 6 mi (10 km) e. 4697 Hwy 12, RR 1 C0B 1Y0. **Facility:** A selection of cozy cottages is featured on the expansive grounds of this pleasant property overlooking the bay. 5 units. 1 three-bedroom suite. 4 cottages. 2 stories (no elevator), interior/exterior corridors. **Parking:** on-site. **Terms:** open 6/15-9/15, office hours 8 am-9 pm, 3 night minimum stay, 30 day cancellation notice, weekly rates available, pets (in cottages). **Amenities:** hair dryers. **Leisure Activities:** playground. **Cards:** MC, VI.
Free Special Amenities: local telephone calls and newspaper.

SOME UNITS

ROSENEATH

———— WHERE TO STAY ————

BRUDENELL FAIRWAY CHALETS
▽▽▽▽▽
Cottage

All Year   2P: $850-$1490   XP: $10   **Phone:** (902)652-2900
Location: Jct Rt 4 and 3, 4 mi (6 km) e on Rt 3. Located in a quiet rural area. 1068 Georgetown Rd C0A 1L0 (PO Box 30, GEORGETOWN). Fax: 902/838-2129. **Facility:** A choice of cottages, all with gas grills and screened porches, is offered at this pleasant property. 14 cottages. 1 story, exterior corridors. **Parking:** on-site.
Terms: office hours 8 am-10 pm, check-in 4 pm, 30 day cancellation notice-fee imposed, weekly rates available, package plans. **Amenities:** irons, hair dryers. **Pool(s):** heated outdoor. **Leisure Activities:** rental bicycles, playground, horseshoes, volleyball. **Guest Services:** complimentary laundry. **Cards:** MC, VI.

RODD BRUDENELL RIVER-A RODD SIGNATURE RESORT
▽▽▽▽
Resort
Large-scale Hotel

                                                   Phone: (902)652-2332
6/1-9/30   1P: $196-$246   2P: $196-$246   XP: $10   F16
5/15-5/31 & 10/1-10/15   1P: $131-$181   2P: $131-$181   XP: $10   F16
Location: Jct Rt 4 and 3, 3.3 mi (5.5 km) e on Rt 3. Located in Brudenell River Provincial Park. (PO Box 67, CARDIGAN, C0A 1G0). Fax: 902/652-2886. **Facility:** The resort, on spacious, manicured grounds overlooking a river and golf courses, offers pleasant hotel rooms, rustic chalets and roomy cottages. 181 units. 109 one-bedroom standard units. 6 one-bedroom suites ($167-$283), some with whirlpools. 50 cabins ($87-$178) and 16 cottages ($167-$536), some with whirlpools. 1-3 stories, interior/exterior corridors. **Parking:** on-site. **Terms:** open 5/15-10/15, 3 day cancellation notice-fee imposed, package plans, pets ($10 extra charge). **Amenities:** voice mail, hair dryers. *Some:* irons. **Dining:** Club 19-Fun Food Drink, Stillwaters-Fine Food & Spirits, see separate listings. **Pool(s):** heated outdoor, heated indoor, wading. **Leisure Activities:** sauna, whirlpool, rental canoes, rental sailboards, 2 lighted tennis courts, rental bicycles, hiking trails, playground, spa. *Fee:* boat dock, golf-45 holes, horseback riding. **Guest Services:** gift shop, valet laundry. **Business Services:** meeting rooms, PC. **Cards:** AX, DC, MC, VI. *(See color ad p 359)*

ROSENEATH BED & BREAKFAST
▽▽▽▽
Historic Bed
& Breakfast

All Year   1P: $90-$95   2P: $95-$99   **Phone:** 902/838-4590
Location: Off Rt 4, follow signs. Located in a quiet rural area. (RR 6, CARDIGAN, C0A 1G0). Fax: 902/838-4590. **Facility:** Gardens, a veranda and a tranquil riverfront setting distinguish this 1868 farmhouse-turned-bed and breakfast. Smoke free premises. 4 units. 3 one- and 1 two-bedroom standard units. 2 stories (no elevator), interior corridors. *Bath:* combo or shower only. **Parking:** on-site. **Terms:** 14 day cancellation notice-fee imposed, [BP] meal plan available, no pets allowed (owner's cats on premises). **Amenities:** hair dryers. **Leisure Activities:** bicycles, hiking trails. **Guest Services:** TV in common area, complimentary evening beverages, coin laundry, wireless Internet. **Business Services:** PC. **Cards:** MC, VI.

———— WHERE TO DINE ————

CLUB 19-FUN FOOD DRINK
▽▽▽
Canadian
DS, JC, MC, VI.

Lunch: $6-$14   **Dinner:** $9-$17   **Phone:** 902/652-2332
Location: Jct Rt 4 and 3, 3.3 mi (5.5 km) e on Rt 3; in Rodd Brudenell River-A Rodd Signature Resort. **Hours:** Open 5/15-10/31; 6:30 am-9 pm. **Reservations:** accepted. **Features:** In a lovely location overlooking the golf course, the casual, pub-style restaurant offers a wide selection of Canadian fare for breakfast, lunch or dinner. Patio dining is a nice option in season. Casual dress; cocktails. **Parking:** on-site. **Cards:** AX, DC,

STILLWATERS-FINE FOOD & SPIRITS
▽▽▽▽
Canadian

Dinner: $24-$36   **Phone:** 902/652-2332
Location: Jct Rt 4 and 3, 3.3 mi (5.5 km) e on Rt 3; in Rodd Brudenell River-A Rodd Signature Resort. **Hours:** Open 6/1-9/30; 6 pm-11 pm. Closed: Mon. **Reservations:** required. **Features:** The cozy, bistro-style dining room affords a lovely view of the golf course and the Brudenell River through its glass walls. The chef prepares fresh local seafood and meat entrees with a creative flair. The selection of wines and cocktails is ample.
Casual dress; cocktails. **Parking:** on-site. **Cards:** AX, DC, DS, JC, MC, VI.

RUSTICOVILLE

———— WHERE TO DINE ————

DAYBOAT PEI
▽▽▽▽
Canadian

Lunch: $8-$14   **Dinner:** $14-$25   **Phone:** 902/963-3833
Location: On Rt 6; at Oyster Bed Bridge. 5033 Rustico Rd C0A 1N0. **Hours:** Open 6/1-10/26; noon-9 pm. **Reservations:** suggested, for dinner. **Features:** Patrons can sit either on the large deck or in the comfortable, airy dining room to enjoy the view of the Wheatley River and surrounding hills. The menu selection includes just-off-the-boat seafood, quality meats and fresh produce. Casual dress; cocktails.
Parking: on-site. **Cards:** AX, MC, VI.

ST. ANN pop. 100

———— WHERE TO DINE ————

ST. ANN'S CHURCH LOBSTER SUPPERS
▽▽▽▽
Seafood
Cards: MC, VI.

Dinner: $20-$36   **Phone:** 902/621-0635
Location: On Rt 224, midway between Stanley Bridge and Hunter River. **Hours:** Open 6/15-9/30; 4 pm-8:30 pm. Closed: Sun. **Features:** Since 1964, the restaurant has delivered fine, flavorful lobster dinners accompanied by salad, chowder, mussels, dessert and coffee. The congenial atmosphere is welcoming to families. The professional staff provides courteous, attentive service. Casual dress; cocktails. **Parking:** on-site.

ST. PETERS

―――― WHERE TO STAY ――――

GREENWICH GATE LODGE **Phone: 902/961-3496**
▽▽▽ All Year 1P: $79-$119 2P: $79-$119 XP: $5
Motel **Location:** Jct Rt 2 and 16; centre. Rt 2 C0A 2A0 (Box 14). Fax: 902/961-3342. **Facility:** 12 one-bedroom standard units, some with kitchens and/or whirlpools. 1 story, exterior corridors. **Parking:** on-site. **Terms:** office hours 7 am-10 pm, 7 day cancellation notice, package plans, small pets only. **Amenities:** hair dryers. **Guest Services:** wireless Internet. **Cards:** AX, DC, MC, VI.

SOME UNITS
(ASK) (S/D) 🐾 🍴 🗙 ☕ / 🛏 🖥 /

THE INN AT ST. PETERS **Phone: (902)961-2135**
(CAA) (SAVE) 7/1-9/23 [MAP] 1P: $315-$340 2P: $365-$390 XP: $75 F11
▽▽▽▽▽ 5/25-6/30 [MAP] 1P: $295-$315 2P: $340-$365 XP: $75 F11
 9/24-10/8 [MAP] 1P: $290-$315 2P: $340-$365 XP: $75 F11
Country Inn **Location:** Jct Rt 16 and 313, 0.6 mi (1 km) w on Rt 313; in The Inn at St. Peters. 1668 Greenwich Rd C0A 2A0. Fax: 902/961-2238. **Facility:** A splendid bay and garden view can be enjoyed from private decks at the inn's spacious, tastefully decorated guest rooms. 16 one-bedroom standard units. 1 story, exterior corridors. **Parking:** on-site. **Terms:** open 5/25-10/8, 2 night minimum stay - seasonal, 7 day cancellation notice-fee imposed, small pets only ($10 extra charge, in limited units). **Amenities:** video library, voice mail, hair dryers. **Dining:** restaurant, see separate listing. **Leisure Activities:** bicycles. **Guest Services:** wireless Internet. **Cards:** MC, VI. **Free Special Amenities: full breakfast and high-speed Internet.**

🐾 🍴 🍸 ☕/M 🗙 (VCR) 🛏 ▣
FEE

―――― WHERE TO DINE ――――

THE INN AT ST. PETERS DINING **Phone: 902/961-2135**
ROOM Lunch: $12-$16 Dinner: $26-$36
(CAA) **Location:** Jct Rt 16 and 313, 0.6 mi (1 km) w on Rt 313; in The Inn at St. Peters. 1668 Greenwich Rd C0A 2A0. **Hours:** Open 5/20-10/31; 7-9:30 am, 11:30-2 & 5-9 pm. **Reservations:** suggested. **Features:** The bright
▽▽▽▽ and airy dining room affords splendid views of St. Peters Bay and the landscaped grounds. Service is attentive yet relaxed. Fine ingredients, fresh local produce, seafood, meats and the chef's skill merge to
Canadian create a memorable meal. Dressy casual; cocktails. **Parking:** on-site. **Cards:** MC, VI. **Country Inn** 🍸

RICK'S FISH'N'CHIPS & SEAFOOD HOUSE Lunch: $4-$8 Dinner: $5-$10 **Phone: 902/961-3438**
▽▽ **Location:** Jct Rt 2 and 16; centre. Rt 2 C0A 2A0. **Hours:** Open 5/15-9/30; 11 am-10 pm; to 7 pm, Fri & Sat-9 pm
Canadian off season. **Features:** The popular seafood take-out bar offers indoor and outdoor seating. Portions are ample, and the French fries are hand-cut on site. Casual dress; beer & wine only. **Parking:** on-site.
Cards: MC, VI. 🍷

SOURIS pop. 1,248

―――― WHERE TO STAY ――――

ROLLO BAY INN *Book at AAA.com* **Phone: (902)687-3550**
▽▽ ▽▽▽ 5/1-9/1 1P: $89-$600 2P: $99-$600 XP: $10 F12
 9/2-10/14 1P: $70-$475 2P: $80-$475 XP: $10 F12
Small-scale Hotel 10/15-4/30 1P: $65-$475 2P: $75-$475 XP: $5 F12
Location: 2.5 mi (4 km) w on Hwy 2. Located in a rural area. (RR 1, C0A 2B0). Fax: 902/687-3570. **Facility:** Smoke free premises. 20 one-bedroom standard units, some with efficiencies. 2 stories (no elevator), interior/exterior corridors. **Parking:** on-site. **Terms:** weekly rates available. **Guest Services:** wireless Internet. **Business Services:** PC. **Cards:** AX, DS, MC, VI.

SOME UNITS
🗙 / 🛏 🖥

―――― *The following lodging was either not evaluated or did not* ――――
meet AAA rating requirements but is listed for your information only.

THE MATTHEW HOUSE INN **Phone: 902/687-3461**
(fyi) Not evaluated. **Location:** Centre. 15 Breakwater St C0A 2B0. Facilities, services, and decor characterize a mid-range property.

―――― WHERE TO DINE ――――

BLUEFIN RESTAURANT Lunch: $6-$9 Dinner: $9-$15 **Phone: 902/687-3271**
▽▽▽ ▽▽▽ **Location:** Just s of Main St; centre. 10 Federal Ave C0A 2B0. **Hours:** 6:30 am-10 pm; to 7 pm off season, Sun from 7:30 am. Closed major holidays. **Features:** The spacious, country-style diner has booth seating and
Canadian pleasant servers. Well-prepared home-style cooking includes fresh breads and pastries baked daily. Casual dress; cocktails. **Parking:** on-site. **Cards:** AX, MC, VI. 🍸

SOUTH RUSTICO

―――― WHERE TO STAY ――――

―――― *The following lodging was either not evaluated or did not* ――――
meet AAA rating requirements but is listed for your information only.

BARACHOIS INN **Phone: 902-963-2194**
(fyi) Not evaluated. **Location:** On Rt 143; centre. 2193 Church Rd C1A 7M4 (RR 3, HUNTER RIVER, C0A 1N0). Facilities, services, and decor characterize a mid-range property.

STANLEY BRIDGE

——— WHERE TO STAY ———

INN AT THE PIER   **Phone:** (902)886-3126

(CAA) (SAVE)   6/28-9/4 [ECP]   1P: $139-$239   2P: $139-$239   XP: $10   F3
                5/1-6/27 & 9/5-10/30 [ECP] 1P: $89-$189   2P: $89-$189   XP: $10   F3
◊◊◊◊◊   **Location:** On Rt 6, 3.6 mi (6 km) w of Cavendish; centre. 9796 Cavendish Rd C0A 1E0. Fax: 902/886-3126.
Small-scale Hotel   **Facility:** Smoke free premises. 17 units. 15 one-bedroom standard units, some with whirlpools. 2 one-
bedroom suites with whirlpools. 2 stories (no elevator), interior/exterior corridors. **Parking:** on-site.
Terms: open 5/1-10/30, office hours 7 am-11 pm, check-in 4 pm, cancellation fee imposed, weekly rates
available, package plans. **Amenities:** irons, hair dryers. **Pool(s):** heated outdoor. **Leisure Activities:** whirlpool, boat dock,
snorkeling & rental equipment, parasailing, kayaks. **Guest Services:** coin laundry, wireless Internet. **Business Services:**
meeting rooms. **Cards:** AX, DC, MC, VI. **Free Special Amenities: expanded continental breakfast and local telephone
calls.**

SOME UNITS
⊇ ⊠ ⊠ ▱ / ⊟ ⊡ /

——— WHERE TO DINE ———

CARR'S OYSTER BAR RESTAURANT & LOUNGE   **Lunch:** $7-$22   **Dinner:** $10-$30   **Phone:** 902/886-3355
◊◊◊◊   **Location:** At Rt 6 and 238. Campbellton Rd C0A 1E0. **Hours:** Open 5/20-10/31; 11 am-9 pm.
Seafood   **Reservations:** accepted. **Features:** On the harbourfront, the restaurant focuses its menu on fresh seafood
but also prepares such comfort foods as burgers and sandwiches. Patrons of this casual spot can relax
either indoors or out on the deck. Casual dress; cocktails. **Parking:** on-site. **Cards:** MC, VI.   (K)

STRATFORD pop. 6,314

——— WHERE TO STAY ———

——— *The following lodging was either not evaluated or did not* ———
meet AAA rating requirements but is listed for your information only.

SOUTHPORT MOTEL   **Phone:** 902/569-2287
(fyi)   Did not meet all AAA rating requirements for locking devices in some guest rooms at time of last
Motel   evaluation. **Location:** Trans-Canada Hwy 1, just s on Stratford Rd, then 1.2 mi (2 km) e of Charlottetown over Bridge.
20 Stratford Rd C1B 1T5. Facilities, services, and decor characterize a basic property.

SUMMERSIDE pop. 14,654

——— WHERE TO STAY ———

CAIRNS MOTEL   **Phone:** 902/436-5841
◊◊◊   6/15-8/25   1P: $59-$69   2P: $59-$69
       8/26-11/30   1P: $47-$56   2P: $47-$56   XP: $2   F20
Motel   5/1-6/14   1P: $47-$54   2P: $47-$54   XP: $2   F20
Location: 1.3 mi (2.4 km) e on Hwy 11. 721 Water St E C1N 4J2. **Facility:** 15 one-bedroom standard units. 1
story, exterior corridors. *Bath:* combo or shower only. **Parking:** on-site, winter plug-ins. **Terms:** open 5/1-11/30, office hours 7:30
am-10 pm. **Amenities:** hair dryers. **Cards:** AX, MC, VI.

⊠ ☎ ⊟

CLARK'S SUNNY ISLE MOTEL   **Phone:** 902/436-5665
◊◊◊   6/15-9/30   1P: $50-$63   2P: $50-$63   XP: $5   D12
       5/1-6/14 & 10/1-10/30 1P: $46-$52   2P: $46-$52   XP: $5   D12
Motel   **Location:** 1.4 mi (2.4 km) e on Hwy 11. 720 Water St E C1N 4J1. **Facility:** 21 one-bedroom standard units. 1
story, exterior corridors. **Parking:** on-site. **Terms:** open 5/1-10/30. **Amenities:** hair dryers. **Guest Services:**
wireless Internet. **Business Services:** PC. **Cards:** AX, DC, MC, VI.

⊠ ☎ ⊟ ⊡

ECONO LODGE   *Book great rates at AAA.com*   **Phone:** (902)436-9100
◊◊◊ ◊◊◊   6/16-9/30   1P: $100-$130   2P: $100-$130   XP: $10   F18
           1/1-4/30   1P: $95-$115   2P: $95-$115   XP: $10   F18
Small-scale Hotel   5/1-6/15 & 10/1-12/31 1P: $90-$110   2P: $90-$110   XP: $10   F18
Location: Jct Hwy 1A and 2, 3.1 mi (5 km) w on Hwy 2. Located in a rural area. 80 All Weather Hwy C1N 4P3.
Fax: 902/436-8805. **Facility:** 40 one-bedroom standard units, some with efficiencies. 1 story, interior corridors. **Parking:** on-site.
Terms: small pets only. **Amenities:** hair dryers. **Pool(s):** heated indoor. **Guest Services:** wireless Internet. **Business
Services:** meeting rooms. **Cards:** AX, DC, DS, MC, VI. *(See color ad card insert)*

SOME UNITS
(ASK) (SD) 🐾 ⑪ ⊻ ⊇ ▱ / ⊠ ⊟ /

**THE LOYALIST LAKEVIEW RESORT &
  CONFERENCE CENTRE**   *Book great rates at AAA.com*   **Phone:** (902)436-3333
◊◊◊◊   6/1-9/30   1P: $142-$199   2P: $142-$199   XP: $10   F18
        5/1-5/31 & 10/1-4/30 1P: $102-$116   2P: $102-$116   XP: $10   F18
Small-scale Hotel   **Location:** Centre of downtown. 195 Harbour Dr C1N 5R1. Fax: 902/436-4304. **Facility:** 103 one-bedroom
standard units, some with whirlpools. 3 stories, interior corridors. **Parking:** on-site. **Terms:** 14 day
cancellation notice. **Amenities:** video library, voice mail, irons, hair dryers. **Dining:** Crown & Anchor Tavern, Prince William
Dining Room, see separate listings. **Pool(s):** heated indoor. **Leisure Activities:** sauna, exercise room. *Fee:* bicycles. **Guest
Services:** gift shop, valet laundry, wireless Internet. **Business Services:** meeting rooms, PC. **Cards:** AX, DC, MC, VI.
(See color ad on TourBookMark)

SOME UNITS
(ASK) (SD) ⑪ ⊻ 🄼 ⊇ ⊠ (VCR) ▱ / ⊠ ⊟ ⊡ /

QUALITY INN GARDEN OF THE GULF   *Book great rates at AAA.com*   Phone: (902)436-2295

(CAA) (SAVE)

	5/31-9/30	1P: $144-$194	2P: $144-$194	XP: $10	F18
	5/1-5/30 & 10/1-4/30	1P: $86-$114	2P: $86-$114	XP: $10	F18

Motel

Location: 1 mi (1.6 km) e on Hwy 11. 618 Water St C1N 2V5 (PO Box 1627). Fax: 902/432-2915. **Facility:** 94 one-bedroom standard units, some with whirlpools. 2 stories (no elevator), interior/exterior corridors. *Bath:* combo or shower only. **Parking:** on-site. **Terms:** [BP] meal plan available, package plans, pets (in selected units). **Amenities:** voice mail, hair dryers. *Some:* irons. **Pool(s):** heated outdoor, heated indoor. **Leisure Activities:** golf-9 holes, golf club rentals, limited exercise equipment. **Guest Services:** sundries, valet laundry, wireless Internet. **Business Services:** meeting rooms. **Cards:** AX, MC, VI. *(See color ad card insert)*

SOME UNITS

🅂🄳 🛏 📶 ➿ 🖥 / ✖ VCR 🗄 🖨 /
FEE

SLEMON PARK HOTEL & CONFERENCE CENTRE   Phone: (902)432-1780

(CAA) (SAVE)

	1/1-4/30	1P: $95	2P: $105	XP: $10	F18
	5/1-12/31	1P: $90	2P: $100	XP: $10	F18

Small-scale Hotel

Location: On Rt 2, 3 mi (5 km) w at Summerside Airport. 12 Redwood Ave C0B 1T0. Fax: 902/436-4523. **Facility:** 119 units. 76 one-bedroom standard units, some with whirlpools. 43 one-bedroom suites ($110-$115) with efficiencies (no utensils). 2 stories (no elevator), interior corridors. *Bath:* combo or shower only. **Parking:** on-site. **Terms:** package plans, pets ($200 deposit, in limited units). **Amenities:** high-speed Internet, voice mail, hair dryers. **Dining:** 6:30 am-8 pm, Fri & Sat-9 pm, cocktails. **Business Services:** meeting rooms. **Cards:** AX, DC, MC, VI. **Free Special Amenities:** local telephone calls and high-speed Internet.

SOME UNITS

🅂🄳 🛏 📶 🍽 Ⓨ 🔌ⓜ 🖥 🖳 / ✖ 🗄 🖨 /
FEE

——— WHERE TO DINE ———

BROTHERS TWO RESTAURANT   **Lunch:** $8-$14   **Dinner:** $10-$21   Phone: 902/436-9654

Location: 1 mi (1.6 km) e on Hwy 11. 618 Water St E C1N 4K2. **Hours:** 11:30 am-10 pm, Sun-9 pm; hours vary off season. Closed: 12/25. **Reservations:** suggested. **Features:** The atmosphere is casual and upbeat in the three dining rooms and on the enclosed deck. Family-owned since 1971, the restaurant delivers such delicious selections as pizza and preparations of pasta, seafood and steak. Service is friendly and fast. In season, this place offers the popular Feast Dinner Theatre. Casual dress; cocktails; entertainment. **Parking:** on-site. **Cards:** AX, DC, MC, VI.

Canadian

Ⓨ

CHINA STAR RESTAURANT   **Lunch:** $5-$10   **Dinner:** $8-$18   Phone: 902/888-3228

Location: At Summer St; centre. 265 Water St C1N 1K8. **Hours:** 11:30 am-11 pm, Fri-3 am, Sat-2 am. Closed: 12/25, 12/26. **Reservations:** accepted. **Features:** Guests are seated in either of two pleasant dining sections to browse the menu of Cantonese and Szechuan entrees, including combination plates and daily lunch specials. Casual dress; cocktails. **Parking:** street. **Cards:** MC, VI.

Chinese

CROWN & ANCHOR TAVERN   **Lunch:** $6-$11   **Dinner:** $12-$21   Phone: 902/436-3333

Location: Centre of downtown; in The Loyalist Lakeview Resort & Conference Centre. 195 Harbour Dr C1N 5R1. **Hours:** 11 am-11 pm, Fri & Sat-midnight. **Features:** A nice port in a storm, the restaurant offers guests casual, friendly service and a menu that centers on traditional pub fare. Among offerings are fish and chips, burgers and stir-fries. Casual dress; cocktails. **Parking:** on-site. **Cards:** AX, DC, MC, VI.

Canadian

Ⓨ

GENTLEMAN JIM'S RESTAURANT   **Lunch:** $6-$12   **Dinner:** $11-$19   Phone: 902/888-2647

(CAA)

Location: Across from the County Fair Mall; centre. 480 Granville St C1N 4K6. **Hours:** 9:30 am-9 pm, Fri & Sat-10 pm. Closed: 12/25, 12/26. **Reservations:** accepted. **Features:** A country theme, with antique lanterns and pictures of islands and ferries, weaves through the casual, family-oriented restaurant. Seafood chowder and rib steak represent traditional surf and turf fare. The coconut cream pie delights the taste buds. Casual dress; cocktails. **Parking:** on-site. **Cards:** AX, DC, MC, VI.

Canadian

PRINCE WILLIAM DINING ROOM   **Lunch:** $8-$15   **Dinner:** $14-$24   Phone: 902/436-3333

Location: Centre of downtown; in The Loyalist Lakeview Resort & Conference Centre. 195 Harbour Dr C1N 5R1. **Hours:** 7 am-2 & 5-10 pm, Sun 7 am-2 & 4-9 pm; hours may vary off season. **Reservations:** accepted. **Features:** In the evening, soft candlelight enhances the elegant atmosphere of the attractive dining room. The menu includes fresh local seafood, prime cuts of meat and some pasta dishes. Service is relaxed and friendly. Casual dress; cocktails. **Parking:** on-site. **Cards:** AX, DC, MC, VI.

Canadian

Ⓨ

STARLITE DINER AND DAIRY BAR   **Lunch:** $5-$10   **Dinner:** $7-$13   Phone: 902/436-7752

Location: Jct Hwy 1A and 11. 810 Water St C1N 4J6. **Hours:** Open 5/1-10/21 & 4/15-4/30; 7 am-10 pm; hours vary off season. **Features:** Patrons experience a flashback to the '50s in this upbeat, rock 'n' roll diner. Great hamburgers, seafood platters and sandwiches ground the menu. Shakes and floats have satisfied sugar cravings since 1959. The commercial location borders the highway. Casual dress; beer & wine only. **Parking:** on-site. **Cards:** MC, VI.

Canadian

TIGNISH pop. 831

——— WHERE TO STAY ———

DRIFTWOOD COUNTRY COTTAGES   Phone: 902/882-2617

	5/1-8/31	1P: $165-$195	2P: $165-$195	XP: $10	F12
	9/1-4/30		2P: $99-$146	XP: $10	F12

Cottage

Location: 2.5 mi (4 km) n on Rt 12. (Box 423, C0B 2B0). Fax: 902/882-3144. **Facility:** These spacious, chalet-style executive cottages border the ocean; all have screened porches and fireplaces. 6 cottages, some with whirlpools. 2 stories (no elevator), exterior corridors. **Parking:** on-site. **Terms:** check-in 4 pm, 30 day cancellation notice, weekly rates available. **Amenities:** *Some:* DVD players. **Guest Services:** coin laundry, wireless Internet. **Cards:** AX, MC, VI.

SOME UNITS

✖ 🐾 🗄 🖨 🖥 / VCR

TIGNISH HERITAGE INN & GARDENS
Phone: 902/882-2491

◈◈ ◈◈	6/16-9/15 [CP]	1P: $70-$110	2P: $70-$110	XP: $10	F6
	5/15-6/15 & 9/16-10/15 [CP]	1P: $60-$110	2P: $60-$110	XP: $10	F6

Small-scale Hotel   **Location:** Adjacent to St Simon and St Jude Church; centre. 206 Maple St C0B 2B0 (PO Box 398). Fax: 902/882-2500. **Facility:** Smoke free premises. 17 units. 15 one-bedroom standard units. 2 one-bedroom suites. 3 stories (no elevator), interior corridors. *Bath:* combo or shower only. **Parking:** on-site. **Terms:** open 5/15-10/15, office hours 7 am-11 pm, weekly rates available. **Amenities:** hair dryers. **Cards:** AX, MC, VI.

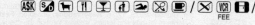

WEST POINT

——— **WHERE TO STAY** ———

——— *The following lodging was either not evaluated or did not* ———
meet AAA rating requirements but is listed for your information only.

WEST POINT LIGHTHOUSE
Phone: 902/859-3605

[fyi]   Not evaluated. **Location:** Oceanfront. On Rt 14; centre. RR 2 O'Leary C0B 1V0. Facilities, services, and decor characterize a mid-range property.

WOOD ISLANDS

——— **WHERE TO STAY** ———

MEADOW LODGE MOTEL
Phone: (902)962-2022

◈	7/1-8/31	1P: $74-$93	2P: $74-$93	XP: $7	F6
	5/18-6/30 & 9/1-9/30	1P: $61-$77	2P: $61-$77	XP: $7	F6

Motel   **Location:** 1 mi (1.6 km) nw of Wood Islands ferry terminal. Trans-Canada Hwy 1, Civic #313 C0A 1B0. Fax: 902/962-2017. **Facility:** 18 units. 16 one- and 2 two-bedroom standard units, some with kitchens. 1 story, exterior corridors. **Parking:** on-site. **Terms:** open 5/18-9/30. **Cards:** MC, VI.

WOODSTOCK

——— **WHERE TO STAY** ———

RODD MILL RIVER RESORT   *Book great rates at AAA.com*
Phone: (902)859-3555

◈◈ ◈◈	6/1-9/30	1P: $106-$211	2P: $106-$211	XP: $10	F16
	5/15-5/31, 10/1-10/15 & 1/20-3/25	1P: $91-$170	2P: $91-$170	XP: $10	F16

Resort   **Location:** On Rt 136, just e of jct Rt 2. Located in Mill River Provincial Park. Rt 180 C0B 1V0 (PO Box 399, O'LEARY).
Small-scale Hotel   Fax: 902/859-2486. **Facility:** The hotel, which overlooks a golf course, offers recreational facilities. 90 units. 87 one-bedroom standard units. 2 one- and 1 two-bedroom suites ($150-$293), some with kitchens. 3 stories (no elevator), interior corridors. **Parking:** on-site. **Terms:** open 5/15-10/15 & 1/20-3/25, check-in 4 pm, 3 day cancellation notice-fee imposed, [BP] & [MAP] meal plans available, package plans, small pets only. **Amenities:** video library (fee), irons, hair dryers. **Dining:** The Hernewood Dining Room, see separate listing. **Pool(s):** heated indoor. **Leisure Activities:** sauna, whirlpool, waterslide, rental canoes, marina, 4 tennis courts (2 lighted), racquetball courts, cross country skiing, ice skating, tobogganing, recreation programs, rental bicycles, hiking trails, playground, exercise room. *Fee:* golf-18 holes, massage. **Guest Services:** gift shop, wireless Internet. **Business Services:** meeting rooms. **Cards:** AX, DC, DS, MC, VI. *(See color ad p 359)*

SOME UNITS

FEE

——— **WHERE TO DINE** ———

THE HERNEWOOD DINING ROOM   **Lunch:** $7-$14   **Dinner:** $10-$22   **Phone:** 902/859-3555

◈◈ ◈◈   **Location:** On Rt 136, just e of jct Rt 2; in Rodd Mill River Resort. Rt 180 C0B 1V0. **Hours:** Open 5/1-10/15 & 2/1-3/31; 7 am-2 & 5-10 pm; to 9 pm off season. **Reservations:** accepted. **Features:** The delightful location
Canadian   overlooks the golf course, and the views are particularly good from the seasonal deck. The menu outlines a fine selection of fresh seafood and meat entrees, all served in ample portions. Casual dress; cocktails. **Parking:** on-site. **Cards:** AX, DC, DS, JC, MC, VI.

Québec

Île-aux-Coudres / © MTOQ
Marc Archambault

Some municipalities in Quebec have or soon will combine with neighboring cities. These mergers will eliminate existing cities and may affect street names, addresses and political boundaries referenced in this guide. For further information, please contact Quebec governing agencies or the local CAA club.

ALMA pop. 25,918

——— WHERE TO STAY ———

COMFORT INN *Book great rates at AAA.com*   **Phone:** (418)668-9221

6/21-9/3	1P: $90-$135	2P: $100-$145	XP: $10 F18
5/1-6/20 & 9/4-4/30	1P: $80-$108	2P: $90-$118	XP: $10 F18

Small-scale Hotel **Location:** On Hwy 169; centre of town. 870 ave du Pont S G8B 2V8. Fax: 418/668-4549. **Facility:** 60 one-bedroom standard units. 2 stories (no elevator), interior corridors. **Parking:** on-site, winter plug-ins. **Terms:** [CP] meal plan available, pets (in smoking units). **Amenities:** irons, hair dryers. **Guest Services:** valet laundry, wireless Internet. **Cards:** AX, DC, DS, JC, MC, VI. *(See color ad card insert)*

SOME UNITS

HOTEL MOTEL LES CASCADES   **Phone:** (418)662-6547

9/5-4/30	1P: $62-$85	2P: $69-$92	XP: $7 F6
6/24-9/4	1P: $75-$80	2P: $82-$87	XP: $7 F6
5/1-6/23	1P: $56-$75	2P: $62-$83	XP: $7 F6

Motel **Location:** On Hwy 169, just n of bridge; centre. 140 ave du Pont N G8B 5C2. Fax: 418/668-6547. **Facility:** 58 one-bedroom standard units, some with whirlpools. 2 stories (no elevator), interior/exterior corridors. **Parking:** on-site, winter plug-ins. **Terms:** small pets only. **Amenities:** *Some:* honor bars. **Business Services:** meeting rooms. **Cards:** MC, VI.

SOME UNITS

HOTEL UNIVERSAL   **Phone:** (418)668-5261

5/1-10/31	1P: $84-$144	2P: $84-$144	XP: $10 F18
11/1-4/30	1P: $62-$132	2P: $62-$132	XP: $10 F18

Large-scale Hotel **Location:** Centre. 1000 boul des Cascades G8B 3G4. Fax: 418/668-9161. **Facility:** 71 one-bedroom standard units, some with whirlpools. 4 stories, interior corridors. **Parking:** on-site. **Terms:** check-in 4 pm, [AP], [BP], [CP] & [MAP] meal plans available, package plans. **Dining:** Restaurant Le Bordelais, see separate listing. **Leisure Activities:** whirlpools, snowmobiling, bicycles, limited exercise equipment, spa. **Guest Services:** valet laundry, wireless Internet. **Business Services:** conference facilities, administrative services (fee), PC. **Cards:** AX, DC, DS, MC, VI. **Free Special Amenities:** full breakfast and high-speed Internet.

SOME UNITS

——— WHERE TO DINE ———

CHEZ MARIO TREMBLAY-BAR-RESTAURANT   **Lunch:** $8-$10   **Dinner:** $9-$35   **Phone:** 418/668-7231

Steak & Seafood **Location:** Just s of rue St-Joseph; centre. 534 ave Collard ouest G9B 1N2. **Hours:** 10 am-11 pm, Fri & Sat-midnight. **Reservations:** accepted. **Features:** This popular restaurant and bar—co-owned by former pro hockey player and coach Mario Tremblay—serves up great pub fare, including AAA Alberta steaks, seafood, ribs, chicken and pizza. Try the delicious house-prepared sugar pie. A display of Montreal Canadiens memorabilia adorns the walls. Casual dress; cocktails. **Parking:** on-site. **Cards:** AX, DC, MC, VI.

RESTAURANT LE BORDELAIS   **Lunch:** $9-$14   **Dinner:** $16-$33   **Phone:** 418/668-7419

French **Location:** Centre; in Hotel Universal. 1000 boul des Cascades ouest G8B 3G4. **Hours:** 7 am-10 pm, Sat & Sun 8 am-11 pm. **Reservations:** suggested. **Features:** The comfortable hotel restaurant offers something for everyone on a varied menu of fine French cuisine, Canadian-Chinese food, lighter pub-style dishes and children's meals. Interesting selections include guinea fowl, beef filet, stuffed chicken, Charlevoix veal, magret of duck, lamb and a fresh fish of the day. Dressy casual; cocktails. **Parking:** on-site. **Cards:** AX, DS, MC, VI.

RESTO ROBERTO   **Lunch:** $7-$13   **Dinner:** $8-$26   **Phone:** 418/662-2191

Italian **Location:** On Hwy 169. 11 rue Scott est G8B 1B6. **Hours:** 24 hours. **Reservations:** accepted. **Features:** The family-friendly pizzeria has a comfortable, casual decor, and its varied menu is sure to please everyone. In addition to gourmet and traditional pizzas, the menu lists egg rolls, French onion soup, chicken cooked over charcoal, burgers, ribs, combination platters, pasta dishes, coquilles St. Jacques, fish and chips, smoked meat, club sandwiches, fajitas and hot submarine sandwiches. Casual dress; cocktails. **Parking:** on-site. **Cards:** AX, MC, VI.

ANJOU —See Montreal p. 480.

Lodging Reservation and Deposit Definitions

Reservation:

A temporary hold on lodgings, usually until 4 or 6 p.m. on the arrival date.

Reservation Confirmation:

Once the reservation process is complete, a "confirmation number" is assigned to the guest for future reference. When ample notice is given, a copy of the reservation details and confirmation number is mailed to the guest.

Credit Card Guaranteed Reservation:

When reserved lodgings have been secured with a credit card number, the room will be held for the first night regardless of arrival time, but will be billed to the credit card if the guest fails to arrive at all (is a "no show"). Credit card guarantees usually pertain to the first night only.

Reservation Deposit:

These funds are collected from the guest in advance of arrival to secure reserved lodgings. A reservation deposit can be in the form of cash, check, money order, credit card transaction or other means to transfer funds. One or more days' payment may be required depending on the length of the stay.

Prepaid Reservation:

Reserved lodgings that are fully paid in advance of arrival.

Cancellation Policy:

Published terms/conditions set by lodging by which the guest can cancel a reservation and recover all, or a portion of, the deposit/full payment. Sometimes a "service charge" or "cancellation fee" is levied regardless of how far in advance the reservation was cancelled.

Cancellation Number:

Upon receipt of a cancellation, it is customary for lodgings to assign a "cancellation number" that is given to the caller for future reference.

One coupon per room per stay. Valid on each night of stay; no copies or facsimiles accepted.

Not valid for groups or in conjunction with any other discount, promotion or special event. Subject to availability.

Coupon has no cash value. 2007CAA AC-QC

One coupon per room per stay. Valid on each night of stay; no copies or facsimiles accepted.

Not valid for groups or in conjunction with any other discount, promotion or special event. Subject to availability.

Coupon has no cash value. 2007CAA AC-QC

One coupon per room per stay. Valid on each night of stay; no copies or facsimiles accepted.

Not valid for groups or in conjunction with any other discount, promotion or special event. Subject to availability.

Coupon has no cash value. 2007CAA AC-QC

One coupon per room per stay. Valid on each night of stay; no copies or facsimiles accepted.

Not valid for groups or in conjunction with any other discount, promotion or special event. Subject to availability.

Coupon has no cash value. 2007CAA AC-QC

------ **WHERE TO STAY** ------

AUBERGE RIPPLECOVE INN

CAA [SAVE]
Country Inn
▼▼▼ ▼▼▼▼

6/22-10/9	1P: $157-$331	2P: $175-$375	XP: $65	D12
10/10-4/30	1P: $135-$275	2P: $153-$310	XP: $65	D12
5/1-6/21	1P: $129-$270	2P: $149-$303	XP: $65	D12

Phone: (819)838-4296

Location: Hwy 55, exit 21, 5 mi (8 km) s on Rt 141. 700 Ripplecove Rd J0B 1C0. Fax: 819/838-5541. **Facility:** An interesting mix of styles characterizes this upscale lakefront inn surrounded by well-tended lawns and gardens. 34 units. 26 one-bedroom standard units. 5 one-bedroom suites ($308-$415) with whirlpools. 1 vacation home ($400-$500) and 2 cottages ($400-$500). 3 stories (no elevator), interior corridors. **Bath:** combo or shower only. **Parking:** on-site, winter plug-ins. **Terms:** check-in 4 pm, age restrictions may apply, 14 day cancellation notice, [AP], [BP], [CP] & [MAP] meal plans available, package plans. **Amenities:** voice mail. Some: CD players, honor bars, irons. **Dining:** restaurant, see separate listing. **Pool(s):** 2 heated outdoor. **Leisure Activities:** whirlpool, boating, canoeing, paddleboats, sailboats, boat dock, fishing, kayaks, lighted tennis court, cross country skiing, snowmobiling, ice skating, snowshoeing, skate rentals, bicycles, spa. Fee: Saturday lake cruises. **Guest Services:** valet laundry, wireless Internet. **Business Services:** meeting rooms, business center. **Cards:** AX, MC, VI. **Free Special Amenities:** newspaper and early check-in/late check-out.

SOME UNITS

[❤️] [🏊] [✕] / [✕] [VCR] [🛗] [🔲] [▭] /

------ **WHERE TO DINE** ------

AUBERGE RIPPLECOVE INN DINING ROOM   *Menu on AAA.com*

CAA
▼▼▼ ▼▼▼▼
French

Lunch: $13-$23   **Dinner:** $52-$85   **Phone:** 819/838-4296

Location: Hwy 55, exit 21, 5 mi (8 km) s on Rt 141; in Auberge Ripplecove Inn. 700 Ripplecove Rd J0B 1C0. **Hours:** 8 am-10, noon-2 & 6-9:30 pm. Closed: for lunch weekdays 10/7-5/1. **Reservations:** suggested. **Features:** Overlooking Lake Massawippi, the upscale dining room and outdoor terrace are favorite spots for an elegant, sophisticated experience. The innovative menu includes such artfully presented selections as veal sweetbreads, Eastern Townships duck, filet of beef, rack of lamb, seasonal lobster, fresh fish and game. Semi-formal attire; cocktails. **Parking:** on-site. **Cards:** AX, MC, VI. **Country Inn**

[Ⓨ]

BAIE-COMEAU pop. 23,079

------ **WHERE TO STAY** ------

COMFORT INN   *Book great rates at AAA.com*

▼▼ ▼▼
Small-scale Hotel

1/1-4/30	1P: $107-$118	2P: $117-$128	XP: $10	F18
6/1-9/30	1P: $107-$117	2P: $117-$127	XP: $10	F18
5/1-5/31 & 10/1-12/31	1P: $103-$114	2P: $113-$124	XP: $10	F18

Phone: (418)589-8252

Location: On Rt 138. 745 boul Lafleche G5C 1C6. Fax: 418/589-8752. **Facility:** 61 one-bedroom standard units. 2 stories (no elevator), interior corridors. **Parking:** on-site, winter plug-ins. **Terms:** small pets only (must be supervised). **Amenities:** irons, hair dryers. **Guest Services:** valet laundry, wireless Internet. **Cards:** AX, DC, DS, MC, VI. *(See color ad card insert)*

SOME UNITS

[ASK] [S🐾] [🛏] [🍴] [▭] / [✕] [🛗] /
FEE

ECONO LODGE BAIE-COMEAU   *Book great rates at AAA.com*

▼▼ ▼▼
Motel

6/1-9/3	1P: $87	2P: $97	XP: $10	F12
9/4-4/30	1P: $84	2P: $94	XP: $10	F12
5/1-5/31	1P: $82	2P: $92	XP: $10	F12

Phone: (418)589-7835

Location: On Rt 138; centre. 1060 boul Lafleche G5C 2W9. Fax: 418/589-2041. **Facility:** 39 one-bedroom standard units. 1 story, exterior corridors. **Parking:** on-site, winter plug-ins. **Terms:** office hours 6 am-midnight, check-in 4 pm, 14 day cancellation notice. **Amenities:** high-speed Internet, hair dryers. Some: DVD players, irons. **Cards:** AX, MC, VI. *(See color ad card insert)*

SOME UNITS

[ASK] [S🐾] [🍴] [▭] / [✕] [🛗] /
FEE

L'AUBERGE LE PETIT CHATEAU

▼▼▼▼▼
Bed & Breakfast

All Year [CP]	1P: $76-$118	2P: $86-$132	XP: $10	F

Phone: 418/295-3100

Location: On Rt 138. 2370 boul Lafleche G5C 1E4. Fax: 418/295-3225. **Facility:** This contemporary-style property has good-size rooms with the charm of a country inn; phone for seasonal closures. 12 one-bedroom standard units. 2 stories, interior corridors. **Parking:** on-site, winter plug-ins. **Terms:** office hours 7 am-11 pm. **Amenities:** hair dryers. **Guest Services:** wireless Internet. **Business Services:** meeting rooms. **Cards:** AX, DC, MC, VI.

SOME UNITS

[🍴] [🛗] / [✕] [🎬] /

------ *The following lodging was either not evaluated or did not meet AAA rating requirements but is listed for your information only.* ------

HOTEL LE MANOIR

[fyi]

Phone: 418/296-3391

Not evaluated. **Location:** Rt 138, 4.4 km e, follow signs. 8 ave Cabot G4Z 1L8. Facilities, services, and decor characterize a mid-range property.

BAIE-ST-PAUL pop. 7,290

------ WHERE TO STAY ------

AUBERGE LA PIGNORONDE — *Book great rates at AAA.com* — Phone: (418)435-5505
CAA SAVE | All Year | 1P: $65-$158 | 2P: $70-$158 | XP: $20 | D12
Location: Rt 138, 0.8 mi (1.3 km) w of jct Rt 362. 750 boul Mgr-de-Laval G3Z 2V5. Fax: 418/435-2779
Facility: This modern country inn offers good-sized comfortable rooms, some with superb views of the picturesque Charlevoix coast. 28 units. 27 one-bedroom standard units. 1 one-bedroom suite ($230) with
Country Inn | whirlpool. 3 stories (no elevator); interior corridors. *Bath:* combo or shower only. **Parking:** on-site.
Terms: 15 day cancellation notice-fee imposed, [BP] & [MAP] meal plans available. **Amenities:** hair dryers.
Dining: 7 am-10 & 6-8 pm, cocktails. **Pool(s):** heated indoor. **Leisure Activities:** hiking trails, shuffleboard. **Guest Services:**
valet laundry, area transportation. **Business Services:** meeting rooms. **Cards:** AX, DC, MC, VI. **Free Special Amenities:** local
telephone calls and newspaper. *(See color ad p 385)*
SOME UNITS

AUBERGE LE CORMORAN — Phone: (418)435-6030
CAA SAVE | 6/15-9/3 [BP] | 1P: $84-$134 | 2P: $89-$139 | XP: $20 | D11
| 9/4-10/7 [BP] | 1P: $72-$134 | 2P: $77-$139 | XP: $20 | D11
| 10/8-4/30 [BP] | 1P: $72-$124 | 2P: $77-$129 | XP: $20 | D11
| 5/1-6/14 [BP] | 1P: $72-$122 | 2P: $77-$127 | XP: $20 | D11
Bed & Breakfast | **Location:** 1.1 mi (1.8 km) s on rue Ste-Anne from jct Rt 362. Located in a quiet area. 196 rue Ste-Anne G3Z 1P8.
Fax: 418/435-5970. **Facility:** 10 one-bedroom standard units, some with whirlpools. 2 stories (no elevator);
interior corridors. *Bath:* combo or shower only. **Parking:** on-site, winter plug-ins. **Terms:** off-site registration, cancellation fee
imposed, [MAP] meal plan available, package plans. **Pool(s):** heated outdoor. **Leisure Activities:** *Fee:* boat dock, massage.
Cards: MC, VI. **Free Special Amenities:** full breakfast and high-speed Internet.

AUX PORTES DU SOLEIL — Phone: 418/435-3540
CAA SAVE | 6/29-9/4 | 1P: $69-$79 | 2P: $82-$102 | XP: $12 | F6
| 12/26-3/30 | 1P: $59-$75 | 2P: $69-$102 | XP: $12 | F6
| 9/5-10/20 | 1P: $55-$69 | 2P: $69-$92 | XP: $12 | F6
| 5/18-6/28 | 1P: $55-$69 | 2P: $59-$79 | XP: $12 | F6
Motel | **Location:** On Rt 362, 0.5 mi (0.8 km) s of jct Rt 138. One side of the place de la Lumiere G3Z 1Y7. Fax: 418/435-3542.
Facility: 17 units. 15 one-bedroom standard units. 1 one- and 1 two-bedroom suites ($118-$188). 1 story;
exterior corridors. *Bath:* combo or shower only. **Parking:** on-site, winter plug-ins. **Terms:** open 5/18-10/20 & 12/26-3/30,
cancellation fee imposed, [ECP] meal plan available, package plans. **Amenities:** hair dryers. *Some:* DVD players, CD players.
Dining: 7-10 am; also 6-10 pm 12/25-4/1, cocktails. **Leisure Activities:** whirlpools, motorcycle and snowmobile shelter. **Guest
Services:** gift shop, coin laundry, wireless Internet. **Business Services:** PC. **Cards:** MC, VI. **Free Special Amenities:**
expanded continental breakfast and high-speed Internet.
SOME UNITS

HOTEL BAIE-SAINT-PAUL — Phone: 418/435-3683
CAA SAVE | 6/24-9/3 | 1P: $109 | 2P: $114 | XP: $10 | F16
| 12/24-4/30 | 1P: $84 | 2P: $89 | XP: $10 | F16
| 9/4-12/23 | 1P: $74 | 2P: $79 | XP: $10 | F16
| 5/1-6/23 | 1P: $64 | 2P: $69 | XP: $10 | F16
Small-scale Hotel | **Location:** On Rt 138, 0.3 mi (0.5 km) e of Rt 362. 911 boul Mgr-de-Laval G3Z 1A1. Fax: 418/435-5652. **Facility:** 62
one-bedroom standard units, some with whirlpools. 2 stories, interior corridors. **Parking:** on-site, winter
plug-ins. **Terms:** [AP], [BP] & [MAP] meal plans available, package plans, small pets only ($5 extra charge). **Amenities:** hair
dryers. **Dining:** 6 am-9 pm; to 10 pm 7/15-8/31, cocktails. **Leisure Activities:** snowmobiling, motorcycle and snowmobile
shelter, exercise room, spa. **Guest Services:** wireless Internet. **Business Services:** meeting rooms, PC. **Cards:** AX, DC,
MC, VI.
SOME UNITS
FEE

------ WHERE TO DINE ------

AUBERGE LA MAISON OTIS DINING ROOM — **Dinner:** $48 — Phone: 418/435-2255
Location: Centre; in Auberge La Maison Otis. 23 rue St-Jean-Baptiste G3Z 1M2. **Hours:** 6 pm-8:30 pm.
Reservations: suggested. **Features:** Country inn charm punctuates the comfortable stone-walled dining
Regional French | room in a quaint village. The chef blends interesting flavors in creative preparations of regional food for the
multicourse menu. The atmosphere is relaxed. Casual dress; cocktails. **Parking:** on-site. **Cards:** MC, VI.
Country Inn

AU PIERRE-NARCISSE RESTAURANT-BAR — **Lunch:** $7-$12 — **Dinner:** $12-$22 — Phone: 418/435-2056
Location: Just w of rue Ste-Anne; centre. 41 rue Ambroise-Fafard G3Z 2J2. **Hours:** 8 am-9:30 pm; 11 am-2 & 4-
9:30 pm, Sat & Sun from 4 pm 11/1-05/31. Closed: 12/25. **Reservations:** suggested. **Features:** The casual
Canadian | eatery is in a cozy inn that has been operated by the same family for generations. Wholesome food tops a
menu that includes pasta, burgers, steak, fish, ribs, pizza, salad and steaks. Casual dress; cocktails.
Parking: on-site. **Cards:** MC, VI.

LA MAISON D'AFFINAGE MAURICE DUFOUR — **Dinner:** $22-$33 — Phone: 418/435-5692
Location: 1.5 mi (2.5 km) n of Rt 138. 1339 boul Mgr-de-Laval G3Z 2X6. **Hours:** Open 5/15-10/31; 6 pm-10 pm.
Reservations: required. **Features:** In a high-quality cheese factory, this upscale dining room affords scenic
French | views of surrounding farmland. The menu lists dishes made from superior regional produce, with several
entrees and desserts incorporating award-winning house-produced cheeses, including Ciel de Charlevoix
and Migneron. Guests might sample salmon tartare, foie gras, duck confit, cheese raclette, breast of chicken or fillet of beef.
Visitors to the cheese factory may reserve a place at afternoon wine and cheese tastings. Casual dress. **Parking:** on-site.
Cards: MC, VI.

Charlevoix
CharlevoixTourism.com

AUBERGE LA PIGNORONDE ⬦⬦⬦

A few minutes away from downtown Baie-Saint-Paul. We offer a warm welcome, comfortable surroundings, fine dining and an outstanding wine list. Enjoy our indoor pool with easy access to the terrace and spectacular landscaped grounds with a magnificent view of the river and Isle-aux-Coudres. Three panoramic dining rooms for your mealtime pleasure.

750, Boul. Mgr-De Laval
BAIE-SAINT-PAUL
1 888 554-6004
aubergelapignoronde.com

from CA **$70** to **$230**
plus tax, lodging only
Subject to availibility

HÔTEL BAIE-SAINT-PAUL ⬦⬦⬦

At Hôtel Baie-Saint-Paul, we've thought of everything for your Charlevoix vacation. With 62 air conditioned rooms, our establishment upholds a tradition for quality and cleanliness. Conveniently located close to numerous attractions & activities. Le Gourmet Restaurant, bar/lounge and health center, sauna and fitness room. Numerous packages: golf, cruises, whalewatching, Grands-Jardins & Hautes-Gorges-de-la-Rivière-Malbaie National Parks, Massif Ski, snowmobile, etc.

911, Boul. Mgr-De Laval
BAIE-SAINT-PAUL
1 800 650-3683
hotelbaiestpaul.com

from CA **$64** to **$114**
plus tax, lodging only
Subject to availibility

FAIRMONT LE MANOIR RICHELIEU ⬦⬦⬦⬦

With its outstanding 27-hole golf course, the Fairmont Le Manoir Richelieu, which celebrated its centennial in 1999, remains Charlevoix's flagship hotel. From its cliff-top perch overlooking the majestic St. Lawrence, this international-calibre resort creates the perfect marriage of nature's soothing charms with an unparalleled tradition of hospitality.

181, Richelieu
LA MALBAIE
1 800 441-1414
fairmont.com/richelieu

from CA **$143** to **$299**
plus tax, lodging only
Subject to availibility

RESTAURANT AU DETOUR | **Lunch:** $7-$23 | **Dinner:** $7-$23 | **Phone:** 418/435-6116

▼▼▼
Canadian
Location: On Rt 138. 770 boul Mgr-de-Laval G3Z 2V5. **Hours:** Open 5/2-9/30; 6 am-8 pm. **Reservations:** accepted. **Features:** Home-style cooking is offered at this roadside diner offering superb views of the scenic Charlevoix coast. Choose from "tourtiere" meat pie, pastas, steak, seafood, sandwiches, burgers and hot dogs. For dessert, try the sugar pie. Casual dress; cocktails. **Parking:** on-site.
Cards: MC, VI.

RESTAURANT LE MOUTON NOIR | **Lunch:** $9-$24 | **Dinner:** $11-$29 | **Phone:** 418/240-3030

▼▼ ▼▼
French
Location: Centre. 43 rue Ste-Anne G3Z 1N9. **Hours:** 11:30 am-2:30 & 5:30-8:30 pm, Fri-9:30 pm, Sat 5:30 pm-9:30 pm; seasonal hours vary. **Closed:** 11/1-12/20 & 1/2-2/14. **Reservations:** suggested. **Features:** Regional produce inspires a varied menu that includes escargot, bison-stuffed ravioli and Quebec lamb and veal, as well as preparations of venison, steak, duck and seafood. The mood is cheerful and upbeat, both in the dining room and on the sunny summer patio. Casual dress; cocktails. **Parking:** on-site. **Cards:** AX, MC, VI.

BEAUPORT —See Quebec p. 546.

BEAUPRE —See Quebec p. 546.

BECANCOUR pop. 11,051

──────── **WHERE TO STAY** ────────

AUBERGE GODEFROY | *Book at AAA.com* | | | **Phone:** (819)233-2200

▼▼▼▼ | All Year | 1P: $145 | 2P: $165 | XP: $20 | F12

Small-scale Hotel
Location: Hwy 55, exit 176 southbound, 0.6 mi (1 km) n on boul Port Royal, then 0.3 mi (0.5 km) e; exit northbound, 0.5 mi (0.8 km) n on ave Godefroy. 17575 boul Becancour G9H 1A5. **Fax:** 819/233-2288. **Facility:** 71 units. 67 one-bedroom standard units, some with whirlpools. 4 one-bedroom suites, some with efficiencies. 3 stories, interior corridors. **Parking:** on-site, winter plug-ins. **Terms:** 7 day cancellation notice, package plans, $2 service charge. **Amenities:** honor bars, irons, hair dryers. *Some:* CD players. **Dining:** Le Godefroy, see separate listing. **Pool(s):** heated indoor. **Leisure Activities:** saunas, whirlpool, steamroom, snowmobiling, bicycles, hiking trails, exercise room, spa, horseshoes, volleyball. **Guest Services:** valet laundry, wireless Internet. **Business Services:** meeting rooms, fax. **Cards:** AX, CB, DC, DS, JC, MC, VI.

SOME UNITS
(ASK) (S◻) (††) (🛋) (🏊) (✕) (💻) / (✕) (VCR) (🛏) /
FEE

──────── **WHERE TO DINE** ────────

LE GODEFROY | **Lunch:** $13-$21 | **Dinner:** $17-$36 | **Phone:** 819/233-2200

▼▼▼▼
French
Location: Hwy 55, exit 176 southbound, 0.6 mi (1 km) n on boul Port Royal, then 0.3 mi (0.5 km) e; exit northbound, 0.5 mi (0.8 km) n on ave Godefroy; in Auberge Godefroy. 17575 boul Becancour G9H 1A5. **Hours:** 7 am-9 pm. **Reservations:** suggested. **Features:** This comfortable hotel dining room is known for its fine regional cuisine, a popular Sunday brunch and its lunch buffets. Menu items include regional fish and seafood, poultry, beef, pork, sweetbreads and an 8-course tasting menu. Casual dress; cocktails. **Parking:** on-site. **Cards:** AX, CB, DC, JC, MC, VI.

(Y)

BELOEIL —See Montreal p. 481.

BERTHIERVILLE pop. 3,939

──────── **WHERE TO STAY** ────────

DAYS INN BERTHIERVILLE | *Book great rates at AAA.com* | | | **Phone:** (450)836-1621

▼▼ ▼▼ | 6/17-10/15 [ECP] | 1P: $98-$140 | 2P: $108-$165 | XP: $15 | F18
| 5/1-6/16 [ECP] | 1P: $88-$140 | 2P: $98-$165 | XP: $10 | F18
Small-scale Hotel | 1/16-4/30 [ECP] | 1P: $88-$140 | 2P: $98-$165 | XP: $12 | F18
| 10/16-1/15 [ECP] | 1P: $82-$140 | 2P: $92-$165 | XP: $10 | F18
Location: Hwy 40, exit 144. Located adjacent to truck stop. 760 rue Gadoury J0K 1A0. **Fax:** 450/836-1578. **Facility:** 60 one-bedroom standard units, some with whirlpools. 3 stories, interior/exterior corridors. **Parking:** on-site, winter plug-ins. **Terms:** check-in 4 pm, cancellation fee imposed, package plans, 14% service charge, small pets only. **Amenities:** irons, hair dryers. *Some:* honor bars. **Guest Services:** valet laundry, wireless Internet. **Business Services:** meeting rooms, PC. **Cards:** AX, DC, DS, MC, VI.

SOME UNITS
(ASK) (S◻) (🛏) (†|•) (Y) (💻) / (✕) (VCR) (🛏) (📺) /

──────── **WHERE TO DINE** ────────

ST-HUBERT | **Lunch:** $7-$20 | **Dinner:** $7-$20 | **Phone:** 450/836-1777

▼▼ ▼▼
Canadian
Location: Hwy 40, exit 144. 1091 ave Gilles-Villeneuve J0K 1A0. **Hours:** 11 am-11 pm, Fri & Sat-1 am. **Closed:** 12/25. **Reservations:** accepted. **Features:** The pleasantly decorated family-friendly restaurant serves affordable chicken dinners, ribs, club sandwiches, chicken wings, salads, soups and hot chicken sandwiches. The children's menu includes animal nuggets. Casual dress; cocktails. **Parking:** on-site.
Cards: AX, DC, MC, VI.

(Y)

BONAVENTURE pop. 2,756

———— WHERE TO STAY ————

———— *The following lodging was either not evaluated or did not* ————
meet AAA rating requirements but is listed for your information only.

RIOTEL CHATEAU BLANC   **Phone:** 418/534-3336
[fyi]   Did not meet all AAA rating requirements for some public areas at time of last evaluation. **Location:** On Rt
              132; centre. 98 ave Port Royal G0C 1E0. Facilities, services, and decor characterize a mid-range property.
Small-scale Hotel

BOUCHERVILLE —See Montreal p. 481.

BROMONT pop. 4,808

———— WHERE TO STAY ————

AUBERGE DU CHATEAU BROMONT   **Phone:** 450/534-3133
              All Year   1P: $90-$120   2P: $90-$120
              Location: Hwy 10, exit 78, 1.8 mi (2.8 km) w on boul Bromont, then just n on rue Champlain; in Station Touristique
Small-scale Hotel Bromont. 95 rue Montmorency J2L 2J1. Fax: 450/534-3933. **Facility:** 49 one-bedroom standard units. 3 stories
(no elevator), interior corridors. *Bath:* combo or shower only. **Parking:** on-site. **Terms:** check-in 4 pm,
cancellation fee imposed, [AP], [BP] & [CP] meal plans available, package plans, $2 service charge. **Amenities:** hair dryers.
Pool(s): outdoor, wading. **Leisure Activities:** lighted tennis court. **Guest Services:** valet laundry, area transportation, wireless
Internet. **Business Services:** meeting rooms. **Cards:** AX, DC, DS, MC, VI.
                                                                                          SOME UNITS
[ASK] [🍴] [🍸] [➰] [🛏] [🖥] / [✕] /

CHATEAU BROMONT RESORT HOTELS   **Phone:** 450/534-3433
              All Year   1P: $149-$180   2P: $149-$180   XP: $20   F17
              Location: Hwy 10, exit 78, 1.6 mi (2.5 km) s on boul Bromont, then 0.8 mi (1.2 km) w on rue Champlain (toward ski hill).
Large-scale Hotel 90 rue Stanstead J2L 1K6. Fax: 450/534-0514. **Facility:** 164 units. 162 one-bedroom standard units, some
with whirlpools. 2 one-bedroom suites ($300) with whirlpools. 3 stories, interior corridors. *Bath:* combo or
shower only. **Parking:** on-site, winter plug-ins. **Terms:** check-in 4 pm, 2 night minimum stay, cancellation fee imposed, [AP],
[BP], [CP] & [MAP] meal plans available, package plans. **Amenities:** video games (fee), dual phone lines, voice mail, safes,
honor bars, irons, hair dryers. *Some:* DVD players, CD players, high-speed Internet. **Dining:** Restaurant Quatre Canards, see
separate listing. **Pool(s):** heated outdoor, heated indoor. **Leisure Activities:** saunas, whirlpools, steamrooms, racquetball court,
exercise room, spa. **Guest Services:** gift shop, area transportation, wireless Internet. **Business Services:** conference facilities,
PC. **Cards:** AX, DC, DS, MC, VI.
                                                                                          SOME UNITS
[🍴] [🍸] [🏋] [➰] [✕] [🎥] [🖥] / [✕] [🛏] /

HOTEL LE MENHIR   **Phone:** (450)534-3790
              All Year   1P: $79-$159   2P: $89-$169   XP: $10   F13
              Location: Hwy 10, exit 78, 1.6 mi (2.7 km) s. 125 boul Bromont J2L 2K7. Fax: 450/534-1933. **Facility:** 41 one-
Small-scale Hotel bedroom standard units, some with efficiencies and/or whirlpools. 3 stories (no elevator), interior/exterior
corridors. **Parking:** on-site. **Terms:** cancellation fee imposed, package plans, pets ($15 extra charge, 1st
floor units). **Amenities:** *Some:* hair dryers. **Pool(s):** heated indoor. **Leisure Activities:** whirlpool. **Guest Services:** valet
laundry, wireless Internet. **Business Services:** meeting rooms, PC, fax (fee). **Cards:** AX, DS, MC, VI.
                                                                                          SOME UNITS
[ASK] [SD] [🛏] [🍴] [🍸] [➰] [🛏] [🖥] / [✕] [VCR] /
                                                                                          FEE

LE ST-MARTIN BROMONT HOTEL & SUITES   *Book great rates at AAA.com*   **Phone:** 450/534-0044
[CAA] [SAVE]   All Year [ECP]   1P: $129-$289   2P: $129-$289   XP: $20   F12
              Location: Hwy 10, exit 78. 111 boul du Carrefour J2L 3L1. Fax: 450/534-0049. **Facility:** 41 units. 38 one-
              bedroom standard units, some with whirlpools. 3 one-bedroom suites. 3 stories, interior corridors. *Bath:*
Small-scale Hotel combo or shower only. **Parking:** on-site. **Terms:** package plans, $2 service charge. **Amenities:** *Some:*
high-speed Internet (fee), voice mail, honor bars, irons, hair dryers. **Pool(s):** heated outdoor. **Leisure
Activities:** whirlpool, exercise room. **Guest Services:** valet laundry. **Business Services:** meeting rooms.
Cards: AX, MC, VI. **Free Special Amenities:** expanded continental breakfast and high-speed Internet.
                                                                                          SOME UNITS
[➰] / [✕] [🍴] [W] [🔒] [🛏] [🖥] [🖥] /

———— WHERE TO DINE ————

MICRO-BRASSERIE BROUEMONT RESTAURANT   **Lunch:** $9-$10   **Dinner:** $10-$20   **Phone:** 450/534-0001
              Location: Hwy 10, exit 78, 1.4 mi (2.3 km) s. 107 boul Bromont J2L 2K7. **Hours:** 11 am-10 pm, Fri-midnight, Sat
              noon-midnight, Sun noon-10 pm. Closed: 1/1, 12/25. **Reservations:** accepted. **Features:** Microbrewed
Canadian   beers are served in the casual atmosphere of the rural village eatery. A fireplace keeps the dining room cozy
              during the ski season. The menu lists sandwiches, soups, grilled chicken, steaks, sausage and burgers. The
terrace opens seasonally. Casual dress; cocktails. **Parking:** on-site. **Cards:** AX, DC, JC, MC, VI.

RESTAURANT L'ETRIER   **Dinner:** $14-$35   **Phone:** 450/534-3562
              Location: Hwy 10, exit 78, 0.3 mi (0.5 km) s on boul Bromont, then just e. 547 rue Shefford (CP 86) J2L 1B9. **Hours:** 5
              pm-10 pm. Closed: 1/1, 9/3, 12/25; also Mon-Wed 9/5-5/31 & 1 week in April & Sept.
Steak & Seafood **Reservations:** accepted. **Features:** Overlooking nearby ski hills, the casual eatery, named for the French
              word for "stirrup," has a rustic country decor with wood walls and a fireplace. Live music is performed most
weekends, and the terrace opens seasonally. Steak and seafood top a menu that includes chicken supreme, flambeed ribs,
salmon, Pernod-flavored scampi and flambeed shrimp. Casual dress; cocktails. **Parking:** on-site. **Cards:** MC, VI.

RESTAURANT QUATRE CANARDS   **Lunch:** $18   **Dinner:** $23-$50   **Phone:** 450/534-3433

▼▼▼

French

Location: Hwy 10, exit 78, 1.6 mi (2.5 km) s on boul Bromont, then 0.8 mi (1.2 km) w on rue Champlain (toward ski hill); in Chateau Bromont Resort Hotels. 90 rue Stanstead J2L 1K6. **Hours:** 7-10:30 am, 11:30-2 & 6-10 pm. **Reservations:** suggested. **Features:** The comfortable, well-appointed hotel restaurant presents a varied menu of fine French cuisine that makes use of quality regional produce. Specialties include Lake Brome duck, loin of deer, marinated trout and yellow perch filets, salmon tournedos, rack of lamb, Charlevoix veal and steamed lobster. Casual dress; cocktails. **Parking:** on-site. **Cards:** AX, DC, DS, MC, VI.

ST-HUBERT   **Lunch:** $8-$12   **Dinner:** $8-$21   **Phone:** 450/534-0223

▼▼

Canadian

Location: Hwy 10, exit 78. 8 boul Bromont J2L 1A9. **Hours:** 11 am-11 pm. **Reservations:** accepted. **Features:** The pleasantly decorated family-friendly restaurant serves affordable chicken dinners, ribs, club sandwiches, chicken wings, salads, soups and hot chicken sandwiches. The children's menu includes animal nuggets. Casual dress; cocktails. **Parking:** on-site. **Cards:** AX, MC, VI.

BROSSARD —See Montreal p. 482.

CARLETON-ST-OMER pop. 4,010

—————— WHERE TO STAY ——————

HOSTELLERIE BAIE BLEUE

▼▼ ▼▼

Motel

			Phone: (418)364-3355
7/1-8/31	1P: $110-$185	2P: $110-$185	XP: $17 F5
5/1-6/30 & 9/1-10/20	1P: $75-$130	2P: $75-$130	XP: $10 F5

Location: On Hwy 132. 482 boul Perron G0C 1J0 (CP 3009). Fax: 418/364-6165. **Facility:** 95 one-bedroom standard units, some with whirlpools. 3 stories (no elevator), exterior corridors. **Parking:** on-site, winter plug-ins. **Terms:** open 5/1-10/20, [MAP] meal plan available, package plans, $2 service charge, small pets only (in designated units). **Amenities:** hair dryers. **Dining:** La Seigneurie Dining Room/Hostellerie Baie Bleue, see separate listing. **Pool(s):** heated outdoor. **Leisure Activities:** lighted tennis court, hiking trails. *Fee:* bicycles. **Guest Services:** valet laundry, area transportation (fee). **Business Services:** meeting rooms, PC (fee).   SOME UNITS

(ASK) ⬛ ⬛ 🐾 ⎢¶ ⬛ 🍸 ⬛ ⇆ ⬛ ⬛ ⬛ ⬛ ⬛ / ⬛ /

—————— WHERE TO DINE ——————

LA SEIGNEURIE DINING
ROOM/HOSTELLERIE BAIE BLEUE   **Dinner:** $15-$33   **Phone:** 418/364-3355

Ⓐ

▼▼▼▼

Regional Steak & Seafood

Location: On Hwy 132; in Hostellerie Baie Bleue. 482 boul Perron G0C 1J0. **Hours:** Open 5/1-10/31 & 6-9 pm. **Reservations:** suggested. **Features:** Soft classical music, draped windows and attractive furnishings add to the restaurant's romantic ambience. Main courses include Atlantic salmon, seafood bouillabaisse, lamb chops in fresh thyme sauce, pork filet, rib steak in cognac and black pepper sauce and boiled lobster. The restaurant may be open occasionally, only by reservation, in off season. Casual dress; cocktails. **Parking:** on-site. **Cards:** AX, DC, MC, VI.

CHAMBLY —See Montreal p. 484.

CHARLESBOURG —See Quebec p. 547.

CHATEAU-RICHER —See Quebec p. 547.

CHELSEA pop. 6,036

—————— WHERE TO DINE ——————

RESTAURANT LES FOUGERES   *Menu on AAA.com*   **Lunch:** $12-$25   **Dinner:** $27-$32   **Phone:** 819/827-8942

Ⓐ

▼▼ ◆ ▼▼

French

Location: On Rt 105, 1.2 mi (2 km) n of Old Chelsea. 783 Rt 105 J9B 1P1. **Hours:** 11 am-10 pm, Sat & Sun from 10 am. Closed: 7/1, 12/24-12/26; also Mon-Thurs 3/1-3/21 & Easter Mon. **Reservations:** suggested. **Features:** The relaxed and elegant country dining room treats patrons to superb food pairings on a menu that includes fresh fish, Prince Edward Island scallops, shrimp, grain-fed chicken, sweetbreads, lamb and venison. The service is refined. Casual dress; cocktails. **Parking:** on-site. **Cards:** AX, DC, MC, VI.

CHICOUTIMI pop. 60,008

—————— WHERE TO STAY ——————

CENTRE DE CONGRES ET HOTEL LA
SAGUENEENNE   *Book at AAA.com*

▼▼▼▼

Small-scale Hotel

			Phone: (418)545-8326
7/1-8/31	1P: $119-$172	2P: $129-$172	XP: $10 F17
5/1-6/30 & 9/1-4/30	1P: $104-$166	2P: $114-$166	XP: $10 F17

Location: Just w of jct Rt 175 (boul Talbot); in Saguenay sector. Located in a commercial area. 250 des Sagueneens G7H 3A4. Fax: 418/545-6577. **Facility:** 118 units. 115 one-bedroom standard units. 3 one-bedroom suites. 4 stories, interior corridors. **Parking:** on-site, winter plug-ins. **Terms:** cancellation fee imposed, [BP] & [CP] meal plans available, $2 service charge, small pets only. **Amenities:** voice mail, safes, irons, hair dryers. **Pool(s):** heated indoor, saltwater. **Leisure Activities:** sauna, whirlpools, steamroom, exercise room. **Guest Services:** valet laundry, wireless Internet. **Business Services:** conference facilities, business center. **Cards:** AX, CB, MC, VI.   SOME UNITS

(ASK) ⬛ ⬛ 🐾 ⎢¶ ⬛ 🍸 ⬛ ⬛ ⇆ ⬛ ⬛ / ⬛ ⬛ ⬛ /

COMFORT INN　　*Book great rates at AAA.com*　　　　　　　　Phone: (418)693-8686

	6/25-9/15	1P: $89-$120	2P: $99-$130	XP: $10	F18
	5/1-6/24 & 9/16-12/31	1P: $77-$90	2P: $87-$110	XP: $10	F18
	1/1-4/30	1P: $80-$93	2P: $90-$103	XP: $10	F18

Small-scale Hotel **Location:** Jct Rt 170, 1.8 mi (2.8 km) n. 1595 boul Talbot G7H 4C3. Fax: 418/693-8015. **Facility:** 81 one-bedroom standard units. 2 stories, interior corridors. **Parking:** on-site, winter plug-ins. **Terms:** weekly rates available. **Amenities:** irons, hair dryers. **Guest Services:** valet laundry, wireless Internet. **Cards:** AX, CB, DC, DS, JC, MC, VI. *(See color ad card insert)*

SOME UNITS
ASK SD 🛏 🍴 🖥 📷 📺 / ✕ VCR 🔌 📠 /
FEE

LE MONTAGNAIS-HOTEL & CENTRE DE CONGRES　　　　　　Phone: 418/543-1521

　　　　　　　　　　　　　　Property failed to provide current rates
Location: On Rt 175. 1080 boul Talbot G7H 3B6. Fax: 418/543-2149. **Facility:** 296 units. 288 one-bedroom standard units. 8 one-bedroom suites with whirlpools. 2-6 stories, interior/exterior corridors. **Parking:** on-
Large-scale Hotel site. **Amenities:** video library (fee), high-speed Internet, voice mail, irons, hair dryers. *Some:* safes. **Pool(s):** heated outdoor, heated indoor. **Leisure Activities:** saunas, whirlpool, lifeguard on duty, miniature golf, tennis court, playground, exercise room, spa, shuffleboard. **Guest Services:** gift shop, valet laundry. **Business Services:** meeting rooms, administrative services (fee), PC.

SOME UNITS
🍴 🍷 🏊 ✕ 🖥 / ✕ VCR 🔌 /

──────── *The following lodging was either not evaluated or did not* ────────
meet AAA rating requirements but is listed for your information only.

HOTEL DU FJORD　　　　　　　　　　　　　　　　　　　　Phone: 418/543-1538

[fyi] Not evaluated. **Location:** Just s of Rt 372 (boul Saguenay). 241 rue Morin G7H 4X8. Facilities, services, and decor characterize a mid-range property.

──────── **WHERE TO DINE** ────────

LA BOUGRESSE　　　　Lunch: $10-$16　　　　Dinner: $18-$35　　　Phone: 418/543-3178

Location: Corner of rue Hotel Dieu; centre. 260 rue Riverin G7H 4R4. **Hours:** 11 am-11 pm, Sat & Sun from 4:30 pm. Closed major holidays. **Reservations:** suggested. **Features:** Wholesome, reasonably priced food—
French such as Quebec veal, steak and fries, sweetbreads, mussels, lamb and filet mignon—is the restaurant's clear strength. The stylish contemporary bistro boasts a lively atmosphere. Service is pleasant and professional. Casual dress; cocktails. **Parking:** on-site. **Cards:** AX, DC, MC, VI.

RESTAURANT LE PRIVILEGE　　　　　　Dinner: $33-$35　　　　　　Phone: 418/698-6262

(CAA) **Location:** On Rt 372, 0.3 mi (0.5 km) se of rue Universite. 1623 boul St-Jean-Baptiste G7H 7Y9. **Hours:** 6:30 pm-9 pm. Closed: 1/1, 12/24, 12/25; also Sun & Mon. **Reservations:** suggested. **Features:** A large French-Canadian family once lived in the country-style home, which now functions as an elegant dining room. The
Nouvelle French space may be small, but flavors are huge in interestingly prepared and artfully presented selections of quail, guinea fowl, partridge, lamb, sweetbreads, fresh fish, veal and foie gras. Although this place is not licensed to serve alcohol, guests can visit a local wine shop where the menu is registered to select appropriate vintages. Reservations are strongly recommended. Dressy casual. **Parking:** on-site. **Cards:** MC, VI.

ST-HUBERT　　　　Lunch: $7-$20　　　　Dinner: $7-$20　　　Phone: 418/545-4104

Location: Centre. 939 boul Talbot G7H 4B5. **Hours:** 11 am-11 pm, Thurs-Sat to midnight. Closed: for dinner 12/25. **Features:** The pleasantly decorated family-friendly restaurant serves affordable chicken dinners, ribs,
Canadian club sandwiches, chicken wings, salads, soups and hot chicken sandwiches. The children's menu includes animal nuggets. Casual dress; cocktails. **Parking:** on-site. **Cards:** AX, DC, MC, VI.

🍷

COTEAU-DU-LAC pop. 5,573

──────── **WHERE TO DINE** ────────

CHEZ LES DE VILLEMURE　　　　　　Dinner: $17-$36　　　　　　Phone: 450/763-5743

Location: Hwy 20, exit 17, 0.6 mi (1 km) s. 7 rue Principale J0P 1B0. **Hours:** 5 pm-9:30 pm. Closed: Mon & Tues.
Reservations: suggested. **Features:** Decorated with flowers, fireplaces and wood accents, the small, cozy
French restaurant exudes a warm, country-style ambience. Interesting regional preparations of ostrich, bison, duck, deer and veal liver combine with fresh fish, roast beef and steak dishes on the diverse menu. The family-run restaurant has been in operation since 1946. Casual dress; cocktails. **Parking:** street. **Cards:** MC, VI.

COTE-ST-LUC —*See Montreal p. 484.*

COWANSVILLE pop. 12,032

──────── **WHERE TO STAY** ────────

DAYS INN-COWANSVILLE　　*Book great rates at AAA.com*　　　　Phone: 450/263-7331

| | 6/16-10/22 & 12/18-4/30 [BP] | 1P: $90-$120 | 2P: $90-$120 | XP: $10 | F12 |
| | 5/1-6/15 & 10/23-12/17 [BP] | 1P: $70-$100 | 2P: $70-$100 | XP: $10 | F12 |

Small-scale Hotel **Location:** Hwy 10, exit 68, 9.9 mi (15.9 km) s on Rt 139. 111 place Jean-Jacques Bertrand J2K 3R5. Fax: 450/263-7335. **Facility:** 32 one-bedroom standard units, some with whirlpools. 3 stories (no elevator), interior corridors. **Parking:** on-site. **Terms:** package plans, small pets only ($15 fee, in designated units). **Amenities:** video library (fee), irons, hair dryers. *Some:* high-speed Internet. **Leisure Activities:** *Fee:* massage. **Guest Services:** coin laundry, wireless Internet. **Business Services:** meeting rooms. **Cards:** AX, DC, DS, MC, VI.

SOME UNITS
ASK SD 🛏 🍴 🍷 🖥 / ✕ VCR 🔌 /
FEE　　　　　　FEE

— WHERE TO DINE —

RESTAURANT LE MCHAFFY   **Lunch:** $12-$17   **Dinner:** $24-$26   **Phone:** 450/266-7700

▼▼▼▼   **Location:** 0.6 mi (1 km) se of rue de Sud; centre. 351 rue Principale J2K 1J4. **Hours:** noon-2 & 5:30-9 pm, Sat
French   5:30 pm-10 pm. **Closed:** Sun, Mon, 12/23-1/9 & 11/1-11/7. **Reservations:** suggested. **Features:** Guests
    dine on fine regional cuisine in the parlor of a vintage rural home. The menu lists black-striped bass, sea
    scallops, pan-seared foie gras, organic grilled pork, rack of lamb and selections of wild game, including red
deer, rabbit and squab. Casual dress; cocktails. **Parking:** on-site. **Cards:** MC, VI.

DANVILLE pop. 4,301

— WHERE TO DINE —

RESTAURANT LE TEMPS DES
   CERISES   **Lunch:** $9-$18   **Dinner:** $17-$23   **Phone:** 819/839-2818
(CAA)   **Location:** Village centre; 0.4 mi (0.7 km) n on rue Daniel-Johnson from jct Rt 116, then just e. 79 rue du Carmel J0A
    1A0. **Hours:** 11:30 am-1:30 & 5:30-9 pm, Sat & Sun from 5:30 pm. **Closed:** 1/2-1/16 & Sun 10/15-6/15.
▼▼▼▼   **Reservations:** accepted. **Features:** In a renovated rural church, the informal dining room serves creative
Regional French   regional cuisine and delicious desserts. Casual dress; cocktails. **Parking:** on-site. **Cards:** AX, DC, MC, VI.

DOLLARD-DES-ORMEAUX —See Montreal p. 484.

DORVAL —See Montreal p. 484.

DRUMMONDVILLE pop. 46,559

— WHERE TO STAY —

BEST WESTERN HOTEL UNIVERSEL   *Book great rates at AAA.com*   **Phone:** (819)478-4971

(CAA) (SAVE)	6/23-9/1	1P: $129-$399	2P: $139-$409	XP: $10	F18
	9/2-4/30	1P: $109-$319	2P: $119-$329	XP: $10	F18
▼▼▼▼	5/1-6/22	1P: $99-$299	2P: $109-$301	XP: $10	F18

Small-scale Hotel   **Location:** Hwy 20, exit 177, just s on boul St-Joseph, then just e. 915 rue Hains J2C 3A1. **Fax:** 819/474-6604. **Facility:** 115 units. 112 one-bedroom standard units, some with whirlpools. 3 one-bedroom suites. 4 stories, interior corridors. *Bath:* combo or tub only. **Parking:** on-site, winter plug-ins. **Terms:** check-in 4 pm, [AP], [BP], [CP], [ECP] & [MAP] meal plans available, package plans, small pets only (1st floor designated units). **Amenities:** voice mail, irons, hair dryers. **Dining:** Restaurant La Verriere, see separate listing. **Pool(s):** heated indoor. **Leisure Activities:** whirlpool, snowmobiling. **Guest Services:** valet laundry, wireless Internet. **Business Services:** conference facilities. **Cards:** AX, DC, DS, MC, VI. **Free Special Amenities:** local telephone calls and high-speed Internet.
(See color ad below)

SOME UNITS
[S/D] [🐕] [🍴] [➰] [🎦] [💻] / [✕] [🔌] [🖥] /
FEE

COMFORT INN   *Book great rates at AAA.com*   **Phone:** (819)477-4000

▼▼ ▼▼	6/24-9/6 [CP]	1P: $93-$110	2P: $104-$121	XP: $10	F18
	1/1-4/30 [CP]	1P: $87-$104	2P: $98-$115	XP: $10	F18
Small-scale Hotel	9/7-12/31 [CP]	1P: $85-$102	2P: $96-$113	XP: $10	F18
	5/1-6/23 [CP]	1P: $84-$101	2P: $95-$112	XP: $10	F18

Location: Hwy 20, exit 177, 0.3 mi (0.5 km) s on boul St-Joseph, then just w. 1055 rue Hains J2C 6G6. **Fax:** 819/477-0930. **Facility:** 59 one-bedroom standard units. 2 stories (no elevator), interior corridors. **Parking:** on-site, winter plug-ins. **Terms:** pets (on ground floor smoking units). **Amenities:** voice mail, irons. *Some:* hair dryers. **Guest Services:** valet laundry, wireless Internet. **Business Services:** meeting rooms. **Cards:** AX, DC, DS, MC, VI. *(See color ad card insert)*

SOME UNITS
[ASK] [S/D] [🐕] [🍴] [💻] / [✕] [🔌] /
FEE

HOTEL & SUITES LE DAUPHIN

Phone: (819)478-4141

▼▼▼▼

6/25-4/30	1P: $102-$117	2P: $112-$127	XP: $12	F18
5/1-6/24	1P: $100-$115	2P: $110-$125	XP: $10	F18

Small-scale Hotel **Location:** Hwy 20, exit 177, 0.8 mi (1.3 km) s. 600 boul St-Joseph J2C 2C1. Fax: 819/478-7549. **Facility:** 121 one-bedroom standard units, some with kitchens and/or whirlpools. 1-2 stories, interior/exterior corridors. **Parking:** on-site, winter plug-ins. **Terms:** check-in 4 pm, package plans. **Amenities:** voice mail, irons, hair dryers. **Pool(s):** heated indoor. **Leisure Activities:** exercise room, spa. **Guest Services:** valet and coin laundry, wireless Internet. **Business Services:** meeting rooms. **Cards:** AX, CB, DC, DS, JC, MC, VI.

SOME UNITS
ASK 🅂🄳 📶 🍽 ⓨ 🛳 🅗 📺 / ✕ 📷 /
FEE

QUALITY SUITES   *Book great rates at AAA.com*

Phone: (819)472-2700

▼▼▼▼

6/23-9/2 [ECP]	1P: $110-$230	2P: $120-$240	XP: $10	F18
5/1-6/22 & 9/3-4/30 [ECP]	1P: $90-$200	2P: $100-$210	XP: $10	F18

Small-scale Hotel **Location:** Hwy 20, exit 175, just s. 2125 rue Canadien J2C 7V8. Fax: 819/472-2704. **Facility:** 71 units. 43 one-bedroom standard units, some with whirlpools. 28 one-bedroom suites. 4 stories, interior corridors. **Parking:** on-site. **Terms:** package plans, small pets only ($10 fee, 1st floor units). **Amenities:** video library (fee), DVD players, CD players, voice mail, irons, hair dryers. **Pool(s):** heated indoor. **Leisure Activities:** whirlpool, exercise room. **Guest Services:** coin laundry. **Business Services:** meeting rooms, business center. **Cards:** AX, DC, DS, MC, VI. **(See color ad card insert)**

SOME UNITS
ASK 🅂🄳 🐾 🍽+ ⓨ 🛳 ✕ 🅗 📺 📺 / VCR /
FEE   FEE

─────── **WHERE TO DINE** ───────

RESTAURANT LA VERRIERE

Lunch: $10-$20   **Dinner:** $17-$24   **Phone:** 819/478-4971

▼▼▼▼
French
DC, MC, VI.

Location: Hwy 20, exit 177, just s on boul St-Joseph, then just e; in Best Western Hotel Universel. 915 rue Hains J2C 3A1. **Hours:** 6:30 am-10 pm, Sat-Mon from 7 am. **Reservations:** accepted. **Features:** The casually elegant hotel restaurant offers a menu of regional French cuisine including filet mignon, frogs' legs, breast of chicken, veal, duck, crab legs, wild game and pasta. Casual dress; cocktails. **Parking:** on-site. **Cards:** AX,

RESTAURANT NORMANDIN

Lunch: $5-$12   **Dinner:** $5-$12   **Phone:** 819/472-7522

▼▼ ▼▼
Canadian
Cards: AX, DC, MC, VI.

Location: On Hwy 143. 130 boul St-Joseph J2C 2A8. **Hours:** 6 am-midnight, Thurs-2 am, Fri & Sat-3 am. Closed: 12/25. **Reservations:** accepted. **Features:** The family restaurant prepares affordable comfort foods that include roasted chicken, hot chicken sandwiches, pasta, burgers and fries. Take-out service, a children's menu and cutely decorated desserts are among other offerings. Casual dress. **Parking:** on-site.

ROTISSERIE SCORES

Lunch: $7-$20   **Dinner:** $7-$20   **Phone:** 819/478-5455

▼▼ ▼▼
Barbecue

Location: Hwy 20, exit 177, 0.3 km s. 120 boul St-Joseph J2C 8J5. **Hours:** 11 am-11 pm. Closed: 12/25. **Reservations:** accepted, weekdays. **Features:** The chain of family restaurants offers a varied menu that includes rotisserie chicken, ribs, salad-bar items, sandwiches, poutine, and sugar, lemon or pecan pies. Casual dress; cocktails. **Parking:** on-site. **Cards:** AX, MC, VI.

ⓨ

ST-HUBERT

Lunch: $7-$20   **Dinner:** $7-$20   **Phone:** 819/477-6622

▼▼ ▼▼
Canadian
Cards: AX, DC, MC, VI.

Location: Hwy 20, exit 177. 125 boul St-Joseph J2C 2A5. **Hours:** 11 am-11 pm, Fri & Sat-midnight. Closed: 12/25. **Reservations:** accepted. **Features:** The pleasantly decorated family-friendly restaurant serves affordable chicken dinners, ribs, club sandwiches, chicken wings, salads, soups and hot chicken sandwiches. The children's menu includes animal nuggets. Casual dress; cocktails. **Parking:** on-site.

ⓨ

FORESTVILLE pop. 3,748

─────── **WHERE TO STAY** ───────

ECONO LODGE   *Book great rates at AAA.com*

Phone: (418)587-2278

▼▼ ▼▼

6/13-9/8	1P: $100-$115	2P: $110-$120	XP: $10	F18
5/1-6/12 & 9/9-4/30	1P: $90-$100	2P: $100-$110	XP: $10	F18

Motel **Location:** On Rt 138; centre. 5 Rt 138 est G0T 1E0. Fax: 418/587-4662. **Facility:** 55 one-bedroom standard units. 1 story, interior/exterior corridors. **Parking:** on-site, winter plug-ins. **Terms:** check-in 4 pm, [CP] meal plan available, package plans. **Amenities:** hair dryers. *Some:* high-speed Internet. **Dining:** Le Danube Bleu, see separate listing. **Guest Services:** coin laundry, wireless Internet. **Business Services:** meeting rooms. **Cards:** AX, CB, DC, DS, MC, VI. **(See color ad card insert)**

SOME UNITS
ASK 🅂🄳 🍽 ⓨ 📺 / ✕ 🄺 🅗 /

─────── **WHERE TO DINE** ───────

LE DANUBE BLEU

Lunch: $8-$16   **Dinner:** $10-$30   **Phone:** 418/587-2278

▼▼ ▼▼
Seafood

Location: On Rt 138; centre; in Econo Lodge. 5 Rt 138 G0T 1E0. **Hours:** 5 am-11 pm, Fri & Sat-midnight. **Reservations:** accepted. **Features:** The house specialty catamaran combines cod, sole, halibut, crab, shrimp and scallops in a visually appealing dish. Steak, pasta, seafood sandwiches and fried or roasted chicken round out the menu. A salad bar is offered. The diner has been family-run since 1956, and the adjacent upscale lounge is a popular nightlife spot. Casual dress; cocktails. **Parking:** on-site. **Cards:** AX, DS, MC, VI.

ⓨ

GASPE pop. 14,932

—— WHERE TO STAY ——

MOTEL ADAMS
Phone: (418)368-2244

▼▼ ▼▼
Motel

All Year   1P: $89-$109   2P: $99-$129   XP: $10   F18
Location: Corner of rue Jacques Cartier; centre. 20 rue Adams G4X 2R8 (CP 6391). Fax: 418/368-6963. **Facility:** 96 one-bedroom standard units. 2 stories (no elevator), interior/exterior corridors. **Parking:** on-site, winter plug-ins. **Terms:** check-in 4 pm. **Amenities:** hair dryers. **Dining:** Adams Restaurant, see separate listing. **Guest Services:** wireless Internet. **Business Services:** meeting rooms, PC. **Cards:** AX, DC, DS, MC, VI.

SOME UNITS

🍴 📷 🔒 🖥 / ✕ VCR 📠 /
FEE

The following lodging was either not evaluated or did not meet AAA rating requirements but is listed for your information only.

HOTEL DES COMMANDANTS
Phone: 418/368-3355

[fyi]   Not evaluated. **Location:** Rt 132, 0.3 mi (0.5 km) e of bridge; centre. 178 rue de la Reine G4X 1T6. Facilities, services, and decor characterize a mid-range property.

—— WHERE TO DINE ——

ADAMS RESTAURANT
Lunch: $8-$20   **Dinner:** $8-$24   **Phone:** 418/368-4949

▼▼ ▼▼
Canadian

MC, VI.

Location: Corner of rue Jacques Cartier; centre; in Motel Adams. 20 rue Adams G4X 2R8. **Hours:** 6 am-9 pm. **Reservations:** suggested. **Features:** The family-run diner serves a variety of wholesome meals at great prices. Menu items include fresh fish, other seafood, hamburgers, pasta, salads and sandwiches. House-prepared pies are a wise choice for dessert. Casual dress; cocktails. **Parking:** on-site. **Cards:** AX, DS,

🍸

RESTAURANT MAREE SOLEIL
Lunch: $9-$15   **Dinner:** $15-$30   **Phone:** 418/368-0013

▼▼ ▼▼
French

Location: Rt 132, 0.3 mi (0.5 km) e of bridge; centre; in Hotel des Commandants. 178 rue de la Reine G4X 2T6. **Hours:** 6-10 am, 11:30-2:30 & 5:30-10 pm, Sat 7 am-11 & 5:30-10 pm, Sun 7 am-1 & 5:30-9:30 pm. Closed: 1/1, 12/25. **Reservations:** suggested. **Features:** French cuisine and maritime produce influence the menu of the comfortable, country-elegant restaurant. On the menu are Atlantic salmon filets, cod, shrimp, salmon tartare, mussels and fries, scallops, milk-fed veal cutlets, gourmet pizza, rib-eye steaks, grain-fed breast of chicken, calves liver, flank steak and pasta. Dressy casual; cocktails. **Parking:** on-site. **Cards:** AX, MC, VI.

🍸

GATINEAU pop. 234,679

—— WHERE TO STAY ——

BEST WESTERN CARTIER HOTEL & CONFERENCE
CENTRE   *Book great rates at AAA.com*
Phone: (819)770-8550

(CAA) (SAVE)

▼▼▼▼

Small-scale Hotel

5/1-10/31   1P: $159-$209   2P: $159-$209   XP: $5   F17
1/1-4/30   1P: $134-$164   2P: $134-$164   XP: $5   F17
11/1-12/31   1P: $129-$159   2P: $129-$159   XP: $5   F17
Location: Between rue St-Laurent and St-Etienne, just e of Alexandria Bridge; in Hull sector. 131 rue Laurier J8X 3W3. Fax: 819/770-9705. **Facility:** 133 units. 124 one-bedroom standard units, some with kitchens. 9 one-bedroom suites ($209-$219). 9 stories, interior corridors. **Parking:** on-site (fee). **Terms:** check-in 4 pm, [AP], [BP], [CP], [ECP] & [MAP] meal plans available, $2 service charge. **Amenities:** voice mail, irons, hair dryers. **Dining:** 7 am-1 & 5-10 pm. **Pool(s):** heated indoor. **Leisure Activities:** exercise room. **Guest Services:** valet laundry, wireless Internet. **Business Services:** meeting rooms, business center. **Cards:** AX, CB, DC, DS, JC, MC, VI. **Free Special Amenities:** local telephone calls and high-speed Internet.

SOME UNITS

📶 🍴 🏊 🖥 / ✕ 🔒 📠 /

CHATEAU CARTIER RELAIS-RESORT
Phone: (819)778-0000

(CAA) (SAVE)

▼▼▼▼

Resort
Large-scale Hotel

All Year   1P: $139-$259   2P: $139-$259   XP: $20   F17
Location: On Rt 148, 0.6 mi (1 km) w of Champlain Bridge; in Aylmer sector. 1170 chemin Aylmer J9H 7L3. Fax: 819/777-2518. **Facility:** The resort features a spa and extensive recreational facilities. 129 units. 39 one-bedroom standard units, some with whirlpools. 90 one-bedroom suites. 6 stories, interior corridors. **Parking:** on-site. **Terms:** check-in 4 pm, cancellation fee imposed, package plans. **Amenities:** voice mail, irons, hair dryers. **Dining:** Sam Snead's Bar & Grill, see separate listing. **Pool(s):** heated indoor. **Leisure Activities:** saunas, whirlpools, steamrooms, cross country skiing, ice skating, tobogganing, bike path, squash court, hiking trails, exercise room, spa, volleyball. Fee: golf-18 holes, 2 lighted tennis courts, racquetball courts, snowshoeing, aerobic instructions, bicycles. **Guest Services:** sundries, valet laundry, wireless Internet. **Business Services:** conference facilities, business center. **Cards:** AX, DC, MC, VI. **Free Special Amenities:** local telephone calls and high-speed Internet.

SOME UNITS

🍴 🏊 ✕ 📷 🔒 🖥 / ✕ /

CLARION HOTEL & CONFERENCE CENTER   *Book great rates at AAA.com*
Phone: (819)568-5252

▼▼▼▼

Small-scale Hotel

1/1-4/30   1P: $113-$133   2P: $113-$133   XP: $10   F16
5/1-12/31   1P: $109-$129   2P: $109-$129   XP: $10   F16
Location: Hwy 50, exit 139, 1 mi (1.6 km) se on boul Maloney ouest (Hwy 148), then just sw. 111 rue Bellehumeur J8T 6K5. Fax: 819/568-0753. **Facility:** 116 units. 115 one-bedroom standard units, some with whirlpools. 1 one-bedroom suite ($156-$182) with whirlpool. 2 stories (no elevator), interior corridors. **Parking:** on-site, winter plug-ins. **Terms:** [CP] meal plan available, package plans, pets ($45 fee). **Amenities:** voice mail, irons, hair dryers. *Some:* dual phone lines, safes, honor bars. **Pool(s):** heated outdoor. **Leisure Activities:** Fee: saunas, exercise room, massage. **Guest Services:** sundries, valet laundry, tanning studio, wireless Internet. **Business Services:** conference facilities, business center. **Cards:** AX, DC, DS, MC, VI. *(See color ad card insert)*

SOME UNITS

(ASK) 📶 🐾 🍴 🍸 🏊 ✕ 📷 🖥 / ✕ 📠 /
FEE

COMFORT INN GATINEAU
Book great rates at AAA.com
Phone: (819)243-6010

CAA SAVE

6/23-10/31 [CP]	1P: $110-$150	2P: $120-$160	XP: $10 F17
5/1-6/22 & 11/1-4/30 [CP]	1P: $100-$140	2P: $110-$150	XP: $10 F17

Location: Hwy 50, exit 140, 1.3 mi (2 km) e. 630 boul La Gappe J8T 9Z6. **Fax:** 819/243-4668. **Facility:** 80 one-bedroom standard units. 2 stories (no elevator), interior corridors. **Parking:** on-site, winter plug-ins. **Terms:** check-in 4 pm, pets (on ground floor). **Amenities:** irons, hair dryers. **Guest Services:** valet laundry, wireless Internet. **Cards:** AX, CB, DC, DS, JC, MC, VI. *(See color ad card insert)*

Small-scale Hotel

SOME UNITS

FOUR POINTS BY SHERATON & CONFERENCE
CENTRE GATINEAU-OTTAWA
Book great rates at AAA.com
Phone: (819)778-6111

CAA SAVE

All Year	1P: $99-$195	2P: $99-$195	XP: $20 F18

Location: Corner of rue Victoria, across from Canadian Museum of Civilization; in Hull sector. 35 rue Laurier J8X 4E9. **Fax:** 819/778-3647. **Facility:** 201 units. 194 one-bedroom standard units. 7 one-bedroom suites ($150-$300). 9 stories, interior corridors. **Parking:** on-site (fee). **Terms:** small pets only. **Amenities:** video games (fee), high-speed Internet, dual phone lines, voice mail, irons, hair dryers. **Dining:** 6:30 am-10 pm, cocktails. **Pool(s):** heated indoor. **Leisure Activities:** whirlpool, exercise room. **Guest Services:** gift shop, valet laundry. **Business Services:** conference facilities, business center. **Cards:** AX, DC, DS, JC, MC, VI. **Free Special Amenities:** newspaper and high-speed Internet. *(See color ad p 5)*

Large-scale Hotel

SOME UNITS

HILTON LAC LEAMY
Book great rates at AAA.com
Phone: (819)790-6444

All Year	1P: $150-$280	2P: $150-$280	XP: $20 F18

Large-scale Hotel
Location: Adjacent to Casino du Lac Leamy; in Hull sector. 3 boul du Casino J8Y 6X4. **Fax:** 819/790-6408. **Facility:** In addition to impressive banquet rooms, this upscale casino hotel built in 2001 has elegant guest rooms with marble baths and one or two beds. 349 units. 314 one-bedroom standard units. 35 one-bedroom suites ($260-$2500), some with whirlpools. 20 stories, interior corridors. **Parking:** on-site and valet. **Terms:** [AP] & [BP] meal plans available, package plans, $2 service charge. **Amenities:** CD players, dual phone lines, voice mail, safes, honor bars, irons, hair dryers. **Fee:** video games, high-speed Internet. **Dining:** Le Baccara, see separate listing. **Pool(s):** heated outdoor, heated indoor, 2 wading. **Leisure Activities:** sauna, whirlpools, steamrooms, boat dock, 2 lighted tennis courts, cross country skiing, bicycles, playground, exercise room, spa, game room. **Fee:** ice skating. **Guest Services:** gift shop, valet laundry, wireless Internet. **Business Services:** conference facilities, business center. **Cards:** AX, CB, DC, DS, JC, MC, VI. *(See color ad p 395)*

SOME UNITS

FEE

HOLIDAY INN PLAZA LA CHAUDIERE
GATINEAU-OTTAWA
Book great rates at AAA.com
Phone: (819)778-3880

CAA SAVE

All Year	1P: $105-$159	2P: $105-$159	XP: $15 F17

Location: 0.5 mi (0.8 km) w of Portage Bridge at Rt 148 and rue Montcalm; in Hull sector. 2 rue Montcalm J8X 4B4. **Fax:** 819/778-7324. **Facility:** 232 units. 221 one-bedroom standard units. 11 one-bedroom suites, some with kitchens. 14 stories, interior corridors. **Parking:** on-site (fee) and street. **Terms:** package plans, 15% service charge, pets ($35 fee, must be attended). **Amenities:** video games (fee), voice mail, safes, irons, hair dryers. *Some:* high-speed Internet. **Dining:** 6:30 am-10 pm, cocktails. **Pool(s):** heated indoor. **Leisure Activities:** saunas, whirlpool, exercise room. **Guest Services:** gift shop, valet laundry, wireless Internet. **Business Services:** conference facilities, business center. **Cards:** AX, DC, DS, JC, MC, VI. **Free Special Amenities:** newspaper and high-speed Internet. *(See color ad card insert)*

Large-scale Hotel

SOME UNITS

FEE   FEE

HOTEL LES SUITES VICTORIA
Phone: (819)777-8899

All Year	1P: $90-$95	2P: $90-$95

Location: 0.3 mi (0.5 km) e on rue Laurier from Portage Bridge, just n; in Hull sector. 1 rue Victoria J8X 1Z6. **Fax:** 819/777-2211. **Facility:** 39 units. 16 one-bedroom standard units with efficiencies. 23 one-bedroom suites ($109-$125) with kitchens, some with whirlpools. 3 stories, interior corridors. **Parking:** on-site. **Terms:** check-in 4 pm. **Amenities:** voice mail, irons, hair dryers. *Some:* dual phone lines. **Guest Services:** valet and coin laundry. **Business Services:** meeting rooms. **Cards:** AX, DC, DS, MC, VI.

Small-scale Hotel

SOME UNITS

FEE

MOTEL CASINO
Phone: 819/776-8888

CAA SAVE

All Year	1P: $69-$79	2P: $89	XP: $10 F11

Location: Hwy 50, exit 134, just n on rue Montcalm; in Hull sector. 275 boul St-Joseph J8Y 3Y2. **Fax:** 819/776-5843. **Facility:** 25 one-bedroom standard units, some with whirlpools. 2 stories, interior corridors. **Parking:** on-site, winter plug-ins. **Amenities:** hair dryers. **Guest Services:** area transportation-casino. **Cards:** AX, DC, MC, VI.

Motel

SOME UNITS

RAMADA PLAZA MANOIR DU CASINO
Book great rates at AAA.com
Phone: (819)777-7538

CAA SAVE

All Year [BP]	1P: $135-$169	2P: $145-$179	XP: $15 F18

Location: Hwy 5, exit 3 (boul du Casino), follow signs; in Hull sector. 75 rue Edmonton J8Y 6W9. **Fax:** 819/777-0277. **Facility:** 174 one-bedroom standard units with whirlpools. 3 stories, interior corridors. **Parking:** on-site, winter plug-ins. **Terms:** check-in 4 pm, package plans. **Amenities:** voice mail, irons, hair dryers. *Some:* DVD players, CD players, dual phone lines, safes. **Dining:** 7 am-10:30 pm, cocktails, also, Le Biftheque, see separate listing. **Pool(s):** heated indoor. **Leisure Activities:** saunas, whirlpool. **Guest Services:** gift shop, valet laundry, beauty salon, wireless Internet. **Business Services:** meeting rooms, PC. **Cards:** AX, DC, MC, VI. **Free Special Amenities:** full breakfast and high-speed Internet. *(See color ad p 395)*

Small-scale Hotel

SOME UNITS

FEE   FEE

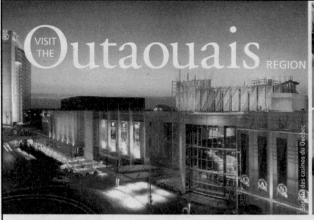

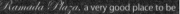

Turn Right for Member Savings

Right now, that is.
Turn to the back of the book
for special coupon savings!

Members save every day, at home and away, with AAA/CAA Show Your Card & Save® discounts on everything from movie tickets to car rental. Visit your AAA/CAA club office or AAA.com/save for details.

And now ... turn to the brand-new **Savings Section** at the back of the book for additional, limited-time bonus values from hotels, restaurants, and attractions. Enjoy extra perks exclusively for AAA/CAA members.

AAA.com

WHERE TO DINE

CHEZ CORA

Canadian modern.

Lunch: $7-$11   **Phone:** 819/771-3561

Location: Corner of rue St-Joseph; centre; in Hull Sector. 1 rue Gamelin J8Y 1V4. **Hours:** 6 am-3 pm, Sun from 7 am. **Reservations:** accepted. **Features:** Although this place specializes in breakfast, it offers a varied daytime menu that includes bacon, eggs, sausages, crepes, grilled cheese, sandwiches, freshly prepared quiches, salads, fruit platters and freshly squeezed juices. The family-friendly dining room is casual and modern. Casual dress; beer & wine only. **Parking:** on-site. **Cards:** AX, DC, MC, VI.

KELSEY'S

Canadian

Lunch: $7-$23   **Dinner:** $7-$23   **Phone:** 819/561-0983

Location: Centre. 740 boul Maloney ouest J8T 8K7. **Hours:** 11 am-11 pm, Thurs-midnight, Fri & Sat-1 am. Closed: 12/25. **Reservations:** accepted. **Features:** A fun, relaxed atmosphere and tasty menu of casual fare make the restaurant a popular favorite with locals. Diners might start a meal with some tempting appetizers, such as wings, loaded potato skins or nachos, and follow them with an old-time favorite, such as a burger, wrap, pizza or pasta dish. For a heartier meal, it's hard to beat pork back ribs or a steak. The diverse menu has broad appeal. Casual dress; cocktails. **Parking:** on-site. **Cards:** AX, CB, DC, DS, JC, MC, VI. 🍽

LE BACCARA

French

Menu on AAA.com   **Dinner:** $29-$58   **Phone:** 819/772-6210

Location: Hwy 5, exit 3 (boul du Casino); in Casino du Lac Leamy; in Hull sector. 1 boul du Casino J8Y 6W3. **Hours:** 5:30 pm-11 pm. **Reservations:** suggested. **Features:** Atop Casino du Lac Leamy, the dining room has a bank of oversized windows that afford a view of the distant Ottawa skyline. Custom table settings, fine crystal stemware and arguably the most attentive and intuitive service in all of Quebec make this a favorite place for special occasions. Also adding to the experience are wonderful contemporary French cuisine and the soothing sounds of the harpist. As guests pass the open kitchen, they can watch the detailed attention given to food preparation. Semi-formal attire; cocktails; entertainment. **Parking:** on-site and valet. **Cards:** AX, DC, MC, VI.

LE BIFTHEQUE

Steak House

Lunch: $7-$20   **Dinner:** $10-$20   **Phone:** 819/777-3727

Location: Hwy 5, exit 3 (boul du Casino), follow signs; in Hull sector; in Ramada Plaza Manior du Casino. 75 rue Edmonton J8Y 6W9. **Hours:** 7 am-10 pm, Wed & Thurs-10:30 pm, Sun 8 am-10 pm. **Reservations:** accepted. **Features:** The restaurant satisfies the cravings of folks in the mood for a sizzling steak. Huge portions of traditional steakhouse fare-including fine steaks, prime rib and seafood selections-keep locals coming back. Among starters are shrimp cocktail, French onion soup and escargots. Meals come with a tasty house salad and the ever-popular biftheque croutons. Diners should arrive with a hearty appetite. Casual dress; cocktails. **Parking:** on-site. **Cards:** AX, CB, DC, DS, JC, MC, VI. 🍽

MAISON SAMORN

Thai

Lunch: $8-$15   **Dinner:** $12-$20   **Phone:** 819/595-0232

Location: Corner rue Victoria; in Hull sector. 53 rue Kent J8X 3J9. **Hours:** 11:30 am-2 & 5-10 pm, Mon-2 pm, Sat 5 pm-10 pm. Closed: Sun & 12/23-1/10. **Reservations:** accepted. **Features:** Thai cuisine is served in a cozy, informal dining room. Among specialties are jumbo shrimp, Pad Thai, fried rice with seafood, salmon in red curry and a choice of soups. Casual dress; cocktails. **Parking:** on-site. **Cards:** MC, VI.

RESTAURANT LE TARTUFFE

Regional French

Lunch: $15-$19   **Dinner:** $29-$39   **Phone:** 819/776-6424

Location: Corner of rue Papineau. 133 Notre-Dame-de-L'Ile J8X 3T2. **Hours:** 11:30 am-2 & 5:30-10 pm, Sat from 5:30 pm. Closed major holidays; also Sun & 12/23-1/2. **Reservations:** suggested. **Features:** The vintage Victorian home serves fine regional cuisine, including creative preparations of grilled salmon, braised corn-fed chicken, roasted Barbarie duck breast, stuffed rabbit, roasted red deer, grilled veal chops, Alberta beef and rack of lamb. Casual dress. **Parking:** street. **Cards:** AX, CB, DC, DS, JC, MC, VI.

RISTORANTE FIORENTINA

Italian

Lunch: $10-$15   **Dinner:** $11-$25   **Phone:** 819/770-7273

Location: Just ne of rue Montcalm; in Hull sector. 189 boul St-Joseph J8Y 3X2. **Hours:** 11 am-11 pm, Sat from 4 pm, Sun 4 pm-10 pm. Closed: 12/24, 12/25. **Reservations:** accepted. **Features:** The cozy 1896 Victorian-style home houses several comfortable dining rooms where guests can relax and enjoy a wide variety of home-style dishes. Casual dress; cocktails. **Parking:** on-site. **Cards:** AX, DC, MC, VI.

ST-HUBERT

Canadian

Lunch: $7-$20   **Dinner:** $7-$20   **Phone:** 819/643-4419

Location: Centre. 357 boul Maloney ouest J8P 3W1. **Hours:** 11 am-11 pm, Thurs-Sat to midnight. Closed: 12/25; also for dinner 12/24. **Reservations:** accepted. **Features:** The pleasantly decorated family-friendly restaurant serves affordable chicken dinners, ribs, club sandwiches, chicken wings, salads, soups and hot chicken sandwiches. The children's menu includes animal nuggets. Casual dress; cocktails. **Parking:** on-site. **Cards:** AX, DC, MC, VI. 🍽

SAM SNEAD'S BAR & GRILL

Steak House

Lunch: $8-$25   **Dinner:** $8-$25   **Phone:** 819/776-7956

Location: On Rt 148, 0.6 mi (1 km) w of Champlain Bridge; in Aylmer sector; in Chateau Cartier Relais-Resort. 1170 chemin Aylmer J9H 5E1. **Hours:** 6:30 am-10 pm. **Reservations:** suggested. **Features:** Named for a former PGA golfer and decorated with golf memorabilia, the chain restaurant lets patrons unwind after a day on the links or other outdoor activity at the upscale resort. Grade A steaks, including filet mignon, are grilled over maple wood. Also on the menu are fajitas, smoked ribs, lobster tail, pizza, pasta, fish, burgers and sandwiches. The pub is a nice stop for a casual drink. Casual dress; cocktails. **Parking:** on-site. **Cards:** AX, DC, MC, VI. 🍽

STERLING

Steak & Seafood

Lunch: $15-$43   **Dinner:** $19-$69   **Phone:** 819/568-8788

Location: Hwy 50, exit 139, 0.6 mi (1 km) se on boul Maloney ouest (Rt 148), then 1.3 (2.1 km) sw on Greber. 835 rue Jacques-Cartier J8T 2W3. **Hours:** 11 am-11 pm, Sat & Sun from 5 pm. Closed: 12/25. **Reservations:** accepted. **Features:** This vintage waterfront home houses a stylish and contemporary steak and seafood restaurant. Start with a serving of beef tartare, oysters on the half shell, caviar, smoked salmon or duck foie gras terrine. Main courses include clams, snow crab, grilled lobster, fresh fish, veal rib chops, filet mignon, porterhouse or rib steak. Casual dress; cocktails. **Parking:** on-site. **Cards:** AX, DC, MC, VI. 🍽

GEORGEVILLE

——— WHERE TO STAY ———

AUBERGE GEORGEVILLE   Phone: (819)843-8683

CAA SAVE

Historic
Country Inn

All Year [MAP]   1P: $175-$230   2P: $250-$325   XP: $100
Location: Hwy 10, exit 118, 12.8 mi (20.5 km) s on Rt 141 and 247. Located in a quiet rural area. 71 chemin Channel J0B 1T0. Fax: 819/843-5045. **Facility:** Sheltering trees hide this charming 1889 Victorian inn, where in warmer months a flower garden blooms in view of the veranda. Smoke free premises. 9 units. 8 one-bedroom standard units. 1 one-bedroom suite ($325-$380). 3 stories (no elevator), interior corridors. **Bath:** combo or shower only. **Parking:** on-site. **Terms:** 2 night minimum stay - weekends, 15 day cancellation notice-fee imposed, [BP] meal plan available, package plans. **Amenities:** CD players. *Some:* DVD players, irons, hair dryers. **Dining:** restaurant, see separate listing. **Leisure Activities:** ice skating, snowshoe trail, badminton, croquet, bicycles, horseshoes. **Guest Services:** complimentary evening beverages, valet laundry. **Business Services:** meeting rooms. **Cards:** AX, MC, VI. **Free Special Amenities: local telephone calls and newspaper.**

SOME UNITS

🍴 ⚒ ✖ ☎ / 🅿 VCR /

——— WHERE TO DINE ———

AUBERGE GEORGEVILLE DINING ROOM   *Menu on AAA.com*   **Dinner:** $51   Phone: 819/843-8683

CAA

French

Location: Hwy 10, exit 118, 12.8 mi (20.5 km) s on Rt 139 and 147; in the Auberge Georgeville. 71 rue Principale J0B 1T0. **Hours:** 8 am-10 & 5:30-9 pm, Sat & Sun 8 am-11 & 5:30-9 pm. Closed: 12/24, 12/25; also Mon, Tues 12/1-5/1 except holidays. **Reservations:** required. **Features:** The cozy, intimate dining rooms are in a charming historic country inn. The five-course table d'hote includes innovative regional dishes with an accent on seasonal offerings. Guests may enjoy breast of Brome Lake duckling, wild Atlantic salmon, spiced loin of lamb, grain-fed veal, roasted Hemmingford pork, snow crab cakes and game liver terrine. Dressy casual; cocktails. **Parking:** on-site. **Cards:** AX, MC, VI. **Country Inn**

🍸

GRANBY pop. 44,121

——— WHERE TO STAY ———

HOTEL CASTEL & SPA CONFORT   Phone: (450)378-9071

Small-scale Hotel

6/1-4/30   1P: $95-$110   2P: $105-$140   XP: $10
5/1-5/31   1P: $75-$90   2P: $85-$105   XP: $10
Location: On Rt 112, 0.6 mi (1 km) e of jct Rt 139; Hwy 10, exit 68. 901 rue Principale J2G 2Z5. Fax: 450/378-9930. **Facility:** 136 units. 133 one-bedroom standard units, some with whirlpools. 3 one-bedroom suites ($170-$300) with whirlpools. 5 stories, interior corridors. **Parking:** on-site, winter plug-ins. **Terms:** check-in 4 pm, cancellation fee imposed, [MAP] meal plan available, package plans, no pets allowed (except during pet shows). **Amenities:** voice mail. *Some:* DVD players, CD players, irons, hair dryers. **Pool(s):** heated outdoor. **Leisure Activities:** whirlpools, playground, exercise room, shuffleboard. *Fee:* massage. **Guest Services:** valet laundry, wireless Internet. **Business Services:** conference facilities. **Cards:** AX, DC, DS, MC, VI.

SOME UNITS

ASK 🍴 🍸 🛏 ⚒ / ✖ VCR 🔌 🖥 💻 / .FEE

ST-CHRISTOPHE HOTEL BOUTIQUE & SPA   Phone: (450)405-4782

CAA SAVE

Small-scale Hotel

7/1-10/15 [BP]   1P: $139-$369   XP: $20   F12
10/16-4/30 [BP]   1P: $129-$339   XP: $20   F12
5/1-6/30 [BP]   1P: $119-$329   XP: $20   F12
Location: On Rt 112; centre. 255 rue Denison est J2H 2R4. Fax: 450/405-4756. **Facility:** Smoke free premises. 48 units. 45 one-bedroom standard units, some with whirlpools. 3 one-bedroom suites, some with whirlpools. 5 stories, interior corridors. **Parking:** on-site. **Terms:** cancellation fee imposed, package plans. **Amenities:** high-speed Internet, voice mail, irons, hair dryers. *Some:* DVD players. **Dining:** 7 am-9 pm, cocktails. **Pool(s):** heated indoor, saltwater. **Leisure Activities:** whirlpool, spa. **Guest Services:** sundries, valet laundry. **Business Services:** meeting rooms, fax (fee). **Cards:** AX, MC, VI. **Free Special Amenities: continental breakfast and high-speed Internet.**

🍴 🍸 🛏 ✖ 🔌 💻

——— WHERE TO DINE ———

CHEZ CORA   **Lunch:** $7-$11   Phone: 450/375-6199

Canadian

Location: Centre; in Les Galeries Granby. 15 rue Simonds N J2J 2P5. **Hours:** 6 am-3 pm, Sun from 7 am. **Reservations:** accepted, Mon-Fri. **Features:** Although this place specializes in breakfast, it offers a varied daytime menu that includes bacon, eggs, sausages, crepes, grilled cheese, sandwiches, freshly prepared quiches, salads, fruit platters and freshly squeezed juices. The family-friendly dining room is casual and modern. Casual dress; beer & wine only. **Parking:** on-site. **Cards:** AX, DC, MC, VI.

RESTAURANT FAUCHEUX   **Lunch:** $14-$21   **Dinner:** $32-$40   Phone: 450/777-2320

French

Location: Just n of rue Principale; corner of Ottawa; centre. 53-2 Dufferin J2G 4W8. **Hours:** 11:30 am-1:30 & 6-8:45 pm. Closed: 12/24-12/26; also Sun, Mon, first 3 weeks in Aug & 1/1-1/10. **Reservations:** suggested. **Features:** An understated elegance punctuates the relaxed dining room. Creative, market-sensitive cuisine includes such specialties as sweetbreads, crepes, smoked or roasted salmon, duck, quail, rack of lamb, foie gras and Quebec veal. The wait staff provides attentive, gracious service. Parking is in the back via rue Ottawa. Dressy casual; cocktails. **Parking:** on-site. **Cards:** AX, DC, MC, VI.

ST-HUBERT   **Lunch:** $7-$20   **Dinner:** $7-$20   Phone: 450/378-4657

Canadian

Location: On Rt 112; centre. 940 rue Principale J2G 2Z4. **Hours:** 11 am-11 pm, Fri & Sat-midnight. Closed: 12/25. **Reservations:** accepted. **Features:** The pleasantly decorated family-friendly restaurant serves affordable chicken dinners, ribs, club sandwiches, chicken wings, salads, soups and hot chicken sandwiches. The children's menu includes animal nuggets. Casual dress; cocktails. **Parking:** on-site. **Cards:** AX, DC, MC, VI.

GRAND-MERE pop. 13,179

—— WHERE TO STAY ——

AUBERGE LE FLORES
Phone: 819/538-9340

▼▼▼▼
Country Inn

Property failed to provide current rates
Location: Hwy 55 N, exit 220, follow signs. 4291 50 ieme Ave G9T 1A6. Fax: 819/538-1884. **Facility:** In a rural setting, the cozy cottage offers country-elegant guest rooms, fine dining, well-kept grounds and a health club. 34 one-bedroom standard units. 2 stories (no elevator), interior corridors. **Parking:** on-site. **Amenities:** hair dryers. **Pool(s):** heated outdoor. **Leisure Activities:** snowmobiling, spa. *Fee:* saunas, whirlpools. **Guest Services:** wireless Internet. **Business Services:** meeting rooms.

🍴 🍸 🏊 ⊗ ✕

AUBERGE SANTE DU LAC DES NEIGES
Phone: (819)533-4518

▼▼▼
Country Inn

All Year [BP] 1P: $105-$185 2P: $125-$215 XP: $60 F12
Location: Hwy 55, exit 220, follow signs. Located in a quiet area. 100 Lac des Neiges G9T 5K5. Fax: 819/533-4727. **Facility:** A spa enhances this contemporary country inn, which is 15 minutes off the main highway; grounds feature a private lake and wooded areas. Smoke free premises. 11 one-bedroom standard units, some with whirlpools. 2 stories (no elevator), interior corridors. *Bath:* combo or shower only. **Parking:** on-site. **Terms:** age restrictions may apply, cancellation fee imposed, package plans. **Amenities:** hair dryers. **Pool(s):** heated indoor. **Leisure Activities:** sauna, whirlpool, boating, canoeing, paddleboats, fishing, tennis court, cross country skiing, ice skating, hiking trails, spa. **Guest Services:** complimentary laundry. **Business Services:** meeting rooms. **Cards:** AX, JC, MC, VI.

SOME UNITS
ASK SD 🍴 🍸 🏊 ⊗ ✕ Z / 🅺 📺 VCR /

GRENVILLE-SUR-LA-ROUGE pop. 1,315

—— WHERE TO STAY ——

HOTEL DU LAC CARLING
Phone: (450)533-9211

Ⓐ SAVE
▼▼▼▼
Resort
Large-scale Hotel

All Year 1P: $140-$170 2P: $170-$220 XP: $50
Location: 3.1 mi (5 km) n. 2255 Rt 327 nord J0V 1B0. **Facility:** Find manicured grounds, upscale common areas, a marble-bottom swimming pool, a luxury spa and indoor tennis courts at this hotel. 99 one-bedroom standard units, some with whirlpools. 3 stories, interior corridors. **Parking:** on-site, winter plug-ins. **Terms:** 30 day cancellation notice-fee imposed, package plans, $3 service charge, small pets only ($20 deposit). **Amenities:** video library, safes, honor bars, irons, hair dryers. *Some:* DVD players, CD players. **Dining:** Restaurant L'If, see separate listing. **Pool(s):** heated indoor. **Leisure Activities:** saunas, whirlpools, boating, canoeing, paddleboats, fishing, kayaks, 2 lighted indoor tennis courts, racquetball court, squash court, tennis equipment, cross country skiing, snowmobiling, ice skating, tobogganing, ski equipment, bicycles, hiking trails, exercise room, spa, sports court. *Fee:* golf-18 holes, dog sleigh rides, snowmobiles, ATV, horseback riding. **Guest Services:** gift shop, valet laundry, wireless Internet. **Business Services:** conference facilities, business center. **Cards:** AX, DC, MC, VI. **Free Special Amenities:** newspaper.

SOME UNITS
SD 🛏 🍴 ♿ 🏊 ⊗ 💻 / ✕ VCR 📶 📷 /
FEE

—— WHERE TO DINE ——

RESTAURANT L'IF
Lunch: $5-$14 **Dinner: $9-$19** **Phone: 450/533-9211**

Ⓐ
▼▼▼
French

Location: 3.1 mi (5 km) n; in Hotel du Lac Carling. 2255 Rt 327 nord J0V 1B0. **Hours:** 7 am-10, noon-2 & 6-9:30 pm. **Reservations:** required. **Features:** In an upscale hotel adjacent to a golf course, the elegant dining room makes its mark with fine regional cuisine, including filet of trout, pan-fried scallops, oven-roasted, free-range chicken breast, braised lamb shank, pan-fried beef tenderloin, pan-fried Barbarie duck and Boileau deer. Semi-formal attire; cocktails. **Parking:** on-site. **Cards:** AX, CB, DC, JC, MC, VI.

HUDSON —*See Montreal p. 485.*

HULL pop. 66,246—*See GATINEAU.*

ILE AUX COUDRES

—— WHERE TO STAY ——

HOTEL MOTEL LA ROCHE PLEUREUSE
Phone: (418)438-2734

▼▼ ▼▼▼
Small-scale Hotel

7/1-9/4 1P: $79-$102 2P: $94-$140 XP: $5 F6
5/1-6/30 & 9/5-10/31 1P: $60-$86 2P: $80-$122 XP: $5 F6
Location: On Ile aux Coudres, 3.6 mi (5.8 km) e of ferry dock, follow signs; in la Baleine sector; access by ferry boat. 2901 chemin des Coudriers G0A 3S0. Fax: 418/438-2471. **Facility:** 87 one-bedroom standard units, some with whirlpools. 1-2 stories, interior/exterior corridors. **Parking:** on-site. **Terms:** open 5/1-10/31, 3 day cancellation notice, [AP], [CP] & [MAP] meal plans available, package plans, 15% service charge. **Pool(s):** heated outdoor. **Leisure Activities:** lighted tennis court, recreation programs in summer, rental bicycles, spa, shuffleboard. **Guest Services:** gift shop. **Business Services:** meeting rooms, PC. **Cards:** AX, CB, DC, DS, JC, MC, VI.

SOME UNITS
🍴 🍸 🏊 ⊗ ✕ / 🅺 /

ILE D'ORLEANS (See map and index starting on p. 517)

—— WHERE TO STAY ——

AUBERGE CHAUMONOT
Phone: 418/829-2735

▼▼▼ ▼▼▼
Country Inn

MC, VI.

5/1-10/31 [CP] 1P: $99-$169 2P: $109-$179 XP: $49 F5
Location: On Rt 368; in municipality of St-Francois. 425 chemin Royal G0A 3S0. **Facility:** 8 one-bedroom standard units. 3 stories (no elevator), interior corridors. **Parking:** on-site. **Terms:** open 5/1-10/31, [MAP] meal plan available. **Amenities:** hair dryers. **Pool(s):** outdoor. **Business Services:** meeting rooms, fax. **Cards:** AX,

🍴 🍸 🏊 ⊗ Z 💻

(See map and index starting on p. 517)

AUBERGE LA GOELICHE

Phone: (418)828-2248   **12**

6/23-9/3	1P: $151-$188	2P: $188-$225	XP: $32	D11
5/1-6/22 & 9/4-10/31	1P: $131-$188	2P: $168-$225	XP: $32	D11
11/1-4/30	1P: $101-$158	2P: $128-$185	XP: $32	D11

Country Inn

Location: 3.1 mi (5 km) w on Rt 368 from bridge, follow signs; in municipality of Ste-Petronille. 22 chemin du Quai G0A 4C0. Fax: 418/828-2745. **Facility:** Most of this contemporary country inn's upscale, individually decorated rooms overlook the St. Lawrence River. 16 units. 14 one-bedroom standard units, some with whirlpools. 2 two-bedroom suites. 2 stories (no elevator), interior corridors. *Bath:* combo or shower only. **Parking:** on-site. **Terms:** 30 day cancellation notice-fee imposed, [AP] & [MAP] meal plans available, package plans. **Amenities:** hair dryers. *Some:* honor bars, irons. **Pool(s):** outdoor. **Leisure Activities:** cross country skiing. **Guest Services:** valet laundry. **Business Services:** meeting rooms. **Cards:** AX, DC, MC, VI.

SOME UNITS

The following lodging was either not evaluated or did not meet AAA rating requirements but is listed for your information only.

AUBERGE LE CANARD HUPPE

Phone: 418/828-2292

[fyi]

Not evaluated. **Location:** From 1st traffic light off Pont de Ile d'Orleans, 3.8 mi (6 km) se. Located on a small island. 2198 chemin Royal G0A 3Z0. Facilities, services, and decor characterize a mid-range property.

———— WHERE TO DINE ————

LE MOULIN DE SAINT-LAURENT

Lunch: $9-$14   Dinner: $15-$26   Phone: 418/829-3888   **11**

(CAA)

French

Historic

Location: In municipality of St-Laurent; on Rt 368, 7.5 mi (12 km) se of Ile d'Orleans bridge. 754 chemin Royal G0A 3Z0. **Hours:** Open 5/1-10/15; 11:30 am-2:30 & 5:30-8:30 pm. **Reservations:** suggested. **Features:** The 18th-century flour mill boasts stone walls, attractive plants and flowers, a cozy summer terrace and pleasant views of a nearby waterfall. Smoked fish, chicken liver pate and game terrine top a menu that also features breast of chicken, salmon, scallops, quail, filet mignon, lamb and veal. Belgian waffles satisfy for dessert. A lighter lunch menu is available. Casual dress; cocktails. **Parking:** on-site. **Cards:** AX, DC, MC, VI.

RESTAURANT LE CANARD HUPPE

Lunch: $20-$29   Dinner: $35-$45   Phone: 418/828-2292

French

Country Inn

Location: From 1st traffic light off Pont de Ile d'Orleans, 3.8 mi (6 km) se; in Auberge Le Canard Huppe. 2198 chemin Royal G0A 3Z0. **Hours:** 8 am-9 pm; from 6 pm 1/1-3/15. **Reservations:** required, required 1/1-3/15. **Features:** In a pleasant country inn, the informal dining room is a nice spot for relaxing over superbly presented fine French cuisine, including chicken, quail, smoked or marinated duck, smoked salmon, veal, sweetbreads, Matane shrimps, filet mignon and Atlantic salmon. Casual dress; cocktails. **Parking:** on-site. **Cards:** AX, DC, MC, VI.

JONQUIERE pop. 54,842

———— WHERE TO STAY ————

HOLIDAY INN SAGUENAY CONVENTION CENTRE

Book great rates at AAA.com   Phone: (418)548-3124

7/1-8/31	1P: $129-$159	2P: $129-$159
5/1-6/30 & 9/1-4/30	1P: $109-$129	2P: $109-$129

Large-scale Hotel

Location: Hwy 70, exit 39, just ne, follow signs. Located next to a mall. 2675 boul du Royaume G7S 5B8. Fax: 418/548-1638. **Facility:** 155 units. 153 one-bedroom standard units. 2 one-bedroom suites. 10 stories, interior corridors. **Parking:** on-site, winter plug-ins. **Terms:** cancellation fee imposed. **Amenities:** voice mail, irons, hair dryers. *Some:* dual phone lines. **Dining:** Restaurant Cote Jardin, see separate listing. **Pool(s):** heated outdoor. **Leisure Activities:** snowmobiling, exercise room, spa. **Guest Services:** valet laundry, wireless Internet. **Business Services:** conference facilities, administrative services (fee), PC. **Cards:** AX, CB, DC, DS, JC, MC, VI.

SOME UNITS

FEE

The following lodging was either not evaluated or did not meet AAA rating requirements but is listed for your information only.

AUBERGE VILLA PACHON

Phone: 418/542-3568

[fyi]

Not evaluated. **Location:** Jct Hwy 372 est, 0.3 mi (0.4 km) w on Hwy 170 W (boul du Royaume), then just ne. 1904 rue Perron G7X 9P3. Facilities, services, and decor characterize a mid-range property.

———— WHERE TO DINE ————

AUBERGE VILLA PACHON RESTAURANT

Dinner: $40-$56   Phone: 418/542-3568

French

Country Inn

Location: Jct Hwy 372 est, 0.3 mi (0.4 km) w on Hwy 170 W (boul du Royaume), then just ne; in Auberge Villa Pachon. 1904 rue Perron G7X 9P3. **Hours:** 6 pm-10 pm. Closed: Sun & Mon. **Reservations:** suggested. **Features:** Fine French cuisine is served in an elegantly restored Tudor-style country inn. The chef's creations highlight fresh regional produce. Among choices are pan-seared foie gras, smoked salmon, rack of lamb, pheasant, milk-fed veal, duck, sweetbreads, beef fillet and venison. The chef is recognized as a "grand master" in the preparation of cassoulet, a white bean specialty offered only by advance request. Casual dress; cocktails. **Parking:** on-site. **Cards:** AX, DC, MC, VI.

LE ST-CYRIAC RESTO-CHAMPETRE

Dinner: $30-$42   Phone: 418/547-5728

(CAA)

Quebecois

Location: 4.8 mi (8 km) se of Hwy 170, follow sign; in L'Hotellerie Cepal Villegiature. 3350 rue St-Dominique G7X 7W8. **Hours:** Open 5/1-12/31; 5 pm-9 pm. **Reservations:** suggested. **Features:** The elegant country dining room is adorned with historic photographs and affords beautiful nature views through large windows. Fine regional cuisine centers on Angus beef, poultry, game, fresh seafood and a number of items prepared with popular Saguenay-region blueberries. Casual dress; cocktails. **Parking:** on-site. **Cards:** AX, DC, MC, VI.

RESTAURANT COTE JARDIN   **Lunch:** $8-$30   **Dinner:** $8-$30   **Phone:** 418/548-3124

▼▼▼   **Location:** Hwy 70, exit 39, just ne, follow signs; in Holiday Inn Saguenay Convention Centre. 2675 boul du Royaume
G7S 5B8. **Hours:** 6:30 am-2 & 5-10 pm. **Reservations:** suggested. **Features:** This casual hotel dining room

French   offers a reliable menu of steak, seafood, fresh fish, pasta and chicken. Service is friendly. Casual dress;
cocktails. **Parking:** on-site. **Cards:** AX, DC, MC, VI.   🍸

RESTAURANT LE BERGERAC   **Lunch:** $12-$15   **Dinner:** $30-$40   **Phone:** 418/542-6263

▼▼▼   **Location:** Hwy 170 W, 1.2 mi (2 km) s on boul Harvey, just e on St-Dominique, just n on rue St-Thomas, then just w on
St-Simon; behind hardware store. 3919 rue St-Jean G7X 3J5. **Hours:** 11 am-2 & 6-10 pm, Sat from 6 pm. Closed:

Nouvelle French   1/1, 12/24, 12/25; also Sun & Mon. **Reservations:** required. **Features:** The intimate, turn-of-the-20th-
century house is appointed with country-style decor. The atmosphere is relaxed. Three- to five-course table
d'hote menus lay out innovative meat, fish and game specialties prepared by the chef/owner. The wine list is impressive. Casual
dress; cocktails. **Parking:** on-site. **Cards:** AX, MC, VI.

ST-HUBERT   **Lunch:** $7-$20   **Dinner:** $7-$20   **Phone:** 418/542-0363

▼▼   **Location:** Centre. 3657 boul Harvey G7X 3A9. **Hours:** 11 am-10 pm, Thurs-Sat to midnight, Sun-11 pm. Closed:
12/25. **Reservations:** accepted. **Features:** The pleasantly decorated family-friendly restaurant serves

Canadian   affordable chicken dinners, ribs, club sandwiches, chicken wings, salads, soups and hot chicken
sandwiches. The children's menu includes animal nuggets. Casual dress; cocktails. **Parking:** on-site.
Cards: AX, DC, MC, VI.   🍸

KIRKLAND —See Montreal p. 486.

LA BAIE pop. 19,940

——— **WHERE TO STAY** ———

AUBERGE DES 21   **Phone:** (418)697-2121

▼▼▼	5/1-10/31	1P: $120-$195	2P: $130-$205	XP: $10	F11
11/1-4/30	1P: $90-$175	2P: $100-$185	XP: $10	F11

Country Inn   **Location:** Just e via rue Bagot (Hwy 170 E). 621 rue Mars G7B 4N1. Fax: 418/544-3360. **Facility:** This
contemporary country inn offers a well-equipped spa and upscale guest rooms, some with views of the bay.
31 units. 30 one-bedroom standard units, some with whirlpools. 1 one-bedroom suite ($175-$250). 2 stories (no elevator),
interior corridors. **Parking:** on-site, winter plug-ins. **Terms:** [MAP] meal plan available, 15% service charge. **Amenities:** hair
dryers. **Dining:** Restaurant Le Doyen, see separate listing. **Pool(s):** heated outdoor, saltwater. **Leisure Activities:** bicycles,
spa. **Guest Services:** valet laundry, wireless Internet. **Business Services:** meeting rooms, PC. **Cards:** AX, MC, VI.

SOME UNITS

🍴 🏊 💻 / ✕ VCR 🛎 🖨 /

——— **WHERE TO DINE** ———

RESTAURANT LE DOYEN   **Lunch:** $15   **Dinner:** $25-$28   **Phone:** 418/697-2121

(CAA)   **Location:** Just e via rue Bagot (Hwy 170 E); in Auberge des 21. 621 rue Mars G7B 4N1. **Hours:** 7 am-10, noon-1:30
& 5-9 pm. Closed: 12/25. **Reservations:** suggested. **Features:** Overlooking the beautiful Saguenay River,

▼▼▼   the elegant dining room is decorated in a contemporary style. Attentive service and pleasantly presented
dishes make for a memorable dining experience at the upscale country inn. Menu highlights include terrine

Regional French   of guinea fowl, rabbit, grilled veal, caribou, Atlantic salmon and smoked trout. Dressy casual; cocktails.
Parking: on-site. **Cards:** AX, DC, MC, VI. **Country Inn**   🍸

LAC-BEAUPORT —See Quebec p. 548.

LAC-BROME (KNOWLTON) pop. 5,100

——— **WHERE TO STAY** ———

AUBERGE KNOWLTON   **Phone:** 450/242-6886

▼▼▼   All Year   1P: $100   2P: $120-$135   XP: $25

Location: Corner of Hwy 104 and Rt 243; centre. 286 chemin Knowlton J0E 1V0. Fax: 450/242-1055. **Facility:** In

Country Inn   the heart of a lively Victorian village, this remodeled hotel offers stylish rooms and modern amenities. 12
one-bedroom standard units. 3 stories (no elevator), interior corridors. **Parking:** on-site. **Terms:** office hours
8 am-9 pm, [BP] meal plan available, package plans, small pets only. **Amenities:** hair dryers. **Dining:** Le Relais Restaurant-
Bistro, see separate listing. **Guest Services:** gift shop, wireless Internet. **Business Services:** meeting rooms. **Cards:** AX,
MC, VI.

SOME UNITS

🐾 🍴 ✕ / 🏋 /

AUBERGE LA BELLE ESCAPADE   **Phone:** 450/243-5532

▼▼   All Year   1P: $85-$115   2P: $95-$125   XP: $30   D6

Location: Hwy 10, exit 90, 7.6 mi (12.1 km) s on Rt 243, then 1.4 mi (2.2 km) w. 562 Knowlton Rd (Rt 104) J0E 1V0.

Historic   **Facility:** This quaint, Victorian-style home offers elegant, country-style rooms, on-site fine dining and a

Country Inn   heated pool surrounded by pretty gardens. Smoke free premises. 4 one-bedroom standard units, some with
whirlpools. 2 stories (no elevator), interior corridors. **Bath:** combo, shower or tub only. **Parking:** on-site.
Terms: 15 day cancellation notice-fee imposed, [MAP] meal plan available, package plans. **Pool(s):** heated outdoor. **Business
Services:** PC. **Cards:** AX, MC, VI.

(ASK) 🅢 🍴 🏊 ✕ 🏋 📺 ☎

AUBERGE LAKEVIEW INN

CAA SAVE

Historic
Country Inn

Phone: (450)243-6183

11/1-4/30	1P: $143-$189	2P: $304-$339	XP: $55	D12
5/1-10/31	1P: $121-$160	2P: $228-$288	XP: $55	D12

Location: Centre. 50 rue Victoria J0E 1V0. Fax: 450/243-0602. **Facility:** The small but charming rooms in this restored 1874 Victorian inn are furnished with reproduction period pieces. Designated smoking area. 28 one-bedroom standard units, some with whirlpools. 3 stories (no elevator), interior corridors. *Bath:* combo or shower only. **Parking:** on-site. **Terms:** check-in 4 pm, 2 night minimum stay - weekends, 14 day cancellation notice, package plans. **Amenities:** video library, hair dryers. *Some:* DVD players, CD players, irons. **Dining:** 7:30 am-10 pm; Sunday brunch, restaurant, see separate listing. **Pool(s):** heated outdoor. **Leisure Activities:** exercise room. **Guest Services:** wireless Internet. **Business Services:** meeting rooms, PC. **Cards:** AX, DC, MC, VI.

SOME UNITS

 / VCR /

AUBERGE QUILLIAMS INN

CAA SAVE

Country Inn

Phone: (450)243-0404

6/17-10/8	1P: $150-$275	2P: $150-$275	XP: $25	D12
5/1-6/16 & 10/9-4/30	1P: $139-$260	2P: $139-$260	XP: $25	D12

Location: Hwy 10, exit 90, 3.1 mi (4.9 km) s on Rt 243. 572 chemin Lakeside J0E 1R0. Fax: 450/243-0770. **Facility:** Private balconies adjoin all rooms at this contemporary country inn, which overlooks a scenic lake; some rooms feature a fireplace. 38 units. 34 one-bedroom standard units, some with efficiencies. 4 one-bedroom suites ($229-$275) with efficiencies and whirlpools. 3 stories (no elevator), interior corridors. **Parking:** on-site. **Terms:** check-in 4 pm, 3 day cancellation notice-fee imposed, [MAP] meal plan available, package plans. **Amenities:** dual phone lines, safes, honor bars, irons, hair dryers. *Some:* DVD players (fee). **Dining:** Restaurant Auberge Quilliams, see separate listing. **Pool(s):** heated outdoor, small heated indoor, lap. **Leisure Activities:** saunas, whirlpool, beach access, rental paddleboats, boat dock, fishing, cross country skiing, snowmobiling. *Fee:* canoes, sailboats, kayak. **Guest Services:** wireless Internet. **Business Services:** meeting rooms. **Cards:** AX, DC, DS, MC, VI.

SOME UNITS

/ VCR /
FEE

------- **WHERE TO DINE** -------

THE AUBERGE LAKEVIEW INN DINING ROOM

CAA

French

Menu on AAA.com

Dinner: $28-$35

Phone: 450/243-6183

Location: Centre; in Auberge Lakeview Inn. 50 rue Victoria J0E 1V0. **Hours:** 6 pm-10 pm. **Reservations:** suggested. **Features:** The restaurant serves French and International cuisine in its elegant, 19th-century-style dining room. Local produce wakes up the flavors in creative preparations of meat, fish and poultry. Dressy casual; cocktails. **Parking:** on-site. **Cards:** AX, DC, DS, JC, MC, VI. Country Inn

LE RELAIS RESTAURANT-BISTRO

Canadian

Lunch: $9-$18

Dinner: $18-$28

Phone: 450/242-2232

Location: Corner of Hwy 104 and Rt 243; centre; in Auberge Knowlton. 286 chemin Knowlton J0E 1V0. **Hours:** 8 am-10 pm; 5 pm-9 pm, Thurs-Sat to 10 pm 11/1-6/1. Closed: 12/25; also for dinner 12/24. **Reservations:** suggested. **Features:** Regional cuisine and some pub foods are prepared at the charming country town's relaxed hotel bistro. On the varied menu are French onion soup, mussels, salmon, fish and chips, fried clams, roast chicken, steak and sandwiches. Apple crisp is worth trying for dessert. Casual dress. **Parking:** on-site. **Cards:** MC, VI.

RESTAURANT AUBERGE QUILLIAMS

CAA

French

Menu on AAA.com

Lunch: $11-$20 Dinner: $20-$40 Phone: 450/243-0404

Location: Hwy 10, exit 90, 3.1 mi (4.9 km) s on Rt 243. 572 chemin Lakeside J0E 1R0. **Hours:** 7 am-10 pm, Fri & Sat-midnight. Closed: for dinner 12/24. **Reservations:** suggested. **Features:** In an upscale Eastern Townships inn, the sophisticated restaurant emphasizes quality regional produce in such preparations as Lake Brome duck, striped sea bass, rabbit, Angus beef, pan-seared ostrich, yellowfin tuna, veal and rack of lamb. Visitors may view the vast wine cellar with its own wine tasting area and private dining room. Dressy casual; cocktails. **Parking:** on-site. **Cards:** AX, DC, MC, VI.

LACHINE —*See Montreal p. 486.*

LA MALBAIE pop. 4,000

------- **WHERE TO STAY** -------

AUBERGE DES 3 CANARDS

CAA SAVE

Small-scale Hotel

Book great rates at AAA.com

Phone: (418)665-3761

All Year	2P: $115-$335	XP: $45	F6

Location: On Rt 362, 2.6 mi (4.1 km) w of jct Rt 138; located in Pointe-au-Pic sector. 115 Cote Bellevue G5A 1Y2. Fax: 418/665-4727. **Facility:** Designated smoking area. 49 units. 48 one-bedroom standard units, some with whirlpools. 1 cottage. 2 stories (no elevator), interior/exterior corridors. **Parking:** on-site, winter plug-ins. **Terms:** 7 day cancellation notice-fee imposed, package plans. **Amenities:** voice mail, irons, hair dryers. **Dining:** restaurant, see separate listing. **Pool(s):** heated outdoor. **Leisure Activities:** putting green, lighted tennis court, cross country skiing, snowmobiling, croquet, shuffleboard. *Fee:* massage. **Business Services:** meeting rooms. **Cards:** AX, MC, VI.

SOME UNITS

ECONO LODGE

Small-scale Hotel

Book great rates at AAA.com

Phone: (418)665-3733

6/21-9/3	1P: $109	2P: $119	XP: $15	F17
5/1-6/20	1P: $85-$95	2P: $95-$105	XP: $10	F17
9/4-4/30	1P: $79-$89	2P: $89-$99	XP: $10	F17

Location: On Rt 362, just w of jct Rt 138. 625 boul de Comporte G5A 1T1 (CP 5027). Fax: 418/665-7758. **Facility:** 17 one-bedroom standard units. 3 stories (no elevator), interior corridors. **Parking:** on-site, winter plug-ins. **Terms:** cancellation fee imposed, [AP], [BP], [CP] & [MAP] meal plans available, package plans. **Amenities:** hair dryers. **Guest Services:** wireless Internet. **Business Services:** meeting rooms. **Cards:** AX, CB, DC, DS, MC, VI. *(See color ad card insert)*

SOME UNITS

ASK / X /

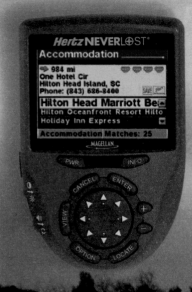

Find Hotels As Easy As 1-2-3-4-5!

For reliable hotel stays matched to your needs, every time, use AAA/CAA's valuable two-part rating system:

- First, rest assured that *every* hotel designated **AAA/CAA Approved** upholds qualities important to members – cleanliness, service, and value.

- Focus your selection using the descriptive one-to-five **AAA/CAA Diamond Ratings** assigned exclusively to Approved properties to help you match your expectations.

Find AAA/CAA Approved and Diamond rated properties in the TourBook® listings, in print and on aaa.com. Look for the AAA/CAA logo on signage and billboards.

Read about **AAA/CAA Diamond Ratings** on page 20-21 or visit aaa.com/Diamonds.

FAIRMONT LE MANOIR RICHELIEU *Book great rates at AAA.com* **Phone:** (418)665-3703

(CAA) (SAVE) All Year 2P: $143-$233 XP: $30 F18

Location: On Rt 362, 2.6 mi (4.1 km) w of jct Rt 138. Located adjacent to a casino. 181 rue Richelieu G5A 1X7.

Classic Historic Resort
Large-Scale Hotel

Fax: 418/665-3093. **Facility:** This family-friendly riverfront resort is adjacent to a golf course; the on-site recreational facilities are extensive. 405 units. 370 one-bedroom standard units. 35 one-bedroom suites ($450-$1200), some with whirlpools. 5 stories, interior corridors. **Parking:** on-site and valet. **Terms:** check-in 4 pm, cancellation fee imposed, [AP], [CP] & [MAP] meal plans available, pets ($25 extra charge). **Amenities:** voice mail, safes, honor bars, irons, hair dryers. *Fee:* video games, high-speed Internet. *Some:* CD players, dual phone lines. **Dining:** 4 restaurants, 7 am-midnight, cocktails, also, Le Charlevoix, see separate listing, entertainment. **Pool(s):** 2 heated outdoor, heated indoor, 2 wading, saltwater. **Leisure Activities:** sauna, whirlpools, steamroom, 3 lighted tennis courts, ice skating, recreation programs, badminton, bocci, petanque, rental bicycles, hiking trails, exercise room, spa, shuffleboard, volleyball. *Fee:* charter fishing, golf-27 holes, miniature golf, snowmobiling, heated snowmobile garage, skis, snowshoes. **Guest Services:** gift shop, valet laundry. **Business Services:** conference facilities, business center. **Cards:** AX, DC, DS, MC, VI. **Free Special Amenities:** local telephone calls and newspaper. *(See color ad card insert & p 385)*

SOME UNITS

(S D) (icons) / (X) (VCR) (icon) /
FEE   FEE

LA MAISON DES BERGES DU SAINT-LAURENT **Phone:** 418/665-2742

(icons)	7/1-8/31 [BP]	1P: $65-$125	2P: $65-$125	XP: $15	D14
Historic Bed & Breakfast	9/1-4/30 [BP]	1P: $55-$105	2P: $55-$105	XP: $15	D14
	5/1-6/30 [BP]	1P: $55-$100	2P: $55-$100	XP: $15	D14

Location: Just off Rt 362, 1.8 mi (2.9 km) w of jct Rt 138; in Pointe-au-Pic sector. 830 rue Richelieu G5A 2X3. **Fax:** 418/665-2742. **Facility:** Overlooking the riverfront road, this cozy village cottage has pleasant, well-maintained guest rooms, four of which afford river views. 9 one-bedroom standard units. 3 stories (no elevator), interior corridors. *Bath:* combo or shower only. **Parking:** on-site. **Terms:** age restrictions may apply, package plans. **Cards:** AX, JC, MC, VI.

SOME UNITS

(X) (Z) / (X) (W) /

LA PINSONNIERE *Book at AAA.com* **Phone:** (418)665-4431

(icons)	5/1-1/7	1P: $350-$500	2P: $350-$500	XP: $60
Country Inn	1/8-4/30	1P: $300-$485	2P: $300-$485	XP: $60

Location: Just off Rt 138, follow signs; in Cap-a-L'Aigle sector. 124 rue St-Raphael G5A 1X9. **Fax:** 418/665-7156. **Facility:** Manicured grounds surround this riverfront estate, which features spacious, luxurious rooms with whirlpools and attractive gas fireplaces. 17 units. 16 one-bedroom standard units with whirlpools. 1 two-bedroom suite ($700-$800) with whirlpool. 2 stories, interior corridors. *Bath:* combo or shower only. **Parking:** on-site. **Terms:** check-in 4 pm, 2-3 night minimum stay - weekends, 15 day cancellation notice-fee imposed, [MAP] meal plan available, package plans. **Amenities:** voice mail, safes, honor bars, irons, hair dryers. *Some:* DVD players, CD players, high-speed Internet. **Dining:** Restaurant de La Pinsonniere, see separate listing. **Pool(s):** heated indoor. **Leisure Activities:** sauna, tennis court, cross country skiing, snowmobiling. *Fee:* massage. **Guest Services:** valet laundry, wireless Internet. **Business Services:** meeting rooms, PC. **Cards:** AX, MC, VI.

SOME UNITS

(icons) / (VCR)
FEE

——— *The following lodging was either not evaluated or did not* ———
meet AAA rating requirements but is listed for your information only.

AUBERGE DES PEUPLIERS **Phone:** 418/665-4423

(fyi) Not evaluated. **Location:** Just off Rt 138; in Cap-a-L'Aigle sector. 381 rue St-Raphael G5A 2N8. Facilities, services, and decor characterize a mid-range property.

——— **WHERE TO DINE** ———

AUBERGE DES 3 CANARDS DINING ROOM **Dinner:** $55 **Phone:** 418/665-3761

(icons)
French

Location: On Rt 362, 2.6 mi (4.1 km) w of jct Rt 138; in Auberge des 3 Canards. 115 cote Bellevue G5A 1Y2. **Hours:** 7 am-11 & 5:30-9:30 pm. **Reservations:** suggested. **Features:** Fine regional cuisine is served in the charming dining room of an elegant country hotel. The menu lists such choices as veal medallions, sweetbreads, salmon, duck and beef. Guests may toast breads at a self-serve grill in the fireplace. Casual dress; cocktails. **Parking:** on-site. **Cards:** AX, MC, VI. **Country Inn**

(Y)

LE CHARLEVOIX **Dinner:** $36-$49 **Phone:** 418/665-3703

(CAA)
(icons)
French

Location: On Rt 362, 2.6 mi (4.1 km) w of jct Rt 138; in Fairmont Le Manoir Richelieu. 181 rue Richelieu G5A 1X7. **Hours:** 6 pm-9 pm. **Features:** In a classic luxury hotel, the upscale restaurant showcases the finest in regional cuisine and makes creative use of fresh local ingredients. Most tables afford memorable views of the river and manicured grounds. Dressy casual; cocktails. **Parking:** on-site and valet. **Cards:** AX, DS, JC, MC, VI.

(& M) (Y)

RESTAURANT DE LA PINSONNIERE **Lunch:** $12-$40 **Dinner:** $42-$50 **Phone:** 418/665-4431

(icons)
French

Location: Just off Rt 138, follow signs; in Cap-a-L'Aigle sector; in La Pinsonniere. 124 rue St-Raphael G5A 1X9. **Hours:** 8-10:30 am, 11:30-3:30 & 6-9:30 pm. **Reservations:** suggested. **Features:** Grilled scallops, halibut, Quebec lamb and pork, milk-fed veal, roast squab, duck and Atlantic salmon are representative of the haute Quebecois cuisine with some Asian influences. The wine list is extensive and live music is offered most nights in the elegant, comfortable dining room, which affords lovely river views. During summer, the terrace is a cozy place for light lunches. Dressy casual; cocktails. **Parking:** on-site. **Cards:** AX, DS, MC, VI. **Country Inn**

(Y)

RESTAURANT L'ALLEGRO **Lunch:** $6-$16 **Dinner:** $15-$34 **Phone:** 418/665-2595

(icons)
Italian

Location: Centre; in Pointe-au-Pic sector. 990 rue Richelieu G5A 2X3. **Hours:** 11 am-2 & 5-9 pm, Sat & Sun 5 pm-10 pm. **Reservations:** suggested. **Features:** The cheerful and lively corner bistro—with its sunny summer terrace—is a favorite spot for affordably priced pasta and pizza. Prices include the gratuity. Casual dress; cocktails. **Parking:** on-site. **Cards:** AX, DC, MC, VI.

(K)

L'ANCIENNE-LORETTE —*See Quebec p. 548.*

LA POCATIERE pop. 4,518

———— WHERE TO STAY ————

MOTEL LE POCATOIS
Phone: 418/856-1688

▼▼▼ ▼▼▼
Motel

Property failed to provide current rates

Location: Hwy 20, exit 439, 0.5 mi (0.8 km) s. 235 Rt 132 G0R 1Z0. **Fax:** 418/856-1688. **Facility:** 21 one-bedroom standard units, some with whirlpools. 2 stories, interior/exterior corridors. **Parking:** on-site, winter plug-ins. **Terms:** small pets only. **Amenities:** high-speed Internet, hair dryers. *Some:* irons. **Guest Services:** valet laundry. **Business Services:** meeting rooms.

SOME UNITS

🐾 🍴 🍸 / ⊠ 🔋 💻 /

LASALLE —*See Montreal p. 486.*

LAVAL —*See Montreal p. 486.*

LENNOXVILLE pop. 4,963

———— WHERE TO STAY ————

LA PAYSANNE MOTEL & HOTEL
Phone: 819/569-5585

(CAA) (SAVE)
▼▼▼ ▼▼▼
Motel

All Year 1P: $70-$106 2P: $70-$106 XP: $10 D18

Location: On Rt 143. 42 rue Queen J1M 1H9. **Fax:** 819/569-4294. **Facility:** 29 one-bedroom standard units. 1-2 stories (no elevator), interior/exterior corridors. *Bath:* combo or shower only. **Parking:** on-site, winter plug-ins. **Terms:** 7 day cancellation notice. **Dining:** 7-10 am. **Pool(s):** heated outdoor. **Guest Services:** sundries, wireless Internet. **Business Services:** meeting rooms. **Cards:** MC, VI. **Free Special Amenities:** local telephone calls and high-speed Internet.

SOME UNITS

🆂🅳 🐾 🍴 🍸 🏊 / ⊠ 🔋 /

———— WHERE TO DINE ————

LE CAFE FINE GUEULE Lunch: $7-$15 Phone: 819/346-0031

▼▼▼ ▼▼▼
Canadian

Location: On Rt 143. 170 rue Queen J1M 1J9. **Hours:** Open 5/1-7/15 & 9/5-4/30; 11 am-2 pm. Closed major holidays; also Sat-Mon. **Reservations:** suggested. **Features:** Hardwood floors and white walls with simple stencil work give the small, quiet dining room an easy, laid-back feel. Logically presented dishes, including a handful of Italian and French choices, are fresh and flavorful. Family-oriented service is friendly. Casual dress; cocktails. **Parking:** street. **Cards:** VI.

SEBBY'S PUB & GRILL *Menu on AAA.com* Lunch: $7-$10 Dinner: $12-$30 Phone: 819/569-9755

(CAA)
▼▼▼ ▼▼▼
Steak House

Location: On Rt 143, just s of jct Rt 108. 83 rue Queen J1M 1J3. **Hours:** 10:30 am-10 pm, Fri-11 pm, Sat 6 am-10 pm, Sun 6:30 am-10 pm. Closed: for dinner 12/24 & 12/31. **Reservations:** suggested. **Features:** Lending to the feel of a vintage steakhouse are a country pub, red-checkered tablecloths and rustic, wood-trimmed walls. The straightforward menu pleases patrons with a selection of AA-AAA grade steaks, barbecue ribs, club sandwiches, chicken, salads and brochettes. Casual dress; cocktails. **Parking:** on-site. **Cards:** AX, MC, VI.

LES EBOULEMENTS pop. 1,027

———— WHERE TO STAY ————

———— *The following lodgings were either not evaluated or did not* ———— *meet AAA rating requirements but are listed for your information only.*

AUBERGE DE NOS AIEUX
Phone: 418/635-2405

(fyi) Not evaluated. **Location:** Just s of Rt 362. 183 rue Principale G0A 2M0. Facilities, services, and decor characterize a mid-range property.

AUBERGE LE SUROUET
Phone: 418/635-1401

(fyi) Not evaluated. **Location:** On Rt 362. 195 rue Village G0A 2MO (CP 88, G0A 2M0). Facilities, services, and decor characterize a mid-range property.

———— WHERE TO DINE ————

AUBERGE ET RESTAURANT LE SUROUET Lunch: $12-$20 Dinner: $30-$45 Phone: 418/635-1401

▼▼▼ ▼▼▼
French

Location: On Rt 362; in Auberge Le Surouet. 195 rue Village G0A 2M0. **Hours:** 8-10 am, 11:30-2 & 6-8 pm. **Reservations:** suggested. **Features:** The decor is soft and graceful in the relaxed restaurant. Original ingredients flavor dishes of fine French cuisine. Diners can enjoy anything from a light luncheon to a comprehensive five-course prix-fixe dinner. The terrace is a nice spot for after-dinner drinks. Dressy casual; cocktails. **Parking:** on-site. **Cards:** AX, DC, MC, VI.

LEVIS —*See Quebec p. 549.*

L'ILE-PERROT —*See Montreal p. 489.*

L'ISLET pop. 3,866

WHERE TO STAY

AUBERGE DES GLACIS

Phone: 418/247-7486

Historic Country Inn

All Year [BP]   1P: $115-$155   2P: $130-$210   XP: $80
Location: 2.1 mi (3.3 km) e on chemin Lamartine est from jct Rt 285, then 0.3 mi (0.5 km) n. Located in a quiet area. 46 Rt de la Tortue G0R 1X0. Fax: 418/247-7182. **Facility:** Built in 1841, this restored stone flour mill is in a clearing near a river; a terrace, a small private lake and fine dining await guests. 10 one-bedroom standard units. 3 stories (no elevator), interior corridors. *Bath:* combo or shower only. **Parking:** on-site. **Terms:** office hours 7 am-11 pm, 7 day cancellation notice-fee imposed, [CP] & [MAP] meal plans available, package plans. **Amenities:** hair dryers. **Leisure Activities:** cross country skiing, snowmobiling, bicycles, hiking trails. *Fee:* massage. **Business Services:** meeting rooms. **Cards:** AX, MC, VI.

SOME UNITS

🍴 🍽 ⊠ ✕ ☎ 🖵 / 🍳 🅿 🖥 /

AUBERGE LA MARGUERITE

Phone: 418/247-5454

Historic Bed & Breakfast

6/21-10/31 [BP]	1P: $64-$114	2P: $78-$128	XP: $25 D6
5/1-6/20 [BP]	1P: $58-$103	2P: $75-$117	XP: $20 D6
11/1-4/30 [BP]	1P: $54-$91	2P: $68-$105	XP: $20 D6

Location: On Rt 132, 0.6 mi (1 km) e of jct Rt 285; centre. 88 des Pionniers est G0R 2B0. Fax: 418/247-7725. **Facility:** This well-maintained historic house, built in 1810, is centered in town and features a backyard with a garden. Smoke free premises. 8 one-bedroom standard units. 2 stories (no elevator), interior corridors. *Bath:* shower only. **Parking:** on-site. **Terms:** office hours 7 am-11 pm, 5 day cancellation notice, package plans, no pets allowed (owner's dog on premises). **Amenities:** hair dryers. **Business Services:** PC. **Cards:** MC, VI.

SOME UNITS

✕ ☎ / 🖥 /

AUBERGE LA PAYSANNE

Property failed to provide current rates

Phone: 418/247-7276

Condominium

Location: On Rt 132, 2.6 mi (4.2 km) e, jct Rt 285; centre. 497 des Pionniers est G0R 2B0. Fax: 418/247-7278. **Facility:** These very-good-size, modern, one-bedroom condo units face a pretty seafront marsh; the upscale guest rooms have a comfortable seating area. 12 one-bedroom suites. 2 stories (no elevator), exterior corridors. **Parking:** on-site. **Terms:** office hours 8 am-midnight, pets ($15 extra charge). **Amenities:** hair dryers. **Business Services:** meeting rooms.

SOME UNITS

🛏 🍳 🖥 🖵 / ✕ /
FEE

LONGUEUIL —See Montreal p. 490.

LOUISEVILLE pop. 7,622

WHERE TO STAY

GITE DU CARREFOUR ET MAISON HISTORIQUE
J.I.L. HAMELIN

Phone: (819)228-4932

Historic Bed & Breakfast

All Year   1P: $60   2P: $80-$90   XP: $25   D12
Location: On Rt 138; Hwy 40, exit 174 westbound; exit 166 eastbound; centre. Located in a rural area. 11 ave St-Laurent ouest J5V 1J3. Fax: 819/228-4932. **Facility:** Built in 1898 in neo-Queen Anne style, this architectural standout is furnished with high-quality antiques. Designated smoking area. 5 one-bedroom standard units. 2 stories (no elevator), interior corridors. *Bath:* some shared or private. **Parking:** on-site, winter plug-ins. **Terms:** small pets only (owner's cat on premises). **Amenities:** *Some:* hair dryers. **Guest Services:** complimentary laundry.

ASK 🛏 📶 ✕ 🍳 🅿 ☎

MAGOG pop. 14,283

——— WHERE TO STAY ———

AUBERGE MEMPHRE   Phone: 819/847-2222

Property failed to provide current rates

Small-scale Hotel

Location: Hwy 10, exit 118, 1 mi (1.6 km) s on Rt 141. 1007 Merry N J1X 2G9. **Fax:** 819/847-3648. **Facility:** 73 one-bedroom standard units. 3 stories, interior corridors. *Bath:* combo or shower only. **Parking:** on-site. **Terms:** check-in 4 pm. **Amenities:** hair dryers. **Pool(s):** heated indoor. **Business Services:** meeting rooms.

SOME UNITS

——— WHERE TO DINE ———

ST-HUBERT   **Lunch:** $7-$20   **Dinner:** $7-$20   Phone: 819/847-3366

Canadian

Location: Hwy 10, exit 118. 1615 chemin Riviere-aux-Cerises J1X 3W3. **Hours:** 11 am-10 pm, Tues-Thurs to 11 pm, Fri & Sat-midnight. **Closed:** 12/25. **Reservations:** accepted. **Features:** The pleasantly decorated family-friendly restaurant serves affordable chicken dinners, ribs, club sandwiches, chicken wings, salads, soups and hot chicken sandwiches. The children's menu includes animal nuggets. Casual dress; cocktails. **Parking:** on-site. **Cards:** AX, DC, MC, VI.

MANIWAKI pop. 3,571

——— WHERE TO STAY ———

CHATEAU LOGUE HOTEL-GOLF-RESORT   Phone: (819)449-4848

| | All Year | 1P: $119-$214 | 2P: $119-$214 | XP: $10 | F16 |

Resort
Small-scale Hotel

Location: On Rt 107, 0.6 mi (1 km) ne of Rt 105. 12 rue Comeau J9E 2R8. **Fax:** 819/441-1370. **Facility:** This contemporary mini-resort includes an 1887 stone manor featuring meeting space and a forestry museum. 51 one-bedroom standard units, some with whirlpools. 3 stories, interior corridors. **Parking:** on-site, winter plug-ins. **Terms:** check-in 4 pm, cancellation fee imposed, package plans. **Amenities:** dual phone lines, hair dryers. **Dining:** Le Poste de Traite-Trading Post, see separate listing. **Pool(s):** heated indoor. **Leisure Activities:** sauna, whirlpool, boat dock, fishing, cross country skiing, snowmobiling, hiking trails, exercise room, spa. **Fee:** boats, canoes, charter fishing, golf-9 holes. **Guest Services:** gift shop, valet laundry. **Business Services:** meeting rooms. **Cards:** AX, MC, VI.

SOME UNITS

——— WHERE TO DINE ———

LE POSTE DE TRAITE-TRADING POST   **Lunch:** $7-$22   **Dinner:** $16-$38   Phone: 819/449-4848

Quebecois

Location: On Rt 107, 0.6 mi (1 km) ne of Rt 105; in Chateau Logue Hotel-Golf-Resort. 12 rue Comeau J9E 2R8. **Hours:** 7 am-10 pm, Sun-Wed to 9 pm. **Reservations:** suggested. **Features:** The restaurant entrance is decorated like a vintage trading post—a job once fulfilled by the adjacent 1887 stone heritage building and inn. Wagon wheels, rural artwork and a wood ceiling complete the cozy country decor. Representative of fine regional cuisine are pork tenderloin, rack of lamb, grilled New York strip steak, black pepper steak, breast of duck with liver pate, red deer, sliced caribou, chicken supreme, pasta, fresh fish and seafood. Casual dress; cocktails. **Parking:** on-site. **Cards:** AX, CB, DC, MC, VI.

MARIA pop. 2,458

——— WHERE TO STAY ———

HOTEL HONGUEDO   Phone: 418/759-3488

Property failed to provide current rates

Small-scale Hotel

Location: On Rt 132, in town centre. 548 boul Perron G0C 1Y0 (CP 1038). **Fax:** 418/759-5849. **Facility:** 60 one-bedroom standard units, some with whirlpools. 2 stories (no elevator), interior/exterior corridors. **Parking:** on-site. **Terms:** small pets only. **Amenities:** hair dryers. **Some:** high-speed Internet, irons. **Pool(s):** heated outdoor. **Guest Services:** valet and coin laundry. **Business Services:** meeting rooms.

SOME UNITS

MATANE pop. 11,635

——— WHERE TO STAY ———

MOTEL LA MARINA   Phone: (418)562-3234

| | 5/21-10/15 | 1P: $50-$92 | 2P: $55-$92 | XP: $7 | F12 |

Motel

Location: On Rt 132. 1032 ave du Phare ouest G4W 3M9 (CP 64). **Fax:** 418/562-2802. **Facility:** 43 one-bedroom standard units, some with efficiencies. 1 story, exterior corridors. *Bath:* combo or shower only. **Parking:** on-site. **Terms:** open 5/21-10/15, small pets only. **Pool(s):** heated outdoor. **Cards:** AX, CB, DC, DS, JC, MC, VI.

SOME UNITS

QUALITY INN MATANE   *Book great rates at AAA.com*   Phone: (418)562-6433

| | 5/1-9/1 | 1P: $99-$159 | 2P: $109-$169 | XP: $15 | F18 |
| | 9/2-4/30 | 1P: $79-$119 | 2P: $89-$129 | XP: $15 | F18 |

Small-scale Hotel

Location: On Rt 132. 1550 ave du Phare ouest G4W 3M6. **Fax:** 418/562-9214. **Facility:** 70 one-bedroom standard units, some with whirlpools. 2 stories (no elevator), interior/exterior corridors. **Parking:** on-site, winter plug-ins. **Terms:** 7 day cancellation notice, $2 service charge. **Amenities:** voice mail, irons, hair dryers. **Some:** CD players, dual phone lines. **Fee:** DVD players. **Dining:** 6:20 am-1 & 5-9 pm, cocktails. **Pool(s):** heated outdoor. **Leisure Activities:** sauna, playground, exercise room. **Guest Services:** valet laundry, wireless Internet. **Business Services:** meeting rooms, PC. **Cards:** AX, CB, DC, DS, JC, MC, VI. **Free Special Amenities:** early check-in/late check-out and high-speed Internet. *(See color ad card insert)*

SOME UNITS

AUBERGE LA SEIGNEURIE   Phone: 418/562-0021
[fyi]   Not evaluated. **Location:** Centre. 621 ave St-Jerome G4W 3M9. Facilities, services, and decor characterize a mid-range property.

RIOTEL MATANE   Phone: 418/566-2651
[fyi]   Not evaluated. **Location:** On Rt 132; centre. 250 ave du Phare est G4W 3N4. Facilities, services, and decor characterize a mid-range property.

——— **WHERE TO DINE** ———

RESTAURANT LE RAFIOT   **Lunch:** $7-$12   **Dinner:** $8-$26   Phone: 418/562-8080
◆◆◆ ◆◆◆   **Location:** Centre; on Rt 132. 1415 ave du Phare ouest G4W 3N3. **Hours:** 11 am-2 & 5-9 pm, Sat & Sun from 5
pm. Closed: 12/25; also Sun 9/15-6/1. **Reservations:** accepted. **Features:** A nautical theme punctuates the
Seafood   decor of this casual pub and restaurant, which specializes in seafood, including Matane shrimp, sole,
mussels, crab and lobster. Also on the menu are chicken, ribs, pasta, thin-crust pizzas and salads. The
seasonal terrace is popular in summer. Casual dress; cocktails. **Parking:** on-site. **Cards:** AX, MC, VI.   ⬭

MATAPEDIA pop. 707

——— **WHERE TO DINE** ———

HOTEL MOTEL RESTIGOUCHE DINING ROOM   **Lunch:** $5-$15   **Dinner:** $16-$28   Phone: 418/865-2155
◆◆◆ ◆◆◆   **Location:** On Rt 132; centre. 5 rue des Saumons G0J 1V0. **Hours:** Open 5/1-10/31; 7 am-2 & 5-10 pm; 7 am-9,
noon-1:30 & 6-8 pm 9/1-10/15. **Reservations:** accepted. **Features:** Near the southern entrance to the
Seafood   scenic Matapedia Valley, the motel restaurant delivers home-style preparations of seafood, including locally
caught salmon. A relaxed atmosphere prevails in the charming, comfortable, lodge-style dining room.
Casual dress; cocktails. **Parking:** on-site. **Cards:** AX, DC, MC, VI.   ⬭

MONTEBELLO pop. 1,039

——— **WHERE TO STAY** ———

AUBERGE MONTEBELLO   *Book great rates at AAA.com*   Phone: (819)423-0001
(CAA) (SAVE)   5/1-10/31 [BP]   1P: $129-$169   2P: $169-$209   XP: $20   F17
          11/1-4/30 [BP]   1P: $109-$149   2P: $149-$189   XP: $20   F17
◆◆◆ ◆◆◆   **Location:** On Rt 148; centre. 676 rue Notre-Dame J0V 1L0. Fax: 819/423-0002. **Facility:** 44 units. 43 one-
bedroom standard units. 1 one-bedroom suite. 4 stories (no elevator), interior corridors. *Bath:* shower only.
Small-scale Hotel   **Parking:** on-site. **Terms:** package plans, $2 service charge. **Amenities:** voice mail, hair dryers. *Some:*
high-speed Internet. **Dining:** 7 am-10:30 & 5:30-9:30 pm, Sat & Sun 8:30 am-noon & 5:30-9:30 pm.
Pool(s): heated outdoor. **Leisure Activities:** petanque, pentanque, spa, horseshoes. *Fee:* boat dock. **Guest Services:** valet
and coin laundry, wireless Internet. **Business Services:** meeting rooms, PC (fee). **Cards:** AX, MC, VI.
Free Special Amenities: newspaper and high-speed Internet.
⬚ 🍴 ⬭ 🏊 ✕ ✕ ▭

FAIRMONT LE CHATEAU MONTEBELLO   *Book great rates at AAA.com*   Phone: (819)423-6341
(CAA) (SAVE)   All Year   1P: $189-$289   2P: $189-$289   XP: $30   F17
◆◆◆◆ ◆◆◆◆   **Location:** On Rt 148. 392 rue Notre-Dame J0V 1L0. Fax: 819/423-1133. **Facility:** The three original buildings of
this classic castle, which dates to 1930, were constructed with 10,000 red-cedar logs. 211 units. 204 one-
Resort   bedroom standard units, some with whirlpools. 7 one-bedroom suites ($259-$369). 3 stories, interior
Large-scale Hotel   corridors. **Parking:** on-site and valet. **Terms:** check-in 4 pm, 2 night minimum stay - seasonal and/or
weekends, 3 day cancellation notice-fee imposed, pets ($35 extra charge). **Amenities:** video games (fee),
CD players, voice mail, honor bars, irons, hair dryers. *Some: Fee:* high-speed Internet. **Dining:** 2
restaurants, 7 am-5 & 5:30-11 pm, cocktails, also, Aux Chantignoles, see separate listing. **Pool(s):** outdoor, heated indoor.
Leisure Activities: saunas, whirlpools, lifeguard on duty, fishing, 8 tennis courts (2 indoor, 8 lighted), cross country skiing, ice
skating, badminton, off road vehicle, hiking trails, playground, exercise room, spa, basketball, horseshoes, shuffleboard,
volleyball. *Fee:* boats, marina, charter fishing, pontoon boats, golf-18 holes, miniature golf, snowmobiling, curling, croquet,
Landrover driving school, bicycles, horseback riding, game room. **Guest Services:** gift shop, valet laundry, wireless Internet.
Business Services: conference facilities, business center. **Cards:** AX, CB, DC, DS, JC, MC, VI. *(See color ad card insert)*

SOME UNITS
🐾 🍴 ⬭ 🛎 🏊 ✕ 🏋 ▭ / ✕ VCR ▤ /
FEE   FEE FEE

——— **WHERE TO DINE** ———

AUX CHANTIGNOLES   **Lunch:** $14-$25   **Dinner:** $22-$40   Phone: 819/423-6341
◆◆◆ ◆◆◆   **Location:** On Rt 148; in Fairmont Le Chateau Montebello. 392 rue Notre-Dame J0V 1L0. **Hours:** 7 am-10 pm.
Features: Within the charming and luxurious Chateau Montebello, the dining room presents a menu of fine
French   regional cuisine, much of it French-influenced. Reservations are a must for non-hotel guests. Dressy casual;
cocktails. **Parking:** on-site. **Cards:** AX, CB, DC, DS, JC, MC, VI.

MONT-LAURIER pop. 7,365

─────── WHERE TO STAY ───────

COMFORT INN   *Book great rates at AAA.com*   **Phone:** 819/623-6465
All Year   1P: $98   2P: $108   XP: $10   F
Location: On Hwy 117; centre. 700 boul A-Paquette J9L 1L4. **Fax:** 819/623-9404. **Facility:** 41 one-bedroom
Small-scale Hotel   standard units, some with whirlpools. 2 stories, interior/exterior corridors. *Bath:* combo or shower only.
Parking: on-site, winter plug-ins. **Terms:** [BP] meal plan available, package plans. **Amenities:** irons, hair
dryers. **Dining:** La Cage aux Sports, see separate listing. **Leisure Activities:** snowmobiling, exercise room. **Guest Services:**
valet laundry, wireless Internet. **Business Services:** meeting rooms. **Cards:** AX, MC, VI. **(See color ad card insert)**

SOME UNITS
(ASK) ⊤⊤ 🖵 / ✕ 🔒 /

─────── WHERE TO DINE ───────

LA CAGE AUX SPORTS   **Lunch:** $7-$13   **Dinner:** $8-$21   **Phone:** 819/623-6435
Location: On Hwy 117; centre; in Comfort Inn. 700 boul A-Paquette J9L 1L4. **Hours:** 6:30 am-10:30 pm, Thurs &
Fri-11:30 pm, Sat 7 am-11:30 pm, Sun 7 am-10:30 pm. **Closed:** 12/25; also for breakfast 1/1 & 12/26.
Canadian   **Reservations:** accepted. **Features:** This popular Quebec chain of sports bars presents a menu of pub
foods, including ribs, chicken, burgers, salads, crispy fries, pasta and tasty desserts. Guests might begin the
meal with a basket of freshly popped popcorn as they check out the sports memorabilia. Children are welcomed. Casual dress;
cocktails. **Parking:** on-site. **Cards:** AX, DC, MC, VI.
⊤

PLACE MONT-LAURIER PIZZERIA   **Lunch:** $5-$10   **Dinner:** $11-$21   **Phone:** 819/623-2597
Location: On Hwy 117; centre. 457 boul A-Paquette J9L 1K7. **Hours:** 11 am-midnight, Fri & Sat-2 am. **Closed:**
1/1, 12/25. **Reservations:** suggested. **Features:** The menu lists simple, well-prepared comfort foods,
Italian   including many traditional Greek and Italian dishes. Pizza, pasta, brochettes, seafood, steak and roast
chicken are among choices. The decor reflects the style of a modern diner, with lots of greenery and large
windows. Casual dress; cocktails. **Parking:** on-site. **Cards:** DC, MC, VI.
⊤

MONTMAGNY pop. 11,654

─────── WHERE TO STAY ───────

MANOIR DES ERABLES   *Book at AAA.com*   **Phone:** (418)248-0100
6/1-10/31   1P: $99-$160   2P: $99-$160   XP: $20   F12
5/1-5/31 & 11/1-4/30   1P: $99-$120   2P: $99-$120   XP: $20   F12
Country Inn   **Location:** Hwy 20, exit 376, 1.4 mi (2.2 km) e on Rt 228, 0.9 mi (1.5 km) e. 220 boul Tache est (Rt 132) G5V 1G5.
Fax: 418/248-9507. **Facility:** Built in 1814, the grounds are a Victorian-style building that dates to 1814, a stone
manor house and a nine-room motel. 24 units. 23 one-bedroom standard units, some with whirlpools. 1 one-bedroom suite
($250-$275). 3 stories (no elevator), interior/exterior corridors. *Bath:* combo or shower only. **Parking:** on-site. **Terms:** office
hours 7:30 am-10 pm, check-in 4 pm, 10 day cancellation notice, [MAP] meal plan available, package plans, small pets only
($15 extra charge, in motel units). **Amenities:** hair dryers. *Some:* irons. **Dining:** restaurant, see separate listing. **Pool(s):**
heated outdoor. **Leisure Activities:** snowmobiling, spa. *Fee:* bicycles. **Guest Services:** wireless Internet. **Business Services:**
meeting rooms, PC, fax. **Cards:** AX, DC, MC, VI.

SOME UNITS
🛏 ⊤⊤ ⇌ ✕ ✕ 🖵 / (𝕏) /
FEE

─────── WHERE TO DINE ───────

MANOIR DES ERABLES DINING ROOM   *Menu on AAA.com*   **Lunch:** $18-$25 **Dinner:** $36-$58 **Phone:** 418/248-0100
Location: Hwy 20, exit 376, 1.4 mi (2.2 km) e on Rt 228, 0.9 mi (1.5 km) e; in Manoir des Erables. 220 boul Tache est
(Rt 132) G5V 1G5. **Hours:** 7:30 am-10 & 6-9:30 pm; also noon-1 pm Mon-Fri 6/24-9/5. **Closed:** 12/25; also for
dinner 12/24. **Reservations:** suggested. **Features:** Built in 1814, the lovely Victorian-style manor exudes
Quebecois   charm and sophistication. The gastronomic menu highlights fine Quebecois cuisine and features roasted
salmon, grilled tuna, larded sturgeon, quail or guinea fowl, stuffed rabbit, walleye filet, veal chops and beef
sirloin. Appetizers include game terrine, marinated salmon and smoked sturgeon. An excellent selection of
wines and cheeses is offered. Dressy casual; cocktails. **Parking:** on-site. **Cards:** AX, DC, MC, VI. **Country Inn**
⊤

RESTAURANT NORMANDIN   **Lunch:** $5-$12   **Dinner:** $5-$12   **Phone:** 418/248-3667
Location: On Hwy 132. 25 boul Tache E G5V 1B6. **Hours:** 6 am-midnight, Thurs-2 am, Fri & Sat-3 am. **Closed:**
12/25. **Reservations:** accepted. **Features:** The family restaurant prepares affordable comfort foods that
Canadian   include roasted chicken, hot chicken sandwiches, pasta, burgers and fries. Take-out service, a children's
menu and cutely decorated desserts are among other offerings. Casual dress. **Parking:** on-site. **Cards:** AX,
DC, MC, VI.

IF YOU ONLY KNEW

how much I've saved
with my CAA membership card.

Once you start saving money with your CAA membership card, you'll tell everyone you know! Save on everything from flowers and clothes to hotel rooms and theme park tickets. You'll receive immediate savings, or at some locations in Canada, will earn CAA Dollars - simply by presenting your CAA membership card.

CAA's Show Your Card & Save® program provides you with savings at over 150,000 participating merchant locations around the world.
Who knew I could save so much?

Destination Montréal
pop. 1,039,534

*I*f you're looking for a *haute* time try Montréal, a cosmopolis whose amenities rival those of any city. And, Montréal does it with *élan*.

*T*he shopping for goods from antiques to *haute couture* is marvelous. Food choices range from East Indian to French *haute cuisine*. And the live entertainment possibilities are world-class and seemingly endless.

© Andre Jenny

Bonsecours Market Montréal in the Old Port of Montréal. This building has been at the heart of Montréal since 1847.

A street market in Old Montréal. Shoppers employ the time-tested methods of sniff and pinch to gather the ingredients for *cuisine québécoise.*

© Buddy Mays Travel
Stock Photography

Sidewalk café in Montréal
Fine cuisine and summer sunshine make *al fresco* dining a favorite pastime.

© Tourisme Montréal / Stéphan Poulin

© age fotostock / SuperStock

Les Cours Mont-Royal, Montréal.
In the heart of downtown, this artistically sophisticated, upscale mall caters to those with traditional as well as trendy tastes. (See mention page 191)

See Downtown map page 414

Laval

Anjou Boucherville

Outremont Longueil Beloeil Mont-St-Hilaire

St-Laurent Westmount St-Hubert-De-Rivere-Du-Loup
Côte-St-Luc Brossard
Verdun Chambly
Lachine Montréal-Ouest
LaSalle

See Vicinity map page 420

© MTOQ / Robin Edgar

Rafting on the Lachine Rapids in Montréal.
Bicyclists along a 7-mile path watch recreational rafters ply the waterways that protected Montréal for 3 centuries. (See listing page 188)

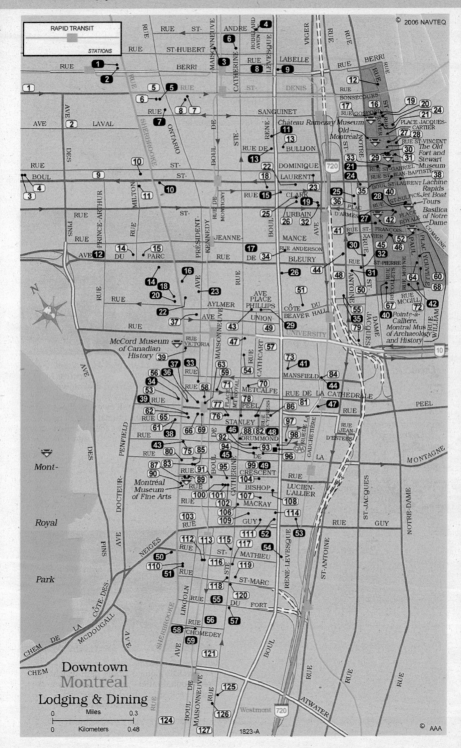

© 2006 NAVTEQ

RAPID TRANSIT

STATIONS

Château Ramezay Museum
Old Montréal

The Old Fort and Stewart Museum

Lachine Rapids Jet Boat Tours

Basilica of Notre Dame

Pointe-à-Callière, Montral Mus of Archaeology and History

McCord Museum of Canadian History

Mont-

Royal

Park

Montréal Museum of Fine Arts

Downtown
Montréal
Lodging & Dining

Miles
0   0.3

Kilometers
0   0.48

Westmont

1823-A

© AAA

Downtown Montreal

This index helps you "spot" where approved accommodations and restaurants are located on the corresponding detailed maps. Lodging rate ranges are for comparison only and show the property's high season; rates are per night, unless only weekly (W) rates are available. Restaurant rate range is for dinner, unless only lunch (L) is served. Turn to the listing page for more detailed rate information and consult display ads for special promotions.

Spotter/Map Page Number	OA	DOWNTOWN MONTREAL - Lodgings	Diamond Rating	Rate Range High Season	Listing Page
1 / p. 414	ⓐ	DoubleTree Plaza Hotel Downtown - see color ad p 434	◈◈◈	$169-$269 SAVE	434
2 / p. 414		La Presidence Hotel and Suites	◈◈◈	$159-$189	445
3 / p. 414	ⓐ	Auberge Le Pomerol	◈◈	$127-$205 SAVE	430
4 / p. 414	ⓐ	Hotel Manoir des Alpes	◈◈	$85-$130 SAVE	442
5 / p. 414	ⓐ	Auberge Le Jardin d'Antoine - see color ad p 428	◈◈	$105-$176 SAVE	430
6 / p. 414	ⓐ	Hotel Gouverneur Place Dupuis - see color ad p 439	◈◈◈	$129-$209 SAVE	440
7 / p. 414	ⓐ	All Suite VIP Loft	◈◈	$89-$139 SAVE	428
8 / p. 414		Hotel Lord Berri	◈◈	$145-$165	442
9 / p. 414	ⓐ	Hotel Le Roberval	◈◈	$129-$179 SAVE	441
10 / p. 414	ⓐ	Hotel Godin	◈◈	$159-$339 SAVE	439
11 / p. 414	ⓐ	Days Inn Montreal Downtown - see color ad p 433	◈◈◈	$142-$172 SAVE	433
12 / p. 414	ⓐ	New Residence Hall/McGill University - see color ad p 449	◈◈	$89-$170 SAVE	450
13 / p. 414	ⓐ	Holiday Inn Express Hotel & Suites - see color ad card insert	◈◈◈	$109-$350 SAVE	436
14 / p. 414	ⓐ	Quality Hotel Downtown Montreal - see color ad card insert	◈◈	$139-$340 SAVE	451
15 / p. 414	ⓐ	Hotel Travelodge Montreal Centre - see color ad p 444	◈◈	$109-$149 SAVE	444
16 / p. 414		Courtyard by Marriott Montreal	◈◈◈	Failed to provide	431
17 / p. 414	ⓐ	Hyatt Regency Montreal - see color ad p 445	◈◈◈	$169-$359 SAVE	444
18 / p. 414	ⓐ	L'Appartement Hotel	◈◈	$140-$160 SAVE	445
19 / p. 414	ⓐ	Holiday Inn Select Montreal-Centre Ville (Dwtn Conv Ctr) - see color ad card insert, p 438	◈◈◈	$159-$229 SAVE	438
20 / p. 414	ⓐ	Four Points by Sheraton Montreal Centre-Ville - see color ad p 435, p 5	◈◈◈	$149-$235 SAVE	435
21 / p. 414	ⓐ	Marriott SpringHill Suites	◈◈◈	$185-$205 SAVE	449
22 / p. 414	ⓐ	Holiday Inn Montreal-Midtown - see color ad card insert	◈◈◈	$119-$179 SAVE	436
23 / p. 414	ⓐ	Delta Montreal - see color ad p 433	◈◈◈	$159-$289 SAVE	434
24 / p. 414	ⓐ	All Suite VIP Saint-Jacques	◈◈◈	$120-$350 SAVE	428
25 / p. 414	ⓐ	Hotel Place d'Armes - see color ad p 443	◈◈◈	$230-$270 SAVE	443
26 / p. 414	ⓐ	Hotel La Tour Centre-Ville	◈◈◈	$125-$145 SAVE	440
27 / p. 414	ⓐ	Le Saint-Sulpice Hotel Montreal	◈◈◈◈	$265-$495 SAVE	447
28 / p. 414	ⓐ	Hotel Nelligan - see color ad p 442	◈◈◈	$230-$270 SAVE	443
29 / p. 414	ⓐ	Le Square Phillips Hotel & Suites - see color ad p 448	◈◈◈	$160-$232 SAVE	447
30 / p. 414	ⓐ	XIXe siecle Hotel Montreal	◈◈◈	$159-$495 SAVE	457
31 / p. 414	ⓐ	Hotel InterContinental Montreal - see color ad p 440	◈◈◈◈	$179-$575 SAVE	440
32 / p. 414		Hotel Le St-James	◈◈◈◈	$400-$475	441

Spotter/Map Page Number	OA	DOWNTOWN MONTREAL - Lodgings (continued)	Diamond Rating	Rate Range High Season	Listing Page
33 / p. 414		Hotel Le Germain	◆◆◆	$250-$330	441
34 / p. 414	ⓐ	**Best Western Ville-Marie Hotel & Suites**	◆◆◆	$139-$395 SAVE	430
35 / p. 414	ⓐ	**W Montreal**	◆◆◆◆	$179-$289 SAVE	457
36 / p. 414	ⓐ	**Hotel Omni Mont-Royal**	◆◆◆◆	$189-$329 SAVE	443
37 / p. 414	ⓐ	**Marriott Residence Inn-Montreal Centre-ville/Downtown**	◆◆◆	$195-$475 SAVE	449
38 / p. 414	ⓐ	**Sofitel Montreal**	◆◆◆◆	$285-$530 SAVE	457
39 / p. 414	ⓐ	**Hotel Le Cantlie Suites** - see color ad p 441	◆◆◆	$139-$499 SAVE	441
40 / p. 414		Hotel Gault	◆◆◆	$349-$749	438
41 / p. 414	ⓐ	**Fairmont The Queen Elizabeth** - see color ad card insert	◆◆◆◆	$189-$499 SAVE	434
42 / p. 414		Hotel St-Paul	◆◆◆	$279	444
43 / p. 414		The Ritz-Carlton, Montreal	◆◆◆◆	$225-$625	457
44 / p. 414	ⓐ	**Hilton Montreal Bonaventure** - see color ad p 436	◆◆◆◆	$179-$269 SAVE	436
45 / p. 414	ⓐ	**Loews Hotel Vogue**	◆◆◆◆	$206-$428 SAVE	448
46 / p. 414	ⓐ	**Best Western Hotel Europa**	◆◆	$149-$200 SAVE	430
47 / p. 414	ⓐ	**Marriott Chateau Champlain**	◆◆◆◆	$279 SAVE	449
48 / p. 414	ⓐ	**Le Centre Sheraton** - see color ad p 5, p 445	◆◆◆◆	$199-$599 SAVE	446
49 / p. 414	ⓐ	**Novotel Montreal Centre** - see color ad p 450	◆◆◆	$119-$289 SAVE	450
50 / p. 414	ⓐ	**Chateau Versailles Hotel** - see color ad p 431	◆◆◆	$209-$254 SAVE	431
51 / p. 414	ⓐ	**Le Meridien Versailles-Montreal** - see color ad p 431	◆◆◆	$149-$219 SAVE	446
52 / p. 414	ⓐ	**Hotel Maritime Plaza** - see color ad p 446	◆◆◆	$149-$350 SAVE	442
53 / p. 414	ⓐ	**Days Hotel** - see color ad p 432	◆◆◆	$149-$400 SAVE	432
54 / p. 414	ⓐ	**Le Nouvel Hotel** - see color ad p 447	◆◆◆	$169-$399 SAVE	446
55 / p. 414		Hotel Le Saint-Malo	◆◆	Failed to provide	442
56 / p. 414	ⓐ	**Clarion Hotel & Suites Downtown** - see color ad card insert	◆◆◆	$155-$169 SAVE	431
57 / p. 414	ⓐ	**Hotel du Fort** - see color ad p 439	◆◆◆	$149-$189 SAVE	438
58 / p. 414		La Tour Belvedere Apartment Hotel	◆◆	$119-$142	445
59 / p. 414	ⓐ	**Residence Inn by Marriott Montreal Westmount** - see color ad p 450	◆◆◆	$119-$189 SAVE	457
		DOWNTOWN MONTREAL - Restaurants			
1 / p. 414		L'Express	◆◆	$13-$21	466
2 / p. 414		Laloux	◆◆◆	$25-$39	463
3 / p. 414		Coco Rico	◆	$5-$8	460
4 / p. 414		Schwartz's Montreal Hebrew Delicatessen	◆	$5-$15	469
5 / p. 414		L'Amere a Boire	◆◆	$6-$9	463
6 / p. 414		La Sila Restaurant	◆◆◆	$12-$35	463
7 / p. 414		Restaurant Fou d'Asie	◆◆	$10-$20	467
8 / p. 414		Zyng Nouillerie	◆◆	$8-$12	470
9 / p. 414	ⓐ	**Maestro S.V.P.**	◆◆◆	$15-$37	466
10 / p. 414		Globe Restaurant	◆◆◆	$26-$49	461

Spotter/Map Page Number	OA	**DOWNTOWN MONTREAL - Restaurants (continued)**	Diamond Rating	Rate Range High Season	Listing Page
⑪ / p. 414		Med Grill	♦♦♦	$24-$40	466
⑫ / p. 414		Restaurant Pierre du Calvet	♦♦♦	$28-$49	468
⑬ / p. 414		Restaurant le Piemontais	♦♦♦	$17-$42	468
⑭ / p. 414		El Gitano	♦♦	$17-$30	461
⑮ / p. 414		Chez Gautier	♦♦♦	$15-$35	460
⑯ / p. 414		Le Restaurant La Boucherie	♦♦♦	$18-$45	465
⑰ / p. 414		Le Club Chasse et Peche	♦♦♦	$27-$32	464
⑱ / p. 414		Deer Garden Jardin du Cerf	♦♦	$5-$8	460
⑲ / p. 414		Chez l'Epicier Restaurant Bar a Vin	♦♦♦	$37-$40	460
⑳ / p. 414		Version Laurent Godbout	♦♦♦	$19-$26	470
㉑ / p. 414		L'Usine de Spaghetti du Vieux-Montreal	♦♦	$9-$19	466
㉒ / p. 414		La Maison V.I.P.	♦♦	$8-$11	463
㉓ / p. 414		Cali Restaurant	♦	$5-$9	459
㉔ / p. 414		La Menara	♦♦♦	$40	463
㉕ / p. 414		Jardin de Jade-Poon Kai Restaurant	♦♦	$12-$13	462
㉖ / p. 414		La Maison Kam Fung	♦♦	$9-$18	463
㉗ / p. 414		Restaurant La Maree	♦♦♦	$35-$49	468
㉘ / p. 414	CAA	**Chez Queux**	♦♦♦	$24-$36	460
㉙ / p. 414		Galiano's Pasta & Bar	♦♦	$13-$32	461
㉚ / p. 414		Les 3 Brasseurs	♦♦	$9-$21	465
㉛ / p. 414		Restaurant Les Remparts	♦♦♦	$22-$34	468
㉜ / p. 414	CAA	**Chez Chine**	♦♦♦	$19-$45	460
㉝ / p. 414	CAA	**Restaurant du Vieux-Port**	♦♦♦	$14-$35	467
㉞ / p. 414		Le Latini	♦♦♦	$24-$40	464
㉟ / p. 414		Creperie Chez Suzette	♦♦	$11-$25	460
㊱ / p. 414		Aix Cuisine du Terroir	♦♦♦	$26-$34	458
㊲ / p. 414		House of Jazz/Maison de Jazz	♦♦	$13-$30	462
㊳ / p. 414		Le Steak frites St-Paul	♦♦	$22-$30	465
㊵ / p. 414	CAA	**Restaurant Verses**	♦♦♦	$20-$40	468
㊶ / p. 414		Na Go Ya Restaurant	♦♦♦	$15-$25	467
㊷ / p. 414	CAA	**S-Le Restaurant**	♦♦♦	$22-$48	469
㊸ / p. 414		Soupebol	♦♦	$7-$14	469
㊹ / p. 414		Fourquet Fourchette du Palais	♦♦	$15-$25	461
㊺ / p. 414	CAA	**Bonaparte**	♦♦♦	$20-$33	459
㊻ / p. 414		Casa de Mateo	♦♦	$17-$25	459
㊼ / p. 414		Guido Angelina	♦♦	$9-$25	462
㊽ / p. 414	CAA	**Toque!**	♦♦♦♦♦	$24-$44	469
㊾ / p. 414		Restaurant Julien	♦♦♦	$19-$36	467
㊿ / p. 414	CAA	**Restaurant Les Continents**	♦♦♦♦	$19-$36	468
(51) / p. 414		Briskets Montreal	♦♦	$7-$16	459

Spotter/Map Page Number	OA	DOWNTOWN MONTREAL - Restaurants (continued)	Diamond Rating	Rate Range High Season	Listing Page
52 / p. 414		Stash Cafe	◆◆	$11-$17	469
53 / p. 414		Zawedeh Restaurant	◆◆◆	$16-$35	470
54 / p. 414		Les 3 Brasseurs	◆◆	$9-$21	465
55 / p. 414		Otto Ristorante-Bar	◆◆◆	$25-$42	467
56 / p. 414		Zen Chinese Cuisine	◆◆◆	$18-$32	470
57 / p. 414		Le Restaurant Club Lounge 737	◆◆◆	$27-$46	465
58 / p. 414		Restaurant Sho-dan Concept Japonais	◆◆◆	$14-$26	468
60 / p. 414	CAA	**Gibby's**	◆◆◆	$27-$48	461
61 / p. 414	CAA	**Renoir**	◆◆◆	$34-$46	467
62 / p. 414		Garcon!	◆◆◆	$28-$34	461
63 / p. 414		L'Orchidee Chine Restaurant Chinois	◆◆◆	$13-$30	466
64 / p. 414		Les Pyrenees Restaurant	◆◆◆	$18-$30	465
65 / p. 414		Le Taj Restaurant	◆◆◆	$9-$18	465
66 / p. 414		Cavalli Ristorante-Bar	◆◆◆	$25-$40	459
67 / p. 414		Boris Bistro	◆◆	$12-$19	459
68 / p. 414		Restaurant La Gargote	◆◆	$16-$24	467
69 / p. 414		L'Entrecote Saint-Jean	◆◆	$17-$21	464
70 / p. 414		Dunns Famous Delicatessen	◆◆	$10-$21	461
71 / p. 414		Guy & Dodo Morali	◆◆◆	$13-$49	462
72 / p. 414		Holder Restaurant-Bar	◆◆	$16-$27	462
73 / p. 414	CAA	**The Beaver Club**	◆◆◆◆	$30-$48	458
75 / p. 414	CAA	**Le Cafe de Paris**	◆◆◆	$29-$48	463
76 / p. 414		Ferreira Cafe	◆◆◆	$30-$40	461
77 / p. 414		Carlos and Pepes	◆◆	$6-$20	459
78 / p. 414		Reuben's Restaurant-Delicatessen	◆◆	$7-$26	469
79 / p. 414		Le Tour de Ville	◆◆◆	$45	465
80 / p. 414		Cafe Holt	◆◆	$15-$22	459
81 / p. 414		Cafe Republique Restaurant Bar	◆◆	$9-$25	459
82 / p. 414		Restaurant L'Actuel	◆◆◆	$16-$43	467
83 / p. 414		Katsura Japanese Restaurant	◆◆◆	$16-$50	462
84 / p. 414	CAA	**Le Castillon**	◆◆◆	$8-$35	464
85 / p. 414		Lo Stivale D'Oro	◆◆	$17-$41	466
86 / p. 414		Le Piment Rouge	◆◆◆	$20-$38	465
87 / p. 414	CAA	**Troika Restaurant**	◆◆◆	$23-$41	470
88 / p. 414	CAA	**Mister Steer**	◆◆	$9-$20	466
89 / p. 414	CAA	**Restaurant L'Autre Saison**	◆◆◆	$25-$49	468
90 / p. 414		Le Cafe des Beaux-Arts	◆◆	$16-$22	464
91 / p. 414	CAA	**Newtown Restaurant**	◆◆◆◆	$30-$42	467

Spotter/Map Page Number	OA	DOWNTOWN MONTREAL - Restaurants (continued)	Diamond Rating	Rate Range High Season	Listing Page
92 / p. 414		Ristorante Le Medusa	▼▼▼	$15-$35	469
93 / p. 414		Le Boeuf Angus	▼▼	$24-$60	463
94 / p. 414		Europea Restaurant	▼▼▼	$24-$41	461
95 / p. 414		Wienstein and Gavinos Pasta Bar Factory Co Ltd	▼▼	$10-$30	470
96 / p. 414		Il Campari Centro	▼▼▼	$18-$35	462
97 / p. 414		Decca 77 Restaurant	▼▼▼	$24-$45	460
98 / p. 414		La Queue de Cheval Bar & Steakhouse	▼▼▼	$30-$56	463
99 / p. 414		Rosalie Restaurant	▼▼▼	$18-$35	469
100 / p. 414		Le Milsa Rotisserie Bresilienne	▼▼	$17-$26	464
101 / p. 414		Maison de Cari	▼▼	$12-$18	466
102 / p. 414		Mesa 14	▼▼	$9-$18	466
103 / p. 414		Bice Ristorante	▼▼▼	$24-$38	458
104 / p. 414		Le Chrysantheme	▼▼▼	$15-$20	464
106 / p. 414		Restaurant La Belle Province	▼	$4-$6	467
107 / p. 414		Bishoku Japanese Restaurant	▼▼▼	$15-$30	459
108 / p. 414		Restaurant Sho-dan Concept Japonais	▼▼▼	$14-$26	468
109 / p. 414		La Baguette D'Ivoire	▼▼	$15-$23	462
110 / p. 414		Ristorante Bronte	▼▼▼	$26-$33	469
111 / p. 414		Chez La Mere Michel	▼▼▼	$20-$27	460
112 / p. 414		Au Bistro Gourmet	▼▼	$17-$28	458
113 / p. 414		Restaurant La Pizzella	▼▼▼	$15-$20	468
115 / p. 414		3 Amigos Resto-Bar	▼▼	$7-$20	458
116 / p. 414		Bocca D'Oro	▼▼▼	$16-$32	459
117 / p. 414		Le Paris Restaurant Francais	▼▼	$18-$31	464
118 / p. 414		Restaurant Kalinka	▼▼	$9-$18	467
119 / p. 414		Alpenhaus Restaurant	▼▼	$13-$24	458
120 / p. 414		Restaurant U & Me	▼▼	$5-$9	468
121 / p. 414		Guido Angelina	▼▼▼	$9-$25	462
		WESTMOUNT - Restaurants			
124 / p. 414		Miso	▼▼	$10-$30	496
125 / p. 414		Chine Toque	▼▼▼	$8-$15	496
126 / p. 414		Kaizen Sushi Bar & Restaurant	▼▼▼	$14-$29	496
127 / p. 414		Taverne sur le Square	▼▼▼	$14-$45	497

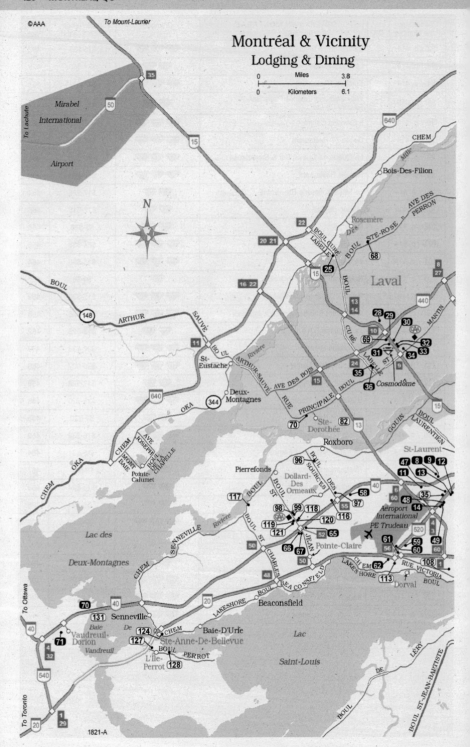

© AAA

To Mount-Laurier

Montréal & Vicinity
Lodging & Dining

Miles 3.8
Kilometers 6.1

To Lachute

Mirabel International Airport

To Ottawa

To Toronto

Bois-Des-Filion

Rosemère

Laval

Cosmodôme

St-Eustache

Deux-Montagnes

Ste-Dorothée

Roxboro

St-Laurent

Pierrefonds

Dollard-Des Ormeaux

Aéroport International PE Trudeau

Pointe-Claire

Dorval

Lac des Deux-Montagnes

Senneville

Beaconsfield

Baie-D'Urfe

Ste-Anne-De-Bellevue

Vaudreuil-Dorion

Vandreuil

L'île-Perrot

Lac Saint-Louis

Pointe-Calumet

1821-A

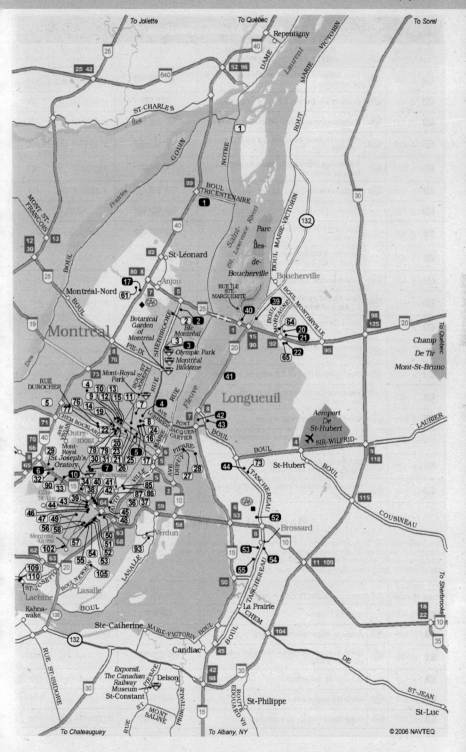

To Joliette
To Québec
To Sorel

Repentigny

25 42

640

25

ST-CHARLES
Îles

52 96

DAME

Laurent

MARIE

VICTORIN

GOUIN

NOTRE

40

1

BOUL
TRICENTENAIRE

89

1

MONT ST.
FRANCOIS

12
30

13

40

Saint-

Lawrence

River

(St. Lawrence River)

Parc
Îles-
de-
Boucherville

BOUL MARIE-VICTORIN

132

30

125

98

82

St-Léonard

Anjou

80 8

17
61

7

Montréal-Nord

RUE ILE-
STE-
MARGUERITE

40

BOUL MONTARVILLE

39

ROUT

Boucherville

20

19

BOUL

25

Montréal

Botanical
Garden
of
Montréal

PIE-IX

SHERBROOKE

BOUL ST JOSEPH

RUE

Bfc
Montréal

2   **2**

3   **3**
Olympic Park
Montréal
Biodôme

Mont-Royal
Park

41

Longueuil

8

73

64

20
21

92

90

15

1

20

95

125

Champ
De Tir
Mont-St-Bruno

To Québec

65

22

LAURIER

Aéroport
De
St-Hubert
SIR-WILFRID-

RUE
DUROCHER

5

76
9

4

10 13
12 15 11

14
19

AVE
LORIMIER

7

4

MARIE

7

8

PONT

42

43

8

9
118

CHEM ROCKLAND

71

77

22

AVE

BOUL

BOUL

TASCHEREAU

115

COUSINEAU

70
66

40

Outre-
mont

78 79
23

20

St-Hubert

44

73

St-Hubert

29
65

6
32

90

Mont-
Royal
St Joseph's
Oratory

30 31 21
26

5

25 17

JACQUES-
CARTIER

PIERRE-

52

33

Westmount

39

34 40 41
38

42

AUTO

85

87 86

28

27

44

6
53

CAA

52

Brossard

Côte
St-Luc

46

43

Montréal-
Ouest

44

64

36 37

8

10

53

53

54

11 109

To Sherbrooke

47 49
56 58

57

50 51
52

48

VILLE

58

59

DUPUY

AVE

2

10

Verdun

LASALLE

55

TASCHEREAU

18
22

10

62
109
110

102

63

55

54

53

105

20

NEW

93

68
63

BOUL

50

35

St-JOSEPH

Lachine
Kahna-
wake

138

BOUL

La Prairie

DE

To Sherbrooke

St-Jean

Ste-Catherine

MARIE-VICTORIN

BOUL

CHEM

104

35

132

Candiac

45

RUE ST-ISIDORE

30

Exporail.
The Canadian
Railway
Museum
St-Constant

Delson

PIERRE

42
98

30

ROUTE VII
EDOUARD

St-Philippe

St-Jean

St-Luc

15

To Chateauguay

To Albany, NY

© 2006 NAVTEQ

✈ Airport Accommodations

Spotter/Map Page Number	OA	PIERRE ELLIOTT TRUDEAU INTERNATIONAL AIRPORT	Diamond Rating	Rate Range High Season	Listing Page
61 / p. 420	CAA	Best Western Aeroport de Montreal, 1 km s of terminal	◈◈◈	$134-$199 SAVE	484
59 / p. 420	CAA	Comfort Inn Dorval, 1.5 km s of terminal	◈◈	$130-$154 SAVE	485
58 / p. 420	CAA	Hampton Inn & Suites, 10 km nw of airport	◈◈◈	$150-$190 SAVE	485
60 / p. 420	CAA	Hilton Montreal Aeroport, 0.3 mi (1.2 km) to terminal	◈◈◈	$139-$329 SAVE	485
62 / p. 420	CAA	Travelodge Montreal-Trudeau Airport, 1.2 km s of terminal	◈◈	$109-$225 SAVE	485
31 / p. 420	CAA	Radisson Hotel Laval, 25 km ne of terminal	◈◈◈	$109-$179 SAVE	488
29 / p. 420		Sheraton Laval Hotel, 25 km ne of airport	◈◈◈	$109-$259	488
9 / p. 420		Courtyard Marriott Montreal Airport, 3 mi (5 km) ne of terminal	◈◈◈	$119-$229	471
11 / p. 420		Days Inn & Conference Center Montreal Airport, 6 km e of terminal	◈◈◈	$159-$280	471
47 / p. 420	CAA	Econo Lodge, 3.5 km e of terminal	◈◈	$69-$99 SAVE	494
13 / p. 420	CAA	Four Points by Sheraton Montreal Airport, 5.5 km e of terminal	◈◈◈	$119-$169 SAVE	471
14 / p. 420		Hilton Garden Inn Montreal/Dorval, 3.5 km e of terminal	◈◈◈	$111-$145	471
12 / p. 420	CAA	Holiday Inn Montreal-Airport, 5.5 km e of terminal	◈◈◈	$104-$169 SAVE	471
49 / p. 420	CAA	Quality Hotel Dorval, 3.5 km e of terminal	◈◈◈	$127 SAVE	494
8 / p. 420		Residence Inn Montreal Airport, 3 mi (5 km) from terminal	◈◈◈	Failed to provide	475
67 / p. 420	CAA	Comfort Inn, 8 km e of airport	◈◈	$89-$195 SAVE	492
66 / p. 420	CAA	Holiday Inn Pointe-Claire Montreal Aeroport, 8 km e of airport	◈◈◈	$119-$229 SAVE	492
65 / p. 420	CAA	Quality Suites Montreal Aeroport, Pointe-Claire, 8 km e of airport	◈◈◈	$99-$169 SAVE	492
48 / p. 420	CAA	Ramada Montreal Airport Hotel, 3.5 km e of terminal	◈◈	$139-$169 SAVE	495

Montreal and Vicinity

This index helps you "spot" where approved accommodations and restaurants are located on the corresponding detailed maps. Lodging rate ranges are for comparison only and show the property's high season; rates are per night, unless only weekly (W) rates are available. Restaurant rate range is for dinner, unless only lunch (L) is served. Turn to the listing page for more detailed rate information and consult display ads for special promotions.

Spotter/Map Page Number	OA	MONTREAL - Lodgings	Diamond Rating	Rate Range High Season	Listing Page
1 / p. 420		Hotel Le Prestige	◈◈	$86-$150	473
2 / p. 420	CAA	Auberge Royal Versailles Hotel	◈◈◈	$105-$139 SAVE	471
3 / p. 420	CAA	Hotel Auberge Universel Montreal - see color ad p 472	◈◈◈	$125-$155 SAVE	472
4 / p. 420		Auberge de la Fontaine	◈◈◈	$133-$249	470
5 / p. 420	CAA	Anne Ma Soeur Anne Hotel-Studio	◈◈	$80-$150 SAVE	470
6 / p. 420	CAA	Hotel Ruby Foo's - see color ad p 472	◈◈◈	$159-$174 SAVE	473

Spotter/Map Page Number	OA	MONTREAL - Lodgings (continued)	Diamond Rating	Rate Range High Season	Listing Page
7 / p. 420		Hotel Terrasse Royale	◈◈	Failed to provide	473
8 / p. 420		Residence Inn Montreal Airport	◈◈◈	Failed to provide	475
9 / p. 420		Courtyard Marriott Montreal Airport	◈◈◈	$119-$229	471
10 / p. 420	ⒶⒶ	Quality Hotel Midtown - see color ad card insert	◈◈◈	$99-$250 [SAVE]	474
11 / p. 420		Days Inn & Conference Center Montreal Airport	◈◈◈	$159-$280	471
12 / p. 420	ⒶⒶ	Holiday Inn Montreal-Airport - see color ad card insert	◈◈◈	$104-$169 [SAVE]	471
13 / p. 420	ⒶⒶ	Four Points by Sheraton Montreal Airport - see color ad p 5	◈◈◈	$119-$169 [SAVE]	471
14 / p. 420		Hilton Garden Inn Montreal/Dorval	◈◈◈	$111-$145	471
		MONTREAL - Restaurants			
① / p. 420		Restaurant Auberge du Cheval Blanc	◈◈◈	$18-$40	478
② / p. 420		Ristorante La Dora	◈◈	$9-$23	479
③ / p. 420		Le Stadium Club Restaurant & Bar	◈◈◈	$11-$32	477
④ / p. 420		Tapeo-Bar a Tapas	◈◈	$4-$15	480
⑤ / p. 420		Dunns Famous	◈◈	$7-$20	476
⑦ / p. 420		Lezvos	◈◈	$11-$22	477
⑧ / p. 420		La Fonderie	◈◈	$16-$32	476
⑨ / p. 420		Soy	◈◈	$9-$17	480
⑩ / p. 420		Restaurant Il Piatto Della Nonna	◈◈	$15-$27	479
⑪ / p. 420		La Binerie Mont-Royal	◈	$7-$11	476
⑫ / p. 420		Wilensky's Light Lunch Inc	◈	$5-$10(L)	480
⑬ / p. 420		Thai Grill	◈◈	$10-$28	480
⑭ / p. 420		Arahova Souvlaki	◈◈	$11-$16	475
⑮ / p. 420		La Chronique	◈◈◈◈	$28-$38	476
⑯ / p. 420		Restaurant Au Pied de Cochon	◈◈◈	$12-$36	478
⑰ / p. 420		Khyber Pass Cuisine Afghane	◈◈	$15-$30	476
⑲ / p. 420		Milos Restaurant	◈◈◈	$30-$42	478
⑳ / p. 420		Restaurant Juni	◈◈◈	$21-$35	479
㉑ / p. 420		Restaurant Chez Doval	◈◈	$9-$20	479
㉒ / p. 420		Lindos Psaropoula	◈◈	$17-$30	477
㉓ / p. 420		Beauty's Luncheonette	◈◈	$10-$30(L)	475
㉔ / p. 420		Area	◈◈◈	$21-$34	475
㉕ / p. 420		Moishe's Steak House	◈◈◈	$26-$52	478

Spotter/Map Page Number	OA	MONTREAL - Restaurants (continued)	Diamond Rating	Rate Range High Season	Listing Page
26 / p. 420		Cafe Santropol	▼▼	$8-$12	475
27 / p. 420	CAA	Restaurant Helene de Champlain	▼▼▼	$24-$40	479
28 / p. 420	CAA	Nuances	▼▼▼▼▼	$39-$45	478
29 / p. 420	CAA	Rib 'n Reef Steakhouse	▼▼▼	$21-$58	479
30 / p. 420		Pizzafiore	▼▼	$8-$16	478
31 / p. 420		Nickels Restaurant	▼▼	$9-$20	478
32 / p. 420		Gibeau Orange Julep	▼	$5-$10	476
33 / p. 420		Le Grill Midtown	▼	$6-$16	477
34 / p. 420		Chez Benny	▼	$6-$17	476
35 / p. 420		Cote St-Luc Bar-B-Q	▼▼	$7-$11	476
36 / p. 420		Hot Spot Restaurant	▼▼	$6-$15	476
37 / p. 420		Restaurant & Taverne Magnan	▼▼	$15-$27	478
38 / p. 420		Quartier Perse	▼▼	$11-$23	478
39 / p. 420		Cote St-Luc Bar-B-Q	▼▼	$7-$10	476
40 / p. 420		Lezvos West	▼▼▼	$11-$22	477
41 / p. 420		Village Szechuan	▼▼	$10-$15	480
42 / p. 420		Mesquite	▼▼	$9-$25	477
43 / p. 420		Monkland Tavern	▼▼	$14-$26	478
44 / p. 420		St-Viateur Bagel & Cafe	▼▼	$5-$12	479
45 / p. 420		Tehran Restaurant	▼▼	$12-$18	480
46 / p. 420		Au Messob d'Or-Cuisine Ethiopienne	▼▼	$15-$30	475
47 / p. 420		Le Maistre	▼▼▼	$21-$24	477
48 / p. 420		Chalet Bar-B-Q Rotisserie	▼▼	$8-$10	476
49 / p. 420		B & M Restaurant	▼▼	$8-$27	475
50 / p. 420		Restaurant Momesso	▼	$5-$11	479
51 / p. 420		B & M Restaurant	▼▼	$6-$19	475
52 / p. 420		Asean Garden	▼▼	$10-$19	475
53 / p. 420		La Louisiane	▼▼	$9-$30	477
54 / p. 420		Alex H. Restaurant	▼▼	$15-$24	475
55 / p. 420		Le Coin d'Asie	▼▼	$10-$19	477
56 / p. 420		Restaurant Ganges	▼▼▼	$9-$15	479
57 / p. 420		Tchang Kiang Restaurant	▼▼	$10-$20	480
58 / p. 420		Bratwurst Restaurant	▼	$5-$8	475
		ANJOU - Lodgings			
17 / p. 420	CAA	Quality Hotel East - see color ad card insert	▼▼	$137-$148 SAVE	480

Spotter/Map Page Number	OA	ANJOU - Restaurant	Diamond Rating	Rate Range High Season	Listing Page
61 / p. 420		Il Pazzesco	◈◈◈	$12-$34	481
		BOUCHERVILLE - Lodgings			
20 / p. 420		Comfort Inn - see color ad card insert	◈◈	$145-$175	481
21 / p. 420	CAA	**Hotel WelcomINNS - see color ad p 481**	◈◈◈	$130-$150 SAVE	482
22 / p. 420	CAA	**Hotel Mortagne**	◈◈◈	$199-$350 SAVE	482
		BOUCHERVILLE - Restaurants			
64 / p. 420		Bistro Le Tire-Bouchon	◈◈◈	$17-$30	482
65 / p. 420		Madisons New York Grill & Bar	◈◈	$9-$35	482
		ROSEMERE - Lodgings			
25 / p. 420		Hotel Le Rivage	◈◈◈	$89-$134	493
		LAVAL - Lodgings			
28 / p. 420	CAA	**Best Western Chateauneuf Laval**	◈◈◈	$79-$159 SAVE	486
29 / p. 420		Sheraton Laval Hotel - see color ad p 5	◈◈◈	$109-$259	488
30 / p. 420	CAA	**Hotel Hilton Montreal-Laval**	◈◈◈	$109-$259 SAVE	487
31 / p. 420	CAA	**Radisson Hotel Laval - see color ad p 488**	◈◈◈	$109-$179 SAVE	488
32 / p. 420		Comfort Inn - see color ad card insert	◈◈	$112-$132	487
33 / p. 420	CAA	**Quality Suites Laval - see color ad card insert**	◈◈	$139-$162 SAVE	488
34 / p. 420	CAA	**Le St-Martin Hotel & Suites - see color ad p 448**	◈◈◈	$129 SAVE	488
35 / p. 420		Econo Lodge - see color ad card insert	◈◈	$74-$144	487
36 / p. 420	CAA	**Hampton Inn & Suites-Laval**	◈◈◈	$109-$154 SAVE	487
		LAVAL - Restaurants			
68 / p. 420		Restaurant le Saint-Christophe	◈◈◈◈	$36-$55	489
69 / p. 420		Ristorante Giotto	◈◈◈	$15-$28	489
70 / p. 420		Le Mitoyen	◈◈◈◈	$25-$32	489
		LONGUEUIL - Lodgings			
39 / p. 420		Days Inn Longueuil	◈◈	$87-$105	490
40 / p. 420	CAA	**Hotel Gouverneur Ile-Charron**	◈◈◈	$129 SAVE	490
41 / p. 420	CAA	**Holiday Inn Montreal-Longueuil - see color ad card insert**	◈◈◈	$139-$189 SAVE	490
42 / p. 420	CAA	**Sandman Hotel Montreal-Longueuil - see color ad p 451**	◈◈◈	$200-$270 SAVE	491
43 / p. 420		Hotel Le Dauphin Montreal Longueuil	◈◈◈	$99-$129	490
44 / p. 420	CAA	**Motel La Siesta - see color ad p 490**	◈◈	$89-$150 SAVE	490
		LONGUEUIL - Restaurant			
73 / p. 420		Homard Plus	◈◈	$13-$35	491
		ST-LAURENT (MONTREAL) - Lodgings			
47 / p. 420	CAA	**Econo Lodge - see color ad card insert**	◈◈	$69-$99 SAVE	494
48 / p. 420	CAA	**Ramada Montreal Airport Hotel - see color ad p 474**	◈◈	$139-$169 SAVE	495
49 / p. 420	CAA	**Quality Hotel Dorval - see color ad card insert**	◈◈◈	$127 SAVE	494
		BROSSARD - Lodgings			
52 / p. 420	CAA	**Quality Inn & Suites - see color ad card insert**	◈◈◈	$126-$168 SAVE	483

Spotter/Map Page Number	OA	BROSSARD - Lodgings (continued)	Diamond Rating	Rate Range High Season	Listing Page
53 / p. 420	ⓐ	**Best Western Hotel National -** see color ad p 429	◈◈◈	$99-$139 [SAVE]	482
54 / p. 420		Comfort Inn - see color ad card insert	◈◈	$100-$120	482
55 / p. 420		Econo Lodge Montreal - Brossard	◈◈	$110-$165	483
		DORVAL - Lodgings			
58 / p. 420	ⓐ	**Hampton Inn & Suites -** see color ad p 4, p 435	◈◈◈	$150-$190 [SAVE]	485
59 / p. 420	ⓐ	**Comfort Inn Dorval -** see color ad card insert	◈◈	$130-$154 [SAVE]	485
60 / p. 420	ⓐ	**Hilton Montreal Aeroport**	◈◈◈	$139-$329 [SAVE]	485
61 / p. 420	ⓐ	**Best Western Aeroport de Montreal -** see color ad p 429	◈◈◈	$134-$199 [SAVE]	484
62 / p. 420	ⓐ	**Travelodge Montreal-Trudeau Airport -** see color ad p 451	◈◈	$109-$225 [SAVE]	485
		DORVAL - Restaurant			
113 / p. 420		Rotisserie Scores	◈◈	$8-$20	485
		POINTE-CLAIRE - Lodgings			
65 / p. 420	ⓐ	**Quality Suites Montreal Aeroport, Pointe-Claire -** see color ad card insert	◈◈◈	$99-$169 [SAVE]	492
66 / p. 420	ⓐ	**Holiday Inn Pointe-Claire Montreal Aeroport** - see color ad card insert, p 438	◈◈◈	$119-$229 [SAVE]	492
67 / p. 420	ⓐ	**Comfort Inn -** see color ad card insert	◈◈	$89-$195 [SAVE]	492
		POINTE-CLAIRE - Restaurants			
116 / p. 420		40 Westt Steakhouse	◈◈◈	$26-$56	493
117 / p. 420		Le Gourmand	◈◈◈	$19-$46	493
118 / p. 420		Le Chambertin	◈◈◈	$20-$35	493
119 / p. 420		Scarolies Pasta Imporium	◈◈	$10-$23	493
120 / p. 420		Arahova Souvlaki	◈◈	$10-$15	493
121 / p. 420		Moe's Deli & Bar	◈◈	$10-$18	493
		VAUDREUIL-DORION - Lodgings			
70 / p. 420	ⓐ	**Chateau Vaudreuil Suites Hotel -** see color ad p 430	◈◈◈◈	$200-$550 [SAVE]	495
71 / p. 420		Super 8	◈◈	$105-$200	495
		VAUDREUIL-DORION - Restaurant			
131 / p. 420	ⓐ	**Villa D'Este**	◈◈◈	$12-$35	496
		OUTREMONT - Restaurants			
76 / p. 420		Restaurant Christophe	◈◈◈	$30-$58	492
77 / p. 420		Le Paris Beurre	◈◈◈	$18-$25	492
78 / p. 420		Restaurant Chez Leveque	◈◈◈	$17-$34	492
79 / p. 420		Restaurant Lemeac	◈◈◈	$17-$34	492
		STE-DOROTHEE - Restaurant			
82 / p. 420		Dunns Famous	◈◈	$7-$20	495
		WESTMOUNT - Restaurants			
85 / p. 420		Bistro on the Avenue	◈◈◈	$10-$25	496
86 / p. 420		Vago Cucina Italiana	◈◈◈	$13-$42	497
87 / p. 420		Restaurant Mess Hall Bistro-Bar	◈◈◈	$13-$34	497

Spotter/Map Page Number	OA	COTE-ST-LUC - Restaurant	Diamond Rating	Rate Range High Season	Listing Page
90 / p. 420		Ernie & Ellie's Restaurant	◈◈	$11-$18	484
		VERDUN - Restaurant			
93 / p. 420		Villa Wellington	◈◈	$8-$19	496
		DOLLARD-DES-ORMEAUX - Restaurants			
96 / p. 420		Hymie's sur le grill	◈◈◈	$9-$34	484
97 / p. 420		Restaurant Aikawa	◈◈◈	$12-$26	484
98 / p. 420		Restaurant New Kam Shing	◈◈	$16-$23	484
99 / p. 420		Momesso Caffe	◈◈	$6-$12	484
		MONTREAL-OUEST - Restaurant			
102 / p. 420		Bistro Westminster	◈◈	$16-$22	491
		LASALLE - Restaurant			
105 / p. 420	🅐	**Boccacinos**	◈◈	$9-$22	486
		LACHINE - Restaurants			
108 / p. 420		Resto-Bar 12	◈◈	$9-$25	486
109 / p. 420		Restaurant Topaze	◈◈	$9-$19	486
110 / p. 420		Ristorante Il Fornetto	◈◈◈	$10-$30	486
		STE-ANNE-DE-BELLEVUE - Restaurant			
124 / p. 420		Le Surcouf	◈◈◈	$15-$35	493
		L'ILE-PERROT - Restaurants			
127 / p. 420		Smoke Meat Pete	◈	$7-$22	489
128 / p. 420	🅐	**Vieux Kitzbuhel Restaurant**	◈◈◈	$17-$32	489

DOWNTOWN MONTREAL　(See map and index starting on p. 414)

———— WHERE TO STAY ————

ALL SUITE VIP LOFT　*Book great rates at AAA.com*　　　　　**Phone:** (514)448-4848　

CAA SAVE	11/3-4/30	1P: $89-$109	2P: $99-$139	XP: $7	D17
	5/1-11/2	1P: $79-$99	2P: $89-$126	XP: $10	D17

Location: Just w of rue St-Denis. 329 rue Ontario est H2X 1H7. Fax: 514/448-4849. **Facility:** Smoke free premises. 10 one-bedroom standard units, some with whirlpools. 3 stories (no elevator), interior corridors. Small-scale Hotel *Bath:* combo, shower or tub only. **Parking:** street. **Terms:** 2 night minimum stay - weekends, 5 day cancellation notice, weekly rates available, package plans, small pets only ($15 extra charge). **Amenities:** DVD players, CD players, voice mail, hair dryers. *Some:* fax, safes. **Guest Services:** complimentary laundry, wireless Internet. **Cards:** AX, CB, DC, DS, JC, MC, VI. **Free Special Amenities: local telephone calls and high-speed Internet.**

SOME UNITS

ALL SUITE VIP SAINT-JACQUES　*Book great rates at AAA.com*　　　**Phone:** (514)667-5052　

CAA SAVE	6/1-10/1	1P: $120-$280	2P: $140-$350	XP: $30	F10
	5/1-5/31 & 1/1-4/30	1P: $90-$280	2P: $110-$300	XP: $30	F10
	10/2-12/31	1P: $100-$250	2P: $120-$290	XP: $30	F10

Location: Corner of boul St-Laurent. 10 rue Saint Jacques ouest H2Y 2V5. Fax: 514/673-0016. **Facility:** 37 units. Small-scale Hotel 10 one-bedroom standard units with kitchens. 15 one-, 10 two- and 2 three-bedroom suites ($400-$800) with kitchens. 11 stories, interior corridors. **Parking:** on-site (fee). **Terms:** office hours 8:30 am-11:30 pm, 3 day cancellation notice-fee imposed, package plans. **Amenities:** DVD players, CD players, high-speed Internet, voice mail, safes, irons, hair dryers. **Dining:** 7 am-11 pm, cocktails. **Pool(s):** heated indoor. **Leisure Activities:** exercise room, sun deck. **Guest Services:** valet and coin laundry. **Business Services:** meeting rooms. **Cards:** AX, DC, MC, VI.

SOME UNITS

(See map and index starting on p. 414)

AUBERGE LE JARDIN D'ANTOINE　　　　　　　　　　　　**Phone:** (514)843-4506　**5**
CAA SAVE　5/1-10/31 [ECP]　　1P: $105-$176　　2P: $105-$176　　XP: $15　　F12
　　　11/1-4/30 [ECP]　　1P: $95-$166　　2P: $95-$166　　XP: $15　　F12
◆◆◆　**Location:** Just s of rue Sherbrooke. Located in the Latin Quarter. 2024 rue St-Denis H2X 3K7. Fax: 514/281-1491.
　　　Facility: 25 units. 19 one-bedroom standard units, some with whirlpools. 6 one-bedroom suites with
Small-scale Hotel　whirlpools. 4 stories (no elevator), interior/exterior corridors. *Bath:* combo or shower only. **Parking:** on-site.
　　　Terms: 3 day cancellation notice-fee imposed. **Amenities:** high-speed Internet, hair dryers. *Some:* DVD
players. **Guest Services:** wireless Internet. **Business Services:** PC. **Cards:** AX, CB, DC, DS, JC, MC, VI.
Free Special Amenities: expanded continental breakfast and high-speed Internet. *(See color ad p 428)*

SOME UNITS

AUBERGE LE POMEROL　　　　　　　　　　　　　　　**Phone:** (514)526-5511　**3**
CAA SAVE　5/1-10/31 [ECP]　　1P: $127-$185　　2P: $147-$205　　XP: $20　　F12
　　　11/1-4/30 [ECP]　　1P: $90-$153　　2P: $110-$173　　XP: $20　　F12
◆◆◆　**Location:** Just e of rue St-Hubert. 819 de Maisonneuve est H2L 1Y7. Fax: 514/523-0143. **Facility:** Housed within
　　　a historic building, this small boutique hotel offers stylish guest rooms and many modern amenities. 27 one-
Historic　bedroom standard units, some with whirlpools. 4 stories, interior corridors. *Bath:* combo or shower only.
Small-scale Hotel　**Parking:** on-site (fee). **Terms:** age restrictions may apply, cancellation fee imposed, package plans.
　　　Amenities: high-speed Internet, hair dryers. *Some:* CD players, safes, irons. **Dining:** 7 am-10, noon-3 & 5-
11 pm. **Guest Services:** wireless Internet. **Business Services:** meeting rooms, PC, fax (fee). **Cards:** AX, CB, DC, DS, MC, VI.
Free Special Amenities: expanded continental breakfast and high-speed Internet.

SOME UNITS

BEST WESTERN HOTEL EUROPA　*Book great rates at AAA.com*　　**Phone:** (514)866-6492　**46**
CAA SAVE　1/1-4/30　　　1P: $149-$200　　2P: $149-$200　　XP: $15　　F
　　　5/1-12/31　　　1P: $149-$189　　2P: $149-$189　　XP: $15　　F
◆◆◆　**Location:** Between rue Ste-Catherine and boul Rene-Levesque. 1240 rue Drummond H3G 1V7. Fax: 514/861-4089.
　　　Facility: 178 units. 176 one-bedroom standard units, some with whirlpools. 1 one- and 1 two-bedroom
Small-scale Hotel　suites ($350-$1000) with efficiencies, some with kitchens and/or whirlpools. 6 stories, interior corridors.
　　　Parking: on-site (fee) and street. **Terms:** [BP] meal plan available, package plans. **Amenities:** voice mail,
irons, hair dryers. **Dining:** 2 restaurants, 6:30-11 am, 11:30-2:30 & 5-10 pm, Fri & Sat-11 pm. **Leisure Activities:** saunas,
whirlpool, exercise room. *Fee:* billiards. **Guest Services:** valet laundry, wireless Internet. **Business Services:** meeting rooms,
PC (fee). **Cards:** AX, DC, DS, JC, MC, VI. **Free Special Amenities: room upgrade and preferred room (each subject to
availability with advance reservations).**

SOME UNITS

BEST WESTERN VILLE-MARIE HOTEL & SUITES　*Book great rates at AAA.com*　**Phone:** (514)288-4141　**34**
CAA SAVE　5/1-10/31　　　1P: $139-$395　　2P: $139-$395　　XP: $10　　F12
　　　11/1-4/30　　　1P: $99-$209　　2P: $99-$209　　XP: $10　　F12
◆◆◆◆　**Location:** Corner of rue Peel and rue Sherbrooke. 3407 rue Peel H3A 1W7. Fax: 514/288-3021. **Facility:** 171 units.
　　　167 one-bedroom standard units. 1 one- and 3 two-bedroom suites, some with kitchens and/or whirlpools.
Small-scale Hotel　21 stories, interior corridors. **Parking:** valet and street. **Amenities:** voice mail, irons, hair dryers. *Some:*
　　　Fee: DVD players. **Dining:** 6:30 am-10 pm, cocktails, also, Zawedeh Restaurant, see separate listing.
Leisure Activities: exercise room. **Guest Services:** gift shop, valet laundry, wireless Internet. **Business Services:** meeting
rooms, business center. **Cards:** AX, DC, DS, MC, VI. **Free Special Amenities: newspaper and room upgrade (subject to
availability with advance reservations).**

SOME UNITS

(See map and index starting on p. 414)

CHATEAU VERSAILLES HOTEL   *Book great rates at AAA.com*   Phone: (514)933-3611   [50]

(CAA) [SAVE]

5/1-10/31 [CP]	1P: $209-$229	2P: $234-$254	XP: $25	F17
11/1-4/30 [CP]	1P: $169-$189	2P: $194-$214	XP: $25	F17

Historic
Small-scale Hotel

Location: Corner rue St-Mathieu. 1659 rue Sherbrooke ouest H3H 1E3. Fax: 514/933-8401. **Facility:** In-room dining and evening turn-down service are offered at this stylish boutique hotel in a historic downtown graystone building. 65 units. 64 one-bedroom standard units, some with whirlpools. 1 one-bedroom suite with whirlpool. 4 stories (no elevator), interior corridors. **Parking:** valet and street. **Terms:** package plans, small pets only ($15 extra charge, must remain caged and supervised). **Amenities:** video games (fee), CD players, voice mail, safes, honor bars, irons, hair dryers. *Some:* high-speed Internet, dual phone lines. **Leisure Activities:** sauna, limited exercise equipment. **Guest Services:** valet laundry, wireless Internet. **Business Services:** meeting rooms, PC (fee). **Cards:** AX, CB, DC, DS, JC, MC, VI. **Free Special Amenities: expanded continental breakfast and newspaper.** *(See color ad below)*

SOME UNITS

CLARION HOTEL & SUITES DOWNTOWN   *Book great rates at AAA.com*   Phone: (514)931-8861   [56]

(CAA) [SAVE]

7/1-10/31	1P: $155-$169	2P: $155-$169	XP: $15	F16
5/1-6/30	1P: $135-$155	2P: $135-$155	XP: $15	F16
11/1-4/30	1P: $130-$145	2P: $130-$145	XP: $15	F16

Large-scale Hotel

Location: Between rue du Fort and ave Atwater. 2100 boul de Maisonneuve ouest H3H 1K6. Fax: 514/931-7726. **Facility:** 266 units. 166 one-bedroom standard units with kitchens. 99 one- and 1 two-bedroom suites with kitchens, some with whirlpools. 23 stories, interior corridors. **Parking:** on-site (fee) and street. **Terms:** 2-3 night minimum stay - seasonal. **Amenities:** *Some:* voice mail, irons, hair dryers. **Dining:** 7 am-11 pm, cocktails. **Leisure Activities:** saunas, whirlpool, pool privileges, exercise room. **Guest Services:** valet and coin laundry, wireless Internet. **Business Services:** meeting rooms, PC. **Cards:** AX, DC, DS, MC, VI. **Free Special Amenities: newspaper and high-speed Internet.** *(See color ad card insert)*

SOME UNITS

COURTYARD BY MARRIOTT MONTREAL   *Book great rates at AAA.com*   Phone: 514/844-8855   [16]

Property failed to provide current rates

Large-scale Hotel

Location: Between rue Bleury and City Councillors. 410 rue Sherbrooke ouest H3A 1B3. Fax: 514/844-0912. **Facility:** Smoke free premises. 181 units. 157 one-bedroom standard units. 24 one-bedroom suites. 26 stories, interior corridors. **Parking:** valet and street. **Amenities:** voice mail, irons, hair dryers. *Some:* safes. **Pool(s):** heated indoor. **Leisure Activities:** whirlpool, exercise room, spa. **Guest Services:** valet and coin laundry, wireless Internet. **Business Services:** meeting rooms, administrative services (fee), PC.

SOME UNITS

(See map and index starting on p. 414)

DAYS HOTEL　*Book great rates at AAA.com*　Phone: (514)938-4611　53

 5/1-10/31　1P: $149-$400　2P: $149-$400　XP: $10　F12
11/1-4/30　1P: $95-$225　2P: $95-$225　XP: $10　F12

Large-scale Hotel　**Location:** Just s of boul Rene-Levesque. 1005 rue Guy H3H 2K4. Fax: 514/938-8718. **Facility:** 205 units. 199 one-bedroom standard units. 6 one-bedroom suites ($220-$400) with whirlpools. 7 stories, interior corridors. *Bath:* combo or shower only. **Parking:** on-site (fee). **Terms:** cancellation fee imposed, [AP], [BP] & [CP] meal plans available, small pets only ($15 fee). **Amenities:** voice mail, irons, hair dryers. *Fee:* video games, high-speed Internet. *Some:* dual phone lines. **Dining:** 7 am-11 pm, Sat-1 am, cocktails. **Pool(s):** heated outdoor. **Leisure Activities:** sauna, whirlpool, exercise room, spa. **Guest Services:** gift shop, valet laundry, wireless Internet. **Business Services:** meeting rooms, business center. **Cards:** AX, DS, MC, VI. **Free Special Amenities:** newspaper and room upgrade (subject to availability with advance reservations). *(See color ad below)*

SOME UNITS

(See map and index starting on p. 414)

DAYS INN MONTREAL DOWNTOWN   *Book great rates at AAA.com*   **Phone:** (514)393-3388   **11**

CAA SAVE

| 5/1-10/31 | 1P: $142-$172 | 2P: $142-$172 | XP: $10 | F17 |
| 11/1-4/30 | 1P: $92-$122 | 2P: $92-$122 | XP: $10 | F17 |

Small-scale Hotel

Location: Corner of rue de l'Hotel de Ville. 215 boul Rene-Levesque est H2X 1N7. Fax: 514/395-9999. **Facility:** 123 units. 104 one-bedroom standard units. 19 one-bedroom suites ($179-$300). 8 stories, interior corridors. *Bath:* combo or shower only. **Parking:** on-site (fee). **Terms:** check-in 4 pm, cancellation fee imposed, [AP] & [CP] meal plans available, package plans. **Amenities:** voice mail, irons, hair dryers. *Some:* CD players, high-speed Internet, safes. **Dining:** 6:30 am-10 pm. **Guest Services:** valet laundry, wireless Internet. **Business Services:** meeting rooms, business center. **Cards:** AX, DC, DS, MC, VI. **Free Special Amenities:** newspaper and high-speed Internet. *(See color ad below)*

SOME UNITS

(See map and index starting on p. 414)

DELTA MONTREAL   *Book great rates at AAA.com*   Phone: (514)286-1986 [23]

(CAA) (SAVE)

5/1-10/31	1P: $159-$289	2P: $159-$289	XP: $20	F18
11/1-4/30	1P: $139-$289	2P: $139-$289	XP: $20	F18

Location: Corner of rue City Councillors. 475 ave President-Kennedy H3A 1J7. Fax: 514/284-4342. **Facility:** 456
Large-scale Hotel units. 453 one-bedroom standard units. 3 one-bedroom suites, some with whirlpools. 23 stories, interior
corridors. **Parking:** on-site (fee) and valet. **Terms:** small pets only ($30 fee). **Amenities:** voice mail, irons,
hair dryers. *Fee:* video games, high-speed Internet. *Some:* CD players, dual phone lines, honor bars.
Dining: 7 am-11 pm, cocktails, entertainment. **Pool(s):** heated indoor. **Leisure Activities:** saunas, whirlpool, 2 squash courts,
kids playroom, exercise room, spa. **Guest Services:** gift shop, valet laundry. **Business Services:** conference facilities,
business center. **Cards:** AX, CB, DC, DS, MC, VI. *(See color ad p 433)*

SOME UNITS

 (icon row) FEE / VCR FEE

DOUBLETREE PLAZA HOTEL DOWNTOWN   Phone: (514)842-8581 [1]

(CAA) (SAVE)

9/1-10/31	1P: $169-$269	2P: $169-$269	XP: $20	F18
5/1-8/31	1P: $149-$249	2P: $149-$249	XP: $20	F18
11/1-4/30	1P: $139-$239	2P: $139-$239	XP: $20	F18

Location: Between rue Berri and St-Hubert. 505 rue Sherbrooke est H2L 4N3. Fax: 514/842-8910. **Facility:** 319
Large-scale Hotel units. 311 one-bedroom standard units. 8 one-bedroom suites. 24 stories, interior corridors. **Parking:** on-site
(fee) and valet. **Terms:** cancellation fee imposed, [ECP] & [MAP] meal plans available, package plans, small
pets only ($25 fee). **Amenities:** CD players, dual phone lines, voice mail, irons, hair dryers. *Some:* DVD players (fee), safes,
honor bars. **Dining:** 6:30 am-10:30 pm, cocktails. **Pool(s):** heated indoor. **Leisure Activities:** saunas, whirlpool, exercise room.
Fee: massage. **Guest Services:** gift shop, valet laundry, wireless Internet. **Business Services:** conference facilities, business
center. **Cards:** AX, CB, DC, DS, JC, MC, VI. **Free Special Amenities: newspaper and room upgrade (subject to availability
with advance reservations).** *(See color ad below)*

SOME UNITS

(icon row) FEE / VCR FEE

FAIRMONT THE QUEEN ELIZABETH   *Book great rates at AAA.com*   Phone: (514)861-3511 [41]

(CAA) (SAVE)

All Year   1P: $189-$499   2P: $189-$499

Location: Between rue University and Mansfield. 900 boul Rene-Levesque ouest H3B 4A5. Fax: 514/954-2258.
Facility: The luxurious hotel, which features added amenities in its business-class units, has access to an
underground mall; a few guest rooms are small. 1039 units. 950 one-bedroom standard units. 87 one- and 2
Large-scale Hotel two-bedroom suites ($499-$2999). 21 stories, interior corridors. **Parking:** on-site (fee) and valet.
Terms: check-in 4 pm, cancellation fee imposed, package plans, small pets only ($25 extra charge).
Amenities: video games (fee), dual phone lines, voice mail, honor bars, irons, hair dryers. *Some:* CD players, safes. *Some:* DVD
players, high-speed Internet. **Dining:** 2 restaurants, 6:30 am-11 pm, also, The Beaver Club, see separate listing. **Pool(s):**
heated indoor, wading. **Leisure Activities:** whirlpool, steamrooms. *Fee:* massage. **Guest Services:** gift shop, valet laundry,
wireless Internet. **Business Services:** conference facilities, business center. **Cards:** AX, DC, DS, JC, MC, VI.
(See color ad card insert)

SOME UNITS

(icon row) FEE / VCR FEE FEE FEE

(See map and index starting on p. 414)

FOUR POINTS BY SHERATON MONTREAL CENTRE-VILLE *Book great rates at AAA.com*

Phone: (514)842-3961   **20**

	1P: $149-$235	2P: $159-$235	XP: $20	F17
5/1-10/15	1P: $139-$215	2P: $139-$215	XP: $20	F17
10/16-4/30				

Large-scale Hotel

Location: Between rue Durocher and Aylmer. 475 rue Sherbrooke ouest H3A 2L9. Fax: 514/842-0945. **Facility:** 196 units. 133 one-bedroom standard units. 63 one-bedroom suites, some with efficiencies and/or whirlpools. 20 stories, interior corridors. **Parking:** valet and street. **Terms:** cancellation fee imposed, [AP], [BP] & [CP] meal plans available, package plans, 3% service charge, small pets only (must remain caged). **Amenities:** video games (fee), voice mail, irons, hair dryers. *Some:* DVD players. **Dining:** 2 restaurants, 6:30 am-10:30 pm; to 11 pm in summer. **Leisure Activities:** saunas, pool privileges, outdoor terrasse, exercise room. **Guest Services:** valet laundry, wireless Internet. **Business Services:** meeting rooms, business center. **Cards:** AX, CB, DC, DS, MC, VI. **Free Special Amenities:** newspaper and high-speed Internet. *(See color ad below & p 5)*

SOME UNITS FEE

(See map and index starting on p. 414)

HILTON MONTREAL BONAVENTURE   *Book great rates at AAA.com*   **Phone:** (514)878-2332

(CAA) (SAVE)

5/1-10/31	1P: $179-$269	2P: $179-$269	XP: $20 F18
1/1-4/30	1P: $169-$239	2P: $169-$239	XP: $20 F18
11/1-12/31	1P: $149-$239	2P: $149-$239	XP: $20 F18

Location: Corner of Mansfield and de la Gauchetiere. Located atop the convention center. 900 rue de La Gauchetiere
Large-scale Hotel W H5A 1E4. **Fax:** 514/878-3881. **Facility:** Corporate rooms in this downtown hotel have marble entrance foyers, ergonomic desk chairs and marble bathroom counters; there is a rooftop garden. 395 units. 383 one-bedroom standard units. 12 one-bedroom suites. 3 stories, interior corridors. **Parking:** on-site (fee) and valet. **Terms:** [BP] & [CP] meal plans available, package plans. **Amenities:** dual phone lines, voice mail, honor bars, irons, hair dryers. *Fee:* video games, high-speed Internet. *Some:* fax, safes. **Dining:** 2 restaurants, 6:30 am-11 pm, cocktails, also, Le Castillon, see separate listing. **Pool(s):** heated outdoor. **Leisure Activities:** vacation station for children, exercise room. *Fee:* massage. **Guest Services:** gift shop, valet laundry, wireless Internet. **Business Services:** conference facilities, business center. **Cards:** AX, CB, DC, DS, JC, MC, VI. *(See color ad below)*

SOME UNITS

FEE FEE

HOLIDAY INN EXPRESS HOTEL & SUITES   *Book great rates at AAA.com*   **Phone:** (514)448-7100   🔞

(CAA) (SAVE)

All Year [ECP]   1P: $109-$350   XP: $15   F18

Location: Corner de Bullion. 155 boul Rene-Levesque est H2X 3Z8. **Fax:** 514/448-7101. **Facility:** 161 units. 40 one-bedroom standard units. 115 one- and 6 two-bedroom suites. 8 stories, interior corridors. **Parking:** valet and street. **Terms:** pets ($100 fee). **Amenities:** video games (fee), high-speed Internet, dual phone lines,
Small-scale Hotel voice mail, irons, hair dryers. *Some:* safes. **Leisure Activities:** exercise room. **Guest Services:** valet and coin laundry. **Business Services:** meeting rooms, business center. **Cards:** AX, CB, DC, DS, JC, MC, VI. **Free Special Amenities:** expanded continental breakfast and high-speed Internet. *(See color ad card insert)*

SOME UNITS

FEE

HOLIDAY INN MONTREAL-MIDTOWN   *Book great rates at AAA.com*   **Phone:** 514/842-6111   ㉒

(CAA) (SAVE)

All Year   1P: $119-$179   2P: $119-$179   XP: $15   F17

Location: Between rue Bleury and City Councillors. 420 rue Sherbrooke ouest H3A 1B4. **Fax:** 514/842-9381. **Facility:** 487 units. 481 one-bedroom standard units. 6 one-bedroom suites ($275-$900), some with kitchens. 19 stories, interior corridors. **Parking:** valet and street. **Terms:** package plans, small pets only
Large-scale Hotel ($35 fee). **Amenities:** voice mail, safes, irons, hair dryers. *Some:* high-speed Internet, honor bars. **Dining:** 6 am-midnight, cocktails. **Pool(s):** heated indoor. **Leisure Activities:** saunas, whirlpool, exercise room. *Fee:* massage. **Guest Services:** gift shop, valet and coin laundry, wireless Internet. **Business Services:** meeting rooms, business center. **Cards:** AX, CB, DC, DS, JC, MC, VI. **Free Special Amenities:** newspaper and high-speed Internet. *(See color ad card insert)*

SOME UNITS

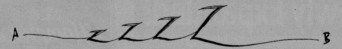
FEE

(See map and index starting on p. 414)

HOLIDAY INN SELECT MONTREAL-CENTRE VILLE
(DWTN CONV CTR)   *Book great rates at AAA.com*   Phone: (514)878-9888   **19**

ⒶⒶⒶ ⓈⒶⓋⒺ

5/1-10/31	1P: $159-$229	2P: $159-$229	XP: $20 F18
11/1-4/30	1P: $139-$219	2P: $139-$219	XP: $20 F18

Location: Corner of rue St-Urbain. Located in Chinatown, across from convention center. 99 ave Viger ouest H2Z 1E9. Fax: 514/878-6341. **Facility:** 235 units. 229 one-bedroom standard units. 6 one-bedroom suites. 8 stories, Large-scale Hotel interior corridors. **Parking:** on-site (fee). **Terms:** [BP] & [CP] meal plans available, package plans. **Amenities:** voice mail, irons, hair dryers. *Some:* honor bars. **Dining:** Chez Chine, see separate listing. **Pool(s):** heated indoor. **Leisure Activities:** sauna, whirlpool, exercise room, spa. **Guest Services:** gift shop, valet and coin laundry, beauty salon, wireless Internet. **Business Services:** conference facilities, business center. **Cards:** AX, CB, DC, DS, JC, MC, VI. *(See color ad card insert & below)*

SOME UNITS

🅢⃝ 🍴 ⓐ ⓂⒼ 🅐⃝ 🔄 ⓧ 🎦 🖥 / ⓧ 🎥 🅑⃝ /
FEE

HOTEL DU FORT   *Book great rates at AAA.com*   Phone: (514)938-8333   **57**

ⒶⒶⒶ ⓈⒶⓋⒺ

5/1-9/30 [ECP]	1P: $149-$189	2P: $149-$189	XP: $25 F12
10/1-4/30 [ECP]	1P: $149-$179	2P: $149-$179	XP: $25 F12

Location: Corner of rue Ste-Catherine ouest. 1390 rue du Fort H3H 2R7. Fax: 514/938-2078. **Facility:** 124 units. 105 one-bedroom standard units. 19 one-bedroom suites ($179-$249). 19 stories, interior corridors. Small-scale Hotel **Parking:** on-site. **Terms:** check-in 4 pm. **Amenities:** video games (fee), voice mail, safes, irons, hair dryers. *Some:* CD players, high-speed Internet (fee), dual phone lines. **Leisure Activities:** exercise room. **Guest Services:** valet laundry. **Business Services:** meeting rooms, business center. **Cards:** AX, DC, JC, MC, VI. **Free Special Amenities:** expanded continental breakfast and newspaper. *(See color ad p 439)*

SOME UNITS

🍴 ⓐ 🎦 🅑⃝ 🖾 🖥 / ⓧ 🎥 /

HOTEL GAULT   *Book at AAA.com*   Phone: 514/904-1616   **40**

▽▽▽   All Year [BP]   1P: $349-$749   2P: $349-$749   XP: $40   F12

Location: Just s of rue Notre-Dame. Located in Old Montreal. 449 rue Ste-Helene H2Y 2K9. Fax: 514/904-1717. Small-scale Hotel **Facility:** 29 one-bedroom standard units, some with efficiencies. 5 stories, interior corridors. *Bath:* combo or shower only. **Parking:** valet. **Terms:** cancellation fee imposed, package plans, pets ($20 extra charge). **Amenities:** video library (fee), DVD players, CD players, high-speed Internet, voice mail, safes, honor bars, irons, hair dryers. **Leisure Activities:** exercise room. *Fee:* massage, off-site spa privileges. **Guest Services:** sundries, valet laundry, wireless Internet. **Business Services:** meeting rooms, business center. **Cards:** AX, DC, DS, MC, VI.

SOME UNITS

🐾 🍴 24⃝ 🕊 ⓐ / ⓧ 🅑⃝ 🖾 🖥 /
FEE

(See map and index starting on p. 414)

HOTEL GODIN

Small-scale Hotel

Book great rates at AAA.com

Phone: (514)843-6000

All Year   1P: $159-$339   2P: $159-$339   XP: $30   F12
Location: Corner of boul St-Laurent. 10 rue Sherbrooke ouest H2X 4C9. Fax: 514/843-6810. **Facility:** 136 units. 130 one-bedroom standard units, some with efficiencies. 6 one-bedroom suites ($259-$509). 5 stories, interior corridors. *Bath:* combo or shower only. **Parking:** valet. **Terms:** cancellation fee imposed, pets ($50 fee). **Amenities:** high-speed Internet (fee), dual phone lines, voice mail, safes, honor bars, irons, hair dryers. *Some:* DVD players (fee). **Dining:** 7 am-10 pm, Sat & Sun 8 am-11 pm. **Leisure Activities:** exercise room. *Fee:* esthetic services, massage. **Guest Services:** gift shop, valet laundry, beauty salon. **Business Services:** meeting rooms, PC (fee). **Cards:** AX, DC, JC, MC, VI. **Free Special Amenities:** local telephone calls and newspaper.

SOME UNITS

   / /
FEE

(See map and index starting on p. 414)

HOTEL GOUVERNEUR PLACE DUPUIS

Book great rates at AAA.com   **Phone: (514)842-4881**   **6**

(CAA) (SAVE)   All Year [CP]   1P: $129-$209   2P: $129-$209   XP: $20   F17

▼▼▼▼ **Location:** Between boul de Maisonneuve and rue Ste-Catherine. 1415 rue St-Hubert H2L 3Y9. Fax: 514/842-1584. **Facility:** 352 units. 345 one-bedroom standard units. 7 one-bedroom suites. 30 stories, interior corridors. *Bath:* combo or shower only. **Parking:** on-site (fee). **Terms:** package plans. **Amenities:** video games (fee), Large-scale Hotel   voice mail, irons, hair dryers. *Some:* DVD players, CD players, high-speed Internet, dual phone lines, safes, indoor. **Leisure Activities:** saunas, exercise room. **Guest Services:** valet laundry. **Business Services:** conference facilities, business center. **Cards:** AX, DC, DS, JC, MC, VI. **Free Special Amenities: continental breakfast and local telephone calls.** *(See color ad p 439)*

[🍴] [🍸] [🏋] [🏊] [🐾] [💻] / [✕] [VCR] [🛁] /
                                       FEE   FEE

HOTEL INTERCONTINENTAL MONTREAL

Book great rates at AAA.com   **Phone: (514)987-9900**   **31**

(CAA) (SAVE)   All Year   1P: $179-$575   2P: $179-$575   F18

▼▼▼ ▼▼▼ **Location:** Corner of rue St-Pierre. Located in Old Montreal. 360 rue St-Antoine ouest H2Y 3X4. Fax: 514/847-8550. **Facility:** This full-service hotel, which is convenient to the convention center, offers luxuriously appointed guest rooms and common areas. 357 units. 334 one-bedroom standard units. 23 one-bedroom suites, some Large-scale Hotel   with whirlpools. 26 stories, interior corridors. **Parking:** valet and street. **Terms:** cancellation fee imposed, package plans, 3% service charge, small pets only ($30 fee). **Amenities:** dual phone lines, voice mail, safes, honor bars, irons, hair dryers. *Fee:* video games, high-speed Internet. *Some:* DVD players (fee), CD players, fax. **Dining:** 2 restaurants, 6:30 am-10:30 pm; to 1 am in summer, also, Restaurant Les Continents, see separate listing. **Pool(s):** heated indoor. **Leisure Activities:** saunas, steamroom, exercise room. *Fee:* massage. **Guest Services:** sundries, valet laundry, wireless Internet. **Business Services:** conference facilities, business center. **Cards:** AX, CB, DC, DS, JC, MC, VI. **Free Special Amenities: newspaper.** *(See color ad below)*

                                                    SOME UNITS
[🛁] [🍴] [24↑] [🍸] [🏋] [🏊] [✕] [🐾] [💻] / [✕] [VCR] [🛁] [🖥] /
FEE   FEE

HOTEL LA TOUR CENTRE-VILLE

Book great rates at AAA.com   **Phone: (514)866-8861**   **26**

(CAA) (SAVE)   5/1-10/31   1P: $125-$145   2P: $125-$145   XP: $12   F17
             11/1-4/30   1P: $102-$121   2P: $102-$121   XP: $12   F17

▼▼ **Location:** Corner of rue de Bleury. 400 boul Rene-Levesque ouest H2Z 1V5. Fax: 514/866-7257. **Facility:** 148 Condominium   units. 59 one-bedroom standard units with kitchens. 89 one-bedroom suites with kitchens. 17 stories, interior corridors. **Parking:** on-site (fee). **Terms:** 3% service charge, small pets only. **Amenities:** voice mail, irons, hair dryers. **Dining:** 2 restaurants, 7 am-11 pm. **Pool(s):** heated indoor. **Leisure Activities:** saunas, exercise room. **Guest Services:** sundries, valet and coin laundry. **Business Services:** meeting rooms, PC (fee). **Cards:** AX, DC, MC, VI. **Free Special Amenities: newspaper.**

                                                   SOME UNITS
[🐾] [🍴] [🍸] [🏊] [🛁] [💻] / [✕] [🖥] /

(See map and index starting on p. 414)

HOTEL LE CANTLIE SUITES   *Book great rates at AAA.com*   Phone: (514)842-2000   **39**
(CAA) (SAVE)   All Year   1P: $139-$499   2P: $149-$499   XP: $25   F12
▼▼▼   **Location:** Between rue Stanley and Peel. 1110 rue Sherbrooke ouest H3A 1G9. Fax: 514/844-7808. **Facility:** 252 units. 171 one-bedroom standard units, some with efficiencies or kitchens. 77 one- and 4 two-bedroom suites ($199-$499), some with efficiencies or kitchens. 28 stories, interior corridors. **Parking:** valet and
Large-scale Hotel   street. **Terms:** cancellation fee imposed. **Amenities:** *Some:* CD players. *Fee:* DVD players, high-speed Internet. **Dining:** 7 am-midnight, cocktails. **Pool(s):** heated outdoor. **Leisure Activities:** exercise room.
Guest Services: valet and coin laundry, wireless Internet. **Business Services:** meeting rooms, business center. **Cards:** AX, CB, DC, DS, MC, VI. **Free Special Amenities:** newspaper. *(See color ad below)*

SOME UNITS
(icons) FEE FEE

HOTEL LE GERMAIN   *Book at AAA.com*   Phone: (514)849-2050   **33**
▼▼▼   5/1-9/30 [ECP]   1P: $250-$330   2P: $250-$330   XP: $25   F12
10/1-4/30 [ECP]   1P: $230-$290   2P: $230-$290   XP: $25   F12
Small-scale Hotel   **Location:** Just n of ave President-Kennedy. 2050 rue Mansfield H3A 1Y9. Fax: 514/849-1437. **Facility:** 101 units. 99 one-bedroom standard units. 2 one-bedroom suites, some with kitchens. 16 stories, interior corridors.
Bath: combo or shower only. **Parking:** valet and street. **Terms:** cancellation fee imposed, pets ($30 extra charge, must be supervised). **Amenities:** CD players, dual phone lines, voice mail, honor bars, irons, hair dryers. *Some:* DVD players, high-speed Internet (fee). **Leisure Activities:** exercise room. *Fee:* massage. **Guest Services:** valet laundry, wireless Internet. **Business Services:** meeting rooms, PC. **Cards:** AX, DC, MC, VI.

SOME UNITS
(ASK icons) FEE FEE

HOTEL LE ROBERVAL   *Book great rates at AAA.com*   Phone: (514)286-5215   **9**
(CAA) (SAVE)   5/1-10/31 [CP]   1P: $129-$179   2P: $129-$179   XP: $15   F12
▼▼▼   11/1-4/30 [CP]   1P: $99-$149   2P: $99-$149   XP: $15   F12
Condominium   **Location:** Corner of rue Berri. 505 boul Rene-Levesque est H2L 5B6. Fax: 514/286-7548. **Facility:** 76 units. 33 one-bedroom standard units, some with kitchens. 43 one-bedroom suites, some with efficiencies or kitchens. 6 stories, interior corridors. **Parking:** on-site (fee). **Terms:** check-in 4 pm. **Amenities:** high-speed Internet, voice mail, hair dryers. **Guest Services:** valet and coin laundry. **Business Services:** meeting rooms, PC. **Cards:** AX, DC, DS, MC, VI. **Free Special Amenities:** continental breakfast and high-speed Internet.

SOME UNITS
(icons)

HOTEL LE ST-JAMES   *Book at AAA.com*   Phone: (514)841-3111   **32**
▼▼▼ ▼▼▼   All Year   1P: $400-$475   2P: $400-$475   XP: $50   F18
Location: Corner of rue St-Pierre. Located in Old Montreal. 355 rue St-Jacques ouest H2Y 1N9. Fax: 514/841-1232.
Historic   **Facility:** The historic 1870 building, which once housed the Merchants' Bank, features outstanding exterior
Small-scale Hotel   stonework and luxurious interiors. 61 units. 50 one-bedroom standard units. 8 one- and 3 two-bedroom suites ($575-$5000), some with kitchens. 12 stories, interior corridors. *Bath:* combo or shower only.
Parking: valet. **Terms:** small pets only. **Amenities:** video library, CD players, high-speed Internet (fee), dual phone lines, voice mail, safes, honor bars, irons, hair dryers. *Some:* DVD players. **Leisure Activities:** exercise room, spa. **Guest Services:** valet laundry, wireless Internet. **Business Services:** meeting rooms, PC. **Cards:** AX, CB, DC, DS, JC, MC, VI.

SOME UNITS
(ASK icons)

(See map and index starting on p. 414)

HOTEL LE SAINT-MALO   Phone: 514/931-7366   **55**
♦♦♦   *Property failed to provide current rates*
            Location: Just s of boul de Maisonneuve. 1455 rue du Fort H3H 2C2. Fax: 514/227-5376. **Facility:** 13 one-
Small-scale Hotel   bedroom standard units. 4 stories (no elevator), interior corridors. *Bath:* combo or shower only. **Parking:** on-
            site (fee). **Terms:** small pets only. **Amenities:** voice mail, irons, hair dryers. **Guest Services:** valet laundry,
wireless Internet.

SOME UNITS
🐕 🖵 /☒/

HOTEL LORD BERRI   *Book at AAA.com*   Phone: (514)845-9236   **8**
♦♦♦   5/1-10/31   1P: $145-$165   2P: $145-$165   XP: $15   F12
               11/1-4/30   1P: $129-$149   2P: $129-$149   XP: $15   F12
Small-scale Hotel   **Location:** Between boul Rene-Levesque and rue Ste-Catherine. 1199 rue Berri H2L 4C6. Fax: 514/849-9855.
Facility: 154 units. 148 one-bedroom standard units. 6 one-bedroom suites. 10 stories, interior corridors.
Parking: on-site (fee). **Amenities:** video games (fee), voice mail, hair dryers. *Some:* DVD players, CD players, irons. **Guest
Services:** gift shop, valet laundry, wireless Internet. **Business Services:** meeting rooms, administrative services (fee).
Cards: AX, CB, DC, MC, VI.

SOME UNITS
🍽 🍸 📷 🖥 🖵 /☒/

HOTEL MANOIR DES ALPES   Phone: 514/845-9803   **4**
ⒶⒶ 〔SAVE〕   5/1-10/31   1P: $85-$110   2P: $90-$130   XP: $10
               11/1-4/30   1P: $80-$100   2P: $85-$120   XP: $10
♦♦♦   **Location:** Just s of rue Ste-Catherine. 1245 rue St-Andre H2L 3T1. Fax: 514/845-9886. **Facility:** 29 one-bedroom
               standard units, some with whirlpools. 3 stories (no elevator), interior corridors. *Bath:* combo or shower only.
Small-scale Hotel   **Parking:** on-site. **Terms:** cancellation fee imposed. **Amenities:** hair dryers. **Guest Services:** wireless
               Internet. **Business Services:** meeting rooms, PC, fax (fee). **Cards:** AX, JC, MC, VI.
Free Special Amenities: continental breakfast and local telephone calls.

SOME UNITS
/☒/

HOTEL MARITIME PLAZA   *Book great rates at AAA.com*   Phone: (514)932-1411   **52**
ⒶⒶ 〔SAVE〕   5/1-10/15   1P: $149-$350   2P: $149-$350   XP: $15   F11
               10/16-4/30   1P: $139-$350   2P: $139-$350   XP: $15   F11
♦♦♦♦   **Location:** Corner of boul Rene-Levesque; centre. 1155 rue Guy H3H 2K5. Fax: 514/932-0446. **Facility:** 214 units.
               211 one-bedroom standard units, some with efficiencies. 3 one-bedroom suites with efficiencies. 14 stories,
Large-scale Hotel   interior corridors. **Parking:** on-site (fee). **Terms:** cancellation fee imposed. **Amenities:** video games (fee),
voice mail, safes, irons, hair dryers. *Some:* high-speed Internet (fee). **Dining:** 6:30-11 am, 11:30-2 & 5-10
pm, cocktails. **Pool(s):** heated indoor. **Leisure Activities:** sun deck, exercise room. **Guest Services:** gift shop, valet laundry,
wireless Internet. **Business Services:** meeting rooms, administrative services (fee). **Cards:** AX, DC, DS, MC, VI.
(See color ad p 446)

SOME UNITS
🆂ᴰ 🍽 ⊟ 🏊 📷 🖵 /☒/ VCR 🗎 📠 /

(See map and index starting on p. 414)

HOTEL NELLIGAN *Book great rates at AAA.com* Phone: (514)788-2040 **28**

(CAA) (SAVE) All Year [ECP] 1P: $230-$270 2P: $230-$270 XP: $25 F12
Location: Corner of rue St-Sulpice. 106 rue St-Paul ouest H2Y 1Z3. Fax: 514/788-2041. **Facility:** Many luxury services are offered at this upscale Old Montreal hotel, which has large, stylish rooms with high-end furnishings and modern amenities. 63 units. 61 one-bedroom standard units, some with whirlpools. 2 one-
Small-scale Hotel bedroom suites ($330-$1200) with whirlpools. 5 stories, interior corridors. **Parking:** valet and street. **Terms:** cancellation fee imposed, [AP], [BP] & [CP] meal plans available, package plans. **Amenities:** CD players, high-speed Internet, dual phone lines, voice mail, safes, honor bars, irons, hair dryers. *Some:* DVD players (fee). **Dining:** Restaurant Verses, see separate listing. **Leisure Activities:** rooftop terrace, exercise room. *Fee:* massage. **Guest Services:** complimentary evening beverages, valet laundry, area transportation-downtown. **Business Services:** PC. **Cards:** AX, CB, DC, DS, JC, MC, VI. **Free Special Amenities:** expanded continental breakfast and newspaper.
(See color ad p 442)
SOME UNITS
🅂ⅅ 🍴 ⓨ ⊠ ⊠ ⍅ / Ⓥ🄲🅁 / FEE

HOTEL OMNI MONT-ROYAL *Book great rates at AAA.com* Phone: (514)284-1110 **36**

(CAA) (SAVE) 5/16-10/31 1P: $189-$329 XP: $35 F
  5/1-5/15 1P: $179-$299 XP: $35 F
  11/1-4/30 1P: $159-$269 XP: $35 F
Location: Corner of rue Peel. 1050 rue Sherbrooke ouest H3A 2R6. Fax: 514/845-3025. **Facility:** The hotel, which
Large-scale Hotel offers luxurious furnishings and elegant banquet rooms, is in a fashionable area near shops and attractions. 300 units. 271 one-bedroom standard units. 29 one-bedroom suites ($319-$1899). 31 stories, interior corridors. **Parking:** on-site (fee) and valet. **Terms:** 7 day cancellation notice, [AP], [BP] & [CP] meal plans available, package plans, small pets only ($50 extra charge). **Amenities:** CD players, dual phone lines, voice mail, safes, honor bars, irons, hair dryers. *Some:* DVD players, fax. **Dining:** 6:30 am-11 pm, cocktails, also, Zen Chinese Cuisine, see separate listing. **Pool(s):** heated outdoor. **Leisure Activities:** sauna, whirlpool, steamrooms, aerobics, yoga, exercise room, spa. **Guest Services:** gift shop, valet laundry, wireless Internet. **Business Services:** conference facilities, business center. **Cards:** AX, CB, DC, DS, MC, VI. **Free Special Amenities:** newspaper and early check-in/late check-out.
SOME UNITS
🅂ⅅ 🛏 🍴 ❷❹ ⓨ ⛛ ⍉ ⊼ ⊠ ⍅ / ⊠ Ⓥ🄲🅁 🔲 🖥 / FEE FEE

HOTEL PLACE D'ARMES *Book great rates at AAA.com* Phone: (514)842-1887 **25**

(CAA) (SAVE) All Year [ECP] 1P: $230-$270 2P: $230-$270 XP: $25 F12
Location: Corner of rue St-Jacques. Located in Old Montreal. 55 rue St-Jacques H2Y 3X2. Fax: 514/842-6469.
Facility: This restored hotel in scenic Old Montreal offers luxurious rooms, spacious suites and a posh spa just a stone's throw from the Notre Dame Basilica. Designated smoking area. 135 units. 123 one-bedroom
Historic standard units, some with whirlpools. 12 one-bedroom suites ($330-$1200) with whirlpools. 8 stories, interior
Small-scale Hotel corridors. *Bath:* combo or shower only. **Parking:** valet. **Terms:** cancellation fee imposed, [AP], [BP] & [CP] meal plans available, package plans. **Amenities:** CD players, high-speed Internet, dual phone lines, voice mail, safes, honor bars, irons, hair dryers. *Some:* DVD players. **Dining:** Aix Cuisine du Terroir, see separate listing. **Leisure Activities:** sun deck, limited exercise equipment, spa. *Fee:* steamroom. **Guest Services:** valet laundry, area transportation, wireless Internet. **Business Services:** meeting rooms, PC. **Cards:** AX, CB, DC, DS, JC, MC, VI. **Free Special Amenities:** expanded continental breakfast and newspaper. *(See color ad below)*
SOME UNITS
🅂ⅅ 🍴 ⓨ ⎙ ⊠ ⊠ / Ⓥ🄲🅁 / FEE

(See map and index starting on p. 414)

HOTEL ST-PAUL *Book at AAA.com*

| | | | | Phone: (514)380-2222 | 42 |

5/1-10/31 [CP]   1P: $279   2P: $279   XP: $35   F12
11/1-4/30 [CP]   1P: $209   2P: $209   XP: $35   F12

Small-scale Hotel **Location:** Corner of rue St-Paul. Located in Old Montreal. 355 rue McGill H2Y 2E8. Fax: 514/380-2200. **Facility:** 120 units. 96 one-bedroom standard units. 24 one-bedroom suites. 10 stories, interior corridors. **Parking:** valet. **Terms:** cancellation fee imposed, small pets only. **Amenities:** CD players, high-speed Internet, dual phone lines, voice mail, fax, safes, honor bars, irons, hair dryers. *Some:* DVD players. **Leisure Activities:** exercise room. *Fee:* massage. **Guest Services:** valet laundry, wireless Internet. **Business Services:** meeting rooms, business center. **Cards:** AX, DC, MC, VI.

SOME UNITS
(ASK) (SO) (☞) (Y) (📷) (💻) / (✕) /

HOTEL TRAVELODGE MONTREAL CENTRE *Book great rates at AAA.com*

| | | | | Phone: (514)874-9090 | 15 |

(CAA) (SAVE)
5/1-10/31 [CP]   1P: $109-$149   2P: $109-$149   XP: $15   F16
1/1-4/30 [CP]   1P: $99-$139   2P: $99-$139   XP: $15   F16
11/1-12/31 [CP]   1P: $99-$129   2P: $99-$129   XP: $15   F16

Location: Between rue Clark and St-Urbain. Located in Chinatown. 50 boul Rene-Levesque ouest H2Z 1A2. Small-scale Hotel Fax: 514/874-0907. **Facility:** 244 one-bedroom standard units. 11 stories, interior corridors. *Bath:* combo or shower only. **Parking:** on-site (fee). **Terms:** [AP] & [BP] meal plans available, package plans, $3 service charge, small pets only. **Amenities:** voice mail, hair dryers. *Some:* high-speed Internet. **Dining:** 7-11 am. **Guest Services:** gift shop, valet laundry, wireless Internet. **Business Services:** meeting rooms. **Cards:** AX, DC, DS, MC, VI. **Free Special Amenities:** expanded continental breakfast and high-speed internet. *(See color ad below)*

SOME UNITS
(SO) (☞) (🍴) (💻) / (✕) (📦) (📦) /

HYATT REGENCY MONTREAL *Book great rates at AAA.com*

| | | | | Phone: (514)982-1234 | 17 |

(CAA) (SAVE)
5/1-10/31   1P: $169-$359   2P: $169-$359   XP: $25   F18
11/1-4/30   1P: $149-$279   2P: $149-$279   XP: $25   F18

Location: Corner of rue Ste-Catherine. Located next to shopping mall. 1255 Jeanne-Mance H5B 1E5. Fax: 514/285-1243. **Facility:** 605 units. 572 one-bedroom standard units. 33 one-bedroom suites. 12 Large-scale Hotel stories, interior corridors. **Parking:** valet. **Terms:** cancellation fee imposed. **Amenities:** video games (fee), dual phone lines, voice mail, irons, hair dryers. *Some:* CD players, fax. *Fee:* DVD players. **Dining:** 6:30 am-11:30 pm, cocktails. **Pool(s):** heated indoor. **Leisure Activities:** saunas, exercise room. *Fee:* massage. **Guest Services:** gift shop, valet laundry, wireless Internet. **Business Services:** conference facilities, business center. **Cards:** AX, CB, DC, DS, JC, MC, VI. *(See color ad p 445)*

SOME UNITS
(🍴) (Y) (&M) (🏊) (✕) (📷) (💻) / (✕) (VCR) (📦) (📦) /
                                    FEE   FEE

(See map and index starting on p. 414)

L'APPARTEMENT HOTEL   *Book great rates at AAA.com*   Phone: (514)284-3634   [18]

CAA SAVE

5/1-10/31 [ECP]	1P: $140-$160	2P: $140-$160	XP: $15 F17
11/1-4/30 [ECP]	1P: $127-$147	2P: $127-$147	XP: $15 F17

Condominium   **Location:** Corner of rue Durocher. 455 rue Sherbrooke ouest H3A 1B7. Fax: 514/287-1431. **Facility:** 126 units. 56 one-bedroom standard units with kitchens. 56 one- and 14 two-bedroom suites ($149-$227) with kitchens. 16 stories, interior corridors. **Parking:** on-site (fee). **Terms:** weekly rates available, small pets only (must remain caged). **Amenities:** high-speed Internet, voice mail, irons, hair dryers. **Pool(s):** heated indoor. **Leisure Activities:** saunas, sun deck, limited exercise equipment. **Guest Services:** valet and coin laundry. **Business Services:** business center. **Cards:** AX, CB, DC, DS, JC, MC, VI. **Free Special Amenities:** expanded continental breakfast and high-speed Internet.

SOME UNITS

🅂🄳 🐕 🍴 🚲 ✕ 🎥 🖥 🖨 💻 / ✕ VCR /

LA PRESIDENCE HOTEL AND SUITES   *Book at AAA.com*   Phone: (514)842-9988   [2]

9/1-10/31	1P: $159-$189	2P: $159-$189	XP: $20 F18
5/1-8/31 & 1/1-4/30	1P: $139-$169	2P: $139-$169	XP: $20 F18
11/1-12/31	1P: $129-$159	2P: $129-$159	XP: $20 F18

Condominium   **Location:** Between rue Berri and St-Hubert. Located in the same building as Plaza Hotel Centre-Ville Downtown. 505 rue Sherbrooke est H2L 4N3. Fax: 514/842-9541. **Facility:** These one- and two-bedroom upscale condos include access to the facilities and services of an adjacent hotel. 52 units. 44 one- and 8 two-bedroom suites with kitchens, some with whirlpools. 24 stories, interior corridors. **Parking:** on-site (fee) and valet. **Terms:** cancellation fee imposed, package plans, small pets only ($25 fee, must be attended). **Amenities:** CD players, high-speed Internet, voice mail, irons, hair dryers. *Some:* DVD players (fee). **Pool(s):** heated indoor. **Leisure Activities:** saunas, whirlpool, exercise room. *Fee:* massage. **Guest Services:** gift shop, valet and coin laundry. **Business Services:** conference facilities, PC (fee). **Cards:** AX, CB, DC, DS, JC, MC, VI.

SOME UNITS

ASK 🅂🄳 🐕 🍴 24 🍸 🏋 🚲 ✕ 🎥 🖥 🖨 💻 / ✕ VCR /
    FEE   FEE

LA TOUR BELVEDERE APARTMENT HOTEL   *Book at AAA.com*   Phone: (514)935-9052   [58]

All Year	1P: $119-$142	2P: $134-$142	XP: $15 F16

Condominium   **Location:** Between Lambert-Closse and Chomedey. 2175 boul de Maisonneuve ouest H3H 1L5. Fax: 514/935-9532. **Facility:** 150 units. 75 one-bedroom standard units with kitchens. 74 one- and 1 two-bedroom suites with kitchens. 21 stories, interior corridors. **Parking:** on-site (fee) and street, winter plug-ins. **Terms:** weekly rates available. **Amenities:** high-speed Internet (fee), voice mail, safes, irons, hair dryers. **Pool(s):** heated indoor. **Leisure Activities:** saunas, exercise room. **Guest Services:** valet and coin laundry. **Cards:** AX, DC, DS, MC, VI.

SOME UNITS

ASK 🅂🄳 🍴 🚲 🎥 🖥 🖨 💻 / ✕ VCR /
                                                                 FEE

(See map and index starting on p. 414)

LE CENTRE SHERATON   *Book great rates at AAA.com*   Phone: (514)878-2000   **48**
(CAA) (SAVE)   5/1-10/20   1P: $199-$599   2P: $199-$599   XP: $40   F17
   10/21-4/30   1P: $169-$599   2P: $169-$599   XP: $40   F17
▼▼▼ ▼▼▼   **Location:** Between rue Drummond and Stanley. 1201 boul Rene-Levesque ouest H3B 2L7. Fax: 514/878-3958.
   Facility: This full-service high-rise offers luxurious guest rooms, many with commanding views of the city;
Large-scale Hotel conference facilities are extensive. 825 units. 791 one-bedroom standard units. 34 one-bedroom suites,
   some with whirlpools. 37 stories, interior corridors. *Bath:* combo or shower only. **Parking:** on-site (fee) and
valet. **Terms:** cancellation fee imposed. **Amenities:** dual phone lines, voice mail, safes, honor bars, irons, hair dryers. *Fee:*
video games, high-speed Internet. *Some:* DVD players, CD players, fax. **Dining:** 6:30 am-10:30 pm, cocktails. **Pool(s):** heated
indoor. **Leisure Activities:** saunas, whirlpool, exercise room, spa. **Guest Services:** gift shop, valet laundry, beauty salon,
wireless Internet. **Business Services:** conference facilities, business center. **Cards:** AX, CB, DC, DS, JC, MC, VI.
Free Special Amenities: newspaper. *(See color ad p 5 & p 445)*

SOME UNITS

🛏️ 🍴 24 📺 ♿ 📱 🐾 🏊 ✕ 🎥 💻 / ✕ VCR 🔌 / FEE

LE MERIDIEN VERSAILLES-MONTREAL   *Book great rates at AAA.com*   Phone: (514)933-8111   **51**
(CAA) (SAVE)   5/1-10/31   1P: $149-$219   2P: $149-$219   XP: $20   F17
   11/1-4/30   1P: $129-$219   2P: $129-$219   XP: $20   F17
▼▼▼▼   **Location:** Corner of rue St-Mathieu. 1808 rue Sherbrooke ouest H3H 1E5. Fax: 514/933-6867. **Facility:** 107 units.
Small-scale Hotel 14 stories, interior corridors. **Parking:** valet and street. **Terms:** [AP], [BP], [CP] & [ECP] meal plans
available, package plans, pets ($15 extra charge, must remain caged and supervised). **Amenities:** video
games (fee), CD players, voice mail, safes, honor bars, irons, hair dryers. *Some:* dual phone lines. **Dining:** Ristorante Bronte,
see separate listing. **Leisure Activities:** exercise room. **Guest Services:** valet laundry, wireless Internet. **Business Services:**
meeting rooms, fax. **Cards:** AX, CB, DC, DS, JC, MC, VI. **Free Special Amenities: newspaper.** *(See color ad p 431)*

SOME UNITS

🛏️ 🍴 ♿ 🎥 💻 / ✕ 🔌 📠 / FEE

LE NOUVEL HOTEL   *Book great rates at AAA.com*   Phone: 514/931-8841   **54**
(CAA) (SAVE)   5/1-10/31   1P: $169-$389   2P: $179-$399   XP: $20   F16
   11/1-4/30   1P: $159-$229   2P: $169-$239   XP: $20   F16
▼▼▼▼   **Location:** Corner of rue St-Mathieu. 1740 boul Rene-Levesque ouest H3H 1R3. Fax: 514/931-5581. **Facility:** 172
   units. 171 one-bedroom standard units, some with efficiencies. 1 one-bedroom suite with kitchen. 8-12
Large-scale Hotel stories, interior corridors. **Parking:** on-site (fee). **Terms:** [BP] meal plan available. **Amenities:** video games
   (fee), voice mail, safes, irons, hair dryers. *Some:* DVD players. **Dining:** 7 am-10:30 pm, cocktails. **Pool(s):**
outdoor. **Leisure Activities:** exercise room, spa. *Fee:* sauna, whirlpool, steamroom. **Guest Services:** gift shop, valet laundry,
beauty salon. **Business Services:** conference facilities, PC (fee). **Cards:** AX, DC, DS, MC, VI. **Free Special Amenities:**
newspaper and high-speed Internet. *(See color ad p 447)*

SOME UNITS

🍴 📺 🐾 ✕ 🎥 💻 / ✕ VCR 🔌 📠 / FEE

(See map and index starting on p. 414)

LE SAINT-SULPICE HOTEL MONTREAL

CAA SAVE

🔷🔷🔷🔷

Small-scale Hotel

Book great rates at AAA.com

6/1-10/31 [CP]	1P: $265-$495	2P: $265-$495	XP: $25	F18
5/1-5/31 [CP]	1P: $205-$335	2P: $205-$335	XP: $25	F18
11/1-4/30 [CP]	1P: $175-$285	2P: $175-$285	XP: $25	F18

Phone: (514)288-1000   27

Location: Just n of rue St-Paul. 414 rue St-Sulpice H2Y 2V5. Fax: 514/288-0077. **Facility:** This condo-hotel behind Basilica of Notre Dame offers studio and one- or two-bedroom suites, luxury services, an exercise room and a fine dining room. 108 units. 26 one-bedroom standard units with efficiencies. 80 one- and 2 two-bedroom suites with efficiencies, some with whirlpools. 6 stories, interior corridors. **Parking:** valet and street. **Terms:** [AP] meal plan available, small pets only ($40 fee). **Amenities:** video games (fee), high-speed Internet, dual phone lines, voice mail, safes, honor bars, irons, hair dryers. *Some:* DVD players, CD players, fax. **Dining:** S-Le Restaurant, see separate listing. **Leisure Activities:** sauna, exercise room, spa. **Guest Services:** valet laundry, wireless Internet. **Business Services:** meeting rooms, business center. **Cards:** AX, DC, DS, MC, VI. **Free Special Amenities: expanded continental breakfast and high-speed Internet.**

SOME UNITS

🛏️ 🍴 24ⁿ Ⓨ ✕ 🐾 🔒 📷 📺 / ✕ /
FEE

LE SQUARE PHILLIPS HOTEL & SUITES

CAA SAVE

🔷🔷🔷

Small-scale Hotel

Book great rates at AAA.com

5/1-10/31 [CP]	1P: $160-$232	2P: $160-$232	XP: $15	F18
11/1-4/30 [CP]	1P: $139-$198	2P: $139-$198	XP: $15	F18

Phone: (514)393-1193   29

Location: Between rue Ste-Catherine and boul Rene-Levesque. 1193 Place Phillips H3B 3C9. Fax: 514/393-1192. **Facility:** 160 units. 114 one-bedroom standard units with kitchens. 16 one- and 30 two-bedroom suites with kitchens. 10 stories, interior corridors. **Parking:** valet and street. **Terms:** cancellation fee imposed, pets (must remain caged). **Amenities:** video games (fee), high-speed Internet, dual phone lines, voice mail, irons, hair dryers. *Some:* DVD players, CD players. **Dining:** 7 am-9 pm, Fri & Sat-10 pm, Sun 8 am-8:30 pm. **Pool(s):** heated indoor. **Leisure Activities:** sun deck, exercise room. **Guest Services:** sundries, valet and coin laundry. **Business Services:** business center. **Cards:** AX, CB, DC, DS, JC, MC, VI. **Free Special Amenities: expanded continental breakfast and newspaper.** *(See color ad p 448)*

SOME UNITS

Ⓢ🄳 🛏️ 🍴 🐾 📽️ 🔒 📷 📺 / ✕ VCR /

(See map and index starting on p. 414)

LOEWS HOTEL VOGUE   *Book great rates at AAA.com*   Phone: (514)285-5555   **45**

5/1-11/10	1P: $206-$428	2P: $206-$428	XP: $35 F17
11/11-4/30	1P: $152-$284	2P: $152-$284	XP: $35 F17

Location: Between rue Ste-Catherine and boul de Maisonneuve. 1425 rue de la Montagne H3G 1Z3.
Fax: 514/849-8903. **Facility:** Marble-tiled bathrooms add an elegant touch to accommodations at this hotel
Large-scale Hotel in the heart of downtown. 142 units. 126 one-bedroom standard units with whirlpools. 16 one-bedroom
suites ($269-$2000) with whirlpools. 9 stories, interior corridors. **Parking:** valet and street. **Terms:** package
plans, small pets only. **Amenities:** DVD players, CD players, dual phone lines, voice mail, safes, honor bars, irons, hair dryers.
Fee: video games, high-speed Internet. **Dining:** 7 am-11 pm. **Leisure Activities:** exercise room. *Fee:* massage. **Guest
Services:** gift shop, valet laundry, wireless Internet. **Business Services:** conference facilities, business center. **Cards:** AX, DC,
DS, MC, VI. **Free Special Amenities:** newspaper and high-speed Internet.

SOME UNITS

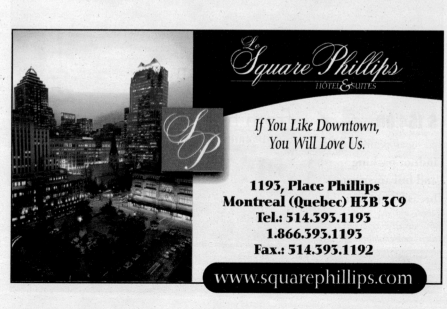

(See map and index starting on p. 414)

MARRIOTT CHATEAU CHAMPLAIN *Book great rates at AAA.com* **Phone:** (514)878-9000 **47**

CAA SAVE

	5/1-10/27	1P: $279	2P: $279	XP: $30	F18
	10/28-12/31 & 3/30-4/30	1P: $249	2P: $249	XP: $30	F18
	1/1-3/29	1P: $239	2P: $239	XP: $30	F18

Location: Corner of rue Peel and de la Gauchetiere. 1 Place du Canada H3B 4C9. Fax: 514/878-6761.
Large-scale Hotel Facility: This upscale property offers underground access to malls and the subway, and most of its rooms provide a commanding view of the city. Smoke free premises. 611 units. 591 one-bedroom standard units. 5 one-, 14 two- and 1 three-bedroom suites. 36 stories, interior corridors. **Parking:** on-site (fee) and valet. **Terms:** [BP] meal plan available, package plans. **Amenities:** voice mail, honor bars, irons, hair dryers. *Some:* DVD players, CD players, high-speed Internet, dual phone lines. **Dining:** 7 am-11 pm, cocktails, entertainment. **Pool(s):** heated indoor. **Leisure Activities:** saunas, whirlpool, steamrooms, exercise room, spa. **Guest Services:** gift shop, valet laundry, wireless Internet. **Business Services:** conference facilities, business center. **Cards:** AX, CB, DC, DS, JC, MC, VI. **Free Special Amenities:** newspaper and high-speed Internet.

SOME UNITS

[icons] / VCR /

MARRIOTT RESIDENCE INN-MONTREAL CENTRE-VILLE/DOWNTOWN *Book great rates at AAA.com* **Phone:** (514)982-6064 **37**

CAA SAVE

	5/1-10/31 [BP]	1P: $195-$475	2P: $195-$475	XP: $20	F17
	4/1-4/30 [BP]	1P: $165-$445	2P: $165-$445	XP: $20	F17
	1/1-3/31 [BP]	1P: $159-$435	2P: $159-$435	XP: $20	F17
	11/1-12/31 [BP]	1P: $155-$435	2P: $155-$435	XP: $20	F17

Small-scale Hotel Location: Between rue Sherbrooke and boul de Maisonneuve. 2045 rue Peel H3A 1T6. Fax: 514/844-8361.
Facility: Smoke free premises. 190 units. 171 one-bedroom standard units, some with efficiencies or kitchens. 19 one-bedroom suites with kitchens. 24 stories, interior corridors. **Parking:** on-site (fee). **Terms:** small pets only ($100 fee). **Amenities:** video library, video games (fee), voice mail, irons, hair dryers. *Some:* DVD players, CD players. **Pool(s):** heated indoor. **Leisure Activities:** exercise room. **Guest Services:** sundries, valet and coin laundry, wireless Internet. **Business Services:** meeting rooms, business center. **Cards:** AX, CB, DC, DS, JC, MC, VI. **Free Special Amenities:** full breakfast and high-speed Internet.

SOME UNITS

[icons] SD FEE / VCR /

MARRIOTT SPRINGHILL SUITES *Book great rates at AAA.com* **Phone:** (514)875-4333 **21**

CAA SAVE

	6/23-10/27 [BP]	1P: $185-$205	2P: $185-$205	XP: $15	F18
	5/1-6/22 [BP]	1P: $149-$167	2P: $149-$167	XP: $15	F18
	10/28-4/30 [BP]	1P: $135-$153	2P: $135-$153	XP: $15	F18

Location: Jct St Laurent Blvd and Notre-Dame, just se. 445 rue St-Jean-Baptiste H2Y 2Z7. Fax: 514/875-4331.
Small-scale Hotel Facility: Smoke free premises. 124 one-bedroom standard units. 6 stories, interior corridors. **Parking:** valet.
Terms: 5 night minimum stay - seasonal, package plans. **Amenities:** video games (fee), high-speed Internet, dual phone lines, voice mail, irons, hair dryers. *Some:* DVD players (fee). **Dining:** 11:30 am-11 pm; closed Sun & Mon 11/15-4/30, cocktails, nightclub. **Pool(s):** small heated indoor. **Leisure Activities:** whirlpool, exercise room, spa. **Guest Services:** sundries, valet and coin laundry. **Business Services:** meeting rooms, business center. **Cards:** AX, DC, DS, MC, VI. **Free Special Amenities:** full breakfast and newspaper.

SOME UNITS

[icons] / VCR / FEE

(See map and index starting on p. 414)

NEW RESIDENCE HALL/MCGILL UNIVERSITY
Phone: 514/398-3471 **12**
CAA SAVE
5/15-8/13 [CP] 1P: $89-$170 XP: $25 F
Large-scale Hotel
Location: Corner of rue Prince-Arthur. 3625 ave du Parc H2X 3P8. Fax: 514/398-4521. **Facility:** 421 units. 408 one-bedroom standard units. 13 one-bedroom suites with efficiencies (no utensils). 15 stories, interior corridors. *Bath:* combo or shower only. **Parking:** on-site (fee). **Terms:** open 5/15-8/13, cancellation fee imposed. **Amenities:** high-speed Internet, voice mail, irons, hair dryers. *Some:* safes. **Dining:** 7:30-10:30 am. **Leisure Activities:** *Fee:* game room. **Guest Services:** coin laundry. **Business Services:** conference facilities. **Cards:** AX, MC, VI. **Free Special Amenities:** continental breakfast and high-speed Internet.
(See color ad p 449)

SOME UNITS

NOVOTEL MONTREAL CENTRE *Book great rates at AAA.com* Phone: (514)861-6000 **49**
CAA SAVE
All Year 1P: $119-$289 2P: $119-$289 XP: $20 F16
Large-scale Hotel
Fax: 514/861-0992. **Facility:** 228 units. 226 one-bedroom standard units. 2 one-bedroom suites, some with whirlpools. 9 stories, interior corridors. **Parking:** on-site (fee). **Terms:** small pets only. **Amenities:** video games (fee), high-speed Internet, dual phone lines, voice mail, honor bars, irons, hair dryers. *Some:* safes. **Dining:** 6 am-midnight, cocktails. **Leisure Activities:** exercise room. **Guest Services:** valet laundry. **Business Services:** meeting rooms, business center. **Cards:** AX, DC, DS, MC, VI. **Free Special Amenities:** newspaper and early check-in/late check-out. *(See color ad below)*
Location: Between rue Ste-Catherine and boul Rene-Levesque. 1180 rue de la Montagne H3G 1Z1.

SOME UNITS

FEE

(See map and index starting on p. 414)

QUALITY HOTEL DOWNTOWN MONTREAL

CAA SAVE ▼▼ ▼▼
Small-scale Hotel

Book great rates at AAA.com

Phone: 514/849-1413 **14**

5/31-6/30	1P: $139-$330	2P: $149-$340	XP: $20	F16
5/1-5/30 & 7/1-10/15	1P: $119-$169	2P: $129-$179	XP: $10	F16
10/16-4/30	1P: $89-$139	2P: $99-$149	XP: $10	F16

Location: Between rue Sherbrooke and Milton. 3440 ave du Parc H2X 2H5. Fax: 514/849-6564. **Facility:** 140 one-bedroom standard units. 8 stories, interior corridors. **Parking:** on-site (fee). **Terms:** [AP], [BP], [CP] & [ECP] meal plans available, package plans, small pets only ($25 fee, in smoking units). **Amenities:** high-speed Internet (fee), irons, hair dryers. **Guest Services:** valet laundry. **Business Services:** PC (fee). **Cards:** AX, CB, DC, DS, JC, MC, VI. *(See color ad card insert)*

SOME UNITS

🅂🄳 [icons] FEE / ⊠ 🅱 🖨 / FEE FEE

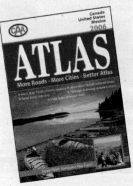

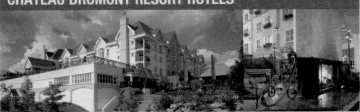

Pets are part of the family... take 'em along!

Traveling With Your Pet offers tips and guidelines for pet travel, with over 13,000 pet-friendly AAA/CAA- Rated® lodgings. Also, find places to take your pet with a wide variety of dog parks, campgrounds and attractions throughout North America.

Purchase AAA/CAA publications at participating AAA/CAA club offices, on aaa.com/barnesandnoble and in fine book stores.

(See map and index starting on p. 414)

RESIDENCE INN BY MARRIOTT MONTREAL WESTMOUNT   *Book great rates at AAA.com*

CAA SAVE

Phone: (514)935-9224   59

6/1-10/31 [BP]	1P: $119-$189	2P: $119-$189	XP: $20	F18
1/1-4/30 [BP]	1P: $113-$157	2P: $113-$157	XP: $20	F18
5/1-5/31 & 11/1-12/31 [BP]	1P: $109-$151	2P: $109-$151	XP: $20	F18

Location: Just e of rue Atwater. 2170 ave Lincoln H3H 2N5. **Fax:** 514/935-5049. **Facility:** Smoke free premises.
Small-scale Hotel 218 units. 67 one-bedroom standard units, some with efficiencies or kitchens. 135 one- and 16 two-bedroom suites ($109-$309), some with efficiencies or kitchens. 19 stories, interior corridors. **Parking:** on-site (fee) and street. **Terms:** pets ($105 fee). **Amenities:** high-speed Internet, voice mail, irons, hair dryers. **Pool(s):** heated indoor. **Leisure Activities:** saunas, exercise room. **Guest Services:** sundries, valet and coin laundry. **Business Services:** meeting rooms, PC. **Cards:** AX, DC, JC, MC, VI. **Free Special Amenities:** full breakfast and high-speed Internet.
(See color ad p 450)

THE RITZ-CARLTON, MONTREAL   *Book at AAA.com*

Phone: (514)842-4212   43

5/1-10/28	1P: $225-$625	2P: $225-$625	XP: $40	D14
4/12-4/30	1P: $225-$295	2P: $225-$295	XP: $40	D14
10/29-4/11	1P: $135-$199	2P: $135-$199	XP: $40	D14

Classic Historic **Location:** Corner de la Montagne. 1228 rue Sherbrooke ouest H3G 1H6. **Fax:** 514/842-3383. **Facility:** The historic
Large-scale Hotel hotel, renowned for its Old World ambience, offers luxurious and spacious guest rooms in close proximity to upscale shops. Smoke free premises. 229 units. 194 one-bedroom standard units. 28 one- and 7 two-bedroom suites. 9 stories, interior corridors. **Parking:** valet and street. **Terms:** [AP] & [CP] meal plans available, package plans, 3% service charge, pets ($150 fee). **Amenities:** dual phone lines, voice mail, safes, honor bars, irons, hair dryers. *Fee:* video games, high-speed Internet. *Some:* DVD players, CD players. **Dining:** Le Cafe de Paris, see separate listing. **Leisure Activities:** exercise room. *Fee:* massage. **Guest Services:** gift shop, valet laundry, beauty salon. **Business Services:** conference facilities, business center. **Cards:** AX, CB, MC, VI.

SOME UNITS

SOFITEL MONTREAL   *Book great rates at AAA.com*

CAA SAVE

Phone: (514)285-9000   38

6/1-10/31	1P: $285-$530	2P: $285-$530	XP: $30	F12
5/1-5/31	1P: $285-$420	2P: $285-$420	XP: $30	F12
11/1-4/30	1P: $195-$420	2P: $195-$420	XP: $30	F12

Location: Corner of rue Stanley. 1155 rue Sherbrooke ouest H3A 2N3. **Fax:** 514/289-1155. **Facility:** Featuring a
Small-scale Hotel luxurious lobby, this newer hotel offers accommodations with excellent duvets, modern amenities and elegant bathrooms. 258 units. 241 one-bedroom standard units. 17 one-bedroom suites ($325-$2000). 16 stories, interior corridors. *Bath:* combo or shower only. **Parking:** valet and street. **Amenities:** CD players, dual phone lines, voice mail, safes, honor bars, irons, hair dryers. *Fee:* video games, high-speed Internet. *Some:* fax. **Dining:** Renoir, see separate listing. **Leisure Activities:** sauna, library, exercise room. *Fee:* massage. **Guest Services:** valet laundry. **Business Services:** conference facilities, business center. **Cards:** AX, DC, DS, MC, VI.

SOME UNITS

W MONTREAL   *Book great rates at AAA.com*

CAA SAVE

Phone: (514)395-3100   35

All Year	1P: $179-$289	2P: $179-$289	XP: $30	F18

Location: Corner of rue St-Antoine. 901 Square-Victoria H2Z 1R1. **Fax:** 514/395-3150. **Facility:** Opened in 2004,
this upscale hotel faces Square Victoria and features youthful design, plus a few cool-looking bar areas and a chic restaurant. Smoke free premises. 152 one-bedroom standard units. 10 stories, interior corridors.
Large-scale Hotel *Bath:* combo or shower only. **Parking:** valet and street. **Terms:** cancellation fee imposed, package plans, small pets only ($100 fee, $25 extra charge). **Amenities:** DVD players, CD players, high-speed Internet (fee), dual phone lines, voice mail, safes, honor bars, irons, hair dryers. **Dining:** 7 am-10 pm, cocktails, also, Otto Ristorante-Bar, see separate listing. **Leisure Activities:** exercise room, spa. **Guest Services:** valet laundry, wireless Internet. **Business Services:** meeting rooms, business center. **Cards:** AX, DC, DS, MC, VI. **Free Special Amenities:** newspaper.

XIXE SIECLE HOTEL MONTREAL   *Book great rates at AAA.com*

CAA SAVE

Phone: (514)985-0019   30

All Year	1P: $159-$495	2P: $159-$495	XP: $25	F12

Location: Between rue St-Jean and rue St-Pierre. Located in Old Montreal. 262 rue St-Jacques ouest H2Y 1N1.
Fax: 514/985-0059. **Facility:** 59 units. 57 one-bedroom standard units, some with whirlpools. 2 one-bedroom suites with whirlpools. 4 stories, interior corridors. **Parking:** valet. **Terms:** 2 night minimum stay -
Small-scale Hotel weekends, cancellation fee imposed, [CP] meal plan available, pets ($50 fee). **Amenities:** dual phone lines, voice mail, irons, hair dryers. *Some:* DVD players, CD players. **Dining:** 7-11 am. **Leisure Activities:** *Fee:* massage. **Guest Services:** valet laundry, wireless Internet. **Business Services:** meeting rooms. **Cards:** AX, DC, MC, VI. **Free Special Amenities:** newspaper and preferred room (subject to availability with advance reservations).

SOME UNITS

The following lodgings were either not evaluated or did not meet AAA rating requirements but are listed for your information only.

AUBERGE DU VIEUX-PORT

[fyi]

Phone: 514/876-0081

Historic
Small-scale Hotel
Did not meet all AAA rating requirements for locking devices in some guest rooms at time of last evaluation. **Location:** Just e of rue St-Gabriel; in Old Port district. 97 rue de la Commune est H2Y 1J1. Facilities, services, and decor characterize a mid-range property.

DELTA CENTRE-VILLE

[fyi]

Phone: 514/879-1370

Large-scale Hotel
Did not meet all AAA rating requirements for locking devices in some guest rooms at time of last evaluation on 04/13/2004. **Location:** Corner of rue St-Antoine. 777 rue University H3C 3Z7. Facilities, services, and decor characterize a mid-range property.

(See map and index starting on p. 414)

HOSTELLERIE PIERRE DU CALVET A.D. 1725

Phone: 514/282-1725

[fyi]

Historic
Small-scale Hotel

Did not meet all AAA rating requirements for locking devices in some guest rooms at time of last evaluation on 11/21/2005. **Location:** Corner of rue St-Paul. 405 rue Bonsecours H2Y 3C3. Facilities, services, and decor characterize a mid-range property.

——— **WHERE TO DINE** ———

3 AMIGOS RESTO-BAR   **Lunch:** $5-$12   **Dinner:** $7-$20   **Phone:** 514/939-3329   (115)

Mexican

Location: Just e of St-Mathieu. 1657 Ste-Catherine ouest H3H 1L9. **Hours:** 11 am-midnight, Fri & Sat-1 am. Closed: 12/25. **Features:** The lively restaurant and pub specializes in affordably priced Mexican and Tex-Mex dishes, including burritos, tacos and fajitas in chicken, lamb, beef and vegetarian varieties. Daily specials also are prepared. Celebrity caricatures adorn a colorful wall mural. Casual dress; cocktails. **Parking:** street. **Cards:** AX, MC, VI.

AIX CUISINE DU TERROIR   **Lunch:** $11-$17   **Dinner:** $26-$34   **Phone:** 514/904-1201   (36)

French

Location: Corner of rue St-Jacques; in Hotel Place d'Armes. 711 Cote de la Place d'Armes H2Y 2X6. **Hours:** 6 am-2:30 & 5:30-10:30 pm, Sat & Sun 6 am-11:30 & 5:30-10:30 pm. **Reservations:** accepted. **Features:** In a chic boutique hotel in Old Montreal, the fashionable restaurant specializes in "cuisine du terroir": dishes prepared with such fresh regional produce as salmon, foie gras, game and Angus beef. High-quality Quebec cheeses and desserts flavored with local maple syrup and Valrhona chocolate round out the menu. Casual dress; cocktails. **Parking:** valet and street. **Cards:** AX, DC, JC, MC, VI.

ALPENHAUS RESTAURANT   **Lunch:** $6-$13   **Dinner:** $13-$24   **Phone:** 514/935-2285   (119)

Swiss

Location: Corner of Ste-Catherine. 1279 rue St-Marc H3H 2E8. **Hours:** 11:30 am-3 & 5:30-10 pm, Thurs & Fri 11:30 am-10:30 pm, Sat 4:30 pm-10:30 pm, Sun 5:30 pm-10 pm. Closed: 12/25; also for lunch major holidays. **Reservations:** suggested. **Features:** Swiss and European specialties include bourguignonne, Swiss cheese or Chinese fondue, sausage, Wiener schnitzel and veal dishes. The cozy mountain lodge decor, which incorporates a fireplace, adds to the ambience. A pianist performs most Friday to Sunday evenings. Casual dress; cocktails. **Parking:** on-site (fee) and street. **Cards:** AX, DC, MC, VI.

AU BISTRO GOURMET   **Lunch:** $10   **Dinner:** $17-$28   **Phone:** 514/846-1553   (112)

French

Location: Between boul de Maisonneuve and ave Lincoln. 2100 rue St-Mathieu H3H 2J4. **Hours:** 11:30 am-2:30 & 5:30-10 pm. Closed major holidays. **Reservations:** accepted. **Features:** In a restored graystone building, the cozy and casual restaurant serves fine French cuisine at affordable prices. Among specialties are preparations of lamb, fresh fish, veal liver, poultry and kidneys. For those with a sweet tooth, a table of desserts awaits. Casual dress; cocktails. **Parking:** street. **Cards:** MC, VI.

BAR-B BARN   **Lunch:** $9-$20   **Dinner:** $9-$20   **Phone:** 514/931-3811

Barbecue

Location: Between boul Rene-Levesque and rue Ste-Catherine. 1201 rue Guy H3H 2K5. **Hours:** 11:30 am-10 pm, Fri & Sat-11 pm. Closed: 12/25; also Mon. **Reservations:** accepted. **Features:** Rustic barn wood adorns the walls of the family restaurant. Specialties include slow-roasted chicken and pork ribs, as well as the popular ribs-and-chicken combination dish. Casual dress; cocktails. **Parking:** on-site. **Cards:** AX, DC, MC, VI.

BATON ROUGE   **Lunch:** $8-$29   **Dinner:** $9-$29   **Phone:** 514/931-9969

Canadian

Location: Just s of boul Rene-Levesque. 1050 rue de la Montagne H3G 1Y8. **Hours:** 11 am-11 pm, Fri & Sat-midnight. Closed: 1/1, 12/25. **Reservations:** accepted. **Features:** Burnished wood, leather seats, brick walls, brass accents and muted lighting give this lively restaurant and pub a clubby atmosphere. House specialties are premium-grade steaks and baby back ribs, but patrons also might opt for a burger, salad, sandwich or dish of pasta, chicken or grilled fresh fish. Flavors abound in meats cooked over the wood-burning grill. This is an ideal spot to meet before or after shopping, theater or a local sporting or concert event. Casual dress; cocktails. **Parking:** on-site. **Cards:** AX, DC, MC, VI.

THE BEAVER CLUB   *Menu on AAA.com*   **Lunch:** $16-$30   **Dinner:** $30-$48   **Phone:** 514/861-3511   (73)

French

Location: Between rue University and Mansfield; in Fairmont The Queen Elizabeth. 900 boul Rene-Levesque ouest H3B 4A5. **Hours:** noon-2 & 6-10 pm, Sat from 6 pm. Closed: Sun, Mon & for lunch 6/24-9/15. **Reservations:** suggested. **Features:** The city landmark boasts an international menu that dabbles in Canadian and French cuisine. Outstanding presentation marks such dishes as grilled caribou and scampi and shrimp tempura in a sauce of black beans and ginger. Service is professional. Dressy casual; cocktails. **Parking:** on-site (fee) and valet. **Cards:** AX, DC, DS, JC, MC, VI.

BICE RISTORANTE   **Dinner:** $24-$38   **Phone:** 514/937-6009   (103)

Italian

Location: Just e of rue Guy. 1504 rue Sherbrooke ouest H3G 1L3. **Hours:** 6 pm-11 pm. Closed: 12/25, 12/26. **Reservations:** suggested. **Features:** The fashionable Sherbrooke Street restaurant prepares excellent pasta dishes, chicken and fresh seafood, including delicious octopus. Youthful servers are polite and refined. Dressy casual; cocktails. **Parking:** valet. **Cards:** AX, DC, MC, VI.

(See map and index starting on p. 414)

BISHOKU JAPANESE RESTAURANT   **Lunch:** $9-$17   **Dinner:** $15-$30   **Phone:** 514/876-0056   107

Japanese

Location: Between Ste-Catherine and boul Rene-Levesque. 1184 rue Bishop H3G 2E3. **Hours:** 11:30 am-2:30 & 5:30-10 pm, Fri-11 pm, Sat 5:30 pm-11 pm. Closed major holidays; also Sun. **Reservations:** accepted. **Features:** Japanese cuisine can be savored at tables or at the sushi bar. Sushi specialties include sushi pizza, shrimp tempura, salmon with avocado and fried soft-shelled crab. Also offered are a dozen sashimi selections. Sushi-sashimi combination platters lay out a good variety. Casual dress; cocktails. **Parking:** street. **Cards:** AX, DC, JC, MC, VI.

BOCCA D'ORO   **Lunch:** $11-$18   **Dinner:** $16-$32   **Phone:** 514/933-8414   116

Italian

Location: Between Maisonneuve and rue Ste-Catherine. 1448 rue St-Mathieu H3H 2H9. **Hours:** noon-11 pm. Closed: 1/1, 12/25; also Sun. **Reservations:** suggested. **Features:** Family-owned and operated, the casually upscale restaurant focuses its menu on seafood, steak, veal, game and fowl. Lots of plants and a solarium roof add to the relaxed feel of the dining room. A nice selection of wine complements the meals. Dressy casual; cocktails. **Parking:** on-site and street. **Cards:** AX, DC, MC, VI.

BONAPARTE   **Lunch:** $15-$29   **Dinner:** $20-$33   **Phone:** 514/844-4368   45

French

Location: Just n of rue St-Paul; in Auberge Bonaparte. 447 rue St-Francois Xavier H2Y 2T1. **Hours:** noon-2:30 & 5:30-10:30 pm. **Reservations:** suggested. **Features:** The lively and sophisticated dining room presents a varied menu of innovative French-influenced dishes, including mushroom ravioli in butter cream sauce with sage, lobster stew flavored with vanilla, beef tartare, rack of lamb in a port wine sauce and wild boar marinated in red wine. The service is refined. Dressy casual; cocktails. **Parking:** street. **Cards:** AX, DC, MC, VI. **Historic**

BORIS BISTRO   **Lunch:** $12-$19   **Dinner:** $12-$19   **Phone:** 514/848-9575   67

French

Location: Just n of rue St-Paul. 465 rue McGill H2Y 2H1. **Hours:** 11:30 am-10 pm, Thurs & Fri-11 pm, Sat noon-11 pm, Sun noon-10 pm. Closed: 2 weeks for Christmas. **Reservations:** required. **Features:** This bustling bistro features live Brazilian music some nights. The interesting menu includes the house specialty: duck (duck sandwich, duck confit, duck risotto), as well as grilled trout, cold beet soup, pasta, beef or tuna tartare, steak and fries. The treed seasonal terrace is a popular spot in summer. Casual dress; cocktails. **Parking:** street. **Cards:** AX, MC, VI.

BRISKETS MONTREAL   **Lunch:** $7-$16   **Dinner:** $7-$16   **Phone:** 514/878-3641   51

Deli/Subs
Sandwiches

Location: Just s of boul Rene-Levesque. 1073 Beaver Hall Hill H2Z 1S5. **Hours:** 11 am-8 pm. Closed: Sat & Sun 11/1-4/30. **Reservations:** accepted. **Features:** This family-friendly downtown restaurant offers something for everyone, including Montreal-style smoked meat on rye, pasta, ostrich burgers, hamburgers, subs, chicken, beef liver, sausages, poutine, steaks, souvlaki, bagel and lox, club sandwiches, club rolls, soup and salad. Casual dress; cocktails. **Parking:** street. **Cards:** AX, DC, JC, MC, VI.

CAFE HOLT   **Lunch:** $15-$22   **Dinner:** $15-$22   **Phone:** 514/282-3750   80

Coffee/Espresso

Location: Corner of de la Montagne; in Holt Renfrew. 1300 rue Sherbrooke ouest H3G 1H9. **Hours:** 10 am-6 pm, Thurs & Fri-9 pm, Sat-5 pm, Sun noon-5 pm. Closed: 1/1, 12/25. **Reservations:** accepted. **Features:** This stylish cafe and sandwich shop is at street level in the Holt-Renfrew luxury department store. The specialty is "tartine-style" open-faced sandwiches prepared with gourmet ingredients, including pricey imported Poilane bread baked daily in Paris and flown in. Patrons also enjoy tasty salads, freshly squeezed juices, specialty coffees, martinis and a choice of delicious desserts, a few of which are prepared with the gourmet Poilane bread. Casual dress; cocktails. **Parking:** street. **Cards:** AX, DC, MC, VI.

CAFE REPUBLIQUE RESTAURANT BAR   **Lunch:** $9-$25   **Dinner:** $9-$25   **Phone:** 514/875-1200   81

French

Location: Between rue Ste-Catherine and boul Rene-Levesque. 1200 rue Peel H3B 2T6. **Hours:** 8 am-1:30 am, Sat & Sun from 9 am. Closed: 1/1. **Reservations:** suggested. **Features:** This trendy downtown bistro offers steaks, salad, pasta, fish and some seafood dishes. Casual dress; cocktails. **Parking:** street. **Cards:** AX, DC, MC, VI.

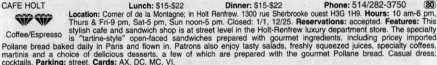

CALI RESTAURANT   **Lunch:** $5-$9   **Dinner:** $5-$9   **Phone:** 514/876-1064   23

Vietnamese

Location: Located in Chinatown; just n of rue St-Antoine. 1011 boul St-Laurent H2Z 1J4. **Hours:** 10 am-10 pm. Closed: 1/1, 12/25. **Reservations:** not accepted. **Features:** The simply decorated Vietnamese diner serves affordable Tonkinese soup and traditional dishes. Casual dress; beer & wine only. **Parking:** street.

CARLOS AND PEPES   **Lunch:** $6-$11   **Dinner:** $6-$20   **Phone:** 514/288-3090   77

Mexican

Location: Between boul de Maisonneuve and rue Ste-Catherine. 1420 rue Peel H3A 1S8. **Hours:** 11:30 am-1 am, Fri & Sat-3 am, Sun-12:30 am. Closed: 12/25. **Features:** The lively restaurant and bar lures guests with inexpensive food and a popular happy hour. Daily specials are affordable. Casual dress; cocktails. **Parking:** street. **Cards:** AX, DC, MC, VI.

CASA DE MATEO   **Lunch:** $12-$25   **Dinner:** $17-$25   **Phone:** 514/844-7448   46

Mexican

Location: Just s of rue Notre-Dame; in Old Montreal. 438 rue St-Francois Xavier H2Y 2T3. **Hours:** 11:30 am-10:30 pm. **Reservations:** suggested. **Features:** Ceramic suns and tiles, blown glassware and weekend live music lend to the restaurant's upbeat mood. Grilled fish and homemade enchiladas stand out on a menu of traditional Mexican fare. Casual dress; cocktails. **Parking:** street. **Cards:** AX, DC, MC, VI.

CAVALLI RISTORANTE-BAR   **Lunch:** $25-$33   **Dinner:** $25-$40   **Phone:** 514/843-5100   66

Italian

Location: Just n of boul de Maisonneuve. 2040 rue Peel H3A 2R4. **Hours:** noon-3 & 6-11 pm, Thurs-midnight, Sat 6 pm-11 pm. Closed: 1/1, 12/25; also Sun. **Reservations:** accepted. **Features:** The popular and stylish bar area—backlit with hot pink panels—sets the tone for this bustling and upscale Italian bistro. The youthful servers are well attired and proficient. The menu features fine Italian and Mediterranean cuisine with a strong focus on pasta and the freshest of fish and seafood. Dessert presentations are excellent. Casual dress; cocktails. **Parking:** street. **Cards:** AX, DC, MC, VI.

(See map and index starting on p. 414)

CHEZ CHINE
(AAA)

Chinese

Lunch: $15-$25 Dinner: $19-$45 Phone: 514/878-9888 [32]
Location: Corner of rue St-Urbain; in Holiday Inn Select Montreal-Centre Ville (Dwtn Conv Ctr). 99 ave Viger ouest W H2Z 1E9. **Hours:** 7-10:30 am, 11-2:30 & 6-9:30 pm. **Reservations:** accepted. **Features:** A full-sized Chinese pagoda is the centerpiece of the elegant hotel dining room, set around a soothing goldfish pond. Fine Chinese cuisine is at the heart of a menu that also includes buffet, luncheons and a limited selection of Continental dishes. Smartly attired servers are attentive. Casual dress; cocktails. **Parking:** on-site (fee). **Cards:** AX, CB, DC, DS, JC, MC, VI.

CHEZ CORA

Canadian

Lunch: $8-$11 Phone: 514/286-6171
Location: Between Ste-Catherine and de boul Maisonneuve. 1425 rue Stanley H3A 1P4. **Hours:** 6 am-3 pm, Sun from 7 am. **Closed:** 1/1, 12/25. **Reservations:** accepted. **Features:** Although this place specializes in breakfast, it offers a varied daytime menu that includes bacon, eggs, sausages, crepes, grilled cheese, sandwiches, freshly prepared quiches, salads, fruit platters and freshly squeezed juices. The family-friendly dining room is casual and modern. Casual dress. **Parking:** street. **Cards:** AX, DC, MC, VI.

CHEZ GAUTIER

French

Lunch: $8-$25 Dinner: $15-$35 Phone: 514/845-1245 [15]
Location: Corner of rue Milton. 3487 ave du Parc H2X 2H6. **Hours:** 11:30 am-11 pm, Sat from 9 am. **Closed:** Sun & 12/23-1/3. **Reservations:** suggested. **Features:** The lovely French bistro specializes in such classics as steak tartare, blood sausage ("boudin noir"), veal liver, "bavette" of beef, rib steak and fries, salads, burgers and fresh fish. After eating, guests can stroll into the Belgian-style bakery for take-out delicacies. Casual dress; cocktails. **Parking:** valet and street. **Cards:** AX, MC, VI.

CHEZ LA MERE MICHEL

Traditional French

Dinner: $20-$27 Phone: 514/934-0473 [111]
Location: Between boul Rene-Levesque and rue Ste-Catherine. 1209 rue Guy H3H 2K5. **Hours:** 5:30 pm-10:30 pm. **Closed:** 12/25; also Sun. **Reservations:** suggested. **Features:** The long-established restaurant delivers fine, classic French cuisine served by a knowledgeable, tuxedoed staff. Country accents lend to the formality of the dining rooms. Food preparations are complex, creative and splashed with interesting color. Dressy casual; cocktails. **Parking:** street. **Cards:** AX, DC, JC, MC, VI.

CHEZ L'EPICIER RESTAURANT BAR A VIN

French

Lunch: $14-$18 Dinner: $37-$40 Phone: 514/878-2232 [19]
Location: Just w of rue Bonsecours; facing Bonsecours Market in Old Montreal. 311 rue St-Paul est H2Y 1H3. **Hours:** 11:30 am-10 pm, Sat & Sun from 5:30 pm. **Closed:** major holidays. **Reservations:** accepted. **Features:** French and Asian influences give comfort foods a new twist at this casually elegant stone-walled Old Montreal eatery and wine bar. Menus are printed on paper bags, and water is served from milk bottles. The menu of fine cuisine may include selections such as Arctic char, milk-fed veal carpaccio, snail shepherd's pie and Parmesan oil ravioli. Specialty gourmet items, cheeses, sauces, oils and sorbets can be carried out. The 2,000-bottle cellar includes many private imports and specialty wines. Casual dress; cocktails. **Parking:** street. **Cards:** AX, DC, MC, VI.

CHEZ QUEUX
(AAA)

French

Lunch: $12-$19 Dinner: $24-$36 Phone: 514/866-5194 [28]
Location: Corner of St-Paul E and Place Jacques-Cartier. 158 rue St-Paul H2Y 1G6. **Hours:** 11:30 am-2:30 & 5-10 pm, Sat & Sun from 5 pm. **Closed:** Mon. **Reservations:** suggested. **Features:** In a historic 1862 stone building, the restaurant is quaint and sophisticated, with original stone walls, wood paneling and wood-beam ceilings. Flambees prepared tableside, rack of lamb, scampi, sweetbreads, fresh fish and seafood are representative of menu selections. Service is professional. Casual dress; cocktails. **Parking:** street. **Cards:** AX, DC, JC, MC, VI. **Historic**

COCO RICO

Portuguese

Lunch: $5-$8 Dinner: $5-$8 Phone: 514/849-5554 [3]
Location: Just n of rue Roy. 3907 boul St-Laurent H2W 1X9. **Hours:** 9 am-10 pm. **Closed:** 1/1, 12/25. **Reservations:** not accepted. **Features:** Halfway down the block, the undeniable aroma of rotisserie-roasted chicken provides a strong hint that this simple diner is nearby. Patrons may also enjoy ribs, sandwiches and fries. Casual dress. **Parking:** street.

CREPERIE CHEZ SUZETTE

French

Lunch: $11-$25 Dinner: $11-$25 Phone: 514/874-1984 [35]
Location: Just e of boul St-Laurent. 3 rue St-Paul est H2Y 1E9. **Hours:** 11:30 am-9 pm, Sat 10:30 am-10:30 pm, Sun 10:30 am-8 pm. **Reservations:** suggested. **Features:** This charming "creperie" overlooks a scenic Old Montreal street and serves a variety of 30 freshly prepared crepes, Chinese and cheese fondues, as well as sandwiches. For dessert, try a fruit crepe. The wine list is affordable as there is only a minimal mark-up above the restaurant's purchase price. Casual dress; cocktails. **Parking:** street. **Cards:** MC, VI.

DECCA 77 RESTAURANT

French

Lunch: $18-$35 Dinner: $24-$45 Phone: 514/934-1077 [97]
Location: Corner of boul Rene-Levesque. 1077 rue Drummond H3B 4X4. **Hours:** 11:30 am-2:30 & 5:30-10:30 pm, Sat from 5:30 pm. **Closed:** 1/1, 12/25, 12/26. **Reservations:** suggested. **Features:** A short walk from the Bell Centre arena, this stylish and upscale restaurant has a posh lounge area. The menu features market-fresh cuisine, including foie gras "torchon," grilled beef strip, roasted guinea hen, pasta, lobster, fresh fish and game specialties. The wine list is impressive. Casual dress; cocktails. **Parking:** valet and street. **Cards:** AX, DC, MC, VI.

DEER GARDEN JARDIN DU CERF

Chinese

Lunch: $5-$8 Dinner: $5-$8 Phone: 514/861-1056 [18]
Location: Just n of boul Rene-Levesque. 1162 boul St-Laurent H2X 2S5. **Hours:** 11 am-11 pm. **Closed:** Tues. **Reservations:** accepted. **Features:** Great food at low prices is what patrons of the simple Chinatown diner can expect. The menu lists Cantonese, Szechuan and Thai specialties. The wide variety of dishes includes noodles, rice, soups, seafood and poultry. Casual dress. **Parking:** street.

(See map and index starting on p. 414)

DUNNS FAMOUS DELICATESSEN
Lunch: $10-$21   **Dinner:** $10-$21   **Phone:** 514/395-1927   ⑦⓪

Deli/Subs Sandwiches

Location: Just s of rue Ste-Catherine. 1249 rue Metcalfe H3B 2V5. **Hours:** 24 hours. **Reservations:** accepted. **Features:** This traditional deli specializes in Montreal-style smoked meat on rye, grilled steaks, latkes, chopped liver and club rolls. For dessert, try the cheesecake. Casual dress; cocktails. **Parking:** street. **Cards:** AX, DC, MC, VI.

EGGSPECTATION
Lunch: $7-$15   **Phone:** 514/842-3447

Canadian

Location: Corner of rue de la Montagne. 1313 boul de Maisonneuve ouest H3G 2R9. **Hours:** 6 am-5 pm, Sun-4 pm. **Closed:** 1/1, 12/25. **Reservations:** accepted, weekends. **Features:** The menu lists dozens of all-day breakfast possibilities, including eggs in a bagel, Bretonne-style crepes, eggs Benedict, pancakes, French toast and waffles. Salads, burgers, sandwiches, pasta, chicken, fish and steak, as well as specialty coffees and a variety of freshly squeezed juices, round out the offerings. Casual dress; cocktails. **Parking:** street. **Cards:** AX, DC, MC, VI.

EL GITANO
Lunch: $10-$15   **Dinner:** $17-$30   **Phone:** 514/843-8212   ⑭

Spanish

Location: Between rue Prince-Arthur and Milton. 3507 ave du Parc H2X 2H8. **Hours:** noon-10 pm, Sat & Sun from 5 pm. **Closed:** 1/1, 12/24, 12/25. **Reservations:** accepted. **Features:** This informal Mediterranean restaurant specializes in Spanish and Portuguese food, including almost a dozen varieties of paella. Pasta, steak, seafood and fresh fish are also featured along with live Flamenco dancers on Saturday evenings beginning at 8:30 p.m. Casual dress; cocktails. **Parking:** street. **Cards:** AX, MC, VI.

EUROPEA RESTAURANT
Lunch: $24   **Dinner:** $24-$41   **Phone:** 514/398-9229   ⑨④

Mediterranean

Location: Between rue Ste-Catherine and boul Rene-Levesque. 1227 rue de la Montagne H3G 1Z2. **Hours:** noon-2 & 6-10:30 pm, Sat & Sun from 6 pm. **Closed:** 12/25. **Reservations:** accepted. **Features:** Located in a vintage downtown greystone building, this upscale restaurant boasts a stylish decor and seasonal terrace. The menu features beautifully garnished contemporary French dishes, including pan-seared foie gras, Arctic char, filet mignon, stuffed quail, lobster ravioli, Kamouraska-region Quebec lamb, Boileau-region deer and milk-fed veal. Multi-course tasting menus are available as well as a la carte selections. Casual dress; cocktails. **Parking:** street. **Cards:** AX, DC, MC, VI.

FERREIRA CAFE
Lunch: $24-$40   **Dinner:** $30-$40   **Phone:** 514/848-0988   ⑦⑥

Portuguese

Location: Between boul de Maisonneuve and rue Ste-Catherine. 1446 rue Peel H4K 1Y2. **Hours:** noon-3 & 6-11 pm, Thurs & Fri-11:30 pm, Sat 5:30 pm-midnight. **Closed:** 1/1, 7/1, 12/24, 12/25; also 12/31 & Sun. **Reservations:** required. **Features:** The upscale Portuguese bistro offers great food and refined service. Menu specialties include grilled sardines, filet mignon, oysters, fresh fish, calamari, poached salmon and rack of lamb. An excellent variety of ports is featured. Dressy casual. **Parking:** on-site and street. **Cards:** AX, DC, MC, VI.

FOURQUET FOURCHETTE DU PALAIS
Lunch: $10-$25   **Dinner:** $15-$25   **Phone:** 514/789-6370   ④④

Quebecois

Location: Corner of rue de Bleury. 265 rue St-Antoine ouest H2Z 1H5. **Hours:** 11:30 am-4 pm, Thurs & Fri-9 pm, Sat 5 pm-9 pm. **Closed** major holidays; also Sun. **Reservations:** accepted. **Features:** In a contemporary steel and glass convention center, the relaxed family restaurant is furnished in decor typical of early settler dwellings. Traditional New French seafood, game, meat and chicken delicacies make up the a la carte menu. Microbrewed beers are incorporated into some dishes. Casual dress; beer & wine only. **Parking:** on-site (fee). **Cards:** AX, DC, MC, VI.

GALIANO'S PASTA & BAR
Lunch: $9-$15   **Dinner:** $13-$32   **Phone:** 514/861-5039   ②⑨

Italian

Location: Just n of rue St-Paul est. 410 rue St-Vincent H2Y 3A5. **Hours:** noon-midnight, Fri & Sat-1 am; to 10 pm, Fri & Sat-11 pm 10/1-5/1. **Closed:** 12/25. **Reservations:** accepted. **Features:** Italian cuisine is served in the casual, stone-walled dining room in historic Old Montreal. Casual dress; cocktails. **Parking:** street. **Cards:** AX, DC, MC, VI.

GARCON!
Lunch: $18-$31   **Dinner:** $28-$34   **Phone:** 514/843-4000   ⑥②

French

Location: Between Peel and Stanley. 1112 rue Sherbrooke ouest H3A 1G6. **Hours:** 11:30 am-2 & 6-10 pm, Fri-10:30 pm, Sat 10 am-2 & 6-10:30 pm, Sun 10 am-2:30 & 6-10 pm; Saturday & Sunday brunch. **Reservations:** suggested. **Features:** Thickly padded leather chairs, plush banquettes, stylish lighting and an upscale bar area characterize the chic hotel restaurant. Innovative contemporary French cuisine makes use of many high-quality regional ingredients and some exotic items. Diners can try quail stuffed with veal, Quebec loin of lamb, pan-seared scallops, foie gras, Boileau deer, milk-fed tenderloin and halibut in truffle butter. Dressy casual; cocktails. **Parking:** street. **Cards:** AX, MC, VI.

GIBBY'S
Dinner: $27-$48   **Phone:** 514/282-1837   ⑥⓪

Steak & Seafood

Location: Just e of rue McGill; in Old Montreal. 298 Place d'Youville H2Y 2B6. **Hours:** 5 pm-11 pm, Sat 4:30 pm-11:30 pm. **Reservations:** suggested. **Features:** Home-smoked salmon and rack of lamb stand out on a menu of mostly tried-and-true steak, fresh fish and seafood preparations, which are served in ample portions. Desserts—such as tart Key lime pie, cheesecake and creme brulee—are delightful. The garden terrace offers seasonal seating. Casual dress; cocktails. **Parking:** valet and street. **Cards:** AX, CB, DC, DS, JC, MC, VI. **Historic**

GLOBE RESTAURANT
Dinner: $26-$49   **Phone:** 514/284-3823   ①⓪

International

Location: Just s of Prince-Arthur. 3455 boul St-Laurent H2X 2T6. **Hours:** 6 pm-11 pm, Thurs-Sat to midnight. **Closed:** 12/24, 12/25. **Reservations:** suggested. **Features:** On the trendy and bustling St-Laurent strip, the upbeat and stylish restaurant supplies its youthful clientele with a steady diet of fine international cuisine. The diverse menu includes pan-seared foie gras, pasta, risotto, breast of chicken, steak tartare, Angus beef and fresh fish. Casual dress; cocktails. **Parking:** valet and street. **Cards:** AX, DC, MC, VI.

(See map and index starting on p. 414)

GUIDO ANGELINA   Lunch: $9-$25   Dinner: $9-$25   Phone: 514/393-3808   47
Italian
Location: Between ave McGill-College and rue University. 690 rue Ste-Catherine ouest H3B 1B9. **Hours:** 11 am-10 pm, Thurs & Sat-11 pm. Closed: 12/25. **Reservations:** accepted. **Features:** Twenty choices of fresh pasta stand out among the restaurant's affordable choices, including seafood platters, steaks, pork, lamb chops, memorable strawberry cheesecake and 10 choices of thin-crust pizza. The lively, informal setting owes to the prime downtown location. Casual dress; cocktails. **Parking:** street. **Cards:** AX, MC, VI.

GUIDO ANGELINA   Lunch: $9-$25   Dinner: $9-$25   Phone: 514/228-5225   121
Italian
Location: Corner of rue Atwater. 2313 rue Ste-Catherine ouest H3H 1N2. **Hours:** 11 am-11 pm, Fri & Sat-midnight. Closed: 12/25, 12/26. **Reservations:** accepted. **Features:** Twenty choices of fresh pasta stand out on an affordable menu that also includes seafood platters, steaks, piglet, lamb chops and 10 choices of pizza. The open kitchen, a take-out counter and friendly, prompt servers. The restaurant is in the former Montreal Forum arena, where the Montreal Canadiens won numerous Stanley Cups. Casual dress; cocktails. **Parking:** on-site (fee). **Cards:** AX, DC, MC, VI.

GUY & DODO MORALI   Lunch: $16-$29   Dinner: $13-$49   Phone: 514/842-3636   71
French
Location: Between boul de Maisonneuve and rue Ste-Catherine. 1444 rue Metcalfe H3A 1T5. **Hours:** 11 am-10 pm, Sat 6 pm-11 pm. Closed: Sun. **Reservations:** suggested. **Features:** The elegant bistro is known for gracious service and upscale bistro cuisine. On the menu are duck confit, scampi, coquilles St. Jacques, lobster in bearnaise sauce and fresh fish, including Dover sole. Delectable desserts include creme brulee, tarte tatin and ile flottant (a "floating island" of meringue surrounded by caramel-custard sauce). Dressy casual; cocktails. **Parking:** on-site (fee). **Cards:** AX, DC, MC, VI.

HOLDER RESTAURANT-BAR   Lunch: $16-$27   Dinner: $16-$27   Phone: 514/849-0333   72
French
Location: Just n of rue St-Paul. 407 rue McGill H2Y 2G3. **Hours:** 11:30 am-11 pm, Sat from 5:30 pm, Sun 5:30 pm-10 pm. Closed: 1/1, 12/25. **Reservations:** accepted. **Features:** The spirited Old Montreal bistro has high ceilings, copper-toned walls, tall pillars and colorful light fixtures. Guests dine casually on such choices as tartares, oxtail shepherd's pie, veal, liver, osso buco, fish and chips, clams, mussels and pasta. Sugar pie is a good dessert option. Casual dress; cocktails. **Parking:** street. **Cards:** AX, DC, MC, VI.

HOUSE OF JAZZ/MAISON DE JAZZ   Lunch: $8-$16   Dinner: $13-$30   Phone: 514/842-8656   37
American
Location: Corner of President-Kennedy. 2060 rue Aylmer H3A 2E3. **Hours:** 11:30 am-1 am, Fri-2:30 am, Sat 6 pm-2:30 am, Sun 6 pm-midnight. Closed major holidays. **Reservations:** suggested. **Features:** Nightly live jazz has made this place a local landmark since 1980. Rib and chicken dishes are specialties on a menu that also lists potato skins, chicken wings and Caesar salad. Guests can choose from a variety of tasty desserts and temptingly aromatic amaretto coffee. Casual dress; cocktails. **Parking:** on-site (fee) and street. **Cards:** AX, DC, DS, MC, VI.

IL CAMPARI CENTRO   Lunch: $14-$22   Dinner: $18-$35   Phone: 514/868-1177   96
Italian
Location: Just n of boul Rene-Levesque. 1177 rue de la Montagne H3G 1Z2. **Hours:** 11:30 am-11 pm, Sat 5 pm-11:30 pm. Closed major holidays; also 12/22-1/6. **Reservations:** suggested. **Features:** Smartly attired servers deliver fine traditional dishes in the vintage downtown graystone. The varied menu lists fresh pasta, chicken parmigiana, tuna carpaccio, veal, fish and seafood, accompanied by rich sauces. Casual dress; cocktails. **Parking:** street. **Cards:** AX, CB, DC, DS, JC, MC, VI.

JARDIN DE JADE-POON KAI RESTAURANT   Lunch: $8-$9   Dinner: $12-$13   Phone: 514/866-3127   25
Chinese
Location: Just w of rue Clark. 67 rue de la Gauchetiere ouest H2Z 1C2. **Hours:** 11 am-11 pm, Fri & Sat-midnight. **Reservations:** accepted. **Features:** The lunch and dinner buffet special is one of the best deals in Chinatown. Multiple buffet items include selections of Szechuan, Cantonese and Canadian-Chinese dishes. Dim sum is served daily. Casual dress; cocktails. **Parking:** street. **Cards:** AX, DC, MC, VI.

KATSURA JAPANESE RESTAURANT   Lunch: $10-$20   Dinner: $16-$50   Phone: 514/849-1172   83
Japanese
Location: Between rue Sherbrooke and boul de Maisonneuve. 2170 rue de la Montagne H3G 1Z7. **Hours:** 11:30 am-2:30 & 5:30-9:30 pm, Fri-10:30 pm, Sat 5:30 pm-10:30 pm, Sun 5:30 pm-9 pm. Closed major holidays. **Reservations:** suggested. **Features:** The upscale restaurant houses a sushi bar, a comfortable dining area and private dining rooms. Staff members dressed in Asian attire serve a wide variety of high-quality sushi and sashimi. Casual dress; cocktails. **Parking:** street. **Cards:** AX, DC, MC, VI.

THE KEG STEAKHOUSE & BAR   Dinner: $15-$30   Phone: 514/871-9093
Canadian
Location: Just e of boul St-Laurent. 25 rue St-Paul est H2Y 1G2. **Hours:** 5 pm-10:30 pm, Fri-11:30 pm, Sat 4 pm-11:30 pm, Sun 4 pm-10:30 pm. Closed: 12/25. **Reservations:** suggested. **Features:** Known for its mesquite-grilled steaks and fun, laid-back atmosphere, the steak house is a longtime favourite with the local crowd. In addition to great beef, the traditional menu lists seafood, grilled chicken, hickory ribs and pasta dishes. Casual dress; cocktails. **Parking:** street. **Cards:** AX, DC, MC, VI.

LA BAGUETTE D'IVOIRE   Lunch: $8-$10   Dinner: $15-$23   Phone: 514/932-7099   109
Asian
Location: Between rue Ste-Catherine and boul Rene-Levesque. 1242 rue Mackay H3G 2H4. **Hours:** 11 am-2:30 & 5-10:30 pm, Fri-11:30 pm, Sat 5 pm-11:30 pm, Sun 5 pm-10:30 pm. Closed: for lunch on holidays. **Reservations:** accepted. **Features:** A graystone duplex in a popular downtown neighborhood houses the casual restaurant, which specializes in Vietnamese, Szechuan and Thai dishes. The menu includes Tonkinese soup, Cantonese-style spicy cuttlefish, basil beef, beef with black beans, sweet and sour pork, vegetables with greens, mango chicken, duck with ginger, General Tao chicken, Imperial chicken and lemongrass chicken. Casual dress; cocktails. **Parking:** street. **Cards:** AX, MC, VI.

See map and index starting on p. 414)

A CAGE AUX SPORTS   Lunch: $8-$23   Dinner: $8-$23   Phone: 514/288-1115
▼▼▼   Location: Just e of rue McGill; in Old Montreal. 395 rue Le Moyne H2Y 1Y5. Hours: 11 am-11 pm. Closed: 12/25;
Canadian   also Sun. Reservations: accepted. Features: This popular Quebec chain of sports bars presents a pub
food menu of ribs, chicken, burgers, salads, crispy fries, pasta and tasty desserts. Guests begin their meal
with a basket of freshly popped popcorn in a setting marked by sports memorabilia. Children are welcomed.
asual dress; cocktails. Parking: street. Cards: AX, DC, MC, VI.

A CAGE AUX SPORTS   Lunch: $8-$23   Dinner: $8-$23   Phone: 514/878-2243
▼▼▼   Location: Just w of rue Crescent. 1437 boul Rene-Levesque H3G 1T7. Hours: 11 am-11 pm, Thurs-Sat to
midnight; 11 am-10 pm, Thurs-Sat to 11 pm 6/23-9/12. Closed: 12/25. Reservations: suggested.
Canadian   Features: This popular Quebec chain of sports bars presents a menu of pub foods, including ribs, chicken,
burgers, salads, crispy fries, pasta and tasty desserts. Guests might begin the meal with a basket of freshly
opped popcorn as they check out the sports memorabilia. Children are welcomed. Casual dress; cocktails. Parking: on-site.
ards: AX, MC, VI.

ALOUX   Lunch: $12-$39   Dinner: $25-$39   Phone: 514/287-9127   [2]
▼▼▼   Location: Corner of rue Laval. 250 ave des Pins est H2W 1P3. Hours: 11:30 am-2:30 & 5:30-10:30 pm, Thurs &
French   Fri-11:30 pm, Sat 5:30 pm-11:30 pm, Sun 5:30 pm-10:30 pm. Closed: 1/1, 12/24, 12/25. Features: Attentive
service and innovative regional cuisine characterize the elegant yet informal dining room in a pleasant
residential neighborhood. Menu options include snow crab flan, mussels with sweetbreads in orange-Pernod
eduction, vanilla-flavored halibut, pan-seared yellowfin tuna, beef tournedos, Nunavut caribou, large shrimp in liqueur sauce
nd roasted veal chops. Dressy casual; cocktails. Parking: street. Cards: AX, DC, MC, VI.

A MAISON KAM FUNG   Lunch: $9-$13   Dinner: $9-$18   Phone: 514/878-2888   [26]
▼▼▼   Location: Just s of boul Rene-Levesque. 1111 rue St-Urbain H2Z 1X6. Hours: 7 am-3 & 5-10 pm.
Chinese   Reservations: suggested. Features: Diners can pick and choose from dishes that servers continually
wheel past tables during dim sum, the Chinese equivalent of brunch. The food is authentic and the selection
outstanding. House specialties include Peking duck, General Tao chicken and lobster served ginger- or
antonese-style. Casual dress; cocktails. Parking: on-site (fee). Cards: AX, DC, MC, VI.

A MAISON V.I.P.   Lunch: $8-$11   Dinner: $8-$11   Phone: 514/861-1943   [22]
▼▼▼   Location: Corner de la Gauchetiere; in Chinatown. 1077 rue Clark H2Z 1K3. Hours: 11:30 am-4 am.
Chinese   Reservations: accepted. Features: This casual, modestly decorated restaurant is a popular spot for
affordable Cantonese and Szechuan dishes. A 20-minute wait at the door is not uncommon on busy nights,
even when reservations are made. Casual dress; cocktails. Parking: street. Cards: MC, VI.

A MENARA   Dinner: $40   Phone: 514/861-1989   [24]
▼▼▼   Location: Just e of boul St-Laurent. 256 rue St-Paul est H2Y 1G9. Hours: 5 pm-midnight, Fri & Sat-2 am.
Moroccan   Reservations: required. Features: This restaurant transports guests downstairs from the cobbled streets of
Old Montreal into a Morrocan oasis of spirited music, lively dancers, rich red fabrics and canopied ceilings.
The menu features exotic Moroccan preparations of fish, lamb and quail, as well as Arabian spiced soup,
ouscous, and a "tajine" (stew) of chicken, meat or shrimps. For dessert, try a delicious pastry with mint tea. Casual dress;
ocktails; entertainment. Parking: street. Cards: AX, MC, VI.

'AMERE A BOIRE   Lunch: $6-$9   Dinner: $6-$9   Phone: 514/282-7448   [5]
▼▼▼   Location: Just s of rue Ontario. 2049 rue St-Denis H2X 3K4. Hours: noon-2:30 & 4:30-11 pm, Sun-9 pm.
International   Reservations: accepted. Features: The casual brew pub faces a lively street and features not only quality
home-brewed beers but also international pub food, including beer-flavored fish and chips; tapas; gravlax;
beef, vegetarian or lamb burgers; spanakopita; moussaka; quesadillas; bar snacks; and Quebec cheeses.
asual dress; beer & wine only. Parking: street. Cards: AX, MC, VI.

A QUEUE DE CHEVAL BAR & STEAKHOUSE   Lunch: $22-$37   Dinner: $30-$56   Phone: 514/390-0090   [98]
▼▼▼   Location: Corner of Drummond St. 1221 boul Rene-Levesque ouest H3G 1T1. Hours: 11:30 am-2:30 & 5:30-10:30
Steak & Seafood   pm, Thurs & Fri-11:30 pm, Sat 5:30 pm-11:30 pm, Sun 5:30 pm-10:30 pm. Closed: 1/1, 12/24, 12/25; also
12/31. Reservations: suggested. Features: An extensive variety of wines complements thoughtful
preparations of dry-aged prime beef, veal and such seafood as jumbo shrimp, red snapper and swordfish.
he downtown graystone faces Molson Centre. Service is gracious and refined. Casual dress; cocktails; entertainment.
arking: valet and street. Cards: AX, DC, MC, VI.

A SILA RESTAURANT   Lunch: $8-$24   Dinner: $12-$35   Phone: 514/844-5083   [6]
▼▼▼   Location: Between rue Sherbrooke and Ontario. 2040 rue St-Denis H2X 3K7. Hours: 11:30 am-2:30 & 5-11 pm,
Italian   Sat & Sun from 5 pm. Closed: 12/31-1/7. Reservations: suggested. Features: Milk-fed veal scaloppine and
poached salmon with chives and red peppercorns represent selections of Italian cuisine. The dining room is
cozy and intimate, while the seasonal sidewalk terrace, facing a lively street, is more informal. Homemade
esserts, including chestnut cake, are delicious. Limited client parking is available. Casual dress; cocktails. Parking: on-site and
treet. Cards: AX, DC, MC, VI.

E BOEUF ANGUS   Lunch: $10-$26   Dinner: $24-$60   Phone: 514/868-1666   [93]
▼▼▼   Location: Just s of rue Ste-Catherine. 1218 rue Drummond H3G 1V7. Hours: 11 am-midnight. Closed: for lunch
Steak & Seafood   during major holidays. Reservations: accepted. Features: Angus beef is the specialty at the cozy pub-style
steakhouse in the heart of downtown. Lamb, fresh seafood, pasta and grilled chicken dishes round out the
menu. Casual dress; cocktails. Parking: street. Cards: AX, DS, MC, VI.

E CAFE DE PARIS   Lunch: $16-$35   Dinner: $29-$48   Phone: 514/842-4212   [75]
CAA   Location: Corner de la Montagne; in The Ritz-Carlton, Montreal. 1228 rue Sherbrooke ouest H3G 1H6. Hours: 7 am-
11 & noon-4:30 pm, Fri & Sat also 6:30 pm-10 pm. Reservations: suggested. Features: Patrons can enjoy
▼▼▼   opulent decor and refined service in the dining room of Montreal's landmark luxury downtown hotel, The
French   Ritz-Carlton. In warmer weather, a table on the garden terrace overlooking the duck pond is a must. Dressy
casual; cocktails. Parking: valet and street. Cards: AX, DC, DS, MC, VI. Historic

(See map and index starting on p. 414)

LE CAFE DES BEAUX-ARTS Lunch: $16-$22 Dinner: $16-$22 Phone: 514/843-3233
▼▼▼ ▼▼▼
French
Location: Between rue Bishop and Crescent; in the Montreal Museum of Fine Arts. 1384 rue Sherbrooke ouest H3 1J5. **Hours:** 11 am-2:30 pm, Wed 11 am-2 & 6-9 pm. Closed: Mon. **Reservations:** accepted. **Features:** Th dual-purpose eatery encompasses an upscale bistro-style dining room and a self-serve cafeteria. Th cafeteria offers lighter fare, while the dining room menu centers on such innovative French-inspired mea as duck confit, steak tartare, grilled salmon, filet mignon, guinea-fowl salad and seared scallops. Soup lovers may want to tr French onion soup encased in crispy melted cheese. Casual dress; cocktails. **Parking:** street. **Cards:** AX, DC, MC, VI.

LE CASTILLON *Menu on AAA.com* Lunch: $8-$25 Dinner: $8-$35 Phone: 514/878-2992
(AAA)
▼▼▼
Continental
Location: Corner of Mansfield and de la Gauchetiere; in Hilton Montreal Bonaventure. 900 rue de la Gauchetiere H5 1E4. **Hours:** 6 am-2:30 & 6-11 pm. **Reservations:** suggested. **Features:** Rack of lamb with a touch of Dijo mustard is representative of fine French cuisine on the sophisticated restaurant's menu. A lighter bist menu and popular lunch buffet are other options. Career servers are smartly attired and helpful. A waterfa and garden lend to the seasonal terrace's appeal. Casual dress; cocktails. **Parking:** on-site (fee) and vale **Cards:** AX, CB, DC, DS, JC, MC, VI.

LE CHRYSANTHEME Lunch: $12-$16 Dinner: $15-$20 Phone: 514/397-1408
▼▼▼ ▼▼▼
Chinese
Location: Between rue Ste-Catherine and boul Rene-Levesque. 1208 rue Crescent H3G 2A9. **Hours:** 11:30 am-2:3 & 5:30-10 pm, Sat-11 pm, Sun 5:30 pm-10 pm. Closed: 1/1, 12/24, 12/25; also for lunch Mon & all day Mc 6/1-9/30; days may vary 7/1-7/31 & 12/1-12/31. **Reservations:** suggested. **Features:** Specializing Szechuan and Peking cuisine, the restaurant delivers such flavorful dishes as sauteed shrimp wi snowpeas and basil, pepper chicken with crispy spinach, orange beef and peanut butter dumplings. Dishes are seasoned to tr diner's taste. Casual dress; cocktails. **Parking:** street. **Cards:** AX, DC, MC, VI.

LE CLUB CHASSE ET PECHE Lunch: $18-$29 Dinner: $27-$32 Phone: 514/861-1112
▼▼▼
French
Location: Just n of rue St-Paul. 423 rue St-Claude H2Y 3B6. **Hours:** noon-2 & 6-10:30 pm, Sat from 6 pr Closed: 1/1, 12/25; also Sun & Mon. **Reservations:** accepted. **Features:** The restaurant's name translate to "Hunting and Fishing Club," and the decor evokes an elegant country hunting lodge, with rough woo beams and stone semi-basement walls. Table settings are refined. The sophisticated menu brings togethe creatively presented surf and turf items, such as lobster, pork, veal, duck, fresh fish, foie gras and scallops. Casual dres cocktails. **Parking:** street. **Cards:** AX, DC, MC, VI.

LE COMMENSAL Lunch: $9-$16 Dinner: $9-$16 Phone: 514/845-262
▼▼ ▼▼
Vegetarian
Location: Just s of rue Ontario. 1720 rue St-Denis H2X 3K8. **Hours:** 11 am-10:30 pm, Thurs-Sat to 11 pr Closed: 1/1, 12/25. **Reservations:** accepted. **Features:** An upscale self-service buffet features an extensiv selection of creative hot and cold items, such as leek pot pie, sweet potato kasha and lasagna, plus variety of desserts, everything of which is exclusively vegetarian. The pleasant, contemporary surrounding change often as new paintings are displayed. Casual dress; beer & wine only. **Parking:** street. **Cards:** AX, MC, VI.

LE COMMENSAL Lunch: $9-$16 Dinner: $9-$16 Phone: 514/871-148
▼▼ ▼▼
Vegetarian
Location: Corner of rue Ste-Catherine. 1204 ave McGill College H3B 4J8. **Hours:** 11:30 am-10 pm. Closed: 1/ 12/25. **Reservations:** accepted. **Features:** An upscale self-service buffet features an extensive selection creative hot and cold items, such as leek pot pie, sweet potato kasha and lasagna, plus a variety desserts, everything of which is exclusively vegetarian. The pleasant, contemporary surroundings chang often as new paintings are displayed. Casual dress; beer & wine only. **Parking:** street. **Cards:** AX, MC, VI.

LE LATINI Lunch: $14-$37 Dinner: $24-$40 Phone: 514/861-3166
▼▼▼ ▼▼▼
Italian
Location: Corner of boul Rene-Levesque ouest. 1130 rue Jeanne Mance H2Z 1L7. **Hours:** 11:30 am-3 & 5:30-11: pm, Sat 5 pm-11 pm, Sun 4 pm-11 pm. Closed: 12/24-1/6. **Reservations:** suggested. **Features:** Fireplace a glassed atrium and a garden add to the informal elegance of the contemporary restaurant. The changi menu centers on seafood. An extensive selection of wine is displayed. Terrace seating is hard to come by season. Casual dress; cocktails. **Parking:** valet and street. **Cards:** AX, DC, MC, VI.

LE MILSA ROTISSERIE BRESILIENNE Dinner: $17-$26 Phone: 514/985-0777
▼▼▼ ▼▼▼
Brazilian
Location: Between boul de Maisonneuve and rue Ste-Catherine. 1445A rue Bishop H3G 2E4. **Hours:** 5:30 pm-clos Closed: 1/1, 12/24, 12/25; also 12/31. **Reservations:** accepted. **Features:** Near Concordia University, th lively downtown restaurant is memorable for its nightly Brazilian dancers and its all-you-can-eat grilled me special. Meats—which include filet mignon, rib steak, Brazilian-cut strip loin, turkey, chicken, bacon, lan and pork—are brought to the table on a spit and sliced onto diners' plates. Other main courses include trout and salmon. F dessert, try grilled pineapple. Casual dress; cocktails. **Parking:** street. **Cards:** AX, DC, MC, VI.

L'ENTRECOTE SAINT-JEAN Lunch: $17-$21 Dinner: $17-$21 Phone: 514/281-6492
▼▼ ▼▼
French
Location: Just n of boul de Maisonneuve ouest. 2022 rue Peel H3A 2W5. **Hours:** 11:30 am-11 pm, Sat & Sun fro 5 pm. Closed: 12/24-1/6. **Features:** The casual, Paris-influenced bistro specializes in a table d'hote menu rib steak served with flavorful Dijon mustard sauce, matchstick fries, soup, a walnut-garnished salad a delicious chocolate-drizzled profiteroles for dessert. Casual dress; cocktails. **Parking:** street. **Cards:** A DC, MC, VI.

LE PARIS RESTAURANT FRANCAIS Lunch: $12-$23 Dinner: $18-$31 Phone: 514/937-4898
▼▼ ▼▼
French
Location: Just w of rue St-Mathieu. 1812 rue Ste-Catherine ouest H3H 1M1. **Hours:** noon-3 & 5:30-10:30 pm, Fri Sat-11 pm, Sun 5:30 pm-10:30 pm. Closed: 1/1, 12/24, 12/25. **Reservations:** accepted. **Features:** operation downtown since 1956, the small, informal French bistro serves many old classics, includi boudin noir (black pudding), veal kidneys, steak and fries, cheese omelets, perch filets, poule au pot, ve brains, filet of pork, sweetbreads and Chilean sea bass. For dessert, try the meringue floating island, creme caramel or one the selection of ice creams. Casual dress; cocktails. **Parking:** street. **Cards:** AX, DC, MC, VI.

(See map and index starting on p. 414)

E PIMENT ROUGE   Lunch: $20-$24   Dinner: $20-$38   Phone: 514/866-7816   86
▼▼▼▼   **Location:** Between rue Ste-Catherine and boul Rene-Levesque. 1170 rue Peel H3B 4P2. **Hours:** 11:45 am-11 pm,
Fri-11:30 pm, Sat noon-11:30 pm, Sun noon-11 pm. Closed: for lunch on major holidays.
Chinese   **Reservations:** suggested. **Features:** The focus of the refined restaurant's menu is on fine Szechuan
cuisine. Carefully prepared dishes include tasty General Tao's chicken, crispy duck, orange beef, Szechuan
shrimp and beef with mango strips in Kahlua sauce. The comfortable dining room is appointed with attractive furnishings. The
wine cellar brims with appropriate vintages. Dressy casual; cocktails. **Parking:** no self-parking. **Cards:** AX, CB, DC, DS, JC,
MC, VI.

E RESTAURANT CLUB LOUNGE 737   Lunch: $13-$46   Dinner: $27-$46   Phone: 514/397-0737   57
▼▼▼▼   **Location:** Corner of boul de Maisonneuve and rue University. 1 Place Ville-Marie, Suite 4340 H3B 5E4. **Hours:** 11:30
am-2:30 & 5:30-11 pm, Sat from 5:30 pm. Closed major holidays; also Sun & Mon. This elegant
French   dining room and lounge sits atop Place Ville Marie, a modern 40-storey skyscraper offering impressive
downtown views, especially at night. One floor below is a popular nightclub. The menu features impressive
appetizers, wild game, meats, fresh fish and seafood. Casual dress; cocktails. **Parking:** on-site. **Cards:** AX, DC, MC, VI.

E RESTAURANT LA BOUCHERIE   Lunch: $14-$35   Dinner: $18-$45   Phone: 514/866-1515   16
▼▼▼▼   **Location:** Between ave Bonsecours and rue St-Claude. 343 rue St-Paul est H2Y 1H3. **Hours:** 11:30 am-2 & 5:30-
10:30 pm. Closed major holidays; also Sun & for dinner Mon. **Reservations:** accepted. **Features:** This
French   casual Old Montreal bistro features gracious service and a tasty French-style menu that includes escargots,
tartares, fresh fish, rack of lamb, filet mignon, frogs' legs, "tourtiere" meat pie, surf 'n' turf and the popular
steak with fries. Casual dress; cocktails. **Parking:** street. **Cards:** AX, DC, JC, MC, VI.

ES 3 BRASSEURS   Lunch: $9-$21   Dinner: $9-$21   Phone: 514/788-6333   54
▼▼▼   ▼▼▼   **Location:** Just e of McGill College. 732 Rue Ste-Catherine ouest H3B 1B9. **Hours:** 11 am-close.
Reservations: accepted. **Features:** The lively brew pub specializes in home-brewed beers, beer cocktails
Canadian   and a pizza-like dish called flammekueche ("flamm," for short). Hailing from Alsace, France, this dish
features a thin baked crust topped with gourmet ingredients including Quebec cheeses, bacon, onions, sour
cream, feta cheese, smoked meat and pesto. The menu also lists salads, sandwich wraps, French onion soup, croque
monsieur, baby back ribs and steak. Patrons can view brewery equipment through a glass wall. Casual dress; cocktails.
Parking: street. **Cards:** AX, DC, MC, VI.

ES 3 BRASSEURS   Lunch: $9-$21   Dinner: $9-$21   Phone: 514/788-6100   30
▼▼▼   ▼▼▼   **Location:** Just e of boul St-Laurent; in Old Montreal. 105 rue St-Paul E H2Y 1G7. **Hours:** 11 am-close. Closed: for
lunch 12/25. **Reservations:** accepted. **Features:** The lively brew pub specializes in home-brewed beers,
Canadian   beer cocktails and a pizza-like dish called "flammekueche" ("flamm," for short). Hailing from Alsace, France,
this dish features a thin baked crust topped with gourmet ingredients including Quebec cheeses, bacon,
onions, sour cream, feta cheese, smoked meat and pesto. The menu also lists salads, sandwich wraps, French onion soup,
croque monsieur, baby back ribs and steak. Patrons can view brewery equipment through a glass wall. Casual dress; cocktails.
Parking: street. **Cards:** AX, MC, VI.

ES PYRENEES RESTAURANT   Lunch: $8-$13   Dinner: $18-$30   Phone: 514/842-5566   64
▼▼▼▼   **Location:** Just e of rue St-Pierre. 320 rue St-Paul ouest H2Y 2A3. **Hours:** 11:30 am-3:30 & 5-10:30 pm, Sat &
Sun from 5 pm. **Reservations:** accepted. **Features:** Bullfight prints and a traditional tapas bar stand out in
Basque   the decor of this casually elegant Old Montreal restaurant. Representative of Catalonian dishes are
piccoulet Catalonian meatballs, Basque-style squid, Toulouse-style cassoulet, assorted tapas, breast of
duck, seafood marmite, paella and wild boar stew. Casual dress; cocktails. **Parking:** street. **Cards:** AX, DC, MC, VI.

E STEAK FRITES ST-PAUL   Lunch: $13-$20   Dinner: $22-$30   Phone: 514/842-0972   38
▼▼▼   ▼▼▼   **Location:** Corner of boul Laurent. 12 rue St-Paul ouest H2Y 2Y3. **Hours:** 11 am-10 pm, Sat 4 pm-11 pm, Sun 4
pm-10 pm. Closed: 12/25. **Reservations:** suggested. **Features:** The lively and informal bistro specializes in
Steak House   steak with thin matchstick fries, but also prepares rack of lamb, grilled shrimp, shrimp cocktail, filet mignon,
rib steaks, calamari, escargots, smoked salmon and onion soup. Rich chocolate sauce tops the classic
profiterole pastry. Casual dress; cocktails. **Parking:** street. **Cards:** AX, DC, MC, VI.

E TAJ RESTAURANT   Lunch: $9-$18   Dinner: $9-$18   Phone: 514/845-9015   65
▼▼▼▼   **Location:** Between rue Sherbrooke and boul de Maisonneuve. 2077 rue Stanley H3A 1R7. **Hours:** 11:30 am-2:30 &
5-10:30 pm, Fri-11 pm, Sat 5 pm-11 pm, Sun noon-2:30 & 5-10:30 pm. Closed: 1/1, 12/25; also for lunch
Indian   1/1. **Reservations:** suggested. **Features:** The tastefully decorated restaurant is a popular place for East
Indian cuisine, including many vegetarian selections. Tasty veggie samosa is served with mint yogurt and
spiced carrots. The prix fixe dinner menu is a favorite of many regulars. Casual dress; cocktails. **Parking:** on-site (fee) and
street. **Cards:** AX, DC, MC, VI.

E TOUR DE VILLE   Dinner: $45   Phone: 514/879-4777   79
▼▼▼▼   **Location:** Corner of rue St-Antoine; in Delta Centre-Ville. 777 rue University H3C 3Z7. **Hours:** 5 pm-11 pm, Sun 9
am-2 pm. Closed: Mon-Thurs. **Reservations:** suggested. **Features:** Guests can enjoy breathtaking views of
French   Montreal's major landmarks from every table in the revolving rooftop restaurant. The gourmet buffet delivers
a tempting array of cold and hot choices, such as smoked salmon, duck and veal. Service is attentive and
professional. Dressy casual; cocktails. **Parking:** on-site (fee). **Cards:** AX, DC, DS, JC, MC, VI.

(See map and index starting on p. 414)

L'EXPRESS
Lunch: $13-$21   Dinner: $13-$21   Phone: 514/845-5333
French
Location: Between Duluth and Roy. 3927 rue St-Denis H2W 2M4. **Hours:** 8 am-3 am, Sat 10 am-2 am, Sun am-1 am. **Closed:** 12/25. **Reservations:** required. **Features:** The lively bistro has been a Montreal favourite since 1980. Steak tartare and fresh seafood are specialties on a menu that also includes poultry, mea salads, meat pies and caviar. Diners can select from an a la carte menu for lunch and dinner. Reservation are a must. Casual dress; cocktails. **Parking:** street. **Cards:** AX, DC, MC, VI.

L'ORCHIDEE CHINE RESTAURANT CHINOIS
Lunch: $13-$19   Dinner: $13-$30   Phone: 514/287-1878
Chinese
Location: Corner of boul de Maisonneuve ouest. 2017 rue Peel H3A 1T6. **Hours:** noon-2 & 5:30-10 pm, Sat 5:3 pm-10:30 pm. **Closed:** 1/1, 12/24, 12/25; also Sun. **Reservations:** accepted. **Features:** In the downtow business core, the upscale, comfortable restaurant specializes in fine Chinese cuisine. Dressy casua **Parking:** valet and street. **Cards:** AX, CB, DC, DS, JC, MC, VI.

LO STIVALE D'ORO
Lunch: $14-$17   Dinner: $17-$41   Phone: 514/844-8714
Italian
Location: Between rue Sherbrooke and boul de Maisonneuve. 2150 rue de la Montagne H3G 1Z7. **Hours:** 11:30 an 2:30 & 5-11 pm, Sat & Sun from 4:30 pm. Closed major holidays; also 1/2 & for lunch holiday **Reservations:** accepted. **Features:** The monthly changing menu lists pasta, veal and seafood specialtie Rustic touches—such as a cozy fireplace and lots of brick and stone—decorate the century-old hous Tantalizing desserts include tiramisu, cakes and creme caramel. Casual dress; cocktails. **Parking:** street. **Cards:** AX, DC MC, VI.

L'USINE DE SPAGHETTI DU VIEUX-MONTREAL
Lunch: $9-$19   Dinner: $9-$19   Phone: 514/866-0963
Italian
Location: Just e of Place Jacques-Cartier; in Old Montreal. 273 rue St-Paul est H2Y 1H1. **Hours:** 11 am-10 pm; am-3 pm, Fri-Sun to 10 pm 11/15-3/15. Closed: for dinner 12/24. **Reservations:** accepted. **Features:** In 19th-century stone-walled building that once housed the Rasco Hotel, the family restaurant prepares a grea variety of inexpensive pasta dishes, including several spaghetti variations, fettuccine, cannelloni an lasagna. Also on the menu are broiled shrimp, sauteed mushrooms, grilled Italian sausage, crab cakes and daily special Legend has it that Charles Dickens, while visiting Montreal in 1842, sat in a back room and wrote the liner notes to "A Tale Two Cities". Casual dress; cocktails. **Parking:** street. **Cards:** AX, MC, VI.

MAESTRO S.V.P.   *Menu on AAA.com*   Lunch: $8-$16   Dinner: $15-$37   Phone: 514/842-6447
Seafood
Location: Just n of rue Prince-Arthur. 3615 boul St-Laurent H2X 1V5. **Hours:** 11 am-11 pm, Sat & Sun from 4 pm Closed: 1/1, 12/25. **Reservations:** suggested. **Features:** Musical instruments decorate the walls of th stylish, elegant dining room, in which the upbeat sounds of jazz enhance the cozy feel. The restaurant known locally for its year-round oyster bar. Servers are friendly and technically proficient. Valet parking available Thursday through Saturday evenings and live music most Thursdays and Sundays. Casual dres cocktails. **Parking:** street. **Cards:** AX, DC, MC, VI.

MAISON DE CARI
Lunch: $9-$11   Dinner: $12-$18   Phone: 514/845-0326
Indian
Location: Between rue Ste-Catherine and boul de Maisonneuve. 1433 Bishop St H3G 2E4. **Hours:** noon-2:30 & 11 pm, Sun from 4 pm. Closed: 1/1, 12/25. **Reservations:** accepted. **Features:** The quaint curry hous serves delicious Northern Indian cuisine with a few Southern dishes. Tandoori preparations and a full rang of curry specialties are piquant and tasty. Draft beer includes British, Scottish and Irish selections. Casu dress; cocktails. **Parking:** street. **Cards:** AX, DC, MC, VI.

MED GRILL
Dinner: $24-$40   Phone: 514/844-0027
French
Location: At Milton. 3500 boul St-Laurent H2X 2V1. **Hours:** 6 pm-11:30 pm. Closed: 1/1, 12/25; also Sun winter. **Reservations:** suggested. **Features:** Youthful servers deliver creatively prepared dishes of fil mignon, rack of lamb, poultry, foie gras and fresh fish. Dessert favorites include creme brulee, sorbets an French pastries. The stylish environment bustles with energy in a neighborhood known for its lively nightlif Casual dress; cocktails. **Parking:** valet and street. **Cards:** AX, DC, MC, VI.

MESA 14
Lunch: $7-$9   Dinner: $9-$18   Phone: 514/284-0344
Mexican
Location: Between rue Sherbrooke and boul de Maisonneuve. 1425 rue Bishop H3G 2E4. **Hours:** 11:30 am-10 p Tues-Thurs to 11 pm, Fri & Sat-midnight, Sun 3 pm-10 pm. Closed: 12/24, 12/25. **Reservations:** accepte **Features:** In the heart of Montreal's nightclub area, the casual eatery prepares affordable Mexican dishe including burritos, tacos and sizzling fajita platters. Casual dress; cocktails. **Parking:** street. **Cards:** AX, D JC, MC, VI.

MIKES RESTAURANT
Lunch: $8-$12   Dinner: $14-$24   Phone: 514/393-995
Canadian
Location: Just s of rue Notre-Dame; in Old Montreal. 425 Place Jacques-Cartier H2Y 3B3. **Hours:** 7 am-9 pm, Fri Sat-1 am. **Reservations:** accepted. **Features:** This popular family-friendly restaurant specializes in pizz and hot submarine sandwiches, along with fries, burgers, soup, salads, pasta, grilled meats and seafoo An excellent variety of colorful desserts rounds out the offerings. Casual dress; cocktails. **Parking:** stree **Cards:** AX, CB, DC, DS, JC, MC, VI.

MIKES RESTAURANT
Lunch: $8-$14   Dinner: $8-$14   Phone: 514/395-222
Canadian
Location: Just e of rue Crescent. 1348 rue Ste-Catherine ouest H3G 1P5. **Hours:** 7 am-midnight, Thurs-1 am, F & Sat-3 am. **Reservations:** accepted. **Features:** This popular family-friendly chain specializes in pizza an hot submarine sandwiches, along with fries, burgers, poutine, soup, salads, sandwiches and pasta. Take-o service is available. Casual dress; cocktails. **Parking:** street. **Cards:** AX, CB, DC, DS, JC, MC, VI.

MISTER STEER
Lunch: $9-$20   Dinner: $9-$20   Phone: 514/866-3233
American
Location: Between Drummond and Stanley sts. 1198 Ste-Catherine ouest H3B 1K1. **Hours:** 8 am-10 pm, Thurs- pm, Fri & Sat-midnight. Closed: 12/25. **Reservations:** suggested. **Features:** In business since 1958, th family restaurant ages its steaks on the premises and prepares fresh steer burgers daily. Suzie Q curly frie and chargrilled chicken also please hungry patrons. For dessert, it's hard to beat the simple sundae Casual dress; cocktails. **Parking:** street. **Cards:** MC, VI.

(See map and index starting on p. 414)

NA GO YA RESTAURANT   **Lunch:** $9-$11   **Dinner:** $15-$25   **Phone:** 514/845-5864   **41**
▼▼▼ ▼▼▼
Asian   **Location:** Corner of rue St-Francois-Xavier. 140 rue Notre-Dame ouest H2Y 1T1. **Hours:** 11:30 am-3 & 5-9 pm, Thurs & Fri-10 pm, Sat 5 pm-10 pm. Closed: 12/25; also Sun. **Reservations:** accepted. **Features:** An ornate graystone facade fronts the casually elegant Old Montreal dining room and sushi bar. The menu features sushi, sashimi, Korean-style barbecue ribs and tableside grills. Sushi is freshly prepared, and servers are friendly and efficient. Casual dress; cocktails. **Parking:** street. **Cards:** AX, DC, MC, VI.

NEWTOWN RESTAURANT   **Dinner:** $30-$42   **Phone:** 514/284-6555   **91**
(CAA)
▼▼▼ ▼▼▼
Mediterranean   **Location:** Corner of boul de Maisonneuve. 1476 rue Crescent H3G 2B6. **Hours:** 5:30 pm-11 pm. **Reservations:** suggested. **Features:** The trendy, upscale dining room—downstairs from a dance club and upstairs from a popular lounge—has a lively, youthful ambience. Mediterranean dishes reflect superb presentations and feature excellent quality fresh fish, meats and seafood. The wine list is comprehensive. The restaurant is co-owned by Quebec race-car driver Jacques Villeneuve. Dressy casual; cocktails. **Parking:** street. **Cards:** AX, DC, DS, MC, VI.
⦙

OTTO RISTORANTE-BAR   **Lunch:** $20-$30   **Dinner:** $25-$42   **Phone:** 514/395-3183   **55**
▼▼▼ ▼▼▼
Mediterranean   **Location:** Corner of rue St-Antoine; in W Montreal. 901 Square Victoria H2Z 1R1. **Hours:** 7 am-11 pm. **Reservations:** suggested. **Features:** Trendy decor and glamorous service is outshined by a menu of fine Mediterranean cuisine, including fresh fish, seasonal seafood, steak and lamb. Desserts are memorable. The atmosphere is chic, especially in the posh red booths in front of a wall decorated with shimmering seashells. Casual dress; cocktails. **Parking:** valet. **Cards:** AX, DC, MC, VI.
⦙

RENOIR   **Lunch:** $28   **Dinner:** $34-$46   **Phone:** 514/285-9000   **61**
(CAA)
▼▼▼ ▼▼▼
French   **Location:** Corner of rue Stanley; in Sofitel Montreal. 1155 rue Sherbrooke ouest H3A 2N3. **Hours:** 6 am-10:30 pm. **Reservations:** suggested. **Features:** The stylish, elegant hotel dining room has a fresh, youthful feel. The decor includes some architectural relics from the renowned Van Horne mansion. Creative food preparations include grilled Maine lobster, Atlantic cod fish, Alberta sirloin beef, pastilla of duck and lemon- and herb-roasted chicken. Creme brulee or chocolate cake is worth a try for dessert. Dressy casual; cocktails. **Parking:** valet and street. **Cards:** AX, CB, DC, DS, MC, VI.
⦙

RESTAURANT DU VIEUX-PORT   **Lunch:** $8-$16   **Dinner:** $14-$35   **Phone:** 514/866-3175   **33**
(CAA)
▼▼▼ ▼▼▼
Steak & Seafood   **Location:** Corner of St-Gabriel; in the Old Port district. 39 rue St-Paul est H2Y 1G2. **Hours:** 11:30 am-11 pm, Fri & Sat-midnight. **Reservations:** accepted. **Features:** Lobster, steaks, seafood and fresh fish are served in the informal Old Montreal restaurant, which occupies a vintage building. Casual dress; cocktails. **Parking:** street. **Cards:** AX, DC, MC, VI. **Historic**
⦙

RESTAURANT FOU D'ASIE   **Lunch:** $7-$15   **Dinner:** $10-$20   **Phone:** 514/281-0077   **7**
▼▼▼ ▼▼▼
Asian   **Location:** Just s of rue Ontario. 1732 rue St-Denis H2X 3K6. **Hours:** 11 am-2:30 & 5-10 pm, Sat & Sun from 4 pm. Closed major holidays. **Reservations:** suggested. **Features:** This casual split-level dining room has many tables overlooking lively rue St-Denis, in addition to seating in a bright atrium area and on the seasonal terrace. The menu features Asian dishes, including sushi, noodles, spring rolls, chicken teriyaki, seafood, meats and several Vietnamese specialties. Casual dress; cocktails. **Parking:** street. **Cards:** AX, DC, MC, VI.

RESTAURANT JULIEN   **Lunch:** $19-$32   **Dinner:** $19-$36   **Phone:** 514/871-1581   **49**
▼▼▼ ▼▼▼
French   **Location:** Just s of rue Ste-Catherine. 1191 ave Union H3B 3C3. **Hours:** 11:30 am-3 & 5-10:30 pm, Sat from 5:30 pm. Closed major holidays; also Sun. **Reservations:** suggested. **Features:** The elegant downtown bistro features some classic dishes, including steak and fries, chicken supreme, steak tartare, scallops, beef bavette, veal, liver, sweetbreads, magret of duck, tuna, salmon and pasta. A garden terrace opens seasonally. Casual dress; cocktails. **Parking:** street. **Cards:** AX, CB, DC, DS, JC, MC, VI.

RESTAURANT KALINKA   **Lunch:** $9-$18   **Dinner:** $9-$18   **Phone:** 514/932-3403   **118**
▼▼▼ ▼▼▼
Russian   **Location:** Just n of rue Ste-Catherine. 1409 rue St-Marc H3H 2G4. **Hours:** noon-10 pm, Fri-1 am, Sat 5 pm-1 am. Closed: 1/1; also Sun. **Reservations:** suggested. **Features:** This small and intimate eatery specializes in authentic Russian food including chicken Kiev, beef stroganoff, brochettes of chicken or pork, steaks, schnitzel, borcht soup, dumplings and crepes. Live musicians perform Friday and Saturday evenings. Casual dress; cocktails. **Parking:** on-site. **Cards:** AX, MC, VI.

RESTAURANT LA BELLE PROVINCE   **Lunch:** $4-$6   **Dinner:** $4-$6   **Phone:** 514/398-9507   **106**
▼▼▼
Canadian   **Location:** Just w of rue Crescent. 1444 rue Ste-Catherine ouest H3G 1R3. **Hours:** 6 am-midnight, Thurs-1 am, Fri & Sat-4 am, Sun noon-11 pm. Closed: 1/1, 12/24, 12/25. **Reservations:** not accepted. **Features:** The favored specialty of the provincial fast food chain is poutine (fries served with curd cheese and gravy), but patrons can sample many inexpensive menu items. Among them are steamed or toasted hot dogs, smoked meat, hamburgers, subs, gyro sandwiches and chicken. Casual dress; beer only. **Parking:** street.

RESTAURANT L'ACTUEL   **Lunch:** $16-$29   **Dinner:** $16-$43   **Phone:** 514/866-1537   **82**
▼▼▼ ▼▼▼
Belgian   **Location:** Between rue Ste-Catherine and boul Rene-Levesque; across from Square Dorchester. 1194 rue Peel H3B 2T6. **Hours:** 11:30 am-10 pm, Wed-Fri to 10:30 pm, Sat 5 pm-10:30 pm. Closed major holidays; also Sun & 12/23-1/2. **Reservations:** suggested. **Features:** The restaurant specializes in Belgian beer and dishes, particularly mussels, seafood and steak. Second-floor dining is elegant and sophisticated, while the first floor retains a casual feel. For dessert, indulge in the profiteroles with chocolate sauce. Casual dress; cocktails. **Parking:** on-site. **Cards:** AX, DC, MC, VI.
⦙

RESTAURANT LA GARGOTE   **Lunch:** $17-$20   **Dinner:** $16-$24   **Phone:** 514/844-1428   **68**
▼▼▼ ▼▼▼
French   **Location:** Corner of rue St-Pierre facing Place d'Youville. 351 Place d'Youville H2Y 2B7. **Hours:** noon-2 & 5:30-10 pm. Closed major holidays; also 12/23-1/3 & Sun 1/4-5/15. **Reservations:** accepted. **Features:** The Old Montreal restaurant serves French cuisine prepared from market-fresh ingredients. Casual dress; cocktails. **Parking:** street. **Cards:** AX, MC, VI.

(See map and index starting on p. 414)

RESTAURANT LA MAREE   **Lunch:** $18-$20   **Dinner:** $35-$49   **Phone:** 514/861-9794   27

French   **Location:** In Old Montreal. 404 Place Jacques-Cartier H2Y 3B2. **Hours:** noon-3 & 5:30-11 pm, Sat & Sun noon-11 pm. **Reservations:** suggested. **Features:** Among the elegant restaurant's seafood specialties are lobster with tomatoes and basil, Dover sole and striped bass with fennel. Velvet curtains and high-back chairs are among touches that reflect a Louis XIII influence. Some meals are prepared tableside. The dessert menu changes often. On weekends from May through September, the terrace is open for lunch. Casual dress. **Parking:** street. **Cards:** AX, DC, DS, JC, MC, VI. **Historic**

RESTAURANT LA PIZZELLA   **Lunch:** $15-$20   **Dinner:** $15-$20   **Phone:** 514/939-3030   113

Italian   **Location:** Between boul de Maisonneuve and ave Lincoln. 2080 rue St-Mathieu H3H 2J4. **Hours:** 11:30 am-close Closed: Sun. **Reservations:** suggested. **Features:** Tasty fettuccine primavera is representative of menu selections at the cozy restaurant, a favorite, upscale spot for fresh pasta, gourmet pizza and Mediterranean specialties. Knowledgeable servers adeptly answer questions about the choices. Casual dress; cocktails. **Parking:** street. **Cards:** AX, MC, VI.

RESTAURANT L'AUTRE SAISON   **Dinner:** $25-$49   **Phone:** 514/845-0058   89

French   **Location:** Between boul de Maisonneuve and rue Sherbrooke. 2137 rue Crescent H3G 2C1. **Hours:** 5 pm-11 pm. Closed: 6/24, 12/24-12/26 & 1/1-1/26. **Reservations:** suggested. **Features:** This casually upscale dining room, located in an historic Crescent Street greystone, offers gracious service and a French-style menu that includes pan-seared foie gras, escargots, mussels, French onion soup, rack of lamb, veal, steaks, salmon scampis and surf 'n' turf. Casual dress; cocktails. **Parking:** street. **Cards:** AX, DC, MC, VI.

RESTAURANT LE PIEMONTAIS   **Lunch:** $17-$42   **Dinner:** $17-$42   **Phone:** 514/861-8122   13

Italian   **Location:** Corner of boul Rene-Levesque. 1145A rue de Bullion H2X 2Z2. **Hours:** 11 am-midnight, Sat from 5 pm Closed: Sun & 7/15-8/7. **Features:** The elegant restaurant serves fine Italian cuisine in a relaxed dining room staffed by genuinely friendly and refined servers. Dressy casual; cocktails. **Parking:** on-site **Cards:** AX, DC, DS, MC, VI.

RESTAURANT LES CONTINENTS   **Lunch:** $16-$27   **Dinner:** $19-$36   **Phone:** 514/847-8729   50

Regional Continental   **Location:** Corner of rue St-Pierre; in Hotel InterContinental Montreal. 360 rue St-Antoine ouest H2Y 3X4. **Hours:** 6:30 am-2:30 & 6-10:30 pm. **Reservations:** suggested. **Features:** Seafood, meats, chicken, fresh fish, game and pasta are the basis for wonderfully flavorful cuisine. The decor is elegant and the ambience sophisticated in the comfortable hotel dining room. Dressy casual; cocktails. **Parking:** on-site (fee) and valet. **Cards:** AX, DC, DS, JC, MC, VI.

RESTAURANT LES REMPARTS   **Lunch:** $16-$20   **Dinner:** $22-$34   **Phone:** 514/392-1649   31

French   **Location:** Just e of rue St-Gabriel; in Old Port district; in Auberge du Vieux-Port. 93 rue de la Commune est H2Y 1J1 **Hours:** 7-10 am, 11:30-3 & 5:30-10 pm, Sat & Sun 7 am-11 & 6-10:30 pm. Closed: 1/1, 12/24, 12/25 **Reservations:** suggested. **Features:** Fresh fish and game are specialties at the elegant French restaurant in the Auberge du Vieux-Port hotel, facing the popular Old Port district of Old Montreal. A rooftop terrace is good for warm-weather dining and viewing summer fireworks presentations. Casual dress; cocktails. **Parking:** valet and street. **Cards:** AX, DC, DS, JC, MC, VI.

RESTAURANT PIERRE DU CALVET   **Dinner:** $28-$49   **Phone:** 514/282-1725   12

French   **Location:** Corner of rue St-Paul. 405 rue Bonsecours H2Y 3C3. **Hours:** 6 pm-10 pm. Closed: 1/1, 12/25; also 2-3 weeks in Jan. **Reservations:** accepted. **Features:** Fine French cuisine is served in the lavish dining room of a historic home and inn that dates backs to 1725. Benjamin Franklin once visited the property. Dressy casual; cocktails. **Parking:** street. **Cards:** AX, DC, MC, VI. **Historic**

RESTAURANT SHO-DAN CONCEPT JAPONAIS   **Lunch:** $11-$34   **Dinner:** $14-$26   **Phone:** 514/871-0777   108

Japanese   **Location:** Just w of rue Bishop. 1425 boul Rene-Levesque H3G 1T7. **Hours:** 11:30 am-2:30 & 5-10 pm, Tues & Wed-10:30 pm, Thurs & Fri-11 pm, Sat 5 pm-11 pm. Closed: Sun. **Reservations:** suggested **Features:** This chic sushi-bar offers an extensive choice of sushi, sashimi and sushi maki menu items and many flavorful eye-catching specialty dishes, including a few dessert sushi selections. Dressy casual; cocktails. **Parking:** street. **Cards:** AX, DC, MC, VI.

RESTAURANT SHO-DAN CONCEPT JAPONAIS   **Lunch:** $11-$18   **Dinner:** $14-$26   **Phone:** 514/987-9987   58

Japanese   **Location:** Between rue Sherbrooke and boul de Maisonneuve. 2020 rue Metcalfe H3A 1X8. **Hours:** 11:30 am-2:30 & 5-10:30 pm, Thurs & Fri-11 pm, Sat 5 pm-11 pm. Closed: 12/25; also Sun & lunch on holidays **Reservations:** accepted. **Features:** This stylish and comfortable sushi-bar offers an extensive choice of sushi, sashimi and sushi maki menu items and many flavorful eye-catching specialty dishes, including a chef's special and a few dessert sushi selections. Casual dress; cocktails. **Parking:** street. **Cards:** AX, DC, MC, VI.

RESTAURANT U & ME   **Lunch:** $5-$9   **Dinner:** $5-$9   **Phone:** 514/931-0081   120

Chinese   **Location:** Corner of rue St-Marc. 1900 rue Ste-Catherine ouest H3H 1M4. **Hours:** 11 am-3 pm. **Reservations:** required. **Features:** It's hard to beat the great prices at the Asian fast-food diner, which specializes in freshly prepared Cantonese and Szechuan dishes. Among menu offerings are hearty noodle soups, Thai-style fried rice, chicken in black bean sauce, beef with curry, pad thai, Cantonese chow mein and Peking-style noodles with vegetables. Casual dress; beer & wine only. **Parking:** on-site.

RESTAURANT VERSES   **Lunch:** $14-$22   **Dinner:** $20-$40   **Phone:** 514/788-4000   40

French   **Location:** Corner of rue St-Sulpice; in Hotel Nelligan. 100 rue St-Paul ouest H2Y 1Z3. **Hours:** 6:30 am-10:30 pm **Reservations:** suggested. **Features:** In an elegant Old Montreal boutique hotel, the upscale bistro and bar presents a menu of French-inspired regional cuisine, including Quebec lamb, breast of duck, Boileau deer, guinea fowl, red snapper, Arctic char, risotto and giant ravioli. Dressy casual; cocktails. **Parking:** valet. **Cards:** AX, CB, DC, DS, MC.

See map and index starting on p. 414)

REUBEN'S RESTAURANT-DELICATESSEN   **Lunch:** $7-$26   **Dinner:** $7-$26   **Phone:** 514/866-1029   [78]

▼▼▼   **Location:** Corner of Peel. 1116 Ste-Catherine St W H3B 1H4. **Hours:** 6:30 am-midnight, Thurs-Sat to 1:30 am.
Deli/Subs   Closed: 12/25. **Reservations:** accepted. **Features:** The downtown delicatessen has comfortable, vinyl-
Sandwiches   padded booths and specializes in Montreal smoked meat, steak and pizza. For dessert, try a hearty slice of
delicious cheesecake. Casual dress; cocktails. **Parking:** street. **Cards:** AX, DC, MC, VI.

RISTORANTE BRONTE   **Dinner:** $26-$33   **Phone:** 514/934-1801   [110]

▼▼▼   **Location:** Corner of rue St-Mathieu; in Le Meridien Versailles-Montreal. 1800 rue Sherbrooke ouest H3H 1E5.
Italian   **Hours:** 6 pm-11 pm. Closed: 12/25; also Sun & Mon. **Reservations:** suggested. **Features:** Fresh-market
cuisine with an Italian flair is served up in this upbeat and very stylish hotel restaurant. Homemade pasta,
including house specialties ravioli and cannelloni, are popular items on a menu that includes veal, fresh fish
and venison. The upscale bar area has comfortable banquette seating. Casual dress; cocktails. **Parking:** on-site (fee) and valet.
Cards: AX, DC, DS, MC, VI.

RISTORANTE LE MEDUSA   **Lunch:** $15-$35   **Dinner:** $15-$35   **Phone:** 514/878-4499   [92]

▼▼▼   **Location:** Just n of boul Rene-Levesque. 1224 rue Drummond H3G 1V7. **Hours:** noon-11 pm, Sat from 5 pm.
Italian   Closed major holidays; also Sun & 12/24-1/2. **Reservations:** suggested. **Features:** The casually upscale
eatery focuses on Italian preparations of fresh pasta, meat and seafood, which are served by the
personable staff. Casual dress; cocktails. **Parking:** street. **Cards:** AX, DC, MC, VI.

ROSALIE RESTAURANT   **Lunch:** $12-$25   **Dinner:** $18-$35   **Phone:** 514/392-1970   [99]

▼▼▼   **Location:** Just s of rue Ste-Catherine. 1232 rue de la Montagne H3G 1Z1. **Hours:** noon-3 & 6-11 pm, Thurs-
French   midnight, Sat & Sun 6 pm-midnight. **Reservations:** suggested. **Features:** Chic, contemporary decor
complements an innovative menu of modern French cuisine, including roasted duck, fresh fish, beef filets,
pork, pasta, smoked or poached salmon, beef tartare and rabbit. For dessert, try some apple pie, chocolate
mousse, creme brulee or chocolate torte cake. A seasonal terrace with stainless steel tables is popular in summer. Casual
dress; cocktails. **Parking:** valet. **Cards:** AX, DC, MC, VI.

ST-HUBERT   **Lunch:** $6-$12   **Dinner:** $7-$20   **Phone:** 514/866-0500

▼▼   **Location:** Corner of rue Stanley; in Gare Windsor Train Station. 1180 rue de la Gauchetiere ouest H3B 2S2. **Hours:** 11
Barbecue   am-9 pm, Wed-10 pm, Thurs & Fri-11 pm, Sat-10 pm. Closed: 12/25. **Reservations:** suggested.
Features: The pleasantly decorated family-friendly restaurant serves affordable chicken dinners, ribs, club
sandwiches, chicken wings, salads, soups and hot chicken sandwiches. The children's menu includes
animal nuggets. Casual dress; cocktails. **Parking:** street. **Cards:** AX, DC, MC, VI.

SCHWARTZ'S MONTREAL HEBREW
DELICATESSEN   **Lunch:** $5-$15   **Dinner:** $5-$15   **Phone:** 514/842-4813   [4]

▼   **Location:** Just n of rue Roy. 3895 boul St-Laurent H2W 1X9. **Hours:** 9 am-12:30 am, Fri-1 am, Sat-2:30 am.
Deli/Subs   **Reservations:** not accepted. **Features:** The casual delicatessen-diner is a favorite for Montreal-style
Sandwiches   smoked meat sandwiches and other deli standards, including smoked turkey, steaks grilled over a hardwood
fire, latkes, liver and kosher dills. Take-out service is available. Casual dress. **Parking:** street.

-LE RESTAURANT   **Lunch:** $16-$25   **Dinner:** $22-$48   **Phone:** 514/350-1155   [42]

(AAA)   **Location:** Just n of rue St-Paul; in Le Saint-Sulpice Hotel Montreal. 125 rue St-Paul ouest H3Y 1Z5. **Hours:** 6 am-11
▼▼▼   pm. **Reservations:** suggested. **Features:** A French grill menu of fresh seafood and grilled imported fish is
French   bolstered by other offerings of rack of lamb, veal and steak. Adding to the atmosphere are helpful servers
and a decor that incorporates rich, wood-trimmed walls, elegant table settings and an informal lounge.
Casual dress; cocktails. **Parking:** valet. **Cards:** AX, DC, MC, VI.

SOUPEBOL   **Lunch:** $7-$14   **Dinner:** $7-$14   **Phone:** 514/282-8388   [43]

▼▼   **Location:** Just s of rue Ste-Catherine. 1245 rue du Square-Phillips H3B 3E9. **Hours:** 11 am-9 pm. Closed: 12/25.
Asian   **Reservations:** accepted. **Features:** This stylish downtown diner specializes in Asian cuisine. Menu items
include Tonkinese soups, sushi, grilled meats, seafood and Cantonese chow mein. Casual dress; cocktails.
Parking: street. **Cards:** AX, DC, MC, VI.

STASH CAFE   **Lunch:** $10-$16   **Dinner:** $11-$17   **Phone:** 514/845-6611   [52]

▼▼   **Location:** Corner of rue St-Francois-Xavier. 200 rue St-Paul ouest H2Y 1Z9. **Hours:** 11:30 am-10 pm, Sat noon-11
Polish   pm, Sun noon-10 pm. Closed: 3/24; also 12/23-12/26. **Reservations:** suggested. **Features:** In a historic
stone building, the informal Old Montreal restaurant is appointed with colorful European publicity posters
and oak church pews. The refreshing menu features authentic Polish specialties, including pierogi, placki
(Polish pancakes), bigos (cabbage stew with meat, sausage and mushrooms), golabki (cabbage rolls), Polish sausages, potato
salad and pork cutlets. A selection of imported and local beers is offered. For dessert, try nalesniki (a cheese-filled pancake).
Casual dress; cocktails. **Parking:** street. **Cards:** AX, DC, MC, VI.

TOQUE!   **Dinner:** $24-$44   **Phone:** 514/499-2084   [48]

(AAA)   **Location:** Corner of rue Ste-Antoine. 900 Place Jean-Paul Riopelle H2Z 2B2. **Hours:** 5:30 pm-10:30 pm. Closed:
▼▼▼▼   Sun, Mon & 12/23-1/6. **Reservations:** suggested. **Features:** The spacious and stylish dining room has an
French   upscale feel that appeals to the professional downtown crowd that frequents the restaurant. Guest-oriented
servers are knowledgeable and gracious. The food is exquisite—superb in preparation, presentation and,
especially, taste. Owners take great care to use the highest quality regional meat, fish and seafood. The
"Bas-du-Fleuve" lamb, Havre St-Pierre scallops and the pan-seared foie gras are highlights. A multi-course
tasting menu is available. Dressy casual; cocktails. **Parking:** on-site (fee). **Cards:** AX, DC, MC, VI.

(See map and index starting on p. 414)

TROIKA RESTAURANT   Dinner: $23-$41   Phone: 514/849-9333   87

CAA

Russian

Location: Just below rue Sherbrooke; opposite Museum of Fine Arts. 2171 rue Crescent H3G 2C1. **Hours:** 5 pm-1 pm. Closed: 12/25; also Sun. **Reservations:** suggested. **Features:** Chicken Kiev, beef stroganoff and wil boar are representative of Russian and Czarist cuisine on the elegant restaurant's tempting menu. A wide selection of imported caviars, imported Siberian teas and flavored vodkas is available. For dessert, opt fc the tasty crepes. Live music is performed nightly. Dressy casual; cocktails; entertainment. **Parking:** stree **Cards:** AX, DC, MC, VI.

VERSION LAURENT GODBOUT   Lunch: $21   Dinner: $19-$26   Phone: 514/871-9135   20

Mediterranean

Location: Corner of rue du Marche Bonsecours. 295 rue St-Paul est H2Y 1H3. **Hours:** 11:30 am-2 & 5:30-10 pm Sat & Sun from 5:30 pm. **Reservations:** suggested. **Features:** Named for its renowned chef, this "boutique concept" Old Montreal restaurant features creatively presented and memorable Mediterranean cuisine. A decor elements, from the dishes to the furnishings, are available for purchase. The menu includes such items as focaccia, cold-cut platter, sardines, sausage, fried clams, mussels, beef ribs, chicken, orzo, milk-fed veal, bio-raise salmon, lobster and about a dozen choices of cheeses from Portugal, Italy and Spain. Casual dress; cocktails. **Parking:** stree **Cards:** AX, DC, MC, VI.

WIENSTEIN AND GAVINOS PASTA BAR FACTORY
CO LTD   Lunch: $10-$14   Dinner: $10-$30   Phone: 514/288-2231   95

Italian

Location: Between rue Ste-Catherine and boul de Maisonneuve. 1434 rue Crescent H3G 2B6. **Hours:** 11 am midnight, Thurs-Sat to 1 am. Closed: 12/25. **Reservations:** accepted. **Features:** The atmosphere i hopping in the trendy bistro-style pasta bar, which sits on the downtown nightclub strip. Diners can choose from a wide selection of freshly prepared pizzas and pasta, as well as meats and salads. The seasona terrace is comfortable and breezy. Casual dress; cocktails. **Parking:** on-site (fee) and street. **Cards:** AX, DC, MC, VI.

ZAWEDEH RESTAURANT   Lunch: $8-$30   Dinner: $16-$35   Phone: 514/288-4141   53

Lebanese

Location: Corner of rue Peel and rue Sherbrooke; in Best Western Ville-Marie Hotel & Suites. 3407 rue Peel H3A 1G5 **Hours:** 6:30 am-11, noon-2:30 & 5-10 pm, Fri & Sat-12:30 am. **Reservations:** suggested. **Features:** The cozy hotel dining room offers polite service and a menu of authentic Lebanese cuisine including hummus tabbouleh, baba ghanoush, falafel, cheese rolls, Lebanese sausage, fatouche salad, stuffed vine leaves shish taouk, brochettes of beef kafta or filet mignon. Regional menu items include poached salmon, chicken supreme, bee medallions and lamb. For dessert, try the syrupy baklava. Casual dress; cocktails. **Parking:** valet and street. **Cards:** AX, DC DS, MC, VI.

ZEN CHINESE CUISINE   Lunch: $18-$25   Dinner: $18-$32   Phone: 514/499-0801   56

Chinese

Location: Corner of rue Peel; in Hotel Omni Mont-Royal. 1050 rue Sherbrooke ouest H3A 2R6. **Hours:** 11:30 am 2:30 & 5:30-10 pm, Sat 5:30 pm-10:30 pm, Sun 11:30 am-3 & 5:30-10:30 pm. **Reservations:** suggested **Features:** Such traditional dishes as orange beef and Szechuan chicken are representative of menu choices. The all-you-can-eat selection is a good value. Minimalist decor—with metal chairs, curved walls and modern colors—gives the dining room a trendy, upscale feel. Servers are efficient and friendly. Dressy casual; cocktails **Parking:** on-site (fee) and valet. **Cards:** AX, DC, MC, VI.

ZYNG NOUILLERIE   Lunch: $8-$12   Dinner: $8-$12   Phone: 514/284-2016   8

Asian

Location: Just s of rue Ontario. 1748 rue St-Denis H2X 3K6. **Hours:** 11:30 am-10 pm. **Reservations:** accepted **Features:** The relaxed, stylish eatery serves Asian soups and fresh noodle dishes. Guests walk up to glass refrigerator and choice their noodles, spices, vegetables and meat (or vegetarian alternative), and the chef then prepares the meal. Casual dress; cocktails. **Parking:** street. **Cards:** MC, VI.

MONTREAL pop. 1,039,534   (See map and index starting on p. 420)

─────── **WHERE TO STAY** ───────

ANNE MA SOEUR ANNE HOTEL-STUDIO   Phone: 514/281-3187   5

CAA SAVE

Small-scale Hotel

5/1-10/31	1P: $80-$140	2P: $90-$150	XP: $15
11/1-4/30	1P: $70-$125	2P: $80-$140	XP: $15

Location: Just s of rue Rachel. 4119 rue St-Denis H2W 2M7. Fax: 514/281-1601. **Facility:** 15 one-bedroon standard units with efficiencies. 3 stories (no elevator), interior/exterior corridors. **Parking:** stree **Terms:** [CP] meal plan available. **Amenities:** high-speed Internet, hair dryers. **Guest Services:** wireless Internet. **Business Services:** meeting rooms. **Cards:** AX, MC, VI. **Free Special Amenities:** continenta breakfast and newspaper.

AUBERGE DE LA FONTAINE   *Book at AAA.com*   Phone: (514)597-0166   4

Bed & Breakfast

5/1-10/15 [ECP]	1P: $133-$229	2P: $153-$249	XP: $20	F1
10/16-4/30 [ECP]	1P: $109-$209	2P: $119-$219	XP: $20	F1

Location: Corner of rue Chambord. Located in a residential area, across from Parc Lafontaine. 1301 rue Rachel es H2J 2K1. Fax: 514/597-0496. **Facility:** Complimentary snacks are available in the shared kitchen of this inn style B&B set in a pleasant residential district facing popular Parc Lafontaine. 21 units. 20 one-bedroom standard units, som with whirlpools. 1 one-bedroom suite with whirlpool. 3 stories (no elevator), interior corridors. *Bath:* combo or shower only **Parking:** on-site and street. **Terms:** cancellation fee imposed, package plans. **Amenities:** hair dryers. *Some:* CD players, high speed Internet, irons. **Guest Services:** valet laundry, wireless Internet. **Business Services:** meeting rooms, PC. **Cards:** AX MC, VI.

SOME UNITS

(See map and index starting on p. 420)

AUBERGE ROYAL VERSAILLES HOTEL · *Book great rates at AAA.com* · Phone: 514/256-1613 · **2**

5/1-10/31	1P: $105-$139	2P: $105-$139	XP: $10 · F18
11/1-4/30	1P: $85-$119	2P: $85-$119	XP: $10 · F18

Small-scale Hotel

Location: Rt 138, 0.3 mi (0.4 km) w of Hwy 25. Located next to Radisson metro station. 7200 rue Sherbrooke est H1N 1E7. Fax: 514/256-5150. **Facility:** 132 units. 128 one-bedroom standard units, some with whirlpools. 4 one-bedroom suites with whirlpools. 2 stories, interior/exterior corridors. **Parking:** on-site, winter plug-ins. **Amenities:** voice mail, hair dryers. *Some:* DVD players, CD players, irons. **Dining:** 7 am-10 pm, cocktails. **Pool(s):** heated outdoor. **Guest Services:** gift shop, valet laundry, wireless Internet. **Business Services:** meeting rooms, business center. **Cards:** AX, DC, MC, VI. **Free Special Amenities: local telephone calls and high-speed Internet.**

SOME UNITS

COURTYARD MARRIOTT MONTREAL AIRPORT · *Book great rates at AAA.com* · Phone: (514)339-5333 · **9**

5/16-4/30	1P: $119-$229	2P: $119-$229	XP: $20 · F12
5/1-5/15	1P: $109-$199	2P: $109-$199	XP: $20 · F12

Small-scale Hotel

Location: Hwy 40, exit 65 (boul Cavendish), 0.3 mi (0.5 km) w on north side service road, then just n on rue Beaulac. 7000 Place Robert-Joncas H4M 2Z5. Fax: 514/339-2788. **Facility:** Smoke free premises. 160 one-bedroom standard units, some with whirlpools. 6 stories, interior corridors. *Bath:* combo or shower only. **Parking:** on-site. **Terms:** [AP] meal plan available. **Amenities:** video games (fee), high-speed Internet, voice mail, irons, hair dryers. **Pool(s):** heated indoor. **Leisure Activities:** whirlpool, exercise room, game room. **Guest Services:** sundries, valet and coin laundry, area transportation, wireless Internet. **Business Services:** conference facilities, business center. **Cards:** AX, DC, MC, VI.

DAYS INN & CONFERENCE CENTER MONTREAL AIRPORT · *Book great rates at AAA.com* · Phone: (514)332-2720 · **11**

6/2-6/30	1P: $159-$280	2P: $159-$280	XP: $10 · F16
5/1-6/1	1P: $119-$139	2P: $119	XP: $10 · F16
7/1-4/30	1P: $119	2P: $119	XP: $10 · F16

Small-scale Hotel

Location: Hwy 40, exit 62, just w on south side service road; in St-Laurent sector. 4545 Cote Vertu ouest H4S 1C8. Fax: 514/332-4512. **Facility:** 92 one-bedroom standard units. 3 stories, interior corridors. **Parking:** on-site, winter plug-ins. **Terms:** [AP] & [CP] meal plans available, package plans, 3% service charge. **Amenities:** video games (fee), voice mail, irons, hair dryers. **Pool(s):** outdoor. **Leisure Activities:** exercise room. **Guest Services:** valet laundry, wireless Internet. **Business Services:** conference facilities, PC. **Cards:** AX, DC, DS, MC, VI.

SOME UNITS

FOUR POINTS BY SHERATON MONTREAL AIRPORT · *Book great rates at AAA.com* · Phone: (514)344-1999 · **13**

All Year	1P: $119-$169	2P: $119-$169	XP: $10 · F18

Large-scale Hotel

Location: Hwy 520, exit 5 eastbound on south side service road; exit westbound to rue Ness, follow signs for rue Hickmore and Hwy 520 E; in St-Laurent sector. 6600 Cote-de-Liesse H4T 1E3. Fax: 514/344-6720. **Facility:** 222 units. 209 one-bedroom standard units. 13 one-bedroom suites, some with whirlpools. 9 stories, interior corridors. *Bath:* combo or shower only. **Parking:** on-site. **Terms:** [AP], [BP] & [CP] meal plans available, package plans. **Amenities:** video games (fee), high-speed Internet, dual phone lines, voice mail, safes, honor bars, irons, hair dryers. **Dining:** 6:30 am-11 pm, cocktails. **Pool(s):** heated indoor. **Leisure Activities:** saunas, whirlpool, waterslide, exercise room. **Guest Services:** gift shop, valet laundry, airport transportation-Pierre Elliott Trudeau International Airport, area transportation-train station, wireless Internet. **Business Services:** conference facilities, business center. **Cards:** AX, CB, DC, DS, JC, MC, VI. **Free Special Amenities: newspaper and room upgrade (subject to availability with advance reservations).** *(See color ad p 5)*

SOME UNITS

HILTON GARDEN INN MONTREAL/DORVAL · *Book great rates at AAA.com* · Phone: (514)788-5120 · **14**

All Year	1P: $111-$145	2P: $111-$145	XP: $15 · F

Small-scale Hotel

Location: Hwy 520, exit 4 eastbound on south side service road; exit 4 (Montee de Liesse) westbound; in St-Laurent sector. 7880 Cote-de-Liesse H4T 1E7. Fax: 514/788-5025. **Facility:** 160 one-bedroom standard units. 4 stories, interior corridors. **Parking:** on-site. **Terms:** cancellation fee imposed, weekly rates available, [AP] & [BP] meal plans available, package plans. **Amenities:** video games (fee), high-speed Internet, dual phone lines, voice mail, safes, irons, hair dryers. **Pool(s):** indoor. **Leisure Activities:** whirlpool, exercise room. **Guest Services:** sundries, valet and coin laundry, area transportation. **Business Services:** conference facilities, business center. **Cards:** AX, CB, DC, DS, MC, VI.

SOME UNITS

HOLIDAY INN MONTREAL-AIRPORT · *Book great rates at AAA.com* · Phone: (514)739-3391 · **12**

All Year	1P: $104-$169	XP: $10 · F17

Small-scale Hotel

Location: Hwy 520, exit 5 eastbound on south side service road; exit westbound to rue Ness, follow signs for rue Hickmore and Hwy 520 E; in St-Laurent sector. 6500 Cote-de-Liesse H4T 1E3. Fax: 514/739-6591. **Facility:** 278 units. 276 one-bedroom standard units, some with whirlpools. 2 one-bedroom suites with kitchens. 2 stories, interior/exterior corridors. **Parking:** on-site. **Terms:** cancellation fee imposed, pets ($35 fee). **Amenities:** video games (fee), voice mail, irons, hair dryers. *Some:* high-speed Internet, safes. **Dining:** 6:30 am-11 pm, cocktails, entertainment. **Pool(s):** outdoor, heated indoor, wading. **Leisure Activities:** saunas, whirlpool, exercise room. *Fee:* massage, game room. **Guest Services:** gift shop, valet laundry, airport transportation-Pierre Elliott Trudeau International Airport, area transportation-train station, wireless Internet. **Business Services:** meeting rooms, business center. **Cards:** AX, CB, DC, DS, JC, MC, VI. **Free Special Amenities: newspaper and room upgrade (subject to availability with advance reservations).** *(See color ad card insert)*

SOME UNITS

(See map and index starting on p. 420)

HOTEL AUBERGE UNIVERSEL MONTREAL   *Book great rates at AAA.com*   Phone: (514)253-3365   **3**

CAA SAVE

	6/22-9/1	1P: $125-$155	2P: $125-$155	XP: $10	F1
	5/1-6/21 & 9/2-10/21	1P: $111-$129	2P: $111-$129	XP: $10	F1
	10/22-4/30	1P: $99-$119	2P: $99-$119	XP: $10	F1

Location: Corner of rue Viau; just e of Botanical Garden and Olympic Stadium. 5000 rue Sherbrooke est H1V 1A1
Large-scale Hotel Fax: 514/253-9958. **Facility:** 228 units. 223 one-bedroom standard units, some with whirlpools. 5 one bedroom suites ($200-$499), some with whirlpools. 7 stories, interior corridors. **Parking:** on-site, winter plug-ins. **Terms:** [AP] & [BP] meal plans available, package plans. **Amenities:** video games (fee), voice mail, irons, hair dryers *Some:* dual phone lines. **Dining:** Le Stadium Club Restaurant & Bar, see separate listing. **Pool(s):** heated outdoor, heated indoor. **Leisure Activities:** sauna, whirlpool, exercise room. **Guest Services:** gift shop, valet laundry. **Business Services** conference facilities, business center. **Cards:** AX, DC, DS, MC, VI. **Free Special Amenities:** full breakfast and loca telephone calls. *(See color ad below)*

SOME UNITS

(See map and index starting on p. 420)

HOTEL LE PRESTIGE   *Book at AAA.com*   **Phone:** (514)640-5500   **1**
♦♦♦♦ ♦♦♦♦   All Year   1P: $86-$150   2P: $96-$150   XP: $10   F12
🔻🔻   **Location:** Hwy 40, exit 87, 0.6 mi (1 km) s on boul du Tricentenaire, then just w. Located in the east end
Small-scale Hotel commercial/industrial area. 12555 Sherbrooke St est H1B 1C8. Fax: 514/640-5499. **Facility:** 72 one-bedroom
           standard units, some with whirlpools. 3 stories, interior corridors. **Parking:** on-site, winter plug-ins.
Terms: cancellation fee imposed. **Pool(s):** outdoor. **Guest Services:** valet laundry. **Business Services:** meeting rooms.
Cards: AX, DC, DS, MC, VI.
                                                                          SOME UNITS
                                                           🍽️ 🏊 📶 / 🚫 /

HOTEL RUBY FOO'S   *Book great rates at AAA.com*   **Phone:** (514)731-7701   **6**
ⒶⒶ (SAVE)   All Year   1P: $159-$174   2P: $159-$174   XP: $15   F18
🔻🔻🔻   **Location:** Hwy 15, exit 69, east side service road. 7655 boul Decarie H4P 2H2. Fax: 514/731-7158. **Facility:** 198
           one-bedroom standard units, some with efficiencies. 4 stories, interior corridors. **Parking:** on-site.
Small-scale Hotel video games, high-speed Internet. **Dining:** 3 restaurants, 7 am-11 pm, Fri-midnight, Sat-1 am. **Pool(s):**
           Terms: [AP], [BP], [CP], [ECP] & [MAP] meal plans available. **Amenities:** voice mail, irons, hair dryers. *Fee:*
           heated outdoor. **Leisure Activities:** saunas, whirlpool, exercise room, spa. **Guest Services:** gift shop, valet
laundry, barber shop, beauty salon. **Business Services:** conference facilities. **Cards:** AX, DC, DS, MC, VI.
Free Special Amenities: local telephone calls and high-speed Internet. *(See color ad p 472)*
                                                                          SOME UNITS
                                    🅂 🍽️ 🍸 📶 🏊 🚫 📷 📠 / 🚫 📶 📠 /
                                                                              FEE

HOTEL TERRASSE ROYALE   **Phone:** 514/739-6391   **7**
♦♦♦♦ ♦♦♦♦   Property failed to provide current rates
🔻🔻   **Location:** Just n of chemin Queen-Mary. 5225 chemin Cote-des-Neiges H3T 1Y1. Fax: 514/342-2512. **Facility:** 56
Small-scale Hotel units. 21 one-bedroom standard units. 35 one-bedroom suites, some with efficiencies or kitchens. 6 stories,
           interior corridors. **Parking:** on-site (fee). **Amenities:** voice mail, irons, hair dryers. **Leisure**
Activities: exercise room. **Guest Services:** gift shop, coin laundry, wireless Internet.
                                                                          SOME UNITS
                                    🍽️ / 🚫 [VCR] 📶 📷 📠 /

(See map and index starting on p. 420)

QUALITY HOTEL MIDTOWN   *Book great rates at AAA.com*   Phone: (514)739-3800   10

5/1-9/1	1P: $99-$250	2P: $99-$250	XP: $10	F12
9/2-4/30	1P: $89-$250	2P: $89-$250	XP: $10	F12

Location: On east side service road for Hwy 15 (Decarie Expwy); corner of ave Plamondon. 6445 boul Decarie H3W 3E1. Fax: 514/739-5616. **Facility:** 100 one-bedroom standard units, some with whirlpools. 3-6 stories, interior corridors. **Parking:** on-site. **Terms:** [CP] meal plan available, package plans. **Amenities:** high-speed Internet, voice mail, irons, hair dryers. *Some:* DVD players. **Dining:** 7 am-2 & noon-10 pm, Fri-2 pm, Sat from 6 pm, also, Le Grill Midtown, see separate listing. **Leisure Activities:** exercise room. **Guest Services:** coin laundry. **Business Services:** meeting rooms, PC. **Cards:** AX, DC, DS, MC, VI. **Free Special Amenities:** expanded continental breakfast and high-speed Internet. *(See color ad card insert)*

Small-scale Hotel

SOME UNITS

186 guestrooms & suites
Free High Speed Internet
Complimentary shuttle to/from P.E.Trudeau airport
Outdoor swimming pool (seasonal-June-August)

RAMADA

15 banquet & conference rooms
VENEZIA (Italian cuisine)
Ten minutes from downtown
Exercise room

7300 Côte de Liesse
St. Laurent, Quebec

www.ramadamontreal.com

Tel.: 514.733.8818
Fax: 514.733.9889

(See map and index starting on p. 420)

RESIDENCE INN MONTREAL AIRPORT   *Book great rates at AAA.com*   Phone: 514/336-9333   **8**
Property failed to provide current rates
Small-scale Hotel   **Location:** Hwy 40, exit 65 (Cavendish boul), then 0.3 mi (0.5 km) w on northside service road, then just n on rue Beaulac. 6500 Place Robert-Joncas H4M 2Z5. Fax: 514/336-1168. **Facility:** Smoke free premises. 169 units. 120 one-bedroom standard units with efficiencies. 44 one- and 5 two-bedroom suites with efficiencies. 6 stories, interior corridors. *Bath:* combo or shower only. **Parking:** on-site. **Terms:** pets ($100 fee). **Amenities:** video games (fee), high-speed Internet, voice mail, irons, hair dryers. **Pool(s):** heated indoor. **Leisure Activities:** whirlpool, exercise room, game room. **Guest Services:** sundries, valet and coin laundry, area transportation, wireless Internet. **Business Services:** conference facilities, business center.

SOME UNITS

🛬 FEE 🐾 🛎 🍽 ⚓ 📷 🏊 ✂ ✕ 📷 🔒 📺 💻 / VCR /

──────── **WHERE TO DINE** ────────

ALEX H. RESTAURANT   **Lunch:** $10-$14   **Dinner:** $15-$24   Phone: 514/487-5444   **54**
Italian   **Location:** Just w of rue Draper. 5862 rue Sherbrooke ouest H4A 1X5. **Hours:** 11:30 am-2:30 & 5:30-10 pm, Sat & Sun from 5:30 pm. Closed: Mon 12/25-4/15. **Reservations:** accepted. **Features:** Italian and French food are the specialties at the affordable family-run restaurant in the suburban borough of Notre-Dame-de-Grace. A chalkboard announces daily specials, which may include stuffed chicken, pork, lamb brochettes, magret of duck, veal liver, kidneys Dijonnaise and pasta. No alcohol is sold on the premises, but guests may bring their own wine. Casual dress. **Parking:** street. **Cards:** MC, VI.

ARAHOVA SOUVLAKI   **Lunch:** $7-$11   **Dinner:** $11-$16   Phone: 514/274-7828   **14**
Greek   **Location:** Between ave du Parc and rue Jeanne-Mance. 256 St-Viateur ouest H2V 1X9. **Hours:** 10:30 am-2 am, Fri & Sat-5 am. Closed: 12/25. **Reservations:** accepted. **Features:** Souvlaki and gyro pitas, as well as other Greek specialties, can be eaten in the casual eatery's dining room or taken out. Casual dress; cocktails. **Parking:** street. **Cards:** MC, VI.

AREA   **Dinner:** $21-$34   Phone: 514/890-6691   **24**
French   **Location:** Between boul de Maisonneuve and rue Ste-Catherine. 1429 rue Amherst H2L 3L2. **Hours:** 6 pm-11 pm. Closed: 1/1, 12/25; also Sun & Mon. **Features:** In Montreal's trendy gay village, the small, stylish dining room has a youthful feel. Items on a menu of exciting modern cuisine are seasoned with a creative blend of herbs and spices. The menu includes pan-seared foie gras, yellowfin tuna and tasty appetizers such as tempura shrimp in mango chutney. Casual dress; cocktails. **Parking:** street. **Cards:** AX, DS, MC, VI.

ASEAN GARDEN   **Lunch:** $10-$19   **Dinner:** $10-$19   Phone: 514/487-8868   **52**
Asian   **Location:** Corner of Melrose. 5828 rue Sherbrooke ouest H4A 1X3. **Hours:** 11:30 am-2:30 & 5-11 pm, Fri & Sat-11 pm. **Reservations:** accepted. **Features:** The popular Asian restaurant is known for its Szechuan, Thai and sushi dishes, as well as for dim sum. The dining area is comfortable and relaxed, with party rooms available for groups. Worth trying are peanut butter dumplings, hot and sour soup, chicken satay, General Tao chicken, crispy duck, Szechuan-style shrimp and curried lamb. Casual dress; cocktails. **Parking:** street. **Cards:** MC, VI.

AU MESSOB D'OR-CUISINE ETHIOPIENNE   **Dinner:** $15-$30   Phone: 514/488-8620   **46**
Ethiopian   **Location:** Corner of Harvard. 5690 ave Monkland H4A 1E4. **Hours:** 5 pm-10:30 pm. Closed: 1/1, 12/25; also Mon. **Reservations:** accepted. **Features:** In a pleasant residential neighborhood, the simply decorated eatery specializes in Ethiopian cuisine. Traditional moist rolls of ingera bread are used for hand-dipping into a delicious platter of small pureed dishes of seasoned vegetables, lamb, beef or chicken. Some like it hot, but many dishes are offered with mild spices. Casual dress; cocktails. **Parking:** street. **Cards:** MC, VI.

B & M RESTAURANT   **Lunch:** $6-$19   **Dinner:** $6-$19   Phone: 514/484-3717   **51**
Canadian   **Location:** Corner of Melrose. 5800 rue Sherbrooke ouest H4A 1X3. **Hours:** 11 am-2 am. Closed: 12/25. **Reservations:** not accepted. **Features:** The popular family restaurant offers a variety of foods, including pizza, burgers, rotisserie and fried chicken, veal cutlets, pasta, salads, submarine sandwiches, smoked meat, souvlaki, brochettes, steak and seafood, Chinese dishes, hamburgers and poutine, a snack of fries doused in cheese curds and gravy. Casual dress; cocktails. **Parking:** street. **Cards:** AX, MC, VI.

B & M RESTAURANT   **Lunch:** $8-$27   **Dinner:** $8-$27   Phone: 514/488-1555   **49**
Canadian   **Location:** Corner of boul Grand. 6200 Somerled Ave H3X 2B3. **Hours:** 7 am-10 pm, Fri-11 pm, Sat 9 am-11 pm, Sun 9 am-10 pm. Closed: 12/25. **Reservations:** accepted. **Features:** The popular family restaurant serves a variety of foods, including pizza, rotisserie and fried chicken, veal cutlets, pasta, salads, submarine sandwiches, smoked meat, souvlaki, brochettes, steak, seafood, Chinese dishes, hamburgers and poutine, a snack of fries doused in cheese curds and gravy. Casual dress; cocktails. **Parking:** street. **Cards:** AX, MC, VI.

BEAUTY'S LUNCHEONETTE   **Lunch:** $10-$30   Phone: 514/849-8883   **23**
Canadian   **Location:** Corner of rue St-Urbain. 93 rue Mont-Royal ouest H2T 2S5. **Hours:** 7 am-4 pm, Sat-5 pm, Sun 8 am-5 pm. Closed: 12/25. **Reservations:** not accepted. **Features:** In the Plateau Mont-Royal district, the well-known breakfast and lunch restaurant has earned a regular clientele by offering wholesome food, such as omelets, bagels with lox or cream cheese, bacon with eggs, sausages and great fresh-pressed orange juice. On weekends, expect a 10- to 15-minute wait at the door, even with a reservation. Casual dress; beer & wine only. **Parking:** street. **Cards:** AX, DC, MC, VI.

BRATWURST RESTAURANT   **Lunch:** $5-$8   **Dinner:** $5-$8   Phone: 514/484-8072   **58**
German   **Location:** Just w of rue Hingston. 6107 rue Sherbrooke ouest H4A 1Y4. **Hours:** noon-9 pm. **Reservations:** not accepted. **Features:** The simple West End diner serves quality grilled Bavarian sausages on rye with all the trimmings. Sausage choices include knackwurst, weisswurst, schublig and debreciner, while the trimmings are of the sauerkraut, potato salad and crisp, golden Swiss-style "rosti" potato varieties. Casual dress; cocktails. **Parking:** street. **Cards:** AX, DC, DS, MC, VI.

CAFE SANTROPOL   **Lunch:** $8-$12   **Dinner:** $8-$12   Phone: 514/842-3110   **26**
Canadian   **Location:** Corner of rue Duluth. 3990 rue St-Urbain H2W 1T7. **Hours:** 11:30 am-midnight. Closed: 1/1, 12/25. **Features:** The lively, eclectic cafe offers health-conscious meals, such as gourmet sandwiches, vegetarian chili, fruit juices, creative desserts and a wide variety of quality teas and fair-trade organic coffees. A seasonal garden terrace is also provided. Casual dress. **Parking:** street.

🍴

(See map and index starting on p. 420)

CHALET BAR-B-Q ROTISSERIE　　　Lunch: $6-$9　　　Dinner: $8-$10　　　Phone: 514/489-7235　　(48)
Barbecue
Location: Just w of boul Decarie. 5456 rue Sherbrooke ouest H4A 1V9. **Hours:** 11 am-10 pm, Fri & Sat-midnight. **Reservations:** accepted. **Features:** The simply decorated family restaurant is a favourite for broiled chicken cooked on a rotisserie over hardwood coals. Meals are served with barbecue sauce, a toasted roll and freshly cut fries. Casual dress; beer & wine only. **Parking:** on-site. **Cards:** MC, VI.

CHEZ BENNY　　　Lunch: $6-$17　　　Dinner: $6-$17　　　Phone: 514/735-1836　　(34)
Kosher
Location: Just e of boul Decarie. 5071 chemin Queen Mary H3W 1X4. **Hours:** 11 am-11 pm. Closed: Jewish holidays; closed for Sabbath (Fri after sunset-Sat after sunset). **Features:** The busy glatt kosher cafeteria focuses on Israeli-style fast food: schnitzel, smoked meat, shish taouk, hot dogs, burgers, mixed grill and a salad bar. Honey pastry tastes great for dessert. Patrons pick up a tray, order at the counter, move down the line to collect their order from the kitchen staff and then seat themselves. Casual dress; beer only. **Parking:** street. **Cards:** MC, VI.

COTE ST-LUC BAR-B-Q　　　Lunch: $7-$11　　　Dinner: $7-$11　　　Phone: 514/737-5007　　(35)
Barbecue
Location: Hwy 520 W, exit Hickmore, just w on north side service road; in St-Laurent sector. 6971 Cote-de-liesse ouest H4T 1Z3. **Hours:** 11 am-10 pm, Wed-Sat to 11 pm, Sun 4 pm-10 pm. Closed: 1/1, 12/25. **Reservations:** accepted. **Features:** The family restaurant specializes in charcoal-broiled barbecue chicken as well as club sandwiches, brochettes, salads and chicken noodle soup. Take-out orders are welcomed. Casual dress; beer & wine only. **Parking:** on-site. **Cards:** AX, CB, DC, JC, MC, VI.

COTE ST-LUC BAR-B-Q　　　Lunch: $7-$10　　　Dinner: $7-$10　　　Phone: 514/488-4011　　(39)
Barbecue
Location: Just w of boul Decarie. 5403 Cote St-Luc Rd H3X 2X3. **Hours:** 11 am-11 pm. Closed: 12/25. **Reservations:** not accepted. **Features:** A city favorite since 1953, the family restaurant specializes in charcoal-broiled barbecue chicken. Takeout orders are welcomed. Casual dress; wine only. **Parking:** street. **Cards:** AX, MC, VI.

DUNNS FAMOUS　　　Lunch: $7-$20　　　Dinner: $7-$20　　　Phone: 514/385-1927　　(5)
Deli/Subs
Sandwiches
Location: Hwy 40, exit boul L'Acadie, then 0.6 mi (1 km) n; in Marche Central Shopping Centre. 1029 rue du Marche-Central H4N 1J8. **Hours:** 11 am-midnight, Sun & Mon-11 pm. Closed: 1/1, 12/25. **Reservations:** accepted. **Features:** This suburban delicatessen specializes in Montreal-style smoked meat on rye, grilled steaks, latkes, matzo ball soup, chopped liver and club rolls. For dessert, cheesecake is hard to beat. Casual dress; cocktails. **Parking:** on-site. **Cards:** MC, VI.

GIBEAU ORANGE JULEP　　　Lunch: $5-$10　　　Dinner: $5-$10　　　Phone: 514/738-7486　　(32)
Canadian
Location: Corner of rue Pare. 7700 boul Decarie H4P 2H4. **Hours:** 8 am-midnight; 24 hours 6/1-8/31. **Features:** In a three-story building shaped like an orange, the family-friendly fast-food restaurant is easy to spot from the Decarie expressway. Not surprisingly, the house specialty is frothy, fresh-squeezed, sweetened orange juice. This also is a good place to grab an inexpensive burger, hot dog and fries. On Wednesday and Thursday nights, vintage and custom cars drop by. Casual dress; **Parking:** on-site.

HOT SPOT RESTAURANT　　　Lunch: $6-$15　　　Dinner: $6-$15　　　Phone: 514/937-7768　　(36)
Caribbean
Location: Corner of rue Laporte. 3901 rue St-Jacques ouest H4C 1H7. **Hours:** 7 am-11 pm. **Reservations:** accepted. **Features:** This modest diner is a hot spot for authentic Caribbean food. The breakfast menu offers callalou (spinach), saltfish, eggs, plantains, yams and dumplings. At lunch and dinner, guests may sample cow foot stew, ackee or escovich fish, roasted goat and a choice of chicken done five ways (curried, jerk, stewed, barbecued or fried). Quench your thirst with a ginger beer, horse tonic or cucumber june-plum juice. Late-night delivery and take-out is offered as well as live music some nights. Casual dress; cocktails. **Parking:** street. **Cards:** VI.

KHYBER PASS CUISINE AFGHANE　　　Dinner: $15-$30　　　Phone: 514/844-7131　　(17)
Ethnic
Location: Corner of rue Berri. 506 ave Duluth est H2L 1A7. **Hours:** 5 pm-11 pm. **Reservations:** accepted. **Features:** The simple dining room has tightly spaced tables with enchanting Afghanistan motifs and music. Inexpensive menu items include Afghan kebab brochettes—made with filet mignon, chicken, lamb or quail—as well as braised leg of lamb, basmati rice and mint coriander salad. Yogurt flavored with Afghan spices is a popular dessert. Casual dress. **Parking:** street. **Cards:** VI.

LA BINERIE MONT-ROYAL　　　Lunch: $7-$11　　　Dinner: $7-$11　　　Phone: 514/285-9078　　(11)
Quebecois
Location: Just w of rue St-Denis. 367 rue Mont-Royal est H2T 1R1. **Hours:** 6 am-8 pm, Sat & Sun 7:30 am-3 pm. Closed major holidays; also 7/11-7/31. **Features:** Representative of dishes at the diner are French-Canadian tourtiere meat pie and baked beans. Casual dress; beer only. **Parking:** street.

LA CHRONIQUE　　　Lunch: $25　　　Dinner: $28-$38　　　Phone: 514/271-3095　　(15)
International
Location: Between ave du Parc and rue St-Urbain. 99 rue Laurier ouest H2T 2N6. **Hours:** noon-2:30 & 5-10 pm, Sat from 6 pm. Closed major holidays; also Sun & Mon. **Reservations:** required. **Features:** Internationally-influenced fine Quebec cuisine is served in this small stylish dining room. The exciting menu bursts with creative food pairings and eye-catching presentations. Some weekends feature only a multi-course prix fixe menu. A la carte menu items include fresh fish, pan-seared foie gras with a duck confit brioche, stuffed rabbit with red onions and scalloped potatoes, deer with potato crepe and grilled portabellas, and blackened duck with grilled shrimp. The service is refined. Dressy casual; cocktails. **Parking:** street. **Cards:** AX, MC, VI.

LA FONDERIE　　　Dinner: $16-$32　　　Phone: 514/524-2100　　(8)
Fondue
Location: Between Boyer and de Mentana sts. 964 Rachel St E H2J 2J3. **Hours:** 5 pm-11 pm. Closed: 12/24, 12/25; also 6/24. **Reservations:** suggested. **Features:** Fond of fondue? For 22 years La Fonderie has been satisfying the palates of Montrealers with its successful fondues. However, if fondue is not your thing La Fonderie also offers steak, lamb, fish and seafood selections. Casual dress; cocktails. **Parking:** street. **Cards:** AX, DC, MC, VI.

(See map and index starting on p. 420)

LA LOUISIANE
♦♦♦
Cajun
Dinner: $9-$30   **Phone:** 514/369-3073   [53]
Location: 0.4 mi (0.6 km) w of the Decarie Expwy; corner of rue Regent. 5850 rue Sherbrooke ouest H4A 1X5. **Hours:** 5:30 pm-10 pm, Fri & Sat-11 pm, Sun-9:30 pm. Closed: 1/1, 12/25. **Reservations:** not accepted. **Features:** The popular Cajun restaurant does not accept individual reservations, so a short wait is to be expected on busy nights. Among menu selections are hush puppies, sweet potato fries, chicken wings, coconut beer shrimp, barbecue shrimp, shrimp or crawfish etouffee, crab cakes, blackened catfish, jambalaya, red bean soup gumbo and Southern pasta dishes. Casual dress; cocktails. **Parking:** street. **Cards:** AX, CB, DC, DS, MC.

LE COIN D'ASIE
♦♦ ♦♦
Vietnamese
Lunch: $6-$17   **Dinner:** $10-$19   **Phone:** 514/482-4035   [55]
Location: Just e of rue Hampton. 6020 rue Sherbrooke ouest H4A 1X9. **Hours:** 11:30 am-2:30 & 5-10 pm, Sat & Sun from 5 pm. Closed: 1/1, 12/24, 12/25; also Mon. **Reservations:** suggested. **Features:** Casually elegant surroundings make diners cozy at the West End dining room, where the menu centers on Vietnamese and other Asian dishes. Among examples are Tonkinese soup, seafood and fish, grilled meats, imperial rolls, fried won tons, sizzling platters, ginger chicken, salt-and-pepper calamari, Vietnamese steak, beef chop suey, fried rice with barbecue pork, noodles and several shrimp dishes. Casual dress; cocktails. **Parking:** street. **Cards:** MC, VI.

LE COMMENSAL
♦♦ ♦♦
Vegetarian
Lunch: $11-$17   **Dinner:** $11-$17   **Phone:** 514/733-9755
Location: Just n of chemin Queen Mary. 5199 chemin de la Cote des Neiges H3T 1Y1. **Hours:** 11 am-9 pm, Thurs-Sat to 10 pm. Closed: 1/1, 12/25. **Reservations:** accepted. **Features:** An upscale self-service buffet features an extensive selection of creative hot and cold items, such as leek pot pie, sweet potato kasha and lasagna, plus a variety of desserts, everything of which is exclusively vegetarian. The pleasant, contemporary surroundings change often as new paintings are displayed. Casual dress; beer & wine only. **Parking:** street. **Cards:** MC, VI.

LE GRILL MIDTOWN
♦♦
Kosher
Lunch: $6-$16   **Dinner:** $6-$16   **Phone:** 514/739-3800   [33]
Location: On east side service road for Hwy 15 (Decarie Expwy); corner of ave Plamondon; in Quality Hotel Midtown. 6445 boul Decarie H3W 3E1. **Hours:** noon-9 pm, Fri-sunset. Closed: Sat & Jewish holidays. **Reservations:** not accepted. **Features:** This Israeli-style cafeteria features glatt kosher comfort foods, including hamburgers, fried brochettes, hotdogs, mixed grill, onion rings, grilled vegetables and a wide selection of chicken dishes. Apple or cherry pie are available for dessert, and there is a children's menu. Order and pay at the counter and wait at your table for the order to arrive. Casual dress. **Parking:** on-site. **Cards:** AX, DC, DS, MC, VI.

LE MAISTRE
♦♦ ♦♦
French
Lunch: $13-$15   **Dinner:** $21-$24   **Phone:** 514/481-2109   [47]
Location: Corner of rue Harvard. 5700 ave Monkland H4A 1E6. **Hours:** 5:30 pm-10 pm, Fri also 11:30 am-2 pm. Closed: 1/1, 12/24, 12/25. **Reservations:** suggested. **Features:** This residential townhouse offers a quaint dining room operated by a French couple. Menu offerings include duck confit, fresh fish, filet of beef, lamb, veal, pork, kidneys, sweetbreads and some game specialties. Desserts are delicious and creatively presented. Casual dress. **Parking:** street. **Cards:** AX, DC, MC, VI.

LE STADIUM CLUB RESTAURANT & BAR
♦♦ ♦♦
Italian
Lunch: $11-$15   **Dinner:** $11-$32   **Phone:** 514/253-5195   [3]
Location: Corner of rue Viau; just e of Botanical Garden and Olympic Stadium. 5000 rue Sherbrooke est H1V 1A1. **Hours:** 7 am-11 pm. **Reservations:** accepted. **Features:** This casual and stylish hotel restaurant impresses patrons with its views of the nearby Olympic Stadium. The menu features a variety of fine Italian dishes, steak and seafood. Seating is offered at tables and in more comfortable and intimate booths. Casual dress; cocktails. **Parking:** on-site. **Cards:** AX, DC, MC, VI.

LEZVOS
♦♦ ♦♦
Mediterranean
Dinner: $11-$22   **Phone:** 514/523-8722   [7]
Location: Just w of rue Brebeuf. 1227A ave Mont-Royal est H2J 1Y2. **Hours:** 5 pm-10 pm, Fri & Sat-11 pm. Closed: Sun. **Reservations:** accepted. **Features:** This lively and casual taverna in a trendy neighborhood has tightly spaced tables and a tasty menu of Mediterranean delights including grilled, fresh seafood. Reservations are strongly recommended. Casual dress; cocktails. **Parking:** street. **Cards:** DC, MC, VI.

LEZVOS WEST
♦♦ ♦♦
Mediterranean
Dinner: $11-$22   **Phone:** 514/484-0400   [40]
Location: Just s of boul Monkland. 4235A boul Decarie H4A 3K4. **Hours:** 5 pm-10 pm, Fri & Sat-11 pm. **Reservations:** accepted. **Features:** This stylish and comfortable restaurant near the popular Monkland village offers a menu of Mediterranean dishes including grilled, fresh seafood. Casual dress; cocktails. **Parking:** street. **Cards:** DC, MC, VI.

LINDOS PSAROPOULA
♦♦ ♦♦
Greek
Lunch: $8-$15   **Dinner:** $17-$30   **Phone:** 514/271-2130   [22]
Location: Just n of ave Fairmount. 5258 ave du Parc H2V 4G7. **Hours:** noon-3 & 5-midnight, Sat-Mon from 5 pm. Closed: 1/1, 12/25. **Reservations:** suggested. **Features:** The traditional taverna features authentic Greek music and food. Freshwater and saltwater fish, such as delicious grilled red snapper, stand out as specialties on a menu that also includes meat dishes and tempting appetizers. Service is attentive. Casual dress; cocktails. **Parking:** valet and street. **Cards:** AX, DC, MC, VI.

MESQUITE
♦♦ ♦♦
South Barbecue
Lunch: $9-$13   **Dinner:** $9-$25   **Phone:** 514/487-5066   [42]
Location: Corner of rue Notre-Dame-de-Grace. 3857 boul Decarie H4A 3J6. **Hours:** 11 am-3 & 5-10:30 pm. Closed: 12/25. **Reservations:** suggested. **Features:** On the western outskirts of the city, the casual eatery treats guests to Southern barbecue, including ribs, chicken, deep-fried hush puppies, brisket, catfish, fresh salmon, pork and shrimp. A slice of Mississippi mud pie is a sweet meal-ender. Casual dress; cocktails. **Parking:** street. **Cards:** MC, VI.

(See map and index starting on p. 420)

MILOS RESTAURANT   **Lunch:** $30-$42   **Dinner:** $30-$42   **Phone:** 514/272-3522   19
Greek
Location: Between ave Fairmount and St-Viateur. 5357 ave du Parc H2V 4G9. **Hours:** noon-3 & 5:30-midnight, Sat & Sun from 5:30 pm. Closed: 1/1, 12/25; also for lunch major holidays. **Reservations:** suggested. **Features:** The trendy taverna features Mediterranean-style decor, comfortable surroundings and a lively atmosphere. At the heart of the menu are skillful preparations of an excellent variety of fresh fish. Grilled octopus salad with capers is superb. Casual dress; cocktails. **Parking:** valet and street. **Cards:** AX, DC, MC, VI.

MOISHE'S STEAK HOUSE   **Lunch:** $18-$29   **Dinner:** $26-$52   **Phone:** 514/845-1696   25
Steak & Seafood
Location: Between rue Pine and Duluth. 3961 boul St-Laurent H2W 1Y4. **Hours:** 11:30 am-2:30 & 5:30-11 pm, Sat from 5 pm. Closed: 1/1, 12/25; also for lunch holidays. **Reservations:** suggested. **Features:** A favorite of Montrealers, the established restaurant bustles with activity, especially on weekends. The atmosphere is upscale for a steakhouse, with quality table settings and dark-wood wine cabinets. For dessert, try a delicious French pastry. Dressy casual; cocktails. **Parking:** on-site. **Cards:** AX, DC, MC, VI.

MONKLAND TAVERN   **Lunch:** $10-$20   **Dinner:** $14-$26   **Phone:** 514/486-5768   43
California
Location: Corner of Old Orchard Ave. 5555 Monkland Ave H4A 1E1. **Hours:** 11:30 am-3 & 6-11 pm, Sat & Sun from 6 pm. Closed: 12/24-12/26; also 12/31. **Reservations:** not accepted. **Features:** The popular neighborhood bistro exudes a warm, lively aura. Fresh pasta and salmon are specialties on a menu of California-style dishes, including a variety of salads and gourmet sandwiches. A good selection of microbrewed beers is offered. Seating on the seasonal terrace is hard to come by during warm weather. Children are not admitted. Casual dress; cocktails. **Parking:** street. **Cards:** AX, DC, MC, VI.

NICKELS RESTAURANT   **Lunch:** $9-$20   **Dinner:** $9-$20   **Phone:** 514/735-7622   31
Canadian
Location: Just n of Queen Mary. 5252 chemin Cote-des-Neiges H3T 1X8. **Hours:** 6 am-midnight, Fri-2 am, Sat & Sun 7 am-midnight. **Reservations:** accepted. **Features:** This Quebec chain of delicatessens specializes in Montreal-style smoked meat sandwiches, as well as pasta, burgers, fish, salads and seafood. Casual dress; cocktails. **Parking:** street. **Cards:** AX, MC, VI.

NUANCES   *Menu on AAA.com*   **Dinner:** $39-$45   **Phone:** 514/392-2708   28
French
Location: S on pont Champlain, follow signs from Montreal; on 5th floor of Casino de Montreal. 1 ave du Casino H3C 4W7. **Hours:** 5:30 pm-11 pm, Fri & Sat-11:30 pm. **Reservations:** suggested. **Features:** Like an oasis, the contemporary dining room sits atop the Casino de Montreal. Unlike patrons busy at the gaming tables, diners in search of haute cuisine will always turn up winners here. Every table offers a view of the city skyline. Most servers are extremely knowledgeable about the food and wine selections. Many waiters are trained sommeliers. Semi-formal attire; cocktails. **Parking:** valet. **Cards:** AX, CB, DC, DS, JC, MC, VI.

PIZZAFIORE   **Lunch:** $8-$16   **Dinner:** $8-$16   **Phone:** 514/735-1555   30
Italian
Location: Just e of chemin Cote-des-Neiges. 3518 Lacombe Ave H3T 1M1. **Hours:** 11 am-10:30 pm. Closed: 12/24, 12/25; also 12/31. **Reservations:** accepted. **Features:** This popular family pizzeria offers a variety of more than 30 types of oven-baked pizzas, as well as calzones, pasta, chicken parmigiana, lasagna, veal scallopine and panini with Italian sausage. Casual dress; cocktails. **Parking:** street. **Cards:** AX, DC, MC, VI.

QUARTIER PERSE   **Lunch:** $11-$23   **Dinner:** $11-$23   **Phone:** 514/488-6367   38
Persian
Location: Corner of rue Monkland. 4241 boul Decarie H4A 3K4. **Hours:** 11:30 am-10 pm, Fri-11 pm, Sat 5 pm-11 pm, Sun 5 pm-10 pm. **Features:** This casual diner is an ideal place to sample inexpensive Persian cuisine including kebabs of chicken, filet mignon or lamb. A seasonal exterior terrace is available. Casual dress; cocktails. **Parking:** street. **Cards:** MC, VI.

RESTAURANT & TAVERNE MAGNAN   **Lunch:** $8-$20   **Dinner:** $15-$27   **Phone:** 514/935-9647   37
Steak & Seafood
Location: Corner of Charlevoix. 2602 rue St-Patrick H3K 1B8. **Hours:** 11 am-11 pm, Sun-10 pm. Closed: 12/25. **Reservations:** accepted. **Features:** Roast beef, Angus rib steaks, pigs' knuckles and grilled seafood are specialties at the informal eatery, which includes a boisterous tavern and a separate casual dining room downstairs. Casual dress; cocktails. **Parking:** on-site. **Cards:** AX, DC, MC, VI.

RESTAURANT AUBERGE DU CHEVAL BLANC   **Lunch:** $11-$15   **Dinner:** $18-$40   **Phone:** 514/642-4091   1
French
Location: Corner of 85ieme ave; in Pointe-aux-Trembles district. 15760 rue Notre-Dame est H1A 1X5. **Hours:** 11:30 am-2:30 & 5:30-10 pm, Sat & Sun from 5:30 pm. Closed: Mon & Tues. **Reservations:** suggested. **Features:** Diners range from lively groups to quiet couples at this intimate family-run, east-end restaurant. The menu of fine food specializes in French cuisine, steaks and game specialties, including Boileau red deer, duck, rabbit and bison. Other menu highlights include ostrich, Charlevoix veal, filet mignon, rib steaks, fish and seafood. Live music is performed Thursday to Saturday evenings. Casual dress. **Parking:** on-site. **Cards:** AX, MC, VI.

RESTAURANT AU PIED DE COCHON   **Dinner:** $12-$36   **Phone:** 514/281-1114   16
Quebecois
Location: Just w of rue St-Hubert. 536 rue Duluth est H2L 1A9. **Hours:** 5 pm-midnight. Closed: 12/24, 12/25; also 1/2 & Mon. **Reservations:** suggested. **Features:** The casual eatery strips away traditional fine-cuisine formality. Fresh, high-quality ingredients factor into such dishes as duck with foie gras, which is cooked in a can and opened at the table; poutine (fries, curd cheese, foie gras and gravy); pied de cochon (pig's feet) stuffed with foie gras; and venison tartare. The fine wine list includes by-the-glass and bottle choices. Fresh seafood is kept on ice before cooking and then carefully prepared and served on multi-tiered dishes. Casual dress; cocktails. **Parking:** street. **Cards:** AX, MC, VI.

(See map and index starting on p. 420)

RESTAURANT CHEZ DOVAL   Lunch: $9-$20   Dinner: $9-$20   Phone: 514/843-3390   ㉑
Portuguese
Location: Just e of boul St-Laurent. 150 Marie-Anne est H2W 1A5. **Hours:** 8 am-11 pm, Sun from 9 am. Closed: 1/1, 12/25. **Reservations:** suggested. **Features:** Varied preparations of Portuguese-style fare are cooked on a wood-burning grill. The casual eatery's menu features grilled sardines, chicken, steak with eggs, calamari, shrimp and brochettes. Casual dress; cocktails. **Parking:** street. **Cards:** AX, DC, MC, VI.

RESTAURANT GANGES   Lunch: $7-$10   Dinner: $9-$15   Phone: 514/488-8850   ㊉
Indian
Location: Just e of rue Hingston. 6079 rue Sherbrooke ouest H4A 1Y2. **Hours:** 11:45 am-2 & 5-10 pm, Sun from 5 pm. Closed: 12/25. **Reservations:** accepted. **Features:** Amid casually elegant surroundings on the western outskirts of Montreal, well-attired servers promptly deliver Indian dishes seasoned with fresh herbs and spices. The menu includes tender tandoori chicken, fish and shrimp courses, biryanis (rice with vegetables or chicken), naan bread and tasty lamb, beef and chicken curries. Casual dress; cocktails. **Parking:** street. **Cards:** AX, MC, VI.
ⓨ

RESTAURANT HELENE DE
CHAMPLAIN   Lunch: $15-$21   Dinner: $24-$40   Phone: 514/395-2424   ㉗
(AAA)

French
Location: From Jacques-Cartier Bridge, exit at Parc Jean-Drapeau, follow signs. 200 Tour de l'Isle H3C 4G8. **Hours:** 11:30 am-2:30 & 5:30-10 pm, Fri & Sat 5:30 pm-11 pm. Closed: 1/1; also for dinner Mon & Tues & for lunch major holidays. **Reservations:** suggested. **Features:** The cozy restaurant is set in a historic, stone-walled mansion on the former Expo '67 site, adjacent to the former U.S. pavilion. Menu highlights include Quebec veal, fish, beef and chicken. Casual dress; cocktails. **Parking:** on-site. **Cards:** AX, DC, MC, VI.
ⓨ

RESTAURANT IL PIATTO DELLA NONNA   Lunch: $9-$14   Dinner: $15-$27   Phone: 514/843-6069   ⑩
Italian
Location: Between rue Fairmount and Laurier. 5171 boul St-Laurent H2T 1R9. **Hours:** noon-2 & 6-10 pm, Thurs & Fri-11 pm, Sat 6 pm-11 pm, Sun 6 pm-9:30 pm. Closed: 1/1, 12/25, 12/26; also 12/27, 1/2 & 1/3. **Reservations:** accepted. **Features:** A simple decor of wood tables and chairs give diners their first hint that the focus here is on affordable preparations of home-style Italian food. The service is friendly and familial. Casual dress; cocktails. **Parking:** street. **Cards:** MC, VI.

RESTAURANT JUNI   Lunch: $21-$29   Dinner: $21-$35   Phone: 514/276-5864   ⑳
Japanese
Location: Just w of rue St-Urbain. 156 rue Laurier ouest H2T 2N7. **Hours:** 11:30 am-2 & 6-10 pm, Fri & Sat-11 pm. Closed: 1/1, 12/25; also Mon for lunch. **Reservations:** suggested. **Features:** Artfully presented sushi stands out on a fine menu that also includes dishes inspired by French, Italian and Mediterranean flavors. Guests can sample California rolls, a Peking duck appetizer and tasty preparations of sea urchin, eel, salmon, yellowfin tuna, king crab and soft-shell crab. The service is attentive and the atmosphere casual at this stylish restaurant. Casual dress; cocktails. **Parking:** street. **Cards:** AX, DC, MC, VI.

RESTAURANT MOMESSO   Lunch: $5-$11   Dinner: $5-$11   Phone: 514/484-0005   ㊿
Deli/Subs
Sandwiches
Location: Just w of ave Girouard. 5562 Upper Lachine Rd H4A 2A7. **Hours:** 7 am-10 pm, Thurs & Fri-11 pm, Sat 8 am-11 pm. Closed major holidays; also Sun & 7/15-7/30. **Reservations:** accepted, for dinner. **Features:** The simple diner tops steak and sausage subs with just enough hot sauce to elicit a smile. Other popular items include veggie and chicken subs, pizza, hamburgers and poutine. Hearty breakfasts are served every day except Sunday. Casual dress; cocktails. **Parking:** street.

RIB 'N REEF STEAKHOUSE   Lunch: $21-$30   Dinner: $21-$58   Phone: 514/735-1601   ㉙
(AAA)

Steak House
Location: Hwy 15, exit Jean-Talon on east side service road. 8105 boul Decarie H4P 2H5. **Hours:** 11:30 am-11 pm, Sun from 4 pm. Closed: for dinner 12/24 & for lunch 12/25. **Reservations:** suggested. **Features:** High-quality preparations of prime steak, roast beef, lobster and fresh fish make up most of the menu at the cozy steakhouse. Comfortable, upscale decor characterizes the restaurant, a local landmark since 1961. Dressy casual; cocktails. **Parking:** valet. **Cards:** AX, DC, JC, MC, VI.
ⓨ

RISTORANTE LA DORA   Lunch: $9-$23   Dinner: $9-$23   Phone: 514/255-8841   ②
Italian
Location: Corner of rue Arcand; 1.5 mi (2.5 km) e of the Olympic Stadium. 6837 rue Sherbrooke est H1N 1C7. **Hours:** 11:30 am-10 pm, Fri & Sat-11 pm. Closed: Sun; 12/23-1/1. **Reservations:** suggested. **Features:** Near the Olympic stadium, the popular, casual restaurant, family-run since 1940, specializes in quality food. On the menu are many selections of pasta, as well as breaded veal, mussels, fish and other seafood. The walls are white plaster, the tables tightly spaced and the wood chairs unpadded, evoking the charm of a traditional trattoria. Casual dress; cocktails. **Parking:** on-site. **Cards:** AX, DC, MC, VI.

ST-HUBERT   Lunch: $7-$20   Dinner: $7-$20   Phone: 514/844-9521
Canadian
Location: Just s of Mont-Royal. 4462 rue St-Denis H2J 2L1. **Hours:** 11 am-11 pm, Fri & Sat-midnight. Closed: 12/25. **Reservations:** accepted. **Features:** The pleasantly decorated family-friendly restaurant serves affordable chicken dinners, ribs, club sandwiches, chicken wings, salads, soups and hot chicken sandwiches. The children's menu includes animal nuggets. Casual dress; cocktails. **Parking:** on-site. **Cards:** AX, DC, MC, VI.

ST-VIATEUR BAGEL & CAFE   Lunch: $5-$12   Dinner: $5-$12   Phone: 514/487-8051   ㊹
Deli/Subs
Sandwiches
Location: Corner of rue Oxford. 5629 Monkland Ave H4A 1E2. **Hours:** 6:30 am-11 pm. Closed: 3/24, 12/25. **Features:** The bustling, stylish cafe serves legendary Montreal bagels baked in a wood-burning oven, using the same recipe as the original St-Viateur Street bagel shop, in operation since 1957. The menu lists varied bagel sandwiches, salads, specialty coffees and tempting desserts. A popular outdoor terrace opens seasonally. Casual dress; cocktails. **Parking:** street. **Cards:** MC, VI.

SCORES ROTISSERIE   Lunch: $6-$20   Dinner: $6-$20   Phone: 514/255-6060
Barbecue
Location: Just e of rue Viau; facing Olympic Village. 5350 rue Sherbrooke est H1V 1A1. **Hours:** 11 am-11 pm. Closed: 12/25. **Reservations:** accepted. **Features:** The chain of family restaurants presents a varied menu that includes rotisserie chicken, ribs, salad-bar items, sandwiches, poutine and sugar, lemon or pecan pie. Casual dress; cocktails. **Parking:** on-site. **Cards:** AX, MC, VI.

(See map and index starting on p. 420)

SOY | **Lunch:** $7-$14 | **Dinner:** $9-$17 | **Phone:** 514/499-9399 (9)

Asian

Location: Just n of ave Fairmount. 5258 boul St-Laurent H2T 1S1. **Hours:** 11:30 am-9:30 pm, Fri-10:30 pm, Sat 5 pm-10:30 pm, Sun 5 pm-9:30 pm. Closed: Mon. **Reservations:** accepted. **Features:** Eclectic yet casual decor fills the dining room, where patrons sit down to such Asian dishes as pork dumplings, won ton ravioli with peanut sauce, Szechuan duck with crepes, beef kalbi, crispy shrimp, grilled portobello mushrooms and hot-and-sour or spicy vermicelli soup. Affordable dishes, which are ideal for sharing, are brought to the table in the Chinese tradition: when each is ready rather than all together. Lunch specials include soup, rice, an entree, biscuit and tea or coffee. Casual dress; cocktails. **Parking:** street. **Cards:** AX, MC, VI.

TAPEO-BAR A TAPAS | **Lunch:** $4-$15 | **Dinner:** $4-$15 | **Phone:** 514/495-1999 (4)

Spanish

Location: Just e of rue Berri. 511 de Villeray est H2R 1H5. **Hours:** noon-3 & 5:30-11 pm, Sat from 5:30 pm. Closed: Mon, Sun, 12/23-1/7 & 8/15-8/31. **Reservations:** suggested. **Features:** Spanish matador paintings adorn the walls of the lively European-style tapas bar, where affordable appetizer-size dishes include seared tuna, octopus salad, sardines, calamari, paella, braised ribs, matchstick fries and seasonal fish and seafood. For dessert, creme brulee is a classic. Seating is offered at table or the counter. Casual dress; cocktails. **Parking:** on-site and street. **Cards:** MC, VI.

TCHANG KIANG RESTAURANT | **Lunch:** $6-$10 | **Dinner:** $10-$20 | **Phone:** 514/487-7744 (57)

Sichuan

Location: Just w of ave Hampton. 6066 rue Sherbrooke ouest H4A 1Y1. **Hours:** 11 am-2 & 5-10 pm, Sat & Sun from 5 pm. Closed: Mon, 7/7-7/30 & 12/22-1/7. **Reservations:** suggested. **Features:** The casual dining room serves an appealing variety of Szechuan and Peking specialties, including moo shoo duck, General Tao chicken, lemon chicken, orange beef, crispy spinach shrimp, Singapore noodles, Peking shrimp, curry pork, Imperial spiced chicken and fresh-ginger beef. Casual dress; cocktails. **Parking:** street. **Cards:** AX, DC, JC, MC, VI.

TEHRAN RESTAURANT | **Lunch:** $12-$18 | **Dinner:** $12-$18 | **Phone:** 514/488-0400 (45)

Middle Eastern

Location: Corner of Grey. 5065 boul de Maisonneuve ouest H4A 1Y9. **Hours:** noon-10 pm. **Reservations:** accepted, Fri-Sun. **Features:** Varied Iranian dishes are prepared at the casual diner in a residential neighborhood facing the Vendome subway station. Thick lentil soup, basmati rice with red currants and marinated chicken in tomato sauce are highlights on an affordable menu that also includes filet mignon and chicken brochettes. Yogurt soda and Iranian tea are good thirst-quenchers. Casual dress. **Parking:** street.

THAI GRILL | **Lunch:** $10-$17 | **Dinner:** $10-$28 | **Phone:** 514/270-5566 (13)

Thai

Location: Corner of ave Laurier. 5101 boul St-Laurent H2T 1R9. **Hours:** 11:30 am-2:30 & 5-11 pm, Thurs-Sat to midnight, Sun 5 pm-11 pm. Closed: 12/25. **Reservations:** suggested. **Features:** The trendy, sophisticated restaurant is a cozy place in which to sample a wide variety of Thai dishes, ranging from spicy to mild. Seafood selections, such as bass and red snapper, and curried noodles are representative of menu choices. Casual dress; cocktails. **Parking:** street. **Cards:** AX, DC, DS, MC, VI.

VILLAGE SZECHUAN | **Lunch:** $7-$15 | **Dinner:** $10-$15 | **Phone:** 514/488-0096 (41)

Sichuan

Location: Just s of ave Monkland. 4242 boul Decarie H4A 3K3. **Hours:** 11 am-10:30 pm. Closed: 12/25. **Reservations:** accepted. **Features:** Just off the Decarie Expressway near the trendy Monkland village, this casual Chinese restaurant offers many affordably priced dishes including an array of Szechuan favorites. Casual dress; cocktails. **Parking:** street. **Cards:** AX, MC, VI.

WILENSKY'S LIGHT LUNCH INC | **Lunch:** $5-$10 | **Phone:** 514/271-0247 (12)

Deli/Subs Sandwiches

Location: Just w of boul St-Laurent. 34 ave Fairmount ouest H2T 2M1. **Hours:** 9 am-4 pm. Closed major holidays; also Sat, Sun & 2 weeks in July. **Reservations:** not accepted. **Features:** Family run since 1932, the vintage corner delicatessen served as a location for the 1974 film The Apprenticeship of Duddy Kravitz, starring Richard Dreyfuss. The decor remains virtually untouched. Patrons can take a seat at the counter and enjoy a Wilensky special sandwich made with salami, bologna and a choice of cheese or nosh on a chopped egg sandwich, half-sour dill pickles, karnatzel or an all-beef hot dog. **Parking:** street.

The following restaurant has not been evaluated by AAA but is listed for your information only.

RESTAURANT CAFETERIA | **Phone:** 514/849-3855

fyi

Not evaluated. **Location:** Corner of rue Prince-Arthur. 3581 boul St-Laurent H2X 2T6. **Features:** On a trendy street renowned for its nightlife, the bistro and bar is an ideal place to experience life on "The Main." The varied menu features daily specials of market-fresh cuisine, including fish, chicken, seafood and meat dishes, including filet mignon. Hearty breakfasts are served each morning. At lunchtime, the menu centers on lighter fare, including salads and burgers. In later evening, the bar does brisk business, and a busy party atmosphere prevails.

The Montreal Vicinity

ANJOU pop. 38,015 (See map and index starting on p. 420)

WHERE TO STAY

QUALITY HOTEL EAST | *Book great rates at AAA.com* | **Phone:** (514)493-6363 (17)

CAA SAVE

6/7-9/30	1P: $137-$143	2P: $143-$148	XP: $5	F18
1/1-4/30	1P: $136-$141	2P: $141-$146	XP: $5	F18
5/1-6/6 & 10/1-12/31	1P: $132-$137	2P: $137-$143	XP: $5	F18

Small-scale Hotel

Location: Hwy 40, exit 78, just n on boul Langelier, 0.4 mi (0.7 km) e on rue Jarry, then s; in Anjou sector. 8100 ave Neuville H1J 2T2. Fax: 514/493-6412. **Facility:** 157 one-bedroom standard units. 9 stories, interior corridors. **Parking:** on-site, winter plug-ins. **Terms:** cancellation fee imposed, package plans. **Amenities:** irons, hair dryers. **Dining:** 6:30 am-10:30 pm, Sat & Sun from 7:30 am, cocktails. **Guest Services:** valet laundry, wireless Internet. **Business Services:** meeting rooms. **Cards:** AX, CB, DC, DS, JC, MC, VI. *(See color ad card insert)*

SOME UNITS

FEE FEE

(See map and index starting on p. 420)

──────── WHERE TO DINE ────────

IL PAZZESCO   Lunch: $11-$30   Dinner: $12-$34   Phone: 514/353-3801   61
▼▼▼   **Location:** Hwy 40 est, exit 78, just n to rue Jarry, then 0.7 km e; in Anjou sector. 7031 rue Jarry est H1J 1G3.
Italian   **Hours:** 11 am-11 pm, Thurs-Sat to midnight, Sun 4 pm-10 pm. **Closed:** 1/1, 3/24, 12/25.
Reservations: accepted. **Features:** For casually upscale dining and a great variety of pasta, seafood and meat dishes, this is the place. A large mural depicting musicians adorns the wall, and servers are friendly and prompt. Dressy casual. **Parking:** on-site. **Cards:** AX, MC, VI.

BELOEIL pop. 19,053

──────── WHERE TO STAY ────────

The following lodging was either not evaluated or did not meet AAA rating requirements but is listed for your information only.

HOSTELLERIE RIVE GAUCHE   Phone: 450/467-4477
[fyi]   Did not meet all AAA rating requirements for some guest rooms at time of last evaluation on 10/27/2004.
Small-scale Hotel   **Location:** Hwy 20, exit 112, just sw. 1810 boul Richelieu J3G 4S4. Facilities, services, and decor characterize a mid-range property.

──────── WHERE TO DINE ────────

RESTAURANT RIVE GAUCHE   Lunch: $11-$19   Dinner: $25-$40   Phone: 450/467-4477
▼▼▼   **Location:** Hwy 20, exit 112, just sw; in Hostellerie Rive Gauche. 1810 boul Richelieu J3G 4S4. **Hours:** 7:30 am-10 &
French   11:30-9:30 pm. **Reservations:** suggested. **Features:** Hanging plants and a cozy fireplace decorate the bright, glass-enclosed atrium. The restaurant offers splendid views of the Richelieu River and Mont-St-Hilaire. A table d'hote menu is available for dinner. Sunday brunch draws a good crowd. Casual dress; cocktails. **Parking:** on-site. **Cards:** AX, DC, MC, VI.   [Y]

BOUCHERVILLE pop. 36,253   (See map and index starting on p. 420)

──────── WHERE TO STAY ────────

COMFORT INN   *Book great rates at AAA.com*   Phone: (450)641-2880   20
▼▼▼

	1P	2P	XP	
6/1-9/30	1P: $145-$165	2P: $155-$175	XP: $10	F18
1/1-4/30	1P: $120-$140	2P: $130-$150	XP: $10	F18
5/1-5/31 & 10/1-12/31	1P: $115-$135	2P: $125-$145	XP: $10	F18

Motel   **Location:** Hwy 20, exit 92, just n. 96 boul de Mortagne J4B 5M7. Fax: 450/641-2677. **Facility:** 100 one-bedroom standard units. 2 stories, interior corridors. **Parking:** on-site, winter plug-ins. **Terms:** small pets only (in smoking units).
Amenities: irons, hair dryers. **Guest Services:** valet laundry, wireless Internet. **Cards:** AX, CB, DC, DS, JC, MC, VI.
(See color ad card insert)

SOME UNITS

[ASK] [S🅳] [🛏] [🍴] [🐾] [📺] /[⊠]/

(See map and index starting on p. 420)

HOTEL MORTAGNE   *Book great rates at AAA.com*   Phone: (450)655-9966   22

(CAA) (SAVE)

All Year   1P: $199-$350   2P: $199-$350   XP: $20   F12

Location: Hwy 20, exit 93 eastbound; exit 92 westbound, take overpass to southside, then just s. 1228 rue Nobel J4B 5H1. Fax: 450/655-9946. **Facility:** 130 units. 120 one-bedroom standard units, some with whirlpools. 10 one-bedroom suites. 6 stories, interior corridors. *Bath:* combo or shower only. **Parking:** on-site.

Large-scale Hotel **Terms:** check-in 4 pm, cancellation fee imposed, package plans. **Amenities:** high-speed Internet (fee), voice mail, safes, irons, hair dryers. **Pool(s):** heated indoor. **Leisure Activities:** sauna, whirlpool, exercise room, spa. **Guest Services:** gift shop, valet laundry. **Business Services:** conference facilities, administrative services (fee), PC. **Cards:** AX, DC, DS, MC, VI. **Free Special Amenities:** local telephone calls and high-speed Internet.

SOME UNITS

HOTEL WELCOMINNS   *Book great rates at AAA.com*   Phone: (450)449-1011   21

(CAA) (SAVE)

1/1-4/30   1P: $130-$150   2P: $130-$150   XP: $15   F17
5/1-12/31   1P: $125-$145   2P: $125-$145   XP: $15   F17

Location: Hwy 20, exit 92, just n. 1195 rue Ampere J4B 7M6. Fax: 450/449-1799. **Facility:** 116 units. 114 one-bedroom standard units. 2 one-bedroom suites. 3 stories, interior/exterior corridors. **Parking:** on-site, winter

Small-scale Hotel plug-ins. **Terms:** package plans. **Amenities:** video games (fee), high-speed Internet, voice mail, irons, hair dryers. *Some:* honor bars. **Pool(s):** heated indoor. **Leisure Activities:** sauna, whirlpool, limited exercise equipment. **Guest Services:** valet and coin laundry. **Business Services:** meeting rooms. **Cards:** AX, CB, DC, DS, MC, VI. **Free Special Amenities:** continental breakfast and high-speed Internet. *(See color ad p 481)*

SOME UNITS

——— WHERE TO DINE ———

BISTRO LE TIRE-BOUCHON   Lunch: $17-$30   Dinner: $17-$30   Phone: 450/449-6112   64

French

Location: Hwy 20, exit 92, just n; in Place de Mortagne. 141 boul de Mortagne J4B 6G4. **Hours:** 11 am-2 & 6-10 pm, Sat from 6 pm. Closed major holidays; also Sun & Mon. **Reservations:** suggested. **Features:** Bistro-style cuisine includes selections from many regions of France. Confit of peppered duck is served with roasted potatoes and julienne carrots. Among other house specialties are veal, salmon and terrine foie gras. Rich woods, warm fabrics and elegant table settings give the dining room an air of sophistication. Dressy casual; cocktails. **Parking:** on-site. **Cards:** AX, DC, MC, VI.

LE BIFTHEQUE   Lunch: $8-$15   Dinner: $10-$27   Phone: 450/449-3388

Steak House

Location: Hwy 20, exit 92, just n. 100 boul de Mortagne J4B 4M7. **Hours:** 11:30 am-10 pm, Wed & Thurs-10:30 pm, Fri & Sat-11 pm. **Reservations:** accepted. **Features:** The restaurant satisfies the cravings of folks in the mood for a sizzling steak. Huge portions of traditional steakhouse fare-including fine steaks, prime rib and seafood selections-keep locals coming back. Among starters are shrimp cocktail, French onion soup and escargots. Meals come with a tasty house salad and the ever-popular biftheque croutons. Diners should arrive with a hearty appetite. Casual dress; cocktails. **Parking:** on-site. **Cards:** AX, CB, DC, DS, JC, MC, VI.

MADISONS NEW YORK GRILL & BAR   Lunch: $9-$35   Dinner: $9-$35   Phone: 450/449-1221   65

Steak & Seafood

Location: Hwy 20, exit 92. 1190 rue Volta J4B 7A2. **Hours:** 11 am-11 pm, Fri-midnight, Sat 4 pm-midnight, Sun 4 pm-11 pm. **Closed:** 12/25. **Reservations:** accepted. **Features:** This casual pub and steakhouse has comfortable chairs and private leather-upholstered booths. The grill menu lists fresh seafood, filet mignon, rib steaks, milk-fed veal, roast beef, ribs, grilled chicken, burgers, giant shrimp, shrimp cocktail, salmon salad, Caesar salad and a choice of sandwiches, including club, crab and red tuna. Casual dress; cocktails. **Parking:** on-site. **Cards:** AX, MC, VI.

ST-HUBERT   Lunch: $7-$20   Dinner: $7-$20   Phone: 450/449-9366

Canadian

Location: Hwy 132, exit Montarville. 500 rue Albanel J4B 2Z6. **Hours:** 11 am-11 pm. **Features:** The pleasantly decorated family-friendly restaurant serves affordable chicken dinners, ribs, club sandwiches, chicken wings, salads, soups and hot chicken sandwiches. The children's menu includes animal nuggets. Casual dress; cocktails. **Parking:** on-site. **Cards:** AX, DC, MC, VI.

BROSSARD pop. 65,026   (See map and index starting on p. 420)

——— WHERE TO STAY ———

BEST WESTERN HOTEL NATIONAL   *Book great rates at AAA.com*   Phone: (450)466-6756   53

(CAA) (SAVE)

5/1-10/31   1P: $99-$129   2P: $115-$139   XP: $15   F17
11/1-4/30   1P: $99-$119   2P: $110-$129   XP: $15   F17

Location: Rt 134, 0.8 mi (1.3 km) w of Hwy 10, exit boul Taschereau ouest. Located in a commercial area. 7746 boul Taschereau J4X 1C2. Fax: 450/671-8179. **Facility:** 114 one-bedroom standard units, some with whirlpools. 2

Small-scale Hotel stories, interior corridors. **Parking:** on-site, winter plug-ins. **Terms:** package plans, $2 service charge, pets (small dogs only, $25 extra charge, must remained caged). **Amenities:** voice mail, irons, hair dryers. **Pool(s):** heated indoor. **Leisure Activities:** sauna, exercise room. **Guest Services:** wireless Internet. **Business Services:** meeting rooms. **Cards:** AX, DC, DS, MC, VI. **Free Special Amenities:** continental breakfast and high-speed Internet. *(See color ad p 429)*

SOME UNITS
FEE   FEE

COMFORT INN   *Book great rates at AAA.com*   Phone: (450)678-9350   54

1/1-4/30   1P: $100-$110   2P: $110-$120   XP: $10   F18
5/1-10/13   1P: $100-$107   2P: $105-$117   XP: $10   F18
10/14-12/31   1P: $97-$104   2P: $107-$114   XP: $10   F18

Small-scale Hotel **Location:** Rt 134, 0.9 mi (1.5 km) w of Hwy 10, exit boul Taschereau ouest. 7863 boul Taschereau J4Y 1A4. Fax: 450/678-4099. **Facility:** 100 one-bedroom standard units. 2 stories, interior corridors. **Parking:** on-site, winter plug-ins. **Terms:** cancellation fee imposed, pets ($10 extra charge). **Amenities:** irons, hair dryers. **Guest Services:** valet laundry, wireless Internet. **Business Services:** meeting rooms. **Cards:** AX, DC, DS, MC, VI. *(See color ad card insert)*

SOME UNITS
FEE   FEE

(See map and index starting on p. 420)

ECONO LODGE MONTREAL - BROSSARD   *Book great rates at AAA.com*   **Phone:** 450/466-2186   [55]

6/21-9/3 [CP]	1P: $110-$165	2P: $110-$165	XP: $10 F
5/1-6/20 & 9/4-4/30 [CP]	1P: $95-$135	2P: $95-$135	XP: $10 F

Motel   **Location:** Rt 134, 1.4 mi (2.3 km) w of Hwy 10, exit boul Taschereau ouest. 8350 boul Taschereau J4X 1C2. Fax: 450/466-3722. **Facility:** 74 one-bedroom standard units, some with efficiencies and/or whirlpools. 2-3 stories (no elevator), interior/exterior corridors. *Bath:* combo or shower only. **Parking:** on-site, winter plug-ins. **Terms:** check-in 4 pm. **Amenities:** hair dryers. *Some:* irons. **Pool(s):** outdoor. **Guest Services:** wireless Internet. **Cards:** AX, CB, DC, DS, MC, VI.

SOME UNITS

(ASK) (SD) (🛜) (🏊) (💻) / (✕) (🔌) (📷) /

QUALITY INN & SUITES   *Book great rates at AAA.com*   **Phone:** (450)671-7213   [52]

(CAA) (SAVE)   5/1-10/31 [ECP]   1P: $126-$168   2P: $139-$168   XP: $15   F17
 11/1-4/30 [ECP]   1P: $119-$148   2P: $129-$148   XP: $15   F17

Small-scale Hotel   **Location:** Rt 134, 0.3 mi (0.4 km) e of jct Hwy 10, exit boul Taschereau est. Located in a commercial area. 6680 boul Taschereau J4W 1M8. Fax: 450/671-7041. **Facility:** 102 units. 93 one-bedroom standard units, some with whirlpools. 9 one-bedroom suites ($199-$395), some with whirlpools. 3 stories, interior corridors. **Parking:** on-site. **Amenities:** voice mail, irons, hair dryers. **Dining:** 11:30 am-2:30 & 5-11 pm, Sat & Sun from 5 pm, cocktails. **Pool(s):** outdoor. **Leisure Activities:** exercise room. **Guest Services:** valet laundry, wireless Internet. **Business Services:** meeting rooms. **Cards:** AX, DC, DS, MC, VI. **Free Special Amenities:** continental breakfast and high-speed Internet. *(See color ad card insert)*

SOME UNITS

(SD) (🍴) (🍷) (🏊) (💻) / (✕) (VCR) (🔌) (📷) /

———— WHERE TO DINE ————

CHEZ CORA   **Lunch:** $7-$11   **Phone:** 450/672-7371

Canadian   **Location:** Hwy 10, exit Taschereau, just e. 3 Place du Commerce J4W 2Z6. **Hours:** 6 am-3 pm, Sun from 7 am. Closed: 1/1, 12/25. **Reservations:** accepted, Mon-Fri. **Features:** Although this place specializes in breakfast, it offers a varied daytime menu that includes bacon, eggs, sausages, crepes, grilled cheese, sandwiches, freshly prepared quiches, salads, fruit platters and freshly squeezed juices. The family-friendly dining room is casual and modern. Casual dress. **Parking:** on-site. **Cards:** AX, DC, MC, VI.

ST-HUBERT   **Lunch:** $7-$20   **Dinner:** $7-$20   **Phone:** 450/676-7910

Canadian   **Location:** Hwy 10, exit boul Taschereau, then e. 6325 boul Taschereau J4Z 1A5. **Hours:** 11 am-10 pm, Tues-Thurs to 11 pm, Fri & Sat-midnight. Closed: 12/25. **Reservations:** accepted. **Features:** The pleasantly decorated family-friendly restaurant serves affordable chicken dinners, ribs, club sandwiches, chicken wings, salads, soups and hot chicken sandwiches. The children's menu includes animal nuggets. Casual dress; cocktails. **Parking:** on-site. **Cards:** AX, DC, MC, VI.

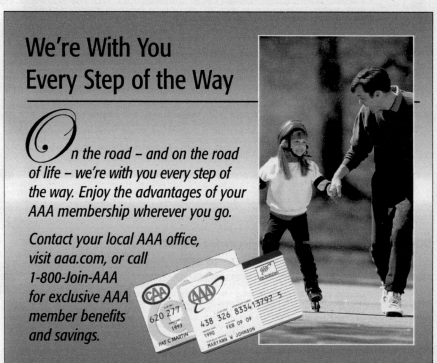

CHAMBLY pop. 20,342

——— WHERE TO DINE ———

FOURQUET FOURCHETTE   **Lunch:** $11-$18   **Dinner:** $14-$20   **Phone:** 450/447-6370
▼▼▼ ▼▼▼   **Location:** Adjacent to Fort Chambly. 1887 Bourgogne Ave J3L 1Y8. **Hours:** 11:30 am-10 pm, Sun from 10:30 am.
            Closed: 12/24, 12/25; also Mon & Tues 9/5-6/15. **Reservations:** suggested. **Features:** Adjacent to historic
Quebecois   Fort Chambly, the relaxed family restaurant is furnished in decor typical of early settler dwellings. Traditional
            Quebec cuisine can be sampled from an a la carte menu that features seafood, game, meat and chicken
delicacies. Many microbrewed beers are available. Casual dress; beer only. **Parking:** on-site. **Cards:** AX, DC, MC, VI.   Ⓨ

COTE-ST-LUC pop. 30,244   (See map and index starting on p. 420)

——— WHERE TO DINE ———

ERNIE & ELLIE'S RESTAURANT   **Lunch:** $8-$12   **Dinner:** $11-$18   **Phone:** 514/344-4444   ⑨⓪
▼▼▼ ▼▼▼   **Location:** Just e of Hwy 15 (Decarie Expwy); corner of Vezina; in Decor Decarie Shopping Mall. 6900 Decarie boul H3X
            2T8. **Hours:** 11 am-10 pm, Fri-sunset, Sat sunset-10 pm. **Closed:** Jewish holidays.
Kosher   **Reservations:** suggested. **Features:** In a shopping mall, the glatt kosher restaurant prepares kosher
            Chinese dishes, rib steaks, roasted chicken, chicken soup, ribs, sandwiches, split franks, grilled fish and
burgers. This place closes for Sabbath observance. Take-out service is available. Casual dress; cocktails. **Parking:** on-site.
Cards: AX, DC, MC, VI.

DOLLARD-DES-ORMEAUX pop. 48,206   (See map and index starting on p. 420)

——— WHERE TO DINE ———

CHEZ CORA   **Lunch:** $8-$11   **Phone:** 514/421-0783
▼▼▼ ▼▼▼   **Location:** Hwy 40, exit 55 (boul des Sources), then just n; in les Promenades des Sources. 3339-B Des Sources H9B
            1Z8. **Hours:** 6 am-3 pm, Sun from 7 am. **Closed:** 1/1, 12/25. **Reservations:** not accepted.
Canadian   **Features:** Although this place specializes in breakfast, it offers a varied daytime menu that includes bacon,
            eggs, sausages, crepes, grilled cheese, sandwiches, freshly prepared quiches, salads, fruit platters and
freshly squeezed juices. The family-friendly dining room is casual and modern. Casual dress. **Parking:** on-site. **Cards:** AX, DC,
MC, VI.

HYMIE'S SUR LE GRILL   **Lunch:** $9-$21   **Dinner:** $9-$34   **Phone:** 514/683-0011   ⑨⑥
▼▼▼ ▼▼▼   **Location:** Corner of rue Anselme-Lavighe, 1.9 mi (3 km) n of Hwy 40. 4705 boul des Sources H8Y 3C6. **Hours:** 11:30
            am-10 pm, Fri-11 pm, Sat 5 pm-11 pm, Sun 5 pm-10 pm. **Closed:** 12/25. **Reservations:** suggested.
Steak House   **Features:** The feel of downtown emanates from the suburban steakhouse, which is decorated with chic and
            stylish accents. The menu features prime rib, baby back ribs, veal chops, a variety of steaks, burgers,
gourmet sandwiches and delicious desserts. Casual dress; cocktails. **Parking:** on-site. **Cards:** AX, MC, VI.

MOMESSO CAFFE   **Lunch:** $6-$12   **Dinner:** $6-$12   **Phone:** 514/626-7177   ⑨⑨
▼▼▼ ▼▼▼   **Location:** Hwy 40, exit 52 (St-Jean nord), 1 km n; in Blue Haven Shopping Centre. 3669 boul St-Jean H9G 1X2.
            Hours: 11 am-10 pm, Thurs-Sat to 11 pm. **Reservations:** accepted. **Features:** The family-run restaurant is
Deli/Subs   owned and managed by Sergio Momesso, who once played professional hockey for the Montreal
Sandwiches   Canadiens. The suburban spot is a great place to get a sub, including the favorite steak and sausage sub
            sandwich with hot sauce. Other items include veggie and chicken subs, panini Italian sandwich, pizza,
hamburgers and poutine. Imported Segafredo espresso coffee is served. Casual dress; cocktails. **Parking:** on-site.
Cards: MC, VI.

RESTAURANT AIKAWA   **Lunch:** $10-$18   **Dinner:** $12-$26   **Phone:** 514/684-4333   ⑨⑦
▼▼▼ ▼▼▼   **Location:** Hwy 40, exit 55 (boul des Sources), just n, then just e; in shopping mall. 55 ave Brunswick 1P7.
            Hours: 11 am-2:30 & 5:30-9:30 pm, Sat 5:30 pm-10 pm. **Closed:** 12/25. **Reservations:** accepted.
Japanese   **Features:** This chic sushi bar offers an extensive choice of sushi, sashimi and sushi maki menu items and
            many flavorful eye-catching specialty dishes, including a few dessert sushi selections. Delivery is available.
Casual dress; cocktails. **Parking:** on-site. **Cards:** AX, DC, MC, VI.

RESTAURANT NEW KAM SHING   **Lunch:** $7-$12   **Dinner:** $16-$23   **Phone:** 514/626-1219   ⑨⑧
▼▼▼ ▼▼▼   **Location:** Hwy 40, exit 52, 0.8 (1.3 km) n. 3811 boul St-Jean H9G 1X2. **Hours:** 11:30 am-2:30 & 4-10:30 pm,
            Thurs & Fri 11:30 pm-11 pm, Sat noon-11 pm, Sun noon-10 pm. **Reservations:** accepted.
Asian   **Features:** Teriyaki and tempura dishes, as well as fresh-tasting sushi, make up the heart of the restaurant's
            menu. Servers and chefs dressed in kimonos, attractive Asian motifs and Japanese music playing in the
background contribute to the atmosphere. Casual dress; cocktails. **Parking:** on-site. **Cards:** AX, MC, VI.

DORVAL pop. 17,600   (See map and index starting on p. 420)

——— WHERE TO STAY ———

BEST WESTERN AEROPORT DE MONTREAL   *Book great rates at AAA.com*   **Phone:** (514)631-4811   ⑥①
Ⓒ Ⓢ   All Year [CP]   1P: $134-$199   2P: $134-$199   XP: $10   F17
▼▼▼ ▼▼▼   **Location:** Jct Hwy 20 and 520; follow signs for Pierre Elliott Trudeau International Airport. 13000 Cote de Liesse H9P
            1B8. Fax: 514/631-7305. **Facility:** 173 units. 171 one-bedroom standard units, some with whirlpools. 2 one-
            bedroom suites. 3 stories, interior corridors. **Parking:** on-site, winter plug-ins. **Terms:** 2-3 night minimum
Large-scale Hotel   stay - seasonal. **Amenities:** high-speed Internet, voice mail, irons, hair dryers. **Dining:** 2 restaurants, open 6 am-
            2 & 5-10 pm, cocktails. **Pool(s):** small heated indoor. **Leisure Activities:** exercise room. **Fee:** sauna,
massage. **Guest Services:** valet laundry, airport transportation-Pierre Elliott Trudeau International Airport, area transportation-
train station. **Business Services:** meeting rooms, business center. **Cards:** AX, DC, DS, MC, VI. **Free Special Amenities:**
continental breakfast and high-speed Internet. *(See color ad p 429)*

SOME UNITS
🚻 🍴 Ⓨ 🏊 ⊠ 🖥 / ⊠ 📶 🛄 /

(See map and index starting on p. 420)

COMFORT INN DORVAL   *Book great rates at AAA.com*   Phone: (514)636-3391   [59]

CAA SAVE	5/1-10/31 [CP]	1P: $130-$142	2P: $154	XP: $10	F14
	1/1-4/30 [CP]	1P: $122-$133	2P: $134-$148	XP: $10	F14
	11/1-12/31 [CP]	1P: $118-$130	2P: $130-$144	XP: $10	F14

Location: Hwy 520, exit 2 eastbound; exit 1 westbound, 0.2 mi (0.3 km) along service road to ave Marshall, follow to
Small-scale Hotel ave Michel-Jasmin. 340 ave Michel-Jasmin H9P 1C1. Fax: 514/636-9495. **Facility:** 98 one-bedroom standard
units. 2 stories, interior corridors. **Parking:** on-site, winter plug-ins. **Terms:** pets (in smoking units).
Amenities: irons, hair dryers. **Guest Services:** valet and coin laundry, airport transportation-Pierre Elliott International,
wireless Internet. **Cards:** AX, DC, JC, MC, VI. *(See color ad card insert)*

SOME UNITS

HAMPTON INN & SUITES   *Book great rates at AAA.com*   Phone: (514)633-8243   [58]

CAA SAVE	5/1-11/30 [ECP]	1P: $150-$180	2P: $160-$190
	12/1-4/30 [ECP]	1P: $140-$165	2P: $150-$175

Location: Hwy 40, exit 55, 0.5 mi (0.8 km) e of boul Sources on south side service road. 1900 route Transcanadienne
(Hwy 40) H9P 2N4. Fax: 514/633-5985. **Facility:** 143 one-bedroom standard units. 4 stories, interior corridors. High-
Small-scale Hotel speed Internet, dual phone lines, voice mail, irons, hair dryers. *Some:* video games (fee). **Pool(s):** heated
indoor. **Leisure Activities:** exercise room. **Guest Services:** sundries, valet and coin laundry, airport transportation-Pierre Elliott
Trudeau International Airport, area transportation-train station, wireless Internet. **Business Services:** conference facilities,
business center. **Cards:** AX, CB, DC, DS, JC, MC, VI. **Free Special Amenities: expanded continental breakfast and high-
speed Internet.** *(See color ad p 4 & p 435)*

SOME UNITS

HILTON MONTREAL AEROPORT   *Book great rates at AAA.com*   Phone: (514)631-2411   [60]

CAA SAVE	6/1-6/30	1P: $139-$329	2P: $139-$329	XP: $20	F18
	5/1-5/31 & 7/1-4/30	1P: $119-$269	2P: $119-$269	XP: $20	F18

Location: Just n of Hwy 520 on northside service road at airport entrance. 12505 boul Cote-de-Liesse H9P 1B7.
Fax: 514/631-0192. **Facility:** 486 units. 481 one-bedroom standard units. 3 one- and 2 two-bedroom suites.
Large-scale Hotel 2-4 stories, interior corridors. *Bath:* combo or shower only. **Parking:** on-site (fee). **Terms:** cancellation fee
imposed, [BP] meal plan available, package plans, pets ($25 fee, must remain caged). **Amenities:** dual
phone lines, voice mail, irons, hair dryers. *Fee:* video games, high-speed Internet. *Some:* honor bars. **Dining:** 3 restaurants, 6
am-1 am, Sat & Sun from 6:30 am, cocktails. **Pool(s):** heated indoor/outdoor. **Leisure Activities:** saunas, whirlpool,
steamroom, exercise room. *Fee:* massage. **Guest Services:** gift shop, valet laundry, airport transportation-Pierre Elliott Trudeau
International Airport, wireless Internet. **Business Services:** conference facilities, business center. **Cards:** AX, DC, DS, MC, VI.
Free Special Amenities: newspaper and early check-in/late check-out.

SOME UNITS
FEE   FEE

TRAVELODGE MONTREAL-TRUDEAU AIRPORT   *Book great rates at AAA.com*   Phone: (514)631-4537   [62]

CAA SAVE	5/1-10/31 [ECP]	1P: $109-$225	2P: $109-$225	XP: $10	F17
	11/1-4/30 [ECP]	1P: $109-$149	2P: $109-$149	XP: $10	F17

Location: Hwy 20, exit 54 westbound, just s on boul Fenelon to ave Dumont, follow to chemin Herron; exit 56
eastbound, 1.1 mi (1.7 km) along service road. 1010 chemin Herron H9S 1B3. Fax: 514/631-1562. **Facility:** 108
Small-scale Hotel units. 78 one-bedroom standard units, some with efficiencies. 30 one-bedroom suites ($129-$250) with
efficiencies. 2-3 stories, interior corridors. *Bath:* combo or shower only. **Parking:** on-site. **Terms:** pets ($40
deposit, in smoking units). **Amenities:** video games (fee), high-speed Internet, voice mail, irons, hair dryers. **Leisure
Activities:** saunas, whirlpool, exercise room. **Guest Services:** sundries, valet and coin laundry, airport transportation-Pierre
Elliott Trudeau International Airport, area transportation-train station, wireless Internet. **Business Services:** meeting rooms, PC,
fax (fee). **Cards:** AX, CB, DC, DS, JC, MC, VI. **Free Special Amenities: expanded continental breakfast and high-speed
Internet.** *(See color ad p 451)*

SOME UNITS
FEE

—————— **WHERE TO DINE** ——————

ROTISSERIE SCORES   Lunch: $8-$20   Dinner: $8-$20   Phone: 514-636-6060   [113]

Location: Hwy 20, exit 55, just s. 444 ave Dorval H9S 3H7. **Hours:** 11 am-11 pm. Closed: 12/25.
Reservations: accepted. **Features:** The chain of family restaurants offers a varied menu that includes
rotisserie chicken, ribs, salad-bar items, sandwiches, poutine and sugar, lemon or pecan pie. Diners can
Canadian quench their thirst with a fruit smoothie. Casual dress; cocktails. **Parking:** on-site. **Cards:** AX, CB, DC, DS,
JC, MC, VI.

HUDSON pop. 4,796

—————— **WHERE TO DINE** ——————

CLEMENTINE   Lunch: $18-$45   Dinner: $18-$45   Phone: 450/458-8181

Location: Centre of village. 398 chemin Main J0P 1H0. **Hours:** 11:30 am-2:30 & 5:30-10:30 pm. Closed: 1/1,
12/25; also Sun & Mon. **Features:** The cozy restaurant is in the heart of a semi-rural suburban village. The
French dining room in the vintage residence is elegantly decorated, and the service is friendly. Representative of
French-influenced regional cuisine are duck foie gras, lobster mousse, rack of lamb, pheasant,
sweetbreads, ostrich, deer medallions and filet mignon. For dessert, try chocolate mousse or raspberry cake. Dressy casual;
cocktails. **Parking:** on-site. **Cards:** AX, MC, VI.

KIRKLAND

——— WHERE TO DINE ———

KELSEY'S
Canadian

Lunch: $7-$23   **Dinner:** $7-$23   **Phone:** 514/630-3321
Location: Hwy 40, exit Ste-Marie, just n; in Colisee Mall area. 3000 rue Jean-Yves H9J 2R6. **Hours:** 11 am-midnight. Closed: 12/25. **Reservations:** accepted. **Features:** A fun, relaxed atmosphere and tasty menu of casual fare make the restaurant a popular favorite with locals. Diners might start a meal with some tempting appetizers, such as wings, loaded potato skins or nachos, and follow them with an old-time favorite, such as a burger, wrap, pizza or pasta dish. For a heartier meal, it's hard to beat pork back ribs or a steak. The diverse menu has broad appeal. Casual dress; cocktails. **Parking:** on-site. **Cards:** AX, CB, DC, DS, JC, MC, VI.

MONTANA'S COOKHOUSE
Steak House

Lunch: $8-$15   **Dinner:** $14-$22   **Phone:** 514/426-5035
Location: Hwy 40, exit Ste-Marie, just n; in Colisee Mall area. 3100 rue Jean-Yves H9J 2R6. **Hours:** 11 am-midnight. Closed: 12/25. **Reservations:** accepted. **Features:** Pine boards, exposed beams, a fireplace and Western gear displayed about the dining room give the feeling of a back-country setting. The menu lists hearty portions of comfort fare, such as Yankee pot roast. While the focus is on steaks, ribs and chicken, some seafood entrees also are among offerings. Service is efficient and friendly. Cocktails. **Parking:** on-site. **Cards:** AX, CB, DC, DS, JC, MC, VI.

ST-HUBERT
Canadian

Lunch: $7-$20   **Dinner:** $7-$20   **Phone:** 514/695-2064
Location: Between Hwy 20 and 40. 2939 boul St-Charles H9H 3B5. **Hours:** 11 am-11 pm, Fri & Sat-midnight. Closed: 12/25. **Reservations:** accepted. **Features:** The pleasantly decorated family-friendly restaurant serves affordable chicken dinners, ribs, club sandwiches, chicken wings, salads, soups and hot chicken sandwiches. The children's menu includes animal nuggets. Casual dress; cocktails. **Parking:** on-site. **Cards:** AX, DC, MC, VI.

LACHINE pop. 40,222 (See map and index starting on p. 420)

——— WHERE TO DINE ———

RESTAURANT TOPAZE
Steak & Seafood

Lunch: $6-$15   **Dinner:** $9-$19   **Phone:** 514/634-7044   (109)
Location: Just e of 25ieme Ave on the riverfront; in Lachine sector. 2166 rue St-Joseph H8S 2N7. **Hours:** 11 am-11 pm, Fri & Sat-midnight. Closed: 12/25. **Reservations:** accepted. **Features:** This suburban, waterfront restaurant and bar overlooks a pretty park and serves up a varied menu of steaks, seafood, burgers, pasta and salad. Terrace seating is ideal during the warm summer months. Casual dress; cocktails. **Parking:** on-site. **Cards:** AX, JC, MC, VI.

RESTO-BAR 12
Steak & Seafood

Lunch: $5-$11   **Dinner:** $9-$25   **Phone:** 514/637-1212   (108)
Location: Hwy 20, exit 32 ave, then 0.5 km s; in Lachine sector. 625 32ieme Ave H8T 3G6. **Hours:** 7 am-midnight, Thurs-Sat to 3 am. Closed: 1/1; also 12/24. **Reservations:** accepted. **Features:** This brasserie-style bar and restaurant is a great place to grab a pitcher of draft beer and enjoy inexpensive pub food, including prime quality steaks, burgers, pasta and chicken. Le Douze (French for Number 12) is named for the jersey number of retired Montreal Canadiens hockey star Yvan Cournoyer, who once owned the restaurant. Casual dress; cocktails. **Parking:** on-site. **Cards:** AX, DC, MC, VI.

RISTORANTE IL FORNETTO
Italian

Lunch: $10-$30   **Dinner:** $10-$30   **Phone:** 514/637-5253   (110)
Location: Corner of 19th Ave; lakefront; in Lachine sector. 1900 boul St-Joseph H8S 2N5. **Hours:** 11:30 am-11:30 pm. Closed: 1/1, 12/25. **Reservations:** suggested. **Features:** The suburban lakefront restaurant prepares affordable wood-oven-baked pizzas, salads and dishes of fresh pasta, meat and seafood. An excellent espresso finishes the meal with style. Casual dress; cocktails. **Parking:** street. **Cards:** AX, CB, DC, DS, JC, MC, VI.

LASALLE pop. 73,983 (See map and index starting on p. 420)

——— WHERE TO DINE ———

BOCCACINOS
Italian

Menu on AAA.com   **Lunch:** $9-$22   **Dinner:** $9-$22   **Phone:** 514/366-0999   (105)
Location: Just e of boul Lapierre; in Lasalle sector. 7333 boul Newman H8N 2K3. **Hours:** 6 am-midnight, Fri-2 am, Sat 7 am-2 am, Sun 7 am-midnight. Closed: 12/25. **Reservations:** accepted. **Features:** The casual chain presents a menu of affordable Italian dishes, including freshly prepared pizza, pasta, chicken, steaks, sandwiches, soups and salads. Casual dress; cocktails. **Parking:** on-site. **Cards:** AX, DC, MC, VI.

LAVAL pop. 343,005 (See map and index starting on p. 420)

——— WHERE TO STAY ———

BEST WESTERN CHATEAUNEUF LAVAL
Small-scale Hotel

Book great rates at AAA.com   **Phone:** (450)681-9000   28

	All Year	1P: $79-$139	2P: $79-$159	XP: $15	F16

Location: Hwy 15, exit 10, just n on east side service road. 3655 Autoroute des Laurentides H7L 3H7. Fax: 450/681-2501. **Facility:** 70 one-bedroom standard units, some with whirlpools. 3 stories, interior corridors. **Parking:** on-site. **Terms:** [AP], [BP], [ECP] & [MAP] meal plans available, package plans. **Amenities:** voice mail, irons, hair dryers. *Some:* high-speed Internet. **Dining:** 6:30 am-2 & 4-9 pm, Sat 6:30 am-1 & 5-8:30 pm, Sun 6 am-1 pm, cocktails. **Pool(s):** heated indoor. **Leisure Activities:** pool table. **Guest Services:** valet laundry, wireless Internet. **Business Services:** conference facilities, business center. **Cards:** AX, DC, DS, MC, VI. **Free Special Amenities:** continental breakfast and local telephone calls.

SOME UNITS

(See map and index starting on p. 420)

COMFORT INN
Book great rates at AAA.com   Phone: (450)686-0600   **32**

5/1-10/15	1P: $112-$121	2P: $123-$132	XP: $10	F18
1/1-4/30	1P: $110-$121	2P: $121-$132	XP: $10	F18
10/16-12/31	1P: $105-$116	2P: $116-$127	XP: $10	F18

Small-scale Hotel **Location:** Hwy 15, exit 8 (boul St-Martin), e on boul St-Martin, 0.4 mi (0.7 km) n on boul Le Corbusier, then w on boul Tessier. 2055 Autoroute des Laurentides H7S 1Z6. Fax: 450/686-9311. **Facility:** 120 one-bedroom standard units. 2 stories (no elevator), interior corridors. **Parking:** on-site, winter plug-ins. **Terms:** cancellation fee imposed, package plans, small pets only (in smoking units). **Amenities:** irons, hair dryers. **Guest Services:** valet laundry, wireless Internet. **Business Services:** meeting rooms. **Cards:** AX, CB, DC, DS, JC, MC, VI. *(See color ad card insert)*

SOME UNITS
ASK SD 🛏 🍴 🍸 🎬 💻 / ✕ VCR 🔲 /
FEE

ECONO LODGE
Book great rates at AAA.com   Phone: (450)681-6411   **35**

All Year [CP]	1P: $74-$84	2P: $89-$144	XP: $10	F18

Small-scale Hotel **Location:** Hwy 15, exit 8 (boul St-Martin) northbound; exit 10 southbound, 1.3 mi (2 km) w on boul St-Martin ouest, then 0.3 mi (0.5 km) n. Located in a commercial area. 1981 boul Cure-Labelle H7T 1L4. Fax: 450/681-4447. **Facility:** 101 one-bedroom standard units, some with whirlpools. 2 stories (no elevator), interior/exterior corridors. **Parking:** on-site, winter plug-ins. **Terms:** check-in 4 pm. **Amenities:** voice mail. **Pool(s):** outdoor. **Business Services:** meeting rooms. **Cards:** AX, DC, MC, VI. *(See color ad card insert)*

SOME UNITS
ASK SD 🛏 🍴 ➰ CTV / ✕ 🔲 💻 /

HAMPTON INN & SUITES-LAVAL
(CAA) (SAVE)   *Book great rates at AAA.com*   Phone: (450)687-0010   **36**

All Year [BP]	1P: $109-$149	2P: $114-$154

Small-scale Hotel **Location:** Hwy 15, exit 8 (boul St-Martin) northbound; exit 10 southbound, 1.4 mi (2.3 km) w on boul St-Martin ouest, then just n. 1961 boul Cure-Labelle H7T 1L4. Fax: 450/687-0100. **Facility:** 104 one-bedroom standard units, some with whirlpools. 5 stories, interior corridors. **Parking:** on-site. **Terms:** small pets only. **Amenities:** video games (fee), high-speed Internet, dual phone lines, voice mail, irons, hair dryers. **Pool(s):** heated indoor. **Leisure Activities:** exercise room. **Guest Services:** sundries, coin laundry, wireless Internet. **Business Services:** business center. **Cards:** AX, DC, DS, JC, MC, VI. **Free Special Amenities:** expanded continental breakfast and high-speed Internet.

SOME UNITS
SD 🛏 🍴 ➰ 🎬 💻 / ✕ 🔲 💻 /

HOTEL HILTON MONTREAL-LAVAL
(CAA) (SAVE)   *Book great rates at AAA.com*   Phone: (450)682-2225   **30**

All Year	1P: $109-$259	2P: $109-$259	XP: $20	F18

Large-scale Hotel **Location:** Hwy 15, exit 8 (boul St-Martin) northbound; exit 10 southbound. 2225 Autoroute des Laurentides H7S 1Z6. Fax: 450/682-8492. **Facility:** 169 one-bedroom standard units, some with whirlpools. 10 stories, interior corridors. **Parking:** on-site. **Terms:** [AP], [BP] & [CP] meal plans available, package plans, 3% service charge. **Amenities:** dual phone lines, voice mail, honor bars, irons, hair dryers. *Fee:* video games, high-speed Internet. *Some:* fax. **Dining:** 6:30 am-10:30 pm, Sat from 7 am; Sunday brunch, cocktails. **Pool(s):** heated indoor. **Leisure Activities:** whirlpool, steamroom, exercise room. *Fee:* massage. **Guest Services:** sundries, valet laundry. **Business Services:** conference facilities, administrative services (fee), PC. **Cards:** AX, DC, DS, JC, MC, VI.

SOME UNITS
SD 🍴 🍸 ➰ ✕ 🎬 💻 / ✕ /

(See map and index starting on p. 420)

LE ST-MARTIN HOTEL & SUITES　*Book great rates at AAA.com*　Phone: (450)902-3000　**34**

CAA SAVE

5/1-9/30 [ECP]　　　1P: $129　　　2P: $129　　　XP: $12　　F8
10/1-4/30 [ECP]　　　1P: $119　　　2P: $119　　　XP: $12　　F8

Small-scale Hotel

Location: Hwy 15, exit 8 (boul St-Martin) northbound; exit 10 southbound, just e. 1400 rue Maurice-Gauvin H7S 2P1. Fax: 450/902-3030. **Facility:** 116 units. 110 one-bedroom standard units, some with whirlpools. 6 one-bedroom suites ($149-$169) with kitchens. 3-6 stories, interior corridors. *Bath:* combo or shower only. **Parking:** on-site, winter plug-ins. **Amenities:** high-speed Internet (fee), voice mail, honor bars, irons, hair dryers. **Leisure Activities:** whirlpools, exercise room. **Guest Services:** valet laundry, wireless Internet. **Business Services:** meeting rooms, business center. **Cards:** AX, DC, MC, VI. **Free Special Amenities: expanded continental breakfast and high-speed Internet.***(See color ad p 448)*

SOME UNITS

QUALITY SUITES LAVAL　*Book great rates at AAA.com*　Phone: (450)686-6777　**33**

CAA SAVE

5/1-10/15 [CP]　　　1P: $139-$151　　2P: $151-$162　　XP: $10　　F18
1/1-4/30 [CP]　　　　1P: $133-$139　　2P: $142-$150　　XP: $10　　F18
10/16-12/31 [CP]　　1P: $128-$135　　2P: $139-$146　　XP: $10　　F18

Small-scale Hotel

Location: Hwy 15, exit 8 (boul St-Martin), 0.4 mi (0.7 km) n on boul Le Corbusier, w on boul Tessier. 2035 Autoroute des Laurentides H7S 1Z6. Fax: 450/686-4371. **Facility:** 115 units. 6 one-bedroom standard units. 109 one-bedroom suites. 3 stories, interior corridors. **Parking:** on-site, winter plug-ins. **Terms:** cancellation fee imposed, package plans, small pets only (in smoking units). **Amenities:** irons, hair dryers. *Some:* honor bars. **Guest Services:** valet laundry, wireless Internet. **Business Services:** meeting rooms, business center. **Cards:** AX, CB, DC, DS, JC, MC, VI. *(See color ad card insert)*

SOME UNITS

FEE

RADISSON HOTEL LAVAL　*Book great rates at AAA.com*　Phone: (450)682-9000　**31**

CAA SAVE

All Year　　　　　1P: $109-$169　　2P: $119-$179　　　　　　　　F18

Location: Hwy 15, exit 10, follow signs. Located adjacent to shopping centre. 2900 boul Le Carrefour H7T 2K9. Fax: 450/687-6616. **Facility:** 175 one-bedroom standard units. 6 stories, interior corridors. **Parking:** on-site.

Large-scale Hotel

Terms: [BP] & [CP] meal plans available, package plans. **Amenities:** video games (fee), high-speed Internet, dual phone lines, voice mail, irons, hair dryers. **Dining:** 6:30 am-midnight, cocktails, also, La Cage aux Sports, see separate listing. **Pool(s):** heated indoor. **Leisure Activities:** exercise room. **Guest Services:** valet laundry, wireless Internet. **Business Services:** meeting rooms, business center. **Cards:** AX, CB, DC, DS, JC, MC, VI. *(See color ad below)*

SOME UNITS

FEE

SHERATON LAVAL HOTEL　*Book great rates at AAA.com*　Phone: (450)687-2440　**29**

All Year　　　　　1P: $109-$259　　2P: $109-$259　　XP: $20　　F18

Location: Hwy 15, exit 10. 2440 Autoroute des Laurentides H7T 1X5. Fax: 450/687-0655. **Facility:** 241 units. 235 one-bedroom standard units, some with whirlpools. 6 one-bedroom suites ($169-$359) with whirlpools. 7 stories, interior corridors. **Parking:** on-site. **Terms:** [AP], [BP] & [CP] meal plans available, package plans.

Large-scale Hotel

Amenities: dual phone lines, voice mail, honor bars, irons, hair dryers. *Fee:* video games, high-speed Internet. *Some:* fax. **Dining:** Ristorante Giotto, see separate listing. **Pool(s):** heated indoor. **Leisure Activities:** whirlpool, steamroom, exercise room, spa. **Guest Services:** gift shop, valet laundry, beauty salon, wireless Internet. **Business Services:** conference facilities, business center. **Cards:** AX, DC, MC, VI. *(See color ad p 5)*

SOME UNITS

(See map and index starting on p. 420)

——— WHERE TO DINE ———

CHEZ CORA

▼▼ ▼▼
Canadian

Lunch: $7-$11 ·   **Phone:** 450/681-3403

Location: Hwy 15, exit 8 (boul St-Martin) northbound; exit 10 southbound, 1.3 mi (2 km) w on boul St-Martin ouest, then 0.6 mi (1 km) n. 2369 boul Cure-Labelle H7T 1R3. **Hours:** 6 am-3 pm, Sun from 7 am. **Closed:** 1/1, 12/25. **Reservations:** accepted. **Features:** Although this place specializes in breakfast, it offers a varied daytime menu that includes bacon, eggs, sausages, crepes, grilled cheese, sandwiches, freshly prepared quiches, salads, fruit platters and freshly squeezed juices. The family-friendly dining room is casual and modern. Casual dress. **Parking:** on-site. **Cards:** AX, DC, MC, VI.

KELSEY'S

▼▼▼▼ ▼▼
Canadian

Lunch: $7-$23   **Dinner:** $7-$23   **Phone:** 450/978-9388

Location: Hwy 15, exit boul St-Martin, 0.6 mi (1 km) e; in Carrefour Laval shopping area. 2565 boul Daniel-Johnson H7T 1S8. **Hours:** 11 am-11 pm, Thurs-midnight, Fri & Sat-1 am. **Closed:** 12/25. **Reservations:** accepted. **Features:** A fun, relaxed atmosphere and tasty menu of casual fare make the restaurant a popular favorite with locals. Diners might start a meal with some tempting appetizers, such as wings, loaded potato skins or nachos, and follow them with an old-time favorite, such as a burger, wrap, pizza or pasta dish. For a heartier meal, it's hard to beat pork back ribs or a steak. The diverse menu has broad appeal. Casual dress; cocktails. **Parking:** on-site. **Cards:** AX, CB, DC, DS, JC, MC, VI.

LA CAGE AUX SPORTS

▼▼▼▼
Canadian

Lunch: $8-$21   **Dinner:** $8-$21   **Phone:** 450/688-8244

Location: Hwy 15, exit 10, follow signs. Located adjacent to shopping centre; in Radisson Hotel Laval. 2900 boul Le Carrefour H7T 2K9. **Hours:** 11 am-midnight, Thurs-Sat to 1 am. **Closed:** 1/1, 12/25. **Reservations:** accepted. **Features:** This popular Quebec chain of sports bars presents a menu of pub favorites, including ribs, burgers, salads, crispy fries, pasta and tasty desserts. Guests might begin the meal with a basket of freshly popped popcorn as they check out the sports memorabilia. Children are welcomed. Casual dress; cocktails. **Parking:** on-site. **Cards:** AX, MC, VI.

LE COMMENSAL

▼▼▼▼
Vegetarian

Lunch: $8-$15   **Dinner:** $8-$15   **Phone:** 450/978-9124

Location: Hwy 15, exit 9 northbound, 0.3 mi (0.5 km) w; exit 10 southbound. 3180 boul St-Martin ouest H7T 1A1. **Hours:** 11 am-10:30 pm, Sun-Wed to 9:30 pm. **Closed:** 1/1, 12/25. **Reservations:** accepted. **Features:** An upscale self-service buffet features an extensive selection of creative hot and cold items, such as leek pot pie, sweet potato kasha and lasagna, plus a variety of desserts, everything of which is exclusively vegetarian. The pleasant, contemporary surroundings change often as new paintings are displayed. Casual dress; beer & wine only. **Parking:** on-site. **Cards:** AX, DC, MC, VI.

LE MITOYEN

▼▼▼ ▼▼▼▼
French

Dinner: $25-$32   **Phone:** 450/689-2977   (70)

Location: Hwy 15, exit 9, 5.1 mi (8.5 km) w on boul St-Martin, just off Rt 148; adjacent to Place Publique Park. 652 Place Publique H7X 1G1. **Hours:** 6 pm-10 pm, Fri & Sat-11 pm. **Closed:** 12/24-12/26; also 6/24 & Mon. **Reservations:** suggested. **Features:** Seasonal and regional produce is emphasized in creative, artfully prepared specialties, including Atlantic salmon, deer, caribou, rack of lamb, ostrich and scallops. The eight-course degustation menu is a celebration of haute cuisine. The elegant country dining room is suitable for relaxed, intimate meals. Dressy casual; cocktails. **Parking:** on-site. **Cards:** AX, DC, MC, VI.

RESTAURANT LE SAINT-CHRISTOPHE

▼▼▼▼ ▼▼
French

Lunch: $19-$24   **Dinner:** $36-$55   **Phone:** 450/622-7963   (68)

Location: Hwy 15, exit 16, 1.7 mi (2.7 km) e. 94 boul Ste-Rose est H7L 1K4. **Hours:** noon-2:30 & 5:30-10 pm. **Closed:** Sun & Mon. **Reservations:** required. **Features:** Traditional fine French cuisine is presented in the elegant parlors of a 1912 red-brick home. Service is friendly and attentive. A seasonal terrace faces lovely gardens. The menu features such specialties as foie gras, cassoulet, sweetbreads and filet mignon. Casual dress; cocktails. **Parking:** on-site. **Cards:** AX, MC, VI.

RISTORANTE GIOTTO

▼▼▼▼ ▼▼
Italian

Dinner: $15-$28   **Phone:** 450/687-2440   (69)

Location: Hwy 15, exit 10; in Sheraton Laval Hotel. 2440 Autoroute des Laurentides H7T 1X5. **Hours:** 5:30 pm-11:30 pm. **Reservations:** suggested. **Features:** The posh hotel dining room offers authentic Italian cuisine including pasta, meat, fish and seafood dishes. Dressy casual; cocktails. **Parking:** on-site. **Cards:** AX, DC, MC, VI.

ST-HUBERT

▼▼▼▼ ▼▼
Canadian

Lunch: $7-$20   **Dinner:** $7-$20   **Phone:** 450/687-4170

Location: Hwy 15, exit boul St-Martin. 3325 boul St-Martin ouest H7N 5B5. **Hours:** 11 am-11 pm, Fri & Sat-midnight. **Closed:** 12/25. **Reservations:** accepted. **Features:** The pleasantly decorated family-friendly restaurant serves affordable chicken dinners, ribs, club sandwiches, chicken wings, salads, soups and hot chicken sandwiches. The children's menu includes animal nuggets. Casual dress; cocktails. **Parking:** on-site. **Cards:** AX, DC, MC, VI.

L'ILE-PERROT pop. 9,375   (See map and index starting on p. 420)

——— WHERE TO DINE ———

SMOKE MEAT PETE

▼▼▼
Canadian

Lunch: $7-$22   **Dinner:** $7-$22   **Phone:** 514/425-6068   (127)

Location: Hwy 20, exit boul Perrot, just se. 283 1ere ave J7V 5A1. **Hours:** 9 am-11 pm, Thurs-Sat to 1 am. **Closed:** 1/1, 12/25; also 6/24, last week in Feb & first week in Mar. **Reservations:** not accepted. **Features:** Fans of this diner say you "can't beat Pete's meat." The house specialty is Montreal-style smoked meat but the varied menu includes other deli and fast-food favorites like grilled steaks, latkes and burgers. The seasonal terrace is popular in summer. Live blues music performed nightly from Thursday to Saturday. Casual dress; beer & wine only. **Parking:** on-site.

VIEUX KITZBUHEL RESTAURANT   *Menu on AAA.com*   **Lunch:** $10-$20

(AAA)

▼▼▼▼
Austrian

Dinner: $17-$32   **Phone:** 514/453-5521   (128)

Location: Jct Hwy 20, 0.9 mi (1.5 km) s. 505 boul Perrot J7V 3H4. **Hours:** 11 am-11 pm. **Closed:** 10/8, 12/24-12/26; also Mon. **Reservations:** accepted. **Features:** This romantic lakeside country inn dining room has oak-panelled walls and authentic European food, including many Austrian specialties. The menu features wild game, lamb, wiener schnitzel and house-prepared desserts. Dressy casual. **Parking:** on-site. **Cards:** AX, DC, MC, VI.

LONGUEUIL pop. 128,016   (See map and index starting on p. 420)

──────── WHERE TO STAY ────────

DAYS INN LONGUEUIL   *Book great rates at AAA.com*   Phone: (450)677-8911   **39**

	1P: $87-$95	2P: $95-$105	XP: $10	F12
5/1-9/30	1P: $76-$86	2P: $86-$96	XP: $10	F12
10/1-4/30				

Small-scale Hotel **Location:** Hwy 20/Rt 132, exit 15 eastbound, follow signs for boul Marie-Victorin est; exit 90 westbound from Pont-Tunnel Louis-Hippolyte-Lafontaine. Located in a suburban area. 2800 boul Marie-Victorin J4G 1P5. Fax: 450/677-2591. **Facility:** 65 one-bedroom standard units, some with whirlpools. 3 stories (no elevator), interior corridors. **Parking:** on-site, winter plug-ins. **Terms:** 3 day cancellation notice, small pets only. **Amenities:** hair dryers. *Some:* irons. **Guest Services:** wireless Internet. **Cards:** AX, DC, MC, VI.

SOME UNITS
(ASK) (SD) (🛏) (🍴) (🍸) (💻) / (X) /

HOLIDAY INN MONTREAL-LONGUEUIL   *Book great rates at AAA.com*   Phone: (450)646-8100   **41**

(CAA) (SAVE)

| 5/1-10/31 | 1P: $139-$189 | 2P: $139-$189 | XP: $15 | F18 |
| 11/1-4/30 | 1P: $119-$169 | 2P: $119-$169 | XP: $15 | F18 |

Location: Rt 132, exit 11. 900 rue St-Charles est J4H 3Y2. Fax: 450/646-7786. **Facility:** 141 one-bedroom standard units. 6 stories, interior corridors. **Parking:** on-site. **Terms:** cancellation fee imposed, package

Small-scale Hotel plans. **Amenities:** voice mail, irons, hair dryers. **Dining:** 6:30 am-10 pm, Sat & Sun from 7:30 am, cocktails. **Pool(s):** heated indoor. **Leisure Activities:** whirlpool, exercise room. **Guest Services:** gift shop, valet laundry, wireless Internet. **Business Services:** meeting rooms, administrative services (fee). **Cards:** AX, DC, DS, MC, VI. **Free Special Amenities:** newspaper and high-speed Internet. *(See color ad card insert)*

SOME UNITS
(SD) (🍴) (🍸) (🏊) (💪) (💻) / (X) (🛏) /

HOTEL GOUVERNEUR ILE-CHARRON   *Book great rates at AAA.com*   Phone: (450)651-6510   **40**

(CAA) (SAVE)

| All Year | 1P: $129 | 2P: $129 | XP: $20 | F17 |

Location: Hwy 25 S, exit 1 (Ile-Charron), just e. 2405 Ile-Charron J4G 1R6. Fax: 450/651-6990. **Facility:** 125 units. 123 one-bedroom standard units. 2 one-bedroom suites. 6 stories, interior corridors. **Parking:** on-site. **Terms:** package plans. **Amenities:** video games (fee), voice mail, irons, hair dryers. *Some:* honor bars.

Large-scale Hotel **Dining:** 6:30 am-10 pm, cocktails. **Pool(s):** outdoor. **Leisure Activities:** boat dock, heliport, volleyball. **Guest Services:** valet laundry, wireless Internet. **Business Services:** conference facilities. **Cards:** AX, DC, MC, VI.

SOME UNITS
(SD) (🍴) (🍸) (🏊) (X) (💪) (💻) / (X) (🛏) /
FEE

HOTEL LE DAUPHIN MONTREAL LONGUEUIL   *Book at AAA.com*   Phone: (450)646-0110   **43**

| 5/1-11/30 | 1P: $99-$129 | 2P: $99-$129 | XP: $10 | F18 |
| 12/1-4/30 | 1P: $90-$129 | 2P: $99-$129 | XP: $10 | F18 |

Small-scale Hotel **Location:** Rt 132, exit 8 (Metro Longueuil), 0.3 mi (0.5 km) se on Place Charles-Lemoyne. 1055 boul St-Laurent ouest J4K 1E1. Fax: 450/646-7718. **Facility:** 80 units. 77 one-bedroom standard units. 3 one-bedroom suites with whirlpools. 6 stories, interior corridors. **Parking:** on-site, winter plug-ins. **Terms:** package plans. **Amenities:** video library, DVD players, CD players, high-speed Internet, voice mail, safes, irons, hair dryers. **Guest Services:** PC. **Cards:** AX, MC, VI.

SOME UNITS
(ASK) (🍴) (VCR) (💪) (🛏) (💻) / (X) (📷) /

MOTEL LA SIESTA   Phone: 450/671-7555   **44**

(CAA) (SAVE)

5/1-9/11 [BP]	1P: $89-$150	2P: $89-$150	XP: $10	F16
9/12-11/30 [BP]	1P: $69-$150	2P: $69-$150	XP: $10	F16
12/1-4/30 [BP]	1P: $59-$150	2P: $59-$150	XP: $10	F16

Motel **Location:** Rt 134 (boul Taschereau), 2.8 mi (4.4 km) e of jct Hwy 10, exit 8E; 2.5 mi (4 km) w of jct Rt 132, exit 8; in Greenfield Park sector. Located in a busy commercial area. 3179 boul Taschereau est J4V 2H4. Fax: 450/671-0834. **Facility:** 49 one-bedroom standard units, some with whirlpools. 2 stories, exterior corridors. **Parking:** on-site, winter plug-ins. **Amenities:** *Some:* CD players. **Guest Services:** valet and coin laundry. **Cards:** AX, MC, VI. **Free Special Amenities:** full breakfast and local telephone calls. *(See color ad below)*

SOME UNITS
(🍴) (🛏) / (X) (VCR) /

(See map and index starting on p. 420)

SANDMAN HOTEL MONTREAL-LONGUEUIL   *Book great rates at AAA.com*   Phone: (450)670-3030   42

(CAA) (SAVE)   All Year   1P: $200-$270   2P: $200-$270   XP: $10   F18
Location: Hwy 20, exit 7, 0.5 mi (0.8 km) n on boul Lafayette. 999 de Serigny J4K 2T1. Fax: 450/670-5928.
Facility: 214 units. 213 one-bedroom standard units. 1 one-bedroom suite. 17 stories, interior corridors.
Parking: on-site. **Terms:** package plans. **Amenities:** high-speed Internet (fee), voice mail, irons, hair
Large-scale Hotel dryers. *Some:* dual phone lines. **Dining:** 6:30 am-2 & 4-10 pm, cocktails. **Pool(s):** heated indoor. **Leisure**
Activities: sauna, exercise room. **Guest Services:** gift shop, valet laundry. **Business Services:** conference
facilities, business center. **Cards:** AX, CB, DC, MC, VI. **Free Special Amenities:** newspaper and high-speed Internet.
(See color ad p 451)

SOME UNITS

(S) (YA) (Y) (&M) (swim) (pet) (video) / (X) (fridge) /
FEE

─────── **WHERE TO DINE** ───────

HOMARD PLUS   Lunch: $7-$13   Dinner: $13-$35   Phone: 450/678-7583   73
Location: Rt 134 (boul Taschereau), 2.4 mi (4 km) e on jct Hwy 10, exit 8E; 2.6 mi (4.4 km) w of jct Rt 132, exit 8; in
Greenfield Park sector. 3319 boul Taschereau est J4V 2H5. **Hours:** 11 am-midnight, Sun from 10 am.
Steak & Seafood **Reservations:** suggested. **Features:** Convenient to nearby hotels, this casual seafood restaurant offers
fresh lobster plus fish n' chips, crabs, raw oysters, steaks and a salad bar. Casual dress; cocktails. **Parking:**
on-site. **Cards:** AX, DC, MC, VI.   (Y)

KELSEY'S   Lunch: $7-$23   Dinner: $7-$23   Phone: 450/468-3939
Location: Hwy 132, exit Roland-Therrien; centre. 1175 chemin du Tremblay J4N 1R4. **Hours:** 11 am-11 pm, Thurs-
midnight, Fri & Sat-1 am. Closed: 12/25. **Reservations:** accepted. **Features:** A fun, relaxed atmosphere
Canadian and tasty menu of casual fare make the restaurant a popular favorite with locals. Diners might start a meal
with some tempting appetizers, such as wings, loaded potato skins or nachos, and follow them with an old-
time favorite, such as a burger, wrap, pizza or pasta dish. For a heartier meal, it's hard to beat pork back ribs or a steak. The
diverse menu has broad appeal. Casual dress; cocktails. **Parking:** on-site. **Cards:** AX, CB, DC, DS, JC, MC, VI.   (Y)

LE COMMENSAL   Lunch: $7-$15   Dinner: $7-$15   Phone: 450/676-1749
Location: Rt 134 (boul Taschereau), corner of ave Auguste; in Greenfield Park sector. 4817 boul Taschereau J4V 2J1.
Hours: 11:30 am-9:30 pm, Thurs-Sat to 10 pm. Closed: 1/1, 12/25. **Reservations:** accepted. **Features:** An
Vegetarian upscale self-service buffet features an extensive selection of creative hot and cold items, such as leek pot
pie, sweet potato kasha and lasagna, plus a variety of desserts, everything of which is exclusively
vegetarian. The pleasant, contemporary surroundings change often as new paintings are displayed. Casual dress; beer & wine
only. **Parking:** on-site. **Cards:** MC, VI.

ST-HUBERT   Lunch: $7-$20   Dinner: $7-$20   Phone: 450/646-4447
Location: Centre; in Place Longueuil. 825 rue St-Laurent ouest J4K 2V1. **Hours:** 11 am-11 pm, Fri & Sat-midnight.
Reservations: accepted. **Features:** The pleasantly decorated family-friendly restaurant serves affordable
Canadian chicken dinners, ribs, club sandwiches, chicken wings, salads, soups and hot chicken sandwiches. The
children's menu includes animal nuggets. Casual dress; cocktails. **Parking:** on-site. **Cards:** AX, DC,
MC, VI.
(Y)

MONTREAL-NORD pop. 83,600

─────── **WHERE TO DINE** ───────

The following restaurant has not been evaluated by AAA
but is listed for your information only.

DIC ANN'S HAMBURGERS
(fyi) Not evaluated. **Location:** Just n of rue Monselet; in Montreal-Nord sector. 10910 boul Pie-IX H1H 4B3.
Features: This popular fast-food diner specializes in small flat spicy hamburgers. Dine in or take out.

MONTREAL-OUEST (See map and index starting on p. 420)

─────── **WHERE TO DINE** ───────

BISTRO WESTMINSTER   Lunch: $10-$12   Dinner: $16-$22   Phone: 514/484-0513   102
Location: Just n of rue Sherbrooke. 49 rue Westminster N H4X 1Y8. **Hours:** 11 am-10 pm, Sat & Sun from 5 pm.
Closed: 12/25, 12/26; also 1/2. **Reservations:** suggested. **Features:** The casual neighborhood bistro
International specializes in international cuisine but prepares a few classic pub-style dishes centered on fresh seafood,
steak, pasta and sandwiches. Themed menus are presented during special events. Cheesecake is a good
dessert choice. Casual dress; cocktails. **Parking:** street. **Cards:** AX, DC, MC, VI.

MONT-ST-HILAIRE pop. 14,270

─────── **WHERE TO STAY** ───────

MANOIR ROUVILLE-CAMPBELL   Phone: 450/446-6060
5/1-9/30   1P: $147-$227   2P: $147-$227   XP: $15   F12
10/1-4/30   1P: $137-$215   2P: $137-$215   XP: $15   F12
Classic Historic **Location:** Hwy 20, exit 113, 3.8 mi (6 km) s on Rt 133. 125 chemin des Patriotes sud J3H 3G5. Fax: 450/446-4878.
Country Inn **Facility:** French and English gardens grace the grounds, and upscale appointments adorn the rooms of this
Tudor-style inn on the Richelieu River. 25 units. 24 one-bedroom standard units. 1 one-bedroom suite. 3
stories (no elevator), interior corridors. **Parking:** on-site, winter plug-ins. **Terms:** 10 day cancellation notice-fee imposed,
package plans. **Amenities:** irons, hair dryers. *Some:* CD players. **Dining:** La Table du Manoir, see separate listing. **Pool(s):**
heated outdoor. **Leisure Activities:** boat dock. **Guest Services:** valet laundry. **Business Services:** conference facilities.
Cards: AX, MC, VI.

(YA) (swim) (X) (video)

─── **WHERE TO DINE** ───

LA TABLE DU MANOIR   **Lunch:** $16-$23   **Dinner:** $30-$40   **Phone:** 450/446-6060
Location: Hwy 20, exit 113, 3.8 mi (6 km) s on Rt 133; in Manoir Rouville-Campbell. 125 chemin des Patriotes sud J3H 3G5. **Hours:** 7 am-11:30, noon-2 & 5:30-9 pm, Sat-10 pm. **Reservations:** suggested. **Features:** Guinea fowl and smoked salmon are specialties at the small, intimate restaurant, a favorite romantic spot for couples. The dining room affords views of the gardens and the Richelieu River. Sunday brunch is especially popular. Dressy casual; cocktails. **Parking:** on-site. **Cards:** AX, MC, VI.

French

OUTREMONT pop. 22,933 (See map and index starting on p. 420)

─── **WHERE TO DINE** ───

LE PARIS BEURRE   **Lunch:** $12-$21   **Dinner:** $18-$25   **Phone:** 514/271-7502   77
Location: Between ave Champagneur and ave Bloomfield; in Outremont sector. 1226 ave Van Horne H2V 1K3. **Hours:** 11:30 am-10 pm, Fri-10:30 pm, Sat 5:30 pm-10:30 pm, Sun 5:30 pm-10 pm. Closed: for lunch most holidays. **Reservations:** suggested. **Features:** The chic, casual bistro is located on a trendy shopping street. The menu of southwestern French cuisine boasts a number of bistro classics like beef tartare, lamb chops, duck "magret," duck confit, cassoulet, salmon and filet mignon. Dessert include a classic creme brulee. Casual dress; cocktails. **Parking:** on-site. **Cards:** MC, VI.

French

RESTAURANT CHEZ LEVEQUE   **Lunch:** $16-$30   **Dinner:** $17-$34   **Phone:** 514/279-7355   78
Location: Between rue Hutchison and Durocher; in Outremont sector. 1030 rue Laurier ouest H2V 2K8. **Hours:** 8 am-midnight, Sat & Sun from 10:30 am. **Reservations:** suggested. **Features:** The cosmopolitan bistro is a charming, lively spot for fine French cuisine and gracious service. The menu changes frequently to offer only the freshest of seasonal specialties, such as oysters, crab, lobster, shrimp and wild game. Dressy casual; cocktails. **Parking:** street. **Cards:** AX, DC, MC, VI.

French

RESTAURANT CHRISTOPHE   **Dinner:** $30-$58   **Phone:** 514/270-0850   76
Location: Between Bloomfield and de l'Epee; in Outremont sector. 1187 Van Horne Ave H2V 1K1. **Hours:** 6 pm-10 pm. Closed: 1/2, Sun, Mon, 7/12-7/31 & 12/23-12/30. **Reservations:** suggested. **Features:** Modern French influences are evident on a menu of abundant fresh fish selections, including salmon and tuna. Veal, venison and some shellfish round out the choices. The restaurant founder was once a private chef for the late French President Francois Mitterrand. The lively dining room is swathed in youthful contemporary decor. Casual dress. **Parking:** street. **Cards:** MC, VI.

French

RESTAURANT LEMEAC   **Lunch:** $16-$34   **Dinner:** $17-$34   **Phone:** 514/270-0999   79
Location: Just w of ave du Parc; in Outremont sector. 1045 ave Laurier ouest H2V 2L1. **Hours:** noon-midnight, Thurs & Fri-1 am, Sat 10:30 am-1 am, Sun 10:30 am-midnight. Closed: 1/1, 12/25. **Reservations:** suggested. **Features:** On a fashionable shopping street, the elegant bistro breathes new life into classic French-style recipes. Diners can enjoy braised short ribs, thick grilled pork chops, rack of lamb, rillettes pate, veal liver, asparagus risotto, magret of duck, black pudding and kidneys. For dessert, sample lemon pie, chocolate mousse or one of the house-prepared sorbets. In the summer, the outdoor terrace is the place to be. Casual dress; cocktails. **Parking:** street. **Cards:** AX, DC, MC, VI.

French

POINTE-CLAIRE pop. 29,286 (See map and index starting on p. 420)

─── **WHERE TO STAY** ───

COMFORT INN   *Book great rates at AAA.com*   **Phone:** (514)697-6210   67

5/1-10/31 [ECP]	1P: $89-$195	2P: $89-$195	XP: $5	F18
11/1-4/30 [ECP]	1P: $79-$195	2P: $79-$195	XP: $5	F18

Location: Hwy 40, exit 52, just s. Located in a suburban area. 700 boul St-Jean H9R 3K2. Fax: 514/697-6934. **Facility:** 100 one-bedroom standard units. 2 stories (no elevator), interior corridors. **Parking:** on-site, winter plug-ins. **Terms:** weekly rates available, 3% service charge, pets (in ground floor smoking units). **Amenities:** voice mail, irons, hair dryers. *Some:* dual phone lines. **Guest Services:** valet laundry, airport transportation-Pierre Elliott Trudeau International Airport, wireless Internet. **Cards:** AX, CB, DC, DS, JC, MC, VI. *(See color ad card insert)*

Small-scale Hotel

SOME UNITS
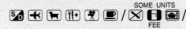
FEE

HOLIDAY INN POINTE-CLAIRE MONTREAL
AEROPORT   *Book great rates at AAA.com*   **Phone:** (514)697-7110   66

All Year	1P: $119-$199	2P: $199-$229	XP: $10	F18

Location: Hwy 40, exit 52, south side service road. Located in a suburban area. 6700 Transcanadienne H9R 1C2. Fax: 514/697-4145. **Facility:** 308 units. 304 one-bedroom standard units. 4 one-bedroom suites. 15 stories, interior corridors. **Parking:** on-site. **Terms:** [AP], [BP] & [CP] meal plans available, package plans. **Amenities:** video games (fee), high-speed Internet, voice mail, irons, hair dryers. **Dining:** 6:30 am-2 & 6-10 pm, Sat & Sun from 7 am, cocktails. **Pool(s):** heated indoor. **Leisure Activities:** saunas, whirlpool, exercise room. *Fee:* 2 squash courts, massage, game room. **Guest Services:** gift shop, valet and coin laundry, airport transportation-Pierre Elliott Trudeau International Airport, wireless Internet. **Business Services:** meeting rooms, business center. **Cards:** AX, CB, DC, DS, JC, MC, VI. *(See color ad card insert & p 438)*

Large-scale Hotel

SOME UNITS

QUALITY SUITES MONTREAL AEROPORT,
POINTE-CLAIRE   *Book great rates at AAA.com*   **Phone:** (514)426-5060   65

5/1-9/30	1P: $99-$159	2P: $109-$169	XP: $10	F18
10/1-4/30	1P: $99-$149	2P: $109-$159	XP: $10	F18

Location: Hwy 40, exit 52 eastbound, south side service road; westbound, follow signs for boul St-Jean sud and Hwy 40 est to access south side service road. 6300 Rt Transcanadienne H9R 1B9. Fax: 514/426-8263. **Facility:** 161 units. 6 one-bedroom standard units. 155 one-bedroom suites. 8 stories, interior corridors. **Parking:** on-site, winter plug-ins. **Terms:** [BP] meal plan available, package plans, pets (in smoking units). **Amenities:** high-speed Internet, voice mail, irons, hair dryers. **Dining:** 6:30 am-11 pm, cocktails. **Leisure Activities:** exercise room. **Guest Services:** valet and coin laundry, airport transportation-Pierre Elliott Trudeau International Airport, wireless Internet. **Business Services:** meeting rooms, PC (fee). **Cards:** AX, CB, DC, DS, JC, MC, VI. *(See color ad card insert)*

Small-scale Hotel

SOME UNITS

(See map and index starting on p. 420)

──────── **WHERE TO DINE** ────────

40 WESTT STEAKHOUSE
▼▼▼▼
Steak & Seafood
Lunch: $19-$26   Dinner: $26-$56   Phone: 514/428-9378   116
Location: Hwy 40, exit 53 (boul des Sources), just nw. 2305 boul Transcanadienne H9R 5Z5. **Hours:** 11:30 am-2:30 & 5:30-10:30 pm, Thurs-Sat to 11:30 pm. Closed: 12/24, 12/25. **Reservations:** suggested. **Features:** Stone surfaces, rich wood moldings, high ceilings, elegant mirrors and etched glass highlight the decor of this upscale suburban steakhouse. The high quality menu features prime cuts of steak, as well as an array of fresh fish and seafood. A butcher shop on the premises sells steaks for take-out. Casual dress; cocktails. **Parking:** on-site. **Cards:** AX, DC, MC, VI.

ARAHOVA SOUVLAKI
▼▼▼
Greek
Lunch: $6-$10   Dinner: $10-$15   Phone: 514/695-1100   120
Location: Hwy 40, exit 52, 0.3 mi (0.5 km) n. 301 boul Brunswick H9R 4Y2. **Hours:** 10:30 am-2 am, Fri & Sat-5 am. **Reservations:** accepted. **Features:** Greek specialties, such as souvlaki, gyro pitas, moussaka and grilled fish and seafood, are served in a casual atmosphere. Casual dress; cocktails. **Parking:** on-site. **Cards:** AX, MC, VI.

BAR-B BARN
▼▼
Barbecue
Lunch: $9-$20   Dinner: $9-$20   Phone: 514/683-0225
Location: Hwy 40, exit 55, just n. 3300 boul des Sources H9B 1Z7. **Hours:** 11 am-9 pm, Fri-10 pm, Sat-10:30 pm. Closed: 12/25; also Mon. **Reservations:** accepted. **Features:** Rustic barn wood adorns the walls of the family restaurant. Specialties include slow-roasted chicken and pork ribs, as well as the popular ribs-and-chicken combination dish. Casual dress; cocktails. **Parking:** on-site. **Cards:** AX, DC, MC, VI.

CHEZ CORA
▼▼
Canadian
Lunch: $8-$13   Phone: 514/630-8104
Location: Hwy 40, exit 52, just se; in shopping mall. 183J boul Hymus H9R 1E9. **Hours:** 6 am-3 pm, Sun from 7 am. Closed: 12/25. **Reservations:** not accepted. **Features:** Although this place specializes in breakfast, it offers a varied daytime menu that includes bacon, eggs, sausages, crepes, grilled cheese, sandwiches, freshly prepared quiches, salads, fruit platters and freshly squeezed juices. The family-friendly dining room is casual and modern. Casual dress. **Parking:** on-site. **Cards:** AX, DC, MC, VI.

LE CHAMBERTIN
▼▼▼▼
French
Lunch: $13-$18   Dinner: $20-$35   Phone: 514/695-0620   118
Location: Hwy 40, exit 52, 0.3 mi (0.5 km) n, then just e on boul Brunswick. 9 Place Frontenac H9R 4Z7. **Hours:** 11:30 am-2:30 & 5-10 pm, Sat from 5 pm. Closed: 7/1, 12/25, 12/26; also Sun. **Reservations:** accepted. **Features:** In operation since 1980, the upscale restaurant presents a menu of prime rib, fresh fish, seafood and steaks. Social dinner and dancing evenings are held regularly. Dressy casual; cocktails. **Parking:** on-site and valet. **Cards:** AX, DC, MC, VI.

LE GOURMAND
▼▼▼▼
French
Lunch: $17-$23   Dinner: $19-$46   Phone: 514/695-9077   117
Location: Hwy 20, exit 49, 0.7 mi (1.1 km) s on ave Cartier, then just w. 42 rue Ste-Anne H9S 4P8. **Hours:** 11:30 am-3 & 5:30-10 pm, Sat from 5:30 pm. Closed: 1/1; also Sun. **Reservations:** suggested. **Features:** This cozy restaurant is located in a historic former blacksmith shop built in 1848. The menu of French cuisine includes chicken breast, filet mignon, rack of lamb, smoked salmon, fresh fish, veal scallopine, linguini with shrimp, duck "magret" and a mixed grill of lamb chops, shrimp and sausages. Casual dress; cocktails. **Parking:** street. **Cards:** AX, DC, MC, VI.

MOE'S DELI & BAR
▼▼▼
Canadian
Lunch: $9-$12   Dinner: $10-$18   Phone: 514/426-8247   121
Location: Hwy 40, exit 52, 1.3 mi (2 km) n; in Colonades Pointe-Claire Shopping Centre. 940 boul St-Jean H9R 5N8. **Hours:** 7 am-11 pm, Fri & Sat-midnight. Closed: 12/25. **Reservations:** accepted. **Features:** The atmosphere is busy and noisy in the energetic restaurant, especially during peak lunch times. The varied menu lists pasta, hamburgers, pizza, steaks and the house specialty smoked meat sandwiches. Portion sizes are generous. Casual dress; cocktails. **Parking:** on-site. **Cards:** AX, DC, MC, VI.

SCAROLIES PASTA IMPORIUM
▼▼▼
Italian
Lunch: $9-$14   Dinner: $10-$23   Phone: 514/694-8611   119
Location: Hwy 40, exit 52, just n. 950 boul St-Jean H9R 5N8. **Hours:** 11 am-11 pm, Fri & Sat-midnight. **Reservations:** suggested. **Features:** Italian dishes are the specialty at the casual, popular eatery in a suburban strip mall. Daily specials are offered along with such popular staples as freshly prepared veal scaloppine, linguine, ravioli, leg of lamb, Atlantic salmon and stuffed chicken. Casual dress; cocktails. **Parking:** on-site. **Cards:** AX, DC, MC, VI.

ROSEMERE pop. 13,391 (See map and index starting on p. 420)

──────── **WHERE TO STAY** ────────

HOTEL LE RIVAGE
▼▼▼▼
Small-scale Hotel
All Year   2P: $89-$134   XP: $10   Phone: 450/437-2171   25
                                          F
Location: Hwy 15, exit 14, 2.4 mi (4 km) e. 125 boul Cure-Labelle J7A 2G9. Fax: 450/437-3005. **Facility:** 65 units. 63 one-bedroom standard units, some with whirlpools. 1 vacation home ($359-$500) and 1 cottage, some with whirlpools. 2 stories (no elevator), interior corridors. **Parking:** on-site. **Terms:** [CP] meal plan available, small pets only. **Amenities:** hair dryers. *Some:* DVD players, CD players, irons. **Pool(s):** heated outdoor. **Leisure Activities:** whirlpool. **Guest Services:** valet and coin laundry. **Business Services:** meeting rooms, fax. **Cards:** AX, DC, MC, VI.

SOME UNITS
🐾 🛏 📞 / ✕ 📼 🖨 /

STE-ANNE-DE-BELLEVUE pop. 5,062 (See map and index starting on p. 420)

──────── **WHERE TO DINE** ────────

LE SURCOUF
▼▼▼
French
Lunch: $10-$16   Dinner: $15-$35   Phone: 514/457-6699   124
Location: In centre of village. 51 rue Ste-Anne H9X 1L5. **Hours:** 11:30 am-2 & 5:30-9:30 pm, Sat & Mon from 5:30 pm. Closed: 12/25; also Sun & 1st week of March. **Reservations:** suggested. **Features:** Fine French cuisine is prepared in an elegant and charming vintage home near the shores of the St. Lawrence and adjacent to John Abbott College campus. The dining room exudes romance, while the menu highlights rack of lamb, red deer, sweetbreads and fresh fish. Casual dress; cocktails. **Parking:** on-site (fee). **Cards:** AX, DC, MC, VI.

ST-HUBERT-DE-RIVERE-DU-LOUP

———— WHERE TO DINE ————

ST-HUBERT
▼▼ ▼▼
Canadian
MC, VI.

Lunch: $7-$20　　**Dinner:** $7-$20　　**Phone:** 450/443-8774
Location: Centre. 5885 boul Cousineau J3Y 7P5. **Hours:** 11 am-10 pm, Thurs-Sat to 11 pm. Closed: 12/25. **Reservations:** accepted. **Features:** The pleasantly decorated family-friendly restaurant serves affordable chicken dinners, ribs, club sandwiches, chicken wings, salads, soups and hot chicken sandwiches. The children's menu includes animal nuggets. Casual dress; cocktails. **Parking:** on-site. **Cards:** AX, DC,

ST-JEROME pop. 54,060

———— WHERE TO STAY ————

COMFORT INN & SUITES　　*Book great rates at AAA.com*　　　**Phone:** 450/438-8000
▼▼▼ ▼▼　　All Year [ECP]　　1P: $99-$117　　2P: $99-$117　　XP: $15　　F18
Small-scale Hotel
Location: Hwy 15, exit 43E (Centre-ville), just e to Carrefour St-Jerome. 255-8 de Martigny ouest J7Y 2G4. Fax: 450/438-7005. **Facility:** 85 one-bedroom standard units, some with whirlpools. 3 stories, interior corridors. *Bath:* combo or shower only. **Parking:** on-site. **Terms:** cancellation fee imposed, package plans. **Amenities:** video library (fee), DVD players, CD players, high-speed Internet, voice mail, irons, hair dryers. **Leisure Activities:** exercise room. **Guest Services:** valet laundry, wireless Internet. **Business Services:** meeting rooms, PC. **Cards:** AX, CB, DC, DS, JC, MC, VI. *(See color ad card insert)*

SOME UNITS

HOTEL BEST WESTERN ST-JEROME　　*Book great rates at AAA.com*　　**Phone:** (450)438-1155
(CAA) (SAVE)　　All Year [BP]　　1P: $106　　2P: $111　　XP: $5　　F17
▼▼▼ ▼▼ ▼▼
Small-scale Hotel
Location: Hwy 15, exit 43E (Centre-ville), just e on de Martigny. Located in a quiet area. 420 rue Mgr-Dubois J7Y 3L8. Fax: 450/438-9440. **Facility:** 50 one-bedroom standard units. 2 stories (no elevator), interior corridors. **Parking:** on-site, winter plug-ins. **Terms:** check-in 4 pm. **Amenities:** voice mail, honor bars, irons, hair dryers. *Some:* DVD players, CD players. **Dining:** 7-10:30 am, 11:30-2 & 5-10 pm, Sat 8 am-11 & 5-9 pm, Sun 8 am-1 & 5-9 pm, cocktails. **Pool(s):** heated outdoor. **Guest Services:** valet laundry, wireless Internet. **Business Services:** meeting rooms, PC. **Cards:** AX, MC, VI. **Free Special Amenities: full breakfast and high-speed Internet.**

SOME UNITS

———— WHERE TO DINE ————

ROTISSERIE SCORES
▼▼ ▼▼
Barbecue

Lunch: $6-$20　　**Dinner:** $8-$25　　**Phone:** 450/432-2060
Location: Hwy 15, exit 43E (Centre-ville), just e to Carrefour St-Jerome. 255 de Martigny, #7 J7Y 2G4. **Hours:** 11 am-11 pm. **Reservations:** accepted. **Features:** The chain of family restaurants offers a varied menu that includes rotisserie chicken, ribs, salad-bar items, sandwiches, poutine and sugar, lemon or pecan pie. Casual dress; cocktails. **Parking:** on-site. **Cards:** AX, MC, VI.

ST-LAURENT (MONTREAL)　(See map and index starting on p. 420)

———— WHERE TO STAY ————

ECONO LODGE　　*Book great rates at AAA.com*　　　**Phone:** (514)735-5702　 **47**
(CAA) (SAVE)　　All Year　　1P: $69-$89　　2P: $79-$99　　XP: $10　　F12
▼▼ ▼▼
Small-scale Hotel
Location: Hwy 520 E, exit Hickmore, take underpass n to rue Griffith, then just e; hotel entrance on rue Griffith, just n of north side service road (Cote-de-Liesse); in St-Laurent sector. 6755 Cote-de-Liesse H4T 1E5. Fax: 514/340-9278. **Facility:** 76 one-bedroom standard units, some with whirlpools. 2 stories (no elevator), interior corridors. **Parking:** on-site, winter plug-ins. **Terms:** cancellation fee imposed, package plans. **Amenities:** irons, hair dryers. **Guest Services:** valet and coin laundry, wireless Internet. **Business Services:** meeting rooms, PC. **Cards:** AX, DC, DS, JC, MC, VI. **Free Special Amenities: continental breakfast and high-speed Internet.** *(See color ad card insert)*

SOME UNITS

FEE　FEE

NOVOTEL MONTREAL AEROPORT　　　　　**Phone:** 514/337-3222
(fyi)
Small-scale Hotel
Property failed to provide current rates
Too new to rate, opening scheduled for November 2006. **Location:** Hwy 40, exit 58. 2529 boul Alfred Nobel H4S 1C8. Fax: 514/337-9222. **Amenities:** 120 units, pets, restaurant, refrigerators, pool. *(See color ad p 473)*

QUALITY HOTEL DORVAL　　*Book great rates at AAA.com*　　**Phone:** (514)731-7821　 **49**
(CAA) (SAVE)　　All Year　　1P: $127　　2P: $127　　XP: $10　　F12
▼▼▼ ▼▼
Small-scale Hotel
Location: Hwy 520, exit 4 eastbound on south side service road; exit 4 (Montee-de-Liesse) westbound; in St-Laurent sector. 7700 Cote-de-Liesse H4T 1E7. Fax: 514/731-7267. **Facility:** 159 one-bedroom standard units. 4 stories, interior corridors. **Parking:** on-site. **Amenities:** video games (fee), high-speed Internet, voice mail, safes, irons, hair dryers. **Dining:** 6:30 am-2 & 6-11:30 pm, cocktails. **Pool(s):** heated outdoor. **Leisure Activities:** saunas, whirlpools, exercise room. **Guest Services:** sundries, valet and coin laundry, airport transportation-Pierre Elliott Trudeau International Airport, area transportation-within 5 km. **Business Services:** meeting rooms, business center. **Cards:** AX, CB, DC, DS, JC, MC, VI. *(See color ad card insert)*

SOME UNITS

FEE

(See map and index starting on p. 420)

RAMADA MONTREAL AIRPORT HOTEL   *Book great rates at AAA.com*   Phone: (514)733-8818   **48**

CAA SAVE

| 5/1-9/30 | 1P: $139-$159 | 2P: $149-$169 | XP: $10 | F17 |
| 10/1-4/30 | 1P: $119-$129 | 2P: $129-$139 | XP: $10 | F17 |

Location: Hwy 520, exit 4 eastbound on south side service road; exit Montee-de-Liesse westbound. 7300 Cote-de-Liesse H4T 1E7. Fax: 514/733-9889. **Facility:** 186 units. 183 one-bedroom standard units. 3 one-bedroom

Large-scale Hotel   suites. 2 stories, interior corridors. **Parking:** on-site, winter plug-ins. **Terms:** 7 day cancellation notice-fee imposed. **Amenities:** video games (fee), voice mail, irons, hair dryers. **Dining:** 6:30 am-11 pm, Sat & Sun 7:30 am-11:30 & 4-11 pm, cocktails. **Pool(s):** outdoor. **Leisure Activities:** exercise room. **Guest Services:** valet and coin laundry, airport transportation-Pierre Elliott Trudeau International Airport, wireless Internet. **Business Services:** conference facilities, administrative services (fee), PC. **Cards:** AX, MC, VI. **Free Special Amenities:** local telephone calls and high-speed Internet. *(See color ad p 474)*

SOME UNITS
FEE FEE FEE

——— **WHERE TO DINE** ———

LE BIFTHEQUE   Lunch: $7-$20   Dinner: $10-$20   Phone: 514/739-6336

Steak House   **Location:** Hwy 520 W, exit Hickmore; in St-Laurent sector. 6705 Cote-de-Liesse H4T 1E5. **Hours:** 11:30 am-10:30 pm. **Reservations:** accepted. **Features:** The restaurant satisfies the cravings of folks in the mood for a sizzling steak. Huge portions of traditional steakhouse fare-including fine steaks, prime rib and seafood selections-keep locals coming back. Among starters are shrimp cocktail, French onion soup and escargots. Meals come with a tasty house salad and the ever-popular biftheque croutons. Diners should arrive with a hearty appetite. Casual dress; cocktails. **Parking:** on-site. **Cards:** AX, CB, DC, DS, JC, MC, VI.

STE-DOROTHEE   (See map and index starting on p. 420)

——— **WHERE TO DINE** ———

DUNNS FAMOUS   Lunch: $7-$20   Dinner: $7-$20   Phone: 450/689-2525   **82**

Deli/Subs
Sandwiches   **Location:** 0.6 mi (1 km) n of boul Samson, from Hwy 13; in Mega Centre Ste-Dorothee; off westside service road. 2260 Autoroute Chomedey H7X 4G8. **Hours:** 11 am-11 pm. Closed: 1/1, 12/25. **Reservations:** accepted. **Features:** This suburban delicatessen specializes in Montreal-style smoked meat on rye, grilled steaks, latkes, matzo ball soup, chopped liver and club rolls. For dessert, cheesecake is hard to beat. Casual dress; cocktails. **Parking:** on-site. **Cards:** MC, VI.

STE-JULIE   pop. 28,580

——— **WHERE TO DINE** ———

RESTAURANT NORMANDIN   Lunch: $5-$12   Dinner: $5-$12   Phone: 450/922-9221

Canadian   **Location:** Just s of Hwy 20. 2001 rue Nobel J3E 1W6. **Hours:** 6 am-midnight, Thurs-2 am, Fri & Sat-3 am. Closed: 12/25. **Reservations:** accepted. **Features:** The family restaurant prepares affordable comfort foods that include roasted chicken, hot chicken sandwiches, pasta, burgers and fries. Take-out service, a children's menu and cutely decorated desserts are among other offerings. Casual dress; cocktails. **Parking:** on-site. **Cards:** AX, DC, MC, VI.

VAUDREUIL-DORION   pop. 18,500   (See map and index starting on p. 420)

——— **WHERE TO STAY** ———

CHATEAU VAUDREUIL SUITES HOTEL   *Book great rates at AAA.com*   Phone: (450)455-0955   **70**

CAA SAVE

| All Year | 1P: $200-$550 | 2P: $200-$550 | XP: $10 | F18 |

Location: Hwy 40, exit 36 westbound; exit 35 eastbound. 21700 Trans-Canada Hwy 40 J7V 8P3. Fax: 450/455-6617. **Facility:** On manicured grounds, this modern chateau-style hotel affords views of Lac des Deux Montagnes; guest rooms and public areas are luxuriously appointegetd. 116 units. 2 one-bedroom standard units with

Large-scale Hotel   whirlpools. 114 one-bedroom suites, some with whirlpools. 6 stories, interior corridors. **Parking:** on-site, winter plug-ins. **Terms:** cancellation fee imposed, package plans, 15% service charge. **Amenities:** voice mail, safes, honor bars, irons, hair dryers. *Fee:* video games, high-speed Internet. *Some:* DVD players, CD players, fax. **Dining:** Villa D'Este, see separate listing. **Pool(s):** heated indoor. **Leisure Activities:** whirlpool, steamroom, rental boats, rental canoes, rental paddleboats, boat dock, fishing, 2 tennis courts, ice skating, rental bicycles, playground, exercise room, volleyball. *Fee:* massage. **Guest Services:** gift shop, valet laundry. **Business Services:** conference facilities, business center. **Cards:** AX, DC, DS, MC, VI. **Free Special Amenities:** newspaper and preferred room (subject to availability with advance reservations). *(See color ad p 430)*

SOME UNITS

SUPER 8   *Book at AAA.com*   Phone: (450)424-8898   **71**

5/1-9/1 [CP]	1P: $105-$179	2P: $110-$200	XP: $10	F16
3/1-4/30 [CP]	1P: $98-$159	2P: $105-$179	XP: $10	F16
9/2-11/30 [CP]	1P: $98-$159	2P: $98-$179	XP: $10	F16
12/1-2/29 [CP]	1P: $90-$159	2P: $90-$169	XP: $10	F16

Small-scale Hotel   **Location:** Hwy 40, exit 35, just s on ave St Charles, 0.3 mi (0.4 km) w on boul de la Cite-des-Jeunes, then just n. 3200 Felix-Leclerc J7V 8W5. Fax: 450/424-9089. **Facility:** 56 one-bedroom standard units, some with whirlpools. 4 stories, interior corridors. **Parking:** on-site. **Amenities:** high-speed Internet, hair dryers. **Pool(s):** small heated indoor. **Leisure Activities:** whirlpool. **Business Services:** meeting rooms. **Cards:** AX, DC, JC, MC, VI.

SOME UNITS

(See map and index starting on p. 420)

——— **WHERE TO DINE** ———

CHEZ CORA

▼▼▼ ▼▼▼

Canadian

Casual dress. **Parking:** on-site. **Cards:** AX, DC, MC, VI.

Lunch: $7-$11   **Phone:** 450/424-2220
Location: On Hwy 20. 84 boul Harwood J7V 1X8. **Hours:** 6 am-3 pm, Sun from 7 am. Closed: 1/1, 12/25.
Reservations: accepted. **Features:** Although this place specializes in breakfast, it offers a varied daytime menu that includes bacon, eggs, sausages, crepes, grilled cheese, sandwiches, freshly prepared quiches, salads, fruit platters and freshly squeezed juices. The family-friendly dining room is casual and modern.

ST-HUBERT

▼▼ ▼▼

Canadian

MC, VI.

Lunch: $7-$20   **Dinner:** $7-$20   **Phone:** 450/455-0409
Location: Hwy 40, exit 35. 601 ave St-Charles J7V 7H4. **Hours:** 11 am-11 pm, Fri & Sat-midnight. Closed: 12/25.
Reservations: accepted. **Features:** The pleasantly decorated family-friendly restaurant serves affordable chicken dinners, ribs, club sandwiches, chicken wings, salads, soups and hot chicken sandwiches. The children's menu includes animal nuggets. Casual dress; cocktails. **Parking:** on-site. **Cards:** AX, DC,

---

VILLA D'ESTE

Italian

DS, MC, VI.

Lunch: $8-$35   **Dinner:** $12-$35   **Phone:** 450/455-0955   [131]
Location: Hwy 40, exit 36 westbound; exit 35 eastbound; in Chateau Vaudreuil Suites Hotel. 21700 Trans-Canada Hwy 40 J7V 8P3. **Hours:** 6 am-11 pm. **Reservations:** suggested. **Features:** Elegant decor and an exceptional lake view enhance the dining experience in the casually upscale restaurant. The menu focuses on fine Italian cuisine, which is backed by an impressive selection of imported wines. Live band entertainment accompanies dinner and dancing on Friday and Saturday evenings. Weekday lunch buffets and a popular Sunday brunch are other offerings. Semi-formal attire; cocktails. **Parking:** on-site and valet. **Cards:** AX, DC,

---

——— *The following restaurant has not been evaluated by AAA* ———
but is listed for your information only.

DIC ANN'S HAMBURGERS

[fyi]

Not evaluated. Location: On Hwy 20; centre. 280 boul Harwood J7V 1Y5. **Features:** This popular fast-food diner specializes in small flat spicy hamburgers. Dine in or take out.

VERDUN pop. 60,564   (See map and index starting on p. 420)

——— **WHERE TO DINE** ———

VILLA WELLINGTON

▼▼ ▼▼

Peruvian

Lunch: $8-$19   **Dinner:** $8-$19   **Phone:** 514/768-0102   [93]
Location: Corner of 2nd Ave; in Verdun sector. 4701 rue Wellington H4G 1X2. **Hours:** 11 am-10 pm. Closed: 12/25; also Mon. **Reservations:** accepted. **Features:** South American handicrafts decorate this casual eatery, within walking distance of de l'Eglise subway station in a vibrant blue-collar neighborhood. The menu boasts hearty portions of affordable Peruvian dishes, including grilled fish, steak, seasoned rice, seafood, stews, grilled chicken, calamari and marinated seafood salad. Casual dress; cocktails. **Parking:** street. **Cards:** MC, VI.

WESTMOUNT pop. 19,727   (See maps and indexes starting on p. 414, 420)

——— **WHERE TO DINE** ———

BISTRO ON THE AVENUE

▼▼▼

French

street. **Cards:** AX, DS, MC, VI.

Lunch: $10-$17   **Dinner:** $10-$25   **Phone:** 514/939-6451   [85]
Location: Between rue Sherbrooke and rue Ste-Catherine. 1362 Greene Ave H3Z 2B1. **Hours:** 11:30 am-10:30 pm, Thurs-Sat to 11 pm. Closed: 1/1, 12/24, 12/25; also 12/31. **Reservations:** suggested. **Features:** On a popular commercial strip in an upscale neighborhood, the chic bistro offers gourmet burgers and sandwiches, fresh grilled fish, chicken, pasta and a variety of salads. Casual dress; cocktails. **Parking:**

CHINE TOQUE

▼▼▼

Chinese

street. **Cards:** AX, DC, MC, VI.

Lunch: $8-$15   **Dinner:** $8-$15   **Phone:** 514/989-5999   [125]
Location: Just w of ave Atwater. 4050 rue Ste-Catherine ouest H3Z 1P2. **Hours:** 11:30 am-2:30 & 5:30-10 pm; Sat & Sun from 5:30 pm. Closed major holidays. **Reservations:** suggested. **Features:** This downtown dining room offers fine Chinese cuisine in an appealing atmosphere. The menu includes Szechuan pork, Cantonese duck, crispy orange beef, General Tao chicken, shrimp in a black bean sauce, chicken dumplings with peanut butter sauce and Singapore-style rice noodles. Take-out is available. Casual dress; cocktails. **Parking:**

KAIZEN SUSHI BAR & RESTAURANT

▼▼▼

Japanese

street. **Cards:** AX, MC, VI.

Lunch: $12-$32   **Dinner:** $14-$29   **Phone:** 514/707-8744   [126]
Location: Between ave Wood and ave Greene. 4075 rue Ste-Catherine ouest H3Z 3J8. **Hours:** 11:30 am-2:30 & 5:30-10:30 pm, Fri-11 pm, Sat noon-2:30 & 5:30-11 pm, Sun 5:30 pm-10:30 pm. Closed: 1/1, 12/25. **Reservations:** suggested. **Features:** Guests can dine at a private table or join others at the Japanese-style sushi bar, where a talented chef prepares fresh sushi dishes. Amid the stylish and upscale decor, patrons order a variety of sushi and sashimi dishes, in addition to teriyaki beef, chicken and shrimp. Dressy casual; cocktails. **Parking:**

MISO

▼▼ ▼▼

Japanese

Lunch: $10-$16   **Dinner:** $10-$30   **Phone:** 514/908-6476   [124]
Location: Corner of rue Atwater. 4000 rue Ste-Catherine ouest H3Z 1P1. **Hours:** 11 am-3 & 5-10 pm. Closed: 12/25. **Reservations:** accepted. **Features:** This stylish Asian restaurant faces the old Montreal Forum Arena (now an entertainment complex) and features a vast selection of freshly prepared sushi and sashimi. Casual dress; cocktails. **Parking:** street. **Cards:** AX, MC, VI.

(See maps and indexes starting on p. 414, 420)

RESTAURANT MESS HALL BISTRO-BAR   **Lunch:** $13-$24   **Dinner:** $13-$34   **Phone:** 514/482-2167   **87**
Location: Just w of rue Victoria. 4858 rue Sherbrooke ouest H3Z 1H1. **Hours:** 11:30 am-4 & 5-11 pm, Sun from 5
pm. Closed: 1/1, 12/25. **Reservations:** suggested. **Features:** The casually upscale Westmount eatery
Continental   serves market-fresh dishes that exhibit Italian and French influences. Guests choose from among pasta
dishes, gourmet burgers, calamari, pork, fresh fish, steak and sandwiches. The seasonal terrace is popular
in summer. Casual dress; cocktails. **Parking:** street. **Cards:** AX, DC, MC, VI.

TAVERNE SUR LE SQUARE   **Lunch:** $10-$25   **Dinner:** $14-$45   **Phone:** 514/989-9779   **127**
Location: Corner of rue Ste-Catherine and Westmount Square Shopping Mall. 1 Westmount Square H3Z 2P9.
Hours: 11:30 am-3 & 6-11 pm, Sat from 6 pm. Closed major holidays; also Sun. **Reservations:** suggested.
Continental   **Features:** In Westmount Square shopping mall, the upscale bistro serves market-fresh cuisine, including a
selection of lighter meals at lunchtime. Among menu offerings are steak and fries, fresh fish, meat chops,
macaroni, grilled tuna sandwiches, salads, burgers and fish and chips. Dressy casual; cocktails. **Parking:** on-site. **Cards:** AX,
MC, VI.

VAGO CUCINA ITALIANA   **Lunch:** $13-$22   **Dinner:** $13-$42   **Phone:** 514/846-1414   **86**
Location: Just s of rue Sherbrooke. 1336 ave Greene H3Z 2B1. **Hours:** 11:45 am-11 pm, Sat from 5 pm. Closed:
Sun, 12/24-1/7. **Reservations:** accepted. **Features:** On fashionable Greene Avenue, the upscale bistro
Italian   offers seating in both the main dining room and in a bright atrium. The menu lines up a strong variety of
pasta dishes and several Italian specialties, such as chicken Marsala. Cherries jubilee is a tempting ender.
Casual dress; cocktails. **Parking:** street. **Cards:** AX, DC, MC, VI.

Fête des Neiges / © Tourisme Montréal

This ends listings for the Montreal Vicinity.
The following page resumes the alphabetical listings of cities in Quebec.

MONTREAL-NORD —See Montreal p. 491.

MONTREAL-OUEST —See Montreal p. 491.

MONT-ST-HILAIRE —See Montreal p. 491.

MONT-TREMBLANT CENTRE DE VILLEGIATURE pop. 8,352

——— WHERE TO STAY ———

AUBERGE LE LUPIN BED & BREAKFAST　　　　　　　　　　　　　**Phone: (819)425-5474**

▽▽▽▽　　All Year　　　　　　　　　1P: $80-$145　　　　2P: $95-$150
　　　　Location: Centre. 127 rue Pinoteau J8E 1G2. Fax: 819/425-6079. **Facility:** This welcoming log home has
Bed & Breakfast　spacious rooms ideal for small families, is just 0.6 mi (1 km) from the ski hill and is within walking distance
　　　　of public beaches. Smoke free premises. 9 one-bedroom standard units. 2 stories (no elevator), interior
corridors. **Bath:** combo or shower only. **Parking:** on-site. **Terms:** 2 night minimum stay - weekends, 21 day cancellation notice,
[BP] meal plan available, package plans, no pets allowed (owner's pets on premises). **Amenities:** hair dryers. Some: CD
players. **Leisure Activities:** beach access, cross country skiing, playground. **Guest Services:** complimentary laundry, wireless
Internet. **Cards:** AX, DC, JC, MC, VI.

SOME UNITS

CHATEAU BEAUVALLON　　*Book great rates at AAA.com*　　　　　　**Phone: (819)681-6611**

(CAA) (SAVE)　All Year　　　　　　1P: $209-$479　　　2P: $209-$479　　　XP: $39
　　　　Location: Hwy 117, exit 119, 4 mi (6.4 km) e. 6385 Montee-Ryan J8E 1S5. Fax: 819/681-1941. **Facility:** The
▽▽▽▽　upscale condo-hotel offers luxurious one-, two- and three-bedroom condos just outside the resort village, in
　　　　a quiet wooded area on a small lake. Smoke free premises. 70 units. 42 one-, 22 two- and 6 three-bedroom
Condominium　suites, some with efficiencies or kitchens. 3 stories, interior corridors. **Parking:** on-site and valet, winter
　　　　plug-ins. **Terms:** 1-2 night minimum stay - weekends, 7 day cancellation notice-fee imposed, [CP], [ECP] &
[MAP] meal plans available, package plans, 2% service charge. **Amenities:** CD players, high-speed Internet, dual phone lines,
voice mail, safes, irons, hair dryers. **Dining:** Bon Vivant Grill, see separate listing. **Pool(s):** heated outdoor, heated indoor,
wading. **Leisure Activities:** sauna, whirlpool, putting green, hiking trails, exercise room, game room. *Fee:* massage. **Guest
Services:** valet and coin laundry, area transportation-within 30 km. **Business Services:** meeting rooms, PC. **Cards:** AX, DC,
DS, MC, VI. **Free Special Amenities:** expanded continental breakfast and early check-in/late check-out.

FEE

CLUB TREMBLANT L'HOTEL DU LAC　　*Book at AAA.com*　　　　　**Phone: 819/425-8781**

▽▽▽▽　12/16-1/2 [MAP]　　　　1P: $212-$323　　　2P: $324-$528
　　　　1/3-4/30　　　　　　　1P: $219-$269　　　2P: $219-$269
Resort　　5/1-9/3　　　　　　　1P: $159-$269　　　2P: $159-$269
Condominium　9/4-12/15　　　　　1P: $159-$169　　　2P: $159-$169
　　　　Location: Hwy 117, exit 119 (Montee Ryan), 5.4 mi (9 km) e, 0.5 mi (0.9 km) n on chemin Principale, then 0.5 mi (0.9
km) e on chemin du lac Tremblant nord. 121 rue Cuttle J8E 1B9. Fax: 819/425-5617. **Facility:** The hotel, on an elevated site
overlooking a lake, offers accommodations with fireplaces, full kitchens and modern amenities. 100 units. 33 one-, 65 two- and
2 three-bedroom suites with kitchens, some with whirlpools. 2-3 stories (no elevator), interior/exterior corridors. **Parking:** on-
site, winter plug-ins. **Terms:** check-in 4:30 pm, 15 day cancellation notice-fee imposed, [AP], [BP] & [MAP] meal plans available,
package plans. **Amenities:** voice mail, irons, hair dryers. **Pool(s):** heated outdoor, heated indoor. **Leisure Activities:** sauna,
whirlpools, boating, canoeing, paddleboats, boat dock, fishing, miniature golf, 3 tennis courts, cross country skiing, ice skating,
recreation programs, hiking trails, jogging, playground, exercise room, spa, volleyball. *Fee:* waterskiing, charter fishing, downhill
skiing, game room. **Guest Services:** gift shop, valet laundry, area transportation, beauty salon. **Business Services:** meeting
rooms, business center. **Cards:** AX, CB, DC, DS, JC, MC, VI.

SOME UNITS

COMFORT INN & SUITES MONT-TREMBLANT　　*Book great rates at AAA.com*　　**Phone: (819)429-6000**

(CAA) (SAVE)　12/21-1/6　　　　　1P: $149-$219　　　2P: $149-$219　　　XP: $15　　F17
　　　　5/1-12/20 & 1/7-4/30　1P: $79-$169　　　2P: $79-$169　　　XP: $15　　F17
▽▽▽▽　**Location:** On Rt 117, 0.5 mi (0.8 km) ne of St-Jovite village. 860 rue LaLonde (CP 4598) J8E 1A1.
　　　　Fax: 819/429-6001. **Facility:** 94 one-bedroom standard units. 3 stories, interior corridors. **Bath:** combo or
Small-scale Hotel　shower only. **Parking:** on-site, winter plug-ins. **Terms:** check-in 4 pm, 2 night minimum stay - weekends,
　　　　package plans, $2 service charge. **Amenities:** video library (fee), DVD players, irons, hair dryers. **Pool(s):**
heated indoor. **Leisure Activities:** whirlpool, snowmobiling. **Guest Services:** coin laundry, area transportation (fee)-ski hills,
wireless Internet. **Business Services:** meeting rooms, PC. **Cards:** AX, DC, DS, MC, VI. **Free Special Amenities: continental
breakfast and high-speed Internet.** *(See color ad card insert)*

SOME UNITS

COUNTRY INN & SUITES BY CARLSON　　*Book at AAA.com*　　　　**Phone: (819)681-5555**

▽▽▽▽　12/16-4/30 [BP]　　　1P: $129-$499　　　2P: $129-$499　　　XP: $15　　F18
　　　　5/1-12/15 [BP]　　　　1P: $119-$299　　　2P: $119-$299　　　XP: $15　　F18
Condominium　**Location:** In Mont-Tremblant Resort centre. 160 chemin Cure-Deslauriers J8E 1T1. Fax: 819/681-5556.
　　　　Facility: These suites and single rooms offer quality furnishings and a charming mix of country and
contemporary. 139 units. 54 one-bedroom standard units. 85 one-bedroom suites with kitchens. 4 stories, interior corridors.
Parking: on-site. **Terms:** check-in 4 pm, 2-5 night minimum stay - seasonal, cancellation fee imposed, package plans, 3%
service charge. **Amenities:** video games (fee), high-speed Internet, voice mail, irons, hair dryers. **Pool(s):** heated outdoor.
Leisure Activities: sauna, whirlpool, rental paddleboats, fishing, cross country skiing, recreation programs, hiking trails,
jogging, playground, limited exercise equipment. *Fee:* boats, canoes, sailboats, windsurfing, waterskiing, charter fishing, golf-36
holes, 6 lighted tennis courts, downhill skiing, ice skating, bicycles, massage. **Guest Services:** valet and coin laundry, area
transportation, wireless Internet. **Cards:** AX, DC, DS, MC, VI.

SOME UNITS

CRYSTAL INN

▽▽▽

Bed & Breakfast

All Year [BP]   1P: $59-$69   2P: $78-$98   XP: $25

Phone: 819/681-7775

Location: Jct Hwy 117 N, exit 119 (Montee Ryan), 0.5 mi (0.8 km) e on Montee Ryan. 100 rue Joseph-Thibault J8E 2G4. Fax: 819/681-7775. **Facility:** A gemstone theme governs upscale guest rooms, which are painted in bold colors and include Memory Foam mattresses, upscale bedding and bathrobes. Smoke free premises. 4 one-bedroom standard units. 2 stories (no elevator), interior corridors. *Bath:* some shared or private. **Parking:** on-site, winter plug-ins. **Terms:** 10 day cancellation notice-fee imposed. **Amenities:** CD players, hair dryers. **Leisure Activities:** whirlpool.

SOME UNITS

✕ 🏋 ☎ / 📺 📼 /

ERMITAGE DU LAC MT TREMBLANT

(CAA) (SAVE)

▽▽▽

Condominium

All Year [ECP]   1P: $149-$389   XP: $20   F12

Phone: (819)681-2222

Location: In Mont-Tremblant Resort centre. 150 Cure-Deslauriers J8C 1E9. Fax: 819/681-2223. **Facility:** Most of these luxurious studio, one-, two- or three-bedroom condos have a fireplace and balcony. All have either an efficiency or full kitchen area. Smoke free premises. 69 units. 22 one-bedroom standard units, some with efficiencies. 35 one-, two- and 6 three-bedroom suites ($169-$1259), some with efficiencies or kitchens. 5 stories, interior corridors. *Bath:* combo or shower only. **Parking:** on-site. **Terms:** check-in 4 pm, 31 day cancellation notice-fee imposed, package plans. **Amenities:** video games (fee), CD players, high-speed Internet, voice mail, irons, hair dryers. **Pool(s):** heated outdoor. **Leisure Activities:** sauna, whirlpool, limited beach access, rental paddleboats, fishing, cross country skiing, recreation programs, hiking trails, jogging, playground, exercise room. *Fee:* boats, canoes, sailboats, windsurfing, charter fishing, golf-36 holes, 6 lighted tennis courts, downhill skiing, ice skating, bicycles. **Guest Services:** valet and coin laundry. **Business Services:** meeting rooms. **Cards:** AX, CB, DC, DS, JC, MC, VI. **Free Special Amenities:** expanded continental breakfast and newspaper.

⑤🅳 🍴 ➳ ✕ ✕ 🎦 🖥 🖨 🖨

FAIRMONT TREMBLANT

(CAA) (SAVE)

▽▽▽▽▽

Resort
Large-scale Hotel

12/21-4/30   1P: $199-$619   2P: $199-$619   XP: $50   F17
5/1-12/20   1P: $189-$369   2P: $189-$369   XP: $50   F17

Phone: (819)681-7000

Location: In Mont-Tremblant Resort centre. 3045 chemin de la Chapelle J8E 1B1. Fax: 819/681-7099. **Facility:** This full-service hotel and spa offers ski-in/ski-out facilities along with well-appointed meeting space and a restaurant. 314 units. 259 one-bedroom standard units. 55 one-bedroom suites, some with efficiencies or kitchens. 7 stories, interior corridors. **Parking:** valet. **Terms:** check-in 4 pm, 2 night minimum stay - weekends, cancellation fee imposed, package plans, 3% service charge. **Amenities:** voice mail, safes, honor bars, irons, hair dryers. *Fee:* video games, high-speed Internet. *Some:* CD players. **Dining:** 3 restaurants, 7 am-midnight, cocktails. **Pool(s):** heated outdoor, heated indoor. **Leisure Activities:** sauna, whirlpools, steamrooms, rental boats, cross country skiing, hiking trails, exercise room, spa. *Fee:* canoes, paddleboats, sailboats, windsurfing, fishing, charter fishing, golf-36 holes, 8 lighted tennis courts, downhill skiing, ice skating, bicycles. **Guest Services:** gift shop, valet and coin laundry. **Business Services:** conference facilities, business center. **Cards:** AX, DC, DS, MC, VI.

SOME UNITS

⑤🅳 🍴 24🍴 ☀ 🙅 🄼 🍽 ➳ ✕ 🎦 🖨 / ✕ 🖨 /

HOMEWOOD SUITES BY HILTON-MONT-TREMBLANT

▽▽▽▽

Condominium

Book great rates at AAA.com

12/21-4/30   1P: $169-$475   2P: $169-$759   XP: $30   F17
5/1-12/20   1P: $129-$235   2P: $129-$325   XP: $30   F17

Phone: (819)681-0808

Location: In Mont-Tremblant Resort centre. 3035 de la Chapelle J8E 1E1. Fax: 819/681-0331. **Facility:** Three buildings with brightly colored roofs house these one- to three-bedroom condo units in the center of a ski resort village. 103 units. 24 one-bedroom standard units with kitchens. 68 one- and 11 two-bedroom suites with kitchens. 3-5 stories, interior corridors. **Parking:** on-site. **Terms:** check-in 4 pm, 14 day cancellation notice, package plans, 3% service charge. **Amenities:** high-speed Internet, dual phone lines, voice mail, irons, hair dryers. **Leisure Activities:** rental paddleboats, cross country skiing, recreation programs, hiking trails, jogging, playground. *Fee:* boats, canoes, sailboats, windsurfing, waterskiing, fishing, charter fishing, golf-36 holes, 6 lighted tennis courts, downhill skiing, bicycles, massage. **Guest Services:** gift shop, valet and coin laundry, area transportation. **Business Services:** meeting rooms. **Cards:** AX, DC, DS, MC, VI.

SOME UNITS

(ASK) ⑤🅳 🍴 🙅 ✕ 🖨 🖨 🖥 / ✕ /

HOTEL QUINTESSENCE

(CAA) (SAVE)

▽▽▽▽

Small-scale Hotel

All Year   1P: $289-$1839   2P: $289-$1839   XP: $60   D6

Phone: (819)425-3400

Location: Hwy 117 N, exit 119 (Montee Ryan), 6 mi (10 km) e to Mont-Tremblant Resort centre. 3004 chemin de la Chapelle J8E 1E1. Fax: 819/425-3480. **Facility:** This lakefront boutique hotel and spa, on three acres of private grounds, has spacious, luxurious rooms with marble bathrooms and romantic fireplaces. 31 units. 25 one-bedroom standard units with whirlpools. 5 one-bedroom suites with whirlpools. 1 cottage. 4 stories, interior corridors. **Parking:** valet. **Terms:** check-in 4 pm, 2 night minimum stay - seasonal and/or weekends, cancellation fee imposed, weekly rates available, package plans, pets ($150 fee, in designated units). **Amenities:** CD players, high-speed Internet, dual phone lines, voice mail, safes, honor bars, irons, hair dryers. *Some:* DVD players. **Dining:** 2 restaurants, 7 am-10:30 pm, cocktails, also, Q Restaurant & Winebar, see separate listing. **Pool(s):** heated outdoor. **Leisure Activities:** sauna, whirlpool, steamroom, beach access, rental canoes, boat dock, ice skating, exercise room, spa. *Fee:* sunset boat cruise in a 1910 antique boat. **Guest Services:** valet laundry, area transportation-ski hill, wireless Internet. **Business Services:** meeting rooms, PC. **Cards:** AX, DC, DS, MC, VI. **Free Special Amenities:** newspaper and high-speed Internet.

SOME UNITS

🛏 🍴 24🍴 ☀ 🙅 ➳ ✕ ✕ 🎦 🖨 / 📼 /
FEE

LA CHOUETTE CONDOS

▽▽▽

Condominium

Property failed to provide current rates

Phone: 819/681-3000

Location: In Mont-Tremblant Resort centre. 140 chemin de la Montagne J9E 1T1. Fax: 819/681-5920. **Facility:** 29 units. 6 one-bedroom standard units with kitchens. 19 one- and 4 two-bedroom suites with kitchens. 3 stories (no elevator), exterior corridors. **Parking:** on-site. **Terms:** off-site registration, check-in 4 pm. **Amenities:** voice mail, irons, hair dryers. *Some:* DVD players, CD players. **Pool(s):** heated outdoor. **Leisure Activities:** rental paddleboats, fishing, cross country skiing, recreation programs, hiking trails, jogging, playground. *Fee:* boats, canoes, sailboats, windsurfing, waterskiing, charter fishing, golf-36 holes, 6 lighted tennis courts, downhill skiing, ice skating, bicycles. **Guest Services:** valet and coin laundry.

SOME UNITS

🍴 ➳ ✕ 🖨 🖨 / 📼 /

LA TOUR DES VOYAGEURS

Phone: (819)681-2000

CAA SAVE

12/22-3/24	1P: $149-$299	2P: $149-$299
6/22-12/21 & 3/25-4/30	1P: $99-$159	2P: $99-$159
5/1-6/21	1P: $99-$129	2P: $99-$129

Condominium

Location: In Mont-Tremblant Resort centre. 160 chemin Cure-Deslauriers J8E 1T1 (1000 chemin des Voyageurs). **Fax:** 819/681-5931. **Facility:** This property is in the center of the resort village and offers studios and one- and two-bedroom condos. 220 units. 109 one-bedroom standard units, some with kitchens. 92 one- and 19 two-bedroom suites with kitchens. 4 stories, interior corridors. **Parking:** on-site. **Terms:** check-in 4 pm, 15 day cancellation notice-fee imposed, package plans, 3% service charge. **Amenities:** video games (fee), high-speed Internet, voice mail, irons, hair dryers. **Dining:** 7 am-10 pm. **Pool(s):** heated outdoor. **Leisure Activities:** sauna, whirlpools, rental paddleboats, fishing, ice skating, recreation programs, hiking trails, jogging, playground, exercise room. *Fee:* boats, canoes, sailboats, windsurfing, waterskiing, charter fishing, golf-36 holes, miniature golf, 6 lighted tennis courts, downhill skiing, bicycles, massage. **Guest Services:** gift shop, valet and coin laundry, area transportation. **Business Services:** meeting rooms. **Cards:** AX, DS, JC, MC, VI.

SOME UNITS

LE GRAND LODGE MONT-TREMBLANT

Book great rates at AAA.com

Phone: (819)425-2734

CAA SAVE

| All Year | 1P: $120-$640 | 2P: $120-$640 | XP: $25 |
| | | | F17 |

Resort
Small-scale Hotel

Location: On Rt 327, 0.3 mi (0.4 km) s of Montee Ryan. 2396 rue Labelle J8E 1T8. **Fax:** 819/425-9725. **Facility:** This upscale hotel, in close proximity to a golf course and ski hill, features a log-beamed lobby and spacious guest rooms. Designated smoking area. 112 units. 11 one-bedroom standard units. 97 one- and 4 two-bedroom suites with kitchens. 4 stories, interior corridors. **Parking:** on-site, winter plug-ins. **Terms:** check-in 4 pm, 2-5 night minimum stay - seasonal and/or weekends, 8 day cancellation notice-fee imposed, [AP], [BP] & [MAP] meal plans available, package plans, small pets only ($25 fee, in designated units). **Amenities:** video games (fee), voice mail, irons, hair dryers. **Dining:** 7 am-10 pm, cocktails. **Pool(s):** heated indoor. **Leisure Activities:** sauna, whirlpool, steamrooms, canoeing, paddleboats, fishing, kayaks, 4 tennis courts, cross country skiing, ice skating, billiards, playground, exercise room, spa, horseshoes, volleyball, game room. *Fee:* downhill skiing, bicycles. **Guest Services:** gift shop, valet and coin laundry, area transportation-Tremblant ski area. **Business Services:** conference facilities, business center. **Cards:** AX, CB, DC, DS, JC, MC, VI.

FEE

LE LODGE DE LA MONTAGNE

Phone: (819)681-2000

CAA SAVE

12/22-3/24	1P: $149-$299	2P: $149-$299
6/22-12/21 & 3/25-4/30	1P: $99-$159	2P: $99-$159
5/1-6/21	1P: $99-$129	2P: $99-$129

Condominium

Location: In Mont-Tremblant Resort centre. 140 Au pied de la Montagne J8E 1T1 (1000 chemin des Voyageurs). **Fax:** 819/681-5920. **Facility:** Many of these condo units have fireplaces and are convenient to ski hills, village shops and nightlife. 137 units. 61 one-bedroom standard units, some with kitchens. 60 one- and 16 two-bedroom suites with kitchens. 5 stories, interior corridors. **Bath:** combo or shower only. **Parking:** on-site. **Terms:** check-in 4 pm, 15 day cancellation notice-fee imposed, package plans, 3% service charge. **Amenities:** video games (fee), high-speed Internet, voice mail, irons, hair dryers. **Pool(s):** heated outdoor. **Leisure Activities:** sauna, whirlpools, rental paddleboats, fishing, cross country skiing, recreation programs, hiking trails, jogging, exercise room. *Fee:* boats, canoes, sailboats, windsurfing, waterskiing, charter fishing, golf-36 holes, 6 lighted tennis courts, downhill skiing, ice skating, bicycles, massage. **Guest Services:** valet and coin laundry, area transportation. **Business Services:** meeting rooms. **Cards:** AX, CB, DC, DS, JC, MC, VI.

SOME UNITS

LE SOMMET DES NEIGES

Book great rates at AAA.com

Phone: (819)681-2000

CAA SAVE

12/22-3/24	1P: $229-$599	2P: $229-$599
3/25-4/30	1P: $199-$359	2P: $199-$359
6/22-12/21	1P: $199-$259	2P: $199-$259
5/1-6/21	1P: $159-$199	2P: $159-$199

Small-scale Hotel

Location: In Mont-Tremblant Resort centre. 1000 chemin des Voyageurs J8E 1T1. **Fax:** 819/681-5950. **Facility:** Smoke free premises. 115 units. 22 one-, 50 two- and 43 three-bedroom suites with kitchens, some with whirlpools. 4 stories, interior corridors. **Parking:** on-site. **Terms:** check-in 4 pm, 15 day cancellation notice-fee imposed, package plans, 3% service charge. **Amenities:** video games (fee), high-speed Internet, voice mail, irons, hair dryers. **Pool(s):** heated outdoor. **Leisure Activities:** sauna, whirlpool, rental paddleboats, fishing, cross country skiing, recreation programs, library, hiking trails, jogging, playground, exercise room, game room. *Fee:* boats, canoes, sailboats, windsurfing, waterskiing, charter fishing, golf-36 holes, miniature golf, 6 lighted tennis courts, downhill skiing, ice skating, bicycles, massage. **Guest Services:** valet and coin laundry, area transportation. **Business Services:** meeting rooms. **Cards:** AX, DS, JC, MC, VI.

LE WESTIN RESORT & SPA

Book great rates at AAA.com

Phone: (819)681-8000

CAA SAVE

| 10/27-4/30 | 1P: $179-$449 | 2P: $179-$449 | XP: $40 | F12 |
| 5/1-10/26 | 1P: $169-$339 | 2P: $169-$339 | XP: $40 | F12 |

Large-scale Hotel

Location: In Mont-Tremblant Resort centre; Hwy 117 N, exit 119 (Montee Ryan), 6 mi (10 km) e, follow signs. 100 chemin Kandahar J8E 1E2. **Fax:** 819/681-8001. **Facility:** In the Mont-Tremblant ski village, at the foot of the slopes, the hotel offers luxuriously appointed, spacious accommodations. Smoke free premises. 125 units. 54 one-bedroom standard units. 56 one- and 15 two-bedroom suites, some with efficiencies, kitchens and/or whirlpools. 6 stories, interior corridors. **Parking:** on-site (fee) and valet. **Terms:** check-in 4 pm, 30 day cancellation notice-fee imposed, package plans, 3% service charge. **Amenities:** dual phone lines, voice mail, safes, irons, hair dryers. *Fee:* video games, high-speed Internet. **Dining:** 7 am-11 pm, cocktails, also, Le Restaurant U, see separate listing. **Pool(s):** heated outdoor. **Leisure Activities:** sauna, whirlpool, rental boats, rental canoes, rental paddleboats, rental sailboats, cross country skiing, hiking trails, playground, exercise room, spa. *Fee:* fishing, charter fishing, golf-18 holes, 8 lighted tennis courts, downhill skiing, ice skating, bicycles. **Guest Services:** valet and coin laundry, area transportation (fee)-area attractions. **Business Services:** meeting rooms, administrative services (fee). **Cards:** AX, DC, MC, VI. *(See color ad p 5)*

MARRIOTT RESIDENCE INN MONT-TREMBLANT

▼▼▼▼

Small-scale Hotel

Phone: (819)681-4000

1/6-4/30 [CP]	1P: $175-$679	2P: $175-$679	XP: $30	F17
12/16-1/5 [CP]	1P: $175-$679	2P: $175-$679	XP: $60	F17
5/1-10/31 [CP]	1P: $109-$309	2P: $109-$339	XP: $30	F17
11/1-12/15 [CP]	1P: $109-$309	2P: $109-$309	XP: $30	F17

Location: In Mont-Tremblant Resort centre. 170 chemin du Cure Deslauriers J0T 1Z0. **Fax:** 819/681-4099. **Facility:** Smoke free premises. 127 units. 35 one-bedroom standard units. 92 one-bedroom suites with kitchens. 3 stories, interior corridors. **Parking:** on-site. **Terms:** check-in 4 pm, 3 day cancellation notice, 30 day in season. **Amenities:** video games (fee), high-speed Internet, voice mail, irons, hair dryers. **Pool(s):** heated outdoor. **Leisure Activities:** rental paddleboats, fishing, cross country skiing, hiking trails, jogging, exercise room. *Fee:* boats, canoes, sailboats, windsurfing, waterskiing, charter fishing, golf-36 holes, miniature golf, 6 lighted tennis courts, downhill skiing, ice skating, bicycles, massage. **Guest Services:** valet and coin laundry. **Business Services:** meeting rooms. **Cards:** AX, DC, DS, JC, MC, VI.

(ASK) ⊟ 🍽 ⊡ 🛶 ⊠ ✕ 📹 🛄 🖨 🖵

PLACE ST-BERNARD

(CAA) (SAVE)

◇

▼▼▼▼

Condominium

Phone: (819)681-2000

12/22-3/24	1P: $149-$299	2P: $149-$299
6/22-12/21 & 3/25-4/30	1P: $99-$159	2P: $99-$159
5/1-6/21	1P: $99-$129	2P: $99-$129

Location: In Mont-Tremblant Resort centre. 135 chemin Kandahar J8E 1T1 (1000 chemin des Voyageurs). **Fax:** 819/681-5982. **Facility:** Most of these spacious studio, one- and two-bedroom units, in the center of the resort village, have fireplaces; a few units have a second-level loft. 115 units. 33 one-bedroom standard units, some with kitchens. 67 one-, 14 two- and 1 three-bedroom suites with kitchens. 3 stories, interior corridors. **Parking:** on-site. **Terms:** off-site registration, check-in 4 pm, 15 day cancellation notice-fee imposed, package plans, 3% service charge. **Amenities:** video games (fee), high-speed Internet, voice mail, irons, hair dryers. **Pool(s):** heated indoor. **Leisure Activities:** sauna, whirlpools, rental paddleboats, fishing, cross country skiing, recreation programs, hiking trails, jogging, playground. *Fee:* boats, canoes, sailboats, windsurfing, waterskiing, charter fishing, golf-36 holes, miniature golf, 6 lighted tennis courts, downhill skiing, ice skating, bicycles. **Guest Services:** valet and coin laundry. **Cards:** AX, CB, DC, DS, JC, MC, VI.

SOME UNITS

⊟🍽 🛶 🛁 ⊠ 📹 / ✕ 🛄 🖨 /
FEE

The following lodgings were either not evaluated or did not meet AAA rating requirements but are listed for your information only.

GRAY ROCKS

[fyi]

Resort
Large-scale Hotel

Phone: 819/425-2771

Did not meet all AAA rating requirements for locking devices in some guest rooms at time of last evaluation on 06/29/2006. **Location:** Rt 117 N, exit 119 (Montee Ryan), 3.1 mi (5 km) e, 1 mi (1.7 km) s on Rt 327. 2322 rue Labelle J8E 1T8. Facilities, services, and decor characterize a mid-range property.

TREMBLANT SUNSTAR MOUNTAIN VACATION
HOME RENTALS

[fyi]

Condominium

Phone: 819/681-4717

Did not meet all AAA rating requirements for locking devices in some guest rooms at time of last evaluation on 03/24/2005. **Location:** Centre; below clock tower. 1000 chemin des Voyageurs J8E 1T1. Facilities, services, and decor characterize a mid-range property.

WHERE TO DINE

AUX TRUFFES

(CAA)

▼▼▼ ◇

French

Lunch: $15-$30   **Dinner:** $28-$45   **Phone:** 819/681-4544

Location: In Mont-Tremblant Resort centre. 3035 chemin de la Chapelle J8E 1B1. **Hours:** 11:30 am-3:30 & 6-10 pm; from 6 pm 10/1-6/24. **Reservations:** suggested. **Features:** Quality ingredients flavor such creatively presented dishes as foie gras, game and fowl specialties, veal sweetbreads and fresh fish. An extensive selection of fine international wine is available. Casual dress; cocktails. **Parking:** on-site (fee). **Cards:** AX, JC, MC, VI.

BON VIVANT GRILL

▼▼▼

French

Lunch: $9-$26   **Dinner:** $11-$26   **Phone:** 819/681-6488

Location: Hwy 117, exit 119, 4 mi (6.4 km) e. 6385 Montee-Ryan J8E 1S5. **Hours:** 7-10:30 am, 11-2:30 & 6-10 pm, Sat & Sun 7 am-2:30 & 6-10 pm; seasonal hours vary. **Reservations:** suggested. **Features:** This casually elegant hotel restaurant serves pleasantly presented dishes of regional cuisine, including lamb, beef, pasta and seafood. Lighter menu items include fish and chips, burgers, pizza, club sandwiches and lunch salads topped with an optional grilled item. Casual dress; cocktails. **Parking:** on-site. **Cards:** AX, DC, MC, VI.

⊡

BULLSEYE

▼▼▼ ◇

Steak House

Lunch: $10-$20   **Dinner:** $26-$50   **Phone:** 819/681-2855

Location: In Mont-Tremblant Resort centre. 118 Kandahar (CP 2609) J8E 1B1. **Hours:** 11 am-11 pm. **Reservations:** accepted. **Features:** At the foot of the ski slopes, the Western-themed steakhouse has a lively pub area for casual dining and an elegant evening dining room. The menu lists filet mignon, New York sirloin, rack of lamb, surf and turf, grilled salmon, Thai chicken, chicken quesadillas, burgers and salads, as well as children's fare. Casual dress; cocktails. **Parking:** street. **Cards:** AX, CB, DC, DS, MC, VI.

⊡

CREPERIE CATHERINE

▼▼▼

French

Lunch: $10-$20   **Dinner:** $10-$20   **Phone:** 819/681-4888

Location: In Mont-Tremblant Resort centre. 113 chemin Kandahar J8E 1A1. **Hours:** 7:30 am-9 pm, Fri & Sat-10 pm. **Reservations:** not accepted. **Features:** In a cozy wood cottage in the heart of the resort village, the lovely creperie prepares crepes (thin pancakes) before guests' eyes in an open kitchen. Meal supplements include salad, escargots and French onion soup. Casual dress; cocktails. **Parking:** on-site. **Cards:** AX, DC, MC, VI.

FAT MARDIS

Cajun

Lunch: $10-$25   **Dinner:** $10-$25   **Phone:** 819/681-2439

Location: In Mont-Tremblant Resort centre. 3035 ch de la Chapelle J8E 1E1. **Hours:** 11 am-11 pm. **Reservations:** not accepted. **Features:** This popular restaurant and bar is at the foot of the ski slopes and focuses on Cajun fare, including Louisiana-style po' boy sandwiches, gumbo, crab cakes, burgers, chicken wings, beer-battered halibut fish and chips, blackened catfish, sweet potato fries and AAA Angus steaks. The decor replicates the style of a vintage Bourbon Street burlesque nightclub and includes upholstered booths ideal for intimate dining. Casual dress; cocktails. **Parking:** on-site (fee). **Cards:** AX, DC, JC, MC, VI.

LA FORGE BAR & GRILL

Canadian

Lunch: $10-$25   **Dinner:** $19-$48   **Phone:** 819/681-4900

Location: In Mont-Tremblant Resort centre. 3041 ch de la Chapelle J8E 1B1. **Hours:** 11 am-close. **Reservations:** suggested. **Features:** Located at the foot of the ski hill, this restaurant has a casual pub-bistro downstairs and a finer dining room upstairs. The menu features meats, game and seafood cooked over a maplewood grill. The dining experience is bolstered by an impressive wine list. Salads, pub food and tasty desserts round out the menu. Dressy casual; cocktails. **Parking:** on-site. **Cards:** AX, DC, MC, VI.

LA TABLE ENCHANTEE

French

Dinner: $14-$36   **Phone:** 819/425-7113

Location: On Rt 117, 0.4 mi (0.7 km) n of Montee Ryan. 1842 Rt 117 J8E 2Y2. **Hours:** 5 pm-10 pm. Closed: Sun, Mon, 5/1-5/31 & 11/1-11/30. **Reservations:** suggested. **Features:** Fiddlehead greens, meatballs, game meats, sirloin steak, clam chowder, Matane shrimp and wild mushrooms are among savory selections on a menu of regional specialties. Old pictures, plants and flowers all contribute to the dining room's country appearance. Homemade desserts are irresistible. The neatly attired staff provides casual yet efficient service. Casual dress; cocktails. **Parking:** on-site. **Cards:** AX, MC, VI.

LE RESTAURANT U

Japanese

Dinner: $25-$40   **Phone:** 819/681-4141

Location: In Mont-Tremblant Resort centre; Hwy 117 N, exit 119 (Montee Ryan), 6 mi (10 km) e, follow signs; in Le Westin Resort & Spa. 100 chemin Kandahar J8E 1E2. **Hours:** 6 pm-11 pm. **Reservations:** suggested. **Features:** In the village, the upscale, stylish restaurant offers a variety of imported sakes to complement dozens of choices of freshly prepared sushi, sashimi and maki. Casual dress; cocktails. **Parking:** on-site (fee) and valet. **Cards:** AX, DC, MC, VI.

LES ARTISTES

French

Lunch: $12-$28   **Dinner:** $15-$45   **Phone:** 819/681-4606

Location: In Mont-Tremblant Resort centre. 116 chemin Kandahar J0T 2H0. **Hours:** 5 pm-10:30 pm, Sat & Sun from 11 am. Closed: 11/11-11/20. **Reservations:** accepted. **Features:** Decorated with displays of original artwork, the lively bistro presents a menu of tasty favorites, such as beef bavette, beef bourguignon, French onion soup, rack of lamb, seafood pasta, filet mignon, salmon, duck foie gras, as well as calamari, a Parisian-style club sandwich and pasta. For dessert, chocolate profiteroles merit a try. The summer terrace is ideal for people-gazing. A kid's menu is offered. Casual dress; cocktails. **Parking:** no self-parking. **Cards:** AX, DC, MC, VI.

MICROBRASSERIE LA DIABLE

International

Lunch: $9-$23   **Dinner:** $9-$23   **Phone:** 819/681-4546

Location: In Mont-Tremblant Resort centre. 1000 chemin de Voyageurs J8E 1B1. **Hours:** 11:30 am-10 pm. **Reservations:** not accepted. **Features:** The jovial country pub features beers brewed on the premises and a menu of international dishes, including European sausages, chicken cordon bleu, Quebec poutine, grilled salmon, pasta, chicken brochettes, steaks and baby back ribs. Youngsters can order from the children's menu. Casual dress; cocktails. **Parking:** on-site. **Cards:** AX, DC, MC, VI.

MOE'S BAR & GRILL

Canadian

Lunch: $6-$12   **Dinner:** $6-$26   **Phone:** 819/425-9821

Location: On Hwy 117; in St-Jovite Village; in Club de Vacances Tremblant. 340 Rt 117 J8E 2X3. **Hours:** 11:30 am-10:30 pm, Fri & Sat-11:30 pm. Closed: 1/1, 12/25. **Features:** In a rural mountain village, this outpost of the regional chain prepares such Canadian pub foods as Montreal-style smoked meat, steaks, fish, pizza, burgers, calamari and French onion soup. Casual dress; cocktails. **Parking:** on-site. **Cards:** AX, DC, MC, VI.

PIZZATERIA TREMBLANT

Italian

Lunch: $9-$15   **Dinner:** $9-$15   **Phone:** 819/681-4522

Location: In Mont-Tremblant Resort centre. 118 chemin Kandahar J8E 1B1. **Hours:** 11:30 am-11 pm; seasonal hours vary. **Reservations:** not accepted. **Features:** This casual family-friendly restaurant at the centre of the resort village has a separate bar area and a seasonal terrace. The menu features a choice of 26 thin-crust pizzas, focaccia, Italian grilled sandwiches, calzones and pasta. Casual dress; cocktails. **Parking:** no self-parking. **Cards:** AX, DC, MC, VI.

Q RESTAURANT & WINEBAR

French

Lunch: $11-$27   **Dinner:** $18-$48   **Phone:** 819/425-3400

Location: Hwy 117 N, exit 119 (Montee Ryan), 6 mi (10 km) e to Mont-Tremblant Resort centre; in Hotel Quintessence. 3004 chemin de la Chapelle J8E 1E1. **Hours:** 7 am-10:30 pm. **Reservations:** accepted. **Features:** The luxurious boutique-hotel restaurant offers table seating in the posh wine bar, in the upscale dining room, at the chef's table off the kitchen or in the wine-sampling dining area in the wine cellar. Examples of innovative regional French cuisine may include pan-seared foie gras, truffle-flavored lobster bisque, warm oysters, halibut, red mullet, lobster tail, organic duck, rabbit, Angus beef, rack of lamb and quail. A seafood raw bar and lighter bistro menu round out the vast offerings. Casual dress; cocktails. **Parking:** valet. **Cards:** AX, DC, MC, VI.

RESTAURANT BAR TERRASSE ANTIPASTO

Italian

Lunch: $9-$27   **Dinner:** $9-$27   **Phone:** 819/425-7580

Location: Centre; in St-Jovite sector. 855 rue de St-Jovite J8E 3J8. **Hours:** 11 am-11 pm. **Features:** In the town's original train station and bedecked in decor fitting of the location, the family restaurant delivers hearty food—from wood-oven pizzas and pasta dishes to preparations of veal and chicken. Food is inexpensive, and portions are generous. Casual dress; cocktails. **Parking:** on-site. **Cards:** AX, MC, VI.

RESTAURANT LE CHEVAL DE JADE   *Menu on AAA.com*   **Dinner:** $26-$33   **Phone:** 819/425-5233

(AAA)

▼▼▼

French

Location: Just ne of Hwy 117 N; centre; in St-Jovite sector. 688 rue de St-Jovite J8E 3J8. **Hours:** 5:30 pm-10 pm. Closed: Wed, 11/1-11/30 & 4/23-4/30. **Reservations:** suggested. **Features:** This cozy rural cottage has country elegant decor and is a perfect spot to enjoy fine French-influenced cuisine. In addition to the main menu, the six- and eight-course tasting menus are popular choices. Sample pan-seared foie gras, bouillabaisse, scallops, tiger prawns flambeed in the dining room, Tilapia fish, red tuna, filet mignon, duck "magret," red deer carpaccio and fish soup prepared with fresh fish imported from France. Service is refined. The seasonal terrace is popular in summer. Casual dress; cocktails. **Parking:** on-site. **Cards:** AX, DC, MC, VI.   ⓧⓒ

MONT-TREMBLANT (ST-JOVITE) pop. 3,955

—— WHERE TO DINE ——

RESTAURANT LA RIPAILLE   **Dinner:** $18-$33   **Phone:** 819/425-5785

▼▼ ▼▼

French

Location: Centre; in sector St-Jovite. 839 rue de St-Jovite J8E 3J8. **Hours:** 5 pm-close. Closed: 11/1-11/30 & 2 weeks in April or May. **Reservations:** suggested. **Features:** In 1904, the property housed the village's first bank. Antique furniture, candles and linens decorate the country-style dining room, while flower boxes line the outdoor terrace. The varied menu includes selections of salmon, ostrich, duck, deer, lamb, steak and scallops. Casual dress; cocktails. **Parking:** street. **Cards:** AX, MC, VI.

MORIN HEIGHTS pop. 2,575

—— WHERE TO DINE ——

L'HERITAGE RESTAURANT   **Dinner:** $19-$39   **Phone:** 450/226-2218

▼▼▼

Swiss

Location: Hwy 15 N; centre. 11 Baker J0R 1H0. **Hours:** 5:30 pm-10:30 pm; Sun from noon 6/1-10/1. Closed: Mon & Tues. **Reservations:** suggested. **Features:** The restaurant is a former bakery, and meals are prepared on a vintage wood-burning stove. The menu comprises Swiss, French and Canadian dishes, such as Swiss raclette, breaded veal cordon bleu and smoked trout prepared on the premises. Regional and imported selections make up the wine list. Meat is roasted on a spit on Sundays during the summer season. Casual dress; cocktails. **Parking:** on-site. **Cards:** AX, MC, VI.

NEW RICHMOND pop. 7,760

—— WHERE TO STAY ——

HOTEL LE FRANCIS   **Phone:** (418)392-4485

▼▼▼

Small-scale Hotel

6/1-9/30	1P: $119-$139	2P: $129-$149	XP: $10	F12
10/1-4/30	1P: $92-$102	2P: $102-$112	XP: $10	F12
5/1-5/31	1P: $89-$99	2P: $99-$109	XP: $10	F12

Location: Just s of Rt 132. 210 chemin Pardiac G0C 2B0. Fax: 418/392-4819. **Facility:** 38 one-bedroom standard units, some with whirlpools. 2 stories (no elevator), interior/exterior corridors. *Bath:* combo or shower only. **Parking:** on-site, winter plug-ins. **Terms:** cancellation fee imposed, [AP] & [CP] meal plans available, small pets only ($10 extra charge). **Amenities:** hair dryers. *Some:* high-speed Internet, irons. **Pool(s):** outdoor. **Leisure Activities:** whirlpool, fishing, cross country skiing, snowmobiling, bicycles, hiking trails. **Guest Services:** valet laundry, wireless Internet. **Business Services:** meeting rooms. **Cards:** AX, DC, DS, MC, VI.

SOME UNITS

ⒶⓈⓀ 🛏 ⑪ 🍸 🏊 ✕ 🖥 / ✕ ⓧ 📠 /
FEE

NORTH HATLEY pop. 746

—— WHERE TO STAY ——

AUBERGE MANOIR LE TRICORNE   **Phone:** (819)842-4522

▼▼▼

Historic Bed & Breakfast

5/1-10/31	1P: $115-$205	2P: $135-$250	XP: $35	F
11/1-4/30	1P: $95-$135	2P: $115-$250	XP: $35	F

Location: Rt 108, 1.3 mi (2 km) n on chemin McFarland, follow signs. Located in a quiet rural area. 50 chemin Gosselin J0B 2C0. Fax: 819/842-2692. **Facility:** Surrounded by 90 acres of woodlands, this historic country inn offers fireplaces and whirlpools in many of its attractively decorated guest rooms. Smoke free premises. 17 one-bedroom standard units, some with whirlpools. 2 stories (no elevator), interior corridors. *Bath:* combo or shower only. **Parking:** on-site. **Terms:** age restrictions may apply, 7 day cancellation notice-fee imposed, [BP] meal plan available. **Amenities:** hair dryers. **Pool(s):** heated outdoor. **Leisure Activities:** sauna, cross country skiing, snowmobiling, hiking trails. **Business Services:** meeting rooms. **Cards:** AX, MC, VI.

SOME UNITS

🏊 ✕ ✕ ⓦ 🅩 / 📠 🖥 /

MANOIR HOVEY (HOVEY MANOR)   **Phone:** (819)842-2421

(AAA) (SAVE)

▼▼▼▼

Classic Historic Country Inn

6/22-10/7 [MAP]	1P: $203-$431	2P: $290-$616	XP: $140	
5/1-6/21 & 10/8-4/30 [MAP]	1P: $175-$346	2P: $250-$495	XP: $140	

Location: Hwy 55, exit 29, 7.5 mi (12 km) e on Rt 108 E. 575 chemin Hovey J0B 2C0. Fax: 819/842-2248. **Facility:** Nestled on scenic lakefront grounds, this 1900 manor house features luxurious accommodations with stylish bathrooms. Designated smoking area. 39 units. 37 one-bedroom standard units, some with efficiencies and/or whirlpools. 2 cottages ($393-$550). 3 stories (no elevator), interior/exterior corridors. *Bath:* combo or shower only. **Parking:** on-site, winter plug-ins. **Terms:** check-in 4 pm, 2 night minimum stay - weekends, age restrictions may apply, 14 day cancellation notice-fee imposed, [AP] meal plan available, package plans. **Amenities:** CD players, voice mail, hair dryers. *Some:* DVD players, irons. **Dining:** restaurant, see separate listing. **Pool(s):** heated outdoor. **Leisure Activities:** boating, canoeing, paddleboats, boat dock, fishing, kayaks, sailboard equipment, lighted tennis court, cross country skiing, ice skating, exercise room. *Fee:* fishing guides, lake cruises, massage. **Guest Services:** valet laundry. **Business Services:** meeting rooms, PC. **Cards:** AX, DC, MC, VI. **Free Special Amenities:** local telephone calls and high-speed Internet.

SOME UNITS

⑪ 🏄 🏊 ✕ ✕ 🖥 / (VCR) 📠 🖥 /

───────── **WHERE TO DINE** ─────────

MANOIR HOVEY (HOVEY MANOR)
DINING ROOM

Lunch: $11-$18	**Dinner:** $58-$97	**Phone:** 819/842-2421

(CAA)

French

Location: Hwy 55, exit 29, 7.5 mi (12 km) e on Rt 108; in Manoir Hovey (Hovey Manor). 575 chemin Hovey J0B 2C0. **Hours:** 8 am-10, noon-2 & 6-9:30 pm; to 10 pm in summer; call for lunch hours 4/1-4/30 & 11/1-11/30. **Reservations:** suggested. **Features:** The seasonally changing menu delivers innovative, contemporary French cuisine. Views of the lake and gardens are sublime from the intimate dining room. The restaurant may close for two weeks in November. Dressy casual; cocktails. **Parking:** on-site. **Cards:** AX, DC, JC, MC, VI. **Country Inn**

PILSEN RESTAURANT & PUB

Lunch: $10-$16	**Dinner:** $10-$27	**Phone:** 819/842-2971

American

Location: Centre. 55 rue Principale J0B 2C0. **Hours:** 11:30 am-10 pm; to 8 pm 11/15-4/1. Closed: 12/25; also for dinner 12/24. **Reservations:** suggested. **Features:** Food is consistently good in the bright and airy, family-friendly restaurant and pub. A good selection of microbrewed and imported beers complements dishes on the table d'hote menu. The summer terrace overlooks the river, which is frequented by ducks. Casual dress; cocktails. **Parking:** on-site. **Cards:** AX, MC, VI.

ORFORD pop. 1,987

───────── **WHERE TO STAY** ─────────

ESTRIMONT SUITES & SPA

All Year [ECP]	1P: $165-$289	2P: $173-$297	XP: $34 F12

(CAA) (SAVE)

Small-scale Hotel

Phone: (819)843-1616

Location: Hwy 10, exit 118, follow signs to Orford Park. 44 ave de L J1X 6J3. Fax: 819/843-4909. **Facility:** 91 units. 88 one-bedroom standard units, some with whirlpools. 2 one- and 1 two-bedroom suites with kitchens and whirlpools. 3 stories, interior corridors. **Parking:** on-site. **Terms:** check-in 4 pm, [BP] & [MAP] meal plans available, package plans. **Amenities:** voice mail, hair dryers. **Dining:** 7:30 am-11 & 6-10 pm; noon-2 pm by reservation, cocktails. **Pool(s):** heated outdoor, heated indoor. **Leisure Activities:** sauna, whirlpool, 2 lighted tennis courts, racquetball court, cross country skiing, snowmobiling, rental bicycles, playground, spa, sports court. **Guest Services:** gift shop, valet laundry, wireless Internet. **Business Services:** conference facilities. **Cards:** AX, MC, VI. **Free Special Amenities: newspaper and high-speed Internet.**

SOME UNITS

🍽 🍸 🛥 🐾 ⊠ 📶 ▱ / ⊠ 📼 ▱ /
FEE   FEE

HOTEL CHERIBOURG *Book great rates at AAA.com*

All Year	1P: $136-$246	2P: $136-$246	XP: $20 F18

(CAA) (SAVE)

Small-scale Hotel

Phone: (819)843-3308

Location: Hwy 10, exit 118, 1.9 mi (3 km) n on Hwy 141. 2603 chemin du Parc J1X 8C8. Fax: 819/843-2639. **Facility:** 131 units. 114 one-bedroom standard units, some with kitchens and/or whirlpools. 4 one-bedroom suites ($196-$246) with kitchens and whirlpools. 13 cottages ($910-$1715), some with whirlpools. 2-3 stories (no elevator), interior/exterior corridors. **Parking:** on-site, winter plug-ins. **Terms:** check-in 4 pm, [AP] & [MAP] meal plans available, package plans. **Amenities:** voice mail, irons, hair dryers. *Some:* video games (fee). **Dining:** 7 am-9:30 pm, cocktails. **Pool(s):** outdoor, heated indoor. **Leisure Activities:** saunas, whirlpool, 2 lighted tennis courts, ice skating, badminton, rental bicycles, playground, exercise room, spa, sports court, volleyball. **Guest Services:** valet laundry. **Business Services:** conference facilities, administrative services (fee), PC. **Cards:** AX, DC, MC, VI.

SOME UNITS

[S] [D] 🍽 🍸 🛥 ⊠ 📶 ▱ / ⊠ 🎮 📶 ▱ /

MANOIR DES SABLES HOTEL & GOLF *Book great rates at AAA.com*

All Year	1P: $147-$246	2P: $147-$295	XP: $20 F18

(CAA) (SAVE)

Resort
Large-scale Hotel

Phone: (819)847-4747

Location: Hwy 10, exit 118, 1.3 mi (2 km) n on Rt 141. 90 ave des Jardins J1X 6M6. Fax: 819/847-3519. **Facility:** Guests of the resort stay in tastefully furnished rooms, many of which have private balconies that afford views of the lake and nearby ski hills. 141 units. 114 one-bedroom standard units. 27 one-bedroom suites ($252-$272) with whirlpools. 3 stories, interior corridors. **Parking:** on-site, winter plug-ins. **Terms:** check-in 4 pm, cancellation fee imposed, [AP] & [MAP] meal plans available, package plans, 15% service charge. **Amenities:** video games (fee), voice mail, irons, hair dryers. *Some:* safes, honor bars. **Dining:** 2 restaurants, 7 am-10 pm, cocktails. **Pool(s):** outdoor, heated indoor. **Leisure Activities:** saunas, whirlpools, rental boats, rental canoes, rental paddleboats, boat dock, fishing, 4 tennis courts (2 lighted), cross country skiing, ice skating, tobogganing, snowshoeing, Saturday night winter sleigh rides, badminton, pool table, table tennis, hiking trails, playground, exercise room, spa, volleyball. **Fee:** golf-27 holes, hiking & biking tours, bicycles, game room. **Guest Services:** gift shop, valet laundry, wireless Internet. **Business Services:** conference facilities, PC (fee), fax. **Cards:** AX, DC, MC, VI.

SOME UNITS

🍽 🍸 🛗 🛥 ⊠ 🎮 ▱ / ⊠ 📶 ▱ /

───────── **WHERE TO DINE** ─────────

LA MERISE

Dinner: $10-$25	**Phone:** 819/843-6288

French

Location: Hwy 10, exit 118, 1.1 mi (1.8 km) n on Rt 141. 2329 chemin du Parc J1X 7A2. **Hours:** 5 pm-10 pm. Closed: 12/24, 12/25; also call for days 10/1-6/30. **Reservations:** suggested, weekends in season. **Features:** French cooking emphasizes fresh produce, local products and garden grown herbs. The specialities include crepes, pasta, meats, fresh fish and seafood. The seasonal Sunday brunch is popular, as is the sunny summer terrace. Collages created by the owner/artist decorate the walls of the late-19th-century cottage's dining room. Casual dress; cocktails. **Parking:** on-site. **Cards:** MC, VI. **Historic**

RESTAURANT LE CHATEAUBRIAND

Lunch: $9-$19	**Dinner:** $41-$52	**Phone:** 819/843-6000

French

Location: Hwy 10, exit 118, 1.3 mi (2 km) n on Hwy 141; in Auberge Au Lion d'Or Conference & Spa. 2240 chemin du Parc J1X 7A2. **Hours:** 8-10 am, 11-2 & 5-9 pm. **Reservations:** required. **Features:** Rich wood walls, elegant table settings and a stone fireplace form the backdrop for the country inn's dining room. The varied menu of fine regional cuisine lists flambeed steak, salmon, sea bass, duck, sweetbreads, scallops, beef tenderloin, wild boar, lamb, pheasant, guinea fowl and deer. Casual dress; cocktails. **Parking:** on-site. **Cards:** AX, CB, DC, DS, JC, MC, VI. **Country Inn**

OUTREMONT —See Montreal p. 492.

PAPINEAUVILLE pop. 2,247

——— WHERE TO DINE ———

LA TABLE DE PIERRE DELAHAYE   **Lunch:** $16   **Dinner:** $27-$36   **Phone:** 819/427-5027

French

Location: On Rt 148; centre. 247 rue Papineau J0V 1R0. **Hours:** Open 5/1-1/1 & 2/1-4/30; 11:30 am-2 & 5:30-9 pm, Sat from 5:30 pm. Closed: 12/25; also Mon & Tues. **Reservations:** suggested. **Features:** Guests can settle into the quaint, country-style dining room to enjoy quality dishes of market-fresh food, such as perch served with whipped potatoes and parsnips. A small hallway separates two stylish dining rooms decorated with chandeliers and simple draperies. Casual dress; cocktails. **Parking:** on-site. **Cards:** MC, VI.

RESTAURANT LE LOUIS-JOSEPH   **Lunch:** $9-$14   **Dinner:** $9-$39   **Phone:** 819/427-5866

Canadian

Location: On Rt 148; centre. 300 rue Papineau J0V 1R0. **Hours:** 11 am-10 pm. Closed: 12/24-12/26. **Reservations:** suggested. **Features:** Guests can gather around the rural restaurant's cozy fireplace to sample tasty Canadian-style comfort foods, including steak, seafood, pasta, pizza, barbecue chicken and hot chicken sandwiches. Casual dress; cocktails. **Parking:** street. **Cards:** MC, VI.

PASPEBIAC pop. 3,326

——— WHERE TO STAY ———

AUBERGE DU PARC INN   **Phone:** 418/752-3355

Property failed to provide current rates

Small-scale Hotel

Location: On Rt 132; centre. 68 boul Gerard D Levesque ouest G0C 2K0 (CP 40). Fax: 418/752-6406. **Facility:** 32 one-bedroom standard units. 1 story, exterior corridors. **Parking:** on-site, winter plug-ins. **Terms:** open 5/1-11/26 & 1/29-4/30. **Amenities:** hair dryers. **Pool(s):** heated outdoor, small heated indoor, saltwater. **Leisure Activities:** saunas, beach access, putting green, tennis court, exercise room, spa, shuffleboard. **Guest Services:** gift shop.

SOME UNITS

PERCE pop. 3,614

——— WHERE TO STAY ———

AU PIC DE L'AURORE   **Phone:** (418)782-2151

7/10-8/23	1P: $100-$135	2P: $100-$135	XP: $15 F
5/26-7/9	1P: $59-$105	2P: $59-$105	XP: $15 F
8/24-9/29	1P: $59-$80	2P: $59-$80	XP: $15 F

Cottage

Location: 1.2 mi (2 km) e from village. 1 Rt 132 G0C 2L0 (PO Box 339). Fax: 418/782-2151. **Facility:** 32 units. 13 one-bedroom standard units, some with efficiencies. 1 one-bedroom suite with efficiency. 1 vacation home ($110-$215) and 17 cottages. 1 story, exterior corridors. **Parking:** on-site. **Terms:** open 5/26-9/29, office hours 7:30 am-10 pm, check-in 4 pm, small pets only ($25 fee). **Amenities:** hair dryers. *Some:* DVD players (fee), CD players, irons. **Guest Services:** coin laundry, wireless Internet. **Business Services:** meeting rooms. **Cards:** AX, MC, VI.

SOME UNITS

HOTEL LA NORMANDIE   **Phone:** (418)782-2112

7/1-8/31	1P: $119-$239	2P: $119-$239	XP: $12 F12
5/20-6/30 & 9/1-10/12	1P: $79-$189	2P: $79-$189	XP: $12 F12

Small-scale Hotel

Location: Centre. 221 Rt 132 ouest G0C 2L0 (CP 129). Fax: 418/782-2337. **Facility:** Smoke free premises. 45 one-bedroom standard units. 3 stories (no elevator), interior corridors. **Parking:** on-site. **Terms:** open 5/20-10/12, package plans, small pets only ($50 fee, in designated units). **Amenities:** hair dryers. *Some:* DVD players, irons. **Dining:** La Normandie Dining Room, see separate listing. **Business Services:** meeting rooms. **Cards:** MC, VI. *(See color ad below)*

SOME UNITS

HOTEL-MOTEL LA COTE SURPRISE

Phone: (418)782-2131

7/1-8/31	2P: $75-$125	XP: $15	F5
10/16-4/30	2P: $75-$105	XP: $15	F5
5/1-6/30	2P: $60-$105	XP: $15	F5
9/1-10/15	2P: $60-$75	XP: $15	F5

Small-scale Hotel

Location: On Rt 132, 0.4 mi (0.7 km) w of village. 367 Rt 132 ouest G0C 2L0 (CP 159). Fax: 418/782-2626. **Facility:** 36 one-bedroom standard units. 2 stories (no elevator), interior/exterior corridors. **Parking:** on-site. **Terms:** cancellation fee imposed, package plans. **Amenities:** hair dryers. *Some:* irons. **Leisure Activities:** playground. **Business Services:** meeting rooms, PC. **Cards:** MC, VI.

SOME UNITS

HOTEL/MOTEL LE MIRAGE

Phone: (418)782-5151

7/11-8/26	1P: $120-$168	2P: $120-$168	XP: $10	F12
5/7-7/10	1P: $68-$92	2P: $75-$95	XP: $10	F12
8/27-10/20	1P: $68-$92	2P: $75-$95	XP: $14	F12

Motel

Location: On Rt 132. 288 Rt 132 ouest G0C 2L0 (CP 159). Fax: 418/782-5536. **Facility:** 67 one-bedroom standard units. 2 stories (no elevator), exterior corridors. **Parking:** on-site. **Terms:** open 5/7-10/20, small pets only. **Amenities:** hair dryers. **Pool(s):** heated outdoor. **Leisure Activities:** tennis court. **Guest Services:** valet laundry, wireless Internet. **Business Services:** meeting rooms. **Cards:** AX, DC, MC, VI. *(See color ad below)*

SOME UNITS

HOTEL MOTEL MANOIR DE PERCE

Phone: 418/782-2022

5/15-10/15	1P: $66-$158	2P: $66-$158	XP: $10	F12

Small-scale Hotel

Location: Centre. 212 Rt 132 G0C 2L0 (CP 160). Fax: 418/782-5195. **Facility:** 40 one-bedroom standard units. 2 stories (no elevator), interior/exterior corridors. **Parking:** on-site. **Terms:** open 5/15-10/15, [MAP] meal plan available, package plans, small pets only ($25 fee). **Amenities:** hair dryers. **Dining:** restaurant, see separate listing. **Leisure Activities:** *Fee:* charter fishing, bicycles. **Guest Services:** coin laundry, wireless Internet. **Business Services:** meeting rooms. **Cards:** AX, DC, DS, MC, VI.

SOME UNITS
FEE

RIOTEL PERCE OCEAN FRONT RESORT

Phone: (418)782-2166

6/19-10/8	1P: $99-$199	2P: $99-$199	XP: $15	F18

Small-scale Hotel

Location: Centre. 261 Rt 132 G0C 2L0 (CP 190). Fax: 418/782-5323. **Facility:** 88 units. 87 one-bedroom standard units, some with efficiencies. 1 one-bedroom suite with efficiency. 2 stories (no elevator), interior/exterior corridors. **Parking:** on-site. **Terms:** open 6/19-10/8, office hours 7 am-11 pm, [AP], [BP], [CP] & [MAP] meal plans available. **Amenities:** hair dryers. *Some:* irons. **Dining:** Riotel Perce Ocean Front Resort Dining Room, see separate listing. **Leisure Activities:** whirlpool, beach access, playground, exercise room. **Guest Services:** coin laundry. **Business Services:** meeting rooms. **Cards:** AX, DC, DS, MC, VI.

SOME UNITS

—— WHERE TO DINE ——

CAFE COULEURS
Location: On Rt 132; 18 km ne of Perce Village. 1004 Rt 132 est G0C 1A0. **Lunch:** $8-$12 **Dinner:** $8-$12 **Phone:** 418/645-2745
Hours: Open 6/5-9/25; 9 am-7 pm. **Reservations:** accepted. **Features:** The cozy cafe and art gallery is owned by painter Gilles Cote, whose artwork adorns the walls along with the works of many regional painters. The menu specialty is waffles with scallops in wine sauce or with a mousse of shrimp or smoked salmon. Also offered are soups, salads, shrimp salad, sandwiches, cheese bagels with smoked salmon, seafood pate and duck confit. For dessert, try an artfully garnished dessert waffle. Specialty coffees include espresso. Casual dress. **Parking:** on-site.
Cards: AX, DC, MC, VI.

Coffee/Espresso

HOTEL MOTEL MANOIR DE PERCE
DINING ROOM
Location: Centre. 212 Rt 132 G0C 2L0. **Dinner:** $18-$45 **Phone:** 418/782-2022
Hours: Open 5/15-10/15; 7 am-10:30 & 5:30-9:30 pm. **Reservations:** accepted. **Features:** In a village motel, the cozy, comfortable family-run dining room features a full array of fresh regional seafood, including salmon pie, fried cod tongues, poached cod, halibut, red deer, surf and turf, lobster and seafood bouillabaisse. Casual dress; cocktails. **Parking:** on-site. **Cards:** AX, CB, DC, DS, MC, VI.

Seafood

LA NORMANDIE DINING ROOM
Location: Centre; in Hotel La Normandie. 221 Rt 132 G0C 2L0. **Dinner:** $25-$48 **Phone:** 418/782-2112
Hours: Open 6/1-10/31; 6 pm-9 pm; also breakfast buffet 7:30-10 am. **Reservations:** suggested. **Features:** Tastefully furnished and decorated, the stylish dining room overlooks Perce Rock and Bonaventure Island. The atmosphere is upscale and comfortable. Tempting preparations include lobster, roasted stuffed quail, chicken supreme with maple glaze, braised pork, grilled beef sirloin, grilled breast of duck and guinea fowl. Casual dress; cocktails. **Parking:** on-site. **Cards:** MC, VI.

Regional French

LA TABLE DE GEORGES PREVEL
Location: On Rt 132; in Perce St-Georges de-Malbaie; in Auberge Fort Prevel. 2053 boul Douglas G0C 2X0. **Dinner:** $19-$42 **Phone:** 418/368-2281
Hours: Open 6/15-9/21; 7:30 am-10 & 6-9 pm. **Reservations:** suggested. **Features:** A jazzy atmosphere punctuates the pleasant, bistro-style restaurant, which overlooks the scenic ocean. The focus is on gourmet meals prepared with market-fresh products, such as cod-liver pate, goat cheese, sweetbreads, scallops, cod tongues, seafood crepes, lobster, caribou, lamb and salmon smoked on the premises. Casual dress; cocktails. **Parking:** on-site. **Cards:** AX, DC, MC, VI.

Canadian

LE CAFE CHAMPETRE
Location: On Rt 132; in Place Charles-Robin. 164-B Rt 132 G0C 2L0. **Lunch:** $6-$15 **Dinner:** $6-$15 **Phone:** 418/782-2036
Hours: Open 6/1-10/15; 6:30 am-11 pm. **Reservations:** accepted. **Features:** This family-friendly diner near the Perce harbor offers a menu of fish, seafood and Canadian fast-food, including lobster rolls, cod pie, hot chicken, burgers, salads, all-day breakfasts and sandwiches. Casual dress; beer & wine only. **Parking:** on-site. **Cards:** MC, VI.

Canadian

LE FOURNAND BAKERY AND CAFE
Location: Centre. 194 Rt 132 ouest G0C 2L0. **Lunch:** $4-$7 **Dinner:** $4-$7 **Phone:** 418/782-2211
Hours: Open 5/1-10/30; 7 am-9 pm; to 10 pm 7/1-8/20. **Reservations:** not accepted. **Features:** The village cafe-bakery offers both a take-out counter and a casual seating area with a seasonal terrace. The affordable menu includes fresh breads, cheeses, sandwiches, salad, tourtiere meat pies, baked beans, quiches and pizza. Fresh desserts include French pastries, sugar pie, muffins, croissants, brioches and danishes, as well as specialty coffee and tea. Casual dress. **Parking:** street.

Bakery/Desserts

RESTAURANT LA MAISON DU
PECHEUR/CAFE DE L'ATLANTIQUE
Location: Centre; at wharf. 155 Place du Quai G0C 2L0. **Lunch:** $13-$45 **Dinner:** $13-$45 **Phone:** 418/782-5331
Hours: Open 6/1-10/15; 7:30 am-midnight. **Reservations:** suggested. **Features:** Next to the port area where tour boats depart, the waterfront restaurant focuses on local seafood, including the specialty cod tongues in sea urchin butter. Menu highlights include lobster, snails, salmon tartare, snow crab, grilled ocean perch or catfish, mussels, shrimp and delicious maplewood-oven pizzas. Home-style pies and cakes are made on the premises. The owner maintains a caged reserve of fresh lobsters on the sea bottom off the shores of Perce. Casual dress; cocktails. **Parking:** on-site. **Cards:** AX, DC, DS, MC, VI.

Seafood

RESTAURANT L'AUBERGE DU GARGANTUA
Location: 1 mi (1.6 km) n on Rt des Failles from jct Hwy 132. 222 Rt des Failles G0C 2L0. **Dinner:** $29-$40 **Phone:** 418/782-2852
Hours: Open 5/15-10/15; 4 pm-10 pm. **Reservations:** suggested. **Features:** The renowned mountaintop restaurant and inn offers a comfortable, country-home feel and spectacular sunset views. Cuisine "bourgeoisie" centers on extremely generous portions of local seafood. Each meal begins with a hearty platter of salads, pates and snails. Hosts entertain diners with a collection of vintage LPs. Casual dress; cocktails. **Parking:** on-site. **Cards:** MC, VI.

French

RIOTEL PERCE OCEAN FRONT
RESORT DINING ROOM
Menu on AAA.com
Location: Centre; in Riotel Perce Ocean Front Resort. 261 Rt 132 G0C 2L0. **Dinner:** $13-$30 **Phone:** 418/782-2166
Hours: Open 6/6-9/30; 7 am-9:30 & 6-9 pm. **Reservations:** suggested. **Features:** The bright, airy dining room affords great views of Bonaventure Island and Perce Rock. Menu highlights include regional fare such as shrimp, chicken, fish and steak. During summer, the outdoor terrace is a popular gathering spot. The dessert selection is varied. Casual dress; cocktails. **Parking:** on-site. **Cards:** AX, DC, DS, MC, VI.

Regional
Quebecois

PETIT-SAGUENAY pop. 849

—— WHERE TO STAY ——

AUBERGE DU JARDIN
Phone: (418)272-3444
5/1-11/4 & 12/8-4/30   1P: $98-$162   2P: $98-$162   XP: $15   D5
Location: On Rt 170; centre. 71 boul Dumas G0V 1N0. Fax: 418/272-3174. **Facility:** 12 one-bedroom standard
Country Inn   units, some with whirlpools. 2 stories (no elevator), interior/exterior corridors. **Parking:** on-site, winter plug-ins. **Terms:** open 5/1-11/4 & 12/8-4/30, cancellation fee imposed, [BP] meal plan available, package plans.
Amenities: hair dryers. **Leisure Activities:** hiking trails. **Guest Services:** coin laundry. **Business Services:** meeting rooms.
Cards: AX, MC, VI.

SOME UNITS

PIKE RIVER

—— WHERE TO STAY ——

AUBERGE-INN LA SUISSE
Phone: (450)244-5870
5/1-12/31 [ECP]   1P: $80   2P: $90   XP: $35   D
1/1-4/30 [ECP]   1P: $70   2P: $80   XP: $35   D
Location: 1.4 mi (2.2 km) n from town centre. 119 Rt 133 J0J 1P0. Fax: 450/244-5181. **Facility:** 4 one-bedroom
Country Inn   standard units. 2 stories (no elevator), interior corridors. *Bath:* shower only. **Parking:** on-site, winter plug-ins.
Terms: 7 day cancellation notice-fee imposed, [AP] meal plan available. **Amenities:** hair dryers.
Dining: Restaurant La Suisse, see separate listing. **Leisure Activities:** walking trail. **Cards:** AX, MC, VI.
Free Special Amenities: expanded continental breakfast and local telephone calls.

—— WHERE TO DINE ——

RESTAURANT LA SUISSE   **Lunch:** $7-$12   **Dinner:** $19-$28   **Phone:** 450/244-5870
Location: 1.4 mi (2.2 km) n from town centre; in Auberge-Inn La Suisse. 119 Rt 133 J0J 1P0. **Hours:** 11 am-11 pm.
Closed: Mon & Tues. **Reservations:** accepted. **Features:** The atmosphere is far from hurried in the laid-
Swiss   back restaurant, which occupies a quaint, pleasant inn near Lake Champlain and area wineries. Raclette
and fondues are specialties on a menu of Swiss-European cuisine. Eclectic, country-style pieces painted by
the owner and her daughter adorn the walls. Casual dress; cocktails. **Parking:** on-site. **Cards:** AX, MC, VI.

PLESSISVILLE pop. 6,756

—— WHERE TO STAY ——

MOTEL A LA CLAIRE FONTAINE
Phone: 819/362-6388
All Year   1P: $40-$65   2P: $45-$75   XP: $5   F6
Location: Rt 165, 0.6 mi (1 km) e on Rt 116, follow signs. 2165 rue St-Calixte G6L 1S2. Fax: 819/362-2544.
Motel   **Facility:** 27 one-bedroom standard units. 1 story, exterior corridors. **Parking:** on-site, winter plug-ins.
Terms: small pets only. **Amenities:** *Some:* high-speed Internet. **Guest Services:** complimentary laundry.
Business Services: meeting rooms, PC. **Cards:** AX, MC, VI.

SOME UNITS

POINTE-AU-PERE pop. 4,171

—— WHERE TO STAY ——

AUBERGE LA MAREE DOUCE
Phone: 418/722-0822
Property failed to provide current rates
Location: On Rt 132. 1329 boul Ste-Anne G5M 1W2. Fax: 418/723-4512. **Facility:** This circa 1860 Victorian inn
Historic   offers pleasantly decorated rooms. Accommodations are available also in a cottage or in the annex built in
Country Inn   1996. 9 units. 8 one-bedroom standard units. 1 one-bedroom suite. 1-2 stories (no elevator), interior/exterior
corridors. **Parking:** on-site. **Terms:** open 5/15-10/1. **Amenities:** hair dryers. **Business Services:** meeting
rooms.

SOME UNITS

POINTE-CLAIRE —See Montreal p. 492.

PORTNEUF pop. 1,436

—— WHERE TO STAY ——

HOTEL LE PORTNEUVOIS
Phone: 418/286-6400
Property failed to provide current rates
Location: Hwy 40, exit 261, then 0.3 mi (0.5 km) s on rue Provencher. 101 rue Simeon-Delisle G0A 2Y0.
Small-scale Hotel   Fax: 418/286-6460. **Facility:** 22 one-bedroom standard units, some with whirlpools. 2 stories (no elevator),
interior corridors. **Parking:** on-site, winter plug-ins. **Terms:** small pets only. **Amenities:** high-speed Internet.
Some: DVD players, hair dryers. **Guest Services:** valet laundry. **Business Services:** meeting rooms.

SOME UNITS

FEE

Destination Québec
pop. 169,076

Québec may be a walled city, but it welcomes visitors with open arms and Old World hospitality. The result is *joie de vivre.*

What is the recipe for this joy of living? Pleasant surroundings, pleasant company and great food. And Québec provides the latter in abundance, at sidewalk eateries and four diamond restaurants. *Bon appétite!*

© age fotostock / SuperStock

Street scene, Québec.
Soft sunset hues transform prosaic stair-step buildings into a scene worthy of a French Impressionist's canvas.

© Andre Jenny

La Fresque des Quartier Petit-Champlain at 102 rue du Petit-Champlain in Vieux-Québec. This mural recounts the history of this Cap-Blanc neighborhood and the fortitude of the people who built and rebuilt it. (See listing page 213)

See Vicinity map page 517

St-Catherine-de-la-Jacques-Cartier

L'Ancienne-Lorette

307

40

40

Places included in this AAA Destination City:

Al fresco dining, Québec.
Whether it's indoor or outdoor
dining, the *cuisine* is *magnifique.*

*Tobogganing on Dufferin
Terrace, Québec.*
Snow, speed and smiles are
guaranteed on the toboggan run
during Festival d'hiver (Winter
Carnival). (See mention
page 209)

St-Ferréol-les-Neiges●

Lac-Beauport

Château-Richer ● ● Beaupré

**See Downtown
map page 512**

Charlesbourg

Beauport

Lévis

Ste-Foy ● St-Romuald

Sillery

Québec

Festive face painting, Québec.
Summer sunshine and smiles
run rampant during the Québec
International Summer Festival.
(See mention page 220)

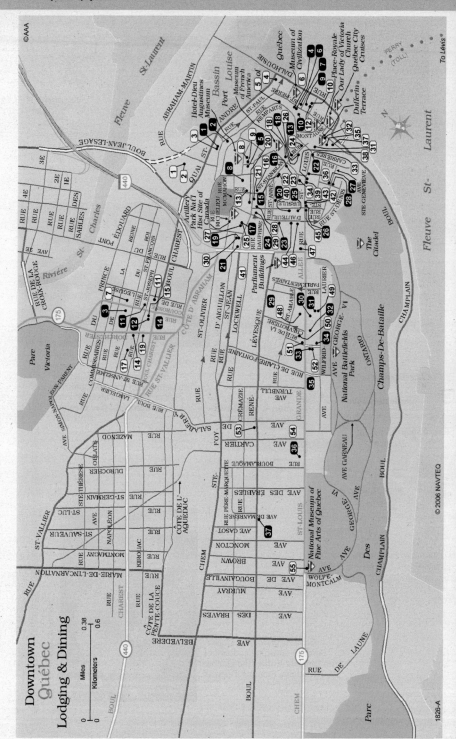

Downtown
Québec
Lodging & Dining

©AAA

©2006 NAVTEQ

1826-A

Downtown Quebec

This index helps you "spot" where approved accommodations and restaurants are located on the corresponding detailed maps. Lodging rate ranges are for comparison only and show the property's high season; rates are per night, unless only weekly (W) rates are available. Restaurant rate range is for dinner, unless only lunch (L) is served. Turn to the listing page for more detailed rate information and consult display ads for special promotions.

Spotter/Map Page Number	OA	DOWNTOWN QUEBEC - Lodgings	Diamond Rating	Rate Range High Season	Listing Page
1 / p. 512	CAA	Hotel des Coutellier	▽▽	$150-$210 SAVE	528
2 / p. 512		Hotel Le Saint-Paul	▽▽	$99-$209	531
3 / p. 512	CAA	Best Western City Centre/Centre-Ville - see color ad p 521	▽▽▽	$169-$319 SAVE	523
4 / p. 512	CAA	Les Immeubles Charlevoix Courtier-St-Pierre	▽▽▽	$600-$650 SAVE	534
5 / p. 512	CAA	L'Hotel du Vieux Quebec - see color ad p 534	▽▽	$144-$284 SAVE	534
6 / p. 512	CAA	Auberge Saint-Pierre	▽▽▽	$129-$325 SAVE	522
7 / p. 512		Hotel 71	▽▽▽	$180-$325	525
8 / p. 512	CAA	Hotel Manoir Victoria - see color ad p 532	▽▽▽	$149-$309 SAVE	531
9 / p. 512	CAA	Auberge Saint-Antoine	▽▽▽▽	$309 SAVE	522
10 / p. 512	CAA	Hotel Le Priori	▽▽▽	$179-$499 SAVE	528
11 / p. 512		Holiday Inn Select Quebec City-Downtown	▽▽▽	Failed to provide	525
12 / p. 512	CAA	Hotel Royal William	▽▽▽	$169-$239 SAVE	532
13 / p. 512	CAA	Hotel Sainte-Anne	▽▽▽	$149-$319 SAVE	533
14 / p. 512	CAA	Auberge L'Autre Jardin	▽▽▽	$109-$164 SAVE	522
15 / p. 512		Hotel Marie-Rollet - see color ad p 532	▽▽	$65-$155	531
16 / p. 512	CAA	Hotel Clarendon - see color ad p 526	▽▽▽	$159-$289 SAVE	528
17 / p. 512	CAA	L'Hotel du Capitole	▽▽▽	$180-$270 SAVE	534
18 / p. 512		Auberge du Tresor - see color ad p 522	▽	$90-$135	521
19 / p. 512		Courtyard Marriott Quebec	▽▽▽	Failed to provide	523
20 / p. 512		Hotel Champlain Vieux-Quebec	▽▽▽	$139-$269	525
21 / p. 512		Hotel Palace Royal	▽▽▽	$139-$489	532
22 / p. 512	CAA	Fairmont Le Chateau Frontenac - see color ad card insert	▽▽▽▽	$249-$549 SAVE	524
23 / p. 512	CAA	Hotel Manoir d'Auteuil	▽▽▽	$99-$219 SAVE	531
24 / p. 512	CAA	Hilton Quebec - see color ad p 525	▽▽▽▽	$99-$329 SAVE	524
25 / p. 512	CAA	Hotel L'Ermitage	▽▽	$119-$169 SAVE	531
26 / p. 512	CAA	Hotel Le Clos St-Louis	▽▽▽	$220-$300 SAVE	528
27 / p. 512	CAA	Hotel Chateau Bellevue - see color ad p 527	▽▽	$119-$249 SAVE	526
28 / p. 512	CAA	Le Chateau de Pierre - see color ad p 533	▽▽	$115-$155 SAVE	533
29 / p. 512	CAA	Delta Quebec - see color ad p 524	▽▽▽	$140-$315 SAVE	524
30 / p. 512		Hotel Manoir LaFayette	▽▽	$109-$229	531
31 / p. 512	CAA	Hotel Chateau Laurier Quebec - see color ad p 527	▽▽▽	$129-$339 SAVE	526
32 / p. 512	CAA	Hotel Chateau Grande-Allee	▽▽	$109-$179 SAVE	526
33 / p. 512		Bed & Breakfast Manoir Mon Calme	▽▽▽	Failed to provide	522
34 / p. 512	CAA	Loews Le Concorde - see color ad p 535	▽▽▽▽	$109-$309 SAVE	534
35 / p. 512		Hotel Manoir de la Tour	▽▽	$79-$169	531

Spotter/Map Page Number	OA	DOWNTOWN QUEBEC - Lodgings (continued)	Diamond Rating	Rate Range High Season	Listing Page
36 / p. 512		Auberge du Quartier	◈◈	$79-$159	521
37 / p. 512		Appartements La Pergola	◈◈	Failed to provide	521
		DOWNTOWN QUEBEC - Restaurants			
1 / p. 512		Aviatic Club	◈◈◈	$14-$32	537
2 / p. 512		Charbon Steakhouse	◈◈	$18-$40	537
3 / p. 512		Moss Bistro Belge	◈◈	$17-$22	539
4 / p. 512		Restaurant Laurie Raphael	◈◈◈◈	$21-$56	541
5 / p. 512		Restaurant l'Echaude	◈◈◈	$29-$35	541
6 / p. 512		Restaurant Le Cafe du Monde	◈◈	$14-$18	541
7 / p. 512		Restaurant Anh Dao	◈◈	$10	540
8 / p. 512	🅐	**Portofino Bistro Italiano**	◈◈	$14-$25	540
9 / p. 512		Pub St-Patrick	◈◈	$7-$22	540
10 / p. 512		Restaurant Initiale	◈◈◈◈	$32-$45	540
11 / p. 512		Yuzu Sushi-Bar	◈◈◈	$22-$42	542
12 / p. 512	🅐	**Panache Restaurant**	◈◈◈◈	$43-$45	539
13 / p. 512		Le Patriarche	◈◈◈	$22-$33	539
14 / p. 512		Le Postino Bistro-Bar	◈◈	$10-$20	539
15 / p. 512		Restaurant Le Sainte-Victoire	◈◈◈	$18-$25	541
16 / p. 512	🅐	**Saint Alexandre Pub**	◈◈	$10-$20	542
17 / p. 512		Restaurant L'Utopie	◈◈◈	$22-$30	542
18 / p. 512	🅐	**D'Orsay Restaurant Pub**	◈◈	$9-$23	538
19 / p. 512		Resto Bar Le Downtown	◈◈	$10-$20	542
20 / p. 512		Pizzeria d'Youville	◈◈	$12-$18	539
21 / p. 512		Restaurant Cafe d'Europe	◈◈	$27-$29	540
22 / p. 512	🅐	**Restaurant La Cremaillere**	◈◈◈	$18-$44	540
23 / p. 512		Le Charles Baillairge	◈◈◈	$18-$34	538
24 / p. 512	🅐	**Restaurant Gambrinus**	◈◈◈	$23-$36	540
25 / p. 512		Ristorante Il Teatro	◈◈◈	$26-$32	542
26 / p. 512	🅐	**Auberge du Tresor**	◈◈◈	$19-$35	537
27 / p. 512		Restaurant La Pointe des Ameriques	◈◈	$10-$22	540
28 / p. 512		Au Petit Coin Breton Creperie Restaurant	◈◈	$12-$22	537
29 / p. 512		L'Entrecote Saint-Jean	◈◈	$11-$24	539
30 / p. 512		Restaurant Que Sera Sera	◈◈◈	$17-$32	542
31 / p. 512	🅐	**Creperie Le Petit Chateau**	◈◈	$5-$22	538
32 / p. 512	🅐	**Restaurant Le Marie Clarisse**	◈◈◈	$29-$32	541
33 / p. 512	🅐	**Le Champlain**	◈◈◈◈	$27-$43	538
34 / p. 512	🅐	**Cafe de la Paix**	◈◈	$20-$32	537
35 / p. 512		Le Lapin Saute	◈◈	$25-$31	539
36 / p. 512	🅐	**Restaurant Le Continental**	◈◈◈	$22-$42	541
37 / p. 512		Cafe Bistro Le Diable aux Anges	◈◈	$11-$27	537

Spotter/Map Page Number	OA	DOWNTOWN QUEBEC - Restaurants (continued)	Diamond Rating	Rate Range High Season	Listing Page
㊳ / p. 512	CAA	**Restaurant aux Anciens Canadiens**	◇◇	$26-$62	540
㊴ / p. 512		Restaurant au Parmesan	◇◇	$10-$30	540
㊵ / p. 512		Restaurant Le Saint Amour	◇◇◇	$30-$48	541
㊶ / p. 512	CAA	**Le Veau d'or**	◇◇	$8-$14	539
㊷ / p. 512	CAA	**Restaurant L'Omelette**	◇◇	$6-$19	541
㊸ / p. 512	CAA	**Cafe de Paris**	◇◇	$20-$30	537
㊹ / p. 512	CAA	**Elysee Mandarin**	◇◇◇	$12-$22	538
㊺ / p. 512		Pizzeria Primavera Bistro Italiano	◇◇	$11-$25	540
㊻ / p. 512		Apsara	◇◇	$13-$15	537
㊼ / p. 512		Restaurant Le Parlementaire	◇◇◇	$12-$28(L)	541
㊽ / p. 512	CAA	**Restaurant Louis Hebert**	◇◇◇	$23-$26	541
㊾ / p. 512	CAA	**La Closerie**	◇◇◇	$18-$35	538
㊿ / p. 512		Le Paris-Brest	◇◇◇	$23-$36	539
51 / p. 512		Ginko Restaurant Japonais	◇◇	$10-$28	538
52 / p. 512		L'Astral - see color ad p 535	◇◇	$20-$55	538
53 / p. 512		Trattoria La Scala	◇◇	$8-$19	542
54 / p. 512		Le Graffiti Resto Cite	◇◇◇	$12-$34	539
55 / p. 512		Cafe Restaurant du Musee	◇◇	$15-$17	537

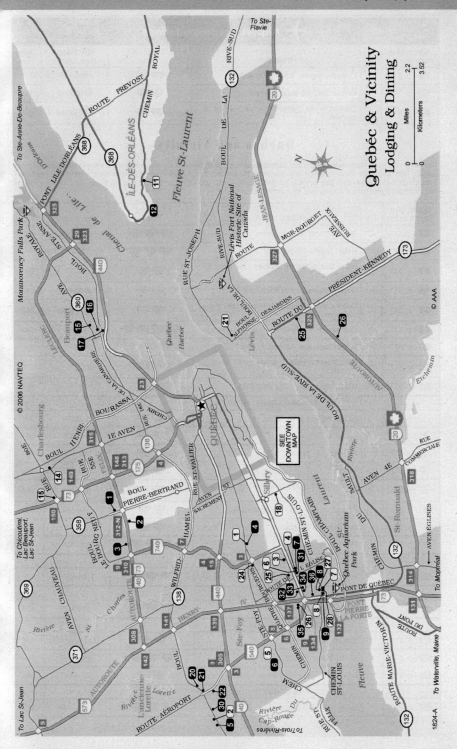

Quebéc & Vicinity
Lodging & Dining

✈ Airport Accommodations

Spotter/Map Page Number	OA	QUEBEC	Diamond Rating	Rate Range High Season	Listing Page
21 / p. 517		Chateau Repotel, 1.8 km s of airport	◆◆	$76-$92	548
22 / p. 517		Comfort Inn, 1.8 km s of airport	◆◆	$110-$145	548
5 / p. 517		Comfort Inn de l'Aeroport-Hamel, 5 km sw of terminal	◆◆	$103-$145	543

Quebec and Vicinity

This index helps you "spot" where approved accommodations and restaurants are located on the corresponding detailed maps. Lodging rate ranges are for comparison only and show the property's high season; rates are per night, unless only weekly (W) rates are available. Restaurant rate range is for dinner, unless only lunch (L) is served. Turn to the listing page for more detailed rate information and consult display ads for special promotions.

Spotter/Map Page Number	OA	QUEBEC - Lodgings	Diamond Rating	Rate Range High Season	Listing Page
1 / p. 517		Hotel & Suites Normandin	◆◆◆	$99-$169	543
2 / p. 517		Hotel Dauphin Quebec City	◆◆◆	$89-$99	543
3 / p. 517	CAA	**Hotel Quality Suites Quebec** - see color ad card insert	◆◆	$130-$190 SAVE	543
4 / p. 517	CAA	**Hotel Universel** - see color ad p 533	◆◆	$128-$148 SAVE	544
5 / p. 517		Comfort Inn de l'Aeroport-Hamel - see color ad card insert	◆◆	$103-$145	543
6 / p. 517	CAA	**Chateau Bonne Entente** - see color ad p 523	◆◆◆◆	$209-$499 SAVE	542
7 / p. 517	CAA	**Hotel Classique** - see color ad p 528	◆◆◆	$129-$229 SAVE	543
8 / p. 517	CAA	**Best Western Hotel L'Aristocrate** - see color ad p 513	◆◆◆	$135-$195 SAVE	542
9 / p. 517	CAA	**Hotel Sepia** - see color ad p 513	◆◆◆	$119-$179 SAVE	543
		QUEBEC - Restaurants			
① / p. 517		La Brochetterie Chez Greco	◆◆	$10-$20	544
② / p. 517		Jardin de Tang	◆◆	$13-$20	544
③ / p. 517		Au Petit Coin Breton	◆◆	$9-$20	544
④ / p. 517		Cosmos	◆◆	$11-$22	544
⑤ / p. 517	CAA	**Monte Cristo Resto Lounge** - see color ad p 523	◆◆◆◆	$18-$40	545
⑥ / p. 517		Restaurant La Pointe des Ameriques	◆◆	$10-$25	545
⑦ / p. 517		Le Manoir du Spaghetti	◆◆	$8-$18	544
⑧ / p. 517		Restaurant Le Galopin	◆◆◆	$25-$35	545
		ILE D'ORLEANS - Lodgings			
12 / p. 517		Auberge La Goeliche	◆◆◆	$151-$225	400
		ILE D'ORLEANS - Restaurant			
⑪ / p. 517	CAA	**Le Moulin de Saint-Laurent**	◆◆◆	$15-$26	400
		BEAUPORT - Lodgings			
15 / p. 517		Gite du Vieux-Bourg	◆◆	Failed to provide	546
16 / p. 517		Ambassadeur Hotel & Suites	◆◆◆	$99-$300	546
17 / p. 517		Comfort Inn - see color ad card insert	◆◆	$95-$195	546
		L'ANCIENNE-LORETTE - Lodgings			
20 / p. 517		Times Hotel & Suites	◆◆◆	$129-$194	549

Spotter/Map Page Number	OA	L'ANCIENNE-LORETTE - Lodgings (continued)	Diamond Rating	Rate Range High Season	Listing Page
21 / p. 517		Chateau Repotel	◆◆	$76-$92	548
22 / p. 517		Comfort Inn	◆◆	$110-$145	548
		LEVIS - Lodgings			
25 / p. 517		Econo Lodge - see color ad card insert	◆◆	$99-$175	550
26 / p. 517		Comfort Inn - see color ad card insert	◆◆	$110-$170	549
		LEVIS - Restaurant			
21 / p. 517	CAA	**Restaurant L'Intimiste**	◆◆◆	$23-$39	550
		STE-FOY - Lodgings			
30 / p. 517		Hotel Quebec Inn	◆◆◆	$83-$173	551
31 / p. 517		Hotel Lindbergh	◆◆◆	$140-$320	551
32 / p. 517		Hotel Gouverneur Quebec-Sainte-Foy	◆◆◆	$115-$250	551
33 / p. 517		Hotel Plaza Quebec	◆◆◆	$107-$207	551
34 / p. 517		Sir Wilfrid Auberge Sainte-Foy	◆◆	$126-$310	551
35 / p. 517		Hotel Clarion Quebec - see color ad card insert	◆◆◆	$99-$350	550
36 / p. 517		L'Hotel Quebec	◆◆◆	$99-$249	551
		STE-FOY - Restaurants			
24 / p. 517		Cafe Pates a Tout	◆	$5-$9	552
25 / p. 517		Bistango	◆◆◆	$13-$30	552
26 / p. 517		Paris Grill Brasserie Francaise	◆◆	$10-$21	552
27 / p. 517	CAA	**Restaurant La Fenouilliere -** see color ad p 513	◆◆◆◆	$23-$31	552
28 / p. 517	CAA	**Ristorante Michelangelo**	◆◆◆◆	$18-$40	552
		CHARLESBOURG - Restaurants			
14 / p. 517		Le Manoir du Spaghetti	◆◆	$8-$18	547
15 / p. 517		Da Cortina	◆◆◆	$16-$33	547
		SILLERY - Restaurant			
18 / p. 517		Paparazzi	◆◆	$13-$28	553

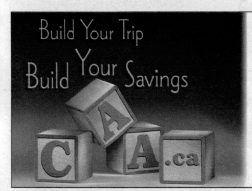

DOWNTOWN QUEBEC   (See map and index starting on p. 512)

────── WHERE TO STAY ──────

APPARTEMENTS LA PERGOLA

Property failed to provide current rates

Phone: 418/681-1428   37

Condominium

Location: Between aves Moncton and des Erables. Located in a busy residential area. 405 boul Rene-Levesque ouest G1S 1S2. Fax: 418/684-7627. **Facility:** 6 units. 1 one-bedroom standard unit with kitchen. 4 one- and 1 two-bedroom suites with kitchens. 2-3 stories (no elevator), interior corridors. **Parking:** on-site, winter plug-ins. **Terms:** small pets only. **Amenities:** CD players. *Some:* DVD players, voice mail, irons, hair dryers. **Guest Services:** coin laundry.

AUBERGE DU QUARTIER   *Book at AAA.com*

Phone: (418)525-9726   36

5/1-6/30 & 10/10-4/30 [CP]	1P: $79-$149	2P: $89-$159	XP: $20	F5
7/1-10/9 [CP]	1P: $79-$129	2P: $89-$139	XP: $20	F5

Historic
Small-scale Hotel

Location: Between aves Bourlamaque and Cartier. 170 Grande Allee ouest G1R 2G9. Fax: 418/521-4891. **Facility:** Attractive rooms that range from small to spacious are offered at this restored 19th-century residence. Smoke free premises. 15 one-bedroom standard units. 3 stories (no elevator), interior corridors. *Bath:* combo or shower only. **Parking:** on-site. **Terms:** cancellation fee imposed, package plans. **Amenities:** CD players, irons, hair dryers. **Guest Services:** valet laundry. **Business Services:** PC (fee). **Cards:** AX, MC, VI.

SOME UNITS

AUBERGE DU TRESOR

Phone: 418/694-1876   18

5/1-10/31	1P: $90-$110	2P: $105-$135	XP: $15	F12
11/1-4/30	1P: $80-$100	2P: $90-$115	XP: $10	F12

Historic
Small-scale Hotel

Location: Corner of rue du Tresor. Located in Old Quebec. 20 rue Ste-Anne G1R 3X2. Fax: 418/694-0563. **Facility:** Overlooking the scenic Chateau Frontenac in the heart of Old Quebec, this red-roofed heritage inn stands on a property first inhabited in 1640. 21 one-bedroom standard units. 3 stories (no elevator), interior corridors. *Bath:* combo or shower only. **Parking:** street. **Terms:** [AP] & [BP] meal plans available, package plans. **Dining:** restaurant, see separate listing. **Guest Services:** valet laundry. **Cards:** AX, DC, JC, MC, VI. *(See color ad p 522)*

SOME UNITS

(See map and index starting on p. 512)

AUBERGE L'AUTRE JARDIN

Phone: (418)523-1790   **14**

(CAA) (SAVE)

5/1-10/15 & 2/1-2/17 [ECP]	1P: $109-$149	2P: $124-$164	XP: $15	F6
10/16-1/31 [ECP]	1P: $89-$132	2P: $101-$144	XP: $12	F6
2/18-4/30 [ECP]	1P: $89-$132	2P: $101-$144	XP: $15	F6

Bed & Breakfast   **Location:** Between rue Dorchester and rue de la Couronne. 365 boul Charest est G1K 3H3. Fax: 418/523-9735. **Facility:** Operated by a non-profit organization, this lodging has contemporary, stylish rooms in a prime neighborhood on the northwest cusp of downtown Quebec. 27 units. 24 one-bedroom standard units, some with whirlpools. 3 one-bedroom suites ($153-$197) with whirlpools. 3 stories (no elevator), interior corridors. *Bath:* combo or shower only. **Parking:** street. **Terms:** check-in 4 pm, cancellation fee imposed, package plans. **Amenities:** dual phone lines, hair dryers. **Leisure Activities:** garden terrace. **Guest Services:** gift shop, valet laundry, wireless Internet. **Business Services:** meeting rooms, PC. **Cards:** AX, DC, DS, JC, MC, VI. **Free Special Amenities: expanded continental breakfast and high-speed Internet.**

SOME UNITS
[⋕⁺] / [✕] [VCR] [▪] /

AUBERGE SAINT-ANTOINE   *Book great rates at AAA.com*

Phone: (418)692-2211   **9**

(CAA) (SAVE)

6/1-10/31	2P: $309	XP: $30	F13
5/1-5/31 & 11/1-4/30	2P: $249	XP: $30	F13

Historic
Small-scale Hotel   **Location:** Corner of rue Dalhousie. Located in Old Port area. 8 rue St-Antoine G1K 4C9. Fax: 418/692-1177. **Facility:** Old Quebec artifacts decorate corridors of this restored 19th-century maritime warehouse with a variety of large, upscale and stylish rooms. 94 units. 89 one-bedroom standard units, some with efficiencies and/or whirlpools. 5 one-bedroom suites. 5 stories, interior corridors. *Bath:* combo or shower only. **Parking:** on-site (fee) and valet. **Terms:** check-in 4 pm, package plans, pets (dogs only, $150 fee). **Amenities:** high-speed Internet, voice mail, safes, honor bars, irons, hair dryers. *Some:* DVD players (fee), CD players, fax. **Dining:** 6:30 am-11 pm, cocktails, also, Panache Restaurant, see separate listing. **Leisure Activities:** movie theatre. *Fee:* massage. **Guest Services:** valet laundry, wireless Internet. **Business Services:** meeting rooms, business center. **Cards:** AX, DC, MC, VI. **Free Special Amenities: newspaper and high-speed Internet.**

SOME UNITS
[🛏] [⋕] [Y] [♿] [▬] / [✕] [VCR] [▪] [▭] /
FEE   FEE

AUBERGE SAINT-PIERRE   *Book great rates at AAA.com*

Phone: (418)694-7981   **6**

(CAA) (SAVE)

5/1-10/31 [BP]	1P: $129-$325	2P: $129-$325	XP: $25	F
11/1-4/30 [BP]	1P: $129-$299	2P: $129-$299	XP: $25	F

Historic
Small-scale Hotel   **Location:** Between rue de la Barricade and rue St-Antoine. Located in Old Port area. 79 rue St-Pierre G1K 4A3. Fax: 418/694-0406. **Facility:** Modern amenities and a full breakfast are among the draws at this upscale hotel set in a restored 1821 building; some luxury services are offered. Smoke free premises. 41 one-bedroom standard units, some with whirlpools. 4 stories, interior corridors. *Bath:* combo or shower only. **Parking:** valet. **Terms:** cancellation fee imposed, package plans. **Amenities:** voice mail, irons, hair dryers. *Some:* DVD players, CD players, dual phone lines. **Leisure Activities:** *Fee:* massage. **Guest Services:** complimentary evening beverages, valet laundry, wireless Internet. **Business Services:** meeting rooms, PC. **Cards:** AX, DC, DS, JC, MC, VI. **Free Special Amenities: full breakfast and high-speed Internet.**

SOME UNITS
[⋕⁺] [📶] [✕] [▬] / [VCR] [▪] /
FEE

BED & BREAKFAST MANOIR MON CALME

Phone: 418/523-2714   **33**

Property failed to provide current rates

Historic Bed
& Breakfast   **Location:** Corner of Cours du Generale-De Montcalm. 549 Grande Allee est G1R 2J5. **Facility:** This handsome Victorian house offers spacious, tastefully decorated rooms within walking distance of restaurants and Old Quebec. Smoke free premises. 5 one-bedroom standard units. 3 stories (no elevator), interior corridors. *Bath:* combo or shower only. **Parking:** on-site. **Amenities:** irons, hair dryers. **Guest Services:** coin laundry.

SOME UNITS
[✕] [🅩] / [▬] /

(See map and index starting on p. 512)

BEST WESTERN CITY CENTRE/CENTRE-VILLE   *Book great rates at AAA.com*   Phone: (418)649-1919   **3**

(CAA) SAVE	7/1-8/27	1P: $169-$299	2P: $189-$319	XP: $15	F16
◆◆◆	8/28-10/9	1P: $139-$239	2P: $159-$269	XP: $15	F16
	5/1-6/30	1P: $149-$199	2P: $169-$249	XP: $15	F16
	10/10-4/30	1P: $119-$189	2P: $139-$249	XP: $15	F16

Large-scale Hotel Location: Corner of rue du Roi. 330 rue de la Couronne G1K 6E6. Fax: 418/529-4411. **Facility:** 180 one-bedroom standard units, some with whirlpools. 6 stories, interior corridors. **Parking:** on-site (fee) and street. **Terms:** check-in 3:30 pm, 7 day cancellation notice, package plans. **Amenities:** voice mail, safes, irons, hair dryers. *Some:* high-speed Internet. **Dining:** 7 am-2 & 5-10 pm, cocktails. **Pool(s):** heated indoor. **Leisure Activities:** whirlpool, limited exercise equipment. **Guest Services:** valet laundry, wireless Internet. **Business Services:** meeting rooms, PC. **Cards:** AX, DC, DS, MC, VI. **Free Special Amenities:** local telephone calls and high-speed Internet. *(See color ad p 521)*

SOME UNITS

FEE   FEE

COURTYARD MARRIOTT QUEBEC   *Book great rates at AAA.com*   Phone: 418/694-4004   **19**

Property failed to provide current rates

◆◆◆ **Location:** Corner of ave Honore-Mercier; in Old Quebec, facing Place d'Youville. 850 Place d'Youville G1R 3P6. **Large-scale Hotel** Fax: 418/694-4007. **Facility:** Smoke free premises. 111 units. 101 one-bedroom standard units. 10 one-bedroom suites, some with whirlpools. 8 stories, interior corridors. **Parking:** on-site (fee) and valet. **Terms:** check-in 4 pm. **Amenities:** video games (fee), high-speed Internet, voice mail, irons, hair dryers. **Dining:** Restaurant Que Sera Sera, see separate listing. **Leisure Activities:** whirlpool, exercise room. *Fee:* massage. **Guest Services:** sundries, valet and coin laundry, wireless Internet. **Business Services:** meeting rooms, PC, fax (fee).

(See map and index starting on p. 512)

DELTA QUEBEC — *Book great rates at AAA.com* — Phone: (418)647-1717 — ㉙

7/1-10/31	1P: $140-$315	2P: $140-$315	XP: $20 F
5/1-6/30	1P: $125-$295	2P: $125-$295	XP: $20 F
11/1-4/30	1P: $100-$230	2P: $100-$230	XP: $20 F

Location: Just w of boul Honore-Mercier. 690 boul Rene-Levesque est G1R 5A8. Fax: 418/647-2146. **Facility:** 377 units. 376 one-bedroom standard units. 1 one-bedroom suite ($200-$950). 12 stories, interior corridors. **Parking:** on-site (fee) and valet. **Terms:** package plans. **Amenities:** video games (fee), voice mail, irons, hair dryers. *Some:* CD players, high-speed Internet (fee), honor bars. **Dining:** 7 am-10 pm, cocktails. **Pool(s):** heated outdoor. **Leisure Activities:** saunas, whirlpool, exercise room. *Fee:* massage. **Guest Services:** gift shop, valet laundry. **Business Services:** conference facilities, business center. **Cards:** AX, DC, DS, JC, MC, VI. *(See color ad below)*

SOME UNITS

FAIRMONT LE CHATEAU FRONTENAC — *Book great rates at AAA.com* — Phone: 418/692-3861 — ㉒

7/1-10/15	1P: $249-$549	2P: $249-$549	XP: $30 F17
12/24-4/30	1P: $199-$449	2P: $199-$449	XP: $30 F17
5/1-6/30	1P: $249-$399	2P: $249-$399	XP: $30 F17
10/16-12/23	1P: $199-$299	2P: $199-$299	XP: $30 F17

Location: In Old Quebec. 1 rue des Carrieres G1R 4P5. Fax: 418/692-1751. **Facility:** Turrets and verdigris copper roofs distinguish this landmark chateau; constructed in 1893, it has a commanding river view. 617 units. 587 one-bedroom standard units, some with whirlpools. 22 one- and 8 two-bedroom suites, some with whirlpools. 21 stories, interior corridors. **Parking:** on-site (fee) and valet. **Terms:** check-in 4 pm, 2 night minimum stay - seasonal, cancellation fee imposed, [BP] meal plan available, package plans, small pets only ($25 extra charge). **Amenities:** video games (fee), voice mail, irons, hair dryers. *Some:* CD players, DVD players, high-speed Internet. **Dining:** 3 restaurants, 6 am-11 pm, also, Le Champlain, see separate listing. **Pool(s):** heated indoor, wading. **Leisure Activities:** whirlpool, steamrooms, ice skating, exercise room, spa. *Fee:* toboggan slide, CD music library on Fairmont Gold floors. **Guest Services:** gift shop, valet laundry, wireless Internet. **Business Services:** conference facilities, business center. **Cards:** AX, CB, DC, DS, JC, MC, VI. *(See color ad card insert)*

SOME UNITS
FEE — FEE

HILTON QUEBEC — *Book great rates at AAA.com* — Phone: (418)647-2411 — ㉔

6/10-10/13	1P: $99-$309	2P: $119-$329	XP: $25 F
5/1-6/9 & 10/14-4/30	1P: $99-$229	2P: $119-$249	XP: $25 F

Location: Corner of Honore-Mercier. Located next to convention centre and shopping complex. 1100 boul Rene-Levesque est G1K 7K7. Fax: 418/647-6488. **Facility:** The luxury high-rise hotel offers excellent city views and many luxury services. Some guest rooms are not spacious. 571 units. 535 one-bedroom standard units. 36 one-bedroom suites ($395-$1255). 23 stories, interior corridors. **Parking:** on-site (fee) and valet. **Terms:** package plans, $2 service charge, small pets only ($25 fee). **Amenities:** dual phone lines, voice mail, honor bars, irons, hair dryers. *Fee:* video games, high-speed Internet. **Dining:** 7 am-11 pm; from 6:45 am 6/15-9/30, cocktails. **Pool(s):** heated outdoor. **Leisure Activities:** sauna, exercise room. *Fee:* massage. **Guest Services:** gift shop, valet laundry, tanning facilities, wireless Internet. **Business Services:** conference facilities, business center. **Cards:** AX, CB, DC, DS, JC, MC, VI. **Free Special Amenities:** newspaper. *(See color ad p 525)*

SOME UNITS
FEE — FEE

(See map and index starting on p. 512)

HOLIDAY INN SELECT QUEBEC CITY-DOWNTOWN *Book great rates at AAA.com*   **Phone:** 418/647-2611   ⓫
Property failed to provide current rates
▼▼▼▼ **Location:** Corner of rue St-Joseph est. 395 rue de la Couronne G1K 7X4. Fax: 418/640-0666. **Facility:** 238 units.
234 one-bedroom standard units. 4 one-bedroom suites. 18 stories, interior corridors. **Parking:** on-site (fee)
Large-scale Hotel and street. **Amenities:** video games (fee), voice mail, irons, hair dryers. *Some:* dual phone lines. **Pool(s):**
heated indoor. **Leisure Activities:** sauna, exercise room. **Guest Services:** gift shop, valet and coin laundry, wireless Internet.
Business Services: conference facilities, business center.

SOME UNITS
🍴 🍸 🏊 🎮 💻 / ✕ VCR 🛗 🖨 /
FEE FEE FEE

HOTEL 71 *Book at AAA.com*   **Phone:** (418)692-1171   ❼
                        5/1-10/31 [CP]   1P: $180-$325   2P: $180-$325   XP: $25   F
▼▼▼   11/1-4/30 [CP]   1P: $165-$275   2P: $165-$275   XP: $25   F
Small-scale Hotel **Location:** Just e of Cote de la Montagne; in Old Port sector. 71 rue St-Pierre G1K 4A4. Fax: 418/692-0669.
Facility: Smoke free premises. 40 units. 36 one-bedroom standard units. 4 one-bedroom suites. 7 stories,
interior corridors. *Bath:* combo or shower only. **Parking:** valet. **Terms:** cancellation fee imposed, package plans.
Amenities: video library, DVD players, CD players, high-speed Internet, dual phone lines, voice mail, safes, irons, hair dryers.
Leisure Activities: exercise room. *Fee:* massage. **Guest Services:** valet laundry, wireless Internet. **Business Services:**
meeting rooms, business center. **Cards:** AX, DC, DS, MC, VI.

(A$K) 🍴 🍸 ✕

HOTEL CHAMPLAIN VIEUX-QUEBEC *Book great rates at AAA.com*   **Phone:** (418)694-0106   ⓴
                        6/22-9/30 [BP]   1P: $139-$269   2P: $139-$269   XP: $20   F10
▼▼▼   5/1-6/21 [BP]   1P: $129-$239   2P: $129-$239   XP: $20   F10
                        10/29-4/30 [BP]   1P: $99-$209   2P: $99-$209   XP: $20   F10
Small-scale Hotel 10/1-10/28 [BP]   1P: $129   2P: $129   XP: $20   F10
Location: Between rue Ste-Angele and St-Stanislas. Located in Old Quebec. 115 rue Ste-Anne G1R 3X6. Fax: 418/692-1959. **Facility:** 50
one-bedroom standard units, some with efficiencies (utensils extra charge) and/or whirlpools. 5 stories, interior corridors.
Parking: on-site (fee), winter plug-ins. **Terms:** cancellation fee imposed, package plans. **Amenities:** dual phone lines, hair
dryers. **Guest Services:** valet laundry, wireless Internet. **Cards:** AX, DC, DS, JC, MC, VI.

(A$K) 🅢 ✕ 🛗 💻

(See map and index starting on p. 512)

HOTEL CHATEAU BELLEVUE   *Book great rates at AAA.com*   **Phone:** (418)692-2573   **27**

CAA SAVE

7/1-10/14	1P: $119-$249	2P: $119-$249	XP: $20	F17
5/1-6/30	1P: $89-$209	2P: $89-$209	XP: $20	F17
10/15-4/30	1P: $74-$184	2P: $74-$184	XP: $20	F17

Historic Small-scale Hotel

Location: Corner of ave Ste-Genevieve. Located in Old Quebec. 16 rue de la Porte G1R 4M9. **Fax:** 418/692-4876. **Facility:** This 1848 building overlooks Parc des Gouverneurs in Old Quebec; small to good-size rooms have attractive furnishings and comfortable bedding. 58 one-bedroom standard units. 4 stories, interior corridors. **Bath:** combo or shower only. **Parking:** on-site. **Terms:** check-in 4 pm, [AP], [BP], [CP] & [ECP] meal plans available. **Amenities:** voice mail, hair dryers. *Some:* high-speed Internet. **Leisure Activities:** *Fee:* massage. **Guest Services:** valet laundry, wireless Internet. **Business Services:** PC. **Cards:** AX, CB, DC, DS, JC, MC, VI. **Free Special Amenities:** newspaper and high-speed Internet. *(See color ad p 527)*

SOME UNITS

/ ⊠ /

HOTEL CHATEAU GRANDE-ALLEE   *Book great rates at AAA.com*   **Phone:** (418)647-4433   **32**

CAA SAVE

2/1-2/17	1P: $109-$179	2P: $109-$179	XP: $15	F11
5/1-10/14	1P: $109-$169	2P: $109-$169	XP: $15	F11
10/15-1/31 & 2/18-4/30	1P: $99-$159	2P: $99-$159	XP: $15	F11

Historic Small-scale Hotel

Location: Corner of de la Chevrotiere. 601 rue Grande Allee est G1R 2K4. **Fax:** 418/649-7553. **Facility:** A bustling district of sidewalk cafes surrounds this Victorian-era stone house. 30 one-bedroom standard units. 1-3 stories (no elevator), interior corridors. **Parking:** on-site (fee), winter plug-ins. **Terms:** cancellation fee imposed, [ECP] meal plan available, package plans. **Amenities:** video library (fee). *Some:* DVD players, hair dryers. **Dining:** noon-2:30 & 5-10 pm, cocktails. **Guest Services:** valet laundry, wireless Internet. **Business Services:** PC. **Cards:** AX, CB, DC, DS, JC, MC, VI. **Free Special Amenities:** high-speed Internet.

SOME UNITS

⊞ ⊤ / ⊠ /

HOTEL CHATEAU LAURIER QUEBEC   *Book great rates at AAA.com*   **Phone:** (418)522-8108   **31**

CAA SAVE

7/1-10/14	1P: $129-$339	2P: $129-$339	XP: $20	F17
5/1-6/30	1P: $119-$289	2P: $119-$289	XP: $20	F17
10/15-4/30	1P: $94-$239	2P: $94-$239	XP: $20	F17

Historic Small-scale Hotel

Location: Corner of Grande Allee est. 1220 Place George-V ouest G1R 5B8. **Fax:** 418/524-8768. **Facility:** Guest rooms in a variety of sizes are all handsomely furnished in a classic style at this well-located downtown hotel. 168 units. 165 one-bedroom standard units, some with whirlpools. 3 one-bedroom suites ($339-$1039). 5 stories, interior corridors. **Bath:** combo or shower only. **Parking:** on-site (fee) and valet, winter plug-ins. **Terms:** check-in 4 pm, [AP], [BP], [CP] & [ECP] meal plans available. **Amenities:** voice mail, safes, irons, hair dryers. *Some:* CD players, high-speed Internet. **Dining:** La Closerie, see separate listing. **Leisure Activities:** exercise room. *Fee:* massage. **Guest Services:** sundries, valet laundry, wireless Internet. **Business Services:** meeting rooms, PC. **Cards:** AX, CB, DC, DS, JC, MC, VI. **Free Special Amenities:** newspaper and high-speed Internet. *(See color ad p 527)*

SOME UNITS

⊞ ⊛ ▭ / ⊠ � ⊟ /
FEE

(See map and index starting on p. 512)

HOTEL CLARENDON *Book great rates at AAA.com* — Phone: (418)692-2480 — **16**

CAA SAVE | 5/1-10/20 & 2/1-2/16 | 1P: $159-$289 | 2P: $159-$289 | XP: $20 | F12
| 10/21-1/31 & 2/17-4/30 | 1P: $109-$229 | 2P: $109-$229 | XP: $20 | F12

Location: Corner of rue des Jardins. Located in Old Quebec. 57 rue Ste-Anne G1R 3X4. Fax: 418/692-4652. **Facility:** Within walking distance to many attractions in Old Quebec, the well-restored, historic hotel offers
Historic — upscale rooms and a range of luxury services. 143 one-bedroom standard units, some with whirlpools. 6
Small-scale Hotel — stories, interior corridors. **Parking:** valet. **Terms:** check-in 4 pm, [BP] & [MAP] meal plans available,
package plans. **Amenities:** video games (fee), voice mail, irons, hair dryers. *Some:* CD players. **Dining:** Le
Charles Baillairge, see separate listing. **Leisure Activities:** exercise room. *Fee:* massage. **Guest Services:** sundries, valet
laundry, wireless Internet. **Business Services:** meeting rooms, PC. **Cards:** AX, CB, DC, DS, JC, MC, VI.
(See color ad p 526)

SOME UNITS
〔image of amenity icons〕

HOTEL DES COUTELLIER *Book great rates at AAA.com* — Phone: (418)692-9696 — **1**

CAA SAVE | 6/22-10/14 [CP] | 1P: $150-$190 | 2P: $170-$210 | XP: $10 | F17
| 10/15-4/30 [CP] | 1P: $120-$170 | 2P: $130-$180 | XP: $10 | F17
| 5/1-6/21 [CP] | 1P: $110-$160 | 2P: $120-$170 | XP: $10 | F17

Location: Corner rue St-Andre. Facing Marche du Vieux-Port. 253 rue St-Paul G1K 3W5. Fax: 418/692-4050.
Small-scale Hotel — **Facility:** 24 one-bedroom standard units, some with whirlpools. 4 stories, interior corridors. **Parking:** street.
Terms: package plans. **Amenities:** voice mail, honor bars, irons, hair dryers. *Some:* DVD players, CD
players. **Dining:** Moss Bistro Belge, see separate listing. **Guest Services:** valet laundry, wireless Internet. **Business Services:**
meeting rooms, PC. **Cards:** AX, DC, DS, MC, VI. **Free Special Amenities: continental breakfast and high-speed Internet.**

SOME UNITS
〔image of amenity icons〕
FEE

HOTEL LE CLOS ST-LOUIS *Book great rates at AAA.com* — Phone: (418)694-1311 — **26**

CAA SAVE | 5/1-11/1 [CP] | 1P: $220-$300 | 2P: $220-$300 | XP: $25
| 11/2-4/30 [CP] | 1P: $195-$255 | 2P: $195-$255 | XP: $25

Location: Just e of rue Ste-Ursule; in Old Quebec. 69 rue St-Louis G1R 3Z2. Fax: 418/694-9411. **Facility:** This
beautifully restored Victorian-style residence in the heart of Old Quebec offers luxurious guest rooms ideal
Historic — for a romantic getaway. Smoke free premises. 18 units. 17 one-bedroom standard units, some with
Small-scale Hotel — whirlpools. 1 one-bedroom suite ($255-$280) with whirlpool. 4 stories (no elevator). **Parking:** on-site (fee).
Terms: 2 night minimum stay - seasonal and/or weekends, 14 day cancellation notice-fee imposed,
package plans. **Amenities:** hair dryers. **Guest Services:** complimentary laundry, wireless Internet. **Business Services:** PC.
Cards: AX, MC, VI. **Free Special Amenities: expanded continental breakfast and high-speed Internet.**

〔image of amenity icons〕

HOTEL LE PRIORI *Book great rates at AAA.com* — Phone: (418)692-3992 — **10**

CAA SAVE | 6/1-8/31 | 1P: $179-$499 | 2P: $179-$499 | XP: $25 | F5
| 9/1-10/31 | 1P: $159 | 2P: $159 | XP: $25 | F5
| 5/1-5/31 | 1P: $149 | 2P: $149 | XP: $25 | F5
| 11/1-4/30 | 1P: $139 | 2P: $139 | XP: $25 | F5

Location: Between Cote de la Montagne and rue St-Antoine. Located in Old Port area. 15 Sault-au-Matelot G1K 3Y7.
Small-scale Hotel — Fax: 418/692-0883. **Facility:** Decor with post-modern influences distinguishes this hotel set in a restored
18th-century stone building. 26 units. 21 one-bedroom standard units, some with whirlpools. 2 one- and 3
two-bedroom suites with whirlpools. 3-4 stories, interior/exterior corridors. *Bath:* combo or shower only. **Parking:** street.
Terms: package plans. **Amenities:** voice mail, irons, hair dryers. *Some:* CD players. **Dining:** 7-10 am, 11:30-2 & 6-10 pm, Sat
7:30 am-noon & 6-10 pm, Sun 7-10:30 am, 11:30-2 & 6-10 pm, cocktails. **Leisure Activities:** *Fee:* massage. **Guest Services:**
valet laundry. **Business Services:** meeting rooms. **Cards:** AX, DC, DS, JC, MC, VI. **Free Special Amenities: expanded
continental breakfast and high-speed Internet.**

SOME UNITS
〔image of amenity icons〕

(See map and index starting on p. 512)

HOTEL L'ERMITAGE

Phone: (418)694-0968   **25**

CAA SAVE

	5/1-10/14 & 2/1-2/17	1P: $119-$169	2P: $119-$169	XP: $15	F11
	2/18-4/30	1P: $109-$169	2P: $109-$169	XP: $15	F11
	10/15-1/31	1P: $99-$159	2P: $99-$159	XP: $15	F11

Historic Small-scale Hotel
Location: Corner of des Ursulines. Located in Old Quebec. 60 rue Ste-Ursule G1R 4E6. Fax: 418/694-0458. **Facility:** Guest rooms have high ceilings; two have balconies. 10 one-bedroom standard units. 3 stories (no elevator), interior corridors. **Parking:** street. **Terms:** off-site registration, cancellation fee imposed, [ECP] meal plan available, package plans. **Amenities:** hair dryers. **Guest Services:** valet laundry. **Cards:** AX, CB, DC, DS, JC, MC, VI. **Free Special Amenities: high-speed Internet.**

SOME UNITS

HOTEL LE SAINT-PAUL   *Book at AAA.com*

Phone: (418)694-4414   **2**

| | 5/1-11/1 | 1P: $99-$199 | 2P: $119-$209 | XP: $25 | D17 |
| | 11/2-4/30 | 1P: $89-$179 | 2P: $99-$189 | XP: $25 | D17 |

Small-scale Hotel
Location: Corner of rue du Marche-du-Vieux Port. 229 1/2 rue St-Paul G1K 3W3. Fax: 418/694-0889. **Facility:** 27 units. 26 one-bedroom standard units. 1 one-bedroom suite with whirlpool. 3 stories, interior corridors. **Parking:** street. **Terms:** cancellation fee imposed, package plans. **Amenities:** hair dryers. **Guest Services:** valet laundry, wireless Internet. **Business Services:** meeting rooms. **Cards:** AX, DC, DS, MC, VI.

SOME UNITS

HOTEL MANOIR D'AUTEUIL   *Book great rates at AAA.com*

Phone: (418)694-1173   **23**

CAA SAVE

| | 5/1-11/1 [CP] | 1P: $99-$199 | 2P: $99-$219 | XP: $15 | D12 |
| | 11/2-4/30 [CP] | 1P: $79-$189 | 2P: $89-$189 | XP: $10 | D12 |

Historic Bed & Breakfast
Location: Corner of rue Ste-Anne. Located in Old Quebec. 49 rue d G1R 4C2. Fax: 418/694-0081. **Facility:** Art Deco-style woodwork is featured in this 1835 hotel. Smoke free premises. 16 one-bedroom standard units. 4 stories (no elevator), interior corridors. *Bath:* combo or shower only. **Parking:** street. **Terms:** 2 night minimum stay - seasonal, package plans. **Amenities:** irons, hair dryers. **Leisure Activities:** ski & bike lockers. **Guest Services:** valet laundry, wireless Internet. **Business Services:** meeting rooms, PC. **Cards:** AX, MC, VI.

SOME UNITS

HOTEL MANOIR DE LA TOUR   *Book at AAA.com*

Phone: (418)525-6276   **35**

| | 7/1-10/9 [CP] | 1P: $79-$159 | 2P: $89-$169 | XP: $20 | F5 |
| | 5/1-6/30 & 10/10-4/30 [CP] | 1P: $69-$134 | 2P: $79-$144 | XP: $20 | F5 |

Small-scale Hotel
Location: Corner of ave Tache. 385 rue Grande-Allee est G1R 2H8. Fax: 418/525-0020. **Facility:** 12 one-bedroom standard units, some with whirlpools. 3 stories (no elevator), interior corridors. *Bath:* combo or shower only. **Parking:** on-site (fee). **Terms:** office hours 7 am-10:30 pm, cancellation fee imposed. **Amenities:** hair dryers. **Guest Services:** valet laundry. **Cards:** AX, MC, VI.

SOME UNITS

HOTEL MANOIR LAFAYETTE   *Book great rates at AAA.com*

Phone: (418)522-2652   **30**

	7/1-10/14	1P: $109-$229	2P: $109-$229	XP: $20	F17
	5/1-6/30	1P: $99-$209	2P: $99-$209	XP: $20	F17
	10/15-4/30	1P: $84-$169	2P: $84-$169	XP: $20	F17

Historic Small-scale Hotel
Location: Between rue d'Artigny and de la Chevrotiere. 661 rue Grande Allee est G1R 3X4. Fax: 418/522-4400. **Facility:** This restored Victorian near restaurants and nightclubs offers small, well-decorated rooms. 53 one-bedroom standard units. 5 stories, interior corridors. **Parking:** on-site. **Terms:** check-in 4 pm, [AP], [BP], [CP] & [ECP] meal plans available. **Amenities:** voice mail, irons, hair dryers. **Leisure Activities:** *Fee:* massage. **Guest Services:** valet laundry, wireless Internet. **Business Services:** meeting rooms. **Cards:** AX, CB, DC, DS, JC, MC, VI.

SOME UNITS

HOTEL MANOIR VICTORIA   *Book great rates at AAA.com*

Phone: (418)692-1030   **8**

CAA SAVE

| | 5/1-10/20 | 1P: $149-$309 | 2P: $149-$309 | XP: $30 | F18 |
| | 10/21-4/30 | 1P: $109-$269 | 2P: $109-$269 | XP: $30 | F18 |

Small-scale Hotel
Location: Corner of rue St-Jean. Located in Old Quebec, across from the hospital. 44 Cote du Palais G1R 4H8. Fax: 418/692-3822. **Facility:** 156 units. 154 one-bedroom standard units, some with whirlpools. 2 one-bedroom suites, some with whirlpools. 6 stories, interior corridors. **Parking:** valet and street. **Amenities:** video games (fee), high-speed Internet, voice mail, honor bars, irons, hair dryers. **Dining:** 2 restaurants, 7 am-11 pm, cocktails. **Pool(s):** heated indoor. **Leisure Activities:** sauna, exercise room, spa. **Guest Services:** valet laundry, wireless Internet. **Business Services:** meeting rooms, PC (fee). **Cards:** AX, CB, DC, DS, JC, MC, VI. **Free Special Amenities: high-speed Internet.** *(See color ad p 532)*

SOME UNITS

HOTEL MARIE-ROLLET

Phone: 418/694-9271   **15**

| | All Year | 1P: $65-$155 | 2P: $65-$155 | XP: $10 | |

Historic Small-scale Hotel
Location: Corner of rue Pierre-Olivier-Chauveau. Located in Old Quebec. 81 rue Ste-Anne G1R 3X4. **Facility:** Vintage pieces and some antiques furnish this intimate 1876 hotel. Smoke free premises. 10 one-bedroom standard units. 4 stories (no elevator), interior corridors. *Bath:* combo or shower only. **Parking:** street. **Terms:** 3 day cancellation notice-fee imposed. **Guest Services:** valet laundry. **Cards:** AX, MC, VI.

(See color ad p 532)

(See map and index starting on p. 512)

HOTEL PALACE ROYAL   Phone: 418/694-2000   **21**

| | 7/14-10/14 | 1P: $139-$489 | 2P: $139-$489 | XP: $20 | F12 |
| | 5/1-7/13 & 10/15-4/30 | 1P: $119-$389 | 2P: $119-$389 | XP: $20 | F12 |

Large-scale Hotel   **Location:** Corner rue St-Jean. 775 ave Honore-Mercier G1R 6A5. Fax: 418/380-2553. **Facility:** 234 units. 96 one-bedroom standard units, some with whirlpools. 138 one-bedroom suites, some with whirlpools. 10 stories, interior corridors. **Parking:** on-site (fee) and valet. **Terms:** check-in 4 pm, cancellation fee imposed, package plans. **Amenities:** high-speed Internet (fee), dual phone lines, voice mail, irons, hair dryers. Some: DVD players (fee). **Pool(s):** heated indoor. **Leisure Activities:** sauna, whirlpool, exercise room. Fee: massage. **Guest Services:** gift shop, valet laundry, tanning facilities, wireless Internet. **Business Services:** conference facilities, business center. **Cards:** AX, DC, DS, MC, VI.

SOME UNITS

(A$K) 🍴 🍷 🛗 🏊 ✕ 🛢 💻 / ✕ (VCR)
FEE

HOTEL ROYAL WILLIAM   *Book great rates at AAA.com*   Phone: (418)521-4488   **12**

	7/1-10/31	1P: $169-$239	2P: $169-$239	XP: $30	F
	11/1-4/30	1P: $169-$189	2P: $169-$189	XP: $30	F
	5/1-6/30	1P: $149-$189	2P: $149-$189	XP: $30	F

Small-scale Hotel   **Location:** On Rt 440. 360 boul Charest est G1K 3H4. Fax: 418/521-6868. **Facility:** Smoke free premises. 44 one-bedroom standard units, some with whirlpools. 5 stories, interior corridors. **Bath:** combo or shower only. **Parking:** on-site (fee) and street, winter plug-ins. **Terms:** cancellation fee imposed, package plans. **Amenities:** DVD players, CD players, high-speed Internet, dual phone lines, voice mail, safes, honor bars, irons, hair dryers. **Dining:** Restaurant Le Sainte-Victoire, see separate listing. **Leisure Activities:** limited exercise equipment. Fee: massage. **Guest Services:** valet laundry. **Business Services:** meeting rooms, business center. **Cards:** AX, CB, DC, DS, JC, MC, VI. **Free Special Amenities:** local telephone calls and high-speed Internet.

🅂🄳 🍴 ✕ 💻

(See map and index starting on p. 512)

HOTEL SAINTE-ANNE   Book great rates at AAA.com   **Phone:** (418)694-1455   **13**

CAA SAVE
▽▽▽▽▽
Small-scale Hotel

5/1-10/31	1P: $149-$299	2P: $149-$319	XP: $20	F17
11/1-4/30	1P: $89-$249	2P: $89-$249	XP: $20	F17

Location: Just w of rue du Tresor. Located in Old Quebec. 32 rue Ste-Anne G1R 3X3. Fax: 418/692-4096. **Facility:** Smoke free premises. 28 one-bedroom standard units. 4 stories, interior corridors. *Bath:* combo or shower only. **Parking:** street. **Terms:** cancellation fee imposed, [BP], [CP] & [MAP] meal plans available, package plans. **Amenities:** high-speed Internet, hair dryers. **Dining:** 7 am-11 pm; closed 11/1-5/1, cocktails. **Leisure Activities:** *Fee:* massage. **Guest Services:** valet laundry, wireless Internet. **Business Services:** meeting rooms. **Cards:** AX, MC, VI. **Free Special Amenities: newspaper and high-speed Internet.**

[$D] [†1] [♈] [✕] [🖥] [💻]

LE CHATEAU DE PIERRE   **Phone:** (418)694-0429   **28**

CAA SAVE
▽▽ ▽▽
Historic
Small-scale Hotel

5/1-10/31	1P: $115-$145	2P: $135-$155	XP: $10
11/1-4/30	1P: $95-$135	2P: $95-$135	XP: $10

Location: Between rue Laporte and des Grisons. Located in Old Quebec. 17 ave Ste-Genevieve G1R 4A8. Fax: 418/694-0153. **Facility:** This restored, mid-1800s Victorian dwelling is near the parc des Gouverneurs in Old Quebec; find small to large units and a walled garden courtyard. 14 one-bedroom standard units. 3 stories (no elevator), interior corridors. *Bath:* combo or shower only. **Parking:** street. **Terms:** cancellation fee imposed. **Amenities:** hair dryers. **Guest Services:** valet laundry. **Cards:** AX, MC, VI. **Free Special Amenities: local telephone calls.** *(See color ad below)*

[†1] [✕] [💻]

(See map and index starting on p. 512)

LES IMMEUBLES CHARLEVOIX
COURTIER-ST-PIERRE
Phone: 418/692-2116 **4**

CAA SAVE

Condominium

All Year   2P: $600-$650   XP: $100
Location: Just w of rue de la Barricade; in Old Port District. 85 rue St-Pierre G1K 3Z7 (179 rue St-Paul, QUEBEC, G1K 3W2). Fax: 418/692-1996. **Facility:** These upscale Old Port studio condos, with kitchens, face the Museum of Civilization; reservations are required and check-ins are by appointment. 4 one-bedroom standard units with kitchens. 3 stories (no elevator), interior corridors. *Bath:* combo or shower only. **Parking:** on-site. **Terms:** office hours 9 am-5 pm, off-site registration, check-in 5 pm, 2 night minimum stay, cancellation fee imposed. **Amenities:** irons, hair dryers. **Guest Services:** coin laundry. **Cards:** MC, VI.

L'HOTEL DU CAPITOLE   *Book great rates at AAA.com*
Phone: (418)694-4040 **17**

CAA SAVE

Small-scale Hotel

5/27-10/13	1P: $180-$270	2P: $180-$270	XP: $30 F
10/14-4/30	1P: $131-$203	2P: $131-$203	XP: $30 F
5/1-5/26	1P: $122-$194	2P: $122-$194	XP: $30 F

Location: Corner of des Glacis. Located in Old Quebec, facing Place d'Youville. 972 rue St-Jean G1R 1R5. Fax: 418/694-1916. **Facility:** 40 one-bedroom standard units, some with whirlpools. 4 stories, interior corridors. **Parking:** valet and street. **Terms:** weekly rates available, [AP] meal plan available, package plans. **Amenities:** video library, CD players, honor bars, irons, hair dryers. **Dining:** Ristorante Il Teatro, see separate listing. **Leisure Activities:** 2 concert halls. **Guest Services:** valet laundry, wireless Internet. **Business Services:** meeting rooms. **Cards:** AX, DC, DS, MC, VI. **Free Special Amenities:** local telephone calls and high-speed Internet.

SOME UNITS

L'HOTEL DU VIEUX QUEBEC   *Book great rates at AAA.com*
Phone: (418)692-1850 **5**

CAA SAVE

Small-scale Hotel

6/1-10/14	1P: $144-$284	2P: $144-$284	XP: $10 F6
5/1-5/31 & 10/15-4/30	1P: $94-$184	2P: $94-$184	XP: $10 F6

Location: Corner of rue de l'Hotel-Dieu. Located in Old Quebec. 1190 rue St-Jean G1R 1S6. Fax: 418/692-5637. **Facility:** 41 one-bedroom standard units, some with whirlpools. 5 stories, interior corridors. *Bath:* combo or shower only. **Parking:** street. **Amenities:** hair dryers. **Dining:** 11:30 am-11 pm, cocktails. **Guest Services:** gift shop, valet laundry. **Business Services:** meeting rooms. **Cards:** AX, DC, MC, VI. **Free Special Amenities: continental breakfast and local telephone calls.** *(See color ad below)*

SOME UNITS

LOEWS LE CONCORDE   *Book great rates at AAA.com*
Phone: (418)647-2222 **34**

CAA SAVE

Large-scale Hotel

All Year   1P: $109-$309   2P: $109-$309   XP: $20   F17
Location: Corner of Grande Allee est. 1225 Cours du General-de-Montcalm G1R 4W6. Fax: 418/647-4710. **Facility:** The hotel's spacious, luxurious rooms offer added amenities, two-line telephones and commanding views; a revolving restaurant sits atop the building. 404 units. 386 one-bedroom standard units. 16 one- and 2 two-bedroom suites ($209-$1250), some with whirlpools. 29 stories, interior corridors. **Parking:** on-site (fee) and valet. **Terms:** cancellation fee imposed, package plans. **Amenities:** dual phone lines, voice mail, safes, honor bars, irons, hair dryers. *Some:* DVD players, CD players, high-speed Internet (fee). **Dining:** 6:30 am-midnight, also, L'Astral, see separate listing, entertainment. **Pool(s):** heated outdoor. **Leisure Activities:** saunas, whirlpool, exercise room. **Guest Services:** gift shop, valet laundry, wireless Internet. **Business Services:** conference facilities, business center. **Cards:** AX, DC, DS, JC, MC, VI. *(See color ad p 535)*

SOME UNITS

FEE

(See map and index starting on p. 512)

─────── *The following lodging was either not evaluated or did not* ───────
meet AAA rating requirements but is listed for your information only.

HOTEL DOMINION 1912   **Phone:** 418/692-2224
[fyi]   Did not meet all AAA rating requirements for locking devices in some guest rooms at time of last evaluation
            on 04/20/2005. **Location:** Corner rue St-Paul. 126 rue St-Pierre G1K 4A8. Facilities, services, and decor characterize
Historic   an upscale property.
Small-scale Hotel

─────── **WHERE TO DINE** ───────

APSARA   **Lunch:** $11-$15   **Dinner:** $13-$15   **Phone:** 418/694-0232   **46**
▼▼▼▼▼   **Location:** Corner of rue St-Louis; in Old Quebec. 71 rue d'Auteuil G1R 4C3. **Hours:** 11:30 am-2 & 5:30-11 pm, Sat
Asian   & Sun from 5:30 pm. **Closed:** 12/24. **Reservations:** accepted. **Features:** The restaurant delivers authentic
             preparations of Cambodian, Vietnamese and Thai cuisine. For dessert, try the banana, apple or pineapple
             deep-fried beignets. The attractive decor has an Asian feel, as do the servers, who dress in ethnic attire.
The historic stone building is near St. Louis gate in Old Quebec. Casual dress; cocktails. **Parking:** street. **Cards:** AX, DC,
MC, VI. **Historic**

AUBERGE DU TRESOR   **Lunch:** $10-$18   **Dinner:** $19-$35   **Phone:** 418/694-1876   **26**
(AAA)   **Location:** Corner of rue du Tresor; in Old Quebec; in Auberge du Tresor. 20 rue Ste-Anne G1R 3X2. **Hours:** 7 am-
▼▼▼▼   2:30 & 5-10:30 pm. **Reservations:** suggested. **Features:** On the ground floor of a late 17th-century
French   building, the restaurant boasts attractive woodwork and stained glass. House specialties are beef
             Wellington, Dover sole and flambeed crepes. Couples seeking upscale dining enjoy polished, friendly
             service. Valet parking is available most summer evenings. Casual dress; cocktails. **Parking:** street.
             Cards: AX, DC, JC, MC, VI. **Historic**   ⅄

AU PETIT COIN BRETON CREPERIE RESTAURANT   **Lunch:** $9-$15 **Dinner:** $12-$22 **Phone:** 418/694-0758   **28**
▼▼▼▼▼   **Location:** Corner of rue Ste-Ursule; in Old Quebec. 1029 rue St-Jean G1R 1R9. **Hours:** 11 am-9 pm, Sat 9 am-11
Continental pm, Sun 9 am-9 pm. **Closed:** for dinner 12/24. **Reservations:** accepted. **Features:** Eighty choices of
             French-style crepes line the menu at the charming family restaurant in Old Quebec. The servers' costumes
             and vintage decor reflect the style of Old France. The menu lists crepes bretonnes, stuffed crepes, French
onion soup, salads and delicious dessert crepes, including crepes Suzette. Casual dress; cocktails. **Parking:** street. **Cards:** AX,
DC, JC, MC, VI.

AVIATIC CLUB   **Lunch:** $9-$16   **Dinner:** $14-$32   **Phone:** 418/522-3555   **①**
▼▼▼▼▼   **Location:** In Gare du Palais (train station); just e of boul Jean-Lesage. 450 Gare du Palais G1K 3X2. **Hours:** 11:30
International am-10:30 pm, Thurs & Fri-11 pm, Sat 5 pm-11 pm, Sun 5 pm-10:30 pm. **Closed:** 1/1, 1/2, 12/24, 12/25; also 1/2.
             Reservations: accepted. **Features:** International specialties include lightly seared and thinly sliced salmon,
             served with mashed potatoes and freshly cooked vegetables. The diverse, seasonally updated menu lists
an array of Asian dishes, such as sushi, tempura, sauteed spicy shrimp, chicken or beef, wok stir-fry, chicken teriyaki, General
Tao chicken, orange beef and beef or salmon tartare. Casual dress; cocktails. **Parking:** on-site. **Cards:** AX, DC, MC, VI.   ⅄

CAFE BISTRO LE DIABLE AUX ANGES   **Lunch:** $10-$15   **Dinner:** $11-$27   **Phone:** 418/692-3888   **37**
▼▼▼ ▼▼▼   **Location:** Near Place Royale; in Old Port area. 28 boul Champlain G1K 4H5. **Hours:** 8 am-11 pm, Sat & Sun-
Canadian   midnight; days may vary in winter. **Reservations:** accepted. **Features:** In the popular Old Port area of lower
             Quebec, the restaurant entertains diners with live music on Friday and Saturday evenings. Seafood
             specialties include mussels prepared in a variety of styles, shrimp, grill specialties, fresh salmon filet and the
seafood platter. Among other choices are steak and fries, pasta, flavorful French onion soup, European-style pizza, chicken
shish kebab and filet mignon. Casual dress; cocktails. **Parking:** street. **Cards:** AX, DC, MC, VI. **Historic**

CAFE DE LA PAIX   **Lunch:** $10-$16   **Dinner:** $20-$32   **Phone:** 418/692-1430   **34**
(AAA)   **Location:** Corner of rue St-Louis; in Old Quebec. 44 rue des Jardins G1R 4L7. **Hours:** 11:30 am-2:30 & 5-11 pm.
▼▼▼▼▼   **Closed:** 12/24, 12/25. **Reservations:** suggested, weekends. **Features:** The menu is built around
French   preparations of seafood, veal, lamb, steak and house specialty seasonal game: quail, guinea fowl, duck,
             caribou and pheasant. Table d'hote specials are presented at lunch and dinner. The uniformed staff provides
             attentive service. Live music is featured most nights. Casual dress; cocktails. **Parking:** valet. **Cards:** AX,
             DC, DS, JC, MC, VI. **Historic**

CAFE DE PARIS   **Lunch:** $10-$14   **Dinner:** $20-$30   **Phone:** 418/694-9626   **43**
(AAA)   **Location:** Between rue des Jardins and rue Ste-Ursule; in Old Quebec. 66 rue St-Louis G1R 3Z3. **Hours:** Open 5/1-
▼▼▼▼▼   11/15 & 3/15-4/30; 11 am-11 pm. **Reservations:** suggested. **Features:** In the heart of Old Quebec, the
French   restaurant is a tourist favorite for casual dining. Closely spaced tables make for a bustling experience. The
             menu outlines a variety of French and Italian dishes, including pasta. A strolling musician plays in the
             evening. Casual dress; cocktails. **Parking:** valet. **Cards:** AX, DC, DS, JC, MC, VI. **Historic**

CAFE RESTAURANT DU MUSEE   **Lunch:** $10-$14   **Dinner:** $15-$17   **Phone:** 418/644-6780   **55**
▼▼▼ ▼▼▼   **Location:** Just s of Grande Allee rue Wolfe-Montcalm. 1 rue Wolfe-Montcalm G1R 5H3. **Hours:** 10 am-5 pm, Wed-9
Quebecois   pm; to 6 pm, Wed-9 pm 6/1-9/6. **Closed:** 12/25; also Mon. **Reservations:** suggested. **Features:** The
             atmosphere is bright and contemporary in the simply decorated casual dining outlet within the Quebec
             Museum. The menu lists dishes with French and Quebecois influences, such as sweetbread in fruit sauce,
mushrooms in puff pastry and Quebec roast pork. Lighter lunch fare includes grilled sandwiches and salads. For dessert, try
creme brulee with a specialty coffee. Casual dress; cocktails. **Parking:** on-site (fee). **Cards:** AX, DC, DS, MC, VI.

CHARBON STEAKHOUSE   **Lunch:** $10-$20   **Dinner:** $18-$40   **Phone:** 418/522-0133   **②**
▼▼▼▼▼   **Location:** Just e of boul Jean-Lesage; in Gare du Palais Train Station. 450 Gare du Palais G1K 3X2. **Hours:** 11:30
     am-11 pm, Sat & Sun from 5 pm. **Closed:** 12/24 & 1/2. **Reservations:** suggested. **Features:** The
Steak & Seafood steakhouse specializes in Canadian AAA-grade steak and seafood cooked over charcoal. Among specialties
             are prime rib of beef, grilled shrimp, baby back ribs, surf 'n' turf platters, Atlantic salmon and a variety of
steaks, including filet mignon, New York cut, rib and porterhouse T-bone. The casual, comfortable dining room is in a vintage
downtown train station. Free indoor parking for up to 2.5 hours is available. Casual dress; cocktails. **Parking:** on-site.
Cards: AX, DC, DS, JC, MC, VI.   ⅄

(See map and index starting on p. 512)

CREPERIE LE PETIT CHATEAU
Lunch: $5-$22   Dinner: $5-$22   Phone: 418/694-1616   (31)

Location: Next to the Fairmont Chateau Frontenac; in Old Quebec. 5 rue St-Louis G1R 3Y8. **Hours:** 7:30 am-10 pm, Fri & Sat-10:30 pm. **Reservations:** accepted. **Features:** Adjacent to the historic Chateau Frontenac, the casual creperie offers 60 affordable varieties of crepes. The seasonal terrace is a popular dining spot. Live music is featured some evenings. Casual dress; cocktails. **Parking:** street. **Cards:** MC, VI.

French

D'ORSAY RESTAURANT PUB
Lunch: $9-$15   Dinner: $9-$23   Phone: 418/694-1582   (18)

Location: Corner of rue des Jardins; in Old Quebec. 65 rue de Buade G1R 4A2. **Hours:** 11:30 am-midnight. **Reservations:** suggested. **Features:** The restaurant has a lively upscale bar area and an all-ages dining room in which patrons savor international preparations of steak, pasta, seafood and salads. Dressy casual; cocktails. **Parking:** street. **Cards:** AX, CB, DC, MC, VI.

International

ELYSEE MANDARIN
Lunch: $8-$11   Dinner: $12-$22   Phone: 418/692-0909   (44)

Location: Between rue St-Louis and Ste-Anne; in Old Quebec. 65 rue d'Auteuil G1R 4C2. **Hours:** 11:30 am-2 & 6-10:30 pm, Thurs-Sat to 11:30 pm. **Closed:** 12/24, for lunch 12/25 & 1/1. **Reservations:** suggested. **Features:** Buddhist statues decorate the lobby of the charming converted Victorian graystone. Wonton with sesame sauce, shrimp toast, spicy duck, orange beef and three varieties of spring rolls are among Szechuan specialties. Service is well-timed and attentive. Casual dress; cocktails. **Parking:** street. **Cards:** AX, DC, JC, MC, VI. **Historic**

Chinese

GINKO RESTAURANT JAPONAIS
Lunch: $10-$15   Dinner: $10-$28   Phone: 418/524-2373   (51)

Location: Corner of rue De Senezergue. 560 Grande Allee est G1R 2K1. **Hours:** 11:30 am-2:30 & 5-10:30 pm, Sat & Sun from 5 pm. **Closed:** 1/1, 12/25. **Reservations:** accepted. **Features:** On the lively Grand-Allee strip, the casual restaurant features a menu of Asian favorites, including sushi, stir-fried noodles, grilled salmon, chicken teriyaki, vegetable tempura, miso soup, grilled filet mignon, tiger shrimp, black cod and Japanese pizza. A fine selection of saki is available. Guests may reserve one of the teppanyaki tables, where a chef prepares food before their eyes on a hot grill. Seating also can be had in a few private tatami rooms. Casual dress; cocktails. **Parking:** street. **Cards:** AX, JC, MC, VI.

Japanese

LA CLOSERIE
Lunch: $12-$25   Dinner: $18-$35   Phone: 418/523-9975   (49)

Location: Corner of Grande Allee est; in Hotel Chateau Laurier Quebec. 1210 Place George-V ouest G1R 5B8. **Hours:** 7 am-11 pm. **Reservations:** suggested. **Features:** This hotel restaurant facing the lively Grande-Allee strip offers two dining options under one historic roof: a casual bistro and a fine dining room. The fine dining room offers a multi-course tasting menu as well as a la carte items that include duck confit, Atlantic salmon, jumbo shrimps, guinea fowl, breast of duck, beef tenderloin, pan-seared foie gras and sweetbreads. Casual dress; cocktails. **Parking:** on-site (fee) and valet. **Cards:** AX, DC, MC, VI.

French

L'ASTRAL
Lunch: $10-$20   Dinner: $20-$55   Phone: 418/647-2222   (52)

Location: Corner of Grande Allee est; in Loews Le Concorde. 1225 Cours du General-de-Montcalm G1R 4W6. **Hours:** 11:45 am-3 & 6-11 pm, Sun from 10 am. **Reservations:** suggested. **Features:** The revolving rooftop restaurant affords spectacular views of Quebec. International influences flavor preparations of such regional specialties as Charlevoix veal, Atlantic salmon and Quebec pork. For a Sunday treat, take advantage of the splendid brunch. Casual dress; cocktails. **Parking:** on-site (fee) and valet. **Cards:** AX, DC, DS, JC, MC, VI.

French

(See color ad p 535)

LE CHAMPLAIN
Menu on AAA.com   Dinner: $27-$43   Phone: 418/692-3861   (33)

Location: In Old Quebec; in Fairmont Le Chateau Frontenac. 1 rue des Carrieres G1R 4P5. **Hours:** 6 pm-10 pm, Sun 10 am-2 & 6-10 pm. **Closed:** Mon mid-Oct to beginning of May for dinner. **Reservations:** suggested. **Features:** A dining room staff attired in 17th-century costumes contributes to the semiformal Old World ambience of the historic landmark hotel. Menu highlights include foie gras, rack of lamb, salmon and game specialties. Beef chateaubriand is just one of several dishes flambeed in dramatic fashion tableside. The multicourse tasting menu offers the chef a chance to dazzle guests with delicacies. For dessert, try one of the heavenly souffles. The wine list is superb. Semi-formal attire; cocktails. **Parking:** on-site and valet. **Cards:** AX, DC, DS, JC, MC, VI. **Historic**

French

LE CHARLES BAILLAIRGE
Lunch: $7-$19   Dinner: $18-$34   Phone: 418/692-2480   (23)

Location: Corner of rue des Jardins; in Hotel Clarendon. 57 rue Ste-Anne G1R 3X4. **Hours:** 7-10:30 am, 11:30-2 & 6-9:30 pm, Sat 7 am-11 & 6-10 pm, Sun 7 am-11 & 6-9:30 pm. **Reservations:** suggested. **Features:** On historic rue Ste-Anne in Old Quebec, the upscale hotel restaurant highlights French-inspired regional cuisine, including preparations of seafood, lamb, steaks and salads. Casual dress. **Parking:** valet. **Cards:** AX, CB, DC, DS, JC, MC, VI.

French

LE COCHON DINGUE
Lunch: $8-$13   Dinner: $17-$22   Phone: 418/523-2013

Location: Just e of rue Cartier. 46 boul Rene-Levesque ouest G1R 2A4. **Hours:** 7 am-10 pm, Fri-11 pm, Sat 8 am-11 pm, Sun 8 am-10 pm. **Closed:** for dinner 12/24. **Reservations:** accepted. **Features:** The lively bistro prepares more than 20 choices for breakfast, in addition to lunch and dinner menus. On the breakfast menu are Canadian bacon and eggs, eggs Benedict, maple syrup with pancakes or French toast, a variety of omelets and fresh fruit plates and juices. Breakfast is served until 3 pm on weekends. Lunch and dinner specialties include mussels, steak with fries, pasta, salad and sandwiches. Casual dress; cocktails. **Parking:** street. **Cards:** AX, DC, DS, JC, MC, VI.

French

LE COCHON DINGUE
Lunch: $9-$14   Dinner: $10-$18   Phone: 418/692-2013

Location: Located in Old Quebec. 46 boul Champlain G1K 4H7. **Hours:** 7 am-11 pm, Fri-midnight, Sat 8 am-midnight, Sun 8 am-11 pm; to 11 pm 9/5-6/20. **Reservations:** suggested. **Features:** The lively Old Quebec bistro faces the ferry boat port and serves classic steak and fries, pasta, sandwiches, salads and mussels. Fine wines are available by the glass, and the seasonal terrace is in high demand during the summer months. On the breakfast menu are Canadian bacon and eggs, eggs Benedict, maple syrup with pancakes or French toast, a variety of omelets and fresh fruit plates and juices. Casual dress; cocktails. **Parking:** street. **Cards:** AX, DC, MC, VI.

French

(See map and index starting on p. 512)

LE COMMENSAL Lunch: $7-$15 Dinner: $7-$15 Phone: 418/647-3733
Vegetarian **Location:** Between Saint-Augustin and Dufferin-Montmorency autoroute. 860 rue St-Jean G1R 1R3. **Hours:** 11 am-9 pm, Thurs-9:30 pm, Fri-10 pm. **Closed:** 1/1, 12/25. **Reservations:** accepted. **Features:** An upscale self-service buffet features an extensive selection of creative hot and cold items, such as leek pot pie, sweet potato kasha and lasagna, plus a variety of desserts, everything of which is exclusively vegetarian. The pleasant, contemporary surroundings change often as new paintings are displayed. Casual dress. **Parking:** street. **Cards:** AX, MC, VI.

LE GRAFFITI RESTO CITE Lunch: $11-$17 Dinner: $12-$34 Phone: 418/529-4949 54
French **Location:** Just n of Grande-Allee. 1191 ave Cartier G1R 2S9. **Hours:** 11:30 am-2:30 & 5-11 pm, Sun 9:30 am-3 & 5-11 pm. **Closed:** 12/25. **Reservations:** suggested. **Features:** In a charming and fashionable shopping district, the bistro-style restaurant offers market cuisine that proudly features Quebec lamb, duck and quail. Items such as pasta, tartare and venison reveal French and Italian influences. Casual dress; cocktails. **Parking:** on-site. **Cards:** AX, DC, MC, VI.

LE LAPIN SAUTE Lunch: $10-$14 Dinner: $25-$31 Phone: 418/692-5325 35
French **Location:** In Old Quebec. 52 rue du Petit Champlain G1K 4H4. **Hours:** 11 am-10 pm, Fri-11 pm, Sat 9 am-11 pm, Sun 9 am-10 pm. **Reservations:** suggested. **Features:** The lively cafe prepares a mix of French bistro cuisine and American fare. Menu items include croque monsieur, grilled salmon sandwiches, pasta, hamburgers, shoestring fries, rabbit cannelloni, rabbit liver and kidneys, and steaks. Casual dress; cocktails. **Parking:** no self-parking. **Cards:** AX, MC, VI.

L'ENTRECOTE SAINT-JEAN Lunch: $11-$24 Dinner: $11-$24 Phone: 418/694-0234 29
French **Location:** Corner of rue d'Auteuil. 1011 rue St-Jean G1R 1R8. **Hours:** 11:30 am-11 pm, Sat from 5 pm, Sun 5 pm-10 pm. **Closed:** 1/1, 12/24, 12/25. **Reservations:** accepted. **Features:** The casual bistro specializes in a table d'hote menu of rib steak served with flavorful Dijon mustard sauce, matchstick fries, soup, a walnut-garnished salad and delicious chocolate-drizzled profiteroles for dessert. The menu also includes croque monsieur, lamb, veal, chicken and fish. Casual dress; cocktails. **Parking:** street. **Cards:** AX, DC, MC, VI.

LE PARIS-BREST Lunch: $12-$17 Dinner: $23-$36 Phone: 418/529-2243 50
French **Location:** Jct Grande Allee and de la Chevrotiere. 590 Grande Allee est G1R 2K5. **Hours:** 11:30 am-2:30 & 5:30-11 pm, Sat & Sun from 5:30 pm. **Reservations:** suggested. **Features:** Wood accents, spotlights and attractive art give the contemporary restaurant a sophisticated ambience. Frog legs, rack of lamb, steak tartare, beef tenderloin and beef Wellington are representative of cuisine on the diverse menu. Also offered are preparations of fresh pasta, fish and seafood. The outdoor terrace bustles during summer. Casual dress; cocktails. **Parking:** valet and street. **Cards:** AX, DC, MC, VI.

LE PATRIARCHE Lunch: $11-$22 Dinner: $22-$33 Phone: 418/692-5488 13
French **Location:** Just n of rue St-Jean; in Old Quebec. 17 rue St-Stanislas G1R 4G7. **Hours:** 11:30 am-2 & 5:30-10:30 pm, Sat-Mon from 5:30 pm. **Closed:** 1/2-1/21. **Reservations:** accepted. **Features:** The restaurant's stone walls, which date back to 1827, provide a touch of history to accompany the fine French food, which is served elegantly at tightly spaced tables. The menu includes game specialties (such as caribou), foie gras, escargots, sea bass, Atlantic scallops, monkfish, milk-fed beef and Quebec lamb. Casual dress; cocktails. **Parking:** valet. **Cards:** AX, MC, VI.

LE POSTINO BISTRO-BAR Lunch: $10-$20 Dinner: $10-$20 Phone: 418/647-0000 14
Mediterranean **Location:** Corner of rue Dorchester. 296 rue St-Joseph est G1K 3A9. **Hours:** 11 am-10 pm, Sat & Sun from 8 am. **Closed:** 1/1, 12/25; also 12/31, for dinner Sun & Mon 1/3-4/30. **Reservations:** accepted. **Features:** Located in a historic greystone that once housed a post office, this chic bistro features a Mediterranean menu that includes a choice of pastas, Angus beef, braised lamb, salmon steaks, veal cutlets, chicken parmigiana and a duck confit salad. Casual dress; cocktails. **Parking:** street. **Cards:** AX, DC, MC, VI.

LE VEAU D'OR Lunch: $8-$10 Dinner: $8-$14 Phone: 418/525-7371 41
CAA
Northern Italian **Location:** Corner of Saint-Augustin. 801 rue St-Jean G1R 1R2. **Hours:** 11 am-2 & 5-11 pm, Sat 5 pm-10 pm, Sun 4:30 pm-10 pm. **Closed:** 1/1, 12/25; also for lunch 12/26-12/31. **Reservations:** accepted. **Features:** Overlooking a lively street just outside the walls of Old Quebec, the casual Italian restaurant prepares fresh veal as its specialty in variations to suit every taste: veal Marsala, Parmesan, Milanese, normande, cordon bleu, butter-lemon or a l'anglaise, in addition to veal brains and liver. A wide selection of pasta, fresh fish and seafood rounds out the menu of affordable items. Casual dress; cocktails. **Parking:** street. **Cards:** AX, DC, MC, VI.

MOSS BISTRO BELGE Lunch: $17-$22 Dinner: $17-$22 Phone: 418/692-0233 3
Belgian **Location:** Corner rue St-Andre; in Hotel des Coutellier. 255 rue St-Paul G1K 3W5. **Hours:** 11 am-11 pm, Sun from 9 am; from 9 am 5/1-10/31. **Closed:** 1/1, 12/24, 12/25. **Features:** The stylish bistro specializes in mussels prepared 14 ways and offers Belgian chocolate desserts and 40 varieties of imported and local beers. Casual dress; cocktails. **Parking:** street. **Cards:** AX, DC, MC, VI.

PANACHE RESTAURANT Lunch: $14-$20 Dinner: $43-$45 Phone: 418/692-1022 12
CAA
Quebecois **Location:** Corner of rue Dalhousie; in Auberge Saint-Antoine. 8 rue St-Antoine G1K 4C9. **Hours:** 6:30-10:30 am, 11:30-2 & 6-10 pm, Sat & Sun 7 am-11 & 6-10 pm. **Reservations:** suggested. **Features:** This stylish fine dining room, located in an historic stone-walled hotel in Old Quebec, in Old Port area, features fine Quebecoise cuisine with panache. Main courses may be complemented by side dishes ordered separately. Exciting and skillfully prepared dishes include Mauricie region sweetbreads, Magdalen Islands lobster and scallops, Atlantic halibut, free-range chicken, Alberta beef, pan-seared foie gras, duckling and clams. Casual dress; cocktails. **Parking:** on-site and valet. **Cards:** AX, DC, MC, VI.

PIZZERIA D'YOUVILLE Lunch: $9-$13 Dinner: $12-$18 Phone: 418/694-0299 20
Italian **Location:** Corner rue d'Auteuil; in old Quebec. 1014 rue St-Jean G1R 1R6. **Hours:** 11 am-11 pm. **Closed:** 12/25. **Reservations:** accepted. **Features:** This cozy and lively family eatery serves Italian specialties, including pizza, pasta, meats and seafood. The decor incorporates the original stone and brick of this historic Old Quebec building. Casual dress; cocktails. **Parking:** street. **Cards:** AX, DC, MC, VI.

(See map and index starting on p. 512)

PIZZERIA PRIMAVERA BISTRO ITALIANO   Lunch: $10-$18   Dinner: $11-$25   Phone: 418/694-0030   45
Italian
Location: Corner rue Ste-Ursule; in Old Quebec. 73 rue St-Louis G1R 3Z2. **Hours:** noon-10:30 pm; seasonal hours may vary. **Closed:** 1/1, 12/25. **Reservations:** suggested. **Features:** Rich woods and contemporary colors brighten the bistro, which resides in the heart of Old Quebec. The light Italian menu lists a good selection of wood-oven pizzas, in addition to meats, pasta and salads. Casual dress; cocktails. **Parking:** street. **Cards:** AX, MC, VI. **Historic**

PORTOFINO BISTRO ITALIANO   *Menu on AAA.com*   Lunch: $11-$14 Dinner: $14-$25 Phone: 418/692-8888   8
Italian
Location: In Place Livernois, at angle of rue St-Jean; in Old Quebec. 54 rue Couillard G1R 3T3. **Hours:** 11 am-11:30 pm. **Closed:** 12/24, 12/25. **Reservations:** suggested. **Features:** A lively feel punctuates the contemporary Italian bistro in Old Quebec. Menu highlights include pizza baked in a wood-burning oven, as well as homemade pasta, veal and fish dishes. Nightly live music lends to the atmosphere. Valet parking is available at lunch and dinner. Casual dress. **Parking:** on-site (fee) and valet. **Cards:** AX, CB, DC, DS, JC, MC, VI.

PUB ST-PATRICK   Lunch: $9-$12   Dinner: $7-$22   Phone: 418/694-0618   9
Canadian
Location: Corner of rue Cote de la Fabrique; in Old Quebec. 1200 rue St-Jean G1R 1S8. **Hours:** 8 am-1 am; from 11:30 am 10/16-6/22. **Reservations:** accepted. **Features:** Ambience abounds as local and imported beer flows within the historic stone walls of the boisterous Old Quebec Irish pub and hears music is heard on some nights. Such standard pub foods as fish and chips, sandwiches, pasta and steak line the menu. The pub's vaulted ceilings date to 1749, and the wine cellar boasts 300 selections. Private rooms are available. Casual dress; cocktails; entertainment. **Parking:** street. **Cards:** AX, MC, VI.   🍸

RESTAURANT ANH DAO   Lunch: $10   Dinner: $10   Phone: 418/529-8881   7
Vietnamese
Location: Corner of rue de Lasalle. 325 rue de la Couronne G1K 6E7. **Hours:** 11 am-3 & 5-11 pm, Sat & Sun from 5 pm. **Reservations:** accepted. **Features:** In the St-Roch neighborhood, the casual diner serves affordably priced Vietnamese and Thai dishes, including Asian-style fondues, seafood, caribou, chicken, beef, noodles, fish, shrimp and beef Tonkinese soups. Diners may bring their own wine. No alcohol is sold on the premises. Casual dress. **Parking:** street.

RESTAURANT AU PARMESAN   Lunch: $10-$15   Dinner: $10-$30   Phone: 418/692-0341   39
Italian
Location: Between rue des Jardins and du Parloir; in Old Quebec. 38 rue St-Louis G1R 3Z1. **Hours:** noon-midnight. **Closed:** 12/24, 12/25. **Reservations:** suggested. **Features:** A favorite of locals, the established, bistro-style restaurant bustles with activity. A blend of French and Italian dishes, such as fettuccine Alfredo, characterize a varied menu that includes selections of steak and seafood. Service is friendly and attentive from start to finish. Nightly live music lends to the atmosphere. Casual dress; cocktails. **Parking:** valet. **Cards:** AX, DC, DS, JC, MC, VI.

RESTAURANT AUX ANCIENS CANADIENS   Lunch: $15   Dinner: $26-$62   Phone: 418/692-1627   38
Quebecois
Location: Corner of rue des Jardins; in Old Quebec. 34 rue St-Louis G1R 4P3. **Hours:** noon-10 pm; to 9 pm 10/1-5/31. **Closed:** 1/1 & 12/25 from 5 pm. **Reservations:** suggested. **Features:** Built in 1676, the city's oldest house is a charming spot in which to savor hearty traditional Quebecois cuisine, including game specialties. A collection of firearms and artisans' tools serves as decor. Try lamb stew, sturgeon or tourtiere meat pie. Casual dress; cocktails. **Parking:** no self-parking. **Cards:** AX, DC, MC, VI. **Historic**

RESTAURANT CAFE D'EUROPE   Lunch: $12-$15   Dinner: $27-$29   Phone: 418/692-3835   21
Continental
Location: Corner of rue St-Jean; in Old Quebec. 27 rue Ste-Angele G1R 4G5. **Hours:** 11:30 am-2 & 5-10:30 pm, Sat & Sun from 5 pm. **Closed:** 12/24, 12/25. **Reservations:** suggested. **Features:** Mobile cooking sideboards let diners watch their salads, tartares and fresh pasta being made. Mahogany furnishings, ceramic floors and a brass bar enhance the quaint, intimate interior. Food borrows from French and Italian influences. Valet parking is free in the evenings. Casual dress; cocktails. **Parking:** street. **Cards:** AX, DC, DS, JC, MC, VI. **Historic**

RESTAURANT GAMBRINUS   Lunch: $10-$16   Dinner: $23-$36   Phone: 418/692-5144   24
Continental
Location: Corner of rue Ste-Anne, facing Chateau Frontenac; in Old Quebec. 15 rue du Fort G1R 3W9. **Hours:** 11:30 am-2:30 & 5-11 pm; Sat & Sun from 5 pm. **Reservations:** suggested. **Features:** Lots of greenery, mahogany and brass accents are distinctive touches in the upscale dining room. Market-fresh ingredients and artful presentation add to the taste and appeal of such specialties as rack of lamb, seafood, caribou filet and lobster bisque. Casual dress; cocktails. **Parking:** valet and street. **Cards:** AX, DC, DS, JC, MC, VI.

RESTAURANT INITIALE   Lunch: $16-$23   Dinner: $32-$45   Phone: 418/694-1818   10
French
Location: Corner of rue Cote-de-la-Montagne; in Old Port. 54 rue St-Pierre G1K 4A1. **Hours:** 11:30 am-1:30 & 6-9 pm, Sat from 6 pm. **Closed:** Sun. **Reservations:** suggested. **Features:** Stylish fabrics, ornate crown moldings and high-back chairs decorate the contemporary dining room in scenic Old Quebec. Creative French dishes are served on lovely china. Patrons can sample seared tuna, Bay of Fundy salmon, sweetbreads, grilled tuna, stuffed rabbit, breast of quail, smoked salmon, roasted scallops, Quebec lamb, Arctic char, grilled beef, foie gras, breast of duckling and veal medallions. Private dining rooms and a chef's tasting table are seating options. Dressy casual; cocktails. **Parking:** street. **Cards:** AX, DC, JC, MC, VI.

RESTAURANT LA CREMAILLERE   Lunch: $15-$20   Dinner: $18-$44   Phone: 418/692-2216   22
Continental
Location: Between rue des Jardins and rue Pierre-Olivier-Chauvreau; in Old Quebec. 73 rue Ste-Anne G1R 3X4. **Hours:** 11:30 am-2:30 & 5-11 pm, Sat & Sun from 5 pm. **Reservations:** suggested. **Features:** Lovely plasterwork and an elegant staircase bring charm to this upscale and historic Old Quebec restaurant. Fine French and Italian preparations of beef, seafood, pasta, lamb and veal make up the menu. Service is attentive and capable. Casual dress; cocktails. **Parking:** valet. **Cards:** AX, MC, VI. **Historic**

RESTAURANT LA POINTE DES AMERIQUES   Lunch: $10-$14   Dinner: $10-$22   Phone: 418/694-1199   27
Italian
Location: Just e of rue des Glacis. 964 rue St-Jean G1R 1R5. **Hours:** 11 am-11 pm, Fri & Sat-midnight. **Closed:** 1/1, 12/25. **Reservations:** suggested. **Features:** Pizza, pasta, salads and fajitas are among the varied menu items offered at the casually stylish restaurant and bar. Casual dress; cocktails. **Parking:** street. **Cards:** AX, MC, VI.   🍸

(See map and index starting on p. 512)

RESTAURANT LAURIE RAPHAEL   Lunch: $16-$25   Dinner: $21-$56   Phone: 418/692-4555   ④
Quebecois
Location: Corner of rue St-Andre; in Old Port area. 117 rue Dalhousie G1K 9C8. **Hours:** 11:30 am-2 & 5:30-10 pm, Sat from 5:30 pm. Closed: 1/1, 12/25; also Sun, Mon & 1/1-1/14. **Reservations:** suggested. **Features:** Stylish, refined decor grounds the comfortable, lively dining room in the scenic Old Port district. The innovative, modern menu of haute Quebecois cuisine features pan-seared foie gras, yellowfin tuna, quail, filet mignon, scallops, deer, caribou, veal, lamb and ostrich. All food presentations are eye-catching, especially the desserts. The seasonal terrace is popular in summer. Dressy casual; cocktails. **Parking:** on-site (fee). **Cards:** AX, DC, MC, VI.

RESTAURANT LE CAFE DU MONDE   Lunch: $12-$16   Dinner: $14-$18   Phone: 418/692-4455   ⑥
French
Location: Corner of St-Andre; in Old Port; in cruise ship terminal. 84 rue Dalhousie G1K 4B2. **Hours:** 11:30 am-11 pm, Sat & Sun from 9:30 am. **Reservations:** suggested. **Features:** With tightly spaced tables, entertaining servers and a lively and bustling clientele of locals and tourists, the restaurant is an ideal spot to experience the cuisine and charm of a classic French-style bistro. Such dishes as confit of duck and sweetbreads are wonderfully flavorful. The weekend brunch draws a hungry, laid-back crowd. This place overlooks the popular harbor area of Old Quebec's lower section. Casual dress; cocktails. **Parking:** on-site. **Cards:** AX, DC, DS, MC, VI.

RESTAURANT L'ECHAUDE   Lunch: $10-$19   Dinner: $29-$35   Phone: 418/692-1299   ⑤
French
Location: Just e of rue de la Barricade; in Old Port area. 73 rue du Sault-au-Matelot G1K 3Y9. **Hours:** 11:30 am-2:30 & 5:30-10 pm, Sat from 5:30 pm, Sun from 10:30 am. Closed: 1/1, 12/24, 12/25; also 12/31. **Reservations:** suggested. **Features:** Pasta, steak, fish and seasonal seafood are on the menu at the casual French restaurant. Casual dress; cocktails. **Parking:** street. **Cards:** AX, DC, MC, VI.

RESTAURANT LE CONTINENTAL   Lunch: $11-$22   Dinner: $22-$42   Phone: 418/694-9995   ㊱
French
Location: Opposite Chateau Frontenac; in Old Quebec. 26 rue St-Louis G1R 3Y9. **Hours:** noon-11 pm, Sat & Sun from 6 pm. Closed: 12/24, 12/25. **Reservations:** suggested. **Features:** Sweetbreads, orange duckling, rack of lamb, flambes and shrimp Newberg flambe are outstanding choices from a sophisticated menu. Windows on the north side overlook a beautiful garden. Warm colors, subdued lighting and candles add to the romantic aura. Semi-formal attire; cocktails. **Parking:** valet. **Cards:** AX, DC, DS, JC, MC, VI.

RESTAURANT LE MARIE CLARISSE   Lunch: $14-$22   Dinner: $29-$32   Phone: 418/692-0857   ㉜
Seafood
Location: At funicular; in Old Port. 12 Petit Champlain G1K 4H4. **Hours:** 11:30 am-10 pm; 11:30 am-2:30 & 6-9 pm, Sat & Sun from 6 pm 11/1-4/15. Closed: 1/5-1/15. **Reservations:** required, 11/1-4/30; suggested 5/1-10/31. **Features:** The decor incorporates original historic stone walls and a small outdoor terrace adjacent to a stone staircase that leads to Old Quebec. The focus of the menu is on fine, fresh seafood, most notably smoked fish and delicious escargot. Casual dress; cocktails. **Parking:** no self-parking. **Cards:** AX, DC, MC, VI. **Historic**

RESTAURANT LE PARLEMENTAIRE   Lunch: $12-$28   Phone: 418/643-6640   ㊼
Regional French
Location: On Grande Allee corner of ave Honore Mercier; in Quebec's National Assembly. Hotel du Parlement Porte G1A 1A3. **Hours:** 8 am-2:30 pm. Closed major holidays; also Sat & Sun. **Reservations:** suggested. **Features:** Guests must produce identification and pass through a metal detector before entering the provincial legislature building, which is home to the ornate, Beaux-Arts dining room. The menu is a showcase for fine regional Quebec cuisine, including pork, rainbow trout, Nunavut caribou, poultry, smoked deer and seasonal seafood, as well as cheeses, wines, ciders and microbrewed beers. On weekdays, the restaurant serves hearty French-Canadian breakfasts. Uniformed servers are informal and friendly. Casual dress; cocktails. **Parking:** street. **Cards:** AX, MC, VI. **Historic**

RESTAURANT LE SAINT AMOUR   Lunch: $14-$26   Dinner: $30-$48   Phone: 418/694-0667   ㊵
French
Location: Just s of rue Ste-Anne. 48 rue Ste-Ursule G1R 4E2. **Hours:** 11:30 am-2:15 & 6-10:30 pm, Sat & Sun from 6 pm. **Reservations:** suggested. **Features:** Diners are seated either at tables in a posh atrium or in an intimate parlor at the upscale Old Quebec restaurant. Fine regional produce factors into innovative preparations of tuna, salmon, game, beef, lamb, seafood and pan-seared foie gras. Iced wine and artfully decorated desserts are delightful meal complements. Dressy casual; cocktails. **Parking:** valet. **Cards:** AX, DC, MC, VI.

RESTAURANT LE SAINTE-VICTOIRE   Lunch: $12-$16   Dinner: $18-$25   Phone: 418/525-5656   ⑮
French
Location: On Rt 440; in Hotel Royal William. 380 boul Charest est G1K 3H4. **Hours:** 7-10 am, 11:30-2 & 5-9 pm, Thurs & Fri-10 pm, Sat 8 am-noon & 5-10 pm, Sun 8 am-noon. **Reservations:** suggested. **Features:** The lively, upscale bistro features live music, original artwork, comfortable seating and a menu of French-influenced regional cuisine, including selections of fresh fish, veal, lamb, pheasant and pasta. Casual dress; cocktails. **Parking:** valet and street. **Cards:** AX, DC, DS, JC, MC, VI.

RESTAURANT L'OMELETTE   Lunch: $6-$19   Dinner: $6-$19   Phone: 418/694-9626   ㊷
Canadian
Location: Just e of rue Ste-Ursule; in Old Quebec. 66 rue St-Louis G1R 3Z3. **Hours:** Open 5/1-11/15 & 3/15-4/30; 7 am-10:30 pm. Closed: for dinner 3/15-4/15; for dinner Mon & Tues 4/15-5/15. **Reservations:** accepted. **Features:** As the name suggests, the restaurant's focus is on breakfast food: omelets, crepes and pancakes. However, the menu also has plenty of other selections, including pork chops, fish, veal, chicken brochettes, pizza, subs, sandwiches and seafood. The 1827 house boasts a bright, cheerful atmosphere. Casual dress; cocktails. **Parking:** valet and street. **Cards:** AX, DC, DS, JC, MC, VI. **Historic**

RESTAURANT LOUIS HEBERT   *Menu on AAA.com*   Lunch: $11-$17   Dinner: $23-$26   Phone: 418/525-7812   ㊽
French
Location: Between rue d'Artigny and La Chevrotiere. 668 Grande Allee est G1R 2K5. **Hours:** 7:30-11 am, 11:30-3 & 5:30-11 pm. Closed: Sat & Sun for breakfast, for lunch 10/1-4/30. **Reservations:** suggested. **Features:** Bright, elegant and airy, the restaurant has a few cozy corners for more intimate dining. Guests can relax on the sidewalk terrace to observe the Main Street hustle and bustle. Eye-catching presentations characterize dishes of market-fresh meat and seafood. Casual dress; cocktails. **Parking:** valet and street. **Cards:** AX, DC, DS, JC, MC, VI.

(See map and index starting on p. 512)

RESTAURANT L'UTOPIE
French

Lunch: $14-$19   Dinner: $22-$30   Phone: 418/523-7878   (17)

Location: Just e of rue Caron. 226 1/2 rue St-Joseph est G1K 3A9. **Hours:** 11:30 am-2 & 6-10 pm, Mon from 6 pm. Closed: 1/1, 12/24, 12/25; also Sun. **Features:** Birch tree-trunk partitions, a glassed front wine cellar and a high angled ceiling stand out in the decor of the stylish restaurant, which serves contemporary French cuisine. Guests can request multicourse tasting menus paired with wines or order a la carte. Selections might include East Coast scallops, veal sweetbreads, prime cuts of beef, foie gras and fresh, seasonal seafood. Fine Quebec cheeses are a nice way to end the meal. Casual dress; cocktails. **Parking:** street. **Cards:** AX, DC, MC, VI.

RESTAURANT QUE SERA SERA
French

Lunch: $12-$18   Dinner: $17-$32   Phone: 418/692-3535   (30)

Location: Corner of ave Honore-Mercier; in Old Quebec, facing Place d'Youville; in Courtyard Marriott Quebec. 850 Place d'Youville G1R 3P6. **Hours:** 6:30 am-10:30 pm, Sat 7 am-12:30 & 4-11 pm, Sun 7 am-12:30 & 4-10:30 pm. **Reservations:** accepted. **Features:** In the lobby of an upscale hotel, the stylish, two-level restaurant offers elegant surroundings and fine modern French cuisine. On the creative menu are guinea fowl, roasted quail, white Charlevoix fowl, veal tagliatelle, angel hair pasta, fresh fish, yellowfin tuna, caribou steaks, beef filet and rump steak. Service is gracious. Casual dress; cocktails. **Parking:** on-site (fee) and valet. **Cards:** AX, DC, MC, VI.

RESTO BAR LE DOWNTOWN
French

Lunch: $10-$20   Dinner: $10-$20   Phone: 418/521-3363   (19)

Location: Corner of rue Dorchester. 299 rue St-Joseph est G1K 3B1. **Hours:** 11:30 am-10:30 pm, Sat & Sun 5 pm-10 pm. Closed: 1/1, 12/25. **Reservations:** suggested. **Features:** The comfortable downtown pub and restaurant serves steak pasta, steak tartare, fish and Angus beef. Casual dress; cocktails. **Parking:** street. **Cards:** AX, DC, MC, VI.

RISTORANTE IL TEATRO
Italian

Lunch: $15-$20   Dinner: $26-$32   Phone: 418/694-9996   (25)

Location: Corner of des Glacis; in L'Hotel du Capitole. 972 rue St-Jean G1R 1R5. **Hours:** 7 am-close. **Reservations:** suggested. **Features:** Just outside the walls of Old Quebec, the casual bistro serves fine Italian cuisine. Casual dress; cocktails. **Parking:** valet and street. **Cards:** AX, DC, MC, VI.

SAINT ALEXANDRE PUB   *Menu on AAA.com*   Lunch: $10-$20   Dinner: $10-$20   Phone: 418/694-0015   (16)
Canadian

Location: Just e of the St-Jean gate; in Old Quebec. 1087 rue St-Jean G1R 1S3. **Hours:** 11:30 am-3:30 & 5-10 pm, Fri & Sat-3 am. **Reservations:** suggested. **Features:** The lively pub in Old Quebec sets the bar high with its choice of 20 scotches and 200 selections of beer, including 20 on tap. On the menu are steak and kidney pie, burgers, fish and chips, pasta and salads. Musicians perform some evenings. Casual dress; cocktails. **Parking:** street. **Cards:** AX, DC, MC, VI.

TRATTORIA LA SCALA
Italian

Lunch: $8-$19   Dinner: $8-$19   Phone: 418/529-8457   (53)

Location: Between rue Cartier and rue de Salaberry. 31 boul Rene-Levesque ouest G1R 2A3. **Hours:** 11:30 am-2 & 5-10 pm, Fri & Sat-3 am. Closed: 12/25. **Reservations:** suggested. **Features:** The relaxed downtown trattoria prepares a variety of authentic Italian dishes. Casual dress; cocktails. **Parking:** valet and street. **Cards:** AX, DC, MC, VI.

YUZU SUSHI-BAR
Japanese

Lunch: $10-$20   Dinner: $22-$42   Phone: 418/521-7253   (11)

Location: Corner of boul Charest est. 438 rue de l'Eglise G1K 6H8. **Hours:** 11:30 am-2:30 & 5-10 pm, Fri-11 pm, Sat 5 pm-11 pm, Sun 5 pm-10 pm. **Reservations:** accepted. **Features:** A youthful ambiance permeates this chic sushi bar decorated with bonsai plants, contemporary seating and a glassed wine cellar. The menu features a variety of freshly prepared sushi and sashimi garnished with fresh ginger, wasabi and soy sauce. Dishes of chicken, shrimp and grilled salmon round out the menu along with creatively garnished desserts. The seasonal terrace is ideal for summer people watching. Casual dress; cocktails. **Parking:** street. **Cards:** AX, DC, MC, VI.

QUEBEC pop. 169,076   (See map and index starting on p. 517)

———— WHERE TO STAY ————

BEST WESTERN HOTEL L'ARISTOCRATE   *Book great rates at AAA.com*   Phone: (418)653-2841   8

	6/22-9/2	1P: $135-$195	2P: $135-$195	XP: $10	F17
	9/3-10/7	1P: $125-$175	2P: $125-$175	XP: $10	F17
	5/1-6/21	1P: $115-$165	2P: $115-$165	XP: $10	F17
	10/8-4/30	1P: $99-$159	2P: $99-$159	XP: $10	F17

Small-scale Hotel **Location:** Hwy 73, exit 133 (chemin St-Louis); in Ste-Foy sector. 3100 chemin St-Louis G1W 1R8. Fax: 418/653-8525. **Facility:** 100 one-bedroom standard units, some with whirlpools. 2 stories (no elevator), interior corridors. **Parking:** on-site, winter plug-ins. **Terms:** package plans. **Amenities:** high-speed Internet, voice mail, irons, hair dryers. **Dining:** Restaurant La Fenouilliere, see separate listing. **Pool(s):** heated outdoor. **Leisure Activities:** limited exercise equipment. **Guest Services:** valet laundry, area transportation-Old Quebec, wireless Internet. **Business Services:** meeting rooms. **Cards:** AX, CB, DC, DS, MC, VI. **Free Special Amenities:** local telephone calls and high-speed Internet. *(See color ad p 513)*

SOME UNITS

CHATEAU BONNE ENTENTE   *Book great rates at AAA.com*   Phone: (418)653-5221   6

	7/16-10/16	1P: $209-$499	2P: $209-$499	XP: $20	F12
	5/1-7/15 & 10/17-4/30	1P: $169-$499	2P: $169-$499	XP: $20	F12

Small-scale Hotel **Location:** Hwy 540 (Autoroute Duplessis), exit chemin Ste-Foy, just w; in Ste-Foy sector. 3400 chemin Ste-Foy G1X 1S6. Fax: 418/653-3098. **Facility:** Common areas at this country inn include a lively lounge, elegant restaurant and luxury spa; guest rooms are luxuriously appointed. 165 units. 126 one-bedroom standard units, some with whirlpools. 39 one-bedroom suites ($299-$799) with whirlpools. 3 stories, interior corridors. *Bath:* combo or shower only. **Parking:** on-site and valet, winter plug-ins. **Terms:** cancellation fee imposed, package plans. **Amenities:** voice mail, safes, honor bars, irons, hair dryers. *Some:* DVD players, CD players, high-speed Internet, dual phone lines. **Dining:** 7 am-11 pm; 6:30 am-9:30 pm 10/16-5/31, also, Monte Cristo Resto Lounge, see separate listing. **Pool(s):** heated outdoor. **Leisure Activities:** sauna, whirlpools, badminton, bicycles, jogging, exercise room, spa, volleyball. **Guest Services:** gift shop, valet laundry, area transportation-Old Quebec, wireless Internet. **Business Services:** conference facilities, business center. **Cards:** AX, CB, MC, VI. **Free Special Amenities:** full breakfast. *(See color ad p 523)*

SOME UNITS

(See map and index starting on p. 517)

COMFORT INN DE L'AEROPORT-HAMEL *Book great rates at AAA.com*   Phone: (418)872-5038   **5**

| | 7/1-9/30 | 1P: $103-$135 | 2P: $123-$145 | XP: $10 | F18 |
| | 1/1-4/30 | 1P: $93-$113 | 2P: $103-$133 | XP: $10 | F18 |
Small-scale Hotel | 5/1-6/30 & 10/1-12/31 | 1P: $83-$103 | 2P: $93-$123 | XP: $10 | F18 |

Location: Hwy 138, 0.9 mi (1.5 km) w of boul Duplessis. 7320 boul Wilfrid-Hamel G2G 1C1 (boul Wilfrid-Hamel). Fax: 418/872-1905. **Facility:** 79 one-bedroom standard units. 2 stories (no elevator), interior corridors. **Parking:** on-site, winter plug-ins. **Terms:** package plans, pets (in smoking units). **Amenities:** irons, hair dryers. **Guest Services:** valet laundry, wireless Internet. **Cards:** AX, CB, DC, DS, JC, MC, VI. *(See color ad card insert)*

SOME UNITS

(ASK) (S/D) (🛏) (📶+) (🏋) (💻) / (✕) (📠) /

FOUR POINTS BY SHERATON QUEBEC *Book great rates at AAA.com*   Phone: (418)627-8008

(CAA) (SAVE) All Year   1P: $120-$155   2P: $120-$155   XP: $10   F17

Location: Hwy 73, exit 154, just e; in Charlesbourg sector. 7900 rue du Marigot G1G 6T8. Fax: 418/627-3658. Large-scale Hotel **Facility:** Smoke free premises. 102 units. 54 one-bedroom standard units. 48 one-bedroom suites ($235-$335), some with whirlpools. 4 stories, interior corridors. **Parking:** on-site. **Terms:** cancellation fee imposed, [AP], [BP], [CP] & [MAP] meal plans available, package plans, $2 service charge. **Amenities:** dual phone lines, voice mail, irons, hair dryers. **Dining:** Le Griffe Restaurant & Bar, see separate listing. **Pool(s):** heated outdoor. **Leisure Activities:** cross country skiing, snowmobiling, ice skating, snowmobile shelter, gym privileges. *Fee:* golf-18 holes. **Guest Services:** sundries, valet laundry, wireless Internet. **Business Services:** meeting rooms, business center. **Cards:** AX, MC, VI. **Free Special Amenities:** local telephone calls and high-speed Internet.

SOME UNITS

(🍴) (⛷) (✕) (✕) (🏋) (💻) / (📠) (📠) /

HOTEL & SUITES NORMANDIN *Book at AAA.com*   Phone: (418)622-1611   **1**

| | 6/11-10/13 [ECP] | 1P: $99-$139 | 2P: $109-$169 | XP: $15 | F13 |
| | 5/1-6/10 [ECP] | 1P: $89-$119 | 2P: $99-$149 | XP: $15 | F13 |
Small-scale Hotel | 10/14-4/30 [ECP] | 1P: $89-$119 | 2P: $95-$145 | XP: $15 | F13 |

Location: Hwy 40, exit 312N eastbound to boul Pierre-Bertrand, then n to rue Bouvier; exit 312N westbound, just w on rue Bouvier. 4700 boul Pierre-Bertrand G2J 1A4. Fax: 418/622-9277. **Facility:** 130 units. 127 one-bedroom standard units, some with whirlpools. 3 one-bedroom suites ($159-$269) with whirlpools. 4 stories, interior corridors. **Parking:** on-site, winter plug-ins. **Terms:** cancellation fee imposed. **Amenities:** irons, hair dryers. *Some:* CD players, high-speed Internet, dual phone lines, honor bars. **Leisure Activities:** exercise room. **Guest Services:** valet and coin laundry, area transportation, wireless Internet. **Business Services:** meeting rooms, business center. **Cards:** AX, DC, JC, MC, VI.

SOME UNITS

(🍴) (🏋) (💻) / (✕) (VCR) (📠) /

HOTEL CLASSIQUE *Book great rates at AAA.com*   Phone: (418)658-2793   **7**

(CAA) (SAVE) 7/16-10/20   1P: $129-$219   2P: $139-$229   XP: $10   F12
5/1-7/15 & 10/21-4/30   1P: $119-$189   2P: $119-$189   XP: $10   F12

Location: Corner of ave de Germain-des-Pres; in Ste-Foy sector. 2815 boul Laurier G1V 4H3. Fax: 418/658-6816. Large-scale Hotel **Facility:** 264 units. 208 one-bedroom standard units. 49 one- and 7 two-bedroom suites ($179-$289), some with efficiencies or kitchens (utensils extra charge). 13 stories, interior corridors. **Parking:** on-site. **Terms:** package plans. **Amenities:** voice mail, irons, hair dryers. *Some:* CD players, high-speed Internet. **Dining:** 7 am-11 pm, also, Cosmos, Restaurant La Pointe des Ameriques, see separate listings. **Pool(s):** heated indoor. **Leisure Activities:** *Fee:* massage, exercise room privileges. **Guest Services:** gift shop, valet and coin laundry, wireless Internet. **Business Services:** conference facilities, PC, fax (fee). **Cards:** AX, CB, DC, MC, VI. **Free Special Amenities:** high-speed Internet. *(See color ad p 528)*

SOME UNITS

(S/D) (🍴) (🍸) (⛷) (📶+) (💻) / (✕) (📠) (📠) /

HOTEL DAUPHIN QUEBEC CITY *Book at AAA.com*   Phone: (418)688-3888   **2**

| | 5/1-10/31 [ECP] | 1P: $89-$99 | 2P: $89-$99 | XP: $10 | F18 |
| | 11/1-4/30 [ECP] | 1P: $79-$89 | 2P: $79-$89 | XP: $10 | F18 |

Small-scale Hotel **Location:** Hwy 40, exit 312S (Pierre-Bertrand sud), just w of Rt 358; in Vanier sector. 400 rue Marais G1M 3R1. Fax: 418/688-1485. **Facility:** 83 one-bedroom standard units, some with whirlpools. 3 stories, interior corridors. **Parking:** on-site, winter plug-ins. **Terms:** package plans. **Amenities:** CD players, high-speed Internet, voice mail, cafes, irons, hair dryers. **Guest Services:** valet and coin laundry. **Business Services:** meeting rooms, PC. **Cards:** AX, DC, JC, VI.

SOME UNITS

(ASK) (📶+) (&M) (VCR) (🏋) (📠) (💻) / (✕) /

HOTEL QUALITY SUITES QUEBEC *Book great rates at AAA.com*   Phone: (418)622-4244   **3**

(CAA) (SAVE) 7/15-10/14 [CP]   1P: $130-$180   2P: $140-$190   XP: $15   F18
6/15-7/14 [CP]   1P: $115-$170   2P: $125-$180   XP: $15   F18
5/1-6/14 & 10/15-4/30 [CP]   1P: $105-$160   2P: $115-$170   XP: $15   F18

Location: Hwy 40, exit 312N (Pierre-Bertrand nord), 1.3 mi (2 km) w of jct Rt 358. 1600 rue Bouvier G2K 1N8. Small-scale Hotel Fax: 418/622-4067. **Facility:** 119 units. 12 one-bedroom standard units. 107 one-bedroom suites. 3 stories, interior corridors. **Parking:** on-site, winter plug-ins. **Terms:** package plans, small pets only. **Amenities:** irons, hair dryers. **Leisure Activities:** exercise privileges. **Guest Services:** valet and coin laundry, wireless Internet. **Business Services:** meeting rooms, PC. **Cards:** AX, CB, DC, DS, JC, MC, VI. *(See color ad card insert)*

SOME UNITS

(S/D) (🛏) (🏋) (🏋) (💻) / (✕) (📠) (📠) /

HOTEL SEPIA *Book great rates at AAA.com*   Phone: (418)653-4941   **9**

(CAA) (SAVE) 6/22-9/2   1P: $119-$179   2P: $119-$179   XP: $10   F16
9/3-10/7   1P: $109-$149   2P: $109-$149   XP: $10   F16
5/1-6/21 & 10/8-4/30   1P: $99-$139   2P: $99-$139   XP: $10   F16

Small-scale Hotel **Location:** Hwy 73, exit 133 (chemin St-Louis); in Ste-Foy sector. 3135 chemin St-Louis G1W 1R9. Fax: 418/653-0774. **Facility:** 81 one-bedroom standard units, some with whirlpools. 2 stories (no elevator), interior corridors. **Parking:** on-site, winter plug-ins. **Terms:** cancellation fee imposed, package plans. **Dining:** Restaurant Le Galopin, see separate listing. **Pool(s):** heated outdoor. **Leisure Activities:** exercise room privileges. **Guest Services:** valet laundry, area transportation-Old Quebec, wireless Internet. **Business Services:** meeting rooms, PC. **Cards:** AX, DC, DS, MC, VI. **Free Special Amenities:** newspaper and high-speed Internet. *(See color ad p 513)*

SOME UNITS

(🍴) (⛷) (📠) (💻) / (✕) (VCR) (📠) /
FEE

(See map and index starting on p. 517)

HOTEL UNIVERSEL Phone: (418)653-5250

CAA SAVE

7/1-8/31	1P: $128-$148	2P: $128-$148	XP: $15
5/1-6/30 & 9/1-4/30	1P: $98-$108	2P: $98-$108	XP: $15

Small-scale Hotel

Location: Hwy 73, exit 137, 1.4 mi (2.3 km) e on chemin des Quatre-Bourgeois; in Ste-Foy sector. Located across fro the university. 2300 chemin Ste-Foy G1V 1S5. Fax: 418/653-4486. **Facility:** 127 one-bedroom standard uni some with efficiencies or kitchens. 3 stories (no elevator), interior/exterior corridors. **Parking:** on-site, win plug-ins. **Terms:** check-in 4 pm, [AP], [BP] & [CP] meal plans available, small pets only (in limited unit **Amenities:** hair dryers. **Dining:** La Brochetterie Chez Greco, see separate listing. **Pool(s):** heated indoor. **Leisu Activities:** saunas. **Guest Services:** valet laundry, airport transportation-Jean-Lesage Airport, area transportation-Ste-Foy Tra Station, wireless Internet. **Business Services:** meeting rooms. **Cards:** AX, DC, DS, JC, MC, VI. **Free Special Amenities:** loc telephone calls. *(See color ad p 533)*

SOME UNITS

--------- **WHERE TO DINE** ---------

AU PETIT COIN BRETON **Lunch:** $9-$20 **Dinner:** $9-$20 **Phone:** 418/653-6051

Continental

Location: Corner of rue de Quen, just n of boul Laurier; in Ste-Foy sector. 2600 boul Laurier G1V 4T3. **Hours:** 7 a 10 pm, Wed-10:30 pm, Thurs-Sat to midnight. **Closed:** for dinner 12/24 & for lunch 12/2 **Reservations:** suggested. **Features:** The restaurant is in a suburban commercial building, but the serve costumes and the decor evoke the style of Old France. Eighty varieties of French-style crepes are offere including crepes bretonnes. Some are prepared tableside. The menu also features salads, French onion soup, omelets, piz crepes, filet of sole, pasta and tasty dessert crepes. Casual dress; cocktails. **Parking:** on-site. **Cards:** AX, MC, VI.

CHEZ CORA **Lunch:** $7-$11 **Phone:** 418/663-676

Canadian

Location: Hwy 440, exit Francois-de-Laval, just e; in Beauport sector. 417 boul Ste-Anne G1E 3L4. **Hours:** 6 am pm, Sun from 7 am. **Closed:** 12/25. **Reservations:** accepted, Mon-Fri. **Features:** Although this plac specializes in breakfast, it offers a varied daytime menu that includes bacon, eggs, sausages, crepes, grill cheese, sandwiches, freshly prepared quiches, salads, fruit platters and freshly squeezed juices. The famil friendly dining room is casual and modern. Casual dress; beer & wine only. **Parking:** on-site. **Cards:** AX, DC, MC, VI.

CHEZ CORA **Lunch:** $7-$11 **Phone:** 418/626-795

Canadian

Location: Hwy 40, exit 312 (Pierre-Bertrand nord), then just e. 710 rue Bouvier G2J 1C2. **Hours:** 6 am-3 pm, S from 7 am. **Closed:** 1/1, 12/25. **Reservations:** accepted. **Features:** Although this place specializes breakfast, it offers a varied daytime menu that includes bacon, eggs, sausages, crepes, grilled chees sandwiches, freshly prepared quiches, salads, fruit platters and freshly squeezed juices. The family-frienc dining room is casual and modern. Casual dress; beer & wine only. **Parking:** on-site. **Cards:** AX, MC, VI.

COSMOS **Lunch:** $9-$22 **Dinner:** $11-$22 **Phone:** 418/652-2001

Continental

Location: Corner of ave de Germain-des-Pres; in Hotel Classique; in Ste-Foy sector. 2813 boul Laurier G1V 2L **Hours:** 7 am-midnight. **Closed:** 12/24, 12/25. **Reservations:** accepted. **Features:** This stylish ho restaurant and pub features wholesome foods like 12 choices of pasta, French onion soup, poutir burgers, smoked salmon, cheese platters, pizzas, gourmet hotdogs, salads, nachos, grilled chicken, ve parmigiana and filet mignon. A large breakfast menu is available. Casual dress; cocktails. **Parking:** on-site. **Cards:** AX, D MC, VI.

JARDIN DE TANG **Lunch:** $9-$13 **Dinner:** $13-$20 **Phone:** 418/877-8737

Chinese

Location: 0.5 mi (0.8 km) w of boul Duplessis (Rt 540); in Ste-Foy sector. 7272 boul Wilfrid-Hamel G2C 1C **Hours:** 11 am-10 pm, Thurs-Sat to 11 pm, Sun 9 am-10 pm. **Closed:** 12/24. **Reservations:** accepte **Features:** The family-friendly buffet displays a large selection of Canadian-style Chinese dishes, includi won ton soup, egg rolls, noodles, seafood, chow mein, fried rice and frogs' legs. The a la carte menu lis additional Chinese dishes, such as Cantonese lobster, General Tao chicken and a sizzling seafood platter. Take-out and delive service are available. Casual dress; cocktails. **Parking:** on-site. **Cards:** AX, JC, MC, VI.

LA BROCHETTERIE CHEZ GRECO **Lunch:** $8-$12 **Dinner:** $10-$20 **Phone:** 418/652-0319

Greek

Location: Hwy 73, exit 137, 1.4 mi (2.3 km) e on chemin des Quatre-Bourgeois; in Ste-Foy sector; in Hotel Universel; Ste-Foy sector. 2300 chemin Ste-Foy G1V 1S5. **Hours:** 11 am-2:30 & 4:30-11 pm, Tues & Wed-10 pm. Close 12/24, 12/25. **Reservations:** suggested. **Features:** The atmosphere is lively, and diners can bring their ow wine—what better way to sample a menu of specialties that includes varied kebabs, Greek salad, tzatz and souvlaki with filet mignon or chicken. For dessert, a sweet serving of baklava is sure to please. Casual dress. **Parking:** o site. **Cards:** MC, VI.

LE BIFTHEQUE **Lunch:** $7-$20 **Dinner:** $10-$20 **Phone:** 418/871-171

Steak House

Location: Hwy 73, exit boul Wilfrid-Hamel. 5050 boul Wilfrid-Hamel G2E 5X5. **Hours:** 11:30 am-10 pm, Wed Thurs-10:30 pm, Fri & Sat-11 pm. **Closed:** for lunch 12/25. **Reservations:** accepted. **Features:** T restaurant satisfies the cravings of folks in the mood for a sizzling steak. Huge portions of traditiona steakhouse fare-including filet steaks, prime rib and seafood selections-keep locals coming back. Amor starters are shrimp cocktail, French onion soup and escargots. Meals come with a tasty house salad and the ever-popul biftheque croutons. Diners should arrive with a hearty appetite. Casual dress; cocktails. **Parking:** on-site. **Cards:** AX, CB, DS, JC, MC, VI.

LE GRIFFE RESTAURANT & BAR **Lunch:** $10-$20 **Dinner:** $18-$25 **Phone:** 418/627-800

Continental

Location: Hwy 73, exit 154, just e; in Charlesbourg sector. 7900 rue du Marigot G1G 6T8. **Hours:** 7 am-10 p **Reservations:** accepted. **Features:** A safari motif adds zing to the stylish decor of this casual hot restaurant. The menu lists Continental cuisine inspired by many Quebec regional products, including por duck confit, steak, chicken, pasta and fresh fish. Casual dress; cocktails. **Parking:** on-site. **Cards:** AX, MC, VI.

LE MANOIR DU SPAGHETTI **Lunch:** $8-$18 **Dinner:** $8-$18 **Phone:** 418/659-5628

Italian

Location: Just e of Pont Pierre-Laporte; in Ste-Foy sector. 3077 chemin St-Louis G1W 1R6. **Hours:** 11 am-11 p Closed: 1/1, 12/24, 12/25. **Reservations:** accepted. **Features:** The family restaurant specializes in multip varieties of spaghetti and other Italian dishes. Casual dress; cocktails. **Parking:** on-site. **Cards:** AX, D MC, VI.

(See map and index starting on p. 517)

MONTE CRISTO
RESTO LOUNGE

Menu on AAA.com   **Lunch:** $12-$25   **Dinner:** $18-$40   **Phone:** 418/650-4550   ⑤

Mediterranean

Location: Hwy 540 (Autoroute Duplessis), exit chemin Ste-Foy, just w; in Ste-Foy sector; in Chateau Bonne Entente. 3400 chemin Ste-Foy G1X 1S6. **Hours:** 6:30 am-10 pm; from 7 am 6/24-9/5. **Reservations:** suggested. **Features:** Modern Mediterranean cuisine is served in an elegant, contemporary dining room and lounge. The menu lists such dishes as lobster Thermidor, grilled black bass, calf sweetbreads with prawns and porcini, filet mignon, rib steaks, rack of lamb, grilled swordfish and roasted scallops. Guests may start their meal with a choice of tapas or creative cocktails. Dressy casual; cocktails. **Parking:** on-site. **Cards:** AX, DC, DS, MC, VI. *(See color ad p 523)*

RESTAURANT LA POINTE DES AMERIQUES   **Lunch:** $9-$13   **Dinner:** $10-$25   **Phone:** 418/658-2583   ⑥

Italian

Location: Corner of ave de Germain-des-Pres; in Hotel Classique. 2815 boul Laurier G1V 4H3. **Hours:** 11:30 am-11 pm, Fri & Sat-11:30 pm. Closed: 12/25. **Reservations:** accepted. **Features:** Pizza, pasta, salads, fajitas and Thai curry are among the varied menu items offered at the casually stylish restaurant and bar. Casual dress; cocktails. **Parking:** on-site. **Cards:** AX, DC, MC, VI.

RESTAURANT LE GALOPIN   **Lunch:** $12-$16   **Dinner:** $25-$35   **Phone:** 418/652-0991   ⑧

Regional French

Location: Hwy 73, exit 133 (chemin St-Louis); in Ste-Foy sector; in Hotel Sepia. 3135 chemin St-Louis G1W 1R9. **Hours:** 7 am-2 & 5-10 pm. Closed: 12/25. **Reservations:** suggested. **Features:** A wide range of regional products, with a heavy focus on game, is used to create innovative, market-sensitive cuisine. Flavorful choices include fillet of pork, salmon tartare, sweetbreads, seafood stew, rabbit and beef mignon. The decor and table settings are upscale. Seating on the summer terrace is popular. Dressy casual; cocktails. **Parking:** on-site. **Cards:** AX, DC, MC, VI.

RESTAURANT NORMANDIN   **Lunch:** $5-$12   **Dinner:** $5-$12   **Phone:** 418/653-4844

Canadian

Location: Ste-Foy sector. 2500 chemin Ste-Foy G1W 1R8. **Hours:** 6 am-midnight, Thurs-2 am, Fri & Sat-3 am. Closed: 12/25. **Reservations:** accepted. **Features:** The family restaurant prepares affordable comfort foods that include roasted chicken, hot chicken sandwiches, pasta, burgers and fries. Take-out service, a children's menu and cutely decorated desserts are among other offerings. Casual dress; cocktails. **Parking:** street. **Cards:** AX, DC, MC, VI.

RESTAURANT NORMANDIN   **Lunch:** $5-$12   **Dinner:** $5-$12   **Phone:** 418/627-1265

Canadian

Location: Hwy 358, exit rue Bouvier. 986 rue Bouvier G2J 1A3. **Hours:** 24 hours. Closed: 12/25. **Reservations:** accepted. **Features:** The family restaurant prepares affordable comfort foods that include roasted chicken, hot chicken sandwiches, pasta, burgers and fries. Take-out service, a children's menu and cutely decorated desserts are among other offerings. Casual dress; cocktails. **Parking:** street. **Cards:** AX, DC, MC, VI.

RESTAURANT NORMANDIN   **Lunch:** $5-$12   **Dinner:** $5-$12   **Phone:** 418/681-0207

Canadian

Location: Jct Hwy 440 and 138. 709 boul Charest ouest G1K 3H4. **Hours:** 6 am-midnight, Thurs-2 am, Fri & Sat-3 am. Closed: 12/25. **Reservations:** accepted. **Features:** The family restaurant prepares affordable comfort foods that include roasted chicken, hot chicken sandwiches, pasta, burgers and fries. Take-out service, a children's menu and cutely decorated desserts are among other offerings. Casual dress; cocktails. **Parking:** street. **Cards:** AX, DC, MC, VI.

RESTAURANT NORMANDIN   **Lunch:** $5-$12   **Dinner:** $5-$12   **Phone:** 418/842-6601

Canadian

Location: On Hwy 369; Neufchatel sector. 2355 boul Bastien G2B 1B3. **Hours:** 6 am-midnight, Thurs-2 am, Fri & Sat-3 am. Closed: 12/25. **Reservations:** accepted. **Features:** The family restaurant prepares affordable comfort foods that include roasted chicken, hot chicken sandwiches, pasta, burgers and fries. Take-out service, a children's menu and cutely decorated desserts are among other offerings. Casual dress; cocktails. **Parking:** street. **Cards:** AX, DC, MC, VI.

ST-HUBERT   **Lunch:** $7-$20   **Dinner:** $7-$20   **Phone:** 418/650-1234

Canadian

Location: Hwy 73, exit boul Laurier; in Ste-Foy sector. 2905 boul Laurier G1V 2M2. **Hours:** 11 am-11 pm, Wed & Thurs-midnight, Fri & Sat-1 am. Closed: 12/25. **Reservations:** accepted. **Features:** The pleasantly decorated family-friendly restaurant serves affordable chicken dinners, ribs, club sandwiches, chicken wings, salads, soups and hot chicken sandwiches. The children's menu includes animal nuggets. Casual dress; cocktails. **Parking:** on-site. **Cards:** AX, DC, MC, VI.

The following restaurant has not been evaluated by AAA but is listed for your information only.

LE COCHON DINGUE   **Phone:** 418/684-2013

fyi   Not evaluated. **Location:** Between chemin St-Louis and boul Laurier; in Sillery sector. 1326 ave Maguire G1T 1Z3. **Features:** The diverse menu at the relaxed restaurant centers on French bistro cuisine.

The Quebec Vicinity

BEAUPORT pop. 72,813   (See map and index starting on p. 517)

——— WHERE TO STAY ———

AMBASSADEUR HOTEL & SUITES   *Book at AAA.com*   Phone: (418)666-2828   **16**
▼▼▼ ▼▼▼   7/1-10/16   1P: $99-$300   2P: $99-$300   XP: $10   F17
                     5/1-6/30 & 10/17-4/30   1P: $90-$300   2P: $90-$300   XP: $10   F17
Small-scale Hotel   **Location:** Hwy 440, exit Francois-de-Laval, just e; in Beauport sector. 321 boul Ste-Anne G1E 3L4.
Fax: 418/666-2775. **Facility:** 93 one-bedroom standard units, some with whirlpools. 4 stories, interio
corridors. *Bath:* combo or shower only. **Parking:** on-site. **Terms:** [AP] & [CP] meal plans available, package plans.
Amenities: voice mail, irons, hair dryers. **Leisure Activities:** saunas, exercise room. **Guest Services:** valet laundry, beauty
salon, wireless Internet. **Business Services:** meeting rooms. **Cards:** AX, CB, DC, DS, MC, VI.

                                                                                         SOME UNITS
                                                              (ASK) (S⃝D) [📶] [🍴] [🖥] / [✕] [🛁] /
                                                                                         FEE FEE

COMFORT INN   *Book great rates at AAA.com*   Phone: (418)666-1226   **17**
▼▼▼ ▼▼▼   5/1-10/15   1P: $95-$150   2P: $95-$195   XP: $10   F18
                     10/16-4/30   1P: $95-$120   2P: $95-$145   XP: $10   F18
Small-scale Hotel   **Location:** Hwy 440, exit Francois-de-Laval. 240 boul Ste-Anne G1E 3L7. Fax: 418/666-5088. **Facility:** 80 one-
bedroom standard units. 2 stories, interior corridors. **Parking:** on-site, winter plug-ins. **Amenities:** irons, hair
dryers. **Guest Services:** valet laundry, wireless Internet. **Cards:** AX, DC, DS, JC, MC, VI. *(See color ad card insert)*

                                                                                         SOME UNITS
                                                              (ASK) (S⃝D) [🛏] [🍴+] [🖥] / [✕] [🛁] /

GITE DU VIEUX-BOURG   Phone: 418/661-0116   **15**
▼▼ ▼▼   Property failed to provide current rates
                     Location: Hwy 440, exit Francois-de-Laval, just n, then 0.3 mi (0.5 km) e; in Beauport sector. 492 ave Royale G1E 1Y1.
Bed & Breakfast   Fax: 418/661-0116. **Facility:** Smoke free premises. 4 one-bedroom standard units, some with kitchens. 2
stories (no elevator), interior corridors. *Bath:* some shared or private, combo or shower only. **Parking:** on-
site. **Terms:** check-in 4 pm. **Amenities:** hair dryers. **Pool(s):** outdoor. **Leisure Activities:** horseshoes. **Guest Services:**
complimentary laundry.

                                                                                         SOME UNITS
                                      [🛏] [🍴+] [≋] [✕] / [🍴] [W] [🏊] [🛁] [🖥] [🖥] /

BEAUPRE pop. 2,761

——— WHERE TO STAY ———

AUBERGE LA CAMARINE   *Book great rates at AAA.com*   Phone: 418/827-5703
(CAA) (SAVE)   11/16-4/30   1P: $125-$200   2P: $125-$200   XP: $10
                     5/1-11/15   1P: $100-$170   2P: $100-$170   XP: $10
▼▼▼ ▼▼▼   **Location:** On Hwy 138, 0.9 mi (1.5 km) w of jct Hwy 360. 10947 boul Ste-Anne G0A 1E0. Fax: 418/827-5430.
Country Inn   **Facility:** On landscaped grounds atop a small hill, this upscale country inn offers attractive, comfortable
guest rooms, many with fireplaces and balconies. 31 one-bedroom standard units, some with whirlpools. 3
stories (no elevator), interior corridors. **Parking:** on-site, winter plug-ins. **Terms:** cancellation fee imposed,
[AP], [BP], [CP] & [MAP] meal plans available, package plans, small pets only. **Amenities:** hair dryers. **Dining:** 7:30 am-10:30 &
6-10:30 pm. **Guest Services:** complimentary laundry, wireless Internet. **Business Services:** meeting rooms, PC. **Cards:** AX,
MC, VI. **Free Special Amenities:** newspaper and early check-in/late check-out.

                                                                                         SOME UNITS
                                                              [🛏] [Y] [🍴] / [✕] [🍴] [🛁] /

CHALETS MONT STE-ANNE   Phone: (418)827-5776
▼▼▼ ▼▼▼   12/1-4/30   2P: $250
                     5/1-11/30   2P: $140
Condominium   **Location:** On Hwy 138, 2.3 mi (3.7 km) e on Hwy 360; just w on Beau Mont. 1 rue Beau Soleil G0A 1E0.
Fax: 418/827-5984. **Facility:** These attractive and comfortable one- to five-bedroom condos are at the base
of a popular and scenic ski hill. 38 units. 24 two- and 14 three-bedroom suites with kitchens, some with whirlpools. 2 stories (no
elevator), exterior corridors. **Parking:** on-site. **Terms:** check-in 6 pm, 2 night minimum stay, 45 day cancellation notice-fee
imposed, package plans. **Leisure Activities:** DVD players, CD players, irons. **Leisure Activities:** snowmobiling, ice skating, hiking
trails. *Fee:* downhill & cross country skiing. **Guest Services:** complimentary laundry, wireless Internet. **Business Services:** PC.
Cards: AX, DS, MC, VI. *(See color ad p 523)*

                                                                                         SOME UNITS
                                                    [✕] [AC] [VCR] [🛁] [🖥] [🖥] / [✕] /

CHATEAU MONT SAINTE ANNE   *Book great rates at AAA.com*   Phone: (418)827-5211
(CAA) (SAVE)   12/1-4/30   1P: $159-$269   2P: $159-$269   XP: $20   F18
                     5/1-11/30   1P: $139-$259   2P: $139-$259   XP: $20   F18
▼▼▼ ▼▼▼   **Location:** Hwy 360, 2.3 mi (3.7 km) ne from jct Hwy 138. 500 boul du Beau-Pre G0A 1E0. Fax: 418/827-5072.
Resort   **Facility:** The resort, which caters to skiers and other outdoor enthusiasts, offers spacious rooms with
Large-scale Hotel   kitchenettes and balconies. Smoke free premises. 240 units. 231 one-bedroom standard units, some with
efficiencies or kitchens (utensils extra charge). 9 one-bedroom suites ($289-$449) with kitchens. 6 stories,
interior corridors. **Parking:** on-site, winter plug-ins. **Terms:** check-in 4 pm, 7 day cancellation notice-fee
imposed, [BP] & [MAP] meal plans available, package plans, pets ($20 fee, in designated units). **Amenities:** voice mail, hair
dryers. *Some:* CD players, irons. **Dining:** 2 restaurants, 6 am-10 pm, cocktails, also, Le Beau Regard, see separate listing.
Pool(s): heated outdoor, heated indoor, 2 wading. **Leisure Activities:** sauna, whirlpools, steamroom, ice skating, dog sleds,
sleigh rides, snowshoes, recreation programs, croquet, paragliding, petanque, canyoning, hiking trails, playground, exercise
room, spa, volleyball. *Fee:* kayaks, downhill & cross country skiing, snowmobiling, bicycles, horseback riding, game room.
Guest Services: gift shop, valet and coin laundry, area transportation, wireless Internet. **Business Services:** conference
facilities, administrative services (fee), PC. **Cards:** AX, CB, DC, DS, JC, MC, VI. **Free Special Amenities:** room upgrade
(subject to availability with advance reservations) and high-speed Internet.

                                                                                         SOME UNITS
                              (S⃝D) [🛏] [🍴] [Y] [🎿] [≋] [✕] [✕] [🛁] [🖥] [🖥] / [VCR] [🖥] /
                              FEE

HOTEL VAL DES NEIGES   *Book great rates at AAA.com*   Phone: 418/827-5711

(CAA) (SAVE)

All Year	1P: $89	2P: $89	XP: $20	F17

Location: Just off Hwy 360. 201 rue Val-des-Neiges G0A 1E0. Fax: 418/827-5997. **Facility:** 111 one-bedroom Large-scale Hotel standard units, some with whirlpools. 4 stories, interior corridors. **Parking:** on-site, winter plug-ins. **Terms:** check-in 4 pm, cancellation fee imposed, [AP], [BP] & [MAP] meal plans available, package plans, pets ($20 extra charge). **Amenities:** voice mail, irons, hair dryers. *Some:* CD players. **Dining:** 2 restaurants, 7 am-10 pm, cocktails. **Pool(s):** heated indoor. **Leisure Activities:** saunas, whirlpool, tennis court, snowmobiling, hiking trails, spa, shuffleboard. *Fee:* game room. **Guest Services:** valet laundry, area transportation-ski hill, wireless Internet. **Business Services:** conference facilities. **Cards:** AX, CB, DC, DS, MC, VI. **Free Special Amenities:** high-speed Internet.

SOME UNITS

VILLAGE TOURISTIQUE MONT STE-ANNE   Phone: 418/827-2002

(CAA) (SAVE)

12/22-1/4	1P: $204-$524	2P: $204-$524	XP: $20	F13
2/18-4/30	1P: $194-$524	2P: $194-$524	XP: $20	F13
1/5-2/17	1P: $114-$384	2P: $114-$384	XP: $20	F13
5/1-12/21	1P: $99-$279	2P: $99-$279	XP: $20	F13

Condominium   **Location:** Hwy 138 E, exit 360. 1000 boul du Beau-Pre G0A 1E0. Fax: 418/827-6666. **Facility:** These large, upscale condos are located at the foot of the ski hill and are equipped with fireplaces. Heated indoor parking is available. 60 units. 35 one-bedroom standard units with efficiencies, some with whirlpools. 16 one- and 9 two-bedroom suites with kitchens, some with whirlpools. 5 stories, interior corridors. **Parking:** on-site. **Terms:** check-in 4 pm, 2 night minimum stay - seasonal, 30 day cancellation notice, in winter-fee imposed, package plans. **Amenities:** video library, DVD players, CD players, irons, hair dryers. **Dining:** 11 am-10 pm, cocktails. **Leisure Activities:** ice skating, rental bicycles, hiking trails. *Fee:* downhill & cross country skiing. **Guest Services:** gift shop, coin laundry. **Business Services:** meeting rooms. *Fee:* administrative services, PC. **Cards:** AX, DC, MC, VI.

WHERE TO DINE

GRANGE A JOE   Lunch: $7-$11   Dinner: $7-$20   Phone: 418/827-4647

Canadian

Location: On Hwy 138; centre. 10998 boul Ste-Anne G0A 1E0. **Hours:** 7 am-9 pm, Fri & Sat-10 pm, Sun-8 pm. **Closed:** 1/1, 12/25. **Reservations:** accepted. **Features:** This family-friendly diner, in business since 1974, offers a variety of affordable meals, including pasta, burgers, pizza, brochettes, fish, "tourtiere" meat pie and crepes. Casual dress; cocktails. **Parking:** on-site. **Cards:** AX, DC, MC, VI.

LE BEAU REGARD   Dinner: $25-$34   Phone: 418/827-5211

French

Location: Hwy 360, 2.3 mi (3.7 km) ne from jct Hwy 138; in Chateau Mont Sainte-Anne. 500 boul Beau-Pre G0A 1E0. **Hours:** 7 am-11 & 6-10 pm. **Reservations:** suggested. **Features:** An upscale ski resort is the setting for the elegant yet casual dining room. The menu features fine French-influenced regional cuisine, including guinea-fowl, pork, lamb, beef, smoked trout, deer, sweetbreads, snow crab and fresh fish. Gourmet theme buffets are offered nightly during the winter ski season. Casual dress; cocktails. **Parking:** on-site. **Cards:** AX, CB, DC, DS, JC, MC, VI.

CHARLESBOURG pop. 70,310   (See map and index starting on p. 517)

WHERE TO DINE

DA CORTINA   Lunch: $18-$24   Dinner: $16-$33   Phone: 418/622-3833   (15)

Northern Italian

Location: Jct Hwy 73, exit 150, just n on ave Doucet; in Charlesbourg sector. 615 80 E rue ouest G1L 2M3. **Hours:** 11:30 am-2:30 & 5:30-10 pm, Sat from 5:30 pm. **Closed:** 12/25; also 12/24 & Sun except Mothers Day and Easter. **Reservations:** suggested. **Features:** The restored, two-story Victorian mansion has large windows, attractive greenery and views of the Quebec City skyline. Pasta, veal and fish selections include delicious salmon steak drizzled with fruit sauce and served with noodles and vegetables. Among other dishes are veal liver, fried calamari, beef filet, and saffron farfalle. A seasonal outdoor terrace is available. Casual dress; cocktails. **Parking:** on-site. **Cards:** AX, DC, MC, VI.

LE MANOIR DU SPAGHETTI   Lunch: $8-$18   Dinner: $8-$18   Phone: 418/627-0161   (14)

Italian

Location: Corner of 76ieme rue; centre; in Charlesbourg sector. 7685 1er Ave G1H 2Y1. **Hours:** 11 am-10 pm, Wed-10:30 pm, Thurs-Sat to 11 pm. **Closed:** 1/1, 12/24, 12/25. **Features:** The comfortable family restaurant prepares varieties of spaghetti and other pastas. Casual dress; cocktails. **Parking:** on-site. **Cards:** AX, DC, MC, VI.

CHATEAU-RICHER pop. 3,442

WHERE TO STAY

AUBERGE BAKER   Phone: (418)666-5509

12/16-4/30 [BP]	1P: $94-$130	2P: $99-$135	XP: $20	D12
6/11-10/15 [BP]	1P: $80-$120	2P: $95-$125	XP: $20	D12
10/16-12/15 [BP]	1P: $74-$105	2P: $75-$125	XP: $20	D12
5/1-6/10 [BP]	1P: $70-$105	2P: $75-$125	XP: $20	D12

Bed & Breakfast

Location: 3.1 mi (5 km) e, just off Hwy 138 via private road. 8790 ave Royale G0A 1N0. Fax: 418/824-4412. **Facility:** Designated smoking area. 8 units. 6 one-bedroom standard units, some with whirlpools. 1 vacation home ($160-$320) and 1 cottage. 2 stories (no elevator), interior/exterior corridors. *Bath:* combo or shower only. **Parking:** on-site, winter plug-ins. **Terms:** 14 day cancellation notice, package plans. **Amenities:** hair dryers. *Some:* irons. **Dining:** restaurant, see separate listing. **Leisure Activities:** cross country skiing, snowmobiling. **Guest Services:** coin laundry, wireless Internet. **Business Services:** meeting rooms. **Cards:** AX, DC, MC, VI.

SOME UNITS

——— WHERE TO DINE ———

RESTAURANT BAKER
(AA)
~~~~~~
Regional French

| | Lunch: $14-$41 | Dinner: $14-$41 | Phone: 418/824-447 |

Location: 3.1 mi (5 km) e, just off Hwy 138 via private road; in Auberge Baker. 8790 ave Royale G0A 1N0. **Hours:** 1 am-9 pm. **Reservations:** suggested. **Features:** The cozy, circa 1840 farmhouse is appointed with country style decor and has a laid-back atmosphere. Preparations of game are the specialty on a menu of traditiona Quebecois and fine French cuisine that also includes duck confit, blood sausage ("boudin noir"), lamb an veal. Casual dress; cocktails. **Parking:** on-site. **Cards:** AX, DC, MC, VI. **Historic**

LAC-BEAUPORT pop. 5,519

——— WHERE TO STAY ———

AUBERGE QUATRE TEMPS
~~~~~~
Country Inn

Phone: (418)849-448

5/1-6/21 & 9/4-12/20	1P: $110-$140	2P: $110-$140	XP: $15	F1
6/22-9/3 & 12/21-4/30	1P: $140	2P: $140	XP: $15	F1

Location: Hwy 73 N, exit 157, 4.1 mi (6.5 km) e on boul du Lac. 161 chemin Tour du Lac G0A 2C0 Fax: 418/849-6123. **Facility:** On the shores of scenic Lac Beauport, this upscale lodging offers rooms wit balconies, as well as a few one-bedroom suites with exterior entrances. 34 units. 27 one-bedroom standard units wit whirlpools. 7 one-bedroom suites with whirlpools, some with efficiencies. 3 stories (no elevator), interior/exterior corridors **Parking:** on-site, winter plug-ins. **Terms:** cancellation fee imposed, [AP], [BP] & [MAP] meal plans available, package plans **Amenities:** hair dryers. *Some:* high-speed Internet. **Pool(s):** outdoor, heated indoor. **Leisure Activities:** limited beach access cross country skiing, snowmobiling, ice skating, hiking trails, spa, volleyball. *Fee:* paddleboats, windsurfing. **Guest Services** complimentary laundry. **Business Services:** meeting rooms, PC. **Cards:** AX, DC, MC, VI.

SOME UNITS
[YI] [Y] [🏋] [🏊] [⊠] / [⊠] [🏌] [VCR] [🔌] [📷] [▯] /

——— *The following lodging was either not evaluated or did not* ——— *meet AAA rating requirements but is listed for your information only.*

MANOIR ST-CASTIN
[fyi]
Historic
Country Inn

Phone: 418/841-400

Did not meet all AAA rating requirements for locking devices in some guest rooms at time of last evaluatio on 03/09/2006. **Location:** Hwy 73 N, exit 157, 3.4 mi (5.5 km) e. 99 chemin Tour du Lac G0A 2C0. Facilities, services and decor characterize a mid-range property.

——— WHERE TO DINE ———

ARCHIBALD MICROBRASSERIE RESTAURANT
~~~~~~
Canadian

| | Lunch: $6-$17 | Dinner: $13-$19 | Phone: 418/841-222 |

Location: Hwy 73 N, exit 157, then 1.9 mi (3.3 km) e. 1021 boul du Lac G0A 2C0. **Hours:** 11 am-2 am. Closed 12/25. **Reservations:** accepted. **Features:** The wood-beamed interior resembles a rustic hunting lodge an is adorned with a hanging canoe and a stuffed animal above the bar. Preservative-free beers are brewed o the premises and the menu of pub food includes burgers, Angus beef, ribs, mussels in beer sauce an veal liver, lamb, gourmet pizza, fish, salad and pasta. The seasonal terrace is a good place to enjoy the rural scenery. Casua dress; cocktails. **Parking:** on-site. **Cards:** AX, DC, MC, VI.

[Y]

LE TIFFANY RESTO-BAR
~~~~~~
French

| | Lunch: $14-$16 | Dinner: $20-$35 | Phone: 418/841-494 |

Location: Hwy 73 N, exit 157, 3.4 mi (5.5 km) e ; in Manoir St-Castin. 99 chemin Tour du Lac G0A 2C0. **Hours:** 7 10:30 am, 11-2:30 & 5-9 pm. **Reservations:** suggested. **Features:** The pleasant dining room, bar an summer terrace look out over Lac-Beauport. The menu focus is on French cuisine, with such well-prepare dishes as filet mignon and beef Wellington. Diners flock here for Sunday brunch. Service is professional an attentive. Casual dress; cocktails. **Parking:** on-site. **Cards:** AX, DC, MC, VI.

[Y]

L'ANCIENNE-LORETTE pop. 15,929 (See map and index starting on p. 517)

——— WHERE TO STAY ———

CHATEAU REPOTEL *Book at AAA.com*
~~~~~~
Small-scale Hotel

Phone: (418)872-1111 [2]

7/1-10/14	1P: $76-$82	2P: $86-$92	XP: $10	F1
10/15-4/30	1P: $76-$82	2P: $76-$82	XP: $10	F1
5/1-6/30	1P: $74-$80	2P: $74-$80	XP: $10	F1

Location: Jct boul Duplessis and Wilfrid-Hamel (Hwy 138). 6555 boul Wilfrid-Hamel G2E 5W3. Fax: 418/872-5989 **Facility:** 100 one-bedroom standard units, some with whirlpools. 4 stories, interior corridors. **Parking:** on-site, winter plug-ins **Terms:** [CP] meal plan available. **Amenities:** hair dryers. *Some:* honor bars. **Guest Services:** valet laundry, wireless Interne **Business Services:** meeting rooms. **Cards:** AX, DC, JC, MC, VI.

SOME UNITS
[📶] [🍴] / [⊠] [🔌] /

COMFORT INN *Book great rates at AAA.com*
~~~~~~
Small-scale Hotel

Phone: (418)872-5900 [2]

6/16-9/15	1P: $110-$135	2P: $115-$145	XP: $10	F1
1/1-4/30	1P: $108-$129	2P: $118-$139	XP: $10	F1
5/1-6/15 & 9/16-12/31	1P: $105-$127	2P: $115-$137	XP: $10	F1

Location: Jct boul Duplessis and Wilfrid-Hamel (Hwy 138). 1255 boul Duplessis G2G 2B4. Fax: 418/872-0550 **Facility:** 59 one-bedroom standard units. 2 stories (no elevator), interior corridors. **Parking:** on-site, winter plug-ins **Terms:** small pets only. **Amenities:** voice mail, irons, hair dryers. **Guest Services:** valet laundry. **Cards:** AX, CB, DC, DS, JC MC, VI.

SOME UNITS
[ASK] [S🔒] [🛏] [🍴] [▯] / [⊠] [🔌] /
FEE

(See map and index starting on p. 517)

TIMES HOTEL & SUITES   *Book at AAA.com*   Phone: (418)877-7788   **20**

6/22-9/30 [ECP]	1P: $129-$179	2P: $129-$194	XP: $15	F11
5/1-6/21 & 10/1-4/30 [ECP]	1P: $119-$139	2P: $119-$154	XP: $15	F11

Small-scale Hotel   **Location:** Just e of autoroute 540 (boul Duplessis). 6515 boul Wilfrid-Hamel G2E 5W3. Fax: 418/877-3333. **Facility:** Smoke free premises. 112 units. 103 one-bedroom standard units. 9 one-bedroom suites with whirlpools. 5 stories, interior corridors. **Parking:** on-site, winter plug-ins. **Terms:** package plans. **Amenities:** high-speed Internet, voice mail, irons, hair dryers. *Some:* safes. **Pool(s):** small heated indoor. **Leisure Activities:** exercise room. *Fee:* massage. **Guest Services:** valet and coin laundry, wireless Internet. **Business Services:** meeting rooms, business center. **Cards:** AX, MC, VI.

SOME UNITS

----------- WHERE TO DINE -----------

LA CAGE AUX SPORTS   **Lunch:** $8-$23   **Dinner:** $8-$23   Phone: 418/872-3000

Canadian   **Location:** Just e of boul Duplessis. 6476 boul Wilfrid-Hamel ouest G2E 2J1. **Hours:** 11 am-11 pm, Thurs-Sat to midnight. Closed: 1/1, 12/25. **Reservations:** accepted. **Features:** This popular Quebec chain of sports bars presents a menu of pub foods, including ribs, chicken, burgers, salads, crispy fries, pasta and tasty desserts. Guests might begin the meal with a basket of freshly popped popcorn as they check out the sports memorabilia. Children are welcomed. Casual dress; cocktails. **Parking:** on-site. **Cards:** AX, DC, MC, VI.

LEVIS   (See map and index starting on p. 517)

----------- WHERE TO STAY -----------

COMFORT INN   *Book great rates at AAA.com*   Phone: (418)835-5605   **26**

6/18-9/30	1P: $110-$160	2P: $120-$170	XP: $15	F18
5/1-6/17	1P: $95-$129	2P: $105-$149	XP: $12	F18
10/1-4/30	1P: $85-$115	2P: $95-$135	XP: $10	F18

Small-scale Hotel   **Location:** Hwy 20, exit 325S eastbound; exit 325 westbound. 10 du Vallon est G6V 9J3. Fax: 418/835-9054. **Facility:** 100 one-bedroom standard units. 2 stories (no elevator), interior corridors. **Parking:** on-site, winter plug-ins. **Terms:** package plans, pets (1st floor smoking units). **Amenities:** irons, hair dryers. **Guest Services:** valet laundry, wireless Internet. **Cards:** AX, CB, DC, DS, JC, MC, VI. *(See color ad card insert)*

SOME UNITS

(See map and index starting on p. 517)

ECONO LODGE   *Book great rates at AAA.com*   Phone: (418)837-8841   **25**

▼▼▼ ▼▼▼

6/16-9/2	1P: $99-$175	2P: $109-$175	XP: $10
9/3-12/31	1P: $79-$149	2P: $84-$149	XP: $10
5/1-6/15 & 1/1-4/30	1P: $74-$125	2P: $79-$125	XP: $10

Motel

Location: Hwy 20, exit 325S eastbound; exit 325 westbound. 208 boul President-Kennedy G6V 9J6. Fax: 418/838-1150. **Facility:** 27 one-bedroom standard units. 2 stories (no elevator), interior corridors. **Parking:** on-site, winter plug-ins. **Amenities:** hair dryers. *Some:* irons. **Leisure Activities:** snowmobiling. **Guest Services:** wireless Internet. **Cards:** AX, DC, MC, VI. *(See color ad card insert)*

SOME UNITS

(ASK) (SD) (📶+) (🎥) (🖥) (💻) / (✕) (📷) /

──── **WHERE TO DINE** ────

CHEZ CORA   Lunch: $7-$11   Phone: 418/838-1444

▼▼▼ ▼▼▼

Location: On Rt 132; centre. 4970 boul de la Rive-Sud G6V 4Z6. **Hours:** 6 am-3 pm, Sun from 7 am. Closed: 12/25. **Reservations:** accepted, Mon-Fri. **Features:** Although this place specializes in breakfast, it offers a varied daytime menu that includes bacon, eggs, sausages, crepes, grilled cheese, sandwiches, freshly prepared quiches, salads, fruit platters and freshly squeezed juices. The family-friendly dining room is casual and modern. Casual dress; beer & wine only. **Parking:** on-site. **Cards:** AX, DC, MC, VI.

Canadian

RESTAURANT L'INTIMISTE   Lunch: $10-$17   Dinner: $23-$39   Phone: 418/838-2711   **21**

(CAA)

Location: Just e of boul Alphonse-Desjardins; in Old Levis. 35 ave Begin G6V 4B8. **Hours:** 11 am-2 & 5-10 pm, Sat 5 pm-11 pm, Sun 5 pm-10 pm. Closed: 12/24-12/26; also Sun 1/1-3/15. **Reservations:** suggested. **Features:** The comfortable, upscale dining room in Old Levis presents a menu of game, pork, duck, quail, lamb, filet mignon and seafood preparations. The ferry boat dock for trips into Old Quebec is a short drive away. Casual dress; cocktails. **Parking:** street. **Cards:** AX, MC, VI.

▼▼▼ ▼▼▼
French

(🍸)

ST-HUBERT   Lunch: $7-$20   Dinner: $7-$20   Phone: 418/835-1234

▼▼▼ ▼▼▼

Location: Centre. 49 C Rt Kennedy G6V 4Z1. **Hours:** 11 am-1 am, Wed & Thurs-midnight, Fri & Sat-1 am. Closed: 12/25. **Reservations:** accepted. **Features:** The pleasantly decorated family-friendly restaurant serves affordable chicken dinners, ribs, club sandwiches, chicken wings, salads, soups and hot chicken sandwiches. The children's menu includes animal nuggets. Casual dress; cocktails. **Parking:** on-site. **Cards:** AX, DC, MC, VI.

Canadian

(🍸)

STE-CATHERINE-DE-LA-JACQUES-CARTIER pop.

──── **WHERE TO STAY** ────

AUBERGE-STATION TOURISTIQUE DUCHESNAY   *Book great rates at AAA.com*   Phone: (418)875-2711

(CAA) (SAVE)

6/23-10/13	1P: $113-$174	2P: $113-$174	XP: $20	F18
1/6-4/30	1P: $109-$162	2P: $109-$162	XP: $20	F18
5/1-6/22 & 10/14-1/5	1P: $89-$142	2P: $89-$142	XP: $20	F18

▼▼▼ ▼▼▼

Resort
Large-scale Hotel

Location: On Rt 367. 143 Rt Duchesnay G0A 3M0. Fax: 418/875-2868. **Facility:** The vast, outdoorsy resort has attractive public areas, and rooms are set in three separate pavilions; many recreational options are available. Smoke free premises. 88 units. 85 one-bedroom standard units. 3 one-bedroom suites ($198-$242) with whirlpools. 2-3 stories (no elevator), interior/exterior corridors. *Bath:* combo or shower only. **Parking:** on-site. **Terms:** check-in 4 pm, 2 night minimum stay - seasonal and/or weekends, cancellation fee imposed, [AP], [BP] & [MAP] meal plans available, package plans. **Amenities:** voice mail, hair dryers. *Some:* CD players, high-speed Internet, honor bars. **Dining:** 7 am-9 pm. **Pool(s):** heated indoor. **Leisure Activities:** sauna, whirlpool, lifeguard on duty, limited beach access, boat dock, ice skating, recreation programs, petanque, hiking trails, playground, exercise room, horseshoes, shuffleboard, volleyball, game room. *Fee:* canoes, paddleboats, kayak, cross country skiing, snowmobiling, tobogganing, winter tubing, bicycles. **Guest Services:** coin laundry, wireless Internet. **Business Services:** meeting rooms, PC. **Cards:** AX, MC, VI.

SOME UNITS

(🍴) (🍸) (🅜) (🏊) (✕) (✕) (🎥) (💻) / (🍳) (🖥) /

──── **WHERE TO DINE** ────

RESTAURANT NORMANDIN   Lunch: $5-$12   Dinner: $5-$12   Phone: 418/875-1014

▼▼▼ ▼▼▼

Location: On Hwy 40, 1.9 mi (3 km) w of jct Hwy 540. 4756 boul Fossambault G0A 3M0. **Hours:** 6 am-midnight, Thurs-2 am, Fri & Sat-3 am. Closed: 12/25. **Reservations:** accepted. **Features:** The family restaurant prepares affordable comfort foods that include roasted chicken, hot chicken sandwiches, pasta, burgers and fries. Take-out service, a children's menu and cutely decorated desserts are among other offerings. Casual dress. **Parking:** on-site. **Cards:** AX, DC, MC, VI.

Canadian

STE-FOY pop. 72,547   (See map and index starting on p. 517)

──── **WHERE TO STAY** ────

HOTEL CLARION QUEBEC   *Book great rates at AAA.com*   Phone: (418)653-4901   **35**

▼▼▼▼

7/1-10/16	1P: $99-$350	2P: $99-$350	XP: $15	F17
5/1-6/30 & 10/17-4/30	1P: $95-$300	2P: $95-$300	XP: $15	F17

Large-scale Hotel

Location: Hwy 73, exit 136 (Hochelaga ouest); in Ste-Foy sector. 3125 boul Hochelaga G1V 4A8. Fax: 418/653-1836. **Facility:** 228 units. 222 one-bedroom standard units. 6 one-bedroom suites with whirlpools. 12 stories, interior corridors. **Parking:** on-site, winter plug-ins. **Terms:** [AP] meal plan available, package plans. **Amenities:** video games (fee), voice mail, irons, hair dryers. *Some:* CD players, honor bars. **Pool(s):** small heated indoor. **Leisure Activities:** sauna, exercise room, spa. **Guest Services:** gift shop, valet and coin laundry, area transportation, wireless Internet. **Business Services:** conference facilities, PC, fax. **Cards:** AX, CB, DC, DS, MC, VI. *(See color ad card insert)*

SOME UNITS

(ASK) (SD) (🛏) (🍴) (🍸) (⚓) (✕) (🎥) (💻) / (✕) (VCR) (🖥) /
FEE

(See map and index starting on p. 517)

HOTEL GOUVERNEUR QUEBEC-SAINTE-FOY

Book at AAA.com Phone: (418)651-3030 **32**

| | 5/1-10/15 | 1P: $115-$250 | 2P: $115-$250 | XP: $20 | F17 |
| | 10/16-4/30 | 1P: $99-$250 | 2P: $99-$250 | XP: $20 | F17 |

Large-scale Hotel **Location:** Corner of rue Lavigerie; in Ste-Foy sector. 3030 boul Laurier G1V 2M5. Fax: 418/651-6797. **Facility:** 320 units. 317 one-bedroom standard units, some with whirlpools. 3 one-bedroom suites, some with whirlpools. 2-4 stories (no elevator), interior/exterior corridors. **Parking:** on-site. **Terms:** [AP], [BP] & [CP] meal plans available, package plans, small pets only ($50 fee, must remain caged). **Amenities:** video games (fee), voice mail, irons, hair dryers. *Some:* high-speed Internet (fee). **Pool(s):** heated outdoor. **Leisure Activities:** exercise room. *Fee:* massage. **Guest Services:** gift shop, valet laundry, beauty salon; wireless Internet. **Business Services:** conference facilities, business center. **Cards:** AX, DC, MC, VI.

SOME UNITS

ASK 🐄 🍴 🍸 🏊 🎥 💻 / ✕ 📱 / FEE

HOTEL LINDBERGH

Phone: 418/653-4975 **31**

| | 7/1-9/30 | 1P: $140-$310 | 2P: $150-$320 | XP: $10 | D3 |
| | 5/1-6/30 & 10/1-4/30 | 1P: $125-$250 | 2P: $135-$260 | XP: $10 | D3 |

Small-scale Hotel **Location:** Between rue d'Eglise and Germain Despres. 2825 boul Laurier G1V 2L9. Fax: 418/651-8805. **Facility:** 124 one-bedroom standard units, some with whirlpools. 4 stories, interior corridors. *Bath:* combo or shower only. **Parking:** on-site. **Terms:** 10 day cancellation notice. **Amenities:** voice mail, irons, hair dryers. *Some:* high-speed Internet (fee), dual phone lines. **Pool(s):** heated outdoor. **Guest Services:** valet and coin laundry, wireless Internet. **Business Services:** meeting rooms, PC (fee). **Cards:** AX, DC, DS, MC, VI.

SOME UNITS

ASK 🍴 🍸 🏊 💻 / ✕ 📱 /

HOTEL PLAZA QUEBEC

Phone: (418)658-2727 **33**

| | All Year | 1P: $107-$207 | 2P: $107-$207 | XP: $20 | F11 |

Large-scale Hotel **Location:** Hwy 73 nord, exit boul Laurier, just e; in Ste-Foy sector. 3031 boul Laurier G1V 2M2. Fax: 418/658-6587. **Facility:** 233 units. 230 one-bedroom standard units. 3 one-bedroom suites ($125-$400) with whirlpools. 7 stories, interior corridors. **Parking:** on-site. **Terms:** check-in 4 pm, cancellation fee imposed, [AP] & [BP] meal plans available, package plans. **Amenities:** high-speed Internet (fee), voice mail, irons, hair dryers. **Pool(s):** heated indoor. **Leisure Activities:** sauna, whirlpool, exercise room. **Guest Services:** gift shop, valet laundry, tanning facilities, wireless Internet. **Business Services:** conference facilities. *Fee:* administrative services, PC. **Cards:** AX, DC, DS, MC, VI.

SOME UNITS

🍴 🍸 🏊 ✕ 💻 / ✕ 📱 🍽 / FEE

HOTEL QUEBEC INN

Phone: 418/872-9831 **30**

| | All Year | 1P: $83-$163 | 2P: $93-$173 | XP: $10 | F12 |

Small-scale Hotel **Location:** 0.6 mi (1 km) w of Hwy 540 (Autoroute Duplessis). 7175 boul Hamel ouest G2G 1B6. Fax: 418/872-1336. **Facility:** 135 one-bedroom standard units, some with whirlpools. 2 stories (no elevator), interior/exterior corridors. **Parking:** on-site. **Terms:** check-in 4 pm, package plans. **Amenities:** voice mail, irons, hair dryers. *Some: Fee:* high-speed Internet. **Pool(s):** heated indoor. **Leisure Activities:** sauna, whirlpool, snowmobiling, exercise room, spa. **Guest Services:** valet and coin laundry, beauty salon. **Business Services:** conference facilities. **Cards:** AX, CB, DC, DS, MC, VI.

SOME UNITS

ASK 🍴 🍸 🏊 ✕ 💻 / ✕ 📱 / FEE

L'HOTEL QUEBEC

Phone: 418/658-5120 **36**

| | 7/16-8/31 | 1P: $99-$249 | 2P: $99-$249 | XP: $15 | D10 |
| | 5/1-7/15 & 9/1-4/30 | 1P: $99-$179 | 2P: $99-$179 | XP: $15 | D10 |

Small-scale Hotel **Location:** Hwy 73 nord, exit boul Laurier, just e; in Ste-Foy sector. 3115 ave des Hotels G1W 3Z6. Fax: 418/658-4504. **Facility:** 204 units. 184 one-bedroom standard units. 20 one-bedroom suites, some with efficiencies and/or whirlpools. 6 stories, interior/exterior corridors. **Parking:** on-site. **Terms:** check-in 4 pm, [AP] meal plans available, package plans. **Amenities:** high-speed Internet (fee), voice mail, irons, hair dryers. **Pool(s):** heated indoor, saltwater. **Leisure Activities:** sauna, whirlpool, playground, exercise room, spa, game room. **Guest Services:** valet laundry. **Business Services:** PC (fee). **Cards:** AX, DS, MC, VI.

SOME UNITS

ASK 🍴 🍸 🏊 ✕ 💻 / ✕ 📱 🍽 / FEE

SIR WILFRID AUBERGE SAINTE-FOY

Phone: (418)651-2440 **34**

	7/1-9/30	1P: $126-$300	2P: $136-$310	XP: $10	D12
	10/1-4/30	1P: $101-$250	2P: $111-$260	XP: $10	D12
	5/1-6/30	1P: $101-$250	2P: $111-$250	XP: $10	D12

Small-scale Hotel **Location:** Hwy 73 nord, exit boul Laurier, just e; in Ste-Foy sector. 3055 boul Laurier G1V 4X2. Fax: 418/651-2111. **Facility:** 106 units. 104 one-bedroom standard units, some with whirlpools. 1 one- and 1 two-bedroom suites, some with whirlpools. 3 stories, interior/exterior corridors. *Bath:* combo or shower only. **Parking:** on-site. **Terms:** 10 day cancellation notice. **Amenities:** voice mail, irons, hair dryers. *Some:* high-speed Internet (fee). **Pool(s):** heated outdoor. **Guest Services:** valet and coin laundry, wireless Internet. **Business Services:** meeting rooms, PC (fee). **Cards:** AX, DC, DS, MC, VI.

SOME UNITS

ASK 🏊 💻 / ✕ 📱 🍽 /

(See map and index starting on p. 517)

──────── **WHERE TO DINE** ────────

BISTANGO　　　　　　　**Lunch:** $10-$16　　　　**Dinner:** $13-$30　　　　**Phone:** 418/658-8780　　㉕
French
Location: Just n of boul Laurier; in Ste-Foy sector; in Hotel Germain-des-Pres. 1200 ave Germain-des-Pres G1W 3M7. **Hours:** 7-10 am, 11:30-3 & 5:30-11 pm, Sat 8 am-11 & 5:30-11 pm, Sun 8 am-2 & 5:30-10 pm. Closed: 12/24. **Reservations:** suggested. **Features:** A lively bistro atmosphere infuses the casual, stylish eatery. Representative of menu selections are salmon tartare, cannelloni and lamb shank with couscous and tomato sauce. Dessert choices are appealing in appearance. Service is gracious. Casual dress; cocktails. **Parking:** on-site and street. **Cards:** AX, DC, MC, VI.

CAFE PATES A TOUT　　　　**Lunch:** $5-$9　　　　**Dinner:** $5-$9　　　　**Phone:** 418/651-8284　　㉔
Italian
Location: Jct Autoroute du Vallon; in Les Halles de Ste-Foy; in Ste-Foy sector. 2500 chemin des Quatre-Bourgeois G1V 4P9. **Hours:** 8:30 am-7 pm, Wed-Fri to 9 pm, Sun-6 pm. Closed: 1/1, 12/25. **Features:** There's nothing pretentious about this place—a fast food counter in a small, indoor food market. Fresh pasta and sauces go into such dishes as linguine, fettuccine Alfredo and lasagna. The breakfast menu includes bacon, eggs, pancakes and French toast. Casual dress. **Parking:** on-site. **Cards:** MC, VI.

CHEZ CORA　　　　　　**Lunch:** $7-$11　　　　　　　　　**Phone:** 418/650-5205
Canadian
Location: 0.3 mi (0.5 km) n of boul Laurier; in Ste-Foy sector. 1020 Rt de l G1V 3V9. **Hours:** 6 am-3 pm, Sun from 7 am. Closed: 1/1, 12/25. **Reservations:** accepted. **Features:** Although this place specializes in breakfast, it offers a varied daytime menu that includes bacon, eggs, sausages, crepes, grilled cheese, sandwiches, freshly prepared quiches, salads, fruit platters and freshly squeezed juices. The family-friendly dining room is casual and modern. Casual dress. **Parking:** on-site. **Cards:** AX, MC, VI.

PARIS GRILL BRASSERIE FRANCAISE　　　**Lunch:** $10-$13　　**Dinner:** $10-$21　　**Phone:** 418/658-4415　　㉖
French
Location: Hwy 73, exit 136 (boul Hochelaga ouest); in Ste-Foy sector. 3121 boul Hochelaga ouest G1W 2P9. **Hours:** 11 am-10 pm, Fri-11 pm, Sat 9 am-11 pm, Sun 9 am-10 pm. **Reservations:** accepted. **Features:** This French-style brasserie pub in suburban Quebec features a mix of pub foods and bistro favourites. The house specialty is Alsacian pie (a thin-crust pizza topped with fresh cream, small lardons, sweet onions and cheese). Also choose from Angus beef with fries, Toulouse sausage, chicken or lamb kebabs, calf's liver, pork chops, filet mignon tartar, sauteed tartar steak, fish casserole, "croque monsieur," salmon cooked on a cedar plank, grilled tuna, mussels, duck confit rolls, and poutine. Casual dress; cocktails. **Parking:** on-site. **Cards:** AX, DC, MC, VI.

RESTAURANT LA FENOUILLIERE　　　**Lunch:** $16-$20　　**Dinner:** $23-$31　　**Phone:** 418/653-3886　　㉗
(CAA)
French
Location: Hwy 73, exit 133 (chemin St-Louis); in Ste-Foy sector; in Best Western Hotel L'Aristocrate. 3100 chemin St-Louis G1W 1R8. **Hours:** 7-11 am, 11:30-2 & 5:30-10 pm. **Reservations:** suggested. **Features:** A typical dinner at the upscale restaurant might include a choice of Atlantic salmon, red tuna, scallops, snow crab or pork filets. The overall dining experience is lively yet refined. Casual dress; cocktails. **Parking:** on-site. **Cards:** AX, DC, MC, VI. *(See color ad p 513)*

RESTAURANT LA TANIERE　　　　　　**Dinner:** $20-$45　　　　　　　**Phone:** 418/872-4386
French
Location: Jct Hwy 540, 2 mi (3.4 km) w on boul Wilfred-Hamel, then 2.5 mi (4.1 km) n; in Ste-Foy sector. 2115 rang Ste-Ange G2E 3L9. **Hours:** 6 pm-9:30 pm. Closed: 1/1, 12/24, 12/25; also Mon, Tues, 1/1-1/15 & 7/18-7/28. **Reservations:** suggested. **Features:** In an elegant rural home decorated with stuffed wild game, the intimate restaurant presents an impressive and varied menu that includes several varieties of foie gras. Flavorful specialties of wild game—including bison, elk, red deer, ostrich, caribou and wild boar—are what set this place apart. The owner/chef displays his talents through creative tasting menus. Casual dress; cocktails. **Parking:** on-site. **Cards:** AX, DC, MC, VI.

RISTORANTE MICHELANGELO　　*Menu on AAA.com*　**Lunch:** $20-$24 **Dinner:** $18-$40 **Phone:** 418/651-6262　㉘
(CAA)
Italian
Location: Corner of ave des Hotels; in Ste-Foy sector. 3111 chemin St-Louis G1W 1R6. **Hours:** 11:30 am-2:30 & 5:30-11 pm, Sat from 5:30 pm. Closed: 1/2, 12/24, 12/25. Sun & for lunch some holidays. **Reservations:** suggested. **Features:** Art Deco-inspired style punctuates the inviting and stylish dining room. Service is superior in all aspects. The menu of fine Italian cuisine lists risotto, steak tartare, seafood platter, milk-fed veal and exquisite pasta dishes, such as wonderful manicotti with tomato sauce. Dressy casual; cocktails. **Parking:** valet. **Cards:** AX, DC, MC, VI.

ST-FERREOL-LES-NEIGES pop. 2,014

──────── **WHERE TO STAY** ────────

CHALETS MONTMORENCY CONDOMINIUMS　　　　　　　　　　**Phone:** (418)826-2600
(CAA) (SAVE)
Condominium
| All Year | 1P: $89-$129 | 2P: $89-$129 | XP: $15 | F17 |

Location: On Hwy 360. 1768 ave Royale G0A 3R0. Fax: 418/826-1123. **Facility:** 33 units. 10 one-bedroom standard units with efficiencies, some with whirlpools. 10 one-, 5 two- and 8 three-bedroom suites ($129-$199), some with kitchens and/or whirlpools. 2 stories (no elevator), exterior corridors. **Parking:** on-site, winter plug-ins. **Terms:** check-in 4 pm, weekly rates available, package plans, pets (dogs only, $25 extra charge). **Amenities:** hair dryers. **Pool(s):** small outdoor, heated indoor. **Leisure Activities:** sauna, whirlpool, snowmobiling, mountain bike trails, hiking trails. *Fee:* downhill & cross country skiing. **Guest Services:** complimentary laundry, area transportation (fee)-ski hill. **Business Services:** PC. **Cards:** MC, VI. **Free Special Amenities:** room upgrade and preferred room (each subject to availability with advance reservations).

SOME UNITS

CHALETS-VILLAGE MONT-SAINTE-ANNE **Phone: (418)826-3331**
All Year 2P: $550-$4950
Location: On north side of Hwy 360; village center. 1815 boul Les Neiges G0A 3R0. Fax: 418/826-3331.
Historic Cottage **Facility:** These varied houses, some 200 years old, are in a village-like setting at the base of the mountain. 13 cottages, some with whirlpools. 2-3 stories, exterior corridors. **Parking:** on-site, winter plug-ins.
Terms: check-in 5 pm, 2-7 night minimum stay, 90 day cancellation notice-fee imposed, weekly rates available, package plans, small pets only ($50-$100 fee, in designated unit). **Amenities:** irons, hair dryers. **Leisure Activities:** cross country skiing, snowmobiling, ice skating, recreation programs. *Fee:* downhill skiing. **Guest Services:** complimentary laundry. **Business Services:** meeting rooms. **Cards:** MC, VI.

SOME UNITS

FEE

ST-ROMUALD pop. 10,825

——— **WHERE TO DINE** ———

RESTAURANT NORMANDIN **Lunch:** $5-$12 **Dinner:** $5-$12 **Phone:** 418/839-5861
Location: On Hwy 132. 2080 boul de la Rive-Sud G6W 2S6. **Hours:** 6 am-midnight, Thurs-2 am, Fri & Sat-3 am.
Canadian Closed: 12/25. **Reservations:** accepted. **Features:** The family restaurant prepares affordable comfort foods that include roasted chicken, hot chicken sandwiches, pasta, burgers and fries. Take-out service, a children's menu and cutely decorated desserts are among other offerings. Casual dress; cocktails. **Parking:** on-site. **Cards:** AX, DC, MC, VI.

SILLERY pop. 11,909 (See map and index starting on p. 517)

——— **WHERE TO DINE** ———

PAPARAZZI **Lunch:** $10-$16 **Dinner:** $13-$28 **Phone:** 418/683-8111 ⑱
Location: Between chemin St-Louis and boul Laurier; in Sillery sector. 1363 ave Maguire G1T 1Z2. **Hours:** 11:30 am-2:30 & 5-10 pm, Fri-11 pm, Sat & Sun from 5:30 pm. Closed: 12/24, 12/25. **Reservations:** accepted.
Italian **Features:** The informal suburban restaurant entices guests with Italian dishes and a sushi bar. Representative of menu offerings are preparations of pasta, meat, shrimp and tuna, as well as salmon tartare, foie gras and veal ravioli. Casual dress; cocktails. **Parking:** street. **Cards:** AX, CB, DC, DS, JC, MC, VI.

Parliament Buildings / © Andre Jenny

This ends listings for the Quebec Vicinity.
The following page resumes the alphabetical listings of cities in Quebec.

RIGAUD pop. 6,552

───── WHERE TO STAY ─────

HOWARD JOHNSON *Book at AAA.com*
Property failed to provide current rates
Phone: 450/458-7997

Small-scale Hotel
Location: Hwy 40, exit 17, then just ne. 93 Rt 201 J0P 1P0. **Fax:** 450/458-5563. **Facility:** Smoke free premises. 28 one-bedroom standard units, some with whirlpools. 2 stories (no elevator), interior corridors. **Parking:** on-site. **Terms:** check-in 4 pm, small pets only ($10 extra charge). **Amenities:** voice mail, hair dryers. **Guest Services:** wireless Internet. **Business Services:** meeting rooms. *Fee:* PC, fax.

SOME UNITS
FEE

───── WHERE TO DINE ─────

RESTAURANT RUBE
Lunch: $8-$19   **Dinner:** $12-$30   **Phone:** 450/458-5369
Steak & Seafood
Location: Hwy 40, exit 17, 0.6 mi (1 km) s. 147 Rt 201 J0P 1P0. **Hours:** 10 am-close. **Reservations:** suggested. **Features:** Steak and seafood top the menu of the lively pub and restaurant in a rural area. The atrium dining room affords pretty views of the forest. Patrons can sample filet mignon, New York steak, rack of lamb, surf and turf, Wiener schnitzel, chicken cod, sandwiches and salads. Casual dress; cocktails. **Parking:** on-site. **Cards:** AX, DC, MC, VI.

RIMOUSKI pop. 31,305

───── WHERE TO STAY ─────

COMFORT INN *Book great rates at AAA.com*
Phone: (418)724-2500

7/1-8/31 [CP]	1P: $120-$135	2P: $130-$150	XP: $10	F
6/1-6/30 [CP]	1P: $110-$120	2P: $120-$135	XP: $10	F
5/1-5/31 & 9/1-4/30 [CP]	1P: $105-$115	2P: $115-$125	XP: $10	F

Small-scale Hotel
Location: On Rt 132. 455 boul St-Germain ouest G5L 3P2. **Fax:** 418/724-6050. **Facility:** 80 one-bedroom standard units. 2 stories (no elevator), interior corridors. **Parking:** on-site, winter plug-ins. **Amenities:** irons, hair dryers. *Some: Fee:* DVD players. **Guest Services:** valet laundry, wireless Internet. **Cards:** AX, DC, MC, VI. *(See color ad card insert)*

SOME UNITS
FEE   FEE   FEE

HOTEL L'EMPRESS
Phone: 418/723-6944

5/1-6/21	1P: $105	2P: $105	XP: $10	F18
6/22-4/30	1P: $85	2P: $85	XP: $10	F18

Small-scale Hotel
Location: Hwy 20, exit 614, 2.1 mi (3.4 km) n. 360 Montee Industrielle & Commerciale G5M 1X1. **Fax:** 418/722-7710. **Facility:** 60 one-bedroom standard units, some with whirlpools. 2 stories, interior corridors. **Parking:** on-site, winter plug-ins. **Terms:** 7 day cancellation notice, [AP] & [CP] meal plans available, package plans. **Amenities:** high-speed Internet, hair dryers. **Dining:** 6 am-2 & 5-9 pm, Sat & Sun from 7 am, also, Restaurant L'Empress, see separate listing. **Leisure Activities:** snowmobiling. **Cards:** AX, CB, DC, DS, MC, VI. **Free Special Amenities:** local telephone calls and high-speed Internet.

SOME UNITS

HOTEL RIMOUSKI *Book at AAA.com*
Phone: 418/725-5000

7/1-8/31	1P: $112-$132	2P: $122-$142	XP: $10	F17
5/1-6/30 & 9/1-4/30	1P: $102-$122	2P: $112-$132	XP: $10	F17

Large-scale Hotel
Location: On Rt 132, corner of rue Julien-Rehel. 225 boul Rene-Lepage est G5L 1P2. **Fax:** 418/725-5725. **Facility:** 185 units. 138 one-bedroom standard units. 47 one-bedroom suites ($122-$142), some with whirlpools. 5 stories, interior corridors. **Parking:** on-site, winter plug-ins. **Terms:** 15 day cancellation notice. **Amenities:** voice mail, irons, hair dryers. *Some:* DVD players, video games (fee), CD players, high-speed Internet, dual phone lines, honor bars. **Pool(s):** heated indoor. **Leisure Activities:** sauna, whirlpool, waterslide, exercise room, spa. *Fee:* miniature golf. **Guest Services:** valet and coin laundry, wireless Internet. **Business Services:** conference facilities, business center. **Cards:** AX, DC, DS, MC, VI.

SOME UNITS
FEE

───── WHERE TO DINE ─────

RESTAURANT L'EMPRESS
Lunch: $8-$20   **Dinner:** $8-$30   **Phone:** 418/721-2222
Seafood
Location: Hwy 20, exit 614, 2.1 mi (3.4 km) n. 360 Montee Industrielle & Commerciale G5M 1X1. **Hours:** 6 am-2 & 4:30-9 pm, Sat & Sun 7 am-2 & 4-9 pm. **Reservations:** accepted. **Features:** This casual hotel eatery offers both table service and a self-serve cafeteria counter. While the house specialty is fish and seafood, including mussels and lobster, the menu is rounded out with other comfort foods like pork chops and roast beef. Breakfast specials include a selection of crepes. Casual dress; cocktails. **Parking:** on-site. **Cards:** MC, VI.

RESTAURANT NORMANDIN
Lunch: $5-$12   **Dinner:** $5-$12   **Phone:** 418/723-7233
Canadian
Location: On Rt 132, corner ave Leonidas. 405 boul Jessop G5L 1M9. **Hours:** 6 am-midnight, Thurs-1 am, Fri & Sat-3 am. **Reservations:** accepted. **Features:** The family restaurant prepares affordable comfort foods that include roasted chicken, hot chicken sandwiches, pasta, burgers and fries. Take-out service, a children's menu and cutely decorated desserts are among other offerings. Casual dress; cocktails. **Parking:** on-site. **Cards:** AX, DC, MC, VI.

ST-HUBERT
Lunch: $7-$20   **Dinner:** $7-$20   **Phone:** 418/723-4419
Canadian
Location: On Rt 132; centre. 185 boul Rene-Lepage est G5L 1P2. **Hours:** 10:30 am-10 pm. **Closed:** 12/25. **Reservations:** accepted. **Features:** The pleasantly decorated family-friendly restaurant serves affordable chicken dinners, ribs, club sandwiches, chicken wings, salads, soups and hot chicken sandwiches. The children's menu includes animal nuggets. Casual dress; cocktails. **Parking:** on-site. **Cards:** AX, DC, MC, VI.

RIVIERE-DU-LOUP pop. 17,772

———— WHERE TO STAY ————

COMFORT INN
Book great rates at AAA.com

Phone: (418)867-4162

7/1-8/31 [ECP]	1P: $110-$160	2P: $120-$170	XP: $10	F17
5/1-6/30 & 9/1-4/30 [ECP]	1P: $90-$110	2P: $100-$120	XP: $10	F17

Small-scale Hotel **Location:** Hwy 20, exit 507, just se; Hwy 85, exit 96 (Fraserville); follow signs. 85 boul Cartier G5R 4X4. Fax: 418/867-1687. **Facility:** 69 one-bedroom standard units. 2 stories (no elevator), interior corridors. **Parking:** on-site, winter plug-ins. **Terms:** pets (in smoking units). **Amenities:** irons, hair dryers. **Guest Services:** valet laundry. **Cards:** AX, CB, DC, DS, JC, MC, VI. *(See color ad card insert)*

SOME UNITS
(ASK) (SD) 🐕 🍴 🎥 💻 / ✕ 🛢 🖥 /

DAYS INN RIVIERE-DU-LOUP
Book great rates at AAA.com

Phone: (418)862-6354

7/1-9/3 [CP]	1P: $125-$185	2P: $125-$185	XP: $10	F17
5/1-6/30 & 9/4-4/30 [CP]	1P: $99-$145	2P: $99-$145	XP: $10	F17

Small-scale Hotel **Location:** Hwy 20, exit 503, 0.6 mi (1 km) e on Rt 132. 182 rue Fraser G5R 1C8. Fax: 418/862-7688. **Facility:** 50 units. 42 one-bedroom standard units, some with whirlpools. 8 cottages ($109-$155). 1-2 stories (no elevator), exterior corridors. **Parking:** on-site, winter plug-ins. **Terms:** package plans, pets ($10 extra charge). **Amenities:** irons, hair dryers. **Pool(s):** heated outdoor. **Guest Services:** valet laundry, wireless Internet. **Cards:** AX, DC, MC, VI. **Free Special Amenities:** continental breakfast and high-speed Internet.

SOME UNITS
(SD) 🐕 🍴 🏊 🛢 💻 / ✕ 🖥 /
FEE

ECONO LODGE
Book great rates at AAA.com

Phone: (418)867-8221

7/13-9/5 [CP]	1P: $99-$129	2P: $109-$169	XP: $15	F17
5/1-7/12 & 9/6-4/30 [CP]	1P: $89-$119	2P: $99-$159	XP: $15	F17

Small-scale Hotel **Location:** Hwy 20, exit 507, then just ne. 61 boul Cartier G5R 5Z3. Fax: 418/867-3092. **Facility:** 62 units. 56 one-bedroom standard units, some with suites ($99-$169). 3 stories, interior corridors. **Parking:** on-site, winter plug-ins. **Terms:** package plans, pets ($20 extra charge). **Amenities:** high-speed Internet, hair dryers. *Some:* DVD players. **Pool(s):** heated indoor. **Leisure Activities:** whirlpool, hiking trails, exercise room. **Guest Services:** valet laundry. **Business Services:** meeting rooms. **Cards:** AX, CB, DC, DS, JC, MC, VI. *(See color ad card insert)*

SOME UNITS
(ASK) (SD) 🍴 🏊 🎥 ✕ 💻 / 🛢 🖥 /
FEE

HOTEL LEVESQUE

Phone: (418)862-6927

7/1-8/31	1P: $119-$139	2P: $129-$149	XP: $15	F18
9/1-4/30	1P: $89-$119	2P: $99-$129	XP: $15	F18
5/1-6/30	1P: $79-$119	2P: $89-$129	XP: $15	F18

Small-scale Hotel **Location:** Hwy 20, exit 503, 0.8 mi (1.2 km) e on Rt 132. 171 rue Fraser G5R 1E2. Fax: 418/867-5827. **Facility:** 84 one-bedroom standard units, some with whirlpools. 2 stories (no elevator), interior corridors. **Parking:** on-site, winter plug-ins. **Terms:** [BP] & [MAP] meal plans available, package plans. **Amenities:** voice mail. *Some:* high-speed Internet, safes. **Dining:** La Terrasse, see separate listing. **Pool(s):** heated outdoor. **Leisure Activities:** saunas, whirlpool, snowmobiling, bicycles, playground, spa. **Guest Services:** sundries, valet laundry, wireless Internet. **Business Services:** conference facilities, administrative services (fee), PC. **Cards:** AX, DC, MC, VI. **Free Special Amenities:** newspaper and high-speed Internet.

SOME UNITS
🍴 🏊 ✕ 💻 / ✕ (VCR) 🛢 /
FEE

MOTEL AU VIEUX PILOTEUX

Phone: 418/867-2635

6/15-9/15	1P: $85-$145	2P: $85-$145	XP: $10	D10
5/1-6/14 & 9/16-4/30	1P: $60-$75	2P: $75-$90	XP: $10	D10

Motel **Location:** Hwy 20, exit 503, then 0.6 mi (1 km) e on Rt 132. 185 rue Fraser G5R 1E2. Fax: 418/867-1409. **Facility:** 23 one-bedroom standard units. 1 story, exterior corridors. **Parking:** on-site, winter plug-ins. **Terms:** cancellation fee imposed. **Amenities:** hair dryers. *Some:* high-speed Internet, irons. **Pool(s):** heated outdoor. **Leisure Activities:** snowmobiling, playground. **Guest Services:** valet laundry. **Cards:** AX, DC, MC, VI. **Free Special Amenities:** local telephone calls and high-speed Internet.

SOME UNITS
(SD) 🔌 🍴 🏊 🛢 / ✕ (VCR) /

———— WHERE TO DINE ————

LA TERRASSE

Lunch: $10-$20   **Dinner:** $18-$40   **Phone:** 418/862-6927

French **Location:** Hwy 20, exit 503, 0.8 mi (1.2 km) e on Rt 132; in Hotel Levesque. 171 rue Fraser G5R 1E2. **Hours:** 7 am-2 & 5:30-9 pm. **Reservations:** suggested. **Features:** An example of creative, market-fresh cuisine is the excellent smoked salmon. The menu also lists beef, pork and veal preparations. The small, pleasant dining room is elegantly appointed with sophisticated furnishings. Service is warm and attentive. Dressy casual; cocktails. **Parking:** on-site. **Cards:** AX, DC, MC, VI.

🍸

LE NOVELLO

Lunch: $10-$16   **Dinner:** $14-$17   **Phone:** 418/862-9895

Italian **Location:** 0.6 mi (1 km) w on Rt 132. 169 rue Fraser G5R 1E2. **Hours:** 11:30 am-2 & 5-9 pm, Sat & Sun from 5:30 pm. Closed: 12/24, 12/25. **Reservations:** accepted. **Features:** A moderately upscale appeal punctuates the casual, family-friendly bistro, which prepares thin-crust European-style pizza, veal and fresh pasta. Casual dress; cocktails. **Parking:** on-site. **Cards:** AX, DC, MC, VI.

RESTAURANT LE ST-PATRICE

Lunch: $10-$14   **Dinner:** $18-$24   **Phone:** 418/862-9895

French **Location:** Hwy 20, exit 503, 0.6 mi (1 km) e on Rt 132. 169 rue Fraser G5R 1E2. **Hours:** 11:30 am-2 & 5-9 pm, Sat from 5 pm, Sun 10 am-1 & 5-9 pm. Closed: 12/24, 12/25. **Reservations:** suggested. **Features:** The bright, open dining room—with an atrium that overlooks the grounds—is a great spot for casual dining. Among regional dishes are veal medallions, Kamouraska lamb, poached Atlantic salmon, seafood stew, rabbit and stuffed pasta. Under the same roof are adjoining restaurants serving Italian, bistro and traditional Quebecois fare. Cocktails. **Parking:** on-site. **Cards:** AX, DC, MC, VI.

RESTAURANT NORMANDIN

▽▽▽ ◆◆
Canadian

Lunch: $5-$15 **Dinner:** $5-$15 **Phone:** 418/867-1366
Location: Hwy 20, exit 507, just s. 83 boul Cartier G5R 2N1. **Hours:** 24 hours. **Reservations:** accepted. **Features:** The family restaurant prepares affordable comfort foods that include roasted chicken, hot chicken sandwiches, pasta, burgers and fries. Take-out service, a children's menu and cutely decorated desserts are among other offerings. Casual dress; cocktails. **Parking:** on-site. **Cards:** AX, MC, VI.

RESTAURANT O'GENTILLERIES

▽▽▽ ◆◆
Canadian

Lunch: $9-$14 **Dinner:** $14-$20 **Phone:** 418/860-4419
Location: Hwy 20, exit 503, then 1 km e, on Rt 132. 183 rue Fraser G5R 1E2. **Hours:** 6 am-9 pm. Closed: 12/25. **Reservations:** accepted. **Features:** This cozy creperie offers 17 varieties of crepes as well as salads, sandwiches, fajitas and soups. For breakfast, there are 72 meals from which to choose. Casual dress; cocktails. **Parking:** on-site. **Cards:** MC, VI.

ST-HUBERT

▽▽▽ ◆◆
Canadian
MC, VI.

Lunch: $7-$20 **Dinner:** $7-$20 **Phone:** 418/867-1830
Location: Hwy 20, exit 507. 80 boul Cartier G5R 2M9. **Hours:** 11 am-11 pm. Closed: 12/25. **Reservations:** accepted. **Features:** The pleasantly decorated family-friendly restaurant serves affordable chicken dinners, ribs, club sandwiches, chicken wings, salads, soups and hot chicken sandwiches. The children's menu includes animal nuggets. Casual dress; cocktails. **Parking:** on-site. **Cards:** AX, DC,

ROBERVAL pop. 10,906

——— **WHERE TO STAY** ———

HOTEL CHATEAU ROBERVAL

(CAA) (SAVE)
▽▽▽▽
Large-scale Hotel

Book great rates at AAA.com **Phone:** (418)275-7511

5/1-8/31	1P: $139	2P: $139	XP: $10	F18
9/1-4/30	1P: $119	2P: $119	XP: $10	F18

Location: On Hwy 169; centre. 1225 boul Marcotte G8H 2P1. Fax: 418/275-6853. **Facility:** 124 one-bedroom standard units, some with whirlpools. 3 stories, interior corridors. **Parking:** on-site, winter plug-ins. **Terms:** cancellation fee imposed, weekly rates available, package plans, $2 service charge, small pets only. **Amenities:** voice mail, hair dryers. *Some:* DVD players, irons. **Dining:** Restaurant L'Abordage, see separate listing. **Pool(s):** heated indoor. **Leisure Activities:** whirlpool, snowmobiling, snowmobile shelter. *Fee:* massage. **Guest Services:** valet laundry, wireless Internet. **Business Services:** conference facilities, PC. **Cards:** AX, MC, VI. **Free Special Amenities:** local telephone calls and high-speed Internet.

SOME UNITS
[S/D] 🛏 🍴 🍸 ⊠ ⊠ / ⊠ VCR 🔌 🖥 /
FEE

——— **WHERE TO DINE** ———

RESTAURANT L'ABORDAGE

▽▽▽▽
Quebecois

Lunch: $9-$12 **Dinner:** $16-$26 **Phone:** 418/275-7511
Location: On Hwy 169; centre. 1225 boul Marcotte G8H 2P1. **Hours:** 7 am-2 & 5-10 pm. **Reservations:** suggested. **Features:** The informal hotel restaurant presents a menu of affordable regional cuisine, including Lac-St-Jean tourtiere (meat pie), ouananiche (a regional fish), salmon, scallops, shrimp, supreme of chicken, Alberta filet mignon, sandwiches and children's dishes. Minaki, a popular blueberry-based aperitif, is a treat. Casual dress; cocktails. **Parking:** on-site. **Cards:** AX, DS, MC, VI.

🍸

ROSEMERE —See Montreal p. 493.

ROUYN-NORANDA pop. 28,270

——— **WHERE TO STAY** ———

BEST WESTERN ALBERT CENTRE-VILLE

▽▽▽
Small-scale Hotel

Book great rates at AAA.com **Phone:** 819/762-3545

All Year	1P: $82-$103	2P: $82-$103	XP: $10	F12

Location: Centre. 84 Principale Ave J9X 4P2. Fax: 819/762-7157. **Facility:** 50 one-bedroom standard units, some with whirlpools. 3 stories, interior corridors. **Parking:** on-site. **Terms:** 7 day cancellation notice, package plans. **Amenities:** irons, hair dryers. *Some: Fee:* DVD players. **Leisure Activities:** exercise room. **Guest Services:** valet laundry, wireless Internet. **Business Services:** meeting rooms. **Cards:** AX, MC, VI.

SOME UNITS
🍴 🍸 🖥 / ⊠ VCR 🔌
FEE FEE

COMFORT INN

▽▽▽
Small-scale Hotel

Book great rates at AAA.com **Phone:** (819)797-1313

All Year [CP]	1P: $80-$100	2P: $90-$110	XP: $10	F

Location: On Rt 117, 2.5 mi (4 km) s from town centre. 1295 rue Lariviere J9X 6M6. Fax: 819/797-9683. **Facility:** 79 one-bedroom standard units. 2 stories (no elevator), interior corridors. **Parking:** on-site, winter plug-ins. **Terms:** pets (in designated units). **Amenities:** voice mail, irons, hair dryers. **Guest Services:** valet laundry, wireless Internet. **Business Services:** meeting rooms. **Cards:** AX, DC, DS, MC, VI. *(See color ad card insert)*

SOME UNITS
(ASK) [S/D] 🛏 🍴 🖥 / ⊠ 🔌

ST-ANTOINE-DE-TILLY pop. 1,417

——— **WHERE TO STAY** ———

MANOIR DE TILLY

▽▽▽
Country Inn

Book at AAA.com **Phone:** (418)886-2407

All Year	1P: $121-$277	2P: $136-$307	XP: $30	D10

Location: Jct Hwy 20, exit 291, 5.3 mi (8.5 km) n on Rt 273; centre. Located in a quiet area. 3854 chemin de Tilly G0S 2C0. Fax: 418/886-2595. **Facility:** This contemporary inn, which overlooks the St. Lawrence River, includes a manor house built in 1786. 30 one-bedroom standard units, some with whirlpools. 3 stories (no elevator), interior corridors. **Parking:** on-site, winter plug-ins. **Terms:** check-in 4 pm, 3 day cancellation notice-fee imposed, [AP], [BP] & [MAP] meal plans available, package plans, small pets only ($25 extra charge). **Amenities:** hair dryers. **Leisure Activities:** spa. **Guest Services:** valet laundry, wireless Internet. **Business Services:** meeting rooms. **Cards:** AX, DC, MC, VI.

SOME UNITS
[S/D] 🛏 🍴 ⊠ / 🔌 /
FEE

ST-DENIS-SUR-RICHELIEU pop. 2,183

———— WHERE TO DINE ————

LES CHANTERELLES DU RICHELIEU   **Dinner: $20-$25**   **Phone: 450/787-1167**

▼▼▼▼▼   **Location:** Hwy 20, exit 113, just s of jct Rt 137 on Rt 133 N. 611 chemin des Patriotes J0H 1K0. **Hours:** Open 5/1-12/31 & 3/15-4/30; 5 pm-9 pm, Sun also 11 am-1 pm. Closed: Mon & Tues. **Reservations:** suggested.

French   **Features:** Fine regional French cuisine is served in a 1905 Victorian-style home. Among specialties are guinea fowl, quail, Quebec veal, filet mignon, sweetbreads and fresh fish. Dressy casual; cocktails. **Parking:** on-site. **Cards:** DC, MC, VI.

ST-DONAT pop. 3,444

———— WHERE TO STAY ————

HOTEL MONTCALM   **Phone: (819)424-1333**

▼▼▼▼ ▼▼▼▼   All Year   1P: $94-$125   2P: $98-$140   XP: $10   F18

           Location: 2.8 mi (4.4 km) s on Rt 125 from jct Rt 329, then 1.3 mi (2 km). Located in a quiet area. 251 chemin Fusey

Resort   J0T 2C0 (CP 299). **Fax:** 819/424-3622. **Facility:** The hotel is in a scenic setting on a lake on which no

Large-scale Hotel   motorized boating is permitted. 32 units. 24 one-bedroom standard units. 8 cottages ($175-$325). 3 stories (no elevator), interior corridors. *Bath:* some combo or shower only. **Parking:** on-site, winter plug-ins. **Terms:** check-in 4 pm, 3 day cancellation notice-fee imposed, weekly rates available, [BP] & [MAP] meal plans available, package plans, no pets allowed (in cottages only). **Amenities:** irons, hair dryers. **Pool(s):** heated indoor. **Leisure Activities:** saunas, boating, canoeing, paddleboats, windsurfing, fishing, 2 lighted tennis courts, cross country skiing, snowmobiling, bicycles, hiking trails, exercise room, spa, shuffleboard. *Fee:* downhill skiing. **Guest Services:** sundries, area transportation. **Business Services:** meeting rooms, PC (fee). **Cards:** AX, DC, MC, VI.

SOME UNITS

（ASK）（S/D）（¶¶）（Y）（≈）（⊠）（⊼）／（⊠）（🕿）（🖥）（🖥）（🖥）／

STE-ADELE

———— WHERE TO STAY ————

HOTEL LE CHANTECLER   *Book great rates at AAA.com*   **Phone: (450)229-3555**

(CAA) (SAVE)   All Year [BP]   1P: $139-$210   2P: $150-$220   XP: $32   F18

    Location: Hwy 15, exit 67 northbound, 0.8 mi (1.3 km) n on boul Ste-Adele, just w on rue Morin, then 0.4 mi (0.6 km) n; exit 69 southbound, 0.9 mi (1.5 km) sw on Hwy 370, then 0.4 mi (0.6 km) n. 1474 chemin Chantecler J8B 1A2.

▼▼▼▼▼▼   **Fax:** 450/229-5593. **Facility:** This four-season family resort near a major ski hill and bike path offers

Resort   cottages and a fieldstone hotel with standard rooms and kitchen suites. 215 units. 181 one-bedroom

Large-scale Hotel   standard units, some with whirlpools. 28 one-bedroom suites with whirlpools, some with kitchens. 6 cottages. 2-7 stories (no elevator), interior/exterior corridors. **Parking:** on-site. **Terms:** 1-2 night minimum stay - seasonal and/or weekends, cancellation fee imposed, [AP] & [MAP] meal plans available, package plans. **Amenities:** voice mail, irons, radios. *Some:* video games (fee), honor bars. **Dining:** 7 am-10 pm, cocktails, entertainment. **Pool(s):** heated indoor. **Leisure Activities:** saunas, whirlpool, lifeguard on duty, rental boats, rental canoes, rental paddleboats, golf-9 holes, 6 lighted tennis courts, petanque, downhill & cross country skiing, snowmobiling, ice skating, tobogganing, sleigh rides, recreation programs, squash courts, hiking trails, exercise room, spa, horseshoes, shuffleboard, volleyball. *Fee:* kayak, horseback riding, game room. **Guest Services:** gift shop, valet laundry, area transportation-ski hill Chantecler. **Business Services:** conference facilities, administrative services (fee). **Cards:** AX, CB, DC, DS, JC, MC, VI.

SOME UNITS

（S/D）（¶¶）（Y）（≈）（⊠）（⊡）（🖥）／（⊠）（⊼）（VCR）（🖥）（🖥）／
FEE

HOTEL MONT-GABRIEL   *Book great rates at AAA.com*   **Phone: (450)229-3547**

(CAA) (SAVE)   12/22-4/30   1P: $109-$195   2P: $109-$195   XP: $15   F

    9/16-10/15   1P: $119-$179   2P: $119-$179   XP: $15   F

▼▼▼▼ ▼▼▼▼   10/16-12/21   1P: $96-$179   2P: $96-$179   XP: $15   F

    5/1-9/15   1P: $96-$179   2P: $96-$179   XP: $20   F

Resort   **Location:** Hwy 15, exit 64, 1.3 mi (2 km) w. 1699 chemin Mont-Gabriel J8B 1A5. **Fax:** 450/229-7034. **Facility:** The

Large-scale Hotel   family resort has good- to very good-sized guestrooms and a choice of three cottages. Resort facilities include downhill skiing, golf and tennis. 130 units. 126 one-bedroom standard units, some with whirlpools. 1 vacation home and 3 cottages, some with whirlpools. 3 stories (no elevator), interior/exterior corridors. **Parking:** on-site. **Terms:** check-in 4 pm, 14 day cancellation notice-fee imposed, [AP] & [MAP] meal plans available, package plans, $2 service charge. **Amenities:** voice mail, irons, hair dryers. **Dining:** 2 restaurants, 7 am-10 pm. **Pool(s):** heated outdoor, heated indoor. **Leisure Activities:** sauna, whirlpools, 6 tennis courts, cross country skiing, snowmobiling, tobogganing, recreation programs, hiking trails, playground, exercise room, spa. *Fee:* golf-18 holes, downhill skiing, tubing in winter, dog sleigh, skates, snowshoes, game room. **Guest Services:** gift shop, wireless Internet. **Business Services:** meeting rooms, PC. **Cards:** AX, MC, VI.

SOME UNITS

（S/D）（¶¶）（Y）（≈）（⊠）（⊼）（🖥）／（⊠）／
FEE

L'EAU A LA BOUCHE   *Book at AAA.com*   **Phone: (450)229-2991**

▼▼▼▼ ▼▼▼▼   All Year   1P: $155-$300   2P: $185-$330

    Location: Hwy 15, exit 67, 2.8 mi (4.5 km) n on Rt 117. Located in a quiet area. 3003 boul Ste-Adele J8B 2N6.

Country Inn   **Fax:** 450/229-7573. **Facility:** In a picturesque mountain setting, this country inn features luxurious rooms that are individually decorated with designer touches. 21 one-bedroom standard units, some with whirlpools. 3 stories (no elevator), interior corridors. **Parking:** on-site. **Terms:** check-in 4 pm, 2 night minimum stay - weekends, 14 day cancellation notice-fee imposed, [BP] & [MAP] meal plans available, package plans. **Amenities:** voice mail, irons, hair dryers. *Some:* CD players. **Dining:** restaurant, see separate listing. **Pool(s):** small heated outdoor. **Leisure Activities:** sauna, whirlpool, steamroom, hiking trails. **Guest Services:** valet laundry, wireless Internet. **Business Services:** meeting rooms, PC. **Cards:** AX, DC, MC.

SOME UNITS

（¶¶）（Y）（≈）（⊠）（⊠）（🖥）／（VCR）／

LE CHATEAU SAINTE-ADELE *Book at AAA.com* **Phone:** 450/229-9192

▼▼ ▼▼
Small-scale Hotel

Property failed to provide current rates

Location: Hwy 15, exit 67 northbound, 2.8 mi (4.5 km) n on Rt 117; exit 69 southbound, just n. 3080 boul Ste-Adele J8B 2N5. **Fax:** 450/229-6332. **Facility:** 47 units. 39 one-bedroom standard units, some with efficiencies and/or whirlpools. 8 one-bedroom suites with whirlpools. 2-3 stories (no elevator), interior corridors. **Parking:** on-site. **Amenities:** hair dryers. **Pool(s):** outdoor, heated indoor. **Leisure Activities:** snowmobiling, exercise room. **Business Services:** meeting rooms.

SOME UNITS

〔▯▮〕〔▼〕〔➤〕〔▭〕 / 〔✕〕〔▮〕〔▱〕 /

────── **WHERE TO DINE** ──────

CHEZ MILOT **Lunch:** $7-$25 **Dinner:** $14-$31 **Phone:** 450/229-2838

▼▼ ▼▼
French

Location: Corner of rue Notre-Dame. 958 rue Valiquette J8B 2M3. **Hours:** 11:30 am-2 & 5-10 pm, Fri-11 pm, Sat & Sun 11 am-2 & 5-10 pm. Closed: 12/25. **Reservations:** accepted. **Features:** A good selection of wines complements such dishes as the specialty mussels—as well as rack of lamb, pasta, veal, steak, chicken and seafood. Waffles, cakes and creme brulee beckon from the dessert menu. The charming terrace is covered and heated. Casual dress; cocktails. **Parking:** on-site. **Cards:** AX, DC, MC, VI.

RESTAURANT LA CLEF DES CHAMPS **Dinner:** $22-$36 **Phone:** 450/229-2857

▼▼▼ ▼▼
French

Location: Hwy 15, exit 69, 0.6 mi (1 km) e. 875 chemin Pierre-Peladeau J8B 1Z3. **Hours:** 5 pm-11 pm. Closed: Mon 9/6-6/30; may close 3 weeks in April. **Reservations:** suggested. **Features:** The small, family-run restaurant reposes in a lovely Laurentian hillside setting. Gourmet cuisine includes a noteworthy selection of game specialties. Saturday diners can sample the degustation. Creme brulee and assorted cakes are excellent desserts. Casual dress; cocktails. **Parking:** on-site. **Cards:** AX, DC, MC, VI.

〔▼〕

RESTAURANT L'EAU A LA BOUCHE **Dinner:** $38-$52 **Phone:** 450/229-2991

▼▼▼ ▼▼▼
French

Location: Hwy 15, exit 67, 2.8 mi (4.5 km) n on Rt 117; in L'Eau A La Bouche. 3003 boul Ste-Adele J8B 2N6. **Hours:** 6 pm-9 pm, Fri & Sat-9:30 pm. **Reservations:** suggested. **Features:** The internationally recognized chef puts heart and soul into preparations of French-influenced regional cuisine. Notable dishes include pan-seared scallops, foie gras, swordfish filet, roasted rack of lamb, venison and Quebec pork tenderloin. Dressy casual; cocktails. **Parking:** on-site. **Cards:** AX, DC, MC, VI. **Country Inn**

STE-AGATHE-DES-MONTS pop. 7,116

────── **WHERE TO DINE** ──────

CREPERIE LA QUIMPERLAISE **Lunch:** $7-$30 **Dinner:** $7-$30 **Phone:** 819/326-1776

▼▼ ▼▼
Canadian

Location: Corner of rue St-Louis; centre. 11 chemin Tour du Lac J8C 1A6. **Hours:** 4:30 pm-10 pm, Sat & Sun from 11 am. Closed: 12/25; also Mon & Tues. **Reservations:** suggested. **Features:** Comfortable decor enhances the casual dining room. The house specialty is crepes, of which specials are posted daily. The menu also features large salads, fondue, soup, steak and lots of fresh seafood, including delicious coquille St. Jacques. Casual dress; cocktails. **Parking:** on-site. **Cards:** AX, MC, VI.

STE-ANNE-DE-BEAUPRE pop. 2,752

────── **WHERE TO STAY** ──────

COMFORT SUITES *Book great rates at AAA.com* **Phone:** (418)827-1570

All Year [CP]	1P: $139-$170	2P: $139-$170	XP: $10	F18

(CAA) (SAVE)
▼▼▼ ◆
Small-scale Hotel

Location: On Hwy 138. 9800 boul Ste-Anne G0A 3C0. **Fax:** 418/827-1601. **Facility:** 47 one-bedroom suites with efficiencies. 3 stories, interior corridors. **Parking:** on-site, winter plug-ins. **Terms:** check-in 4 pm, cancellation fee imposed. **Amenities:** irons, hair dryers. **Guest Services:** coin laundry, wireless Internet. **Business Services:** meeting rooms, PC. **Cards:** AX, DC, DS, MC, VI. **Free Special Amenities:** continental breakfast and high-speed Internet. *(See color ad and card insert)*

SOME UNITS

〔Sᴅ〕〔▮▸〕〔▮〕〔▱〕〔▭〕 /〔✕〕/

MANOIR STE-ANNE **Phone:** 418/827-8383

6/23-9/10	1P: $75-$85	2P: $95-$125	XP: $10	F13
12/24-4/30	1P: $75-$85	2P: $85-$115	XP: $10	F13
9/11-12/23	1P: $55-$75	2P: $75-$95	XP: $10	F13
5/1-6/22	1P: $55-$65	2P: $65-$85	XP: $10	F13

(CAA) (SAVE)
▼▼ ▼▼
Motel

Location: On Hwy 138. 9776 boul Ste-Anne G0A 3C0. **Fax:** 418/827-8400. **Facility:** 27 one-bedroom standard units. 2 stories (no elevator), exterior corridors. **Parking:** on-site, winter plug-ins. **Terms:** check-in 4 pm, cancellation fee imposed, [CP] meal plan available, small pets only. **Leisure Activities:** snowmobiling. *Fee:* snowmobile shelter. **Guest Services:** coin laundry. **Business Services:** meeting rooms. **Cards:** AX, CB, DC, DS, MC, VI. **Free Special Amenities:** continental breakfast and local telephone calls.

SOME UNITS

〔🛏〕〔▮▸〕〔▭〕 /〔✕〕〔▮〕〔▱〕 /

────── **WHERE TO DINE** ──────

RESTAURANT LE MARIE BEAUPRE **Lunch:** $7-$10 **Dinner:** $7-$19 **Phone:** 418/827-3446

▼▼ ▼▼
Canadian

Location: On Hwy 138. 9749 boul Ste-Anne G0A 3C0. **Hours:** 6 am-11 pm, Fri & Sat-2 am. Closed: 12/25. **Reservations:** accepted. **Features:** Near Ste-Anne-de-Beaupre shrine, the restaurant serves divine family food, including burgers, salads, rib steaks, club sandwiches, roasted chicken, hot chicken sandwiches and chicken pot pie. No meal is complete without dessert, and some winners here include coconut cream pie, sugar pie, apple turnovers and ice cream sundaes. Casual dress; cocktails. **Parking:** on-site. **Cards:** AX, DC, MC, VI.

STE-ANNE-DE-BELLEVUE —See Montreal p. 493.

STE-ANNE-DES-MONTS pop. 5,511

—————— WHERE TO STAY ——————

MOTEL BEAURIVAGE
Phone: (418)763-2291

(CAA) (SAVE)

▼▼▼ ▼▼▼
Motel

6/21-8/31	1P: $60-$140	2P: $75-$160	XP: $10	F12
5/1-6/20 & 9/1-10/15	1P: $50-$100	2P: $55-$110	XP: $10	F12

Location: Just off Rt 132. 245 1ere ave ouest G4V 1E3. Fax: 418/763-7434. **Facility:** 47 units. 46 one-bedroom standard units, some with efficiencies. 1 cottage. 1 story, interior/exterior corridors. *Bath:* combo or shower only. **Parking:** on-site. **Terms:** open 5/1-10/15, office hours 7 am-11 pm, small pets only. **Amenities:** irons, hair dryers. **Dining:** 6:30-10 am, Sat & Sun-noon. **Leisure Activities:** miniature golf, playground. **Guest Services:** wireless Internet. **Cards:** AX, MC, VI.

SOME UNITS

[icons]

—————— *The following lodging was either not evaluated or did not* ——————
meet AAA rating requirements but is listed for your information only.

GITE DU MONT-ALBERT
Phone: 418-763-2288

(fyi)

Not evaluated. **Location:** On Rt 299; in Parc de la Gaspesie. 2001 Rt du Parc G4V 2E4. Facilities, services, and decor characterize a mid-range property.

—————— WHERE TO DINE ——————

RESTAURANT GITE DU MONT-ALBERT   *Menu on AAA.com*   **Lunch:** $17-$21   **Dinner:** $33-$39   **Phone:** 418/763-2288

(CAA)

▼▼▼ ▼▼▼
Canadian

Location: On Rt 299; in Parc de la Gaspesie; in Gite du Mont-Albert. 2001 Rt du Parc G4V 2E4. **Hours:** Open 5/1-10/29 & 12/20-4/30; 7 am-9:30, noon-2 & 6-9 pm, Sun 7 am-9:30 & 6-9 pm; Sunday brunch by reservation, 11 am & 1 pm. **Reservations:** suggested. **Features:** The tranquil, forested surroundings set the scene for this romantic dining room overlooking Mont-Albert, a scenic mountain that loses its snow caps for a few weeks each summer. Casual dress; cocktails. **Parking:** on-site. **Cards:** AX, DC, MC, VI.

[icon]

STE-CATHERINE-DE-LA-JACQUES-CARTIER —See Quebec p. 550.

STE-DOROTHEE —See Montreal p. 495.

STE-FLAVIE pop. 919

—————— WHERE TO DINE ——————

CAPITAINE HOMARD   **Lunch:** $9-$30   **Dinner:** $9-$30   **Phone:** 418/775-8046

▼▼▼ ▼▼▼
Seafood

Location: On Rt 132, 1.5 mi (2.5 km) w of village. 180 Rt de la Mer G0J 2L0. **Hours:** Open 5/1-9/30; 11 am-11 pm. **Reservations:** required, 5/1-6/30 & 9/1-9/30. **Features:** The casual, seafront restaurant delivers specialties of fresh boiled lobster, seafood bouillabaisse, seafood crepes, fried clams, mussels, surf 'n' turf, lobster club sandwiches and maplewood-smoked salmon. A red tin roof sits atop the white, wood-shingled exterior. The dining room decor is decidedly nautical, with fish nets and fishing apparel strung from the ceiling. After dining, guests may shop for a maritime souvenir in the gift shop or purchase fresh fish and seafood in the fish market. Casual dress; cocktails. **Parking:** on-site. **Cards:** AX, DC, MC, VI.

[icons]

STE-FOY —See Quebec p. 550.

STE-JULIE —See Montreal p. 495.

STE-MARGUERITE-ESTEREL pop. 1,600

—————— WHERE TO DINE ——————

LE BISTRO A CHAMPLAIN   **Dinner:** $22-$48   **Phone:** 450/228-4988

▼▼▼ ▼▼▼ ▼▼▼ ▼▼▼
Regional French

Location: Hwy 15, exit 69, 7.8 mi (12.5 km) e on Rt 370. 75 chemin Masson J0T 1L0. **Hours:** 6 pm-10 pm. Closed: 12/24, 12/25; also Tues 11/1-4/15, Mon. **Reservations:** suggested. **Features:** The restored general store now functions as an upscale traditional Quebec dining room, decorated with magnificent works of modern art by Riopelle. Complex and eclectic dishes line a menu complemented by an exceptional wine list. Presentations are creative. Tours of the owner's vast wine cellar are offered. Casual dress; cocktails. **Parking:** on-site. **Cards:** AX, DC, JC, MC, VI.

[icon]

STE-MARIE pop. 11,320

—————— WHERE TO DINE ——————

RESTAURANT NORMANDIN   **Lunch:** $5-$12   **Dinner:** $5-$12   **Phone:** 418/387-3874

▼▼▼ ▼▼▼
Canadian

Location: Between Hwy 73 and 173. 525 route Cameron G6E 1B1. **Hours:** 6 am-midnight, Thurs-2 am, Fri & Sat-3 am. Closed: 12/25. **Reservations:** accepted. **Features:** The family restaurant prepares affordable comfort foods that include roasted chicken, hot chicken sandwiches, pasta, burgers and fries. Take-out service, a children's menu and cutely decorated desserts are among other offerings. Casual dress. **Parking:** on-site. **Cards:** AX, DC, MC, VI.

STE-MARTHE pop. 1,094

———— WHERE TO STAY ————

AUBERGE DES GALLANT   **Phone:** 450/459-4241
▼▼▼ All Year   1P: $119-$229   2P: $130-$250   XP: $25   F16
Country Inn **Location:** 5.3 mi (8.5 km) w on chemin St-Henri from Hwy 201. 1171 chemin St-Henri J0P 1W0. **Fax:** 450/459-4667.
Facility: A trout pond is the centerpiece of lovely gardens surrounding this contemporary country inn, which offers many rooms with balconies and fireplaces. Smoke free premises. 25 one-bedroom standard units, some with whirlpools. 2 stories (no elevator), interior corridors. **Parking:** on-site, winter plug-ins. **Terms:** 2 night minimum stay - weekends, 14 day cancellation notice-fee imposed, [AP], [BP], [CP] & [MAP] meal plans available, package plans, small pets only ($25 fee). **Amenities:** voice mail, irons, hair dryers. **Dining:** restaurant, see separate listing. **Pool(s):** heated outdoor. **Leisure Activities:** sauna, cross country skiing, bicycles, hiking trails, playground, exercise room, spa, volleyball. **Guest Services:** valet laundry. **Business Services:** meeting rooms, PC. **Cards:** AX, MC, VI.

SOME UNITS
🅵 🍴 ➰ 🗙 ✕ 💻 / VCR
FEE

———— WHERE TO DINE ————

AUBERGE DES GALLANT DINING ROOM   **Lunch:** $16-$27   **Dinner:** $21-$55   **Phone:** 450/459-4241
▼▼▼ **Location:** 5.3 mi (8.5 km) w on chemin St-Henri from jct Hwy 201; in Auberge des Gallant. 1171 chemin St-Henri J0P
Regional French 1W0. **Hours:** 8 am-10 pm, Sat-11 pm, Sun-9 pm. **Reservations:** suggested. **Features:** Regional menu selections include fresh fish, seafood, veal and lamb. The dining room has the cozy, quiet ambience of a casual country inn. Guests can enjoy unhurried relaxation and good food during the restaurant's Sunday brunch. Casual dress; cocktails. **Parking:** on-site. **Cards:** AX, DC, MC, VI. **Country Inn**   ⓨ

ST-FAUSTIN-LAC-CARRE pop. 1,600

———— WHERE TO STAY ————

MOTEL SUR LA COLLINE   **Phone:** (819)688-2102
▼▼ 12/16-4/30 [CP]   1P: $80-$152   2P: $80-$152   XP: $15   F12
    6/16-10/15 [CP]   1P: $70-$152   2P: $70-$152   XP: $15   F12
Motel 5/1-6/15 & 10/16-12/15 [CP]   1P: $60-$152   2P: $60-$152   XP: $15   F12
Location: On Rt 117, 2.5 mi (4 km) n of exit for city. 357 Rt 117 J0T 1J2. **Fax:** 819/688-2582. **Facility:** 27 one-bedroom standard units, some with efficiencies and/or whirlpools. 1-2 stories, interior/exterior corridors. *Bath:* combo or shower only. **Parking:** on-site, winter plug-ins. **Terms:** 2 night minimum stay - weekends, 15 day cancellation notice-fee imposed, package plans, small pets only ($15 extra charge). **Amenities:** *Some:* hair dryers. **Pool(s):** heated outdoor. **Cards:** AX, DC, DS, MC, VI.

SOME UNITS
(ASK) SⒹ 🛏 ➰ 🅟 💻 / ✕ 🖼 /
FEE

———— WHERE TO DINE ————

LE P'TIT STOP   **Lunch:** $4-$8   **Dinner:** $4-$8   **Phone:** 819/688-3111
▼ **Location:** On Rt 117. 1176 Rt 117 J0T 1J3. **Hours:** Open 5/1-10/30 & 12/21-4/30; 11 am-8 pm, Fri & Sun-9 pm.
Canadian Closed: 1/1, 12/25. **Reservations:** not accepted. **Features:** The roadside diner serves hamburgers made from 100 percent fresh beef, as well as grilled cheese, hot dogs and poutine (fries with curd cheese and gravy). Patrons place their order at the counter and then wait to have it brought to their table. Casual dress.
Parking: on-site.

ST-FELICIEN pop. 10,622

———— WHERE TO STAY ————

HOTEL DU JARDIN   **Phone:** (418)679-8422
(CAA) (SAVE) 5/1-9/30   1P: $139-$190   2P: $149-$190   XP: $10   F19
           10/1-4/30   1P: $95-$190   2P: $105-$190   XP: $10   F19
▼▼▼ **Location:** On Hwy 167. 1400 boul du Jardin G8K 2N8. **Fax:** 418/679-4459. **Facility:** 85 one-bedroom standard
Large-scale Hotel units, some with whirlpools. 6 stories, interior corridors. **Parking:** on-site, winter plug-ins. **Terms:** [CP] & [MAP] meal plans available. **Amenities:** hair dryers. *Some:* DVD players, irons. **Dining:** L'Oasis, see separate listing. **Pool(s):** heated indoor. **Leisure Activities:** sauna, whirlpool, snowmobiling, exercise room, spa. **Guest Services:** valet laundry. **Business Services:** conference facilities, PC. **Cards:** AX, DC, MC, VI. **Free Special Amenities:** local telephone calls and high-speed Internet.

SOME UNITS
🛏 🍴 ⓨ ➰ 🗙 / ✕ VCR 🅟 💻 /

———— WHERE TO DINE ————

L'OASIS   **Lunch:** $9-$13   **Dinner:** $17-$30   **Phone:** 418/679-8422
(CAA) **Location:** On Hwy 167; in Hotel du Jardin. 1400 boul du Jardin G8K 2N8. **Hours:** 6:30-10 am, 11:30-1:30 & 5:30-
▼▼▼ 10 pm. Closed: for lunch 7/1-8/31. **Reservations:** suggested. **Features:** This comfortable hotel dining room
French offers fine regional cuisine, including a multi-course tasting menu. Dishes include three styles of mussels, escargots, filet mignon, Chateaubriand beef, salmon, scallops, scampis, smoked trout, Saguenay-style "tourtiere" meat pie, pasta and club sandwiches. Dressy casual; cocktails. **Parking:** on-site. **Cards:** AX, MC, VI.   ⓨ

ST-FERREOL-LES-NEIGES —See Quebec p. 552.

ST-GEORGES (BEAUCE) pop. 20,100

——— WHERE TO STAY ———

COMFORT INN *Book great rates at AAA.com*   **Phone:** (418)227-1227
(CAA) (SAVE)   All Year   1P: $80-$135   2P: $85-$165   XP: $10   F12
Motel   **Location:** On Rt 173, just n of jct Rt 204 W. Located on busy thoroughfare. 16525 boul Lacroix G5Y 2G2. **Fax:** 418/228-6208. **Facility:** 51 units. 47 one-bedroom standard units, some with whirlpools. 4 one-bedroom suites, some with kitchens. 3 stories (no elevator); interior/exterior corridors. *Bath:* combo or shower only. **Parking:** on-site, winter plug-ins. **Terms:** package plans, small pets only ($25 extra charge). **Amenities:** voice mail, hair dryers. *Some:* irons. **Dining:** 11 am-11 pm, Fri & Sat-midnight, cocktails. **Guest Services:** valet laundry, wireless Internet. **Business Services:** meeting rooms. **Cards:** AX, DC, DS, MC, VI.
(See color ad card insert)

SOME UNITS
(S)(fee) 🛏 🍴 🍽 💻 / ✕ 🔌 🖥 / FEE   FEE

GOUVERNEUR HOTEL ST-GEORGES   *Book at AAA.com*   **Phone:** 418/228-6607
Property failed to provide current rates
Small-scale Hotel   **Location:** Just w on 118ieme rue from Rt 173; centre. 11531 1ere Ave G5Y 2C7. **Fax:** 418/227-4253. **Facility:** 55 units. 53 one-bedroom standard units, some with whirlpools. 2 one-bedroom suites. 2 stories, interior corridors. *Bath:* combo or shower only. **Parking:** on-site. **Amenities:** irons, hair dryers. **Dining:** Mondo Resto Bar, see separate listing. **Leisure Activities:** exercise room. *Fee:* massage. **Guest Services:** valet laundry. **Business Services:** meeting rooms, business center.

SOME UNITS
🍴 🍽 💻 / ✕ (VCR) 🖥 / FEE

——— WHERE TO DINE ———

LA TABLE DU PERE NATURE   **Lunch:** $10-$15   **Dinner:** $23-$30   **Phone:** 418/227-0888
Regional French   **Location:** Corner of 107th est rue, just w of jct Rt 173. 10735 1ere Ave G5Y 2B8. **Hours:** 11:30 am-2 & 6-10 pm, Sat from 6 pm, Sun 5 pm-9 pm. **Closed:** 12/24, 12/25. **Reservations:** suggested. **Features:** An excellent variety of wines complements flavorful and creative presentations of lamb, Atlantic salmon, lobster, filet mignon, milk-fed veal and Quebec pork. Plants, fresh flowers, candles and interesting art enhance the romantic ambience of the intimate dining room, set in a colorful windmill. The terrace opens seasonally. Casual dress; cocktails. **Parking:** on-site. **Cards:** AX, DC, MC, VI.

MONDO RESTO BAR   **Lunch:** $7-$24   **Dinner:** $7-$24   **Phone:** 418/228-4133
Italian   **Location:** Just w on 118ieme rue from Rt 173; centre; in Gouverneur Hotel St-Georges. 11615 1re Ave G5Y 2C7. **Hours:** 7 am-11 pm, Thurs-midnight, Fri-4 am, Sat 8 am-4 am, Sun 8 am-11 pm. **Reservations:** accepted. **Features:** The casual restaurant focuses its menu on light meals. Among offerings are delicious wood-oven pizzas, pasta, steaks, salads, stir-fries, scampi, shrimp, chicken supreme and veal. Casual dress; cocktails. **Parking:** street. **Cards:** AX, DC, MC, VI.   🍽

ST-HUBERT   **Lunch:** $6-$12   **Dinner:** $7-$20   **Phone:** 418/227-0001
Canadian   **Location:** On Rt 173, just n of jct Rt 204 W. 16505 boul Lacroix G5Y 2G2. **Hours:** 11 am-11 pm, Fri & Sat-1 am. **Reservations:** accepted. **Features:** The pleasantly decorated family-friendly restaurant serves affordable chicken dinners, ribs, club sandwiches, chicken wings, salads, soups and hot chicken sandwiches. The children's menu includes animal nuggets. Casual dress; cocktails. **Parking:** on-site. **Cards:** AX, DC, MC, VI.   🍽

ST-HONORE-DE-TEMISCOUATA pop. 804

——— WHERE TO STAY ———

MOTEL JASPER   **Phone:** 418/497-2322
   5/1-10/31   1P: $60-$68   2P: $68-$74   XP: $6   D3
   11/1-4/30   1P: $56-$60   2P: $64-$68   XP: $6   D3
Motel   **Location:** On Rt 185. 657 Rt 185 G0L 3K0. **Fax:** 418/497-1522. **Facility:** 12 one-bedroom standard units. 1 story, exterior corridors. **Parking:** on-site. **Terms:** [AP] meal plan available, small pets only. **Amenities:** *Some:* DVD players, hair dryers. **Cards:** AX, JC, MC, VI.

SOME UNITS
(ASK) (S)(fee) 🛏 🍴 / ✕ (VCR) 🌀 🖥 /

ST-HUBERT-DE-RIVERE-DU-LOUP —See Montreal p. 494.

ST-HYACINTHE pop. 38,739

——— WHERE TO STAY ———

HOTEL DES SEIGNEURS SAINT-HYACINTHE   *Book at AAA.com*   **Phone:** (450)774-3810
   All Year   1P: $110-$300   2P: $110-$300   XP: $15   F18
Large-scale Hotel   **Location:** Hwy 20, exit 130S, just e on rue Gauvin from boul Laframboise. 1200 rue Johnson J2S 7K7. **Fax:** 450/774-2060. **Facility:** 290 units. 279 one-bedroom standard units, some with whirlpools. 11 one-bedroom suites ($225-$375) with whirlpools, some with kitchens. 13 stories, interior corridors. **Parking:** on-site, winter plug-ins. **Terms:** [AP], [BP] & [MAP] meal plans available, package plans, pets (in designated areas). **Amenities:** video games (fee), voice mail, hair dryers. *Some:* high-speed Internet (fee), irons. **Dining:** Restaurant Les Quatre Saisons, see separate listing. **Pool(s):** heated outdoor, heated indoor. **Leisure Activities:** sauna, whirlpool, racquetball court, snowmobiling, limited exercise equipment. **Guest Services:** gift shop, valet laundry, wireless Internet. **Business Services:** conference facilities. **Cards:** AX, DC, DS, MC, VI.

SOME UNITS
(ASK) (S)(fee) 🛏 🍴 🍽 🏊 ✕ 📷 💻 / ✕ (VCR) 🖥 / FEE

HOTEL LE DAUPHIN ST-HYACINTHE

▼▼▼▼ All Year **1P:** $79-$89 **2P:** $89-$99 **XP:** $10 F18

Phone: (450)774-4418

Location: Hwy 20, exit 130S, 0.3 mi (0.5 km) s on boul Laframboise, then e on rue Gauvin. Located next to Convention Small-scale Hotel Centre. 1250 rue Johnson ouest J2S 7K7. Fax: 450/774-3291. **Facility:** 76 one-bedroom standard units, some with efficiencies and/or whirlpools. 2 stories, interior corridors. **Parking:** on-site, winter plug-ins. **Amenities:** high-speed Internet, voice mail, safes, irons, hair dryers. **Guest Services:** sundries, valet and coin laundry. **Business Services:** meeting rooms, PC. **Cards:** AX, MC, VI.

SOME UNITS

(ASK) (Y|+) (🐾) (🖥) (💻) / (✕) (💼) /

———— WHERE TO DINE ————

CHEZ CORA

▼▼▼ ▼▼ **Lunch:** $7-$11 **Phone:** 450/778-2000

Location: Hwy 20, exit 130, just w on boul Laframboise, then just n; in mini-mall. 2485 boul Casavant J2S 7E5. Canadian **Hours:** 6 am-3 pm, Sun from 7 am. Closed: 12/25. **Reservations:** accepted. **Features:** Although this place specializes in breakfast, it offers a varied daytime menu that includes bacon, eggs, sausages, crepes, grilled cheese, sandwiches, freshly prepared quiches, salads, fruit platters and freshly squeezed juices. The family-friendly dining room is casual and modern. Casual dress. **Parking:** on-site. **Cards:** AX, DC, MC, VI.

LE PARVIS DINING ROOM

▼▼▼▼ **Lunch:** $9-$23 **Dinner:** $15-$30 **Phone:** 450/774-2200

Location: Centre. 1295 rue Girouard ouest J2S 2Z2. **Hours:** 11:30 am-2 & 5:30-9 pm, Sat & Mon from 5:30 pm. French Closed: Sun. **Reservations:** suggested. **Features:** The stylishly converted basement of an 1878 church is a quaint place in which to enjoy a romantic, intimate dining experience. Seafood pasta, cod fillets in butter-lemon sauce, sweetbreads, New York-cut pepper steak and raspberry duck are representative of menu selections. Dinner theater packages are available in summer. Open Sunday by reservation only. Casual dress; cocktails. **Parking:** on-site. **Cards:** AX, MC, VI.

RESTAURANT LES QUATRE SAISONS

▼▼▼▼ **Lunch:** $18-$20 **Dinner:** $20-$30 **Phone:** 450/774-3810

Location: Hwy 20, exit 130S, just e on rue Gauvin from boul Laframboise; in Hotel des Seigneurs Saint-Hyacinthe. French 1200 rue Johnson J2S 7K7. **Hours:** 7-10:30 am, 11:30-2 & 5:30-10 pm. **Reservations:** suggested. **Features:** The casually elegant dining room overlooks the interior atrium, which is lush with foliage. Representative of fine French cuisine are stuffed salmon, guinea fowl, breast of duck, sweetbreads, pork, beef and seafood. A buffet is set up at lunch. Casual dress; cocktails. **Parking:** on-site. **Cards:** AX, DC, DS, MC, VI.

(Y)

RESTO LE FOUR

▼▼▼ ▼▼ **Lunch:** $6-$12 **Dinner:** $7-$25 **Phone:** 450/774-3687

Location: Hwy 20, exit 130S, then just s on boul Laframboise. 1350 rue Gauvin J2S 8J4. **Hours:** 11 am-10 pm, Fri-11 pm, Sat 2 pm-11 pm, Sun 10 am-10 pm. Closed: 12/25. **Reservations:** accepted. **Features:** The family-Canadian friendly diner serves budget-friendly Canadian comfort foods—including wood-oven pizza, steak, seafood and pasta—and well as traditional fast foods and offerings from the salad and soup bar. A pub area is separate from the main dining space. Casual dress; cocktails. **Parking:** on-site. **Cards:** AX, DC, MC, VI.

(Y)

ST-HUBERT

▼▼▼ ▼▼ **Lunch:** $7-$20 **Dinner:** $7-$20 **Phone:** 450/774-7770

Location: Hwy 20, exit 130, just w. 1250 rue Gauvin J2S 7X5. **Hours:** 11 am-11 pm, Thurs-Sat to midnight. Canadian Closed: 12/25. **Reservations:** accepted. **Features:** The pleasantly decorated family-friendly restaurant serves affordable chicken dinners, ribs, club sandwiches, chicken wings, salads, soups and hot chicken sandwiches. The children's menu includes animal nuggets. Casual dress; cocktails. **Parking:** on-site. **Cards:** AX, DC, MC, VI.

(Y)

TI-PERE RESTAURANT

▼ **Lunch:** $5-$18 **Dinner:** $7-$18 **Phone:** 450/773-0415

Location: Hwy 20, exit 130S, 0.5 mi (0.8 km) s. 2995 boul Laframboise J2S 4Z3. **Hours:** 11 am-1 am, Fri & Sat-2 Barbecue am. **Reservations:** accepted. **Features:** The simple diner specializes in roasted chicken, spaghetti, sandwiches, chicken wings and salad. For dessert, try sugar or pecan pie. Casual dress; cocktails. **Parking:** on-site. **Cards:** MC, VI.

ST-JEAN-PORT-JOLI pop. 3,372

———— WHERE TO STAY ————

AUBERGE DU FAUBOURG

▼▼ ▼▼ 5/1-10/10 **1P:** $89-$105 **2P:** $89-$105 **XP:** $20 F12

Phone: 418/598-6455

Location: 1.4 mi (2.4 km) w on Rt 132 from jct Rt 204; Hwy 20, exit 414. 280 ave de Gaspe ouest (Rt 132) G0R 3G0. Motel Fax: 418/598-3302. **Facility:** 75 units. 68 one-bedroom standard units. 7 cottages ($220). 2 stories (no elevator), exterior corridors. **Parking:** on-site. **Terms:** open 5/1-10/10, check-in 4 pm, 10 day cancellation notice-fee imposed, [AP], [BP] & [MAP] meal plans available, package plans, small pets only (dogs only, $15 extra charge, in designated units). **Dining:** restaurant, see separate listing. **Pool(s):** outdoor. **Leisure Activities:** rental bicycles, spa. **Business Services:** meeting rooms. **Cards:** AX, MC, VI.

SOME UNITS

(ASK) (🛏) (Y|) (Y) (🏊) (✕) (🔧) / (🛗) (💻) /
FEE

———— WHERE TO DINE ————

AUBERGE DU FAUBOURG DINING ROOM

▼▼▼▼ **Lunch:** $8-$14 **Dinner:** $30-$38 **Phone:** 418/598-6455

Location: 1.4 mi (2.4 km) w on Rt 132 from jct Rt 204; Hwy 20, exit 414; in Auberge Du Faubourg. 280 ave de Gaspe ouest G0R 3G0. **Hours:** Open 5/1-10/31; 7-10 am, 11:30-2 & 5-8:30 pm, Fri & Sat-10 pm. Regional French **Reservations:** suggested. **Features:** Sunlight pours through many windows to give the riverfront dining room a bright, cheerful feel. The French-influenced menu features many regional products in such dishes as seafood fettuccine, salmon in beurre blanc sauce, duck breast, roasted lamb, beef mignon and a variety of fowl preparations. Casual dress; cocktails. **Parking:** on-site. **Cards:** AX, DC, MC, VI.

ST-JEAN-SUR-RICHELIEU pop. 37,386

─────── **WHERE TO STAY** ───────

COMFORT INN   *Book great rates at AAA.com*   **Phone:** (450)359-4466
▼▼ ▼▼
    1/1-4/30 [ECP]   1P: $99-$169 2P: $99-$169 XP: $10 F18
    5/1-12/31 [ECP]   1P: $94-$149 2P: $94-$149 XP: $10 F18
Small-scale Hotel **Location:** Hwy 35, exit 9, e on rue Pierre-Caisse. 700 rue Gadbois J3A 1V1. Fax: 450/359-0611. **Facility:** 98 one-bedroom standard units. 2 stories, interior corridors. **Parking:** on-site, winter plug-ins. **Terms:** pets (1st floor units). **Amenities:** hair dryers. *Some:* irons. **Pool(s):** heated indoor. **Leisure Activities:** whirlpool, exercise room. **Guest Services:** valet and coin laundry, wireless Internet. **Business Services:** meeting rooms, PC. **Cards:** AX, CB, DC, DS, MC, VI. *(See color ad card insert)*

SOME UNITS
(ASK) (SD) 🛏 🛗 🏊 / ✕ VCR 🔒 🖼 /
             FEE FEE FEE

HOTEL RELAIS GOUVERNEUR
ST-JEAN-SUR-RICHELIEU   *Book at AAA.com*   **Phone:** (450)348-7376
▼▼ ▼▼
    5/1-10/15   1P: $95-$113   XP: $10 F17
    10/16-4/30   1P: $91-$109   XP: $10 F17
Small-scale Hotel **Location:** Hwy 35, exit 7. 725 boul du Seminaire nord J3B 8H1. Fax: 450/348-9778. **Facility:** 110 units. 107 one-bedroom standard units. 3 one-bedroom suites ($119-$180). 8 stories, interior corridors. **Parking:** on-site, winter plug-ins. **Terms:** check-in 4 pm, 30 day cancellation notice-fee imposed, package plans. **Amenities:** hair dryers. *Some:* honor bars, irons. **Pool(s):** heated indoor. **Guest Services:** valet laundry, wireless Internet. **Business Services:** conference facilities, business center. **Cards:** AX, DC, DS, MC, VI.

SOME UNITS
(ASK) (SD) 🛗 🍽 🏊 🐾 💻 / ✕ 🔒 🖼 /
               FEE FEE

─────── **WHERE TO DINE** ───────

LE SAMUEL II   **Lunch:** $17-$21 **Dinner:** $24-$40 **Phone:** 450/347-4353
▼▼▼
    Location: Between rue Foch and St-Charles; centre. 291 rue Richelieu J3B 6Y3. **Hours:** Open 5/1-1/1 & 1/22-4/30;
Nouvelle French 11 am-10 pm, Sat & Sun from 5 pm; 11 am-2 & 5-10 pm, Sat from 5 pm 10/15-4/15. Closed: 12/25; also Sun 9/10 thru 5/1. **Reservations:** suggested. **Features:** The cozy dining room affords lovely views of the river and countryside. House-smoked salmon, grilled Atlantic salmon, wild game, filet mignon and deboned quail are among creative dishes prepared with fresh market ingredients. Dressy casual; cocktails. **Parking:** on-site. **Cards:** AX, DC, MC, VI.

🍸

RESTAURANT L'IMPREVU **Lunch:** $9-$14 **Dinner:** $14-$33 **Phone:** 450/346-2417
▼▼▼
    Location: Corner of rue Laurier; centre. 163 rue St-Jacques J3B 2K4. **Hours:** 10 am-10 pm, Sat & Sun from 4 pm.
French Closed: Sun 1/1-Easter & Mon; may also close 1st week of March. **Reservations:** suggested. **Features:** In the city's historic district, the restaurant delivers imaginative dishes, including preparations of filet mignon, mussels, fish, veal liver, salmon, shrimp and pasta. The lively seasonal terrace offers comfortable, sunny seating. Casual dress; cocktails. **Parking:** on-site. **Cards:** AX, DC, MC, VI.

ST-JEROME —*See Montreal p. 494.*

ST-LAURENT (MONTREAL) —*See Montreal p. 494.*

ST-LIBOIRE pop. 2,829

─────── **WHERE TO STAY** ───────

ECONO LODGE   *Book great rates at AAA.com*   **Phone:** (450)793-4444
▼▼ ▼▼
    6/1-4/30   1P: $90-$110 2P: $100-$120 XP: $10 F18
    5/1-5/31   1P: $67-$99 2P: $76-$109 XP: $10 F18
Small-scale Hotel **Location:** Hwy 20, exit 147, just s. 110 Rang Charlotte J0H 1R0. Fax: 450/793-4449. **Facility:** 36 one-bedroom standard units, some with whirlpools. 1 story, interior corridors. **Parking:** on-site. **Terms:** check-in 4 pm, cancellation fee imposed, package plans, pets ($40 deposit). **Amenities:** irons, hair dryers. **Pool(s):** heated outdoor. **Guest Services:** coin laundry. **Business Services:** meeting rooms. **Cards:** AX, DC, MC, VI. *(See color ad card insert)*

SOME UNITS
(ASK) (SD) 🛏 🍽 🍸 🏊 💻 / ✕ 🔒 /
          FEE

ST-MARC-SUR-RICHELIEU pop. 1,957

─────── **WHERE TO STAY** ───────

HOSTELLERIE LES TROIS TILLEULS & SPA
GIVENCHY   *Book at AAA.com*   **Phone:** (514)856-7787
▼▼ ▼▼
    5/15-10/15   1P: $150-$602 2P: $175-$704 XP: $20 D12
    5/1-5/14 & 10/16-4/30 1P: $130-$500 2P: $155-$500 XP: $20 D12
Small-scale Hotel **Location:** Hwy 20, exit 112, 4.4 mi (7 km) n on Rt 223. 290 rue Richelieu J0L 2E0. Fax: 450/584-3146. **Facility:** Designated smoking area. 41 one-bedroom standard units with whirlpools. 3 stories (no elevator), interior corridors. **Parking:** on-site. **Terms:** check-in 4 pm, cancellation fee imposed, [BP] & [MAP] meal plans available, package plans. **Amenities:** voice mail, safes, irons, hair dryers. **Dining:** restaurant, see separate listing. **Pool(s):** heated indoor, saltwater. **Leisure Activities:** saunas, 2 tennis courts, exercise room, spa. *Fee:* boat dock. **Guest Services:** gift shop, valet laundry, wireless Internet. **Business Services:** meeting rooms, administrative services (fee), PC. **Cards:** AX, DC, MC, VI.

SOME UNITS
🛗 🏊 ✕ ✕ / VCR /
           FEE

——— **WHERE TO DINE** ———

AUBERGE HANDFIELD INN RESTAURANT   Lunch: $8-$15   Dinner: $16-$31   Phone: 450/584-2226
Location: On Rt 223, 6.4 mi (10.3 km) n of jct Hwy 20, exit 112; in Auberge Handfield Inn. 555 rue Richelieu J0L 2E0.
Hours: 8-10:30 am, 11:30-2 & 5-9 pm, Sun 8-10:30 am, 11-3 & 5-9 pm. Closed: Mon 11/17-5/1.
Regional French   **Reservations:** suggested. **Features:** The cozy country inn welcomes diners to enjoy warm service, a rustic dining room and tasty regional food. In addition to tourtiere, ragout and fresh perch, the menu delivers preparations of grilled meat and poultry. Sugar pie is a nice dessert choice. Casual dress; cocktails. **Parking:** on-site.
Cards: AX, DC, DS, MC, VI. **Country Inn**

RESTAURANT LES TROIS TILLEULS   Lunch: $26-$35   Dinner: $20-$59   Phone: 514/856-7787
Location: Hwy 20, exit 112, 4.4 mi (7 km) n on Rt 223. 290 rue Richelieu J0L 2E0. **Hours:** 7:30-10 am, 11:30-2:30
& 6-9 pm. **Reservations:** suggested. **Features:** On the Richelieu River, the elegant dining room has the
French   sophisticated feel of a relaxed country inn. Rack of lamb, cream of vegetable soup and salad of greens with
warm chicken livers are popular menu choices. Many diners visit to savor the Sunday brunch. Casual dress;
cocktails. **Parking:** on-site. **Cards:** AX, DC, MC, VI. **Country Inn**

ST-RAYMOND pop. 8,836

——— **WHERE TO DINE** ———

AUBERGE LA BASTIDE   Lunch: $7-$15   Dinner: $23-$36   Phone: 418/337-3796
Location: 0.5 mi (0.8 km) n of rue St-Jacques; centre. 567 rue St-Joseph G3L 1K8. **Hours:** 11:30 am-1:30 & 6-8
pm, Sun from 9 am; 6 pm-8 pm 9/1-6/1. Closed: Mon. **Reservations:** suggested. **Features:** Fine regional
French   cuisine is offered in this casually elegant country inn. The menu features sweetbreads, lamb, Lake Brome
duck confit, filet of dore, veal filet, guinea fowl, deer, black angus beef. Dressy casual; cocktails. **Parking:**
on-site. **Cards:** AX, CB, MC, VI.

SAINT-SAUVEUR pop. 3,316

——— **WHERE TO STAY** ———

AUBERGE SOUS L'EDREDON   Phone: (450)227-3131

1/1-4/30 [ECP]	1P: $90-$110	2P: $100-$185	XP: $40	D
5/1-12/31 [ECP]	1P: $85-$105	2P: $95-$180	XP: $35	D

Bed & Breakfast   **Location:** Hwy 15, exit 60, 1.1 mi (1.8 km) w on Rt 364, then 0.8 mi (1.4 km) s. 777 rue Principale J0R 1R2.
Fax: 450/227-3131. **Facility:** Smoke free premises. 5 one-bedroom standard units. 2 stories (no elevator),
interior corridors. **Bath:** combo or shower only. **Parking:** on-site, winter plug-ins. **Terms:** 14 day cancellation notice-fee imposed,
package plans. **Pool(s):** heated outdoor. **Leisure Activities:** whirlpool. **Cards:** MC, VI.

SOME UNITS

MANOIR SAINT-SAUVEUR   *Book great rates at AAA.com*   Phone: (450)227-1811

12/22-1/6	1P: $149-$299	2P: $149-$299	XP: $20	F17
1/7-4/30	1P: $115-$299	2P: $115-$299	XP: $20	F17
5/1-12/21	1P: $109-$299	2P: $109-$299	XP: $20	F17

Resort   **Location:** Hwy 15, exit 60, just w. 246 chemin du Lac Millette J0R 1R3. **Fax:** 450/227-8512. **Facility:** Quality
Large-scale Hotel   furnishings and some wood-burning fireplaces enhance these hotel rooms and condo units set in a scenic
ski village. 300 units. 259 one-bedroom standard units, some with whirlpools. 41 one-bedroom suites ($189-
$539), some with kitchens and/or whirlpools. 3-4 stories, interior corridors. **Parking:** on-site. **Terms:** check-
in 4 pm, cancellation fee imposed, [BP] & [MAP] meal plans available, package plans. **Amenities:** voice mail, honor bars, irons,
hair dryers. *Some:* DVD players, CD players, high-speed Internet. **Dining:** 2 restaurants, 7 am-9:30 pm; outdoor terrace 5/1-
9/15, cocktails. **Pool(s):** outdoor, heated indoor, wading. **Leisure Activities:** sauna, whirlpool, steamroom, 2 lighted tennis
courts, playground, spa. **Guest Services:** gift shop, valet laundry, area transportation-ski hill, wireless Internet. **Business
Services:** meeting rooms, PC. **Cards:** AX, DC, MC, VI.

SOME UNITS

FEE   FEE

TRAVELODGE SUITES   *Book at AAA.com*   Phone: (450)227-4628
All Year   1P: $90-$200   2P: $90-$200   XP: $20   F
Location: Hwy 15, exit 60, then just w of jct Rt 364. 190 chemin de la Gare J0R 1R2. **Fax:** 450/227-4628.
Small-scale Hotel   **Facility:** 40 one-bedroom standard units, some with efficiencies, kitchens and/or whirlpools. 3 stories (no
elevator), exterior corridors. **Parking:** on-site. **Terms:** off-site registration, check-in 4 pm, cancellation fee
imposed, package plans. **Amenities:** hair dryers. *Some:* high-speed Internet. **Pool(s):** outdoor. **Business Services:** meeting
rooms. **Cards:** AX, DC, MC, VI.

SOME UNITS

——— **WHERE TO DINE** ———

BENTLEY'S BAR & RESTAURANT   Lunch: $10-$15   Dinner: $10-$24   Phone: 450/227-1851
Location: Centre. 235 rue Principale J0R 1R0. **Hours:** 11 am-10 pm. Closed: 12/25. **Features:** The popular pub
and restaurant is an ideal stop after a day spent outdoors on the mountain. It offers beers on tap, daily
Canadian   specials and a menu that includes grilled salmon, burgers, steaks, ribs, chicken and pasta served with
house-prepared sauces. Casual dress; cocktails. **Parking:** on-site. **Cards:** AX, DC, MC, VI.

CHEZ CORA   Lunch: $7-$11   Phone: 450/227-1077
Location: Hwy 15, exit 60; centre. 10 rue Filion J0R 1R0. **Hours:** 6 am-3 pm, Sun from 7 am. Closed: 1/1, 12/25.
Reservations: accepted, Mon-Sat. **Features:** Although this place specializes in breakfast, it offers a varied
Canadian   daytime menu that includes bacon, eggs, sausages, crepes, grilled cheese, sandwiches, freshly prepared
quiches, salads, fruit platters and freshly squeezed juices. The family-friendly dining room is casual and
modern. Casual dress; beer & wine only. **Parking:** on-site. **Cards:** AX, DC, MC, VI.

CREPERIE A LA GOURMANDISE BRETONNE

Canadian

Lunch: $10-$22   **Dinner:** $10-$22   **Phone:** 450/227-5434

Location: Centre. 396 rue Principale J0R 1R0. **Hours:** 11:30 am-9 pm, Fri & Sat-10 pm. Closed: 1/1, 12/24, 12/25; also 12/31, Mon & Tues 11/1-12/13 & 4/15-5/30. **Reservations:** not accepted. **Features:** In the heart of St-Sauveur Village, the family-oriented restaurant specializes in crepes, which diners can fill with a wide array of ingredients, such as creamy bechamel sauce—a melted cheese. Excellent desserts are served in huge portions. Casual dress; cocktails. **Parking:** on-site. **Cards:** AX, DC, MC, VI.

GIBBYS

Steak & Seafood

Dinner: $20-$45   **Phone:** 450/227-2623

Location: Jct Rt 364 and chemin Turcotte. 414 rue Principale J0R 1R4. **Hours:** 4:30 pm-11 pm, Sat-11:30 pm, Sun 4 pm-11 pm. **Reservations:** suggested. **Features:** Cultivated oysters, lobster and several hearty selections of fresh fish mingle with beef dishes on the traditional menu. Several dining areas have cozy fireplaces, subtle lighting and beamed ceilings. Casual dress; cocktails. **Parking:** on-site. **Cards:** AX, DC, DS, MC, VI.

LE BIFTHEQUE

Canadian

Lunch: $11-$35   **Dinner:** $11-$35   **Phone:** 450/227-2442

Location: On Rt 364; centre. 86 de la Gare J0R 1R3. **Hours:** 4 pm-11 pm, Fri & Sat from 11 am. **Reservations:** suggested. **Features:** The restaurant satisfies the cravings of folks in the mood for a sizzling steak. Huge portions of traditional steakhouse fare-including fine steaks, prime rib and seafood selections-keep locals coming back. Among starters are shrimp cocktail, French onion soup and escargots. Meals come with a tasty house salad and the ever-popular biftheque croutons. Diners should arrive with a hearty appetite. Casual dress; cocktails. **Parking:** on-site. **Cards:** AX, DC, MC, VI.

ST-URBAIN pop. 1,430

——— WHERE TO STAY ———

AUBERGE DU RAVAGE

Country Inn

Phone: 418/665-4400

All Year   **1P:** $139-$187   **2P:** $209-$274

Location: Jct Rt 138, 35.3 mi (56.5 km) n on Rt 381, then 9.5 mi (15.2 km) e on gravel road. CP 156 (Parc-des-Grands-Jardins) G0A 4K0. **Fax:** 418/665-4400. **Facility:** 12 one-bedroom standard units. 2 stories, interior/exterior corridors. *Bath:* shower only. **Parking:** on-site, winter plug-ins. **Terms:** package plans. **Amenities:** hair dryers. **Leisure Activities:** sauna, boating, rental canoes, snowmobiling, rental bicycles, hiking trails, exercise room. *Fee:* charter fishing, cross country skiing, massage. **Guest Services:** coin laundry, area transportation (fee). **Business Services:** meeting rooms, PC. **Cards:** MC, VI.

SALABERRY-DE-VALLEYFIELD pop. 26,170

——— WHERE TO STAY ———

HOTEL PLAZA VALLEYFIELD

Large-scale Hotel

Phone: (450)373-1990

All Year   **1P:** $99-$109   **XP:** $10   **F18**

Location: Corner of rue St-Laurent; centre. 40 ave du Centenaire J6S 3L6. **Fax:** 450/373-1936. **Facility:** 122 units. 120 one-bedroom standard units, some with whirlpools. 2 one-bedroom suites with whirlpools. 9 stories, interior corridors. **Parking:** on-site. **Terms:** weekly rates available, package plans. **Amenities:** video games (fee), hair dryers. *Some:* irons. **Pool(s):** heated indoor. **Leisure Activities:** saunas, whirlpools, steamrooms, exercise room, spa. **Guest Services:** valet and coin laundry, beauty salon. **Business Services:** conference facilities, administrative services (fee), PC. **Cards:** AX, CB, DC, DS, JC, MC, VI.

SOME UNITS

——— WHERE TO DINE ———

ST-HUBERT

Canadian

Lunch: $7-$20   **Dinner:** $7-$20   **Phone:** 450/371-9222

Location: Just s of Rt 201. 1370 boul Mgr-Langlois J6S 1E3. **Hours:** 11 am-11 pm, Fri & Sat-midnight. Closed: 12/25. **Reservations:** accepted. **Features:** The pleasantly decorated family-friendly restaurant serves affordable chicken dinners, ribs, club sandwiches, chicken wings, salads, soups and hot chicken sandwiches. The children's menu includes animal nuggets. Casual dress; cocktails. **Parking:** on-site. **Cards:** AX, DC, MC, VI.

SEPT-ILES pop. 25,200

——— WHERE TO STAY ———

COMFORT INN

Small-scale Hotel

Book great rates at AAA.com   **Phone:** (418)968-6005

	1P	2P	XP	F18
7/1-8/31 [CP]	$115-$125	$125-$135	$10	F18
1/1-4/30 [CP]	$113-$123	$123-$133	$10	F18
5/1-6/30 & 9/1-12/31 [CP]	$110-$120	$120-$130	$10	F18

Location: 2.8 mi (4.5 km) w on Rt 138. 854 boul Laure G4R 1Y7. **Fax:** 418/968-0701. **Facility:** 61 one-bedroom standard units. 2 stories (no elevator), interior corridors. **Parking:** on-site, winter plug-ins. **Terms:** 30 day cancellation notice, package plans. **Amenities:** irons, hair dryers. **Guest Services:** valet laundry, wireless Internet. **Cards:** AX, DC, DS, JC, MC, VI. *(See color ad card insert)*

SOME UNITS

——— **WHERE TO DINE** ———

CHEZ CORA

Canadian

Lunch: $7-$11

Phone: 418/960-0226

Location: On Rt 138; centre. 1006-B rue Laure G4R 5P1. **Hours:** 6 am-3 pm, Sun from 7 am. Closed: 12/25. **Reservations:** accepted. **Features:** Although this place specializes in breakfast, it offers a varied daytime menu that includes bacon, eggs, sausages, crepes, grilled cheese, sandwiches, freshly prepared quiches, salads, fruit platters and freshly squeezed juices. The family-friendly dining room is casual and modern. Casual dress. **Parking:** on-site. **Cards:** AX, DC, MC, VI.

ST-HUBERT

Canadian

Lunch: $7-$20 **Dinner: $7-$20**

Phone: 418/968-9191

Location: On Rt 138. 1005 boul Laure ouest G4R 4S6. **Hours:** 11 am-10 pm. Closed: 12/25. **Reservations:** accepted. **Features:** The pleasantly decorated family-friendly restaurant serves affordable chicken dinners, ribs, club sandwiches, chicken wings, salads, soups and hot chicken sandwiches. The children's menu includes animal nuggets. Casual dress; cocktails. **Parking:** on-site. **Cards:** AX, DC, MC, VI.

SHAWINIGAN pop. 17,535

——— **WHERE TO STAY** ———

AUBERGE ESCAPADE INN

Small-scale Hotel

Phone: (819)539-6911

6/18-4/30 [BP]	1P: $82-$145	2P: $92-$150	XP: $12 F12
5/1-6/17 [BP]	1P: $72-$145	2P: $79-$150	XP: $12 F12

Location: Hwy 55, exit 217, then 0.3 mi (0.5 km) n on Rt 351. 3383 rue Garnier G9N 6R4. **Fax:** 819/539-7669. **Facility:** 40 one-bedroom standard units, some with whirlpools. 2 stories (no elevator), interior/exterior corridors. **Parking:** on-site, winter plug-ins. **Terms:** cancellation fee imposed, package plans, small pets only (in designated units). **Amenities:** video library (fee), DVD players, CD players, irons, hair dryers. **Dining:** 6:30-9:30 am, 11:30-2 & 5-9 pm, Sat 8 am-11 & 5-9 pm, Sun 8-11 am, cocktails. **Leisure Activities:** snowmobiling. **Guest Services:** valet laundry, wireless Internet. **Business Services:** meeting rooms, PC. **Cards:** AX, DC, DS, MC, VI. **Free Special Amenities: full breakfast and high-speed Internet.**

AUBERGE GOUVERNEUR & CENTRE DE CONGRES SHAWINIGAN *Book great rates at AAA.com*

Small-scale Hotel

Phone: (819)537-6000

5/1-10/15	1P: $150-$175	2P: $150-$175	XP: $10 F17
10/16-4/30	1P: $150-$160	2P: $150-$160	XP: $10 F17

Location: Hwy 55 N, exit 211, 2.8 mi (4.4 km) n on Hwy 153, follow signs. 1100 Promenade-du-St-Maurice G9N 1L8. **Fax:** 819/537-6365. **Facility:** 106 units. 104 one-bedroom standard units. 2 one-bedroom suites ($180-$220) with whirlpools. 2 stories (no elevator), interior corridors. **Bath:** combo or shower only. **Parking:** on-site. **Terms:** cancellation fee imposed, package plans, small pets only. **Amenities:** voice mail, honor bars, irons, hair dryers. *Some:* dual phone lines. **Dining:** Grill & Bar Le St-Maurice, see separate listing. **Pool(s):** heated indoor. **Leisure Activities:** whirlpools, snowmobiling, spa, gym privileges. *Fee:* game room. **Guest Services:** valet and coin laundry, wireless Internet. **Business Services:** conference facilities, business center. **Cards:** AX, DC, MC, VI. **Free Special Amenities: local telephone calls and high-speed Internet.**

COMFORT INN & SUITES *Book great rates at AAA.com*

Small-scale Hotel

Phone: (819)536-2000

7/2-9/23 [CP]	1P: $79-$135	2P: $82-$145	XP: $10 F18
5/1-7/1 & 9/24-4/30 [CP]	1P: $69-$119	2P: $72-$121	XP: $10 F18

Location: Hwy 55 N, exit 211, 2.8 mi (4.4 km) n on Hwy 153, then 1.3 mi (2 km) s on Rt 157. 500 boul du Capitaine G9P 5J6. **Fax:** 819/536-2010. **Facility:** 71 units. 68 one-bedroom standard units. 3 one-bedroom suites with whirlpools. 3 stories (no elevator), interior corridors. **Parking:** on-site, winter plug-ins. **Terms:** package plans, small pets only. **Amenities:** high-speed Internet, irons, hair dryers. *Some:* honor bars. *Fee:* DVD players. **Leisure Activities:** exercise room. **Guest Services:** valet and coin laundry. **Business Services:** meeting rooms. **Cards:** AX, MC, VI. **(See color ad card insert)**

——— **WHERE TO DINE** ———

GRILL & BAR LE ST-MAURICE

Canadian

Lunch: $11-$26 **Dinner: $11-$26**

Phone: 819/537-6000

Location: Hwy 55 N, exit 211, 2.8 mi (4.4 km) n on Hwy 153, follow signs; in Auberge Gouverneur & Centre de Congres Shawinigan. 1100 Promenade-du-St-Maurice G9N 1L8. **Hours:** 6:30 am-10 pm, Sun-9 pm. **Reservations:** suggested. **Features:** The upscale hotel restaurant is an ideal place to sample fine regional cuisine, including veal, steaks, salads, pasta, seafood and fresh fish. Casual dress; cocktails. **Parking:** on-site. **Cards:** AX, DC, MC, VI.

LE RESTO-PUB 57

Canadian

Lunch: $6-$25 **Dinner: $6-$25**

Phone: 819/536-2657

Location: Hwy 55 N, exit 211, 2.8 mi (4.4 km) n on Hwy 153, just s on Rt 157. 880 Promenade-du-St-Maurice G9N 6V9. **Hours:** 11 am-10 pm, Fri-11 pm, Sat 8 am-11 pm, Sun 8 am-10 pm. **Reservations:** accepted. **Features:** The family restaurant and pub features 1950s memorabilia and a menu of classic American comfort foods, including burgers, ribs, chicken and steaks. Casual dress; cocktails. **Parking:** street. **Cards:** AX, MC, VI.

SHERBROOKE pop. 75,916

---- WHERE TO STAY ----

COMFORT INN *Book great rates at AAA.com*
Phone: **(819)564-4400**

	6/21-9/1	1P: $96-$122	2P: $106-$132	XP: $10	F17
	9/2-4/30	1P: $88-$97	2P: $98-$124	XP: $10	F17
Small-scale Hotel	5/17-6/20	1P: $87-$114	2P: $97-$124	XP: $10	F17
	5/1-5/16	1P: $81-$112	2P: $91-$122	XP: $10	F17

Location: Hwy 410, exit 4, 0.9 mi (1.5 km) w on Rt 112. 4295 boul Bourque J1N 1S4. Fax: 819/564-7011. **Facility:** 59 one-bedroom standard units. 2 stories (no elevator), interior/exterior corridors. **Parking:** on-site, winter plug-ins. **Terms:** check-in 4 pm, [CP] meal plan available, package plans. **Amenities:** irons, hair dryers. **Guest Services:** valet laundry, wireless Internet. **Cards:** AX, CB, DC, DS, MC, VI. *(See color ad card insert)*

SOME UNITS

DELTA SHERBROOKE HOTEL AND CONFERENCE CENTRE *Book great rates at AAA.com*
Phone: **(819)822-1989**

	All Year	1P: $89-$161	2P: $89-$161	XP: $15	F17

Location: Hwy 410, exit 4E, 0.6 mi (1 km) e on Rt 112. 2685 rue King ouest J1L 1C1. Fax: 819/822-8990. **Facility:** 178 units. 176 one-bedroom standard units, some with whirlpools. 2 one-bedroom suites ($134-$300). 10 stories, interior corridors. **Parking:** on-site. **Terms:** check-in 4 pm, cancellation fee imposed, [BP] [CP] & [MAP] meal plans available, package plans, small pets only. **Amenities:** video games (fee), honor bars, irons, hair dryers. **Dining:** 6:30 am-10 pm, Sat from 7 am, Sun 8 am-9 pm, cocktails. **Pool(s):** heated indoor. **Leisure Activities:** sauna, whirlpool, children's play room, exercise room, spa. **Guest Services:** valet laundry, wireless Internet. **Business Services:** conference facilities, business center. **Cards:** AX, DC, DS, JC, MC, VI. *(See color ad below)*

SOME UNITS

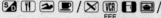

QUALITY HOTEL & SUITES
Phone: **(819)563-4755**

	5/1-10/15	1P: $99-$159	2P: $109-$169	XP: $10	F
	10/16-4/30	1P: $89-$149	2P: $99-$159	XP: $10	F

Location: Hwy 410, exit 4, 0.4 mi (0.6 km) w. 4206 rue King ouest J1L 1V5. Fax: 819/563-3515. **Facility:** 44 one-bedroom standard units, some with whirlpools. 3 stories (no elevator), interior/exterior corridors. **Parking:** on-site, winter plug-ins. **Terms:** cancellation fee imposed. **Amenities:** high-speed Internet, hair dryers. *Some:* voice mail. **Dining:** 6 am-3 pm, cocktails. **Pool(s):** outdoor. **Leisure Activities:** *Fee:* massage. **Guest Services:** sundries, valet laundry, beauty salon, wireless Internet. **Business Services:** meeting rooms. **Cards:** AX, CB, DC, DS, JC, MC, VI. **Free Special Amenities:** full breakfast and high-speed Internet.

SOME UNITS

FEE

---- WHERE TO DINE ----

CHEZ CORA
Lunch: $7-$11
Phone: 819-823-0781

Canadian

Location: On Rt 112; centre. 3200 rue King ouest J1L 1C9. **Hours:** 6 am-3 pm, Sun from 7 am. Closed: 1/1, 12/25. **Reservations:** accepted, Mon-Fri. **Features:** Although this place specializes in breakfast, it offers a varied daytime menu that includes bacon, eggs, sausages, crepes, grilled cheese, sandwiches, freshly prepared quiches, salads, fruit platters and freshly squeezed juices. The family-friendly dining room is casual and modern. Casual dress; beer & wine only. **Parking:** on-site. **Cards:** AX, DC, MC, VI.

DA TONI

Lunch: $11-$15   Dinner: $11-$35   Phone: 819/346-8441

Italian

Location: Corner rue King ouest; downtown. 15 rue Belvedere nord J1H 4A7. **Hours:** 11 am-11 pm, Sat & Sun from 4 pm. Closed: 12/25. **Reservations:** suggested. **Features:** The stylish, contemporary dining room features a glassed wine cellar and elegant table settings. The menu includes French and Italian preparations of pasta, seafood and steaks. The impressive wine list incorporates selections to suit every budget. Casual dress; cocktails. **Parking:** on-site and valet. **Cards:** AX, MC, VI.

LA FALAISE ST-MICHEL

Lunch: $11-$20   Dinner: $29-$42   Phone: 819/346-6339

French

Location: Just n on rue Wellington N, from rue King ouest, then just e on rue Meadow; centre. 100 rue Webster J1H 5N3. **Hours:** 11:30 am-2 & 5:30-9:30 pm, Sat from 5:30 pm. Closed: 1/1, 12/25; also Sun & for dinner Mon. **Reservations:** suggested. **Features:** The spacious, airy dining room has a classic feel. Poached salmon, veal kidneys and sweetbreads are representative of well-prepared French cuisine. Homemade ravioli is served in a sauce that blends sun-dried tomatoes and Parmesan cheese. Dressy casual; cocktails. **Parking:** on-site (fee). **Cards:** AX, DC, MC, VI.

LE CHOU DE BRUXELLES

Dinner: $14-$27   Phone: 819/564-1848

Belgian

Location: Rt 112 (rue King ouest), 0.7 mi (1.1 km) s on J Cartier to rue Galt ouest, then 0.3 mi (0.5 km) e. 1461 rue Galt ouest J1H 2A9. **Hours:** 5 pm-9 pm, Thurs-Sat to 10 pm. Closed: 12/24, 12/25; also last 2 weeks of July. **Reservations:** suggested, weekends. **Features:** The "bring-your-own-wine" establishment specializes in mussels, including a preparation with garlic and Parmesan and mozzarella cheese. Among other menu highlights is veal sweetbread or kidneys served in cream sauce. Wall sconces provide subtle lighting in the upbeat dining room. Well-timed, attentive service satisfies from start to finish. Casual dress. **Parking:** on-site. **Cards:** AX, DC, MC, VI.

RESTAURANT AU P'TIT SABOT

Lunch: $11-$21   Dinner: $16-$26   Phone: 819/563-0262

French

Location: Rt 112 (rue King ouest), near rue Vimy. 1410 rue King ouest J1J 2C2. **Hours:** 11:30 am-2 & 5:30-9 pm, Mon-2 pm. Closed: 12/25; also Sun. **Reservations:** suggested. **Features:** Shades of pink and soft radio music enhance the relaxed mood in the small, comfortable dining room. The limited menu centers on traditional dishes of fish, beef and game, including bison and caribou. Laid out on the dessert tray are such tempting treats as flavorful sugar pie. Casual dress; cocktails. **Parking:** on-site. **Cards:** AX, DC, MC, VI.

RESTAURANT NORMANDIN

Lunch: $5-$12   Dinner: $5-$12   Phone: 819/822-0555

Canadian

Location: On Rt 112. 2707 rue King ouest J1L 1C1. **Hours:** 6 am-midnight, Thurs-2 am, Fri & Sat-3 am. Closed: 12/25. **Reservations:** accepted. **Features:** The family restaurant prepares affordable comfort foods that include roasted chicken, hot chicken sandwiches, pasta, burgers and fries. Take-out service, a children's menu and cutely decorated desserts are among other offerings. Casual dress. **Parking:** on-site. **Cards:** AX, DC, MC, VI.

SCORES ROTISSERIE & COTES LEVEES

Lunch: $5-$11   Dinner: $8-$18   Phone: 819/563-4444

Barbecue

Location: On Rt 112 (rue King ouest), corner of rue Burlington. 2800 rue King ouest J1L 1Y7. **Hours:** 11 am-11 pm, Fri & Sat-midnight. Closed: 12/25. **Reservations:** suggested. **Features:** The chain of family restaurants presents a varied menu that includes rotisserie chicken, ribs, salad-bar items, sandwiches, poutine and sugar, lemon or pecan pie. Casual dress; cocktails. **Parking:** on-site. **Cards:** AX, MC, VI.

ST-HUBERT

Lunch: $7-$20   Dinner: $7-$20   Phone: 819/563-5112

Canadian

Location: Hwy 50, exit rue King. 3070 rue King ouest J1L 1C9. **Hours:** 11 am-11 pm, Fri & Sat-midnight. Closed: 12/25; also for dinner 12/24. **Reservations:** accepted, before 4 pm or after 8 pm. **Features:** The pleasantly decorated family-friendly restaurant serves affordable chicken dinners, ribs, club sandwiches, chicken wings, salads, soups and hot chicken sandwiches. The children's menu includes animal nuggets. Casual dress; cocktails. **Parking:** on-site. **Cards:** AX, DC, MC, VI.

SILLERY —See Quebec p. 553.

SOREL-TRACY pop. 36,786

——— **WHERE TO DINE** ———

ST-HUBERT

Lunch: $7-$20   Dinner: $7-$20   Phone: 450/742-4574

Canadian

Location: On Rt 132. 381 boul Fiset J3P 3R4. **Hours:** 11 am-11 pm, Fri & Sat-midnight. Closed: 12/25. **Reservations:** accepted. **Features:** The pleasantly decorated family-friendly restaurant serves affordable chicken dinners, ribs, club sandwiches, chicken wings, salads, soups and hot chicken sandwiches. The children's menu includes animal nuggets. Casual dress; cocktails. **Parking:** on-site. **Cards:** AX, DC, MC, VI.

TADOUSSAC pop. 870

——— **WHERE TO STAY** ———

DOMAINE DES DUNES

Phone: 418/235-4843

All Year   1P: $100-$130   2P: $100-$130   XP: $15

Cottage

Location: 1.6 mi (2.5 km) se of village via rue des Pionniers. 585 chemin du Moulin a Baude G0T 2A0. **Fax:** 418/235-1512. **Facility:** 10 cottages. 2 stories (no elevator), interior corridors. **Parking:** on-site, winter plug-ins. **Terms:** 30 day cancellation notice-fee imposed. **Amenities:** hair dryers. **Leisure Activities:** snowmobiling, playground, horseshoes, volleyball. **Guest Services:** coin laundry. **Cards:** MC, VI.

HOTEL TADOUSSAC

CAA SAVE

▼▼▼▼

Classic Historic
Large-scale Hotel

5/3-10/8   1P: $119-$239   2P: $119-$284   **Phone: (418)235-4421**

Location: Just off rue des Pionniers; centre. 165 rue Bord de l G0T 2A0. Fax: 418/235-4607. **Facility:** This landmark red-roofed hotel, built in 1942, is located in the heart of a village famous for summer whale-watching tours. Guestrooms are upscale. 149 one-bedroom standard units. 3 stories, interior corridors. **Parking:** on-site. **Terms:** open 5/3-10/8, check-in 4 pm, package plans. **Amenities:** irons, hair dryers. *Some:* DVD players, CD players. **Dining:** 2 restaurants, 7 am-9:30 pm, cocktails, also, Restaurant William, see separate listing. **Pool(s):** heated outdoor. **Leisure Activities:** tennis court, spa, shuffleboard. **Guest Services:** gift shop, valet laundry, area transportation-cruise boats & golf. **Business Services:** conference facilities, business center. **Cards:** AX, CB, DC, DS, JC, MC, VI. **Free Special Amenities:** local telephone calls and newspaper.

SOME UNITS

——— WHERE TO DINE ———

RESTAURANT WILLIAM

CAA

▼▼▼

French

Dinner: $29-$42   **Phone: 418/235-4421**

Location: Just off rue des Pionniers; centre; in Hotel Tadoussac. 165 rue Bord de l'Eau G0T 2A0. **Hours:** Open 5/15-10/15; 6 pm-9 pm. **Reservations:** suggested. **Features:** This small and intimate atrium dining room provides a fine dining option at this family-friendly hotel. The multi-course tasting menu is an excellent way to sample the fine regional cuisine, including sweetbreads, pan-seared foie gras, deer, breast of duck, scallops, lobster, crab and fresh fish. Service is proficient. Casual dress; cocktails. **Parking:** on-site. **Cards:** AX, DC, MC, VI.

THETFORD MINES pop. 16,628

——— WHERE TO STAY ———

COMFORT INN

▼▼

Small-scale Hotel

Book great rates at AAA.com

6/15-9/14 & 1/1-4/30	1P: $114-$119	2P: $124-$129	XP: $10	F18
9/15-12/31	1P: $112-$117	2P: $122-$127	XP: $10	F18
5/1-6/14	1P: $110-$115	2P: $120-$125	XP: $10	F18

Phone: (418)338-0171

Location: On Rt 112. 123 boul Frontenac ouest G6G 7S7. Fax: 418/338-9252. **Facility:** 63 one-bedroom standard units. 2 stories, interior corridors. **Parking:** on-site, winter plug-ins. **Terms:** weekly rates available, [CP] meal plan available, package plans. **Amenities:** irons, hair dryers. **Guest Services:** valet laundry, wireless Internet. **Business Services:** meeting rooms. **Cards:** AX, CB, DC, DS, JC, MC, VI. *(See color ad card insert)*

SOME UNITS

FEE   FEE

——— WHERE TO DINE ———

LA PIZZERIA DU BOULEVARD

▼▼▼ ▼▼▼

Canadian

MC, VI.

Lunch: $7-$10   **Dinner: $8-$25**   **Phone: 418/335-7531**

Location: On Rt 112; centre. 83 boul Frontenac est G6G 1N3. **Hours:** 7 am-midnight, Fri-2 am, Sat 8 am-2 am, Sun 8 am-midnight. Closed: 1/1, 12/25. **Reservations:** accepted. **Features:** The family-friendly diner serves hearty food, including pizza, pasta, hamburgers and fries. For dessert, try a slice of coconut cream pie. Breakfast is served daily. Delivery is available. Casual dress; cocktails. **Parking:** on-site. **Cards:** AX, DC,

---

MIKE'S

▼▼ ▼▼

Canadian

Cards: AX, MC, VI.

Lunch: $6-$9   **Dinner: $10-$22**   **Phone: 418/338-2185**

Location: On Rt 112, centre. 165 boul Frontenac G6G 6K2. **Hours:** 6 am-10 pm, Fri-11 pm, Sat 7 am-11 pm, Sun 7 am-10 pm. **Reservations:** accepted. **Features:** This popular family-friendly restaurant specializes in pizza and hot submarine sandwiches, along with fries, burgers, soup, salads, pasta, grilled meats and seafood. An excellent variety of colorful desserts rounds out the offerings. Casual dress; cocktails. **Parking:** on-site.

ST-HUBERT

▼▼▼ ▼▼▼

Canadian

MC, VI.

Lunch: $7-$20   **Dinner: $7-$20**   **Phone: 418/335-7557**

Location: On Rt 112. 203 boul Frontenac ouest G6G 6K2. **Hours:** 11 am-9 pm, Fri & Sat-11 pm. **Reservations:** accepted. **Features:** The pleasantly decorated family-friendly restaurant serves affordable chicken dinners, ribs, club sandwiches, chicken wings, salads, soups and hot chicken sandwiches. The children's menu includes animal nuggets. Casual dress; cocktails. **Parking:** on-site. **Cards:** AX, DC,

---

TROIS-RIVIERES pop. 46,264

——— WHERE TO STAY ———

COMFORT INN

▼▼▼ ▼▼

Small-scale Hotel

Book great rates at AAA.com

1/1-4/30 [CP]	1P: $81-$102	2P: $92-$112	XP: $10
5/1-9/30 [CP]	1P: $80-$100	2P: $90-$110	XP: $10
10/1-12/31 [CP]	1P: $78-$100	2P: $88-$110	XP: $10

Phone: 819/371-3566

Location: Hwy 55, exit 183 (boul Jean XXIII); 1.3 mi (2 km) n of Laviolette Bridge, then 0.3 mi (0.5 km) e. 6255 rue Corbeil G8Z 4P9. Fax: 819/371-8977. **Facility:** 80 one-bedroom standard units. 2 stories (no elevator), interior corridors. **Parking:** on-site, winter plug-ins. **Amenities:** voice mail, irons, hair dryers. **Guest Services:** valet laundry, wireless Internet. **Business Services:** meeting rooms. **Cards:** AX, MC, VI. *(See color ad card insert)*

SOME UNITS

FEE

DAYS INN   *Book great rates at AAA.com*   **Phone:** (819)377-4444

5/1-10/14 [CP]   1P: $90-$150   2P: $90-$170   XP: $10   F17
            10/15-4/30 [CP]   1P: $80-$150   2P: $80-$170   XP: $10   F17
            Location: Hwy 55, exit 183 (boul Jean XXIII), 0.3 mi (0.5 km) w, then 0.3 mi (0.4 km) n. 3155 boul Saint-Jean G9B
Small-scale Hotel   2M4. Fax: 819/377-3626. **Facility:** 74 units. 73 one-bedroom standard units, some with whirlpools. 1 two-
            bedroom suite ($180) with kitchen. 2 stories (no elevator), interior corridors. **Parking:** on-site. **Terms:** 14
            day cancellation notice, pets ($10 extra charge). **Amenities:** hair dryers. *Some:* irons. **Guest Services:**
valet and coin laundry, wireless Internet. **Business Services:** meeting rooms. **Cards:** AX, MC, VI. **Free Special Amenities:**
continental breakfast and local telephone calls.

SOME UNITS

DELTA TROIS-RIVIERES HOTEL AND CONFERENCE
CENTER   *Book great rates at AAA.com*   **Phone:** (819)376-1991

All Year   1P: $99-$125   XP: $15   F18
            Location: Corner of rue St-Roch; centre. 1620 rue Notre-Dame centre G9A 6E5. Fax: 819/372-5975. **Facility:** 159
Large-scale Hotel   one-bedroom standard units. 12 stories, interior corridors. **Parking:** on-site (fee). **Terms:** [AP], [CP],
            [ECP] & [MAP] meal plans available, pets ($30 fee). **Amenities:** video games (fee), honor bars, irons, hair
dryers. *Some:* DVD players, CD players. **Dining:** Le Troquet, see separate listing. **Pool(s):** heated indoor. **Leisure
Activities:** sauna, whirlpool, steamroom, exercise room. *Fee:* massage. **Guest Services:** gift shop, valet laundry, wireless
Internet. **Business Services:** conference facilities, administrative services (fee), PC. **Cards:** AX, DC, DS, MC, VI.

SOME UNITS

HOTEL DU ROY TROIS-RIVIERES   **Phone:** (819)379-3232

All Year   1P: $70-$125   2P: $75-$125   XP: $5   F6
            Location: On Rt 138, 1.3 mi (2 km) e of Pont Laviolette and jct Hwy 55. Located near a railway crossing. 3600 boul
            Gene H Kruger G9A 4M3. Fax: 819/379-8045. **Facility:** 102 one-bedroom standard units, some with
            whirlpools. 2 stories, interior/exterior corridors. **Parking:** on-site, winter plug-ins. **Terms:** cancellation fee
Small-scale Hotel   imposed, weekly rates available, small pets only. **Amenities:** hair dryers. **Dining:** 7-10:30 am. **Pool(s):**
            outdoor. **Guest Services:** valet laundry, wireless Internet. **Business Services:** meeting rooms, PC.
Cards: AX, DC, MC, VI. **Free Special Amenities:** full breakfast and local telephone calls.

SOME UNITS

HOTEL GOUVERNEUR TROIS-RIVIERES   *Book great rates at AAA.com*   **Phone:** (819)379-4550

5/1-10/15   1P: $94-$154   2P: $94-$154   XP: $15   F17
            10/16-4/30   1P: $92-$152   2P: $92-$152   XP: $15   F17
            Location: Corner of rue Laviolette; centre. 975 rue Hart G9A 4S3. Fax: 819/379-3941. **Facility:** 128 units. 127
            one-bedroom standard units. 1 one-bedroom suite. 6 stories, interior corridors. **Parking:** on-site.
Small-scale Hotel   **Terms:** check-in 4 pm, package plans. **Amenities:** video games (fee), voice mail, irons, hair dryers. *Some:*
            honor bars. **Dining:** 6:30 am-10 pm, Sat from 7 am, Sun 7 am-9 pm, cocktails. **Pool(s):** outdoor. **Leisure
Activities:** exercise room. **Guest Services:** valet laundry, wireless Internet. **Business Services:** conference facilities,
administrative services (fee). **Cards:** AX, DC, DS, JC, MC, VI.

SOME UNITS

FEE FEE

HOTEL LES SUITES DE LAVIOLETTE

Phone: (819)377-4747

All Year   1P: $79-$119   2P: $89-$129   XP: $10   F16

Location: Hwy 55, exit 181; at north end of Laviolette Bridge. 7201 rue Notre-Dame ouest G9B 1W2.

Small-scale Hotel   **Fax:** 819/377-2331. **Facility:** 102 units. 40 one-bedroom standard units, some with whirlpools. 62 one-bedroom suites ($109-$295), some with efficiencies and/or whirlpools. 2 stories (no elevator), interior/exterior corridors. **Parking:** on-site, winter plug-ins. **Terms:** 7 day cancellation notice. **Amenities:** voice mail, irons, hair dryers. *Some:* DVD players (fee), CD players, honor bars. **Pool(s):** heated outdoor. **Leisure Activities:** lighted tennis court, bicycles. **Guest Services:** sundries, coin laundry, area transportation, wireless Internet. **Business Services:** meeting rooms, PC. **Cards:** AX, DC, DS, MC, VI.

SOME UNITS

ASK ⓈⒹ 🏊 🛏 💻 / ✕ VCR / FEE

SUPER 8 MOTEL TROIS-RIVIERES

Phone: (819)377-5881

Ⓐ SAVE

5/1-10/15   1P: $119-$139   2P: $119-$139   XP: $15   F17

10/16-4/30   1P: $111-$131   2P: $111-$131   XP: $15   F17

Location: Hwy 55, exit 183 (boul Jean XXIII), just nw. 3185 boul Jean XXIII G9B 2M4. **Fax:** 819/377-2488.

Small-scale Hotel   **Facility:** 78 one-bedroom standard units, some with whirlpools. 3 stories, interior corridors. **Parking:** on-site, winter plug-ins. **Terms:** [ECP] meal plan available, package plans, pets ($15 extra charge). **Amenities:** high-speed Internet, voice mail, irons, hair dryers. *Some:* video games, dual phone lines. **Pool(s):** heated indoor. **Leisure Activities:** waterslide, exercise room. **Guest Services:** coin laundry, wireless Internet. **Business Services:** meeting rooms, PC. **Cards:** AX, DC, DS, MC, VI. **Free Special Amenities:** expanded continental breakfast and local telephone calls.

SOME UNITS

ⓈⒹ 🐕 🍴 🏊 📹 🛏 🖥 💻 / ✕ / FEE

WHERE TO DINE

AU FOUR A BOIS

Lunch: $8-$14   **Dinner:** $8-$26   **Phone:** 819/373-3686

Location: Corner of rue Hart; centre. 329 rue Laviolette G9A 1V1. **Hours:** 11:30 am-2 & 5-10 pm, Sat from 5 pm. Closed: 1/1, 12/24, 12/25; also Sun & for dinner Mon. **Reservations:** accepted. **Features:** The open dining room has the feel of a warm country home. A cozy fireplace and quaint, covered terrace lend to the informal atmosphere. The menu lays out a wide selection of pizzas prepared in a wood-burning oven, as well as steak, pasta and salad. Casual dress; cocktails. **Parking:** on-site. **Cards:** AX, MC, VI.

Canadian

CASTEL DES PRES RESTAURATION

Lunch: $12-$29   **Dinner:** $12-$29   **Phone:** 819/375-4921

Location: Hwy 55, exit 181, 0.6 mi (1 km) e on Rt 138. 5800 boul Royal G9A 4P2. **Hours:** 11 am-10 pm, Sat from 4:30 pm. Closed: 4/9, 10/8, 12/24, 12/25; also Sun. **Reservations:** accepted. **Features:** Smoked salmon is a flavorful choice on a varied menu that includes mussels, filet mignon, rack of lamb, sweetbreads, steak tartare, pasta, salads, sandwiches and steak with fries. Patrons can choose from seating in the lively bar-area bistro or in the more intimate adjacent dining room. The extensive wine list includes many by-the-glass selections. Terrace tables are popular during the summer. Casual dress; cocktails. **Parking:** on-site. **Cards:** AX, DC, MC, VI.

French

Ⓨ

CHEZ CORA

Lunch: $7-$11   **Phone:** 819/697-2662

Location: On Rt 138; centre. 1350 rue Royale G9A 4J4. **Hours:** 6 am-3 pm, Sun from 7 am. Closed: 1/1, 12/25. **Reservations:** not accepted. **Features:** Although this place specializes in breakfast, it offers a varied daytime menu that includes bacon, eggs, sausages, crepes, grilled cheese, sandwiches, freshly prepared quiches, salads, fruit platters and freshly squeezed juices. The family-friendly dining room is casual and modern. Casual dress. **Parking:** on-site. **Cards:** AX, DC, MC, VI.

Canadian

L'AUBERGE DU LAC ST-PIERRE DINING ROOM

Lunch: $12-$17   **Dinner:** $33-$48   **Phone:** 819/377-5971

Location: On Rt 138; in Pointe-du-Lac sector. 10911 rue Notre-Dame ouest G9B 7Y6. **Hours:** 7:30-11 am, 11:30-1:30 & 6-8:30 pm. Closed: 1/2-1/16. **Reservations:** suggested. **Features:** Patrons can enjoy casual dining in the contemporary country inn's dining room, which overlooks Lac St-Pierre. Eye-catching presentation marks dishes of refined French cuisine, most notably the appetizers. Four- and five-course table d'hote menus are offered. Dressy casual; cocktails. **Parking:** on-site. **Cards:** AX, DC, MC, VI. **Country Inn**

French

Ⓨ

LE TROQUET

Lunch: $8-$20   **Dinner:** $19-$37   **Phone:** 819/372-5979

Location: Corner of rue St-Roch; centre; in Delta Trois-Rivieres Hotel and Conference Center. 1620 rue Notre-Dame Centre G9A 6E5. **Hours:** 6:30 am-9:30 pm, Sat from 7 am. **Reservations:** suggested. **Features:** Colorful art and cherry paneling exemplify the bright, contemporary bistro decor. Preparations of Quebec cuisine include varieties of smoked trout, bison, veal and lamb. The dessert table displays a good selection of temptations. Casual dress; cocktails. **Parking:** on-site. **Cards:** AX, DC, DS, JC, MC, VI.

Canadian

Ⓨ

RESTAURANT LE LUPIN

Lunch: $8-$13   **Dinner:** $21-$32   **Phone:** 819/370-4740

Location: Corner of rue Champlain; centre. 376 rue St-Georges G9A 2K6. **Hours:** 11 am-2 & 5-close, Sat from 5 pm. Closed: Sun & Mon. **Reservations:** accepted. **Features:** In a vintage, two-story Victorian home, the restaurant is a nice spot for casual, comfortable dining. The ever-changing menu centers on traditional French dishes, crepes, mussels, fresh fish, game and fresh pasta. The beautifully presented stuffed crepe is delicious. Casual dress. **Parking:** street. **Cards:** AX, MC, VI.

French

RESTAURANT NORMANDIN

Lunch: $5-$12   **Dinner:** $5-$12   **Phone:** 819/372-0146

Location: On Hwy 157. 580 boul Thibeau G8T 6Z4. **Hours:** 24 hours. Closed: 12/25. **Reservations:** accepted. **Features:** The family restaurant prepares affordable comfort foods that include roasted chicken, hot chicken sandwiches, pasta, burgers and fries. Take-out service, a children's menu and cutely decorated desserts are among other offerings. Casual dress. **Parking:** on-site. **Cards:** AX, DC, MC, VI.

Canadian

RESTAURANT NORMANDIN

Lunch: $5-$12   **Dinner:** $5-$12   **Phone:** 819/372-0146

Location: On Hwy 157. 580 boul Thibeau. **Hours:** 24 hours. Closed: 12/25. **Reservations:** accepted. **Features:** The family restaurant prepares affordable comfort foods that include roasted chicken, hot chicken sandwiches, pasta, burgers and fries. Take-out service, a children's menu and cutely decorated desserts are among other offerings. Casual dress. **Parking:** on-site. **Cards:** AX, DC, MC, VI.

Canadian

RESTAURANT NORMANDIN
Lunch: $5-$12   **Dinner:** $5-$12   **Phone:** 819/691-0507
Location: Just ne of boul des Forges. 1350 boul des Recollets G8Z 4L5. **Hours:** 6 am-midnight, Thurs-2 am, Fri & Sat-3 am. Closed: 12/25. **Reservations:** accepted. **Features:** The family restaurant prepares affordable comfort foods that include roasted chicken, hot chicken sandwiches, pasta, burgers and fries. Take-out
Canadian   service, a children's menu and cutely decorated desserts are among other offerings. Casual dress. **Parking:**
on-site. **Cards:** AX, DC, MC, VI.

ST-HUBERT
Lunch: $7-$20   **Dinner:** $7-$20   **Phone:** 819/375-7521
Location: Hwy 40, exit boul des Forges. 5275 boul des Forges G8Y 4Z3. **Hours:** 11 am-11 pm, Fri & Sat-midnight. Closed: 12/25. **Reservations:** accepted. **Features:** The pleasantly decorated family-friendly restaurant serves affordable chicken dinners, ribs, club sandwiches, chicken wings, salads, soups and hot chicken
Canadian   sandwiches. The children's menu includes animal nuggets. Casual dress; cocktails. **Parking:** on-site.
Cards: MC, VI.

VAL-DAVID pop. 3,819

———— WHERE TO DINE ————

ROTISSERIE AU PETIT POUCET
Lunch: $8-$22   **Dinner:** $11-$22   **Phone:** 819/322-2246
Location: On Hwy 117; in town centre; Hwy 15 N, exit 76. 1030 Rt 117 J0T 2N0. **Hours:** 8 am-10 pm.
Reservations: accepted. **Features:** Maple-smoked ham, baked beans, pigs' knuckles, chicken pot pie,
Quebecois   rainbow trout and meat pie are representative of regional Quebecois comfort foods. The log cabin is appointed with woodwork and antiques that bring out warmth and rustic charm. Homemade fruit and sugar
pies are tempting desserts. A supper buffet is available Saturday and Sunday. Meats and preserves are available at a take-out counter. Casual dress; cocktails. **Parking:** on-site. **Cards:** AX, MC, VI.

VAL-D'OR pop. 22,748

———— WHERE TO STAY ————

COMFORT INN   *Book great rates at AAA.com*   **Phone:** 819/825-9360
Property failed to provide current rates
Location: In town centre. 1665 3ieme Ave J9P 1V9. Fax: 819/825-0419. **Facility:** 80 one-bedroom standard
Small-scale Hotel   units. 2 stories (no elevator), interior corridors. **Parking:** on-site, winter plug-ins. **Amenities:** voice mail, hair dryers. *Some:* irons. **Guest Services:** valet laundry, wireless Internet.
SOME UNITS

HOTEL FORESTEL   **Phone:** (819)825-5660
All Year   1P: $80-$140   2P: $80-$140   XP: $10   F14
Location: On Rt 117. 1001 3ieme ave est J9P 4P8. Fax: 819/825-8849. **Facility:** 91 units. 89 one-bedroom
standard units. 2 one-bedroom suites ($120-$150) with whirlpools. 2 stories, interior corridors. **Parking:** on-
Large-scale Hotel   site, winter plug-ins. **Terms:** check-in 4 pm, package plans. **Amenities:** voice mail, irons, hair dryers. *Some:* DVD players (fee), high-speed Internet. **Dining:** Le Bistro, see separate listing. **Guest Services:** valet laundry, wireless Internet.
Business Services: conference facilities, administrative services (fee), PC. **Cards:** AX, DC, DS, MC, VI.
SOME UNITS
FEE

HOTEL-MOTEL PRELUDE   **Phone:** (819)825-0090
1/1-4/30   1P: $81   2P: $88   XP: $7   F
5/1-12/31   1P: $74   2P: $81   XP: $7   F
Location: On Rt 117 N; in town centre. 1159 3ieme ave J9P 1T7. Fax: 819/825-0094. **Facility:** 26 one-bedroom
Small-scale Hotel   standard units. 2 stories (no elevator), interior/exterior corridors. *Bath:* combo or shower only. **Parking:** on-
site, winter plug-ins. **Terms:** cancellation fee imposed. **Amenities:** hair dryers. **Guest Services:** valet laundry. **Cards:** AX, MC, VI.
SOME UNITS

MOTEL L'ESCALE HOTEL SUITE   **Phone:** 819/824-2711
All Year   1P: $91-$121   2P: $101-$131   XP: $10   F5
Location: In town centre. 1100 rue L J9P 4G8. Fax: 819/825-2145. **Facility:** 70 units. 56 one-bedroom standard
units. 14 one-bedroom suites ($121-$141) with whirlpools. 2 stories (no elevator), interior/exterior corridors.
Small-scale Hotel   **Parking:** on-site, winter plug-ins. **Terms:** package plans, small pets only. **Amenities:** voice mail, irons, hair dryers. *Some:* high-speed Internet, honor bars. **Dining:** Restaurant Le Canon, see separate listing. **Leisure Activities:** snowmobiling. **Guest Services:** valet laundry, wireless Internet. **Business Services:** conference facilities, administrative services (fee). **Cards:** AX, DC, MC, VI.
SOME UNITS

———— WHERE TO DINE ————

LE BISTRO   **Dinner:** $21-$24   **Phone:** 819/825-5660
Location: On Rt 117; in Hotel Forestel. 1001 3ieme ave est J9P 4P8. **Hours:** 5 pm-10 pm.
Reservations: suggested. **Features:** Regional produce inspires the menu of French cuisine, including pork
French   fillets, chicken supreme, rib steak, brook trout, Caesar salad and fine Quebec cheeses. The casually elegant dining room has a lounge area and pretty aquarium. Casual dress; cocktails. **Parking:** on-site. **Cards:** AX,
DS, MC, VI.

PASTA D'ARMANDO   **Lunch:** $7-$28   **Dinner:** $7-$28   **Phone:** 819/874-4419
Location: On Rt 117; centre. 1666 3ieme ave J9P 1W1. **Hours:** 8 am-10 pm, Thurs-Sat to 11 pm. Closed: 12/25.
Reservations: accepted. **Features:** This casual family restaurant features three eateries under one roof:
Italian   Pasta D'Armando, Pizza Planet and "O" Poulet. Lasagna and cannelloni are specialties along with a variety of other pastas, rotisserie chicken, pizza, raclette and fondues. Bring your own wine. Take-out pasta and
sauces are available. Casual dress. **Parking:** on-site. **Cards:** AX, MC, VI.

RESTAURANT LE CANON   Lunch: $10-$14   ·   Dinner: $16-$45   Phone: 819/824-2711
▼▼▼ **Location:** In town centre; in Motel L'Escale Hotel Suite. 1100 rue L'Escale J9P 4G8. **Hours:** 6:30 am-1:30 & 5:30-11
pm, Sat & Sun from 7:30 am. Closed: 1/1, 12/25. **Reservations:** suggested. **Features:** The cozy hotel
Steak & Seafood restaurant has elegant country decor and is one of the best places in town for steak and seafood. Menu
selections include trout, beef brochettes, filet mignon, scallops, shrimp, rack of lamb, roast beef, Chinese
fondue, walleye filet, seafood linguine, grilled lobster tails, scampi, escargots and smoked salmon. For dessert, try cheesecake
or creme caramel. Casual dress; cocktails. **Parking:** on-site. **Cards:** AX; DC, MC, VI.

RESTAURANT PIZZERIA VAL-D'OR   Lunch: $7-$10   Dinner: $7-$10   Phone: 819/825-7111
▼▼▼ **Location:** On Rt 117; centre. 1272 3ieme ave J9P 1V4. **Hours:** 11 am-10 pm, Thurs-Sat to midnight, Sun 11:30
am-10 pm. Closed: 1/1, 12/25. **Reservations:** accepted. **Features:** This popular family restaurant
Canadian specializes in pizza, pasta, burgers, fries, poutine, barbecue chicken and fish and chips. Casual dress;
cocktails. **Parking:** on-site. **Cards:** MC, VI.

VALLEE-JONCTION pop. 1,882
———— WHERE TO DINE ————

RESTAURANT FEUILLE D'ERABLE   Lunch: $8-$20   Dinner: $13-$20   Phone: 418/253-6133
▼▼▼ **Location:** On Rt 173 at jct Rt 112 W; centre. 242 rue Principale G0S 3J0. **Hours:** 7:30 am-9 pm, Mon-2 pm.
Reservations: accepted. **Features:** A large, stained-glass maple leaf adorns the wall of the casual family-
Canadian friendly eatery, which has a second, more upscale dining room where French cuisine is served. Among
wholesome meals are hamburger steak with mashed potatoes, club sandwiches, chicken, steaks, seafood
pasta, fish, pizza and poutine. Themed buffets, take-out service and a salad bar are available. Casual dress; cocktails. **Parking:**
on-site. **Cards:** AX, MC, VI.

VAL-MORIN pop. 2,216
———— WHERE TO DINE ————

CREPERIE BRETONNE AU TOURNESOL   Lunch: $5-$19   Dinner: $5-$19   Phone: 819/322-1401
▼▼▼ **Location:** Hwy 15, exit 76, then just ne. 5825 Rt 117 J0T 2R0. **Hours:** Open 5/1-11/1 & 12/1-4/30; 5 pm-9 pm, Fri
& Sat 11 am-10 pm, Sun 11 am-9 pm. Closed: Mon & Tues, also 2 weeks in April.
French **Reservations:** suggested. **Features:** The beamed ceiling and varnished pine tables of this casual creperie
provide the charm of a quaint ski lodge, where guests may enjoy a variety of freshly prepared Bretagne-
style crepes (thin pancakes). Start your meal with a cheese-topped French onion soup; end it with a delicious fruit dessert
crepe. The crepes are prepared right before your eyes in an open kitchen. Casual dress; cocktails. **Parking:** on-site.
Cards: MC, VI.

VAUDREUIL-DORION —See Montreal p. 495.

VERDUN —See Montreal p. 496.

WAKEFIELD
———— WHERE TO STAY ————

AUBERGE LE MOULIN WAKEFIELD MILL INN & SPA   Phone: 819/459-1838
▼▼▼   Property failed to provide current rates
Location: 0.6 mi (1 km) w of Riverside Dr; centre. 60 chemin Mill J0X 3G0. Fax: 819/459-1697. **Facility:** This
Historic stone-walled inn, adjacent to Gatineau Park, offers upscale guest rooms and fine dining in a scenic rural
Country Inn setting. Smoke free premises. 27 one-bedroom standard units, some with whirlpools. 5 stories, interior
corridors. *Bath:* combo or shower only. **Parking:** on-site. **Terms:** check-in 4 pm. **Amenities:** dual phone
lines, voice mail, hair dryers. *Some:* irons. **Leisure Activities:** whirlpool, cross country skiing, snowmobiling, tobogganing,
hiking trails, spa. **Guest Services:** wireless Internet. **Business Services:** meeting rooms.

SOME UNITS

🍽 ☂ ⊠ ⊠ 🐾 ▣ / VCR /
FEE

WEST BROME
———— WHERE TO STAY ————

AUBERGE & SPA WEST BROME   Phone: (450)266-7552
CAA SAVE All Year   2P: $145-$245   XP: $34   F5
▼▼▼ **Location:** Jct Rt 104, 1.3 mi (2.1 km) s. 128 Rt 139 J0E 2P0. Fax: 450/266-2040. **Facility:** 25 units. 13 one-
bedroom standard units, some with kitchens and/or whirlpools. 12 one-bedroom suites with kitchens. 3
Small-scale Hotel stories (no elevator), interior corridors. **Parking:** on-site, winter plug-ins. **Terms:** office hours 7 am-11 pm, 3
day cancellation notice-fee imposed, [AP], [BP] & [MAP] meal plans available, package plans.
Amenities: voice mail, irons, hair dryers. *Some:* DVD players, CD players. **Dining:** restaurant, see separate
listing. **Pool(s):** heated outdoor. **Leisure Activities:** whirlpool, steamroom, spa. **Guest Services:** valet laundry, wireless
Internet. **Business Services:** meeting rooms, PC. **Cards:** AX, MC, VI. **Free Special Amenities:** full breakfast and high-
speed Internet.

SOME UNITS

🍽 🏠 🏊 ⊠ ⊠ 📺 🐾 / 📁 ▣ /

———— WHERE TO DINE ————

AUBERGE WEST BROME
RESTAURANT   Dinner: $25-$30   Phone: 450/266-7552
CAA **Location:** Jct Rt 104, 1.3 mi (2.1 km) s. 128 Route 139 J0E 2P0. **Hours:** 6 pm-10 pm. **Reservations:** suggested.
Features: The sommelier provides detailed information about wines to complement French-inspired
▼▼▼ choices, such as preparations of Angus beef, fresh fish, Quebec veal and lamb, Atlantic salmon and
seafood. Gracious servers tend to patrons in the charming and elegant country setting. Casual dress;
French cocktails. **Parking:** on-site. **Cards:** AX, DC, MC, VI.

WESTMOUNT —See Montreal p. 496.

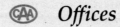 Offices

Cities with main offices are listed in **BOLD TYPE** and toll-free member service numbers in *ITALIC TYPE*.
All are closed Saturdays, Sundays and holidays unless otherwise indicated.
The type of service provided is designated below the name of the city where the office is located:

✦ Auto travel services, including books/maps, marked maps and on-demand TripTik® maps
● Auto travel services, including books/maps, marked maps, but no on-demand TripTik® maps
■ Provides books/maps only. No marked maps or on-demand TripTik® maps available
▲ Travel agency services

NATIONAL OFFICE: 1000 AAA DRIVE, HEATHROW, FLORIDA 32746-5063, (407) 444-7000

NEW BRUNSWICK

FREDERICTON—CAA MARITIMES, 418 YORK ST, E3B 3P7.
MON-FRI 8:30-5:30, THU 8:30-7, SAT 10-1. (506) 452-1987,
(800) 561-8807.●▲

MONCTON—CAA MARITIMES, 60 KING ST, E1C 4M2. MON-FRI
8:30-5:30, THU 8:30-7, SAT 10-1. (506) 857-8225,
(800) 561-8807.●▲

SAINT JOHN—CAA MARITIMES, 378 WESTMORLAND RD, E2J
2G4. MON-FRI 8:30-5, THU 8:30-7, SAT 10-1. (506) 634-1400,
(800) 561-8807.✦▲

NOVA SCOTIA

DARTMOUTH—CAA MARITIMES, 133 ILSLEY AVE UNIT H, B3B
1S9. MON-FRI 8:30-5:30, THU 8:30-7, SAT 10-1. (902) 468-6306,
(800) 561-8807.●▲

HALIFAX—CAA MARITIMES, 3514 JOSEPH HOWE DR STE 5,
B3L 4H7. MON-FRI 8:30-5:30, THU 8:30-7, SAT 10-1.
(902) 443-5530, *(800) 561-8807.*●▲

PRINCE EDWARD ISLAND

CHARLOTTETOWN—CAA MARITIMES, 330 UNIVERSITY AVE,
C1A 4M4. MON-FRI 8:30-5:30, SAT 10-1. (902) 892-1612,
(800) 561-8807.●▲

QUEBEC

BROSSARD—CAA QUEBEC, 3-G PLACE DU COMMERCE #G,
J4W 2Z6. MON-FRI 9-6, THU & FRI 9-8, SAT 10-4.
(514) 861-7575, *(800) 686-9243.*●▲

CHICOUTIMI—CAA QUEBEC, 1100-1700 TALBOT BLVD, G7H
7Z4. MON-FRI 9-5:30, THU 9-8, SAT 9-4. (514) 861-7575,
(800) 686-9243.●▲

GATINEAU—CAA QUEBEC, 101-290 BLVD ST-JOSEPH, J8Y 3Y3.
MON-FRI 9-6, THU 9-8, SAT 10-4. (514) 861-7575,
(800) 686-9243.●▲

LACHENAIE—CAA QUEBEC, 302 MONTEE DES PIONNIERS, J6V
1S6. MON-FRI 10-6, THU & FRI 10-8, SAT 10-5. (514) 861-7575,
(514) 686-9243.✦▲

LAVAL—CAA QUEBEC, 3131 W ST-MARTIN BLVD 100, H7T
2Z5. MON-FRI 9-6, THU & FRI 9-8, SAT 10-4. (514) 861-7575,
(800) 686-9243.●▲

MONTREAL—CAA QUEBEC, 101-1180 DRUMMOND ST, H3G
2R7. MON-FRI 8:30-6, THU & FRI 8:30-7, SAT 10-4.
(514) 861-7575, *(800) 686-9243.*●▲

POINTE-CLAIRE—CAA QUEBEC, 90-1000 ST JEAN BLVD, H9R
5P1. MON-FRI 9-6, THU & FRI 9-8, SAT 10-4. (514) 861-7575,
(800) 686-9243.●▲

QUEBEC—CAA QUEBEC, 444 BOUVIER ST, G2J 1E3. MON-FRI
8:30-5. (418) 624-2424, *(800) 686-9243.*
[Administrative office only]

QUEBEC—CAA QUEBEC, 202-500 BOUVIER ST, G2J 1E3.
MON-FRI 9-5:30, THU & FRI 9-8, SAT 10-4. (514) 861-7575,
(800) 686-9243.✦▲

SHERBROOKE—CAA QUEBEC, 2990 KING W ST, J1L 1Y7.
MON-FRI 9-5:30, THU & FRI 9-8, SAT 10-4. (514) 861-7575,
(800) 686-9243.●▲

STE-FOY—CAA QUEBEC, 133-2600 LAURIER BLVD, G1V 4T3.
MON-FRI 9-5:30, THU & FRI 9-8, SAT 10-4. (514) 861-7575,
(800) 686-9243.●▲

ST-LEONARD—CAA QUEBEC, 7360 LANGELIER BLVD, H1S 3C4.
MON-FRI 9-6, THU & FRI 9-8, SAT 10-4. (514) 861-7575,
(800) 686-9243.●▲

TROIS-RIVIERES—CAA QUEBEC, 4450 DES FORGES BLVD, G8Y
1W5. MON-FRI 9-5:30, THU & FRI 9-8, SAT 10-4.
(514) 861-7575, *(800) 686-9243.*●▲

Population

Canadian population figures—Statistics Canada's 2001 GeoSuite, by permission of Canadian Minister of Industry.

Metric Equivalents Chart

TEMPERATURE

To convert Fahrenheit to Celsius, subtract 32 from the Fahrenheit temperature, multiply by 5 and divide by 9.
To convert Celsius to Fahrenheit, multipy by 9, divide by 5 and add 32.

ACRES

1 acre = 0.4 hectare (ha)   1 hectare = 2.47 acres

MILES AND KILOMETRES

Note: A kilometre is approximately 5/8 or 0.6 of a mile.
To convert kilometres to miles multiply by 0.6.

Miles/Kilometres	Kilometres/Miles
15..........................24.1	30..........................18.6
20..........................32.2	35..........................21.7
25..........................40.2	40..........................24.8
30..........................48.3	45..........................27.9
35..........................56.3	50..........................31.0
40..........................64.4	55..........................34.1
45..........................72.4	60..........................37.2
50..........................80.5	65..........................40.3
55..........................88.5	70..........................43.4
60..........................96.6	75..........................46.6
65..........................104.6	80..........................49.7
70..........................112.7	85..........................52.8
75..........................120.7	90..........................55.9
80..........................128.7	95..........................59.0
85..........................136.8	100..........................62.1
90..........................144.8	105..........................65.2
95..........................152.9	110..........................68.3
100..........................160.9	115..........................71.4

Celsius ° / Fahrenheit °

Celsius °		Fahrenheit °
100	BOILING	212
37		100
35		95
32		90
29		85
27		80
24		75
21		70
18		65
16		60
13		55
10		50
7		45
4		40
2		35
0	FREEZING	32
-4		25
-7		20
-9		15
-12		10
-15		5
-18		0
-21		-5
-24		-10
-27		-15

LINEAR MEASURE

Customary	Metric
1 inch = 2.54 centimetres	1 centimetre = 0.4 inches
1 foot = 30 centimetres	1 metre = 3.3 feet
1 yard = 0.91 metres	1 metre = 1.09 yards
1 mile = 1.6 kilometres	1 kilometre = .62 miles

WEIGHT

If You Know:	Multiply By:	To Find:
Ounces	28.000	Grams
Pounds	0.450	Kilograms
Grams	0.035	Ounces
Kilograms	2.200	Pounds

LIQUID MEASURE

Customary	Metric
1 fluid ounce = 30 millilitres	1 millilitre = .03 fluid ounces
1 cup = .24 litres	1 litre = 2.1 pints
1 pint = .47 litres	1 litre = 1.06 quarts
1 quart = .95 litres	1 litre = .26 gallons
1 gallon = 3.8 litres	

PRESSURE

Air pressure in automobile tires is expressed in kilopascals. Multiply pound-force per square inch (psi) by 6.89 to find kilopascals (kPa).

24 psi = 165 kPa   28 psi = 193 kPa
26 psi = 179 kPa   30 psi = 207 kPa

GALLON AND LITRES

Gallons/Litres		Litres/Gallons	
5..........................19.0	12..........................45.6	10..........................2.6	40..........................10.4
6..........................22.8	14..........................53.2	15..........................3.9	50..........................13.0
7..........................26.6	16..........................60.8	20..........................5.2	60..........................15.6
8..........................30.4	18..........................68.4	25..........................6.5	70..........................18.2
9..........................34.2	20..........................76.0	30..........................7.8	80..........................20.8
10..........................38.0	25..........................95.0	35..........................9.1	90..........................23.4

Approved

The Symbols of Quality

Only properties that meet the strict quality criteria to become CAA/AAA Approved receive a CAA/AAA Diamond rating. This means that every CAA/AAA Approved lodging and restaurant, regardless of its Diamond rating, delivers the basic qualities members require.

Diamond ratings provide an easy way to select quality lodgings and restaurants with the amenities and degree of sophistication you desire.

Each Approved and Diamond rated establishment is visited and thoroughly reviewed by CAA/AAA's professional evaluators.

One Diamond lodgings are basic, no-frills accommodations appealing to the budget-minded. Restaurants offer simple, affordable dining in a casual or self-service style.

Two Diamond lodgings show modest enhancements in décor and amenities. Restaurants are informal yet rise above the ordinary, often well-suited to family dining.

Three Diamond lodgings offer a higher level of physical appeal, comfort and amenities. Restaurants provide a more creative, upscale, adult-oriented experience.

Four Diamond lodgings feature a high level of service amid upscale surroundings. Restaurants offer fine distinctive dining with complex menu offerings and a highly skilled staff.

Five Diamond lodgings offer extraordinary luxury, personalized services, and extensive amenities. Restaurants are world-class, providing innovative cuisine and impeccable service.

For quality assurance, choose only CAA/AAA Approved lodgings and restaurants. Then for a perfect match, select the Diamond rating that best meets your needs.

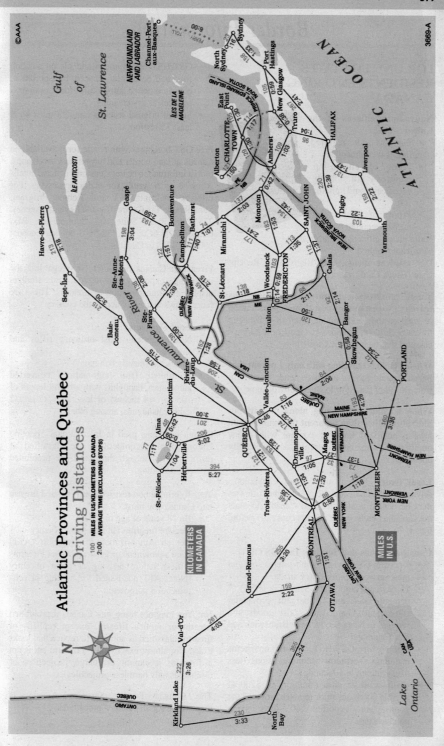

Atlantic Provinces and Québec
Driving Distances

100 MILES IN US/KILOMETERS IN CANADA
2:00 AVERAGE TIME (EXCLUDING STOPS)

Border Information

FOR UNITED STATES RESIDENTS ENTERING CANADA

Native-born citizens of the United States:
- Passport not required (but is recommended)
- Proof of citizenship required (a birth certificate and photo ID)
- Proof of residence may be required

Naturalized citizens: naturalization certificate required

U.S. resident aliens: Alien Registration Receipt Card (Green Card) required

Single parents, grandparents or guardians traveling with a minor must show documentation of legal custody and provide proof of citizenship for each child (the minor's passport or a parent's passport that includes the child).

When a child is traveling with only 1 parent that parent should have a notarized letter of consent from the other parent or legal custody documents.

When a child is traveling alone or with an individual other than a parent the minor should have a notarized letter of consent with phone number(s) from both parents or a custody document.

Legal Issues: Persons with felony convictions, driving while intoxicated records or other offenses may be denied admittance into Canada. Contact the Canadian embassy or nearest consulate before travel.

Canadian Goods and Services Tax (GST):
- 7 percent GST levied on most items sold and most services rendered in Canada
- 15 percent Harmonized Sales Tax (HST) (7 percent GST and 8 percent provincial component) charged on most goods and services in Nova Scotia, New Brunswick and Newfoundland
- Apply for GST/HST rebate on items including short-term accommodations (less than 1 month in 1 location)
- Claim a rebate on a minimum of $200 of eligible purchases prior to taxes provided the goods are exported 60 days from purchase date
- GST/HST rebate not refundable on alcohol, food and beverages, tobacco, transportation, entertainment, automobile fuel and such services as dry cleaning
- Submit original receipts (amount must be at least $50 before tax)

Free GST brochures with rebate form available in Canada at land border and airport duty-free shops, tourist information centers, customs offices, hotels. Allow 4 to 6 weeks for claim processing. For information contact: Visitor Rebate Program, Summerside Tax Centre, Canada Revenue Agency, 275 Pope Road, Suite 104, Summerside, P.E., Canada C1N 6C6; 902-432-5608 outside Canada; 800-668-4748 in Canada.

Firearms: Canada has strict laws regarding the importing, exporting, possession, use, storage, display and transportation of firearms. These are federal laws that apply across the country.

Classes of Firearms:
- Non-restricted (most ordinary rifles and shotguns)
- Restricted (mainly handguns)
- Prohibited (full automatics, converted automatics, handguns with a barrel length of 105 m ($\approx$4 inches) or less, and .25 or .32 caliber handguns, among others)

Certain handguns used in International Shooting Union sporting competition are classified as restricted even though they meet the prohibited handgun definition.

Yes: To bring a non-restricted or restricted firearm into Canada you must:
- Be 18 years of age or older
- Declare firearm(s) at first point of entry
- Get an Authorization to Transport (ATT) from a provincial or territorial Chief Firearms Officer before arriving at point of entry (Note: ATT not issued for hunting or self-protection purposes)

No: You may not bring into Canada a prohibited firearm or replica firearm, except replicas of firearms classified as antiques (a replica that looks exactly, or almost exactly, like a firearm but is not a firearm; it cannot discharge projectiles or discharges only harmless projectiles).

The Canada Border Services Agency is responsible for all customs procedures.

Yes:

- You may import non-restricted firearms for legitimate purposes: sporting or hunting; use in competitions; transit movement; or personal protection against wildlife in remote areas (customs officer must agree that circumstances warrant firearm possession)
- Register weapons with U.S. Customs before departure
- Upon return you must show proof that you had the weapon before departure
- Under certain circumstances individuals and businesses may import firearms

No: Non-residents may not import prohibited items.

Fees (in Canadian funds):

- Non-Resident Firearm Declaration – $50 covers all firearms listed on declaration
- Possession and acquisition license – $60 for non-restricted firearms; valid for 5 years
- Temporary Firearms Borrowing License (for non-residents) – $30; may renew once in a 12-month period at no extra cost; $30 thereafter (800-731-4000)
- Imported firearm registration fee – $25 per firearm registered in Canada

Prohibited: Any large capacity cartridge magazine (limited to 5 rounds for semiautomatic rifles or shotguns, 10 rounds for handguns), any device designed to stop the sound of a firearm, any knife with a blade opened by spring pressure (e.g., switchblade), martial arts weapons (e.g., shuriken (shooting stars), nunchaku sticks), mace, blowguns, hand-held compact crossbows and any other weapons declared prohibited by regulation.

Yes: Hunters may bring in, duty-free, 200 rounds of ammunition; competition participants 1,500 rounds. Must show valid license or declaration to purchase ammunition. If planning to hunt in multiple provinces or territories, you must obtain a hunting license from each one.

No: Firearms forbidden in many of Canada's national and provincial parks, game reserves and adjacent areas.

Parks and Hunting Regulation Information: Newfoundland and Labrador 800-563-6353 or 709-729-2830; Prince Edward Island 888-734-7529 or 902-629-2400; Nova Scotia 800-565-0000 ext 998 or 902-425-5781; New Brunswick 800-561-0123 or 506-789-4982; Quebec 800-363-7777 or 514-873-2015; Ontario 800-668-2746 or 416-314-0944; Manitoba 800-665-0040 or 204-945-3777; Saskatchewan 877-237-2273 or 306-787-2300; Alberta 800-661-8888 or 780-427-4321; British Columbia 800-663-6000 or 250-387-1642; Northwest Territories (Western NWT) 800-661-0788 or 867-873-4059; Nunavut (Eastern NWT) 800-491-7910 or 867-979-1261; Yukon 867-667-5340.

Note: Provinces and territories also have their own laws regulating the transportation of firearms through their areas, usually in connection with their hunting regulations. For further information on the entry of firearms, applying for a license or to obtain authorization to transport a firearm, contact: Canadian Firearms Centre at 800-731-4000.

Personal Baggage:

- Admissible into Canada on a temporary basis without payment of duty and taxes
- Customs may require a refundable security deposit at time of entry
- Deposits not normally required for health- or pleasure-related visits as long as all items are exported at trip's end

Personal baggage that may be taken into Canada on a duty- and tax-free basis includes clothing and personal items, sporting goods, automobiles, vessels, aircraft, snowmobiles, cameras, personal computers, food products and other items appropriate for the purpose and duration of the visit.

Tobacco products – Those meeting age requirements (18 years in Alberta, Manitoba, Northwest Territories and Nunavut, Saskatchewan, Quebec and Yukon Territory; 19 years in other provinces) may bring in 50 cigars, 200 cigarettes, 200 grams of tobacco and 200 tobacco sticks. **Alcohol** – Those meeting age requirements (18 years in Alberta, Manitoba and Quebec; 19 years in other provinces and territories) may bring in limited alcoholic beverages: 40 ounces (1.14 L) of liquor, 1.6 quarts (1.5 L) of wine or 9 quarts (8.6 L) of beer or ale (equivalent to 24 12-ounce bottles or cans).

- Generally, a minimum 24-hour stay is required to transport any liquor or tobacco into Canada

- Amounts exceeding the allowable quantities noted above are subject to federal duty and taxes, and provincial/territorial liquor fees
- Pay provincial fees at customs at the time of entry in all provinces and the Yukon Territory
- Illegal to bring more than the allowable alcohol quantity into the Northwest Territories and Nunavut

Articles purchased at Canadian duty-free shops are subject to U.S. Customs exemptions and restrictions; those purchased at U.S. duty-free shops before entering Canada are subject to duty if brought back into the United States.

Prescription Drugs: Persons requiring medication while visiting Canada are permitted to bring it for their own use. Clearly identify and carry in original packaging with a label listing the drug and its intended use. Have a copy of the prescription and prescribing doctor's phone number.

Gifts: Items not exceeding $60 (CAN) in value, excluding tobacco, alcoholic beverages and advertising matter, taken into or mailed to Canada are allowed free entry. Gifts valued at more than $60 are subject to regular duty and taxes on the excess amount.

Pets and Plants: You must have a certificate for a dog or cat age 3 months and older. It must clearly describe the animal, declare that the animal has been vaccinated

against rabies within the past 36 months, and have a licensed veterinarian signature.

- Collar tags are not sufficient proof of immunization
- Be sure the vaccination does not expire while traveling in Canada
- The certificate is also required to bring the animal back into the United States

Exempt From These Rules: Assist dogs; healthy puppies and kittens under 3 months old with a health certificate, signed by a licensed veterinarian, indicating that the animal is too young to vaccinate.

Plants or plant material must be declared. For information, contact: Canadian Food Inspection Agency (CFIA), 59 Camelot Dr., Ottawa, OT K1A 0Y9; 613-225-2342.

Radio Communication Equipment
- Cell phone, PCS phone, citizens band (CB) or Family Radio Service radio allowed without prior registration
- Use of aircraft, marine or amateur radio allowed without prior authorization
- All other types of radio transmitting stations allowed with authorization letter from Industry Canada's Radiocommun-ication and Broadcasting Regulatory Branch

Special Permits: A CITIES (Convention on International Trade in Endangered Species) permit is required for any endangered species brought into Canada, including those kept as pets, and for any items made from them (e.g., coats, handbags, shoes). For information contact: Environment Canada, Canadian Wildlife Service at 819-997-1840.

An Export Permit may be required to take out of Canada objects more than 50 years old (e.g., fossils, archaeological artifacts, fine and decorative art, technological objects or books and archival material). Contact: Movable Cultural Property Program of Canadian Heritage, 15 Eddy St., 3rd Floor, Hull, Quebec, Canada K1A 0M5; 819-997-7761.

An Import Permit may be required for the importation of clothing, textiles, steel and certain agricultural products in excess of minimum quantities. For information contact: Department of Foreign Affairs and Int'l Trade, Export and Import Controls Bureau, Tower C, 4th Floor, LB Pearson Bldg, 125 Sussex Dr., Ottawa, OT K1A 0G2.

Vehicles
- Vehicles entering Canada for touring, including trailers not exceeding 8 feet 6 inches (2.6 m) in width are generally subject to quick and routine entry procedures.
- To leave or store a car, trailer or other goods in Canada while you leave the country you must pay import duty and taxes or present a valid permit. Canadian Customs officials issue permits at point of entry.
- You may not store a vacation trailer in Canada during the off-season.
- Vehicle registration cards required for Canadian travel.
- If driving a car other than your own, you must have written permission from the owner to use it.
- If driving a rented car, you must possess a copy of the contract.
- A valid U.S. driver's license is valid in Canada for time period specified by the individual provinces and territories.

- In all Canadian provinces and territories it is illegal to use radar detectors.
- Seat belts required for the driver and all passengers throughout Canada.

Headlights: Driving with vehicle headlights on for extended periods after dawn and before dusk is  a statutory requirement in provinces and territories.

- In Alberta, British Columbia, New Brunswick, Ontario and Prince Edward Island, lights must be turned on when light conditions restrict visibility to 500 feet (150 m).
- In Manitoba, lights must be turned on when light conditions restrict visibility to 200 feet (60 m).
- In Alberta, Yukon Territory, Northwest Territories and Nunavut, headlights must remain on at all times.
- Elsewhere in Canada, driving with headlights on during all hours of the day is advised.

FINANCIAL RESPONSIBILITY LAWS IN CANADA

When an accident involves death, injury or property damage, Canadian provinces and territories require evidence of financial responsibility. You may be asked to show this evidence at any time.

U.S. motorists should obtain from their own U.S. insurance companies a yellow Non-Resident Inter-Province Motor Vehicle Liability Insurance Card (accepted as evidence of financial responsibility throughout Canada). Those not carrying proper proof may be subject to a substantial fine (minimum $575). Fine varies in each province. If renting a vehicle, check with the rental car company.

The minimum liability insurance requirement is $200,000 in all provinces and territories except Quebec, which requires $50,000. Should the courts' judgments exceed these figures, motorists held accountable are responsible for paying the full amount.

If traveling in Quebec, discuss your collision, disability and bodily injury coverages with your insurance agent. Since Quebec's minimum requirement does not include bodily injury, coverage of $200,000 or more is recommended. Consider additional coverage (i.e., trip accident policy).

FOR UNITED STATES RESIDENTS RETURNING TO THE UNITED STATES

Everyone who seeks entry into the United States – whether foreign visitors, U.S. citizens, or U.S. lawful permanent residents – must be inspected at the point of entry. Random searches may be conducted by U.S. Customs and Border Protection agents.

U.S. Exemptions for a Stay in Canada No Less Than 48 hours

- You may bring back tax- and duty-free articles not exceeding $800 in retail value
- Any amount over the $800 exemption is subject to duty
- The exemption is allowed once every 30 days
- A family (related persons living in the same household) may combine its exemptions (a family of 6 is entitled to $4,800 worth of goods duty-free on 1 declaration, even if articles claimed by 1 member exceed that individual's $800 amount)
- Exemptions based on fair retail value (keep receipts of all purchases as proof of fair retail value)
- Exemptions apply to articles acquired only for personal or household use or as gifts, but not intended for sale
- The exemption may include 100 cigars, 200 cigarettes and 1 liter of liquor per person over age 21 (customs enforces state liquor laws)
- All articles claimed under this exemption must accompany you on your return

U.S. Exemptions for a Stay in Canada Less Than 48 hours

- You may bring back tax- and duty-free articles not exceeding $200 in retail value
- The exemption may include no more than 50 cigarettes, 10 cigars, 4 fluid ounces (150 milliliters) of alcoholic beverage or 150 milliliters of perfume containing alcohol
- A family may not combine purchases
- If purchases exceed the $200 exemption, you lose the exemption and all purchases become subject to duty
- All goods must be declared
- All articles claimed under this exemption must accompany you on your return

Gifts

- Gifts up to $100 fair retail value may be sent to friends or relatives in the United States provided no recipient receives more than 1 gift per day (need not be included in the $800 exemption)

- Gifts containing tobacco products, alcoholic beverages or perfume containing alcohol valued at more than $5 retail are excluded from this provision
- Write on outside of package the contents, retail value and "Unsolicited Gift"

Prohibited: Articles considered detrimental to the general welfare of the United States are prohibited entry: narcotics and dangerous drugs, drug paraphernalia, obscene articles and publications, seditious or treasonable matter, lottery tickets, hazardous items (fireworks, dangerous toys, toxic or poisonous substances) and switchblade knives. Any goods originating in the following countries are prohibited: Balkans, Burma, Cuba, Iran, Iraq, Liberia, Libya, North Korea, Sudan, Syria and Zimbabwe. Please note embargoes are not limited to these countries.

Restricted items include automobiles, biological materials (disease organisms and vectors for research), ceramic tableware, cultural treasures, firearms and ammunition, articles bearing marks or names copying or simulating trademarked articles or trade names (watches, cameras, perfumes), pirated copies of copyrighted articles (books, CDs, DVDs, audio- and video-tapes, computer programs), agricultural goods (plants and animal products) and pets, wildlife and fish.

You may bring into or take out of the United States an unlimited amount of money, however, if you transport more than $10,000 you must file a Form 4790 with U.S. Customs. Failure to comply can result in civil, criminal and/or forfeiture penalties. Monies include currency, traveler's checks, U.S. or foreign coins in circulation, money orders and negotiable instruments or investment securities in bearer form. For a currency reporting flier contact: U.S. Customs, P.O. Box 7407, Washington, D.C. 20044.

While some agricultural products of Canadian origin (fruits, some plants with phyto-sanitary certificates, meats, etc.) may be brought into the United States, many are restricted to prevent the introduction of plant and animal pests and diseases. All must be declared at the U.S. border. Write to APHIS, Dept. of Agriculture, 6505 Belcrest Rd., Hyattsville, MD 20782, for a free copy of *Traveler's Tips*. Write to U.S. Customs, P.O. Box 7407, Washington, D.C. 20044 for other

helpful leaflets: *Visiting the U.S.: Requirements for Non-Residents*, *Know Before You Go*, *Importing a Car*, and *Pets, Wildlife and U.S. Customs*.

FOR CANADA RESIDENTS ENTERING THE UNITED STATES

Native-born citizens of Canada:
- Passport not required (but is recommended)
- Proof of citizenship required (a birth certificate and photo ID)
- Proof of residence may be required

If traveling to the United States with a child, carry documentation proving your custodial rights. A person under age 18 traveling to the United States alone or with only 1 parent or another adult, must have certified documentation proving that the trip is permitted by both parents.

United States Customs permits Canadian residents to bring, free of duty, for personal use and not intended for sale: clothing, personal items and equipment appropriate to the trip, including 200 cigarettes, 50 cigars or 2 kilograms of tobacco, or proportionate amounts of each, and 1 liter of alcoholic beverage.

Visitors in the United States for at least 72 hours who have not claimed this exemption in the preceding 6 months may bring gifts totaling $100 (US) retail value. Perfume containing alcohol and valued at more than $5 retail, tobacco products and alcoholic beverages excluded from the gift provision.

Use of cell phones and General Radio Service Station (CB) is unrestricted.

FOR CANADA RESIDENTS RETURNING TO CANADA

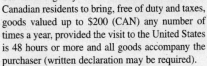

The Canada Border Services Agency allows Canadian residents to bring, free of duty and taxes, goods valued up to $200 (CAN) any number of times a year, provided the visit to the United States is 48 hours or more and all goods accompany the purchaser (written declaration may be required).

You may claim a $50 (CAN) exemption on goods, excluding alcoholic beverages and tobacco products, if returning after an absence of 24 hours or more and are not using any other exemption. If bringing back more than $50 worth of goods, the regular duty and tax rate is levied on the entire value. This exemption may apply any number of times in a year.

If returning after 7 days or more in the United States (not counting departure day from Canada) you may claim up to a $750 (CAN) exemption on goods. Goods, other than alcohol and tobacco products, need not accompany you (written declaration may be required).

Permitted within the $200 and $750 exemptions: up to 50 cigars, 200 cigarettes, 200 tobacco sticks and 200 grams (6.4 oz) of tobacco, and up to 1.14 liters (40 oz) of liquor or 1.5 liters (1.6 qts) of wine or 8.5 liters (9 qts) of beer or ale (or its equivalent of 24 12-ounce bottles or cans). You must meet the minimum age requirement of the province or territory entered to claim alcohol or tobacco products.

Special Tariff: When exceeding the $200 or $750 exemption, a special rate of 7 percent combined duty and taxes is  levied on the next $300 value in goods (except tobacco and alcohol) exceeding the maximum exemptible amounts, provided goods are of U.S origin. Regular duties apply on any additional amount. A 15 percent Harmonized Sales Tax (HST) (7 percent Goods and Services Tax (GST) and 8 percent provincial component) is charged on most goods and services supplied in Nova Scotia, New Brunswick and Newfoundland and Labrador. For information contact the Canada Border Services Agency before departing Canada. All extra goods must accompany you.

All exemptions are individual and may not be combined with those of other people. You may be asked to verify the length of your visit. Dated receipts normally constitute proof. Gifts (excluding alcoholic beverages, tobacco products and advertising matter) up to $60 (CAN) retail may be sent from abroad free of duty or taxes. For gifts valued at more than $60 (CAN), duty and taxes apply to amount exceeding $60. Gifts sent from abroad do not count against personal exemptions; gifts brought back must be included in exemptions.

NATIONAL PARKS ENTRANCE FEES

At Canada's national parks, the basic per person or per family entry fee gives visitors access to the park, scenic outlooks, picnic areas and a variety of facilities. Additional fees are charged for visitors who choose to use other recreational services such as campgrounds, special interpretation programs and golf courses.

To receive a free Parks Canada vacation planner, phone (888) 773-8888. Detailed information about the services, benefits, entry fees and discounts at all national parks and historic sites is available by calling the following numbers:

- (800) 748-7275 for Alberta;

- (902) 426-3436 for Atlantic provinces (Newfoundland and Labrador, New Brunswick, Nova Scotia and Prince Edward Island);

- (604) 513-4777 for British Columbia;

- (888)748-2928 for Manitoba;

- (800) 748-7275 for Saskatchewan;

- (800) 463-6769 for Québec;

- (800) 661-0486 for Yukon Territory.

Points of Interest Index

Index Legend

NB.................................national battlefield	NR.....................................national river
NBP.............................national battlefield park	NS..................................national seashore
NC..............................national cemetery	NWR..............................national wildlife refuge
NF....................................national forest	PHP.........................provincial historic(al) park
NHM...................national historic(al) monument	PHS............................provincial historic(al) site
NHP.......................national historic(al) park	PP..................................provincial park
NHS........................national historic(al) site	SF.......................................state forest
NL...................................national lakeshore	SHM...................state historic(al) monument
NME................................national memorial	SHP.........................state historic(al) park
NMO................................national monument	SHS...........................state historic(al) site
NMP.............................national military park	SME....................................state memorial
NP.......................................national park	SP..state park
NRA...........................national recreation area	SRA...........................state recreation area

⏆ GEM: Points of Interest Offering a *Great Experience for Members*®

EXHIBITS & COLLECTIONS-INDIAN

EXHIBITS & COLLECTIONS-MUSIC

EXHIBITS & COLLECTIONS-RELIGIOUS ITEMS

EXHIBITS & COLLECTIONS-SCIENCE

HISTORIC BUILDINGS & HOUSES

HISTORIC DOCUMENTS, MANUSCRIPTS & RARE BOOKS

HISTORIC SITES

MUSIC HALLS & OPERA HOUSES

NATIONALITIES & ETHNIC AREAS

NATURAL PHENOMENA

[SAVE] *Attraction Admission Discount Index*

Bed & Breakfast Lodgings Index

Some bed and breakfasts listed below might have historical significance. Those properties are also referenced in the Historical index. The indication that continental [CP] or full breakfast [BP] is included in the room rate reflects whether a property is a Bed-and-Breakfast facility.

Country Inns Index

Some of the following country inns can also be considered as bed-and-breakfast operations. The indication that continenta [CP] or full breakfast [BP] is included in the room rate reflects whether a property is a Bed-and-Breakfast facility.

Historical Lodgings & Restaurants Index

Some of the following historical lodgings can also be considered as bed-and-breakfast operations. The indication that continental [CP] or full breakfast [BP] is included in the room rate reflects whether a property is a Bed-and-Breakfast facility.

Historical Lodgings & Restaurants (cont'd)

Resorts Index

Many establishments are located in resort areas; however, the following places have extensive on-premises recreational facilities:

NOVA SCOTIA

ACCOMMODATIONS

PRINCE EDWARD ISLAND

ACCOMMODATIONS

QUEBEC

ACCOMMODATIONS

Comprehensive City Index

Here is an alphabetical list of all cities appearing in this TourBook® guide. Cities are presented by state/province. Page numbers under the POI column indicate where points of interest text begins. Page numbers under the L&R column indicate where lodging and restaurant listings begin.

Comprehensive City Index (cont'd)

Comprehensive City Index (cont'd)

Comprehensive City Index (cont'd)

Simplify. . .
Choose AAA/CAA Approved.

Because AAA/CAA's high standards are based on member input and feedback, choosing hotels that are AAA/CAA Approved and Diamond rated means choosing with confidence. AAA/CAA's professional evaluators have been there and done the research, checking for qualities important to AAA/CAA members – cleanliness, service, and value.

Wherever you travel, choose AAA/CAA Approved and Diamond rated hotels from the TourBook®, in print and on aaa.com!

For more information on AAA/CAA Diamond Ratings, turn to page 20-21 or visit aaa.com/Diamonds.

At 100 kph, if you reach down to change the radio station you can travel the length of a football field.

Stay Focused
Keep your mind on the road.

AAA TourBook® Guide Savings Section

At home and away, your AAA membership entitles you to exclusive savings.

Save every day of the year at thousands of participating AAA Show Your Card & Save® businesses — from hotels and car rental to movie theaters and attractions. Visit one of more than 1,000 club offices or AAA.com/save for national Show Your Card & Save offers or a complete list of savings by location.

Plus, enjoy special limited-time extras and savings at participating Show Your Card & Save lodgings, restaurants, and attractions with the following coupon offers for members.

With so many money-saving opportunities, it pays to be a AAA member!

Members Save With Our Partners

SAVINGS. SELECTION. SATISFACTION.—When contacting one of these lodging partners, you will be given AAA/CAA's best rates for your dates of stay. Your valid membership card must be presented at check-in. Select the chain you want and have your membership card available when making a reservation and checking in. Let the property know if you are dissatisfied with any part of your stay. If the matter cannot be resolved, you are entitled to recompense (see page 17).

Offer good at time of publication; chains and offers may change without notice. Lodging partners offering discounts to AAA/CAA members may vary in Mexico and the Caribbean.

| Visit | Over 1,000 AAA/CAA Offices | Click | AAA.com | Call | 866-AAA-SAVE |

CHOICE HOTELS INTERNATIONAL ™

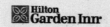

Members Save With Our Partners

These National Show Your Card & Save® partners provide the listed member benefits. Admission tickets that offer greater discounts may be available for purchase at the local AAA/CAA club. A maximum of six tickets is available at the discount price at the gate. Visit AAA.com to discover all the great Show Your Card & Save® discounts in your area.

SeaWorld/Busch Gardens AAA.com/SeaWorld

- Save $5 on 1-day gate admission at SeaWorld, Busch Gardens, and Sesame Place
- Save $3 on 1-day admission at Water Country USA and Adventure Island

- Save 10% on select up-close dining. Reservations are required; visit Guest Relations for details

AAA.com/BuschGardens

Six Flags Theme Parks

- 10% OFF Brunch with Bugs
- 10% OFF merchandise purchases of $15 or more at all Six Flags operated locations.

Universal Orlando AAA.com/Universal

- Save $4 on a 2-day/2-park pass at Universal Orlando's theme parks (savings apply to tickets purchased at the gate)
- Save 10% on select dining and souvenirs at both Universal Orlando theme parks and at select Universal CityWalk Orlando restaurants (excludes Emeril's)

Universal Studios Hollywood

- Save $3 on a 1-day Universal Studios Hollywood pass (savings applies to tickets purchased at the gate) AAA.com/Universal
- Save 10% on select dining and souvenirs at Universal Studios Hollywood and Universal CityWalk

Gray Line
AAA.com/GrayLine

- Save 10% on sightseeing tours of 1 day or less

Landry's Seafood House, The Crab House, Chart House, Muer Seafood Restaurants, Joe's Crab Shack and Aquarium and Downtown Aquarium Restaurants

- 10% discount on food and non-alcoholic beverages at all of the above restaurants.
- 10% discount on novelty merchandise at Joe's Crab Shacks and Aquarium and Downtown Aquarium Restaurants.

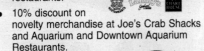

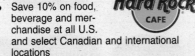

Hard Rock Cafe

- Save 10% on food, beverage and merchandise at all U.S. and select Canadian and international locations

Restaurant Partner Savings applies to AAA/CAA members and up to five guests.

Tanger Outlet Centers www.tangeroutlet.com

- Save up to 20% on total purchase at select merchants with AAA/CAA coupon booklet
- Member BONUS: FREE $5 gift card for each additional Tanger Outlet Center visited after first within same calendar year

- Show membership card and register at the AAA customer service desk when you visit